Marketing Research

An Indian Perspective

NAVAL BAJPAI

ABV-Indian Institute of Information Technology and Management
Gwalior

PEARSON

Delhi • Chennai

Senior Editor—Development: Priya Christopher
Assistant Editor—Acquisitions: Varun Goenka
Editor—Production: M. Balakrishnan

ISBN 978-93-325-3637-1

First Impression

Published by Dorling Kindersley (India) Pvt. Ltd, licensees of Pearson Education in South Asia.

Head Office: 7th Floor, Knowledge Boulevard, A-8(A), Sector 62, Noida 201 309, UP, India.
Registered Office: 11 Community Centre, Panchsheel Park, New Delhi 110 017, India.

Compositor: MAP Systems, Bengaluru.
Printed in India: HT Media Ltd., Noida

In loving memory of my grandfather, late Professor Ramesh Chandra Agnihotri;
and my grandmother, late Mrs Sudha Agnihotri

To my mother, Mrs Chitra Bajpai; my father, Mr P. S. Bajpai;
my sister, Mrs Nidhi Shukla; my wife, Mrs Archana Bajpai;
and my daughters, Aditi and Swasti

Brief Contents

Contents

About the Author

Naval Bajpai is a faculty at the ABV-Indian Institute of Information Technology and Management, Gwalior. He has a multifarious background in industrial, teaching and research fields spanning over a decade and is a lifetime member of the Indian Society for Technical Education.

A postgraduate in statistics, Professor Bajpai did his doctoral research in Management at Pt Ravishankar Shukla University, Raipur. He also earned his master's degree in business administration from the same university and has conducted several management development programmes on organizational behaviour and research methods. With over 40 research papers published in journals of national and international repute, Professor Bajpai is an avid analyst of contemporary work trends in public-sector organizations. He is the author of *Business Statistics*, *Business Research Methods* and *Research Methodology* and the co-author of *Quantitative Analysis* published by Pearson Education, India.

Dr Bajpai has served as a faculty at the Indian Institute of Management Raipur, and the Indian Institute of Foreign Trade, New Delhi. He is a visiting professor at the Institute of Finance Management, Dar es Salaam, Tanzania. He is a UGC NET-qualified faculty actively involved in teaching, research and consultancy in a distinguished career spanning over 18 years.

Preface

Every market researcher or business analyst needs to be aware of marketing research methods. Market researchers will find it difficult to conduct an in-depth analysis in their areas of specialization without a sound knowledge of the scientific process of conducting research. Researchers may consult many books and articles but their knowledge may remain inadequate if they lack the patience to devote the time required to understand research techniques prevailing in the contemporary marketing world. They must remember that little knowledge is dangerous and devote time and energy to understand the essence of research before executing any type of marketing research. This book provides readers with an opportunity to understand the crux of marketing research in a scientific and systematic manner. Market researchers who are potential readers of the book must systematically read all the chapters without resorting to shortcuts such as focusing on only a few chapters. This book deals with real examples from the business world that exemplify market research concepts. For example, it uses the example of consumer attitude or consumer satisfaction to deal with the different dimensions of research. It comes in handy even for a researcher involved in organizational behaviour analysis, as any topic related to employee attitude or employee satisfaction can be dealt with using the same kind of research methodology by merely changing the dimension of study from the business level to the organizational level. Similarly, other research topics related to varied streams, such as psychology, sociology, anthropology, social psychology, etc. can be analysed using the tools and techniques presented here. Broadly, any research related to primary data collection or field data collection can be effectively performed with the help of this book.

A basic prerequisite that any researcher who aims at becoming an expert at market research techniques needs to possess is a sound knowledge of statistical techniques. Thus, before one sets out to read this book, it is advisable to first become familiar with application-oriented statistics. Marketing research is designed using the concepts of statistics. Hence, this book unfolds basic and advanced marketing research methods with the assumption that the readers have prior knowledge of the fundamentals of statistics. For example, common terms in statistics such as average, median, mode, standard deviation, etc. are used throughout this book. Similarly, readers must have a solid knowledge of probability and probability distributions. My books, *Business Statistics* (2009) and *Business Research Methods* (2011), published by Pearson Education, provide tools to understand some of the basic concepts of statistics commonly applied to research methods. It will be a good idea for readers to go through these two books before going through the marketing research methods presented here.

Designed to meet the requirements of students in business schools across India, this book also presents case studies and problems developed using real data gathered from organizations such as the Centre for Monitoring Indian Economy (CMIE) and Indiastat.com. Statistical concepts are explained in a simple manner without going into the derivation of formulas. The only prerequisite to understand these concepts is a basic knowledge of algebra. Clear instructions help readers to use these programs for statistical analysis and interpret the outputs obtained. The focus on interpretation rather than computation develops competencies that will aid students in their future careers as managers. This book guides students to make the best use of marketing research by using a variety of learning tools. Each chapter opens with a list of learning objectives that introduce the reader to the topics covered in the chapter. This is followed by an opening vignette that links theory to actual industry practice. The introductory section in all chapters provides a broad outline of the subject. Scenarios from day-to-day life are used to illustrate complex theories. Problems are provided at the end of important sections to enable students to practice the ideas discussed. Solved examples framed using real data from organizations such as Indiastat. com and CMIE highlight the business applications of marketing research methods. Unsolved numerical problems are designed to strengthen problem-solving skills. A case study at the end of each chapter acquaints the student with an assortment of organizational scenarios that they may encounter in the future.

COVERAGE

This book is divided into six parts consisting of a total of 22 chapters. These six parts are: *Introduction to Marketing Research; Research Design Formulation; Sources and Collection of Data: Descriptive Statistics and Data Analysis; Result Presentation* and *Applications of Marketing Research*. The first and the most important aspect of conducting any research is to define the research problem properly. In addition, the researcher must have a strong background in marketing research and be knowledgeable about the various stages in conducting a scientific research programme. *Part I: Introduction to Marketing Research* comprises two chapters. *Chapter 1: Marketing Research: An Introduction* introduces readers to marketing research. *Chapter 2: Market Research Process Design* explains the stages in the research process and focuses on the sequential steps in conducting research.

Part II: Research Design Formulation consists of three chapters. *Chapter 3: Measurement and Scaling* deals with measurement issues and discusses the various scales for measurement. *Chapter 4: Questionnaire Design* discusses the development of the questionnaire as a research tool. *Chapter 5: Sampling and Sampling Distributions* discusses sampling, types of sampling, sampling and non-sampling errors and sampling distributions.

Part III: Sources and Collection of Data consists of four chapters. *Chapter 6: Secondary Data Sources* focuses exclusively on the sources of secondary data, especially in India. *Chapter 7: Data Collection: Survey and Observation* explains various survey and observation techniques. *Chapter 8: Experimentation* deals with the validity issue, the process of conducting experiments and the classification of experimental designs. *Chapter 9: Fieldwork and Data Preparation* describes the process of gathering data through field work as well as editing, coding, and preparation of the data matrix for statistical analysis.

Part IV: Descriptive Statistics and Data Analysis consists of 11 chapters. *Chapter 10: Descriptive Statistics: Measures of Central Tendency* gives insights into the central tendency of data. *Chapter 11: Descriptive Statistics: Measures of Dispersion* focuses on the various measures of dispersion. *Chapter 12: Statistical Inference: Hypothesis Testing for Single Populations* introduces readers to the hypothesis-testing procedure for single populations. *Chapter 13: Statistical Inference: Hypothesis Testing for Two Populations* discusses the hypothesis-testing procedure for two populations. *Chapter 14: Analysis of Variance and Experimental Designs* deals with the analysis of variance and designs of experiments. *Chapter 15: Hypothesis Testing for Categorical Data (Chi-Square Test)* discusses the chi-square test and its applications. *Chapter 16: Correlation and Simple Regression Analysis* discusses the applications of bivariate correlation and regression. Chapters 17, 18 and 19 focus on the widely used multivariate statistical techniques in the field of marketing research.

Chapter 17: Multivariate Analysis I: Multiple Regression Analysis discusses multiple regression. *Chapter 18: Multivariate Analysis II: Discriminant Analysis and Conjoint Analysis* focuses on discriminant analysis and conjoint analysis. *Chapter 19: Multivariate Analysis III: Factor Analysis, Cluster Analysis, Multidimensional Scaling and Correspondence Analysis* discusses advanced, interdependent multivariate techniques in marketing research such as factor analysis, cluster analysis, multidimensional scaling and correspondence analysis. *Chapter 20: Sales Forecasting* discusses the various techniques of sales forecasting.

Part V: Result Presentation comprises *Chapter 21: Presentation of Result: Report Writing.* This chapter explains the systematic method to present the results of a marketing research project.

Part VI: Applications of Marketing Research includes the final chapter, *Chapter 22: Marketing Mix Research: Product, Price, Place and Promotion Research.* This chapter focuses on the role played by marketing research in making critical decisions regarding the different elements of the marketing mix.

KEY FEATURES

Learning Objectives define the key points in each chapter that need to be focused on while reading the chapter.

LEARNING OBJECTIVES

Upon completion of this chapter, you will be able to:

- Understand the difference between basic and applied research
- Define marketing research
- Understand the roadmap to learn marketing research methods
- Learn how marketing research methods can be used as a decision making tool by the managers
- Understand the marketing research process
- Get a preliminary idea about the use of software for data preparation and data analysis

Research in Action sets the tone for each chapter and focuses on the marketing research methods discussed in the chapter.

RESEARCH IN ACTION: AIR INDIA LTD

Civil aviation is a key contributor to the growth and development of Indian economy and contributes to the sustainable development of trade, commerce, and tourism in the country. This sector provides three categories of services—operations, infrastructure, and regulatory-cum-development. Domestic and international air services are provided by the government-owned airlines and some private airlines. Airport infrastructure facilities are taken care of by the Airport Authority of India. Mumbai and Delhi airports have now been handed over to private enterprise under a Public-Private Partnership (PPP) model.[1]

In July 2009, cash-strapped Air India-Indian Airlines sought an immediate loan of ₹100,000 million from the government along with an annual equity infusion of ₹25,000-30,000 million for the next 4 to 5 years, which will be linked to the induction of new aircrafts into its fleet. In all, the tottering airlines project has a requirement of almost ₹200,000 million.

TABLE 1.1
Income, expenses, and profit after tax of Air India Ltd (from Dec 1999 to Dec 2007) in million rupees

Year	*Income*	*Expenses*	*Profit after tax*
Dec-99	43,895.3	45,640.1	−1744.8
Dec-00	48,342.5	48,718.8	−376.3
Dec-01	53,650.5	54,094.5	−444
Dec-02	50,517.2	50,362.8	154.4
Dec-03	57,062.4	55,723.8	1338.6
Dec-04	62,612.3	61,689	923.3
Dec-05	77,890.2	76,926.6	963.6
Dec-06	93,394.4	93,245	149.4
Dec-07	96,278	100,757.3	−4479.3

Source: Prowess (V. 3.1): Centre for Monitoring Indian Economy Pvt. Ltd, Mumbai.

Marginalia highlight the critical concepts and definitions discussed in each chapter.

1.1 INTRODUCTION

Marketing researchers systematically collect, compile, analyse, and interpret data to provide quality information based on which a decision maker will be able to take a decision in an optimum manner.

The marketing environment is always uncertain and there is a need to handle this uncertainty by developing a pool of information in a scientific manner. Marketing researchers systematically collect, compile, analyse, and interpret data to provide quality information, based on which a decision maker will be able to take a decision in an optimum manner. Market research never operates in vacuum. Decision makers of various organizations face a dilemma because of continuous change in the marketing environment. They happen to be in continuous need to have relevant and objective information for the problem at hand. Information may be provided to decision makers by anyone, but the authenticity of such information would be under suspicion. It is the role of the marketing researcher to conduct research scientifically and hence, provide accurate information to the decision maker. In an uncertain environment, decision makers always remain keen to gather scientific and accurate information that will help them to arrive at an optimum decision.

Solved examples based on real data from industry enable students to learn about statistical methodology and its application.

Example 5.5

The bottled water segment in India has witnessed rapid growth. Institutional users are responsible for 30% sales in the market.[3] If 100 customers are randomly selected, what is the probability that 25 or more customers are institutional users?

Solution Here, $p = 0.30$, $\bar{p} = \frac{25}{100} = 0.25$, and $n = 100$

By substituting all the values in the z formula, we obtain

$$z = \frac{\bar{p} - p}{\sqrt{\frac{pq}{n}}} = \frac{0.25 - 0.30}{\sqrt{\frac{(0.30)(0.70)}{100}}} = -\frac{0.05}{0.0458} = -1.09$$

The z value obtained is -1.09 and the corresponding probability from the normal table is 0.3621, which is the area between sample proportion, 0.25 and the population proportion, 0.30. Figure 5.16 exhibits this area. So, when 100 customers are randomly selected, then the probability that 25 or more customers are institutional users is

$$P(\bar{p} \geq 0.25) = 0.3621 + 0.5000 = 0.8621$$

This result indicates that 86.21% of the time a random sample of 100 customers will consist of 25 or more institutional users.

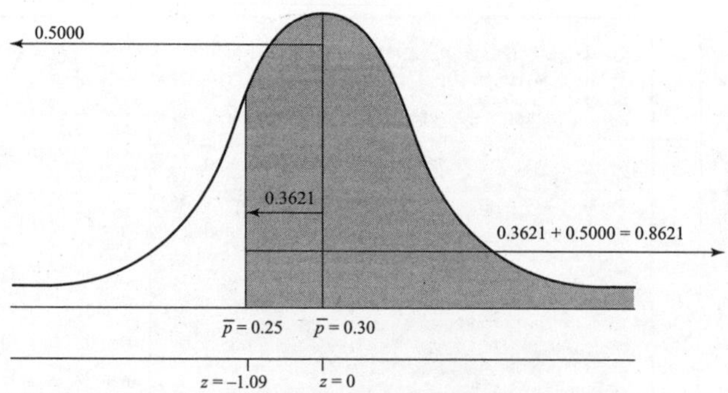

FIGURE 5.16 Shaded area under the normal curve exhibiting the probability that 25 or more customers are institutional users.

Self-Practice Problems provide opportunities for further analysis and practice of the statistical concepts discussed in each chapter.

SELF-PRACTICE PROBLEMS

11D1. Compute sample standard deviation and sample variance for the following series:

45 67 117 180 23 29 89 12 200 280

11D2. Compute sample standard deviation and sample variance for the following data:

x:	50	75	89	110	175	185
f:	11	19	20	21	19	12

11D3. Compute sample standard deviation and sample variance for the following data:

x:	50–100	100–150	150–200	200–250	250–300
f:	10	20	22	23	19

11D4. The table below shows the circlewise number of broadband subscribers as on March 31, 2008. Compute sample standard deviation and sample variance from the data.

State/telecom circle	*Broadband subscribers*	*State/telecom circle*	*Broadband subscribers*
Andaman & Nicobar Islands	1725	Kerala	183,506
Andhra Pradesh	294,111	Maharashtra (including Goa)	809,982
Assam	21,538	Madhya Pradesh (including Chhattisgarh)	112,686
Bihar (including Jharkhand)	52,779	North East	7400
Delhi (including Noida, Gurgaon, Ghaziabad, and Faridabad)	431,377	Orissa	32,321
Gujarat	249,785	Punjab	131,750
Haryana	58,616	Rajasthan	94,110
Himachal Pradesh	12,514	Tamilnadu	499,442
Jammu & Kashmir	13,444	Uttar Pradesh (including Uttaranchal)	170,966
Karnataka	421,392	West Bengal	266,595

Source: www.indiastat.com, accessed October 2008, reproduced with permission.

Problems framed using data from organizations such as **CMIE and Indiastat.com** relate statistical analysis to the business environment in India.

The **Summary** at the end of each chapter recapitulates the main concepts discussed in the chapter.

SUMMARY |

Discriminant analysis is a technique of analysing data when the dependent variable is categorical and the independent variables are interval in nature. The difference between multiple regression and discriminant analysis can be examined in the light of nature of the dependent variable, which happens to be categorical, as compared with metric, as in the case of multiple regression analysis. Two-group discriminant analysis is conducted through the following five-step procedure: problem formulation, discriminant function coefficient estimation, significance of the discriminant function determination, result interpretation, and validity of the analysis determination. When categorical dependent variable has more than two categories, multiple discriminant analysis is performed.

The main objective of the conjoint analysis is to find the attributes of the product, which a respondent mostly prefers. The word conjoint refers to the notion that relative value of any phenomenon (product in most of the cases) can be measured jointly, which may not be measured when taken individually. Conjoint analysis determines the relative importance of various product attributes (attached by the consumers to different product attributes) and the values (utility) attached to different levels of these attributes. Conjoint analysis is conducted through the following five-step procedure: problem formulation, trade-off-data collection, metric versus non-metric input data, result analysis and interpretation, and reliability and validity check.

Discussion Questions test students' understanding of concepts and promote critical thinking.

DISCUSSION QUESTIONS |

1. What do you understand by hypothesis testing?
2. What is the importance of hypothesis testing in managerial decision making?
3. What are the steps in hypothesis testing?
4. Discuss the concept of a two-tailed test in hypothesis testing?
5. When should we consider a one-tailed test for hypothesis testing?
6. What are the two types of errors in hypothesis testing?
7. Explain the z-value approach to hypothesis testing.
8. Explain the p-value approach to hypothesis testing. What is the importance of the p-value approach in terms of modern statistical software available?
9. What is the conceptual framework of the critical value approach to hypothesis testing?

Numerical Problems enhance problem-solving skills and facilitate application of concepts.

NUMERICAL PROBLEMS |

1. A population has mean 40 and standard deviation 10. A random sample of size 50 is taken from the population, what is the probability that the sample mean is each of the following:
   (a) Greater than or equal to 42
   (b) Less than 41
   (c) Between 38 and 43
2. A housing board colony of Gwalior consists of 2000 houses. A researcher wants to know the average income of the households in this housing board colony. The mean income per household is ₹150,000 with standard deviation ₹15,000. A random sample of 200 households is selected by a researcher and analysed. What is the probability that the sample average is greater than ₹160,000?
3. A population proportion is 0.55. A random sample of size 500 is drawn from the population.
   (a) What is the probability that sample proportion is greater than 0.58?
   (b) What is the probability that sample proportion is between 0.5 and 0.6?
4. The government of a newly formed state in India is worried about the rising unemployment rates. It has promoted some finance companies to launch schemes to reduce the rate of unemployment by promoting entrepreneurial skills. A finance company introduced a scheme to finance young graduates to start their own business. Out of 200,000 young graduates, 130,000 accepted the policy and received loans. If a random sample of 20,000 is taken

Significant terms compiled at the end of each chapter as **Key Terms** enable students to dwell on the topics for added familiarity.

KEY TERMS |

Applied research, 5
Basic research, 5
Marketing research, 5
Decision making, 6
Diagnosing problem or opportunity, 10
Problem or opportunity identification, 10
Roadmap to learn marketing research methods, 7

Case Studies drawn from companies across various sectors in India correlate statistical theories to their actual applications in the industry.

CASE STUDY |

Case 4: *Videocon Industries Limited: Opting a Way of Consolidation for Materializing Dreams*

Introduction: An Overview of the Consumer Electronics Industry in India

The consumer electronics industry has been witnessing a remarkable growth over the past few years. The fast-growing segments during the year were colour televisions, air conditioners, DVD players, and home theatre systems. Other segments of consumer electronics and home appliances have also shown a positive growth. The consumer electronics and home appliances industry broadly comprises brown goods, white goods, and small domestic appliances.

Brown goods: colour televisions, CD and DVD players, camcorders, still cameras, video game consoles, HIFI, and home cinema;
White goods: air conditioners, refrigerators, dish washers, drying cabinets, microwave ovens, washing machines, freezers, and so on;
Small domestic appliances: iron, vacuum cleaners, water purifiers, and so on.

The company is primarily into manufacturing and distribution of colour televisions, refrigerators, washing machines, air conditioners, microwave ovens, glass shells, and other components.[1]

Videocon Group: A Major Player in Consumer Electronics

Shri Nandlal Madhavlal Dhoot was the founder of Videocon Group. In early 1980s, through a technical tie up with Toshiba Corporation of Japan, he produced India's first world-class colour television: Videocon. Today, Videocon is a household name across the nation—India's No. 1 brand of consumer elec-

THE TEACHING AND LEARNING PACKAGE

The following resources included with the book are available at www.pearsoned.co.in/navalbajpai:

- An instructors' solution manual that contains solutions for all the problems and case studies in the text.
- PowerPoint lecture slides with chapter outlines that facilitate the teaching process.
- Multiple-choice and true/false questions that are designed to test students' comprehension of key topics.

Naval Bajpai

PART I

Introduction to Marketing Research

CHAPTER 1

Marketing Research: An Introduction

LEARNING OBJECTIVES

Upon completion of this chapter, you will be able to:

- Understand the difference between basic and applied research
- Define marketing research
- Understand the roadmap to learn marketing research methods
- Learn how marketing research methods can be used as a decision making tool by the managers
- Understand the marketing research process
- Get a preliminary idea about the use of software for data preparation and data analysis

RESEARCH IN ACTION: AIR INDIA LTD

Civil aviation is a key contributor to the growth and development of Indian economy and contributes to the sustainable development of trade, commerce, and tourism in the country. This sector provides three categories of services—operations, infrastructure, and regulatory-cum-development. Domestic and international air services are provided by the government-owned airlines and some private airlines. Airport infrastructure facilities are taken care of by the Airport Authority of India. Mumbai and Delhi airports have now been handed over to private enterprise under a Public-Private Partnership (PPP) model.[1]

In July 2009, cash-strapped Air India-Indian Airlines sought an immediate loan of ₹100,000 million from the government along with an annual equity infusion of ₹25,000-30,000 million for the next 4 to 5 years, which will be linked to the induction of new aircrafts into its fleet. In all, the tottering airlines project has a requirement of almost ₹200,000 million.

TABLE 1.1
Income, expenses, and profit after tax of Air India Ltd (from Dec 1999 to Dec 2007) in million rupees

Year	*Income*	*Expenses*	*Profit after tax*
Dec-99	43,895.3	45,640.1	−1744.8
Dec-00	48,342.5	48,718.8	−376.3
Dec-01	53,650.5	54,094.5	−444
Dec-02	50,517.2	50,362.8	154.4
Dec-03	57,062.4	55,723.8	1338.6
Dec-04	62,612.3	61,689	923.3
Dec-05	77,890.2	76,926.6	963.6
Dec-06	93,394.4	93,245	149.4
Dec-07	96,278	100,757.3	−4479.3

Source: Prowess (V. 3.1): Centre for Monitoring Indian Economy Pvt. Ltd, Mumbai.

The merged airline, National Aviation Company of India Ltd (NACIL), accumulated losses of ₹72,000 million till March 2009.[2]

Table 1.1 shows income, expenses, and profit after tax of Air India Ltd (from Dec 1999 to Dec 2007) in million Rupees.

In this situation, a section of employees of Air India have decided to go on a 2-hour strike even as the national carrier is trying to tide over the worst financial crises in its history. The Civil Aviation Minister Mr Praful Patel, termed this strike "unfortunate" and feels that this kind of agitation will create a "wrong impression" among the travelling public and people will consequently shun flying Air India.[3]

One has to understand the reasons for the employees' agitation, at a time Air India is going through historical financial crises. Research is the only tool through which this can be explored. One has to conduct the research in a systematic manner. This chapter deals with the beginning of the research, mainly, defining marketing research, the nature and objective of marketing research, the difference between basic and applied research, marketing research as a decision making tool, and use of statistical software for data preparation and data analysis.

1.1 INTRODUCTION

Marketing researchers systematically collect, compile, analyse, and interpret data to provide quality information based on which a decision maker will be able to take a decision in an optimum manner.

The marketing environment is always uncertain and there is a need to handle this uncertainty by developing a pool of information in a scientific manner. Marketing researchers systematically collect, compile, analyse, and interpret data to provide quality information, based on which a decision maker will be able to take a decision in an optimum manner. Market research never operates in vacuum. Decision makers of various organizations face a dilemma because of continuous change in the marketing environment. They happen to be in continuous need to have relevant and objective information for the problem at hand. Information may be provided to decision makers by anyone, but the authenticity of such information would be under suspicion. It is the role of the marketing researcher to conduct research scientifically and hence, provide accurate information to the decision maker. In an uncertain environment, decision makers always remain keen to gather scientific and accurate information that will help them to arrive at an optimum decision.

Consider the hypothetical example of a multinational company engaged in the manufacturing and selling of toothpaste. The company has got a big client base and has almost 100 million customers in rural and urban India. The company is enjoying a sound market position and willing to enhance the client base by 10 million customers in the next 2 years. After 1 year of fixing this target, the company assessed its performance. An estimation revealed that, instead of enhancing, the client base of the company is surprisingly reduced to approximately 95 million customers. The company management is worried and wants to ascertain where the actual problem lies. Superficially, the problem seems to be the loss of customers and it has to be elaborated and properly addressed.

As discussed, the company has a client base of 100 million customers and the problem and solution can be explored by contacting these customers in a pre-specified and systematic manner. Ultimately, customers will reveal the reason for this change. There is a well-described systematic procedure to obtain information from the customers. This problem must be addressed in various established stages. The company management should contact a marketing researcher. The marketing researcher meets the decision maker of the company and explores the need and dimensions of the proposed research work. The first and most important issue is to define the problem properly. Defining the problem properly is not an easy task. A researcher has to launch a pilot study or an exploratory research to have an insight of the problem. He has to select an appropriate research design and should also focus on developing or adopting a tool (questionnaire) to address the problem. Obviously, the researcher cannot contact all the customers. He has to determine a sample size and suitable sampling techniques to cater to the diverse population of rural and urban India in an optimum manner. Administering the questionnaire to the respondents and executing the related fieldwork is another concern of the researcher. Data coding and data preparation is the next step before launching statistical analysis. As the next step, an appropriate statistical test must be used and the obtained statistical result must be properly interpreted. This obtained information must be conveyed to the decision maker and it is the decision maker who actually takes the final decision.

Thus, conducting research to deal with any problem is a scientific, systematic, and interlinked exercise, which requires sound experience and knowledge. This chapter is an attempt to understand the nature and scope of marketing research methods. The chapter introduces the dimensions of this discussion and is the first step in learning **marketing research** methods systematically and objectively.

Conducting research to deal with any problem is a scientific, systematic, and interlinked exercise, which requires sound experience and knowledge.

1.2 DIFFERENCE BETWEEN BASIC AND APPLIED RESEARCH

The purpose of both basic and **applied research** is to contribute or develop a body of knowledge. **Basic research** is generally not related to a specific problem and its findings cannot be immediately applied. For example, consider a researcher testing the changing motivational factors of Indian buyers, especially after liberalization. The researcher systematically and scientifically conducts the research and presents a theory about the changing motivational factors of Indian buyers. This is actually adding something to the academic body of knowledge that already exists. The existing body of knowledge has already presented some motivational factors for Indian buyers. The researcher believes that with the passage of time these factors have changed, especially after liberalization. By conducting research, the researcher has presented a new set of motivational factors for Indian buyers. This result is very important but is only a guideline and cannot be applied directly for a specific research problem.

Basic research is generally not related to a specific problem and its findings cannot be immediately applied.

Applied research directly addresses the problem at hand. In general, applied research is launched by the firm, agency, or individual facing a specific problem. As in basic research, the researcher adopts a systematic and scientific procedure to conduct the research. Findings are presented to the research sponsor agency or the decision maker. On the basis of the presented findings, the decision maker takes the decision to address the problem. Thus, the difference lies in terms of applying the findings. Basic research is a development or contribution to the theory where the findings are used directly or immediately. Whereas, applied research is organized to address a specific problem and its findings are immediately applied by the decision maker based on their feasibility and sustainability.

Applied research directly addresses the problem at hand. Applied research is launched by the firm, agency, or individual facing a specific problem.

It is important to note that the techniques and procedure for conducting basic and applied research are the same. The procedure is scientific for both basic research and applied research. This scientific procedure is nothing but systematic data collection, compilation, analysis, interpretation, and implication pertaining to any research problem. All the chapters in this book are sequentially knit to deal with the scientific and systematic procedure of conducting marketing research. The approach of conducting the research does not change when dealing with two diverse topics from two different disciplines. For example, consider two topics such as "measuring the job satisfaction of employees" and "measuring the consumer satisfaction for a product." Research methods of these two topics will be almost the same. This means that the researcher has to first identify the problem, develop a theoretical model, prepare a questionnaire and develop hypotheses in the light of a theoretical model, select a sampling method, launch an appropriate data analysis exercise, perform interpretation, and present the finding. For dealing with these two different topics, there will be different approaches to identify the problem and develop the theoretical model through literature. In the first case, for measuring the job satisfaction, a researcher has to explore the literature related to "job satisfaction" and then propose a theoretical model to quantify job satisfaction. In the second case, for measuring consumer satisfaction, a researcher has to explore the literature related to "consumer satisfaction" and then propose a theoretical model to quantify consumer satisfaction. Hence, there will be changes in the aspect of dealing the two different topics, but the basis for conducting the research will remain the same for these two topics. This book will deal with "the basis for conducting the research" through the various chapters in a sequential manner.

1.3 DEFINING MARKETING RESEARCH

Marketing research method is a systematic and scientific procedure of data collection, compilation, analysis, interpretation, and implication pertaining to any marketing problem.

All markets present opportunities and problems. Opportunities are to be explored and problems are to be resolved. Marketing research can be termed as a system that can be used to address such issues. This system, popularly known as marketing research, is a universal phenomenon and is universally applied with some varied regional, geographical, national differences. Tull and Hawkins (1993) have defined marketing research as the function of marketing to provide information that will assist the marketing manager in recognizing and reacting to marketing opportunities and problems. In essence, marketing research exists to help marketing managers make better decisions. It is very difficult to cover all aspects of marketing research through a single definition. The various definitions provided by different scholars are just an attempt to define marketing research concisely. In such an attempt, Parasuraman et al. (2004) define marketing research as a set of techniques and principles for systematically collecting, recording, analysing, and interpreting data that can aid decision makers involved in marketing goods, services and ideas. This definition also focuses on developing a system or systematic approach to collect, record, analyse and interpret data. The key word that distinguishes research from a haphazard gathering of observations is systematic (Luck and Rubin 2008). A researcher has to ensure that a system has been established to address the problems that arise. The system must be such that it can be understood and used by all other researchers. Therefore, there is not only the need to develop a systematic study and understanding but it must also confirm to different universally accepted global parameters.

Another popular definition of marketing research focuses on consumer satisfaction rather than profit maximization. Aaker et al. (2000) stated that a research organization should try to obtain information on consumer needs and gather marketing intelligence to help satisfy these needs efficiently. They defined marketing research as a critical path of such a marketing intelligence system, which helps improve management **decision making** by providing relevant, accurate, and timely information. This marketing intelligence system is in fact a systematic effort to generate relevant, accurate, and timely information. Relevancy, accuracy and timeliness are the factors that propel researchers to take up marketing research as a continuous process.

Marketing research is a systematic and scientific procedure of data collection, compilation, analysis, interpretation, and implication pertaining to any marketing problem. This exercise is launched to provide objective and timely support to the decision maker of a business organization. The definition can be decomposed into five different parts. The first part states that the data collection procedure is scientific and systematic. This means that one cannot collect data haphazardly. Data collection cannot be initiated abruptly.

Data are collected in an organized manner through a well-constructed instrument commonly referred to as the "questionnaire." Developing the questionnaire is also a systematic procedure. In fact, the questionnaire quantifies the theoretical model of the research. One cannot willingly include questions in the questionnaire. The questionnaire measures the variables under the research investigation that have already been taken from the literature. For example, a research problem "brand shift" may have various reasons. The dimensions of probable reasons can be explored through extensive literature survey. The probable reasons may be change in brand equity, lack of brand awareness, problems in distribution channel, ineffective advertisement campaign, and the like. These are surface problems; exploratory research can reveal many other problems of "brand shift." As the next step, the researcher explores each and every factor under investigation and frames questions relevant to each factor. For example, the researcher may take eight different dimensions of a factor namely, "problems in the distribution channel." Each question of the said factor is rated on a 1 to 5 rating scale. Thus, for the factor "problems in the distribution channel," minimum score can be 8 and maximum score can be 40. This is the quantification of the factor "problems in the distribution channel." Likewise, quantification of other factors can be executed. Thus, the questionnaire is a systematic compilation of questions related to all these factors and measures the research phenomenon under investigation. Demographic information is also obtained through the questionnaire in a systematic manner.

Data compilation is also a systematic effort made by the researcher. Data collected from fieldwork may not be ready for analysis. It must be verified, edited, and coded before launching the statistical analysis exercise. Before analysis, data must also be entered in a computer spreadsheet. This exercise must be done carefully. There is a well-defined procedure to handle the misses and inconsistencies in the data matrix.

Data analysis is an integral part of the research process. It is an inferential process where the researcher tries to validate the accuracy of the result obtained from a sample taken from the population. Based on the nature (type) of the data, a researcher applies metric or non-parametric statistical tests. Furthermore, statistical analysis can be classified into univariate statistical analysis, bivariate statistical analysis, and multivariate statistical analysis. Data analysis provides a statistical result. As a next step, the researcher has to interpret the result in the light of the prevailing circumstances. The researcher again takes the help of the literature to substantiate his or her findings. Ultimately, the findings are communicated to the decision maker who actually sponsored the research project. In the light of these well-described findings, the decision maker takes an appropriate decision.

1.4 ROADMAP TO LEARN MARKETING RESEARCH

Students should learn marketing research techniques in a sequential and systematic manner. There is a need to understand that all the chapters incorporated in the book are related to each other and the study of any chapter out of sequence will not provide a scientific understanding of the subject. It has been observed that there is a tendency among students to start with any chapter, which they perceive is of importance to them. For example, taking a short cut, some students directly start with the questionnaire design and then focus on applying any statistical technique without having the base knowledge for applying these sophisticated statistical techniques. The issue becomes more serious when students do not concentrate on the structure of the research. One has to understand that, from problem definition to the questionnaire in the appendix, each and every step is thoroughly linked and interconnected. To understand this link, students should study the subject from Chapter 1 to Chapter 22 in a sequence. Figure 1.1 provides a roadmap to learn marketing research.

For the purpose of understanding, the systematic study of marketing research can be classified into six parts. These six parts of this book are: Introduction to marketing research;

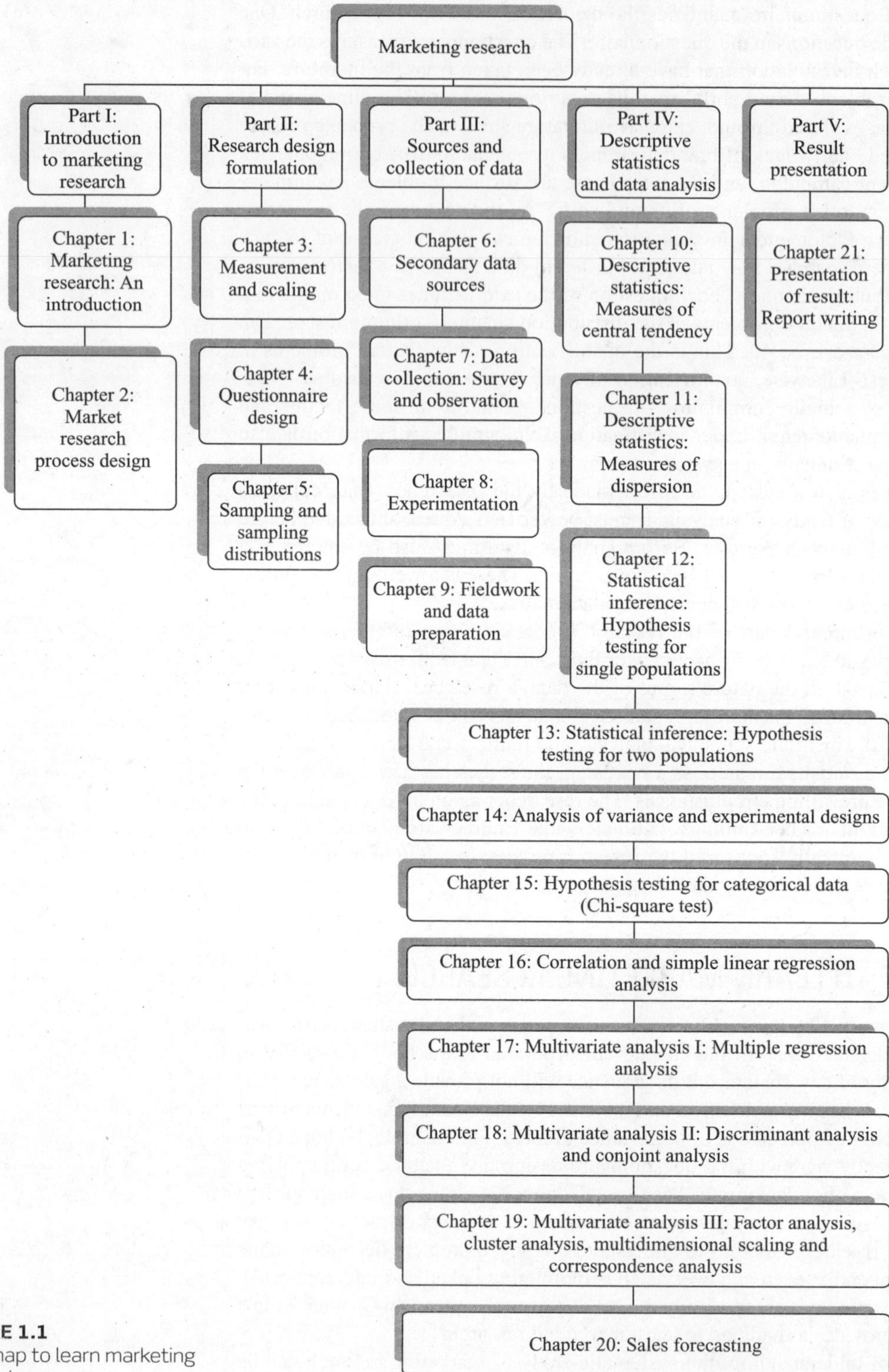

FIGURE 1.1
Roadmap to learn marketing research

research design formulation; sources and collection of data: descriptive statistics and data analysis; result presentation and applications of marketing research.

The first and the most important aspect of conducting any research is to define the research problem properly. In addition, the researcher must have a strong background in marketing research and be knowledgeable about the various stages in conducting a scientific research programme. **Part I: Introduction to Marketing Research** comprises two chapters. **Chapter 1: Marketing Research: An Introduction** introduces readers to marketing research. **Chapter 2: Market Research Process Design** explains the stages in the research process and focuses on the sequential steps in conducting research.

Part II titled **Research Design Formulation** consists of three chapters. **Chapter 3: Measurement and Scaling** deals with measurement issues and discusses the various scales for measurement. **Chapter 4: Questionnaire Design** discusses the development of the questionnaire as a research tool. **Chapter 5: Sampling and Sampling Distribution** discusses sampling, types of sampling, sampling and non-sampling errors and sampling distributions.

Part III entitled **Sources and Collection of Data** consists of four chapters. **Chapter 6: Secondary Data Sources** focuses exclusively on the sources of secondary data, especially in India. **Chapter 7: Data Collection: Survey and Observation** explains various survey and observation techniques. **Chapter 8: Experimentation** deals with the validity issue, the process of conducting experiments and the classification of experimental designs. **Chapter 9: Fieldwork and Data Preparation** describes the process of gathering data through field work as well as editing, coding, and preparation of the data matrix for statistical analysis.

Part IV: Descriptive Statistics and Data Analysis consists of 11 chapters. **Chapter 10: Descriptive Statistics: Measures of Central Tendency** gives insight into the central tendency of data. **Chapter 11: Descriptive Statistics: Measures of Dispersion** focuses on the various measures of dispersion. **Chapter 12: Statistical Inference: Hypothesis Testing for Single Populations** introduces readers to the hypothesis testing procedure for single populations. **Chapter 13: Statistical Inference: Hypothesis Testing for Two Populations** discusses the hypothesis testing procedure for two populations. **Chapter 14: Analysis of Variance and Experimental Designs** deals with the analysis of variance and designs of experiments. **Chapter 15: Hypothesis Testing for Categorical Data** discusses the chi-square test and its applications. **Chapter 16: Correlation and Simple Regression Analysis** discusses the applications of bivariate correlation and regression. Chapters 17, 18 and 19 focus on the widely used multivariate statistical techniques in the field of marketing research. **Chapter 17: Multivariate Analysis I: Multiple Regression Analysis** discusses multiple regression. **Chapter 18: Multivariate Analysis II: Discriminant Analysis and Conjoint analysis** focuses on discriminant analysis and conjoint analysis. **Chapter 19: Multivariate Analysis III: Factor Analysis, Cluster Analysis, Multidimensional Scaling and Correspondence Analysis** discusses advanced, interdependent multivariate techniques in marketing research such as factor analysis, cluster analysis, multidimensional scaling and correspondence analysis. **Chapter 20: Sales Forecasting** discusses the various techniques of sales forecasting.

Part V: Result Presentation comprises **Chapter 21: Presentation of Result: Report Writing**. This chapter explains the systematic method to present the results of a marketing research project.

Part VI: Applications of Marketing Research includes the final chapter, **Chapter 22: Marketing Mix Research: Product, Price, Place and Promotion Research**. This chapter focuses on the role played by marketing research in making critical decisions regarding the different elements of the marketing mix.

1.5 MARKETING RESEARCH: A DECISION MAKING TOOL IN THE HANDS OF MANAGEMENT

Decision making is always a crucial part of any organizational functioning.

Decision making is always the crucial part of any organizational functioning. Decision makers are expected to take the optimum decision in an uncertain environment. In this situation, they take the help of research to aid them in making decisions. Actually, marketing research either provides new information or aids information in the existing body of knowledge. In any way, marketing research generates information that helps a decision maker in making optimum decisions. In the field of marketing research, this valuable information is obtained using the following interrelated steps:

1. **Problem or opportunity identification**
2. **Diagnosing the problem or opportunity**
3. Executing marketing research to explore the solutions
4. Implement presented solutions
5. Evaluate the effectiveness of decision making

These five steps are systematically executed to make the required information available to the decision making authority in the organization. The following section focuses on a brief discussion of these five interrelated stages.

1.5.1 Problem or Opportunity Identification

Any delay in the problem identification and solution implementation; and the opportunity identification and encashment may become harmful to the organization.

The success of any organization depends on its ability to diagnose the problem and solve it immediately. Success also lies in identifying the opportunities and cashing them in the prescribed stipulated time. Any delay in the problem identification and solution implementation; and the opportunity identification and encashment may become harmful to the organization. Hence, timely action is always required.

For example, a company may face problems in supplying the products and services on time and as a result, the brand image would start diluting. This problem requires immediate focus on the management. Similarly, a biscuit manufacturing company may present a productline and diversify into bread and cake manufacturing, to cater to the disposable income in the hands of consumers. The company needs to seek reasonable scientific information before investing in diversification.

1.5.2 Diagnosing the Problem or Opportunity

Diagnosing involves exploring the situation to have a better insight about the situation.

Organizations present these problems or opportunity scenarios to the marketing researchers. Marketing researchers actually diagnose the problem or opportunity. Diagnosing involves exploring the situation to have a better insight about the situation. For example, in the case of a company facing problems in supplying the products and services on time, the marketing researcher can identify where the actual problem zone is located. It may lie in the company's distribution channel—the distributor's end, dealer's end, or the retailer's end, or there may be some other underlying reason for this problem. Similarly, in the second case related to opportunity identification, marketing research can provide the real insight of the productline or the range to be offered to the consumers.

1.5.3 Executing Marketing Research to Explore the Solution

After the identification and diagnosis of the problem, marketing researchers systematically conduct research to present a solution.

After identification and diagnosis of the problem, marketing researchers systematically conduct research to present a solution. A theoretical model is developed with the help of extensive literature survey. Hypotheses are formulated, sample size and sampling procedure are determined, data are collected through a well-designed questionnaire, statistical analysis is executed, and findings are noted.

1.5.4 Implement Presented Solution

Marketing researchers conduct research in consultation with the decision makers of the concerned organization. The findings are presented to the decision maker and he or she analyses these findings in the light of his or her decision range. Decision makers have also got some limitations in terms of their own constraints. A decision maker analyses all these constraints and then takes the appropriate decision in the light of the solutions presented by the marketing researcher.

Marketing researchers conduct research in consultation with the decision makers of the concerned organization.

1.5.5 Evaluate the Effectiveness of Decision Making

A decision can click or it can fail miserably. The decision maker takes the decision in an uncertain environment and its after-effects are examined later. After taking the decision, its effectiveness is examined. This is sometimes referred to as the evaluation research. Decisions may go right or wrong. The after-effects of any decision are systematically examined by the company's management. This examination is also very systematic and explores all dimensions of affectivity in terms of time, cost, and other resources. The best part of the decision is retained and the unsuccessful part is considered for further research. This is a continuous process, as the environmental and organizational circumstances are not constant and vary time to time. Hence, it is very important for the decision maker to continuously receive refined information to make an optimum decision.

After taking a decision, its effectiveness is examined. This is sometimes referred to as evaluation research.

1.6 USE OF SOFTWARE IN DATA PREPARATION AND ANALYSIS

1.6.1 Introduction to MS Excel

MS Excel (a part of the MS Office package), developed by Microsoft Corporation, is a very popular software program and is widely used in most offices, research centres, and academic institutions. Nowadays, managers are expected to use MS Excel on a day-to-day basis. Therefore, a working knowledge of its application is of paramount importance. MS Excel is a fine example of a spreadsheet program and is best suitable for the interactive manipulation of numerical data. To open MS Excel, either double click on the MS Excel icon on the desktop or select **Start ® Programs ® Microsoft Office ® Microsoft Office Excel 2010**. The Microsoft Excel window as shown in Figure 1.2 will appear on the screen.

Many of the techniques of data analysis can be performed on an MS Excel worksheet by using a tool called **Data Analysis**. To access the **Data Analysis** feature, click on the **File/ Options. Excel Options** dialogue box will appear on the screen (as in Figure 1.3).

The **Data Analysis** icon does not appear on this menu, so we need to add it. This can be done by using **Add-Ins** from the **Excel Options** dialogue box. In this dialog box, click on **Add-Ins** from the pull-down menu and select the check box for **Analysis ToolPak** and click on **Go** (as shown in Figure 1.3). **Add-Ins** dialogue box will appear on the screen (Figure 1.4). Check in **Analysis ToolPak** and Click on **OK. Data Analysis** will now be added to the options capability. This process will install the **Data Analysis** feature and this can be used as described in some coming chapters of the book.

FIGURE 1.2
Microsoft Excel window

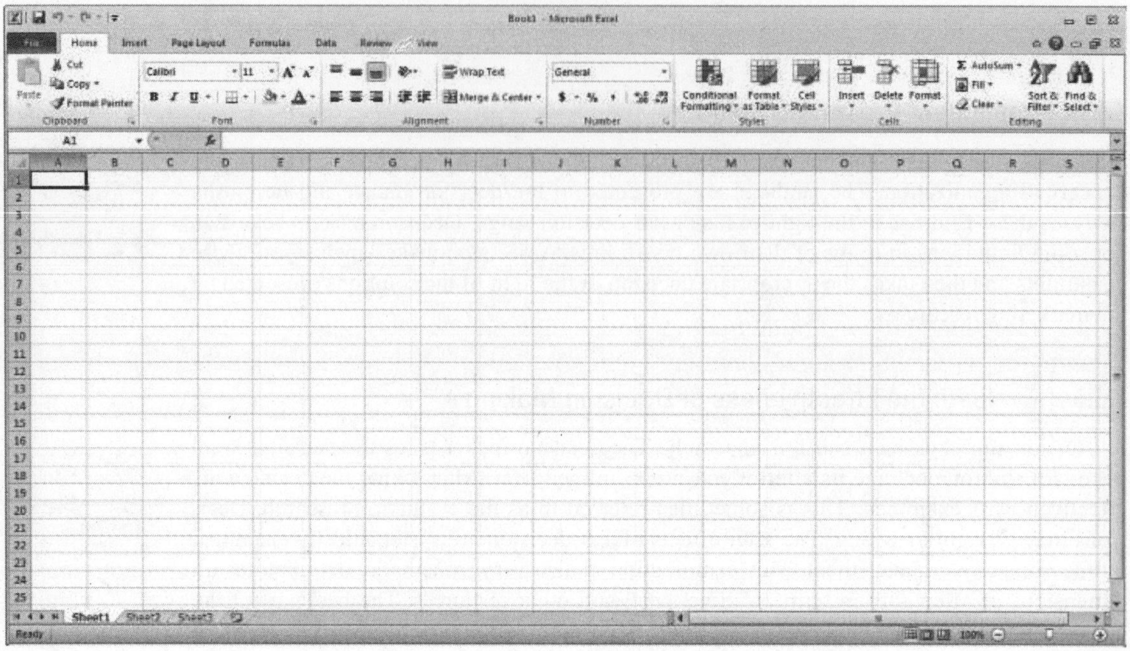

FIGURE 1.3
MS Excel worksheet with Excel Options feature

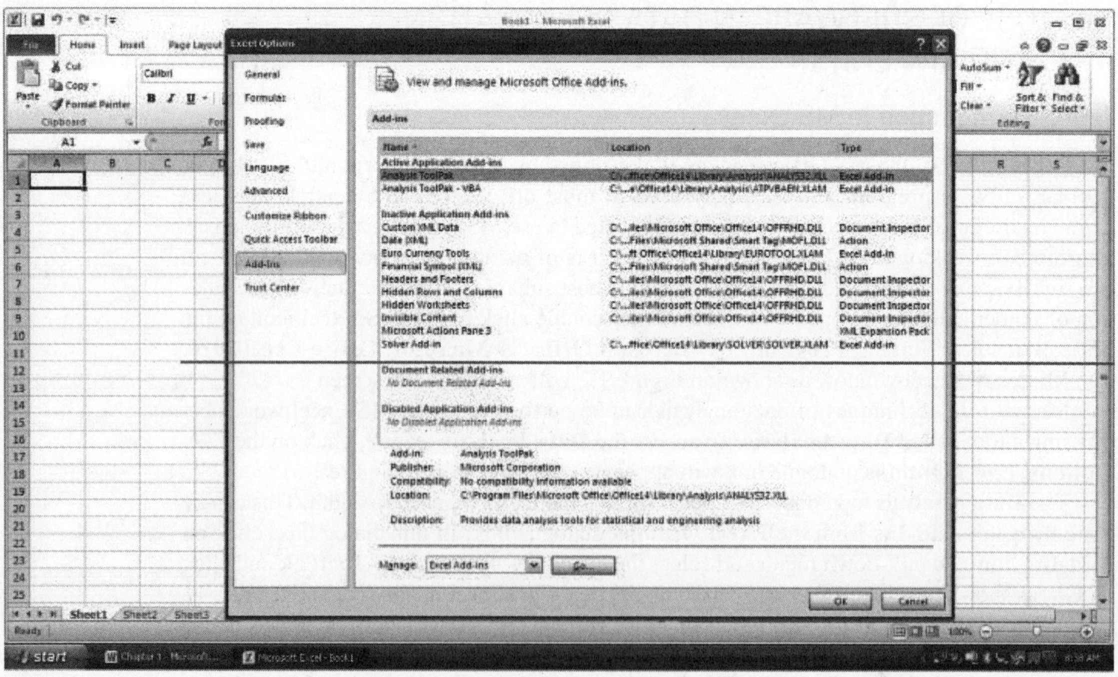

FIGURE 1.4
MS Excel Add-Ins dialog box

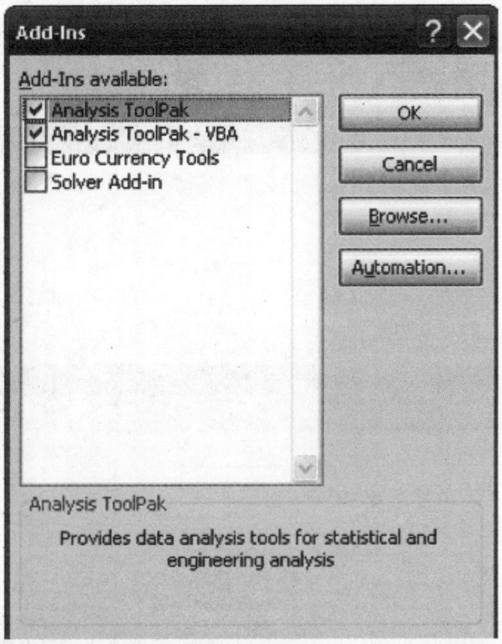

1.6.2 Introduction to Minitab®

To open Minitab, either double click the Minitab icon on the desktop or select **Start → Programs → Minitab → Minitab 16 Statistical software**. The Minitab session/worksheet window as shown in Figure 1.5 will appear on the screen. For entering data, maximize worksheet window as shown in Figure 1.6. Figure 1.6 also shows two column headings—Age and Designation (this can be obtained by typing Age and Designation in the respective columns). Data pertaining to age and designation can be entered manually. Minitab 16 offers an additional feature **Assistant** on top menu bar.

1.6.3 Introduction to SPSS

Norman H. Nie, C. Hadlai (Tex) Hull, and Dale H. Bent developed SPSS in 1968. SPSS is now widely used by colleges and universities all over the world. The success of this software can be understood in light of the company's mission: "Drive the widespread use of data in decision making."

To open SPSS, either double click on the SPSS icon on the desktop or select **Start → programs → IBM SPSS Statistics → IBM SPSS Statistics 21**. The **SPSS Data Editor** window as shown in Figure 1.7 will appear on the screen.

Numeric data can be entered in the **Data Editor** window. The **Data Editor** consists of two parts, **Data View** and **Variable View**. To define data, click on **Variable View** located at the bottom of the **Data Editor** window. The **Variable View** part of the **Data Editor** window is depicted in Figure 1.8.

Variables can be defined using the **Data Editor** (Variable View) window. For example, assume that one wants to define two variables—age and designation. In the first row of the first column, type Age and in the second row of the first column, type Designation (as shown in Figure 1.8). Click on **Data View**; the variables (age and designation) that we have entered

FIGURE 1.5
Minitab session/worksheet window

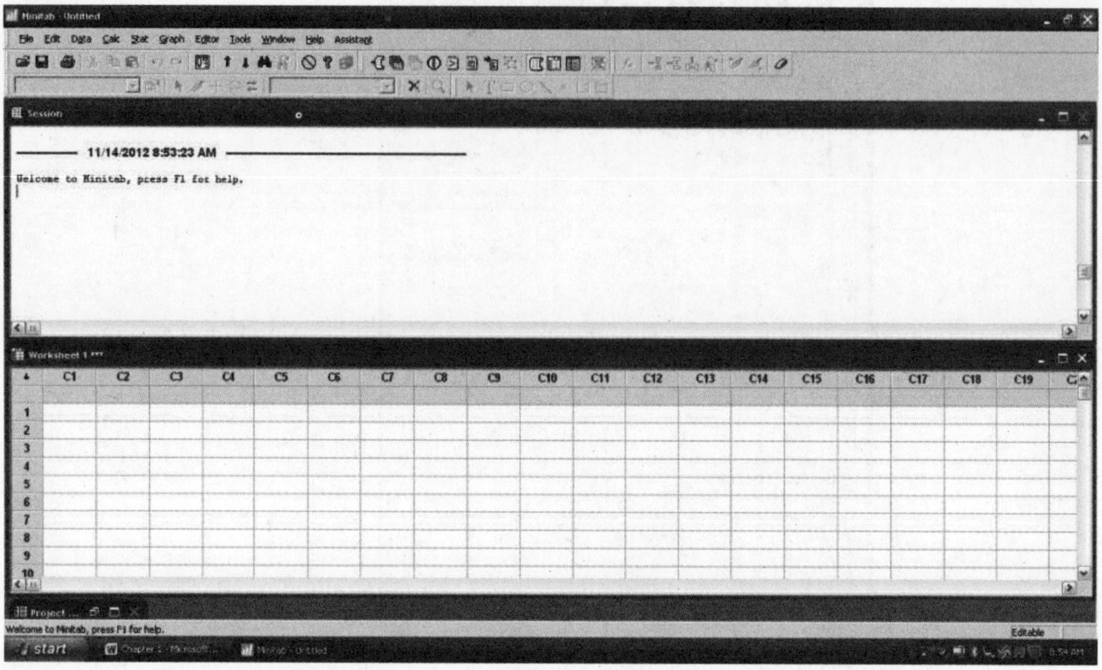

FIGURE 1.6
Minitab worksheet window (in maximized form)

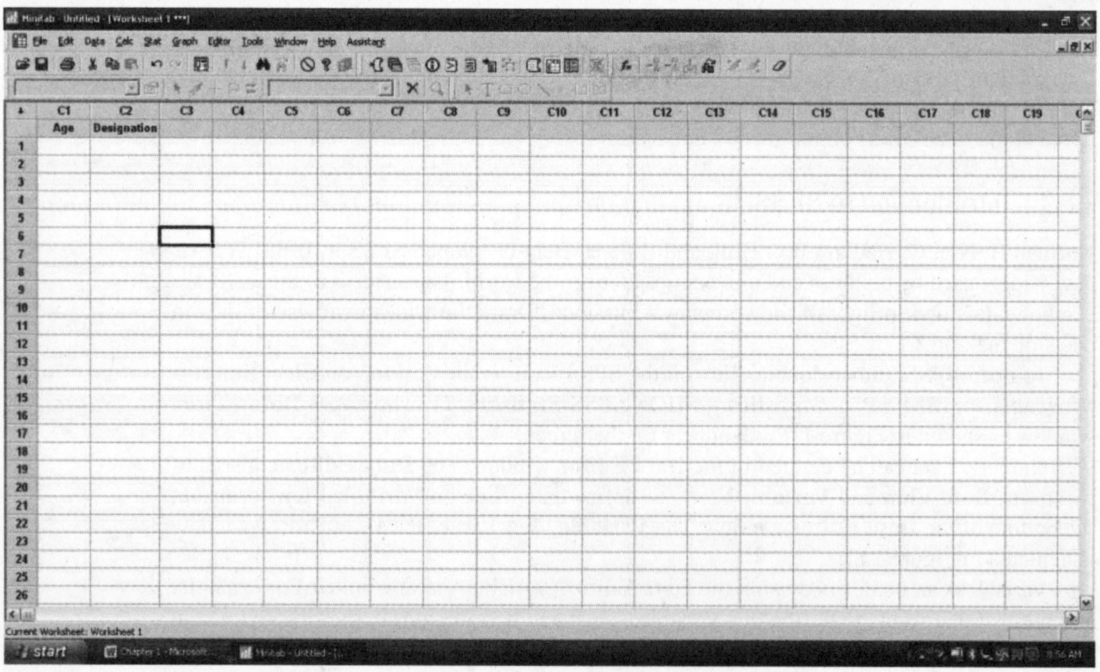

FIGURE 1.7
SPSS Data Editor window

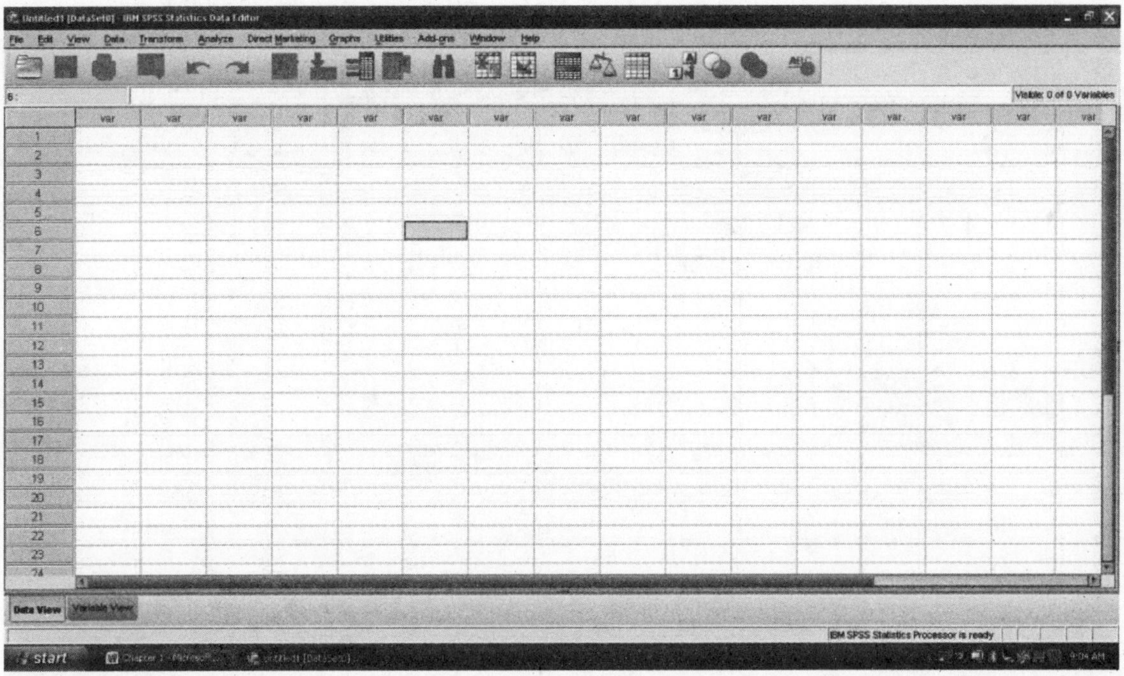

FIGURE 1.8
SPSS Data Editor window (Variable View)

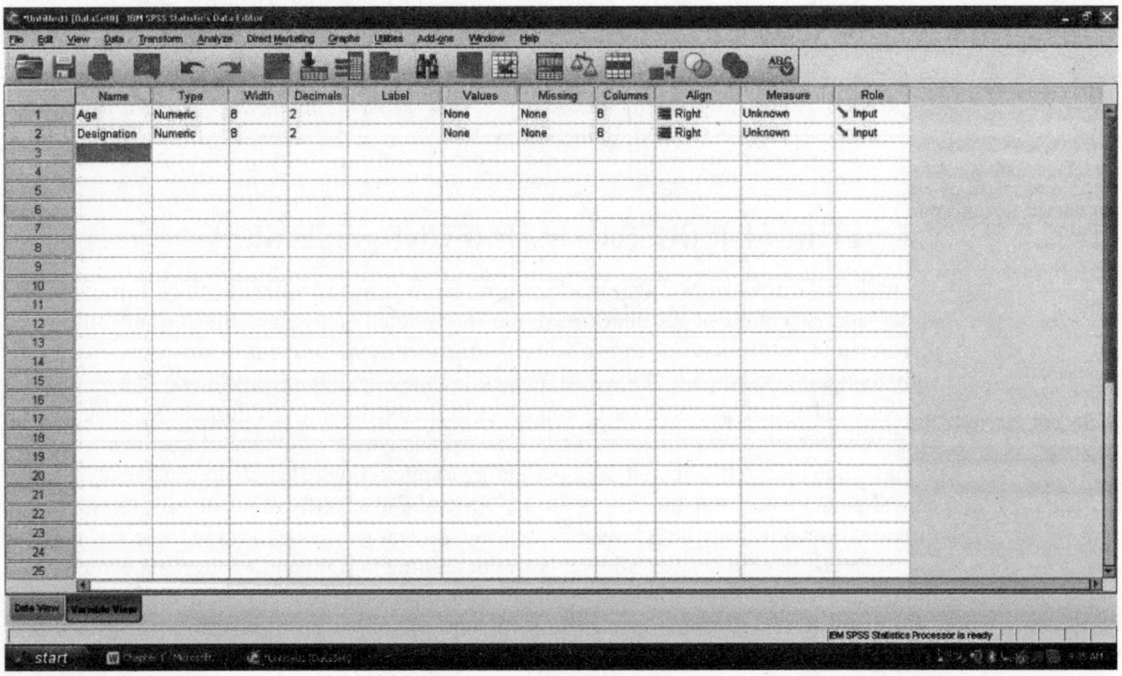

FIGURE 1.9
SPSS Data Editor window with Analyze features

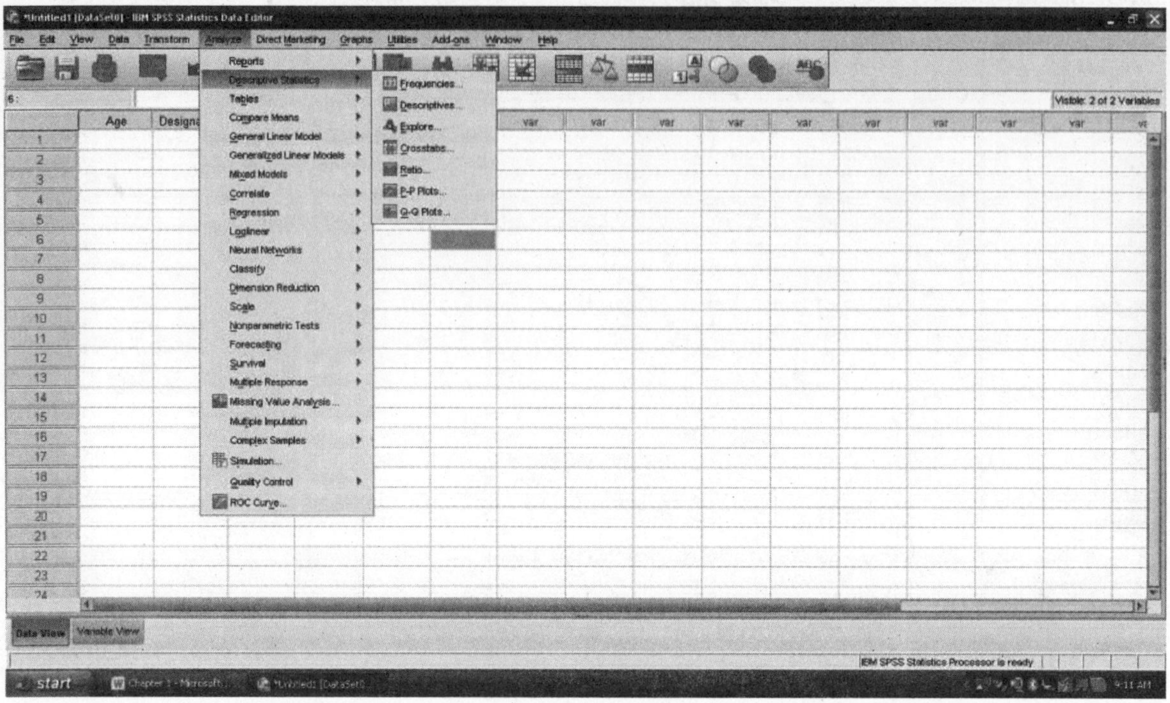

are now the headings for the first two columns. Statistical decision making is based on the analysis of data. SPSS provides a powerful platform for data analysis. The functions on the menu bar, **Data, Transform, Analyze, and Graph**, facilitate a variety of statistical operations. For example, from the menu bar select **Analyze** and note that it provides a wide range of data analysis tools as shown in the Figure 1.9.

1.7 ETHICAL ISSUES IN MARKETING RESEARCH

We will study in Chapter 2 that marketing research is not an isolated study. It requires the systematic execution of all interlinked and interrelated steps. It is the responsibility of a researcher to carry out research in a scientific manner as the findings of any research specifically marketing research will have an impact on many including consumers. The temptation to avoid a step that seems to be unimportant in the beginning can ultimately prove to be a costly mistake. It is very difficult to create an exhaustive list of ethical or unethical practices in marketing research. The literature pertaining to marketing research presents many general ethical guidelines. These guidelines are too general and specifications on how to proceed in different research scenarios are usually missing. A clear guideline to act in a specific marketing research scenario is not available. Issues pertaining to right and wrong can be interpreted in different ways and are also very general in nature. The researcher may also have to deal with many ethical considerations while carrying out research. Marketing research affects five major groups: (1) the researcher, (2) the respondents, (3) the client who requires the information, (4) the consumer and (5) the overall research community. A brief discussion on how marketing research affects these five sections is given below.

Researchers or their representatives sometimes get involved in data falsification practices. Marketing research or any research involves a lot of time. Sometimes, researchers feed false data themselves instead of collecting it from the respondents. They tend to apply this shortcut to wind up the research as early as possible without understanding the long-term implications of this unethical exercise. Cost is also a factor that compels researchers to adopt this unethical practice. The lack of awareness about the implications of this unethical practice may also be a factor that propels researchers into getting involved in this. Researchers need to be properly educated about how this kind of unethical behaviour hurts themselves as well as others. Unbiasedness is the key to conduct any kind of research. Researchers also have the tendency of replacing subjects while conducting their research. This happens when researchers find that getting responses from genuine respondents is relatively more difficult than obtaining it from friends and relatives. They replace respondents with a relatively more comfortable to handle group for their convenience. This ultimately affects the research findings as genuine respondents were not used during the data collection process.

Researchers sometimes also carry out an activity which is referred by them as "intellectual adjustment of data." This situation occurs when a researcher finds it difficult to cater to a pre-specified sample size. Collecting data is a marathon exercise and requires the involvement of many resources. For example, the simple research to determine the preference of consumers for a particular brand requires contacting representative respondents throughout the country as the consumers using the brand are spread throughout country. Suppose, 1,000 is the sample size decided by the researchers. In order to obtain an accurate representation, the researcher needs to select respondents from different town across the country. This mammoth exercise demotivates researchers as it is a very difficult task to execute. So, researchers sometimes tend to take the easy option of contacting only 200 respondents and then adjusting the pattern of responses for the remaining 800 respondents. In this manner, they contact only 20% of the respondents who need to be contacted and adjust the remaining "intellectually" on the basis of the trend noticed in the responses obtained from the 200 respondents. This pattern can be used for all types of data collection methods discussed in some later chapters. Researchers can carry out adjustments in data recording, data cleaning, data feeding and data analysis. Therefore, researchers can behave unethically in all the stages of performing market research. Therefore, it is very important that researchers act ethically to safeguard the interests of the many parties involved.

Respondents act unethically when they provide wrong, careless or ignorant answers. Because marketing research is an activity launched by a marketing research firm, respondents sometimes find it difficult to connect with the cause of the research. Researchers generally prepare long questionnaires for respondents to fill. They conveniently presume that the questions are clear to the respondents and they will be able to justify the answers provided. This presumption leads to the creation of a comfortable environment for the researcher and the researcher does not feel the need to provide an explanation for the difficult questions or provide motivation to researchers. This often leads to the creation of an indifferent attitude among respondents and leads them to provide careless or wrong answers. Respondents randomly pick answers instead of carefully picking the appropriate answers. Continuous insistence on the part of the researcher to fill the questionnaire forces respondents to fill it abruptly. The researcher can ultimately eliminate inconsistencies manually for extreme answers. However, complete random answers by respondent cannot be easily erased. Respondents also provide wrong or biased answers when questions in the questionnaire hurt their personal ego. For example, a question pertaining to the income of a respondent in India can be easily connected with the social status and prestige of the concerned respondent. In such a situation, the possibility is high that the respondent will provide a wrong answer. Sometimes, respondents provide incorrect answers to please the interviewer. An element of mutual trust exists in the relationship between the researcher and the respondent. The researcher must not hide the true purpose of conducting the research and the sponsorship of the research. In addition, the confidentiality of the responses must definitely be maintained. Ethically, the researcher must declare the purpose of the research and ensure that the answers provided are kept confidential.

Sometimes, the clients who use the research information also engage in unethical activity. They seek proposals from various marketing research firms to conduct research. The proposal is the blueprint for the proposed research. This contains necessary information such as the theoretical framework, sample, sampling frame, sampling techniques, questionnaire, proposed research methodology, etc. Some clients use the information provided in the proposal to plan and execute the research themselves or give it another marketing research firm without consulting the firm which has prepared the proposal. Clients also have the tendency of promising all the necessary information when the research begins. But during the research, they become involved with their routine work and tend to ignore the requirements of the marketing research firm. In some cases, clients show a reluctance to accept the findings if the results are not as per their expectations. This happens when clients are not professionals and engage a marketing research firm to satisfy their need for becoming a professional firm. The unethical practices discussed in this section must be curtailed by the clients in order to promote a conducive environment for research.

There are several ethical issues related to consumers too. Sometimes companies try to hide the negative aspects of their products or service discovered during marketing research. They try to mislead consumers as they have already invested a lot in conducting market research for the product. Consumers remain uninformed or less informed about the different characteristics of product or services. As discussed earlier, there is also the possibility of the researcher and the client arriving at a particular finding that suits them both. This mainly happens when a client tries to compare two or more brands including his own with the help of a hired marketing research firm. The consumer ends up becoming a victim because of the unethical association between the client and the marketing research firm. The onus is on the marketing research firm to overcome the influence of the client and check such unethical behaviour.

Marketing research has now emerged as a sought after profession. Important findings of market researchers occupy a place in literature. Any finding by a marketing research firm either substantiates the existing body of knowledge or challenges it by presenting a new theory or understanding. As the findings increasingly secure a place in the academic body of knowledge, a sound and scientific procedure for conducting the research is essential. Any lapse in the adoption of a well-defined procedure that is discussed in this book will ultimately affect everyone including academia. False findings will not only impact current marketing practices but also impact future researchers who rely on past findings and practices to launch their research. Researchers have to fight against the temptation to manipulate data. Research cannot be governed by strict laws and regulations. The researcher's freedom is an important factor in the market research process. Though scientific guidelines have been designed to practice market research, these can be easily boycotted by unethical researchers. Researchers have to take care to ensure that they adhere to ethical practices during the research process. Morality cannot be enforced by law; it is something that every researcher has to follow by instinct. These issues are discussed in detail across various chapters in this book.

REFERENCES |

Aaker, D. A., V. Kumar and G. S. Day (2000). *Marketing Research*, 7th ed., p. 70. John Wiley & Sons.

Luck, A. K. and C. B. Rubin (2008). *Marketing Research*, 7th ed., p. 1. New Delhi: PHI Learning Private Limited.

Parasuraman, A., D. Grewal and R. Krishnan (2004). *Marketing Research*, p. 9. Boston: Houghton Mifflin.

Tull, D. and D. Hawkins (1993). *Marketing Research: Measurement and Method*, 6th ed., p. 4. New York: Macmillan.

SUMMARY |

This chapter presents an introductory discussion about marketing research. Marketing researchers systematically collect, compile, analyse, and interpret data to provide quality information based on which the decision maker will be able to take a decision in an optimum manner. Conducting research to deal with any problem is a scientific, systematic, and interlinked exercise, which requires sound experience and knowledge. This chapter is an attempt to understand the nature and scope of marketing research methods. It introduces the discussion dimensions and is the first step in learning marketing research methods, systematically and objectively.

The purpose of both basic and applied research is to contribute to or develop a body of knowledge. Basic research is generally not related to a specific problem and its findings cannot be immediately applied. Applied research directly addresses the problem at hand. Applied research is launched by the firm, agency, or the individual facing the specific problem.

A marketing research method is a systematic and scientific procedure of data collection, compilation, analysis, interpretation, and implication pertaining to any marketing problem. This exercise is launched to provide objective and timely support to the decision maker of a business organization. In fact, marketing research methods are tools in the hands of a decision maker to make an optimum decision in an environment of uncertainty. The chapter also presents a **roadmap to learn marketing research methods** in a sequential and systematic manner. It also presents an introductory idea about the use of software in data preparation and data analysis.

KEY TERMS |

Applied research, 5
Basic research, 5
Marketing research, 5
Decision making, 6
Diagnosing problem or opportunity, 10
Problem or opportunity identification, 10
Roadmap to learn marketing research methods, 19

NOTES |

1. Prowess (V. 3.1): Centre for Monitoring Indian Economy Pvt. Ltd, Mumbai, accessed Aug. 2009, reproduced with permission.
2. http://timesofindia.indiatimes.com/NEWS/Business/India-Business/Air-India-asks-for-₹-2
3. http://www.hindu.com/2009/07/04/stories/2009070458690100.htm.

DISCUSSION QUESTIONS |

1. What is the difference between basic and applied research?
2. Define marketing research and explain its application in managerial decision making.
3. How can you study marketing research methods in a systematic manner? Explain your answer by presenting a roadmap to learn marketing research methods?

4. Marketing research methods are tools for decision making in the hands of a researcher. Justify the statement.
5. Explain the role and use of statistical software in managerial decision making.

CASE STUDY |

Case 1: *Wipro Limited: A Journey from a Vanaspati Product Manufacturer to an Information Technology Leader*

Introduction

Wipro Ltd was incorporated in 1945 as an oil factory. Later in the 1980s, Wipro entered the information technology sector as a flagship company of the Wipro Group, providing IT services, product engineering, technology infrastructure services, business process outsourcing, consultancy services, and solutions.[1] Wipro Infotech is a leading strategic IT partner for companies across India, the Middle East, and Asia-Pacific, offering integrated IT solutions. Wipro Infotech plans, deploys, sustains, and maintains IT life cycles through total outsourcing consulting services, business solutions, and professional services. Wipro Infotech drives the momentum in various organizations—no matter what domain these organizations are working in.

Culture in Wipro

The culture of Wipro is characterized by the "The Spirit of Wipro" concept. "The Spirit of Wipro" attempts to bring the Wipro culture back to the roots, with which the company started its journey. This concept is not only rooted in current reality, but also conveys what Wipro aspires to be, thus making it future active. Wipro uses three statements to best reflect "The Spirit of Wipro" culture. They are as follows:

Intensity to win: Make customer successful. Team, Innovate, Excel.

Act with sensitivity: Respect for individual. Thoughtful and Responsible.

Unyielding integrity. Delivering on commitments. Honesty and Fairness in action.[2]

Wipro really understands the responsibility of having a strong work culture in the organization. More specifically, Wipro's philosophy of building a strong culture is not limited only to its employees but caters to its clients as well. Wipro has developed an unstructured environment of working by encouraging initiation skills of employees. No doubt, the miraculous success of Wipro is an outcome of inculcation of this kind of unique culture. It is the determination of the employees that constantly drives them to do more. Table 1.01 exhibits profit after tax of Wipro, which itself is a self-explanatory phenomenon of Wipro's success story.

TABLE 1.01
Profit after tax (in million rupees) of Wipro Ltd from March 1999 to March 2008

Year	*Profit after tax (in million rupees)*
Mar-99	1038.5
Mar-00	2430.6
Mar-01	6574.2
Mar-02	8661.1
Mar-03	8132.3
Mar-04	9148.8
Mar-05	14,948.2
Mar-06	20,205
Mar-07	28,421
Mar-08	30,633

Source: Prowess (V. 3.1): Centre for Monitoring Indian Economy Pvt. Ltd, Mumbai.

Revisiting Strategy

To cater to the huge demand from the government of India, Wipro is reworking its strategic framework. Wipro's close competitors, TCS and Infosys, already have an eye on the Unique Identification (UID) Project and large government contracts.

Wipro is revisiting its strategy and game plan with regard to the government business. Highlighting this new strategy, Mr Suresh Vaswani, Joint Chief Officer of Wipro Ltd said, "Government business has been a thrust area for us… But we feel that our plans have been somewhat conservative. We expect the business to be big in this space, and so, the exercise is aimed at leveraging our full capacity in tapping the opportunity." When asked about the company's target regarding government business, Mr Vaswani did not reply directly but said that "reworking the plan would involve building capabilities and solutions proactively to address the market."[3]

Suppose you have joined Wipro as a marketing manager. You have been entrusted with the responsibility of developing a new market. The potential of the market is completely unknown to you. You do not have any data with you to forecast the market and your competitors are also planning to cater to this unexplored market. No doubt, you will have to launch a well-structured research programme to uncover the different layers of this market.

What will be your first step to launch this structured research programme?

As discussed earlier in this case, till date, no research programme has been launched in this market to cater to the potential of the market. In this scenario, how will you build a theoretical model as a basis for conducting this research programme?

NOTES |

1. Prowess (V. 3.1): Centre for Monitoring Indian Economy Pvt. Ltd, Mumbai.
2. http://www.wipro.in/Company/Culture/.
3. http://www.blonnet.com/2009/07/31/stories/2009073151360400.htm.

CHAPTER **2**

Marketing Research Process Design

LEARNING OBJECTIVES

Upon completion of this chapter, you will be able to:

- Understand the steps in conducting research
- Understand the types of research
- Learn the purposes and methods of conducting exploratory research
- Learn about descriptive research and the types of descriptive research
- Have a preliminary idea about causal research
- Establish a difference between exploratory research, descriptive research, and causal research

RESEARCH IN ACTION: LUPIN LTD

Lupin Ltd was established in 1983 and has a wide onshore and offshore presence with its products available in about 70 countries. In terms of overall revenue, the overseas business constitutes about 55%, whereas the remaining are from the domestic market. Lupin has retained a stronghold in India, growing ahead of the industry, and has achieved a formidable position in many segments leveraging its sound marketing prowess and a wide product basket.[1]

On the other side of its growth towards globalization, Lupin commenced forays into Japan, the second largest pharmaceutical market in the world. This has been facilitated through the acquisition of Kyowa Pharmaceuticals of Japan. This was in a series of small and meaningful acquisitions launched by Lupin Ltd in the past few years. In the national scenario, Lupin has graduated from the 10th position in the year 2006 to the 6th position in the Indian pharmaceutical sector, according to IMS ORG (MAT March 2008). This has been contributed by a combination of unique promotional strategies, judicious selection of products, and an extremely motivated team. Lupin is committed to expand and grow on the strength of

TABLE 2.1
Income and profit after tax (in million rupees) of Lupin Ltd from 1999 to 2009

Year	*Income (in million rupees)*	*Profit after tax (in million rupees)*
Mar-99	1108.2	109.3
Mar-00	742.8	94.9
Mar-01	8190.5	519.7
Mar-02	8801.3	721.8
Mar-03	10,128.7	730.7
Mar-04	12,332.8	950.9
Mar-05	12,310.4	822.9
Mar-06	17,335.5	1790
Mar-07	22,155.2	2979.8
Mar-08	28,072.8	4433.8
Mar-09	30,518.5	4169.7

Source: Prowess (V. 3.1), Centre for Monitoring Indian Economy Pvt. Ltd, Mumbai, accessed August 2009, reprinted with permission.

>>>

innovative products, addition of new therapies, and enhanced market reach.[2] The growth and prosperity of Lupin Ltd can be seen from its income and profit after tax (in million rupees) from 1999 to2009 as given in Table 2.1.

It has already been discussed that Lupin Ltd has adopted a policy of launching small and meaningful acquisitions to meet its global player ambition. Dr Desh Bandhu Gupta, Chairman of Lupin Ltd, clearly stated that "As we move closer to our goal of US$ 1 billion we are changing ourselves to set new milestones. We are accelerating our pace to strongly establish Lupin in five of the 10 pharmaceutical markets of the world. We are aiming at generating two third of our revenues from global market."[3] Suppose that Lupin Ltd wants to assess the positioning of its brands in the overseas market then what will be the source of getting some basic information to formulate clear guidelines for the research? How will the company launch exploratory research? What should be the research design? This chapter is an attempt to answer these questions. This chapter mainly focuses on the research design with specific emphasis on exploratory research, descriptive research, and causal research.

2.1 INTRODUCTION

The ability to take an informed decision is generated through a systematic study that is conducted through various interrelated stages.

Research is all about finding something, the absence of which may distort our ability to take informed decisions (Nwokah et al. 2009). The ability to take an informed decision is generated through a systematic study that is conducted through various interrelated stages. To design something, various parts are put together to complete the phenomenon. The same process is done to conduct a research. All the steps in a research are interrelated and no independent activity is launched without considering the decisions on the previous stages. One has to really understand that, from problem identification to presentation of findings, every step is interlinked and interrelated. For example, a research project title or objective is set as "Consumer motivation to purchase a refrigerator: A comparative study between two leading brands." The title of the research project itself introduces the dimensions of these interrelated steps. In the light of the title, a researcher has to first construct a theoretical model of consumer motivation. All other steps such as the questionnaire design, setting the research questions, and setting the hypotheses are related to the title and are interrelated—not independent. **Data analysis** plan is also related to the title. The title clearly suggests that the researcher has to apply z-test for two populations to compare the two population means. This can be further supplemented by other statistical techniques such as simple or multiple regression. The title clearly indicates that z-test for a single population, analysis of variance (ANOVA) techniques, and non-parametric tests cannot be applied. Similarly, if a researcher decides to take a sample size as 300 from both the populations then t test cannot be applied. In short, by framing the objective, a variety of interrelated decisions is also conceptualized. Hence, a researcher cannot separate the interlinked characteristics of the various decisions to be taken while executing any research programme. The following section deals with the marketing research process design to understand the interlinked nature of any research programme.

2.2 MARKETING RESEARCH PROCESS DESIGN

A research design is the detailed blueprint used to guide a research study towards its objective.

Figure 2.1 explains the process of conducting marketing research. A research design is the detailed blueprint used to guide a research study towards its objective (Aaker et al. 2000). In the introductory section, it has already been discussed that the steps in conducting a research programme are interlinked and interrelated. A good research is conducted using 10 steps; they are **problem or opportunity identification**, decision maker and marketing researcher meeting to discuss the problem and opportunity dimensions, defining the **management problem** and subsequently the **research problem**, formal research

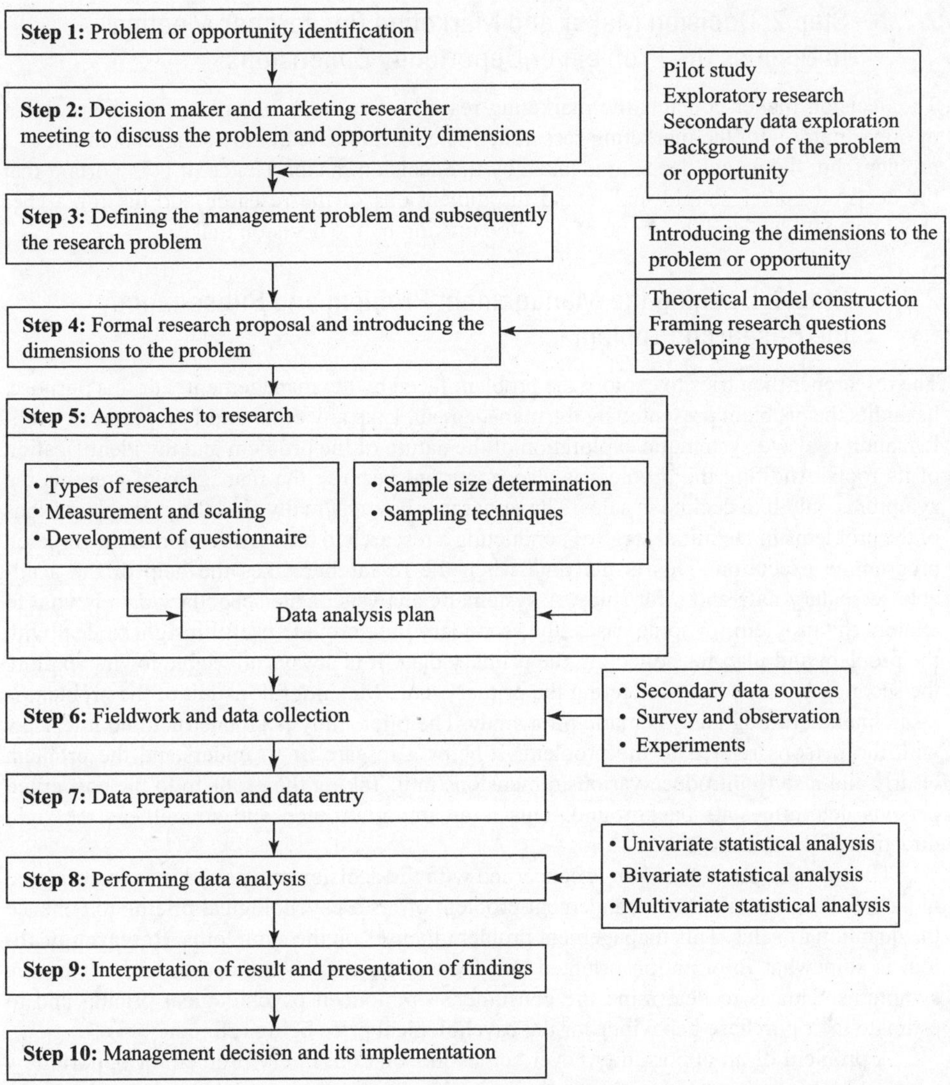

FIGURE 2.1
Marketing research process design

proposal and introducing the dimensions of the problem, **approaches to research**, fieldwork and data collection, data preparation and data entry, performing data analysis, interpretation of result and presentation of findings, and management decision and its implementation.

2.2.1 Step 1: Problem or Opportunity Identification

The process of marketing research starts with the **problem or opportunity identification**. Actually, the management of the company identifies the problem or opportunity in the organization or in the environment. The management can identify the symptoms or the effects of the problem, but to understand the reasons of the problems, a systematic research has to be adopted. This required research should either be executed by a marketing research firm or a marketing researcher.

The process of marketing research starts with the problem or opportunity identification.

2.2.2 Step 2: Decision Maker and Marketing Researcher Meeting to Discuss the Problem or Opportunity Dimensions

The researcher can only suggest solution to a problem, but the actual decision is taken by the decision maker.

The decision maker contacts the marketing research firm and then discusses the problem or opportunity with the marketing researcher. The researcher can only suggest solution to a problem, but the actual decision is taken by the decision maker. Hence, it is important that the decision maker should understand the dimensions of the research and the researcher should also understand the scope of decision making by the decision maker.

2.2.3 Step 3: Defining the Management Problem and Subsequently the Research Problem

The researcher then tries to explore the problem faced by the management. For this purpose, he audits the problem presented by the management. Like any other audit programme, problem audit is also a systematic exploration of the nature of the problem and the identification of its roots. Auditing the problem is also important because the management presents the symptoms only like decline in sales. The researcher has to actually find the probable reasons of the problems in the initial stage of conducting a research to have a direction of the research programme execution. This is the time when the researcher takes the help of the available secondary data and pilot study. A systematic analysis of the secondary data is vital to explore the problem. In some cases, the secondary data provide useful insight to deal with the problem and plan for collecting the primary data. It is always advisable to first explore the secondary data before collecting the primary data. Meaningful insight of the problem is also obtained through a systematic pilot study. The pilot study is an unstructured interview with the persons related to the problem. It helps a researcher to understand the problem clearly and also to introduce various dimensions in it. Taking the problem to the concerned persons determines its background. This is an important step and strengthens the right direction of the research.

The management problem is concerned with the decision maker and is action oriented in nature.

Research problem is somewhat information oriented and focuses mainly on the causes and not on the symptoms.

The **management problem** is concerned with the decision maker and is action oriented in nature. For example, the management problem offers a psychological pricing to enhance the quantum of sales. This management problem focuses on the symptoms. **Research problem** is somewhat information oriented and focuses mainly on the causes and not on the symptoms. This is to determine the consumer's opinion on psychological pricing and to estimate their purchase behaviour for the psychological price being offered.

A problem or an opportunity never comes in isolation. Every problem or opportunity, which a researcher wants to address, has a background. Without understanding the background of the problem or the opportunity, the researchers can neither propose a solution nor will he or she be able to propose suggestions to explore the opportunities available in the environment. There are many factors, such as the company's resources and constraints, legal environment and economic policies of the country in which the company is operating, social and cultural environment, changing technological environment, and so on, which have a decisive role in conducting the research. While framing the research strategies, the researcher has to keep all these and some other local, national, and international impactful surrounding factors in mind. Rather than just defining the problem and start working on it, he or she should have a clear knowledge about the factors that can ultimately influence the study. For example, any researcher conducting a consumer study in India must have the background knowledge of changing consumer aspirations in the post-liberalization era, different status of rural and urban consumers, increasing disposable income, increasing literacy rate, impact of heavy advertisement campaigns, multiple availability of product options, and so on. The consumer study cannot be launched in isolation; all these and many other factors may have a decisive impact on the study.

2.2.4 Step 4: Formal Research Proposal and Introducing the Dimensions to the Problem

Now, the researcher prepares a formal proposal of the research and develops the approaches to the research problem. The first part is to develop a theoretical model to quantify an attitude. For example, to estimate the "buying intentions" for a particular product, first, the researcher has to prepare a theoretical model to measure an attitude like buying intentions. The theory provides a list of decisive factors in buying a particular product. The researcher collects these factors from the literature and then proposes a model containing various factors that are combined to measure the buying intention. Suppose the researcher has decided to take five factors as the antecedents or determinants of the buying intention. These factors are brand image, brand awareness, price, availability, and after-sales services and are treated as the main variables. The researcher explores every factor from the literature in a systematic manner. For example, he has explored the first factor—brand image—and collected seven statements from the literature to characterize it. These seven statements are converted into seven questions and are placed as the first seven questions of the questionnaire. Similarly, to measure the other four factors, five, eight, six, and nine concerned statements have been collected and questions related to these statements are formulated and placed in the questionnaire. In this manner, the questionnaire consists of approximately 35 questions, where each question is designed to measure some phenomenon of interest to the researcher. These questions are now rated on a 1- to 7-point rating scale. Thus, a respondent can score a minimum of 35 and a maximum of 245 to exhibit his buying intention. In fact, this process is adopted to quantify the attitudinal feeling—buying intention—scientifically, which otherwise is difficult to measure. Hence, the theory plays a key role in conceptualizing a research phenomenon. Apart from these five main variables, few other variables such as age, gender, and income also have a determining impact on the buying intention of an individual. These are not the main variables but are referred as the moderating variables, which in combination with the main variables have a reasonable impact on the buying intention. Moderating variables are the second set of independent variables, which a researcher believes to have a significant contributory or contingent impact on the originally assumed cause–effect relationship between the dependent and independent variables. Figure 2.2 shows a theoretical model to measure the buying intentions. As a next step, in the light of the main variables and the moderating variables, the research hypotheses are constituted.

A marketing research problem can be formulated as a broad statement, and its inherent components are to be addressed by the researcher. He or she has to always keep in mind that

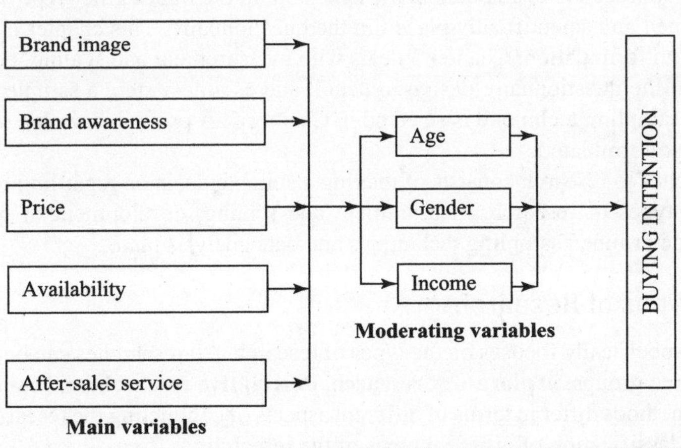

FIGURE 2.2
Theoretical model to measure the buying intention

the broad statement should not be too lengthy or too small. A lengthy statement will unnecessarily mislead the researcher and a shorter statement will not be able to address all the important issues of the research problem. In the previous example of determining the buying intention, brand image, brand awareness, price, availability, and after-sales services are considered as the determining factors. Thus, the main research question can be formulated simply as determining the buying intention for a particular product.

According to the researcher, the buying intention is a research phenomenon that is based on the five factors: brand image, brand awareness, price, availability, and after-sales services. The researcher assumes that after quantification of these independent variables, any enhancement in one of these variables will enhance the buying intention of the consumer. Thus, five hypotheses can be constructed as follows:

Hypothesis 1: "Brand image" has a significant liner impact on the buying intention.
Hypothesis 2: "Brand awareness" has a significant liner impact on the buying intention.
Hypothesis 3: "Price" has a significant liner impact on the buying intention.
Hypothesis 4: "Availability" has a significant liner impact on the buying intention.
Hypothesis 5: "After-sales services" has a significant liner impact on the buying intention.

Definitely, these hypotheses will be statistically tested through a simple regression model in which each of these will be considered as the independent variable and the buying intention will be considered as the dependent variable.

The researcher can also test the combined impact of these five variables on the buying intention. The proposed multiple regression model will be

$$\text{Buying intention} = b_0 + b_1(\text{Brand Image (BI)}) + b_2(\text{Brand Awareness (BA)}) + b_3(\text{price}) + b_4(\text{availability}) + b_5(\text{after-sales}).$$

The corresponding hypothesis may be constructed as follows:

Hypothesis 6: All the five factors in combination have a significant linear impact on the buying intention.

Similarly, three other hypotheses can be constituted to measure the significant impact of the moderating variables. It can be noted that all the nine hypotheses are concerned with the theoretical model proposed in Figure 2.2. Chapter 12 details the hypotheses setting and testing procedures.

2.2.5 Step 5: Approaches to Research

The research approach is formulated in the next step. In the light of the "type of data," questions are framed and scientifically placed in the questionnaire. This chapter is based on the research design formulation, Chapter 3 deals with measurement and scaling, Chapter 4 with the aspects of the questionnaire design in detail, and as a next step, a sample size is determined and a sampling technique is selected in Chapter 5. A preliminary plan related to data analysis is also formulated.

Approaches to research consists of making a suitable decision regarding research components like types of research, measurement and scaling, development of questionnaire, sample size-determined sampling techniques and data analysis plan.

2.2.5.1 Types of Research

All researches can be broadly classified into three groups: exploratory research, descriptive research, and causal research.

This section specifically focuses on the types of research. All researches can be broadly classified into three groups: **exploratory research**, **descriptive research**, and **causal research**. These three methods differ in terms of different aspects of conducting the research. Figure 2.3 exhibits the classification of different types of the research.

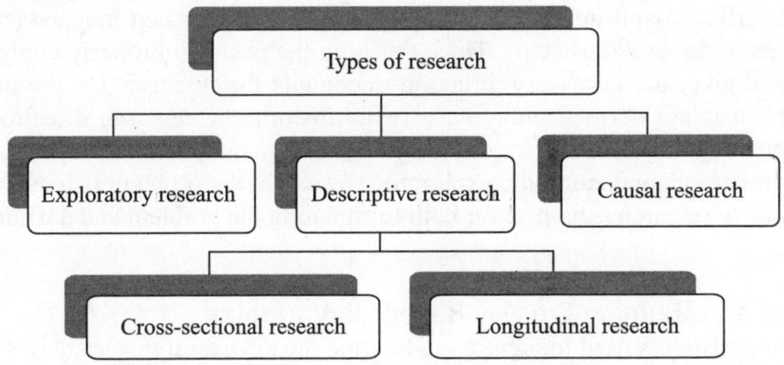

FIGURE 2.3
Classification of different types of research

Exploratory Research

As the name indicates, **exploratory research** is mainly used to explore the insight of the general research problem. It is also used to find out the relevant variables to frame the theoretical model. Decision alternatives are also explored by launching the exploratory research that is purely unstructured and provides an insight to the problem. While conducting a research, the researcher generally faces a problem of not knowing anything about the problem. In this situation, the exploratory research is used to explore the different dimensions of the problem, so that a better understanding of the research framework can be developed. The research procedure is unstructured, qualitative, and flexible and gives all freedom to a researcher to understand the problem. In some cases, the researcher talks to the concerned persons related to the proposed research and generates the required information.

As the name indicates, exploratory research is mainly used to explore the insight of the general research problem.

Findings of the exploratory research are generally not conclusive and require further exploratory or conclusive research. This is required because the exploratory research is unstructured and the sample used to obtain the information is small and mostly determined on the basis of the convenience of the researcher. This is used for the following purposes.

Obtaining Background Information

It has already been discussed that a decision maker presents the problem to a marketing researcher who is supposed to launch the research. Sometimes, it happens that the researcher has got no clues about the problem. In this situation, the researcher has to conduct an exploratory research to know the meaningful insight about the problem. Even if the researcher has the background information about the problem, he or she has to conduct the exploratory research to accumulate the current and relevant information. This could also be ignored for no reason because the nature and dimension of the problem change with time. For example, consider a company established in 1920 that has a rich experience of 90 years and strong brand goodwill. Since the last 50 years, a marketing research firm is associated with the company and has conducted many research programmes. In recent years, the top management of the company has realized that its brand goodwill is diluting and likes to take some corrective actions. It has contacted the marketing research firm to conduct a research and find out the reasons of dilution. Although this research firm has got an experience of 50 years in dealing with the company, it has to conduct an exploratory research to understand the recent and relevant circumstances. There is no rationale why a researcher will be missing the exploratory research.

Even if the researcher has the background information about the problem, he or she has to conduct the exploratory research to accumulate the current and relevant information. This could also be ignored for no reason as the nature and dimension of the problem change with time.

Research Problem Formulation or Defining it More Precisely

The exploratory research is helpful for both formulating the problem and defining it more precisely.

The exploratory research also helps in formulating a research problem. This is the most important aspect of conducting a research. It has already been discussed that the research steps are interlinked and interrelated and no step can be launched independently without considering the previous steps. Thus, defining the problem properly completes half the task, as it gives the necessary direction to conduct the research. On the other hand, if the problem is not defined properly, it really distorts the research direction and the researcher's energy. Hence, it is important to first define the problem properly. It may be possible that before conducting the exploratory research, the problem is loosely defined. The exploratory research is helpful for both formulating the problem and defining it more precisely.

Identifying and Defining the Key Research Variables

Exploratory research is used to identify and define the key research variables.

Exploratory research is used to identify and define the key research variables. In the buying intention example, five variables, such as brand image, brand awareness, price, availability, and after-sales services, have been identified by the researcher. The researcher has conducted an exploratory research and two more local variables, namely, "store employee behaviour" and "location of the store" have also been identified. Hence, the model is further refined and instead of five main variables, now, seven variables have been incorporated in the theoretical model. In addition, the exploratory research has identified "occupation" as another moderating variable—it has a determining impact on "buying intentions" and has been incorporated in the model. The refined model to measure the buying intentions is exhibited in Figure 2.4.

Developing Hypotheses

Exploratory research is also helpful in formulating the hypotheses.

Exploratory research is also helpful in formulating the hypotheses. For example, the theoretical buying intention model can be used to note the difference between the buying intentions for two similar products produced by two different companies. Hence, null hypothesis can be formulated as "there is no difference in the buying intention for the two products." An alternative hypothesis can also be formulated as "there is a significant difference in the buying intention for the two products." Similarly, other relevant hypotheses can be formulated. Chapter 12 specifically deals with the procedure of hypothesis testing.

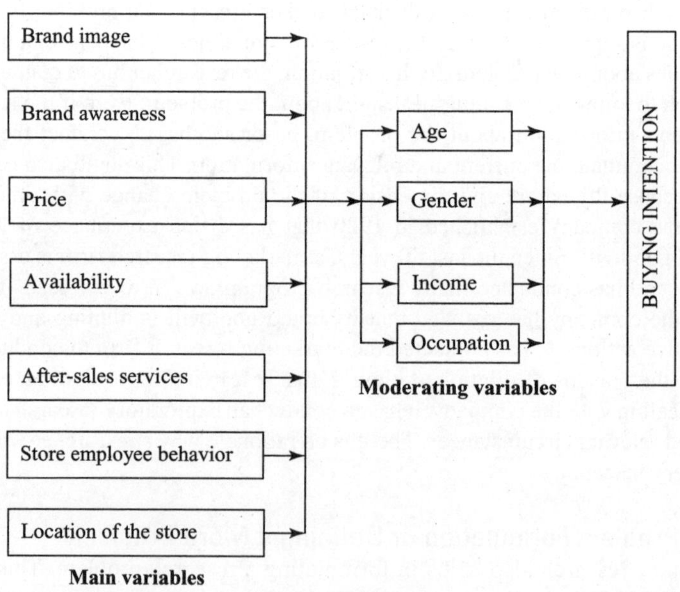

FIGURE 2.4
The refined theoretical model to measure the buying intentions (obtaining inputs from exploratory research)

Methods of Conducting Exploratory Research

The researchers use a variety of methods to conduct the exploratory research. These methods are **secondary data analysis, expert survey, focus group interviews**, depth interview, **case analysis**, and **projective techniques**. Figure 2.5 shows the methods of conducting exploratory research.

The researchers use a variety of methods to conduct the exploratory research. These methods are secondary data analysis, expert survey, focus group interviews, depth interview, case analysis, and projective techniques.

Secondary Data Analysis Secondary data already exist in the environment and are mainly collected for some other purposes. The researchers generally use the secondary data to understand the problem and explore the dimensions of the problem. The secondary data are not only used for problem understanding and exploration but are also used to develop an understanding about the research findings. In recent times, after the introduction of the computers, the Internet, and other computer-related facilities, accessibility to the secondary data has become convenient and easy. In most of the cases, use of the secondary data for the research purpose is time and cost efficient and it really provides an insight to the problem. Considering the importance of the secondary data analysis, Chapter 6 exclusively deals with this topic.

The secondary data are not only used for problem understanding and exploration but are also used to develop an understanding about the research findings.

Expert Survey To get the authentic information about the problem, the researchers sometimes consult the experts of the concerned field. These experts provide authentic and relevant information useful for the research, which otherwise is difficult to obtain. For example, an automobile company would like to penetrate in the rural market segment and would like to understand the requirements of the potential rural customers. Apart from the directly interviewing customers, information can also be obtained from the dealers and retailers who have been operating in this field since long time. Thus, with respect to their continuous interactions with the rural customers, dealers, and retailers, the company can well identify the aspirations and expectations of the rural segment. In addition, the dealers and retailers can provide that category of information, which will not be possible for the researcher to obtain through interviews, as the interviews will make the prospective customers conscious. Although some experts do not directly involve in the selling process, they can also provide substantial information. For example, in the automobile case, engineers, workers, production managers, and consultants can also provide important and categorical information.

To get the authentic information about the problem, the researchers sometimes consult the experts of the concerned field.

Focus Group Interviews Focus groups are widely used in the investigation of applied-research problems and are recognized as distinct research methods (Bender and Ewbank 1994). In a focus group, a small number of individuals are brought together in a room to sit and talk about some topic of interest to the focus group sponsor (Churchill and Iacobucci 2004). In fact, the focus group interview is a qualitative research technique in which a trained moderator leads a small group of participants to an unstructured discussion about the topic of interest. It generally involves 8 to 12 individuals who discuss a particular topic under the direction of a moderator, who promotes the interaction and guides the discussion on the topic of interest (Richter et al. 2007).

In fact, the focus group interview is a qualitative research technique in which a trained moderator leads a small group of participants to an unstructured discussion about the topic of interest.

In a focus group, the participants gather at a centralized location. There are usually 6 to 12 participants discussing a single topic in the presence of the moderator. The moderator

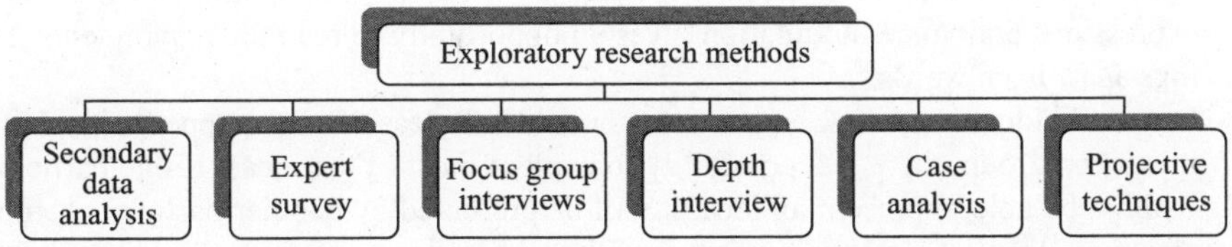

FIGURE 2.5
Methods of conducting exploratory research

introduces the discussion topic and encourages the participants to discuss the topic within the discussion range. In this mode of discussion, the participants are allowed to express their true emotional feelings, anxieties, frustrations, and opinions in a free discussion atmosphere. The focus group provides an opportunity for the researchers to probe the people's emotional reaction to issues that offer further understanding of the target individuals' reaction to the issues, thereby assisting in better understanding of the research finding (Zuckerman-Parker and Shank 2008).

The process of conducting a focus group interview starts with the identification of the problem by the firm. This is the stage when the firm has already identified and defined the problem and a qualitative research is required to explore the different dimensions of the problem. Framing the research objective is not sufficient, a researcher also has to frame the objective of the focus group interview. Although the pattern and discussion of the focus group are unstructured, it does not mean that there will not be any systematic pattern to conduct the focus group interviews. The researcher has to also prepare a questionnaire to have a structured way of obtaining the answers. The participant group involved in the focus group interview technique must have the knowledge about the topic of the discussion as the participants have to take the discussion forward. The participants should also have few similar characteristics, as a diverse group will not be able to generate the required information. It is also important to pre-establish the role of a moderator as he or she is the one who will be encouraging the discussion and will be trying to put the discussion on track. The moderator also intelligently places the discussion point during the discussion and tries to get the information desired by the researcher. Based on these guidelines, the researcher conducts the focus group interview and analyses the findings. As the process is exploratory and qualitative in nature, a careful interpretation is also required. The fact that the participants have an active role in the research process does not, of course, mean that everything can be left to the participants or that everything said should be taken at face value. The researchers need to analyse, conceptualize, and consider the validity of the interpretations made from the data (Heiskanen et al. 2008). He or she has to wind up the whole process of the focus group discussion within a stipulated time that varies from 1 to 3 hours.

The focus group is a popular technique of collecting information in the field of marketing research. The companies in Western countries frequently use focus groups to make the product or services better and desirable from the consumer point of view. The major advantage of the focus group interview is its ease of execution. In addition to being specific to the target group, it also presents an opportunity to analyse the outcome and is inexpensive in nature. The researcher can get the responses through the focus group interview, which is not possible in the structured survey, because it provides an opportunity to express the emotional feelings without any hesitation. The following section presents some of the advantages and disadvantages of the focus group interview technique.

Advantages and Disadvantages of Focus Group Interview Technique It has already been discussed that the focus group research is popular in the field of business and marketing research. The following are some advantages of the focus group research:

- The focus group provides an opportunity to note the natural reaction of the respondents, which is rare in a survey. In addition, a careful examination of their facial expressions and voice modulation gives an opportunity to read the respondents' feelings apart from words.
- In an individual interview, some of the thoughts or ideas can be dropped out, whereas in a focus group, there is a possibility to explore most of the ideas. If one participant will not be able to present an idea, it will be presented by another participant. In this manner, all the important dimensions of the problem are properly addressed.

- An unstructured discussion provides flexibility to the focus group interview technique. The moderator can lead the discussion to the desired direction.
- The presence of many participants really triggers the discussion. A careful selection of participants can lead to some fruitful information.
- The focus group has the biggest advantage in terms of spontaneous responses by the participants. The participants respond to a topic in a natural manner and flow of communication also follows a natural sequence.
- An experienced and effective moderator can control the discussion and generate the relevant information. The effective and required intervention by the moderator results in a channelized discussion in the focus group research.
- Interaction among the group members is an added advantage of the focus groups. Mutual exchange of thoughts stimulates every participant to express their views freely.
- The focus group can generate information fast. Its execution is also fast.

Although the focus group interview technique is popular in the field of business research and marketing research, it is not free from some limitations. The following are some limitations.

- The first drawback of the focus group interview technique is the scientific validity of the findings. The findings are exploratory and qualitative in nature and need to be strengthened by conducting further structured research. Moreover, the statistical validity of the procedure is also under serious doubt as the participant group is small and may not be a true representative of the population.
- The second limitation of the focus group research is the bias because of the moderator and the participants. As the direction and mode of the discussion are based on the moderator, providing a biased approach cannot be easily ruled out by the moderator. The participants who can talk and express well can also divert the real findings of the focus group. One or two individuals dominating in conversation can really distract the discussion. In addition, the analysis is subjective in nature; hence, the findings cannot be cross validated.
- The third drawback of the focus group research lies in its important outcome as findings. No doubt, the focus group presents important information but these are not conclusive. As a matter of drawback of the focus group research, some managers treat the information as conclusive without taking the pain of launching a conclusive research.

Depth Interviews A depth interview is a probing between a highly skilled interviewer and a respondent from the target population to unfold the underlying opinions, motivations, emotions, or feelings of an individual respondent, on a topic generally coined by the researcher. In addition to the focus group interview, the depth interview is also a widely used qualitative research technique for data collection. In the depth interview, one-on-one information is obtained from a member of the target population by a skilled interviewer. Similar to the focus group interview, unstructured and qualitative information is collected in a depth interview also. In the focus group research, the respondents can be influenced by peers and coping with this situation will be difficult for the moderator. In the depth group interview, through a one-on-one interaction process, an interviewer can explore the in-depth information, which is not possible through a focus group interview.

A depth interview is a probing between a highly skilled interviewer and a respondent from the target population to unfold the underlying opinions, motivations, emotions, or feelings of an individual respondent on a topic generally coined by the researcher.

The quality of information obtained through the depth interview is dependent on the skill and experience of the interviewer, hence, a skilled and qualified interviewer is the first pre-requisite of the depth interview technique. The depth interview can last for 30 minutes to 1 hour. As a first step, the interviewer asks some basic and initial information. After passing through this phase, the interviewer adopts an unstructured format of interview. Initial response of the respondent decides the direction of the remaining interview. This probing technique is unstructured because the spontaneous initial response by the respondent is the basis of framing the subsequent questions in the interview and because next question of the interviewer is based on the respondent's reply for the previous question. The sequence of the questions may be as follows: "do you like this product?", "what do you like in this product?", "why do you like this specific feature of the product?", and so on. Probing is used to uncover the deep rooted, deeply instilled hidden feelings of the participants.

Advantages and Disadvantages of Depth Interview It has already been discussed that the focus group research and depth interview are the two most common and widely applied qualitative research techniques in the field of business and marketing research. The following are some advantages of the depth interview technique:

- The depth interviews are especially advantageous when the research topic is sensitive or personal for a respondent. In this type of situation, the respondent always feels comfortable answering the questions from one interviewer rather than from a group.
- One-on-one interviews give greater flexibility to both the respondent and the interviewer. Much revealing and authentic information can be obtained from the depth interview.
- Personal interviews are easily scheduled when compared with the group interviews. Hence, the depth interviews can be arranged much conveniently compared with the focus group interviews.
- The depth interviews can handle some complex topics well, as it is personal in nature.

Like any other research technique, the depth interviews also have some limitations. The following are some limitations.

- Success of the depth interview is completely based on the skill of an interviewer. Searching a skilful and an experienced interviewer is not an easy task.
- Probing by the interviewer can sometimes put the respondent in an uncomfortable situation. The respondent may develop a feeling of being trapped in the situation and may become non-cooperative.
- Continuous interviewing sometimes generates monotony and boredom for the interviewer, which ultimately dilutes the quality of the gathered information.
- Like any other exploratory research technique, the analysis and interpretation of the data are difficult exercises. The reliability of the obtained data is also under serious doubt because there is lack of consistency in conducting the interview in terms of the approach adopted by the interviewer. The depth interviews also lack statistical validity.

A case study research method actually combines the record analysis and observation with individuals and group interviews.

Case Analysis A case study research method actually combines the record analysis and observations from individual and group interviews. The case studies become particularly useful when one needs to understand some particular problem or situation in great depth and when one can identify the cases rich in information (Noor 2008). In the case study research method, the researcher collects the information from various existing sources such as company brochures, sales data, newspaper and magazine articles, direct observation, and so on. This information is combined with the interview data obtained from the participants. Unconstrained by the rigid limits of questionnaires and models, it can lead to new and creative insights, development of new theory, and have high validity with practitioners—the ultimate users of the research (Voss et al. 2002).

When performing a **case analysis**, the researchers select multiple participants to have an opportunity to conduct a cross-case analysis. Mostly, multiple cases are used, but the importance of using a single case in some specific situations cannot be ruled out. The phenomenon is examined under natural settings and data are collected by multiple means.

The case studies are mainly used for the exploration, classification, and hypothesis development stage of the research process. The case study research methodology generally deals with some contemporary issues and is conducted to explore the "why" and the "how" of a research phenomenon.

The major advantage of the case research is its appropriateness to research, an area where few studies have been carried out. The case studies are being conducted to address a real problem; hence, it really provides a sound knowledge base to the existing body of knowledge. Weakness of the case study research includes difficulties in generalizing research result and the subjectivity of the data collection and analysis process (Darke et al. 1998). In addition, the case analysis is time consuming and requires expert interviewers.

Projective Techniques Projective technique is achieved by presenting the respondents with ambiguous verbal or visual stimulus materials, such as bubble cartoons, which they need to make sense of by drawing from their own experiences, thoughts, feelings, and imagination before they can offer a response (Catterall and Ibbotson 2000). The **projective technique** is used to generate the information when the researcher believes that the respondent will or cannot reveal the desired meaningful information by direct questioning. This is particularly useful when the respondent is unwilling to share his feelings because of the requirement of exhibiting socially desirable behaviour or any other reason. In this technique, a respondent is asked to explain the behaviour of another person in a given situation rather than to explain his or her own behaviour. In this process of explaining the behaviour of others, the respondents indirectly project their own behaviour in terms of their inner motivation, beliefs, attitudes, or feelings in a given situation. By explaining the behaviour of the other person in a given situation, the respondent actually describes his or her own behaviour when placed in a given situation. These are the feelings, emotions, attitudes, or opinions that the respondents will not like to share by answering a direct question. The various stimuli used in the projective techniques are intentionally vague and open to different interpretations, in the expectation that the participant will give meaning to the stimuli, which emerges from internal personality processes, and thus enable observation of these processes (Levin-Rozalis 2006).

The projective technique is used to generate the information when the researcher believes that the respondent will or cannot reveal the desired meaningful information by direct questioning.

In the field of marketing research, the projective techniques are broadly classified as **word association**, **completion task**, **construction task**, and **expressive task**. The following section presents a brief discussion of these four techniques.

Word Association Word association provides a technique that facilitates the study and shading of attitudes, which cannot be ordinarily uncovered through standard interview methods (Vicary 1948). In the word association technique, the respondents are required to respond to the presentation of an object by indicating the first word, image, or thought that comes in his or her mind as a response to that object. The researcher observes both the verbal and non-verbal response to the given object. The technique is based on the assumption that the first reflection to the stimuli is the natural and spontaneous reaction and is the inherent attitude, feeling, or emotion about the stimuli.

The word association technique is a special technique to obtain the consumer's response about a particular product or brand. For example, Sony colour television is tested on three words: quality, price, and availability. If the first response of the respondent is "quality" then the unprocessed and spontaneous response to the brand indicates that the quality of the brand is perceived well by the consumer. The word association techniques are also used to unfold brand personification or association of a brand or product with a person or personality type. In this technique, the respondents are presented with various pictures and words and asked to associate it with a particular brand or product. They are

In the word association technique, the respondents are required to respond to the presentation of an object by indicating the first word, image, or thought that comes in his or her mind as a response to that object.

also asked to explain the reasons of their association of the word or picture with a particular brand or product.

The major advantage of the word association technique is its ability to generate a response in a simple manner, more specifically, as fun for the respondents. Subjective interpretation is a major disadvantage of the projective technique. Interpretation of the result of the word association technique is a difficult exercise and has a problem in terms of the individual and subjective interpretation. As a matter of subjectivity in the word association technique, sometimes, the researchers focus on the interpretation of what is not said instead of what is said. The time taken by the respondent to respond to a particular stimulus is also a potential consideration in the interpretation of the feeling of the respondent about the stimuli.

In a completion task, the respondent is presented with an incomplete sentence, story, argument, or conversation and asked to complete it. In the field of marketing research, the two widely used completion task techniques are sentence-completion task and story-completion task.

Completion Task In a **completion task**, the respondent is presented with an incomplete sentence, story, argument, or conversation and asked to complete it. In the field of marketing research, the two widely used completion task techniques are sentence-completion task and story-completion task.

In the sentence-completion task, the respondent is presented with an incomplete sentence and asked to complete it. It is widely applied because this technique generates contextual and brand- or product-specific information. For example, to assess the respondent's feelings about LG air conditioners, the completion task may be, "I use LG air conditioner because it gives me ______________." This is just one example; many incomplete sentences can be constructed to elicit responses from different angles. Another example is, "People who use LG air conditioners are _________."

In the second technique, story completion, the respondents are given an incomplete story, presented the direction to understand the topic but the ending is not known. The respondent is required to complete the story in his own words. In the process of completing the story, the respondent reveals his own emotional feelings about the matter under discussion.

In the construction task technique, the respondent is provided with less initial structure as compared with the completion task where the respondent is provided with an initial structure, and then, he or she completes the task. In the field of marketing research, third-person questioning and bubble drawing (cartoon testing) are two commonly used construction techniques.

Construction Task Construction task is related to the completion task technique with a little difference. In the **construction task** technique, the respondent is provided with less initial structure as compared with the completion task where the respondent is provided with an initial structure, and then, he or she completes the task. In the field of marketing research, third-person questioning and bubble drawing (cartoon testing) are two commonly used construction techniques.

In the third-person questioning technique, the respondents are asked to present their opinion, emotion, attitude, or feeling about the other person in a given situation. He or she is asked to explain how a third person (neighbour or a friend) will act in a given situation. In this manner, he or she reveals his or her own feeling or opinion in the form of a third person without any hesitation because he or she can willingly express the thoughts as he or she does not feel any personal accountability. This technique has one serious limitation—the respondent can describe socially acceptable norm or behaviour instead of his or her own behaviour.

Bubble drawings are also referred as cartoon tests. The bubble drawing uses cartoon characters to exhibit a specific situation related to any problem. These cartoon characters are presented to the researcher in an ambiguous situation that is of interest. For example, in a two-cartoon character situation, one character is looking at the shelf of a departmental store and talking to the second character; indicating a particular product, "What is your opinion about that product?" While explaining the opinion of the second cartoon character, the respondent will actually explain his or her own behaviour. The limitation of this technique is also the same as that of the third-person questioning technique in terms of this technique's assumption that the respondent will describe his own opinion, attitude, or feeling when describing the opinion, attitude, or feeling of others.

Expressive Task In **expressive task** technique, the respondents are asked to role-play, act, or paint a specific (mostly desired by the researcher) concept or situation. In the role-playing technique, the participant is required to act someone else's behaviour in a particular setting. For example, a salesperson playing the role of a sales manager projects himself as a sales manager and behaves like a sales manager. A person playing the role of another person actually exhibits his own expectation for that particular person. This technique is also based on the assumption that the participant playing the role will actually project his or her own feeling when he will be in that role.

In expressive task technique, the respondents are asked to role-play, act, or paint a specific (mostly desired by the researcher) concept or situation. In the role-playing technique, the participant is required to act someone else's behaviour in a particular setting.

Advantages and Disadvantages of Projective Techniques The advantages of these techniques are typically hypothesized to be their ability to get around or under the conscious defences of the research participants and to allow the researchers to gain access to important psychological information of which the respondents are not consciously aware (Boddy 2005). In the consumer domain, the projective techniques are a means for the researchers to transcend communication barriers and illuminate the aspects of consumer experience that may be difficult to study (Steinman 2009). The biggest advantage of the projective technique is its ability to unfold the deep-rooted inner feelings of individuals in an indirect manner, which is not possible to be discovered in a direct manner. When a researcher addresses some personal issues of the individual, there is a high possibility that the individual will intentionally or unintentionally mislead or misinterpret the researcher.

Subjective interpretation of the result is the major disadvantage of any projective technique. Projective profiling techniques produce soft, opinionated data that are open to interpretation, and which has only random relevance to predict the customer behaviour (Yeager 2003). This technique requires highly skilled and experienced interviewers. In addition, sound background, knowledge, and experience of the interpreter are also a prerequisite for using the projective techniques. It is also possible that the participants of the projective technique may not be true representatives of the population.

Descriptive Research

As evident from the name, **descriptive research** is conducted to describe the business or market characteristics. The descriptive research mainly answers who, what, when, where, and how kind of questions. It attempts to address who should be surveyed, what, at what time (pre- and post-type of study), from where (household, shopping mall, market, and so on), and how this information should be obtained (method of data collection). However, descriptive designs are not capable of addressing any of the why questions associated with a given research problem (Hair et al. 2002).

As evident from the name, descriptive research is conducted to describe the business or market characteristics.

Descriptive researches are generally used in segmenting and targeting the market. They are mainly conducted to describe the characteristics of some relevant groups for the research, to understand the demographic and other characteristics of the population, to understand the consumer perception about any product or services, to understand the degree of association between marketing variable, and to make some forecasting about sales, production, or other phenomenon of interest. For example, a consumer durable company has conducted a descriptive research to understand the consumption pattern for its product. Descriptive research has revealed that 80% of the customers are government employees, 10% are businessmen, and the remaining 10% are scattered in different segments of society. The research has also revealed that 70% of the customers are men and 30% are women.

The descriptive research is conducted on the basis of some previous understanding of the research problem and does not completely explore the research phenomenon as in the case of the exploratory research. Unlike the exploratory research, specific hypotheses are formulated before conducting the descriptive research. Hence, this is structured and pre-planned in comparison with the exploratory research. The structural nature of this research provides it a clear direction of information collection. Hence, information obtained from this research is not loosely structured. In short, unlike the exploratory research, it involves a clear definition of the problem, formulation of specific hypotheses, and collection of structured, detailed, and relevant data. It can be further classified into **cross-sectional study** and **longitudinal study**.

Cross-Sectional Study

Cross-sectional research design involves the collection of information from a sample of a population at only one point of time.

Cross-sectional study is popular in the field of business and marketing research. **Cross-sectional** research design involves the collection of information from a sample of a population at only one point of time. In this study, various segments of the population are sampled so that the relationship among the variables may be investigated by cross tabulation (Zikmund 2007). Sample surveys are cross-sectional studies in which the samples happen to be a representative of the population. The cross-sectional study generally involves large samples from the population; hence, they are sometimes referred as "sample surveys."

Longitudinal Study

Longitudinal study involves survey of the same population over a period of time.

Longitudinal study involves survey of the same population over a period of time. There is a well-defined difference between a cross-sectional study and a longitudinal study. In a longitudinal study, the sample remains the same over a period of time. In a cross-sectional design, a representative sample taken from the population is studied at only one point of time. Addressing a question such as, "What is the effectiveness of an advertisement campaign for an air conditioner?" is an example of cross-sectional study. Whereas, "How have consumers changed their opinion about the performance of air conditioner as compared with that last summer?" is an example of longitudinal study. Longitudinal surveys usually combine both extensive (quantitative) and intensive (qualitative) approaches (Ruspini 1999).

In some cases, researchers use the term "panel" instead of longitudinal study. A panel is a sample of respondents who have agreed to provide responses over a specified time interval. Panels are also of two types: traditional panels and omnibus panels. In case of traditional panels, same questions are asked to the respondents on each panel measurement. For example, firms are interested in knowing the change in attitude, opinion, feeling, or emotion of the customers about a particular product over a specific time interval. In this case, brand switching studies are common. In the case of omnibus panels, different set of questions are asked to the respondents on each panel measurement. Hence, different set of information is obtained using omnibus panels. Use of panels is based on the objective of the research and the nature of the problem. Like traditional panels, the omnibus panels are also representatives of the target population and are demographically matched to some extent.

Both the cross-sectional and longitudinal studies have relative advantages and disadvantages. The longitudinal studies are mainly conducted to detect the change in the attitude, opinion, or feeling of the customers. Cross-sectional studies are not capable of detecting change. As discussed, longitudinal studies are conducted on panels. Panel members are generally compensated for their participation in research; hence, data collection is relatively easier in longitudinal study as compared with cross-sectional study. In addition, cross-sectional studies are based on the past-recall capacity of the respondents, which makes the collected data less accurate. In the longitudinal study, the same panel is used for the research, and thus there is no question of testing the past-recall capacity of the consumers. There are at least two major disadvantages of the longitudinal study.

The respondents may not be true representatives of the population (discussed in detail in Chapter 12). Refusal to participate will elicit the inclusion of new respondents in the research, which ultimately generates a response bias. Cross-sectional studies have got a relative superiority in these two aspects. In a cross-sectional design, data are collected only once from a population, and hence, there is no question of response bias. The cross-sectional studies are not designed to generate responses from the same group of respondents over a period of time, thus, there is no issue of non-cooperation by the respondents being studied previously.

Causal Research

Causal research is conducted to identify the cause-and-effect relationship between two or more marketing (or decision) variables. Many marketing decisions are based on the causal relationship between the variables of interest. For example, a cement manufacturing company is working on the assumption that the increase in advertisement expenditure is going to increase the sales of the company. Although this assumption seems to be true, a strict validation of the assumption by conducting a formal research is essentially required. "Concept of causality" is discussed in detail in Chapter 8.

Causal research is conducted to identify the cause-and-effect relationship between two or more marketing (or decision) variables.

As discussed, the descriptive research is able to answer who, what, when, where, and how kind of questions but not the "why" part of the question. The causal research is designed to address the why part of the question. Unlike the exploratory research but similar to the descriptive research, causal research is a well-structured research design. In this design, the independent variables are manipulated in a controlled environment to identify the causal relationship between two or more variables. It discovers the functional relationship between the causal factors and its predicted impact on the dependent variable under the research investigation. Table 2.2 exhibits a comparison of exploratory research, descriptive research, and causal research.

2.2.6 Step 6: Fieldwork and Data Collection

As a next step, fieldwork and data collection activities are planned. An analysis of secondary data sources is also executed to have supporting ideas. It is used in the various stages

TABLE 2.2
A relative comparison of exploratory research, descriptive research, and conclusive research

Comparison parameters	*Exploratory research*	*Descriptive research*	*Conclusive research*
Research objective	Is conducted to understand problem background, identify variables, and develop an understanding about the problem and situation	Is conducted to describe the business or market characteristics	Is designed to understand the cause-and-effect relationship between variables
Problem	Clarifying problem and its component	Problem is clearly defined	Problem is clearly defined
Structure	Unstructured	Structured	Structured
Method	Secondary data analysis, expert survey, focus group interviews, case analysis, and projective techniques	Survey and observation	Experiments
Research findings	Inconclusive	Conclusive	Conclusive

of the research execution. These are also useful in presenting the findings. Chapter 6 is exclusively based on secondary data sources. The researcher has to also decide whether he or she has to go for a survey or has to adopt the observation methods and decide whether the research will be based on the field data collection or it will be a laboratory experiment. Chapter 7 is based on survey and observation techniques, Chapter 8 introduces the various dimensions of experimentation, and Chapter 9 focuses on fieldwork and data preparation process.

2.2.7 Step 7: Data Preparation and Data Entry

There is a specific scientific procedure to deal with the missing data and other problems related to the data-collection process.

After fieldwork, the collected data are in raw format. Before performing data analysis, it is important for a researcher to structure the data. There is a specific scientific procedure to deal with the missing data and other problems related to the data collection process. Chapter 9 details all these aspects of data preparation. After preparing the data, a researcher has to feed it into a computer spreadsheet in a pre-determined manner to execute the data analysis exercise. Preparing this data matrix through the spreadsheet is also a scientific exercise and requires a lot of expertise and experience. In addition to the data preparation exercise, Chapter 9 also explains the process of data entry.

2.2.8 Step 8: Data Analysis

After feeding the data in the spreadsheet, data analysis is launched.

After feeding the data in the spreadsheet, **data analysis** is launched. Chapters 10 to 19 present various sophisticated statistical analytical techniques to execute the data analysis exercise. These include univariate statistical analysis, bivariate statistical analysis, and multivariate statistical analysis. Chapter 10 gives insight into the central tendency of data. Chapter 11 focuses on the various measures of dispersion. Chapter 12 introduces readers to the hypothesis testing procedure for single populations. Chapter 13 discusses the hypothesis testing procedure for two populations. Chapter 14 deals with the analysis of variance and designs of experiments. Chapter 15 discusses the chi-square test and its applications. Chapter 16 discusses the applications of bivariate correlation and regression. Chapter 17 discusses multiple regression. Chapter 18 focuses on discriminant analysis and conjoint analysis. Chapter 19 discusses factor analysis, cluster analysis, multidimensional scaling and correspondence analysis.

2.2.9 Step 9: Interpretation of Result and Presentation of Findings

There is need to interpret the result and present the non-statistical findings derived from the statistical result.

It has been already discussed that after applying data analysis techniques, a statistical result is obtained. There is need to interpret the result and present the non-statistical findings derived from the statistical result. A meaningful interpretation of the result is a skilful activity and is an important aspect of research. The researcher has to determine whether the result of the study is in line with the existing literature. It is also important to present the findings in a scientific manner. The results obtained from the analysis are statistical in nature. At the end, procedure and findings are systematically drafted and Chapter 21 discusses the method to systematically draft research work and results.

2.2.10 Step 10: Management Decision and Its Implementation

The decision maker analyses the findings and takes an appropriate decision in the light of the statistical findings presented by the researcher.

As the last step of conducting a research programme, the findings are conveyed to the decision maker after consultation with the research programmer. The decision maker analyses the findings and takes an appropriate decision in the light of the statistical findings presented by the researcher. This is not a formal part of the research process. Here, it is included as a step of the research process, because it is the decision maker who will ultimately take the decision and is the managerial implication of the research programme.

REFERENCES

Aaker, D. A., V., Kumar and G. S. Day (2000). *Marketing Research*, 7th ed., p 70. Wiley.

Bender, D. E. and D. Ewbank (1994). "The Focus Group as the Tool for Health Research: Issues in Design and Analysis", *Health Transition Review*, 4(1): 63–79.

Boddy, C. (2005). "Projective Techniques in Market Research: Valueless Subjectivity or Insightful Reality", *International Journal of Market Research*, 47(3): 239–54.

Catterall, M. and P. Ibbotson (2000). "Using Projective Techniques in Education Research", *British Educational Research Journal*, 26(2): 245–56.

Churchill Jr, G. A. and D. Iacobucci (2004). *Marketing Research: Methodological Foundation*, 8th ed., p. 98. Singapore: Thomson Asia Pte. Ltd.

Darke, P., G. Shanks and M. Broadbent (1998). "Successfully Completing Case Study Research: Combining Rigour, Relevance and Pragmatism", *Information Systems Journal*, 8: 273–89.

Hair, J. F., R. P. Bush and D. J. Ortinau (2002). *Marketing Research: Within a Changing Information Environment*, p. 41. Tata McGraw-Hill.

Heiskanen, E., K. Jarvela, A. Pulliainen, M. Saastamoinen and P. Timonen (2008). "Qualitative Research and Consumer Policy: Focus Group Discussions as a Forum of Consumer Participation", *The Qualitative Report*, 13(2): 152–72.

Levin-Rozalis, M. (2006). "Using Projective Techniques in the Evaluation of Groups for Children of Rehabilitating Drug Addicts", *Issues in Mental Health Nursing*, 27(5): 519–35.

Noor, K. B. M. (2008). "Case Study: A Strategic Research Methodology", *American Journal of Applied Sciences*, 5(11): 1602–4.

Nwokah, N. G., B. D. Kiabel and A. E. Briggs (2009). "Philosophical Foundations and Research Relevance: Issues for Marketing Information Research", *European Journal of Scientific Research*, 33(3): 429–37.

Richter, J. M., D. J. Bottenberg and K. A. Roberto (2007). "Focus Group: Implication for Programme Evaluation of the Mental Health Services", *The Journal of Behavioural Health Services and Research*, 18(2): 148–53.

Ruspini, E. (1999). "Longitudinal Research and the Analysis of Social Change", *Quality & Quantity*, 33: 219–27.

Steinman, R. B. (2009). "Projective Techniques in Consumer Research", *International Bulletin of Business Administration*, 10 (5): 37–45.

Vicary, J. M. (1948). "Word Association and Opinion Research: 'Advertising'—An Illustrative Example", *Public Opinion Quarterly*, 12(1): 81–98.

Voss, C., N. Tsikriktsis and M. Frohlich (2002). "Case Research in Operations Management", *International Journal of Operations and Production Management*, 22(2): 195–219.

Yeager, J. (2003). "Innovative Motivational Profiling: Comparing Marketing Projective Techniques versus Linguistic Forensic Techniques", *The Qualitative Report*, 8(1): 129–50.

Zikmund, W. G. (2007). *Business Research Methods*, 7th ed., p.187. South-Western Thomson Learning.

Zuckerman-Parker, M. and G. Shank (2008). "The Town Hall Focus Group: A New Format for Qualitative Research Methods", *The Qualitative Report*, 13(4): 630–5.

SUMMARY

The ability to take an informed decision is generated through a systematic study that is conducted through various interrelated stages. A research design is the detailed blueprint used to guide a research study towards its objective. A good research is conducted using the following 10 steps: problem or opportunity identification, decision maker and marketing researcher meeting to discuss the problem and opportunity dimensions, defining the management problem and subsequently the research problem, formal research proposal and introducing the dimensions to the problem, approaches to research, fieldwork and data collection, data preparation and data entry, performing data analysis, interpretation of result and presentation of findings, and management decision and its implementation.

Research may broadly be classified into three groups: exploratory research, descriptive research, and causal research. These three methods differ in terms of different aspects of conducting the research. As the name indicates, exploratory research is mainly used to explore the insight of the general research problem. It is used in obtaining background information, research problem formulation or defining it more precisely, identifying and defining key research variables, and developing hypotheses. The researchers use a variety of methods to conduct exploratory research. These methods are secondary data analysis, expert survey, focus group interviews, case analysis, and projective techniques.

The second type of research, descriptive research, is conducted to describe the business or market characteristics. Descriptive research can be further classified into cross-sectional study and longitudinal study. Cross-sectional research design involves collection of information from a sample of a population at only one point of time. Longitudinal study involves survey of the same population over a period of time. The third type of research, causal research, is conducted to identify the cause-and-effect relationship between two or more marketing (or decision) variables.

KEY TERMS |

Approaches to research, 25
Case analysis, 31
Causal research, 28
Completion task, 35
Construction task, 35
Cross-sectional study, 38
Data analysis, 24
Descriptive research, 28
Expert survey, 31
Exploratory research, 28
Expressive task, 35
Focus group interview, 31
Longitudinal study, 38
Management problem, 24
Problem or opportunity identification, 24
Projective techniques, 31
Research problem, 24
Secondary data analysis, 31
Word association, 35

NOTES |

1. http://www.lupinworld.com/about_index.htm, accessed on August 2009.
2. Prowess (V. 3.1): Centre for Monitoring Indian Economy Pvt. Ltd, Mumbai, accessed August 2009, reprinted with permission.
3. http://www.lupinworld.com/ceo.htm, accessed on August 2009.

DISCUSSION QUESTIONS |

1. What are the steps in marketing research process design?
2. What is the difference between a management problem and a research problem?
3. What are the different types of research?
4. For what purposes, exploratory research is used?
5. What are the uses of main variables and moderating variables in conducting a research?
6. What are the different methods in conducting an exploratory research?
7. What is a focus group interview? Explain the advantages and disadvantages of focus group interviews.
8. What is a depth interview? Explain the advantages and disadvantages of depth interviews.
9. What is the importance of case analysis in understanding and exploring a research problem?
10. What are projective techniques? Explain the different types of projective techniques. Explain the advantages and disadvantages of projective techniques.
11. What is descriptive research and when do researchers conduct it.
12. What is a cross-sectional study?
13. What is a longitudinal study?
14. What is cause–effect relationship in a causal research?

Case 2: *Castrol India Limited: A Journey from Market Growth to Market Saturation*

Introduction

As the story of any other sector in India, the lubricant industry has witnessed growth after 1992 when the lubricant market was deregulated. The lubricant industry in India was mainly dominated by three major public sector companies (Indian Oil Corporation Limited, Bharat Petroleum Corporation Limited, and Hindustan Petroleum Corporation Limited) capturing almost 90% of the market share. This scenario started changing by the year 2004, as the share of these public sectors started shrinking with the major part taken over by a private sector player, Castrol India Limited (CIL). Apart from these four major players, many multinationals have also entered the market to make the competition tougher. The Indian lubricant market, which was mainly driven by three public sector companies, is now operated by 40 players in the market.

There is no doubt that the lubricant industry is witnessing a phenomenal growth in the last few years. Table 2.01 lists the past and future demand for the lubricant industry.

TABLE 2.01
Past and future demand for lubricant industry in million metric tonnes

Year	*Demand (in million metric tonnes)*
2000–2001	1.05
2001–2002	1.14
2002–2003	1.25
2003–2004	1.29
2004–2005	1.33
2005–2006	1.37
2006–2007	1.42
2007–2008	1.47
2008–2009	1.52
2009–2010	1.58
2014–2015	1.92

Source: www.indiastat.com, accessed August 2009, reprinted with permission.

CIL: A Key Player of the Market

The lubricant industry in India is broadly divided into three major sectors: automotive, industrial and marine, and energy applications. The industry is led by four major players: Indian Oil Corporation Limited, Bharat Petroleum Corporation Limited, Hindustan Petroleum Corporation Limited, and CIL. These four companies constitute more than 70% of the total market share. There are several players including global majors operating in the balance 30% of the market, leading to an extremely competitive market. CIL is the subsidiary of Castrol Ltd, an UK-based British Petroleum (BP) group company. In 1979, Castrol amalgamated its business in India with Indrol Lubricants and Specialties Ltd. (A producer of automotive and industrial lubricants.) In 1982, this merged entity was converted into a public limited company. CIL acquired its present name in 1990. Over the years, the foreign parent expanded its stake from 40% in 1979 to 71% as on 30 September 2007.[1]

In the year 2000, Castrol was acquired by BP. It has become the leading brand within BP's lubricant business. Castrol was selected by BP because it was seen as one of the great lubricant brands in the world with a name that is synonymous with superbly engineered products of the highest quality. Its success can be witnessed by its vision and mission, "We will sustainably enhance the profitability of our customers by developing innovative products and services offers. As a result, we will become the manufacturing partner of choice within the Equipment Manufacturing and Industrial Maintenance market spaces."[2] Table 2.02 exhibits sales and profit after tax (in million Rupees) of CIL from Mar-98 to Mar-09.

TABLE 2.02
Sales and profit after tax (in million Rupees) of CIL

Year	*Sales (in million rupees)*	*Profit after tax (in million rupees)*
Mar-98	10,110.6	1581.7
Mar-99	10,894.3	1783.8
Mar-00	12,057.3	2043.8
Mar-01	12,786.6	1344.4
Mar-02	13,935.5	1163.3
Mar-03	13,598.2	1529.2
Mar-04	13,990.1	1373.8
Mar-05	15,651.4	1274.6
Mar-06	17,077.6	1468.1
Mar-07	20,916.8	1544.9
Mar-08	23,044.4	2184.3
Mar-09	26,000.8	2623.7

Source: Prowess (V. 3.1), Centre for Monitoring Indian Economy Pvt. Ltd, Mumbai.

Challenges Faced by CIL

As discussed earlier, Castrol witnessed a tremendous growth rate from 1991 to 1996. The market share of the public sector oil companies decreased from 90% in 1993 to more than 65% in 2004; CIL's market share has gone up from 6% to 20%.[3] After 1996, CIL focused on consolidation and efficiency rather than growth. As a measure of consolidation, CIL has initiated several initiatives such as computerization, total quality management, balanced scorecard performance management system, working capital management, and brand management.

The challenge faced by CIL is to succeed in an industry that has evolved and made the transition from the growth stage to the maturity stage. The period of rapid growth in demand accompanied by rapid expansion in revenues and profit is over. The growth in demand has slowed down because of the factors such as hike in oil prices, introduction of Euro II compliant vehicles, and problems in the agriculture sector. Competition has also increased. New competitors have entered the market—the MNC competitors—and new invigorated public sector units (PSUs) are fighting for market share.[4]

In a multiplayer environment, customers shifting from one brand to another are common. All the companies are coming up with unique offers not only to retain its customers but also to encroach in the customer base of other companies. Suppose CIL is also willing to examine "brand shift" from Castrol to other companies and from other companies to Castrol. What kind of research strategy will it be opting? What should be the steps of this research programme? Make a blue print of this research programme.

NOTES |

1. Prowess (V. 3.1), Centre for Monitoring Indian Economy Pvt. Ltd, Mumbai, accessed August 2009, reprinted with permission.
2. http://www.castrol.com/castrol/sectiongenericarticle.do?categoryId=8278011&contentID=...
3. www.indiastat.com, accessed August 2009, reprinted with permission.
4. Anupam Bawa. (2005): Case Analysis II. *Viklpa*, Vol. 3, No. 3, p. 141.

PART II

Research Design Formulation

CHAPTER 3

Measurement and Scaling

LEARNING OBJECTIVES

Upon completion of this chapter, you will be able to:

- Understand the scale of measurement and four levels of data measurement
- Understand the criteria for good measurement
- Learn about the various established measurement scales used in marketing research
- Understand the factors to be considered in selecting the appropriate measurement scales

RESEARCH IN ACTION: SIEMENS LTD

Siemens Ltd was founded by Werner Von Siemens in 1847 and was incorporated in India in 1957. In India, Siemens Ltd is operational in the field of electrical and electronics engineering. It operates in the business segments such as energy, healthcare, industry, information and communication, lighting, and transportation. In all the areas of its operation, Siemens Ltd provides a range of products and services. In the energy sector, it offers expertise in the areas from power plants to meters. It builds airports and produces contactors for the industry sector. In transportation, the company delivers complete high-speed trains right down to safety relays, and in lighting, it illuminates large stadiums and manufactures small light bulbs. In the healthcare sector, the company executes complete solutions for hospitals and makes hearing aids. In the communication segment, it provides a complete spectrum of products from large public networks to mobile phones. Some of the products manufactured/traded by the company are switchgears, electric motors, generators, control boards, X-ray equipment, electromedical equipment, measuring and control instruments, accessories, and so on.[1]

TABLE 3.1
Sales and profit after tax (in million rupees) of Siemens Ltd from 1995 to 2009

Year	*Sales*	*Profit after tax*
Mar-95	8839.5	351.2
Mar-96	10,597.6	372.4
Mar-98	17,534.8	–1556.3
Mar-99	10,258.2	–560.2
Mar-00	10,838	351.2
Mar-01	11,263.6	840
Mar-02	12,281.9	687.2
Mar-03	13,619.5	865.6
Mar-04	15,110	1393.8
Mar-05	19,155.5	1513.7
Mar-06	29,251.8	2547.5
Mar-07	47,947.1	3601.1
Mar-08	80,582.6	5965.4
Mar-09	86,100.7	5933.3

Source: Prowess (V. 3.1), Centre for Monitoring Indian Economy Pvt. Ltd, Mumbai, accessed August 2009, reprinted with permission.

>>>

Table 3.1 shows sales and profit after tax of Siemens Ltd from 1995 to 2009. The increasing sales figures show the success story of Siemens Ltd over the years. However, Siemens Ltd suffered from some negative growth in 1997–1998 and 1998–1999 (as shown in Table 3.1). The tottering of these two years was converted in sound footing in the later years, and profit after tax revenue of the company began to reach approximately 6000 million rupees in 2007–2008 and 2008–2009.

The projected demand of cellular phones in 2014–2015 is 149 million. This is 24 times higher than that in 2001–2002, when the demand was 6.15 million. Siemens is also a key player in producing cellular phones. As far as market share is concerned, Nokia, Motorola, Samsung, and Philips have 19.6%, 19.5%, 15.7%, and 15.5% of the total market, respectively. Siemens secures the fifth position by having 11.2% of the total market share.[2]

Suppose if Siemens is focusing to increase the size of the market for its product and wants to know one-to-one consumer preference of its product with the first four leading brands of the market, then what kind of rating scale is required to make this comparison? Should the company be using a ranking scale for obtaining its relative ranking? If the answer is yes to both the questions, then what is the way to construct a scientific scale? If the company has decided to launch a new product with some new features, then it has to go for a heavy advertisement before launching the product. The company now wants to measure the "impact of the advertisement." Should the company be using a single-item scale or a multi-item scale or a combination of both? If the company has decided to use a multi-item scale, then what type of scale will be an appropriate choice? What factors should be considered when making a decision regarding selection of a typical scaling technique. This chapter is an attempt to answer all such type of questions; deals with measurement and scaling techniques; and mainly focuses on scales of measurement, four levels of data measurement, various types of scales and their use, and factors to be considered in selecting an appropriate scale.

3.1 INTRODUCTION

In the field of marketing research, a researcher tries to gather information through administering questionnaire. In most of the cases, this information happens to be psychological in nature. For example, a researcher may be interested in knowing the consumer motivation for buying a product, their perception about the product, impact of the advertisement related to the advertisement campaign for that product, and so on. Most of this kind of information is based on the feelings of the consumers and their intended future behaviour. The marketer will always be willing to assess the following: Why a particular product is preferred over the other products? How a consumer evaluates a product with respect to the other leading brands available in the market? And what are his reasons of liking or disliking a particular product? To generate useful data, a researcher has to be careful in assessing what to be measured and how to be measured. In this regard, an expert approach is essentially required. This chapter focuses on the issues related to make an objective measurement and specifically deals with the various types of scaling techniques available in the field of marketing research. As a matter of first discussion, we will discuss a topic of what should be measured?

3.2 WHAT SHOULD BE MEASURED?

"What should be measured" is a complex task to be performed. Measurement objects can be tangible such as the number of people or consumers, or psychological such as attitude or perception measurement. In a nutshell, a researcher attempts to measure either physical or psychological properties of a phenomenon. The measurement of physical properties is not a complex deal, whereas the measurement of psychological properties requires a careful attention of a researcher. For example, consider a marketing researcher willing to address a research question "What motivates a consumer to buy a luxury car." In this case, a researcher has to focus on unfolding the underlying motives of a consumer. Therefore, a researcher has to broadly quantify the research focus on "consumer motivation" to address the above

The measurement of physical properties is not a complex deal, whereas measurement of psychological properties requires a careful attention of a researcher.

research question. What are the ways to get this job done? Is there a uniform way to measure the consumer motivation or does it has different dimensions in terms of measurement? Suppose that a researcher hired by a Company X decides to measure it as below:

Strongly motivated 5
Motivated 4
Neutral 3
Not motivated 2
Not strongly motivated 1

If a consumer has obtained Score 5, then we will say that the consumer is strongly motivated to purchase a new car. This is one way of measurement. Another way that can be adopted is to compare consumer ranks for a luxury car in the light of other brands of luxury cars available in the market. If the research shows third rank for Company X out of seven similar luxury brands, then this technique of measurement indicates Score 3 in terms of Rank 3 secured by the company. In another way of measurement, the researcher will simply ask a question that will you be purchasing a luxury car produced by Company X, say "Yes" or "No." Answers yes and no are coded as 1 and 2, respectively. In this case, the Company X has scored 1. Hence, we can see that the three measuring techniques have measured the phenomenon in three different ways. The quality of the research always depends on the fact that what measurement techniques are adopted by the researcher and how these fit in the prevailing research circumstances. Scientific research always demands "precision." Precise measurement in marketing research requires a careful conceptual definition, an operational definition, and a system of consistent rules for assigning scores and numbers (Zikmund 2007).

The quality of the research always depends on the fact that what measurement techniques are adopted by the researcher and how these fit in the prevailing research circumstances.

3.3 SCALES OF MEASUREMENT

Research is a continuous process. Thousands of researchers are collecting data every day for specific purposes. All the data collected for these purposes cannot be analysed in the same statistical way because the entities represented by the numbers are different. For this purpose, a researcher has to have proper knowledge in the levels of data measurement, represented by numbers that are to be analysed. For example, take two numbers, 2 and 4. These two numbers can be the weights of two particular commodities. Obtaining an average of these two numbers is always possible. However, if these two numbers are the class ranks of two individuals, then the average of these two numbers will have no statistical value. Hence, the same statistical procedure cannot be applied to analyse these two numbers. As a third case, if these two numbers are the serial order numbers of a commodity in a shop, then this is also different from the above two cases. In other words, numbers convey different meanings that are always case specific. Therefore, there is a need to understand the concept of scale of measurement to use an appropriate statistical tool and technique, based on different scales of measurement. The following are the four common data measurement levels used:

- Nominal scale
- Ordinal scale
- Interval scale
- Ratio scale

3.3.1 Nominal Scale

When data are labels or names used to identify the attribute of an element, the nominal scale is used.

If data are labels or names used to identify the attribute of an element, then the **nominal scale** is used. For example, assume that a marketing research company wants to conduct a survey in three towns of India: Bhopal, Nagpur, and Baroda. While compiling the data, the company assigns the Numeric Code "1" to Bhopal, "2" to Nagpur, and "3" to Baroda. In this case, 1, 2, and 3 are the labels used to identify the three different towns. Data show the numeric value, but the scale of measurement is nominal. In other words, we cannot say that the Numeric Code 1 indicates any ranking or any rating; this is only for the sake of convenience in identification. Employee identification numbers, contributory provident fund numbers, personal identification number, and so on are some examples of nominal data. Nominal level measurement is the lowest level of data measurement.

3.3.2 Ordinal Scale

In addition to nominal level data capacities, ordinal scale can be used to rank or order objects.

In addition to the nominal level data capacities, the **ordinal scale** can be used to rank or order objects. For example, a manufacturing company administers a questionnaire to 150 consumers to obtain the consumer perception for one of its products. Each consumer is asked to judge between three given options: excellent, good, or poor. Clearly, excellent is ranked the best and poor the worst, with good ranked between the two. If we want to assign numeric values to these three attributes, "1" can be used for excellent, "2" for good, and "3" for poor. In most cases, when we apply statistical tools and techniques, for the sake of interpretation convenience, rankings are set in reverse. In this case, "1" will be used for poor, "2" for good, and "3" for excellent. Therefore, the lowest number has the lowest ranking and the highest number the highest ranking. While using this kind of ordinal measurement, the company cannot say that the interval between Ranking Points 1 and 2 is equal to the interval between Ranking Points 2 and 3. It can be stated that 1 is superior followed by 2 and 3, or as in the second case, 1, the lowest number, has got the lowest ranking followed by the next two numbers, 2 and 3, as the ranking reference for good and excellent. The exact difference between these numeric values cannot be measured in any of these cases. The nominal and ordinal level data measurements are often used for imprecise measurements such as demographic questions, ranking of items under the study, and so on. This is why these data are termed as non-metric data and are referred as qualitative data.

3.3.3 Interval Scale

In interval level measurement, the difference between the two consecutive numbers is meaningful.

In the **interval level** measurement, the difference between the two consecutive numbers is meaningful. The interval data are always numeric. For example, three students of M.Sc. Statistics have scored 65, 75, and 85 in the subject **reliability** theory. These three students can be rated in terms of their performances. However, the difference in the numbers is also meaningful. The student who secured 85 marks is the highest-ranking performer, whereas the student who secured 65 is the lowest, with the student who secured 75 marks in the middle. In the interval level measurement, the meaningful difference between the two ranking points can be obtained. In the above example, we can also compute that between the highest and the lowest ranking points, the difference is 20 marks.

3.3.4 Ratio Scale

Ratio level measurements possess all the properties of interval data with meaningful ratio of two values.

Ratio level measurements possess all the properties of interval data with meaningful ratio of two values. The ratio scale must contain a zero value that indicates that nothing exists for the variable at zero point. For example, a company markets two toothbrushes priced ₹30 and ₹15, respectively. In the ratio scale, the difference between the two prices, that is, ₹30 – ₹15 = ₹15, can be calculated and is meaningful. With it, we can also say that the price of the first product, ₹30, is two times that of the second product. The interval and ratio level data are collected using some precise instruments. These data are called metric data and are sometimes referred as quantitative data.

3.4 FOUR LEVELS OF DATA MEASUREMENT

Nominal data have the most limited use in terms of the use of analytical and statistical tools and techniques. When compared with the nominal data, the ordinal data allows a researcher to use statistical tools and techniques with some additional features. The interval level data measurement has some additional properties over the nominal and ordinal level data. Researchers can make ratio comparison with the help of ratio level data, and with this data level, any statistical analysis can be performed that can be performed on nominal, ordinal, and interval level data. In terms of using the data level, statistical tools and techniques can be divided into two categories: parametric statistics and non-parametric statistics. Refer *Business Statistics* written by the same author for a detailed discussion of parametric and non-parametric statistics.

The nominal and ordinal level data can be analysed using non-parametric statistics, whereas the interval and ratio level data can be analysed using parametric statistics. In terms of usage, nominal, ordinal, interval, and ratio level data can be placed in an increasing order. Figure 3.1 depicts a comparison of the four levels of data.

In terms of measurement capacity, nominal, ordinal, interval, and ratio level data are placed in an ascending order. This means that the nominal data are the weakest and the ratio data are the strongest in terms of applicability in different statistical tests.

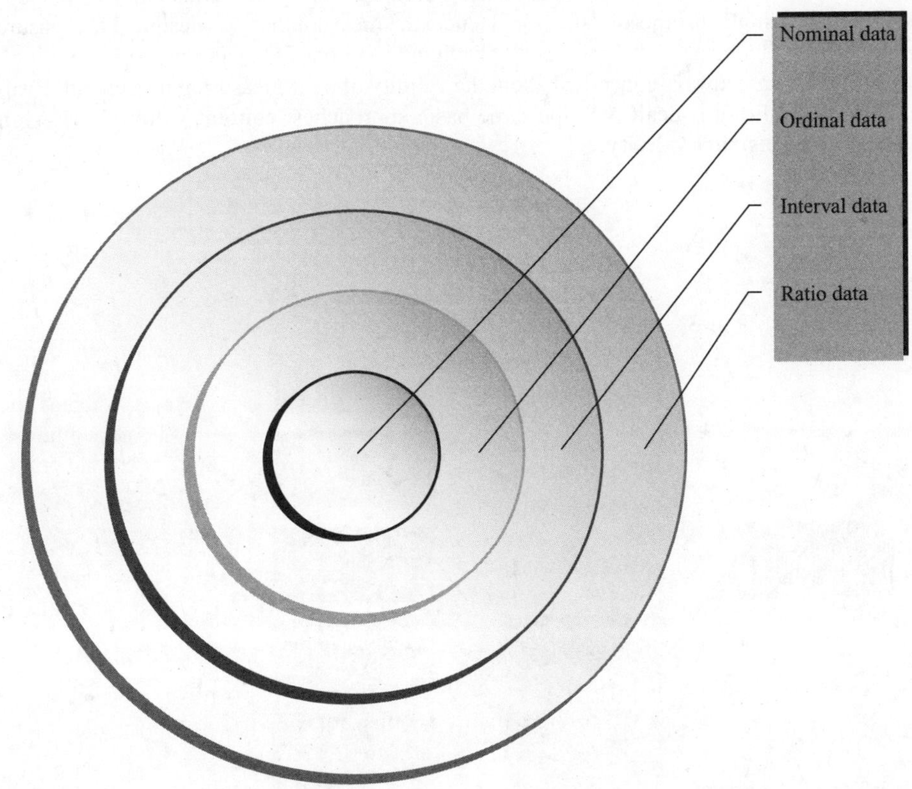

FIGURE 3.1
A comparison between the four levels of data measurement in terms of usage potential

Minitab and SPSS provide a solid platform to conduct non-parametric statistical tests. Run test, Mann-Whitney *U* test, Wilcoxon matched-paired signed rank test, Kruskal-Wallis test, Friedman test, and Spearman's rank correlation are some examples of the non-parametric tests, whereas *z*, *t*, and *F* are examples of some of the commonly used parametric tests. This book largely focuses on parametric tests except for Chapter 15 (χ^2 test is regarded as parametric by some statisticians and non-parametric by some statisticians).

3.5 THE CRITERIA FOR GOOD MEASUREMENT

For scale evaluation, three criteria are generally applied: **validity**, reliability, and **sensitivity**. Figure 3.2 shows the criteria for good measurement. The following section focuses on these three scale-evaluation criteria.

3.5.1 Validity

In fact, validity is the ability of an instrument to measure what is designed to measure.

An attitude measure has validity if it measures what it supposed to measure (Aaker et al. 2000). In fact, **validity** is the ability of an instrument to measure what is designed to measure. It sounds simple that a measure should measure what it is supposed to measure but has a great deal of difficulty in real life. For example, behaviour of employees to measure consumer satisfaction in a big shopping mall is a validity issue. It is always possible that the behaviour of employees is not a determinant of consumer satisfaction rather various other factors such as pricing policies, discount policy, parking facility, and others may be responsible for generating consumer satisfaction. Hence, the measure that was designed to measure consumer satisfaction from "employees' behaviour" may not be a valid measurement tool. The researchers are always concerned about the validity of their measuring instrument. Evaluation of the validity is dealt with the three basic approaches: **content validity**, **criterion validity**, and **construct validity**.

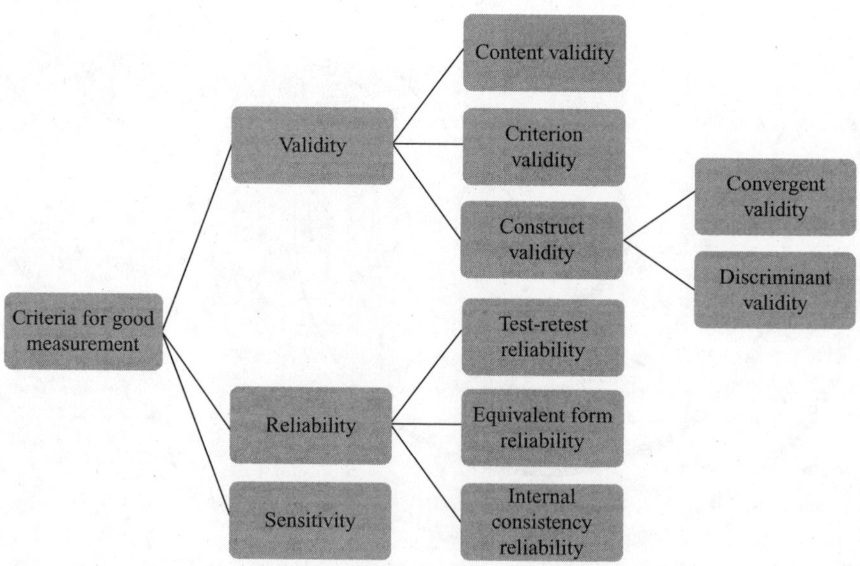

FIGURE 3.2
The criteria for good measurement

3.5.1.1 Content Validity

The **content validation** includes, but is not limited to, careful specification of constructs, review of scaling procedures by content validity judges, and consultation with experts and the members of the population (Vogt et al. 2004). Sometimes, the content validity is also referred as face validity. In fact, the content validity is a subjective evaluation of the scale for its ability to measure what it is supposed to measure. The researchers or the group of experts examine the content of the measuring instrument. When they find that the measuring instrument is able to provide adequate coverage of the concept, then it is said to have the face validity. Thus, a scale measures the same for which it is designed. A researcher first carefully defines the objective of the research and all the relevant dimensions to be used to address the objective of the research. This logical process is by, and largely based on, the logical discretion of a researcher, and for no doubt, it is subjective in nature. As the content validity is subjective in nature, it alone is not a sufficient evaluation criterion. The criterion validity provides a more formal structure to the evaluation process.

In fact, the content validity is a subjective evaluation of the scale for its ability to measure what it is supposed to measure.

3.5.1.2 Criterion Validity

The **criterion validity** is the ability of the variable to predict the key variables or criteria (Lehmann et al. 1998). It involves the determination of whether the scale is able to perform up to the expectation with respect to the other variables or criteria. Criterion variables may include demographic and psychographic characteristics, attitudinal and behavioural measures, or scales obtained from other scales (Malhotra 2004). For example, a researcher has developed a new measuring instrument to assess the consumer satisfaction based on "offering snack during shopping." Now a researcher will be willing to be sure that this new measurement is correlated with the other traditional measures of consumer satisfaction such as price, discount, after-sales services, and so on. In accordance with the time sequence, the criterion validity is classified as a concurrent validity and a predictive validity.

The criterion validity involves the determination of whether the scale is able to perform up to the expectation with respect to the other variables or criteria.

If the data collected from the scale to be evaluated and the data collected on the criterion variables are executed at the same time and are shown to be valid, then it has the concurrent validity. If the new measure is able to predict some future events, then the predictive validity is said to be established. For example, the consumer satisfaction measuring instrument is predictive valid if it is followed by sales in near future.

3.5.1.3 Construct Validity

The construct is the initial concept, notion, question, or hypothesis that determines which data are to be generated and how they are to be gathered.

The **construct validity** is the initial concept, notion, question, or hypothesis that determines which data are to be generated and how they are to be gathered (Golafshani 2003). To evaluate the construct validity, both the theory and the measuring instrument are considered. For example, if a researcher has developed a scale to measure "consumer preference" for a consumer electronics product, then to evaluate construct validity, the researcher will correlate the result obtained by this new measure with the existing well-known measure of the consumer satisfaction. To achieve the construct validity, the researcher must focus on **convergent validity** and **discriminant validity**. The convergent validity is established when the new measure correlates or converges with other similar measures. The literal meaning of correlation or convergence specifically indicates the degree to which the score on one measuring instrument (scale) is correlated with other measuring instrument (scale) developed to measure the same constructs. On the same grounds, the discriminant validity is established when a new measuring instrument has low correlation or non-convergence with the measures of dissimilar concept. The literal meaning of no correlation

A convergent validity is established when the new measure correlates or converges with the other similar measures.

A discriminant validity is established when a new measuring instrument has low correlation or non-convergence with the measures of dissimilar concept.

or non-convergence specifically indicates the degree to which the score on one measuring instrument (scale) is not correlated with the other measuring instrument (scale) developed to measure the different constructs.

To establish the construct validity, a researcher has to establish the convergent validity and discriminant validity. In our country, in the field of marketing research, even theory development is at the infancy stage, and that is why some times validating construct becomes very difficult. In the field of marketing research, there is a scarcity of well-developed measuring instruments that can be applied in all the relevant circumstances. Market researchers try to develop a specific measuring instrument for their own specific marketing objectives. The frequent need of "new" result in adaption of research to different contexts has consequences for validity issue (Brennan et al. 2009). Always searching for a different concept and result has made the availability of widely applicable theoretical models scarce and is really a concern to address the issue of the construct validity or more specifically validity in the field of marketing or business research.

3.5.2 Reliability

Reliability is the tendency of a respondent to respond in the same or in a similar manner to an identical or a near identical question (Burns and Bush 1999). The reliability of a measuring instrument is not directly adversely affected by the systematic errors as these affect the measurement in a systematic way. The reliability is mainly adversely affected by the inconsistent errors as these produce a low reliability in the measuring instruments. A measure is said to be **reliable** when it elicits the same response from the same person when the measuring instrument is administered to that person successively in similar or almost similar circumstances. Reliable measuring instruments provide confidence to a researcher that the transient and situational factors are not intervening in the process, and hence, the measuring instrument is robust. An unreliable measuring instrument is extremely dangerous for a marketing researcher, as it will generate different responses from the respondents who have the same feeling about the phenomenon. There are many reasons to get these kinds of responses, and at a first check, these are verified from the interviewer's end. Probably, instructions as a part of questionnaire may not be clear, question wordings posed by the interviewer may not be the same in each situation, and many more reasons like this. A researcher can adopt three ways to handle the issue of reliability: **test–retest reliability**, **equivalent forms reliability**, and **internal consistency reliability**.

A measure is said to be reliable when it elicits the same response from the same person when the measuring instrument is administered to that person successively in similar or almost similar circumstances.

3.5.2.1 Test–Retest Reliability

To execute the **test–retest reliability**, the same questionnaire is administered to the same respondents to elicit responses in two different time slots. As a next step, the degree of similarity between the two sets of responses is determined. To assess the degree of similarity between the two sets of responses, correlation coefficient is computed. Higher correlation coefficient indicates a higher reliable measuring instrument, and lower correlation coefficient indicates an unreliable measuring instrument.

To execute test-retest reliability, the same questionnaire is administered to the same respondents to elicit responses in two different time slots.

To assess the degree of similarity between the two sets of responses, correlation coefficient is computed. Higher correlation coefficient indicates a higher reliable measuring instrument, and lower correlation coefficient indicates an unreliable measuring instrument.

Test–retest reliability has its own limitations. The first problem a researcher faces is the ideal time interval between the two responses. There is a scope of several problems taking place between the first and the second observations. There is a possibility that the respondent will become sensitive for the subject matter to be investigated, and hence, the second answer will be influenced by his or her sensitivity. There is a possibility that the respondent will answer the same question in the same way because the first session interview memories are not totally erased from his or her mind. There is a great possibility that some external factors such as heavy advertisement by the company may alter the respondent's views about a particular product or situation. Therefore, his or her second answer will be different from his or her first answer because of the environmental changes taken place between the two measurements. In the light of these common problems related to reliability of the measuring instruments, it is often suggested that a researcher should couple his or her test with two other approaches of testing reliability.

3.5.2.2 Equivalent Forms Reliability

In test–retest reliability, a researcher considers personal and situation fluctuation in responses in two different time periods, whereas in the case of considering **equivalent forms reliability**, two equivalent forms are administered to the subjects at two different times. To measure the desired characteristics of interest, two equivalent forms are constructed with different sample of items. Both the forms contain the same type of questions and the same structure with some specific difference. On applying the forms of the measurement device, they may be given one after the other or after a specified time interval, depending on the investigator's interest in stability over time (Green et al. 1999). The reliability is established by computing the correlation coefficient of the results obtained from the two equivalent forms.

In test–retest reliability, a researcher considers personal and situation fluctuation in responses in two different time periods, whereas in the case of considering equivalent forms reliability, two equivalent forms are administered to the subjects at two different times.

3.5.2.3 Internal Consistency Reliability

The **internal consistency reliability** is used to assess the reliability of a summated scale by which several items are summed to form a total score (Malhotra 2004). The basic approach to measure the internal consistency reliability is split-half technique. In this technique, the items are divided into equivalent groups. This division is done on the basis of some predefined aspects as odd versus even number questions in the questionnaire or split of items randomly. After division, responses on items are correlated. High correlation coefficient indicates high internal consistency, and low correlation coefficient indicates low internal consistency. Subjectivity in the process of splitting the items into two parts poses some common problems for the researchers. A very common approach to deal with this problem is **coefficient alpha or Cronbach's alpha**.

Internal consistency reliability is used to assess the reliability of a summated scale by which several items are summed to form a total score.

The **coefficient alpha or Cronbach's alpha** is actually a mean reliability coefficient for all the different ways of splitting the items included in the measuring instruments. As different from correlation coefficient, coefficient alpha varies from 0 to 1, and a coefficient value of 0.6 or less is considered to be unsatisfactory. There is also an argument that the value of Cronbach's alpha should be more than 0.7 for a narrow construct and 0.55–0.7 for a moderately broad construct (Van de Ven and Ferry 1980). A satisfactory Cronbach's alpha value of reliability depends on how a measure is being used (Jung and Goldenson 2007). Nowadays, researchers generally use computer softwares to compute the internal consistency reliability. Many researchers use coefficient alpha or Cronbach's alpha as a measure of internal consistency reliability for **multi-item scales**.

Coefficient alpha or Cronbach's alpha is actually a mean reliability coefficient for all the different ways of splitting the items included in the measuring instruments.

3.5.3 Sensitivity

Sensitivity is the ability of a measuring instrument to measure the meaningful difference in the responses obtained from the subjects included in the study. It is to be noted that the dichotomous categories of response such as yes or no can generate a great deal or variability in the responses. Hence, a scale with many items as a sensitive measure is required. For example, a scale based on five categories of responses, such as "strongly disagree," "disagree," "neither agree nor disagree," "agree," and "strongly agree," presents a more sensitive measuring instrument. To enhance the sensitivity of the measuring instrument, a

Sensitivity is the ability of a measuring instrument to measure the meaningful difference in the responses obtained from the subjects included in the study.

single-question scale must be avoided and a researcher's focus should be on including more relevant items or questions.

3.6 MEASUREMENT SCALES

Comparative scales are based on the direct comparison of stimulus and generally generate some ranking or ordinal data. This is the reason why these scales are sometimes referred as non-metric scales. Non-comparative scaling techniques generally involve the use of a rating sale, and the resulting data are interval or ratio in nature. This is the reason why these scales are referred as monadic scales or metric scales by some marketing researchers.

Marketing or business researchers often use rating scales to measure theoretical constructs such as consumer satisfaction, brand loyalty, and attitude towards a product or service. The debate on the distributional and measurement properties of rating scale data (i.e., ordinal versus interval scale) and the appropriateness of various statistical techniques has continued for the past four decades (Babakus and Ferguson 1988). The discussion of the various scales used by marketing researchers can be dealt on a variety of dimensions such as comparative or non-comparative scales, scales categorized on the level of data measurement, and so on. Comparative scales are based on the direct comparison of stimulus and generally generate some ranking or ordinal data. This is the reason why these scales are sometimes referred as non-metric scales. Non-comparative scaling techniques generally involve the use of a rating sale, and the resulting data are interval or ratio in nature. This is the reason why these scales are referred as monadic scales or metric scales by some marketing researchers. Another way is to deal measurement scales in terms of its capacity of respondent data generation. In this method, the scale can be divided into nominal, ordinal, interval, and ratio scales. This section is an attempt to discuss the various types of scales in the light of items included in the scales. These are **single-item scales**, multi-item scales, and **continuous rating scales**. Figure 3.3 shows the classification of these measurement scales.

3.6.1 Single-Item Scales

As clear from the name, single-item scales measure only one item as a construct.

As clear from the name, the single-item scales measure only one item as a construct. Some of the commonly used single-item scales in the field of marketing research are **multiple-choice scales**, forced-ranking scales, **paired-comparison scales**, **constant-sum scales**,

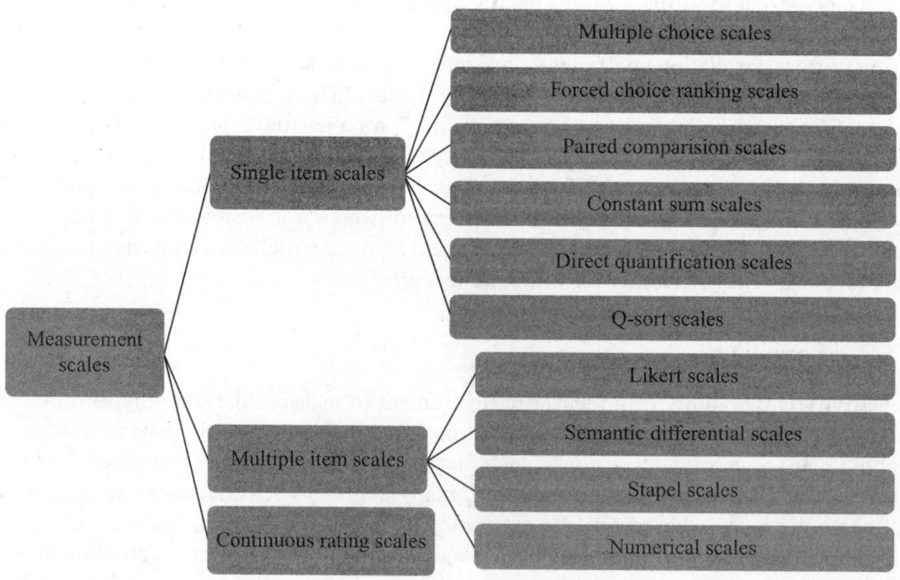

FIGURE 3.3
The classification of measurement scales

direct quantification scales, and **Q-sort scales**. The following section focuses on various common single-item scales.

3.6.1.1 Multiple-Choice Scale

In marketing research, the researchers are interested in collecting some demographic or other information that is nominal in nature. In short, the researcher tries to generate some basic information to conduct his or her research work, and for the sake of convenience or further analysis, he or she codes it by assigning different numbers to different characteristics of interest. This type of measurement is commonly referred as **multiple-choice scale** and results in generating the nominal data. In this type of scale, the researcher poses a single question with multiple response alternatives. For a mere quantification reason, a researcher assigns 1 to the first response, 2 to the second response, and so on. It is important to note that the numbers provide only the nominal information. Some of the examples of the multiple-choice scale are shown in Figure 3.4.

Researcher tries to generate some basic information to conduct his or her research work, and for the sake of convenience or further analysis, he or she codes it by assigning different numbers to different characteristics of interest. This type of measurement is commonly referred as multiple-choice scale and results in generating the nominal data.

It can be seen from Figure 3.4 that all the question responses provide the nominal information. For example, Question 3 seeks the response that in the previous month, which brand of toothpaste you have purchased. This is just the nominal information and does not provide ranking or rating of toothpaste over another brand. Similarly, Question 4 is posed to know about the respondent's occupation. Therefore, the responses are not the respondent's preference about the occupation. This is just a symbolic representation of the respondent's occupation.

3.6.1.2 Forced-Choice Ranking

This is a common type of scaling technique used by many marketing researchers. In the **forced-choice ranking** scaling technique, the respondents rank different objects simultaneously from a list of objects presented to them. For example, as shown in Figure 3.5, in the **forced-choice ranking scale**, a respondent is presented a list of seven brands of colour television available in the Indian market. The respondent is supposed to provide his or her preference of the brands in terms of providing ranking to the different brands. This scaling technique is known as the forced choice because the items or objects on the scale are decided by the scale designer, and the respondent is almost forced to provide his or her ranking from the list of brands included by the scale designer. This scaling technique is also referred as rank-order scaling and results in generating ordinal-level data.

In forced-choice ranking scaling technique, the respondents rank different objects simultaneously from a list of objects presented to them.

Que. (1) Do you own a car?

Yes (1) No (2)

Que. (2) You belong to which region?

Andhra Pradesh (1) Chhattisgarh (2) Madhya Pradesh (3) Gujarat (4) Punjab (5) Bihar (6)

Que. (3) In the previous month, which brand of toothpaste you have purchased?

Colgate (1) Pepsodent (2) Babool (3) Close-up (4)

Que. (4) What is your occupation?

Government service (1) Private service (2) Own business (3) Lawyer (4)

FIGURE 3.4
Examples of multiple-choice scales

Following is the list of some colour television brands available in Indian market. Please rank the brands in order of your preference by assigning 1 to most preferred brand, 2 to next preferred brand, and so forth. Please keep in mind that no two brands should receive the equal rank order.

Brands	Ranking
LG	______
Samsung	______
Sansui	______
Videocon	______
Sony	______
Philips	______

FIGURE 3.5
Example of forced-choice scale

3.6.1.3 Paired-Comparison Technique

As the name indicates, in paired-comparison scaling technique, a respondent is presented a pair of objects or stimulus or brands and the respondent is supposed to provide his or her preference of the object from a pair.

In the field of marketing research, paired comparison is the widely used scaling technique. As the name indicates, in the **paired-comparison scaling** technique, a respondent is presented a pair of objects or stimulus or brands and the respondent is supposed to provide his or her preference of the object from a pair. For example, as shown in Figure 3.6, a respondent is given an option to prefer the brand of his or her preference from a pair of brands. The "+" sign indicates that the column brand is preferred over the row brand and "–" sign indicates that the row brand is preferred over the column brand. The last row indicates the number of times a brand is preferred over other brands in paired comparison. It is clearly shown in this hypothetical example that Usha is the most preferred brand by this particular respondent followed by Khaitan, Bajaj, and Polar.

When n items (objects or brands) are included in the study, a respondent has to make $n(n-1)/2$ paired comparisons.

As can be seen from Figure 3.6, the respondent has made six comparisons to evaluate the four brands included in the study. When n items (objects or brands) are included in the study, a respondent has to make $n(n-1)/2$ paired comparisons. This technique usually generates the ordinal level of data. Data obtained from the paired-comparison scaling technique can be analysed using several techniques. The first technique is already elaborated in terms of the respondent's preference from most preferred to least preferred as shown in Figure 3.5. Sometimes, a researcher uses the "**principle of transitivity**" to analyse the data obtained from a paired-comparison scaling technique. Transitivity is a simple concept that says that if Brand "X" is preferred over Brand "Y" and Brand "Y" is preferred over Brand "Z," then Brand "X" is also preferred over Brand "Z". Paired-comparison scaling technique also has some disadvantages. We have taken a simple example of comparing the four brands. The application of paired-comparison scaling technique becomes difficult when we have some more brands, say 12 brands, to compare. In this manner, we will have about 66 comparisons, and the interpretation will become difficult.

Sometimes, a researcher uses the "principle of transitivity" to analyse the data obtained from a paired-comparison scaling technique. Transitivity is a simple concept that says that if Brand "X" is preferred over Brand "Y" and Brand "Y" is preferred over Brand "Z," then Brand "X" is also preferred over Brand "Z".

3.6.1.4 Constant-Sum Scales

In the constant-sum scaling technique, the respondents allocate points to more than one stimulus objects or object attributes or object properties, such that the total remains a constant sum of usually 10 or 100. Figure 3.7 shows an example of constant-sum scale. It can be seen from the figure that a respondent is required to provide his or her opinion about

Please indicate which of the following electric fan brand you prefer from the pair of brands presented as below:

Brands	Polar	Usha	Bajaj	Khaitan
Polar	*	+	+	+
Usha	–	*	–	–
Bajaj	–	+	*	+
Khaitan	–	+	–	*
Number of times a brand is preferred in a pair	0	3	1	2

"+" indicates that the column brand is preferred over row brand and "–" indicates that the row brand is preferred over column brand.

FIGURE 3.6
Example of paired-comparison scaling technique

Following section presents six attributes about a car. Please indicate your points from 100. More points you will assign will indicate your relative preference for that attribute. The total of all the points should be equal to 100. If you feel that an attribute is not at all important, then please assign 0 for that attribute.

Attributes	Points
Price	**37**
Space	**10**
Interior decoration	**5**
Mileage	**33**
Colour range	**10**
Power steering	**5**
Total	**100**

FIGURE 3.7
Example of a constant-sum scale

six attributes of a car. These attributes are price, space, interior decoration, mileage, colour range, and power steering. The respondent has to provide his or her rating points on these six product attributes, such that the sum of all the scoring points is equal to 100. The sum of all the points should be equal to a predefined constant 100 or 10, which is why this scale is called the **constant-sum scale**. This scaling technique generates the ratio-level data.

In the constant-sum scaling technique, respondents allocate points to more than one stimulus objects or object attributes or object properties, such that the total remains a constant sum of usually 10 or 100.

The application of this scale has two major difficulties. First, this scale cannot be administered to uneducated respondents and small kids. Even when this scale is administered to an educated respondent, there is a high possibility that the respondent may mess the scoring points leading to recalculation. Second problem occurs in dealing with the rounding off situations. Few rounding off situations lead to trade-off, and many rounding off situations lead to cumbersome state of mind for the respondent and the researcher.

3.6.1.5 Direct Quantification Scale

The simplest form of obtaining information is to directly ask a question related to some characteristics of interest resulting in ratio-scaled data. Researchers generally ask a question related to payment intention of consumers. For example, a housing construction company may be interested in knowing the approximate amount a consumer is willing to pay to purchase a new flat. They can ask a simple question, "How much of amount you are willing to pay to purchase a new flat in the coming year?" Similarly, other kinds of ratio-scaled

The simplest form of obtaining information is to directly ask a question related to some characteristics of interest resulting in ratio-scaled data.

How much is your income from sources other than salary?
How many litres of petrol is monthly consumed by using a personal car?
How much of sugar does your family consume in a month?

FIGURE 3.8
Example of a direct quantification scale

information can also be obtained. Figure 3.8 shows an example of the **direct quantification scale** resulting in ratio-scaled data.

The major problem with this approach is dealing with the situation when the respondent does not know the answer. For example, in most of the cases, the respondent will not be able to answer the questions such as how many litres of petrol is monthly consumed by using a personal car? Similarly, there may be many questions related to direct quantification which a respondent is not able to answer and results in no data instead of the interval data or ratio data.

3.6.1.6 Q-Sort Scales

The objective of the Q-sort scaling technique is to quickly classify a large number of objects. In this kind of scaling technique, the respondents are presented with a set of statements, and they classify it on the basis of some predefined number of categories (piles), usually 11.

The objective of the **Q-sort scaling** technique is to quickly classify a large number of objects. In this kind of scaling technique, the respondents are presented with a set of statements, and they classify it on the basis of some predefined number of categories (piles), usually 11. For example, the respondents are given 70 attitudinal statements related to their views on ethical marketing practices by the companies presented on individual cards. The respondents are supposed to categorically place these statement cards into 11 piles ranging from "most strongly agree" to "least strongly agree." Number of cards presented to the respondents should not be less than 60 and should not be more than 120. Sorting is also done in a structured and an unstructured manner. In the structured sorting technique, the allocation of cards in each pile is predetermined, whereas in the unstructured sorting technique, only the number of piles are determined and not the distribution of cards in each pile. Although the distribution of cards results in a roughly normal distribution in most of the structured sorting, there is a debate on analysing the data as the ordinal or interval data.

3.6.2 Multi-Item Scales

Multi-item scaling techniques generally generate some interval type of information. In interval scaling technique, a scale is constructed with the number or description associated with each scale position. Therefore, the respondent's rating on certain characteristics of interest is obtained.

Multi-item scaling techniques generally generate some interval type of information. In interval scaling technique, a scale is constructed with the number or description associated with each scale position. Therefore, the respondent's rating on certain characteristics of interest is obtained. For the majority of researchers, the rating scales are the preferred measuring device to obtain interval (or quasi-interval) data on the personal characteristics (i.e., attitude, preference, and opinions) of the individuals of all kind (Peterson 1997). There are arguments and counter-arguments in favour of both single- and multi-item scales. Peter (1979) argued that the multiple measures are inherently more reliable because they enable computation of correlations between the items. A second argument in favour of the multi-item measures is that a multi-item measure captures more information than that captured by a single-item measure (Bergkvist and Rossiter 2007). The following section discusses some common multi-item scales such as **Likert scales**, **semantic differential scales**, **staple scales**, and **numerical scales**.

3.6.2.1 Summated Scaling Technique: The Likert Scales

The Likert scale is developed by Rensis Likert and is a most common scaling technique in the field of marketing research. In a **Likert scale**, each item response has five rating categories, "strongly disagree" to "strongly agree" as two extremes with "disagree," "neither agree nor disagree," and "agree" in the middle of the scale. Typically, a 1- to 5-point rating scale is used, but few researchers also use another set of numbers such as −2, −1, 0, +1, and +2. The analysis can be done by using either profile analysis or summated analysis. The profile analysis is item-by-item analysis, where the respondent's scores are obtained for each item of the scale, and the analysis is also done on the basis of individual item scores. As another approach, scores are obtained from the respondents, and the sum is obtained across the scale items. After summing, an average is obtained for all the respondents. The summated approach is widely used, which is why the Likert scale is also referred as the **summated scale.**

In a Likert scale, each item response has five rating categories, "strongly disagree" to "strongly agree" as two extremes with "disagree," "neither agree nor disagree," and "agree" in the middle of the scale. Typically, a 1- to 5-point rating scale is used, but few researchers also use another set of numbers such as −2, −1, 0, +1, and +2.

Figure 3.9 presents an example related to discovering the consumer's opinion related to washing machine produced by a multinational company. It can be seen from the figure that the Items 3 and 4 are negative in nature; hence, for these two items, the scale must be reversed. It means that for these two items, strongly disagree should get the Score 5 and strongly agree should get the Score 1. Therefore, for a positive-scale item, strongly agree should have the highest rating point, and for a negative statement, strongly disagree should have the highest rating point and rest of the scale points must be set accordingly. The major advantage of the Likert scale is its ease in construction and comfort in administration. The major disadvantage of the Likert scale is that it takes more time to complete than other itemized rating scales because respondents have to read each statement (Malhotra 2004). Parasuraman et al. (2005) developed a multi-item scale (E-S-QUAL) to measure the service quality delivered by Websites in which online shopping is available for the customers (Figure 3.10). Each item of the scale is rated on a 1- to 5-point rating scale in which 1 indicates strongly disagree and 5 strongly agree.

3.6.2.2 Semantic Differential Scales

Semantic differential scale was developed by Charles Osgood, George Suchi, and Percy Tannenbaum in 1957. The semantic differential is a popular scaling technique that usually takes

FIGURE 3.9
Example of Likert scale

Following are some statements related to washing machine produced by a multinational company. Indicate your answer in terms of your agreement or disagreement on the statement by circling the concerned number as described below:

1 = Strongly disagree 2 = Disagree 3 = Neither agree nor disagree 4 = Agree 5 = Strongly agree

	Strongly disagree	**Disagree**	**Neither agree nor disagree**	**Agree**	**Strongly agree**
1. Price range for the washing machine is appropriate	1	2	3	4	5
2. Product has got innovative features.	1	2	3	4	5
3. After sales services are poor.*	1	2	3	4	5
4. Ad campaign is not attractive.*	1	2	3	4	5
5. Credit policy is highly facilitative.	1	2	3	4	5
6. Sales executives are very cooperative.	1	2	3	4	5
7. Showroom demonstration is appropriate.	1	2	3	4	5

E-S-QUAL

Respondents rated the Website's performance on each scale item using a 5-point scale (1 = strongly disagree and 5 = strongly agree). The items below are grouped by dimensions for expositional convenience; they appeared in a random order on the survey.

Efficiency

EFF 1 This site makes it easy to find what I need.
EFF2 It makes it easy to get anywhere on the site.
EFF3 It enables me to complete a transaction quickly.
EFF4 Information at this site is well organized.
EFF5 It loads its pages fast.
EFF6 This site is simple to use.
EFF7 This site enables me to get on to it quickly.
EFF8 This site is well organized.

System Availability

SYS1 This site is always available for business.
SYS2 This site launches and runs right way.
SYS3 This site does not crash.
SYS4 Pages at this site do not freeze after 1 enter my order information.

Fulfilment

FUL1 It delivers orders when promised.
FUL2 This site makes items available for delivery within a suitable time frame.
FUL3 It quickly delivers what I order.
FUL4 It sends out the items ordered.
FUL5 It has in stock the items the company claims to have.
FUL6 It is truthful about its offering
FUL7 It makes accurate promises about the delivery of the products.

Privacy

PRI1 It protects information about my Web-shopping behaviour.
PRI2 It does not share my personal information with other sites
PRI3 This site protects information about my credit card.

FIGURE 3.10
Multi-item scale (E-S-QUAL) to measure the service quality delivered by Web sites in which online shopping is available for the customers

Source: Parasuraman, A., V. A. Zeithaml and A. Malhotra (2005). "E-S-QUAL: A Multi-Item Scale for Assessing Electronic Service Quality", *Journal of Service Research*, 7(10): 1–21.

The semantic differential scale consists of a series of bipolar adjectival words or phrases placed on the two extreme points of the scale.

Good semantic differential scales keep some negative adjectives and some positive adjectives on the left side of the scale to tackle the problem of the halo effect.

the form of a 5- or 7-point bipolar adjective scale (Garland 1990). The **semantic differential scale** consists of a series of bipolar adjectival words or phrases placed on the two extreme points of the scale. Some researchers prefer bipolar scales, whereas some other researchers prefer unipolar scales. In a bipolar scale, mid-point is the neutral point, whereas in a unipolar scale, the mid-point is simply a point between the two poles.

Figure 3.11 shows an example of a semantic differential scale in which positive adjectives are on the left side of the scale for Items 1, 2, 3, 4, and 7. This is a reason why the highest number of scale, that is, 7, is assigned to the left side of the scale. In contrast to the discussed items, for Items 5 and 6, left side of the scale carries negative adjectives or phrases. This is a reason why lowest rating number 1 is assigned to the left side of the Items 5 and 6. This is a deliberately done exercise because it avoids the halo effect. The halo effect has an adverse impact on the respondent's answer because it is the tendency of a respondent to follow the previous judgment carelessly when all the items have the negative adjectives on the left side of the scale and the positive adjectives on the right. Hence, good semantic differential

Following is the list of bipolar adjectives that explains your feeling about your organization. In this 7- point scale, please tick the choice of your preference.		
Strong (7)	– – – – – – –	(1) Weak
Favourable (7)	– – – – – – –	(1) Unfavourable
Sweet (7)	– – – – – – –	(1) Bitter
Aggressive (7)	– – – – – – –	(1) Submissive
Not intelligent (1)	– – – – – – –	(7) Intelligent
Inequity (1)	– – – – – – –	(7) Equity
Moral (7)	– – – – – – –	(1) Immoral

FIGURE 3.11
Example of semantic differential scale

scales keep some negative adjectives and some positive adjectives on the left side of the scale to tackle the problem of the halo effect. Few researchers and authors place the semantic differential scale in the ordinal scale category because they believe that the weight assignment is arbitrary in nature, whereas others put it in the category of interval scale, assuming that the data generated from this scale are interval in nature.

3.6.2.3 Staple Scales

A staple scale is a variation of the semantic differential scale; however, each item consists of just one word or phrase on which respondents rate the attitude object using a 10-item scale with just numerical labels (Parasuraman et al. 2004). The **staple scale** is generally presented vertically with a single adjective or phrase in the centre of the positive and negative ratings (Figure 3.12).

The staple scale is generally presented vertically with a single adjective or phrase in the centre of the positive and negative ratings.

The biggest advantage of using the staple scale is its ease in administration. A researcher has the convenience of not testing the appropriateness of the two bipolar adjectives, which

Select a plus number or minus number for your opinion about your satisfaction level from a mixer grinder of Company A. Also select a plus number or minus number for your opinion about the advertisement campaign launched by the Company A. For higher level of satisfaction, select a larger plus number with increasing plus numbers for increasing level of satisfaction. For lower level of satisfaction, select a minus number with increasing minus numbers for increasing level of dissatisfaction. Adopt the same procedure for giving your opinion about the effectiveness of advertisement campaign.

+5	+5
+4	+4
+3	+3
+2	+2
+1	+1
Satisfied	**Effectiveness of advertisement campaign**
–1	–1
–2	–2
–3	–3
–4	–4
–5	–5

FIGURE 3.12
Example of staple scale

is a prerequisite while using a semantic differential scale. As with the Likert scale and the semantic differential scale, points are at equidistant position in a staple scale, both physically and numerically, which usually results in the interval-scaled responses.

3.6.2.4 Numerical Scales

Numerical scales provide equal intervals separated by numbers, as scale points to the respondents. These scales are generally 5- or 7-point rating scales.

The Likert scale seeks respondent's responses on verbal description item and the semantic differential scale seeks the respondent's response on a semantic space provided by the bipolar adjective scale. In contrast to these two scales, **numerical scales** provide equal intervals separated by numbers, as scale points to the respondents. These scales are generally 5- or 7-point rating scales. For example, a bicycle manufacturing company is willing to assess the consumers' opinion about the purchase of their new product with new features and high price. A 7-point numerical scale designed to unfold the motive of the consumer's buying intention is shown in Figure 3.13.

Similar to the Likert scale, semantic differential scale, and staple scale, the numerical scale also usually generates interval-scaled responses.

FIGURE 3.13
Example of numerical scale

Would you be buying the new product with new features and high price?

Definitely buy 7 6 5 4 3 2 1 Definitely not buy

3.6.3 Continuous Rating Scales

In a continuous rating scale, the respondents rate the object by placing a mark on a continuum to indicate their attitude. In this scale, the two ends of continuum represent the two extremes of the measuring phenomenon.

In a **continuous rating scale**, the respondents rate the object by placing a mark on a continuum to indicate their attitude. In this scale, the two ends of continuum represent the two extremes of the measuring phenomenon. This scale is also referred as a graphing rating scale and allows a respondent to select his or her own rating point instead of the rating points predefined by the researcher. The respondent's scores are measured in length from one end of the scale to the mark placed by the respondent. This kind of measurement style supports the argument of the researchers who put the scale response data in interval scale data, which is the biggest advantage of using the graphic rating scale. Another advantage of this scale is that it is easy to construct and administer. Inconsistency in placing the marks on a continuum is the major disadvantage of using the graphic rating scale. Figure 3.14 shows an example of continuous rating scale.

The continuous graphing rating scale also uses two pictures at the two ends of the scale to represent two feelings of the respondents especially kids. In this type of scale, the two ends of the scale carry two emotions: very good or very happy and very bad or very unhappy.

FIGURE 3.14
Example of a continuous rating scale

In the following continuum, place your answer by placing an "X" mark. In your opinion, how important is it to exhibit ethical behavior?

Very important ______________________________ Not important

Very important -- Not important

10 20 30 40 50 60 70 80

How do you feel after seeing this toy in a shopping mall?

Very happy Very unhappy

FIGURE 3.15 Example of a continuous graphic rating scale

This type of scale is generally used by the confectionary companies or toy manufacturing companies, as their consumers are usually small kids and they find it difficult to rate using words or phrases. Figure 3.15 shows the example of a graphic rating scale used by a toy manufacturing company.

3.7 FACTORS IN SELECTING AN APPROPRIATE MEASUREMENT SCALE

In the previous section, we have discussed many types of scales. A researcher always faces a dilemma in deciding the type of scale to be used for the research. He or she generally considers six factors in deciding the type of scale to be selected. These six factors are as follows: decision on the basis of objective of conducting a research, decision based on the response data type generated by using a scale, decision based on using single- or multi-item scale, decision based on forced or non-forced choice, decision based on using balanced or unbalanced scale, and decision based on the number of scale points. Figure 3.16 shows some factors in selecting an appropriate measurement scale.

3.7.1 Decision on the Basis of Objective of Conducting a Research

The researchers have versatile and numerous objectives to be focused on. In the field of marketing research, the researches generally try to uncover attitudes of consumer for an object, attitude change for an object, product or product attribute preference, consumer behaviour, consumer satisfaction, purchase intention or purchase behaviour, post-purchase behaviour, and so on. For example, if a company is in the process of launching a new product in a particular geographical area, then the first objective of using any scale is to uncover the purchase intention of the consumer. In addition to obtaining this information, the researcher can also generate other information such as the satisfaction level of consumers from the other products of the company as well as consumer preference for the products of the other companies. Hence, while deciding about the measurement of scale, the research objective must be considered first.

While deciding about the measurement of scale, the research objective must be considered first.

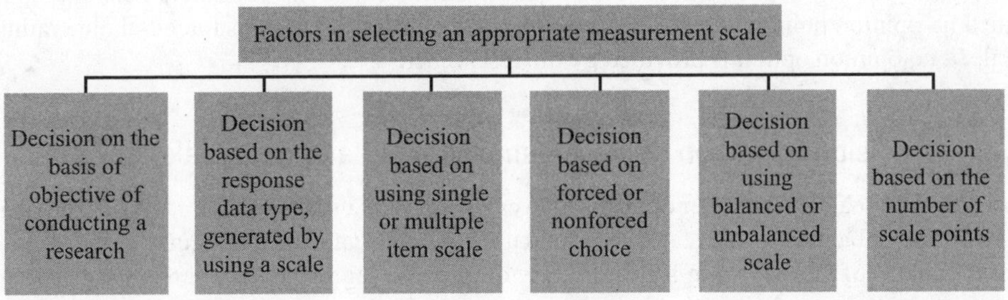

FIGURE 3.16 Factors in selecting an appropriate measurement scale

3.7.2 Decision Based on the Response Data Type Generated by Using a Scale

To get the nominal information, a nominal scale (multiple-choice scales) is used. This kind of demographic information provides a new dimension to research. For example, product preference can always be clubbed with some demographic variables such as age or gender of a consumer. A respondent's attitude significantly varies in the light of differences among the demographic characteristics of respondents. A researcher has to use a ranking scale when he or she is supposed to make comparisons between the two objects or object attributes. The ranking scales are also used to rank different objects simultaneously from a list of objects presented to them. The rating scales are generally used when research focus is to get the respondent's response for an object on a rating continuum usually on a 1- to 5- or 1- to 7-point rating scale. For example, a respondent is presented with the 1- to 5-point rating scale in which 1 is strongly disagree and 5 strongly agree. The respondent is supposed to provide his or her opinion about the service facility statements (items) of a five-star hotel group. Sometimes, a ratio scale is used to obtain direct information such as average income of a group and its comparison with the other groups.

3.7.3 Decision Based on Using Single- or Multi-Item Scale

Single-item scale or multi-item scale or both has its own advocates and opponents in the field of marketing research.

Single-item scale or multi-item scale or both has its own advocates and opponents in the field of marketing research. Proponents of the multi-item scale believe that a single observation may be misleading and lacking in context, thus the multi-item measurement scales can help to overcome these distortions (Glimore and McMullan 2009). Practitioner's preference for single-item measures is not theoretically based but rather is practical, in that single-item measures minimize respondent refusal and reduce data collection and data processing cost (Bergkvist and Rossiter 2007). Based on the research objective, a researcher should take a decision about the single-item or multi-item scale.

3.7.4 Decision Based on Forced or Non-Forced Choice

In a forced-choice rating scale, researchers do not include a "no opinion" option in the scale points, whereas in a non-forced-choice rating scale, a no opinion option is provided by the researcher.

In a forced-choice rating scale, the researchers do not include a "no opinion" option in the scale points. This forces a respondent to provide an opinion even when he has no opinion about the object. In some cases, researchers conduct a research study under the assumption that the respondent will definitely be providing an opinion in terms of selecting a rating point. In such situations, the respondents may sometimes have an undecided attitude and they usually select the mid-point of the scale. This mid-point of the scale is necessarily not the no opinion option and hence biases the result. The respondent's tendency to select the middle option distorts the result, as measures of central tendency such as mean and median of the data tend to shift towards the mid-point. In such a situation, a researcher can incorporate a no opinion point in the scale to avoid biased responses. In a non-forced-choice rating scale, a no opinion option is provided by the researcher.

3.7.5 Decision Based on Using Balanced or Unbalanced Scale

In a balanced scale, the number of favourable and unfavourable categories remains equal, whereas in an unbalanced scale, the favourable and unfavourable categories remain unequal.

In a balanced scale, the number of favourable categories and unfavourable categories remains equal. In an unbalanced scale, favourable and unfavourable categories remain unequal. A balanced scale is of the following form: strongly disagree, disagree, neither agree nor disagree, agree, and strongly agree. Note that in this type of scale, two rating points indicate agreement, two rating points indicate non-agreement and one point is the neutral state (neither agree nor disagree). Hence, this scale is a balanced scale. An unbalanced scale is of the following form: strongly disagree, disagree, agree, strongly agree, and very strongly agree. It can be noted that in the discussed scale, three rating points indicate agreement and only two rating points indicate non-agreement resulting in an unbalanced scale. The respondents have the tendency of rating higher when object is familiar to them or when the object involves "ego" of the respondents. Usually, researchers use a balanced scale with equal number of favourable and unfavourable terms. Sometimes researchers know in advance that the respondents will present a skewed response in favour and non-favour of the research phenomenon. In this case, an unbalanced scale in the direction of skewness may be an appropriate choice. In the case of using an unbalanced rating scale, the researchers have to take this consideration when doing data analysis.

3.7.6 Decision Based on the Number of Scale Points and Its Verbal Description

The researchers generally use a 3-, 5-, 7-, 9-, or 11-point scale. In some rare cases, a 13-point scale is also used. When an object is simple and has no major impact on the respondent's life, a simple 3-point scale can be used. In other case, when the object requires high involvement of the respondent, any scale ranging from 5 to 11 points can be considered by the researcher.

The researchers generally use a 3-, 5-, 7-, 9-, or 11-point scale. In some rare cases, a 13-point scale is also used.

While deciding the number of scale categories, some factors such as handling comfort of respondents, respondent's awareness about the subject matter, and mode of data collection method must be considered. It is obvious that the respondent finds a great deal of difficulty in handling scale categories if these are many. Therefore, based on the researcher's essentiality to include scale categories, too many items in scale categories must be avoided. The respondent's familiarity with the subject matter or objects allows a researcher to include a large number of categories. On the other hand, if the respondent is unaware or little aware about the object or subject matter, the inclusion of a large number of categories must be avoided. Mode of data collection is also a determinant of scale categories. For example, a researcher will be uncomfortable using a large number of categories while administering the questionnaire through a telephone. The telephone method of data collection requires a fewer scale categories.

A scale can have numerical or verbal or pictorial descriptions associated with the scale points. In some cases, researchers label extreme scale points. In some other cases, the researchers label every scale point. As a general rule, the description of the scale point should be close to the concerned point. As another matter of understanding, labelling all the scale points allows a researcher to avoid scale ambiguity. These are the general recommendations, although the final decision is a matter of researcher's wisdom.

REFERENCES

Aaker, D. A., V. Kumar and G. S. Day (2000). *Marketing Research*, 7th ed., p. 597. Wiley, Asia.

Babakus, E. and C. E. Ferguson Jr (1988). "On Choosing the Appropriate Measure of Association When Analyzing Rating Scale Data", *Journal of the Academy of Marketing Science*, 16 (1): 95–102.

Bergkvist, L. and J. R. Rossiter (2007). "The Predictive Validity of Multiple-Item versus Single-Item Measures of the Same Constructs", *Journal of Marketing Research*, XLIV: 175–84.

Brennan, L., J. Camm and J. K. Tanas (2009). "Validity in Market Research Practice: 'New' is not always 'Improved'", *Dermarkt*, 46(1–2): 6–16.

Burns, A. C. and R. F. Bush (1999). *Marketing Research*, 3rd ed., p. 329. Upper Saddle River, NJ: Prentice-Hall.

Garland, R. (1990). "A Comparison of Three Forms of the Semantic Differential", *Marketing Bulletin*, 1: 19–24.

Glimore, A. and R. McMullan (2009). "Scales in Service Marketing Research: A Critique and Way Forward", *European Journal of Marketing*, 43(5/6): 640–51.

Golafshani, N. (2003). "Understanding Reliability and Validity in Qualitative Research", *The Qualitative Report*, 8(4): 597–607.

Green, P. E., D. S. Tull and G. Albaum (1999). *Research for Marketing Decisions*, 5th ed., p. 254. New Delhi, India: Prentice Hall of India Private Limited.

Jung, H. and D. R. Goldenson (2007). "The Internal Consistency and Precedence of Key Process Areas in the Capability Maturity Model for Software", *Empirical Software Engineering*, 13(2): 125–46.

Lehmann, D. R., S. Gupta and J. H. Steckel (1998). *Marketing Research,* p. 255. Addison-Wesley.

Malhotra, N. K. (2004). *Marketing Research: An Applied Orientation*, 4th ed. Pearson Education.

Parasuraman, A., D. Grewal and R. Krishnan (2004). *Marketing Research,* p. 292. Boston, NY: Houghton Mifflin Company.

Parasuraman, A., V. A. Zeithaml and A. Malhotra (2005). "E-S-QUAL: A Multi-Item Scale for Assessing Electronic Service Quality", *Journal of Service Research*, 7(10): 1–21.

Peter, P. J. (1979). "Reliability: A Review of Psychometric Basics and Recent Marketing Practices", *Journal of Marketing Research*, 16: 6–17.

Peterson, R. A. (1997). "A Quantitative Analysis of Rating-Scale Response Variability", *Marketing Letters*, 8(1): 9–21.

Van de Ven, A. H. and D. L. Ferry (1980). *Measuring and Assessing Organizations.* New York, NY: Wiley.

Vogt, D. S., D. W. King and L. A. King (2004). "Focus Group in Psychological Assessment: Enhancing Content Validity by Consulting Members of the Target Population", *Psychological Assessment*, 16(3): 231–43.

Zikmund, W. G. (2007). *Business Research Methods*, 7th ed., p. 294. South-Western Thomson Learning.

SUMMARY |

Precise measurement in marketing research requires a careful conceptual definition, an operational definition, and a system of consistent rules for assigning scores and numbers. For scale evaluation, three criteria are generally applied: validity, reliability, and sensitivity. Validity is the ability of an instrument to measure what it is designed to measure. Evaluation of the validity is done using three basic approaches: content validity, criterion validity, and construct validity. Content validity is a subjective evaluation of the scale for its ability to measure what it is supposed to measure. Criterion validity involves the determination of whether the scale is able to perform up to the expectation with respect to the other variables or criteria. To evaluate construct validity, both the theory and the measuring instrument are considered. To achieve construct validity, a researcher must focus on convergent validity and discriminant validity. A convergent validity is established when the new measure correlates or converges with other similar measures. A discriminant validity is established when a new measuring instrument has low correlation or non-convergence with the measures of dissimilar concept. To establish construct validity, a researcher has to establish convergent validity and discriminant validity.

Reliability is the tendency of a respondent to respond in the same or in a similar manner to an identical or near-identical question. A researcher can adopt three ways to handle the issue of reliability: such as test–re-test reliability, equivalent forms reliability, and internal consistency reliability. For executing test–re-test reliability, the same questionnaire is administered to the same respondents, for eliciting responses in two different time slots. In the case of considering equivalent forms reliability, two equivalent forms are administered to the subjects at two different times. A basic approach to measure the internal consistency reliability is the split-half technique. A common approach to deal with this problem is coefficient alpha or Cronbach's alpha. Coefficient alpha or Cronbach's alpha is a mean reliability coefficient for all the different ways of splitting the items included in the measuring instruments. In contrast to correlation coefficient, coefficient alpha varies from 0 to 1, and a coefficient value of 0.6 or less is considered to be unsatisfactory. Sensitivity is the ability of a measuring instrument to measure a meaningful difference in the responses obtained from the subjects included in the study. This chapter is an attempt to discuss the various types of scales in the light of items included in the scales. These are single-item scales, multi-item scales, and continuous rating scales.

Single-item scales measure only one item as a construct. Multiple-choice scale generates nominal information. In the forced-choice ranking scaling technique, respondents rank different objects simultaneously from a list of objects presented to them. In a paired-comparison scaling technique, a respondent is presented a pair of objects or stimulus or brands and the respondent is supposed to provide his or her preference of the object from a pair. In constant-sum scaling technique, respondents allocate points to more than one stimulus objects or object attributes or object properties, such that the total usually remains a constant sum of 10 or 100. The simplest form of obtaining information is to directly ask a question related to some characteristics of interest resulting in ratio-scaled data. The objective of the Q-sort scaling technique is to quickly classify a large number of objects.

Multi-item scaling techniques usually generate some interval type of information. In a Likert scale, each item response has five rating categories, "strongly disagree" to "strongly agree" as two extremes with "disagree," "neither agree nor disagree," and "agree" in the middle of the scale. Semantic differential scale consists of a series of bipolar adjectival words or phrases placed on the two extreme points of the scale. Staple scale is generally presented vertically with a single adjective or phrase in the centre of positive and negative ratings. Numerical scales provide equal intervals separated by numbers, as scale points to respondents. In continuous rating scale, respondents rate the object by placing a mark on a continuum to indicate their attitude.

A researcher generally considers six factors in deciding the type of scale to be selected. These six factors are as follows: decision on the basis of objective of conducting a research, decision based on the response data type generated by using a scale, decision based on using single- or multi-item scale, decision based on forced or non-forced choice, decision based on using balanced or unbalanced scale, and decision based on the number of scale points.

KEY TERMS |

NOTES |

1. Prowess (V. 3.1), Centre for Monitoring Indian Economy Pvt. Ltd, Mumbai, accessed August 2009, reprinted with permission.
2. www.indiastat.com, assessed in September 2009.

DISCUSSION QUESTIONS |

1. While conducting a research how a researcher will determine what should be measured?
2. What are the four scales of measurement?
3. Establish the difference between nominal scale, ordinal scale, interval scale, and ratio scale. Also, discuss the relative superiority of these scales in the light of their importance for a researcher.
4. What are the criteria for a good measurement?
5. Explain the three basic approaches to deal with the issue of validity in a research.
6. What is reliability? How a researcher can handle the issue of reliability?
7. Write short notes on the following topics:
   - Content validity
   - Criterion validity
   - Construct validity
   - Test–retest reliability
   - Equivalent forms reliability
   - Internal consistency reliability

8. What is sensitivity? How a researcher can handle the issue of sensitivity?
9. What are single-item scales? What are multiple-choice scales, forced-ranking scales, paired-comparison scales, constant-sum scales, direct quantification scales, and Q-sort scales and how these can be used by a marketing researcher?
10. What are multi-item scales? Explain the use and importance of Likert scales, semantic differential scales, staple scales, and numerical scales in the field of marketing research.
11. What is continuous rating scale and under what situation it is applied by a marketing researcher?
12. What are the factors to be considered in selecting a good measurement scale?

CASE STUDY |

Case 3: *Sintex Industries Limited: Grooming with Increased Demand of Plastic*

Introduction: An Overview of the Plastic Industry

The use of plastic in various product manufacturing has provided a substantial base to plastic industry for grooming. The automobile industry is one of the largest consumers of plastic, as it is lightweight, resilient, rust resistant and a good insulator. Earlier, plastic was used only in decorative laminates, but now complete furniture and upholstery are being substituted with plastic. The use of plastic has increased over the years in water and air transport. Fibreglass boats are preferred on account of their lightweight appearance, low maintenance costs, and anti-corrosion. A plastic product provides safety, performance, and value. Plastics have almost substituted glassware and crockery, used in making appliances such as refrigerators, washing machines, televisions, and computers. It has emerged as a key element in modern packaging, used in making artificial body parts such as artificial heart valves, bones, and teeth. Polymers also play a significant role in textiles, with synthetic fibres in vogue and used as substitutes to natural fibres such as cotton, wool, and silk.[1]

Sintex Industries Ltd: A Pioneer in Plastic Industry

The Sintex group is one of the leading providers of plastics and niche textile-related products in India. It caters to the Indian market and has a solid presence spanning nine countries across four continents including countries such as France, Germany, and the USA. Sintex group's clients are scattered across the globe and most of them are parts of Fortune 500 companies list. Established in India in 1931, Sintex has a proven track record of pioneering innovative concepts in plastics and textile sectors in India and an uninterrupted 77 years of dividend payment to its shareholders. Continuous innovation is the foundation of Sintex's success over the years. "Active thinking" drives the company on its path. The innovative ideas are not only limited to products but also implemented in the manufacturing process, markets, and management policies.[2] The company generates 45% of consolidated turnover from building materials such as pre-fabs and monolithic; 40% comes from custom-moulded and plastic composite products; and the remaining 15% is attributed to textiles.[3] The company is highly sucessful and has witnessed a steady increase in income, sales, and profit after tax from 1997–1998 to 2007–2008 as can be seen from Table 3.01. As evident from the table, Sintex industries limited never suffered from losses in the last 11 years. Rather, it has shown tremendous growth rate during this time span. This consistent performance is the foundation of company's overall excellence.

TABLE 3.01
Income, sales, and profit after tax of Sintex Industries Limited from 1997-1998 to 2007-2008

Year	*Income (in million rupees)*	*Sales (in million rupees)*	*Profit after tax (in million rupees)*
Mar-98	1839.9	1821.8	104
Mar-99	2227.8	2203.5	105.5
Mar-00	2445.4	2427	131.6
Mar-01	3320.8	3225.1	241.4
Mar-02	4216.1	4167.9	192.2
Mar-03	4981.9	4916.7	236.8
Mar-04	5946.1	5822.7	336.6
Mar-05	7294.9	7160.8	539.1
Mar-06	9437.8	9144.7	920.2
Mar-07	12,395	12,128	1305.8
Mar-08	18,348.5	17,902.9	2163.3

Source: Prowess (V. 3.1), Centre for Monitoring Indian Economy Pvt. Ltd, Mumbai, accessed September 2009, reprinted with permission.

Opportunities for Indian Plastic Industry

The Indian plastic industry is catalysed by a surging demand in downstream industries such as packaging, automobile, and retail on the one hand and an exponential increase in the middle-class disposable incomes on the other. India's plastic industry expects to capitalize on this optimism through the realities such as a large and expanding domestic market, a burgeoning consuming class with increasing purchasing power, delicensed and deregulated regime, facilitating growth and investment, large processing industry base of more than 22,000 units with the potential for another 40,000 units, low manpower costs, providing an export edge, recent gas finds, enhancing feedstock security and environmental opportunities through water security, energy conservation, and preservation of natural resources. India is the eighth largest plastic consumer in the world with a per capita consumption of around 8 kg—far below the global average of 20 kg. The consumption of recycled plastic constitutes approximately 30% of the total off-take in the country. With the increasing demand in the domestic market, India is expected to be the third largest consumer after the USA and China by 2010 with an expected consumption of 12.5 million metric tonnes (MMT) (a projected componded annual growth rate (CAGR) of 15%), as against 38.9 MMT for the United States and 31.3 MMT for China. The polymer demand in India will be largely dominated by polythene and polypropylene.[1]

Sintex industries are ready to explore growth opportunities. A company that had a single plant for building materials a couple of years ago, Sintex now has five plants for the building material order supply. The company is also planning to enhance the capacity of these plants. Various other measures such as acquisition and innovative product offering are also being taken by the company to cater to the market needs. Suppose the company wants to ascertain consumer attitude for its different brands, then discuss various stages of the research to launch this research programme, define the research problem, discuss the type of the research design used for this research programme, what will be the nature of data for ascertaining consumer attitude? Discuss the scaling techniques used to measure the consumer attitude, and justify your selection of a particular scaling technique.

NOTES |

1. Prowess (V. 3.1), Centre for Monitoring Indian Economy Pvt. Ltd, Mumbai, accessed August 2009, reprinted with permission.
2. http://www.sintex-india.com/aboutus.html, accessed September 2009.
3. http://economictimes.indiatimes.com/Features/Investors-Guide/Sintex-Industries-attractive-f...

CHAPTER 4

Questionnaire Design

LEARNING OBJECTIVES

Upon completion of this chapter, you will be able to:

- Understand the meaning and importance of questionnaire
- Understand three stages of the questionnaire design process
- Learn about pre-construction phase of the questionnaire
- Learn about construction phase of the questionnaire
- Learn about post-construction phase of the questionnaire

RESEARCH IN ACTION: AMBUJA CEMENTS LTD

Gujarat Ambuja Cements was promoted as a joint venture, in 1981, between Gujarat Industrial Investment Corporation and N. S. Sekhsaria. Beginning with a 0.7 million tonne cement plant, the company has grown into a 19.3 million tonne entity through regular capacity additions and acquisitions. It is one of the major cement manufacturers in the country with plants located across Indian Territory, except Southern India. To reflect the geographical presence of the company, its name was changed to Ambuja Cements with effect from April 5, 2007. The cement manufactured by the company is marketed under the tag of "Ambuja Cement," which enjoys a strong brand image. In January 2006, Swiss global cement giant Holcim entered Ambuja Cements by purchasing a 14.8% stake in the company from its promoters. The deal amounted to ₹21,000 million, translating into a consideration of ₹105 per share. The Holcim Group held 45.68% stake in the company as of March 2008.[1]

Ambuja Cements has adopted a unique marketing strategy to fulfil the needs of the end consumer by contacting them directly. Ambuja Cements has built a strong position in smaller towns and rural areas over the last 2 decades. A Fast Moving Consumer Goods (FMCG) approach was adopted to create a wide retail network of small "mom and pop" shops, right down to the taluk/village level. A large sales force works alongside these small dealers to help them promote and sell the brand to the right consumer at the right price. Meanwhile, a team of expert civil engineers works closely with small contractors and masons who undertake construction of single-unit houses in small residential centres. Building a brand on the dusty rural map has its own excitements. Ambuja Cements' people have worked with local communities to demonstrate better construction practices and materials and to build economical and durable structures—not only housing but also rural infrastructure, like check dams, schools, and roads. They have also undertaken training for local people in masonry skills. For example, Gujarat state government has launched an initiative to train tribals in rural areas and has teamed up with Ambuja Cements to start a formal mason training school in Dahod, near Baroda. In Rajasthan, Gujarat Ambuja's Customer Support Group has provided

>>>

mason training as part of a Skill and Entrepreneurship Development Institute initiative, in collaboration with the Ambuja Cement Foundation. Creating an active distribution and customer service network down to this level is certainly a big challenge but a worthwhile investment as it has enabled the company to reap handsome rewards in terms of premium brand recognition and loyalty of the end consumer.[1]

Measures such as adopting an innovative marketing approach, people power approach, induction of fresh talent, continuous expansion strategy, and so on put the company, which started in 1981 when almost many national players were well established, in solid financial base. This fact can be observed from Table 4.1, which gives sales (in million rupees), profit after tax (in million rupees), and forex earnings (in million rupees) of Ambuja Cements Ltd from 1994-1995 to 2008-2009.

Ambuja Cements Ltd has systematically positioned its brand all over the country. As a result, the brand positioning has significantly improved. Suppose the company wants to assess its brand positioning as compared with other leading brands of the country then should the company use comparative scaling techniques or non-comparative scaling techniques? suppose the company has decided to use non-comparative scaling techniques then should it be using itemized rating scales? The company also has to make choices among balanced or unbalanced scale, forced-choice or non-forced-choice scale. Physical form of the scale is also an important decision criterion. Reliability, validity, and sensitivity of the scale are also some of the important factors taken into consideration. This chapter attempts to answer all such questions.

TABLE 4.1
Sales (in million rupees), profit after tax (in million rupees), and forex earnings (in million rupees) of Ambuja Cements Ltd from 1994-1995 to 2008-2009

Year	*Sales*	*Profit after tax*	*Forex earning*
Mar-95	3209.1	624.9	389.2
Mar-96	4292.3	991	504.8
Mar-97	7305.6	1415.6	523.6
Mar-98	9303.5	1321.1	834.1
Mar-99	11,457.8	1301.8	846.9
Mar-00	12,523.4	1505.6	555.5
Mar-01	13,027.8	4278.5	561.1
Mar-02	14,473.2	1929.7	900.6
Mar-03	15,826.3	1789.3	1512.3
Mar-04	20,251	2220.9	2300.9
Mar-05	23,012.8	3367.9	2368.3
Mar-06	30,258.4	4682.9	2722.5
Mar-07	70,167	15,032.5	5208.4
Mar-08	63,962	17,691	2779.4
Mar-09	70,898.9	14,022.7	2285.3

Source: Prowess (V. 3.1), Centre for Monitoring Indian Economy Pvt. Ltd, Mumbai, accessed September 2009, reprinted with permission.

4.1 INTRODUCTION

To conduct surveys, researchers always need a good **questionnaire**. There are some problems in designing good questionnaires because there is no universally accepted rule to be taken as the guideline while preparing the questionnaire. Theories will always enhance the construction of the questionnaire, but the experience of a researcher has a decisive role in the construction of a questionnaire. In the field of marketing research, many interviewers use the same questionnaire to conduct any survey. They cannot use different questionnaires to measure the same characteristics of interest. There must be a common questionnaire for the use of all the interviewers to avoid the bias in the research. A good questionnaire should be designed such that it will be able to fulfil research objective. The construction of the questionnaire has many constraints such as number of questions to be included, order of questions, physical form, and so on. Furthermore, increasing scope of marketing research has given an option to surveying firms to conduct continuous interviewing. Excessive interviewing is also a serious problem to the researchers. Brennan (1992) warned the researchers about the changing public attitude towards survey due to excessive interviewing and "sugging" (selling under the guise of research) in New Zealand. Although the study was conducted in New Zealand, the findings are true for researchers worldwide. Designing does not involve picking questions randomly and abruptly incorporating them into the questionnaire. It is a process based on logic and systematic effort, which is rather scientific in nature.

4.2 WHAT IS A QUESTIONNAIRE?

A **questionnaire** consists of formalized and pre-specified set of questions designed to obtain responses from potential respondents. Questions in the questionnaire reflect the research objective under investigation. For example, suppose a researcher wants to measure consumer attitude for a product and is in the process of designing a questionnaire. To measure the consumer attitude, the researcher has to first quantify the consumer attitude, which inherently is a feeling. The researcher has to collect relevant statements from the literature and then convert them in the form of questions to quantify a feeling such as the consumer's attitude. Finally, he or she prepares a set of questions that ultimately reflect various dimensions of consumer attitude rated on a rating scale. The summated score obtained from each consumer is the consumer attitude score for the concerned respondent. Similarly, any other feeling can be measured using a well-structured questionnaire. Questionnaires are generally situation and culture specific. So, the same questionnaire for measuring attitude cannot be used in all the cultures and situations. Questionnaire design process requires a careful attention to each step as the questionnaire or research instrument should be adapted to the specific cultural environment and should not be biased in terms of any one culture (Malhotra et al. 1996). Following section specifically focuses on the questionnaire design process.

A questionnaire consists of formalized and pre-specified set of questions designed to obtain responses from potential respondents.

4.3 QUESTIONNAIRE DESIGN PROCESS

Designing of the questionnaire is a systematic process. This section explores the systematic process of questionnaire design in three phases: **pre-construction phase**, **construction phase**, and **post-construction phase**. Figure 4.1 shows all these steps.

Designing of the questionnaire is a systematic process.

4.3.1 Phase I: Pre-Construction Phase

Phase I is the **pre-construction phase** of the questionnaire design process. It consists of three steps: specific required information in the light of research objective, an overview of **respondent's characteristics**, and decision regarding selecting an appropriate survey technique.

Phase I is the pre-construction phase of the questionnaire design process. It consists of three steps: specific required information in the light of research objective, an overview of respondent's characteristics, and decision regarding selecting an appropriate survey technique.

4.3.1.1 Specific Required Information in the Light of Research Objective

This is the first and probably most important step of questionnaire design process. A poor conceptualization at this stage will lead to collection of a lot of irrelevant information and, more than that, this will also lead to loss of some relevant information. This will unnecessarily waste researcher's time and energy that is always precious and must be conserved. This also will lead to the increased cost of project in hand. So, the first and the foremost important decision relates to finding the required information through a questionnaire. To generate specific information, the researcher should clearly define the objective and the other research components such as theoretical model, research questions, and hypotheses. Clarity in all these components is very important as these only will provide the base of specific information to be collected through survey. In addition, the exploratory research can be launched to identify relevant research variables.

To generate specific information, the researcher should clearly define the objective and other research components such as theoretical model, research questions, and hypotheses.

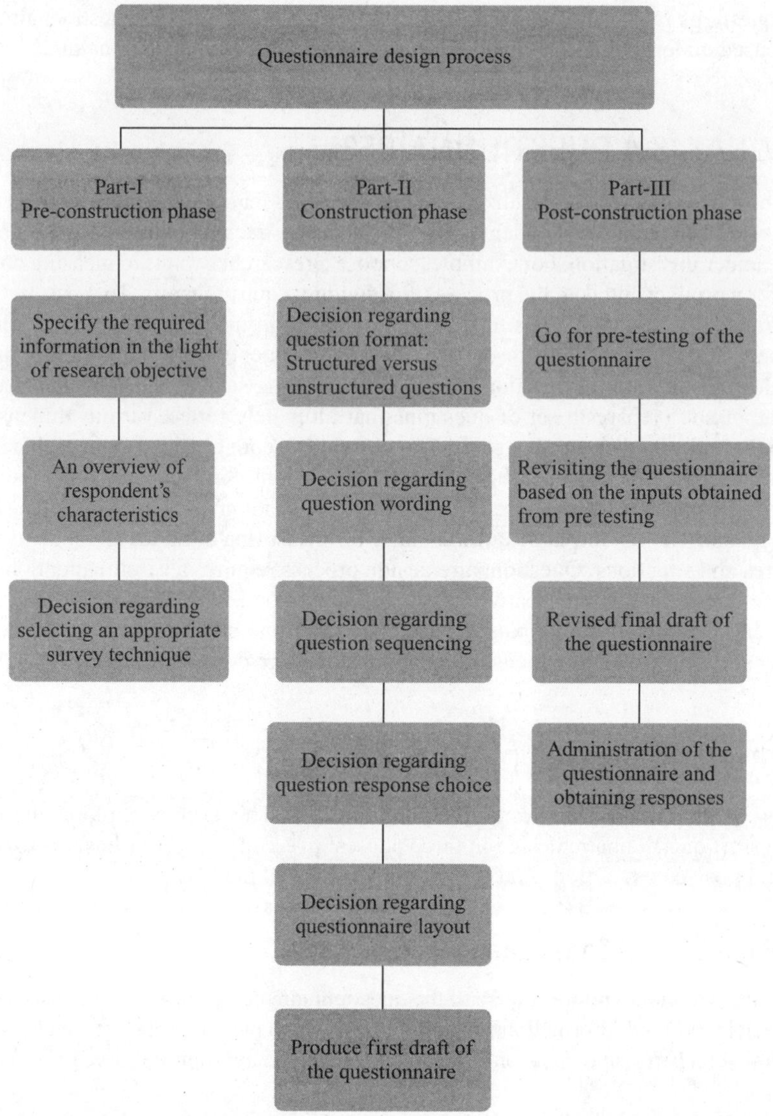

FIGURE 4.1
Steps in questionnaire design process

4.3.1.2 An Overview of Respondent's Characteristics

While collecting the information, an overview of the respondent's characteristics is a vital consideration. A researcher must construct the questionnaire in the light of the respondent's profile.

While collecting the information, an overview of the **respondent's characteristics** is a vital consideration. A researcher must construct the questionnaire in the light of the respondent's profile. For example, "purchase intention" is directly related to purchase capacity of the individuals. A questionnaire discovering purchase intention for a particular product, administered to various respondents without keeping their earning in consideration, will always lead to vague data. Hence, respondent's financial status and accordingly preparation and administration of the questionnaire are the key to generate relevant information. Similarly, while assessing the impact of "new tax policy," the researcher has to contact tax payers or potential tax payers. Simply a random selection from the population and then administration of questionnaire is not going to solve the purpose. Even while constructing a questionnaire, a researcher has to keep the profile of a probable respondent in mind. Various factors such as the respondent's qualification, age, experience, income, marital status, occupation, and so on have a decisive and impactful role in conducting a research. All the respondents may not be alike in all these factors and this is the reason a different profiling and different consideration with respect to this profiling are very important to construct a questionnaire.

4.3.1.3 Decision Regarding Selecting an Appropriate Survey Technique

While constructing a questionnaire, a deep thinking process is required to select an appropriate survey technique. On the basis of the mode of administration, personal interview, telephone interview, mail interview, and electronic interview are commonly used survey techniques. Each of the techniques has its relative advantages and disadvantages. Chapter 7 provides a detailed discussion of various survey and observation techniques and its relative advantages and disadvantages. The questions in the questionnaire must be constructed, sequenced, and placed according to the mode of the survey. For example, a lengthy and difficult-to-answer question must be avoided in a telephone interview method but may be appropriate in personal interview technique.

While constructing a questionnaire, a deep thinking process is required to select an appropriate survey technique.

4.3.2 Phase II: Construction Phase

Phase II is the real **construction phase** of the questionnaire design process. It consists of six steps: decision regarding question format, **structured questions** versus **unstructured questions**; decision regarding **question relevance** and wording; decision regarding **question sequencing**; decision regarding **question response choice**; decision regarding the **questionnaire layout**; and producing **first draft of the questionnaire**.

Phase II is the real construction phase of the questionnaire design process. It consists of six steps: decision regarding question format: structured questions versus unstructured questions, decision regarding question relevance and wording, decision regarding question sequencing, decision regarding question response choice, decision regarding the questionnaire layout, and producing first draft of the questionnaire.

4.3.2.1 Decision Regarding Question Format: Unstructured Versus Structured Questions

Questionnaires use two types of question formats. These are **open-ended questions** and **closed-ended questions**. In the case of a "closed-ended" question, the respondent has to format the judgment to fit the response categories and when "open-ended" questions are used, the judgment has to be verbalized into a preliminary answer (DeLeeuw 2001). The closed-ended question format can be further divided into dichotomous, **multiple-choice questions**, and **scales**. The following sections focus on open-ended questions and closed-ended questions.

Questionnaires use two types of question formats. These are open-ended questions and closed-ended questions.

Open-ended Questions

Open-ended questions are **unstructured questions**. The open-ended questions provide a free-to-answer opportunity to the respondents instead of fixed-response choices. In an open-ended question, a respondent remains free to provide his or her opinion about any topic in his or her own words. While narrating an opinion or attitude, the respondent provides a deep insight about the phenomenon under study. This really helps a researcher to design a questionnaire in a more structured manner. Hence, the open-ended questions are extremely useful for an exploratory research. In addition, these questions provide the respondent an opportunity to freely express his or her feelings and provide an insight into the problem in hand. Here, the researcher must be very cautious that the respondent should not be overburdened with more than what is required. To meet the objective of getting the required range of answer, the researcher can deliberately provide a pre-decided space for writing the answer. This can check the excessive and unimportant writing without mentioning it to the respondent. Following are some examples of the open-ended questions:

> What is your favourite advertisement for a soft drink?
> Who is your favourite business figure?
> What do you think is the most important consumer durable product for a household?

The open-ended questions are unstructured questions. The open-ended questions provide a free-to-answer opportunity to the respondents instead of fixed-response choices.

The open-ended questions also have some serious limitations. One of the major limitations is to handle the interviewer and the interpretation bias. While writing the answers, the interviewers generally use their own way of writing instead of a verbatim answer. This sometimes distorts the main issue and unnecessarily opens the different dimensions that may not be very important for the research. To get the required answer, the researchers are supposed to use tape recorders. Answers to the open-ended questions require a careful interpretation. In any case, it is very difficult to have a subjective interpretation without human bias. Open-ended questions have the tendency to provide an extra importance to the respondents who are more expressive.

In some cases, the respondents do not feel comfortable with the open-ended questions as it requires more effort and time to fill. In general, the respondents do not welcome any survey. The researchers try to motivate the respondents to participate in the survey through various means such as providing incentives. Long and descriptive type of answers really frustrates the respondents and, as a result, they try to avoid it. Even when the respondent has an idea about the matter under investigation, he or she finds a great deal of difficulty in expressing it because there is no response choice available to him or her. In case of a telephone interview, providing the open-ended question may not be a good choice. The open-ended questions are also not good for self-administering questionnaires. The open-ended questions are difficult to code and require a lot of time.

Closed-ended Questions

Closed-ended questions are structured questions. The closed-ended questions provide response alternative to the respondents instead of giving them a free-to-express response option.

Closed-ended questions are **structured questions**. The question structure does matter (Connolly et al. 2005). The closed-ended questions provide response alternative to the respondents instead of giving them a free-to-express response option. The choice offered to the respondents can be either in the form of a rating system or a set of response alternatives. These response alternatives are presented to the respondents and they select the most appropriate one. The closed-ended questionnaires are generally cheaper, more reliable, and faster to code, and analyse the collected data (Swamy 2007).

The closed-ended questions have several advantages. Administration of the closed-ended questionnaire is relatively easy as the need for explaining question dimensions is minimal. The closed-ended questions reduce the respondent's burden as the respondent is provided with the response alternatives and the burden of expressing a feeling or an opinion in his or her own thinking is the least. In this manner, the closed-ended questions motivate the respondents to complete the survey. A structured questionnaire also reduces the interviewer bias as the respondent has to select from a fixed alternative list. As the question is already structured, the interpretation bias is also reduced, which ultimately saves time and cost. Coding and tabulation of data also become very easy as the response alternatives are fixed and the researcher has no burden to create categories from a wide range of different narratives provided by the different respondents.

The questionnaire with closed-ended questions has several disadvantages as well. These questions are very difficult to construct and require some expertise. The researcher has a limitation in terms of providing all the exhaustive alternatives to a respondent and cannot provide a list of 30 possible answers to the respondents. He or she has to go for an extensive study of the subject under study and has to obtain an expert input to provide the most possible alternatives to the questions. This is of course a time- and money-consuming exercise and requires a lot of effort. To cover all the alternatives to the questions, the researchers specify an alternative as "Please specify if any other." When many respondents select this option, the essence of closed-ended question diminishes as the obtained answer must again be categorized by the researcher. As discussed earlier, the closed-ended question format can be further divided into dichotomous, multiple-choice questions, and scales.

Dichotomous Questions

Dichotomous questions have only two response alternatives usually presenting the two extremes "yes" or "no." To make the alternatives balanced, the researchers often present a third neutral alternative "don't know." For example, to boost the sales, a motorbike company has reduced the price and provided "0% interest scheme" to potential purchasers, as a special scheme for 1 year. The company now wants to uncover the purchase intention of the potential customers and asked a dichotomous question with a set of other questions such as

> Do you have plans to purchase a motorbike as the company has reduced the price and offered "0% interest scheme"
>
> Yes ________________
>
> No ________________
>
> Cannot say __________

The researchers also ask dichotomous questions to understand the demographic profile of the respondents. For example, an insurance company has launched a new policy with special features for the children. To understand the response, the company can ask the following dichotomous questions:

1. Please specify your gender.

   Male ___________

   Female _________

2. Is it an attractive policy with special features for kids?

   Yes ________

   No ________

   Cannot say ___________

3. Will you be purchasing this policy this year?

   Yes ________

   No ________

   Cannot say ___________

4. Do you have any other policy related to children?

   Yes ________

   No ________

   Cannot say ___________

Dichotomous questions have only two response alternatives usually presenting the two extremes "yes" or "no."

The main advantage of dichotomous questions is that they are simple to construct and administer. This does not require expertise and requires less time to construct. On the one hand, these questions are easy to code and analyse. Interpretation bias is also less as the responses are less (two or three) and are clear. On the other hand, the disadvantage is that these questions sometimes generate biased responses if the researcher phrases the question in a particular way. Leading questions (discussed later) generally generate biased responses. Another problem with the dichotomous questions is the forced choice available to the respondents in terms of answering yes or no when the researcher has not included a neutral response. To avoid the forced-choice option, if the researcher includes a neutral option, the respondents will conveniently prefer this neutral option and avoid preferring yes or no choices. Malhotra (2004) presented the guidelines to include neutral option in the multiple choice questions. He states that "If a substantial portion of the respondents can be expected to be neutral, include a neutral alternative otherwise do not include the neutral alternative."

Multiple-Choice Questions

While asking **multiple-choice questions**, the researcher presents various answer choices to a respondent and the respondent is supposed to select any one from the options. The multiple-choice questions are also referred as multichotomous questions. A private bank assessing the customer intention to have a relationship with the bank can ask the following multiple choice questions:

1. How do you rate the services offered by the bank?

   Excellent ________

   Very good ________

   Moderate ________

   Just right ________

   Poor ____________

2. How much are you planning to spend in a "fixed deposit scheme" this year?

   Less than ₹20,000

   ₹20,001 to ₹40,000

   ₹40,001 to ₹60,000

   ₹60,001 to ₹80,000

   ₹80,0001 to ₹1,00,000

3. For what time period will you be investing in a "fixed deposit scheme"?

   Less than 1 year

   1 year to 2 years

   2 years to 3 years

   3 years to 4 years

   4 years to 5 years

While asking multiple choice questions, the researcher presents various answer choices to a respondent and the respondent is supposed to select any one from the options.

The advantages of multiple choice questions are same as that of the dichotomous questions. Similar to the dichotomous questions, the multiple choice questions are easy to administer and to get the responses. It also reduces the interpretation bias and leaves little scope for the interviewer bias. These questions are also easy to code and analyse.

The number of alternatives to be provided to the respondents is a key consideration while framing the multiple-choice questions. A researcher should present all the possible mutually exclusive alternatives to the respondents. As discussed already, to make the list exhaustive, an alternative, "if others please specify," must also be included. The order of alternative presented to the respondent is another problem with the multiple-choice questions. The respondents have the tendency of electing the first and the last alternative, specifically the first one. To avoid this problem, a researcher can prepare several sets of questionnaire by changing the order of alternative in each. In this manner, all the alternatives will be having a chance to secure the first-order position as well as all the positions in the order. This helps to overcome the bias in selecting a particular alternative by the respondents from the list of alternatives.

Scales

Scales are also closed-ended questions, where multiple choices are offered to the respondents. Scales are discussed in detail in Chapter 3.

4.3.2.2 Decision Regarding Question Wording

Question wording is a typical and an important aspect of the development of a questionnaire. Negative wording of questions discourages the respondents and decreases the response rate, and even if the respondent responds, it may be a biased answer. The negative wordings impact the process of interpreting the questions, leading at least some respondents to misinterpret how to respond and, thus, reducing or destroying the usefulness of the questions or the series of questions (Johnson et al. 2004). In some cases of conducting personal interviews, the researchers feel that they will be able to overcome the wrong wording during the discussion, but they suggest a different understanding. The effects of question wording on response accuracy did not seem to be moderated by the respondent's knowledge gained via discussion (Bickart et al. 2006). A small change in wording a question can either encourage or discourage the responses. The guideline to evaluate the questions that are to be incorporated in the questionnaire is shown in Figure 4.2.

Negative wording of questions discourages the respondents and decreases the response rate, and even if the respondent responds, it may be a biased answer.

Question Wordings Must be Simple and Easy to Understand

While preparing a questionnaire, the researcher must always be careful as the respondent may be a common person who will not be able to understand the technical language. He or she should use simple, easy to understand, and direct words. What is very simple for the researcher may be very difficult for a common person. So, while assessing the difficulties in understanding the word, a common person's understanding must be taken into consideration instead of that of a group of highly educated persons. For example, instead of asking

While preparing a questionnaire, the researcher must always be careful as the respondent may be a common person who will not be able to understand the technical language.

> What is your **perception** about the new advertisement campaign?

A researcher should frame the same question as

> What is your **view** about the new advertisement campaign?

A respondent may not always be familiar with the word "perception." This word can rather perplex him or her leading to non-response or a misleading answer. Both the situations are not healthy for the research. Instead of using a relatively heavy word such as "perception," a researcher can use a light and easy-to-understand word "view."

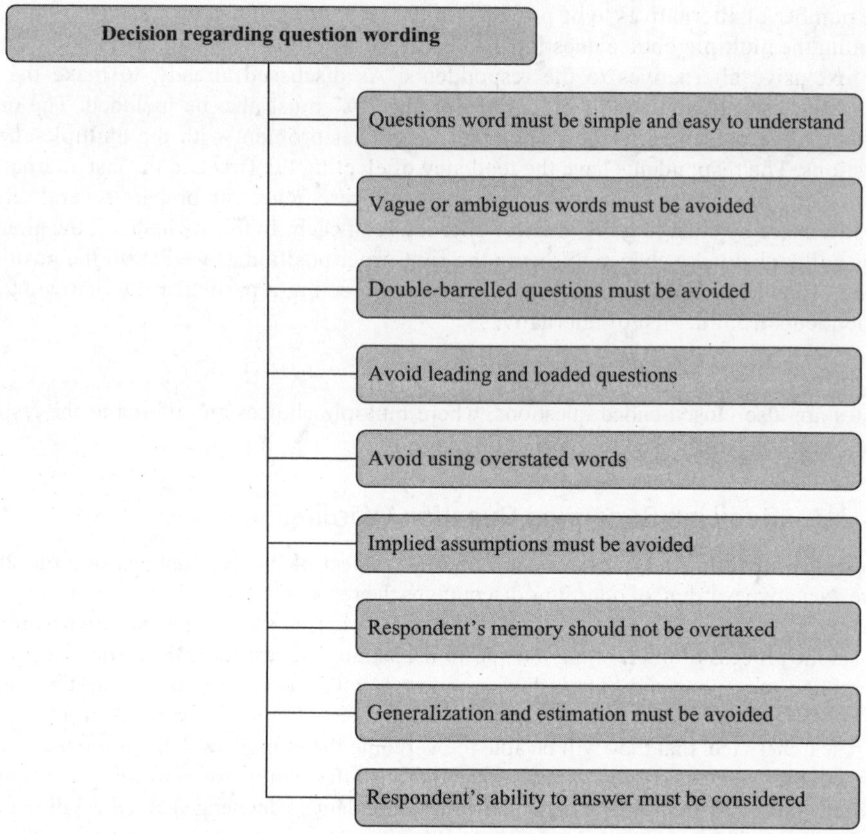

FIGURE 4.2
Decision parameters regarding question wording

Some words such as "often," "occasionally" and "usually," "how long," "how much," and "reasonably well" may be confusing for a respondent as these words specify a specific time frame.

Vague or Ambiguous Words Must be Avoided

Some words such as "often," "occasionally" and "usually," "how long," "how much," and "reasonably well" may be confusing for a respondent because these words specify a specific time frame. In addition, different words may have different meanings for a respondent. For example, the below question to determine consumer intention to spend on shopping in a year generates confusion for a consumer as he or she is not able to decide what the researcher's intention is.

In a year, how much will you spend on shopping?
Very much
Much
Reasonably well
Less
Very less

In this case, the respondent will be using his or her opinion about the question and answer alternatives, and accordingly he or she will be answering the question. A much better way of asking the same question may be as follows:

In a year, how much do you plan to spend on shopping?
Less than 10,000
Less than 20,000
Less than 30,000
Less than 40,000
Less than 50,000

This presents clear options to the respondent, and his or her assessment options are closed as the researcher has given five clear options to get the respondent's intention to spend.

Double-Barrelled Questions Must be Avoided

Double-barrelled questions are those with wordings such as "and" or "or." In a double-barrelled question, a respondent may agree to one part of the question but not to the other part. These questions also pose a situation where the respondent cannot provide his or her answer to the second part of the question without accepting the first part. For example, instead of asking a question

Double-barrelled questions are those with wordings such as "and" or "or." In a double-barrelled question, a respondent may agree to one part of the question but not to the other part.

On weekends, would you prefer an outing with your family and which is your favorite outing spot in the town?

In this type of question, the second part assumes that he or she prefers outing with the family in the weekend without even asking the respondent. Furthermore, the respondent is perplexed if his or her answer is "no" to the first part of the question. Instead of asking this type of double-barrelled question, the researcher can ask this question in two parts:

Que 1: On weekends, would you prefer an outing with your family?
Que 2: If yes, then which is your favourite outing spot in the town?

Dividing the question into two parts avoids confusion for the respondent. Only if the answer to the first question is "yes," the respondent will be attempting the second question. If the answer to the first question is "no," then the respondent will be ignoring the second question and, hence, there will be no confusion in answering the questions.

Avoid Leading and Loaded Questions

A **leading question** is the one which clearly reveals the researcher's opinion about the answer to the question. This is a biased way of presenting a question to get the desired answer. For example, a leading question can be presented as follows:

A leading question is the one which clearly reveals the researcher's opinion about the answer to the question.

Aren't you satisfied with the new feature of the product?

The question is presented in such a manner that the researcher gets a desired answer. A slight emphasis on the word "Aren't you" will change the respondent's answer. More specifically, asking the question such as "Are you satisfied with the new feature of the product?" will be more unbiased way as it gives freedom to the respondent to provide either "yes" or "no" answer.

Identifying the **loaded question** bias in a question requires more judgment because the wording elements in a loaded question allude to the universal belief or rules of behaviour (Burns and Bush 1999). The **loaded questions** are posed to address the inner feeling of the respondent and the response is almost predestinated. For example, a loaded question can be given as follows:

Every patriotic Indian will prefer an Indian brand of soap.

This question is a specific loading question and probably every respondent will like to answer it as "yes" because the question indirectly addresses their feeling of patriotism. Elimination of the words "patriotic Indian" from this question will definitely yield a different answer. The more accurate way of asking the same question is "Every Indian will prefer an Indian brand of soap."

The split-ballot technique involves the construction of a single question in two alternative phrases, and the question based on one phrase is administered to half of the respondents and question based on the other phrase is administered to the other half of the respondents.

A leading question generally emphasizes either the positive or negative aspect of the question. Sometimes, it becomes necessary to ask a question with either the positive or negative aspect. In this situation, a **split-ballot technique** is used to avoid bias due to positive or negative aspect of the question. This technique involves the construction of a single question in two alternative phrases, and the question based on one phrase is administered to half of the respondents and the question based on the other phrase is administered to the other half of the respondents. For example, in a 1 to 5 rating scale, where 1 represents strongly disagree and 5 represents strongly agree, a question measuring the increased use of fully automatic washing machine can be administered to half of the respondents as follows:

A fully automatic washing machine is better than the semi-automatic washing machine.

Reverse phrasing of the same question can be provided to the other group as follows:

A semi-automatic washing machine is better than the fully automatic washing machine.

The split-ballot technique is used with the expectation that two alternative of the same question will be able to generate more accurate summated score as compared to the situation when a single-phrasing question is used.

Avoid Using Overstated Words

It is always better to pose a question in a natural way rather than in a positive or a negative way. Overstatement of words will always bias the individual response. For example, a question related to the purchase of a water purifier with overstatement of words is as follows:

A survey revealed that hepatitis cases are increasing in India due to dirty water drinking. Have you any intentions to purchase a water purifier in the coming 6 months?

The answer will always be overblown due to the first part of the question, which generates a worry in the mind of the respondent and results in a positive answer, which is not possible otherwise. A more poised way of asking the same question is shown below.

Have you any intentions to purchase a water purifier in the coming 6 months, which can protect you from many waterborne diseases.

Implied Assumptions Must be Avoided

While constructing a questionnaire, implied alternatives must always be avoided to avoid unnecessary confusions. For example, the question

> It is always better to pose a question in a natural way rather than in a positive or negative way. Overstatement of words will always bias the individual response.

> Do you think Company "A" should continue with its incentive scheme on bulk purchase?

has an implicit assumption that the discount policy on bulk purchase offered by Company "A" is working excellent and by answering "yes," the company will continue its policy. The respondent assumes that giving a no answer will encourage the company to stop the scheme. Posing this type of question creates a binding on the respondent to provide his answer in a certain pre-determined manner. A more poised approach of asking the same question may be as follows:

> Do you like a discount scheme on bulk purchase, as provided by company "A"?

This way of asking a question emphasizes the discount scheme and seeks the respondent's answer in an indirect manner with reference to Company A's offer.

Respondent's Memory Should Not be Overtaxed

In some situations, a researcher's questions are based on the respondent's memory. The respondents tend to forget the incidents that are not important for them. These incidents may be important for the researcher, and he or she has framed question on these incidents. The following example is a difficult question to answer:

> In the past 2 months, how many times you have eaten ice cream of Brand "X" with your family?

Is is difficult for a respondent to keep a record of eating ice creams in the past 2 months. This is an unnecessary testing of the respondent's memory. Even if he or she provides the answer, it may not be accurate, rather it would be an approximate answer. A more accurate and informal way of asking the above question may be as follows:

> How many times you enjoyed ice cream parties with your family in past 2 months?

Generalization and Estimation Must be Avoided

A researcher should not pose questions that have a generalized answer. Generalization means respondent's belief, "what must happen" or "what should happen." For example, a question related to a new small car purchase in a generalized manner can be as follows:

> Generalization means respondent's belief, "what must happen" or "what should happen."

> While purchasing, will you be discussing the warranty issue with the shop manager?

This question has a generalized answer as every respondent will be seeking for the warranty while purchasing a car whether it is a small or a big one. The more accurate way of asking this question may be

> While purchasing, will you be likely to discuss the warranty issue with the shop manager?

> The questionnaire designing process must always consider that the respondent should not be left with the estimation or computation.

The questionnaire designing process must always consider that the respondent should not be left with the estimation or computation. Most of the respondents are either unwilling to compute or incapable to compute. For example, if a researcher is worried about the fact that the increasing pulse prices will lead to the low consumption of pulse in India in the year 2009–2010, he or she would ask a question

> What is the average per person consumption of pulses by your family in past 6 months?

For a common respondent, this type of question is difficult to answer. Hence, it leads to non-response or a faulty response. To answer this question, a respondent has to first assess the consumption of pulses by his family for past 6 months. Furthermore, to find the average per person consumption, this average must be divided by the number of family members. For response simplicity, this question must be divided into two components as shown below:

> What is the consumption of pulses by your family in the past 6 months?
> How many members are there in your family?

Average per person consumption must be computed by the researcher, and the respondent is left with the provision of answering two simple questions.

Respondent's Ability to Answer Must be Considered

Questions must be designed in the light of the respondent's ability and experience.

Questions must be designed in the light of the respondent's ability and experience. For example, a question targeted to officers older than 55 years to assess the importance of Internet banking is as follows:

> Do you feel that Internet banking is an added advantage for bank customers?

Most of the officers older than 55 years are not comfortable with a new concept like "internet banking." Thus, targeting this question to this respondent segment may not be an appropriate exercise.

Another example is related to a research question concerning the difference in consumer attitude in pre- and post-liberalization period in India. The question may be posed to the concerned respondents as follows:

> Do you find a difference in your purchasing behaviour in pre- and post-liberalization period?

Targeting this question to young respondents may not be an appropriate choice. The first question is that which period will be considered pre-liberalization period and which will be the post-liberalization period. Even if the researcher takes a pre-decided cut-off as before 1998 (when the impact of reforms noticed) as the pre-liberalization period and after 1999 till date as the post-liberalization period, answering for the probable respondents may be a difficult exercise. This is because young respondents were small kids during the pre-liberalization period, and they used to shop with their parents. Hence, seeking their opinion about the purchase behaviour may not be a right step. Targeting this question to the respondents younger than 22 years will provide a misleading answer. Targeting this question to the respondents older than 35 years may be an appropriate way as the respondents of this age group would have been approximately 17–25 years in the pre-liberalization period. In this age group, they may be treated as independent consumers and are able to provide independent answers.

4.3.2.3 Decision Regarding Question Sequencing

Question sequence also plays a key role in generating the respondent's interest and motivation to answer the question. Questions should have a logical sequencing in the questionnaire and should not be placed abruptly. The effects of question order are of two types: context and sequence. Context effects are those of consistency (when responses to the later questions become more congruous due to an earlier stimulus) or contrast (when there is a greater difference due to ordering) (Welch and Swift 1992). To facilitate the responses, a researcher has to follow some logical steps in sequencing the questions in the questionnaire. This arrangement usually requires the considerations as shown in Figure 4.3.

Question sequence also plays a key role in generating the respondent's interest and motivation to answer the question. Questions should have a logical sequencing in the questionnaire and should not be placed abruptly.

Screening Questions

Researchers generally begin with some **screening questions** to make sure that the target respondent is qualified for the interview. For example, if a company wants to assess the impact of "buy one get one free" offer through consumers who availed it through a company showroom in a shopping mall, then it has to conduct a mall intercept interview to know the impact of scheme. In this case, every person who is coming out of the mall cannot be interviewed as there is possibility that he or she may not have visited the showroom. Thus, the first and the basic question to ask is "have you visited the company's showroom?" The "yes" response to this question can open further interviewing process and a "no" response terminates the interview. In some cases, when the researcher is very sure about the qualification status of the respondent, he or she does not incorporate the screening question and starts from some "**opening questions**."

Researchers generally begin with some screening questions to make sure that the target respondent is qualified for the interview.

Opening Questions

The **opening questions** should be simple, encouraging, and trust building. From the research objective point of view, these questions may sometimes be little irrelevant but should be good initiators. These questions should not seek in-depth information and should be as general as possible. For example, a microwave company, trying to assess "shift in consumer attitude" from traditional way of cooking, should ask a first opening question as follows:

The opening questions should be simple, encouraging, and trust building. From the research objective point of view, these questions may sometimes be little irrelevant but should be good initiators.

Are microwave ovens increasingly occupying Indian kitchens?

Traditionally, Indians do not use microwave ovens as a part of their cooking system. With the change in food habits, preparation instruments have also started changing. Thus, the first question focuses on this issue and avoids respondent's confusion and makes him aware about this change without harming his prestige.

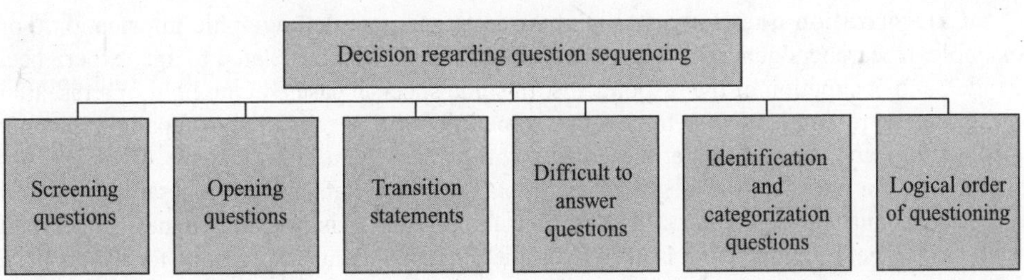

FIGURE 4.3
Decision parameters regarding question sequence

Transition Statements

The movement from one set of questions to another requires transition statements.

A questionnaire contains several questions related to various predetermined variables. The researchers generally collect these variables from extensive literature review. Each variable has a different set of questions. The movement from one set of questions to another set requires **transition statements**. For example, a mineral water bottle manufacturing company is encouraged with the expanding market. The company wants to assess the potential future market and hence conducted a survey on non-users. Its researchers have identified various variables to get the potential use, of which "awareness" and "taste" are important. It has prepared the first 11 questions, with the first five questions based on the "awareness" and the next six questions on "taste." After asking the first set of five questions, a researcher moves to the second set of six questions to get the potential consumer feeling for mineral water taste. Thus, before asking the next set of six questions, a transition statement is required to make the respondent familiar with the coming questions. Hence, a transition statement "Now, I would like to understand your opinion about the mineral water taste" will develop respondent's connectivity for the next set of six questions related to "taste," and he or she will be in a comfortable state of mind to answer these questions.

Difficult to Answer Questions

Difficult to answer, sensitive, or complicated questions should be placed later in the questionnaire. Placing it first will confuse the respondent and he or she will tend to terminate the interview process.

Difficult to answer, sensitive, or complicated questions should be placed later in the questionnaire. Placing it first will confuse the respondent and he or she will tend to terminate the interview process. Start must be fairly simple and encouraging, and difficulties must lie at the later stage to make them comfortable with the interview process. In the process of asking simple questions, first, the respondent develops a rapport with the process and even when there comes a time to respond relatively difficult questions, he or she feels a moral responsibility to wind up the process. This makes him or her feel that he or she has answered many questions and that after attempting these difficult questions the process will be over. At this stage, in personal interview, an interviewer is supposed to motivate and help the respondent to complete the process. Asking difficult questions first in a telephone interview reduces a respondent's interest in the interview process and he or she tends to terminate the interview. Under telephone interview conditions, substantively related questions affect the responses to the target question only when asked first (Schwarz and Hippler 1995).

Identification and Categorization Questions

Identification questions are used to generate some basic identification information such as name, mailing address, office phone number, personal phone number, or cell phone number.

Categorization questions are mainly used to generate demographic information.

The questionnaire consists of some identification and **categorization questions**. **Identification questions** are used to generate some basic identification information such as name, mailing address, office phone number, personal phone number, or cell phone number. A researcher must keep in his mind that if a respondent does not like to provide some information, he should be allowed to do so. For example, some respondents may not be interested in giving his or her personal telephone number or cell phone number to safeguard their privacy. This is important to enhance the credibility of the survey.

Categorization questions are mainly used to generate demographic information. For example, researchers generally want to generate the information related to age, experience, gender, and occupation of the respondents. In some specific cases, in the light of a research objective, the researchers wish to generate some information related to occupation, income, designation, and so on. Sometimes, these categorization information are of paramount importance for a research. Categorization or classification data are the general information collected about the respondents or their households, which is not immediately concerned with the subject of enquiry but is used to divide the respondents into groups for the purpose of analysis or sample validation (Cauter 1956). For example, when the research objective is to determine the impact of age on changing consumer learning, age of the respondents is the key demographic information to be generated during the survey.

Logical Order of Questioning

In a questionnaire, the questions must flow in a logical sequence. There are at least three approaches to suggest the roadmap to place the questions in a logical sequence; they are **funnel technique**, **work technique**, and sections technique. **Funnel technique** suggests asking general questions first and then the specific questions. The general questions allow an interviewer to have knowledge about the respondent's understanding and opinion about the subject matter to be investigated. **Work technique** suggests that difficult-to-answer, sensitive, or complicated questions should be placed later in the questionnaire. Researchers generally place the scaled questions in this category as the respondent has to put much effort to answer these questions compared with simple questions. The third technique is the **section technique** in which questions are placed in different sections with respect to some common base. In general, the research objective itself provides some common base to place the questions in different sections. Construction of questionnaire is mainly a logical discretion of a researcher, such that there is no strict guideline to follow. These three techniques provide a rational thinking platform to a researcher and there is no reason why a researcher cannot use a combination of all the three as guideline to construct a good questionnaire.

Funnel technique suggests asking general questions first and then the specific questions. Work technique suggests that difficult-to-answer, sensitive, or complicated questions should be placed later in the questionnaire. The third technique is the section technique in which questions are placed in different sections with respect to some common base.

4.3.2.4 Decision Regarding Question Response Choice

After deciding about the question format as a closed-ended question, the researcher has to make an important decision about the number of response choices to be presented before the respondent. It is important to understand that too many response choices will burden the respondent and he or she will be perplexed while answering. Few response choices will not be able to cover all ranges of possible alternatives. A researcher keeps only two response choices when a question has to be answered availing two alternatives. For example, in some cases, the response alternatives are reasonable "yes" or "no" or when response alternatives are "male" or "female," two alternatives are sensibly good.

It is important to understand that too many response choices will burden the respondent and he or she will be perplexed while answering. Few response choices will not be able to cover all ranges of possible alternatives.

As a general rule, the researchers present a question with five to seven response alternatives. It is important to understand that in many situations, the response alternatives can be many. For example, "which town you will like to visit in the next summer vacations." As one can understand, the response alternatives may be plenty. In this type of situation, a researcher has to frame the alternatives keeping the research objective in mind. A researcher can include the towns in light of the research objective. As discussed earlier, for opening the options of including other alternatives, a researcher must include an alternative as "please specify if any other."

4.3.2.5 Decision Regarding Questionnaire Layout

Questionnaire layout is important to enhance the response rate. A recent study (Lagarace and Washburn 1995) revealed that a user-friendly format, and to some extent colour, is valuable to increase mail survey response rate. The questionnaire layout plays a key and decisive role in the pattern of answering. The appearance of a questionnaire is particularly important in mail surveys because the instrument, along with the preliminary letter and/or cover letter, must sell itself and convince the recipient to complete and return it (Boser 1990). It has been observed that the respondent emphasizes the questions that are placed at the top of the questionnaire compared with that at the bottom. The first part of any questionnaire is the introduction part. This is a vital part of any questionnaire as it explains

Questionnaire layout is important to enhance the response rate.

in brief the purpose of seeking responses. This also assures the respondents that their responses will be kept confidential so as to motivate and encourage them. Beginning part should also consist of a clear-cut instruction to fill the questionnaire, so that the respondent can navigate his or her way through the questionnaire. A researcher can keep the navigation instructions in boldface and in different font size, so that these will not mingle with the other questions.

The questionnaire should not be very long and should not also be ambiguous. To enhance comfort of the respondent, first few questions can be placed to generate some demographic information. The questionnaire may be divided into several parts, where each part of the questionnaire must have a logical base of incorporating questions. Questions of each part should be properly numbered. Wherever required, coding of questions must also be done. This is equally important to print the questionnaire on a good quality paper. If it has to be photocopied, there must be enough attention to get the photocopies on good quality papers. Bad quality papers are perceived as the diluted seriousness of the research objective by the respondents.

4.3.2.6 Producing First Draft of the Questionnaire

At this stage, a researcher decides about the appearance of the questionnaire as it is of paramount importance to generate a good response.

At this stage, a researcher decides about the appearance of the questionnaire as it is of paramount importance to generate a good response. The questionnaire appearance is particularly important in mail surveys because the instrument, along with the preliminary letter and/or cover letter, must sell itself and convince the recipient to complete and return it (Boser 1990). Printing on a poor quality paper or an unprofessional look of the questionnaire may generate a non-serious feeling among the respondents. So, the questionnaire may be printed on a good quality paper and must have a professional look. The appearance of the front cover on a mail questionnaire and the nature of first questions have been purported to have an important influence on the respondent's decision to complete the questionnaire (Frey 1991). Each question in the questionnaire must be distinctly separated. To reduce the questionnaire length, the researchers may crowd the questions, which enhance the ambiguity, which in turn is more dangerous. Hence, the researchers must be careful to not crowd the questions. Instructions to the answer should be as close as possible to the concerned questions. Font size of the questionnaire must be appropriate. Both too small and too big font sizes hinder easy reading.

Phase III is the post-construction phase of the questionnaire design process. It consists of four steps: pre-testing of the questionnaire, revisiting the questionnaire based on the inputs obtained from the pre-testing, revising final draft of the questionnaire, and administering the questionnaire and obtaining responses.

4.3.3 Phase III: Post-Construction Phase

Phase III is the **post-construction phase** of the questionnaire design process. It consists of four steps: **pre-testing of the questionnaire**, revisiting the questionnaire based on the inputs obtained from the pre-testing, revising final draft of the questionnaire, and administering the questionnaire and obtaining responses.

4.3.3.1 Pre-Testing of the Questionnaire

Pre-testing of the questionnaire involves administering the questionnaire to a small sample of the population to identify and eliminate the potential problems of the questionnaire, if any.

Although the questionnaire is prepared by best experts, it may have some problems that can be identified and removed through pre-testing. **Pre-testing of the questionnaire** involves administering the questionnaire to a small sample of the population to identify and eliminate the potential problems of the questionnaire, if any. Testing a questionnaire can be a time-consuming process, and this stage of questionnaire has often been overlooked in the past in the researcher's eagerness to start collecting data (Williams 2003). Avoiding pre-testing may be a serious miss in the development of a good questionnaire. The pre-test is used to ensure that the questionnaire is appropriate for the survey in terms of structure and language, and it enables the researcher to check that the information obtained from the target population is actually collected through the research instrument (Reynolds and Diamantopoulos 1996).

Now, there exists a question that what method should be adapted to pre-test the questionnaire. Blair and Presser (1992) have put the affectivity of four pre-testing methods in the following order: expert panels, the conventional pre-test, behavioural interaction coding, and cognitive interviews. Expert panel is a group of three research experts who are treated as the respondents of the survey and are supposed to identify the problems with the questionnaire. In a conventional pre-test, a researcher takes a small sample from the population and follows the same procedure of interviewing as he or she is supposed to follow for the final survey. Behavioural interaction coding involves observing the individual behaviour while filling the responses and noting deviation from the standard set of behaviour. Cognitive interviews involve discovering the problems in answering the questions. In this method of pre-testing, the interviewer tries to diagnose the problems that the respondents are facing in understanding the questions or in recalling the answer or any other related problem.

Researchers generally use two common procedures to pre-test: protocol analysis and debriefing. Using protocol analysis, a researcher asks the respondent to "think aloud" while answering the question. In this manner, the researcher is able to read the respondent's mind. His or her response to different questions is noted and analysed. This gives an opportunity to the researcher to correct the questionnaire on the basis of the input. Debriefing is an interview conducted when a respondent has filled the questionnaire. After completing, the respondents are informed that the questionnaire they have just filled was a pre-test questionnaire and are requested to share their views about various dimensions of the questionnaire. They are also requested to find out the problems with the questionnaire, which they realized while filling it.

Pre-testing is done on a small sample collected from the target population. Although there is no magic number that should be sampled during a pre-test, most experts would agree that the sample size should be relatively small—100 or fewer people knowledgeable about the test topic (Shao 2002). Few researchers have a counter argument on this sample size of 100 respondents for the pre-testing. Ordinarily, the pre-test sample size is small, varying from 15 to 30 respondents for the initial testing, depending on the heterogeneity of the target population (Malhotra 2004). Largely, determining the sample size is discretion of a researcher. While taking a decision about the sample size for pre-testing, as a thumb rule, a researcher should keep the nature of population diverse. More heterogeneity in population requires relatively large size of the sample compared with the situation when population is relatively homogeneous.

While taking a decision about the sample size for pre-testing, as a thumb rule, a researcher should keep the nature of population diverse. More heterogeneity in population requires relatively large size of the sample compared with the situation when population is relatively homogeneous.

4.3.3.2 Revisiting the Questionnaire Based on the Inputs Obtained from Pre-Testing

To enhance the accuracy, after incorporating suggestions from the pre-testing, a researcher can go for second pre-testing. It is always possible that the second pre-testing may also reveal some of the problems of the questionnaire. Pre-testing of the questionnaire might have provided many inputs in a subjective manner. At this stage, the researcher must objectively incorporate all the inputs obtained from the pre-testing exercise. All the parameters related to the question wording (as discussed in the previous sections) must be carefully considered. Double-barrelled questions, if any, identified in the pre-testing should be either reconstructed or eliminated. Similar treatment is required for leading or loading questions. If pre-testing has identified any overstatement, it must be corrected. Any question having an implicit assumption or generalization must be reconstructed to make the respondents

To enhance the accuracy, after incorporating suggestions from the pre-testing, a researcher can go for second pre-testing.

comfortable with the questionnaire. The questionnaire should also be able to match the respondent's ability to provide answer. Any question overtaxing the respondent's memory must be either simplified or reconstructed.

Similarly, question sequencing must also be re-examined on the basis of the inputs obtained from the pre-testing. Obtained inputs must be examined in the light of appropriateness of screening questions, opening questions, **transition statements**, difficult to answer questions, identification, and categorization questions. The input must also be examined in the light of accuracy of question format. Necessary changes, if any, must be made related to the questionnaire appearance and layout.

4.3.3.3 Revised Final Draft of the Questionnaire

At this stage, the researcher makes the questionnaire "ready to administer" by eliminating all the minute mistakes and tries to make it error free.

At this stage, the researcher once again carefully examines the questionnaire. Insertions and deletions of the previous stage must be re-checked to provide the desired accuracy. The researcher makes the questionnaire "ready to administer" by eliminating all the minute mistakes and tries to make it error free. After careful examination of all the incorporations obtained from pre-testing, the researcher is now ready to have the final draft of the questionnaire and administers to the sample taken from a target population.

At this stage, the researchers administer the questionnaire to the respondents and obtain the responses. These responses are coded, data are tabulated, and appropriate statistical techniques are applied to analyse the data.

4.3.3.4 Administration of the Questionnaire and Obtaining Responses

At this stage, the researchers administer the questionnaire to the respondents and obtain the responses. These responses are coded, data are tabulated, and appropriate statistical techniques are applied to analyse the data. Chapter 9 describes the data preparation and data coding. Chapters 12–19 open the detailed discussion related to data analysis.

REFERENCES

Bickart B., J. M. Phillips and J. Blair (2006). "The Effects of Discussion and Question Wording on Self and Proxy Reports of Behavioural Frequencies", *Marketing Letters,* 17(3): 167–80.

Blair, J. and S. Presser (1992). "An Experimental Comparison of Alternative Pre-Test Technique: A Note on Preliminary Findings", *Journal of Advertising Research,* 32(2): 2–5.

Boser, J. A. (1990). "Surveying Alumni by Mail: Effect of Booklet/Folder Questionnaire Format and Style of Type on Response Rate", *Research in Higher Education,* 31(2): 149–59.

Brennan, M. (1992). "Threats to Survey Research: Excessive Interviewing and 'Sugging'", *Marketing Bulletin,* 3: 56–62.

Burns, A. C. and R. F. Bush (1999). *Marketing Research,* 3rd ed., p. 355. Upper Saddle River, NJ: Prentice-Hall.

Cauter, T. (1956). "Some Aspects of Classification Data in Market Research", *The Incorporated Statistician,* 6(3/4): (133–44).

Connolly, H. B., J. Corner and S. Bowden (2005). "An Empirical Study of the Impact of Question Structure on Recipient Attitude during Knowledge Sharing", *The Electronic Journal of Knowledge Management,* 32(1): 1–10.

DeLeeuw, E. D. (2001). "Reducing Missing Data in Surveys: An Overview of Methods", *Quality & Quantity,* 35: 147–60.

Frey, J. H. (1991). "The Impact of Cover Design and First Questions on Response Rates for a Mail Survey of Sky Divers", *Leisure Science,* 13(1): 67–76.

Johnson, J. M., D. N. Bristow and K. C. Schneider (2004). "Did You not Understand the Question or Not? An Investigation of Negatively Worded Questions in Survey Research", *Journal of Applied Business Research,* 20(1): 75–86.

Lagarace, R. and J. Washburn (1995). "An Investigation Into the Effect of Questionnaire Format and Color Variations on Mail Survey Response Rates", *Journal of Technical Writing and Communication,* 25(1): 57–70.

Malhotra, N. K., (2004). *Marketing Research: An Applied Orientation*, 4th ed., p. 291. Pearson Education.

Malhotra, N. K., J. Agarwal and M. Peterson (1996). "Methodological Issues in Cross-Cultural Marketing Research", *International Marketing Review,* 13(5): 7–43.

Reynolds, N. and A. Diamantopoulos (1996). "The Effect of Pretest Method on Error Detection Rates", *European Journal of Marketing,* 32(5/6): 480–98.

Schwarz, N. and H. J. Hippler (1995). "Subsequent Questions may Influence Answers to Preceding Questions in Mail Survey", *Public Opinion Quarterly,* 59(1): 93–7.

Shao, A. T. (2002). *Marketing Research: An Aid to Decision Making*, 2nd ed., p. 279. South-Western Thomson Learning.

Swamy, S. (2007). *Usability and Internationalization (LNCS),* Part II. p. 496. Springer Berlin/Heidelberg.

Welch, J. L. and C. O. Swift (1992). "Question Order Effects in Taste Testing of Beverages", *Journal of the Academy of Marketing Science,* 20(3): 265–8.

Williams, A. (2003). "How to … Write and Analyse a Questionnaire", *Journal of Orthodontics,* 30(3): 245–52.

SUMMARY |

To conduct any research, questionnaire is an important tool. A questionnaire consists of formalized and pre-specified set of questions designed to get responses from potential respondents.

Designing of questionnaire is a systematic process consisting of three phases: pre-construction phase, construction phase, and post-construction phase. Phase I is the pre-construction phase of the questionnaire design process. It consists of three steps: specify the required information in the light of research objective, an overview of the respondent's characteristics, and decision regarding selecting an appropriate survey technique. Phase II is the real construction phase of the questionnaire design process. It consists of six steps: decision regarding question format (structured questions vs unstructured questions), decision regarding question relevance and wording, decision regarding question sequencing, decision regarding question response choice, decision regarding questionnaire layout, and producing first draft of the questionnaire. Phase III is the post-construction phase of the questionnaire design process. It consists of four steps: pre-testing of the questionnaire, revisiting the questionnaire based on the inputs obtained from the pre-testing, revising final draft of the questionnaire, and administering the questionnaire and obtaining responses.

NOTE |

1. Prowess (V. 3.1): Centre for Monitoring Indian Economy Pvt. Ltd, Mumbai, accessed September 2009, reprinted with permission.

KEY TERMS |

DISCUSSION QUESTIONS |

1. What is a questionnaire and how can we use the questionnaire as a research tool?
2. What are the steps involved in the questionnaire designing process?
3. What is a pre-construction phase of the questionnaire and what are the steps to be considered for launching the pre-construction phase of the questionnaire?
4. What is a construction phase of the questionnaire and what are the steps to be considered to launch the construction phase of the questionnaire?
5. What are structured and unstructured questions?
6. Write short notes on the following terms:
   - Open-ended questions
   - Closed-ended questions
   - Dichotomous questions
   - Multiple-choice questions
   - Scales
7. What precautions a researcher should consider while wording the questions?
8. What are double-barrelled questions and how do they negatively impact the effectiveness of a questionnaire?
9. What are leading and loaded questions? How these bias responses while administering the questionnaire?
10. Under what circumstances a researcher uses split-ballot techniques?
11. What are the decision parameters a researcher should consider when sequencing the questions?
12. What is the importance of screening questions, opening questions, and transition statement in the questionnaire construction?
13. What is the use of identification questions and categorization questions in construction of a questionnaire?
14. What are the approaches to be considered when a researcher takes a decision about logical order of questioning?
15. How a questionnaire layout makes an impact on the response rate. Is the questionnaire layout important to increase the response rate?
16. What is a post-construction phase of the questionnaire and what are the steps to be considered to launch the post-construction phase of the questionnaire?
17. Is pre-testing questionnaire essential for a questionnaire development process? Why there is a general tendency of the researchers to avoid the pre-testing questionnaire?

CASE STUDY |

Case 4: *Videocon Industries Limited: Opting a Way of Consolidation for Materializing Dreams*

Introduction: An Overview of the Consumer Electronics Industry in India

The consumer electronics industry has been witnessing a remarkable growth over the past few years. The fast-growing segments during the year were colour televisions, air conditioners, DVD players, and home theatre systems. Other segments of consumer electronics and home appliances have also shown a positive growth. The consumer electronics and home appliances industry broadly comprises brown goods, white goods, and small domestic appliances.

Brown goods: colour televisions, CD and DVD players, camcorders, still cameras, video game consoles, HIFI, and home cinema;
White goods: air conditioners, refrigerators, dish washers, drying cabinets, microwave ovens, washing machines, freezers, and so on;
Small domestic appliances: iron, vacuum cleaners, water purifiers, and so on.

The company is primarily into manufacturing and distribution of colour televisions, refrigerators, washing machines, air conditioners, microwave ovens, glass shells, and other components.[1]

Videocon Group: A Major Player in Consumer Electronics

Shri Nandlal Madhavlal Dhoot was the founder of Videocon Group. In early 1980s, through a technical tie up with Toshiba Corporation of Japan, he produced India's first world-class colour television: Videocon. Today, Videocon is a household name across the nation—India's No. 1 brand of consumer electronics and home appliances, trusted by more than 50 million people to improve the quality of life. Videocon Group has a working environment that is driven by performance, strong value base, empowerment, inclusive approach, diversified talent base, and fun filled. This conducive environment is further fostered by creativity and autonomy, equal opportunities, long-term perspective training, and reward. The philosophy of Videocon Group can be well understood from their Vision and Mission statement: "To delight and deliver beyond expectation through ingenious strategy, intrepid entrepreneurship, improved technology, innovative products, insightful marketing and inspired thinking about the future."[2] Table 4.01 exhibits sales and profit after tax (in million rupees) of Videocon Industries Limited from 1994–1995 to 2008–2009.

TABLE 4.01
Sales and profit after tax (in million rupees) of Videocon Industries Limited from 1994-1995 to 2008-2009

Year	*Sales*	*Profit after tax*
Mar-95	11,179.8	864.9
Mar-96	16,387.5	904.4
Mar-97	17,151.3	884.1
Mar-98	21,077.6	1004.7
Mar-99	24,224.4	772.4
Mar-00	30,030	991
Mar-01	32,440.5	1545.2
Mar-03	49,739.3	1720.3
Mar-04	36,015.3	1072.7
Mar-05	40,031	1415.5
Mar-06	56,538.4	4300.4
Mar-07	75,803.3	8188
Mar-08	87,102.6	8587.6
Mar-09	1,01,051.3	8550.1

Source: Prowess (V. 3.1), Centre for Monitoring Indian Economy Pvt. Ltd, Mumbai, accessed September 2009, reprinted with permission.

Some Challenges Before Consumer Electronics Industry

Like any other industry, consumer electronics industry in India is also facing some problems. Some of the common problems are listed below[1]:

- The sharp depreciation of rupee is exerting pressure on the cost of inputs.
- In view of the global slowdown, the consumer sentiments are getting muted as a result of which it is expected that the overall spending may go down and so is the demand for the company's products.
- There is risk of non-adjustment of product mix in line with the market demand or keep pace with the technological changes.
- There is risk of non-adoption/availability of technology.
- There is risk of inability to keep pace with the changes in product design and features.
- The regulatory environment continues to be uncertain, and changes from time to time can delay the projects.
- Poor government spending on rural and small town electrification program and poor distribution network are major concerns.

Some problems related to the industry can be tackled, but those related to the government policies and other external environment are difficult to handle. For smooth growth, the company has to take care of all the challenges internal and external. The Videocon Group is also aware of all these challenges and ready to counter-attack by adopting some strategic changes. Consolidation of various business activities is one way to cope with the environment challenges.

Videocon Group: Changing the Way through Consolidation

K. R. Kim, the former MD of LG Electronics, was appointed as the vice chairman and CEO of Videocon Industries Limited in 2008. From 2008, Mr K. R. Kim is leading the company in the domestic and global operations. While talking about consolidation issue in 2009, Kim told *The Economic Times* "The Videocon Group was very fragmented with many brands and each of them run by a separate team. So, the first job was to consolidate and generate efficiencies. Just to give a perspective, we have reduced the number of branches from 160 across all the brands to just 46. Similarly, the number of warehouses is now down to 50 from close to 200." Kim optimistically added that the key to success lies in changing the organizational culture first and then sales. While talking about the multi-brand strategy of the group, Kim said that a multi-brand strategy has its own advantageous and disadvantageous, but yes, having too many brands can be a problem as it requires marketing investments. Comparing his grand success in LG with Videocon, Kim stated that at Videocon, we are changing the way we did business earlier. As long as we are able to instil the core values of discipline, integrity, and quality, we will be able to meet the targets.[3]

Videocon Group has realized the problems of having a multi-brand strategy. It is willing to meet the challenges posed on the consumer electronics and home appliance business with the discussed consolidation strategy. Suppose Videocon is interested in assessing "brand shift" in its favour as a result of the consolidation strategy then to operate this research programme, it has to address various issues such as should the company be using comparative scaling techniques or non-comparative scaling techniques? If the company decides to use the non-comparative scaling techniques then should it be a continuous scale, Likert scale, semantic differential scale, or staple scale? How will the company decide about the nature and description of the scale? What will be the physical form of the proposed scale? How the company will be able to meet the criteria of reliability, validity, and sensitivity?

NOTES

1. Prowess (V. 3.1), Centre for Monitoring Indian Economy Pvt. Ltd, Mumbai, accessed September 2009, reprinted with permission.
2. http://www.videoconworld.com, accessed September 2009.
3. http://economictimes.indiatimes.com/Openion/Interviews/We-are-changing-the-way-we-did..., accessed September 2009.

CHAPTER 5

Sampling and Sampling Distributions

LEARNING OBJECTIVES

Upon completion of this chapter, you will be able to:

- Understand the importance of sampling
- Differentiate between random and non-random sampling
- Understand the concept of sampling and non-sampling errors
- Understand the concept of sampling distribution and the application of central limit theorem
- Understand sampling distribution of sample proportion

STATISTICS IN ACTION: LARSEN & TOUBRO LTD

The Indian cement industry was delicensed in 1991 as part of the country's liberalization measures. India is the second largest producer of cement in the world after China, which is the largest producer of cement in the world. The total cement production in India in year 2004-2005 was approximately 126.70 million metric tonnes. This figure is expected to touch 265.00 million metric tonnes by 2014-2015. Table 5.1 highlights the past and expected future growth in cement production in India.

Larsen & Toubro (L&T) was incorporated as a limited company in 1946. The company started its business in the non-core cement sector and later diversified into many fields. The company's businesses have been classified into 6 operating divisions: engineering, construction and contracts; engineering and construction (projects); heavy engineering; electrical and electronics; machinery and industrial products, and technology services. It has prepared some proactive plans to combat the slowdown in India's economic growth.[1]

TABLE 5.1
Cement demand: past and future

Year	*Demand (in million metric tonnes)*
2004–2005	126.70
2005–2006	135.45
2006–2007	145.10
2007–2008	155.65
2008–2009	167.35
2009–2010	180.40
2014–2015	265.00

Source: www.indiastat.com, accessed November 2008, reproduced with permission.

Strong infrastructure and industrial growth, buoyant market for the capital goods sector, and a sound risk management framework contributed to the growth of the company. M. L. Naik, Chairman and Managing Director, L&T, stated, "L&T is organized into 15 companies and there is a fairly good hedge

>>>

against a slowdown in any one sector with new operating companies in shipping, power, and railways".[2] Table 5.2 indicates the profit after tax of L&T from 2000–2007.

L&T realizes the importance of customer satisfaction in order to accomplish its ambitious growth plans. Let us assume that L&T wants to ascertain the satisfaction level of its customers. The company has a large customer base. Should the company use a census or a sample to administer the customer satisfaction survey? If it decides to go in for a sample, what is the procedure of sampling that it should apply? If the population is not normal, how can the sampling be justified? This chapter provides the answers to such questions. It discusses the importance of sampling, random and non-random sampling, sampling and non-sampling errors, sampling distribution, and central limit theorem.

TABLE 5.2
Profit after tax of L&T from 2000–2007

Year	*2000*	*2001*	*2002*	*2003*	*2004*	*2005*	*2006*	*2007*
Profit after tax (in million rupees)	3416.3	3150.6	3468.0	4331.0	5327.5	9838.5	10,116.0	14,022.3

Source: Prowess (V. 3.1), Centre for Monitoring Indian Economy Pvt. Ltd, Mumbai, accessed November 2008, reproduced with permission.

5.1 INTRODUCTION

While conducting research, a researcher has to collect data from various sources. We have already discussed that for collecting data, relying on the entire population is neither feasible nor practical. So, a researcher has to select a **sample** instead of going in for a complete census. A researcher faces problems in terms of the procedure of selecting a sample. Statistical inference is based on the information obtained from the sample. On the basis of information obtained from the sample (through sample statistic), an inference about the population (population parameter) is made. In this process, we need to keep in mind that the sample contains only a portion of the population and not the entire population. So, a proper **sampling** method should be used for selecting a sample. In order to make a good estimate of the population characteristics, selecting a reasonably good sampling method is of paramount importance.

This chapter focuses on the various issues related to sampling and sampling distributions. It also presents the distribution of two very important statistics; sample mean and sample proportion. Sample mean and sample proportion are normally distributed under certain conditions. The knowledge of these statistics form the foundation of statistical analysis and inference.

5.2 SAMPLING

A researcher generally takes a small portion of the population for study, which is referred to as sample. The process of selecting a sample from the population is called sampling.

Sampling is the most widely used tool for gathering important and useful information from the population. A researcher generally takes a small portion of the population for study, which is referred to as sample. The process of selecting a sample from the population is called sampling. As a part of the research process, we collect information from the sample, apply statistical tools and techniques for the analysis, and make important interpretations on the basis of statistical analysis. Decisions are then taken on the basis of this interpretation. For example, there are two methods of determining the degree of job satisfaction of a company having 120,000 employees. The first method is to prepare a well-structured questionnaire and administer it to all employees. This method would be very expensive and cumbersome. The second method is to select a representative sample from the population and make decisions on the basis of the information obtained from the sample (after applying all the necessary statistical tools and techniques). Therefore, census is not a practical method of gathering information in many situations because of the time, costs, and other constraints involved. In other words, we can say that sampling is the only practical solution in certain situations.

5.3 WHY IS SAMPLING ESSENTIAL?

We have discussed the advantages of sampling over a complete census. The following points reinforce this statement.

- Sampling saves time.
- Sampling saves money.
- When the research process is destructive in nature, sampling minimizes the destruction.
- Sampling broadens the scope of the study in light of the scarcity of resources.
- It has been noticed that sampling provides more accurate results, as compared to census because in sampling, **non-sampling errors** can be controlled more easily. (The concept of non-sampling errors will be discussed in detail later in this chapter).
- In most cases complete census is not possible and, hence, sampling is the only option left.

5.4 THE SAMPLING DESIGN PROCESS

Sampling design process can be explained by five interrelated steps. These five steps are shown in Figure 5.1.

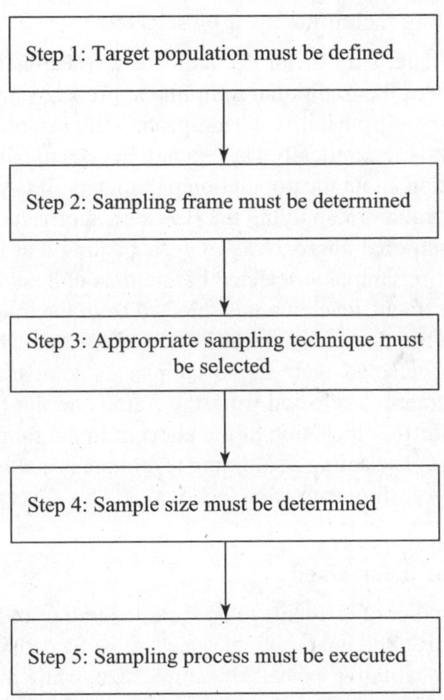

FIGURE 5.1
Steps in sampling design process

Step 1: Target population must be defined

Target population is the collection of the objects which possess the information required by the researcher and about which an inference is to be made.

The target population should be defined in the light of a research objective. **Target population** is the collection of objects, which possess the information required by the researcher and about which an inference is to be made. Improper definition of the target population will lead to misleading results which might prove dangerous for a researcher. Therefore, target population must be defined very carefully. As discussed earlier, the research objective should be the most important factor to be taken into account while deciding on the target population. However, other parameters like time and cost should not be ignored.

Step 2: Sampling Frame must be determined

A researcher takes a sample from a population list, directory, map, city directory, or any other source used to represent the population. This list possesses the information about the subjects and is called the sampling frame.

A researcher takes a sample from a population list, directory, map, city directory, or any other source used to represent the population. This list possesses the information about the subjects and is called the **sampling frame**. It might seem that the target population and the sampling frame are the same, however, in reality, there is a reasonable difference between the two. For understanding this difference, let us take the example of a telephone directory. A telephone directory possesses information about a particular region. When we take a sample on the basis of information available in a directory, there is a possibility that this will not give us true information. It is always possible that few subjects in that region may not have telephones, few subjects may have changed their residence and this information might not have been updated in the telephone directory. Similarly, some subjects may have multiple listings under different names; some subjects may have changed the numbers ever since the directory was printed. **Sampling** is carried out on the sampling frame and not on the target population. Theoretically, the target population and the sampling frame are the same, however, in practice, sampling frame and target population are often different. Over-registered sampling frames contain all the units of target population plus some additional units. Under-registered sampling frames contain fewer units as compared to the target population. A researcher's objective is to minimize the differences between the sampling frame and the target population.

Sampling is carried out from the sampling frame and not from the target population.

Step 3: Appropriate sampling technique must be selected

In sampling with replacement, an element is selected from the frame, required information is obtained, and then the element is placed back in the frame. This way, there is a possibility of the element being selected again in the sample. As compared to this, in sampling without replacement, an element is selected from the frame and not replaced in the frame. This way, the possibility of further inclusion of the element in the sample is eliminated.

Selecting a sampling technique is a crucial decision for a researcher. A researcher has to decide between the Bayesian or the traditional sampling approach, sampling with or without replacement, and whether to use probability or non-probability sampling techniques.

The Bayesian approach is theoretically very sound, but practically not very appealing. It is based on prior information about the population parameters. It is very difficult to obtain the required information essential for applying the Bayesian approach. Hence, its use is very limited in research. The traditional approach is more appealing and is widely used. In the traditional approach, the entire sample is selected before data collection begins.

In sampling with replacement, an element is selected from the frame, the required information is obtained, and then the element is placed back in the frame. This way, there is a possibility of the element being selected again in the sample. As compared to this, in sampling without replacement, an element is selected from the frame and not replaced in the frame. This way, the possibility of further inclusion of the element in the sample is eliminated.

The most important part of selecting a sampling technique is making the choice between **random sampling** and **non-random sampling** techniques. This is very important and is discussed in detail in this chapter.

Step 4: Sample size must be determined

Sample size refers to the number of elements to be included in the study.

Sample size refers to the number of elements to be included in the study. While deciding the sample size, various qualitative and quantitative aspects must be considered. In this section, we are going to discuss the qualitative aspects of sample size, while the quantitative aspects will be discussed later. The nature of research and analysis, number of variables, sample size used for similar kind of study, time, resources, incidence rates, and completion rates are some of the qualitative considerations that need to be taken into account when taking a decision about the sample.

The nature of research and analysis is an important consideration while deciding the sample size. For qualitative research, a small sample size is sufficient. For conclusive research, a larger sample is required. Sophisticated statistical analysis is also a foundation for taking a decision about the sample size. The statistical analysis techniques applied for analysing small and large samples are different. In case of multivariate analysis or when the data is being analysed at the subgroup or segment level, large data are required. Similarly, when data are collected for a large number of variables, large samples are required. The cumulative errors across variables are reduced in a large sample.

Sample size used for similar studies can also be used as a basis for selecting sample size. This is more useful when non-probability sampling techniques are used for the study. Time and resources are the two constraints on which the sample size of every research study is based. Sample size should also be adjusted with respect to factors such as eligible respondents and the completion rate.

Step 5: Sampling process must be executed

The execution of sampling techniques requires detailed specification of target population, sampling frame, sampling techniques, and the sample size. At this stage, each step in the sampling process must be effectively executed.

5.5 RANDOM VERSUS NON-RANDOM SAMPLING

Sampling procedure can be broadly divided into two categories: random and non-random sampling. In **random sampling**, each unit of the population has the same probability (chance) of being selected as part of the sample. In random sampling, the chance factor comes into play in the process of sample selection. For statistical analysis, a random sample is ideal. However, there may be some cases where random sampling is not feasible. In these cases, non-random sampling methods can be good alternatives. As compared to random sampling, in non-random sampling, every unit of the population does not have the same chance of being selected in the sample. In non-random sampling, members of the sample are not selected by chance. Some other factors like familiarity of the researcher with the subject, convenience, etc. are the basis of selection. On the basis of the selection procedure used, random and non-random sampling techniques are referred to as probability and non-probability sampling, respectively. Figure 5.2 depicts the broad classification of random sampling methods and non-random sampling methods.

In random sampling, each unit of the population has the same probability (chance) of being selected as part of the sample.

In non-random sampling, members of the sample are not selected by chance. Some other factors like familiarity of the researcher with the subject, convenience, etc. are the basis of selection.

5.6 RANDOM SAMPLING METHODS

We have discussed that in random sampling methods, every unit of the population has an equal chance of being selected in the sample. As shown in Figure 5.2, the random sampling methods used for selecting samples from the population are as follows:

5.6.1 Simple Random Sampling

In **simple random sampling**, each member of the population has an equal chance of being included in the sample. Simple random sampling is the most common method of selecting a sample from the population. In the simple random sampling method, first, a complete list of

In simple random sampling, each member of the population has an equal chance of being included in the sample.

FIGURE 5.2
Random and non-random sampling methods

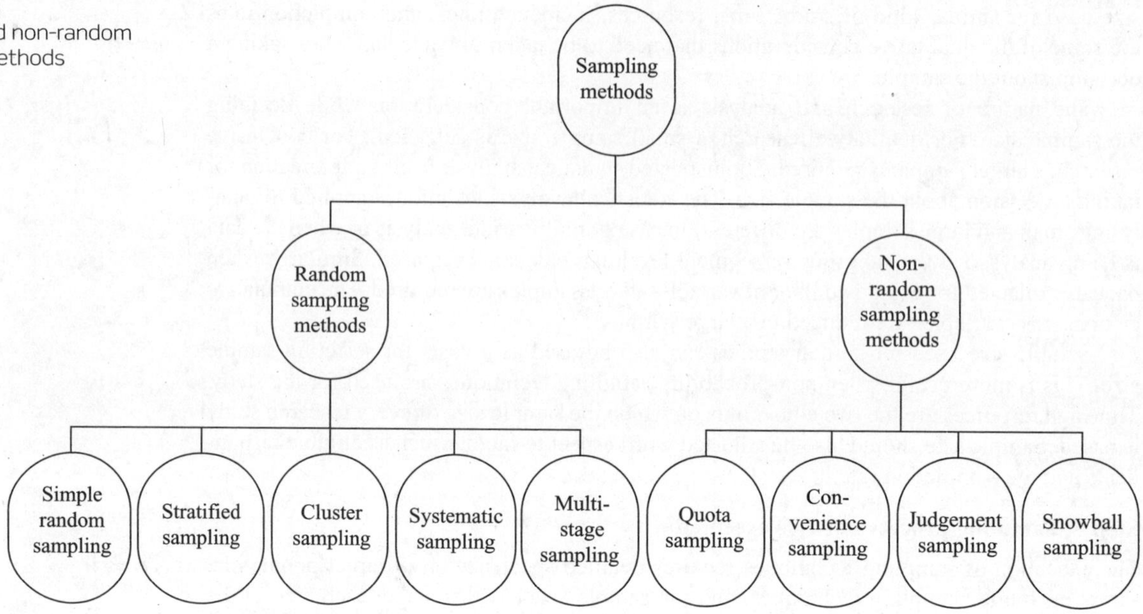

all the members of the population is prepared. Each element is identified by a distinct number (say from 1 to *N*). Then *n* items are selected from a population of size *N*, either using random number tables or the random number generator. Random number generator is usually a computer program that generates random numbers. The random number table has been developed by statisticians. For small populations, simple random sampling is appropriate, but when the population is large, simple random sampling becomes cumbersome. This is because numbering all the members of the population and then selecting items is not an easy task.

Simple random sampling is based on the process of selecting a sample randomly. This does not mean that the randomness allows haphazard selection of samples; it means that the process of selecting a sample should be free from human judgement (bias). In this context, there are two methods of drawing a random sample from the population. These two methods are: (1) the lottery method and (2) the use of random numbers.

In the lottery method, each unit of the population is properly numbered. The numbers are written on different pieces of paper. The pieces of paper are then folded and mixed together in a small box. A sample of our choice can be drawn randomly from the box (by selecting folded papers randomly).

The second method to draw a random sample is to use a random number table. The units of the population are numbered from 1 to *N*. A sample of size *n* has to be then selected. The following example explains the use of random number tables.

Suppose a researcher wants to conduct a survey related to attitude measurement in five companies. He has a list of 25 companies. He wants to select 5 companies out of 25 through the simple random sampling method. The first step is to number each unit of the population. For this purpose, we select as many digits for each unit sampled, as there are in the largest number in the population. For example, if there are 700 members in a population, we select three-digit numbers like 001, 003, 045, 054 for the first, third, forty-fifth and fifty-fourth units, respectively.

A researcher wants to select five companies out of 25, so in this case, each unit of the population is numbered from 1 to 25 with two-digit numbers, as explained earlier. This population contains only 25 companies, so all the numbers greater than 25, that is, (26–99)

TABLE 5.3
A part of the random number table

12651	61646	11769	75109	86996	97669	25757	32535	07122	76763
81769	74436	02630	72310	45049	18029	07469	42341	98173	79260
36737	98863	77240	76251	00654	64688	09343	70278	67331	98729
82861	54371	76610	94934	72748	44124	05610	53750	95938	01485
21325	15732	24127	37431	09723	63529	73977	95218	96074	42138

must be ignored. For example, if a number 58 is selected, it is ignored and the process is continued until a value between 1 to 25 is obtained. Similarly, if the same number occurs the second time, we proceed to another number. Table 5.3 depicts a part of the random number table.

The researcher's objective is to select 5 companies out of 25, so different two-digits numbers must be selected from the table of random numbers. For this, we start from the first pair of digits from the random number table and proceed across the first row until we get the required 5 companies in terms of the different values between 01 and 25. Here, we have started the selection of samples from the first row of the random number table, but it may be done from anywhere in the table.

In Table 5.4, a list of 25 companies is given from which the researcher wants to select 5 companies for his study. The list given in Table 5.4 is not numbered and the list is numbered in Table 5.5 for convenience in sample selection.

From Table 5.3, the first two digit number is 12 which lies between 01 and 25. So, this number can be selected as the first number of choice. The next two numbers are 65 and 16. The number 65 is out of the range of the selection criteria. So, the next two digit number 16 is selected, which is within the range of the selection criteria. In a similar manner, we proceed further and select five two-digit numbers as 12, 16, 11, 09, and 25. In this manner, from Table 5.5, the 12th, 16th, 11th, 09th, and 25th companies are selected in the final sample. So, in this manner the final sample will consist of the following five companies:

Tata Iron and Steel Company Ltd
Maruti Udyog Ltd
Mahanagar Telephone Nigam Ltd
Larsen & Toubro Ltd
Ranbaxy Laborataries Ltd

TABLE 5.4
A list of 25 companies

IndianOil Corporation Ltd
Reliance Industries Ltd
Bharat Sanchar Nigam Ltd
Oil and Natural Gas Corporation Ltd
National Thermal Power Corporation Ltd
Hindustan Petroleum Corporation Ltd
Bharat Petroleum Corporation Ltd
Steel Authority of India Ltd
Larsen & Toubro Ltd
Gas Authority of India Ltd
Mahanagar Telephone Nigam Ltd
Tata Iron & Steel Company Ltd
Tata Motors Ltd
Hindustan Unilever Ltd
Bharat Heavy Electricals Ltd
Maruti Udyog Ltd
Essar Steel Ltd
Videsh Sanchar Nigam Ltd
Grasim Industries Ltd
Bajaj Auto Ltd
Haldia Petrochemicals Ltd
Videocon International Ltd
Wipro Ltd
Sterlite Industries Ltd
Ranbaxy Laboratories Ltd

TABLE 5.5
A numbered list of 25 companies

1	IndianOil Corporation Ltd
2	Reliance Industries Ltd
3	Bharat Sanchar Nigam Ltd
4	Oil & Natural Gas Corporation Ltd
5	National Thermal Power Corporation Ltd
6	Hindustan Petroleum Corporation Ltd
7	Bharat Petroleum Corporation Ltd
8	Steel Authority of India Ltd
9	Larsen & Toubro Ltd
10	Gas Authority of India Ltd
11	Mahanagar Telephone Nigam Ltd
12	Tata Iron & Steel Company Ltd
13	Tata Motors Ltd
14	Hindustan Unilever Ltd
15	Bharat Heavy Electricals Ltd
16	Maruti Udyog Ltd
17	Essar Steel Ltd
18	Videsh Sanchar Nigam Ltd
19	Grasim Industries Ltd
20	Bajaj Auto Ltd
21	Haldia Petrochemicals Ltd
22	Videocon International Ltd
23	Wipro Ltd
24	Sterlite Industries Ltd
25	Ranbaxy Laboratories Ltd

5.6.2 Using MS Excel for Random Number Generation

For several probability distributions, random numbers can be generated by MS Excel. For this, select **Data** from the menu bar and then select **Data Analysis.** From the **Data Analysis** dialog box, select **Random Number Generation**. The required distribution can be selected from the third box of the **Random Number Generation** dialog box. Select the distribution for which the random numbers are to be generated (Figure 5.3). With the selected distribution, the options and the required responses in the **Random Number Generation** dialog box will change accordingly. In each case, the number of variables should be filled in the first box and the number of random numbers to be generated should be filled in the second box (Figure 5.3).

5.6.3 Using Minitab for Random Number Generation

Minitab can also be used for random number generation for various probability distributions. For this purpose, click **Calc/Random Data/Normal**. The **Normal distribution** dialog box as shown in Figure 5.4, will appear on the screen. Note that like normal distribution, any of the probability distributions can be used for random number generation. As shown in Figure 5.4, the random numbers to be generated should be placed in the **Generate rows of data** box. For example, if we want to generate 50 random numbers, we need to place 50 in the box, as shown in Figure 5.4. In **Store in column(s)** box, place the column location where we want to store the random numbers. The required mean and standard deviation can also be placed in the concerned boxes. Like normal distribution, each distribution requires specific parameters. According to the requirement, these parameters can be placed in the concerned boxes and random numbers for concerned specific probability distributions can be generated.

In stratified random sampling, elements in the population are divided into homogeneous groups called strata. Then, researchers use the simple random sampling method to select a sample from each of the strata. Each group is called stratum. In stratified random sampling, stratum should be relatively homogenous and the strata should contrast with each other. This process of dividing heterogeneous populations into relatively homogenous groups is called stratification.

5.6.4 Stratified Random Sampling

Stratified random sampling is based on the concept of homogeneity and heterogeneity. In stratified random sampling, elements in the population are divided into homogeneous groups called strata. Then, researchers use the simple random sampling method to select a sample from each of the strata. Each group is called stratum. In stratified random sampling, stratum should be relatively homogenous and the strata should contrast with each other. This process of dividing heterogeneous populations into relatively homogenous groups is called stratification. In most cases, researchers use demographic variables as the base of stratification.

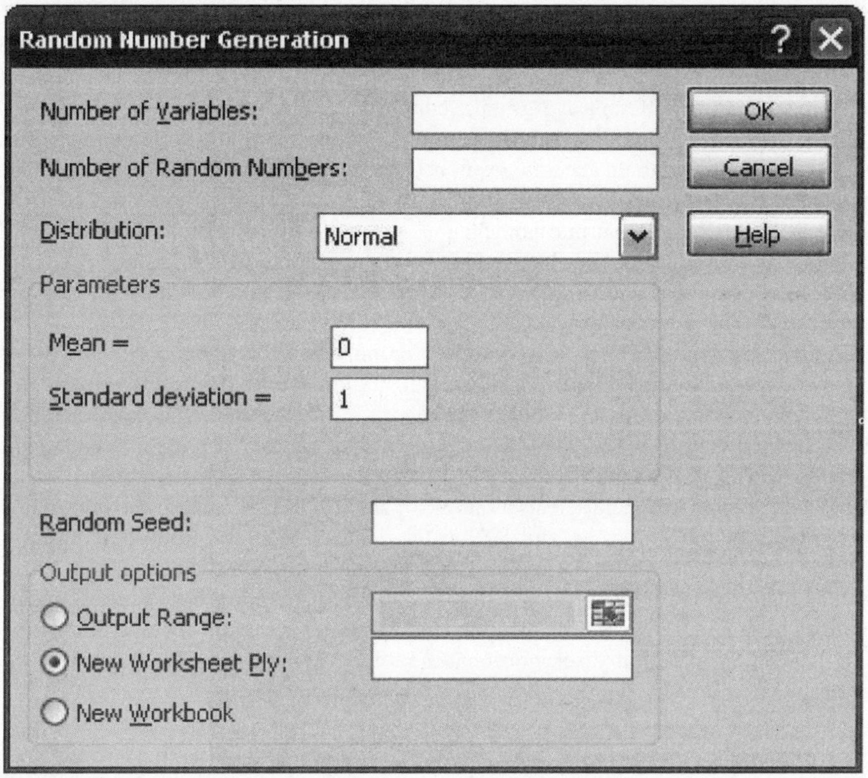

FIGURE 5.3
MS Excel Random Number Generation dialog box (for normal distribution)

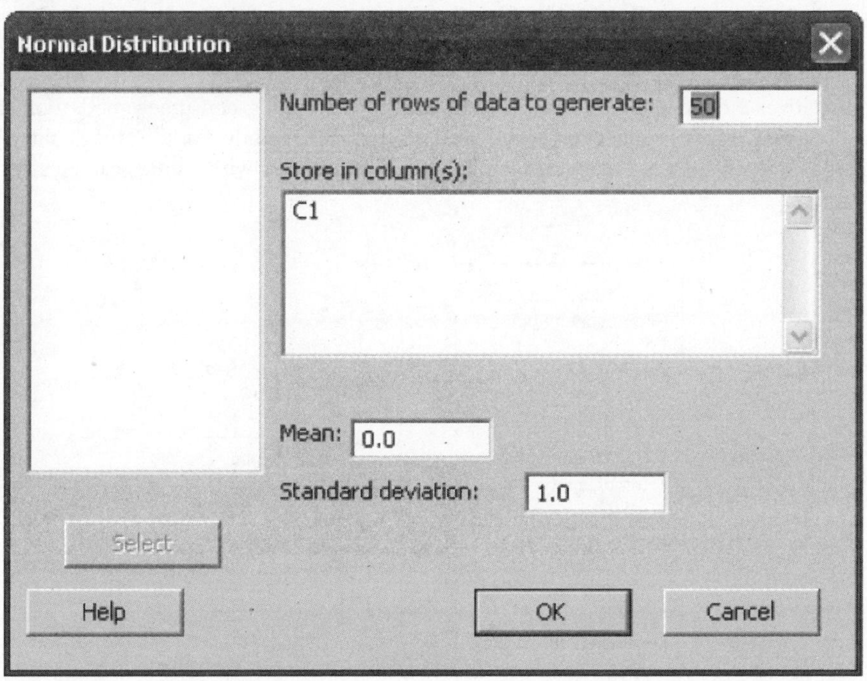

FIGURE 5.4
Minitab Normal Distribution dialog box (for random number generation)

For example, a company that produces perfume wants to know the consumer preference for its newly launched product. For this purpose, company researchers have to select a sample of 1000 consumers from a particular town with a population of 1,000,000. This population contains people from different age groups, education, regions, religion, etc. These groups may have different reasons for preferring a brand. Taking 1000 people randomly from the population will not lead to an accurate result because they may not be true representatives of the population. So, instead of selecting people directly from the population, we need to divide this heterogeneous population into homogenous groups, and then simple random sampling procedure can be used to obtain the samples from these homogenous groups. A researcher has to keep in mind that within each group, homogeneity or alikeness must be present and between the groups, heterogeneity must be present.

In cases where the percentage of sample taken from each stratum is proportionate to the actual percentage of the stratum within the whole population, stratified sampling is termed as proportionate stratified sampling.

Stratified random sampling can be either proportionate or disproportionate. In cases where the percentage of sample taken from each stratum is proportionate to the actual percentage of the stratum within the whole population, stratified sampling is termed as proportionate stratified sampling. For example, suppose in a population, 75% are matriculates, 15% are graduates, and 10% are postgraduates. A researcher uses the stratified random sampling based on educational level and selects a sample of size 1000. This sample is required to have 750 matriculates, 150 graduates, and 100 postgraduates to achieve proportionate stratified sampling. On the other hand, a sample of 600 matriculates, 200 graduates, and 200 postgraduates will lead to disproportionate stratified random sampling. So, in cases, where the sample taken from each stratum is disproportionate to the actual percentage of the stratum within the whole population, disproportionate stratified random sampling occurs. Figure 5.5 exhibits the stratified random sampling based on educational levels.

In cases where the sample taken from each stratum is disproportionate to the actual percentage of the stratum within the whole population, disproportionate stratified random sampling occurs.

In cluster sampling, we divide the population into non-overlapping areas or clusters.

5.6.5 Cluster (or Area) Sampling

In **cluster sampling**, we divide the population into non-overlapping areas or clusters. It might seem as there is no difference between stratified sampling and **cluster sampling**. This is not true; in fact there is a well-defined difference between stratified sampling and cluster sampling. In **stratified sampling**, strata happen to be homogenous but in cluster sampling, clusters are internally heterogeneous. A cluster contains a wide range of elements that are good representatives of the population. For example, a fast-moving-consumer-goods company wants to launch a new product and wants to conduct a market study. For this, the country can be divided into clusters of cities and then individual consumers within cities can be selected

In stratified sampling, strata happen to be homogenous but in cluster sampling, clusters are internally heterogeneous. A cluster contains a wide range of elements and is a good representative of the population.

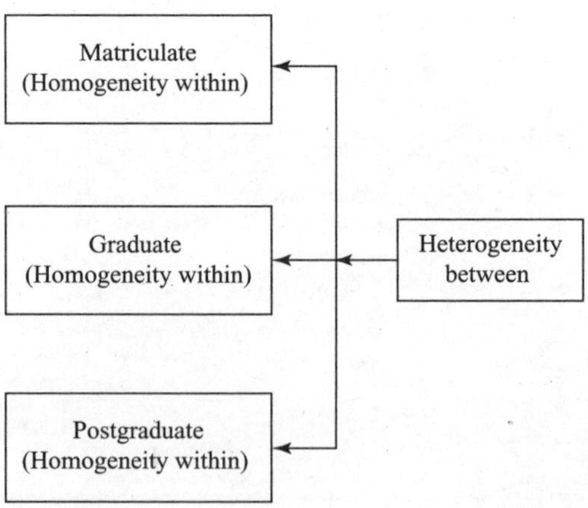

FIGURE 5.5
Stratified random sampling based on educational levels

for the survey. In this case, clusters of cities may be too large for surveying individuals. In order to overcome this difficulty, the city can be divided into clusters of blocks and consumers can be selected randomly from the blocks. This technique of dividing the original cluster into a second set of clusters is called two-stage sampling.

Cluster sampling is very useful in terms of cost and convenience. When compared to stratum in stratified random sampling, clusters are easy to obtain and focus of the study remains on the cluster instead of the entire population, so cost is also reduced in cluster sampling (Figure 5.6). In real life, cluster sampling becomes the only available option because of the unavailability of the sample frame. This does not mean cluster sampling is free from drawbacks. Cluster sampling may be statistically inefficient, in cases where elements of the cluster are similar.

5.6.6 Systematic (or Quasi-Random) Sampling

In **systematic sampling**, sample elements are selected from the population at uniform intervals in terms of time, order, or space. For obtaining samples in systematic sampling, first of all, a sampling fraction is calculated. For example, a researcher wants to take a sample of size 30 from a population of size 900 and he has decided to use systematic sampling for this purpose. As the first step, he has to calculate a sample fraction k, which is equal to $\frac{N}{n}$, where N is the total number of units in the population and n is the sample size.

In systematic sampling, sample elements are selected from the population at uniform intervals in terms of time, order, or space.

So, in this case, sample fraction will be $\frac{900}{30} = 30$. For obtaining the sample, the first member can be selected randomly and after that every 30th member of the population is included in the sample. Suppose the first element 3 is selected randomly and after this, every 30th element, that is, 33rd, 63rd, … element up to a sample size of 30 are included in the sample. For obtaining starting point or the beginning point of the sampling process, a random number table can also be used. In our example $k = 30$, so a researcher can use a random number table to get the first element between 1 and 30.

In systematic sampling, the selection of a sample is very convenient and is cost and time efficient. This is an aspect of systematic sampling which makes it applicable in many situations. However, systematic sampling has certain limitations. In systematic sampling, the first unit is selected randomly and the selection of remaining units is based on the first unit. So, randomness of the selected sample units can be questioned. There can be another problem with systematic sampling; if the data are periodic and the sampling interval is in syncopation with it. For example, consider a list of 250 consumer groups that is a merged list of five

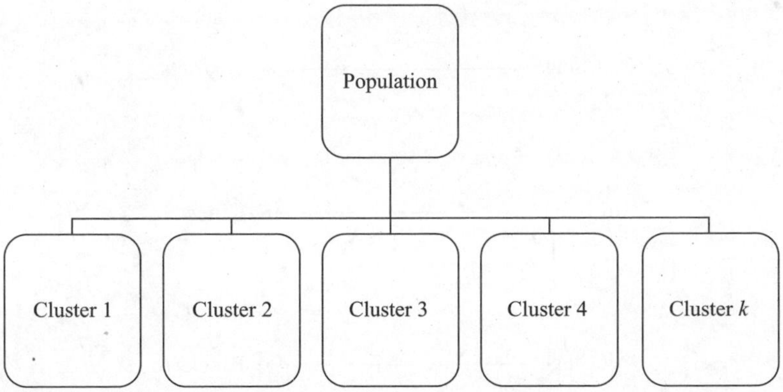

FIGURE 5.6
Diagram for cluster sampling

income classes with 50 consumers in each class. The list of 50 consumers is an ordered list of consumers with some predefined sequence in data. If a researcher uses systematic sampling, then on the basis of the first selected unit, the possibility of including almost all high-income groups, almost all middle-income groups or lower-income groups in the sample cannot be ignored because the original population is arranged in order. Let us assume that, this researcher wants to take a sample of size 10 from the population of size 250. As discussed the sample fraction will be $\frac{250}{10} = 25$. The researcher selects the first unit as the 25th item (randomly) and then selects every 25th unit such as 50th, 75th, 100th, …, 250th unit. As there is some predefined sequence in the data, the possibility of selecting all the 10 units or maximum units from a particular income group cannot be ignored. Systematic sampling is based on the assumption that the source of the population element is random. Systematic sampling is some times known as quasi-random sampling.

5.6.7 Multi-Stage Sampling

As the name indicates, multi-stage sampling involves the selection of units in more than one stage.

As the name indicates, **multi-stage sampling** involves the selection of units in more than one stage. The population consists of primary stage units and each of these primary stage units consists of secondary stage units. In the process of multi-stage sampling, first, a sample is taken from the primary stage units and then a sample is taken from the secondary stage units. For example, a researcher wants to select 200 urban households from the entire country and wants to use multi-stage sampling for this. For this purpose, he may first select 27 states from the country as the primary sampling unit. During the second stage, 50 districts from these 27 states may be selected. Finally, 4 households from each district may be randomly selected. Thus, a researcher will obtain the required 200 urban households in two stages.

Though this type of sampling may be costly, it will be a true representative of the entire population. The number of stages in multi-stage sampling is a matter of the researcher's discretion. On the basis of convenience or the discretion of the researcher, a few stages can be deleted or included in multi-stage sampling. In the previous example, the last stage was at the district level, which may be expensive and inconvenient. So, to avoid this difficulty, two more stages, in terms of cities and blocks can be included in the sampling process. In this manner, stages of the sampling can be as shown in Figure 5.7.

1st Stage → States

2nd Stage → Districts

3rd Stage → Cities

4th Stage → Blocks

FIGURE 5.7
Multi-stage (four stages) sampling

5.7 NON-RANDOM SAMPLING

Sampling techniques where the selection of the sampling units is not based on a random selection process are called **non-random sampling techniques**. In the selection of the sample units, the probability (of being included in the sample) is not used, which is why these techniques are also termed as non-probability sampling techniques. **Quota sampling**, **convenience sampling**, **judgement sampling**, and **snowball sampling** techniques are some of the commonly used non-random sampling techniques.

Sampling techniques where selection of the sampling units is not based on a random selection process are called non-random sampling techniques.

5.7.1 Quota Sampling

Quota sampling in some cases is similar to stratified random sampling. In quota sampling, certain subclasses, such as age, gender, income group, and education level are used as strata. Stratified random sampling is based on the concept of randomly selecting units from the stratum. However, in case of quota sampling, researchers use non-random sampling methods to gather data from one stratum until the required quota fixed by the researcher is fulfilled. A quota is generally based on the proportion of subclasses in the population. For example, a researcher wants to select a sample of 1000 from a population of 50,000. This population contains 10,000 males and 40,000 females. The researcher wants to apply quota sampling and he assigns a quota in the sample according to the population proportion. So, in a sample of 1000 people, the researcher will select 200 males and 800 females as per the population proportion.

In quota sampling, certain subclasses, such as age, gender, income group, and education level are used as strata. Stratified random sampling is based on the concept of randomly selecting units from the stratum. However, in case of quota sampling, a researcher uses non-random sampling methods to gather data from one stratum until the required quota fixed by the researcher is fulfilled.

Quota sampling is a useful technique when there are cost and time constraints. However, the non-random nature of this sampling method is a serious limitation. Obtaining a representative sample in quota sampling is difficult because selection largely depends on the researcher's convenience. In spite of these limitations, quota sampling is useful under certain specified conditions. For example, a researcher wants to stratify the population of different scooter owners in a city, however, he finds it difficult to obtain a list of Bajaj scooter owners. In this case, through quota sampling, the researcher can conduct interviews of all the scooter owners and cast out non-Bajaj scooter owners until the quota of Bajaj scooter owners is filled.

5.7.2 Convenience Sampling

As the name indicates, in convenience sampling, sample elements are selected based on the convenience of a researcher. In this case, the researcher includes samples which are readily available. The focus is on the convenience of the researcher. For example, a marketing research firm wants to survey 2000 consumers for a particular product. It will be more convenient for the firm to interview 2000 customers who come to the mall and look friendly. If a researcher wants to survey 1000 consumers door-to-door in a particular locality, samples can be selected from houses which are near by, houses where people are responsive and friendly, and houses which are in the first floor of an apartment. From the discussion, it is very clear that in convenience sampling, the researcher's convenience is the only basis for selecting sampling units. Hence, this eliminates the chance factor in the sample selection process. It suffers from non-randomness criteria like any other non-random sampling technique.

In convenience sampling, sample elements are selected based on the convenience of a researcher.

5.7.3 Judgement Sampling

In judgement sampling, the selection of the sampling unit is based on the judgement of a researcher. In some cases, researchers believe that they will be able to select a more representative sample by using their judgement, which will be time and cost efficient and more accurate than simple random sampling. This sampling technique also suffers from the limitations

In judgement sampling, selection of the sampling units is based on the judgement of a researcher.

of other non-random sampling techniques. The judgement of the researcher makes the sampling process non-random and, hence, determining **sampling error** is difficult because probabilities are based on non-random selection. In addition, judgement sampling does not provide a basis for comparing the judgement of two different persons. There is no well-defined scientific method which can tell us that how one person's judgement is better than another person's judgement. Generally, judgement sampling is useful when a sample size is small. In case of large samples, the bias from the researcher's end may be high.

5.7.4 Snowball Sampling

In snowball sampling, survey respondents are selected on the basis of referrals from other survey respondents.

In snowball sampling, survey respondents are selected on the basis of referrals from other survey respondents. A snowball collects ice particles when it rolls on ice. Similarly, in snowball sampling, a researcher uses a respondent to collect information about another respondent. When information about the subjects is not directly available, a researcher identifies a person who will be able to provide details of other respondents whose profile will fit the study. Through referrals, respondents can be located easily, which could otherwise be a difficult and expensive exercise. Snowball sampling method also suffers from the non-randomness of the sample selection procedure.

5.8 SAMPLING AND NON-SAMPLING ERRORS

Research is rarely free from errors. During the research process, a researcher collects, tabulates, analyses, and interprets data. The possibility of committing errors cannot be eliminated at any stage in the process. In statistics, these errors can be broadly classified into two categories: sampling errors and non-sampling errors.

5.8.1 Sampling Errors

Sampling error occurs when the sample is not a true representative of the population. In complete enumeration, sampling errors are not present.

Sampling error has the origin in sampling itself. We have already discussed that only a small part of the population, known as sample is taken for the study and all the inferences are based on this small part of the population. When the sample happens to be a true representative of the population, there is no problem. Sampling errors occur when the sample is not a true representative of the population. In complete enumeration, sampling errors are not present because in complete enumeration sampling is not being done.

Sampling errors can occur due to some specific reasons. Some times sampling errors occur due to faulty selection of the sample. For example, in judgement sampling, a researcher can deliberately select a sample to obtain predetermined results. Secondly, some times due to the difficulty in selection a particular sampling unit, researchers try to substitute that sampling unit with another sampling unit which is easy to be surveyed. In this situation, the researcher conveniently substitutes the difficult to approach sampling unit by the easy to approach sampling unit, though the difficult to approach sampling unit is of paramount importance to the study. This leads to sampling errors because the characteristics possessed by the substituted unit are not the same as the original unit. Thirdly, some times researchers demarcate sampling units wrongly and hence, provide scope for committing sampling errors. By selecting a sample randomly, sampling errors can be computed and analysed very easily.

5.8.2 Non-Sampling Errors

All errors other than sampling errors can be includedinthecategoryofnon-sampling errors.

As the name indicates, non-sampling errors are not due to sampling but due to other forces generally present in every research. Broadly, we can say all errors other than sampling errors can be included in the category of non-sampling errors. Non-sampling errors mainly arise at the stages of observation, ascertainment, and processing of data and hence are present in both sampling and complete enumeration. Data obtained in complete enumeration is generally free from sampling errors. However, the data obtained from a sample survey should be treated for both; sampling errors and non-sampling errors. Non-sampling errors can occur at any stage of the sampling or complete census. It is very difficult to prepare an exhaustive list of non-sampling errors. The following are some common non-sampling errors:

5.8.2.1 Faulty Designing and Planning of Survey

The most important part of research is to set objectives. On the basis of these objectives, a researcher prepares the questionnaire. The questionnaire is the primary source of data collection. Some times, the data specification is inconsistent with the objectives of the study and hence, provides scope for committing non-sampling errors. Getting trained and qualified staff for survey is very difficult. Sometimes researchers employ inexperienced and unqualified staff for survey, who commitmistakes during the survey process.

5.8.2.2 Response Errors

Sometimes respondents do not provide pertinent information during the survey. Response errors may be accidental. They may arise due to self-interest or prestige bias of the respondents or due to the bias of the interviewer. Due to these factors respondents furnish wrong information.

5.8.2.3 Non-Response Bias

Non-response errors occur when the respondent is not available at home or the researcher is not in a position to contact him due to some other reason. Non-response errors also occur when respondents refuse to answer certain questions which are important from the researcher's point of view. As a result, it becomes difficult to obtain complete information. Due to this, very important parts of the sample do not provide relevant and required information and this leads to non-sampling errors.

5.8.2.4 Errors in Coverage

When the objectives of the research are not clearly laid down, the possibilities are always high that few sampling units that should not have been included are included in the sample list. Similarly, exclusion of some very important sampling units is also possible. In both the cases, the possibility of committing errors in terms of proper coverage are high. For example, a researcher wants to conduct a survey on the age group of 20–30. However, he will not be able to select the possible respondents until the section of society that the respondents must be chosen from (based on the objectives of the research) is clearly specified. In order to minimize errors of coverage, it must be clearly specified whether respondents must be selected among college students, servicemen, farmers, rural or urban customers, etc.

5.8.2.5 Compiling Error and Publication Error

A researcher can also commit errors during compilation of the data. Various operations of data processing, such as editing and coding of the response, tabulation, and summarization of the data collected during survey can be major sources of errors. Similarly, errors can occur during the presentation and printing of the results.

Statistical techniques are not available to control non-sampling errors. Statistical techniques discussed in this book are based on the assumption that non-sampling errors have not been committed. These non-sampling errors can be controlled, up to one extent, by employing qualified, trained, and experienced personnel and through careful planning and execution of the research study.

5.9 SAMPLING DISTRIBUTION

It has been discussed earlier that a researcher selects a sample and computes the sample statistic in order to make an inference. On the basis of the computed sample statistic, the researcher makes inferences about the population parameter. So, it is important to have a clear understanding about the distribution of the sample statistic. Sample mean is a commonly used statistic in the inferential process. In this section, we will explore sample mean, $\bar{x}$, as the sample statistic. For making sampling distributions clearer, we will take a population with a particular distribution; after this, we will randomly select a sample of given size. The sample mean will be calculated next and finally the distribution of the sample mean will be determined. Let us take a small finite population of size $N = 6$. Elements of the population are as below:

$$25, 30, 35, 40, 45, 50$$

The shape of the distribution of this population is determined by using MS Excel histogram. Figure 5.8 is the MS Excel histogram where class interval is represented by the x axis and frequency by the y axis for a small population of size 6.

From Figure 5.8, the distribution of the population is clear. We want to understand the distribution of sample mean from this population. We take a sample of size 2 from this population with replacement. The result is presented in the following manner:

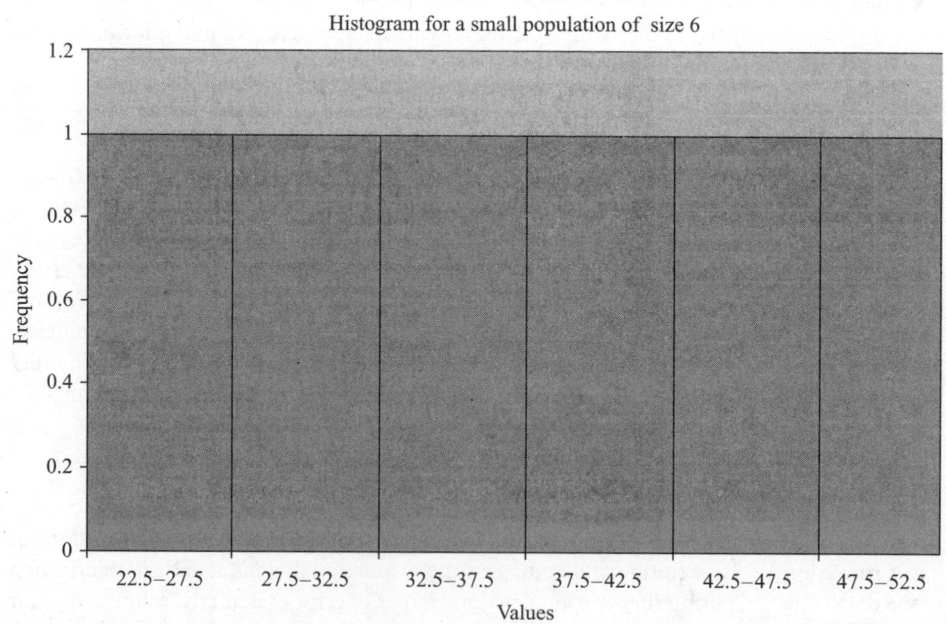

FIGURE 5.8
Histogram produced using MS Excel for a small population of size 6

(25, 25)	(25, 30)	(25, 35)	(25, 40)	(25, 45)	(25, 50)
(30, 25)	(30, 30)	(30, 35)	(30, 40)	(30, 45)	(30, 50)
(35, 25)	(35, 30)	(35, 35)	(35, 40)	(35, 45)	(35, 50)
(40, 25)	(40, 30)	(40, 35)	(40, 40)	(40, 45)	(40, 50)
(45, 25)	(45, 30)	(45, 35)	(45, 40)	(45, 45)	(45, 50)
(50, 25)	(50, 30)	(50, 35)	(50, 40)	(50, 45)	(50, 50)

We want to assess the distribution of mean. The means of each of these samples are as below:

(25)	(27.5)	(30)	(32.5)	(35)	(37.5)
(27.5)	(30)	(32.5)	(35)	(37.5)	(40)
(30)	(32.5)	(35)	(37.5)	(40)	(42.5)
(32.5)	(35)	(37.5)	(40)	(42.5)	(45)
(35)	(37.5)	(40)	(42.5)	(45)	(47.5)
(37.5)	(40)	(42.5)	(45)	(47.5)	(50)

The histogram produced using MS Excel (Figure 5.9) exhibits the shape of the distribution for these sample means. The difference between the shape of the histogram between population and sample means (Figures 5.8 and 5.9) can be noticed easily and this leads to a very important result in inferential statistics. The distribution of sample means taken from the above population tends to be normal. An important question arises as to the shape of the distribution of sample means with differently shaped population distributions. The **central limit theorem** provides an answer to this question.

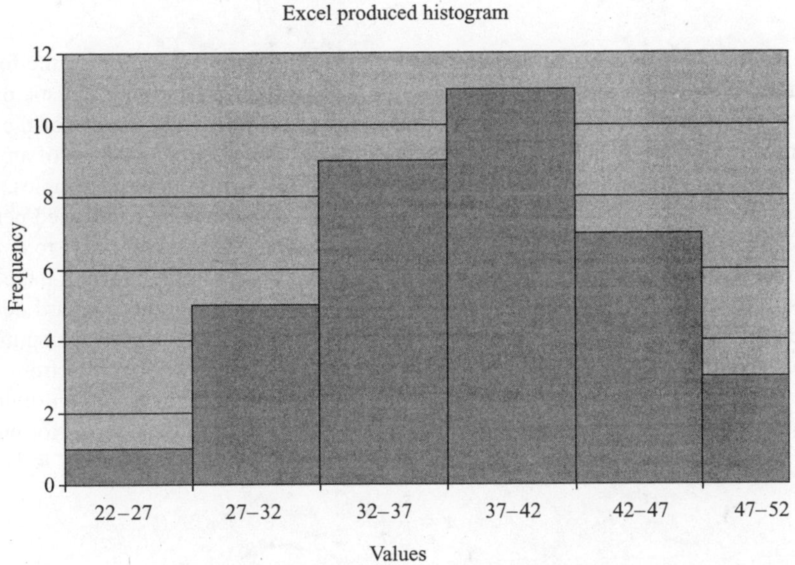

FIGURE 5.9
MS Excel produced histogram for sample means

5.10 CENTRAL LIMIT THEOREM

A population has a mean μ and standard deviation σ. If a sample of size n is drawn from the population, for sufficiently large sample size ($n \geq 30$); the sample means are approximately normally distributed regardless of the shape of the population distribution. If the population is normally distributed, the sample means are normally distributed, for any size of the sample.

According to the central limit theorem, if a population is normally distributed, the sample means for samples taken from that normal population are also normally distributed regardless of sample size. A population has a mean μ and standard deviation σ. If a sample of size n is drawn from the population, for sufficiently large sample size ($n \geq 30$); the sample means are approximately normally distributed regardless of the shape of the population distribution.

Mathematically, it can be shown that the mean of the sample means is the population mean, that is, $\mu = \mu_{\bar{x}}$ and the standard deviation of the sample means is the standard deviation of the population, divided by the square root of the sample size, that is, $\sigma_{\bar{x}} = \frac{\sigma}{\sqrt{n}}$. Central limit theorem is perhaps the most important theorem in statistical inference. The beauty of the central limit theorem lies in the fact that it allows a researcher to use the sample statistic to make an inference about the population parameter, even in cases where we have no idea about the shape of the distribution of the population. Central limit theorem provides a platform to apply normal distribution to many populations when the sample size is sufficiently large ($n \geq 30$). In many situations, a researcher is not sure about the shape of the population distribution. Sometimes, a sample drawn from the population may not be distributed normally. In both the situations, if sample size is sufficiently large ($n \geq 30$), the central limit theorem provides the opportunity of using the properties of normality.

Central limit theorem says that for sufficiently large sample size ($n \geq 30$), the sample means are approximately normally distributed regardless of the shape of the population distribution. For a normally distributed population, sample means are normally distributed for any size of the sample. We have already discussed that the formula of determining z scores, for individual values from a normal distribution is

$$z = \frac{x - \mu}{\sigma}$$

In case where sample means are normally distributed, z formula applied to sample mean will be

$$z = \frac{\bar{x} - \mu_{\bar{x}}}{\sigma_{\bar{x}}}$$

This formula is nothing but the general formula of obtaining z scores. In the formula, the mean of the statistic of interest is $\mu_{\bar{x}}$ and the standard deviation of the statistic of interest is $\sigma_{\bar{x}}$. This standard deviation is sometimes termed as the standard error of the mean. For computing $\mu_{\bar{x}}$, a researcher has to randomly draw all the possible samples of any given size, from the population; then, he has to compute sample mean from these samples. Practically this task is very difficult or some times even impossible within a specified period of time. Very fortunately, $\mu_{\bar{x}}$ is equal to population mean which is relatively easy to compute. In a similar manner, for computing the value of $\sigma_{\bar{x}}$, a researcher has to draw all the possible samples of any given size, from the population and has to compute the standard deviation accordingly. This task also faces the same degree of difficulty because for computing the standard deviation, a researcher has to calculate sample standard deviations from all the possible samples. Fortunately, $\sigma_{\bar{x}}$ is equal to the population standard deviation divided by the square root of the sample size. Substituting these two values in the above z formula, the revised version of the z formula can be presented as below:

$$z = \frac{\bar{x} - \mu}{\frac{\sigma}{\sqrt{n}}}$$

As sample size increases, the standard deviation of the sample mean becomes smaller because the population standard deviation (σ) is divided by the larger values of the square root of the sample size. Example 5.1 explains the application of the central limit theorem clearly.

Example 5.1

The distribution of the annual earnings of the employees of a cement factory is negatively skewed. This distribution has a mean of ₹25,000 and standard deviation of ₹3000. If a researcher draws a random sample of size 50, what is the probability that their average earnings will be more than ₹26,000?

Solution The z formula used for this problem is as below:

$$z = \frac{\overline{x} - \mu}{\frac{\sigma}{\sqrt{n}}}$$

Here, Population mean (μ) = 25,000
Population standard deviation (σ) = 3000
Sample size (n) = 50
Sample mean ($\overline{x}$) = 26,000

By substituting all these values in the z formula, we obtain the z score as below:

$$z = \frac{26{,}000 - 25{,}000}{\frac{3000}{\sqrt{50}}}$$

$$z = 2.35$$

This gives an area of 0.4906 between $z = 0$ to $z = 2.35$. This is an area between mean and 26,000. The required area lies between 26,000 and the area under the right-hand tail. So, the required area under normal curve is

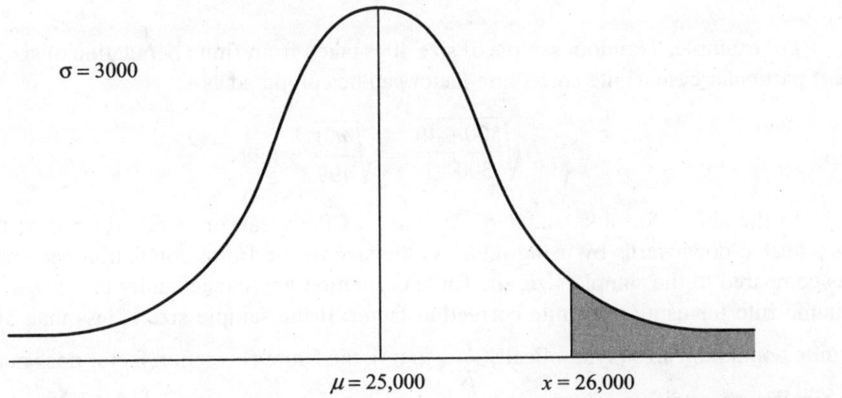

FIGURE 5.10 Probability that the average earnings of employees is more than ₹26,000

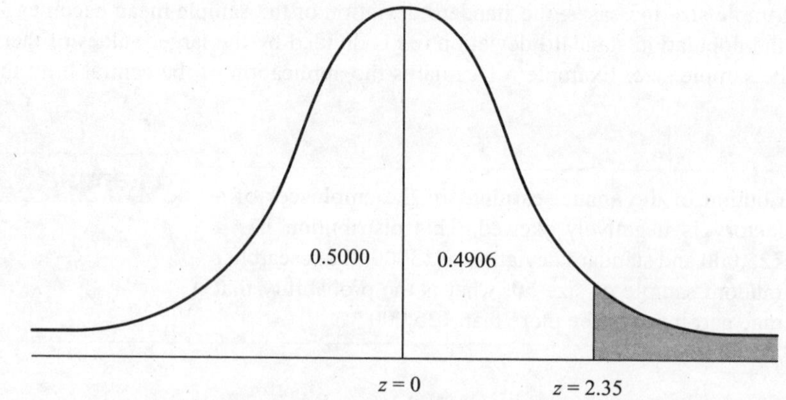

FIGURE 5.11 Corresponding z scores for probability of average earnings more than ₹26,000

(Area between 26,000 and the right hand tail) = (Area between the mean and right hand tail) – (Area between mean and 26,000)

Required area = 0.5000 – 0.4906 = 0.0094

Thus, the probability that the average earning of the sample group is more than ₹26,000 will be 0.94% (as shown in Figures 5.10 and 5.11).

5.10.1 Case of Sampling from a Finite Population

Example 5.1 is based on the assumption that the population is extremely large or infinite. In case of a finite population, a statistical adjustment called finite correction factor can be incorporated into the z formula for sample mean. This correction factor is given by $\sqrt{\frac{(N-n)}{(N-1)}}$. It operates on standard deviation of the sample means, $\sigma_{\bar{x}}$. After applying this finite correction factor, the z formula becomes

$$z = \frac{\bar{x} - \mu}{\frac{\sigma}{\sqrt{n}}\sqrt{\frac{(N-n)}{(N-1)}}}$$

For example, a random sample of size 40 is taken from finite population of size 500. For this particular case, finite correction factor can be computed as

$$\sqrt{\frac{500-40}{500-1}} = \sqrt{\frac{460}{499}} = 0.96$$

In the above formula, standard deviation of the mean or standard error of the mean is adjusted downwards by using 0.96. As the size of the finite population becomes larger, as compared to the sample size, the finite correction approaches unity or 1. There exists a thumb rule for using the finite correction factor. If the sample size is less than 5% of the finite population size (symbolically $\frac{n}{N} < 0.05$), the finite correction factor does not provide a significant modified solution.

SELF-PRACTICE PROBLEMS

5A1. A population has mean 100 and standard deviation 15. From this population, a random sample of size 25 is taken. Compute the following probabilities:
(a) Sample mean is greater than 90
(b) Sample mean is greater than 105
(c) Sample mean is less than 90
(d) Sample mean is less than 105

5A2. A researcher has taken a random sample of size 30 from a normally distributed population which has mean 150 and standard deviation 50. Compute the probability of obtaining sample mean more than 160. Also compute the probability of obtaining a sample mean less than or equal to 160.

5A3. In a big bazaar, the mean expenditure per customer is ₹1850 with a standard deviation of ₹750. If a random sample of 100 customers is selected, what is the probability that the, sample average expenditure per customer for this sample is more than ₹2000.

5.11 SAMPLE DISTRIBUTION OF SAMPLE PROPORTION $\overline{p}$

When data items are measurable such as time, income, weight, height, etc. sample mean can be an appropriate statistic of choice. In cases where research produces countable items such as the number of people in a sample who own cars (and we want to estimate population proportion through sample proportion) the sample proportion can be an appropriate statistic. In many situations, the researcher uses sampling proportion $\overline{p}$ to make the statistical inference about the population proportion p. The process of using sample proportion $\overline{p}$ to make an inference about the population proportion p is exhibited in Figure 5.12.

The sampling distribution of $\overline{p}$ is the probability distribution of all the possible values of the sample proportion $\overline{p}$. The sample proportion can be obtained by dividing the frequency with which a given characteristic occurs in a sample by the number of items in the sample. Symbolically,

$$\text{Sample proportion } \overline{p} = \frac{x}{n}$$

where x is the number of items in a sample possessing the given characteristics and n the number of items in the sample.

The mean of the sample proportion, for all the samples of size n drawn from a population is p (the population proportion) and the standard deviation of the sample proportion is

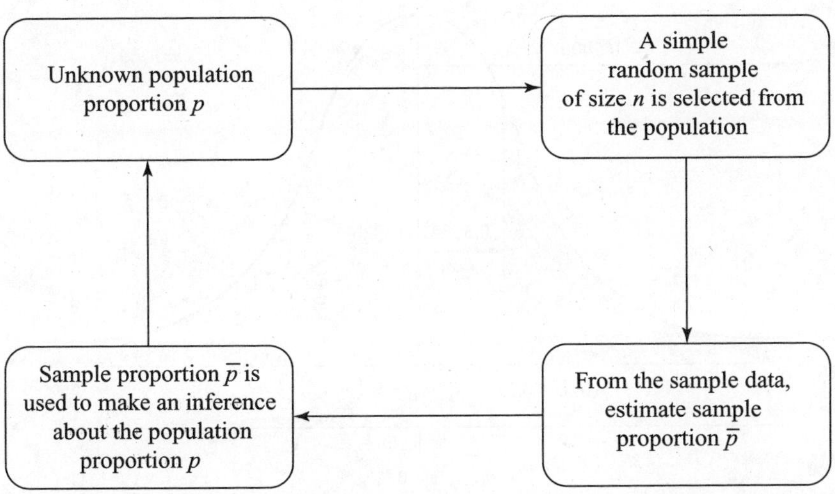

FIGURE 5.12
Using sample proportion $\overline{p}$ to make an inference about the population proportion p

$\sqrt{\dfrac{pq}{n}}$. After obtaining mean and standard deviation of the sample proportion, it is important to understand how a researcher can use the sample proportion in analysis. The concept of central limit theorem can also be applied to the sampling distribution of $\bar{p}$ with certain conditions. For a large sample size, the sampling distribution of $\bar{p}$ can be approximated by a normal probability distribution. Here, we need to understand which sample size can be considered large for applying the central limit theorem. Under two pre-specified circumstances $np \geq 5$ and $nq \geq 5$, the sample distribution of $\bar{p}$ can be approximated by a normal distribution.

The z formula for sample proportion for $np \geq 5$ and $nq \geq 5$ is

$$z = \frac{\bar{p} - p}{\sqrt{\dfrac{pq}{n}}}$$

where $\bar{p}$ is the sample proportion, n the sample size, p the population proportion, and $q = 1 - p$.

Example 5.2

In a population of razor blades, 15% are defective. What is the probability of randomly selecting 90 razor blades and finding 10 or less defective?

Solution

Here, $p = 0.15$, $\bar{p} = \dfrac{10}{90} = 0.11$, and $n = 90$

By substituting all the values in the z formula

$$z = \frac{\bar{p} - p}{\sqrt{\dfrac{pq}{n}}} = \frac{0.11 - 0.15}{\sqrt{\dfrac{(0.15)(0.85)}{90}}} = -\frac{0.04}{0.0376} = -1.06$$

The z value obtained is –1.06 and the corresponding probability from the standard normal table is 0.3554, which is the area between

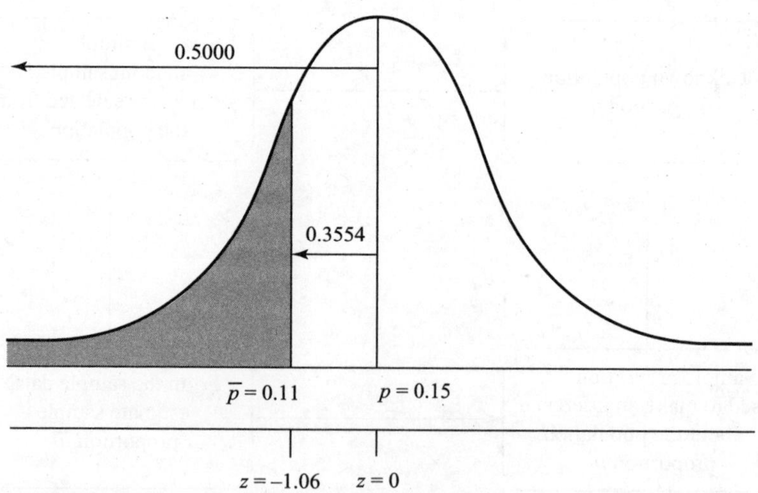

FIGURE 5.13 The probability of randomly selecting 90 razor blades and finding 10 or less defective

sample proportion 0.11 and the population proportion 0.15 (as shown in Figure 5.13). So, the probability of randomly selecting 90 razor blades and finding 10 or less defective is

$$P(\bar{p} \le 0.11) = 0.5000 - 0.3554 = 0.1446$$

This result indicates that 10 or less razor blades will be defective in a random sample of 90 razor blades 14.46% of the time when the population proportion is 0.15.

SELF-PRACTICE PROBLEMS

5B1. The branded mattresses market has four product variants: rubberised coir, polyurethane, rubber foam, and spring mattresses. Rubberised coir mattresses occupy a market share of 63%.[3] What is the probability of randomly selecting 150 customers and finding 90 of them or fewer using rubberised coir mattresses?

5B2. Hindustan Petroleum Company Ltd has an 18% market share in the lubricants market.[3] What is the probability of randomly selecting 120 customers and finding 38 or more HPCL lubricant purchasers?

Example 5.3

In a grocery store, the mean expenditure per customer is ₹2000 with a standard deviation of ₹300. If a random sample of 50 customers is selected, what is the probability that the sample average expenditure per customer is more than ₹2080?

Solution As discussed in the chapter, the z formula is given as below:

$$z = \frac{\bar{x} - \mu}{\frac{\sigma}{\sqrt{n}}}$$

Here, Population mean (μ) = 2,000
Population standard deviation (σ) = 300
Sample size (n) = 50
Sample mean ($\bar{x}$) = 2080

By substituting all these values in the z formula, we get the z score as below:

$$z = \frac{2080 - 2000}{\frac{300}{\sqrt{50}}} = \frac{80}{42.4268} = 1.88$$

$$z = 1.88$$

So, the required area under normal curve is

(Area between $z = 1.88$ and the right-hand tail) = (Area between $z = 0$ and right-hand tail) – (Area between $z = 0$ and $z = 1.88$)

Required area = 0.5000 – 0.4699 = 0.0301

Probability that sample average expenditure per customer is more than ₹2080 is 3.01% as shown in Figure 5.14.

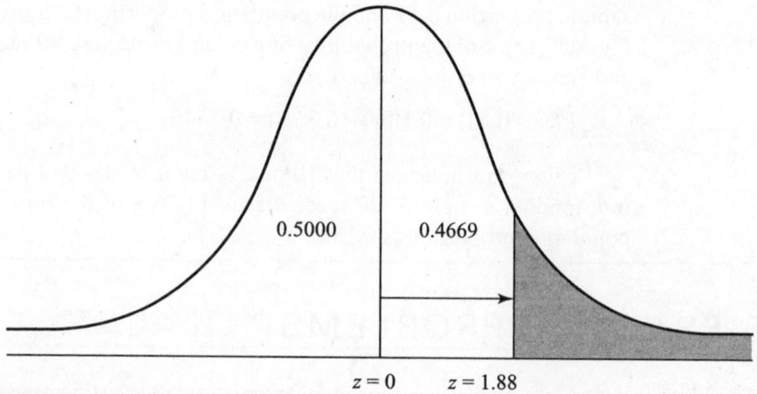

FIGURE 5.14
Shaded area under the normal curve exhibiting the probability that sample average expenditure per customer is more than ₹2080

Example 5.4

For Example 5.3, determine the probability that the sample average expenditure per customer is between ₹2040 and ₹2080.

Solution

In this problem, we have to determine $P(2040 \le \bar{x} \le 2080)$. Sample mean is given as $\bar{x} = 2040$ and $\bar{x} = 2080$.

For 2040, $$z = \frac{2040 - 2000}{\frac{300}{\sqrt{50}}} = \frac{40}{42.4268} = 0.9428$$

For 2080, $z = 1.88$ (computed in Example 5.3)

From Figure 5.15 it is clear that we have to determine the area between $z = 0.94$ and $z = 1.88$

So, the required area under normal curve is

(Area between $z = 0.94$ and $z = 1.88$) = (Area between $z = 0$ and $z = 1.88$) – (Area between $z = 0$ and $z = 0.94$)

$$= 0.4699 - 0.3264 = 0.1435$$

The probability that the sample average expenditure is between ₹2040 and ₹2080 is 0.1435.

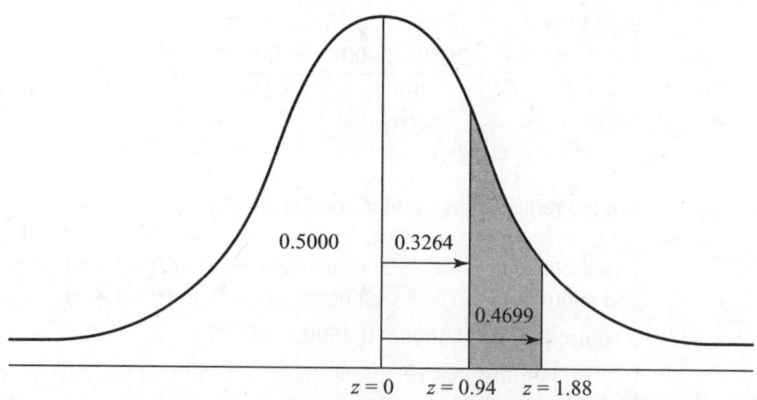

FIGURE 5.15
Shaded area under normal curve exhibiting the probability of sample average expenditure per customer between ₹2040 and ₹2080.

Example 5.5

The bottled water segment in India has witnessed rapid growth. Institutional users are responsible for 30% sales in the market.[3] If 100 customers are randomly selected, what is the probability that 25 or more customers are institutional users?

Solution

Here, $p = 0.30,\ \bar{p} = \dfrac{25}{100} = 0.25$, and $n = 100$

By substituting all the values in the z formula, we obtain

$$z = \frac{\bar{p} - p}{\sqrt{\dfrac{pq}{n}}} = \frac{0.25 - 0.30}{\sqrt{\dfrac{(0.30)(0.70)}{100}}} = -\frac{0.05}{0.0458} = -1.09$$

The z value obtained is −1.09 and the corresponding probability from the normal table is 0.3621, which is the area between sample proportion, 0.25 and the population proportion, 0.30. Figure 5.16 exhibits this area. So, when 100 customers are randomly selected, then the probability that 25 or more customers are institutional users is

$$P(\bar{p} \geq 0.25) = 0.3621 + 0.5000 = 0.8621$$

This result indicates that 86.21% of the time a random sample of 100 customers will consist of 25 or more institutional users.

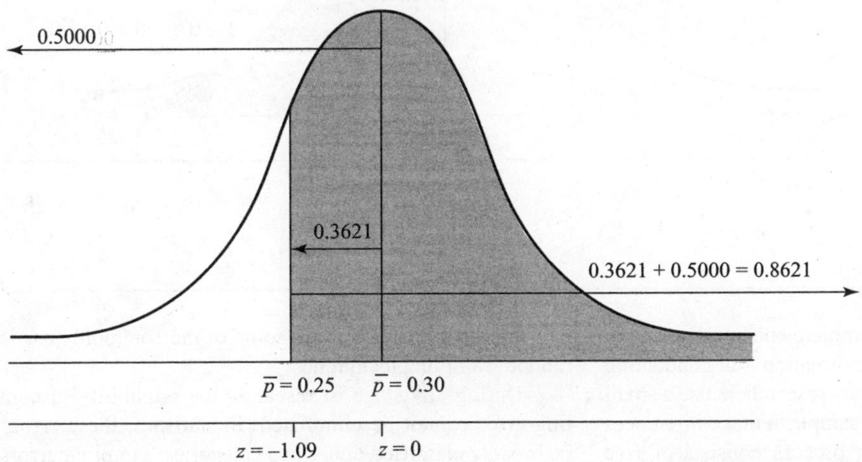

FIGURE 5.16 Shaded area under the normal curve exhibiting the probability that 25 or more customers are institutional users.

Example 5.6

By the year 2014–2015, the telephone instrument industry is estimated to grow by 106.20 million units as compared to 1993–1994 when the total market size was only 3 million units. Bharti Teletech, BPL Telecom, ITI (Indian Telephone Industries), Bharti Systel, Tata Telecom, and Gigrej Telecom are some of the major players in the market. Bharti Teletech has a market share of 24%.[3] If 200 purchasers of telephone instruments are randomly selected, what is the probability that 55 or more are Bharti Teletech customers?

Solution In this example, $p = 0.24$, $\overline{p} = \dfrac{55}{200} = 0.275$, and $n = 200$

By substituting all the values in the z formula

$$z = \frac{\overline{p} - p}{\sqrt{\dfrac{pq}{n}}} = \frac{0.275 - 0.24}{\sqrt{\dfrac{(0.24)(0.76)}{200}}} = \frac{0.035}{0.0301} = 1.16$$

The z value obtained is 1.16 and corresponding probability from the normal table is 0.3770. This is the area between $z = 0$ and $z = 1.16$. So, total area less than 1.16 is equal to $0.5000 + 0.3770 = 0.8770$. Hence, when 200 purchasers of telephone instruments are randomly selected, probability that 55 or more are Bharti Teletech customers is equal to $1 - 0.8770 = 0.1230$ (Figure 5.17).

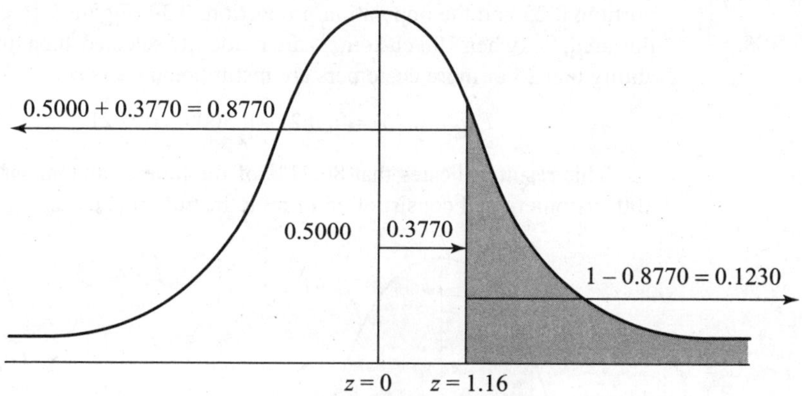

FIGURE 5.17
Shaded area under the normal curve exhibiting the probability that 55 or more are Bharti Teletech customers

SUMMARY |

Due to various reasons, census or complete enumeration is not a feasible approach of obtaining information for conducting research or for any other purpose. Many researchers use a small portion of the population termed as a sample to make inferences about the population. The sampling process consists of five steps, namely determining target population; determining sampling frame; selecting appropriate sampling technique; determining sample size, and execution of the sampling process.

Sampling procedure can be broadly defined in two categories: random and non-random sampling. In random sampling, every unit of the population gets an equal probability of being selected in the sample. In non-random sampling, every unit of the population does not have the same chance of being selected in the sample. Simple random sampling, stratified random sampling, cluster sampling, and systematic sampling are some of the commonly used random sampling methods. Quota sampling, convenience sampling, judgement sampling, and snow ball sampling techniques are some of the commonly used non-random sampling techniques.

During any stage of research, the possibility of committing error cannot be eliminated. In statistics, these errors can be broadly classified under two categories: sampling errors and non-sampling errors. Sampling errors occur when the sample is not a true representative of the population. In complete enumeration, sampling errors are not present. Non-sampling errors are errors that arise not due to sampling but due to other factors in the process. Broadly, we can say that all errors other than sampling errors can be included in the category of non-sampling errors. Faulty designing and planning of the survey, response errors, non-response bias, errors in coverage, compiling, and publication errors are some of the common sources of non-sampling errors.

Sample mean is one of the most commonly used statistic in inferential process. This leads to a very important theorem of inferential statistics: the central limit theorem. Central limit theorem states that for a population with a mean μ and standard deviation σ, if a sample of size n is drawn from the population, for sufficiently large sample size ($n \geq 30$), the sample means are approximately normally distributed regardless of the shape of the population distribution. If the population is normally distributed, the sample means are normally distributed for any size of the sample.

KEY TERMS |

NOTES |

1. Prowess (V. 3.1), Centre for Monitoring Indian Economy Ltd, Mumbai, accessed November 2008, reproduced with permission.
2. www.thehindu.com/2008/05/30/stories/2008053056201700.htm, accessed November 2008.
3. www.indiastat.com, accessed November 2008, reproduced with permission.

DISCUSSION QUESTIONS |

1. What is the difference between a sample and a census, and why is sampling so important for a researcher?
2. Explain the sampling design process.
3. What are sampling and non-sampling errors and how can a researcher control them?
4. Explain the types of probability or random sampling techniques.
5. Explain the types of non-probability or non-random sampling techniques.
6. How do probability sampling techniques or random sampling techniques differ from non-probability sampling techniques or non-random sampling techniques?
7. What is the concept of sampling distribution and also state its importance in inferential statistics?

NUMERICAL PROBLEMS |

1. A population has mean 40 and standard deviation 10. A random sample of size 50 is taken from the population, what is the probability that the sample mean is each of the following:
   (a) Greater than or equal to 42
   (b) Less than 41
   (c) Between 38 and 43
2. A housing board colony of Gwalior consists of 2000 houses. A researcher wants to know the average income of the households in this housing board colony. The mean income per household is ₹150,000 with standard deviation ₹15,000. A random sample of 200 households is selected by a researcher and analysed. What is the probability that the sample average is greater than ₹160,000?
3. A population proportion is 0.55. A random sample of size 500 is drawn from the population.
   (a) What is the probability that sample proportion is greater than 0.58?
   (b) What is the probability that sample proportion is between 0.5 and 0.6?
4. The government of a newly formed state in India is worried about the rising unemployment rates. It has promoted some finance companies to launch schemes to reduce the rate of unemployment by promoting entrepreneurial skills. A finance company introduced a scheme to finance young graduates to start their own business. Out of 200,000 young graduates, 130,000 accepted the policy and received loans. If a random sample of 20,000 is taken

from the population, what is the probability that it exceeds 60% acceptance?

5. A market research firm has conducted a survey and found that 58% of the customers complete their important shopping on Sunday. Suppose 100 customers are randomly selected:
   (a) What is the probability that 45 or more than 45 customers complete their important shopping on Sunday?
   (b) What is the probability that 70 or more than 70 customers complete their important shopping on Sunday?

CASE STUDY |

Case 5: *Air Conditioner Industry in India: Systematic Replacement of the Unorganized Sector by the Organized Sector*

Introduction

The Indian consumer durables industry is estimated to have a total market size of ₹250,000 million. The home appliances industry is estimated to have a size of ₹87,500 million. Refrigerators contribute to the largest share at around ₹38,000 million, followed by room air-conditioners at around ₹27,500 million, and washing machines at ₹14,000 million. The air-conditioner industry enjoys the highest growth in the appliances category and is expected to grow at over 20% in the years to come.[1] Due to the high prices in the organized sector, the unorganized sector was responsible for a lion's share of the total sales until a few years ago. The reduction in excise duties and a decline in import duties have narrowed down the price gap in the unorganized and organized sectors

The share of the unorganized market, which was at 70% in the 1980s has dropped down and is now only 25%.[2] Increasing disposa-ble incomes and the change in lifestyles are some of the factors supporting the upward demand for air conditioners in the country. Table 5.01 exhibits the market share of air-conditioners in different categories and region-wise market share of air-conditioners. Table 5.02 shows the market share of air-conditioners in the organized and unorganized sectors for window and split air-conditioners. As is evident from Table 5.02, metro cities have 60% market share as compared to a group of non-metro cities that have a market share of 40%.

Major Players in the Market

An increased share in the market has allowed various major players to participate in the race for maximizing their own market share. Blue Star, LG, Voltas, Carrier, Amtrex Hitachi, Samsung, National, etc. are some of the major players in the market.

Blue Star, founded in 1949, is one of the major players in the market with an annual turnover of ₹22,700 million. Voltas was founded in 1951 as a collaboration between Tata Sons Ltd and a Swiss firm Volkart Brothers. Voltas's domestic air-conditioning and refrigeration business witnessed a growth in revenue of 48% in 2006–2007 over the previous year. Carrier Aircon, an international major started operations in India in 1986, and established Carrier Refrigeration in 1992. Carrier has become an important player in the market in just a few years.

TABLE 5.01
Market share of air conditioners in different categories and region-wise market share of air conditioners

Market segmentation	
Segment	Share (%)
Domestic	20
Government	15
Corporates/Industry	20
Small Private sector	25
Hospitals	5
Public sector	15
North	37
East	8
West	33
South	22

Source: www.indiastat.com, accessed June 2008, reproduced with permission.

Hitachi Home & Life Solutions (India) Ltd, a subsidiary of Hitachi Home & Life Solutions Inc., Japan was established in 1984. On the basis of consumer research, the company launched an advanced "Logicool" range of ACs. LG Electronics, a major market shareholder has launched its new brand "LG Plasma" which filters out air in four stages. Market giants like National, Samsung, Videocon, and Whirlpool also have a sound footing in the market.

TABLE 5.02
Market share of air-conditioners in the organized and the informal sectors.

Market segmentation		
	Organized	Informal
Windows	75	25
Split	85	15
Metropolitan Cities (7)		60
Non-Metro Cities		40

Source: www.indiastat.com, accessed June 2008, reproduced with permission.

The Indian air-conditioner industry continues to register a growth of over 25%. There is a higher preference for split air-conditioners over window air-conditioners in the Indian market in line with the global trends. The household segment has shown a rapid increase and now accounts for 65% of the total market. The presence of more than 20 players in the market, including a few new entrants, both Indian and Chinese, has ensured that the selling price of air-conditioners has remained steady despite cost pressures.[1]

Suppose you have been appointed as a business analyst by a leading multinational company preparing to enter the air-conditioners segment. You have been assigned the task of analysing the needs of customers with respect to product features:

1. What will be your sampling frame, appropriate sampling techniques, sample size, and sampling process?
2. Will you be using probability sampling technique or non-probability sampling technique and why?
3. What will be your plans to control sampling and non-sampling errors to obtain an accurate result?

NOTES |

1. Prowess (V. 3.1), Centre for Monitoring Indian Economy Pvt. Ltd, Mumbai, accessed November 2008, reproduced with permission.
2. www.indiastat.com, accessed November 2008, reproduced with permission.

PART III

Sources and Collection of Data

CHAPTER 6

Secondary Data Sources

LEARNING OBJECTIVES

Upon completion of this chapter, you will be able to:

- Understand the meaning of primary and secondary data
- Get the insight of benefits and limitations of using secondary data
- Understand the classification of secondary data
- Use different sources of secondary data for a research problem
- Understand the roadmap for using secondary data.

RESEARCH IN ACTION: DATANET INDIA PVT LTD

Datanet India Pvt. Ltd was established as an IT-enabled company in February 2000. It launched its first website indiastat.com on 14 November 2000. Its endeavour is to collect, collate, and compile in ready-to-use socio-economic information about India and its states and to make it available online. Today, indiastat.com is a cluster of 51 sites, including India-specific, sector-specific, and state-specific sites rendering its specific services to the research fraternity from academic, professional, and corporate world with authentic and comprehensive compilation of secondary-level socio-economic statistical data about India and its states on more than 35 variables.[1]

Indiastat.com is the mother site of a cluster of 51 websites delivering socio-economic data about India and its states covering various sectors. The information available online can be used by all the professionals as per their need and discretion. With more than 500,000 comprehensive pages on the net, the site covers a wide range of topics such as agriculture, demographics, market forecast, health, media, economy, crime and social welfare, and so on. Of the 50 associated sites of indiastat.com, 19 sites are sector specific and are listed below.[2]

IndiaAgristat.com	IndiaEnvironstat.com	IndiaSCSTstat.com
IndiaChildrenstat.com	IndiaHealthstat.com	IndiaTourismstat.com
IndiaCrimestat.com	IndiaHousingstat.com	IndiaUrbanstat.com
IndiaDemographics.com	IndiaIndustrystat.com	IndiaWelfarestat.com
IndiaEconomystat.com	IndiaInfrastat.com	IndiaWomenstat.com
IndiaEducationstat.com	IndiaLabourstat.com	
IndiaEnergystat.com	IndiaRuralstat.com	

>>>

The remaining 31 sites are State/Union Territories (UT)-specific and provide comprehensive information on Indian states and its UT covering various socio-economic aspects of the concerned states. These sites are listed as below.[2]

IndiaNationalstat.com	Himachalpradeshstat.com	Orissastat.com
Andhrapradeshstat.com	Jammuandkashmirstat.com	Punjabstat.com
Arunachalpradeshstat.com	Jharkhandstat.com	Rajasthanstat.com
Assamstat.com	Karnatakastat.com	Sikkimstat.com
Biharstat.com	Keralastat.com	Tamilnadustat.com
Chandigarhstat.com	Madhyapradeshstat.com	Tripurastat.com
Chhattisgarhstat.com	Maharashtrastat.com	Uttarakhandstat.com
Delhistat.com	Manipurstat.com	Uttarpradeshstat.com
Goastat.com	Meghalayastat.com	Westbengalstat.com
Gujaratstat.com	Mizoramstat.com	
Haryanastat.com	Nagalandstat.com	

In addition, indiastat.com provides data on various variables at national level. Similar to indiastat.com, various other sites are available that provide data to researchers from various streams. Of this bulky data, how a researcher evaluates the relevant data and uses it at the appropriate level? What are the advantages of using the secondary data? How can we use search engines and Internet for secondary data evaluation? Is there any systematic way of secondary data searching? Apart from indiastat.com, what are the other secondary data sources available in India? This chapter attempts to answer all such type of questions and provides a guideline to use the secondary data sources for research objectively.

6.1 INTRODUCTION

A marketing researcher has to tackle the problem of converting the management question into a research question. To do this, the researcher must have some information readily available before formally starting an experiment or a research. This information is also important to understand different dimensions of a management problem. The readily available data sources also provide an opportunity to access other researcher's work that had similar kind of problems. This provides an opportunity to the researchers to develop their research problems in a more comprehensive manner. The available data sources are also important to identify the relevant variables to be included in the study and to frame the research questions properly. In the modern era, when computer and Internet facility are available everywhere, it is important for a researcher to be focused on the right source of data. It will help him or her to be concentrated on the concerned source and the research energy will not be devoured in searching an available unlimited source or more specifically web source. The quantity of the data will never be a problem for a researcher, but its added features of time and cost efficiencies will be a matter of concern. The chapter begins with the discussion on the difference between the primary and **secondary data**.

The quantity of the data will never be a problem for a researcher, but its added features of time and cost efficiencies will be a matter of concern.

Primary data are mainly collected by a researcher to address the research problem. Secondary data are the data that have already been collected by someone else before the current needs of a researcher.

6.2 MEANING OF PRIMARY AND SECONDARY DATA

Primary data are mainly collected by a researcher to address the research problem. In other words, these are not readily available from various sources, rather the researcher has to systematically collect the data relevant to a pre-specified research problem. **Secondary data**

are the data that have already been collected by someone else before the current needs of a researcher. The present researcher only uses these data with related reference and never collects it from the field. When compared with the **primary data**, secondary data can be collected easily with time and cost efficiency. Both the primary and the secondary data have its own relative advantages and disadvantages. Although the secondary data are readily available and provide a base to tackle the research problem, the importance of the primary data is unquestionable. The arrangement of chapters in this book is mainly based on the primary data. The next section discusses some of the advantages and disadvantages of using the secondary data.

6.3 BENEFITS AND LIMITATIONS OF USING SECONDARY DATA

The main **advantage of using secondary data** sources is that they already exist; therefore, the time spent on the study is considerably less than that on studies that use the primary data collection. The **disadvantages of using secondary data** are related to the fact that their selection and quality, and the methods of their collection, are not under the control of the researcher and that they are sometimes impossible to validate (Sorensen et al. 1996). In some cases, the researchers find great difficulty in collecting the primary data. In such situations, the secondary data provide a base to tackle the problem. It is suggested that the secondary data not only offer advantages in terms of cost and effort, as conventionally described in the research method books, but in certain cases their use may also overcome some of the difficulties that particularly afflict marketing researchers in gathering the primary data (Cowton 1998). There may be cases when the problem is general, such as the demographic structure of a population at a particular region, in such cases there is no meaning in collecting the primary data. The various available secondary data sources such as the indiastat.com, the Centre for Monitoring Indian Economy (CMIE) products, and so on are capable of providing this information and are easily accessible. Similarly, sales, net sales, profit after tax, and many other information related to any company are easily accessible through a well-known data source of CMIE, commonly known as PROWESS. Hence, collecting the primary data for this purpose is meaningless.

The main advantage of using the secondary data sources is that they already exist; therefore, the time spent on the study is considerably less than that on studies that use primary data collection.

Regarding disadvantages, the accuracy of secondary data is most of the time questionable as the researcher is unaware about the pattern of data collection. In addition, the researcher has no control over the data collection pattern. The researcher may try to use the secondary data that are developed for some other purpose in some other time frame in some other circumstances. This poses a great question mark on the currency and relevance of the data in terms of its use in the current problem. Moreover, the secondary data become outdated quickly. It is a big restriction on the frequent use of the secondary data. For example, a consumer attitude study conducted 3 years ago may not be useful today because a lot of developments have taken place in these 3 years, which are not incorporated into the study conducted 3 years ago. The secondary data are not free from the limitations of the original research. Once a researcher decides to use a specific secondary database, he or she is subjected to the methods and limitations chosen by the original researchers, and therefore, it is crucial that the researcher who considers using a secondary database knows its limitations and potentials (Best 1999).

Regarding disadvantages, the accuracy of the secondary data is most of the time questionable as the researcher is unaware about the pattern of data collection. In addition, the researcher has no control over the data collection pattern.

6.4 CLASSIFICATION OF SECONDARY DATA SOURCES

Secondary data sources can be broadly classified into internal and **external secondary data** sources. The **internal secondary data** are generated within the organization and the **external secondary data** are obtained from the sources available outside the organization.

Secondary data sources can be broadly classified into internal and external secondary data sources. The internal secondary data are generated within the organization and the external secondary data are obtained from the sources available outside the organization.

For example, a company's accounting records may be treated as an internal data and are not available to any other company baring some general form of data such as the profit and loss statement of the company, which remain available on the public domain. Sometimes it happens that these data does not remain in an actionable form such as the list of invoice. A researcher has to convert it into an actionable data. The external data are gathered from the data resources available outside the company. For example, a company can generate the data by purchasing various business periodicals and magazines. Nowadays, various electronic resources of data are also available. These data resources are extremely useful in developing a research problem. For example, in the chapter-opening discussion, a detailed discussion of a data resource called indiastat.com is given. This data resource provides innumerable data to the researcher to deal with the problem. This is an online database and can be acquired by the organization by accepting certain payment conditions. The internal secondary data are the internal records of the organization. The external secondary data can be further classified into the following four groups: **books, periodicals, and other published material**; **reports and publication from government sources**; **computerized commercial and other online data sources**; and **media resources** (Figure 6.1).

6.4.1 Books, Periodicals, and Other Published Material

The books, periodicals, and other published material generally available in most of the libraries are big sources of secondary data.

The **books, periodicals, and other published material** generally available in most of the libraries are big sources of secondary data. For example, let us consider that a researcher wants to gather some data on post-independence period of Indian economy. The books, periodicals, and other published material available in some good libraries provide a lot of meaningful information to the researcher to understand all the dimensions of the problem, especially in light of the relevant time period. Now, most of the big libraries in our country are in the process of digitizing the published material. It seems that it will be convenient for a researcher to access any information after a decade, which will be available in a digital form. Libraries also provide access to some good research journals of the country. For example, research journals such as Indian Institute of Management, Ahmedabad Journal, *Vikalpa*; Indian Institute of Management, Bangalore Journal, *Management Review*; Indian Institute of Management, Kolkata Journal, *Decision*; Indian Institute of Management, Lucknow Journal, *Metamorphosis*; Indian Institute of Management, Indore Journal, *Indore Management Journal*; XLRI Jamshedpur Journal, *Prabandhan* and *Management*

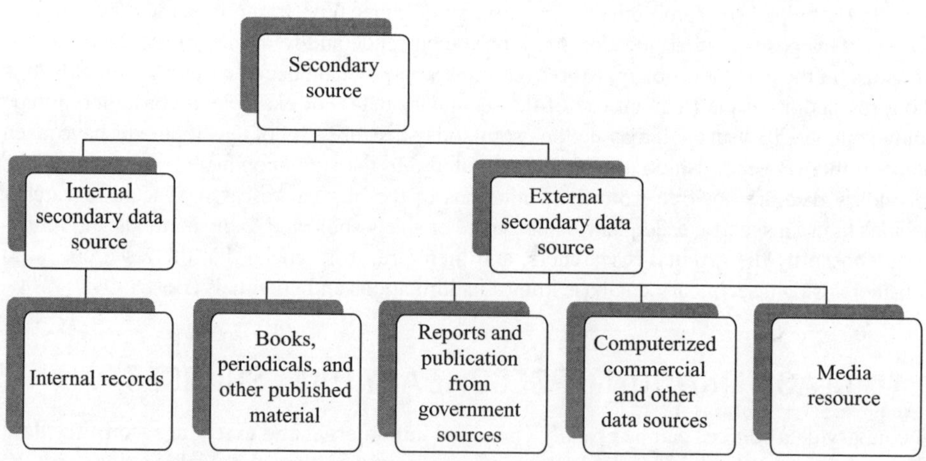

FIGURE 6.1
Classification of secondary data sources

and Labour Studies; Management Development Institute, Gurgaon Journal, *Vision*; Indian Institute of Foreign Trade, New Delhi Journal, *Foreign Trade Review*; and many others provide a lot of authentic and quality information to researchers. Many foreign journals such as the *Harvard Business Review* are also available in most of the libraries of management institutes.

6.4.2 Reports and Publication from Government Sources

Government sources also provide data. The accuracy and quality of these data sources are unquestionable. Hence, most researchers rely on government sources of data to conduct their research programme. Although some relevant information can be obtained from the website of any ministry, central, or state government set-up. Few government set-up specifically provide information. Ministry of Statistics and Programme Implementation, Government of India (http://mospi.gov.in), can provide a lot of information to the researchers. Apart from this, the National Statistics Commission, the Central Statistical Organization, and the National Sample Survey Organization may provide a lot of base data to any researcher. The Office of Registrar General and Census Commissioner, India (http://www.censusindia.gov.in), is also a great source of data and provide a lot of statistical information on different demographics and other characteristics of the people of India. Director General of Commercial Intelligence and Statistics, Ministry of Commerce and Industry, Government of India (http://www.dgciskol.nic.in), mainly collect, compile, and disseminate India's trade statistics and commercial information.

Government sources also provide data. The accuracy and quality of these data sources are unquestionable. Hence, most researchers rely on government sources of data to conduct their research programme.

Reserve Bank of India (http://www.rbi.org.in) established on 1 April 1935 in accordance with the provisions of the Reserve Bank of India Act 1934 provides a lot of information related to the Indian economy. Planning Commission, Government of India (http://planningcommission.gov.in), provides a lot of information related to different 5-year plans and other Indian economical statistics. Labour Bureau, Government of India (http://labourbureau.nic.in), provides a lot of labour statistics information related to the index numbers, annual survey of industries, occupational wage surveys, industrial disputes, unorganized sectors, socio-economic condition of women workers, and minimum wages. As discussed earlier, the list presented in this section is not an exhaustive one, and information can always be obtained from the concerned websites of different departments and set-ups of state governments and Government of India.

6.4.3 Computerized Commercial and Other Data Sources

In India, there are various firms involved in selling data. For example, indiastat.com and CMIE are two private firms involved in the accumulation and selling of the data. The chapter-opening vignette describes the various features of indiastat.com, and the case study given at the end of the chapter discusses the various products and features of the CMIE Pvt. Ltd. Figures 6.2 and 6.3 show the Home Page of indiastat.com and Prowess V. 3.1 (a product of the CMIE), respectively. Similarly, there are many more commercial data sources that provide a lot of data pertaining to the demographic structure of the Indian people, state-wise information, market structure, Indian economy, and so forth on certain pre-specified payment terms and conditions. In India, many researchers either directly use these data sources to handle the problem or use the information available to formulate a well-structured research problem. The data available from these sources are also used by many magazines, news papers, research journals, and so on.

In India, there are various firms involved in selling data. For example, indiastat.com and the CMIE are the two private firms involved in the accumulation and selling of the data.

In India, the Ministry of Human Resource Development has set-up the "Indian National Digital Library in Engineering Sciences and Technology (INDEST) Consortium"

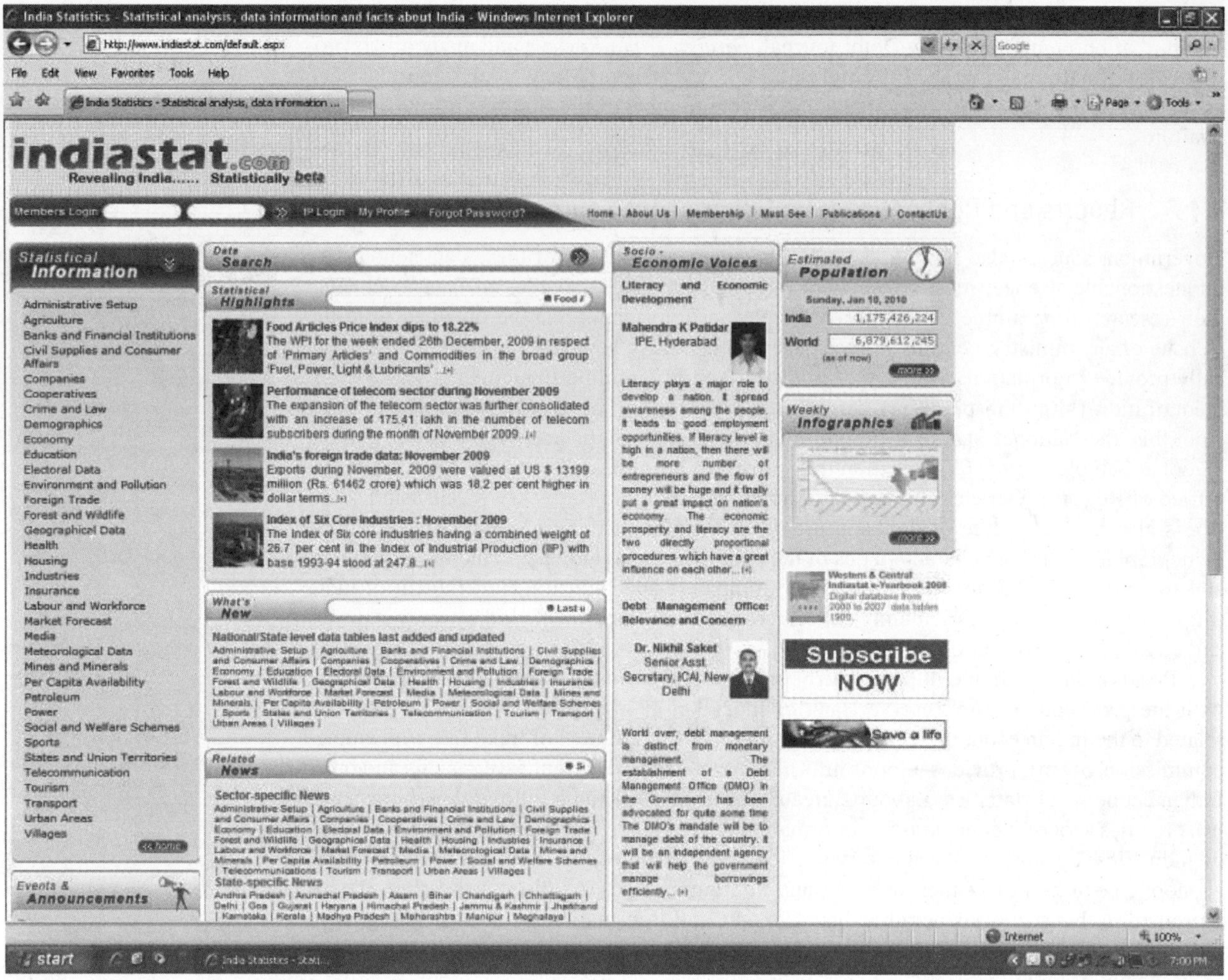

FIGURE 6.2
Home page of indiastat.com

headquartered at IIT, Delhi. The Ministry provides funds required for subscription of electronic resources for 48 institutions including IISc, IITs, NITs, IIMs, and a few other centrally funded government institutions through the consortium headquartered at IIT, Delhi. In addition, 60 government or government-aided engineering colleges and technical departments in the universities have joined the consortium with financial support from the All India Council for Technical Education (AICTE). The INDEST-AICTE consortium also welcomes other institutions to join them on their own to share the benefits it offers in terms of highly discounted rates of subscription and better terms of agreement with the publishers. Three hundred fifty-three engineering colleges and institutions have already joined the consortium on their own. Recently, 457 engineering colleges and institutions have joined under the new self-support schemes.[3] Figure 6.4 shows the Home Page (e-resources) of INDEST. If an institution has subscribed for an e-resource (e.g., EBSCO databases), it can directly open the INDEST e-resources page that provide access to the innumerable text resources.

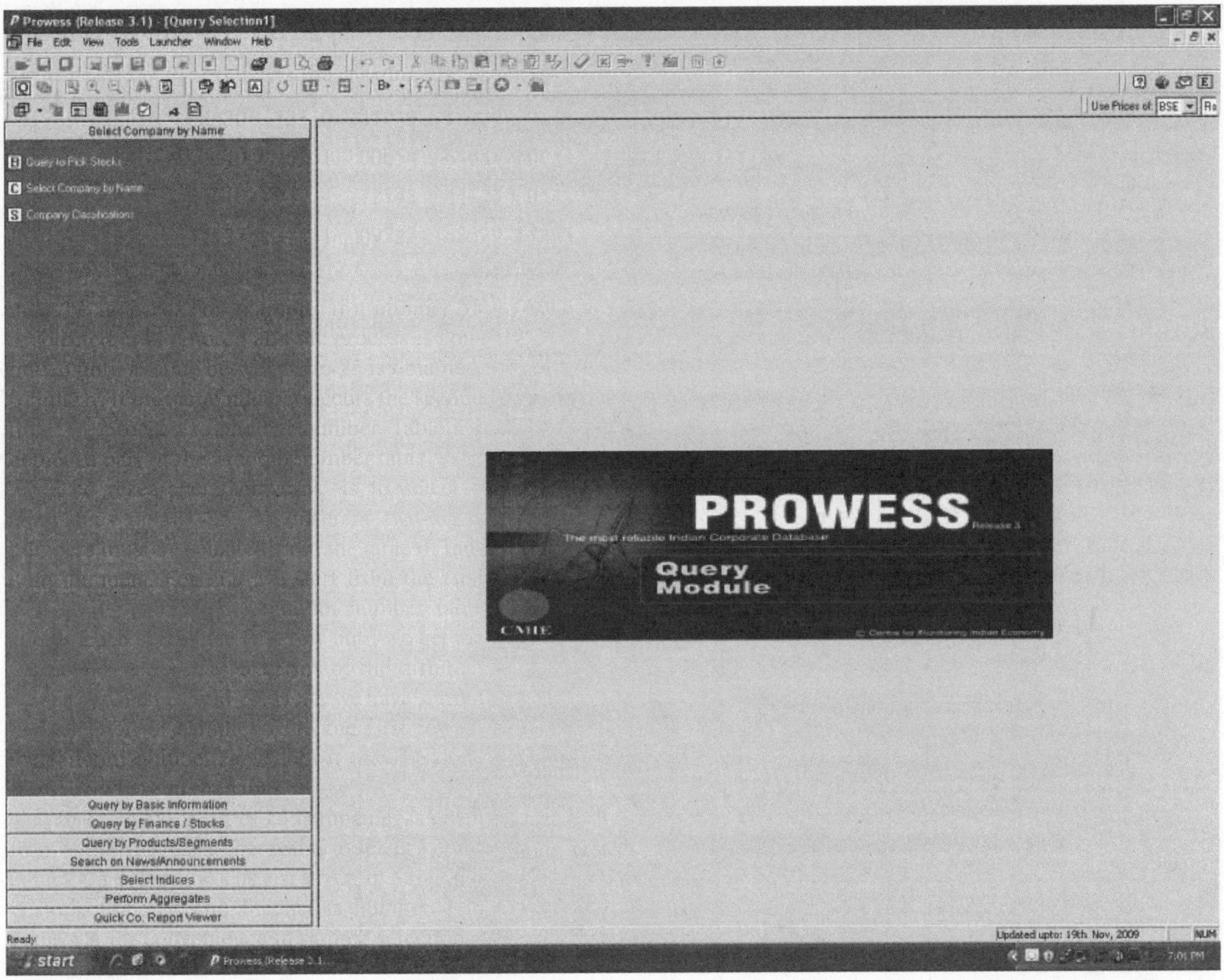

FIGURE 6.3
Home page of Prowess V. 3.1 (a product of the CMIE)

6.4.4 Media Resources

Some relevant and authentic information can also be gathered from the broadcast and print media. Apart from the academic researchers, the print and electronic media frequently conduct researches related to personal life, professional life, life style, change in life style, income status, change in income status, and many other issues. Leading news papers such as *The Economic Times*, *Pioneer*, *The Hindu*, *The Hindustan Times*, *The Indian Express*, *The Telegraph* (Kolkata), *The Asian Age*, *The Hindu Business Line*, *Business Standard*, *The Financial Express*, and many more national and regional newspapers have plentiful information. A researcher can carefully examine these sources of information to shape the research question. Nowadays, e-versions of most of the newspapers are available. This gives an ample opportunity to a researcher to explore the research idea. Apart from the daily newspapers, some magazines such as *India Today*, *Outlook*, *Business India*, *Business Today*, *Competition Success Review*, and so on provide a lot of information related to the current issues. The information available in these sources are generally not useful to make end conclusion, but it helps the researcher to develop an insight about the research problem.

Some relevant and authentic information can also be gathered from the broadcast and print media. Apart from the academic researchers, the print and electronic media frequently conduct researches related to personal life, professional life, life style, change in life style, income status, change in income status, and many other issues.

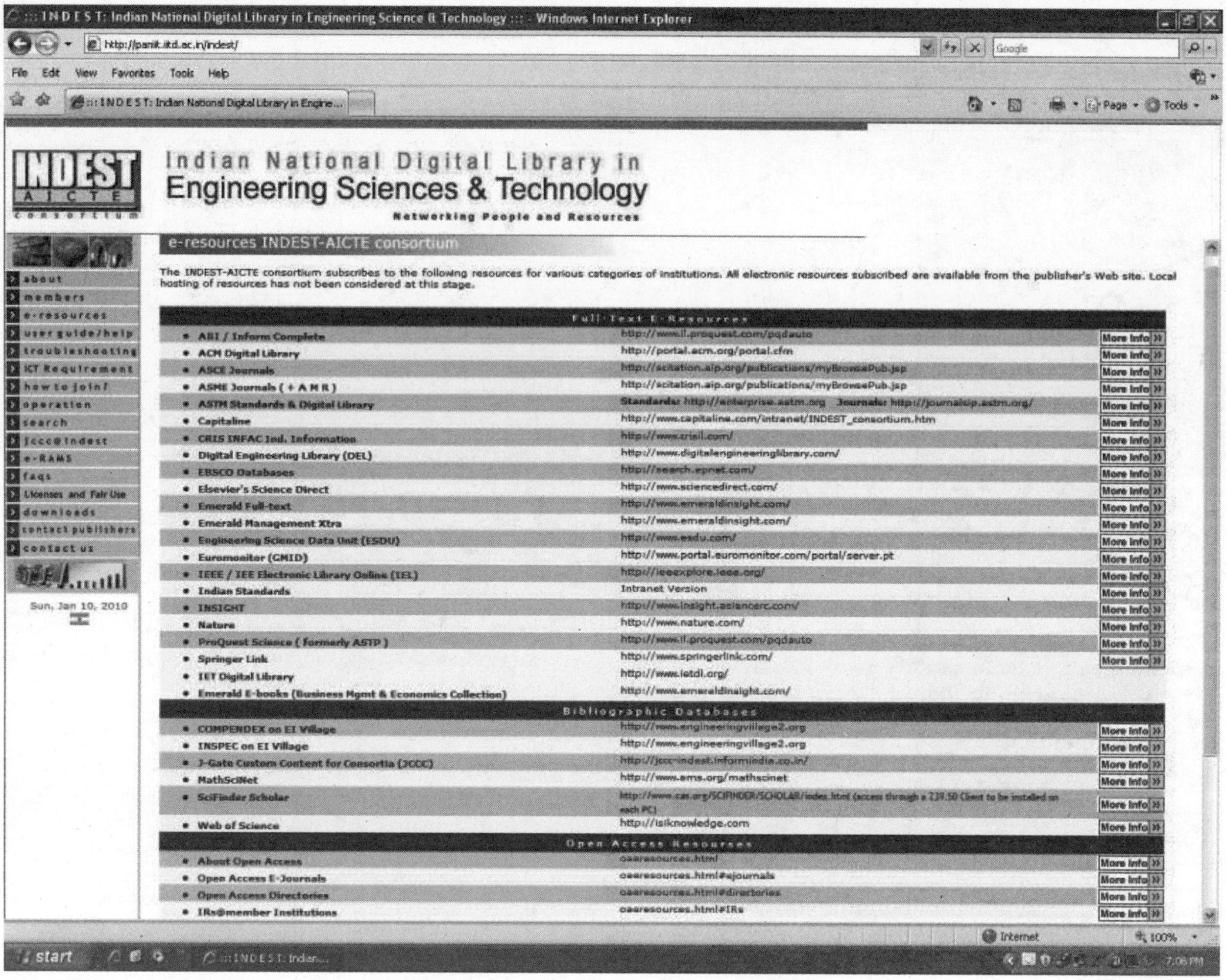

FIGURE 6.4
Home page (e-resources) of INDEST

6.5 ROADMAP TO USE SECONDARY DATA

The secondary data are useful in research, but there is a guideline available to use it. A researcher has to properly follow some pre-defined steps to use the secondary data.

The secondary data are useful in a research, but there is a guideline available to use it. A researcher has to properly follow some pre-defined steps to use the secondary data; Figure 6.5 presents the roadmap for it. The researcher has to consider four steps to use the external secondary data source. As discussed in the previous section, numerous secondary data sources are available. On the one hand, this presents a great opportunity, and on the other hand, this also poses some problems to the researcher. How a researcher can collect data that are useful for the study from the ocean of data available from the variety of sources? This is a million dollar question for any researcher with a research problem. The available secondary data must qualify certain tests and only then the researcher will be able to use it for his or her research problem. As Step 1, the researcher must identify the need of the secondary data for the research. Step 2 is to examine the utility of the internal secondary data sources for the research problem in terms of **objective, relevancy, accuracy, currency, authenticity, dependability, and action ability.** If Step 2 is not supportive then the researcher moves to Step 3. In Step 3, the utility of the external secondary data sources for the research problem

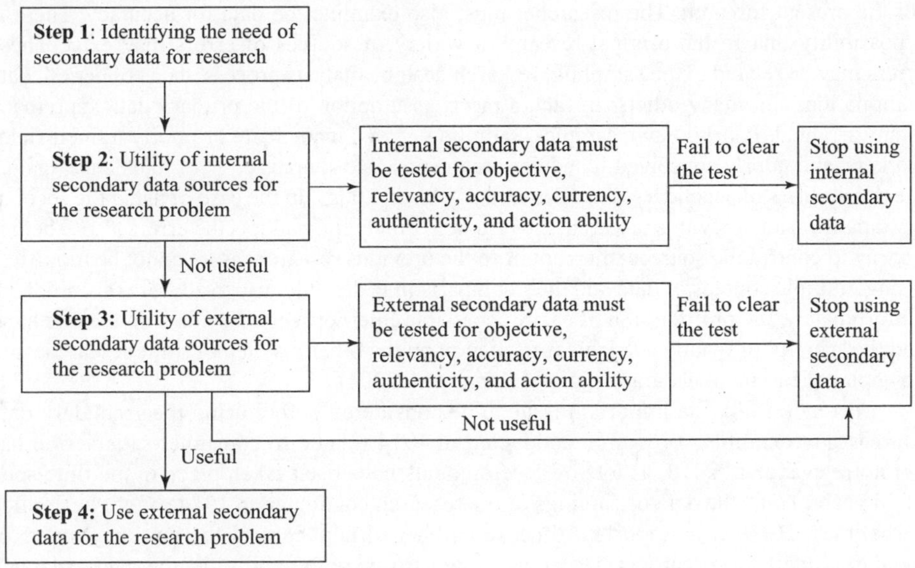

FIGURE 6.5
Roadmap for using secondary data

is examined as in Step 2. If these data qualify Step 3 then the researcher is free to use it as the final step. Let us consider these four steps one by one.

6.5.1 Step 1: Identifying the Need of Secondary Data for Research

As a first step, a researcher must identify the need of using the secondary data for the research. These are generally used to find the already available facts about a phenomenon.

As a first step, a researcher must identify the need of using the secondary data for the research. These are generally used to find the already available facts about a phenomenon. For example, a researcher conducting a research related to export and import has a lot of secondary data, and these can be used effectively to open the dimensions of the research problem. Before going for the primary data collection, the available secondary data related to export and import will provide a clear-cut direction to conduct the research. We have already discussed the importance of model building for the research. The secondary data sources help in developing a theoretical model, which ultimately should be tested statistically. To develop a model, a researcher has to specify the relationship between two or more variables and the secondary data support in specifying this relationship. More sophisticated forecasting techniques use the secondary data to forecast some research variables such as sales, profit, income, and so on. After identifying the need of the secondary data, the researcher has to decide whether an internal or external secondary data source is to be used.

6.5.2 Step 2: Utility of Internal Secondary Data Sources for the Research Problem

As a second step, a researcher has to examine the utility of in-house secondary data in light of objective, relevancy, accuracy, currency, authenticity, dependability, and action ability of the data for the research problem.

As a second step, a researcher has to examine the utility of in-house secondary data in light of **objective, relevancy, accuracy, currency, authenticity, dependability, and action ability of the data** for the research problem. For a specific research, the researchers generally collect data with a pre-defined objective. The data collected for a specific objective solve a specific research problem and may not be useful for other purposes. Hence, before using it for any other purpose, one has to keep in mind the objective of the original researcher. The objective also helps in determining the relevancy of the data in terms of its suitability for the present research. The researcher must also examine the data for accuracy. There is a possibility that in the original research a variety of sources of errors may exist. These errors may be related to the sampling, research design, analysis process, data collection, data compilation, and many others. In fact, a priori assumption of the primary data supremacy is unwarranted. Poorly drawn samples, sampling errors, inadequate or poorly trained field-workers, and poorly conceived schedules are the possible sources of error to balance against the possibilities of secondary data (Boster and Martin 2005). In the case of using the secondary data from any previous research, the researcher inherently adopts the errors also. There is no way to control the sources of errors from the previous research, as it cannot be modified. Using multiple sources of data and their comparison is the only way to address this problem. Unfortunately, the proliferation of easily accessible Internet secondary data on the one hand and the scarcity of readily available information on the other may tempt some researchers to downplay the issue of accuracy (Parasuraman et al. 2004).

Currency is also an important issue to be considered before using the secondary data sources. For example, a research conducted in 1974 related to consumer satisfaction has got no relevance in 2010, as lots of developments have been taken place in the time span of 36 years. Thus, the data or findings of the research conducted in 1974 cannot be applied verbatim in 2010. It is important for a researcher to take care of the currency status of the data. Finally, a researcher has to carefully scrutinize the ability of the data to launch an action. This action may be related to collection, compilation, or analysis part of the data. We have already discussed that four types of data exist. A researcher has to carefully notice what kind of data he or she is collecting and what will be the treatment given to the collected data.

When the data qualify all the above-described tests, It can be used for research without any suspicion or hesitation. However, if it is not able to qualify any of the above testing parameter, the use for the data must immediately be stopped and a researcher must focus on gathering information from the external secondary data sources.

6.5.3 Step 3: Utility of External Secondary Data Sources for the Research Problem

The external secondary data should also be tested for all the parameters as it is done for the primary internal data.

As shown in Figure 6.5, the external secondary data should also be tested for all the parameters as it is done for the internal secondary data. In addition, the authenticity of the external secondary data must also be tested, which was the matter of concern for the in-house generated data. To address the issue of authenticity of the data, a researcher has to determine "who" collected the data. Some research organizations, magazines, books, periodicals, journals, and so on have got high reputation and credibility in the society or concerned field. Government data sources are also authentic. Thus, while using the secondary data, a researcher has to keep in mind the authentic nature of the data.

6.5.4 Step 4: Use External Secondary Data for the Research Problem

After qualifying the first three stages, a researcher finds himself or herself in a comfortable stage to use the data, as he or she is sure that the data are useful for the research problem and there is no harm in using it as it has already been tested for all the discussed parameters.

These guidelines are followed only to use the **secondary data sources for a research purpose**. The final decision is a matter of the researcher's discretion. It is the researcher who will ultimately decide whether the use of secondary data is a facilitator or not. In most of the cases, it is noted that the researchers commonly use it to explore the problem and develop insights into it.

REFERENCES

Best, A. E. (1999). "Secondary Data Bases and Their Use in Outcomes Research: A Review of the Areas Resource File and the Healthcare Cost and Utilization Project", *Journal of Medical Systems*, 23(3): 175–81.

Boster, R. S. and W. E. Martin (2005). "The Value of Primary versus Secondary Data in Interindustry Analysis: A Study on the Economics of the Economic Model", *The Annals of Regional Science*, 6(2): 35–44.

Cowton, C. J. (1998). "The Use of Secondary Data in Business Ethics Research", *Journal of Business Ethics*, 17: 423–34.

Parasuraman, A., D. Grewal and R. Krishnan (2004). *Marketing Research*, p. 98. Boston, NY: Houghton Mifflin Company.

Sorensen, H.T., S. Sabroe and J. Olsen (1996). "A Framework for Evolution of Secondary Data Sources for Epidemiological Research", *International Journal of Epidemiology*, 25(2): 435–42.

SUMMARY

Primary data are mainly collected by a researcher to address the research problem. Secondary data are the data that have already been collected by someone else before the current needs of a researcher. Time and cost efficiencies are the major advantages in collecting the secondary data.

Secondary data sources can be broadly classified into internal and external secondary data sources. The internal secondary data are generated within and are the internal records of the organization, and the external secondary data are obtained from the sources available outside the organization and can be further classified into following four groups: books, periodicals, and other published material; reports and publication from government sources; computerized commercial and other online data sources; and media resources.

Secondary data are useful in research, but there is a guideline available to use it. A researcher has to properly follow some pre-defined steps to use it. These four steps are **identifying the need of secondary data for research, utility of internal secondary data sources for the research problem, utility of external secondary data sources for the research problem**, and use of external secondary data for the research problem.

KEY TERMS

NOTES

1. http://www.indiastat.com/aboutus.aspx, accessed September 2009.
2. http://www.indiastat.com/aboutus/ourwebsites.aspx, accessed September 2009.
3. http://paniit.iitd.ac.in/indest/about.php

DISCUSSION QUESTIONS

1. What is the difference between primary and secondary data?
2. Why a researcher focuses on collecting secondary data when he or she can collect the primary data?
3. What are the major sources of gathering the secondary data? Explain your answer in the light of classification of the secondary data.

4. What is the utility of an internal secondary data source for a researcher?
5. What is the utility of an external secondary data source for a researcher?
6. How reports and publication from government sources are different from the commercial data sources?
7. What is the roadmap of using the secondary data?
8. On what parameters, one can check the utility of an internal secondary data source and an external secondary data source?

CASE STUDY |

Case 6: *Centre for Monitoring Indian Economy Pvt. Ltd: An Independent Economic Think Tank*

Introduction

The Centre for Monitoring Indian Economy (CMIE), established in 1976, is an independent think tank. Its headquarters is located at Mumbai, India. It provides information solution in the form of databases and research reports and has built the largest database on Indian economy and companies. CMIE's "Mission" statement clearly states that "We aim to understand the dynamics of the economy and use this knowledge to help our clients take informed decisions." This is further specified by the "Vision" statement of the company, which clearly states that "To be the most effective source of economic information and knowledge solutions."[1]

The CMIE mainly provides the information databases to its customers. The information products and solutions of the company can be broadly categorized into five groups: macroeconomy, sectoral services, firm-level data services, state analysis services, and customized solutions. Its services are subscribed by thousands of organization in India and abroad. The company's clientele includes various government institutions, educational institutes, corporate companies, and many other individual clients. As discussed earlier, the CMIE offers wide range of products in five different categories.

A brief description of these five different products is given below.[2]

Macroeconomics

Economic Intelligence Service provides an overview and a prognosis of the Indian economy through a **Monthly Review of the Indian Economy** and provides 12 annual volumes of the detailed reference data. The monthly and the 12 volumes are available in print form as well as in PDF file formats. You can conduct your own research using the **Business Beacon**—a database of the macroeconomic time series data. **International Economics** is a database containing macroeconomic time series data on individual countries. Both these databases are updated on a daily basis.

Sectoral Products

Industry Analysis Service provides an incisive analysis of about 100 industries, every month. It contains forecasts and provides a detailed time-series database on the industries. **Indian Harvest** is a database on Indian agriculture while **India Trades** provides detailed data on India's foreign trade. All these databases are updated on a daily basis.

Firm-level Databases

Prowess is a database of over **10,000 Indian companies**. It contains detailed normalized data culled from the audited annual accounts, stock exchanges, company announcements, and so on. It has over **10 years of time series** and is updated with the latest data on a daily basis. **First Source** is a database of over 250,000 companies. It is brief but has a large spread. **CapEx** is a unique database that provides up-to-date information on new investment projects on hand in the country. **Alpha** provides information on mutual funds and there is a monthly report on **Mergers & Acquisitions**.

Regional Services

CMIE produces a monthly review on the **states of India** called the **State Analysis Service**. Each state review is replete with the data, news, comparisons, and the analysis.

i^3 (i-cube)

The i^3 is a comprehensive service. It provides all the **CMIE products** on a dedicated server along with **the services of an information officer**, who helps you access the information efficiently.

Suppose a multinational consumer electronics firm is willing to join the Indian market. The company is aware that many national and multinational players are already operating in India to maximize their profits. These players are operating since decades and have strong footing in the market domain. Their products are well placed in the market and enjoy sound positioning. Despite all these facts, the company knows that the Indian market size is large and tends to enhance larger and larger and has the capacity to provide an opportunity to many brands with different features. The company wants to assess consumer's attitude about the entry of a new brand through a direct research, but before going for the direct research, it is willing to prepare a detailed research report about the status of the consumer electronics industry and its future in India, through the available secondary data source.

Let us consider you as an owner of a marketing research firm and assume that a multinational company firm has contacted you to prepare a detailed report on the consumer electronics market in India. The report must be prepared in light of the market share for various companies of consumer electronics, future demand for different products of consumer electronics, profit after tax, and various other financial parameters of different companies, complete industry analysis, demographics of rural and urban market, government policies, and various other economic parameters (national income, per person income, growth rate, Gross Domestic Production (GDP), and so on). Use Indiastat.com, CMIE products, and other available secondary data sources to prepare the required report on the consumer electronics industry in India. The report must be prepared keeping in mind the company's requirement to launch the primary data survey.

NOTES |

1. http://www.cmie.com/database/?service=about-cmie.htm, accessed September 2009.
2. http://www.cmie.com/database/?service=database-products.htm, accessed September 2009.

CHAPTER 7

Data Collection: Survey and Observation

LEARNING OBJECTIVES

Upon completion of this chapter, you will be able to:

- Learn about survey method of data collection and classification of survey methods
- Understand the comparative evaluation of different survey methods
- Learn about advantages and disadvantages of different survey techniques
- Understand different observation techniques and classification of observation methods
- Learn about advantages and disadvantages of observation

RESEARCH IN ACTION: FORCE MOTORS LTD (BAJAJ TEMPO LTD)

Incorporated in 1958, Force Motors started production of the Hanseat three-wheelers in collaboration with Vidal & Sohn Tempo-Werke, Germany. Force Motors Ltd, owned by the Firodia Group, is a vertically integrated automobile company, with expertise in designing, developing, and manufacturing automotive components, aggregates, and vehicles. Shri N. K. Firodia was the founder of the company. The products of Force Motors can be divided into five product segments viz.: tractors, three-wheelers, light commercial vehicles (LCVs), multi-utility vehicles, and heavy commercial vehicles. Some of the brand names used by the company for their products are Ox and Balwan (tractors); Minidor (three-wheelers); Traveller and Excel (LCVs); and Trax Judo, Trax Gurkha, Trax GAMA, Trax Cruiser, Trax Kargo King (multi-utility vehicles).[1]

This company was earlier known as Bajaj Tempo Ltd. The word "force" in the company's name is not just to show the product of "mass" and "acceleration," but it also reflects the company's value of ethical business, strength in technology, strength in manufacturing, and energy in product development. It is also a binding force in the company's close and mutually beneficial relationships with its customers, dealers, suppliers, and business associates. Force is the dynamism with which the company ventures into the future supported by the array of technical collaborations and business alliances with world leaders such as MAN, Diamler Chrysler, and ZF.[2]

As indicated in Table 7.1 for financial year 2006–2007 and 2007–2008, financial performance was not good. There are some fundamental reasons behind the decrease in profit after tax of the company. The company specializes in the production of fully body built LCVs, including factory built vans and minibuses and hence, the proportion of steel sheets in the bodies of LCVs manufactured by the company is significantly higher than that in the LCVs manufactured by other competing companies. Most of the minibuses built in the country have bodies that are built on drive-away truck chassis by independent bus body builders, where there is a significant price advantage because of differential taxation and other reasons. Two main issues impacting the performance of the company are due to demand preference change and project delays, resulting in delays on new revenue streams.[3]

Abhay Firodia, CMD of Force Motors Ltd, has drawn up plans to aggressively push its new brand that is key to its plans of introducing the new range of medium and heavy commercial vehicles in collaboration with German auto giant, MAN Nutzfahrzeuge.[4] Suppose that Force Motors Ltd wants to assess the views of customers, dealers, suppliers, and business associates on its new branding strategy, and for this purpose it wants to launch a wide survey programme. Should the company be using personal interviews, telephone interviews, mail interviews, or electronic interviews? If it has decided to use the personal interview method for contacting respondent groups, then how will they be contacting the respondent group? What kind of problems an interviewer will be facing while contacting the respondents? How an appropriate contacting method will be selected by the company? For collecting information, should the company follow any observational technique? Is it applicable for collecting the information through the respondents? What are the relative advantages of various survey techniques over others? This chapter focuses on answering all these types of questions.

TABLE 7.1
Sales, net income, and profit after tax (in million rupees) of Force Motors Ltd from 1996-1997 to 2007-2008

Year	*Sales*	*Net income*	*Profit after tax*
Mar-97	6868.5	5916.4	63.9
Mar-98	6218.9	5176	39.3
Mar-99	5476.1	4591	−282.2
Mar-00	6788.3	5684.4	−149.4
Mar-01	6151.1	5188.8	−173.5
Mar-02	6307.3	5218.8	16
Mar-03	8266	7004.7	321.7
Mar-04	1,1117.3	9465.4	442.1
Mar-05	9999.6	8500	27.2
Mar-06	1,0871.3	9236	301.3
Mar-07	1,1438.4	10031.9	−374.9
Mar-08	1,0927	9277.6	−836.5

Source: Prowess (V. 3.1): Centre for Monitoring Indian Economy Pvt. Ltd, Mumbai, accessed September 2009, reprinted with permission.

7.1 INTRODUCTION

The main purpose of any data collection method is to enhance decision-making ability of a decision maker.

The main purpose of any data collection method is to enhance the decision-making ability of a decision maker. Obviously, data collection methods may be many. Broadly, we can classify them into human method of data collection and mechanical method of data collection. No matter what the technique of data collection is, precision is the prime objective of a data collection technique. Human method of data collection involves face-to-face data collection or mail or telephone method. Mechanical methods are also very common these days. Mechanical methods involve computer-generated methods for data collection. "Who" collects the data is not relatively less important than "what" type of data is collected. Data can be broadly classified as primary data and secondary data. We have already discussed secondary source of data collection. This chapter is an attempt to launch a discussion about some primary data collection methods. This chapter focuses on some survey and observation methods of data collection and their relative advantages and disadvantages.

7.2 SURVEY METHOD OF DATA COLLECTION

Survey means gathering information through respondents for any pre-established research objective.

Survey means gathering information through respondents for any pre-established research objective. In most of the scientific research, this information is obtained from a representative sample of the population. In a survey method, a structured questionnaire is given to the respondents and the information is obtained. This information pertains to some demographic characteristics, attitudinal aspects, intentions, and awareness of the respondents participating in survey. Survey also covers overall assessment of a respondent about any object and his or her favourable or unfavourable opinion about it. Decisions are also the topic of research; the focus is not so much on the results of decisions in the past but more on the process by which the respondents evaluate things (Aaker et al. 2000). Measuring the respondent behaviour mainly involves seeking answers of "what," "when," "where," and "how often" about a research phenomenon. For example, a talcum powder company can launch a survey to assess "what" attributes consumers want, "when" they purchase talcum powder, "where" is the source of purchase, and "how often" consumers purchase the product. Further statistical analysis attempts to answer "why" part of the research objective through establishing a "causal" relationship. For example, after obtaining the necessary information through survey, a researcher can develop a causal relationship in terms of "why" a particular brand of talcum powder is preferred over any other brand.

Like any other method of data collection, the survey methods have several advantages and disadvantages. The first advantage of the survey lies in the fact that this method gives an opportunity to the researcher to collect data at one time. The second advantage is its ability to generate some standardized information as the same questionnaire is administered to different respondents more often on same time. In addition, each respondent is also presented with the same categories of responses. For example, a survey to unfold consumer attitude through a structured questionnaire provides similar questions with similar response categories (points in rating scale) to all the respondents. Fixed response options eliminate the variability in responses due to interviewer. This method generates standardized information. Third advantage of the survey method is its suitability for data coding, tabulation, analysis, and interpretation. Especially increasing use of statistical software has made the process of coding, tabulation, analysis, and interpretation relatively much easier. Fourth advantage is the ease in administering the questionnaire.

The survey method of data collection also has some disadvantages. The major disadvantage is to handle the unwillingness of the respondents to provide responses. The unwillingness of the respondents may be due to the reasons such as their unawareness about the survey matter, information such as their income status obtained through the survey may be related to prestige of the respondents, and so on. In such cases, the respondents refuse to cooperate and do not provide any information and sometimes provide wrong information. Second disadvantage of the survey methods is the fact that the individual characteristics of the interviewer or the way of presentation of the questionnaire or the way of asking questions makes a big difference in getting the responses. So, there is a great possibility of variation in the responses as they are generated from different interviewers. In spite of these limitations, this is a widely used technique of data generation in the field of marketing research.

7.3 A CLASSIFICATION OF SURVEY METHODS

This section focuses on a classification of survey methods by the mode of administration. Broadly, the four methods are personal interview, telephone interview, mail interview, and electronic interview. Each of these survey methods can be further classified into different categories by the mode of administration. Figure 7.1 presents a broad classification of survey methods.

> On the basis of the mode of administration, four survey methods are personal interview, telephone interview, mail interview, and electronic interview.

7.3.1 Personal Interview

> As the name indicates, personal interview is a method of data collection through contacting a respondent personally.

As the name indicates, personal interview is a method of data collection through contacting a respondent personally. Naturally, there may be different ways of contacting the subjects (respondents). These ways can be classified on the basis of the respondents to be contacted and the means to contact them. Accordingly, personal interviews can be broadly classified

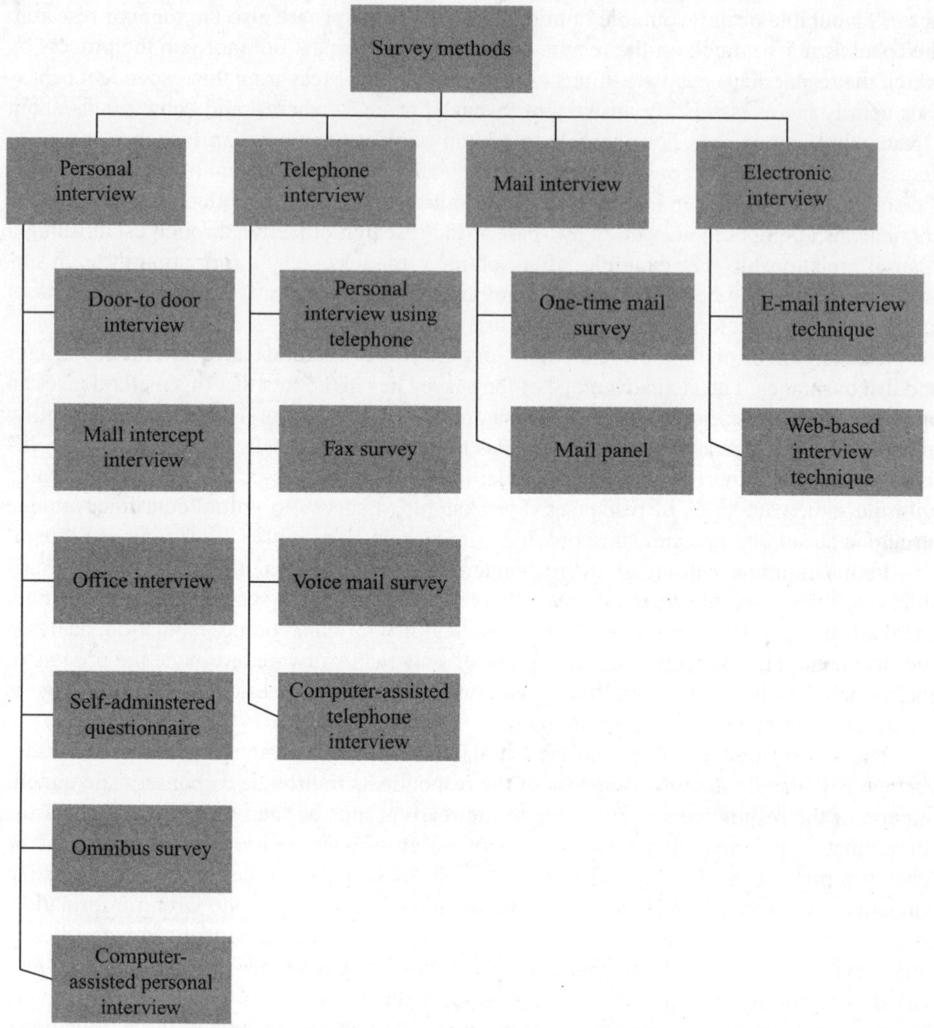

FIGURE 7.1
A broad classification of the survey methods

into six categories: door-to-door interview, mall intercept interview, office interview, self-administered questionnaire, omnibus survey, and computer-assisted interviews.

7.3.1.1 Door-to-Door Interview

Door-to-door interview technique is a traditional technique of getting responses from the respondents at their home.

Door-to-door interview is a traditional technique of getting the responses from the respondents at their home. In this technique, the interviewer contacts the respondents at their home in person and seeks a face-to-face interview. Principally, door-to-door interview technique is ideal as it allows the respondents to provide answers in a familiar, safe, and comfortable home environment. This gives an opportunity to an interviewer to uncover some real facts and figure that otherwise is very difficult to obtain. It sounds well that the respondent must be contacted at home, but it is very difficult in terms of execution. People do not want strangers to enter their homes. Nowadays, people are busy at their work place and their jobs require much time. Hence, generally a respondent does not want to share his or her time at home with anyone. This poses a great deal of difficulty for an interviewer who is supposed to visit the respondent at his or her home when the latter is reluctant to share his or her leisure time with anyone, especially an unknown person. To find an interviewer at his or her door when he or she answers the door bell can be very unpleasant for many individuals as this hinders their routine or leisure activities such as watching a movie with the family. In spite of these difficulties, for demonstration of product at home with interview, in-home product tests and conduction of long in-depth interviews, the door-to-door interview technique is the only viable alternative available to a researcher.

7.3.1.2 Mall Intercept Interview

In mall intercept interview technique, a respondent who actually is a visitor to a shopping mall is intercepted by the interviewer for obtaining responses. The interviewers stationed at the entrance of the shopping mall or any other pre-specified location invite the respondents to participate in a structured interview. After introduction of shopping malls in almost all the big cities in India, this technique of survey has become very popular. Cost-efficient approach of collecting data is a major advantage of this type of interview. In addition, due to the limited coverage space, a researcher can control the interview up to some extent which otherwise is extremely difficult when the respondents are scattered in a big geographic area. A researcher can also use efficiently a big respondent pool available at different mall locations.

In mall intercept interview technique, a respondent who actually is a visitor to the shopping mall is intercepted by the interviewer for obtaining the responses.

Mall intercept interview technique is easy to execute, but it also has some major disadvantages. Principally, the response rate is assumed to be higher, but in practice the response rate happens to be very low. The reason is very simple. The respondents come to the malls for shopping and not for answering the questions. Especially in India, where visiting shopping malls is treated as a fun activity with the family, interruption of any kind is not welcomed by anyone. Sometimes malls are not the true representative of the population as usually mall visitors in countries like India are not the common people. For example, a soap company has introduced a special 2-rupee reduction offer and will like to know the consumer attitude on the price cut. Consumers of soap are in millions and they may welcome the price cut. It is always possible that the mall visitors will be indifferent to this price cut, and assessing their opinion about the price cut would not provide any support in making strategic decision. In mall intercept interview technique, there is a great possibility that the interviewer will try to contact a respondent who looks friendly, and this results in a respondent selection bias. Finally, interview in a crowded place sometimes generates a great difficulty for the researcher.

7.3.1.3 Office Interviews

An interviewer conducts an office interview at the work place of the respondents. When the research objective is to unfold the consumer attitude of any industrial product or services, then probably home interview technique will not be able to generate accurate responses. Office interviews are usually conducted after taking prior appointment from the interviewee. In an organization, various categories of employees can provide a variety of information. A researcher can focus on these different categories of employees to generate the responses in the light of a specific research objective. For example, for assessing the attitude of a user of an industrial product like a big weighing machine, machine operator must be contacted. A manager will not be able to provide the desired information. Similarly, for unfolding the machine purchase intentions, the machine operator will not be able to provide the desired information. For this purpose, a decision maker in the organization must be contacted.

An interviewer conducts an office interview at the work place of the respondents.

7.3.1.4 Self-Administered Questionnaire

In self-administered questionnaire, no interviewer is involved. A series of questions are presented to the respondents without the intervention of the interviewer. For example, hotels

In self-administered questionnaire, no interviewer is involved. A series of questions are presented to the respondents without the intervention of the interviewer.

generally present a series of questions to the respondents to ask about their services. While absence of intervention of the interviewer makes this interview technique bias-free from the interviewer's angle on the one hand, a personal clarification to some of the questions of the survey by the interviewer is completely missing on the other. So, answer to some of the difficult-to-understand questions will always be suspicious as it is affected by the interpretation of the respondent.

7.3.1.5 Omnibus Surveys

Omnibus surveys are regular schedule-based personal interviews where a series of questions are provided by the clients of the survey-conducting company.

Omnibus surveys are regular schedule-based personal interviews where a series of questions are provided by the clients of the survey-conducting company. The schedule of the survey conduction may be weekly, fortnightly, monthly, quarterly, six monthly, yearly, or any other specific time interval decided by the survey-conducting company. The questionnaire consists of a series of questions on some diverse research topics where each set of question is provided by different clients. As a form of continuous marketing research, such surveys are conducted at regular intervals and cover a range of topics, usually for a number of different clients (Marshall 1995). Omnibus surveys have many advantages over other techniques of survey. This technique is cost effective as the cost of conducting the survey is shared by the clients. Second advantage of omnibus surveys is that the procedure of conducting the survey is standardized and schedule based. Expertise of the survey-conducting company facilitates to collect a variety of data based on the need of the researcher. For example, the need of data for before and after study can be easily fulfilled through omnibus survey technique as respondents can be easily tracked. The respondent's unwillingness to answer because of monotony and boredom is a major disadvantage of this survey technique.

7.3.1.6 Computer-Assisted Personal Interviewing (CAPI) Techniques

CAPI is a type of personal interview technique where the respondents provide their response inputs directly through a computer terminal by using a keyboard or a mouse.

Computer-assisted techniques of collecting data have become increasingly popular. CAPI is an increasingly popular method of data collection for large, scale household survey of the general population (Couper 1994). CAPI is a type of personal interview technique where the respondents provide their response inputs directly through a computer terminal by using a keyboard or a mouse. There are several advantages of this survey technique. Graphical display associated with the question presents a good opportunity for the respondents to understand the questions well. This technique also allows catering to the response time a respondent is taking to answer a question. This gives an opportunity to a researcher to understand which questions are difficult to answer. This technique also allows a researcher to incorporate the follow-up questions more easily. The respondents directly provide answers and hence, this technique of conducting survey also provides an option to reduce time spent in data collection and coding. The major disadvantage of this method is the lack of personal touch to the process, which can be provided by the interviewer in a personal interview. Table 7.2 presents the advantages and disadvantages of different personal interview techniques.

7.3.2 Telephone Interview

Telephone interviewing technique can be classified into four categories: personal interview using telephone, fax survey, voice mail survey, and computer-assisted telephone interviewing (CATI).

Increasing popularity and easy availability of telephone facility have changed the survey techniques in the field of marketing research. As the number of telephones increase, it might be expected that the telephone interviews would assume greater role as an approach to data collection (Ibsen and Ballweg 1974). Few researchers (e.g. Wilson 2007) argue that the procedure of data collection through telephone is both reliable and valid compared with the collection through mail questionnaire. Telephone interviewing technique can be classified

TABLE 7.2
Advantages and disadvantages of different personal interview techniques

Type of personal interview method	*Advantages*	*Disadvantages*
Door-to-door interview	Comfort for the respondent, face-to-face interview, ease for product demonstration	Avoidance of strangers at home, reluctance of the respondent to share his or her personal time
Mall intercept interview	Cost-efficient approach of data collection, easy coverage, and big respondent pool	Respondent's reluctance to answer, non-representative sample of respondents
Office interview	Suitable for unfolding the consumer attitude of any industrial product or services	Difficult to get appointment during working hours
Self-administered questionnaire	Free from the interviewer bias	Difficulty in handling explanation of some questions
Omnibus surveys	Cost effective, quick response, and suitable for longitudinal study	Respondent's unwillingness to answer because of monotony and boredom
Computer-assisted personal interview	Graphical display, quick follow-up, less time spent on data collection and coding	Lack of personal touch

into four categories: personal interview using telephone, fax survey, voice mail survey, and computer-assisted telephone interviewing (CATI).

7.3.2.1 Personal Interview Using Telephone

In personal interview using telephone, the interviewers ask a series of questions to the respondents and record the responses on the questionnaire papers. These days most of the telephone interviews are conducted from a centralized location where the telephone lines are specifically set up for conducting the surveys. This method of conducting interview also has various advantages. The telephone interviews when conducted through a central location give an opportunity to a researcher to control the interview process and help the interviewer when required. As compared with the personal interview technique, the telephone interviews are cost efficient as these eliminate the cost incurred in travelling. Personal interview using telephone is not free from limitations. One of the serious limitations of telephone personal interview is the inability of the interviewer to have face-to-face communication with the respondent. A face-to-face communication provides a personal relationship opportunity to an interviewer that completely diminishes when an interviewer talks to a respondent as a stranger. Another limitation of this type of interviewing technique is the "non-response" of the respondent. A common respondent gets plenty of calls on his or her phone or mobile. Hence, in a personal interview using telephone, it becomes very difficult for an interviewer to explain to the respondent the seriousness of his or her survey technique. The respondent finds great deal of difficulty in understanding the importance of the survey as he or she seems to be generally reluctant to receive telephone calls. Explaining some difficult questions is equally difficult for the interviewer. The telephone surveys are also unable to deal with a situation when a product demonstration is extremely important.

In personal interview using telephone, the interviewers ask a series of questions to the respondents and record the responses on the questionnaire papers.

7.3.2.2 Fax Survey

Traditionally, fax messages are treated as urgent, and there is a possibility that the response may be speedy, which is not valid for the mail survey.

Fax machines in organizations are now very common. For quicker response and cheaper cost, many researchers use fax survey. The researchers generally make a phone call intimating the respondents about the survey matter and then send the questionnaire to the respondents by a fax machine. When the researcher does not get any response in a week or two, he makes a follow-up call and tries to get the responses from the respondents. To get a quick response, the researchers generally use the fax survey method. This is a relative advantage of this method over mail survey method as the latter requires more time to get the response. Traditionally, fax messages are treated as urgent, and there is a possibility that the response may be speedy, which is not valid for the mail survey.

There are some disadvantages to the fax survey method. After the widespread penetration of computers with e-mail facility, the use of fax machine as a survey instrument is reducing. In some cases, the quality of the questionnaire received by the respondents happens to be poor through a fax machine. Fax survey method is not suitable for household survey as the fax machines are rarely found in houses. Although it is probably premature to consider fax as a practical means of collecting data from the consumer households, it can be used now for research with industrial, commercial, or institutional respondents (Kumar et al. 2001).

7.3.2.3 Voice Mail Survey

Voice mail survey is a completely automated telephone survey method where fixed-response questions are posed to a respondent through a pre-recorded voice of the professional interviewer and the respondent is supposed to press the telephone buttons to register the responses.

Voice mail survey is a completely automated telephone survey method where fixed-response questions are posed to a respondent through a pre-recorded voice of the professional interviewer and the respondent is supposed to press the telephone buttons to register the responses. The biggest advantage of this method is its ease for the respondent to be able to provide the answer about the questions related to household consumable items. Non-human interaction is the major disadvantage of this method of survey. There is no one to help the respondent when he seeks some clarification related to some of the questions of the questionnaire. In addition, this process is completely mechanical and lacks the personal touch of the interviewer.

7.3.2.4 Computer-Assisted Telephone Interviewing (CATI) Technique

While conducting the CATI, an interviewer sits at computer terminal that shows the questionnaire. The interviewer reads each question displayed on the screen, gets the respondent's answer, and then inputs the responses.

Advances in computer technology allow the telephone interviewers to enter the responses directly into a computer in a process known as "computer-assisted telephone interviewing" (Moghaddam and Moballeghi 2008). While conducting the CATI, an interviewer sits at the computer terminal that shows the questionnaire. The interviewer reads each question displayed on the screen, gets the respondent's answer, and then inputs the responses. This method allows an interviewer to feed the responses directly, in computer, which ultimately saves time and cost and minimizes the mistakes committed by the computer operator when feeding the data. CATI enables one to reach more number of subjects and records the answers instantly, minimizing errors of recording (Ketola and Klockars 1999).

The major disadvantage of the CATI technique is its inability to contact important mobile respondents. Due to their job-related mobility, these respondents find themselves uncomfortable to cope with the CATI. They find themselves comfortable with the e-mail survey technique, as this technique allows them to answer from anywhere any time and does not restrict their freedom. Table 7.3 presents advantages and disadvantages of different telephone interview techniques.

7.3.3 Mail Interview

In a mail survey, the questionnaire is sent to the respondent through mail and the respondent returns the filled questionnaire (providing his opinion about the questions).

In a mail survey, the questionnaire is sent to the respondent through mail and the respondent returns the filled questionnaire (providing his opinion about the questions). In this type

TABLE 7.3
Advantages and disadvantages of the different telephone interview techniques

Type of telephone interview method	*Advantages*	*Disadvantages*
Personal interview using telephone	Control over the interview process when conducted from a central position, cost efficiency	Lack of face-to-face interview, non-response, difficulty in explaining some questions, lacks the product demonstration
Fax survey	Quicker response, cheaper cost, traditional perception of respondents treating fax urgent, useful for industrial, commercial, or institutional respondents	Quality of the questionnaire received by the respondents, unavailability of fax machines in households
Voice mail survey	Suitable for household consumable items	Lacks personal dealing, getting explanation for some questions is difficult
Computer-assisted telephone interview	Reaches a high number of subjects, records the answers instantly minimizing the errors of recording	Unable to contact mobile respondents

of survey method, a questionnaire with a cover letter is sent to the potential respondent. The respondent after filling the questionnaire sends back his replies in an envelope, usually provided by the interviewer. In the mailing survey technique, the rate of return is a matter of concern. Researchers apply many techniques such as providing short questionnaire, providing postage paid return envelopes, and sometimes providing incentives to fill the questionnaire. Some researchers favour providing some incentives to the respondents. Others believe that the incentive type has no impact on the return of the survey (Church 1993). Mail surveys, traditionally known as paper-and-pencil surveys, have several advantages and disadvantages. As far as advantages are concerned, they generally provide accurate results because the respondent has enough time to think and respond. The respondent, if willing, can also take necessary support from other persons and because of the absence of interviewer, bias due to interviewer can also be controlled. Before the use of computers in conducting survey, the mail surveys used to be comparatively cost efficient. Use of computer technology in survey has got an edge over mail survey in terms of cost cutting. Another advantage of the mail survey is its ability to cover an extensive geographic area as compared with the personal interview technique. The use of computer in the survey has also reduced this advantage of mail survey, as the computers can cover relatively high geographical area in low cost. In the disadvantages side, the mail surveys have low response rate as compared with the personal interviewing and telephone interviewing techniques. Return time is not guaranteed in the mail surveys as the respondent may take weeks or months to respond. On the one hand, non-absence of the interviewer reduces the interviewer bias, on the other hand, it eliminates the possibility of explanation of difficult-to-understand question by the interviewer. Inflexibility is another major disadvantage of mail surveys as the answers cannot be altered once mailed. Follow-up is also difficult in these surveys. They can be broadly classified in two categories: one-time mail survey and mail panel.

In some cases, when the interviewer wants only one-time response from the respondent and continuous information gathering is not desired, one-time mail survey is used.

7.3.3.1 One-Time Mail Survey

In some cases, when the interviewer wants only one-time response from the respondent and continuous information gathering is not desired, one-time mail survey is used. Reduced cost as compared with the personal interview is one major advantage of this type of survey. Non-response is a major disadvantage. In a nutshell, the advantages and disadvantages of the one-time mail survey are almost the same as those of the mail surveys.

7.3.3.2 Mail Panel

Mail panel is a group of respondents who have agreed to participate in the survey conducted by the research agencies related to some business issues.

Mail panel is a group of respondents who have agreed to participate in the survey conducted by the research agencies related to some business issues. The researchers create the mail panel to generate continuous responses on certain research issues related to marketing research. To have a representative sample in the panel, the researchers collect a lot of demographic information and other types of information and then make a conscious decision to have right respondent in the panel. As the respondents have already agreed to provide the response, the response rate happens to be high in mail panel survey technique. Through a mail panel, same respondent can be contacted repeatedly and hence, it is an appropriate technique of data collection for a longitudinal research design. Table 7.4 exhibits advantages and disadvantages of different mail interview techniques.

7.3.4 Electronic Interview

There seems to be a consensus that the electronic surveys in general are less expensive than the traditional mail surveys because they do not involve printing, folding, envelope stuffing, and mailing cost.

Electronic interview techniques are basically of two types: e-mail interview and web-based interview. Electronic interview techniques are becoming very popular and will have a key role in marketing research in the near future. This is because of many advantages electronic interviews offer over traditional interview technique. There seems to be a consensus that the electronic surveys in general are less expensive than the traditional mail surveys because they do not involve printing, folding, envelope stuffing, and mailing cost (Cole 2005). In addition, non-involvement of the interviewer eliminates the possibility of bias due to the interviewer. The obtained input data are also of superior quality in this technique. Electronic surveys are also excellent facilitators in launching international and cross-cultural research programmes. Collecting data for international or cross-cultural studies is an expensive and difficult exercise to execute. Deficiencies of traditional survey are exacerbated for research on global competitiveness issues that require international data gathering activities; however, they can be mitigated, if not completely eliminated, by using dynamic web-based survey methods (Bonometti and Tang 2006). Electronic interviews also allow a researcher to have a proper follow-up. The following section discusses two commonly used electronic survey techniques: e-mail interview and web-based interview.

7.3.4.1 E-Mail Interview Technique

In an e-mail interview technique, the researcher sends the questionnaire to the respondents by an e-mail. The respondents key in their answers and send the e-mail back to the researcher.

In an e-mail interview technique, the researcher sends the questionnaire to the respondents by an e-mail. The respondents key in their answers and send the e-mail back to the researcher. As discussed, time and cost efficiency, wide coverage, and quick response are the major advantages of this technique. The major disadvantage is the lack of computer

TABLE 7.4
Advantages and disadvantages of different mail interview techniques

Type of mail interview method	*Advantages*	*Disadvantages*
One-time mail survey	Less cost	Non-response
Mail panel	High response rate, appropriate for longitudinal design	Respondent's unwillingness to answer due to monotony and boredom

TABLE 7.5
Advantages and disadvantages of different electronic interview techniques

Type of electronic interview method	*Advantages*	*Disadvantages*
E-mail interview technique	Time and cost efficiency, wide coverage, quick response, eliminates interviewer bias, easy follow-up	Lack of computer facility penetration in households
Web-based interview techniques	Eliminates interviewer bias, collecting data for international or cross cultural studies are non-expensive, easy follow-up	Computer-literate respondents are less in number, non-representative as only those who have access to computer systems can participate

facility penetration in households. Use of the e-mail interview technique is reducing as the web-based interview techniques are becoming popular.

7.3.4.2 Web-Based Interview Technique

Web-based interview techniques involve posting of the survey material on a particular website. Respondents login the website and provide their answers. Marketing research firms generally maintain databases of respondents who are supposed to participate in the web-based interview technique. In other method of finding the respondents, the research firms contact the respondents and request them to participate in the web-based survey. Andrews et al. (2003) argued that the web-based surveys are superior to the e-mail surveys in many aspects but that e-mail combined, perhaps with offline media, is an excellent vehicle for inviting individuals to participate in the web-based surveys. Inclusion of graphical display and sound in the web-based survey is an advantage over the e-mail interview technique. It has also got all the other advantages of electronic interview techniques. However, web-based surveys are also not free from some noticeable limitations. Inspite of the increasing popularity of computers in day-to-day use, computer-literate respondents are less in number. This makes the sample selection non-representative as only those who have got the access to computer systems can participate. It is very difficult for the interviewer to uncover the profile and status of the respondent, which is a phenomenal fact in conducting any research. Some researchers also claim that some cultural factors seem to be responsible for low response rate for the web surveys as compared with the traditional survey techniques. Al-Subaihi (2008), in a study conducted in Saudi Arabia, found that the restricted use of Web survey is due to some cultural factors (i.e., thoughts among people and across certain gender) and not due to technical infrastructure (geographical coverage). Table 7.5 exhibits advantages and disadvantages of different electronic interview techniques.

Web-based interview techniques involve posting of the survey material on a particular website.

7.4 EVALUATION CRITERIA FOR SURVEY METHODS

As discussed in the previous section, various methods of survey are available. A researcher often faces a dilemma as to which method of survey should be adopted. Hence, it becomes important for the researcher to evaluate all the survey methods on some pre-established criteria. This section presents an evaluation of the survey methods on the basis of 11 parameters: cost, time, response rate, speed of data collection, coverage area, bias due to the interviewer, quantity of data, control over fieldwork, anonymity of the respondent, question posing, and question diversity. Figure 7.2 exhibits evaluation criteria for various survey methods.

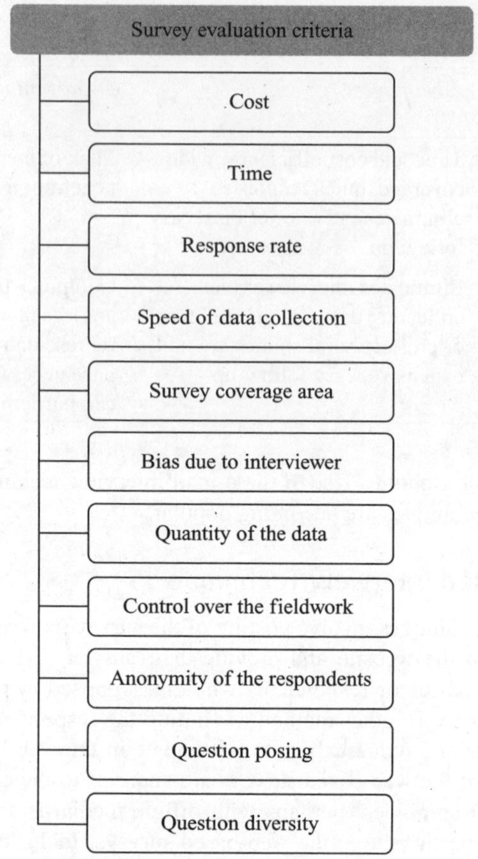

FIGURE 7.2
Evaluation criteria for various survey methods

7.4.1 Cost

In case of personal interview, the cost of conducting survey remains very high. For conducting an interview, the interviewer has to prepare a questionnaire and travel extensively for personally contacting the respondents. This makes the process very costly. This cost is very low in case of conducting personal interview through electronic means. Cost is mainly curtailed due to non-travelling mode of conducting survey. Cost is moderate in case of conducting personal interview by telephone. Few years ago, the cost of conducting personal interview was not as low as in recent times in India. Easy availability of mobiles has changed the scenario like anything. Even cost of making a call is dramatically reducing, making the telephone mode of survey cheaper than mail survey. In India, using government postal services is not very costly. It is a costly affair if the researcher wants to use private courier services. In broad sense, personal interview is the costliest of the four techniques with electronic interview as the cheapest. Telephone interview and mail interview are in between the personal interview and electronic interview in terms of cost.

7.4.2 Time

It is obvious that personal interview technique takes long time to operate and complete. Similarly, mail survey technique also takes more time to complete. Sometimes it takes more time than personal interview as the respondents have no time limit to reply. Though the researcher mentions the time limit, it is ultimately up to the respondent whether he or she will complete and send it on time. Electronic surveys are less time consuming as the mode of operation is electronic and not manual or postal. Telephone survey techniques are moderate to low time consuming. When an interviewer gets immediate response, this technique is less time consuming. In cases where interviewer does not get immediate response from the potential respondent, the technique becomes moderate time consuming. Many times the interviewers make many calls to fix an appointment to conduct surveys. This makes the process time consuming but less time consuming than the personal interview and electronic interview techniques.

7.4.3 Response Rate

For personal interviewing techniques, response rate is usually higher. Telephone interviewing techniques generate moderate to high response rate. This technique faces the problem of non-response or no answer. Response rate in the telephone interviewing technique increases when an interviewer makes a proper follow-up. Response rate of the mail survey can be separately discussed in the light of the response rate of two mailing techniques: one-time mail survey and mail panel. For a typical traditional mail technique, the response rate happens to be very low, but in the mail panel the response rate increases as the interviewer is in continuous touch with the potential respondents. So, for the mail panel survey technique, the response rate is high. Electronic interview techniques have low response rate. Between the two electronic survey techniques, the web-based surveys have lower response rate as compared with that of the e-mail survey technique. It has already been discussed that for enhancing the response rate of the web-based interview techniques, this must be supplemented by traditional mail, e-mail, or any other technique for providing prior information about the purpose of the survey to the respondents.

7.4.4 Speed of Data Collection

In case of personal interview, speed of data collection remains slow, as the interviewer has to spend time with the respondents and then has to devote time for data feeding and compiling. Telephone interview provides an opportunity to collect data at fast rate. Specifically, CATI technique generates data at a very fast rate. Mail interviews are not able to generate data at fast rate. In fact, this survey technique generates data at the lowest rate among the four discussed techniques of survey. In mail survey technique, sometimes the researcher is able to collect data after several weeks or even after several months of launching the interview programme. Electronic survey techniques provide high rate of data collection opportunity. This is even faster for the web-based interview technique than the e-mail interviewing technique. Printing, mailing, data feeding, and other such activities are not there in web-based survey techniques.

7.4.5 Survey Coverage Area

When using personal interview technique, a researcher has to keep a fact in mind that he or she will not be able to cover a wide geographical area. So, for coverage area-wise, the personal interview technique has limited use. As compared with the personal interview technique, remaining three methods, that is, telephone, mail, and web-based interview techniques, provide a wider area coverage option. Covering a wide geographical area may be costly for telephone interview technique and mail interview technique as compared with web-based interview technique. Web-based interview techniques offer a wide range of coverage at low cost.

7.4.6 Bias Due to Interviewer

Bias due to the interviewer is very high in personal interview technique. The interviewer can bias the interview process by intentional wording of questions, wishful and convenient contact to the respondent, and more than that bias the answers while feeding the data. Bias due to the interviewer is moderate in telephone interviewing method. Telephone interviewer can also bias the process by wrong wording and changing the pitch of voice. The remaining two survey methods, mail interview and web-based interviews, are free from the bias due to the interviewer.

7.4.7 Quantity of Data

Personal interviewing technique has the capacity to generate a large amount of data. This technique offers a face-to-face communication opportunity to both the interviewer and the respondents. This facilitates the interview process, and a lot of information can be generated. Remaining three methods, telephone interview, mail interview, and electronic interview, generate moderate quantity of data because these techniques lack face-to-face communication. Out of these three methods, telephone interview has the lowest capacity of data quantity generation because respondent do not feel comfortable answering questions in a lengthy interview. Mail panels can also provide moderate to high quantity of data as the respondents are a pool created by the researcher. Respondents do not feel comfortable with the lengthy questionnaire, hence for getting large amount of data, sending long questionnaire to the respondents has a very limited use.

7.4.8 Control Over Fieldwork

Control over fieldwork is moderate for mall intercept, self-administered questionnaire, omnibus surveys, and computer-assisted personal interviews. This control is often low in door-to-door interview and office interview techniques. Control over fieldwork is moderate in telephone interview techniques. In mail and web-based surveys, fieldwork control problem is eliminated as there is no fieldwork in these techniques.

7.4.9 Anonymity of the Respondent

Anonymity of the respondent is his or her perception that his or her identities will not be disclosed by the interviewer. Personal interviews have the low anonymity of the respondents as most of these offer direct interaction with the respondent. Anonymity of the respondents remains moderate in the telephone interview technique as there is no face-to-face interaction, but there is an interaction that makes the respondent suspicious. Perceived anonymity of the respondents is high in the mail survey as there is no personal or verbal interaction. Web-based interviews have high degree of anonymity of the respondents. As compared with the web-based interviews, e-mails have moderate degree of anonymity of the respondents. In e-mail interaction, the respondents' identity is disclosed when he or she replies.

7.4.10 Question Posing

Question-posing facility is high in personal interview technique, as face-to-face communication acts as a facilitator in posing and explaining questions. This is moderate in the telephone interview technique. Question-posing facility is low in the mail interview techniques and electronic interview techniques, as it never opens an opportunity to have a personal interaction.

TABLE 7.6
Comparative evaluation of various survey methods on different evaluation parameters

Evaluation criteria	*Personal interview*	*Telephone interview*	*Mail interview*	*Electronic interview*
Cost	High	Moderate	Moderate	Low
Time	High	Moderate to low	High	Low
Response rate	High	Moderate	Low/high	Low
Speed of data collection	Slow	Fast	Slow	Fast
Survey coverage area	Narrow	Wide	Wide	Wide
Bias due to interviewer	High	Moderate	None	None
Quantity of the data	High	Moderate	Moderate	Moderate
Control over fieldwork	Moderate to low	Moderate	High	High
Anonymity of the respondent	Low	Moderate	High	Moderate to high
Question posing	High	Moderate	Low	Low
Question diversity	High	Low	Moderate	Moderate to high

7.4.11 Question Diversity

Asking diverse questions is always convenient in personal interviews. In personal interview, the respondent actually sees the questions. Interviewer is also present to help the respondents in making some clarifications related to some difficult questions. This gives an opportunity to ask diverse questions to the interviewer. In telephone interviews, the interviewer cannot ask such diverse questions as the interviewer reads the questions and marks the answers. In this manner, the respondent has limited response options and gets irritated very soon and terminates the interview from his end. Mail interviews provide moderate opportunity for asking diverse questions. This opportunity is moderate because the respondents do not want to fill a long questionnaire, and they are usually reluctant to respond to a lengthy questionnaire. E-mail interview technique gives a limited option to ask diverse questions whereas the web-based interviewing techniques give a good option to ask diverse questions. Table 7.6 presents comparative evaluation of various survey methods on different evaluation parameters.

7.5 OBSERVATION TECHNIQUES

Observation techniques involve watching and recording the behaviour of test subjects or test objects in a systematic manner without interacting with them.

Observation techniques involve watching and recording the behaviour of test subjects or test objects in a systematic manner without interacting with them. So, observations in research are systematic. Systematic observation represents the ultimate in cheap but good research, which enables one to gather free data found in the environment (Demirdjian 2006). While applying observation techniques, the researcher does not communicate with the subjects and acts as a neutral observer. In observation method, the researcher records the behaviour of the test subjects or test objects using a pencil and paper or does videography. Compared with the emphasis on the survey techniques within the marketing discipline, attention to observational data collection methods is relatively rare (Grove and Fisk 1992). Observation does not often appear as a research methodology in the marketing literature: this may be because it is sometimes hard to quantify the outcomes of observational research at the outset or because it is considered as time consuming, or sometimes it may be difficult to generalize the findings

(Boote and Mathews 1999). Observation research can be broadly classified as direct versus **indirect observation**; structured versus **unstructured observation**; disguised versus undisguised observation; and human versus **mechanical observation**.

7.5.1 Direct versus Indirect Observation

In direct observation, the researchers directly observe the behaviour of a subject and record it. In indirect observation, the researcher observes outcome of a behaviour rather than observing the behaviour.

In **direct observation**, the researchers directly observe the behaviour of a subject and record it. For example, for observing purchase behaviour of shopper for a tea packet, a researcher can stand in a big grocery store just aside the shelf that contains tea packets. He can systematically record the behaviour of the shoppers such as their first pick (choice) from the shelf; their preference for the hard pack, jar pack, or poly pack; their inclination for a particular brand; impact of price (as the shopper picks a pack and places it back on the shelf after seeing the price); and so on. In **indirect observation**, the researcher observes outcome of a behaviour rather than observing the behaviour. For example, a researcher can count the number of cups in which tea is consumed in a product demonstration to note the consumer preference for a particular brand or taste.

7.5.2 Structured versus Unstructured Observation

In a structured observation, a clear guideline is provided to the observer as what is to be observed and what is not to be observed. In an unstructured observation, the observer is free to observe what he or she feels is important for a research.

In a **structured observation**, a clear guideline is provided to the observer as what is to be observed and what is not to be observed. In this type of observational technique, observation is being made on a pre-specified format or checklist. This format itself does not consist the observation points that are not important for the researcher. Structured observation is a suitable technique when the research problem is clearly defined and the information needed from the observation is clearly laid down. As the name suggests, in an **unstructured observation**, the observer is free to observe what he feels is important for a research. No pre-specified format or checklist is provided to the observer, and he or she almost makes a discretionary decision on what is to be observed and what must be dropped from the observation. In theory, all the behaviour of the subjects can be recorded, but in practice, the observer applies his discretion.

7.5.3 Disguised versus Undisguised Observation

In disguised observation, the subject happens to be unaware that his or her behaviour or action is being monitored by the observer. In undisguised observation, the subject happens to be aware that he or she is being observed by an observer.

In **disguised observation**, the subject happens to be unaware that his or her behaviour or action is being monitored by the observer. This type of observational technique is especially used because the subjects will exhibit natural behaviour when they are unaware of the fact that they are being observed by an observer. For example, for making a disguised observation in a big shopping mall, an observer may be disguised as a shopper. In **undisguised observation**, the subject happens to be aware that he or she is being observed by an observer. There is a debate among the researchers that the undisguised observation can bias the observation process or not. Few researchers are of the view that the undisguised observation can bias the observation process, others say that the observer effect on the observation process is not long lasting.

7.5.4 Human versus Mechanical Observation

Human observational techniques involve observation of the test subjects or test object by a human being, generally an observer appointed by a researcher. Mechanical observation techniques involve observation by a non-human device.

Human observational techniques involve observation of the test subjects or test object by a human being, generally an observer appointed by a researcher. Advancement in technology and its appropriateness has reduced the burden of human observers. **Mechanical observation** techniques involve observation by a non-human device. These devices are many, for example, video camera, voice recorder, eye-movement recorder, scanners, and so on. In the field of marketing research, use of mechanical device has been becoming increasingly popular as these devices are free from the bias caused by human observer.

7.6 CLASSIFICATION OF OBSERVATION METHODS

Observation methods can be broadly classified into five categories. These are personal observation, mechanical observation, audits, content analysis, and physical trace analysis (Shao 2002). Following section focuses on the discussion of these five different types of observation methods classified by mode of administration. Figure 7.3 exhibits these different observation methods.

Observation methods can be broadly classified into five categories. These are personal observation, mechanical observation, audits, content analysis, and physical trace analysis.

7.6.1 Personal Observation

As the name indicates, in personal observation, an observer actually watches the subject behaviour and makes a record of it. The researcher never tries to alter the behaviour of the subject but just records it as it happens in front of him. The subject may or may not be aware that his behaviour is being observed by the observer. This type of observation is extremely useful when the subjects are small kids. Perception of the observer is conditioned by his knowledge, and therefore he perceives the event to happen in a certain way (Juma'h 2006). Anyway, personal observation is a practical and useful technique to collect data, specifically in cases where other means of data collection are seemingly not advantageous.

As the name indicates, in personal observation, an observer actually watches the subject behaviour and makes a record of it.

7.6.2 Mechanical Observation

Mechanical observation involves the observation of behaviour of the respondents through a mechanical device. This device may be a video camera, a voice recorder, eye-movement recorder, and other such devices. In modern times, many mechanical devices are available to record the behaviour of the subjects. This is especially important when a researcher has to make continuous observation or when a researcher feels that the human observation will not solve the research purpose. For example, a camera can record the actions of a respondent better than any human being. In addition, the camera has the capacity of observing behaviour of the subjects for a long time as compared with the human observer. In some cases, human observation is not possible. For example, when a researcher, in particular will like to measure the emotional reaction of an individual to a stimuli through his eye pupil movement, the human observation is neither feasible nor practical. In this case, an instrument commonly known as eye-movement recorder is used. This instrument has the capacity of measuring eye movement at a rate of 30 readings per second with respect to any stimuli such as advertisement, shelf display, and so on. Obviously, no human being will be able to match the capacity of this instrument.

Mechanical observation involves the observation of behaviour of the respondents through a mechanical device.

7.6.3 Audits

Audit involves examination of particular records or inventory analysis of the items under investigation. In audit analysis, the researchers personally collect the data and usually make the count of the items under investigation. Audit is a highly structured technique and usually is performed personally by an auditor without using a mechanical device. Nowadays

Audit involves examination of particular records or inventory analysis of the items under investigation.

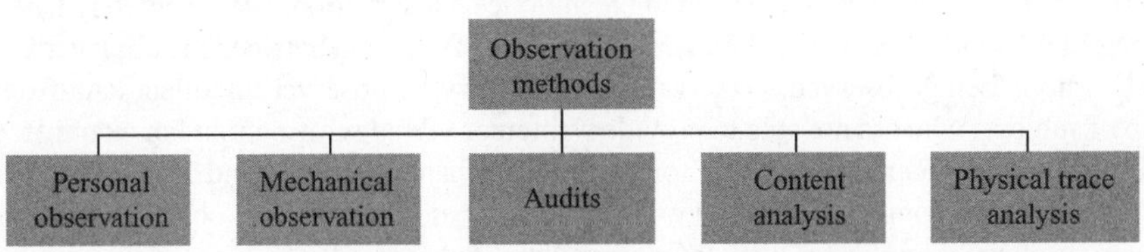

FIGURE 7.3 Classification of observation methods

some mechanical devices are also used to make an audit. For example, modern libraries use bar-coded books and a laser gun to count the number of books in the library. In the field of consumer behaviour, pantry audit is very popular. In pantry audit, the researcher inventories the items in the kitchen of the subjects while making a personal interview. Pantry audits are capable of handling the problem of biased responses of the subjects as their used items can be counted from their pantry. Though, few researchers argue that the presence of items in the pantry does not guarantee that the subjects are using it. In addition, getting in the pantry of the subjects is a difficult exercise because many subjects may not be willing to allow the researcher into their kitchens.

7.6.4 Content Analysis

Content analysis is a research technique used to objectively and systematically make inferences about the intentions, attitudes, and values of individuals by identifying specified characteristics in textual messages.

Content analysis is a research technique used to objectively and systematically make inferences about the intentions, attitudes, and values of individuals by identifying specified characteristics in textual messages (Morris 1994). Content analysis systematically examines the content of communication as an indirect observation and analysis. Malhotra (2004) stated that the unit of analysis may be words (different words or type of words in the message), characters (individuals or objects), themes (propositions), space and time measures (length or duration of the message), or topics (subjects of the message). Marketing researchers generally examine the content of message in print advertisement and electronic advertisement, content analysis for the print articles, and so on. For example, Zhou (2005) has used content analysis to find the usability challenges and cross-cultural difference issues in city tourism website design. By applying content analysis, he examined the content and functions of 55 city tourism websites covering North America, Europe, Asia, Australia, and Africa. Through content analysis, he revealed the apparent differences among countries of different economic level as well as culture and suggested to make websites more effective, efficient, and easy-to-use.

7.6.5 Physical Trace Analysis

Physical trace analysis involves collection of data through physical trace of the subjects in terms of understanding their past behaviour.

Physical trace analysis involves collection of data through physical trace of the subjects in terms of understanding their past behaviour. For example, a researcher can count the number of soft drinks consumed in an annual function of a college to understand the inclination of youth for a particular brand. Physical trace analysis is an indirect method of observation as the behaviour is not directly observed, but the outcome of a behaviour is observed. In some cases, physical trace analysis is very useful. For example, the popularity of a website can be analysed by counting the number of times the users have visited the site.

7.7 ADVANTAGES OF OBSERVATION TECHNIQUES

The most admirable advantage of the observation methods is the collection of data on the basis of actually observed information rather than on the basis of using a measurement scale. Observation also eliminates recall error as the observation is immediately recorded on the place of observation. Influence of the interviewer on getting answers from the respondents is a major limitation of personal interviewing techniques. Observations are completely free from this bias of personal interview technique as there is no interaction between the observer and the subject who is being observed. Observations also allow an observer to collect data from the group of subjects who are not able to provide written or verbal information. For example, a toy manufacturing company making toys for small kids of age between 1 and 5 years will get the response of kids through observation only. In some specific cases, the observation methods prove to be cheaper and faster than other survey methods.

7.8 LIMITATIONS OF OBSERVATION TECHNIQUES

One of the major limitations of the observation techniques is its inability to measure attitude or intentions of the subjects. Another limitation of the observation method is the subjective observation by the observer. A same incident may have three different observations by three different observers. For personal observation, continuous monitoring by the observer is required. Observers often feel fatigue from this long continuous observation, and this results in a biased result. Personal observation techniques require a lot of time and energy to be executed. Disguised observation is sometimes unethical as the subject is unaware that his or her action is being observed by the observer. From a practical standpoint, it is best to view the observation method as a complement to survey methods, rather than to view it as a competitor (Malhotra 2004).

REFERENCES

Aaker, D. A., V. Kumar and G. S. Day (2000). *Marketing Research*, 7th ed., p. 218. Wiley, Asia.

Al-Subaihi, A. A. (2008). "Comparison of Web and Telephone Survey Response Rates in Saudi Arabia", *Electronic Journal of Business Research Methods*, 6(2): 123–32.

Andrews, D., B. Nonnecke and J. Preece (2003). "Conducting Research on Internet: Online Survey Design, Development and Implementation Guidelines", *International Journal of Human–Computer Interaction*, 16(2): 185–210.

Bonometti, R. J. and J. Tang (2006). "A Dynamic Technique for Conducting Online Survey-Based Research", *Competitiveness Review: An International Business Journal Incorporating Journal of Global Competitiveness*, 16(2): 97–105.

Boote, J. and A. Mathews (1999). "'Saying is One Thing; Doing is Another: The Role of Observation in Marketing Research", *Qualitative Market Research: An International Journal*, 2(1): 15–21.

Church, A. H. (1993). "Estimating the Effect of Incentives on Mail Survey Response Rates: A Meta-Analysis", *Public Opinion Quarterly*, 57(1): 62–7.

Cole, S. T. (2005). "Comparing Mail and Web-Based Survey Distribution Methods: Results of Surveys to Leisure Travel Retailers", *Journal of Travel Research*, 43(5): 422–30.

Couper, M. P. (1994). "Interviewer Attitudes Toward Computer Assisted Personal Interviewing (CAPI)", *Social Science Computer Review*, 12(1): 38–54.

Demirdjian, Z. S. (2006). "Inexpensive Research in Marketing: Empowering the Technologically Challenged Entrepreneurs", *Innovative Marketing*, 2(1): 7–14.

Grove, S. J. and R. P. Fisk (1992). "Observational Data Collection Methods for Service Marketing: An Overview", *Journal of the Academy of Marketing Science*, 20(3): 217–24.

Ibsen, C. A. and J. A. Ballweg (1974). "Telephone Interviews in Social Research: Some Methodological Considerations", *Quality and Quantity*, 8(2): 181–92.

Juma'h, A. H. (2006). "Empirical and Realistic Approaches of Research", *Inter Metro Business Journal*, 2(1): 88–108.

Ketola, E. and M. Klockars (1999). "Computer-Assisted Telephone Interview (CATI) in Primary Care", *Family Practice*, 16(2): 179–83.

Kumar, V., D. A. Aaker and G. S. Day (2001). *Essentials of Marketing Research*, 2nd ed., pp. 228. Wiley.

Malhotra, N. K., (2004). *Marketing Research: An Applied Orientation*, 4th ed., p. 189. Pearson Education.

Marshall, D. W. (1995). "Market Research Methods and Scottish Eating Habits", *British Food Journal*, 97(7): 27–31.

Moghaddam, G. G. and M. Moballeghi (2008). "How do we Measure the Use of Scientific Journals? A Note on Research Methodologies", *Scientometrics*, 76(1): 125–33.

Morris, R. (1994). "Computerized Content Analysis in Management Research: A Demonstration of Advantages and Limitations", *Journal of Management*, 20(4): 903–31.

Shao, A. T., (2002). *Marketing Research: An Aid to Decision Making*, 2nd ed., p. 170. South-Western Thomson Learning.

Wilson, T. C. (2007). "Collecting Conjoint Data Through Telephone Interviews", *Journal of the Academy of Marketing Science*, 12(4): 190–9.

Zhou, Q. (2005). "Usability Issues in City Tourism Web Site Design: A Content Analysis", *IEEE International Professional Communication Conference Proceeding*, pp. 789–796.

SUMMARY

This chapter focuses on some survey and observation methods of data collection and their relative advantages and disadvantages. Survey is gathering information through the respondents for any pre-established research objective. On the basis of mode of administration, the survey methods can be broadly classified as personal interview, telephone interview, mail interview, and electronic interview. Personal interview can be further classified into door-to-door interview, mall intercept interview, office interviews, self-administered questionnaire, omnibus surveys, and computer-assisted interviewing techniques. Telephone interviews are classified into personal interview using telephone, fax survey, voice mail survey, and CATI technique. Mail surveys can be broadly classified into two categories: one-time mail survey and mail panel. Two commonly used electronic survey techniques are e-mail interview and web-based interview. Survey methods can be evaluated on the basis of 11 parameters. These are cost, time, response rate, speed of data collection, coverage area, bias due to the interviewer, quantity of data, control over fieldwork, anonymity of the respondent, question posing, and question diversity. Each method of survey has its own advantages and disadvantages with respect to various evaluation parameters.

Observation techniques involve watching and recording the behaviour of test subjects or test objects in a systematic manner without interacting with them. Observation research can be broadly classified as direct versus indirect observation; structured versus unstructured observation; disguised versus undisguised observation; and human versus mechanical observation. Observation methods can be broadly classified into five categories. These are personal observation, mechanical observation, audits, content analysis, and physical trace analysis. Each method of observation also has its own advantages and disadvantages with respect to various evaluation parameters.

KEY TERMS

NOTES

1. Prowess (V. 3.1): Centre for Monitoring Indian Economy Pvt. Ltd, Mumbai, accessed September 2009, reprinted with permission.
2. http://www.forcemotors.com/index.aspx
3. http://forcemotors.com/html/management_d_analysis.aspx
4. http://www.financialexpress.com/news/supreme-court-spikes-rahul-bajaj-plea-against-force-...

DISCUSSION QUESTIONS

1. What is survey method of data collection and when is it used in marketing research?
2. What are different survey methods available for launching a marketing research study? What will be the best method to be adopted? Explain and rationalize your answer.
3. Make a comparative chart to evaluate selection criteria for different survey techniques.
4. What is personal interview technique? Explain different types of personal interview techniques.
5. What are the relative advantages of telephone interview technique over other methods of survey? Explain different types of telephone interview techniques.
6. What is mail interview technique? For a marketing researcher, in what circumstance is this technique suitable?
7. What is the relative advantage of web-based interview technique over e-mail interview technique? Also explain the use and importance of electronic interview technique in recent times.
8. Make an evaluation charts for the different methods of survey with parameters such as cost, time, response rate, speed of data collection, coverage area, bias due to the interviewer, quantity of data, control over fieldwork, anonymity of the respondent, question posing, and question diversity.
9. What is observation? Why observation is not very frequently used by marketing researchers as compared with the survey techniques?
10. Write a short note on following terms:
    - Direct versus indirect observation
    - Structured versus unstructured observation
    - Disguised versus undisguised observation
    - Human versus mechanical observation

11. What is personal observation and under what circumstances is this a preferred option by a marketing researcher?
12. What is the difference between mechanical observation and audit analysis?
13. What is content analysis and what is the major reason of using this as an observation method?
14. What is physical trace analysis and what are the relative advantages of this observation technique over other techniques of observation?
15. What are the advantages and disadvantages of observation techniques?

CASE STUDY |

Case 7: *TVS Motors Company Ltd*

Introduction: Two-Wheeler Industry in India

The two-wheeler category is steadily moving from a discretionary purchase to an essential purchase, especially among the burgeoning Indian middle-class households. Better quality and durability, higher fuel efficiency, new age styling, and features in conjunction with a slew of new product launches and greater finance availability have been the primary drivers of sales in the past years.[1] India secures second-largest position in two-wheeler production. Apart from the discussed facts, inadequacy and poor quality of public transport system in India have pushed the demand of two-wheelers. In India, the two-wheeler industry is highly diversified in terms of presenting a versatile product line. Two-wheeler manufacturers produce different economic models for general public as well as some specific models to cater the different needs of high-income group. Two-wheelers contain scooters, mopeds, and motorcycles. Few years ago the market was dominated by scooter segment, but scenario changed in 1998–1999 when motorcycles took the edge and never looked back. Nowadays, Indian two-wheeler industry is dominated by the motorcycle segment. Hero Honda, Bajaj, TVS Motors, Kinetic Motors, and LML are some of the main players in the Indian two-wheeler industry.

Demand of two-wheelers is increasing day-by-day. In the year 1990–1991, the demand for the two-wheelers was 1.82 million units that grew to 3.83 million units in the year 2000–2001. The projected demand for the two-wheelers in the year 2014–2015 is estimated to reach 16 million units.[2] This is no doubt a rosy picture for the growth of Indian two-wheeler industry. Tables 7.01 and 7.02 present market segmentation and product variation of two-wheelers in India, respectively.

TABLE 7.01
Market segmentation for the two-wheeler industry in four regions of the country

Market segmentation	
Segment	*Share (%)*
North	32
East	9
West	27
South	32

Source: http://www.indiastat.com, accessed September 2009, reproduced with permission.

TABLE 7.02
Product wise market share for the two-wheeler industry in India

Product variation	
Type	*Share (%)*
Motorcycles	66
Scooters	22
Mopeds	11

Source: http://www.indiastat.com, accessed September 2009, reproduced with permission.

TVS Group: A Major Player in Two-Wheeler Market in India

TVS Group was established in 1911 by T. V. Sundram Iyengar. As one of India's largest industrial entities, it epitomizes Trust, Value, and Services. Today TVS Group comprises of over 30 companies, employing more than 40,000 people worldwide and with a turnover in excess of US$ 4 billion. With heavy growth, expansion, and diversification, TVS commands a strong presence in manufacturing two-wheelers, auto component, and computer peripherals. The company also has a vibrant business in the distribution of heavy commercial vehicles, passenger cars, finance, and insurance. Mission statement of the company clearly states, "We are committed to being highly profitable, socially responsible, and leading manufacturer of high value for money, environmentally friendly, lifetime personal transportation products under the TVS brand, for customers predominantly in Asian markets and to provide fulfillment and prosperity for the employees, dealers and suppliers." Company's

TABLE 7.03
Sales, income, and profit after tax and forex earning (in million rupees) of TVS Motors Ltd from 1994-1995 to 2008-2009

Year	*Sales*	*Income*	*Profit after tax*	*Forex earning*
Mar-95	4088.5	4119.2	337.5	64.3
Mar-96	6183.2	6229.1	351.5	44.3
Mar-97	8299.3	8363.2	543.6	114.5
Mar-98	10,186.2	10,398.7	685.4	159.2
Mar-99	13,130.7	13,284.7	817.5	107.2
Mar-00	15,417.7	15,577.5	857.3	164.1
Mar-01	18,209.8	18,408.2	625.7	159.3
Mar-02	22,135.9	22,336.2	539.5	170.4
Mar-03	31,112.8	31,419.6	1293.5	249.7
Mar-04	32,600.1	33,109.5	1377.5	694.8
Mar-05	33,212.5	34,108.9	1389.9	1222
Mar-06	37,317.5	38,179.7	1225	1806.8
Mar-07	44,720.1	45,514.8	662.8	2581
Mar-08	36,835.3	37,849.4	317.7	3344.7
Mar-09	40,089.1	40,894.6	310.8	5241.1

Source: Prowess (V. 3.1): Centre for Monitoring Indian Economy Pvt. Ltd, Mumbai, accessed September 2009, reprinted with permission.

long-term vision can be well understood by its Vision statement comprised of three core values: Driven by the customer, The industry leader, and Global overview.[3]

Opportunities and Threats for TVS Motors Ltd

With the increased affordability among the Indian consumer class, the penetration level grew to 50 vehicles per thousand people. However, this is very low in comparison with countries such as Indonesia (100), Thailand (240), and Malaysia (300). Therefore, growth opportunities are ample in the future. Easy availability of low-cost finance has been a success factor in expanding the customer base in the past. Any restrictions will hamper the growth prospects. TVS Star has established itself as a strong brand in the economy segment and has already sold more than 1.2 million vehicles till date. However, the competition in this segment has been intense with price promotions and new product launches. The company plans to further invest and grow in this segment through continuous innovation and value addition to customers. TVS Apache struck a chord with the younger generation and has become a well-known brand in that segment of customers. However, the sensitivity of this segment to new products is high and a slew of new product launches from competition will act as a deterrent. The company plans to address this threat through a series of variants and new products to keep the excitement growing. Moped category sales is also growing specially in rural areas due to good monsoon in last few years, but a weak monsoon status can reverse the situation.[1] TVS Motors has strategies to meet with challenges posed by the environment. TVS Motors has some long-term plans to meet the challenges and threats.

Responding to shareholder's queries at the Seventh Annual General Meeting in Chennai, Chairman and MD, Venu Srinivasan clearly stated, "All our investments will start paying dividends from this year. We are serious about the addressing the issues raised by the members like better utilization of the loans invested in assets, reducing the cost of operations and improving the returns. We will also looking at tapping renewable energy and other sources to tide over the power shortage and rising cost of the input." Mr Srinivasan stated that TVS Motors has to revitalize its finance entity as the finances for two-wheelers and consumer durables have dried up from banks. He further stated that Indonesia may be a long-term market as TVS has established itself as a quality supplier.[4]

Three-wheeler market is also growing in its own proportion. In the year 2000–2001, market was covered with the demand for 2,14,000 units in a year. This is projected to reach the 6,60,000 units per year in the year 2014–2015.[2] TVS Motors is willing to cater the opportunities of three-wheeler industry. It has launched a three-wheeler brand "TVS King" to capitalize the opportunity present in a three-wheeler market. TVS Motors is willing to add more features in its three-wheeler brand "TVS King" on the basis of customer's response. Assume, having this task in hand, the company decided to use both survey and observation method to collect the required response from the customer. What kind of survey methods should company use to collect the required information? What will be the basis of selecting an appropriate survey technique? What observation method the company should use to collect the information related to adding new features in the product? What should be the base of using survey and observation method?

NOTES |

1. Prowess (V. 3.1): Centre for Monitoring Indian Economy Pvt. Ltd, Mumbai, accessed September 2009, reprinted with permission.
2. http://www.indiastat.com, accessed September 2009, reprinted with permission.
3. http://www.tvsmotor.in/group.asp
4. http://economictimes.indiatimes.com/News/News-By-Industry/Auto/Automobiles/TVS-mot…

CHAPTER 8

Experimentation

LEARNING OBJECTIVES

Upon completion of this chapter, you will be able to:

- Understand the concept of experimentation and causality
- Understand the internal and external validity issues in experimentation
- Understand the threats to internal and external validity in experimentation
- Understand the ways to control extraneous variables
- Understand and compare a laboratory experiment and field experiment
- Understand the concept of experimental designs and deal with various types of experimental designs
- Understand the limitations of experimentation
- Understand the concept of test marketing and different types of test marketing techniques

RESEARCH IN ACTION: BERGER PAINTS INDIA LTD

Berger Paints is the culmination of over seven-decade process of evolution and growth that began in 1923. The company's growth is closely linked with the business and industrial development of modern India. Berger's performance is anchored today in a wide variety of decorative and industrial paints, which continue to gain an increasing share of the highly competitive Indian paint market. Being an ISO 9001 company, the quality products of the company have attained an instant recognition worldwide and continue to meet the quality requirements that are demanded today even in the domestic market.[1]

Berger Paints India Ltd, owned by the Dhingra Group, was incorporated in the year 1923. The company was originally formed by Mr Hadfield, and the Dhingra Group took over it in 1991. The company is engaged in the business of manufacturing and marketing of paints and varnishes in India. Product range of the company includes synthetic enamel, interior and exterior wall coatings, wood finish, and acrylic emulsions. The enamels are marketed in the brand name of Luxol Hi Synthetic, Luxol Satin, Luxol Lustre, and so on. WeatherCoat Longlife and WeatherCoat Smooth 100% Acrylic are the popular brands of exterior wall coatings. The company markets interior wall coatings in five different brand names and offers complete painting solution services in the name of home decor, which includes professional help on the product selection, material delivery, clean up, and supervision. It has launched Lewis Berger ColorBank, which is based on the computerized paint technology, having a range of shades.[2] The success story of the company is witnessed through the income and profit after tax status of the company from 1994-1995 to 2008-2009 (Table 8.1).

>>>

In the financial year 2008-2009, similar to other paint companies, Berger Paints India Ltd has also suffered from the deterioration in profit after tax status. Rising crude oil price and higher interest cost post-September 2008 are some of the reasons. In September 2008, the world economy has taken an abrupt turn affecting the situation in an adverse way. This also has an adverse impact on the performance of some Indian companies and their international operations. Nowadays, many global companies are changing the strategies so as to operate in that part of the globe that is less affected by the environmental adversities, as compared to focus on the part of the globe that is affected highly by the environmental adversities. This may be a very good exercise to pool the losses incurred from one segment of the globe by the another segment.

The Indian companies have also realized the importance of being global and catering market through global operations. Commenting on the profit decline of 2008-2009, Subir Bose, managing director of Berger Paints India Ltd, said, "We will have volume growth but with paint prices now coming down to levels of 2007-08, value growth will be a challenge. Our overseas operations have not been impacted heavily due to recession as our exposure is very small."[3] Assume that Berger Paints has decided to go for a massive brand awareness programme in the overseas market. For formulating a broad research programme, the company has decided to go for experimentation.

How pilot test and conduction of the final test will be operationalized? Which experimental design should be used? Field experiment or laboratory experiment, which model should be used? What will be the relevant variables for testing? How a researcher will be controlling the environment and extraneous variables? This chapter provides an opportunity to answer all such type of questions and attempts to make the readers aware of the complete process of experimentation.

TABLE 8.1
Income and profit after tax (in million rupees) of Berger Paints India Ltd from 1994-1995 to 2008-2009

Year	*Income*	*Profit after tax*
Mar-95	2183.1	68.8
Mar-96	2779.7	98.5
Mar-97	3170.4	143
Mar-98	3529.5	182.4
Mar-99	4355.9	236.3
Mar-00	5111.4	237
Mar-01	5689.2	284.9
Mar-02	6111	313.9
Mar-03	6794.2	334.2
Mar-04	7825.6	440.3
Mar-05	9625	521.2
Mar-06	11,361.9	702.9
Mar-07	13,411.3	830.7
Mar-08	15,436.1	920.8
Mar-09	17,265.2	887.6

Source: Prowess (V. 3.1), Centre for Monitoring Indian Economy Pvt. Ltd, Mumbai, accessed September 2009, reprinted with permission.

8.1 INTRODUCTION

For understanding the concept of experimentation, let us take a simple example of a firm facing a problem of decline in sales. The firm is desperate to understand the reasons of the decline in sales. There may be many factors responsible for this slump such as poor advertisement impact, lack of sales people support, perceived poor quality of the product, lack of motivation for dealers and retailers, poor promotional policies adopted by the company, high turnover rate among sales people, and so on. The company has to understand the main reasons of the decline in sales and must be focused on these reasons to control the slump in sales.

We have already discussed some techniques such as using the secondary data, survey, and observation to collect the data to explore the insights of the problem in hand. These techniques are important to explore the dimensions of the problem in hand but are not able to provide the definitive answer to the research question. These techniques are basically exploratory and descriptive in nature and are not able to answer causal questions. Experimentations are generally used to determine the "causal relationship" between the variables. As discussed in the decline in sales example, there may be various causes of the decline in sales, and we focused on few of these listed earlier. To understand the causal relationship, we take an independent variable "perceived poor quality of the product" as the determinant of research question "decline in sales." Now, it is important to understand that the perceived poor quality of the product is not the only cause of the decline in sales, there may be many more. In addition, the perceived poor quality of the product not always determines the decline in sales; it is only the probabilistic cause in the decline in sales. More specifically, we can never prove that the perceived poor quality of the product is the determinant of the decline in sales; we can only infer that this independent variable may be the reason of the decline in sales.

8.2 DEFINING EXPERIMENTS

Experiments can be defined as the systematic study in which a researcher controls or manipulates one or more independent (experiment) variables to test a hypothesis about the independent variable. **Independent variables** are the variables that are manipulated or controlled by the researcher. As given in Section 8.1, poor advertisement impact, lack of sales people support, perceived poor quality of the product, lack of motivation for dealers and retailers, poor promotional policies adopted by the company, and high turnover rate among sales people are independent variables. On the other hand, **dependent variables** are variables on which a researcher has little or no control over the research process, but the researcher is keen to note a change in it with the corresponding change in the independent variables. In the chapter opening example, sales are the dependent variables. The researcher manipulates the explanatory or independent variable and then observes that the hypothesized dependent variable is affected by the intervention of the researcher or not. During this process of intervention by the researcher, all other independent variables that may confound the relationship between dependent and independent variables are being controlled or eliminated. Hence, the main purpose of the experimentation is to provide an opportunity to the researcher, where he is able to control the research situation for determining the causal relationship between the dependent and independent variables. Tull and Hawkins (1984) stated that the essence of experimentation is the manipulation of one or more variables by the experimenter in such a way that its effect on one or more variables can be measured.

> Experiments can be defined as the systematic study in which a researcher controls or manipulates one or more independent (experiment) variables to test a hypothesis about the independent variable.

> Independent variables are the variables that are manipulated or controlled by the researcher. On the other hand, dependent variables are variables on which a researcher has little or no control over the research process, but the researcher is keen to note a change in it with the corresponding change in independent variables.

Before detailing experimentation, we will first focus on the concept of causality, a prerequisite for experimentation. We do things in the world by exploiting our knowledge of what cause what (Hobbs 2005). In fact, **causality** is a conditional phenomenon between variables in the form "if x, then y." **Causality** is an important aspect of how we construct reality (Cavazza et al. 2007).

> In fact, causality is a conditional phenomenon between variables in the form "if x, then y."

There exist four formal conditions for causality: **covariation, time order of occurrence of variable**, **systematic elimination of other causal variable**, and **experimental designs**. Covariation is the extent to which a caused variable occurs with the causal variable together or vary together as the framed hypothesis under consideration. For example, sales (dependent variable) move upward with the lowered status of the price (independent variable). The second condition, time order of occurrence of variable, explains that the causal variable changes prior to or simultaneously with the caused variable; hence, it cannot occur afterwards. For example, when prices are increased on the first day of the month, sales go down on the remaining days of the month. The third condition, systematic elimination of other causal variables, indicates that the variable being investigated should be the only causal explanation of any change in the dependent variable. For understanding the third condition, let us take the chapter opening example again. The lack of sales people support may be the cause in slump in sales when a researcher is confident that all other possible variables affecting sales, such as poor advertisement impact, perceived poor quality of the product, lack

> There exist four formal conditions for causality: covariation, time order of occurrence of variable, systematic elimination of other causal variable, and experimental designs.

of motivation for dealers and retailers, poor promotional policies adopted by the company, and high turnover rate among sales people, are held constant or otherwise controlled by the researcher. The experimental designs are a set of procedures conducted to state the unequivocally causal nature of the variable. For example, to determine the slump in sales, a formal market test should be designed and conducted.

8.3 SOME BASIC SYMBOLS AND NOTATIONS IN CONDUCTING EXPERIMENTS

To provide the roadmap of understanding the concept of experimentation, it is important to have some prior understanding or knowledge of some basic symbols and notations frequently used in the experimentation.

To provide the roadmap of understanding the concept of experimentation, it is important to have some prior understanding or knowledge of some basic symbols and notations frequently used in the experimentation. Following is the list of some basic symbols and notations used in conducting the experiment:

O = Observation or measurement made on dependent variable as a part of the experiment

X = Exposure of the test unit under investigation to independent variable or experimental manipulation or treatment

EG = Experimental group that is exposed to the experimental manipulation or treatment

CG = Control group participating in the experiment but has no exposure to the experimental manipulation or treatment

R = Random assignment of test units and experimental manipulation or treatments to the groups

M = Match of experimental group and control group on the basis of some concerned related characteristics

The symbols O_1, O_2, O_3, and so on are indications of three or more observations or measurements made on dependent variable as a part of the experiment. Similarly, X_1, X_2, X_3, and so on indicate that the test unit under investigation is exposed to three or more independent variables or experimental manipulation or treatment. The symbols EG_1, EG_2, EG_3, and so on are used to indicate that the experiment has three or more experimental groups. Similarly, the symbols CG_1, CG_2, CG_3, and so on are used to indicate the participation of three or more control groups in the experiment.

8.4 INTERNAL AND EXTERNAL VALIDITY IN EXPERIMENTATION

If the design and structure of a study are such that one can confidently conclude that the independent variable caused systematic changes in the dependent variable, then the study is said to have a high internal validity. On the other hand, if the study gives us plausible alternative interpretation of the observed relationship between the independent and dependent variable, then it is said to have a low internal validity.

The external validity typically refers to the generalizability of the results of a study to other (usually real world) settings or populations.

If the design and structure of a study are such that one can confidently conclude that the independent variable caused systematic changes in the dependent variable, then the study is said to have a high internal validity. On the other hand, if the study gives us a plausible alternative interpretation of the observed relationship between the independent and dependent variable, then it is said to have a low internal validity. The **external validity** typically refers to the generalizability of the results of a study to other (usually real world) settings or populations (Anderson and Bushman 1997).

The internal validity indicates that the manipulation in experimental treatment or independent variable causes an observed effect on the dependent variable. If the observed effect is influenced by the confounding impact of **extraneous variables**, then drawing valid conclusions about the causal relationship between the experimental treatment (independent variable) and dependent variable becomes extremely difficult. The problems of the external validity generally relate to the possibility that a specific, but time limited, set of experimental conditions may not deal with the interpretations of untested variables in the real world

(Zikmund 2007). The lack of external validity puts a researcher in a difficult situation to repeat the experiment for a different set of subjects in different time span. If an experiment lacks the internal validity, then there is no meaning in generalizing the result of the experiment. Factors that are of serious concern for the internal validity of the experiment may also jeopardize the external validity of the experiment. The major source of threat to the internal validity of the experiment is the impact of different extraneous variables.

8.5 THREATS TO THE INTERNAL VALIDITY OF THE EXPERIMENT

The following section focuses on some extraneous variables, such as **history**, **maturation**, **testing**, **instrumentation**, **statistical regression**, **selection bias**, and **mortality**, that seriously jeopardize the internal validity of the experiment.

8.5.1 History

History effect refers to a specific event in the external environment that occurs between the commencements of experiment and when the experiment ends. More specifically, this event in the external environment may influence the subjects during the experiment and has an impact on the first and second measurements. This external event happens to be beyond the control of the researcher. History does not deal with the event occurred before the experiment, rather it deals with the event that occurs during an experiment. For example, a coloured television producer has decided to determine the impact of a new advertisement campaign. The company's researchers have decided to take two measurements, first after 1 week of the launch of the advertisement and second after 15 weeks of launching the advertisement. The company's researchers have taken the first measurement, after 1 week of the launch of the advertisement campaign. In the meantime, in the ninth week of the experiment, another multinational company stepped in the market with the support of a heavy advertisement campaign. Now the second measurement of the company's research team will always be influenced by the introduction of this external event during the experiment. A researcher should try to isolate the effect of history, as he or she is not able to control its impact as it is external and beyond the control of the researcher.

History effect refers to a specific event in the external environment that occurs between the commencements of experiment and when the experiment ends.

8.5.2 Maturation

It is always possible that during the experiment, subjects may mature or change. Therefore, with **time**, a change may be observed in the subjects themselves, but more important, it is not due to the experimental treatment or independent variable. In an experiment, **maturation** takes place when the subjects become older, bored, experienced, or disinterested during the experiment. If a company offers an incentive scheme to enhance the productivity of plant workers, then the company decides to test the level of productivity over 2 years. The productivity of the plant workers may improve over the 2 years because the subjects (plant workers) may become more skilled or more experienced. The increased productivity may not be due to experimental treatment (incentive scheme offered by the company).

In an experiment, maturation takes place when the subjects become older, bored, experienced, or disinterested during the experiment.

8.5.3 Testing

A **testing** effect occurs when a pre-test measurement sensitizes the subjects to the nature of the experiment. As a result, in a post-test measurement, the respondents may react differently when compared with the situation when they were not exposed to the pre-test measurement. This occurs in a before-and-after kind of study when taking a measurement

A testing effect occurs when a pre-test measurement sensitizes the subjects to the nature of the experiment.

before the application of treatment sensitizes respondents and they respond differently as a matter of sensitization to the experiment processes. The measurement before the application of treatment enhances the tendency of the respondents to give a socially desirable answer.

8.5.4 Instrumentation

The instrumentation effect is said to be occurred in an experiment when either the measuring instrument or the observer changes during the experiment.

The **instrumentation** effect is said to be occurred in an experiment when either the measuring instrument or the observer changes during the experiment. In some cases, researchers modify the measuring instruments during the experiment, resulting in instrumentation effect. Sometimes, the researchers present different sets of questionnaire to the respondents to tackle the problem of the testing effect. In doing so, they avoid the testing effect but encounter with the problem of instrumentation effect. The internal validity threatens the experiment when there is a change in the way of asking a question, change in the interviewer, and other procedures used to assess the change in the dependent variable. For example, if two interviewers are engaged in a before-and-after measurement, then there is a possibility that the way of placing and wording questions may be different for these two interviewers and results in the instrumentation effect of the experiment.

8.5.5 Statistical Regression

Statistical regression is the tendency of the subjects with extreme scores to migrate (regress) towards the average scores during the experiment.

Statistical regression is the tendency of the subjects with extreme scores to migrate (regress) towards the average scores during the experiment. For example, in a job satisfaction-measuring survey, few subjects may have scored very satisfied (extreme score) and few subjects may have scored very dissatisfied (extreme score) in the pre-test measurement. There is a strong possibility that in the post-test measurement, attitude of the subjects may change and they will move towards the average scores. This often happens because the respondents with extreme opinion have more space to move towards average over the passage of time. Therefore, under the effect of statistical regression, the change in post-test measurement is not due to the application of treatment but due to the extraneous variable referred as statistical regression.

8.5.6 Selection Bias

Selection bias occurs when an experimental group significantly differs from the target population or control group.

Selection bias occurs when an experimental group significantly differs from the target population or control group. Similarity between the experimental and control groups is extremely important, so that the difference in the result can be attributed to the experimental treatment and not to the difference between the experimental and control groups. A random assignment of the subjects to the experimental and control groups largely solves the problems of the selection bias. The experimental and control groups should be as similar as possible.

8.5.7 Mortality

Mortality effect occurs when the subjects drop out while the experiment is in progress.

Mortality effect occurs when the subjects drop out while the experiment is in progress. The subjects refuse to participate in the experiment because of various reasons such as lack of time, loss of interest in the experiment, and so on. Mortality is a problem because a researcher is not sure that the lost subjects would respond to the experimental treatment in the same manner as the remaining subjects respond. For example, in an experiment related to measure the effect of a new incentive scheme, few subjects of the experimental group will drop out because they do not like the new incentive scheme, and as a result, they have taken a sophisticated way in terms of not participating in the experiment. This will not present an opportunity to a researcher to compare the results of the experimental and control groups without any premeditated bias.

8.6 THREATS TO THE EXTERNAL VALIDITY OF THE EXPERIMENT

As previously discussed, the external validity refers to the ability of an experimental result's generalizability to other populations. We have also discussed that if an experiment lacks the internal validity, then there is no meaning in generalizing the result of the experiment. In other words, the internal validity can be viewed as a necessary, but not sufficient, condition for external validity (Parasuraman et al. 2004). In the following section, we will focus on the four biases, such as **reactive effect, interaction bias, multiple treatment effect**, and **non-representativeness of the samples**, that seriously jeopardize the external validity of an experiment.

8.6.1 Reactive Effect

Reactive effect occurs when the respondents exhibit an unusual behaviour knowing that they are participating in an experiment. Reactive effect is an area of prime concern in a **laboratory experiment** when compared with a **field experiment**, though in the latter, this effect cannot be eliminated. Exhibiting an unusual behaviour, while participating in an experiment, is a natural phenomenon of respondent's behaviour. For example, if a company is willing to determine the purchase behaviour of the consumer in a particular departmental store and has chosen 100 participants for this purpose, then there is a high possibility that these 100 respondents will exhibit an artificial behaviour as being watched by the observer.

Reactive effect occurs when the respondents exhibit an unusual behaviour knowing that they are participating in an experiment.

8.6.2 Interaction Bias

Interaction bias occurs when a pre-test increases or decreases the sensitization of the respondent to the experimental treatment. A reactive bias generates from the experiment as a whole, whereas an interaction bias reflects from the increased or decreased sensitivity of the respondents due to the pre-test exposure of the experimental manipulation.

Interaction bias occurs when a pre-test increases or decreases the sensitization of the respondent to the experimental treatment.

8.6.3 Multiple Treatment Effect

Multiple treatment effect occurs when a participant is exposed to multiple treatments. This is quite obvious that the impact of previous treatments cannot be fully erased from the mind of the respondents. Hence, the impact of any previous treatment on the later treatment cannot be simply ruled out.

Multiple treatment effect occurs when a participant is exposed to multiple treatments.

8.6.4 Non-Representativeness of the Samples

This is mainly a sampling problem. It has also been discussed in the chapter related to sampling that the sample must be a true representative of the population. Sometimes, it happens that a researcher knowingly or unknowingly selects the subjects who may not be a true representative of the population. When this happens in an experiment, it lacks external validity.

Sometimes, it happens that a researcher knowingly or unknowingly selects the subjects who may not be a true representative of the population. When this happens in an experiment, it lacks external validity.

8.7 WAYS TO CONTROL EXTRANEOUS VARIABLES

It has already been discussed that the presence of extraneous variable poses a serious threat to the internal as well as external validity of the experiment. Extraneous variables if present in the experiment affect the result in terms of affecting the dependent variable for the reasons other than the application of experimental treatment. In fact, the extraneous variables confound the result, which is why these are sometimes referred to as confounding variable. The four ways to control the extraneous variable are **randomization**, **matching**, **statistical control**, and **design control**.

8.7.1 Randomization

Randomization refers to the random assignment of the subjects and experimental treatment to experimental group to equally distribute the effect of extraneous variables.

Randomization refers to the random assignment of the subjects and experimental treatment to experimental group to equally distribute the effect of **extraneous variables**. Randomization not fully eliminates the effect of extraneous variable but controls the effect of extraneous variables. In fact, randomization ensures the researcher that the groups are identical with respect to all the variables and the result, which the researcher is observing, is due to the experimental treatment. It is no wonder that the vast majority of the experimentalists recognize randomization as the greatest strength of their research design (Imai et al. 2009).

8.7.2 Matching

When a researcher suspects that the extraneous variables may affect the dependent variable, he or she applies the technique of matching, which involves matching each group on some pertinent characteristics or some pertinent background variables.

When a researcher suspects that the extraneous variables may affect the dependent variable, he or she applies the technique of **matching**, which involves matching each group on some pertinent characteristics or some pertinent background variables. For example, if a research question is to determine the impact of income level on job satisfaction of the employees, it will be very important for a researcher to match the experimental group and the control group on income to get the desired result. Although matching assures a researcher that the subjects on each group are similar on some key background characteristics, a researcher is never sure that the subjects on each group are similar on all the characteristics. As another matter of concern, if matching on some pertinent variable has no affect on the dependent variable, then it unnecessarily devours the energy of a researcher.

8.7.3 Statistical Control

With the help of a statistical control, a researcher measures the effect of extraneous variable and adjusts its impact with a sophisticated statistical analysis.

With the help of a **statistical control**, a researcher measures the effect of extraneous variable and adjusts its impact with a sophisticated statistical analysis. In this context, a statistical technique such as ANCOVA can be applied.

8.7.4 Design Control

Design control suggests the use of an appropriate experimental design to control the effect of extraneous variable.

Design control suggests the use of an appropriate experimental design to control the effect of extraneous variable. Section 8.9 focuses on some special types of experimental designs with its specific features and limitations. A researcher can select an appropriate design on the basis of a careful evaluation of all the experimental designs.

8.8 LABORATORY VERSUS FIELD EXPERIMENT

The laboratory experiment is conducted in a laboratory or artificial setting. A researcher applies or controls the experimental manipulation or treatment in an artificial environment.

Experimental research can be broadly classified into two categories: laboratory experiment and field experiment. The first type of experiment known as the **laboratory experiment** is conducted in a laboratory or artificial setting. A researcher applies or controls the experimental manipulation or treatment in an artificial environment. The laboratory experiment provides an opportunity to a researcher to measure the impact of many independent variables of experimental treatments on dependent variable, which otherwise will be an extremely expensive affair. In addition, bringing consumers into a contrived laboratory gives an opportunity to a researcher to control many extraneous variables. In some experiments, the researcher intends to achieve a higher level of internal validity, the laboratory experiment provides an opportunity to a researcher. So, the main advantage of a laboratory experiment lies in its ability to provide a higher level of internal validity in the experiment. The laboratory experiment also saves time and cost as compared with the field experiment. The major disadvantage of the laboratory experiment is the lack of natural setting in the experiment, and hence, the major concern of the external validity "generalizability" is really a matter of concern. As another matter of concern, in a laboratory experiment, a respondent attempts to guess the purpose of launching the experiment and tends to respond accordingly.

A **field experiment** is conducted in the field or a natural setting. In the field experiment, the effect of experimental manipulation or independent variables on dependent variable is observed in a natural setting. In a field experiment, the respondents are usually unaware that they are being monitored under an experiment and hence tend to be very natural while responding. These experiments are conducted in fields and hence provide a high level of external validity. On the same ground, they do not provide high levels of internal validity. Generalization of experimental result is the biggest advantage of the field experiment. As discussed, the field experiments are organized in a natural setting and are more accurate in terms of applying experimental results in the real world. The major disadvantage of the field experiment is the presence of extraneous variables: it is not only their presence but also their control that is very difficult. In addition, the field experiments are cost inefficient and time consuming as compared with the laboratory experiment.

A field experiment is conducted in the field or a natural setting. In the field experiment, the effect of experimental manipulation or independent variables on dependent variable is observed in a natural setting.

The main objective of experimentation is to detect or confirm the causal relationship between the dependent variable and independent variables and quantify them. In every study, there is a trade-off between internal and external validity. In the early stages of the research, a researcher focuses on maximizing the internal validity to ensure the causal relationship. A marketing decision maker operates in the real world. So, early experimentation should be a field experimentation, and the external validity should be a matter of later concern.

In every study, there is a trade-off between internal and external validity.

8.9 EXPERIMENTAL DESIGNS AND THEIR CLASSIFICATION

An experimental design is a sketch to execute an experiment where a researcher is able to control or manipulate at least one independent variable. The experimental designs can be broadly segregated into two groups: **classical experimental designs** and **statistical experimental designs**. Classical experimental designs consider the impact of only one treatment level of independent variable taken for the study at a time, whereas statistical experimental design considers the impact of different treatment levels of independent (explanatory) variable as well as the impact of two or more independent variables. On the basis of these two factors, the experimental designs can be broadly classified as pre-experimental designs, **post-experimental designs,** quasi-experimental designs, and statistical experimental designs. The first three designs can be placed under the classical experimental design category and the last one can be placed under the statistical experimental design. Figure 8.1 presents a classification of the experimental designs.

An experimental design is a sketch to execute an experiment where a researcher is able to control or manipulate at least one independent variable. The experimental designs can be broadly segregated into two groups: classical experimental designs and statistical experimental designs.

8.9.1 Pre-Experimental Design

Pre-experimental design is an exploratory type of research design and has no control over extraneous factors. These designs cannot be easily put under the category of the experimental designs, because these are not able to establish the cause and effect relationship. These designs are exploratory in nature and are mainly used to frame the hypotheses about the casual relationship and that is why a detailed description of these designs is of paramount importance. Hence, these designs are mainly applied for developing causal relationship

Pre-experimental design is an exploratory type of research design and has no control over extraneous factors.

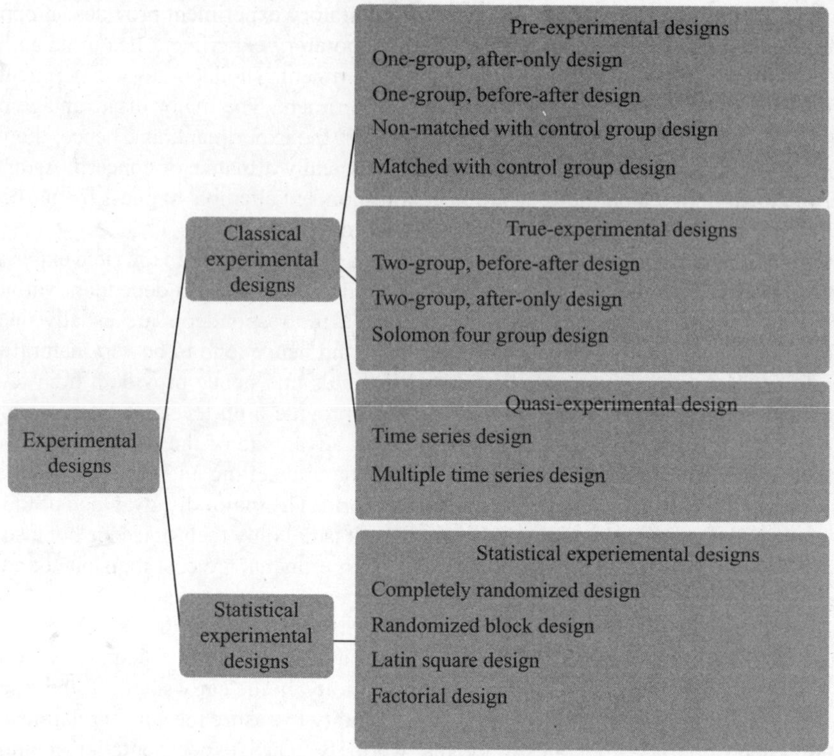

FIGURE 8.1
A classification of experimental designs

hypotheses and not for testing the hypotheses. In addition to this design, further research should be executed to make the researcher firm about the casual relationship between variables. There are four commonly used pre-experimental designs. These are **one-group, after-only design**; **one-group, before-after design**; **non-matched with control group design**, and matched with control group design.

8.9.1.1 One-Group, After-Only Design

One-group, after-only experimental design involves the exposure of single group test unit to a treatment *X* and then taking a single measurement on the dependent variable (*O*).

One-group, after-only design is the most basic experimental design. One-group, after-only experimental design involves the exposure of single group test unit to a treatment *X* and then taking a single measurement on the dependent variable (*O*). For example, a consumer electronics company has launched a heavy advertisement campaign for 2 months. The experiment may be to measure the impact of the advertisement on "purchase intention" of the consumers. Symbolically, this design can be represented as

$$EG \quad X \quad O$$

This design does not provide some valid conclusions due to various problems attached. First, it is not very clear when the experiment group will not be present. Second, the observation may be affected by various extraneous variables like history, maturation, selection, and mortality. In this design, a researcher has a very little control over the impact of various extraneous variables, and hence, this design is mainly used for the exploratory research and not for the conclusive research.

8.9.1.2 One-Group, Before-After Design

One-group, before-after design involves testing the test units twice. The first observation is made without exposing the test units to any treatment, and the second observation is made after exposing the test unit to treatment. As obvious, first observation is symbolized by O_1, and second observation is symbolized by O_2. The treatment effect can be determined as the difference between the first observation and the second observation, that is, $O_1 - O_2$. For example, a company is facing problems due to "low morale" of the employees. For boosting the morale of the employees, the company has organized a 1-week special training programme. Before measurement is the measurement of morale before the training programme. After measurement can be noted after introducing the treatment in terms of providing the training programme. The difference between the measurement before and after the treatments can be computed. Symbolically, this design can be represented as

One-group, before-after design involves testing the test units twice. The first observation is made without exposing the test units to any treatment, and the second observation is made after exposing the test unit to treatment.

$$O_1 \quad X \quad O_2$$

Uncontrolled extraneous variables put the validity of inferences drawn under question mark. "Before measure" may be one of the serious threats, because the respondent group is aware that they are being monitored for the research purpose. Hence, the tendency of giving socially desirable answer may increase. "Mortality impact" may also be one of the problems, because in the second phase of the experiment, some respondents who participated in the first phase will not participate. This design involves a third problem in terms of handling "instrumentation impact." This bias can occur in terms of wording the questions in the second phase of the interview or the interviewer may change in the second phase of the interview.

8.9.1.3 Non-Matched With Control Group Design

Non-matched with control group design involves the introduction of control group in the experiment. This group does not receive any experimental treatment. In this design, the control group is introduced, so that it can be compared with the experimental group. The treatment effect can be determined as the difference between the observations from the experimental group that receives the treatment (O_1) and the observations from the control group that receives no treatment (O_2). Hence, the result of interest is $O_1 - O_2$. For example, to measure the impact of the advertisement, the discussed consumer electronics company may compare the measurement with the group of respondents who have not received any treatment. Symbolically, this design can be represented as

Non-matched with control group design involves the introduction of control group in the experiment. This group does not receive any experimental treatment. In this design, the control group is introduced, so that it can be compared with the experimental group.

$$\begin{array}{lll} EG & X & O_1 \\ CG & & O_2 \end{array}$$

Note that this experimental design is also not able to address two extraneous variables: selection and mortality. Selection bias may appear as the control group may have many characteristics that may not be present in the experimental group but may have serious impact on the experiment. The selection bias may become serious when self-selection occurs in an experiment. It means, members of the experimental group are voluntarily participating in the experiment and are in better condition before the experiment as compared with the members of the control group, who are not voluntarily participating in the experiment. Mortality impact may also be one of the problems as more test units can withdraw themselves from the experimental group as compared with the control group.

To address the problem of selection bias, matched with control group design involves the matching of experimental group and control group on the basis of some relevant characteristics.

8.9.1.4 Matched with Control Group Design

To address the problem of selection bias, **matched with control group design** involves the matching of experimental group and control group on the basis of some relevant characteristics. For example, in our example of measuring, the impact of the advertisement, a researcher can collect the data from both the experimental group and the control group, which are arranged on the basis of some relevant similar characteristic such as same income group or same age group. Symbolically, this design can be represented as

$$\begin{array}{llll} EG & M & X & O_1 \\ CG & M & & O_2 \end{array}$$

M indicates that experimental group and control group are matched on the basis of some relevant characteristics.

"Randomization" is the key of difference between pre-experimental design and true experimental design.

8.9.2 True-Experimental Design

Most of the problems of the **pre-experimental design** (discussed in the previous section) can be tackled with the help of randomization procedure. "Randomization" is the key of difference between pre-experimental design and true experimental design. The randomized experiments are more likely to yield unbiased estimates of causal effects than typical observational studies, because the randomization of treatment makes the treatment and control groups equal on average in terms of all (observed and unobserved) characteristics (Horiuchi et al. 2007). True experimental design involves the random assignment of test units to the experimental group and various treatments to the experimental groups. This random assignment provides an opportunity to neutralize the impact of extraneous variables in the experiment. True experimental designs are commonly classified as two-group, before-after design; **two-group, after-only design**; and **Solomon four-group design**. Following section provides a discussion of these three true experimental designs.

The two-group, before-after design is also known as pre-test-post-test control group design. This design involves the random assignment of test units to either the experimental group or the control group.

8.9.2.1 Two-Group, Before-After Design

Two-group, before-after design is also known as pre-test–post-test control group design. This design involves the random assignment of test units to either the experimental group or the control group. For example, a firm has launched a new advertisement campaign. The firm would like to assess the impact of this new advertisement campaign. A sample of consumers is selected randomly and half of the consumers are randomly assigned to experimental group and other half to the control group. Symbolically, two-group, before-after design can be represented as

$$\begin{array}{lllll} EG & R & O_1 & X & O_2 \\ CG & R & O_3 & & O_4 \end{array}$$

For determining the impact of treatment, the difference between O_1 and O_2 is compared with the difference between O_3 and O_4. The experimental group is treated with both the experimental treatment and extraneous variable. The control group is treated with extraneous variable only and not with the experimental treatment. Let the impact of experimental variable be EV and impact of extraneous variable be UV. Hence, the impact of the experimental treatment can be computed as

$$
\begin{aligned}
O_2 - O_1 &= EV + UV \\
O_4 - O_3 &= UV \\
\hline
O_2 - O_1 &= UV
\end{aligned}
$$

This calculation incorporates all extraneous variables such as history, maturation, testing effect, statistical regression, and instrument variation. Selection bias is well taken care of by randomly assigning units (or treatments) to experimental group or control group. If some respondents refuse to participate, then this design will also suffer from mortality impact.

8.9.2.2 Two-Group, After-Only Design

Two-group, after-only design is similar to the matched with control group design with one difference in terms of assignment of units (or treatments) to experimental group and control group in a random manner. Two-group, after-only design can be symbolically represented as

$$
\begin{array}{llll}
EG & R & X & O_1 \\
CG & R & & O_2
\end{array}
$$

Two-group, after-only design is similar to the matched with control group design with one difference in terms of assignment of units (or treatments) to experimental group and control group in a random manner.

This design is mainly susceptible to two extraneous variables: selection bias and mortality. This design is based on the assumption that the experimental group and control group are similar in terms of pre-treatment measures on the dependent variable. This is because of random assignment of test units to groups. In the absence of any pre-treatment measures, this assumption cannot be verified. As discussed, mortality is always a probable concern of this design. Mortality can exist because a researcher is not very sure that the participants who leave the experimental group are similar to those who leave the control group.

8.9.2.3 Solomon Four-Group Design

To handle the problems of two supplement groups, before-after design is supplemented by an after-only design and is referred to as **Solomon four-group design**. This design is also known as four-group-six-study design. The Solomon four-group design is symbolically represented as

$$
\begin{array}{lllll}
EG & R & O_1 & X & O_2 \\
CG & R & O_3 & & O_4 \\
EG & R & & X & O_5 \\
CG & R & & & O_6
\end{array}
$$

To handle the problems of two supplement groups, before-after design is supplemented by an after-only design and referred to as Solomon four-group design. This design is also known as four-group-six-study design.

This design is rarely used because of its expensive and time consuming nature. Though this design provides various comparison measures of the experimental treatment (X), these comparison measures may be $(O_2 - O_1) - (O_4 - O_3)$, $(O_6 - O_5)$, $(O_2 - O_4)$. An agreement among these measures makes the inference strong. In case of no agreement, it is still possible to measure the interaction and before measure effects $[(O_2 - O_4) - (O_5 - O_6)]$.

8.9.3 Quasi-Experimental Designs

In quasi-experimental design, a researcher lacks full control over the when and whom part of the experiment and often non-randomly selects the group members.

In **quasi-experimental design**, a researcher lacks full control over the when and whom part of the experiment and often non-randomly selects the group members. When the researcher lacks control over these experimental stimuli, the design is regarded as quasi experimental

(Shao 2002). The quasi-experimental designs are useful because these are less expensive and they save time. These designs can also be used when true experimental designs cannot be used. The widely used quasi-experimental designs are **time series designs** and multiple time series designs.

8.9.3.1 Time Series Designs

Time series designs are like One-group, before-after design except that the periodic measurement is employed on the dependent variable for a group of test units. In the time series designs, treatments are either administered by the researcher or it occurs naturally.

Time series designs are like one-group, before-after design except that the periodic measurement is employed on the dependent variable for a group of test units. In the time series designs, treatments are either administered by the researcher or it occurs naturally. Measurement continues after the treatment for the impact of treatment effect. Symbolically, the time series design can be represented as

$$EG \quad O_1O_2O_3O_4 \times O_5O_6O_7O_8$$

From this display, it can be well inferred that the observations are made on a group of test units over time. Then the experimental treatment is introduced, and the reaction of test units to experimental treatment is again observed. In the time series experiment, a researcher has repeated assess to test units. However, the researcher has no control over the exposure schedule of experimental treatment to the test units, though he or she has a control over the time schedule of measurement for measuring the impact of experimental treatment. Figure 8.2 exhibits sales of different companies as measurement before-treatment exposure and after-treatment exposure.

By taking observations before and after the treatment, a researcher can have partial control over the extraneous variables. Selection bias can be reduced by selecting the test units randomly. Maturation can be partially checked because its impact is not valid for O_5 and O_4 but valid for all other observations. Similar argument can be raised to control the extraneous

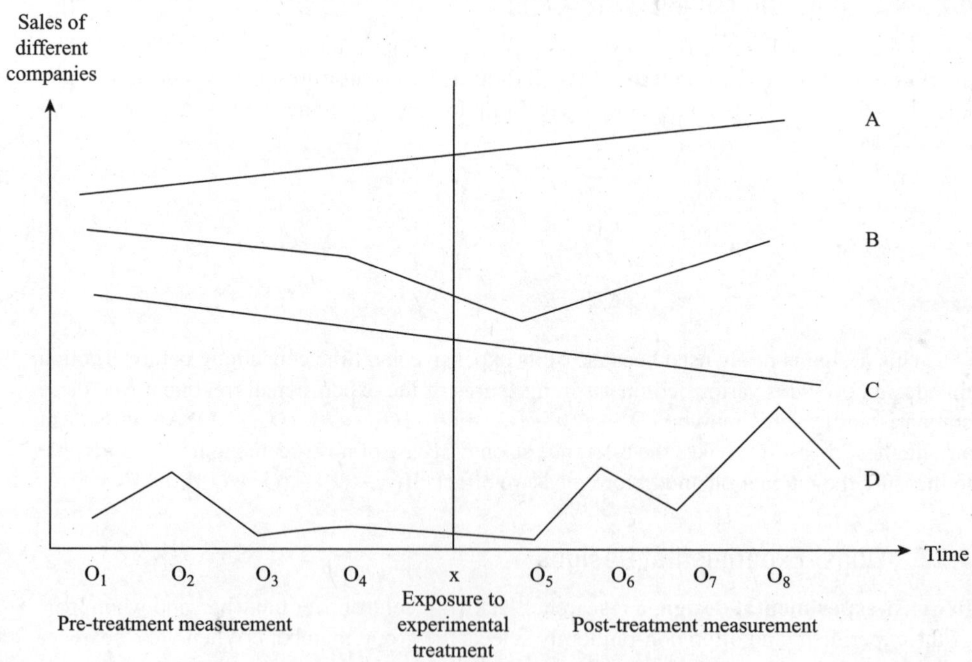

FIGURE 8.2
Time series design

variables like instrumentation and statistical regression. Mortality can be tackled by offering some incentives to respondents.

8.9.3.2 Multiple Time Series Designs

In a **multiple time series design**, another group of test units is incorporated to serve as a control group. This design may be a better alternative as compared with the time series designs subject to a cautious selection of the control group. Multiple time series design can be symbolically represented as

In a multiple time series design, another group of test units is incorporated to serve as a control group. This design may be a better alternative as compared with the time series designs subject to a cautious selection of the control group.

$$\begin{array}{ll} EG & O_1O_2O_3O_4 \times O_5O_6O_7O_8 \\ CG & O_1O_2O_3O_4 \times O_5O_6O_7O_8 \end{array}$$

8.9.4 Statistical Experimental Designs

Statistical experimental designs involve the conduction of a series of experiments to statistically control the extraneous variables and to measure the impact of multiple independent variables. As different from the classical experimental designs, statistical experimental designs allow a researcher to examine the impact of different treatment levels of the experimental variable. These designs also provide an opportunity to determine the impact of two or more independent variables. The most widely and commonly used statistical designs are **completely randomized design**, **randomized block design**, **Latin square design**, and **factorial design**.

Statistical experimental designs involve the conduction of a series of experiments to statistically control the extraneous variables and to measure the impact of multiple independent variables.

The most widely and commonly used statistical designs are completely randomized design, randomized block design, Latin square design, and factorial design.

8.9.4.1 Completely Randomized Design

In a **completely randomized design**, the experimental treatments are randomly assigned to the test units. By randomly assigning treatments to the test units, a researcher tries to check the impact of extraneous variables through manipulation of the treatment variable. For example, a company wants to ascertain the impact of three different price levels on target consumers. The company has taken a random sample of 3000 similar customers and divided them in three randomly constructed groups named as Experimental Groups 1, 2, and 3. The experiment can be symbolically represented as

In a completely randomized design, the experimental treatments are randomly assigned to the test units.

$$\begin{array}{llll} EG_1 & R & X_1 & O_1 \\ EG_2 & R & X_2 & O_2 \\ EG_3 & R & X_3 & O_3 \end{array}$$

where X_1 is the first experiment treatment level. The term "level" refers to the different forms of same independent variable. Similarly, X_2 and X_3 are the second and third experimental levels, respectively. In our example, X_1, X_2, and X_3 are the three different levels of price. The focus of experiment is to compare the effect of three experimental treatments. The statistical technique applied to analyse the result of this type of experimental design is known as "Analysis of Variance" commonly known as ANOVA.

8.9.4.2 Randomized Block Design

Randomized block design involves in random assignment of treatments to the experimental group and control group. A randomized block design is useful when there is one major external variable, such as sales, store size, or income of the respondent that might influence the dependent variable (Malhotra and Dash 2009). For using the randomized block design,

Randomized block design involves in random assignment of treatments to the experimental group and control group.

a researcher splits the test units into similar groups or blocks in light of the external variable such as sales, age, gender, income, experience, occupation, or any other variable that is believed to impact the test units or dependent variable. The purpose of blocking is to make sure that the experimental group and control group are matched closely on the external variable. In fact, the randomized block design is a combination of randomization and matching. Thus, control variable defines groups and the randomized experiment is conducted within each group. A randomized block design can be symbolically represented as

$$
\begin{array}{llll}
EG_1 & R & X & O_1 \\
CG_1 & R & & O_2 \\
EG_2 & R & X & O_3 \\
CG_2 & R & & O_4
\end{array}
$$

For understanding the concept of randomized block design, let us take a simple example of a company that considers the difference in sales in four different "price levels". It is also believed by the company that the geographic regions may also have an impact on the sales. The company has identified three regions of the country, which may provide the difference in sales namely the north region, west region, and east region. In a randomized block design, the treatment assignment to each block of the design is a random process. In our example, four treatments in terms of four different "price levels" are randomly assigned to different cities within each region. The sales (in thousands) results are exhibited in the Table 8.2.

The research question may be do the regions significantly differ in terms of generating sales. The second question may be do the price levels significantly differ in terms of generating sales. This example can be symbolically represented as

$$
\begin{array}{lllll}
 & EG_1 & R & X_1 & O_1 \\
 & EG_2 & R & X_2 & O_2 \\
 & EG_3 & R & X_3 & O_3 \\
\text{North Region} & EG_4 & R & X_4 & O_4 \\
 & EG_5 & R & X_1 & O_5 \\
 & EG_6 & R & X_2 & O_6 \\
 & EG_7 & R & X_3 & O_7 \\
\text{West Region} & EG_8 & R & X_4 & O_8 \\
 & EG_9 & R & X_1 & O_9 \\
 & EG_{10} & R & X_2 & O_{10} \\
 & EG_{11} & R & X_3 & O_{11} \\
\text{East Region} & EG_{12} & R & X_4 & O_{12}
\end{array}
$$

TABLE 8.2
Randomized block design

Treatments	*North Region*	*West Region*	*East Region*	*Row Means*
Price level 1	110	80	78	89.33
Price level 2	95	85	82	87.33
Price level 3	90	75	100	88.33
Price level 4	92	78	84	84.66
Column means	96.75	79.5	86	

8.9.4.3 Latin Square Design

Latin square design allows a researcher to control two external variables (non-interacting) along with the manipulation of independent variable.

We have already discussed that a randomized block design is useful when there is one major external variable, such as sales, store size, or income of the respondent that might influence the dependent variable. Latin square design allows a researcher to control two external variables (non-interacting) along with the manipulation of independent variable. In Latin square design, the test units are grouped according to the two external variables considered in the study. The test units are systematically blocked in two directions provided by two external variables. As different from the randomized block design, in a Latin square design, if we have four treatment levels then we must have four rows and four columns. In the randomized block design example, three different regions provided the basis for difference in sales. Let us assume that another external variable "size of the showroom" may provide the basis for difference in quarterly sales (in million rupees) of the company. In addition, the company has also considered one more region "south region" as the basis for difference in sales volume. The company has four different sizes of showrooms across the country. So, the design based on the two external variables "different regions" and "size of the showroom" will appear as shown in Table 8.3.

Treatments (levels of independent variable) are applied to the cells in such a way that each level of independent variable is applied to each cell only once as exhibited in Table 8.3. In Latin square design, each cell is treated with only one treatment level.

8.9.4.4 Factorial Design

In a factorial design, two or more experimental variables are simultaneously considered.

In many scientific investigations, the main interest is in the study of effects of many factors simultaneously. Factorial designs, especially the two- or three-level factorial designs, are the most commonly used experimental plans for this type of investigations (Xu et al. 2009). In the statistical designs discussed so far, the effect of only one independent (experimental) variable on dependent variable was studied. In a factorial design, two or more experimental variables are simultaneously considered. In a factorial experiment, more than one type of independent variables are varied at a time but in a structured way (Shaw et al. 2002); for example, a fast moving consumer goods company wants to test a new product in 30 cities. Three different customer groups with respect to income: high-income group, middle-income group, and low-income group are to be tested. In addition, two price levels: high price and moderate price are considered in the experiment. Hence, this will be 3 × 2 factorial, as there are three different levels of income and two different treatment levels. So, this design will have the following six experimental groups:

X_1 = High-income group; high price
X_2 = High-income group; moderate price
X_3 = Middle-income group; high price
X_4 = Middle-income group; moderate price
X_5 = Low-income group; high price
X_6 = Low-income group; moderate price

TABLE 8.3
Latin square design

Showroom size	*Regions*				
	North region	*West region*	*East region*	*South region*	*Row means*
Showroom size 1	110(X_1)	90(X_2)	95(X_3)	82(X_4)	94.25
Showroom size 2	115(X_2)	85(X_1)	100(X_4)	75(X_3)	93.75
Showroom size 3	108(X_3)	80(X_4)	105(X_1)	68(X_2)	90.25
Showroom size 4	112(X_4)	82(X_3)	108(X_2)	70(X_1)	93
Column means	111.25	84.25	102	73.75	371.25

X_1 = price level 1, X_2 = price level 2, X_3 = price level 3, and X_4 = price level 4.

TABLE 8.4
Factorial design

Income group	*Price levels (in million rupees)*		
	High price	*Moderate price*	*Row means*
High-income group	110	122	116
Middle-income group	105	135	120
Low-income group	118	143	130.5
Column means	111	133.3333	

Thus, the factorial design can be symbolically represented as

$$EG_1 \quad R \quad X_1 \quad O_1 \quad n=5$$
$$EG_2 \quad R \quad X_2 \quad O_2 \quad n=5$$
$$EG_3 \quad R \quad X_3 \quad O_3 \quad n=5$$
$$EG_4 \quad R \quad X_4 \quad O_4 \quad n=5$$
$$EG_5 \quad R \quad X_5 \quad O_5 \quad n=5$$
$$EG_6 \quad R \quad X_6 \quad O_6 \quad n=5$$

The effect of each independent variable on dependent variable is referred to as the main effect. Hence, the impact of "different income levels" on sales and "price levels" on sales is termed as the main effect. Factorial design also allows a researcher to determine the impact of interaction of independent variables on dependent variables. Interaction takes place when the simultaneous effect of two or more experimental variables is different from the sum of their separate effect. For our example, the factorial design will look like as exhibited in Table 8.4

Thus, in one experiment, the effect of two experimental variables can be determined. The main problem with the factorial design appears with the increase in the number of treatment variables as it makes the design complicated. However, it is often too costly to perform a full factorial experiment, so a fractional factorial design, which is a subset or fraction of a full factorial design, is preferred because it is cost effective (Xu et al. 2009).

8.10 LIMITATIONS OF EXPERIMENTATION

Experimentations have become very popular because they develop a causal relationship between variables, which is otherwise vague in nature. Although experimentations are popular, there are few limitations such as time, cost, **secrecy**, and **implementation problems**.

Because of various factors such as competitive nature of the market, experiments cannot be launched for an unlimited time instead they are framed in light of the time span available to a researcher, which is ultimately decided by the decision maker.

8.10.1 Time

Most of the decision makers in marketing research face the problem of having shortage of time to launch a time-consuming experiment and wait for a long time to complete the experiment. Because of various factors such as the competitive nature of the market, experiments cannot be launched for an unlimited **time** instead they are framed in light of the time span available to a researcher, which is ultimately decided by the decision maker.

8.10.2 Cost

Cost is another constraint in performing an experiment. As discussed, the application of various treatments to the experimental group and control group is an affair that requires huge investment in running and completing experimentation. For achieving higher levels of internal and external validity, higher expenses are required. There is also a possibility that the cost of the experiment may be very high, but it leads to some inaccurate results resulting in non-implementable implications.

Cost is another constraint in performing an experiment.

8.10.3 Secrecy

In any field research, it is not possible for a researcher to hide the intentions of launching a research programme. So, when secrecy is desired by a decision maker, it is not possible in a field experiment. When **secrecy** is also an objective of a researcher or a decision maker, a simulation or a carefully performed laboratory experiment is a feasible alternative.

When secrecy is also an objective of a researcher or a decision maker, a simulation or a carefully performed laboratory experiment is a feasible alternative.

8.10.4 Implementation Problems

The execution of experiments is always a difficult problem to handle. Getting cooperation from the persons involved in the experiment like sales executives, retailers, and wholesalers is very difficult. They are having their own reasons and justifications for not cooperating. The second problem occurs when the subjects of the experimental group develop a communication with the subjects of the control group. Sometimes, finding a control group also becomes very difficult in experimentation. This is particularly possible when there are only few buyers of the product (e.g. a big weighing machine), and they often communicate with each other. Presence of competitors is also a problem in executing an experiment effectively.

The execution of experiments is always a difficult problem to handle. Getting cooperation from the persons involved in the experiment like sales executives, retailers, and wholesalers is very difficult.

8.11 TEST MARKETING

Test marketing means conducting an experiment in a field setting. Companies generally launch test market strategy in selected parts of the market referred to as the test markets. Once able to determine the relationship between independent variable(s) and dependent variable, a national marketing strategy can be adopted by the company. Test marketing is mainly adopted for two important reasons. First, a company will like to determine the sales potential of newly launched product and second, to identify the variations in the marketing mix of a product or services. Test market is a very expensive and time-consuming activity. It is not easy for a producer to launch the new product in a selected area, as it requires million rupees investment. Although many argue the rational of using the test market strategy, it is an extremely useful marketing strategy. Test market also provides an opportunity to the producer to have an input about the consumer and supply chain reaction about the introduction of a new product. Experimental launching of new products is intended to expose problems that otherwise would be undetected until full-scale introductions are underway (Silk and Urban 1978). Test markets are generally classified into four types: standard, controlled, electronic, and simulated. Brief descriptions of these types are given below.

Test marketing means conducting an experiment in a field setting.

8.11.1 Standard Test Market

In standard test market, a company uses its own distribution channel network to test a new product or market mix variables. The main advantage of this type of test marketing can be explained by the fact that it allows a decision maker to evaluate the impact of new product or marketing mix under normal marketing conditions.

In **standard test market**, a company uses its own distribution channel network to test a new product or market mix variables. The main advantage of this type of test marketing can be explained by the fact that it allows a decision maker to evaluate the impact of new product or marketing mix under normal marketing conditions. Although standard test marketing is a time- and cost-consuming process, it provides an opportunity to a marketer to observe the product behaviour in true marketing environment. When a product is launched through standard test market technique, the competitors immediately get an opportunity to assess the marketing strategies of the company that has used the standard test market option. The competitors have been known to take deliberate retaliatory actions to disrupt another firm's test markets, which makes it extremely difficult to untangle the results even by complex model based analysis (Urban 1970).Test duration is a subjective matter that largely depends upon time and cost consideration for the company, probably competitor and consumer response and many other factors.

8.11.2 Controlled Test Market

In controlled test market, a company hires an outside research agency to conduct the study. As compared with the standard test market procedure, this method is less expensive and less time consuming.

In **controlled test market**, a company hires an outside research agency to conduct the study. As compared with the standard test market procedure, this method is less expensive and less time consuming. During the test, the research agency handles the retailer's sale and all other distribution-related activities. The agency also provides the incentives and has a control over the inventory issues. In many cases, data are collected through electronic scanning devices, so that repeat purchase, household penetration, demographics of the consumers, and other buyer related information as well as information related to the first year sales volume are generated.

8.11.3 Electronic Test Market

An electronic test market gathers data from the consumers who agree to carry an identification card that they present when buying goods and services at participating retailers in the selected cities.

An **electronic test market** gathers data from the consumers who agree to carry an identification card that they present when buying goods and services at participating retailers in the selected cities (Hair et al. 2002). The main advantage of this type of test market is the collection of demographic and other purchase behaviour information becomes very easy. On the other hand, the identification card-carrying consumers may not be the true representatives of the whole market as the card-carrying consumers are not being selected randomly.

8.11.4 Simulated Test Market

Simulated test market is an artificial technique of test marketing. A simulated test market occurs in a laboratory, where the potential consumers of a particular product are exposed to a new product or competitive product or any other marketing stimuli.

Simulated test market is an artificial technique of test marketing. A simulated test market occurs in a laboratory, where the potential consumers of a particular product are exposed to a new product or competitive product or any other marketing stimuli. Simulated test market is a technique to determine a consumer's response for a product in a limited time period. Simulated test market uses an artificial setting, where a researcher selects the potential consumers and asks questions related to various features of the product to assess the product's behaviour, when it will be launched in full market. Simulated test marketing is a valid methodology that has been used by the marketing community since the 1960s to forecast the purchase interest of new products and new positioning for existing products (Clancy 2005). The major advantage of simulated test market is that it is less expensive and less time consuming. In addition, to maintain the secrecy about a company's marketing strategy it is also possible to use simulated test market.

REFERENCES

Anderson, C. A. and B. J. Bushman (1997). "External Validity of 'Trivial' Experiments: The Case of Laboratory Aggression", *Review of General Psychology,* 1(1): 19–41.

Cavazza, M., J. Lugrin and M. Buehner (2007). "Causal Perception in Virtual Reality and its Implications for Presence Factors", *Presence: Teleoperators & Virtual Environment,* 16(6): 623–42.

Clancy, K. J., P. Kreig and M. M. Wolf (2005). *Market New Product Successfully,* p. 318. New York, NY: Rowman & Littlefield.

Hair, J. F., R. P. Bush and D. J. Ortinau (2002). *Marketing Research: Within a Changing Information Environment*, Tata McGraw-Hill Publishing Company Limited.

Hobbs, J. R. (2005). "Toward a Useful Concept of Causality for Lexical Semantics", *Journal of Semantics,* 22(2): 181–209.

Horiuchi, Y., K. Imai and T. Taniguchi (2007). "Designing and Analyzing Randomized Experiments: Application to a Japanese Election Survey Experiment", *American Journal of Political Science,* 51(3): 669–87.

Imai, K., G. King and C. Nall (2009). "Rejoinder: Matched Pairs and the Future of Cluster-Randomized Experiments", *Statistical Survey,* 24(1): 65–72.

Malhotra, N. K. and S. Dash (2009). *Marketing Research: An Applied Orientation*, 5th ed., p. 236. India: Dorling Kindersley Pvt. Ltd.

Parasuraman, A., D. Grewal and R. Krishnan (2004). *Marketing Research,* p. 242. Boston, NY: Houghton Mifflin Company.

Shao, A. T., (2002). *Marketing Research: An Aid to Decision Making*, 2nd ed., p. 303. South-Western Thomson Learning.

Shaw, R., M. F. Festing, I. Peers and L. Furlong (2002). "Use of Factorial Designs to Optimize Animal Experiments and Reduce Animal Use", *ILAR Journal*, 43(4): 223–32.

Silk, A. J. and G. L. Urban (1978). "Pre-Test Market Evaluation of New Packaged Goods: A Model and Measurement Methodology", *Journal of Marketing Research,* 15(2): 171–91.

Tull, D. and D. Hawkins (1984). *Marketing Research: Measurement and Method*, 3rd ed. New York, NY: Macmillan.

Urban, G. L. (1970). "SPRINTER Mod III: A Model for Analysis of New Frequently Purchased Consumer Products", *Operation Research,* 18(3): 805–53.

Xu, H., F. K. H. Phoa and W. K. Wong (2009). "Recent Developments in Nonregular Fractional Factorial Designs", *Statistical Surveys,* 3: 18–46.

Zikmund, W. G. (2007). *Business Research Methods*, 7th ed., pp. 273–274. South-Western Thomson Learning.

SUMMARY

Experiments can be defined as the systematic study where a researcher controls or manipulates one or more independent (experiment) variables to test a hypothesis about the independent variable. Independent variables are the variables that are manipulated or controlled by the researcher. On the other hand, dependent variables are variables on which a researcher has little or no control over the research process, but the researcher is keen to note a change in it with the corresponding change in the independent variables. Experiments are based on the concept of causality. In fact, causality is a conditional phenomenon between variables in the form "if x, then y." There exist four formal conditions for causality. These are covariation, time order of occurrence of variable, systematic elimination of other causal variable, and experimental designs.

Internal validity indicates that the manipulation in experimental treatment or independent variable causes observed effect on the dependent variable. Problems of external validity generally relate to the possibility that a specific but time-limited set of experimental conditions may not deal with the interpretations of untested variables in the real world. Some extraneous variables seriously jeopardize internal validity of the experiment. These extraneous variables are history, maturation, testing, instrumentation, statistical regression, selection bias, and mortality. There are four biases that seriously jeopardize the external validity of an experiment. These four factors are reactive effect, interaction bias, multiple treatment effect, and non-representativeness of the samples. The four ways to control the extraneous variable are randomization, matching, statistical control, and design control.

Experimental research can be broadly classified into two categories: laboratory experiment and field experiment. Laboratory experiment is conducted in a laboratory or artificial setting. A field experiment is conducted in the field or a natural setting. An experimental design is a sketch to execute an experiment, where a researcher is able to control or manipulate at least one independent variable. Experimental designs can be broadly segregated into two groups: classical experimental designs and statistical experimental designs. Classical experimental design considers the impact of only one treatment level of independent variable taken for the study at a time, whereas statistical experimental design considers the impact of different treatment levels of independent (explanatory) variable as well as the impact of two or more independent variables. On the basis of these two factors, the experimental designs can be broadly classified into pre-experimental designs, post-experimental designs, quasi-experimental designs, and statistical experimental designs. The first three designs can be placed in the classical experimental design category and the last one under the category of statistical experimental design.

Experimentations have become very popular because they develop a causal relationship between the variables, which is otherwise vague in nature. Although experimentations are popular, there are few limitations such as time, cost, secrecy, and implementation problems. Test marketing means conducting an experiment in a field setting. Test markets are generally classified in four types: standard, controlled, electronic, and simulated.

KEY TERMS |

Causality, 167
Classical experimental designs, 173
Completely randomized design, 179
Controlled test market, 184
Covariation, 167
Dependent variables, 167
Design control, 172
Electronic test market, 184
Experimental designs, 167
Experiments, 167
External validity, 168
Extraneous variables, 168
Factorial design, 179
Field experiment, 171
History, 169
Implementation problems, 182
Independent variables, 167
Instrumentation, 169
Interaction bias, 171
Laboratory experiment, 171
Latin square design, 179
Matching, 172
Matched with control group design, 174
Maturation, 169
Mortality, 169
Multiple time series design, 179
Multiple treatment effect, 171
Non-matched with control group design, 174
Non-representativeness of the samples, 171
One-group, after-only design; 174
One-group, before-after design; 174
Post-experimental designs, 173
Pre-experimental design, 176
Quasi-experimental design, 177
Randomization, 172
Randomized block design, 179
Reactive effect, 171
Secrecy, 182
Selection bias, 169
Simulated test market 184
Solomon four-group design, 176
Standard test market, 184
Statistical control, 172
Statistical experimental designs, 173
Statistical regression, 169
Systematic elimination of other causal variable, 167
Testing, 169
Test marketing, 183
Time, 169
Time order of occurrence of variable, 167
Time series designs, 178
Two-group, after-only design, 176
Two-group, before-after design, 176

NOTES |

1. http://www.bergerpaints.com/profile.php, accessed September 2009.
2. Prowess (V. 3.1): Centre for Monitoring Indian Economy Pvt. Ltd, Mumbai, accessed September 2009, reprinted with permission.
3. http://economictimes.indiatimes.com/News/News-By-Industry/Indl-Goods-/-Svs/Chem-/Fe...

DISCUSSION QUESTIONS |

1. What is experimentation and why is this important for conducting any marketing research?
2. What is causality? Explain the four formal conditions for causality?
3. What are internal and external validity in experimentation?
4. Explain the common threats to internal validity and external validity in an experiment.
5. How can a researcher control the threats to internal and external validity in an experiment.
6. What is the main difference between laboratory experiment and field experiment?

7. What are the various types of experimental designs available for a researcher to conduct research?
8. Write a short note on following terms:
   a. Pre-experimental designs
   b. Post-experimental designs
   c. Quasi-experimental designs
   d. Statistical experimental designs
9. Write a short note on following terms:
   a. Two-group, before-after design
   b. Two-group, after-only design
   c. Solomon four-group design
10. Write a short note on following terms:
    a. Time series design
    b. Multiple time series design
11. Write a short note on following terms:
    a. Completely randomized design
    b. Randomized block design
    c. Latin square design
    d. Factorial design
12. What are the limitations of experimentation?
13. What is the concept of test marketing in marketing research? What are the different kinds of test markets?

CASE STUDY |

Case 8: *Voltas Ltd: A Constituent of Tata Conglomerate*

Introduction: Profile of Tata Group

Tata companies operate in seven business sectors: communications and information technology, engineering, materials, services, energy, consumer products, and chemicals. They are, by and large, based in India and have significant international operations. The total revenue of the Tata companies when taken together was $70.8 billion (around ₹32,53,340 million) in the year 2008–2009. Almost 64.7% of the revenue comes from the business outside India and they employ 3,57,000 people worldwide. The name "Tata" is respected in India since 140 years for its adherence to strong values and business ethics. The major Tata companies are Tata Steel, Tata Motors, Tata Consultancy Services (TCS), Tata Power, Tata Chemicals, Tata Tea, Indian Hotels, and Tata Communications.[1]

Voltas Ltd: A Constituent of Tata Conglomerate

Voltas Ltd, a part of the Tata conglomerate, was incorporated in 1954. In 1951, the collaboration of Tata Sons Ltd with a Swiss firm Volkart Brothers formed "Voltas Ltd." It is India's premier air-conditioning and engineering service providers. Its operations are organized into four independent business specific clusters such as electro-mechanical projects and services, unitary cooling products for comfort and commercial use, engineering agency and services, and others. Voltas Ltd manufactures domestic and industrial air conditioners and refrigerators, commercial refrigerators, water coolers, freezers, forklift trucks, and large water supply pumps. It also undertakes engineering, procurement and construction projects, and electromechanical projects, specializing in heating, ventilation and air conditioning, building management and communication systems, power and lighting, water management, and pollution controls. Voltas Ltd is also actively engaged in the procurement and marketing of air conditioners, textile machinery, machine tools, mining and construction equipment, and industrial chemicals.[2]

Voltas Ltd suffered from some negative profit growth in two consecutive years 1996–1997 and 1997–1998. From the year 1999–2000, the company has not looked back exhibiting continuous growth in sales and profit after tax (Table 8.01). The table shows the sales and profit after tax of the company from 1994–1995 to 2008–2009.

TABLE 8.01
Sales and profit after tax (in million rupees) of Voltas Ltd from 1994-1995 to 2008-2009

Year	*Sales*	*Profit after tax*
Mar-95	8113.7	217.3
Mar-96	9833.1	157
Mar-97	10,413.5	–168.1
Mar-98	11,072.5	–95.6
Mar-99	9953.5	127.9
Mar-00	7913.3	55
Mar-01	8601.3	55.8
Mar-02	9429.7	168.3
Mar-03	12,423.8	255.8
Mar-04	13,419.6	390.3
Mar-05	14,495.5	504.1
Mar-06	19,142.5	704.9
Mar-07	24,648.7	1860.8
Mar-08	30,862.2	2083.7
Mar-09	40,702.9	2525.9

Source: Prowess (V. 3.1): Centre for Monitoring Indian Economy Pvt. Ltd, Mumbai, accessed September 2009, reprinted with permission.

Some Opportunities and Threats for All the Independent Business Clusters of the Company

Electro-mechanical projects and services business of the company may witness many opportunities and threats. Matured domestic market, energy efficient and environment friendly product, and focus on developing in-house manufacturing facility are some of the opportunities for electro-mechanical projects and services business of the company. Longer completion time frames for industrial and infrastructure project, intense competition due to planning of key international players setting up manufacturing facilities for greater cost effectiveness, currency fluctuations especially for the company's operation in the middle east, and fluctuating price of the raw materials are some the threats for the company. While the commitment of engineering product and services segment of the company to projects in coal mining and development of new range of material-handling equipments may be seen as opportunities, the presence of major manufacturers at both global and domestic levels and shrinking sales may be some of the threats. In case of unitary cooling products for comfort and commercial use, reduction in excise duty, taxes and interest rates will act as stimulus for the air-conditioner and refrigeration projects. Awareness of Indian consumers about product and price benefits as well as their awakening to environmental concerns is in the favour of the company. Competitive market with the entry possibility of many national and multinational brands may be a threat to the company.[2] The company has its own plan to utilize cater the opportunities and tackle the challenges of volatile environment of business. Relying on some of the model human resource philosophy and policy is one of the ways to counter the threats posed by the environment.

Human Resource Philosophy and Policy at Voltas Ltd

The cornerstone of Voltas Ltd's human resource management philosophy is the conviction that the well-being of the company and its employees is interdependent, and the most valuable asset for the company is its employees. The company emphasizes on its commitment: to employ the most competent, on the basis of merit; to ensure that every employee is treated with dignity and respect, and in a fair, consistent and equitable manner; to create a stimulating, enabling and supportive work atmosphere and to aid and encourage employees in realizing their full potential.[3] The company's focus on improved employee engagement and ushering in a proactive work culture, through several enterprise level initiatives, have been noteworthy. The employee-contact programmes have helped to obtain valuable feedback and to implement appropriate action plans. The company continues to place emphasis on the enhancement of skills and capabilities of its employees for meeting the future challenges. The key areas of human resource development are training, competency development, and skill enhancement. Career development plans have been evolved for high-potential managers. In addition, the company continued to impart training to its employees, with a major focus on leadership development and managerial effectiveness. A number of internal and external training workshops, courses, and seminars were conducted and an elaborate induction-training programme for fresh graduate engineers, at the entry level, is arranged.[2]

Assume Voltas Ltd wants to attract most talented individuals from the job market, then before going for a wide range of recruitment programme, the company wants to assess its image as "employee friendly" through a well-structured research programme. Suppose the company has appointed you as a marketing researcher. Answers to the following questions would help the company to bring out a successful programme: How a pilot test will be conducted? How will you be using the experimentation? Will it be field experiment or a laboratory experiment? What will be the base of classifying the experimental design? How will you be addressing the issues related to internal and external validity of the experiment? How will you decide about the list of relevant variable to be included in the research study? Explain the strategies to control the environment and extraneous variables. What will be the limitations of the experimentations?

NOTES

1. http://www.tata.com/aboutus/sub_index.aspx?sectid=8hOk5Qq3EfQ=, accessed September 2009.
2. Prowess (V. 3.1): Centre for Monitoring Indian Economy Pvt. Ltd, Mumbai, accessed September 2009, reprinted with permission.
3. http://www.voltas.com/new/corporate/philosophy.html, accessed September 2009.

CHAPTER 9

Fieldwork and Data Preparation

LEARNING OBJECTIVES

Upon completion of this chapter, you will be able to:

- Understand the importance of fieldwork in conducting research
- Understand the steps in fieldwork process
- Understand the meaning and importance of data preparation process
- Understand the steps of data preparation process
- Get a preliminary idea about the tools and techniques of data analysis

RESEARCH IN ACTION: ESCORTS LTD

The Escorts Group is India's leading conglomerates operating in the high-growth sector of the agri-machinery, construction and material-handling equipment, railway equipment, and auto-components. Escort facility has already provided over a million tractors and more than 16,000 construction and material-handling equipments to its highly satisfied customer base. Technology and business collaborations with world leaders over the years, globally competitive engineering capabilities, more than 1600 sales and services outlets, and footprints in more than 40 countries have been instrumental in making Escorts an Indian Multinational.[1] Table 9.1 lists sales, net income, and profit after tax of Escorts Ltd from 1994–1995 to 2008–2009.

There is an increase in the demand for food grains and agricultural products, which is a good opportunity for the company to strengthen its core business. Auto-component market is growing fast and the company has a solid preparation to meet the pace in the market. Modernization plans of the Indian Railway present opportunities to the Railway equipment manufacturing wing of Escorts Ltd. Growth in infrastructure and construction industry also presents opportunities for Escorts Construction Equipment Ltd, a 100% subsidiary of Escorts Ltd. Material-handling equipment business is also growing, specifically road construction equipment segment. Escorts Ltd is ready to explore the opportunities present in the environment.

The company suffered from negative profit after tax in some of the financial years. Situation changed in the year 2008–2009 when the company incurred profit after tax of ₹118.7 million (Table 9.1). Motivated by the turnaround in profit, Escorts Ltd has set an ambitious plan to achieve over billion dollar turnover by 2012. Joint Managing director of Escorts Ltd optimistically stated that "Our mission 2012 is to have a top line between ₹55,000 million and ₹60,000 million, to come from the three core business area." In the financial year 2008–2009, the company had

>>>

made a turnaround profit after tax of ₹118.7 million. Mr Nikhil Nanda highlights the strategy of this turnaround stating that "This profitability was achieved on the back of the improved earnings, structural recognition and greater cost and operational efficiencies".[2]

Assume that to meet the preparation of achieving ambitious target of having over billion dollar turnover by 2012, Escorts wants to assess "purchase intentions" of the consumers with specific reference to a comparison between the "brand equity" of Escorts and other competitors. Suppose the company has organized a well-structured research programme and is at the stage of deciding about the strategy of launching fieldwork. How will the company decide about the initial contact, the way of asking questions from the respondents, recording the responses, and winding up the interviews? Who will be supervising the fieldwork? How will the company be organizing validation and evaluation of the fieldwork? This chapter presents a roadmap to provide all such type of information and focuses on fieldwork and data collection process in a well-organized manner.

TABLE 9.1
Sales, net income, and profit after tax (in million rupees) of Escorts Ltd from 1994-1995 to 2008-2009

Year	*Sales*	*Net income*	*Profit after tax*
Mar-95	13,637.7	12,472.5	509.4
Mar-96	13,417.3	12,746.7	1004.2
Mar-97	15,145.7	14,615.3	1272.4
Mar-98	12,902.5	12,311.6	1298.4
Mar-99	12,214	12,001.1	841.7
Mar-00	14,552.4	14,070.6	1123.7
Mar-01	14,420.9	14,161	1073.8
Mar-02	12,383.5	11,903.1	86
Mar-03	87,73.7	10,902	240.4
Mar-05	12,584.4	11,361.4	−3135.4
Mar-06	13,124.8	17,832.2	390.9
Mar-07	17,945.4	18,643.1	190
Mar-08	21,126.9	20,986.8	−64.4
Mar-09	20,233.9	20,403.5	118.7

Source: Prowess (V. 3.1): Centre for Monitoring Indian Economy Pvt. Ltd, Mumbai, accessed September 2009, reprinted with permission.

9.1 INTRODUCTION

Researchers generally collect marketing research data by means of two options. The researcher can either develop his or her own set-up to generate data from the field or with help of fieldwork agencies. These agencies charge an amount, do the fieldwork, and provide data to the researcher. In marketing research, the fieldwork is an important process and requires a systematic approach. It is the most exciting part of the research that really provides an opportunity to a researcher to have a new thinking and a new way to look at various things. It is just not a simple phenomenon, as commonly perceived by many people. A number of problems arise when researchers send out questionnaires (Meckel et al. 2005). Fieldwork is a challenging job, and these challenges are glaringly apparent when fieldwork scope crosses the national boundaries. In an unfamiliar cross-cultural or transitional socialist context, these challenges range from the application for research visas to request for official data, and the negotiation of relationships with local host institutions and "gatekeepers" (Scott et al. 2006). More or less fieldwork is a specialized technical job and requires a lot of technical expertise. Since the fieldwork context is not considered as known in advance or predictable, but something to be directly experienced by the researcher before any decoding or explanation is possible, the ultimate value of ethnographic enquiry cannot be known in advance (Nilan 2002). Fieldwork is a part of the research, which is not directly controlled by the researcher. Many aspects such as behaviour of a fieldworker, behaviour and cooperation of a respondent, and so on may not be under direct control of the researcher. The importance

Fieldwork is a challenging job and these challenges are glaringly apparent when fieldwork scope crosses the national boundaries.

of field interviews in conducting scientific research cannot be undermined. Field interviews are excellent in providing detailed explanations of best practices and deep understanding of the theory developed (Alam 2005). Hence, an effective planning and beyond that an effective execution of the planning is required by the researcher, and this part of the research should be taken up seriously.

9.2 FIELDWORK PROCESS

Systematic fieldwork is performed using the following seven steps: **job analysis**, **job description**, and **job specification**; **selecting fieldworkers**; **providing training to fieldworkers**; **briefing and sending fieldworkers to field for data collection**; **supervising the fieldwork**; **debriefing** and **fieldwork validation**; and **evaluating and terminating fieldwork**. Figure 9.1 shows the process of fieldwork.

Systematic fieldwork is performed using the following seven steps: job analysis, job description, and job specification; selecting fieldworkers; providing training to fieldworkers; briefing and sending fieldworkers to field for data collection; supervising the fieldwork; debriefing and fieldwork validation; and evaluating and terminating fieldwork.

9.2.1 Job Analysis, Job Description, and Job Specification

Job analysis focuses on different aspects of a job to recruit a suitable person. Job analysis involves assessment of time to complete the job, tasks that can be grouped to constitute a job, job engineering to enhance job holder's performance, required behaviour to perform a job, and identifying individual personality traits to perform a job. It produces information on the job requirements, which is then used in developing job description (a list of what the job entails) and job specification (a list of the job's human requirements or the kind of people to be hired for the job; Dessler 2003).

Job analysis involves assessment of time to complete the job, tasks that can be grouped to constitute a job, job engineering to enhance job holder's performance, required behaviour to perform a job, and identifying individual personality traits to perform a job.

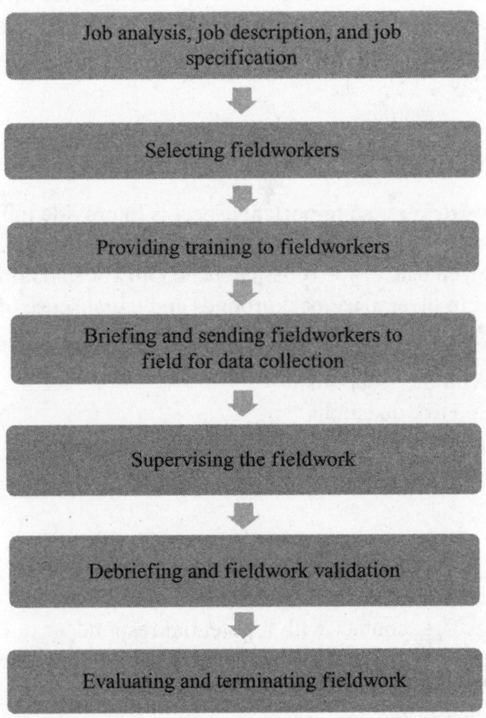

FIGURE 9.1
Seven steps in executing fieldwork

Before recruiting fieldworkers, a researcher should do the job analysis, job description, and job specification. This will clearly lay down the job requirement and the traits of a person required to execute the job. Conducting a research, especially primary data collection, is a difficult exercise. Task becomes more difficult when data collection is done for more than one country. The researcher may suffer from isolation, anxiety, stress, and depression, even in a relatively straightforward fieldwork (Nilan 2002). Same can happen with the fieldworkers, as the job of a fieldworker is equally difficult. Hence, a fieldworker must possess the required traits to perform this difficult task. Job specification provides the list of basic traits required to execute the job.

9.2.2 Selecting a Fieldworker

A researcher who designs a research project rarely collects data. We have already discussed that fieldwork is an important and a crucial stage of conducting research and must be carried out carefully. Thus, the researcher has to recruit someone who is capable of handling the tedious job of fieldwork. Interviewer's background also plays a key role in performing a research effectively. While recruiting a fieldworker, who will be a potential interviewer, the applicant's affiliation and image should be a prime area of focus. Interviewer background includes factors such as interviewer affiliation, interviewer image, respondent–interviewer distance, respondent relevance, and interviewer bias due to inadequate training (Malhotra et al. 1996). Recruiting a good fieldworker is not as easy as it appears. In the field of marketing research, recruiting a qualified and trained fieldworker is a difficult task, especially in countries like India. "Lack of permanency" in job is a major factor that limits finding good, qualified, and trained fieldworkers. Projects are generally tenure based, and the tenure fieldworkers find a great difficulty in getting placed in another employment. Even if research designers find an extremely talented fieldworker, they also find difficulty in providing reemployment to the concerned fieldworker because the funding for the project is also tenure based. However, a qualified, trained, and experienced fieldworker is the backbone of any research programme and a careful recruitment policy is important to conduct research scientifically and effectively.

> However, a qualified, trained, and experienced fieldworker is the backbone of any research programme and a careful recruitment policy is important to conduct research scientifically and effectively.

9.2.3 Providing Training to Fieldworkers

After **selection of fieldworkers**, an important aspect is to provide training to them. Training is a systematic development of knowledge, skills, and attitude required by employees to perform adequately on a given task or job (Olaniyan and Ojo 2008). Training is important as the fieldworkers may be from diversified backgrounds and the purpose of the research is to collect data in a uniform manner. Training of the fieldworkers must cover the following topics:

> Training is important as the fieldworkers may be from diversified backgrounds and the purpose of the research is to collect data in a uniform manner.

- **Initial contact** with the respondent
- Start interview and ask questions
- **Probing** the respondents
- Making a record of respondent's answers
- Come to an end

9.2.3.1 Initial Contact with the Respondent

> Initial contact involves first contact with a potential respondent to convince him or her to join the interview programme.

Initial contact involves first contact with a potential respondent to convince him or her to join the interview programme. It is a crucial stage where a respondent may or may not be ready to participate in the interview; thus, this stage requires a sophisticated handling of the matter specifically when the respondent is unwilling to participate. Skill of interviewer is especially required in encouraging or motivating a potential respondent if he or she is in dilemma in terms of participating in the interview. For example, an interviewer can frame an initial statement as follows.

> Good morning sir, my name is _____ and I am an interviewer appointed by _______ marketing research firm. We are conducting a survey to understand consumer's opinion on a vacuum cleaner. You have been selected as a respondent and we seek your cooperation in conducting the survey. We value your frank opinion and answers.

The interviewer must also be able to convince the potential respondent that the interviews are organized by a professional research agency and not a sales call. This fact is important to explain because most of the respondents will not be able to differentiate between a sales call and a research interview until and unless it is clearly explained to them. When a respondent replies that he or she does not have time, the situation must be handled intelligently, such that an interviewer can ask, "may I know when you will be able to spend time in this week."

9.2.3.2 Start Interview and Ask Questions

Even a well-designed questionnaire can lead to a disaster if the questions are not asked properly by the interviewer. Hence, the fieldworkers must be properly trained to ask questions in an artistic manner. A small deviation from the sequence of asking or a slight emphasis on a particular word or sentence may completely distort the response. Thus, an interviewer should ask questions in a predetermined order and avoid unnecessary emphasis on any specific word or question. The interviewer must read each question slowly, so that the respondent may not have any problem in understanding. If a respondent has any problem in understanding the question, then the interviewer must explain it again. Interviewers have the tendency of completing the answer themselves. It is more common when an interviewer had conducted many interviews and the job becomes monotonous. This generates an unintentional interviewer bias and may be a serious problem later on.

Even a well-designed questionnaire can lead to a disaster if the questions are not asked properly by the interviewer.

9.2.3.3 Probing the Respondents

Probes help motivate the informants, facilitate the flow of an interview, and elicit information but not necessarily in the form of a question (De Leon and Cohen 2005). There may be situations where the respondent is unable to provide a clear answer, the answer is incomplete, or unable to provide an answer. **Probing** involves providing a stimulus to the respondents to clarify, explain, or complete the answer. On-the-spot probing could gather data that would normally be done at a later stage or not at all due to funding or project deadlines (Grim et al. 2006). It actually deals with two situations: first, when a respondent is unable to provide a clear answer or is unable to provide an answer, the interviewer's intervention as probing is essentially required, and second, when the respondent is distracted from the track of interview. It is the responsibility of an interviewer to clarify the answer if there is any ambiguity or track back the interview if it is distracted. Some common probing techniques are given below:

Probing involves providing a stimulus to the respondents to clarify, explain, or complete the answer.

- An interviewer should repeat the question, if needed, which enhances the understanding of the respondent and he replies in a clear manner.
- When an interviewer feels that the respondent is on the right track and has a clear understanding of the question, he must maintain a "**strategic silence**" and allow the

respondent to speak. The interviewer must be able to assess when a respondent needs his or her help and at that point must be able to break the silence.

- When further clarification of the answer is required, an interviewer can repeat the answer and provide an opportunity to the respondent to be more elaborate.
- To facilitate the discussion, an interviewer can ask few neutral questions. For example, to obtain further clarification of the answer, an interviewer can ask a question such as "what do you mean by…?" To make the respondent more elaborate, an interviewer can ask "anything else will you like to tell."

9.2.3.4 Making a Record of the Respondent's Answers

One common way of recoding the questions is to check in the box related to respondent's choice of answer. Answer to unstructured questions must be recorded verbatim and there should not be any variation from respondent's answer while recording.

The analyst who fails to instruct the fieldworkers about the technique of recording answers for one study rarely forgets to do so in the second study (Zikmund 2007). Although the task seems to be simple, the mistakes in the recording are common. At this stage, the interviewer records the respondent's answer. For structured questions, the way of recording the questions differs from researcher to researcher. One common way of recoding questions is to check in the box related to the respondent's choice of answer. Answer to unstructured questions must be recorded verbatim and there should not be any variation from respondent's answer while recording.

9.2.3.5 Come to an End

Before termination of the interview, the fieldworker has to make sure that all the relevant and important information have been obtained.

Before termination of the interview, the fieldworker has to make sure that all the relevant and important information have been obtained. Before winding up, an interviewer should not forget to thank the respondent. Sometimes, the respondents may give some concluding remark, which may not be a part of the interview but may be important from the research point of view; hence this "remark" must be recorded immediately. An interviewer should always keep in mind that he or she has to contact the respondent again. Hence, the scope of this re-contact must not be finished and the interview termination must be friendly.

9.2.4 Briefing and Sending Fieldworkers to Field for Data Collection

Briefing session should be organized for both experienced and inexperienced fieldworkers. A researcher should never take a liberty that briefing is not required because the fieldworker is experienced and trained. It is also important to brief fieldworkers about the objective of the research and the clear purpose of data collection. The researcher must provide required details to the fieldworker. It includes background of the study, purpose of the study, details of the study already conducted by the researcher, and so on. The researcher has to keep in mind that the interviewer should not be provided with too much information, that is, more than what is required. Providing "more than the required" information can bias an interviewer in terms of framing a preconceived notion about the question or response. The researcher must also provide demographic details of the respondents to the fieldworker so as to facilitate the process of obtaining the response. In some of the surveys, the interviewer faces an embarrassing situation before the respondent when he finds himself unable to answer the respondent's query about the research. This inability reduces the interviewer's seriousness and credibility to conduct the interview. In addition, this discourages an interviewer and he starts hesitating to probe. This results in dilution of the quality of the interview. Hence, it is important for a research designer to brief all the required details to the interviewer to avoid such kind of embarrassment. There should be a ready plan to contact the respondents located at different locations. Interviews must be planned in such a way that the expenditure incurred in travelling must be as minimum as possible.

After briefing, the interviewers are sent to the field for data collection. An important point is to implement the plan of sending interviewers alone or accompanied by some associates or supervisors. Travelling plan that has already been decided must be executed effectively. A research designer must decide in advance the number of interviews to be conducted in a day. They must be clearly instructed about their contact plan and movement after contacting a particular respondent. Even when an interviewer has the discretion to randomly select household or subjects, a proper guideline must be issued to avoid selection bias. Research head must also brief about the return plan to fieldworkers.

Briefing session should be organized for both experienced and inexperienced fieldworkers.

9.2.5 Supervising the Fieldwork

Although training and briefing minimize the possibility of committing mistakes during the fieldwork, it is not completely eliminated. Hence, it is not the right time for a researcher to be relaxed as the fieldwork is carried out by the fieldworkers, but it is the right time for effective supervision. A supervisor continuously interacts with the fieldworkers and tries to find out solution to the problem faced by the fieldworkers on the field. A fieldworker might have faced many problems during the fieldwork, and these problems can be predicted in advance only to a certain extent. A few problems cannot be predicted and occur during the fieldwork without any estimation. These problems can occur on a daily basis, and hence these must be dealt and solved on a daily basis. Supervision involves checking the quality parameters, sampling verification, and cheating control.

Supervision involves checking the quality parameters, sampling verification, and cheating control.

9.2.5.1 Checking the Quality Parameters

Researchers always pre-specify the quality parameters. At this stage, a proper supervision is essentially required to find any deviation from these parameters. Supervisors must check whether all the questionnaires are properly filled. They must resolve the problem of an interviewer in terms of finding difficulty in filling answers for a particular question, if any. They must check whether the interviews are on schedule. If there is any deviation from the pre-specified schedule of conducting the interviews, the reasons for the delay must be examined properly and appropriate action must be taken.

Researchers always pre-specify the quality parameters.

9.2.5.2 Sampling Verification

It is important for a researcher to check whether the interviewers are contacting proper subjects. It is a common tendency of an interviewer to replace the concerned subjects with easily available subjects. For example, if an interviewer has contacted a household and the respondent from it is not available then instead of contacting the concerned subject again, the interviewer tries to pick the convenient option by contacting the neighbouring household. This leads to a loss of data being collected as the subject from the neighbouring household may not possess the required characteristics that may be important from the research designer's point of view.

To check the sampling verification, a supervisor has to maintain a day-to-day record. A direct supervision of daily contact, refusal, and postponement is of paramount importance. The supervisor has to clearly check whether the refusal is an actual refusal, because there is a possibility that the interviewer had put the subject in the refusal category due to his or her unavailability or non-cooperation. There should be a daily check on the number of completed interviews. In short, a careful supervision is required to track the interviewers who may otherwise make things happen on the basis of their comfort and convenience.

A careful supervision is required to track the interviewers who may otherwise make things happen on the basis of their comfort and convenience.

9.2.5.3 Cheating Control

The most severe falsifying occurs when the interviewer fills the entire questionnaire himself without contacting the respondent.

Cheating occurs when an interviewer falsifies the interviews. Falsifying means an interviewer can provide false or fake answers to some questions or the entire questionnaire. The most severe falsifying occurs when the interviewer fills the entire questionnaire himself without contacting the respondent. A fair and good selection policy in recruiting legitimate fieldworkers is one of the ways to handle this problem.

9.2.6 Debriefing and Fieldwork Validation

Debriefing involves verification or validation of the responses provided by the fieldworker and evaluation of the fieldwork process.

Debriefing involves verification or validation of the responses provided by the fieldworker and evaluation of the fieldwork process. **Fieldwork validation** is an exercise launched to check whether the fieldworkers have submitted authentic filled questionnaires. To validate the fieldwork, the supervisors generally conduct re-interviews of some of the subjects previously interviewed by the fieldworker. While re-interviewing, the supervisors do not repeat the entire interview, but try to re-check some of the information obtained by the fieldworker. If not a personal re-interview, the supervisors contact the respondents through telephone or postcard to detect whether any false interview has been conducted by the fieldworker. The supervisors generally ask about the quality and length of the interview. They check the demographic information of the respondents, revealed by the fieldworker. The supervisor will be conducting a re-interview for verification; this awareness among the fieldworkers reduces the possibility of falsifying. For a supervisor, there is no quota fixed for re-interview. Conducting re-interview is a matter of researcher's discretion and the researcher or the supervisor ultimately decides the number of re-interviews to be conducted.

9.2.7 Evaluating and Terminating the Fieldwork

It is important to evaluate the fieldwork process.

It is important to evaluate the fieldwork process. In fact, a researcher must supply the evaluation parameters to all the fieldworkers during the training session. The first component of the evaluation may be time and cost of conducting a fieldwork. Time and cost must also be evaluated in the light of quality of data. It is possible that if a fieldworker has devoted less time and the cost of conducting the interview is also low then he or she has not provided a quality data. In this manner, the fieldworker has actually wasted the time and cost in conducting the fieldwork. The other important evaluation parameter is the quality of interviewing. A supervisor must evaluate the quality of interviewing in person or by means of a recorded interview. This involves identifying the individual calibre of a fieldworker to conduct a quality interview in terms of handling various sensitive issues such as introduction of the interviewer, probing, gathering sensitive information, handling respondent's reluctance to answer some questions, and so on. The supervisor also focuses on response rate, especially when it is low. In this case, the supervisor immediately provides support to the fieldworker to enhance the response rate.

At the end of the fieldwork, the supervisor takes care of every aspect of the fieldwork such as the address and telephone number of the respondents and the fieldworker (taking care of the change taken place during the fieldwork). The supervisor thanks the fieldworkers and settles their financial claims. The supervisor also makes a note of the star performers in fieldwork to build a good team of the fieldworkers in the near future.

9.3 DATA PREPARATION

There exist two stages between data collection and interpretation: data preparation and data analysis.

There exist two stages between data collection and interpretation: data preparation and data analysis. Data preparation secures the first place in these two stages. The reason behind it is simple. Data collected by the researchers from the field happens to be in raw format. Before going for analysis, the researcher has to convert raw data into the data format that is ready for data analysis. This section opens the discussion on how data can be prepared to facilitate statistical data analysis.

9.4 DATA PREPARATION PROCESS

The **data preparation process** starts from **preliminary questionnaire screening** followed by data **editing** and data **coding**. After editing and coding, data are entered into the computer spreadsheets, and then **data analysis strategy** is initiated. Data analysis strategies can be further categorized into **descriptive data analysis** and **inferential data analysis**. **Descriptive data analysis** is used to describe the data, whereas inferential statistical analysis is based on use of some sophisticated statistical analysis to estimate the population parameter from sample statistic. **Inferential data analysis** can be classified into **univariate, bivariate, and multivariate data analyses**. Figure 9.2 shows the discussed data preparation process.

9.4.1 Preliminary Questionnaire Screening

Although **preliminary questionnaire screening** takes place during the fieldwork, it is important to re-check the questionnaire. If the researcher has taken the service of any fieldwork agency then it is the responsibility of the concerned agency to take care of these problems during the fieldwork itself. There is a possibility that the questionnaire is technically complete, but there may be few issues that should be addressed by the research designer.

There is a possibility that the questionnaire is technically complete, but there may be few issues that should be addressed by the research designer.

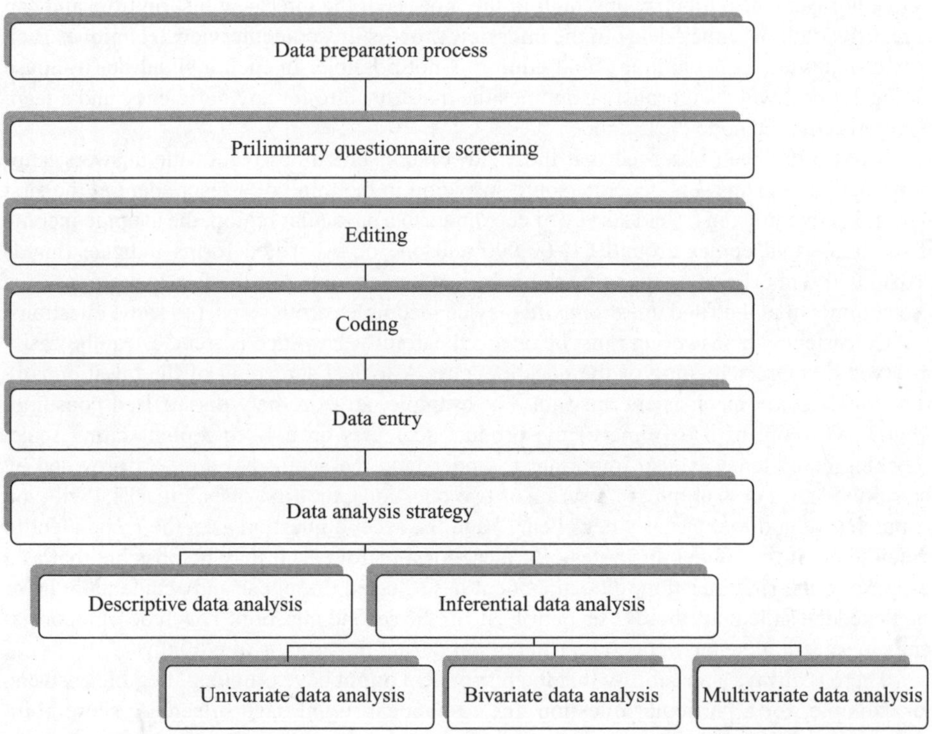

FIGURE 9.2
Data preparation process

Checking of the questionnaire is important, because there is a possibility that few pages of the questionnaire may be missing. Another possibility occurs in terms of irrational consistency in filling the answer on a rating scale. For example, on a 1- to 5-point rating scale, a respondent has chosen the rating point 3 for all the questions. This indicates that the respondent is not serious, and this must be taken care. During the preliminary screening of the questionnaire, the researcher can also identify the understanding of the respondent. This can be done by analysing the answer pattern to different questions. If there is a continuous skipping of some questions or if there is un-rationale selection of rating point as the answer to some questions, this is an indication of lack of understanding of the respondent. If these problems are serious in nature, the research designer can conduct the additional interviews to handle the situation. It is always advisable to take care of all the discussed issues during the fieldwork to avoid additional interview. Practically, some problems do appear even after considering all the precautions. This is the stage of research where the researcher finally addresses all these problems.

9.4.2 Editing

Editing is actually checking of the questionnaire for suspicious, inconsistent, illegible, and incomplete answers visible from careful study of the questionnaire.

Editing is actually checking of the questionnaire for suspicious, inconsistent, illegible, and incomplete answers visible from careful study of the questionnaire. Field editing is a good way to deal with the answering problems in the questionnaire and is usually done by the supervisor on the same day when the interviewer has conducted the interview. Editing on the same day of the interview has various advantages. In the case of any inconsistent or illogical answering, the supervisor can ask the interviewer about it, and the interviewer can also answer well because he or she has just conducted the interview and the possibility of forgetting the incident is minimal. The interviewer can then recall and discuss the answer and situation with the supervisor. In this manner, a logical answer to the question may be arrived. Field editing can also identify any fault in the process of the interview just on time and can be rectified without much delay in the interview process. In some interview techniques such as mail-interviewing technique, field editing is not possible. In such a situation, in-house editing is done, which rigorously examines the questionnaire for any deficiency and a team of experts edit and code these data.

It has often been observed that the fieldworkers sometimes record the answers inappropriately. These answers generate some suspicion in the mind of a respondent at the first glance. For example, in a field survey of customers in a particular region, the average income of the household comes around ₹1, 00,000 and one or two filled forms indicate this as ₹10,00,000. This figure seems to be doubtful and a re-checking of the fact is required. It is also common that the filed questionnaire may be incomplete with respect to some questions.

Consistency in answering must be checked carefully. Few inconsistencies can be easily observed by mere screening of the questionnaire. A logical screening of the questionnaire can provide some inconsistent answers. For example, an extremely dissatisfied consumer providing a score of 5 to some of the product attributes on a 1- to 5-point rating scale. Checking consistency is also important to understand the accidental answers provided by the respondent. For example, in a series of two questions, the first question asks, "will you be purchasing a diesel car or a petrol car?" and the second question asks the respondent to prefer some of the salient attributes of a diesel or a petrol car. It may be possible that as a response to the first question, the respondent has selected diesel car and accidentally he or she ticked the salient attributes of a petrol car for the second question. This type of inconsistency in selecting the answer can be filtered out during the process of editing.

There is always a possibility that the respondent might have provided illegible answers. For example, for a particular question, the respondent might have selected a score point of both 4 and 5. For coding or further data analysis, the researcher essentially requires a single-digit number. Thus, there exists a question, which score point is to be selected, 4, 5, or an average of 4 and 5.

The researcher must examine the pattern of incomplete answers. It is always possible that some questions may be difficult to answer or understand, and there is an apparent pattern in skipping these questions. In some cases, it has also been observed that the respondent skips the first part of the question and answers the second part that actually is connected with the first part of the question. For example, the first question is, "in last year how many times you have gone out of the city for a personal trip" and the second question is, "please state the places where you have gone." It is possible that the respondent has skipped the first part of the question but has mentioned three places as an answer to the second part of the question. This clearly specifies that the respondent has gone out of the city three times as he has mentioned the name of the places as an answer to the second part of the question. This type of incompleteness in the answer can be logically detected and settled down.

9.4.3 Coding

Before performing statistical analysis, a researcher has to prepare data for analysis. This preparation is done by data coding. Coding of data is probably the most crucial step in the analytical process (Sinkovics et al. 2009). Codes or categories are tags or labels for allocating units of meaning to the descriptive or inferential information compiled during a study (Basit 2003). In **coding**, each answer is identified and classified with a numerical score or other symbolic characteristics for processing the data in computers. While coding, researchers generally select a convenient way of entering the data in a spreadsheet (usually MS Excel). The data can be conveniently exported or imported to other software such as Minitab and SPSS. The character of information (points on which the information is collected such as age, gender, etc.) occupies the column position in the spreadsheet with the specific answers to the question entered in a row. Thus, each row of the spreadsheet will indicate the respondent's answers on the column heads.

In coding, each answer is identified and classified with a numerical score or other symbolic characteristics for processing the data in computers.

Coding of open-ended questions is a typical task and must be done carefully. Most of the marketing research questionnaires are generally closed ended and the complexity is minimal as compared with the open-ended questionnaire. Coding alone is not sufficient but the correct coding and intelligent entry with respect to the coding is essentially required. Coding is an essential part of the analysis, but the questions of quality control in the coding process have received little attention (Hruschka et al. 2004). To enhance the quality in the coding exercise, training the persons involved in the coding and **data entry** is important. This is required especially when a researcher has to deal with large number of data in a limited time schedule. Data coders from different background may make the process more difficult. Similarities in knowledge and substance background of coders facilitate equivalence in the process of analysis (Polsa 2007).

Figure 9.3 exhibits a sample questionnaire with coding. The questionnaire is developed to provide some information about toilet soap. Figure 9.4 in the spreadsheet showing data coding and entry of responses for the first 27 respondents belonging to different states. The first column is devoted for respondent identification number and the second column is devoted for the respective state to which the concerned respondent belongs. Question 1 is coded as Q1 and secures Column 3 and Question 2, coded as Q2, occupies Columns 4–10, and consists of seven different questions. These are further coded as Q2(a) to Q2(g) as the heading of Columns 4–10. Thus, the values are checked in the respective columns for the first concerned respondent as "4, 5, 2, 3, 4, 4, and 2" (see Figure 9.4).

Question 3 coded as Q3 occupies Columns 11–16 and asks the respondents to provide their opinion about a particular brand in a list of six, which allows the question to be categorized into six parts each for one particular brand (see Figure 9.3). These are further coded as Q3(a) to Q3(f) as the heading of Columns 11–16. Thus the values are checked in Columns (11–16) for the concerned first respondent as "4, 5, 3, 4, 5, and 3" (see Figure 9.4).

Question 4 seeks respondent's views on product attribute. Questionnaire presents five attributes to be rated on a five-point rating scale with 1 as not at all important and 5 as extremely important (Figure 9.3). These are further coded as Q4(a) to Q4(e) as the heading of Columns 17–21. Thus, the values are checked in Columns (17–21) for the concerned respondents as "4, 2, 2, 5, and 1" (see Figure 9.4).

Questions 5–11 are coded as Q5 to Q11 and occupy the head of Columns 22–28. The respective answers are checked in Columns (22–28) for the concerned first respondent as "4, 4, 3, 4, 6, 1, and 3."

1. Do you use soaps? Yes No {Q1}
2. Please state your degree of agreement with the following statements on a five-point scale, where 1 = strongly disagree; 2 = disagree; 3 = neither agree nor disagree; 4 = agree; 5 = strongly agree

I am very health conscious.	1	2	3	(4)	5	{Q2(a)}
Body cleanliness is very important for me.	1	2	3	4	(5)	{Q2(b)}
I prefer soap with germ-killing ability.	1	(2)	3	4	5	{Q2(c)}
I prefer soap that keeps my skin soft.	1	2	(3)	4	5	{Q2(d)}
I am quality concisions.	1	2	3	(4)	5	{Q2(e)}
Price of a soap bar is a non-issue for me.	1	2	3	(4)	5	{Q2(f)}
Taking bath twice in a day is extremely important for me	1	(2)	3	4	5	{Q2(g)}

3. Following is the list of some famous brands of soap. Please provide your opinion about the brand, where 1 = extremely bad; 2 = bad; 3 = neither bad nor good; 4 = good; 5 = extremely good

Liril	1	2	3	(4)	5	{Q3(a)}
Pears	1	2	3	4	(5)	{Q3(b)}
Dettol	1	2	(3)	4	5	{Q3(c)}
Hamam	1	2	3	(4)	5	{Q3(d)}
Lux	1	2	3	4	(5)	{Q3(e)}
Santoor	1	2	(3)	4	5	{Q3(f)}

4. Following are some of the attributes of soap bar. Please indicate importance of these attributes on a five-point scale, where 1 = not at all important; 2 = important; 3 = I cannot say; 4 = important; 5 = extremely important

Fragrance	1	2	3	(4)	5	{Q4(a)}
Price	1	(2)	3	4	5	{Q4(b)}
Size	1	(2)	3	4	5	{Q4(c)}
Freshens	1	2	3	4	(5)	{Q4(d)}
Colour	(1)	2	3	4	5	{Q4(e)}

5. How often do you bathe in a day? {Q5}

1. Once in 2 days ______ 2. Every alternate day ____ 3. Daily ________
4. Twice in a day ______ 5. More than twice in a day _______

6. How many members are there in your family? {Q6}

1. Single_______ 2. Two members_____ 3. Three members _____
4. Four members______ 5. Five members_____ 6. More than five members_______

7. What is your qualification? {Q7}

1. Matriculate_____ 2. Simple graduate___ 3. Professional degree graduate____
4. Postgraduate___ 5. Doctorate_____

8. What is the nature of your occupation? {Q8}

1. Government job______ 2. Private job_______ 3. Own business______
4. Self-employed____ 5. Consultant________

9. What is your monthly household income? {Q9}

1. Under ₹5000______ 2. ₹5001 to ₹10,000____ 3. ₹10,001 to ₹15,000___
4. ₹15,001 to ₹20,000__ 5. ₹20,001 to ₹25,000__ 6. Over ₹25,000_____

10. What is your marital status? {Q10}

1. Married______ 2. Single_____ 3. Divorced______
4. Spouse is not alive____ 5. Other________

11. What is your age? {Q11}

1. 15 to 25_____ 2. 26 to 35_____ 3. 36 to 45_____
4. 46 to 55_____ 5. 56 to 65____ 6. Above 66____

FIGURE 9.3
Questionnaire with coding

The process of data coding will become clear with the help of MS Excel spreadsheet as shown in Figure 9.4. Similarly, data can be entered for *n* number of respondents.

9.4.3.1 Codebook

A **codebook** contains instructions for coding and information of the variables taken for the study. It also contains variable location in the data set. Even if the questionnaire is pre-coded, coding helps researchers in identifying and locating the variables easily. A codebook generally contains the following information: (1) column number, (2) record number, (3) variable number, (4) variable name, (5) question number, and (6) instructions for coding (Malhotra 2004).

A codebook contains instructions for coding and information of the variables taken for the study.

9.4.4 Data Entry

At this stage, the data are entered in the spreadsheet. This is a crucial stage and is usually done by the computer typist. A careful supervision of the **data entry** is essentially required by the researcher. A re-check of the entire process is also important. A manual re-check of the data entry process can be done for a small set of data, whereas it is difficult and time consuming for the large. In this situation, the researcher can take help of another typist. Difference in entries can be easily pointed out and must be corrected with the help of originally filled questionnaire. After the data entry, the researcher has to launch **data cleaning** exercise.

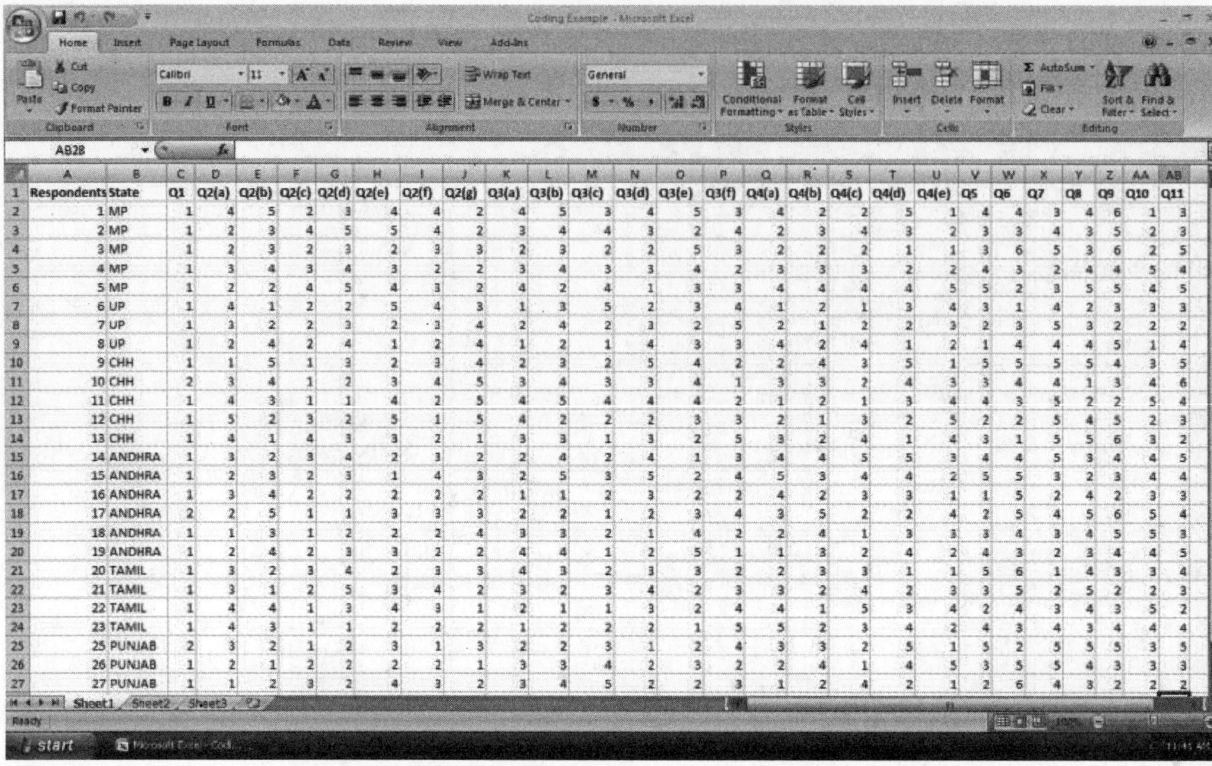

Respondents	State	Q1	Q2(a)	Q2(b)	Q2(c)	Q2(d)	Q2(e)	Q2(f)	Q2(g)	Q3(a)	Q3(b)	Q3(c)	Q3(d)	Q3(e)	Q3(f)	Q4(a)	Q4(b)	Q4(c)	Q4(d)	Q4(e)	Q5	Q6	Q7	Q8	Q9	Q10	Q11
1	MP	1	4	5	2	3	4	4	2	4	5	3	4	5	3	4	2	2	5	1	4	4	3	4	6	1	3
2	MP	1	2	3	4	5	5	4	2	3	4	4	3	2	4	2	3	4	3	2	3	3	4	3	5	2	3
3	MP	1	2	3	2	3	2	3	3	2	3	2	2	5	3	2	2	2	1	1	3	6	5	3	6	2	5
4	MP	1	3	4	3	4	3	2	2	3	4	3	3	4	2	3	3	3	2	2	4	3	2	4	4	5	4
5	MP	1	2	2	4	5	4	3	2	4	2	4	1	3	3	4	4	4	4	5	5	2	3	5	5	4	5
6	UP	1	4	1	2	2	5	4	3	1	3	5	2	3	4	1	2	1	3	4	3	1	4	2	3	3	3
7	UP	1	3	2	2	3	2	3	4	2	4	2	3	2	5	2	1	2	2	3	2	3	5	3	2	2	2
8	UP	1	2	4	2	4	1	2	4	1	2	1	4	3	3	4	2	4	1	2	1	4	4	4	5	1	4
9	CHH	1	1	5	1	3	2	3	4	2	3	2	5	4	2	2	4	3	5	1	5	5	5	5	4	3	5
10	CHH	2	3	4	1	2	3	4	5	3	4	3	3	4	1	3	3	2	4	3	3	4	4	1	3	4	6
11	CHH	1	4	3	1	1	4	2	5	4	5	4	4	4	2	1	2	1	3	4	4	3	5	2	2	5	4
12	CHH	1	5	2	3	2	5	1	5	4	2	2	2	3	3	2	1	3	2	5	2	2	5	4	5	2	3
13	CHH	1	4	1	4	3	3	2	1	3	3	1	3	2	5	3	2	4	1	4	3	1	5	5	6	3	2
14	ANDHRA	1	3	2	3	4	2	3	2	2	4	2	4	1	3	4	4	5	5	3	4	4	5	3	4	4	5
15	ANDHRA	1	2	3	2	3	1	4	3	2	5	3	5	2	4	5	3	4	4	2	5	5	3	2	3	4	4
16	ANDHRA	1	3	4	2	2	2	2	2	1	1	2	3	2	2	4	2	3	3	1	1	5	2	4	2	3	3
17	ANDHRA	2	2	5	1	1	3	3	3	2	2	1	2	3	4	3	5	2	2	4	2	5	4	5	6	5	4
18	ANDHRA	1	1	3	1	2	2	2	4	3	3	2	1	4	2	2	4	1	3	3	3	4	3	4	5	5	3
19	ANDHRA	1	2	4	2	3	3	2	2	4	4	1	2	5	1	1	3	2	4	2	4	3	2	3	4	4	5
20	TAMIL	1	3	2	3	4	2	3	3	4	3	2	3	3	2	2	3	3	1	1	5	6	1	4	3	3	4
21	TAMIL	1	3	1	2	5	3	4	2	3	2	3	4	2	3	3	2	4	2	3	3	5	2	5	2	2	3
22	TAMIL	1	4	4	1	3	4	3	1	2	1	1	3	2	4	4	1	5	3	4	2	4	3	4	3	5	2
23	TAMIL	1	4	3	1	1	2	2	2	1	2	2	2	1	5	5	2	3	4	2	4	3	4	3	4	4	4
25	PUNJAB	2	3	2	1	2	3	1	3	2	2	3	1	2	4	3	3	2	5	1	5	2	5	5	5	3	5
26	PUNJAB	1	2	1	2	2	2	2	1	3	3	4	2	3	2	2	4	1	4	5	3	5	5	4	3	3	3
27	PUNJAB	1	1	2	3	2	4	3	2	3	4	5	2	2	3	1	2	4	2	1	2	6	4	3	2	2	2

FIGURE 9.4
MS Excel spreadsheet exhibiting data coding for toilet soap questionnaire

Data cleaning exercise is undertaken by any researcher to deal with the problem of missing data and illogical or inconsistent entries.

Data cleaning exercise is undertaken by any researcher to deal with the problem of missing data and illogical or inconsistent entries.

9.4.4.1 Data Cleaning

As discussed earlier, data cleaning involves two stages: **handling missing data** and checking data for illogical or inconsistent entries.

Handling Missing Data

Missing data are of two types: first, the data may be missing because the respondent has not provided any answer or has provided a vague answer; second, the data can be missed when the typist fails to type the data, and as a result, the concerned cell is empty.

Missing data are of two types: first, the data may be missing because the respondent has not provided any answer or has provided a vague answer; second, the data can be missed when the typist fails to type it, and as a result, the concerned cell is empty. The second category of missing problem is easy to deal with the help of the computer software solutions such as MS Excel, Minitab, SPSS, and so on, which provide the missing data number clearly. The concerned cell can be identified and the missing data can be re-entered with the help of the original questionnaire.

Dealing with the first category of missing data is relatively difficult. In this case, the data may be missed when a respondent deliberately or unknowing fails to tick an answer. This can be checked during the preliminary screening of the questionnaire stage or the data editing process by contacting the respondent again and getting the individual score for the concerned question. Difficulty occurs when the interviewer is unable to contact the respondent again or even if contacted, the respondent seems to be reluctant to provide an answer to the concerned question. Following are some of the guidelines to deal with such kind of missing data.

Leaving the missing data and performing the analysis: If the number of missing data is not too high then leaving the missing data as it is and performing the analysis is one of the options available to any researcher. Almost all the computer software solutions present the option of performing the analysis leaving the missing data and present the outputs by just mentioning the number of missing entries. A researcher cannot delete or allow the missing data to be a part of the data matrix when the number of missing observations is beyond a permissible limit. Now, there exists an important question, what is the permissible limit? There is no scientific guideline available pertaining to this permissible limit. As a general rule, the missing data should not exceed 10% of the total observations. In such case, deleting or leaving the observation does not solve the purpose.

If the number of missing data is not too high then leaving the missing data as it is and performing the analysis is one of the options available to any researcher.

Substituting a mean value: To deal with the problem of missing data, mean value to the concerned variable can be substituted. For example, for a particular survey, a researcher has collected 100 filled questionnaires. In the preliminary screening of the questionnaire, the researcher has observed that 15 responses pertaining to question 15 are missing. The researcher has re-conducted the interview and could get three responses but 12 are still missing. Now the researcher has an alternate option to deal with the problem of missing data. He can take the mean response of the 88 questions and can substitute it for the missing values. Although this approach is questionable because mean is the centric value, and it has got a poor match with the extreme observations like 1 or 7 in a seven-point rating scale.

To deal with the problem of missing data, mean value to the concerned variable can be substituted.

Case-wise deletion: Using this approach, a researcher can take a decision to discard the subject from the analysis. This approach has got a serious limitation. It will reduce the number of complete responses and the effort invested in data collection will be of no use. It is also possible for the missing data to be in a particular pattern and hence, a particular reason of not filling the answer for a question. Discarding all such subjects from the analysis will leave the subjects who have completed the questionnaire. This will miss an important aspect of the research, "why some respondents have not filled answer to some particular questions." Case-wise deletion is possible when missing data are few, such as one in hundred and when there is no visible systematic pattern in missing data.

Each procedure in handling missing data has its own advantages and disadvantages. Each procedure can result in a different result. This is more possible when missing is not random and a sequence in missing can be detected. It is always advisable to keep the missing as minimum as possible because the procedures used to cope with the problem of missing is the repair process and can never compete with "no missing" situation. Principally, no missing is an ideal situation, but practically it is rare in a research. Hence, while dealing with the missing data, the researcher must examine the pros and cons of each method of handling the missing data and then should choose an appropriate method.

Principally, no missing is an ideal situation, but practically it is rare in a research.

Checking Data for Illogical or Inconsistent Entry

Before performing data analysis, the data must be checked for illogical or inconsistent entry. For example, on a 1- to 7-point rating scale, few respondents have provided entry as 8 and 9. It is illogical, as the rating scale has already been defined as 1 to 7 and the entries cannot be beyond that. This type of error must be detected and appropriate action must be taken. Nowadays, almost all the computer software solutions can detect this type of illogical data entries. Inconsistencies are common in the data set obtained from the respondents. For example, a respondent claims that he or she is a frequent user of Internet banking, and in the next response says that he or she does not have a bank account. This type of inconsistencies must be identified and a corrective action must be initiated.

Before performing data analysis, the data must be checked for illogical or inconsistent entries.

9.5 DATA ANALYSIS

Data analysis exercise cannot be launched independently ignoring the previous steps of the research to deal with the problem.

Analysing data is an important and a scientific procedure and should be well described, documented, and explained (Haring 2008). Data analysis exercise cannot be launched independently ignoring the previous steps of the research to deal with the problem. Data analysis technique is directly linked with the initial stages of conducting a research. For example, consider a research problem as "A comparative study of consumer attitude in two states, Gujarat and Chhattisgarh." After establishing all the steps of the research, a researcher has to consider *z*-test for comparing the population in the two states. A change in the objective of the study as "A comparative study of consumer attitude in three states Gujarat, Chhattisgarh, and Madhya Pradesh" leads to the use of analysis of variance (ANOVA) technique for data analysis as the population has now been increased by one and the researcher should consider the population for three states. Hence, the data analysis technique is dependent on the previous stages of research.

Thus, each statistical analysis technique has its own assumptions, specifications, and abilities to confirm the hypothesized assumptions. All these cannot be applied together, because each technique presents a unique base of use and more or less is distinct from any other statistical technique.

Another important factor in data analysis is the type of data gathered through questionnaire. As already discussed, for nominal and ordinal level of data, non-parametric tests are applied, and for interval and ration level of data, parametric tests are applied. A researcher cannot independently use any of the available technique and apply it on any type of data. These statistical analyses have some underlying assumptions. Before selecting any statistical analysis technique, these assumptions must be examined carefully. Few statistical analyses such as "time series analysis" are better used for predictions, whereas the others such as "multiple regression technique" can be used for prediction and determination of the relationship between the independent and dependent variables. Thus, each statistical analysis technique has its own assumptions, specifications, and abilities to confirm the hypothesized assumptions. All these cannot be applied together, because each technique presents a unique base of use and more or less is distinct from any other statistical technique. Hence, while selecting a tool for the data analysis some considerations are of paramount importance.

A researcher who has a deep knowledge about the analytical and statistical techniques will be able to deal with some advanced and sophisticated statistical techniques, whereas a conservative researcher has some hesitation in using them.

First, data analysis tool must be selected in light of the research objective. Second, the underlying assumptions associated with each analytical tool must be carefully examined and violation of assumptions must be clearly checked. Third, the statistical analysis technique must be selected in the light of scale of measurement. Fourth, nature of research problem also provides a base of selecting a statistical analysis. For example, consider a problem, "impact of age, gender, and income on consumer motive: a comparative study in Delhi and Mumbai". This problem itself clearly states that a researcher has to first apply *z*-test for comparing the population of two states and subsequently apply the regression technique to determine the impact of independent variables, such as age, gender, and income, on a dependent variable consumer motive. Finally, the researcher's interest, background, and knowledge play an important role in selecting a statistical tool. A researcher who has a deep knowledge about the analytical and statistical techniques will be able to deal with some advanced and sophisticated statistical techniques, whereas a conservative researcher has some hesitation in using them.

By and large statistical techniques for analysis can be placed in two categories: univariate and multivariate.

By and large statistical techniques for analysis can be placed in two categories: univariate and multivariate. Univariate statistical techniques are used only when one measurement of each element in the sample is taken or multiple measurement of each element are taken but each variable is analysed independently (Shao 2002). Multivariate statistical techniques can be defined as "a collection of procedures for analysing the association between two or more sets of measurements that were made on each object in one or more samples of objects" (Aaker et al. 2000).

When the data are nominal or ordinal, non-parametric statistical tests are used for data analyses, whereas when they are interval or ratio parametric, statistical tests are used.

On the basis of scale of measurement (type of data), univariate techniques can be further classified into metric and non-metric statistical tests. When the data are nominal or ordinal, non-parametric statistical tests are used for data analyses, whereas when they are interval

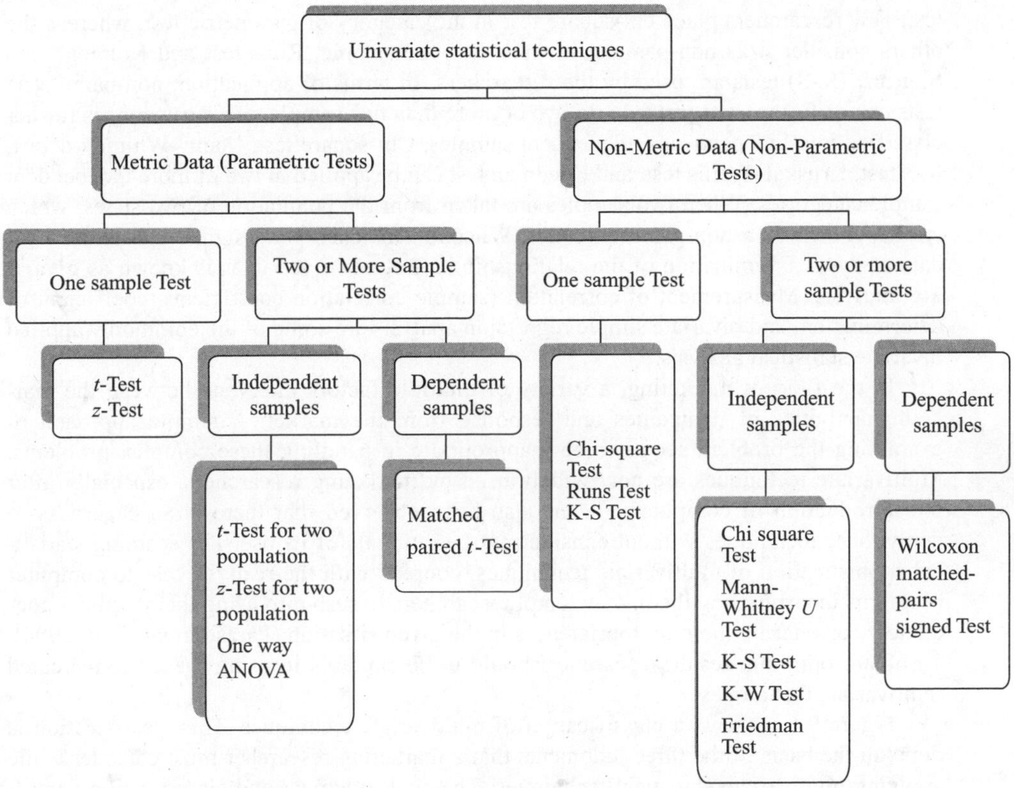

FIGURE 9.5
Classification of univariate statistical techniques

or ratio parametric, statistical tests are used. Parametric tests are the statistical techniques used to test a hypothesis based on some restrictive assumption about the population, whereas non-parametric tests are not dependent on the restrictive normality assumption of the population (Bajpai 2009).

A broad classification of univariate statistical techniques is shown in Figure 9.5. Univariate statistical techniques are categorized on the basis of metric or non-metric data. Type of data whether it is metric or non-metric presents a base for selecting appropriate test statistics. Parametric tests are applied for metric data, and non-parametric tests are applied for non-metric data. Selection of appropriate test statistics is based on one, two, or more than two samples from the population. When one sample is taken from one population, *z*- or *t*-test is applied for data analysis. When the sample size is more than 30 (a large sample), *z*-test statistic is used, and when sample size is less than or equal to 30 *t*-test statistic is used. In the category of parametric tests, two or more samples tests can be further classified on the basis of independent samples or related (dependent) samples category. When two independent samples are taken from two populations and the intention of the researcher is to find the mean difference of the population through sample means, then *z*- and *t*-tests are applied for large and small samples, respectively. When two samples are dependent on each other, matched-paired *t*-test is used. When a researcher wants to compare more than two samples taken from more than two populations, ANOVA technique is used.

Type of data whether it is metric or non-metric presents a base of selecting appropriate test statistics. Parametric tests are applied for metric data and non-parametric tests are applied for non-metric data.

When data are non-parametric (nominal or ordinal data), non-parametric tests are applied. Similar to parametric tests, non-parametric tests can be further classified on the basis of the number of samples. The most important non-parametric test is the chi-square test. Few researchers place chi-square test in the category of parametric test, whereas the others consider it as non-parametric tests. For one sample, Runs test and Kolmogorov–Smirnov (K-S) tests are used by the researchers. In terms of application, non-parametric tests can be further categorized into two or more than two samples. This category is further classified into independent or dependent samples. Chi-square test, Mann–Whitney *U* test, K-S test, Kruskal–Wallis test, and Friedman test can be applied in two or more independent sample categories. When two samples are taken from the population of two states, which are dependent as a non-parametric test, Wilcoxon matched-pairs signed test is used for data analysis. Examination of the relationship between two variables is known as **bivariate analysis**. Measurement of correlation (sample correlation coefficient), coefficient of determination, and bivariate simple regression analysis are some of the commonly applied bivariate statistical analysis.

In the field of marketing, a variety of multiple factors intervene between the marketing activities of companies and response from the market. A simple approach of examining the problem seems to be inappropriate in handling these complex problems. Multivariate techniques are now widely used by marketing researchers, especially after the introduction of computers. It has also been observed that there is an eagerness to apply these techniques without considering the rationale of its use. The seeming statistical sophistication of multivariate techniques, coupled with the ready access to computer programs incorporating them, may tempt researchers to rush into using them without adequately considering their appropriateness in the given situation (Parasuraman et al. 2004). To obtain optimum result, researcher should to be cautious in using these sophisticated multivariate techniques.

Multivariate techniques are now widely used by marketing researchers, especially after the introduction of computers.

Figure 9.6 presents a classification of multivariate techniques. This classification is done on the basis of the three judgments that a marketing researcher must consider while applying multivariate statistical techniques. The first judgment and classification parameter is the dependence of variables, and the second judgment and classification parameter is the "number of variables treated as dependent in a single analysis." The final judgment and classification parameter is the type of data: metric data or non-metric data. ANOVA,

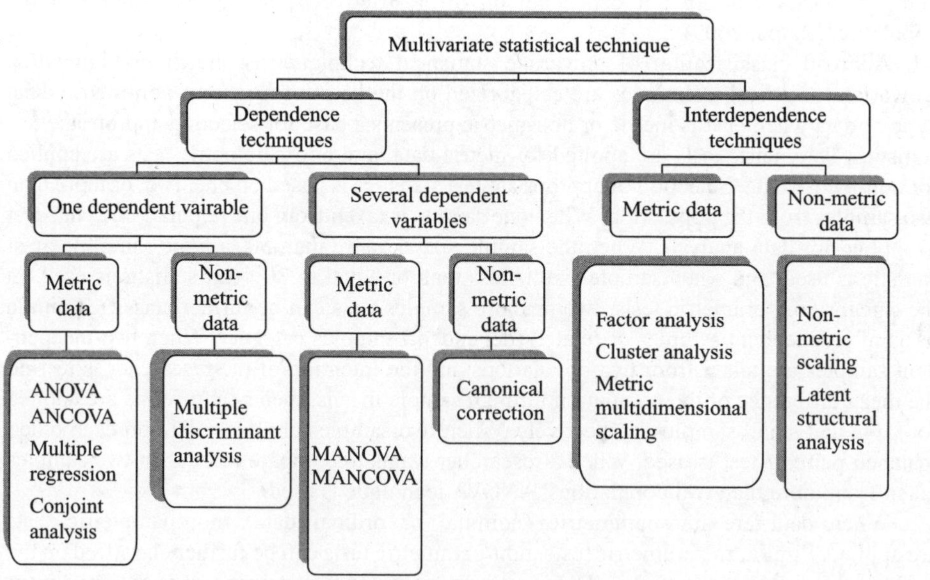

FIGURE 9.6
Classification of multivariate statistical techniques

analysis of covariance (ANCOVA), multiple regression, and conjoint analysis are some of the commonly used dependence techniques, when there is only one dependent variable and the data are metric in nature. Multiple discriminant analysis is a dependence technique when the data are categorical (non-metric) in nature. When there are many dependent variables and the data are metric in nature, multivariate ANOVA and ANCOVA are used as the statistical techniques. When there are many dependent variables and the data are non-metric in nature, canonical correlation is used as the multivariate statistical techniques. Factor analysis, cluster analysis, and metric multidimensional scaling are some of the commonly used interdependence techniques when there is only one dependent variable and the data are metric in nature. Non-metric scaling and latent structural analysis are some of the interdependence techniques, when there is one dependent variable and the data are non-metric in nature.

REFERENCES |

Aaker, D. A., V. Kumar and G. S. Day (2000). *Marketing Research*, 7th ed., p. 436. Wiley.

Alam, I. (2005). "Fieldwork and Data Collection in Qualitative Marketing Research", *Qualitative Market Research: An International Journal,* 8(1): 97–112.

Bajpai, N. (2009). *Business Statistics*, p. 678. Pearson Education.

Basit, T. N. (2003). "Manual or Electronic? The Role of Coding in Qualitative Data Analysis", *Educational Research,* 45(2): 143–53.

De Leon J. P. and J. H. Cohen (2005). "Objects and Walking Probes in Ethnographic Interviewing", *Field Methods,* 17(2): 200–4.

Dessler, G. (2003). *Human Resource Management*, 8th ed., p. 84. Pearson Education Singapore Pte. Ltd.

Grim, B. J., A. H. Harmon and J. C. Gromis (2006). "Focused Group Interviews as an Innovative Quanti-Qualitative Methodology (QQM): Integrating Quantitative Elements into a Qualitative Methodology", *The Qualitative Report,* 11(3): 516–37.

Haring, R. (2008). "Conducting Culturally Appropriate Qualitative Market Research in the Native American Landscape", *Qualitative Market Research: An International Journal,* 11(1): 7–16.

Hruschka, D. J., D. Schwartz, D. C. St. John, E. Picone-Decaro, R. A. Jenkins, and J. W. Carey (2004). "Reliability in Coding Open-Ended Data: Lessons Learned from HIV Behavioral Research", *Field Methods,* 16(3): 307–31.

Malhotra, N. K., (2004). *Marketing Research: An Applied Orientation*, 4th ed., p. 407. Pearson Education.

Malhotra, N. K., J. Agarwal and M. Peterson (1996). "Methodological Issues in Cross-Cultural Marketing Research", *International Marketing Review,* 13(5): 7–43.

Meckel, M., D. Walters and P. Baugh (2005). "Mixed-Modes Surveys Using Mail and Web Questionnaires", *The Electronic Journal of Business Research Methodology,* 3(1): 69–80.

Nilan, P. (2002). "'Dangerous Fieldwork' Re-Examined: The Question of Researcher Subject Position", *Qualitative Research,* 2(3): 363–86.

Olaniyan, D. A. and L. B. Ojo (2008). "Staff Training and Development: A Vital Tool for Organizational Effectiveness", *European Journal of Scientific Research,* 24(3): 326–31.

Parasuraman, A., D. Grewal and R. Krishnan (2004). *Marketing Research*, p. 537. Boston, NY: Houghton Mifflin Company.

Polsa, P. (2007). "Comparability in Cross-Cultural Qualitative Marketing Research: Equivalence in Personal Interviews", *Academy of Marketing Science Review,* 2007(8): 1–18.

Scott, S., F. Miller and K. Lloyd (2006). "Doing Fieldwork in Development Geography: Research Culture and Research Space in Vietnam", *Geographical Research,* 44(1): 28–40.

Shao, A. T. (2002). *Marketing Research: An Aid to Decision Making*, 2nd ed., p. 438. South-Western Thomson Learning.

Sinkovics, R. R., E. Penz and P. N. Ghauri (2009). "Enhancing the Trustworthiness of Qualitative Research in International Business", *Management International Review,* 48(6): 689–714.

Zikmund, W. G. (2007). *Business Research Methods*, 7th ed., p. 441. South-Western Thomson Learning.

SUMMARY

In marketing research, fieldwork is important and requires a systematic approach. Fieldwork is the most exciting part of the research that provides an opportunity to a researcher to have a new thinking and a new way to look at various things. A systematic fieldwork is performed using the following seven steps: job analysis, job description, and job specification; selecting fieldworkers; providing training to fieldworkers; briefing and sending fieldworkers to the field for data collection; supervising the fieldwork; debriefing and fieldwork validation; and evaluating and terminating fieldwork.

There exist two stages between data collection and interpretation, they are data preparation and data analysis. Data preparation secures the first place in these two stages. The data preparation process starts from preliminary questionnaire screening. In the subsequent steps, data editing and data coding are executed. After editing and coding, the data are entered into computer spreadsheets and then the data analysis strategy is initiated. Data analysis strategies can be further categorized into descriptive data analysis and inferential data analysis. Descriptive data analysis is used in describing the data, whereas inferential statistical analysis is based on the use of some sophisticated statistical analysis to estimate the population parameter from sample statistic. Inferential data analysis can be classified into univariate, bivariate, and multivariate data analyses.

KEY TERMS

Briefing, 191
Briefing session, 194
Codebook, 201
Coding, 197
Data analysis strategy, 197
Data cleaning, 201
Data entry, 199
Data preparation process, 197
Debriefing, 191
Descriptive data analysis, 197
Editing, 197
Evaluation and termination of fieldwork, 191
Fieldwork validation, 191
Handling missing data, 202
Inferential data analysis, 197
Initial contact, 192
Job analysis, 191
Job description, 191
Job specification, 191
Preliminary questionnaire screening, 197
Probing, 192
Providing training to fieldworkers, 191
Selection of fieldworkers, 192
Strategic silence, 193
Supervising the fieldwork, 191
Univariate, bivariate, and multivariate data analyses, 197

NOTES

1. http://www.escortsgroup.com/the_group/group_about_us.html
2. http://economictimes.indiatimes.com/News/News-By-Industry/Indl-Goods–Svs/Engineeri…

DISCUSSION QUESTIONS

1. What is fieldwork and how fieldwork is an integral part of conducting any research?
2. Explain the various stages of fieldwork process.
3. What are job analysis, job description, and job specification, and how a researcher can explore these in recruiting good fieldworkers?
4. Why training is essential before sending fieldworkers for data collection?
5. What is the role of briefing, supervising, and debriefing in conducting fieldwork programme?
6. Why fieldwork validation and fieldwork evaluation are essential for a marketing researcher?
7. What are the various steps of data preparation process?
8. What is the role of editing and coding in data preparation process?
9. What are the precautions a researcher has to keep in mind while entering data?
10. Explain data cleaning in the light of handling missing data and checking data for illogical or inconsistent entry.
11. What are the important considerations while performing data analysis?
12. Write a short note on the following terms:
    - Univariate statistical analysis
    - Bivariate statistical analysis
    - Multivariate statistical analysis

CASE STUDY |

Case 9: *ITC: A Long Way Journey from a Pure Tobacco Company to a Well-diversified FMCG Company*

Introduction

The Indian Tobacco Company (ITC) has come a long way from being a pure tobacco company to become a well-diversified fast moving consumer goods (FMCG) company. Slower growth in cigarettes business with the global anti-tobacco movement gaining momentum and the heavy taxation policy followed by the government for cigarettes prompted ITC to diversify into other businesses. Today, it has a strong presence in paperboards, paper and packaging, hotels, and other FMCG products including branded packaged food, apparels, safety matches, agarbattis, greeting cards, and agribusiness. Although manufacturing cigarettes still remains the company's prime economic activity, its share in total sales has come down to 65.8% in 2006–2007.[1]

In 1925, ITC first diversified into packaging and printing. This division contributes around 10% of the company's revenue. ITC entered into hospitality business in 1975 by opening its first hotel in Chennai, "Hotel Chola." Today, the company operates over 70 hotels across India classified under five brands: ITC Hotels - Luxury collection, ITC-Welcomgroup Sheraton Hotels, WelcomHotels, Fortune Hotels, and WelcomHeritage. It is the second largest company in the Indian hotel and restaurant business with a market share of 11.9% (2005–2006). However, the hotel business contributes 4% to the company's gross sales. Table 9.01 exhibits the growth story of ITC through net profit (in million rupees) of ITC Ltd in different quarters.[1]

As one of the valued and prestigious organizations of the country, ITC is perceived to be dedicatedly nation-oriented. Mr Y. C. Deveshwar, Chairman of the ITC Ltd, terms it as the source of inspiration "a commitment beyond the market." He says that "ITC believes that its aspiration to create enduring value for the nation provides the motive force to sustain growing shareholder value. ITC practices this philosophy by not only driving each of its businesses towards international competitiveness but by also consciously contributing to enhancing the competitiveness of the larger value chain which it is a part".[2]

Focus on Hotel Industry

The strong growth witnessed by the Indian hospitality industry in the last few years was driven by increased business traffic and leisure travel in the wake of favourable economic conditions and higher order integration of India with the global economy. The premium segment that accounts for 60% of the hotel industry's revenues grew at an impressive 27% between 2003–2004 and 2007–2008. This growth momentum continued into the first half of the fiscal year 2008–2009 reflected in the growth of the Company's revenues by 14%. The effect of the economic slowdown started to impact from the middle of the year with clampdown on domestic-corporate travel and steep reduction in international travel as a fallout of the global financial crisis. Lack of consumer confidence also adversely affected leisure travel. The situation worsened with the horrific terror strikes at Mumbai, which triggered off negative travel advisories leading to a sharp reduction in occupancies and average room revenues. This cyclical downturn affected the hospitality industry, although the business has been able to demonstrate some resilience during this challenging period. However, the business continues to pursue an aggressive investment-led growth strategy recognizing the inadequate capacity and the longer term potential of this sector.[1]

ITC Ltd has lined up an investment of ₹80,000 million to grow its hotel businesses. Addressing the company's 98th AGM in Kolkata, the chairman of ITC Ltd, Mr Y. C. Deveshwar clearly stated the company's strategy, "We are looking at various opportunities in the hotel space within the country. Senior officials from ITC led by the chief executive of development cell are scouting for the properties in the country. Talks are on with a number of people including real estate developers for acquiring

TABLE 9.01
Net profit (in million rupees) of ITC Ltd in different quarters

Year	*Net profit*
Mar-05	7717.5
Jun-05	5583
Sep-05	5723.3
Dec-05	5368.3
Mar-06	5678.9
Jun-06	6522.8
Sep-06	6796
Dec-06	7174
Mar-07	6506.9
Jun-07	7828.7
Sep-07	7708.7
Dec-07	8307.2
Mar-08	7356.4
Jun-08	7486.7
Sep-08	8027.2
Dec-08	9032.1
Mar-09	8089.9

Source: Prowess (V. 3.1): Centre for Monitoring Indian Economy Pvt. Ltd, Mumbai, accessed September 2009, reprinted with permission.

properties. The hotel business continues to pursue an aggressive investment led growth strategy recognizing the long-term potential of this sector and the need for greater room capacities commensurate with India's economic growth. We are extremely bullish about the hotels business".[3]

Highlighting more details of the hotels business development plan, the senior executive vice president (hotels division) of ITC presented the aim of 2012, "Our plan is to have 100 hotels under the Fortune brand across the country by 2012 with an inventory of around 8,000 rooms." With an optimistic vision he further added, "Leisure travellers comprise around 15–20 per cent of our customers, while the ratio between foreign and domestic customers is 75:25. We are now planning to put more emphasis on attracting domestic visitors in the leisure segment".[4]

As discussed in the case, ITC Ltd wants to attract domestic customers for its hotel business. Suppose that ITC Ltd wants to ascertain aspirations of domestic customers related to hotel facility on some grounds such as food, swimming pool facility, room service, recreation facility, room cleaning facility, and launched an extensive survey programme. How company will organize fieldwork and data collection process? What will be the way of framing questions and how company will decide about the initial contact? What should be the finest way to supervise the fieldwork? How will the company validate and evaluate the fieldwork?

NOTES |

1. Prowess (V. 3. 1): Centre for Monitoring Indian Economy Pvt. Ltd, Mumbai, accessed September 2009, reprinted with permission.
2. http://www.itcportal.com/the_itc_profile/itc_profile.html, accessed September 2009.
3. http://economictimes.indiatimes.com/News/News-By-Industry/Services/Hotels-Restaurant… accessed August 2009.
4. http://www.telegraphindia.com/1090411/jsp/business/story_10806478.jsp accessed October 2009.

PART IV

Descriptive Statistics and Data Analysis

CHAPTER 10

Descriptive Statistics: Measures of Central Tendency

LEARNING OBJECTIVES

Upon completion of this chapter, you will be able to:

- Understand the concept of arithmetic mean, geometric mean, harmonic mean, median, mode, quartiles, percentiles, and deciles
- Compute arithmetic mean, geometric mean, harmonic mean, median, mode, quartiles, percentiles, and deciles
- Use MS Excel, Minitab, and SPSS for computing mathematical averages, positional averages, and partitional values

STATISTICS IN ACTION: RUCHI SOYA LTD

The Indian oilseed industry is ranked fifth in the world, and its edible oil consumption represents 9% of the world consumption. The quantum of edible oil marketed in both packed and branded form, however, has been low considering the overall consumption. This scenario is now changing owing to various factors such as the ever expanding population in the country, the rising disposable income, growing health consciousness, and the vast growth expected in organized retail industry.[1]

In the early 1960s, when Mahadev Shahra went about convincing farmers in Madhya Pradesh (MP) about the potential benefits of growing soya, he never imagined he would be instrumental in kickstarting a small green revolution in the state. He not only introduced but also encouraged soya bean cultivation on a commercial scale. Although his family was in the business of commodities trading, it subsequently entered into the business of ginning and oil milling. The Shahra family's efforts along with that of others resulted in a soya revolution in MP. Today MP is considered the "soya bowl" of the country, and it contributes almost 70% of the total production of soya in the country. Despite all odds, Ruchi Soya is now the largest player in the country in the edible oils and soya foods category.[2] Table 10.1 shows the profit after tax of Ruchi Soya Industries from 2000 to 2007.

TABLE 10.1
Profit after tax from 2000 to 2007

Year	*2000*	*2001*	*2002*	*2003*	*2004*	*2005*	*2006*	*2007*
Profit after tax (in million rupees)	198.5	261.3	273.3	270.1	341.6	435.9	828.2	1007

Source: Prowess (V. 2.6), Centre for Monitoring Indian Economy Pvt. Ltd, Mumbai, accessed July 2008, reproduced with permission.

>>>

Table 10.1 gives a broad picture of the company's performance from 2000 to 2007. Using certain statistical tools such as average, median, mode, etc. we can analyse this data so that more meaningful information can be obtained. This chapter deals with the various mathematical and positional averages. It also describes the process of using MS Excel, Minitab, and SPSS for computing arithmetic mean, geometric mean, harmonic mean, median, mode, quartiles, percentiles, and deciles.

10.1 INTRODUCTION

This chapter focuses on the **measures of central tendency**, and Chapter 11 discusses the measures of dispersion and shape. After the classification and tabulation of data, we need to use a few measures that can reveal the basic features of the data. In statistics, a tool which represents the basic features of data is referred to as an "average." An average value is a single value that describes an entire group of values. In other words, it is a single value within the range of the data that is used to represent all the values in the series. Simply speaking, the average of a statistical series is the value of the variable which is representative of the entire series.

10.2 CENTRAL TENDENCY

The tendency of the observations to concentrate around a central point is known as central tendency.

A **central tendency** is a single value which is used to represent an entire set of data. It is a typical value around which most of the other values cluster. In other words, the tendency of the observations to concentrate around a central point is known as central tendency.

10.3 MEASURES OF CENTRAL TENDENCY

Statistical measures which indicate the location or position of a central value to describe the central tendency of the entire data are called the measures of central tendency.

Statistical measures that indicate the location or position of a central value to describe the central tendency of the entire data are called the **measures of central tendency**. In statistics, there are various types of measures of central tendency, some of which can be broadly classified as follows:

1. Mathematical Averages
   (a) **Arithmetic mean** or mean
      - Simple
      - Weighted
   (b) **Geometric mean**
   (c) **Harmonic mean**
2. **Positional Averages**
   (a) **Median**
   (b) **Mode**
   (c) **Quartiles**
   (d) **Deciles**
   (e) **Percentiles**

An average should possess some basic prerequisites. A brief description of these prerequisites is given below.

10.4 PREREQUISITES FOR AN IDEAL MEASURE OF CENTRAL TENDENCY

Some important characteristics of an ideal measure of central tendency are as follows:

1. It should be rigidly defined.
2. It should be readily comprehensible and easy to calculate.
3. It should be based upon all the observations.
4. It should be suitable for further mathematical treatment.
5. It should be affected as little as possible by the fluctuations of sampling.

There are various measures of central tendency of data. The most common and widely used measure is the arithmetic mean. The following section discusses various mathematical averages and their computation.

10.5 MATHEMATICAL AVERAGES

Methods of computing mathematical averages are classified according to the nature of the data. In classification and tabulation of data, values of the observations can be arranged in any of the following series:

1. Individual series or ungrouped data
2. Discrete frequency distribution
3. Continuous frequency distribution

Individual series is composed of raw (ungrouped) data. Discrete frequency distribution and continuous frequency distribution comprise of grouped data. In discrete frequency distribution, raw data is grouped with frequencies, whereas in continuous frequency distribution, raw data is grouped with frequencies and class interval.

Computation of mathematical averages can also be differentiated according to the nature of the data series. The data series could be in the form of individual series, discrete frequency distribution, or continuous frequency distribution. It is important to note that individual series comprises of raw (ungrouped) data. Discrete frequency distribution and continuous frequency distribution comprise of grouped data. In discrete frequency distribution, the raw data is grouped with frequencies, whereas in continuous frequency distribution; the raw data is grouped with frequencies and class intervals.

10.5.1 Arithmetic Mean

The **arithmetic mean** (AM) of a set of observations is their sum, divided by the number of observations. It is generally denoted by $\bar{x}$ or AM. Population mean is denoted by μ. Therefore,

Arithmetic mean of a set of observations is their sum divided by the number of observations.

$$\text{AM} = \frac{\text{Sum of all the observations}}{\text{Number of observations}}$$

Arithmetic mean is of two types:

- Simple arithmetic mean
- **Weighted arithmetic mean**

10.5.1.1 Calculation of Simple Arithmetic Mean

Arithmetic mean can be computed differently for three different types of series. In other words, arithmetic mean can be computed differently for individual series, discrete frequency distribution, and continuous frequency distribution.

The arithmetic mean of an individual series can be calculated by dividing the sum of the observations by the number of observations.

Computation of arithmetic mean for individual series

The arithmetic mean of an individual series can be calculated by dividing the sum of the observations by the number of observations.

In a series $x_1, x_2, x_3, \ldots x_n$, the arithmetic mean can be calculated by

$$\text{AM} = \frac{x_1 + x_2 + \cdots + x_n}{n} = \frac{1}{n}\sum_{i=1}^{n} x_i$$

To understand the procedure of computing arithmetic mean for an individual series, see Example 10.1.

Example 10.1

A rainwear manufacturing company wants to launch some new products in a new state. The rainfall in the state (in cm) for the past 10 years is given in Table 10.2. Find the average rainfall of the state in the past 10 years.

TABLE 10.2
Rainfall for 10 years (1995–2004)

Year	1995	1996	1997	1998	1999	2000	2001	2002	2003	2004
Rainfall (cm)	110	120	130	135	140	150	160	170	180	190

Solution

For computing average rainfall, we have to first compute the total rainfall in 10 years (see Table 10.3) and then divide this total by the total number of years, 10.

$$\text{AM} = \frac{x_1 + x_2 + \cdots + x_n}{n} = \frac{1}{n}\sum_{i=1}^{n} x_i$$

$$= \frac{1485}{10} = 148.5$$

TABLE 10.3
Total rainfall in ten years

Year	*Rainfall (x)*
1995	110
1996	120
1997	130
1998	135
1999	140
2000	150
2001	160
2002	170
2003	180
2004	190
Total	1485

Hence, the average rainfall in 10 years in the state is 148.5 cm.

Computation of arithmetic mean for discrete frequency distribution

In this type of distribution, every term is multiplied by its corresponding frequency and the total sum of these products is divided by the sum of frequencies. Hence, for a given series $x_1, x_2, x_3, \ldots, x_n$, with corresponding frequencies $f_1, f_2, f_3, \ldots, f_n$, the arithmetic mean AM is given by

Arithmetic mean of a discrete frequency distribution is obtained by multiplying each term by its corresponding frequency and then dividing the sum of these products by the sum of frequencies.

$$\text{AM} = \frac{f_1x_1 + f_2x_2 + \cdots + f_nx_n}{f_1 + \cdots + f_n} = \frac{\sum_{i=1}^{n} f_i x_i}{\sum_{i=1}^{n} f_i}$$

To understand the method of calculating the arithmetic mean for a discrete series, see Example 10.2.

Example 10.2

The weekly earnings of 187 employees of a company is given in Table 10.4. Find the mean of the weekly earnings.

TABLE 10.4
Weekly earning of 187 employees

Weekly earnings (in ₹)	100	120	140	160	180	200	210
Number of employees	5	8	12	16	22	44	80

Solution In a discrete series, each value must be multiplied by its frequency. The next step is to divide the sum of this product by the total sum of the frequencies to arrive at the arithmetic mean (see Table 10.5).

TABLE 10.5
Product of the weekly earnings and number of employees

Weekly earnings (in rupees) (x)	*Number of employees (f)*	*(fx)*
100	5	500
120	8	960
140	12	1,680
160	16	2,560
180	22	3,960
200	44	8,800
210	80	16,800
Total	$\Sigma f = 187$	$\Sigma fx = 35{,}260$

$$\text{AM} = \frac{\sum fx}{\sum f} = \frac{35260}{187} = \text{Rs } 188.55$$

Hence, the average weekly earning is ₹188.55.

Computation of arithmetic mean for continuous frequency distribution

The process of computing arithmetic mean for a continuous frequency distribution is the same as the process of computing arithmetic mean for a discrete series. In a continuous frequency distribution, the class intervals are given. We take the midpoint of each class interval as the value of x. The remaining steps are the same as that for computing the arithmetic mean of a discrete series. The formula given below is used for computing the arithmetic mean for a continuous series:

$$\text{AM} = \frac{f_1x_1 + f_2x_2 + \cdots + f_nx_n}{f_1 + \cdots + f_n} = \frac{\sum_{i=1}^{n} f_ix_i}{\sum_{i=1}^{n} f_i}$$

Example 10.3 explains the procedure of computing arithmetic mean for continuous frequency distribution.

Example 10.3

From Table 10.6, find the arithmetic mean.

TABLE 10.6
Data related to class intervals and frequencies

Class interval	*Frequencies*
0–10	5
10–20	7
20–30	19
30–40	12
40–50	5
50–60	2
60–70	7

Solution

For computing arithmetic mean in a continuous frequency distribution, we need to compute the midpoint of class intervals (x). The midpoints are multiplied by the corresponding frequencies (fx). The sum of this product is obtained and is divided by the sum of frequencies (Table 10.7).

TABLE 10.7
Data given in Table 10.6 arranged with class midpoint, frequencies, and the product of mid-points and frequencies

Size	*Midpoint (x)*	*Frequencies (f)*	*fx*
0–10	5	5	25
10–20	15	7	105
20–30	25	19	475
30–40	35	12	420
40–50	45	5	225
50–60	55	2	110
60–70	65	7	455
Total		$\sum f = 57$	$\sum fx = 1815$

$$\text{AM} = \frac{\sum fx}{\sum f} = \frac{1815}{57} = 31.84$$

10.5.2 Mathematical Properties of Arithmetic Mean

The arithmetic mean is based on all the observations and is capable of further mathematical treatment. It has some very important mathematical properties:

The sum of the deviations of the items from the arithmetic mean is always zero, that is $(x_i - \bar{x}) = 0$.

1. The sum of the deviations of the items from the arithmetic mean is always zero, that is, $\sum(x_i - \bar{x}) = 0$. This property is well explained by Table 10.8:

   here,

$$\sum(x_i - \bar{x}) = 0 = \frac{\sum x_i}{n} = \frac{150}{5} = 30$$

   So, $\Sigma(x_i - \sum(x_i - \bar{x}) = 0) = 0$ (from Table 10.8)

2. The sum of the squares of the deviation of a set of values is minimum when taken from the mean.

   To understand this property, see Table 10.9. The sum of the squares of the deviation from mean (computed as 30) can be computed as in Table 10.9.

TABLE 10.8
Sum of the deviations of the items from the arithmetic mean

x_i	$(x_i - \bar{x})$
10	–20
20	–10
30	0
40	10
50	20
$\Sigma x_i = 150$	$\Sigma(x_i - \bar{x}) = 0$

TABLE 10.9
Sum of the squares of the deviation from mean

x_i	$(x_i - \bar{x})$	$(x_i - \bar{x})2$
10	–20	400
20	–10	100
30	0	0
40	10	100
50	20	400
$\Sigma x = 150$	$\Sigma(x_i - \bar{x}) = 0$	$\Sigma(x_i - \bar{x})^2 = 1000$

In this case, the sum of the squares of the deviation is equal to 1000. If the deviation would be taken from any other value, say 20, then the sum of the squares of the deviations would be greater than 1000 as shown in Table 10.10.

It is clear that when the sum of the square was taken from the arithmetic mean, it was 1000 and when it was taken from any other value, for example, 20 as in Table 10.10, it was 1500, which is greater than 1000. This result can be generalized.

The sum of the squares of the deviation of a set of values is minimum when taken from the mean.

TABLE 10.10
Sum of the squares of the deviation from any value other than mean

x_i	$x_i - 20$	$(x_i - 20)^2$
10	–10	100
20	0	0
30	10	100
40	20	400
50	30	900
$\Sigma x_i = 150$		$\Sigma(x_i - 20)^2 = 1500$

Simple arithmetic means may be combined to form a composite mean.

3. Simple arithmetic means may be combined to form a **composite mean**. The formula for com posite mean is

$$\text{AM} = \frac{n_1\bar{x}_1 + n_2\bar{x}_2 + \cdots + n_k\bar{x}_k}{n_1 + n_2 + \cdots n_k}$$

10.5.3 Merits and Demerits of Arithmetic Mean

No mathematical or positional average is free from merits and demerits. It is important to understand its merits and demerits to have an idea about its appropriate application. Some of the merits and demerits of arithmetic mean are listed below.

10.5.3.1 Merits

1. It is rigidly defined.
2. It is easy to calculate and understand.
3. It is based upon all the observations.
4. It is capable of further algebraic treatment.
5. Arrangement of data in ascending or descending order is not necessary.
6. Of all the averages, arithmetic mean is the least affected by fluctuations of sampling.

10.5.3.2 Demerits

1. It is highly affected by extreme values.
2. It cannot be determined by inspection.
3. When dealing with qualitative characteristics, such as intelligence, honesty, beauty, etc. arithmetic mean cannot be used. In such cases, median can be used.
4. In extremely asymmetrical (skewed) distributions, the arithmetic mean is not a suitable measure.

10.5.4 Weighted Arithmetic Mean

The weighted mean enables us to calculate an average that takes into account the importance of each value to the overall total.

In the computation of arithmetic mean, equal importance is given to all the items of a series. However, there are cases where all the items are not of equal importance, and importance itself is relative by nature. In other words, some items of a series are more important as compared to the other items in the same series. In such cases, it becomes important to assign different weights to different items. The weighted mean can be used to calculate an average that takes into account the importance of each value with respect to the overall total. For example, to get an idea of the change in the cost of living of a certain group of people, a simple mean of the prices of the commodities consumed by them will not be an appropriate tool for measuring average price, as all the commodities may not be of equal importance. For example, wheat, rice, and pulses may be more important when compared with cigarettes, tea, and other luxury items.

10.5.4.1 Computation of Weighted Mean

The formula for calculating weighted mean is

$$\bar{x}_w = \frac{\Sigma wx}{\Sigma w}$$

where x is the value of the item and w the weights attached to the corresponding items.

SELF-PRACTICE PROBLEMS

10A1. Determine the mean from the following series:

23 27 28 25 20 21
34 18 29 21 16

10A2. Determine the mean from the following frequency distribution:

Value	*Frequency*
10	5
27	6
28	8
34	9
55	6
38	5
52	7
40	4
45	3
57	5

10A3. Determine the mean from the following class intervals:

Class interval	*Frequency*
10–20	14
20–30	16
30–40	17
40–50	15
50–60	14
60–70	19
70–80	21
80–90	22
90–100	18
100–110	19

10A4. The following data shows the consumption of primary sources of conventional energy in India from 1996–1997 to 2005–2006. This includes coal, crude petroleum, natural gas, and electricity. Compute the average consumption of coal, crude petroleum, natural gas, and electricity from 1996–1997 to 2005–2006.

Year	*Coal (thousand tonnes)*	*Crude petroleum (thousand tonnes)*	*Natural gas (million cubic metres)*	*Electricity (GWh)*
1996–1997	298, 620	62,870	18, 632	280, 146
1997–1998	306, 824	65, 166	21, 513	296, 749
1998–1999	313, 476	68, 538	22, 489	309, 734
1999–2000	315, 047	85, 964	26, 885	312, 841
2000–2001	341, 220	103, 444	27, 860	316, 600
2001–2002	349, 740	107, 274	28, 037	322, 459
2002–2003	361, 745	112, 559	29, 964	339, 598
2003–2004	379, 405	121, 841	30, 906	360, 937
2004–2005	404, 691	127, 117	30, 775	386, 134
2005–2006	407, 013	130, 109	31, 025	415, 299

Source: www.indiastat.com, accessed October 2008, reproduced with permission.

10A5. IDBI Bank Ltd was incorporated under an act of Parliament in 1964 as a wholly owned subsidiary of the Reserve Bank of India. The main purpose of this move was to monitor and coordinate the activities of financial institutions at the state and national level. IDBI Bank has many products and is mainly involved in providing long-term finance for various projects. The income of IDBI Bank from 1998–1999 to 2006–2007 except 2003–2004 is given below. Compute the average income of the bank from 1998–1999 to 2006–2007(Except 2003–2004).

Year	*Income (in million rupees)*
1998–1999	76,202.1
1999–2000	78,675.6
2000–2001	78,359.1
2002–2002	71,890.1
2002–2003	67,638.1
2004–2005	35,816.4
2005–2006	86,904.9
2006–2007	76,909.9

Source: Prowess (V. 3.1), Centre for Monitoring Indian Economy Pvt.Ltd, Mumbai, accessed 25 September 2008, reproduced with permission.

10A6. Find the arithmetic mean from the following data:

Class interval	*Frequency*
0–20	17
20–40	27
40–60	19
60–80	12
80–100	25
100–120	22
120–140	57

10.5.5 Geometric Mean

Geometric mean is the nth root of the product of n items of a series.

Geometric mean (GM) is the nth root of the product of n items of a series. For example, if there are three items in a series, their geometric mean would be the cube root of the product of all the three items. If these three items are 4, 6, and 9, then their geometric mean, which is generally denoted by G, can be computed as

$$G = \sqrt[3]{4 \times 6 \times 9} = \sqrt[3]{216} = 6$$

In the previous sections, we have seen that average can be calculated differently for various types of distributions. Likewise, geometric mean can also be calculated for three different types of series. These are

1. individual series or ungrouped data;
2. discrete frequency distribution; and
3. continuous frequency distribution.

In the following section, we discuss the computation of geometric mean for these three types of distributions.

10.5.5.1 Computation of Geometric Mean for Individual Series

Suppose an individual series contains n items as $x_1, x_2, x_3, \ldots, x_n$. Then, geometric mean G is defined as

$$G = (x_1 \cdot x_2 \cdots x_n)^{1/n}$$

Taking logarithms on both sides of the above equation, we have

$$\log \mathrm{G} = \frac{1}{n}(\log x_1 + \log x_2 + \cdots + \log x_n)$$

$$\log \mathrm{G} = \frac{1}{n}\sum_{i=1}^{n} \log x_i$$

$$\mathrm{G} = \operatorname{antilog}\left[\frac{1}{n}\sum_{i=1}^{n} \log x_i\right]$$

Example 10.4

The annual rate of growth for a factory for 5 years is 7%, 8%, 4%, 6% and 10% respectively. What is the average rate of growth per annum for this period?

Solution

If the growth in the beginning is 100, then for 5 years, the growth is as given in Table 10.11.

TABLE 10.11
Computation of Geometric mean for Example 10.4

Year	*x*	*log x*
1	100 + 7 = 107	2.0293
2	100 + 8 = 108	2.0334
3	100 + 4 = 104	2.0170
4	100 + 6 = 106	2.0253
5	100 + 10 = 110	2.0413
		$\Sigma \log x = 10.14654$

$$G = \text{antilog } \frac{1}{n}\sum_{i=1}^{n}\log x_i$$

$$= \text{antilog}\left[\frac{10.14654}{5}\right]$$

$$= \text{antilog } (2.0293)$$

$$= 106.98$$

The required average growth rate is 106.98 – 100 = 6.98. Therefore, the average rate of growth percentage per annum is 6.98%.

10.5.5.2 Geometric Mean for Discrete and Continuous Series

If there are n items in a discrete series, $x_1, x_2, x_3, \ldots, x_n$, with $f_1, f_2, f_3, \ldots, f_n$, frequencies, respectively, then N can be defined as the sum of all frequencies, that is, $N = f_1 + f_2 + f_3 + \cdots + f_n$. Then, geometric mean G is given by

$$G = \left[x_1^{f_1} x_2^{f_2} x_3^{f_3} \cdots x_n^{f_n}\right]^{1/N}$$

Taking logarithms on both sides in the above equation, we have

$$\log G = \frac{1}{N}\left[f_1 \log x_1 + f_2 \log x_2 + \cdots + f_n \log x_n\right]$$

$$\log G = \frac{1}{N}\sum_{i=1}^{n}(f_i \log x_i)$$

The above formula can be used for calculating the geometric mean for a discrete frequency distribution. So, geometric mean for a discrete frequency distribution can be obtained by inserting one more column in the solution (as compared to computing geometric mean for an individual series), that is $\sum_{i=1}^{n}(f_i \log x_i)$. Similarly the geometric mean for a continuous series can be obtained by finding out the mid-value of the interval, in the usual way. Practically, geometric mean is widely used for calculating the average rate of growth. For large data sizes, geometric mean can be used to calculate the average rate of growth or depreciation.

10.5.6 Average Rate of Growth

As mentioned earlier, **geometric mean** is commonly used for the calculation of the average rate of growth. For the same purpose, the following formula is used.

Geometric mean is commonly used in the calculation of average rate of growth.

$$P_n = P_0 (1 + r)^n$$

where P_n is the figure at the end of period n, P_0 is the figure at the beginning of the period, r is the average rate of change, and n the length of the period.
Taking logarithms on both the sides of the above equation, we obtain

$$r = \text{anti log}\left[\frac{\log P_n - \log P_0}{n}\right] - 1$$

Example 10.5

The population of a country increased from 360 million to 380 million from 1991 to 1995. Find the average annual growth rate of population.

Solution The formula for calculating the average annual growth rate is

$$\log(1+r) = \left[\frac{\log P_n - \log P_0}{n}\right]$$

$$1 + r = \text{antilog}\left[\frac{\log 380 - \log 360}{4}\right]$$

$$r = \left\{\text{anti}\log\left[\frac{0.0234}{4}\right]\right\} - 1$$

$$= (1.0135–1)$$

$$= 0.0135$$

$$= 1.35\%$$

Hence, the annual growth rate of the population is 1.35%.

10.5.7 Importance of Geometric Mean

Geometric mean is generally used to compute the average in situations where small items are assigned large weights and large items are assigned smaller weights.

We have already studied how the arithmetic mean can be used as a tool for obtaining averages. But what could be the use of geometric mean? What is the need to use geometric mean as an average tool as we already have averages of various types? The answer lies in the fact that geometric mean is generally used in situations where small items are assigned large weights and vice versa. The following are some of the special uses of geometric mean.

1. Geometric mean is useful for calculating the average percentage increase or decrease.
2. In the construction of index numbers, geometric mean is considered to be the best average tool.

Example 10.6 explains the special use of geometric mean as a tool of computing average percentage increase.

Example 10.6

The price of a commodity increased by 8% from 1993 to 1994, 12% from 1994 to 1995, and 76% from 1995 to 1996. The average price increase from 1994 to 1996 is quoted as 28.64% and not 32%. Explain and verify the result.

Solution Here, the average of the percentage increase over a period of 3 years is to be computed. Thus, geometric mean is the most appropriate average tool. The appropriateness of using geometric mean can also be checked by first computing the average of the growth and then by verifying the result. The arithmetic mean of the percentage increases is

$$\bar{x} = \frac{\Sigma x}{n} = \frac{8+12+76}{3} = 32\%$$

However, an average increase of 32% is not the correct answer (as was clarified in the verification part). To obtain the correct answer, the GM of the percentage increase is to be computed (Table 10.12).

TABLE 10.12
Computation of geometric mean for Example 10.6

Year	*Percentaage increase*	*Price level at the end of the year with the preceding year's level as base = 100 (x)*	*log x*
1993–1994	8	108	2.033423755
1994–1995	12	112	2.049218023
1995–1996	76	176	2.245512668
	Total		$\Sigma \log x = 6.328154446$

$$\text{GM} = \text{antilog}\left(\frac{\Sigma \log x}{N}\right) = \text{antilog}\left(\frac{6.328154446}{3}\right) = 128.64266$$

Therefore, the average increase from 1994 to 1996 is 128.64266 – 100 = 28.64266%. Now, we verify the actual situation (Case 1) by comparing it with the situation where the average increase is 32% (arithmetic average, Case 2), and when the average increase is 28.64266% (geometric mean, Case 3).

Verification

Case 1: When the commodity price increases by 8% from 1993 to 1994, 12% from 1994 to 1995 and 76% from 1995 to 1996 (Table 10.13).

TABLE 10.13
Commodity price from 1994 to 1996

Year	*Rate of increase*	*Total increase*	*Price at the end of each year*
1993–1994	8% on 100	8	100 + 8 = 108
1994–1995	12% on 108	12.96	108 + 12.96 = 120.96
1995–1996	76% on 120.96	91.92	120.96 + 91.92 = 212.88

Case 2: When the average increase is 32% (arithmetic mean) per year (Table 10.14).

TABLE 10.14
Average increase in commodity price is 32% (arithmetic mean) per year.

Year	*Rate of increase*	*Total increase*	*Price at the end of each year*
1993–1994	32% on 100	32	100 + 32 = 132
1994–1995	32% on 132	42.24	132 + 42.24 = 174.24
1995–1996	32% on 174.24	55.75	174.24 + 55.75 = 229.99

Case 3: When average increase is 28.64266% (geometric mean) per year (Table 10.15)

TABLE 10.15
Average increase in commodity price is 28.64266% (geometric mean) per year

Year	*Rate of increase*	*Total increase*	*Price at the end of each year*
1993–1994	28.64266% on 100	28.64266	128.64266
1994–1995	28.64266% on 128.64266	36.84667972	165.4893397
1995–1996	28.64266% on 165.4893397	47.40054891	212.88

From Tables 10.13–10.15, it can be seen very easily that in Cases 1 and 3, the price level at the end of the third year is the same. Hence, geometric mean is an appropriate tool of computing average percentage increase.

10.5.8 Merits and Demerits of Geometric Mean

In situations where the average rate of change has to be calculated over a period of several years the use of arithmetic mean leads to a faulty result (as discussed earlier). In such cases, the geometric mean has been found to be an appropriate tool. However, this does not mean that this average tool is free from limitations. The following are some of the merits and demerits of geometric mean.

10.5.8.1 Merits

1. It is rigidly defined.
2. It is useful in dealing with ratios and percentages and can be very well used in determining the rate of increase or decrease.
3. It is suitable for algebraic treatments. If GM_1 and GM_2 are geometric means of two series and n_1 and n_2 are the number of observations of these two series, respectively, then the *combined geometric mean* can be easily calculated by applying the formula
$$GM_{12} = \text{antilog}\left[\frac{n_1 \log GM_1 + n_2 \log GM_2}{n_1 + n_2}\right].$$
4. Some statistical errors such as fluctuation of sampling have the least effect on it.
5. It is based on all the observations.

10.5.8.2 Demerits

1. It is difficult to compute and understand, therefore, its application is limited.
2. For negative and zero values in a series, it is difficult to apply.

SELF-PRACTICE PROBLEMS

10B1. Compute the geometric mean for the following series.

23	25	32	36	39	41
43	21	47	43		

10B2. A firm purchased an old machine for its manufacturing process. The seller claims that the machine will depreciate 40% in the first year, 30% in the second year, 25% in the third year, and 20% in the fourth year. Compute the average depreciation for all 4 years?

10B3. A detergent company launched a new product in the market in 2001–2002 and planned for massive advertisements to promote the product in the market. The percentage increase in sales from 2003–2004 to 2007–2008 is given below. Compute the average percentage increase in sales from 2003–2004 to 2007–2008.

Year	*Percentage increase in sales*
2003–2004	5
2004–2005	8
2005–2006	12
2006–2007	17
2007–2008	25

10B4. The following data gives the production of wheat (in million tonnes) along with percentage coverage under irrigation in India from 1982–1983 to 2003–2004. Calculate the average production of wheat from 1982–1983 to 1992–1993 and 1993–1994 to 2003–2004. Also compute the average percentage coverage under irrigation from 1982–1983 to 1992–1993 and 1993–1994 to 2003–2004.

Year	*Production of wheat (in million tonnes)*	*Percentage coverage under irrigation*
1982–1983	42.79	72.5
1983–1984	45.48	73
1984–1985	44.07	74.5
1985–1986	47.05	74.6
1986–1987	44.32	76.3
1987–1988	46.17	76.8
1988–1989	54.11	79.2
1989–1990	49.85	80.3
1990–1991	55.14	81.1
1991–1992	55.69	83.7
1992–1993	57.21	84.2
1993–1994	59.84	84.8
1994–1995	65.77	85.2
1995–1996	62.1	85.8
1996–1997	69.35	86.2
1997–1998	66.35	85.8
1998–1999	71.29	85.8
1999–2000	76.37	87.2
2000–2001	69.68	88.1
2001–2002	72.77	87.4
2002–2003	65.76	88
2003–2004	72.16	88.4

Source: www.indiastat.com, accessed October 2008, reproduced with permission

10.5.9 Harmonic Mean

The **harmonic mean** of any series is the reciprocal of the arithmetic mean of the reciprocal of the *variate*, that is, the harmonic mean by definition is given by

$$\frac{1}{H} = \text{Arithmetic mean of } \frac{1}{x_1}, \frac{1}{x_2}, \cdots, \frac{1}{x_n}$$

$$\frac{1}{H} = \frac{1}{x_1} + \frac{1}{x_2} + \cdots + \frac{1}{x_n}$$

$$= \frac{1}{n}\sum_{i=1}^{n}\frac{1}{x_i}$$

$$H = \frac{n}{\sum_{i=1}^{n}\frac{1}{x_i}}$$

Like any other measure of central tendency, harmonic mean can also be calculated in three different ways for three types of distributions. In the following section, we discuss how to compute the harmonic mean for

The harmonic mean of any series is the reciprocal of the arithmetic mean of the reciprocal of the variate

1. an individual series;
2. a discrete frequency distribution; and
3. a continuous frequency distribution.

10.5.9.1 Computation of Harmonic Mean for Individual Series

For a series like $x_1, x_2, x_3, \ldots, x_n$, the harmonic mean is given by

$$\frac{1}{H} = \frac{1}{x_1} + \frac{1}{x_2} + \cdots + \frac{1}{x_n}$$

$$= \frac{1}{n}\sum_{i=1}^{n}\frac{1}{x_i}$$

$$H = \frac{n}{\sum_{i=1}^{n}\frac{1}{x_i}}$$

Example 10.7

Calculate the harmonic mean of the following items:
2.0, 1.5, 3.0, 10.0, 250.0, 0.5, 0.905, 0.095, 2000, 0.099

Solution

To compute harmonic mean, we have to first compute the reciprocals of each item as given in Table 10.16.

TABLE 10.16
Computation of harmonic mean for Example 10.7

Size of item (x)	*Reciprocal (1/x)*
2	0.5
1.5	0.6666
3	0.3333
10	0.1
250	0.004
0.5	2
0.905	1.1049
0.095	10.5263
2000	0.0005
0.099	10.1010
$n = 10$	$\sum \frac{1}{x} = 25.3367$

$$\text{HM} = \text{Reciprocal of} \left[\frac{25.3367}{10}\right]$$

= Reciprocal (2.53367)

= 0.39468

10.5.9.2 Computation of Harmonic Mean for Discrete Frequency Distribution and Continuous Frequency Distribution

For a discrete frequency distribution, frequencies are also given with individual values. So, for a discrete frequency distribution, the formula includes these frequencies and takes the form

$$\frac{1}{H} = \frac{\sum_{i=1}^{n} f_i\left(\frac{1}{x_i}\right)}{\sum_{i=1}^{n} f_i}1$$

$$\text{or} \qquad H = \frac{N}{\sum_{i=1}^{n} f_i \left(\frac{1}{x_i} \right)}$$

$$\text{where} \sum_{i=1}^{n} f_i = N$$

In the case of a continuous series, the same formula can be applied and the mid-values of the classes are taken as x_is. Example 10.8 clarifies the procedure for calculating the geometric mean and harmonic mean for a continuous series.

Example 10.8

Table 10.17 shows the salary ranges (in thousand rupees) and the number of employees for a manufacturing firm.

TABLE 10.17
Salary range of the number for employees for a manufacturing firm

Salary range (in thousand rupees)	*Number of employees*
50–60	12
60–70	15
70–80	20
80–90	44
90–100	42
100–110	32
110–120	32
120–130	12
Total	209

Calculate the geometric mean and harmonic mean for the frequency distribution of salaries.

Solution See Table 10.18 for the compution of Geometric mean and Harmonic mean.

TABLE 10.18
Computation of geometric mean and harmonic mean for Example 10. 8

Salary (in thousand rupees)	*Midpoint (x)*	*f*	*f/x*	*log x*	*f·log x*
50–60	55.0	12	0.2181	1.7403	20.8843
60–70	65.0	15	0.2307	1.8129	27.1937
70–80	75.0	20	0.2666	1.8750	37.5012
80–90	85.0	44	0.5176	1.9294	84.8944
90–100	95.0	42	0.4421	1.9777	83.0643
100–110	105.0	32	0.3047	2.0211	64.6780
110–120	115.0	32	0.2782	2.0606	65.9423
120–130	125.0	12	0.096	2.0969	25.1629
Total		209	2.354		409.3211

$$\text{GM} = \text{antilog}\left[\frac{\Sigma f \log x}{N}\right] = \text{antilog}\left[\frac{409.3211}{209}\right]$$

$$= \text{antilog}\,(1.9584) = 90.88$$

$$\text{HM} = \frac{N}{\sum \frac{f}{x}} = \frac{209}{2.354} = 88.78$$

10.5.10 Weighted Harmonic Mean

In some cases, the computation of weighted harmonic mean becomes very important. For example, when a researcher has to compute different distances with different speeds, the average speed can be computed using weighted harmonic mean. The formula for calculating weighted harmonic mean is

$$\text{Weighted harmonic mean} = \frac{\Sigma w}{\Sigma w / x}$$

where x is the value of the item and w the weights attached to the corresponding items.

10.5.11 Importance of Harmonic Mean

Harmonic mean is specifically used in the computation of average speed, average price, average profit, etc. under various conditions.

Harmonic mean is specifically used in the computation of average speed, average price, average profit, etc. under various conditions. The rates which are usually averaged by harmonic mean indicate a relationship between two measuring units which can be reciprocally expressed. For example, if a bus travels 100 km in 4 hours, then its speed can be expressed as

$$\frac{100\text{km}}{4\text{h}} = 25 \text{ kmph}$$

Here, the unit of distance travelled is kilometres and the unit of time is hours. The above equation can be reciprocally expressed as

$$\frac{4\text{h}}{100\text{km}} = 0.4 \text{ hpkm.}$$

So, when the average of different speeds (expressed in kilometres per hour) or the average price of certain commodities (given in per rupee) is to be computed, the harmonic mean is an appropriate averaging tool.

Example 10.9

X started a journey to a village 9 km away from his house. He travelled by car driving at a speed of 40 kmph. After travelling 6 km, the car stopped running. He then travelled by rickshaw at a speed of 10 kmph. After travelling a distance of 2.0 km, he left the rickshaw and covered the remaining distance on foot at a speed of 4 kmph. Find his average speed and verify the calculation.

Solution In this case, weighted arithmetic mean can be computed as

$$\frac{40+10+4}{3} = 18 \text{ kmph}$$

This may not be a correct answer (see verification). The correct answer can be obtained by calculating the harmonic mean (Table 10.19).

The problem can be solved with the help of weighted harmonic mean.

TABLE 10.19
Computation of harmonic mean for Example 10.9

Speed x	*Distance w (km)*	*w/x*
40	6	0.15
10	2	0.2
4	1	0.25
Sum	9	0.6

$$\text{Average speed} = \frac{\Sigma w}{\Sigma w/x} = \frac{9}{0.6} = 15 \text{ kmph}$$

Verification (Table 10.20)

TABLE 10.20
Verification part (actual situation) of Example 10.9

Mode of conveyance	*Distance (Km)*	*Speed (kmph)*	*Time taken (min)*
Car	6.00	40	9
Rickshaw	2.00	10	12
On foot	1	4	15
Total	9		36

Total distance travelled = 9 km

Total time taken = 36 min

In 36 min, he covers 9 km

$$\text{In 60 min, he will cover} = \frac{9}{36} \times 60$$

$$= 15 \text{ km}$$

Hence, x's average speed per hour is 15 kmph which is equal to the computed harmonic mean.

10.5.12 Relationship Between AM, GM, and HM

There exists a defined relationship between arithmetic mean, geometric mean, and harmonic mean. This relationship is

1. AM ≥ GM ≥ HM
   When all the observations are same, the equality sign holds, that is,
   AM = GM = HM (When all the observations are equal).
2. For any two observations,
   $(GM)^2 = (AM) \times (HM)$
   $GM = \sqrt{(AM) \times (HM)}$

Example 10.10 Calculate AM, GM, and HM for the observations 2, 4, 8, 12, and 16, and show that AM > GM > HM.

Solution

$$AM = \frac{\Sigma x}{n} = \frac{2+4+8+12+16}{5} = \frac{42}{5} = 8.4$$

$$GM = \text{antilog } \frac{\Sigma \log x}{n}$$

$$= \text{antilog } \frac{\log 2 + \log 4 + \log 8 + \log 12 + \log 16}{5}$$

$$= \text{antilog } \frac{0.3010 + 0.6021 + 0.9031 + 1.0792 + 1.2041}{5}$$

$$GM = \text{antilog } \left(\frac{4.0895}{5}\right) = \text{antilog } (0.8179) = 6.575$$

$$HM = \frac{n}{\Sigma 1/x}$$

$$= \frac{5}{1.0208}$$

$$= 4.89$$

Thus, we can see that AM > GM > HM.

Example 10.11 The AM of two numbers is 10; the GM of these numbers is 8. Find the HM of these numbers.

Solution We know that

$$(GM)^2 = (AM) \times (HM)$$

$$8^2 = 10 \times HM$$

$$HM = \frac{8^2}{10} = \frac{64}{10} = 6.4$$

10.5.13 Merits and Demerits of Harmonic Mean

Although harmonic mean is based upon all the observations and gives weightage to smaller values, its application is limited because of its shortcomings. It is useful in cases where small items need to be given very high weightage. The following are some of the merits and demerits of harmonic mean.

10.5.13.1 Merits

1. It is based on all the observations.
2. It is suitable for algebraic treatment.
3. It gives more importance to smaller values.

10.5.13.2 Demerits

1. It is difficult to compute.
2. When there are positive and negative values in a series or when one or more items are zero, then it is difficult to compute.
3. It gives more importance to smaller values. This merit of harmonic mean is a demerit in itself. This property of harmonic mean becomes a hindrance in its wide use with regard to economical data.

SELF-PRACTICE PROBLEMS

10C1. Compute the harmonic mean from the following data series:
4.0; 3.5; 5.0; 11.0; 340.0; 0.8; 0.804; 0.0 40; 5000; 0.088.

10C2. Compute the harmonic mean from the following distribution:

Class interval	*Frequency*
0–50	7
50–100	10
100–150	15
150–200	18
200–250	21
250–300	17
300–350	16

10.6 POSITIONAL AVERAGES

Positional averages mainly focus on the position of the value of an observation in the data set

Arithmetic mean, geometric mean, and harmonic mean are all mathematical in nature and are measures of quantitative characteristics of data. To measure the qualitative characteristics of data, other measures of central tendency, namely median and mode are used. **Positional averages**, as the name indicates, mainly focus on the position of the value of an observation in the data set.

10.6.1 Median

The median may be defi ned as the middle or central value of the variable when values are arranged in the order of magnitude.

The **median** of a distribution is the value of the variable that divides it into two equal parts so that one half of the data has values less than the median while the other half has values greater than the median. Median may be defined as the middle or central value of the variable when values are arranged in the order of magnitude. In other words, median is defined as that value of the variable that divides the group into two equal parts, one part comprising all values greater and the other all values lesser than the median.

10.6.2 Calculation of Median

As discussed earlier (Section 10.5), the calculation of median can also be broadly classified into three categories:

1. Median for the individual series.
2. Median for the discrete frequency distribution.
3. Median for the continuous frequency distribution.

10.6.2.1 Computation of Median for the Individual Series

In this type of distribution, data can be arranged in ascending or descending order. If there are n terms (observations) in the data, there can be two cases:

Case 1: If n (number of observations) is odd, then the middle term of the series is the $\left(\frac{n+1}{2}\right)$th term and is the value of the median.

Case 2: If n (number of observations) is even, then there will be two middle terms. These will be the $\frac{n}{2}$th term and $\left(\frac{n}{2}+1\right)$th term. In this case, the arithmetic mean of their value will be considered to be the value of the median.

The following two examples are based on Case 1 (Example 10.12) and Case 2 (Example 10.13) for computing median.

Example 10.12

The consumption of printing paper reams (in units) for the first 11 months of a computer operator is given as

10, 11, 12, 15, 18, 22, 8, 10, 12, 15, 25

Find the median.

Solution

By arranging the data in ascending order, we get the series

8, 10, 10, 11, 12, 12, 15, 15, 18, 22, 25

The number of terms in this series is 11 which is odd.

Hence, the required median (M_d) = value of the $\frac{(11+1)}{2}$th observation

= value of the 6th observation = 12.

Example 10.13

Table 10.21 relates to the monthly salaries of employees (in thousand rupees). Compute the median salary of the employees.

TABLE 10.21
Monthly salaries of employees

Employee	1	2	3	4	5	6	7	8	9	10
Salary	120	135	132	128	148	136	138	151	153	150

Solution

To compute the median, we first arrange the data in ascending order.

120, 128, 132, 135, 136, 138, 148, 150, 151, 153

This data series contains 10 items. As the number of observations in this data series is even, median will be the average of $\frac{n}{2}$th term and $\left(\frac{n}{2}+1\right)$th term, that is, average of $\frac{10}{2}$th term and $\left(\frac{10}{2}+1\right)$th term.

Hence, median will be the average of the 5th and 6th term.

So, median (M_d) is $\frac{136+138}{2}=137$

Thus, the median salary is ₹137,000.

10.6.2.2 Computation of Median for a Discrete Frequency Distribution

In the case of a discrete series, median can be calculated by using the following steps:

1. Arrange the data in ascending or descending order of magnitude.
2. Obtain cumulative frequencies.
3. Size of $\left(\frac{N+1}{2}\right)$th item must be determined, when N is the total of all the frequency, that is, $\sum_{i=1}^{n} f_i = N$.
4. The value for which cumulative frequency includes $\left(\frac{N+1}{2}\right)$th item is taken as the median.

Example 10.14

Calculate the median for the values and frequencies given in Table 10.22.

TABLE 10.22
Values and frequencies for Example 10.14

Value	2	3	4	5	6	7	8	9	10	11	12	13	14	15
Frequency	2	3	8	10	12	16	10	8	6	5	6	4	3	1

Solution

As a first step we calculate the cumulative frequencies (as shown in Table 10.23).

$$\text{Size of } \left(\frac{N+1}{2}\right)\text{th item} = \left(\frac{94+1}{2}\right)\text{th item} = 47.5$$

TABLE 10.23
Computation of median for Example 10.14

Value	*Frequency*	*Cumulative frequency*
2	2	2
3	3	5
4	8	13
5	10	23
6	12	35
7	16	51
8	10	61
9	8	69
10	6	75
11	5	80
12	6	86
13	4	90
14	3	93
15	1	94

Median is the value for which cumulative frequency includes 47.5th value. Cumulative frequency 51 of value 7 includes 47.5th value. Hence the median is 7.

10.6.2.3 Determination of Median for a Continuous Frequency Distribution

As in a discrete frequency distribution, in case of a continuous series also cumulative frequencies are calculated. As a next step the size of $N/2$th item is computed (N being the total frequency). Then, the median class in the cumulative frequencies column where the size of $N/2$th item falls is located. Then, the following formula is applied to calculate median:

$$\text{Median} = l + \frac{(N/2) - c}{f} \times i$$

where l is the lower limit of the median class, N the sum of the frequencies, c the cumulative frequency of the class preceding the median class, and i the width of the median class. Note that in the case of a continuous frequency distribution, the size of $N/2$th item is to be computed. In the case of individual series and discrete frequency distribution, size of the $\left(\frac{N+1}{2}\right)$th item was computed because we wanted to compute specific items or individual values that divides the data into two equal parts. In the case of a continuous frequency distribution, however, the individuality of frequencies is lost and we try to find out a specific point in the curve that divides it into two equal parts (half of the frequencies are on the one side the curve and half the frequencies on the other side of the curve). $N/2$ divides the curve area into two equal parts, not $\left(\frac{N+1}{2}\right)$. Hence, we use $\frac{N}{2}$ instead of $\left(\frac{N+1}{2}\right)$ for the computation of median in a continuous frequency distribution.

Example 10.15

Delta Tiers employed 159 employees for a factory located at Kanpur. The company's management is worried about the high absenteeism rate in the organization. Before taking any corrective action, the management has decided to calculate the median leaves availed by the employees. Table 10.24 shows vacations availed in a year and the number of employees who availed vacations. Compute median from the data.

TABLE 10.24
Vacations availed in a year and the number of employees who availed vacation

Vacations availed in a year	0–10	10–20	20–30	30–40	40–50	50–60	60–70	70–80
Number of employees	2	18	30	45	35	20	6	3

Solution For computing the median, for a continuous frequency distribution we have to compute cumulative frequencies as shown in Table 10.25.

TABLE 10.25
Computation of median for Example 10.15

Vacations availed	*Number of employees (f)*	*Cumulative frequency (cf)*
0–10	2	2
10–20	18	20
20–30	30	50
30–40	45	95
40–50	35	130
50–60	20	150
60–70	6	156
70–80	3	159
Sum	$\sum_{i=1}^{n} f_i = N = 159$	

Here $N = 159$, which is an odd number.

$\frac{N}{2} = \frac{159}{2} = 79.5$, which falls in the class 30–40 (see the row of the cumulative frequency 95 which contains 79.5). Hence the median class is 30–40.

l = lower limit of median class = 30

f = frequency of median class = 45

c = total of all frequencies preceding median class = 50

i = width of class interval of median class = 10

$$\text{Median} = l + \frac{\left(\frac{N}{2}\right) - c}{f} \times i$$

$$= 30 + \frac{\left(\frac{159}{2}\right) - 50}{45} \times 10 = 30 + \frac{79.5 - 50}{45} \times 10$$

$$= 30 + \left(\frac{29.5}{45} \times 10\right) = 30 + \frac{295}{45} = 30 + \frac{59}{9}$$

$$= 30 + 6.55 = 36.55$$

10.6.3 Merits and Demerits of Median

Median has several advantages over mean. More importantly, as compared to arithmetic mean, median is *the least* affected by extreme values. The following is a list of merits and demerits of median.

10.6.3.1 Merits

1. It is well defined, and based on all observations. Therefore, it can be easily computed.
2. Extreme values do not affect the median as strongly as the mean.
3. Median can be computed even when data is of qualitative nature such as colour, honesty, beauty, etc.

10.6.3.2 Demerits

1. As median is a positional average, data must be arranged in order before any calculation can be performed.
2. Median computation can be time-consuming for any data set with a large number of elements.
3. It is not suitable for algebraic treatment.
4. Sometimes it may not be a true representative of data.

SELF-PRACTICE PROBLEMS

10D1. Compute the median for the series given in Problem 10A1.

10D2. Compute the median for the series given in Problem 10A2.

10D3. ICICI Bank is a key bank in India with a solid international presence. In May 2002, it merged with Industrial Credit Investment Corporation of India Limited (ICICI Ltd). Later two more companies, ICICI Personal Financial Services and ICICI Capital Services, came under the umbrella of the merged entity. After the merger ICICI Bank became the second largest bank in India after State Bank of India. The following data gives the quarterly income figures of ICICI Bank from March 2003 to March 2007. Compute the mean and median from the income figures.

Quarter	*Income (in million rupees)*
Mar 2003	30,157.8
Jun 2003	29,527.4
Sep 2003	30,728.8
Dec 2003	30,329.4
Mar 2004	30,036.7
Jun 2004	29,267.6
Sep 2004	30,659.2
Dec 2004	33,196.5
Mar 2005	36,744.6
Jun 2005	42,064.9
Sep 2005	44,408.8
Dec 2005	47,627.8
Mar 2006	55,074.5
Jun 2006	60,496.6
Sep 2006	67,968.2
Dec 2006	75,814.6
Mar 2007	84,955.2

Source: Prowess (V. 3.1), Centre for Monitoring Indian Economy Pvt. Ltd, Mumbai, accessed September 2008, reproduced with permission.

10D4. TVS Srichakra is one of India's leading two- and three-wheeler tyre manufacturing companies. The growth in the automobile industry has contributed to a growth in the tyre industry. The following data depicts the quarterly net sales of TVS Srichakra from June 1998 to March 2007. Find the average net sales and median net sales from the data.

Quarter	*Net sales*
Jun 1998	308.3
Sep 1998	327.6
Dec 1998	329.7
Mar 1999	345.9
Jun 1999	349.3
Sep 1999	358.4
Dec 1999	354.5
Mar 2000	344.6
Jun 2000	372.5
Sep 2000	359.6
Dec 2000	364.1
Mar 2001	347.5
Jun 2001	355.1
Sep 2001	392
Dec 2001	432.9
Mar 2002	442
Jun 2002	492.3
Sep 2002	545.8
Dec 2002	562.9
Mar 2003	479.9
Jun 2003	524.2
Sep 2003	534.3
Dec 2003	491.4
Mar 2004	480.5
Jun 2004	457.3
Sep 2004	458
Dec 2004	543.2
Mar 2005	528.9
Jun 2005	609
Sep 2005	707.8
Dec 2005	767.2
Mar 2006	847.6
Jun 2006	952.2
Sep 2006	1107.2
Dec 2006	1078.3
Mar 2007	1025.8

Source: Prowess (V. 3.1), Centre for Monitoring Indian Economy Pvt. Ltd, Mumbai, accessed September 2008, reproduced with permission.

10D5. An insurance company obtained the following data for accident claims from a particular region. Obtain the median from this data.

Amount of claim (in thousand rupees)	*Frequency*
10–20	13
20–30	15
30–40	25
40–50	36
50–60	45
60–70	32
70–80	23
80–90	17

10.6.4 Mode

Mode is the variate having the maximum frequency in a data series.

Mode is defined as the value that is repeated most often in the data set. It is the value of the variate having the maximum frequency in a data series. The mode of a distribution is the value at the point around which the items tend to be most heavily concentrated. In other words, the value of the variable which occurs most frequently in a distribution is called the mode.

A distribution which has a single mode is called a unimodal distribution, and a distribution which has two modes is called a bimodal distribution.

In a distribution, there may be one, two, or more than two modes. A distribution which has a single mode is called ***unimodal*** distribution and a distribution which has two modes is called a ***bimodal*** distribution (Figures 10.1 and 10.2).

For a frequency distribution, for which a curve is drawn, the mode is the value of the variable at which the curve reaches its *peak* or *maximum*. In a bimodal distribution, we can observe two peaks or two maximum points, which state that these points are higher than the neighbouring values in terms of frequencies with which they are observed. Figures 10.1 and 10.2 exhibit unimodal and bimodal distributions.

The concept of a mode is widely used in production. For example, a shoe manufacturer will produce shoes of a size that will fit the maximum number of customers. A customer who has a large shoe size, say size 11, may find it difficult to buy a shoe that fits him.

Using mode as an average tool, we can overcome some drawbacks of the measures of mathematical average (arithmetic mean) and positional average (median). There are many situations in which arithmetic mean and median fail to reveal the true characteristics of data. For example, in the presence of extreme values in a data series, the arithmetic mean may not be an appropriate averaging tool. Similarly, the median may not be a true representative of data owing to the uneven nature of the distribution. As already discussed, median is the value which divides the data into two equal parts. For example, in a data series consisting of values from 0 to 1000, it is possible that the lower part of the distribution ranges from 0 to 10 and the upper part of the distribution ranges from 10 to 1000. In such a case, the median value 10 is not a true central representative of the data. Both these drawbacks of mean and median may be tackled by using mode, which is the value of the variable which occurs most frequently in a distribution.

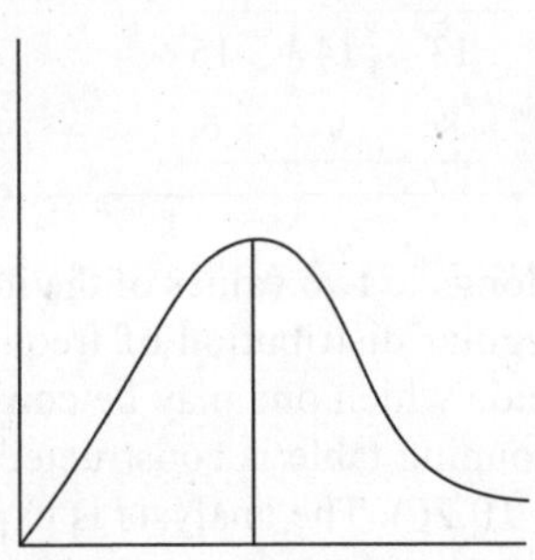

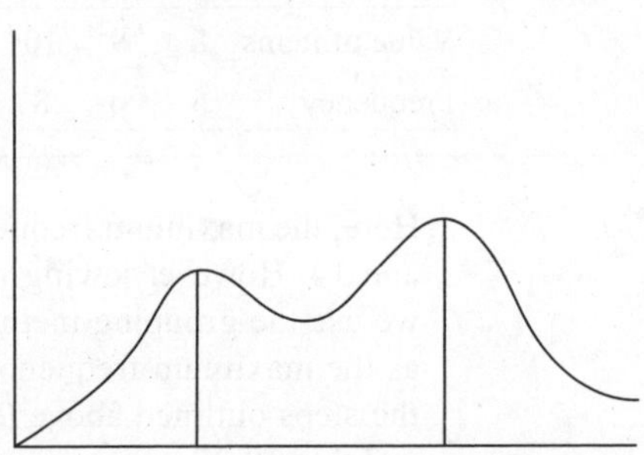

FIGURE 10.1
Unimodal distribution

FIGURE 10.2
Bimodal distribution with two unequal modes

10.6.5 Determination of Mode

Like every other method of determining various averages, mode can also be determined differently in three types of distribution: mode in an individual series, a discrete frequency distribution, and a continuous frequency distribution. As a first case, we take into consideration the mode in an individual series.

10.6.5.1 Computation of Mode for the Individual Series

In the case of an individual series, data is arranged in order and mode can be determined by inspection *only*. The value of the variable (in data series) which occurs the most or the value of the data series with maximum frequency is the mode of the data series. For example, for a series 1, 1, 3, 3, 3, 3, 4, 5, 8, 8, 16, 16 (arranged in the order of magnitude), observation 3 has the maximum frequency 4. Therefore, mode of the series is 3.

10.6.5.2 Computation of Mode for Discrete Frequency Distribution

By this method, mode can be determined very easily (the value with the maximum frequency), but in the case of repeated frequency distribution, irregular distribution, and in cases where maximum frequency occurs in the very beginning or at the end of the distribution, mode cannot be determined by this method. The modal value is determined by applying grouping method. The grouping method can be performed in three steps, which are (1) preparation of grouping table, (2) preparation of analysis table, and (3) finding the mode.

Preparation of grouping table

In a grouping table, normally there are six columns. If necessary more columns may be constructed. The details of these six columns are explained below:

Column 1: Original frequencies (given in the data).
Column 2: Given frequencies are added in twos and the highest total is marked.
Column 3: Leaving the first frequency, the remaining frequencies are added in twos and the highest total is marked.
Column 4: Given frequencies are added in threes and the highest total is marked.
Column 5: Leaving the first frequency, the given frequencies are added in threes.
Column 6: Leaving the first two frequencies, the given frequencies are added in threes.

The preparation of the analysis table and finding the mode are explained with the help of Example 10.16.

Example 10.16

Calculate the mode from the following series:

Value of items	8	9	10	11	12	13	14	15
Frequency	5	6	8	7	9	8	9	6

Solution

Here, the maximum frequency 9 belongs to two values of the items 12 and 14. However, owing to the irregular distribution of frequencies, we use the grouping method to decide which one may be considered as the maximum frequency. The grouping table is constructed as per the steps outlined above (see Table 10.26). The analysis is explained in Table 10.27.

TABLE 10.26
Grouping table for Example 10.16

Value of the items (x)	*Frequency or sum of frequencies* 1	2	3	4	5	6	*Analysis table*	
8	5	11						
9	6		14	19				
10	8	15			21		I	1
11	7		16			**24**	II	2
12	9	**17**		**24**			IIIII	5
13	8		**17**		**26**		IIII	4
14	9	15				23	III	3
15	6							

Note: Bold and underlined numbers indicate the highest total under each column.

TABLE 10.27
Separate analysis table for Example 10.16

Column no.	*Size of items containing maximum frequency* 10	11	12	13	14
1			12		14
2			12	13	
3				13	14
4		11	12	13	
5			12	13	14
6	10	11	12		
Number of items	**1**	**2**	**5**	**4**	**3**

As 12 occurs the maximum number of times (5), the value 12 is the mode.

10.6.5.3 Computation of Mode for Continuous Frequency Distribution

In a continuous frequency distribution, first the modal class is determined. This can be determined either by inspection or by grouping method. The required mode lies within the limits of this modal class and is determined by the following formula:

$$M_0 = l + \frac{f_1 - f_0}{2f_1 - f_0 - f_2} \times i$$

where M_0 is the mode, l the lower limit of the modal class, f_1 the frequency of the modal class, f_0 the frequency of the class preceding the modal class, f_2 the frequency of the class succeeding the modal class, and i the width of the modal class.

The above formula is useful for exclusive and equal class intervals in ascending order. If the mode lies in the first class interval, then f_0 is taken to be zero. If the mode lies in the last class interval, then f_2 is taken to be zero.

10.6.6 Merits and Demerits of Mode

Like the other measures of central tendency, mode has its own advantages and disadvantages. It is widely used in the industry. The following are some common advantages and disadvantages of mode:

10.6.6.1 Merits

1. It is easy to understand and calculate. It can be detected by a mere look at the graph.
2. It is very useful in industries.

10.6.6.2 Demerits

1. It is not based on all the observations.
2. When data sets contain two, three, or many modes, they are difficult to interpret and compare.
3. It is neither based on all the observations nor is it suitable for algebraic treatment.

10.6.7 An Empirical Relation Between Mean, Median, and Mode

The relationship between mean, median, and mode depends upon the shape of the frequency curve; in other words, the relationship between mean, median, and mode depends upon the type of frequency distribution. For a *symmetrical* distribution (Figure 10.3(a)), mean, median, and mode all coincide. That is, mean = median = mode: $\bar{x} = M_d = M_o$. In the case of a negatively (left) skewed curve (Figure 10.3(b)), mean < median < mode, that is $\bar{x} < M_d < M_o$, where as in the case of a positively skewed (right) curve (Figure 10.3(c)), mean > median > mode, that is $\bar{x} > M_d > M_o$.

For a moderately asymmetrical frequency distribution, the empirical relationship between mean, median, and mode is given by Karl Pearson and is defined as

$$\text{Mode} = 3(\text{Median}) - 2(\text{Mean})$$

If any two values are known, the third value can be easily determined.

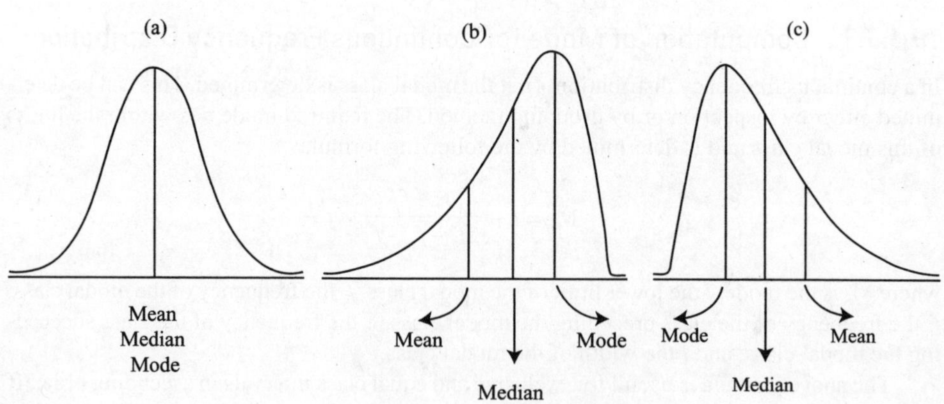

FIGURE 10.3 Comparison between mean, median, and mode for (a) symmetrical, (b) negatively skewed, and (c) positively skewed distribution

SELF-PRACTICE PROBLEMS

10E1. Compute the mode for the series given in Problem 10A1.

10E2. Maruti Suzuki, India's leading company in the passenger car segment, launched various brands to cater to the diverse requirements of the Indian automobile market. In 1983, it captured the market with Maruti 800 model. It has a great national reach in terms of presence in almost all the major cities of every state in the country. The quarterly gross sales of Maruti Suzuki from December 2002 to March 2007 is given below. Compute the average, median, and mode from the table.

Quarter	*Gross sales (in million rupees)*	*Quarter*	*Gross sales (in million rupees)*
Dec 2002	22,579.2	Mar 2005	37,274.1
Mar 2003	26,759.9	Jun 2005	32,247.1
Jun 2003	24,583.5	Sep 2005	37,155.7
Sep 2003	26,105.9	Dec 2005	38,251.4
Dec 2003	27,477.6	Mar 2006	39,799.9
Mar 2004	33,827.4	Jun 2006	36,782.9
Jun 2004	30,055.2	Sep 2006	40,021.3
Sep 2004	32,030.6	Dec 2006	43,077.6
Dec 2004	34,070.7	Mar 2007	51,675

Source: Prowess (V. 3.1), Centre for Monitoring Indian Economy Pvt. Ltd, Mumbai, accessed September 2008, reproduced with permission.

10.7 PARTITION VALUES: QUARTILES, DECILES, AND PERCENTILES

Median is the value which divides the data into two equal parts. **Partition values** are measures that divide the data into several equal parts. There are three type of partition values: quartiles, deciles, and percentiles. *Quartiles* divide data into four equal parts, *deciles* divide data into *ten* equal parts, and *percentiles* divide data into hundred equal parts. The method of computing these partitional values is similar to the method of computing median. The only difference can be observed in terms of location of the partition value.

Partition values are measures that divide the data into several equal parts. Quartiles divide data into 4 equal parts, deciles divide data into 10 equal parts, and percentiles divide data into 100 equal parts.

10.7.1 Quartiles

As discussed earlier, after arranging the data in an ordered sequence, **quartiles** divide the data into four equal parts using three quartiles: Q_1, Q_2, and Q_3. The first quartile is generally denoted by Q_1 and is the value for which 25% of the observations $\left(\frac{n}{4}\right)$ are smaller than Q_1 and 75% of the observations $3\left(\frac{n}{4}\right)$ are larger than Q_1. The third quartile, generally denoted by Q_3, is the value for which 75% of the observations $3\left(\frac{n}{4}\right)$ are smaller than Q_3 and 25% of the observations $\left(\frac{n}{4}\right)$ are larger than Q_3. The second quartile, generally denoted by the Q_2, is the value for which 50% of the observations are smaller than Q_2 and 50% of the observations are larger than Q_2. Hence, the second quartile is nothing but the median. In the following section, we discuss the procedure for calculating quartiles for an individual series, a discrete frequency distribution, and a continuous frequency distribution.

10.7.1.1 First and Third Quartiles for Individual Series

For an individual series, the first and third quartiles can be computed using the following formula:

$$Q_1 = \text{First quartile or lower quartile} = \frac{n+1}{4} \text{ ordered observation}$$

$$Q_3 = \text{Third quartile or upper quartile} = \frac{3(n+1)}{4} \text{ ordered observation}$$

Example 10.17

From the following data, find the first and third quartiles.

Serial No.	1	2	3	4	5	6	7
Daily wages (in hundred rupees)	8	10	15	27	35	42	50

Solution

The first and third quartiles can be computed by applying the formula discussed above. The data is already arranged in an ordered manner:

Q_1 is the size of $\left(\frac{n+1}{4}\right)$th item = size of $\left(\frac{7+1}{4}\right)$th item = size of 2nd item

Hence, $Q_1 = 10$

Q_3 is the size of $3\left(\frac{n+1}{4}\right)$th item = size of $3\left(\frac{7+1}{4}\right)$th item = size of 6th item

Hence, $Q_3 = 42$.

When the number of items are even in a data series, quartiles can be computed differently, as shown in Example 10.18.

Example 10.18

From the following data, find the first and third quartiles.
15 20 30 40 50 64 70 75

Solution

Q_1 is the size of $\left(\frac{n+1}{4}\right)$th item = size of $\left(\frac{8+1}{4}\right)$th item = 2.25th value

Q_1 = 2nd value + 0.25(3rd value – 2nd value) = 20 + 0.25(30 – 20) = 20 + 2.5 = 22.5

Q_3 is the size of $3\left(\frac{n+1}{4}\right)$th item = size of $3\left(\frac{8+1}{4}\right)$th item = 6.75th value

Q_3 = 6th value + 0.75(7th value – 6th value) = 64 + 0.75 (70 – 64) = 64 + 4.5 = 68.5

Hence, first quartile Q_1 = 22.5 and third quartile Q_3 = 68.5.

10.7.1.2 First and Third Quartiles for Discrete Series

The quartiles for a discrete series can also be computed using the formula discussd above. Q_1 is the size of $\left(\frac{N+1}{4}\right)$th item and Q_3 is the size of $3\left(\frac{N+1}{4}\right)$th item. Here, $N = \Sigma f$.

10.7.1.3 First and Third Quartiles for Continuous Series

The first and third quartiles for a continuous series can be computed by applying the formula given below:

$$Q_1 = l + \frac{(N/4) - c}{f} \times i \quad \text{and} \quad Q_3 = l + \frac{(3N/4) - c}{f} \times i$$

where l is the lower limit of the quartile class, f the frequency of the quartile class, i the class interval of the quartile class, c the total of all the frequency below the quartile class, and N the total frequency ($N = \Sigma f$).

The quartile class can be located in the cumulative frequency column, where the size of $\frac{N}{4}$-th and $\frac{3N}{4}$-th item falls.

Example 10.19

Calculate the first and third quartiles from the data given below.

TABLE 10.28
Class and frequencies for Example 10.19

Class	0–5	5–10	10–15	15–20	20–25	25–30	30–35	35–40
Frequency	4	5	6	10	11	9	4	1

Solution As discussed earlier, we know that

$$Q_1 = l + \frac{(N/4) - c}{f} \times i \quad \text{and} \quad Q_3 = l + \frac{(3N/4) - c}{f} \times i$$

where l is the lower limit of the quartile class, f the frequency of the quartile class, i the class interval of the quartile class, c the total of all the frequencies below the quartile class, and N the total frequency ($N = \Sigma f$).

TABLE 10.29
Class, frequencies, and cumulative frequencies for Example 10.19

Class	*Frequency*	*Cumulative frequency*
0–5	4	4
5–10	5	9
10–15	**6**	**15**
15–20	10	25
20–25	11	36
25–30	**9**	**45**
30–35	4	49
35–40	1	50

Here, $\frac{N}{4} = \frac{50}{4} = 12.5$

Hence, lower quartile class is 10–15 (Table 10.29).

$$Q_1 = l + \frac{(N/4) - c}{f} \times i$$

$$= 10 + \frac{12.5 - 9}{6} \times 5$$

$$= 10 + 2.91$$
$$= 12.91$$
$$\left[3\frac{N}{4} = 3 \times \frac{50}{4} = 37.5\right.$$

Hence, upper quartile class is 25 – 30 (Table 10.29)

$$Q_3 = l + \frac{3\ (N/4) - c}{f} \times i$$
$$= 25 + \frac{37.5 - 36}{9} \times 5$$
$$= 25 + 0.83$$
$$= 25.83$$

So, first quartile $Q_1 = 12.91$ and third quartile $Q_3 = 25.83$.

10.7.2 Merits and Demerits of Quartiles

Quartiles are the most widely used measures of non-central locations, but they are not free from drawbacks. While calculating quartiles, the upper 25% and the lower 25% of the data remain unnoticed. However, quartiles are less affected by the presence of extreme values. Hence, quartiles possess some merits as well as some demerits. The following is a list of the merits and demerits of quartiles.

10.7.2.1 Merits

1. It is easy to calculate and simple to understand.
2. Quartiles are less affected by the presence of extreme values.

10.7.2.1 Demerits

1. Quartiles are not based on all the observations. In fact, 50% of the items in any series is ignored. In other words, it does not cover the first 25% and the last 25% items of a series.
2. It is not suitable for further mathematical treatment.
3. Its value is very much affected by sampling fluctuations.

10.7.3 Deciles

In a data series, when observations are arranged in an ordered sequence, deciles divide the data into 10 equal parts.

In a data series, when the observations are arranged in an ordered sequence, **deciles** divide the data into 10 equal parts. In the case of individual series and discrete frequency distribution, the generalized formula for computing deciles is given as

$$D_k = \frac{k(N+1)}{10}$$

where $k = 1, 2, 3, \ldots, 9$ and $N = \sum f$. Hence, $D_1 = \frac{1 \cdot (N+1)}{10}$ and $D_9 = \frac{9 \cdot (N+1)}{10}$

In the case of a continuous frequency distribution, the generalized formula for deciles is given as

$$D_k = l + \frac{(kN/10) - c}{f} \times i$$

where $k = 1, 2, 3, \ldots, 9$. Other symbolic notations are as explained earlier.

10.7.4 Percentiles

In a data series, when observations are arranged in an ordered sequence, **percentiles** divide the data into 100 equal parts. For an individual series and a discrete frequency distribution, the generalized formula for computing percentiles is given as

$$P_k = \frac{k(N+1)}{100}$$

where $k = 1, 2, 3, \ldots, 99$ and $N = \Sigma f$. Hence, $P_1 = \frac{1\cdot(N+1)}{100}$ and $P_{99} = \frac{99\cdot(N+1)}{100}$

In the case of a continuous frequency distribution, the generalized formula for computing percentiles is given as

$$P_k = l + \frac{(kN/100) - c}{f} \times i$$

where $k = 1, 2, 3, \ldots, 99$. Other symbolic notations are as explained earlier.

SELF-PRACTICE PROBLEMS

10F1. Compute mean, median, mode, first and third quartiles, inter-quartile range, and deciles for the data given in Problem 10D3.

10F2. Compute mean, median, mode, first and third quartiles, inter-quartile range, and deciles for the data given in Problem 10D4.

10F3. Compute mean, median, mode, first and third quartiles, inter-quartile range, and deciles for the data given in Problem 10E2.

SUMMARY

A measure of central tendency is a single value which is used to represent an entire set of data. The tendency of the observations to concentrate around a central point is known as central tendency. In statistics, there are various types of measures of central tendencies, some of which may be broadly classified into two groups: mathematical averages and positional Averages. Arithmetic mean, geometric mean, and harmonic mean fall under the category of mathematical averages, and median, mode, quartiles, deciles, and percentiles belong to the category of positional averages.

The arithmetic mean of a set of observations is their sum divided by the number of observations. The weighted mean enables us to calculate an average value that takes into account the importance of each value with respect to the overall total. Geometric mean is the nth root of the product of n items of a series. Geometric mean is useful in calculating the average percentage increase or decrease. Harmonic mean of any series is the reciprocal of the arithmetic mean of the reciprocal of the variate. It has specific applications in the computation of average speed, average price, average profit, etc. under various conditions.

Arithmetic mean, geometric mean, and harmonic mean are mathematical in nature and measures of the quantitative characteristics of data. To measure the qualitative characteristics of data, other measures, namely median, mode, quartiles, and percentiles, are used.

The median of a distribution is the value of the variable which divides it into two equal parts. Mode is the value that is repeated most often in the data set. Partition values are measures of central tendencies which divide the data into several equal parts. Quartiles divide data into 4 equal parts, deciles divide the data into 10 equal parts, and percentiles divide the data into 100 equal parts.

KEY TERMS |

Arithmetic mean, 214
Central tendency, 214
Deciles, 214
Geometric mean, 214
Harmonic mean, 214
Measures of central tendency, 214
Median, 214
Mode, 214
Partition values, 243
Percentiles, 214
Positional averages, 214
Quartiles, 214
Weighted arithmetic mean, 215

NOTES |

1. Prowess (V. 2.6), Centre for Monitoring Indian Economy Pvt Ltd, Mumbai, accessed July 2008, reproduced with permission.
2. www.ruchisoya.com/profile.htm, accessed August 2008.

DISCUSSION QUESTIONS |

1. What is the meaning of measures of central tendency?
2. What are the various measures of central tendency? Describe their relative merits and demerits and their uses.
3. What are the prerequisites for an ideal measure of central tendency?
4. In light of merits and demerits of the measures of central tendency, critically examine each. Which particular measure of central tendency is considered to be the best and why?
5. Define arithmetic mean and weighted mean. Describe their application in the managerial decision-making process.
6. What is the difference between arithmetic mean and weighted arithmetic mean?
7. "Arithmetic mean is the best among all the averages" Justify this statement.
8. What is the concept of geometric mean? State its merits, demerits, uses, and its application in the decision-making process.
9. In what context is there a difference between arithmetic mean and geometric mean, and when is geometric mean useful?
10. What is the concept of harmonic mean? State its merits, demerits, uses, and application in the decision-making process.
11. State the special use of harmonic mean.
12. What is the use of various averages in management or in decision making?
13. "Each average has its own characteristics. It is difficult to say which is the best." Discuss with suitable examples.
14. Write short notes on
    (a) Arithmetic mean and weighted arithmetic mean.
    (b) Median and positional averages.
    (c) Mode and its application in decision making.
    (d) Special use of geometric mean.
    (e) Special use of harmonic mean.
    (f) Relationship between the various types of averages.
15. Prepare a chart on the various types of averages and compare them on various grounds.
16. Define median, and state its merits, demerits, and use in decision making.
17. Define mode. State its merits, demerits, and its application in decision making.
18. What is the empirical relationship between arithmetic mean, median, and mode?
19. What is the meaning of partition or positional values? Write short notes on quartiles, deciles, and percentiles.

NUMERICAL PROBLEMS |

1. Compute the arithmetic average of the marks obtained by 10 students in the subject principles and practices of management.
   48, 32, 56, 67, 40, 42, 41, 38, 36, 45
2. The following data gives the daily wages of workers in a manufacturing company. Find the arithmetic mean.

Daily wages (in hundred rupees)	6	8	10	12	15	18
Number of workers	20	14	7	16	12	2

3. Find the mean from the following distribution:

Income (₹)	30–40	40–50	50–60	60–70	70–80	80–90	90–100
Number of persons	6	12	18	13	9	4	1

4. Compute geometric mean for the data given in Problems 1–3.
5. Compute harmonic mean for the data given in Problems 1–3.
6. Compute median for the data given in Problems 1–3.
7. Compute mode for the data given in Problem 1.
8. Compute first and third quartiles for the data given in Problem 1 and Problem 2.
9. Compute deciles for the data given in Problem 1.
10. Compute percentiles for the data given in Problem 1.

CASE STUDY |

Case 10: *Chemical, Industrial, and Pharmaceutical Laboratories (Cipla): A Leading Player in the Indian Pharmaceutical Industry*

Introduction

Khwaja Abdul Hamied incorporated the Chemical, Industrial, and Pharmaceutical Laboratories, which came to be popularly known as Cipla. Cipla was registered as a public limited company with an authorized capital of ₹60,000 million in 1935.[1] Operations officially started in September 1937 when its first product was launched in the market. The *Sunday Standard* reported, "The birth of Cipla which was launched into the world by Dr K. A. Hamied will be a red lettered day in the annals of industries in Bombay. The first city in India can now boast of a concern, which will supersede all existing firms in the magnitude of its operations"[2].

Product Ranges offered

Cipla's products and services are categorized as prescription, animal health care products, over-the-counter (OTC) products, bulk drugs, and technology services. The prescription division covers medicines for a variety of human diseases. The OTC products manufactured by Cipla include a range of drugs such as analgesics, artificial sweeteners, cosmetics and skin care products, dental care and oral hygiene products, food supplements, toiletries, infant foods, medicated Plasters, etc. The animal health care products are further categorized as per animal groups, herbal specialties, and therapeutic groups. The drugs produced under this category are equine products, poultry products, products for companion animals, and products for livestock. Bulk drugs include active pharmaceutical ingredients and drug intermediates. Technology services provided by Cipla include consulting, project appraisal, engineering, plant supply and commissioning, training, operation management, support, know-how transfer, and quality control.[3]

Moving Forward

The domestic pharmaceutical industry in India grew at more than double the rate, recording a 11% growth in value as per ORG-IMS, compared to 4.2% during 2004–2005. For the first time, the company's turnover crossed the ₹30 billion (see Table 10.01). Once again, this was way more than the overall growth rate of the industry. Cipla now exports to countries in Europe, Australia, Africa, Asia, the Middle East, and North, Central, and South America. The company's steady progress won it the "Express Pharma Pulse Award" for "sustained growth" for 2005–2006. Cipla is one of a handful of companies in India that has consistently increased its turnover and profitability in the past 15 years in a row.[1]

Cipla overtook Ranbaxy and GlaxoSmithKline (GSK) to become the largest pharmaceutical company in the domestic market for the first time in 2007.[3]

TABLE 10.01
Sales turnover of Cipla Ltd from 1989-2006

Year	*Sales (in million rupees)*
1989	971.3
1990	928.9
1991	1,236.4
1992	1,514.0
1993	1,990.3
1994	2,454.7
1995	2,987.1
1996	3,623.6
1997	4,525.8
1998	5,170.8
1999	6,255.4
2000	7,721.4
2001	10,643.1
2002	14,008.1
2003	15,730.2
2004	20,554.3
2005	24,008.9
2006	31,036.2

Source: Prowess (V. 2.6), Centre for Monitoring Indian Economy Pvt. Ltd, accessed September 2008, reproduced with permission.

1. Calculate the average sales of Cipla Ltd for 1989–2006.
2. Calculate the median sales of Cipla Ltd for 1989–2006.
3. Is there any modal value present in the data relating to sales turnover?

NOTES

1. Prowess (V. 3.1), Centre for Monitoring Indian Economy Pvt Ltd, Mumbai, accessed July 2008, reproduced with permission.
2. www.cipla.com/corporateprofile/history.htm, accessed July 2008.
3. www.cipla.com/whatsnews/news.htm, accessed July 2008.

CHAPTER **11**

Descriptive Statistics: Measures of Dispersion

LEARNING OBJECTIVES

Upon completion of this chapter, you will be able to:

- Understand the concept of range, quartile deviation, mean deviation, standard deviation, and variance.
- Compute range, quartile deviation, mean deviation, standard deviation, and variance.
- Understand skewness, kurtosis, and box-and-whisker plots.
- Compute the coefficient of correlation and understand its interpretation.
- Use MS Excel, Minitab, and SPSS for computing range, quartile deviation, mean deviation, standard deviation, skewness, kurtosis, and coefficient of correlation.
- Use Minitab and SPSS for box-and-whisker plot construction.

STATISTICS IN ACTION: DABUR INDIA LTD

Dabur India, was founded by S. K. Burman and started operations initially as a small pharmacy in Kolkota in 1884. Dabur was incorporated as a private limited company in 1936 by the Dabur Group to produce cosmetics and toilet preparations. It became a public limited company in 1986 after a reverse merger with Vidogum limited. The company sells a host of personal care products including hair oil, soap, shampoo, toothpowder, toothpaste, health supplements such as Chyawanprash and honey, digestives, ayurveda-based over-the-counter medicines, and other consumer care products. These products are marketed under the brand Dabur, Vatika, Hajmola, and Anmol and are positioned on the ayurvedic wellness platform.[1]

Dabur responded to the changing dynamics of the business environment in India by appointing its first non-family CEO Ninu Khanna in 1998. The company promotes its brands in the various regional languages of India and is focused on creating special products with a distinct local touch.

The company has been able to sustain its growth momentum in

TABLE 11.1
Net exports of Dabur India Ltd from 1996 to 2007

Year	*1996*	*1997*	*1998*	*1999*	*2000*	*2001*	*2002*	*2003*	*2004*	*2005*	*2006*	*2007*
Net exports (in million rupees)	329.4	447.6	164.9	151.5	286.4	245.4	286.4	331.4	203.6	309.5	211.8	583.2

Source: Prowess (V. 2.6), Centre for Monitoring Indian Economy Pvt. Ltd, Mumbai, accessed July 2008, reproduced with permission.

>>>

key categories like hair care and oral care. Its health supplements reported a 15% growth during the year 2007-2008, whereas its foods business grew by 19%. The Consumer Health Division also marked a turnaround, reporting a 12% growth in the second half of the 2007-2008 fiscal and 5.4% growth for the full year.[2]

Dabur is also keen to maintain and expand its foothold in the international market. It has shown remarkable presence in the Middle East and North African countries and has doubled its business in Pakistan. Table 11.1 lists the net exports of Dabur India Ltd for the past 12 years.

The value of net exports varies greatly over the years with the lowest export at ₹151.5 million in 1999 and the highest export at ₹583.2 million in 2007. The measures of mathematical averages and positional averages alone will not describe this data adequately. We need to have some tools that will measure the scatteredness of data to analyse the variations. This chapter focuses on the various measures of dispersion and measures of shape. The measures of association such as correlation are also discussed in this chapter.

11.1 INTRODUCTION

The meaning of dispersion is "scatteredness."

The various measures of central tendency discussed in Chapter 10 provide information about a particular point of the data set. They give us an idea about the central position of data. If we have two distributions with the same mean, it becomes difficult to ascertain whether the two distributions are identical or different; if these two distributions are different, then it is difficult to ascertain which parameter can be used to measure the difference of these two distributions.

The degree to which numerical data tends to spread around an average value is called variation or dispersion of data.

The meaning of **dispersion** is **"scatteredness."** Suppose we have three distributions with the same mean. Curve A, obtained from the first distribution, is less spread or less scattered than curve B (obtained from the second distribution), and curve A is also less spread or less scattered as compared to curve C, obtained from the third distribution (Figure 11.1). By measures of central tendency, data characteristics cannot be specifically described. If we study mean alone, one important characteristic of the data (scatteredness) will be missed. Additionally, by studying only the mean, we will not be able to measure the difference between these three distributions. The same is true with median and mode, which tells us only one aspect of the data in terms of middle position and value with maximum frequency, respectively. So, a tool is required to measure the scatteredness of the data. The extent or the degree to which data tends to spread around an average is called dispersion or variation. **In other words, the degree to** which numerical data tends to spread around an average value is called variation or dispersion of data. Figure 11.1 exhibits the difference between three distributions having the same mean but different dispersion.

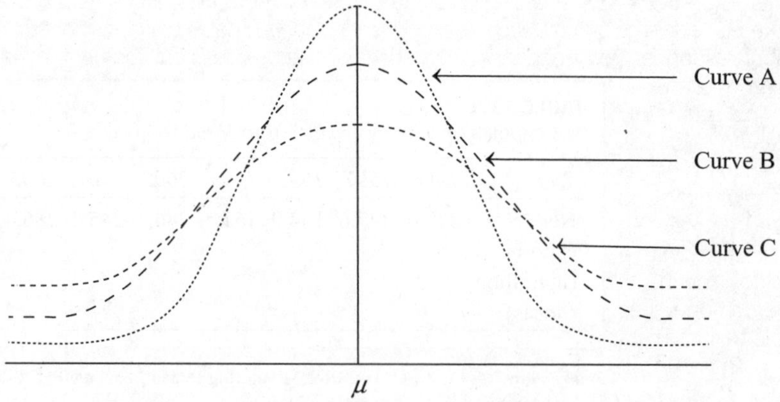

FIGURE 11.1
Three distributions A, B, and C with same mean and different dispersion

11.2 MEASURES OF DISPERSION

Absolute measures of dispersion are presented in the same unit as the unit of distribution. They are useful in comparing two distributions where the unit of data remains the same.

Broadly, statistical techniques that measure dispersion are of two types. In the first category, we study statistical techniques to measure deviation of data value from a measure of central tendency which is usually the mean or median. These statistical techniques are referred to as **measures of dispersion** (or variation or deviation). In the second category, we study statistical techniques to describe the shape of the distribution. These statistical techniques are referred to as **measures of shape**. This section focuses on the measures of dispersion. There are two types of measures of dispersion.

1. *Absolute measures of dispersion*: Absolute measures of dispersion are presented in the same unit as the unit of distribution. For example, if units are rupees, metres, years, etc., then the measure of dispersion will be presented in terms of rupees, metres, and years, respectively. Absolute measures of dispersion are useful in comparing two distributions where the unit of data remains the same. In cases where the two set of data values are expressed in different units, this measure of dispersion is not useful. For example, there cannot be any comparison between metres and rupees.
2. *Relative measures of dispersion*: Relative measures of dispersion are useful in comparing two sets of data which have different units of measurement. These are expressed as the percentage or the coefficient of the **absolute measure of dispersion**. We can say that relative measures of dispersion are pure numbers without unit, and are generally called **coefficient of dispersion**.

11.3 PROPERTIES OF A GOOD MEASURE OF DISPERSION

Like any other measure of central tendency, the measure of dispersion should possess some important prerequisites. The important characteristics that a measure of dispersion should possess are the following:

1. It should be simple to understand and should be rigidly defined.
2. It should be based on all the observations.
3. Fluctuations of sampling should not affect it.
4. It should be suitable for further mathematical treatment.
5. It should not be affected by extreme values.

11.4 METHODS OF MEASURING DISPERSION

In the previous chapter we discussed that only one measure of central tendency is not sufficient to study data. There are various tools for measuring central tendency, such as mean, median, mode, etc., each having some specialty. The same is true of the measures of dispersion. Only one measure of dispersion is not sufficient as its use is case specific. The following are some of the important and widely used methods of measuring dispersion:

- **Range**
- **Interquartile range** and **quartile deviation**
- Mean deviation or average deviation
- **Standard deviation**

11.4.1 Range

Range is the simplest measure of dispersion. It is defined as the difference between the smallest and the greatest values in a distribution. In other words, range is the value of the highest observation – the value of the lowest observation. Symbolically,

$$R = L - S$$

where L is the largest observation, S the smallest observation, and R the range.

Range is an absolute measure of dispersion. The **relative measure of dispersion** for range is called the **coefficient of range** and is calculated by the following formula:

$$\text{Coefficient of range} = \frac{L - S}{L + S}$$

$$= \frac{\text{Largest observation} - \text{Smallest observation}}{\text{Largest observation} + \text{Smallest observation}}$$

As discussed for measures of central tendency, range can also be determined for all three types of distributions: individual series, discrete frequency distribution, and continuous frequency distribution. In the following section, we study the process of determining range for the three types of distribution.

11.4.1.1 Range for Individual Series

The range for an individual series can be obtained by simply subtracting the value of the lowest observation from the value of the highest observation. Example 11.1 explains the procedure of computing range for an individual series.

Example 11.1

Find out the range and its coefficient from the following series.
110, 117, 129, 300, 357, 100, 500, 630, 750

Solution

Range can be computed by subtracting the lowest value of the series from the highest value of the series as shown below:

L = largest observation = 750
S = smallest observation = 100
Range $(R) = L - S = 750 - 100 = 650$

$$\text{Coefficient of range} = \frac{L - S}{L + S} = \frac{650}{850} = 0.764$$

11.4.1.2 Range for Discrete Frequency Distribution

The range for a discrete frequency distribution can also be obtained by applying the same procedure discussed above.

Example 11.2

Calculate range and its coefficient from the following data

x:	10	11	12	13	14	15
f:	8	10	16	20	4	2

Solution

Table 11.2 exhibits values and frequencies. For a discrete frequency distribution, range can be computed by subtracting the lowest value of the series from the highest value of the series as shown below:

TABLE 11.2
Values and frequencies for Example 11.2

x	f
10	8
11	10
12	16
13	20
14	4
15	2

Range $(R) = L - S$

where largest value $L = 15$ and smallest value $S = 10$

Range $(R) = L - S = 15 - 10 = 5.$

$$\text{Coefficient of range} = \frac{15-10}{15+10} = \frac{5}{25} = 0.2$$

11.4.1.3 Range for Continuous Frequency Distribution

Range for a continuous frequency distribution can be obtained by subtracting the lower limit of the lowest class interval from the upper limit of the highest class interval. Range can also be obtained by subtracting the mid-value of the lowest class interval from the mid-value of the highest class interval.

Range for a continuous frequency distribution can be obtained by subtracting the lower limit of the lowest class interval from the upper limit of the highest class interval. Range can also be obtained by subtracting the mid-value of lowest class interval from the mid-value of highest class interval.

Example 11.3

Find out the range and its coefficient in the following series.

x:	10–60	60–120	120–180	180–240	240–300
f:	3	5	6	3	2

Solution Table 11.3 exhibits class interval and frequencies.

TABLE 11.3
Class interval and frequencies for Example 11.3

x	f
10–60	3
60–120	5
120–180	6
180–240	3
240–300	2

As discussed above, range can be obtained by subtracting the lower limit of the lowest class interval from the upper limit of the highest class interval.

Upper limit of the highest class interval $L = 300$

Lower limit of the lowest class interval $S = 10$

Range $(R) = L - S = 300 - 10 = 290$

$$\text{Coefficient of range} = \frac{L-S}{L+S} = \frac{290}{310} = 0.93$$

So, range = 290 and coefficient of range = 0.93

11.4.2 Merits and Demerits of Range

Range is widely applied in the field of statistical quality control. It provides the upper and lower limit in which product quality should fall. If there is any variation from the specified limit provided by range, then the production machinery or the production process needs to be checked. Range is also used in meteorological departments where the difference between maximum temperature and minimum temperature is used to forecast the weather on a particular day. Range calculates the difference between two extreme observations. In this process, the middle part of the data remains ignored. However, calculation of range is very easy. Hence, range possesses some merits as well as some demerits. The following is a list of the merits and demerits of range.

11.4.2.1 Merits

1. It is easy in terms of calculation and understanding.
2. Its computation is based upon two extreme values and thus provides a broad picture of variation in data very quickly.
3. It is rigidly defined.

11.4.2.2 Demerits

1. Range is not based on all the observations of data; rather it focuses on two extreme values.
2. It is highly affected by fluctuations in sampling.
3. Sometimes range cannot explain very clearly the nature or the characteristics of data. For example, if there are two series A and B, such as,

A: 2, 2, 2, 2, 2, 6, 2, 2, 2
B: 1, 2, 3, 4, 5, 1, 2, 3, 4

In terms of dispersion, the difference in the two series can be observed by inspection only. When we take the range of both the series, it comes to 4. Hence, range does not provide a real picture of the dispersion of two series in terms of comparison of two series.

SELF-PRACTICE PROBLEMS

11A1. Find out the range and its coefficient from the following series:

234, 255, 270, 300, 347, 400, 500, 530, 570

11A2. Calculate range and its coefficient from the following data:

x:	30	35	50	60	75	95
f:	10	17	16	11	9	12

11A3. Find out the range and its coefficient for the following series:

x:	10–40	40–70	70–100	100–130	130–160
f:	9	15	16	15	10

11A4. The table below shows the gross import of crude oil and petroleum products in India from 1992–1993 to 2002–2003. Compute the range and the coefficient of range.

Year	*Gross import of crude oil*	*Gross import of petroleum product*
1992–1993	29,247	11,283
1993–1994	30,822	12,076
1994–1995	27,349	13,951
1995–1996	27,342	20,335
1996–1997	33,906	20,265
1997–1998	34,494	22,970
1998–1999	39,808	23,772
1999–2000	57,805	16,608
2000–2001	74,097	9267
2001–2002	78,706	7009
2002–2003	81,989	7228

Source: www.indiastat.com accessed October 2008, reproduced with permission.

11.4.3 Interquartile Range and Quartile Deviation

We have already discussed in Chapter 10 that after arranging the data in an ordered sequence, quartiles divide data into four equal parts. Range as the difference between the highest value and the lowest value is based upon two extreme observations of data and, hence, does not cover all the values of the data distribution. However, this drawback of range can be overcome by using interquartile range. **Interquartile range** is the difference between the third quartile and the first quartile. Symbolically,

Interquartile range the difference between the third quartile and the first quartile.

Interquartile range = $Q_3 - Q_1$

where Q_1= first quartile or lower quartile $= \frac{n+1}{4}$ ordered observation, and Q_3 = third quartile or upper quartile $= \frac{3(n+1)}{4}$ ordered observation.

Quartile deviation or semi-interquartile range can be obtained by dividing the interquartile range by 2.

Sometimes, interquartile range is reduced to the form of quartile deviation or semi-interquartile range, which is obtained by dividing the interquartile range by 2, that is,

Quartile deviation or semi-interquartile range $= \frac{Q_3 - Q_1}{2}$

where Q_3 and Q_1 have their usual meaning. Quartile deviation is an absolute measure of dispersion. Relative measure is called the **coefficient of quartile deviation**. Coefficient of quartile deviation can be used to measure the degree of variation in two different distributions when both have different units of measurement. It is given as

Quartile deviation is an absolute measure of dispersion. Relative measure is called the coefficient of quartile deviation. Coefficient of quartile deviation can be used to measure the degree of variation in two different distributions when both have different units of measurement.

Coefficient of quartile deviation $= \frac{Q_3 - Q_1}{Q_3 + Q_1}$

11.4.3.1 Interquartile Range for Individual Series, Discrete Frequency Distribution, and Continuous Frequency Distribution

In Chapter 10, we have already discussed the procedure for computing first and third quartiles for an individual series, a discrete frequency distribution, and a continuous frequency distribution. The formula for computing interquartile range, semi-interquartile range, and coefficient of quartile deviation is based on first quartile Q_1 and third quartile Q_3. We use Example 11.4 to understand the procedure of computing interquartile range, semi-interquartile range, and coefficient of quartile deviation. Figure 11.2 exhibits range, first quartile, median, third quartile and interquartile range.

Example 11.4

Find the interquartile range, semi-interquartile range, and coefficient of quartile deviation for Examples 10.18 and 10.19 discussed in Chapter 10.

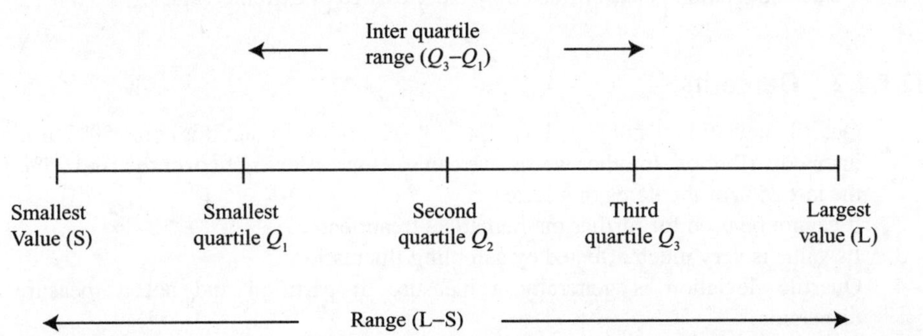

Figure 11.2
Range, first quartile, median, third quartile, and interquartile range

Solution We have already seen that for Example 10.18, discussed in Chapter 10, the first quartile is $Q_1 = 22.5$ and the third quartile is $Q_3 = 68.5$.

Interquartile range $= Q_3 - Q_1 = 46$

Quartile deviation or semi-interquartile range $= \dfrac{Q_3 - Q_1}{2} = 23$

Coefficient of quartile deviation $= \dfrac{Q_3 - Q_1}{Q_3 + Q_1} = 0.505$

For Example 10.19, discussed in Chapter 10, the first and third quartiles are 12.91 and 25.83, respectively. Hence,

Interquartile range $= Q_3 - Q_1 = 12.92$

Quartile deviation or semi-interquartile range $= \dfrac{Q_3 - Q_1}{2} = 6.46$

Coefficient of quartile deviation $= \dfrac{Q_3 - Q_1}{Q_3 + Q_1} = 0.333$

Quartiles for a discrete frequency distribution can be computed in the same way as for individual series. Q_1 is the size of $\left(\dfrac{N+1}{4}\right)th$ item and Q_3 is the size of $3\left(\dfrac{N+1}{4}\right)th$ item, where $N = \Sigma f$. For a continuous frequency distribution, the formula for computing quartiles has already been discussed in Chapter 10.

11.4.4 Merits and Demerits of Quartile Deviation

Quartiles are the most widely used measures of partition but they are not free from drawbacks. While calculating the interquartile range, the upper 25% and the lower 25% of the data remains unnoticed. However, quartiles are less affected by the presence of extreme values. Hence, quartile deviations possess some merits as well as some demerits. The following is a list of the merits and demerits of quartile deviation.

11.4.4.1 Merits

1. It is easy to calculate and simple to understand.
2. Quartile deviation is least affected by the presence of extreme values.

11.4.4.2 Demerits

1. Quartile deviation is not based on all the observations. In fact it ignores 50% of items in any distribution. In other words, we can say that it does not cover the first 25% and the last 25% of the items in a series.
2. It cannot be used for further mathematical treatment.
3. Its value is very much affected by sampling fluctuations.
4. Quartile deviation is generally a measure of partition and not a measure of dispersion.

SELF-PRACTICE PROBLEMS

11B1. Compute interquartile range, semi-interquartile range, and coefficient of quartile deviation from the series given below:

12	17	21	34	35	38
40	47	55	60	67	

11B2. Compute interquartile range, semi-interquartile range, and coefficient of quartile deviation from the distribution given below:

Value	*Frequency*
20	7
29	9
38	10
39	12
55	14
64	20
72	21
80	10
85	7
100	3

11B3. Calculate the first and third quartiles, interquartile range, semi-interquartile range, and coefficient of quartile deviation from the following data

Class:	0–8	8–16	16–24	24–32	32–40	40–48	48–56	56–64
Frequency:	8	9	10	11	12	7	6	4

11B4. Compute the first and third quartiles, interquartile range, semi-interquartile range, and coefficient of quartile deviation from the data given in Problem 11A4.

11.4.5 Mean Absolute Deviation (or Average Absolute Deviation)

In the previous discussion, we noticed that while measuring dispersion, range and quartile deviation do not take into account some parts of the data. It can also be noticed that these positional measures are not based on all the observations. So, in the real sense, scatteredness of the data around an average cannot be measured by range and quartile deviation. There is need for a tool of measurement which considers deviation from central point or deviation from the average. Mean absolute deviation provides this platform.

The **average absolute deviation** is the average scatter of the items in a distribution, from either the mean or the median or the mode, ignoring the signs of deviations. When this deviation is taken from mean, it is called mean absolute deviation. As some of the deviations may be positive and some negative, their algebraic sum may be zero. To avoid this difficulty, the average of absolute deviations from the central value is taken, that is, (+) or (–) signs are ignored. In general, mean or median or mode can be used to calculate deviation from the average value, although mean is usually the most widely used measure of central tendency of taking deviation from the central value. The formula for mean absolute deviation is given as

$$\text{Mean absolute deviation} = \frac{\sum_{i=1}^{n} |(x_i - \bar{x})|}{n}$$

In case deviation is taken from the median, the above formula can be rearranged as

$$\text{Median absolute deviation} = \frac{\sum_{i=1}^{n} |(x_i - M_d|}{n}$$

In case deviation is taken from the mode, the above formula can be rearranged as

$$\text{Mode absolute deviation} = \frac{\sum_{i=1}^{n} |(x_i - M_o|}{n}$$

where $|(x_i - \bar{x})|$, $|(x_i - M_d)|$, $|(x_i - M_o)|$ are absolute deviations from mean, median, and mode, respectively, and n is the number of items in a data series.

Mean absolute deviation is an absolute measure of dispersion. In this context, a relative measure, also known as coefficient of mean absolute deviation, is obtained by the following formula:

$$\text{Coefficient of mean absolute deviation} = \frac{\text{Mean absolute deviation}}{\text{Mean}}$$

Mean absolute deviation can be determined for all types of data distribution such as individual series, discrete frequency distribution, and continuous frequency distribution. The procedure for computing mean, median, and mode has already been described in Chapter 10. For computing mean absolute deviation, as a first step, we have to compute mean and then the sum of absolute deviation of mean from the data values. For obtaining mean absolute deviation, this sum is divided by the number of items. Similarly, by calculating median and mode, median absolute deviation and mode absolute deviation can be obtained.

11.4.5.1 Mean Absolute Deviation for Individual Series

As discussed, the mean absolute deviation for an individual series can be determined by first computing the mean and then the sum of absolute deviation of mean from data values. To obtain mean absolute deviation, this sum is divided by the number of items. Example 11.5 clearly illustrates this procedure.

Example 11.5

Find the mean absolute deviation and coefficient of mean absolute deviation for Example 10.1 discussed in Chapter 10.

Solution

In Example 10.1 in Chapter 10, the average rainfall in 10 years is computed as 148.5 cm. So, mean = 148.5.

Mean absolute deviation and coefficient of mean absolute deviation for Example 3.1 discussed in Chapter 10

Year	*Rainfall* (x_i)	$(x_i - \bar{x})$	$\lvert(x_i - \bar{x})\rvert$
1995	110	–38.5	38.5
1996	120	–28.5	28.5
1997	130	–18.5	18.5
1998	135	–13.5	13.5
1999	140	–8.5	8.5
2000	150	1.5	1.5
2001	160	11.5	11.5
2002	170	21.5	21.5
2003	180	31.5	31.5
2004	190	41.5	41.5
Total			$\Sigma\lvert(x_i - \bar{x})\rvert = 215$

$$\text{Mean absolute deviation} = \frac{\sum_{i=1}^{n}|(x_i - \bar{x})|}{n} = \frac{215}{10} = 21.5$$

$$\text{Coefficient of mean absolute deviation} = \frac{\text{Mean absolute deviation}}{\text{Mean}} = \frac{21.5}{148.5} = 0.1447$$

11.4.5.2 Mean Absolute Deviation for Discrete and Continuous Frequency Distributions

To obtain mean absolute deviation in a discrete frequency distribution, mean must be computed first. Then the absolute deviation of mean from the data values is computed. This absolute deviation of mean is multiplied by the corresponding frequencies of the data values and its sum is obtained. To compute mean absolute deviation, this sum is divided by the sum of all frequencies. So, mean absolute deviation in a discrete frequency distribution is computed as

$$\text{Mean absolute deviation} = \frac{\sum_{i=1}^{n} f_i \left|(x_i - \bar{x})\right|}{\sum_{i=1}^{n} f_i}$$

For continuous frequency distribution also, the mean absolute deviation and coefficient of mean absolute deviation can be obtained using the same formula described above. Here, class midpoints are the values of x_is.

For a discrete distribution, the procedure for computing mean absolute deviation is explained by Example 11.6.

Example 11.6

Find the mean absolute deviation and coefficient of mean absolute deviation for Example 10.2 discussed in Chapter 10.

Solution For Example 10.2, the arithmetic mean is computed as shown below:

$$\text{Arithmetic mean} = \frac{\sum fx}{\sum f} = \frac{35{,}260}{187} = ₹188.55$$

Table 11.4 exhibits some computations for calculating mean absolute deviation and coefficient of mean absolute deviation.

TABLE 11.4
Mean absolute deviation and coefficient of mean absolute deviation for Example 10.2 discussed in Chapter 10

Weekly earnings (in rupees) (x)	*Number of employees (f)*	*Product of the weekly earnings and number of employees (fx)*	$(x_i - \bar{x})$	$\lvert(x_i - \bar{x})\rvert$	$f_i\lvert(x_i - \bar{x})\rvert$
100	5	500	−88.55	88.55	442.75
120	8	960	−68.55	68.55	548.4
140	12	1680	−48.55	48.55	582.6
160	16	2560	−28.55	28.55	456.8
180	22	3960	−8.55	8.55	188.1
200	44	8800	11.45	11.45	503.8
210	80	16,800	21.45	21.45	1716
Total	$\Sigma f = 187$	$\Sigma f x = 35260$		$\Sigma\lvert x_i - \bar{x}\rvert = 275.65$	$\Sigma f_i\lvert x_i - \bar{x}\rvert = 4438.45$

$$\text{Mean absolute deviation} = \frac{\sum_{i=1}^{n} f_i|(x_i - \bar{x})|}{\sum_{i=1}^{n} f_i} = \frac{4438.45}{187} = 23.73$$

$$\text{Coefficient of mean absolute deviation} = \frac{\text{Mean absolute deviation}}{\text{Mean}} = \frac{23.73}{188.5} = 0.1258$$

11.4.6 Merits and Demerits of Mean Absolute Deviation

The serious limitation of mean absolute deviation in terms of its incapability of algebraic treatment has restricted its wide use. Mean absolute deviation is useful in some areas of economics. The following are some of the merits and demerits of mean absolute deviation.

11.4.6.1 Merits

1. It is based on all the observations.
2. Mean absolute deviation is less affected by extreme values.
3. It is easy to calculate and understand.

11.4.6.2 Demerits

1. While taking deviation from average, algebraic signs are ignored and this makes this method non-algebraic.
2. It is not capable of algebraic treatment.
3. Mean absolute deviation is not satisfactory for a skewed distribution.

SELF-PRACTICE PROBLEMS

11C1. Compute mean absolute deviation and coefficient of mean absolute deviation from the following series

25 45 56 67 78 112 120 144 156 178

11C2. Compute mean absolute deviation and coefficient of mean absolute deviation from the following data

x:	50	55	65	80	100	105
f:	10	12	14	15	9	7

11C3. Compute mean absolute deviation and coefficient of mean absolute deviation from the following distribution:

x:	10–50	50–90	90–130	130–170	170–210
f:	6	10	12	13	9

11.4.7 Standard Deviation, Variance, and Coefficient of Variation

The greatest limitation of mean absolute deviation is that the signs of all the deviation from average are taken as positive (absolute) and there is no justification or logical answer for doing this. This limitation of mean absolute deviation has been removed in standard deviation. The concept of standard deviation was first used by Karl Pearson.

11.4.8 Standard Deviation

Standard deviation is the square root of sum of the square deviations of various values from their arithmetic mean divided by the sample size minus one. Population standard deviation is generally denoted by the small Greek letter σ (read as sigma) and sample standard deviation is generally denoted by s. The greater the standard deviation, the greater the magnitude of the values from their mean; smaller the standard deviation, greater the uniformity in the observation. The formula for the calculation of sample standard deviation is

$$\text{Sample standard deviation } (s) = \sqrt{\frac{\sum_{i=1}^{n}(x_i - \bar{x})^2}{n-1}}$$

where $\bar{x}$ is the sample arithmetic mean, n the sample size, and x_i the ith value of the variable x.

The formula used for the calculation of population standard deviation is given as

$$\text{Population standard deviation}(\sigma) = \sqrt{\frac{\sum_{i=1}^{n}(x_i - \mu)^2}{N}}$$

where μ is the population arithmetic mean, x_i the ith value of the variable x, and $N = \Sigma f$. In the above formula (for sample standard deviation), in the denominator part, instead of n, $(n - 1)$ is used because certain desirable mathematical properties possessed by sample statistic s makes it appropriate for statistical inference. However, as the sample size increases, the difference between n and $(n - 1)$ reduces and becomes irrelevant.

Standard deviation is the square root of the sum of square deviations of various values from their arithmetic mean divided by the sample size minus one. Population standard deviation is generally denoted by the small Greek letter s (read as sigma) and sample standard deviation is generally denoted by s.

11.4.9 Variance

Variance is the square of standard deviation. **Sample variance** is the sum of squared deviations of various values from their arithmetic mean divided by the sample size minus one.

$$\text{Sample variance } (s^2) = \frac{\sum_{i=1}^{n}(x_i - \bar{x})^2}{n-1}$$

The formula used for calculation of population variance is given as

$$\text{Population variance } (\sigma^2) = \frac{\sum_{i=1}^{n}(x_i - \mu)^2}{N}$$

where symbols have their usual meanings.

Variance is the square of standard deviation. Sample variance is the sum of squared deviations of various values from their arithmetic mean divided by the sample size minus one.

11.4.10 Coefficient of Variation

Standard deviation is an absolute measure of dispersion. To compare the dispersion of two distributions, the relative measure of standard deviation is used and is referred to as the **coefficient of variation**. Coefficient of variation is equal to standard deviation divided by the arithmetic mean and the resultant multiplied by 100. The **coefficient of variation** is generally denoted by CV. Hence, coefficient of variation is given as

$$\text{Coefficient of variation } (CV) = \frac{\text{Standard deviation}}{\text{Mean}} \times 100 = \frac{\sigma}{\bar{x}} \times 100$$

where $\bar{x}$ is the arithmetic mean and σ the standard deviation. If coefficient of variation is low, the set of data is said to be uniform (consistent) or homogenous. A distribution with lesser CV shows greater consistency, homogeneity, and uniformity whereas a distribution with greater CV is considered more variable than others.

Like any other measure of dispersion, standard deviation and variance can also be calculated for individual series, discrete frequency distribution, and continuous frequency distribution.

To compare the dispersion of two distributions, the relative measure of standard deviation is used and is referred to as the coefficient of variation.

A distribution with lesser CV shows greater consistency, homogeneity, and uniformity, whereas a distribution with greater CV is considered more variable than others.

11.4.10.1 Standard Deviation and Variance for an Individual Series

We have already discussed that for computing standard deviation of any series we have to compute the square root of the sum of square deviations of various values from their arithmetic mean divided by the sample size minus one. Example 11.7 clearly explains the procedure for computing standard deviation for an individual series.

Example 11.7

Find the standard deviation and variance for the data given in Example 11.1.

Solution

The first step in determining standard deviation is to compute the arithmetic mean of the data.

Table 11.5 exhibits some computations for calculating standard deviation and variance for Example 11.7.

TABLE 11.5
Computation of standard deviation and variance for Example 11.1

Series (x)	$(x_i - \bar{x})$	$(x_i - \bar{x})^2$
110	–222.55	49,528.5025
117	–215.55	46,461.8025
129	–203.55	41,432.6025
300	–32.55	1059.5025
357	24.45	597.8025
100	–232.55	54,079.5025
500	167.45	28,039.5025
630	297.45	88,476.5025
750	417.45	174,264.5025
Sum		483,940.2225

$$\text{Arithmetic mean } (\bar{x}) = \frac{\sum x}{n} = \frac{2993}{9} = 332.55$$

$$\text{Sample standard deviation } (s) = \sqrt{\frac{\sum_{i=1}^{n}(x_i - \bar{x})^2}{n-1}} = \sqrt{\frac{483{,}940.2225}{8}} = 245.9523$$

where $\bar{x}$ = arithmetic mean = 332.5, and n = sample size = 9.

$$\text{Sample variance } (s^2) = \frac{\sum_{i=1}^{n}(x_i - \bar{x})^2}{n-1} = 60{,}492.53$$

11.4.10.2 Standard Deviation and Variance for Discrete and Continuous Frequency Distributions

In the case of a discrete series, the formula discussed above will vary slightly. In this case, we have to compute an additional term: $\sum_{i=1}^{n} f_i(x_i - \bar{x})^2$. The formula for sample standard deviation and sample variance for a discrete frequency distribution is given as

$$\text{Sample standard deviation } (s) = \sqrt{\frac{\sum_{i=1}^{n} f_i(x_i - \bar{x})^2}{N-1}} \quad \text{where } N = \sum_{i=1}^{n} f_i$$

$$\text{Sample variance}(s^2) = \frac{\sum_{i=1}^{n} f_i(x_i - \bar{x})^2}{N-1} \quad \text{where } N = \sum_{i=1}^{n} f_i$$

Standard deviation and variance for a continuous frequency distribution can also be computed by applying the same procedure we have adopted for a discrete frequency distribution. For a continuous frequency distribution, class midpoints will be x_i values. Example 11.8 explains the procedure for computing standard deviation and variance for a discrete frequency distribution.

Example 11.8

Find the standard deviation and variance for the data given in Example 11.2.

Solution As discussed in Example 11.7, to compute standard deviation of the data, as a first step, we have to compute arithmetic mean of the data. Table 11.6 exhibits some computations for calculating standard deviation and variance for Example 11.8.

TABLE 11.6
Computation of standard deviation and variance for Example 11.2

x	f	$f.x$	$(x_i - \bar{x})$	$(x_i - \bar{x})^2$	$f_i(x_i - \bar{x})^2$
10	8	80	–2.13	4.5369	36.2952
11	10	110	–1.13	1.2769	12.769
12	16	192	–0.13	0.0169	0.2704
13	20	260	0.87	0.7569	15.138
14	4	56	1.87	3.4969	13.9876
15	2	30	2.87	8.2369	16.4738
Sum	60	728			94.934

$$\text{Arithmetic mean } (\bar{x}) = \frac{\sum fx}{\sum f} = \frac{728}{60} = 12.13$$

$$\text{Standard deviation}(s) = \sqrt{\frac{\sum_{i=1}^{n} f_i(x_i - \bar{x})^2}{N-1}} = \sqrt{\frac{94.934}{59}} = 1.26$$

$$\text{Variance}(s^2) = \frac{\sum_{i=1}^{n} f_i(x_i - \bar{x})^2}{N-1} = \frac{94.934}{59} = 1.60$$

11.4.11 Mathematical Properties of Standard Deviation

Standard deviation has some important properties which enhance its utility in the field of management, economics, etc. The following are some of the important algebraic properties of standard deviation:

1. If n_1 and n_2 are the observations, $\bar{x}_1$ and $\bar{x}_2$ are the means, and σ_1^2 and σ_2^2 are the standard deviations of two sets of data, respectively, then the combined standard deviation σ_{12} is given by

$$d_{12}^2 = \frac{1}{n_1 + n_2}\left[n_1\left(d_1^2 + d_1^2\right) + n_2\left(d_2^2 + d_2^2\right)\right]$$

$$\text{or } \sigma_{12} = \sqrt{\frac{n_1\left(\sigma_1^2 + \sigma_1^2\right) + n_2\left(d_2^2 + d_2^2\right)}{n_1 + n_2}}$$

where $d_1 = \bar{x}_1 - \bar{X} \quad d_2 = \bar{x}_2 - \bar{X}$

$\bar{X}$ = Combined mean $\dfrac{n_1\bar{x}_1 + n_2\bar{x}_2}{n_1 + n_2}$

The above formula can be extended for more than two sets of data. For example, if we have three sets of data, then the combined standard deviation for these three sets of data is given by

$$\sigma_{123} = \sqrt{\frac{n_1\left(\sigma_1^2 + d_1^2\right) + n_2\left(\sigma_2^2 + d_2^2\right) + n_3\left(\sigma_3^2 + d_3^2\right)}{n_1 + n_2 + n_3}}$$

where σ_{123} is the combined standard deviation, $\bar{X}$ the combined mean $\dfrac{n_1\bar{x}_1 + n_2\bar{x}_2 + n_3\bar{x}_3}{n_1 + n_2 + n_3}$

σ_3 the standard deviation of the third set of data, d_3 is $\bar{x}_3 - \bar{X}$, and n_3 the observations for the third set of data. Other symbols have their usual meanings.

2. Standard deviation is independent of change of origin, that is, the value of standard deviation of a series remains unchanged if each variate value is increased or decreased by some constant value. This property of standard deviation will be clearer with the help of the following example:
Suppose for a series x, 10 observations are as given below:
x: 59, 48, 55, 57, 34, 60, 37, 34, 43, 43
Series y is obtained by adding a constant 4 to each observation of x and series z is obtained by subtracting 5 from each of the observation of the series x. For verifying the above property of standard deviation, we determine the standard deviation of the series x, y, and z.
From Figure 11.3 (from MS Excel), it can be observed that $\sigma_x = \sigma_y = \sigma_z$, that is, the value of standard deviation of a series remains unchanged if each variate value is increased or decreased by some constant value.

3. If the value of a variable, say x, is multiplied (or divided) by a constant, then the standard deviation of the new series y (which is obtained by multiplying series x by a constant) and the standard deviation of the new series z (which is obtained by dividing series x by a constant) can be obtained by multiplying (or dividing) the original standard deviation (of series x) by the same constant.

   In the above example we can see that series y is obtained by multiplying series x by 3 and series z is obtained by dividing series x by 3 (Figure 11.4). The standard deviation of series y is obtained by multiplying the standard deviation of series

F6 | =STDEV(B2:B11)

	A	B	C	D	E	F
1	x	y=(x+4)	z=(x-5)			
2	59	63	54			
3	48	52	43			
4	55	59	50		standard deviation for the series x=	10.2632
5	57	61	52			
6	34	38	29		standard deviation for the series y=	10.2632
7	60	64	55			
8	37	41	32		standard deviation for the series z=	10.2632
9	34	38	29			
10	43	47	38			
11	43	47	38			
12						

FIGURE 11.3 MS Excel worksheet exhibiting the computation of standard deviation for series *x*, *y* and *z* (when each variate value is increased or decreased by some constant value for obtaining series *y* and series *z*).

I6

	A	B	C	D	E	F
1	x	y=3x	z=x/3			
2	59	177	19.66667		standard deviation for the series x=	10.2632
3	48	144	16			
4	55	165	18.33333		standard deviation for the series y=	30.78961
5	57	171	19			
6	34	102	11.33333		standard deviation for the series z=	3.421068
7	60	180	20			
8	37	111	12.33333			
9	34	102	11.33333		standard deviation for the series y=	30.78961
10	43	129	14.33333		standard deviation for the series z=	3.421068
11	43	129	14.33333			

Standard deviation obtained by multiplying 10.2632 by 3 (computed as 30.78961) for series *y* and standard deviation obtained by dividing 10.2632 by 3 (computed as 3.421068) for series *z*

This box is obtained by first multiplying a series by 3 (for getting series *y*) and then by dividing series by 3 (for getting series *z*) and then computing standard deviation for these two series separately.

FIGURE 11.4 MS Excel sheet exhibiting computation of standard deviation for series x, y, and z (when each variate value is multiplied or divided by some constant value for obtaining series *y* and series *z*)

x by 3, that is, $\sigma_y = 3\sigma_x$ and standard deviation of series *z* is obtained by dividing standard deviation of series *x* by 3, that is $\sigma_z = \frac{\sigma_x}{3}$.

4. The sum of the squares of the deviation of a set of values is minimum when taken from the mean. This is a reason why standard deviation is always calculated from the arithmetic mean.

11.4.12 Merits and Demerits of Standard Deviation

Standard deviation is a very widely used statistical tool of measuring dispersion. In computing **correlation** and regression, it plays a key role. Standard deviation has wide applications in sampling theory, **skewness**, **kurtosis**, and in tests of hypothesis. Inspite of its limitations, it is regarded as the best measure of dispersion in statistical analysis. The following is a list of merits and demerits of standard deviation.

11.4.12.1 Merits

1. Standard deviation is rigidly defined.
2. It is least affected by fluctuations of sampling.
3. It is suitable for further algebraic treatment.
4. It is a most accepted and widely used measure of dispersion.
5. For two or more groups it is possible to measure the combined standard deviation.

11.4.12.2 Demerits

1. It is difficult to calculate and understand.
2. It gives greater weight to extreme values. For example, two deviations of a series are 2 and 10, their ratio is 1:5, but when we take the square of this deviation, it is 4 and 100 with ratio 1:25.
3. It cannot be used for the comparison of two distributions whose measurement units are different. For example, if the unit of measureent for two distributions are kilograms and rupees, respectively, then comparison on the basis of standard deviation of the two series is not possible.

SELF-PRACTICE PROBLEMS

11D1. Compute sample standard deviation and sample variance for the following series:

45 67 117 180 23 29 89 12 200 280

11D2. Compute sample standard deviation and sample variance for the following data:

x:	50	75	89	110	175	185
f:	11	19	20	21	19	12

11D3. Compute sample standard deviation and sample variance for the following data:

x:	50–100	100–150	150–200	200–250	250–300
f:	10	20	22	23	19

11D4. The table below shows the circlewise number of broadband subscribers as on March 31, 2008. Compute sample standard deviation and sample variance from the data.

State/telecom circle	*Broadband subscribers*	*State/telecom circle*	*Broadband subscribers*
Andaman & Nicobar Islands	1725	Kerala	183,506
Andhra Pradesh	294,111	Maharashtra (including Goa)	809,982
Assam	21,538	Madhya Pradesh (including Chhattisgarh)	112,686
Bihar (including Jharkhand)	52,779	North East	7400
Delhi (including Noida, Gurgaon, Ghaziabad, and Faridabad)	431,377	Orissa	32,321
Gujarat	249,785	Punjab	131,750
Haryana	58,616	Rajasthan	94,110
Himachal Pradesh	12,514	Tamilnadu	499,442
Jammu & Kashmir	13,444	Uttar Pradesh (including Uttaranchal)	170,966
Karnataka	421,392	West Bengal	266,595

Source: www.indiastat.com, accessed October 2008, reproduced with permission.

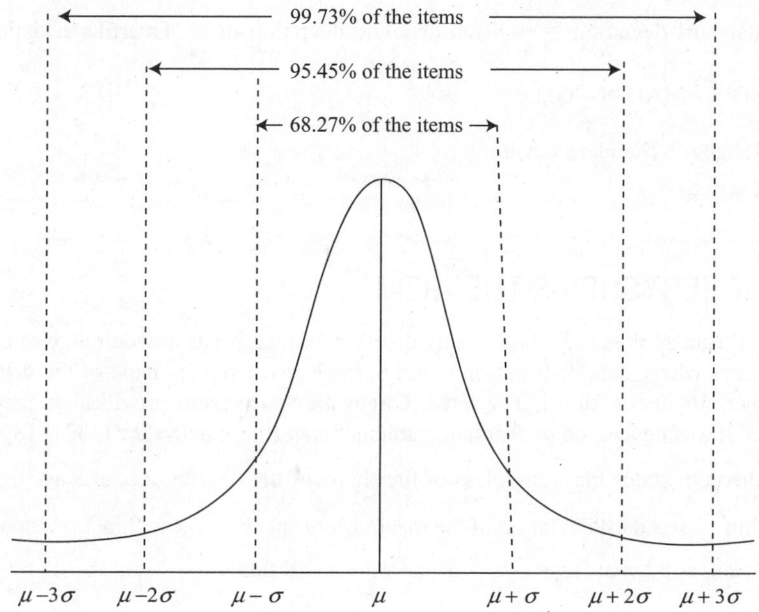

FIGURE 11.5
Area under the normal curve

11.5 EMPIRICAL RULE

For a symmetrical bell-shaped frequency distribution (quite commonly known as a normal distribution), the range within which approximate percentage of values of the distribution are likely to fall within a given number of standard deviation from the mean is determined as below:

$\mu \pm 1\sigma$, that is, mean ±1 standard deviation covers 68.27% of the items in a data set.
$\mu \pm 2\sigma$, that is, mean ±2 standard deviation covers 95.45% of the items in a data set.
$\mu \pm 3\sigma$, that is, mean ±3 standard deviation covers 99.73 of the items in a data set.
Figure 11.5 explains the area under the normal curve.

> $\mu \pm 1\sigma$, that is, mean ±1 standard deviation covers 68.27% of the items in a data set.
> $\mu \pm 2\sigma$, that is, mean ±2 standard deviation covers 95.45% of the items in a data set.
> $\mu \pm 3\sigma$, that is, mean ±3 standard deviation covers 99.73% of the items in a data set.

11.6 EMPIRICAL RELATIONSHIP BETWEEN MEASURES OF DISPERSION

In the case of a symmetrical distribution, the empirical relationship between the various measures of dispersion is given by:

1. Quartile deviation $= \frac{2}{3}$ Standard deviation, that is, $\text{QD} = \frac{2}{3}\sigma$
2. Mean absolute deviation $= \frac{4}{5}$ Standard deviation, that is, $\text{MAD} = \frac{4}{5}\sigma$
3. Quartile deviation $= \frac{5}{6}$ Mean absolute deviation, that is, $\text{QD} = \frac{5}{6}\text{MAD}$
4. 6 Standard deviation = 9 Quartile deviation = 7.5 Mean absolute deviation, that is, $6\sigma = 9$ QD = 7.5 MAD

5. Standard deviation $= \frac{5}{4}$ Mean absolute deviation or $\frac{3}{2}$ Quartile deviation, that is,

$$SD = \frac{5}{4}MAD \text{ or } \frac{3}{2}QD$$

6. Range = 6 Standard deviation

$R = 6\sigma.$

11.7 CHEBYSHEV'S THEOREM

Empirical rule applies only to normally distributed data. It has a wide range of application, but in cases where data distribution is not normal or where the shape of the distribution is not known, its application is restricted. **Chebyshev's theorem** provides an answer to this problem. It was developed by Russian mathematician P. L. Chebyshev (1821–1894). Chebyshev's theorem states that regardless of the shape of the distribution, at least $1-\frac{1}{k^2}$ values fall within $\pm k$ standard deviation of the mean. More specifically, within k standard deviation of the mean, $\mu \pm k\sigma$, at least $1-\frac{1}{k^2}$ of the values will fall.

If $k = 1$, at least $1-\frac{1}{k^2}=1-\frac{1}{1^2}=0$, that is, 0% of the values will fall within $\pm\sigma$ of the mean regardless of the shape of the distribution. Similarly, when $k = 2$, at least $1-\frac{1}{k^2}=1-\frac{1}{2^2}=0.75$, that is, 75% of the values will fall within $\pm 2\ \sigma$ of the mean regardless of the shape of the distribution. For $k = 3$, at least $1-\frac{1}{k^2}=1-\frac{1}{3^2}=0.8889$, that is, 88.9% of the values will fall within $\pm 3\sigma$ of the mean regardless of the shape of the distribution. For $k = 4$, at least $1-\frac{1}{k^2}=1-\frac{1}{4^2}=0.9375$, that is, 93.75% of the values will fall within $\pm 4\sigma$ of the mean regardless of the shape of the distribution. This theorem has its own limitation. For $k = 1$, at least $1-\frac{1}{k^2}=1-\frac{1}{1^2}=0$, that is, 0% of the values will fall within $\pm\sigma$ of the mean. This result does not provide any information.

11.8 MEASURES OF SHAPE

Measures of shape are the tools used for describing the shape of a distribution of the data. This section focuses on two measures of shape: skewness and kurtosis. Box-and-whisker plots are also discussed in this chapter.

11.8.1 Skewness

A distribution of data where the right half is the mirror image of the left half is said to be symmetrical. If the distribution is not symmetrical, it is said to be asymmetrical or skewed.

The distribution of data may or may not be symmetrical. A distribution where the right half is the mirror image of the left half is said to be symmetrical. If the distribution is not symmetrical, it is said to be **asymmetrical or skewed**. Figure 11.6(a) shows a distribution which is left-skewed or negatively skewed, Figure 11.6(b) shows a distribution which is right-skewed or positively skewed, and Figure 11.6(c) shows a distribution which is symmetrical.

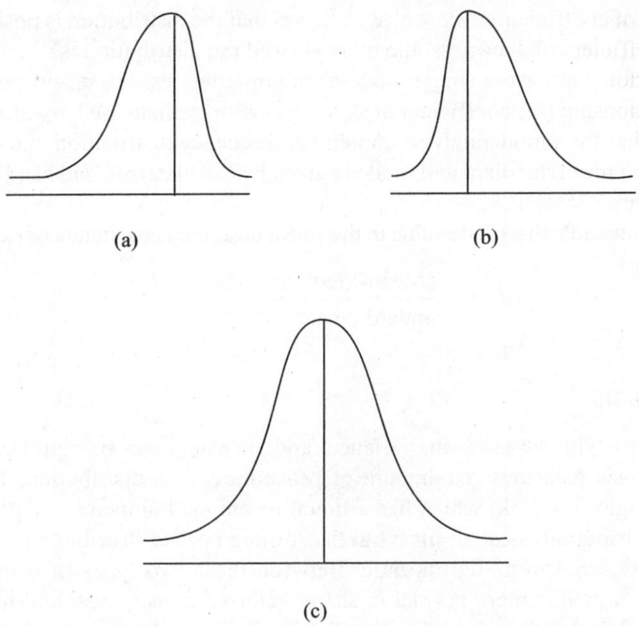

FIGURE 11.6
(a) Left skewed distribution, (b) right skewed distribution, and (c) symmetrical distribution

The concept of skewness is also helpful in understanding the relationship between mean, median, and mode. In the case of a unimodal distribution (distribution having a single peak or mode) that is skewed (either negative or positive), the mode is the peak point of the curve and the median is the middle value of the curve. Mean is located toward the tail of the distribution because mean is affected by all the values of the observations including extreme values. In a symmetric distribution, mean, median, and mode fall at the center of the distribution with no skewness. Figure 10.3 (in Chapter 10) shows the relationship between mean, median, and mode for symmetric, negative skewed and positive skewed distributions, respectively.

11.8.2 Coefficient of Skewness

Karl Pearson developed a method for measuring skewness, referred to as the **Pearsonian coefficient** of skewness. This coefficient compares mean and mode and is divided by standard deviation. Pearsonian **coefficient of skewness** is given as

Karl Pearson developed a method for measuring skewness, referred to as the Pearsonian coefficient of skewness.

$$Sk_p = \frac{\text{Mean} - \text{Mode}}{\text{Standard deviation}} = \frac{\bar{x} - M_o}{\sigma}$$

In theory, there is no limit to the computed value of Pearsonian coefficient of skewness and is a considered demerit. In practice, the formula rarely produces any high value and generally lies in between ±1. Here, it is important to note that for a symmetrical distribution where **mean = median = mode**, that is, $\bar{x} = M_d = M_o$, the Pearsonian coefficient of skewness is computed as zero. For a positively skewed distribution, the coefficient of skewness will have a plus sign and for a distribution that is negatively skewed, the coefficient of skewness will have a minus sign. The actual degree of skewness can be obtained from the numerical value of the coefficient of skewness.

For a symmetrical distribution where mean = median = mode, that is, $\bar{x} = M_d = M_o$, the Pearsonian coefficient of skewness is computed as zero. For a positively skewed distribution, the coefficient of skewness will have a plus sign and for a negatively skewed distribution, the coefficient of skewness will have a minus sign.

For example, a distribution has mean 20, mode 15, and standard deviation 11. Then, the coefficient of skewness can be computed as

$$Sk_p = \frac{\text{Mean} - \text{Mode}}{\text{Standard deviation}} = \frac{20 - 15}{11} = \frac{5}{11} = +0.45$$

A positive sign of coefficient of skewness indicates that the distribution is positively skewed. Greater the coefficient of skewness, the more skewed the distribution is.

A distribution can have a single mode or multiple modes. So, it will be convenient to define this relationship (for coefficient of skewness) with median. We have already discussed in Chapter 10 that for a moderately asymmetrical frequency distribution, the empirical relationship between mean, median, and mode is given by Karl Pearson and can be defined as Mode = 3Median – 2Mean

When we substitute this mode value in the above described coefficient of skewness, we get

$$Sk_{\mathrm{p}} = \frac{3(\text{Mean-Median})}{\text{Standard deviation}} = \frac{3(\bar{x} - M_{\mathrm{d}})}{\sigma}$$

11.8.3 Kurtosis

Kurtosis measures the amount of peakedness of a distribution. A flatter distribution than a normal distribution is called platykurtic. A more peaked distribution than the normal distribution is referred to as leptokurtic. Between these two types of distribution is a distribution which is more normal in shape, referred to as mesokurtic distribution.

Two distributions with same mean, variance, and skewness can be significantly different in shape. **Kurtosis** measures the amount of peakedness of a distribution. The word, kurtosis, has its origin in Greek, which has a literal meaning "humped." A flatter distribution than normal distribution is called **platykurtic**. A more peaked distribution than the normal distribution is referred to as **leptokurtic**. Between these two types of distribution, there is a distribution which is more normal in shape, referred to as a **mesokurtic distribution**. Figure 11.7(a–c) exhibits a **leptokurtic distribution**, a **platykurtic distribution**, and mesokurtic distribution, respectively. A negative kurtosis value implies a platykurtic distribution and a positive kurtosis value implies a leptokurtic distribution.

11.9 THE FIVE-NUMBER SUMMARY

In the **five-number summary**, five numbers—the smallest value, the first quartile, the median, the third quartile, and the largest value are used to summarize data. In the case of a symmetrical distribution, the relationship between the various measures of the five-number summary is expressed as

- the distance from the smallest value to the median and the distance from the median to the largest value remains equal;
- the distance from the smallest value to the first quartile and the distance from the third quartile to the largest value remains equal.

In the case of an asymmetrical distribution, the relationship between the various measures of five-number summary is expressed as follows:

- In a right-skewed distribution, the distance from the median to the largest value is greater than the distance from the smallest value to the median.
- In a right-skewed distribution, the distance from the third quartile to the largest value is greater than the distance from the smallest value to the first quartile.
- In a left-skewed distribution, the distance from the median to the largest value is less than the distance from the smallest value to the median.
- In a left-skewed distribution, the distance from the third quartile to the largest value is less than the distance from the smallest value to the first quartile.

For Example 11.1, smallest value = 100, first quartile = 113.55, median = 300, third quartile = 565, and largest value = 750. These five numbers can be used to assess the shape of the distribution (from Figure 11.8). Figure 11.8 is the Minitab output exhibiting smallest value, first quartile, median, third quartile, and largest value.

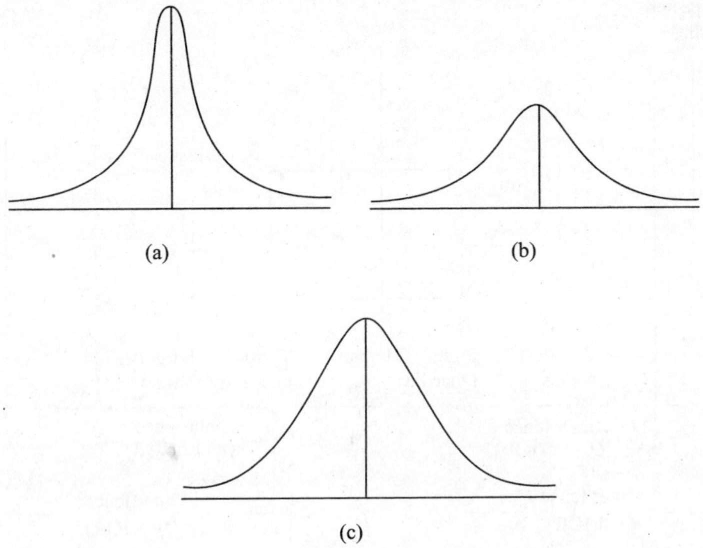

FIGURE 11.7
(a) Leptokurtic distribution, (b) Platykurtic distribution, and (c) Mesokurtic distribution

Descrptive Statistics: Series

Variable	Minimum	Q1	Median	Q3	Maximum	IQR
Series	100.0	113.5	300.0	565.0	750.0	451.5

FIGURE 11.8
Minitab output exhibiting computation of smallest value, first quartile, median, third quartile, and largest value for Example 11.1

The distance from the median to the largest value (750 – 300 = 350) is greater than the distance from the smallest value to the median (300 – 100 = 200). Also the distance from the third quartile to the largest value (750 – 565 = 185) is greater than the distance from the smallest value to the first quartile (113.5 – 100 = 13.5). Therefore, distribution of the data for Example 11.1 is right skewed.

11.10 BOX-AND-WHISKER PLOTS

Box-and-whisker plot is another way to describe a distribution of data (Figure 11.9). In fact, a box-and-whisker plot is a graphical representation of the data based on the five-number summary. Figure 11.10 is a Minitab-produced box-and-whisker plot and Figure 11.11 is an SPSS-produced box-and-whisker plot for Example 11.1. Figure 11.9 explains the elements of a box-and-whisker plot. In the figure, the vertical line within the box represents median. The vertical line at the left side of the box, represents the location of the first quartile and vertical line at the right side of the box represents the location of the third quartile. Interquartile range (*IQR*) is the difference between third quartile (Q_3) and first quartile (Q_1), covers 50% of the data and is equal to length of the box. The distance of 1.5(*IQR*) from the lower and upper quartile is referred to as inner fences. The distance of 3(*IQR*) from the hinges (lower and upper quartile) is referred to as outer fences. Any data value which is in between inner fences and outer fences is marked as suspected outlier. Any data value which is outside the outer fences is marked as outlier.

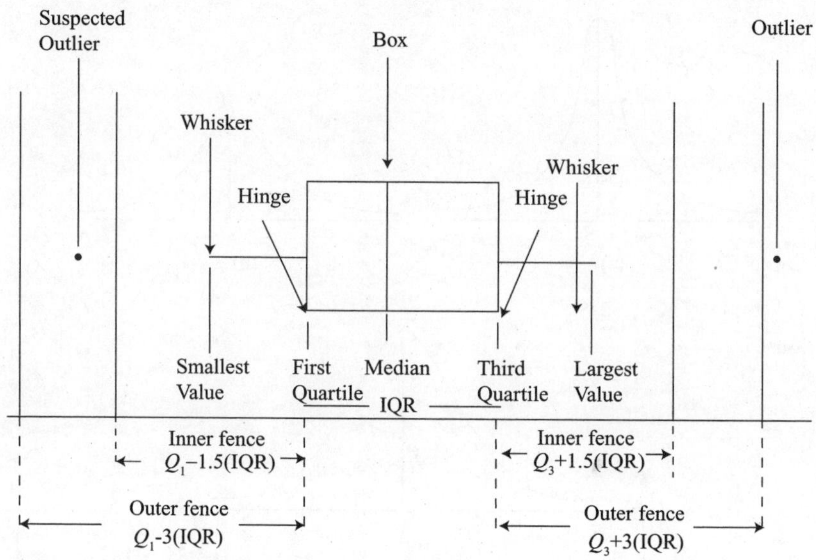

FIGURE 11.9
Elements of box-and-whisker plot

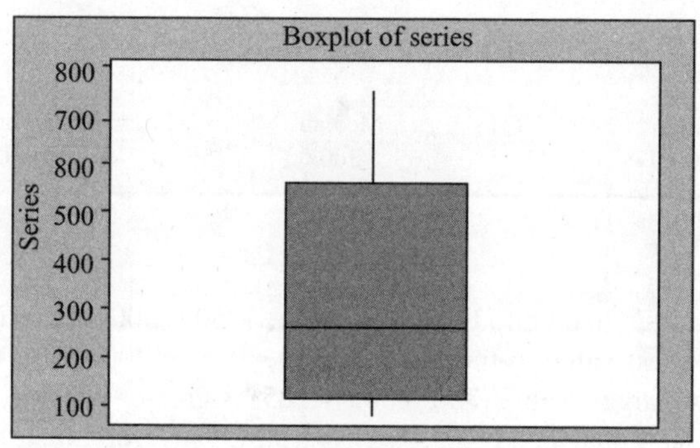

FIGURE 11.10
Box-and-whisker plot for Example 11.1 produced using Minitab

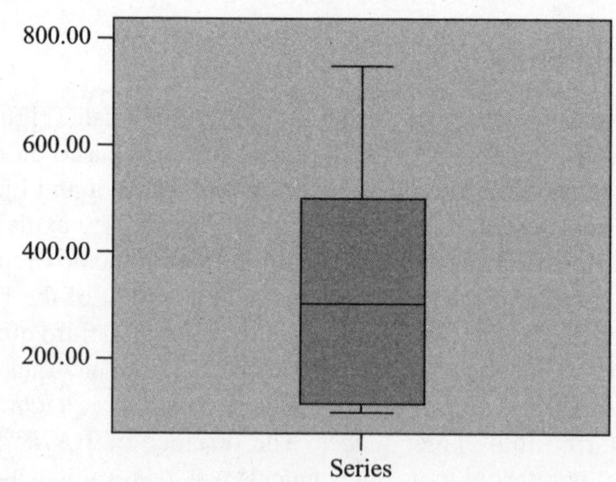

FIGURE 11.11
Box-and-whisker plot for Example 11.1 produced using SPSS

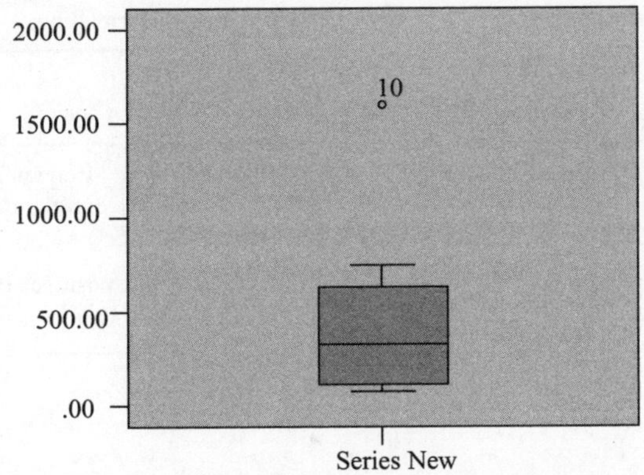

FIGURE 11.12
SPSS produced box-and-whisker plot for Example 11.1 (produced after inserting a new value 1600)

Thus, box-and-whisker plots can be used to identify outliers. They can also be used to determine the skewness of a distribution. If median is located in the left side of the box, then the distribution is right skewed, and if the median is located on the right side of the box, the distribution is left skewed. If the median is located in the middle of the box, then the distribution is symmetrical. The length of the whisker on both the sides of the box can also be used to judge the skewness of the outer values. If the whisker is longest to the right side of the box, then outer data are skewed to the right and vice versa. Figures 11.9–11.11 exhibit a right-skewed distribution. They also show that the outer data are skewed to the right. From Example 11.1, it can be seen that none of the values are outliers. Suppose we introduce one more item as 1600 in the series given in Example 11.1. The box-and-whisker plot (from SPSS) for this new series is given in Figure 11.12. It can be noticed that this new item (10th item of the series, i.e. 1600) is beyond the outer fence ($Q_1 + 3\text{IQR} = 113.5 + 1354.5 = 1468$) of the box-and-whisker plot and marked as an outlier in the box-and-whisker plot as shown in Figure 11.12.

11.10.1 Using Minitab for Box-and-Whisker Plot Construction

Minitab can be used easily for box-and-whisker plot construction. Click **Graph/Box Plot**. The **Box Plot** dialog box will appear on the screen. Click **Simple** and **OK** in the dialog box. The **Box plot – One Y, Simple** dialog box will appear on the screen. Place series (variables) in **Graph variables** box and click **OK**. The Box-and-whisker plot for Example 11.1 as exhibited in Figure 11.10 will appear on the screen.

11.10.2 Using SPSS for Box-and-Whisker Plot Construction

SPSS can also be used easily to construct a box-and-whisker plot. Click **Graph/Legacy Dialogs/Box plot**. The **Boxplot** dialog box will appear on the screen. In this dialog box, select **Simple** and from **Data in Chart Are**, select **Summaries of separate variables** and click **Define**. The **Define Simple Boxplot: Summaries of Separate Variables** dialog box will appear on the screen. Place the variable list in **Boxes Represent** box and click **OK**. The box-and-whisker plot as shown in Figure 11.11 will appear on the screen.

11.11 MEASURES OF ASSOCIATION

Measures of association are statistics for measuring the strength of a relationship between two variables. This chapter focuses on only one measure of association, that is, correlation for two numerical variables.

Measures of association are statistics for measuring the strength of relationship between two variables.

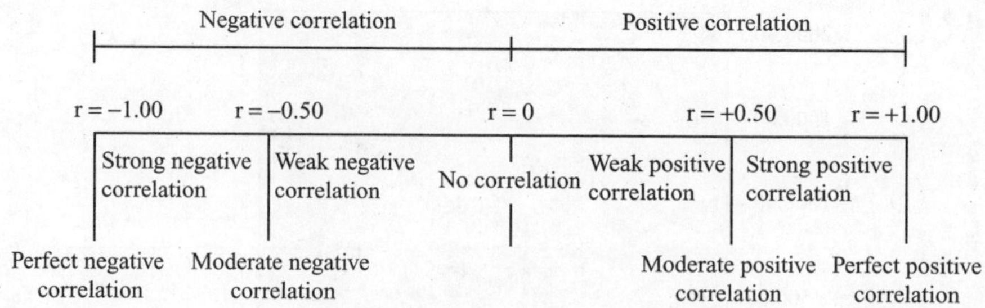

FIGURE 11.13
Interpretation of correlation coefficient

11.11.1 Correlation

Correlation measures the degree of association between two variables.

Correlation measures the degree of association between two variables. For example, a business manager may be interested in knowing the degree of relationship between two variables: sales and advertisement. In this section, we focus on one method of determining correlation between two variables: Karl Pearson's coefficient of correlation.

Karl Pearson's coefficient of correlation is a quantitative measure of the degree of relationship between two variables. Coefficient of correlation lies between +1 and −1.

11.11.2 Karl Pearson's Coefficient of Correlation

Karl Pearson's coefficient of correlation is a quantitative measure of the degree of relationship between two variables. Suppose these variables are x and y, then Karl Pearson's coefficient of correlation is defined as

$$r = \frac{n\sum xy - (\sum x)(\sum y)}{\sqrt{n(\sum x^2) - (\sum x)^2}\sqrt{n(\sum y^2) - (\sum y)^2}}$$

The coefficient of correlation lies in between +1 and −1. Figure 11.13 explains how coefficient of correlation measures the extent of relationship between two variables. Figure 11.14 exhibits the SPSS output for Example 11.9. Figure 11.15 exhibits five examples of correlation coefficient.

Example 11.9

Table 11.7 shows the sales revenue and advertisement expenses of a company for the past 10 months. Find the coefficient of correlation between sales and advertisement.

TABLE 11.7
Sales and advertisement for 10 months

Month	*Jan*	*Feb*	*Mar*	*Apr*	*May*	*Jun*	*Jul*	*Aug*	*Sept*	*Oct*
Advertisement (in thousand rupees)	10	11	12	13	11	10	9	10	11	14
Sales (in thousand rupees)	110	120	115	128	137	145	150	130	120	115

Solution

As discussed, the correlation coefficient between sales and advertisement can be obtained by applying Karl Pearson's coefficient of correlation formula as shown in Table 11.8.

$$r = \frac{n\sum xy - (\sum x)(\sum y)}{\sqrt{n(\sum x^2) - (\sum x)^2}\sqrt{n(\sum y^2) - (\sum y)^2}}$$

TABLE 11.8
Calculation of correlation coefficient between sales and advertisement

Month	*Sales (x)*	*Advertisement (y)*	*xy*	x^2	y^2
Jan	110	10	1100	12,100	100
Feb	120	11	1320	14,400	121
Mar	115	12	1380	13,225	144
Apr	128	13	1664	16,384	169
May	137	11	1507	18,769	121
June	145	10	1450	21,025	100
July	150	9	1350	22,500	81
Aug	130	10	1300	16,900	100
Sept	120	11	1320	14,400	121
Oct	115	14	1610	13,225	196
Sum	1270	111	14,001	162,928	1253

Correlations

		Advertisement	Sales
Advertisement	Pearson correlation	1	–.519
	Sig. (2-tailed)	.	.124
	N	10	10
Sales	Pearson correlation	–.519	1
	Sig. (2-tailed)	–.124	.
	N	10	10

FIGURE 11.14
SPSS output for Example 11.9

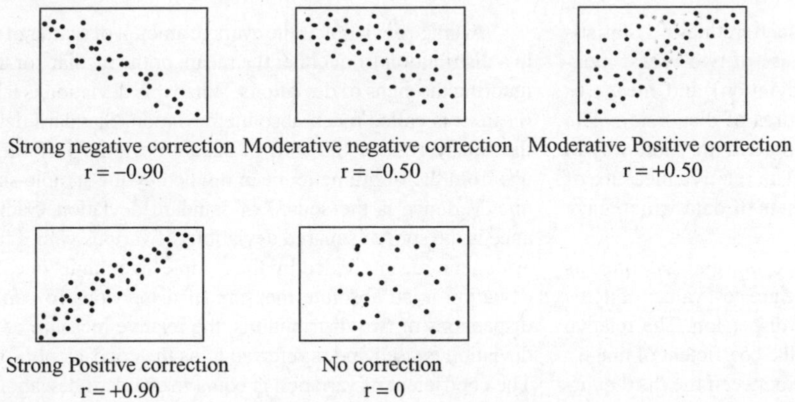

FIGURE 11.15
Five examples of correlation coefficient

$$r=\frac{n\sum xy-(\sum x)(\sum y)}{\sqrt{n(\sum x^2)-(\sum x)^2}\sqrt{n(\sum y^2)-(\sum y)^2}}$$

$$=\frac{10\times 14{,}001-(111)\times(1270)}{\sqrt{10\times(162{,}928)-(1270)^2}\sqrt{10\times(1253)-(111)^2}}$$

$$=\frac{140010-140970}{\sqrt{1{,}629{,}280-1{,}612{,}900}\times\sqrt{12{,}530-12{,}321}}=\frac{-960}{\sqrt{16{,}380}\times\sqrt{209}}$$

$$=\frac{-960}{127.9843\times 14.4568}=\frac{-960}{1850.2434}=-0.51$$

Hence, correlation coefficient between sales and advertisement is –0.51. This indicates that sales and advertisement are negatively correlated to the extent of –0.51. We can conclude that an increase in the expenditure on advertisements will not result in an increase in sales.

SELF-PRACTICE PROBLEMS

11E1. Determine Karl Pearson's coefficient of correlation from the following series:

x	5	8	10	14	17	19	21	22	25	28
y	16	14	10	9	7	6	5	3	3	1

11E2. The table below exhibits the sales and advertisement (in million rupees) of Polar Fan India Ltd. Determine Karl Pearson's coefficient of correlation from the data.

Year	*Sales*	*Advertisement*
Mar 1990	136.1	0.1
Mar 1991	195.3	0.8
Mar 1992	183.9	1.1
Mar 1993	197.6	1
Mar 1994	174.6	0.9
Mar 1995	211	7
Mar 1996	253.5	3.2
Mar 1997	238.9	0.1
Mar 1999	260.9	0.2
Mar 2000	254.8	3.4

Source: Prowess (V. 3.1), Centre for Monitoring Indian Economy Pvt. Ltd, Mumbai, accessed November 2008.

SUMMARY

The literal meaning of dispersion is "scatteredness". Statistical techniques to measure dispersions are of two types: measures of dispersion (or variation or deviation) and measures of shape. There are two types of measures of dispersion. The absolute measure of dispersion is presented in the same way in which the unit of distribution is given. The relative measure of dispersion is useful in comparing two sets of data which have different units of measurement.

Range is the simplest measure of dispersion and is defined as the difference between the smallest and the greatest values of items in a series. It is an absolute measure of dispersion. The relative measure of dispersion for range is called the coefficient of range.

Interquartile range is the difference between the third quartile and the first quartile. It is reduced to the form of quartile deviation or semi-interquartile range, which is obtained by dividing the interquartile range by 2.

Average deviation is the average amount of scatter of the items in a distribution from either the mean, or the median, or the mode, ignoring the signs of deviations. When this deviation is taken from mean, it is called mean absolute deviation. Standard deviation is the square root of the sum of square deviations of various values from their arithmetic mean divided by the sample size minus one. Variance is the square of standard deviation. Sample variance is the sum of squared deviations of various values from their arithmetic mean divided by the sample size minus one. Standard deviation is an absolute measure of dispersion. To compare the dispersions of two distributions, the relative measure of standard deviation is used and is referred to as the coefficient of variation. The coefficient of variation is equal to standard deviation divided by the arithmetic mean and the resultant multiplied by 100.

Standard deviation leads to a very important empirical rule. For a symmetrical bell-shaped frequency distribution, the range within which approximate percentage of values of the distribution are likely to fall within a given number of standard deviation from the mean is determined as $\mu \pm 1\sigma$, that is, mean ± 1 standard deviation covers 68.27% of the items in a data set; $\mu \pm 2\sigma$, that is, mean ± 2 standard deviation covers 95.45% of the items in a data set; $\mu \pm 3\sigma$, that is, mean ± 3 standard deviation covers 99.73% of the items in a data set.

Empirical rule applies only to normally distributed data. It has a wide range of applicability but in cases where data distribution is not normal or where the shape of the distribution is not known, its applicability is restricted. Chebyshev's theorem states that regardless of the shape of the distribution, at least $1-\frac{1}{k^2}$ values fall within $\pm k$ standard deviation of the mean.

Measures of shape are the tools which are used for describing the shape of the data distribution. Karl Pearson developed a method for measuring skewness which is referred to as the Pearsonian coefficient of skewness. This coefficient compares mean and mode, divided by standard deviation. For a positively skewed distribution, the coefficient of skewness will have a plus sign, whereas for a negatively skewed distribution, the coefficient of skewness will have a minus sign. Kurtosis measures the amount of peakedness of a distribution. In five-number summary, five numbers – smallest value, first quartile, median, third quartile, and largest value are used to summarize data. Box-and-whisker plot is another way to describe the distribution of data. In fact, a box-and-whisker plot is a graphical representation of the data based on the five-number summary.

Measures of association are statistics for measuring the strength of relationship between two variables. Correlation measures the association between two variables. Karl Pearson's coefficient of correlation is a quantitative measure of the degree of relationship between two variables.

KEY TERMS |

Absolute measure of dispersion, 253
Average absolute deviation, 259
Box-and-whisker plot, 273
Chebyshev's theorem, 270
Coefficient of skewness, 271
Coefficient of variation, 263
Correlation, 268
Dispersion, 252
Five-number summary, 272
Interquartile range, 253
Kurtosis, 268
Leptokurtic distribution, 272
Measures of association, 275
Measures of dispersion, 253
Measures of shape, 253
Mesokurtic distribution, 272
Platykurtic distribution, 272
Quartile deviation, 253
Range, 253
Relative measure of dispersion, 254
Skewness, 268
Standard deviation, 253
Variance, 263

NOTES |

1. Prowess (V. 2.6), Centre for Monitoring Indian Economy Pvt. Ltd, Mumbai, accessed July 2008, reproduced with permission.
2. www.dabur.com, accessed July 2008.

DISCUSSION QUESTIONS |

1. What is the meaning of dispersion? State its utility.
2. What are the various methods of measuring dispersion? Explain with suitable examples.
3. Describe range, its merits, and demerits and its uses.
4. Explain the concept of interquartile range and quartile deviation.
5. What is the meaning of mean deviation? Explain mean deviation in light of average deviation.
6. What are the merits, demerits, and utility of mean deviation.
7. What is the meaning of standard deviation? Explain why standard deviation is the most preferred and widely used tool of measure of dispersion.
8. What are the merits, demerits, and uses of standard deviation.
9. What are the mathematical properties of standard deviation? State its application in the field of management.
10. What is the concept of coefficient of variation? What is the application of coefficient of variation in the field of management?
11. Explain the main difference between mean deviation and standard deviation.
12. What are measures of shape? Explain the importance of measures of shape in summarizing data.
13. What are measures of association? What is the tool used for measuring the strength of relationship between two variables?

NUMERICAL PROBLEMS

1. The following data lists the average salary in thousand rupees offered to nine students during placement interviews. Find the range and its coefficient from the following series:
   96, 180, 98, 75, 270, 80, 102, 100, 94
2. A company has decided to purchase special shoes for security guards. The following series shows the number of security guards and the required shoe sizes for these guards. Find the range and its coefficient from the following distribution:

Shoe size:	6	7	8	9	10	11
Number of security guards:	7	10	15	13	3	1

3. Find interquartile range, quartile deviation, and its coefficient for the data given in Problem 1.
4. Find interquartile range, quartile deviation, and its coefficient for the data given in Problem 2.
5. Find the mean absolute deviation and coefficient of mean absolute deviation for the data given in Problem 1.
6. Find the mean absolute deviation and coefficient of mean absolute deviation for the data given in Problem 1.
7. Find standard deviation and variance for the data given in Problem 1.
8. Find standard deviation and variance for the data given in Problem 2.
9. The following table shows the sales and expenditure in sales promotion schemes of a company for the past 10 years. Find the coefficient of correlation between sales and expenditure.

Year	*Sales (in thousand rupees)*	*Expenditure in sales promotion schemes (in thousand rupees)*
1995	20	220
1996	25	210
1997	35	280
1998	32	300
1999	40	270
2000	44	350
2001	48	325
2002	50	400
2003	55	375
2004	60	360

CASE STUDY

Case 11: *Hero Honda Motors Ltd: Aiming to Capture the Growing Market in India*

Introduction

Hero Honda Motors Ltd came into existence on 19 January 1984 as a result of a joint venture between India's Hero Group and Japan's Honda Motor Company. During the 1980s, Hero Honda became the first company in India to prove that it was possible to drive a vehicle without polluting the roads. The company introduced new generation motorcycles that set the industry benchmark for fuel thrift and low emission. The legendary "Fill it–Shut it–Forget it" slogan captured the imagination of millions across India. Hero Honda sold millions of bikes on its commitment of increased mileage.[1]

Products Offered by Hero Honda Motors Ltd

The company produces motorcycles and scooters. Some of its brands are Achiever, Karizma, CBZ, Splendor, Super Splendor, Splendor Plus, Glamour, Passion, Passion Plus, CD Deluxe, CD 100 SS, Sleek, and CD Dawn. The company also manufactures spare parts for these two wheelers. It also provides mobile after-sales service to its existing customers.[2]

In urban India, lower taxes and good salary increments across sectors have resulted in an increase in the disposable income in the hands of consumers. A sizeable chunk of GDP now comes from the service sector, which contributes 54% to the country's total GDP. More significantly, the fastest growing segment in the service sector, information technology and IT-enabled services, is being driven by youth.[2] Before the1980s, motorcycles were considered to be the ideal transport medium for rural India. However, in the changing environment, motorcycles are preferred by urban youth because of the attractions of style and speed. The motorcycle market overtook the scooter market in 1998–1999 and this trend seems to be continuing. The changing nature of jobs especially in selling, marketing, etc. low EMIs offered by financial institutions, increasing disposable incomes, and rising fuel prices are some of the factors that have contributed to the increase in the size of the motorcycle market. India could have more than a dozen metropolitan cities by the next decade, and this will throw up its own challenges and opportunities. Hero Honda has already begun seeding the rural market, especially in north and west India, through loan tie-ups with two leading banks, the Punjab State Cooperative Bank and the State Bank of India. Similarly, through a tie-up with the state bank of India, Hero Honda field officers are working directly with the bank branch officers reaching rural credit holders (Kisan credit cards) in specific regions and approaching farmers personally.[2]

An Optimistic Future

According to the 2005 National Council of Applied Economic Research (NCAER) study on India's consuming classes, currently around 20 million Indian families (around 100 million consumers) have an annual income of more ₹200,000 making them ripe candidates for consumer durable purchases. The NCAER data also shows that there are currently twice the number of motorcycle owners in the ₹200,000–500,000 income segment, compared to the ₹90,000–200,000 income segment. Those earning between ₹200,000 and ₹500,000 per year are projected to nearly treble by 2009–2010. Hero Honda expects this income group to be a key constituency for its price and deluxe category motorcycles, which accounts for the bulk of its product portfolio.[2]

Hero Honda believes that the changing demographic profile of India, increasing urbanization, and the empowerment of rural India will add millions of new families to the economic mainstream. This would provide the growth ballast that would sustain Hero Honda in the years to come. As Brijmohan Munjal, chairman of Hero Honda Motors, succinctly points out, "We pioneered India's motorcycle industry, and it is our responsibility now to take the industry to the next level. We will do all it takes to reach there."[1]

Table 11.01 gives the total income of the company from the year 1990 to 2006.

TABLE 11.01
Total income of Hero Honda Motors Limited (1990–2006)

Year	*Total income (in million rupees)*
1990	1523.3
1991	2187.0
1992	2757.3
1993	3134.7
1994	3667.1
1995	5087.6
1996	6187.1
1997	7840.3
1998	11,642.2
1999	15,655.3
2000	22,698.0
2001	32,060.0
2002	45,132.7
2003	51,520.3
2004	67,864.8
2005	86,656.2
2006	101,879.5

Source: Prowess (V. 2.6.), Centre for Monitoring Indian Economy Pvt. Ltd, Mumbai, accessed September 2008, reproduced with permission.

Figure 11.01 is the MS Excel output (**Descriptive Statistics**) and Figure 11.02 is the Minitab output (**Graphical Summary**) of the total income of Hero Honda Motors Ltd. From the output, prepare a detailed statistical report on the success story of the company.

	A	B
1	*Descriptive Statistics*	
2		
3	Mean	27499.61176
4	Standard Error	7768.966788
5	Median	11642.2
6	Mode	#N/A
7	Standard Deviation	32032.27067
8	Sample Variance	1026066364
9	Kurtosis	0.542188703
10	Skewness	1.276985473
11	Range	100356.2
12	Minimum	1523.3
13	Maximum	101879.5
14	Sum	467493.4
15	Count	17
16	Largest(1)	101879.5
17	Smallest(1)	1523.3
18	Confidence Level(95.0%)	16469.47375

FIGURE 11.01
MS Excel output (Descriptive Statistics) of the total income of Hero Honda Motors Ltd from 1990 to 2006

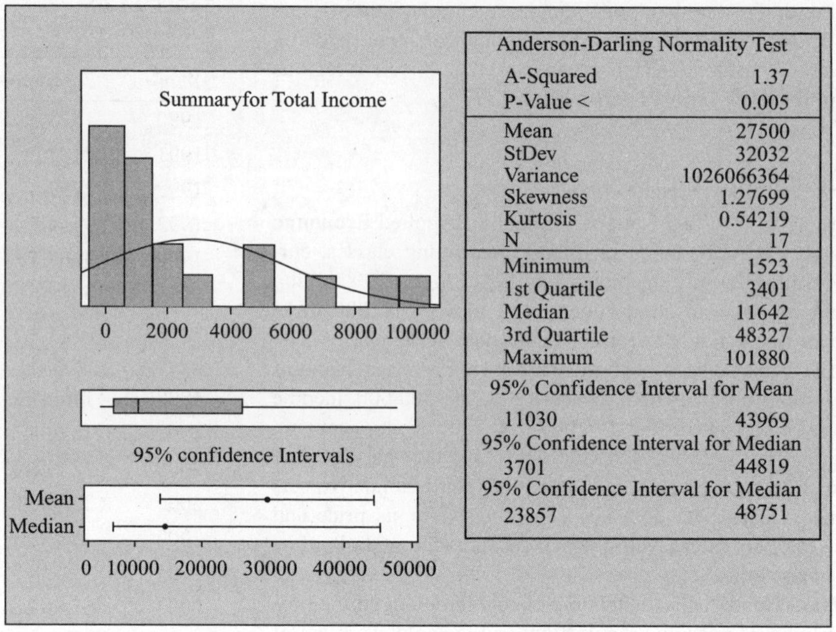

FIGURE 11.02
Minitab output (graphical summary) of the total income of Hero Honda Motors Ltd from 1990 to 2006

NOTES |

1. www.herohonda.com/co_corporate_profile.htm, accessed July 2008.
2. Prowess (V. 2.6), Centre for Monitoring Indian Economy Pvt. Ltd, Mumbai, accessed July 2008, reproduced with permission.

CHAPTER 12

Statistical Inference: Hypothesis Testing for Single Populations

LEARNING OBJECTIVES

Upon completion of this chapter, you will be able to:

- Understand hypothesis-testing procedure using one-tailed and two-tailed tests
- Understand the concepts of Type I and Type II errors in hypothesis testing
- Understand the concept of hypothesis testing for a single population using the *z* statistic
- Understand the concepts of *p*-value approach and critical value approach for hypothesis testing
- Understand the concept of hypothesis testing for a single population using the *t* statistic
- Understand the procedure of hypothesis testing for population proportion

STATISTICS IN ACTION: LIBERTY SHOES LTD

The footwear industry in India contributes significantly to exports and has great potential for growth in the country's new economy. Currently, the share of India in the global footwear market is not that significant. However, if the GDP grows at the current rate and the inflow of foreign investments continue, the Indian footwear industry will become competitive enough to increase its share in the global market. India is the seventh largest exporter of shoes to the USA and has established itself as an exporter of quality leather shoes in the European market.[1] The Indian shoe market is dominated by the informal sector with a market share of 82%, with a meagre 18% market share for the organized sector. The market share of products by price also varies significantly. Low, mid, and high-priced products have a market share of 65%, 32%, and 3% respectively.[2] Bata India, Liberty Shoes, Lakhani India, Nikhil Footwears, Graziella shoes, Mirza Tanners, Relaxo Footwear, Performance shoes, and Aero group are some of the key players in the organized shoe market.

Liberty Shoes Ltd is the only Indian company that is among the top five manufacturers of leather footwear in the world with a turnover exceeding US $100 million. Liberty produces more than 50,000 pairs of footwear daily covering virtually every age group and income category. Its products are marketed across the globe through 150 distributors, 350 exclusive showrooms and over 6000 multi-brand outlets, and sold in thousands every day in more than 25 countries including fashion-driven, quality-obsessed nations such as France, Italy, and Germany.[3] Table 12.1 gives the sales turnover of Liberty Shoes Ltd from 2001 to 2007.

Bata India is the industry leader in the footwear market in India. Suppose Liberty Shoes Ltd wants to ascertain how its products are positioned in the market when compared to previous years. The company can collect data from its

>>>

customers only through the process of sampling. How should a decision maker collect sample data, compute sample statistics, and use this information to ascertain the correctness of the hypothesized population parameter? Also, if Liberty wants to check whether the 18% market share attributed to the organized sector is correct, it can take a sample of consumers, compute sample statistic, and use this information to ascertain the correctness of the hypothesized population parameter. This chapter discusses the concept of hypothesis testing, two-tailed and one-tailed tests of hypothesis testing, concept of Type I and Type II errors in hypothesis testing, concept of hypothesis testing for a single population using *z* statistic, the concept of *p*-value approach and critical value approach for hypothesis testing, the concept of hypothesis testing for a single population using *t* statistic, and the procedure of hypothesis testing for population proportion.

TABLE 12.1
Sales turnover of Liberty Shoes Ltd from 2001–2007

Year	*Sales (in million rupees)*
2001	631.8
2002	729.6
2003	729.7
2004	2061.5
2005	1987.5
2006	2278.9
2007	2416.7

Source: Prowess (V. 3.1) Centre for Monitoring Indian Economy Pvt. Ltd, Mumbai, accessed July 2008, reproduced with permission.

12.1 INTRODUCTION

We know how a sample can be used to develop point and interval estimates for assessing the population parameter (see *Business Statistics*, Bajpai 2009). Statistical inference is based on estimation and **hypothesis testing**. In this chapter, we will continue the discussion of statistical inference in terms of hypothesis testing. Hypothesis testing is the soul of inferential statistics and is a very important tool, which can be used by a marketing researcher to arrive at a meaningful conclusion. The main objective of this chapter is to discuss how hypothesis testing can be conducted around population parameters.

12.2 INTRODUCTION TO HYPOTHESIS TESTING

In diverse fields such as marketing, personnel management, financial management, etc. decision makers might need answers to certain questions in order to take optimum decisions. For example, a marketing manager might be interested in assessing the customer loyalty for a particular product; a personnel manager might be interested in knowing the job satisfaction level of employees; a financial manager might be interested in understanding the financial aspect of the company's retirement scheme, etc. In every case the concerned manager has to make decisions on the basis of the available information and in most cases, information is obtained through sampling. The sample statistic is computed through sampling and it is used to make an inference about the population parameters. These are just examples. In real life, managers encounter many situations where they need to find solutions to problems. As discussed earlier, a complete census is neither practical nor statistically recommended (due to non-sampling errors).

A statistical hypothesis is an assumption about an unknown population parameter.

In order to find out the answers to these questions, a decision maker needs to collect sample data, compute the sample statistic and use this information to ascertain the correctness of the hypothesized population parameter. For this purpose, a researcher develops a "hypothesis" which can be studied and explored. For example, suppose the Vice President (HR) of a company wants to know the effectiveness of a training programme which the company has organized for all its 70,000 employees based at 130 different locations in the country. Contacting all these employees with an effectiveness measurement questionnaire is not feasible. So the Vice President (HR) takes a sample of size 629 from all the different locations in the country. The result that is obtained would not be the result from the entire population but only from the sample. The Vice President (HR) will then set an assumption that "training has not enhanced efficiency" and will accept or reject this assumption through a well-defined statistical procedure known as **hypothesis testing**. A statistical hypothesis is an assumption about an unknown population parameter. Hypothesis testing starts with an assumption termed as "hypothesis" that a researcher makes about a population parameter. We cannot accept or reject the hypothesis on the basis of intuition or on the basis of general information. **Hypothesis testing** is a well-defined procedure which helps us to decide objectively whether to accept or reject the hypothesis based on the information available from the sample.

Hypothesis testing is a well-defined procedure which helps us to decide objectively whether to accept or reject the hypothesis based on the information available from the sample.

Now we need to understand the rationale of hypothesis testing. Drawing a random sample from the population is based on the assumption that the sample will resemble the population. Based on this philosophy, the known sample statistic is used for estimating the unknown population parameter. When a researcher sets a hypothesis or assumption, he assumes that the sample statistic will be close to the hypothesized population parameter. This is possible in cases where the hypothesized population parameter is correct and the sample statistic is a good estimate of the population parameter. In real life, we cannot expect the sample statistic to always be a good estimate of the population parameter. Differences are likely to occur due to sampling and non-sampling errors or due to chance. A large difference between the sample statistic and the hypothesized population parameter raises questions on the accuracy of the sampling technique. In statistical analysis, we use the concept of probability to specify a probability level at which a researcher concludes that the observed difference between the sample statistic and the population parameter is not due to chance.

In statistical analysis, we use the concept of probability to specify a probability level at which a researcher concludes that the observed difference between the sample statistic and the population parameter is not due to chance.

12.3 HYPOTHESIS TESTING PROCEDURE

We have already discussed that hypothesis testing is a well-defined procedure. A sample is selected for estimating the population parameter. Sample statistic is computed from this sample and is used to estimate the population parameter. A systematic procedure needs to be adopted for hypothesis testing. The seven steps in hypothesis testing are shown in Figure 12.1.

Step 1: Set null and alternative hypotheses

The null hypothesis, generally referred to as H_0 (H sub-zero), is the hypothesis which is tested for possible rejection under the assumption that it is true. Theoretically, a null hypothesis is set as no difference or status quo and considered true, until and unless it is proved wrong by the collected sample data. The null hypothesis is always expressed in the form of an equation, which makes a claim regarding the specific value of the population. Symbolically, a null hypothesis is represented as

$$H_0\text{: } \mu = \mu_0$$

where μ is the population mean and μ_0 is the hypothesized value of the population mean. For example, to test whether a population mean is equal to 150, a null hypothesis can be set as "population mean is equal to 150." Symbolically,

$$H_0\text{: } \mu = 150$$

The null hypothesis generally referred by H_0 (H sub-zero), is the hypothesis which is tested for possible rejection under the assumption that is true. Theoretically, a null hypothesis is set as no difference or status quo and considered true, until and unless it is proved wrong by the collected sample data.

The **alternative hypothesis**, generally referred by H_1 (H sub-one), is the logical opposite of the null hypothesis. In other words, when null hypothesis is found to be true, the

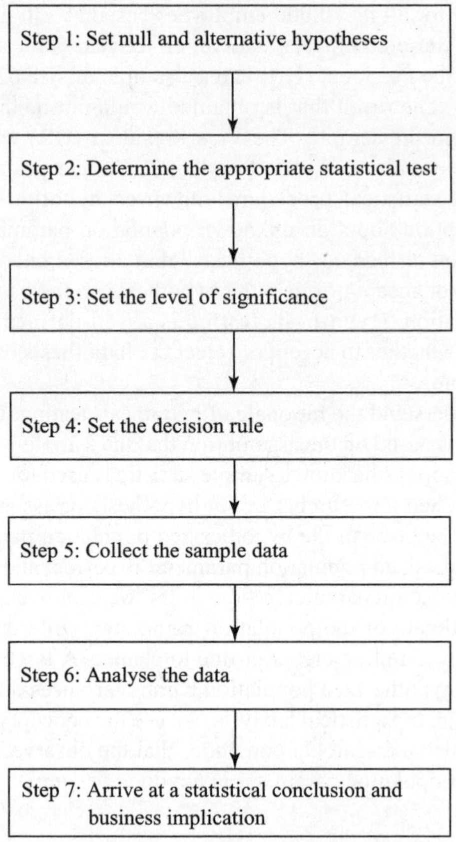

FIGURE 12.1
Seven steps of hypothesis testing

> The alternative hypothesis, generally referred by H_1 (H sub-one), is a logical opposite of the null hypothesis. In other words, when null hypothesis is found to be true, the alternative hypothesis must be false or when the null hypothesis is found to be false, the alternative hypothesis must be true.

alternative hypothesis must be false or when null hypothesis is found to be false, the alternative hypothesis must be true. Symbolically, alternative hypothesis is represented as:

$$H_1: \mu \neq \mu_0$$

Consequently,

$$H_1: \mu < \mu_0$$

$$H_1: \mu > \mu_0$$

For the above example, the alternative hypothesis can be set as "population mean is not equal to 150." Symbolically,

$$H_1: \mu \neq 150$$

This results in two more alternative hypotheses, H_1: $\mu < 150$, which indicates that the population mean is less than 150 and H_1: $\mu > 150$; which indicates that the population mean is greater than 150.

Step 2: Determine the appropriate statistical test

After setting the hypothesis, the researcher has to decide on an appropriate statistical test that will be used for statistical analysis. Type, number, and the level of data may provide a platform for deciding the statistical test. Apart from these, the statistics used in the study (mean, proportion, variance, etc.) must also be considered when a researcher decides on appropriate statistical test, which can be applied for hypothesis testing in order to obtain the best results.

Step 3: Set the level of significance

The **level of significance** generally denoted by α is the probability, which is attached to a null hypothesis, which may be rejected even when it is true. The level of significance is also known as the size of the rejection region or the size of the critical region. It is very important to note that the level of significance must be determined before we draw samples, so that the obtained result is free from the choice bias of a decision maker. The levels of significance which are generally applied by researchers are: 0.01; 0.05; 0.10. The concept of "level of significance" is discussed in detail later in this chapter.

The level of significance, generally denoted by α is the probability, which is attached to a null hypothesis, which may be rejected even when this is true. The level of significance is also known as the size of rejection region or the size of the critical region.

Step 4: Set the decision rule

The next step for the researcher is to establish **a critical region**, which is the area under the normal curve, divided into two mutually exclusive regions (shown in Figure 12.2). These regions are termed as acceptance region (when the null hypothesis is accepted) and the rejection region or critical region (when the null hypothesis is rejected).

If the computed value of the test statistic falls in the acceptance region, the null hypothesis is accepted, otherwise it is rejected. For making a decision regarding the acceptance or rejection of the null hypothesis, a researcher has to determine the critical value which separates the rejection region from the acceptance region. The determination of critical value depends on the size of the rejection region, which is directly related to the risk involved in decision making. In other words, we can say that the size of the rejection region is directly related to the level of precision which a decision maker wants to maintain while estimating the population parameter.

Critical region is the area under the normal curve, divided into two mutually exclusive regions. These regions are termed as acceptance region (when the null hypothesis is accepted) and the rejection region or critical region (when the null hypothesis is rejected).

If the computed value of the test statistic falls under the acceptance region, the null hypothesis is accepted, otherwise it is rejected. For making a decision regarding the acceptance or rejection of the null hypothesis, a researcher has to determine the critical value which separates the rejection region from the acceptance region.

Step 5: Collect the sample data

In this stage of sampling, data are collected and the appropriate sample statistics are computed. The first four steps should be completed before collecting the data for the study. It is not advisable to collect the data first and then decide on the stages of hypothesis testing. We have already discussed the process of sampling in Chapter 5.

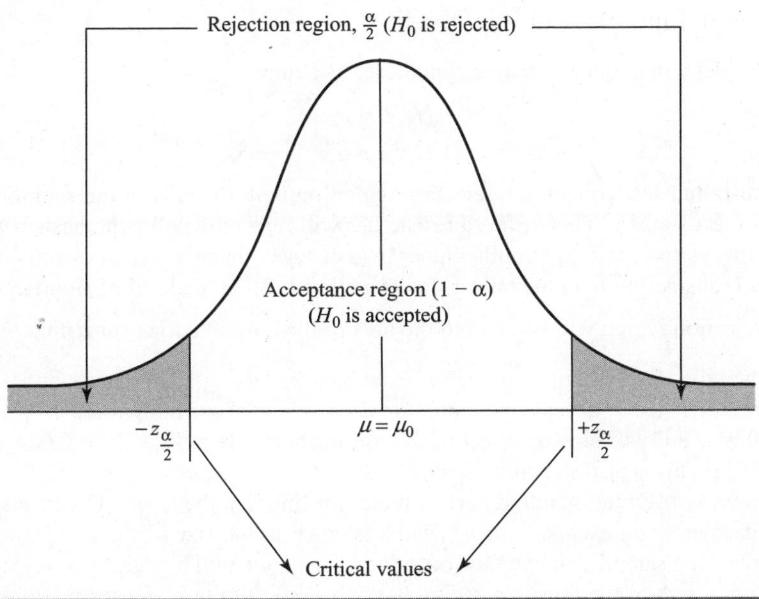

FIGURE 12.2
Acceptance and rejection regions for null hypothesis (two-tailed test)

Step 6: Analyse the data

In this step, the researcher has to compute the test statistic. This involves selection of an appropriate probability distribution for a particular test. For example, when the sample is small ($n < 30$), the use of the normal probability distribution (z) is not an accurate choice. The t distribution needs to be used in this case. Some of the commonly used testing procedures are z, t, F, and χ^2. The selection of a suitable test statistic will be discussed in detail in the succeeding chapters.

Step 7: Arrive at a statistical conclusion and business implication

In this step, the researchers draw a statistical conclusion. A statistical conclusion is a decision to accept or reject a null hypothesis. This depends on whether the computed test statistic falls in the acceptance region or the rejection region. If we test a hypothesis at 5% level of significance and the observed set of results have a probability of less than 5%, we consider that the difference between the sample statistic and the hypothesized population parameter as significant. In this situation, a researcher decides to reject the null hypothesis and accept the alternative hypothesis. On the other hand, if the observed set of results have the probability of more than 5%, we consider the difference between the sample statistic and hypothesized population parameter as not significant. In this situation, a researcher decides to accept the null hypothesis and the alternative hypothesis is automatically rejected.

Statisticians present the information obtained using hypothesis-testing procedure to the decision makers. Decisions are made on the basis of this information. Ultimately, a decision maker decides that a statistically significant result is a substantive result and needs to be implemented for meeting the organization's goals.

12.4 TWO-TAILED AND ONE-TAILED TESTS OF HYPOTHESIS

There are two types of tests of hypothesis. They are two-tailed tests and one-tailed tests of hypothesis. Hypothesis formulation provides a base for test selection. This will be discussed in detail in the succeeding chapters.

12.4.1 Two-Tailed Test of Hypothesis

Two-tailed tests contain the rejection region on both the tails of the sampling distribution of a test statistic. This means a researcher will reject the null hypothesis if the computed sample statistic is significantly higher than or lower than the hypothesized population parameter (considering both the tails, right as well as left).

Let us consider a null and alternative hypotheses as below:

$$H_0: \mu = \mu_0$$
$$H_1: \mu \neq \mu_0$$

A **two-tailed test** contain the rejection region on both the tails of the sampling distribution of a test statistic. This means a researcher will reject the null hypothesis if the computed sample statistic is significantly higher than or lower than the hypothesized population parameter (considering both the tails, right as well as left). If the level of significance is α, then the rejection region will be on both the tails of the normal curve, consisting of $\frac{\alpha}{2}$ area on both the tails of the normal curve. For example, for testing a hypothesis at 5% level of significance, the size of acceptance region on each side of the mean will be 0.475 (0.475 + 0.475 = 0.95), and the size of rejection region on both the tails will be 0.025 (0.025 + 0.025 = 0.05). This is also shown in Figure 12.3.

When we consult the standard normal table, we find that the area 0.475 corresponds to 1.96 standard error on each side of μ_0, which is equal to the size of the acceptance region (0.95% area). If a sample statistic falls outside this area, the null hypothesis is rejected. This is equal to the size of the rejection region (0.05% area). Similarly, for testing a hypothesis

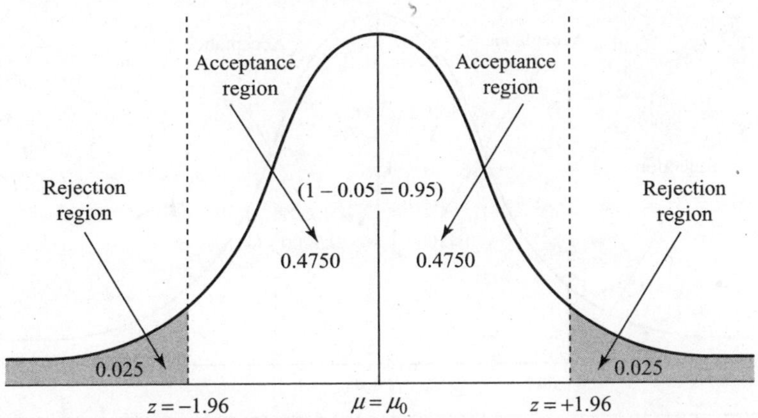

FIGURE 12.3
Acceptance and rejection regions ($\alpha = 0.05$)

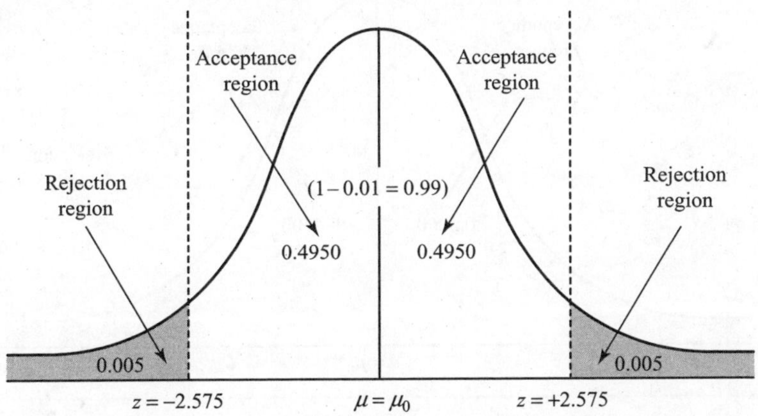

FIGURE 12.4
Acceptance and rejection regions ($\alpha = 0.01$)

at 1% level of significance, the size of the acceptance region on each side of the mean will be 0.495 (0.495 + 0.495 = 0.99) and the size of rejection region on both the tails will be 0.005 (0.005 + 0.005 = 0.01). From the standard normal table, we find that the area 0.495 corresponds to 2.575 standard error on each side of μ_0, and this is equal to the size of the acceptance region (0.99% area). This is shown in Figure 12.4.

When we compare Figures 12.3 and 12.4, a very important result emerges. When we decrease the size of the rejection region (Figure 12.4), the probability of accepting a null hypothesis increases.

One-tailed test contains the rejection region on one tail of the sampling distribution of a test statistic. In case of a left-tailed test, a researcher rejects the null hypothesis if the computed sample statistic is significantly lower than the hypothesized population parameter (considering the left side of the curve in Figure 12.5). In case of a right-tailed test, a researcher rejects the null hypothesis if the computed sample statistic is significantly higher than the hypothesized population parameter (considering the right side of the curve in Figure 12.6).

12.4.2 One-Tailed Test of Hypothesis

Let us consider a null and alternative hypotheses as below:

$$H_0: \mu = \mu_0 \quad \text{and} \quad H_1: \mu < \mu_0 \quad \text{(Left-tailed test)}$$

$$H_0: \mu = \mu_0 \quad \text{and} \quad H_1: \mu > \mu_0 \quad \text{(Right-tailed test)}$$

Unlike the two-tailed test, the **one-tailed test** contains the rejection region on one tail of the sampling distribution of a test statistic. In case of a left-tailed test, a researcher rejects the null hypothesis if the computed sample statistic is significantly lower than the hypothesized population parameter (considering the left side of the curve in Figure 12.5). In the case of a

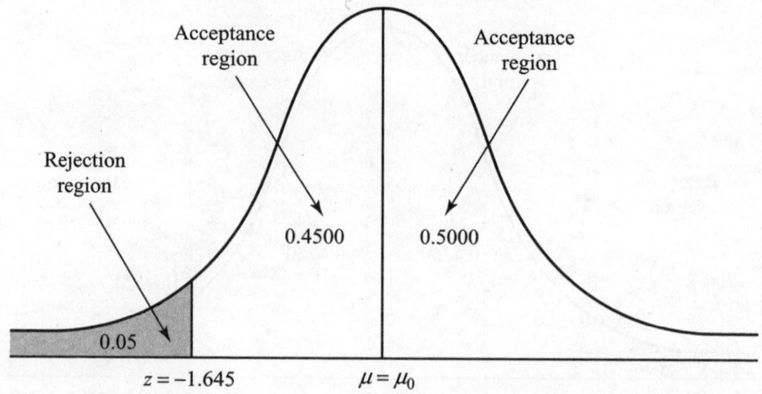

FIGURE 12.5
Acceptance and rejection regions for one-tailed (left) test ($\alpha = 0.05$)

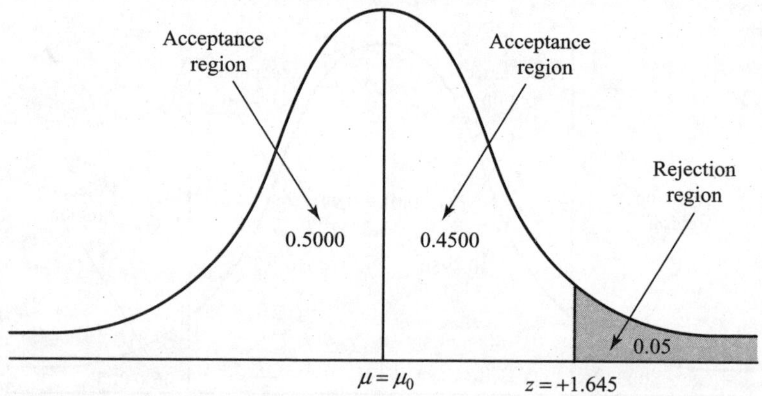

FIGURE 12.6
Acceptance and rejection regions for one-tailed (right) test ($\alpha = 0.05$)

right-tailed test, a researcher rejects the null hypothesis if the computed sample statistic is significantly higher than the hypothesized population parameter (considering the right side of the curve in Figure 12.6). Thus, in a one-tailed test the entire rejection region corresponding to the level of significance (α) is located only in one tail of the sampling distribution of the statistic.

Let us discuss the example which we had taken up in the section discussing "hypothesis testing procedure" with population mean equal to 150. As discussed in this example, the null hypothesis is

$$H_0: \mu = 150$$

A two-tailed alternative hypothesis (population mean is not equal to 150) can be exhibited as below

$$H_1: \mu \neq 150 \text{ (Two-tailed test)}$$

TABLE 12.2
Values of z_a for the most commonly used confidence intervals

Confidence level (1 − α) %	*(α)*	*One-tailed region*	*Two-tailed region*
90%	0.10	±1.28	±1.645
95%	0.05	±1.645	±1.96
99%	0.01	±2.33	±2.575

A one-tailed (left) alternative hypothesis (population mean is less than 150) can be exhibited as below

$$H_1: \mu < 150 \text{ (Left-tailed test)}$$

A one-tailed (right) alternative hypothesis (population mean is more than 150) can be exhibited as below

$$H_0: \mu > 150 \text{ (Right-tailed test)}$$

Table 12.2 shows a summary of certain values at various significance levels for test statistic *z*.

12.5 TYPE I AND TYPE II ERRORS

While testing hypotheses, null hypothesis should be accepted when it is true and null hypothesis should be rejected when it is false. In a real-life situation, the correct decision is not always possible. We know that the hypothesis-testing procedure uses a sample statistic (based on the sample) to arrive at a conclusion about the population parameter. In this process, the possibility of making incorrect decisions about the null hypothesis cannot be ignored. In fact, when a researcher tests statistical hypotheses, there can be four possible outcomes as follows:

1. Rejecting a true null hypothesis (**Type I error**)
2. Accepting a false null hypothesis (**Type II error**)
3. Accepting a true null hypothesis (Correct decision)
4. Rejecting a false null hypothesis (Correct decision)

A Type I error is committed by rejecting a null hypothesis when it is true. The possibility of committing Type I error is called (α) or the level of significance. α is the area under the curve which is in the rejection region beyond the critical values.

1. **A Type I error is committed by rejecting a null hypothesis when it is true.** For example, a quality control manager of a ballpoint pen manufacturing firm finds that 5% pens are defective. For testing the hypothesis, researchers take a random sample of 100 pens and test to find the defective pieces. It is possible that this sample contains the most extreme lots (more than 10% or less than 2%), leading to the rejection of the null hypothesis though the population mean is actually 5%. In this case, the researchers have committed Type I error. The possibility of committing Type I error is called (α) or level of significance. α is the area under the curve which is in the rejection region beyond the critical values. As discussed earlier, some of the most common values of α are 0.10, 0.05, and 0.01.

A Type II error is committed by accepting a null hypothesis, when it is false. The probability of committing Type II error is beta (β).

2. **A Type II error is committed by accepting a null hypothesis when it is false.** In the example related to ballpoint pens, suppose the population mean is 6% defective pieces even though the null hypothesis is 5% defectives. A sample of 100 pens yields 5.2% defectives which falls in the non-rejection region. The researcher does not reject the null hypothesis (he accepts a false null hypothesis). In this situation, a Type II error is committed. The probability of committing type II error is beta (β). Symbolically,

$$\alpha = \text{Probability of committing Type I error}$$
$$\beta = \text{Probability of committing Type II error}$$

We need to examine the relationship between (α) and (β). Type I error is committed by rejecting a null hypothesis when it is true, and Type II error is committed by accepting a null hypothesis when it is false. A researcher cannot commit Type I and Type II errors at the same time on the same hypothesis test. Generally, α and β are inversely related to each other, that is, if α is reduced, β is increased and if β is reduced, α is increased. ($1-\beta$) is the power of the test and measures the probability of rejecting the false null hypothesis. Table 12.3 exhibits the relationship between the two types of errors, confidence level, and the power of a test.

TABLE 12.3
Errors in hypothesis testing and power of the test

Statistical decision	State of nature: H_0 True	H_0 False
Accept H_0	Correct decision with confidence level $(1 - \alpha)$	Type II error, P(Type II error) = β
Reject H_0	Type I error, P(Type I error) = α	Correct decision, Power of the test = $(1 - \beta)$

12.6 HYPOTHESIS TESTING FOR A SINGLE POPULATION MEAN USING THE *z* STATISTIC

Hypothesis testing for large samples ($n \geq 30$) is based on the assumption that the population, from which the sample is drawn, has a normal distribution. As a result, the sampling distribution of mean $\bar{x}$ is also normally distributed. Even when the population is not normal, the sampling distribution of mean $\bar{x}$ for a large sample size is normally distributed, irrespective of the shape of the population (central limit theorem). For testing hypothesis about a single population mean, z formula can be used, if the sample size is large ($n \geq 30$) for any population; for small samples ($n < 30$), if x is normally distributed. As discussed earlier, z formula can be stated as below:

z Formula for a single population mean

$$z = \frac{\bar{x} - \mu}{\dfrac{\sigma}{\sqrt{n}}}$$

where μ is the population mean, σ the population standard deviation, n the sample size, and $\bar{x}$ the sample mean.

Example 12.1

A marketing research firm conducted a survey 10 years ago and found that the average household income of a particular geographic region is ₹10,000. Mr Gupta, who has recently joined the firm as a vice president has expressed doubts about the accuracy of the data. For verifying the data, the firm has decided to take a random sample of 200 households that yield a sample mean (for household income) of ₹11,000. Assume that the population standard deviation of the household income is ₹1200. Verify Mr Gupta's doubts using the seven steps of hypothesis testing. Let $\alpha = 0.05$.

Solution

In the previous section, we have already discussed the seven steps of testing hypothesis. The first step is to establish the null and alternative hypotheses.

Step 1: Set null and alternative hypotheses

In this particular example, the researcher is trying to verify whether there is any change in the average household income within 10 years.

The null hypothesis is set as no difference or status quo, that is, the average household income has not changed. Symbolically, this is given as

$$H_0: \mu = 10{,}000$$

The alternative hypothesis is a logical opposite of the null hypothesis. Hence,

$$H_1: \mu \neq 10{,}000$$

Step 2: Determine the appropriate statistical test

At this stage, an appropriate statistical test must be determined. In this case, sample size is large (≥ 30) and the sample mean is used as a statistic, so the z formula can be used for hypothesis testing. As discussed, z formula for a single population mean is given as

$$z = \frac{\bar{x} - \mu}{\frac{\sigma}{\sqrt{n}}}$$

Step 3: Set the level of significance

The level of significance α is also known as the size of rejection region or the size of the critical region and is 0.05 in this case.

Step 4: Set the decision rule

In the light of the alternative hypothesis, we are clear that this is a case of a two-tailed test (mean household income can be less than 10,000 and can be more than 10,000) and the level of significance is 0.05. As shown in Figure 12.7, the acceptance region covers 95% of the area and the rejection region covers the remaining 5% of the area at the two ends of the distribution. The critical z values can be obtained from the normal table as below:

$$z_{\frac{\alpha}{2}} = \pm 1.96$$

If the computed test statistic is between +1.96 and −1.96, the decision is to accept the null hypothesis and if the computed test statistic is outside ±1.96, the decision is to reject the null hypothesis (accept the alternative hypothesis).

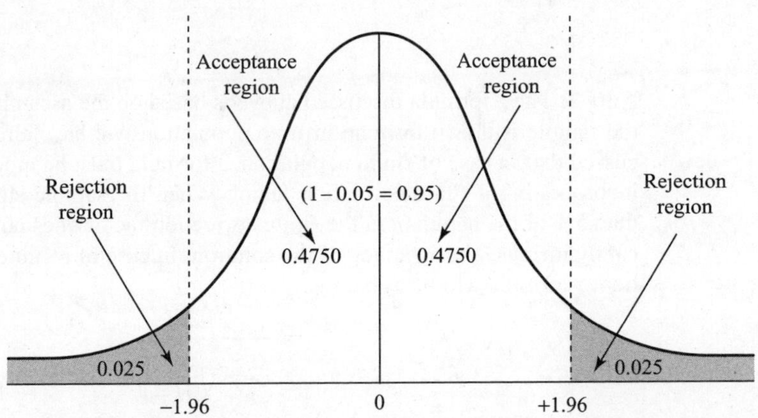

FIGURE 12.7 Acceptance and rejection region ($\alpha = 0.05$)

Step 5: Collect the sample data

At this stage, a researcher collects the data. In this example, a sample of 200 respondents yields a sample mean of ₹11,000.

Step 6: Analyse the data

The value of the sample statistic is calculated in this stage. From the example, $n = 200$, $\bar{x} = 11{,}000$, $\sigma = 1200$, and the hypothesized mean $\mu = 10{,}000$. z formula for a single population mean is as follows:

$$z = \frac{\bar{x} - \mu}{\frac{\sigma}{\sqrt{n}}}$$

By substituting all the values we get: $z = \dfrac{11{,}000 - 10{,}000}{\frac{1200}{\sqrt{200}}} = 11.79$

Step 7: Arrive at a statistical conclusion and business implication

The calculated z value is 11.79, which is greater than +1.96. Hence, the statistical conclusion is to reject the null hypothesis and accept the alternative hypothesis. The calculated z value is also termed as the observed value. So, in this case the observed value of z is 11.79 and the critical value of z is +1.96.

On the basis of hypothesis testing, it can be concluded that the average household income of the particular geographic region is not ₹10,000. Mr Gupta's doubts about this average household income was right. In the last 10 years, the average household income has increased. Since ₹11,000 is only the sample mean, there is no guarantee that all the different samples taken from the population will produce an increase of ₹1000 (confidence is 95%). However, broadly we can conclude that the average household income has increased and now policies of the company must be decided on the basis of this increased household income.

Note 1: In many real-life situations, the population standard deviation remains unknown. In this case, for a large sample size ($n \geq 30$), the population standard deviation (σ) can be replaced by a sample standard deviation (s) and the resulting z formula will be as under:

$$z = \frac{\bar{x} - \mu}{\frac{s}{\sqrt{n}}}$$

Note 2: The z formula discussed above is based on the assumption that the sample is drawn from an infinite population. We have already discussed that in case of finite population, z formula must be modified by incorporating a finite correction factor. When the sample size is less than 5% of the population, the finite correction factor does not significantly increase the accuracy of the solution. In case of a finite population, z formula will be as below:

$$z = \frac{\bar{x} - \mu}{\frac{\sigma}{\sqrt{n}} \times \sqrt{\frac{N - n}{N - 1}}}$$

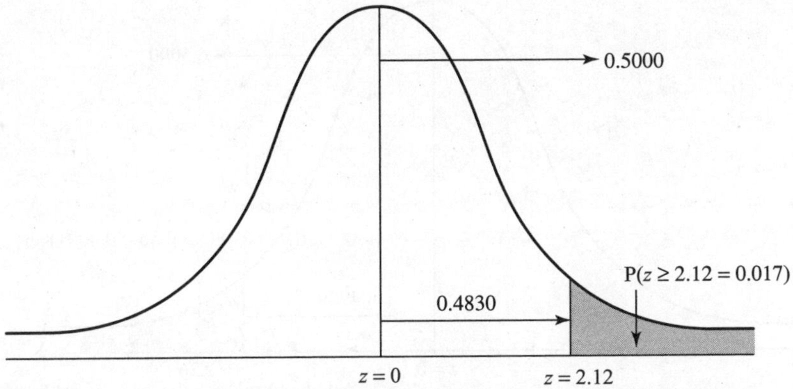

FIGURE 12.8
Probability of $p(z \geq 2.12)$

12.6.1 *p*-Value Approach for Hypothesis Testing

The *p*-value approach for hypothesis testing is used for large samples and is some times referred to as the observed level of significance. This approach is very advantageous especially after the introduction of many statistical software programs. The ***p* value** defines the smallest value of α for which the null hypothesis can be rejected. The decision rule for accepting or rejecting a null hypothesis based on the *p* value is as given below:

Reject the null hypothesis H_0 when the *p* value is $< \alpha$, otherwise, accept the null hypothesis H_0

For example, a researcher conducting a hypothesis test with rejection region on the right tail of the distribution obtains an observed test statistic value of 2.12. From the normal table, the corresponding probability area for *z* value 2.12 is 0.4830. So, the probability of obtaining a *z* value greater than or equal to 2.12 is 0.5000 – 0.4830 = 0.017 (shown in Figure 12.8).

In this case, the *p* value is 0.017. For $\alpha = 0.05$ and $\alpha = 0.1$, this *p* value falls under the rejection region (at $\alpha = 0.05$, $0.017 < 0.05$ and $\alpha = 0.1$, $0.017 < 0.1$), so the null hypothesis will be rejected at 0.05 and 0.1 levels of significance. At $\alpha = 0.01$, the researcher cannot reject the null hypothesis for the value of α equal to 0.017 because $\alpha = 0.01 < 0.017$.

The *p*-value approach of hypothesis testing for large samples is some times referred to as the observed level of significance. The *p*-value defines the smallest value of α for which the null hypothesis can be rejected.

The procedure of calculating the *p* value for a two-tailed test is slightly different. In a two-tailed test, the rejection region falls in both the tails of the normal distribution. For example, at $\alpha = 0.05$, the rejection region is located in both the tail areas of the distribution in terms of 0.025% (0.025 + 0.025 = 0.05) area in both the tails of the distribution. The researcher compares this α value to the computed *p* value for accepting or rejecting the null hypothesis. For this comparison, instead of splitting the α value, we double the *p* value and then compare that *p* value with the α value. In the previous example, the researcher conducted a hypothesis test with rejection region on both the tails of the distribution (two-tailed test) and obtained the observed test statistic as 2.12 and corresponding *p* value as 0.017. So, instead of splitting α value in two parts, the researcher should double the *p* value, that is, $(0.017 \times 2 = 0.034)$. So, for a two-tailed test, this *p* value (0.034) is compared with the α values 0.05 and 0.1. Hence, at $\alpha = 0.05$ and $\alpha = 0.1$, the null hypothesis will be rejected but at $\alpha = 0.01$, the null hypothesis will be accepted $(0.01 < 0.034)$.

Example 12.2

For Example 12.1, use the p-value method to test the hypothesis using $\alpha = 0.01$ as the level of significance. Assume that the sample mean is 10,200.

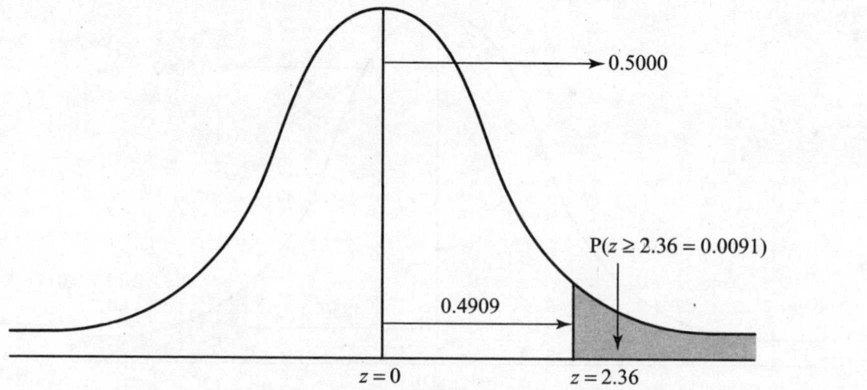

FIGURE 12.9
Probability of $p(z \geq 2.36)$

Solution In the light of this new sample mean $\bar{x}$ = 10,200, the z value can be calculated as below:

$$z = \frac{10,200 - 10,000}{\frac{1200}{\sqrt{200}}} = \frac{200}{84.85} = 2.36$$

The observed test statistic is computed as 2.36. From the normal table, the corresponding probability area for z value 2.36 is 0.4909. So, the probability of obtaining a z value greater than or equal to 2.36 is 0.5000 – 0.4909 = 0.0091 (shown in Figure 12.9). For a two-tailed test, this value is multiplied by 2 (as discussed above). Thus, for a two-tailed test, this value is (0.0091 × 2 = 0.0182). So, the null hypothesis is accepted because (0.01 < 0.0182). It has to be noted that for $\alpha = 0.05$ and $\alpha = 0.1$, the null hypothesis is rejected because 0.0182 < 0.05 and 0.0182 < 0.1.

12.6.2 Critical Value Approach for Hypothesis Testing

In Chapter 5, we have already discussed that z formula for estimating the population mean is given by

$$z = \frac{\bar{x} - \mu}{\frac{\sigma}{\sqrt{n}}}$$

Sample mean $\bar{x}$ can be greater than or less than the population mean. The above formula can also be written as

$$\mu = \bar{x} \pm z \frac{\sigma}{\sqrt{n}}$$

In the critical value approach for hypothesis testing, a critical $\bar{x}$ value, $\bar{x}_c$, and a critical z value, z_c, is determined and placed in the formula. After placing, the formula can be written as

$$\mu = \bar{x}_c \pm z_c \frac{\sigma}{\sqrt{n}}$$

After rearranging, this formula can be written as

$$\pm z_c = \frac{\bar{x}_c - \mu}{\frac{\sigma}{\sqrt{n}}}$$

$$\bar{x}_c = \mu \pm z_c \times \frac{\sigma}{\sqrt{n}}$$

This formula can be used for obtaining the lower and upper critical values. The critical value approach will be clearer with the help of Example 12.3.

Example 12.3

A cable TV network company wants to provide modern facilities to its consumers. The company has five-year old data which reveals that the average household income is ₹120,000. Company officials believe that due to the fast development in the region, the average household income might have increased. The company takes a random sample of 40 households to verify this assumption. From the sample, the average income of the households is calculated as 125,000. From historical data, population standard deviation is obtained as 1200. Use $\alpha = 0.05$ to verify the finding.

Solution The null and alternative hypotheses can be set as below:

$$H_0: \mu = 120{,}000$$
$$H_1: \mu \neq 120{,}000$$

Since the sample size is 40, the *z*-test must be used. The level of significance is taken as $\alpha = 0.05$. Using the critical value formula discussed earlier, we get:

$$\pm z_c = \frac{\bar{x}_c - \mu}{\frac{\sigma}{\sqrt{n}}}$$

$$\pm 1.96 = \frac{\bar{x}_c - 120{,}000}{\frac{1200}{\sqrt{40}}} = \frac{\bar{x}_c - 120{,}000}{189.73}$$

$$\bar{x}_c = 120{,}000 \pm 371.87$$

This gives the lower and upper limits of the rejection region (as shown in Figure 12.10). Hence,

Lower limit $\bar{x}_c = 120{,}000 - 371.87 = 119{,}628.13$

Upper limit $\bar{x}_c = 120{,}000 + 371.87 = 120{,}371.87$

The result indicates that a sample mean of value greater than 120,371.87 and less than 119,628.13 will lead to the rejection of the null hypothesis. In this case, sample mean is calculated as 125,000 which leads to the rejection of the null hypothesis.

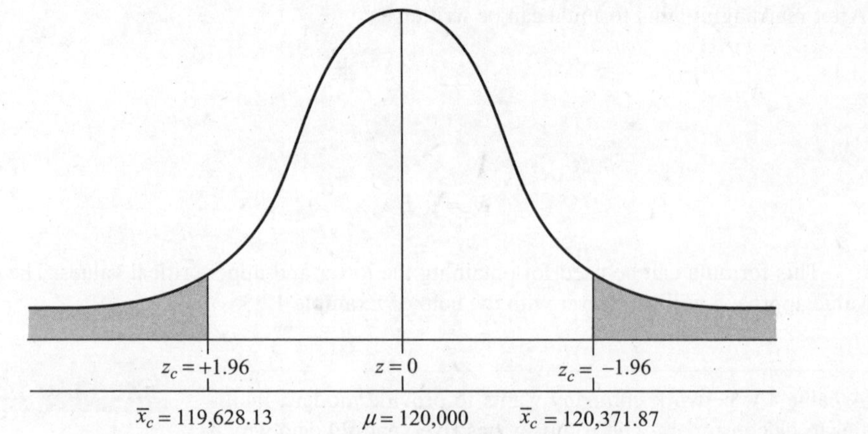

FIGURE 12.10
Critical value method for testing a hypothesis about the population mean for Example 12.3

FIGURE 12.11
Minitab output exhibiting 95% confidence interval for sample mean for Example 12.3

One-sample Z

Test of mu = 120000 vs not = 120000
The assumed standard deviation = 1200

N	Mean	SE Mean	95% CI	Z	P
40	125000	190	(124628, 125372)	26.35	0.0000

Note that for obtaining 95% confidence interval, $z_c \times \frac{\sigma}{\sqrt{n}} = 372$ (371.87 = 372 approximately) is deducted and added from the sample mean 125,000. Hence, the lower limit is obtained as 125,000 – 372 = 124,628 and upper limit is obtained as 125,000 + 372 = 125, 372 (as shown in Figure 12.10). Figure 12.11 is the Minitab output exhibiting 95% confidence interval for sample mean for Example 12.3.

SELF-PRACTICE PROBLEMS

12A1. Use the following data to test the hypotheses

$$H_0: \mu = 50 \quad H_1: \mu \neq 50$$

when sample mean $(\bar{x}) = 55$, sample size $(n) = 80$, population standard deviation $\sigma = 7$, and level of significance $(\alpha) = 0.05$

12A2. Use the p-value approach to test the hypothesis for the data given in 10A1.

12A3. Use the critical value approach to test the hypothesis for the data given in 10A1.

12A4. Use the following data to test the hypotheses

$$H_0: \mu = 105 \quad H_1: \mu < 105$$

when sample mean $(\bar{x}) = 95$, sample size $(n) = 60$, population standard deviation $\sigma = 11$, and level of significance $(\alpha) = 0.10$

12A5. A company conducted a survey in the past and found that the average income of an individual in a particular region is ₹25,000 per year. After a few years, the company feels that this average income may have changed. For verifying this, the company officers have taken a random sample of size 50 and found that the sample mean is ₹40,000. The sample standard deviation is computed as ₹15,000. Use $\alpha = 0.05$ and hypothesis testing procedure to determine whether the average income of an individual has changed.

12.7 HYPOTHESIS TESTING FOR A SINGLE POPULATION MEAN USING THE *t* STATISTIC (CASE OF A SMALL RANDOM SAMPLE WHEN $n < 30$)

We have already discussed that due to time, money, and other constraints, sometimes a researcher may have to take a small sample of size less than 30, that is, $n < 30$. In case of a small sample, z is not the appropriate test statistic. When a researcher draws a small random sample ($n < 30$) to estimate the population mean μ and when the population standard deviation is unknown and the population is normally distributed, t test can be applied. The t test can also be applied to estimate the population mean μ when population standard deviation is unknown using large samples irrespective of the shape of the population. There is a debate on this issue. Some researchers use the t test when the population standard deviation is unknown, irrespective of the sample size. Some other researchers feel that for a large sample size, z distribution is a close approximation of the t distribution even when population standard deviation is unknown. The t formula for testing such a hypothesis is as below:

When a researcher draws a small random sample ($n < 30$) to estimate the population mean μ and when the population standard deviation is unknown and population is normally distributed, t-test can be applied.

$$t = \frac{\bar{x} - \mu}{\frac{s}{\sqrt{n}}}$$

Example 12.4

Royal Tyres has launched a new brand of tyres for tractors and claims that under normal circumstances the average life of the tyres is 40,000 km. A retailer wants to test this claim and has taken a random sample of 8 tyres. He tests the life of the tyres under normal circumstance. The results obtained are presented in Table 12.4.

TABLE 12.4
Life of the sample tyres

Tyres	1	2	3	4	5	6	7	8
km	35,000	38,000	42,000	41,000	39,000	41,500	43,000	38,500

Use $\alpha = 0.05$ for testing the hypothesis.

Solution

Here, the sample size is 8 (less than 30) and the population standard deviation is unknown, so t test can be used for testing the hypo-thesis. The seven steps of hypothesis testing can be performed as below:

Step 1: Set null and alternative hypotheses

Null Hypothesis: H_0: $\mu = 40{,}000$

Alternative Hypothesis: H_1: $\mu \neq 40{,}000$

Step 2: Determine the appropriate statistical test

As discussed earlier, the sample size is less than 30. So, t test will be an appropriate test. The t statistic is given as under

$$t = \frac{\bar{x} - \mu}{\frac{s}{\sqrt{n}}}$$

Step 3: Set the level of significance

The level of significance, that is, α is set as 0.05.

Step 4: Set the decision rule

The t distribution value for a two-tailed test is $t_{0.025,7} = 2.365$ for degrees of freedom 7. So, if the computed t value is outside the ±2. 365 range, the null hypothesis will be rejected; otherwise, it is accepted.

Step 5: Collect the sample data

The data collected from eight samples are as below:

Tyres	1	2	3	4	5	6	7	8
km	35,000	38,000	42,000	41,000	39,000	41,500	43,000	38,500

Step 6: Analyse the data

The sample standard deviation and the sample mean are computed from the sample data at this stage. These are given as below:

Sample standard deviation $(s) = 2618.61$ and Sample mean $(\bar{x}) = 39{,}750$

$\mu = 40{,}000$ and $n = 8$ and $df = n - 1 = 8 - 1 = 7$

The tabular t value is $t_{0.025,7} = 2.365$

The t formula for testing hypothesis is $t = \dfrac{\bar{x} - \mu}{\dfrac{s}{\sqrt{n}}} = \dfrac{39{,}750 - 40{,}000}{\dfrac{2618.61}{\sqrt{8}}}$

$= -0.27$

Step 7: Arrive at a statistical conclusion and business implication

The observed t value is –0.27 which falls in the acceptance region. Hence, null hypothesis cannot be rejected (Figure 12.12). This implies that the evidence from the sample is not sufficient to reject the null hypothesis that the population mean (of average tyre life) is 40,000 km.

As discussed in Step 7, the evidence from the sample is sufficient to accept that the average life of the tyres is 40,000 km. The retailer can quite convincingly tell customers that the company's claim is valid under normal conditions.

Note: As exhibited in the Minitab output given in Figure 12.13, for obtaining 95% confidence interval, ±portion, that is, $z_c \times \dfrac{\sigma}{\sqrt{n}} = 2189.58$ is deducted and added from the sample mean 39,750. Here, the critical value of t has to be placed instead of the value of z_c.

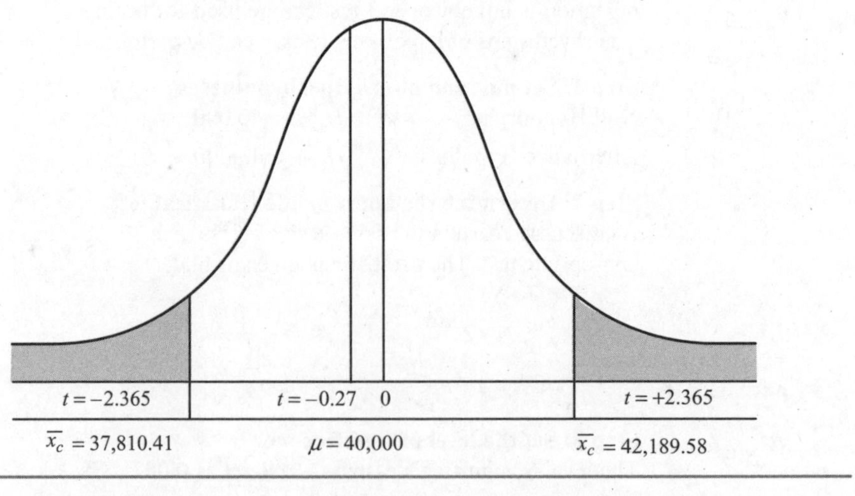

FIGURE 12.12
Computed and critical t values for Example 12.4

One-sample T: Sample

Test of mu = 40000 vs not = 40000

Variable	N	Mean	StDev	SE Mean	95% CI	T	P
Sample	8	39750	2619	926	(37561, 41939)	−0.27	0.795

FIGURE 12.13 Minitab output for Example 12.4

SELF-PRACTICE PROBLEMS

12B1. Use the following data to test the hypotheses

$$H_0: \mu = 25 \quad H_1: \mu \neq 25$$

when sample mean $(\bar{x}) = 30$, sample size $(n) = 15$, population standard deviation $\sigma = 5$, and level of significance $(\alpha) = 0.05$.

12B2. Use the following data to test the hypotheses

$$H_0: \mu = 40 \quad H_1: \mu < 40$$

when sample mean $(\bar{x}) = 35$, sample size $(n) = 20$, sample standard deviation $s = 7$, and level of significance $(\alpha) = 0.01$.

12B3. Suppose that the average price per square feet of commercial land in Raipur is ₹2000. A big real estate company is doubtful about the accuracy of this average price. The company believes that the average price may be on the higher side. The company hires a researcher and he has taken a random sample of 25 land deals in Raipur. From this, the average price per square feet is determined as ₹3000. The sample standard deviation is computed as ₹500. If the researcher has taken the level of significance as 5%, what statistical conclusions can be drawn? State your answer in terms of setting the hypotheses and accepting or rejecting it on the basis of the sample result.

12.8 HYPOTHESIS TESTING FOR A POPULATION PROPORTION

In marketing research, information is generally expressed in terms of proportions. For example, we often read that the market share of a company is 30% or 20% of the customers have switched from one brand to another brand. There are many areas where data is usually expressed in proportions or percentage. Quality defects, consumer preferences, market share, etc. are some of the common examples. This kind of data is highly dynamic in nature. Marketing researchers sometimes want to test the hypothesis about such proportions to check whether these have changed. The concept of central limit theorem can also be applied to the sampling distribution of $\bar{p}$ with certain conditions. In Chapter 11, we discussed the z-test for a population proportion for $np \geq 5$ and $nq \geq 5$. This formula can be presented as below:
z-test for a population proportion for $np \geq 5$ and $nq \geq 5$,

$$z = \frac{\bar{p} - p}{\sqrt{\frac{pq}{n}}}$$

where $\bar{p}$ is the sample proportion, n the sample size, p the population proportion, and $q = 1 - p$.

Example 12.5

The production manager of a company that manufacturers electric heaters believes that atleast 10% of the heaters are defective. For testing his belief, he takes a random sample of 100 heaters and finds that 12 heaters are defective. He takes the level of significance as 5% for testing the hypothesis. Applying the seven steps of hypothesis testing, test his belief.

Solution The seven steps of hypothesis testing can be performed as below:

Step 1: Set null and alternative hypotheses

The null and alternative hypotheses can be stated as below:

$$H_0: p = 0.10$$
$$H_1: p \neq 0.10$$

Step 2: Determine the appropriate statistical test

The z-test for a population proportion for $np \geq 5$ and $nq \geq 5$ will be the appropriate test. This is given as below:

$$z = \frac{\overline{p} - p}{\sqrt{\frac{pq}{n}}}$$

where $\overline{p}$ is the sample proportion, n the sample size, p the population proportion, and $q = 1 - p$.

Step 3: Set the level of significance

The level of significance, that is, α is set as 0.05.

Step 4: Set the decision rule

This will be a two-tailed test with rejection region on both the tails of the distribution. The level of significance is 5%, which shows that the rejection region will occupy 0.025% area on both the sides of the distribution, that is, $z_{0.025} = \pm 1.96$.

Step 5: Collect the sample data

The researcher has taken a random sample of 100 heaters and finds that 12 pieces are defective.

Step 6: Analyse the data

Here, $\overline{p}$ = Sample proportion $= \frac{12}{100} = 0.12$

p = Population proportion = 0.10

$q = 1 - p = 1 - 0.10 = 0.90$

The z statistic for a population proportion for $np \geq 5$ and $nq \geq 5$ can be computed as

$$z = \frac{\overline{p} - p}{\sqrt{\frac{pq}{n}}} = \frac{0.12 - 0.10}{\sqrt{\frac{(0.10) \times (0.90)}{100}}} = \frac{0.02}{0.03} = 0.67$$

Step 7: Arrive at a statistical conclusion and business implication

The observed value of z is in the acceptance region ($0.67 < 1.96$); so, the null hypothesis that the population proportion is 0.10 is accepted. The result that we have obtained from the sample may be due to chance.

The production manager's claim that at least 10% of the products are defective seems to be valid. The manufacturer can plan a marketing strategy taking into account the fact that 10% of the products may be defective.

SELF-PRACTICE PROBLEMS

12C1. Use the following data to test the hypotheses

$$H_0: \mu = 0.30 \quad H_1: \mu \neq 0.30$$

when the characteristics in the sample are (x = 20), sample size (n) = 70, level of significance (α) = 0.05.

12C2. Use the following data to test the hypotheses

$$H_0: \mu = 0.40 \quad H_1: \mu > 0.40$$

when the characteristics in the sample are (x = 45), sample size (n) = 80, and level of significance (α) = 0.05.

12C3. The lighting segment is composed of GLS lamps, fluorescent tubes, and CFL (compact fluorescent lamps). The organized market contributes 60% to the total sales of GLS lamps.[2] A leading national GLS lamps company believes that this market size has increased due to various factors. For verifying this claim, the company's research officer has taken a random sample of 200 GLS lamps purchasers. Out of 200 GLS lamps purchasers, 145 purchasers have purchased from the organized market. At 95% confidence level, test the belief of the company.

SUMMARY |

Hypothesis testing is a well-defined procedure which helps us to decide objectively whether to accept or reject the hypothesis based on the information available from the sample. Hypothesis testing is a well-defined procedure that can be performed using seven steps.

In statistics, two types of hypothesis tests are available. These are known as two-tailed test and one-tailed test of hypothesis. Two-tailed tests contain the rejection region on both the tails of the sampling distribution of a test statistic. As different from a two-tailed test, a one-tailed test contain the rejection region on one tail of the sampling distribution of a test statistic.

A Type I error is committed by rejecting a null hypothesis when it is true. The possibility of committing Type I error is called (α) or level of significance. A Type II error is committed by accepting a null hypothesis when it is false. The probability of committing Type II error is beta (β).

Symbolically,

α = Probability of committing Type I error

β = Probability of committing Type II error

Hypothesis testing can be performed by applying three approaches: the z-value approach, the p-value approach, and the critical value approach. For testing hypothesis about a single population mean, z formula can be used if the sample size is large ($n \geq 30$) for any population and for small samples ($n < 30$) if x is normally distributed. The p value defines the smallest value of α for which the null hypothesis can be rejected. In the critical value approach for hypothesis testing, a critical $\bar{x}$ value, $\bar{x}_c$, and critical z value, z_c, is determined and inserted in the formula. When a researcher draws a small random sample ($n < 30$) to estimate the population mean μ and when the population standard deviation is unknown and the population is normally distributed, the t test can be applied. The z-test can also be used for testing hypothesis about a population proportion with $np \geq 5$ and $nq \geq 5$.

KEY TERMS |

Hypothesis testing, 284
One-tailed test, 289
p Value, 295
Two-tailed test, 288
Type I error, 291
Type II error, 291

NOTES |

1. Prowess (V. 3.1), Centre for Monitoring Indian Economy Pvt. Ltd, Mumbai, accessed July 2008, reproduced with permission.
2. Indiastat.com, accessed August 2008, reproduced with permission.
3. www.libertyshoes.com/about_liberty.asp, accessed August 2008.

DISCUSSION QUESTIONS |

1. What do you understand by hypothesis testing?
2. What is the importance of hypothesis testing in managerial decision making?
3. What are the steps in hypothesis testing?
4. Discuss the concept of a two-tailed test in hypothesis testing?
5. When should we consider a one-tailed test for hypothesis testing?
6. What are the two types of errors in hypothesis testing?
7. Explain the z-value approach to hypothesis testing.
8. Explain the p-value approach to hypothesis testing. What is the importance of the p-value approach in terms of modern statistical software available?
9. What is the conceptual framework of the critical value approach to hypothesis testing?

NUMERICAL PROBLEMS |

1. a. Use the following data for testing the hypotheses mentioned below:

   $$H_0: \mu = 40 \quad H_1: \mu \neq 40$$

   where σ = population standard deviation = 12, n = sample size = 200, $\bar{x}$ = sample mean = 42, and $\alpha = 0.05$

   b. Also use the p-value approach to hypothesis testing.
2. An industrial goods manufacturer claims that the average life of its products is 10 months with a standard deviation of 2 months. For verifying this result, a random sample of 10 products has been taken and the average life is obtained as 11 months. Frame a hypothesis and use 10% level of significance for testing the hypothesis.
3. Use the p-value approach to accept or reject the hypothesis for Problem 2.
4. Consider the following hypothesis:

   $$H_0: \mu = 45 \quad \text{and} \quad H_1: \mu \neq 45$$

   A sample of size 60 is taken, which produces a sample mean as 46. Population standard deviation is 5. Test this hypothesis on the basis of the p-value approach taking the level of significance as $\alpha = 0.01$.
5. For Problem 4, use the critical value approach to accept or reject the hypothesis.
6. Suppose that in the last five years, the average price per 2 bedroom flat in the Vasant Kunj area of New Delhi has been estimated as ₹2,000,000. A real estate company wants to determine whether this data still holds good. The company takes a sample of 20 houses and finds that the average price is ₹2,500,000 with a standard deviation of ₹25,000. Use $\alpha = 0.05$ to test the hypothesis.
7. A mineral water company claims that the average amount of water filled in each of its bottles is 1.108 litres. For verifying this claim, a researcher takes a sample of 25 bottles and measures the quantity of water in each bottle. The results are as follows:

1.191	1.291	1.118	1.117	1.112	1.114	1.117	1.118	1.119
1.112	1.111	1.008	1.007	1.006	1.005	1.006	1.119	1.112
1.111	1.118	1.125	1.114	1.117	1.118	1.192		

   Use $\alpha = 0.05$ to test the hypothesis.

8. An electric bulb manufacturer claims that not more than 5% of its products are defective. For verifying this claim, a client takes a random sample of 200 bulbs and finds that 24 are defective. Test the hypothesis by taking 90% as the confidence level.
9. A company conducted a survey a few years ago and found out that 15% of its employees have two sources of income. The company wants to cross verify this finding since the data is old. For this purpose, the company takes a random sample of 300 employees and finds that 100 employees have two sources of income. Test the hypothesis by taking 95% as the confidence level.

CASE STUDY |

Case 12: *Ice Cream Market in India: Changing Tastes*

Introduction

The ice cream market in India has witnessed a steady growth over the years. The players in the organized sector have slowly eaten into the market share of players from the unorganized market. The per capita consumption of ice creams in India is still a dismal 106 ml per annum against a consumption of 22 litres in the USA.[1] The low consumption in the Indian market provides fresh avenues to ice cream manufacturers to expand the market. The total volume of sales in the ice cream market is projected to touch 330 million litres by 2014.[2]

Leading Players in the Market

Amul, marketed by the Gujarat Cooperative Milk Marketing Federation (GCMF), is the leading brand in the ice cream market in India. The company has expanded the market with a host of new launches, and created brand new segments within ice creams in order to meet its goal of becoming a Rs 10,000 million brand by 2010.[1] Kwality which joined hands with Hindustan Unilever Limited in 1995 to introduce the brand "Kwality Walls" is also a key player in the Indian ice cream industry. Hindustan Unilever has focused its business in the four metros as well as Bangalore and Hyderabad. These six cities claim 65% of the total market share (see Table 12.01).

TABLE 12.01
Market Segmentation

Market segmentation	
Segment	*Share (%)*
North	30
East	10
West	45
South	15
Branded	40
Unbranded	60
Metropolitan Cities (6)	65
Non Metro Cities	35

Source: www.indiastat.com, accessed June 2008, reproduced with permission.

In order to meets its vision of becoming an "Indian MNC in frozen foods," Ahmedabad-based Vadilal Industries Ltd has consolidated and expanded operations to strengthen its network. Mother Dairy, Delhi which was set up in 1974, is the wholly owned subsidiary of the National Dairy Development Board. It launched its ice cream brand in 1995 and has secured 62% of the market share in Delhi and NCR. Arun, a leader in south India, markets through its brand Hatsun Agro Products Ltd. The company controls 56% of the Tamil Nadu market and has a 33% share in the southern market.[1] Dinshaws, a key regional force has also established a sound footing in west India. Table 12.02 depicts the market share of the leading players in the ice cream market. The product variations in the ice cream market are depicted in Table 12.03.

TABLE 12.02
Leading Players in the Ice Cream Market

Leading players	
Company	*Share (%)*
Amul	27
Kwality Wall's	8
Vadilal Industries	7
Mother Dairy	7
Dinshaws	4
Arun	4

Source: www.indiastat.com, accessed June 2008, reproduced with permission.

TABLE 12.03
Product Variations in Ice Creams

Product variation	
Type	*Share (%)*
Vanilla	35
Chocolate	32
About 200 other flavours	33

Source: www.indiastat.com, accessed in June 2008, reproduced with permission.

Entry of Multinationals

Unlike the market for other products, the Indian ice cream market is completely dominated by national players such as Amul, Kwality, Vadilal, and some major regional players like Arun in south India and Dinshaws in west India. Multinationals are also trying to make their presence felt in the market. Movenpick, a famous Swiss brand launched its Blue Bunny brand of ice creams in Mumbai recently. However, high prices and some other global factors have restricted the brand's visibility in India. Baskin Robbins has also plans to bring the world-renowned Dunkin Donuts bakery chain to India. French player Candia, which owns Cream Bell brand has taken the route of joint ventures to enter the market. The ice cream market provides plenty of challenges and opportunities to national as well as multinational players. Both are ready to battle it out to gain control of the market.

Suppose you have joined an organization as a market research analyst. Using the information given in the case and the concept of hypothesis testing presented in this chapter, discuss the following:

1. As per Table 12.01, branded ice creams have captured 40% of the total ice cream market. There is a possibility that heavy advertisement and market penetration might

have changed this figure. Suppose a researcher takes a random sample of size 1680 from the entire country. Out of the 1680 consumers surveyed, 820 consumers say that they purchase branded ice creams. Test the figure of 40% by taking 95% as the confidence level.

2. Table 12.03 gives the information that 35% of the consumers in the market prefer vanilla flavour. Many new players have entered the market with new brands and flavours. Suppose a researcher takes a random sample of 1820 consumers. Out of the 1820 consumers, 420 consumers say that they prefer vanilla over any other flavour. Test the hypothesis that 35% of the consumers prefer vanilla flavour. Take 95% as the confidence level.

3. Table 12.02 gives the information that 4% of the consumers prefer Dinshaws. Suppose the company believes that its market share will grow to 7% after it adopts an aggressive marketing strategy. A researcher has taken a random sample of 2200 consumers and 150 consumers reply that they prefer Dinshaws. Test the hypothesis that 4% of the consumers prefer Dinshaws. Take 95% as the confidence level.

NOTES |

1. "The ice cream punch", Sindhu J.Bhattacharya, *The Hindu Business Line*, available at www.thehindubusinessline.com/catalyst/2004/06/24/stories/2004062400160100.htm, accessed August 2008.
2. www.indiastat.com, accessed August 2008, reproduced with permission.

CHAPTER

13

Statistical Inference: Hypothesis Testing for Two Populations

LEARNING OBJECTIVES

Upon completion of this chapter, you will be able to:

- Test the hypothesis for the difference between two population means using the *z* statistic
- Test the hypothesis for the difference between two population means using the *t* statistic
- Understand the concept of statistical inference of the difference between the means of two related populations (matched samples)
- Test hypothesis for the difference in two population proportions
- Test hypothesis about two population variances (*F* distribution)

STATISTICS IN ACTION: JK PAPER LTD

JK Group, a leading private sector group in India, was founded over 100 years ago. The group is composed of companies with interests in diverse sectors such as automotive tyres and tubes, paper and pulp, cement, oil seals, power transmission systems, hybrid seeds, woollen textiles, readymade apparels, sugar, food, dairy products, and cosmetics, etc. Their products are established brand names as well as market leaders in different segments.[1]

JK Paper Ltd, incorporated in 1960, is engaged in the manufacture and sale of pulp paper, paper board, straw paper, writing and printing paper, and speciality papers. Beyond developing new product applications in order to meet the varying needs of its consumers, the company has invested in several innovative promotional campaigns to communicate the product benefits to its users and channel partners. The company enjoys a price premium in the market as a result of these efforts. The company's leading brands "JK Copier" and "JK Easy Copier" have reinforced their position as the largest and second largest selling brands in the cut-size segment.[2]

Stressing on the importance of branding in the paper industry, Harshpati Singhania, MD, JK Paper Ltd said: "Branding allows better penetration in the market. With a brand there is always a quality assurance. We have realized the importance of branding in the industry and are consciously increasing our share in the branded segment. At present, our branded products share ranges from 60–75%."[3]

This conscious brand-building exercise has ensured sound financial results for the company over the years. Table 13.1 the net income of JK Paper Ltd from 1997 to 2007.

>>>

The company is dedicatedly engaged in a brand building exercise. Let as assume that the company wants to find out the quantitative difference (which will be measured through a well-designed questionnaire of brand equity) between its brand and the competitor's brand. The company entrusts a marketing research firm to complete this task. The marketing research firm administers a questionnaire made up of 10 questions to be rated on a scale from 1 to 5, to 3000 users of JK Paper and 3000 users of its closest competitor. On the basis of these two samples from two different populations, the company is trying to ascertain the difference in brand equity of two populations. There is a well-defined statistical procedure for this. This chapter discusses the hypothesis-testing procedure for two populations in detail. It mainly focuses on testing hypothesis for the difference between two populations mean using the z statistic; testing hypothesis for the difference between two population means using the t statistic; the concept of statistical inference about the difference between the means of two related populations (matched samples); testing hypothesis for the difference in two population proportions, and testing hypothesis about two population variances (F distribution).

TABLE 13.1
Net income of JK Paper Ltd from 1997 to 2007

Year	*Net income (in million rupees)*
1997	1366.0
1998	1279.2
1999	1346.0
2000	1168.7
2001	1338.6
2002	5832.6
2003	5705.6
2004	6151.9
2005	7060.1
2006	6657.0
2007	7670.1

Source: Prowess (V. 3.1), Centre for Monitoring Indian Economy Pvt. Ltd, Mumbai, August 2008, reproduced with permission.

13.1 INTRODUCTION

In the last chapter, we discussed hypothesis-testing procedure for single populations. In the real-world, marketing analysts often encounter situations where they need to test the hypothesis from two populations instead of a single population. For example, a marketing analyst may want to find out the difference between the expenditure patterns of two different geographical regions. In order to achieve this, the analyst has to take two samples from two populations, calculate the means, and compare these means. The techniques for doing this are presented in this chapter. In other words, this chapter will focus on statistical inference in situations involving two or more populations.

We have discussed that the z statistic is used as a tool for statistical inference for large samples and the t statistic is used for small samples. We will be discussing four techniques of analysing data for two populations in this chapter. It is important to note that out of the four techniques, three are based on the assumption that the samples are independent. This assumption explains that the items in two samples taken from the two populations are not related (independent) to each other and any relationship or similarity between two samples is coincidental or due to chance. This chapter also focuses on the statistical technique of analysing data for two related samples.

13.2 HYPOTHESIS TESTING FOR THE DIFFERENCE BETWEEN TWO POPULATION MEANS USING THE z STATISTIC

The difference in two sample means, $\bar{x}_1 - \bar{x}_2$ is normally distributed for large samples (both n_1 and $n_2 \geq 30$), irrespective of the shape of the population.

In this section, we will discuss the difference in means from two samples taken from two populations. On many occasions, a marketing researcher might have to compare two means taken from two different samples from two populations, and make an inference about the difference in the population means of the two populations based on the sample means. For example, a researcher is interested in analysing the difference in consumer satisfaction for a particular product in two cities, Mumbai and Delhi. In order to accomplish this, the researcher collects two different samples from the two cities taken in the study, obtain the two sample means, and then compare these two means. Finally, the researcher draws a conclusion about the population means based on the inference obtained from the sample means.

A question arises as to the validity of procedure of analysing the difference in two samples based on the sample means. The central limit theorem states that the difference in two sample means, $\bar{x}_1 - \bar{x}_2$, is normally distributed for large sample sizes (both n_1 and $n_2 \geq 30$) irrespective of the shape of the populations. Suppose we have two populations with means σ_1 and σ_2. The standard deviation of these two populations is μ_1 and μ_2. The size of the sample taken from these two populations is n_1 and n_2, respectively. Hence, the z formula can be given as below:

z Formula for difference between mean values of two populations (n_1 and $n_2 \geq 30$)

$$z = \frac{(\bar{x}_1 - \bar{x}_2) - (\mu_1 - \mu_2)}{\sqrt{\frac{\sigma_1^2}{n_1} + \frac{\sigma_2^2}{n_2}}}$$

where μ_1 is the mean of Population 1, μ_2 the mean of Population 2, n_1 the size of Sample 1, n_2 the size of Sample 2, σ_1 the standard deviation of Population 1, and σ_2 the standard deviation of Population 2.

The formula given above is applicable when population variances are known. When population variances are unknown and the sample size is large (n_1 and $n_2 \geq 30$), sample variances can be a good approximation of population variances. The z formula for the difference between the mean values of two populations (n_1 and $n_2 \geq 30$) using sample variances can be presented as below:

When population variances are unknown and sample size is large (n_1 and $n_2 \geq 30$), sample variances can be a good approximation of population variances.

z Formula for the difference between mean values of two populations with unknown σ_1^2 and σ_2^2 (n_1 and $n_2 \geq 30$)

$$z = \frac{(\bar{x}_1 - \bar{x}_2) - (\mu_1 - \mu_2)}{\sqrt{\frac{s_1^2}{n_1} + \frac{s_2^2}{n_2}}}$$

where μ_1 is the mean of Population 1, μ_2 the mean of Population 2, n_1 the size of Sample 1, n_2 the size of Sample 2, s_1 the standard deviation of Sample 1, and s_2 the standard deviation of Sample 2.

Example 13.1

Two consumer durables companies market two brands of electric irons A and B, respectively. A researcher has taken a random sample of size 35 from the first company and size 40 from the second company and computed the average life of both the brands in months (average life is shown in Table 13.1(a) and 13.1(b)). Is there a significant difference between the average life of the two brands A and B? Take 95% as the confidence level.

TABLE 13.1(a)
Average life of an electric iron in months (Brand A)

61	62	62	61	62
62	63	63	62	61
60	61	62	64	63
63	62	62	62	64
62	67	64	61	61
61	65	65	62	62
64	62	62	63	60

TABLE 13.1(b)
Average life of an electric iron in months (Brand B)

61	61	65	63	62
62	61	67	62	64
60	63	64	65	62
63	65	62	64	65
64	64	64	61	62
62	66	65	62	63
61	64	63	66	61
60	62	61	63	65

Solution

The solution can be presented using the seven steps of hypothesis testing as below:

Step 1: Set null and alternative hypotheses
The null and alternative hypotheses can be stated as below:

$$H_0: \mu_1 = \mu_2$$

and

$$H_1: \mu_1 \neq \mu_2$$

The above hypotheses can be reframed as

$$H_0: \mu_1 - \mu_2 = 0$$

and

$$H_1: \mu_1 - \mu_2 \neq 0$$

Step 2: Determine the appropriate statistical test
The test statistic is

$$z = \frac{(\bar{x}_1 - \bar{x}_2) - (\mu_1 - \mu_2)}{\sqrt{\frac{s_1^2}{n_1} + \frac{s_2^2}{n_2}}}$$

Step 3: Set the level of significance
α has been specified as 0.05.

Step 4: Set the decision rule

Value of $\alpha = 0.05$. The critical values of z from the z distribution table is ± 1.96. Therefore, the hypothesis will be rejected if the observed value of z is less than -1.96 and greater than $+1.96$.

Step 5: Collect the sample data

The sample data is as follows:

n_1 = Size of Sample 1 = 35

n_2 = Size of Sample 2 = 40

s_1^2 = Variance of Sample 1 = 2.1815

s_2^2 = Variance of Sample 2 = 3.0769

μ_1 = Mean of the Sample 1 = 62.37

μ_2 = Mean of the Sample 2 = 63

Step 6: Analyse the data

The z formula for the difference between the mean values of two populations with unknown σ_1^2 and σ_2^2 and (sample size n_1 and $n_2 \geq 30$) is as below:

$$z = \frac{(\bar{x}_1 - \bar{x}_2) - (\mu_1 - \mu_2)}{\sqrt{\dfrac{s_1^2}{n_1} + \dfrac{s_2^2}{n_2}}} = \frac{(62.37 - 63) - 0}{\sqrt{\dfrac{2.1815}{35} + \dfrac{3.0769}{40}}} = \frac{-0.63}{0.3731} = -1.68$$

Step 7: Arrive at a statistical conclusion and business implication

At 95% confidence level, the critical value obtained from the z distribution table is ± 1.96. The observed value of z is calculated as -1.68 which falls in the acceptance region. Hence, the null hypothesis is accepted and the alternative hypothesis is rejected. The result which we have obtained from the sample (difference between two sample means) may be owing to chance.

Therefore, the statistical evidence is not sufficient to accept the hypothesis that there is a significant difference between the average life of electric irons produced by the two electric iron companies.

SELF-PRACTICE PROBLEMS

13A1. Test the following hypotheses by taking $\alpha = 0.05$

$$H_0: \mu_1 - \mu_2 = 0, \quad H_1: \mu_1 - \mu_2 \neq 0$$

when information about two samples is given as follows:

First Sample

Sample mean $(\bar{x}_1) = 50$, sample size $(n_1) = 70$, sample standard deviation $s_1 = 9$

Second Sample

Sample mean $(\bar{x}_2) = 65$, sample size $(n_2) = 75$, sample standard deviation $s_2 = 10$

13A2. Test the following hypotheses by taking $\alpha = 0.10$

$$H_0: \mu_1 - \mu_2 = 0, \quad H_1: \mu_1 - \mu_2 \neq 0$$

when information about two samples is given as follows:

First Sample

90	101	99	99	96	88	86
97	98	90	92	95	98	91
98	97	92	89	90	93	94
99	94	95	81	99	95	96
100	99	97	82	91	99	100

Second Sample

70	71	73	78	79	78	80	69
66	69	68	70	71	72	73	65
65	70	63	64	65	71	72	73
68	69	70	77	69	64	65	60
68	67	65	67	70	64	65	67

13A3. Test the following hypotheses by taking $\alpha = 0.10$

$$H_0 : \mu_1 - \mu_2 = 0 \quad H_1 : \mu_1 - \mu_2 < 0$$

when information about two samples is given as follows:

First Sample

10	11	12	11	12	10	9	11
13	12	11	13	12	10	9	8
11	10	9	10	14	15	13	12
10	8	9	10	11	13	14	14
12	13	11	14	12	13	10	12

Second Sample

12	11	13	10	9	11	10	12	13
14	13	12	11	10	13	14	13	15
15	16	11	12	14	10	9	8	7
10	11	13	12	9	7	8	10	9
9	11	12	13	14	10	13	11	12

13.3 HYPOTHESIS TESTING FOR THE DIFFERENCE BETWEEN TWO POPULATION MEANS USING THE *t* STATISTIC (CASE OF A SMALL RANDOM SAMPLE, $n_1, n_2 < 30$, WHEN POPULATION STANDARD DEVIATION IS UNKNOWN)

> When sample size is small ($n_1, n_2 < 30$) and samples are independent (not related) and the population standard deviation is unknown, the t statistic can be used to test the hypothesis for difference between two population means.

In the previous section, we discussed hypothesis testing for the difference between two population means using the *z* statistic. This procedure is applicable for large samples, when the population standard deviation is known (when unknown, sample standard deviation can be used in place of population standard deviation). When sample size is small ($n_1, n_2 < 30$) and samples are independent (not related) and population standard deviation is unknown, the *t*-statistic can be used to test the hypothesis for the difference between two population means. This technique is based on the assumption that the characteristic being studied is normally distributed for both the populations. In the previous section, we have arrived at the *z* formula as:

$$z = \frac{(\bar{x}_1 - \bar{x}_2) - (\mu_1 - \mu_2)}{\sqrt{\frac{6_1^2}{n_1} + \frac{6_2^2}{n_2}}}$$

It is assumed that the two population variances are unknown but equal. Therefore, under this assumption, if $\sigma_1^2 = \sigma_2^2 = \sigma$, the *z* formula can be modified as follows:

$$z = \frac{(\bar{x}_1 - \bar{x}_2) - (\mu_1 - \mu_2)}{\sqrt{\frac{\sigma^2}{n_1} + \frac{\sigma^2}{n_2}}} = \frac{(\bar{x}_1 - \bar{x}_2) - (\mu_1 - \mu_2)}{\sigma\sqrt{\frac{1}{n_1} + \frac{1}{n_2}}}$$

Under the assumption that population variances are unknown, σ can be estimated by pooling two sample variances and computing a pooled standard deviation as follows:

$$\sigma = s_{pooled} = \sqrt{\frac{s_1^2(n_1 - 1) + s_2^2(n_2 - 1)}{n_1 + n_2 - 2}}$$

Substituting the value of σ in the *z* formula and replacing *z* by *t*, the *t* formula for testing the difference between two population means assuming equal variances can be stated as below:

$$t = \frac{(\bar{x}_1 - \bar{x}_2) - (\mu_1 - \mu_2)}{\sqrt{\frac{s_1^2(n_1 - 1) + s_2^2(n_2 - 1)}{n_1 + n_2 - 2}}\sqrt{\frac{1}{n_1} + \frac{1}{n_2}}}$$

with $df = n_1 + n_2 - 2$

The t formula presented above is based on the assumption that the population variances are equal. If this is not the case, then the following formula is used:

$$t = \frac{(\bar{x}_1 - \bar{x}_2) - (\mu_1 - \mu_2)}{\sqrt{\frac{s_1^2}{n_1} + \frac{s_2^2}{n_2}}}$$

with

$$df = \frac{\left\{\frac{s_1^2}{n_1} + \frac{s_2^2}{n_2}\right\}^2}{\frac{\left[\frac{s_1^2}{n_1}\right]^2}{n_1 - 1} + \frac{\left[\frac{s_2^2}{n_2}\right]^2}{n_2 - 1}}$$

This formula requires a complex computation of degrees of freedom. Therefore, it may not be attractive for some researches. Some statistical software programs such as MS Excel facilitate the computation of the t-statistic with both the formulas. MS Excel provides two tests—t-test: two samples assuming equal variances using pooled formula and t test: two samples assuming unequal variances using unpooled formula.

Example 13.2

Anmol Constructions is a leading company in the construction sector in India. It wants to construct flats in Raipur and Dehradun, the capitals of the newly formed states of Chhattisgarh and Uttarakhand, respectively. The company wants to estimate the amount that customers are willing to spend on purchasing a flat in the two cities. It randomly selected 25 potential customers from Raipur and 27 customers from Dehradun and posed the question, "how much are you willing to spend on a flat?" The data collected from the two cities is shown in Table 13.2(a) and Table 13.2(b). The company assumes that the intention to purchase of the customers is normally distributed with equal variance in the two cities taken for the study. On the basis of the samples taken for the study, estimate the difference in population means taking 95% as the confidence level.

TABLE 13.2(a)
Proposed expenditure on flats by customers from Raipur (in thousand rupees)

125	155	130
130	145	140
126	140	150
127	165	160
150	135	140
135	130	145
140	165	165
160	170	
120	130	
150	145	

TABLE 13.2(b)
Proposed expenditure on flats by customers form Dehradun (in thousand rupees)

185	145	145
165	150	160
160	155	170
170	160	180
180	145	145
190	140	
170	135	
150	185	
155	180	
160	190	

Solution

The seven steps of hypothesis testing can be performed as below:

Step 1: Set null and alternative hypotheses

The hypotheses for this test are as below:

$$H_0: \mu_1 - \mu_2 = 0$$
$$H_1: \mu_1 - \mu_2 \neq 0$$

Step 2: Determine the appropriate statistical test

We have discussed that under the assumption of equal variance, the t formula can be stated as

$$t = \frac{(\bar{x}_1 - \bar{x}_2) - (\mu_1 - \mu_2)}{\sigma\sqrt{\frac{1}{n_1} + \frac{1}{n_2}}}$$

σ can be estimated by pooling two sample variances and computing pooled standard deviation as follows:

$$\sigma = s_{pooled} = \sqrt{\frac{s_1^2(n_1 - 1) + s_2^2(n_2 - 1)}{n_1 + n_2 - 2}}$$

Step 3: Set the level of significance

α has been specified as 0.05.

Step 4: Set the decision rule

Value of α is 0.05 and the degrees of freedom is 27 + 25 – 2 = 50. The tabular t value is $t_{0.025,\,50} = \pm 2.009$. The null hypothesis will be rejected if the observed value of t is less than –2.009 or greater than +2.009.

Step 5: Collect the sample data

The sample data is as follows:

$$s_1^2 = 203.6410, \quad s_2^2 = 273.0833$$
$$n_1 = 27, \quad n_2 = 25$$
$$\bar{x}_1 = 143.4444, \quad \bar{x}_2 = 162.8$$

Step 6: Analyse the data

By substituting all the values in formula for pooled standard deviation, we get

$$\sigma = s_{pooled} = \sqrt{\frac{(203.6410) \times (26) + (273.0833) \times (24)}{27 + 25 - 2}}$$

$$= \sqrt{\frac{5294.666 + 6553.999}{50}} = \sqrt{236.9733} = 15.39$$

By substituting the value of pooled standard deviation in the t formula, we get

$$t = \frac{(143.4444 - 162.8) - (0)}{15.39\sqrt{\frac{1}{27} + \frac{1}{25}}}$$

$$t = \frac{-19.3556}{4.2715} = -4.53$$

Step 7: Arrive at a statistical conclusion and business implication

The t value from the t distribution table is $t_{0.025,\, 50} = \pm 2.009$ and the observed t value is –4.53. So, the observed t value –4.53 is less than the tabular t value –2.009. Hence, the null hypothesis is rejected and the alternative hypothesis is accepted. This result shows that there is a significant difference in the means of the amounts that customers are willing to spend on a flat in the two cities.

Therefore, Anmol Constructions can plan relatively more expensive flats for Dehradun when compared to Raipur.

Note: Like the z formula, the t formula for difference between mean values of two populations can also be manipulated to produce a formula for constructing confidence intervals for the difference in two population means (for small sample size n_1, $n_2 < 30$). This is also based on the assumption that the population variances are unknown and equal. So, the confidence interval to estimate the difference in two population means for small sample sizes assuming that population variances are unknown and equal can be presented as below:

Confidence interval to estimate the difference in two population means for small sample sizes assuming that population variances are unknown and equal

$$(\bar{x}_1 - \bar{x}_2) - t\sqrt{\frac{s_1^2(n_1-1) + s_2^2(n_2-1)}{n_1+n_2-2}} \times \sqrt{\frac{1}{n_1}+\frac{1}{n_2}} \le \mu_1 - \mu_2$$

$$\le (\bar{x}_1 - \bar{x}_2) + t\sqrt{\frac{s_1^2(n_1-1) + s_2^2(n_2-1)}{n_1+n_2-2}} \times \sqrt{\frac{1}{n_1}+\frac{1}{n_2}}$$

where $df = n_1 + n_2 - 2$

SELF-PRACTICE PROBLEMS

13B1. Test the hypotheses given below by taking $\alpha = 0.05$

$$H_0: \mu_1 - \mu_2 = 0, \quad H_1: \mu_1 - \mu_2 \neq 0$$

Information about two samples is given as under:

First Sample

Sample mean $(\bar{x}_1) = 55$, sample size $n_1 = 10$, sample variance $s_1^2 = 25$

Second Sample

Sample mean $(\bar{x}_2) = 70$, sample size $n_2 = 15$, sample variance $s_2^2 = 36$

Assume that population variances are not equal.

13B2. Test the hypotheses given below by taking $\alpha = 0.10$

$$H_0: \mu_1 - \mu_2 = 0, \quad H_1: \mu_1 - \mu_2 < 0$$

Information about two samples is gives as under:

First Sample

15	17	18	17	17	19	22	21
16	17	18	19	21	15	16	17

Second Sample

10	9	11	12	11	10	11	12	10
11	10	9	8	10	7	9	10	11
10	12							

13.4 STATISTICAL INFERENCE ABOUT THE DIFFERENCE BETWEEN THE MEANS OF TWO RELATED POPULATIONS (MATCHED SAMPLES)

In the previous section, we discussed the process of hypothesis testing and confidence interval construction for independent samples. In this section, we will discuss the hypothesis testing and confidence interval construction for dependent samples or related samples. The procedure of testing hypothesis is also referred to as "matched paired test or *t* test for related samples." For example, the management of a company plagued by poor productivity realizes the need to provide technical training to employees. It hires a researcher to measure the productivity levels of a sample of 25 employees. The productivity levels are measured again after a one-month technical training programme. In this kind of pre-and post-training study, samples which are taken before and after the study cannot be treated as independent because each observation in Sample 1 is related to the observation in Sample 2. The productivity scores obtained before training is related to the scores obtained after training because the two measurements apply to the same person.

In this kind of pre- and post-training study, samples which are taken before and after the study cannot be treated as independent because each observation in sample one is related to the observation in sample two.

For dependent samples or related samples test, it is important that the two samples taken in the study are of the same size. The *t* formula to test the difference between the means of two **related populations** (matched samples) can be presented as below:

For dependent samples or related samples, it is important that the two samples taken in the study are of the same size.

***t* Formula to test the difference between the means of two related populations (matched samples)**

$$t = \frac{\bar{d} - \mu_d}{\frac{s_d}{\sqrt{n}}} \quad \text{with } df = n - 1$$

where n is the number of pairs of difference, $\bar{d}$ the mean sample difference, μ_d the mean population difference, and s_d the standard deviation of the sample difference.

Here, $\bar{d} = \frac{\sum d}{n}$

$$s_d = \sqrt{\frac{\sum (d - \bar{d})^2}{n-1}} = \sqrt{\frac{\sum d^2 - \frac{\left(\sum d\right)^2}{n}}{n-1}} = \sqrt{\frac{\sum d^2}{n-1} - \frac{\left(\sum d\right)^2}{n(n-1)}}$$

Example 13.3

An electronic goods company arranged a special training programme for one segment of its employees. The company wants to measure the change in the attitude of its employees after the training. For this purpose, it has used a well-designed questionnaire, which consists of 10 questions on a 1 to 5 rating scale (1 is strongly disagree and 5 is strongly agree). The company selected a random sample of 10 employees. The scores obtained by these employees are given in Table 13.3.

Use $\alpha = 0.10$ to determine whether there is a significant change in the attitude of employees after the training programme.

TABLE 13.3
Scores obtained by the employees before and after the training

Employees	*Scores before training*	*Scores after training*
1	25	32
2	26	30
3	28	32
4	22	34
5	20	32
6	30	28
7	22	25
8	20	30
9	21	25
10	24	28

Solution

The seven steps of hypothesis testing can be performed as below:

Step 1: Set null and alternative hypotheses

The hypothesis for this test is as below:

$$H_0: \mu_d = 0$$
$$H_1: \mu_d \neq 0$$

Step 2: Determine the appropriate statistical test

The t formula to test the difference between the means of two related populations (matched samples) will be the appropriate statistical test.

$$t = \frac{\bar{d} - \mu_d}{\frac{s_d}{\sqrt{n}}} \quad \text{with } df = n - 1$$

Step 3: Set the level of significance

α has been specified as 0.10.

Step 4: Set the decision rule

Value of α is 0.10 and the degrees of freedom is 9. The tabular t value is $t_{0.05,\,9} = \pm 1.833$. The null hypothesis will be rejected if the observed value of t is less than -1.833 or greater than $+1.833$.

Step 5: Collect the sample data

The sample data and some other calculations are as below:

Employees	*Before training scores*	*After training scores*	*Difference in scores d*	d^2
1	25	32	–7	49
2	26	30	–4	16
3	28	32	–4	16
4	22	34	–12	144
5	20	32	–12	144
6	30	28	2	4
7	22	25	–3	9
8	20	30	–10	100
9	21	25	–4	16
10	24	28	–4	16
Total			–58	514

We know that $\bar{d} = \frac{\sum d}{n} = \frac{-58}{10} = -5.8$

$$s_d = \sqrt{\frac{\sum d^2}{n-1} - \frac{\left(\sum d\right)^2}{n(n-1)}} = \sqrt{\frac{514}{10-1} - \frac{(-58)^2}{10 \times (10-1)}}$$

$$= \sqrt{(57.1111) - (37.3777)} = \sqrt{19.7334} = 4.4422$$

Step 6: Analyse the data

Substituting all the values in the t formula, we get

$$t = \frac{\bar{d} - \mu_d}{\frac{s_d}{\sqrt{n}}} = \frac{-5.8 - 0}{\frac{4.4422}{\sqrt{10}}} = \frac{-5.8}{1.4047} = -4.13$$

Step 7: Arrive at a statistical conclusion and business implication

So, the observed t value –4.13 is less than the tabular t value –1.833. Hence, the null hypothesis is rejected and the alternative hypothesis is accepted. Therefore, it can be concluded that there is a significant difference in the attitude of employees before and after the training.

The special training programme organized by the company has significantly changed the attitude of the employees. Hence, the company should organize this special training programme for all its employees.

Note: The confidence interval formula for statistical inference about the difference between the means of two related populations (matched samples) can be presented as below:

Confidence interval for statistical inference about the difference between the means of two related populations (matched samples)

$$\bar{d} - t\frac{s_d}{\sqrt{n}} \le \mu_d \le \bar{d} + t\frac{s_d}{\sqrt{n}}$$

with $df = n - 1$

SELF-PRACTICE PROBLEMS

13C1. Using $\alpha = 0.05$, for the data given, test the following hypotheses:

$$H_0: \mu_d = 0$$
$$H_1: \mu_d \neq 0$$

Assume that the differences are normally distributed.

Pair	*Sample* 1	*Sample* 2
1	18	16
2	19	15
3	18	17
4	20	15
5	17	18
6	18	14
7	19	17
8	20	15
9	21	16
10	19	18

13C2. Using $\alpha = 0.10$, for the data given, test the following hypotheses:

$$H_0: \mu_d = 0$$
$$H_1: \mu_d > 0$$

Assume that the differences are normally distributed.

Pair	*Sample 1*	*Sample 2*
1	50	45
2	55	47
3	57	48
4	60	46
5	62	49
6	61	42
7	70	43
8	65	45

13C3. A fast moving consumer goods company has organized a training programme to boost the morale of its employees. For measuring effectiveness of the training programme the company has taken a random sample of 7 employees and obtained their training scores (before and after). Assume that the difference is normally distributed. The scores obtained by the employees before and after the training programme are given in the following table:

Employee No.	*Before training*	*After training*
1	30	32
2	29	31
3	28	29
4	32	30
5	27	28
6	31	30
7	32	31

Using $\alpha = 0.01$, test the hypothesis to ascertain whether the training has boosted the morale of the employees.

13.5 HYPOTHESIS TESTING FOR THE DIFFERENCE IN TWO POPULATION PROPORTIONS

It has already been discussed that in many real life situations, researchers are interested in measuring the difference between two population proportions. For example, a researcher might want to compare the market share of a product in two different markets. On the basis of the difference in sample proportions, a researcher can estimate the difference in population proportions. The statistic used for comparing the difference in sample proportions is $\bar{p}_1 - \bar{p}_2$, where $\bar{p}_1$ and $\bar{p}_2$ are the sample proportions from Sample 1 and Sample 2, respectively.

On the basis of the difference in sample proportions, a researcher can estimate the difference in population proportions. The statistic used for comparing the difference in sample proportions is $\bar{p}_1 - \bar{p}_2$, where $\bar{p}_1$ and $\bar{p}_2$ are the sample proportions from Sample 1 and Sample 2, respectively.

The difference in sample proportions, $\bar{p}_1 - \bar{p}_2$, is based on the assumption that the difference between two population proportions $p_1 - p_2$ is normally distributed. The standard deviation of the difference of proportion is given by

$$\sigma_{\bar{p}_1 - \bar{p}_2} = \sqrt{\frac{p_1 \times (1 - p_1)}{n_1} + \frac{p_2 \times (1 - p_2)}{n_2}} = \sqrt{\frac{p_1 \times q_1}{n_1} + \frac{p_2 \times q_2}{n_2}}$$

This information can be used for developing the z formula for the difference in population proportions.

z Formula for the difference in population proportions

$$z = \frac{(\bar{p}_1 - \bar{p}_2) - (p_1 - p_2)}{\sqrt{\frac{p_1 \times q_1}{n_1} + \frac{p_2 \times q_2}{n_2}}}$$

where $\bar{p}_1$ is the proportion from the first sample, $\bar{p}_2$ the proportion from the second sample, p_1 the proportion from the first population, p_2 the proportion from the second population, n_1 the size of the first sample, n_2 the size of the second sample, $q_1 = (1 - p_1)$, and $q_2 = (1 - p_2)$.

This formula is based on the prior knowledge of the values of p_1 and p_2. Population proportions are not always known. In this case, we combine two sample proportions $\bar{p}_1$ and $\bar{p}_2$ to get an unbiased estimate of the population proportion using a weighted average to produce p_w. Using this concept, the modified z formula can be presented as under:

z Formula for the difference in population proportions

$$z = \frac{(\bar{p}_1 - \bar{p}_2) - (p_1 - p_2)}{\sqrt{(p_w \times q_w)\left(\frac{1}{n_1} + \frac{1}{n_2}\right)}}$$

where

$$\bar{p}_1 = \frac{x_1}{n_1} \Rightarrow x_1 = n_1\bar{p}_1$$

$$p_w = \frac{x_1 + x_2}{n_1 + n_2} = \frac{n_1\bar{p}_1 + n_2\bar{p}_2}{n_1 + n_2} \quad \text{and} \quad q_w = 1 - p_w$$

Example 13.4

There has been a fundamental shift in Indian economy after 1991. All business sectors including the banking sector have been affected by the liberalization and privatization measures of the government. Due to heavy competition, Indian public sector banks have also adopted consumer-friendly policies such as extending service time for their customers. On one hand, changes introduced by the banks enhance the quality of services; however, on the other hand, they are also responsible for generating stress among employees. A researcher wants to assess the stress levels of bank employees. The researcher has selected two banks, A & B for this purpose. The working hours of Bank A are from 10 a.m to 3.30 p.m and the working hours of Bank B are from 8.00 a.m to 8.00 p.m. The researcher has randomly selected 40 employees from Bank A and 10 of them have indicated high stress levels. The researcher has also randomly selected 50 employees from Bank B and 22 of them have indicated high stress levels. Does this indicate that the stress levels of employees of Bank B are significantly higher. Test the hypothesis by taking 99% as the confidence level.

Solution

The seven steps of hypothesis can be performed as below:

Step 1: Set null and alternative hypotheses

Sample 1 is the sample of Bank A employees and Sample 2 is the sample of Bank B employees. p_1 is the proportion of Bank A employees who have reported high stress levels and p_2 is the proportion of Bank B employees who have reported high stress levels, then the hypotheses for this test are below:

$$H_0 : p_1 - p_2 = 0$$
$$H_1 : p_1 - p_2 < 0$$

Step 2: Determine the appropriate statistical test

z Formula for the difference in population proportions

$$z = \frac{(\bar{p}_1 - \bar{p}_2) - (p_1 - p_2)}{\sqrt{(p_w \times q_w)\left(\frac{1}{n_1} + \frac{1}{n_2}\right)}}$$

where $\bar{p}_1 = \frac{x_1}{n_1} \Rightarrow x_1 = n_1\bar{p}_1$

Similarly, $\bar{p}_2 = \frac{x_2}{n_2} \Rightarrow x_2 = n_2\bar{p}_2$

Hence, $p_w = \frac{x_1 + x_2}{n_1 + n_2} = \frac{n_1\bar{p}_1 + n_2\bar{p}_2}{n_1 + n_2}$ and $q_w = 1 - p_w$

Step 3: Set the level of significance
α has been specified as 0.01.

Step 4: Set the decision rule
Value of $\alpha = 0.01$. The tabular z value is ±2.575. From the alternative hypothesis, $p_1 < p_2$, it is very clear that this is a left-tailed test. The null hypothesis will be rejected if the observed value of z is less than –2.575.

Step 5: Collect the sample data
The sample information is as below:

For Bank A: $n_1 = 40$ and $\bar{p}_1 = \frac{x_1}{n_1} = \frac{10}{40} = 0.25$

For Bank B: $n_1 = 50$ and $\bar{p}_2 = \frac{x_2}{n_2} = \frac{22}{50} = 0.44$

Step 6: Analyse the data
Placing the values in z-formula, we get

$$z = \frac{(\bar{p}_1 - \bar{p}_2) - (p_1 - p_2)}{\sqrt{(p_w \times q_w)\left(\frac{1}{n_1} + \frac{1}{n_2}\right)}} = \frac{(0.25 - 0.44) - 0}{\sqrt{(0.3555 \times 0.6445)\left(\frac{1}{40} + \frac{1}{50}\right)}}$$

$$= \frac{-0.19}{\sqrt{0.0103}} = \frac{-0.19}{0.1015} = -1.87$$

where $\bar{p}_1 = \frac{x_1}{n_1} \Rightarrow x_1 = n_1\bar{p}_1$

$$p_w = \frac{x_1 + x_2}{n_1 + n_2} = \frac{n_1\bar{p}_1 + n_2\bar{p}_2}{n_1 + n_2} = \frac{(40) \times (0.25) + (50) \times (0.44)}{40 + 50}$$

$$= \frac{10 + 22}{90} = \frac{32}{90} = 0.3555$$

and $q_w = 1 - p_w = 1 - 0.3555 = 0.6445$

Step 7: Arrive at a statistical conclusion and business implication
Therefore, the observed z value –1.87 is greater than the tabular z value –2.575. Hence, the null hypothesis is accepted and the alternative hypothesis is rejected. Therefore, it can be concluded that a significantly higher proportion of employees from Bank B do not suffer from high stress levels. The result obtained from the sample may be due to chance.

It is important to note that by changing the level of significance for the test, the alternative hypothesis is accepted. Hence, we cannot ignore the high stress levels of employees due to their long working hours and efforts should be taken to launch stress management programmes.

SELF-PRACTICE PROBLEMS

13D1. Test the hypotheses mentioned below:

$$H_0: p_1 - p_2 = 0$$
$$H_1: p_1 - p_2 \neq 0$$

Use $\alpha = 0.05$ and the following information related to samples:

Sample 1: $n_1 = 120 \quad x_1 = 35$

Sample 2: $n_2 = 150 \quad x_2 = 40$

where x is the number of desired characteristics of interest in the sample.

13D2. Test the hypotheses mentioned below:

$$H_0: p_1 - p_2 = 0$$
$$H_1: p_1 - p_2 > 0$$

Use $\alpha = 0.01$ and the following information related to samples:

Sample 1: $n_1 = 100 \quad x_1 = 45$

Sample 2: $n_2 = 160 \quad x_2 = 50$

where x is the number of desired characteristics of interest in the sample.

13D3. Test the hypotheses mentioned below:

$$H_0: p_1 - p_2 = 0$$
$$H_1: p_1 - p_2 < 0$$

Use $\alpha = 0.05$ and the following information related to samples:

Sample 1: $n_1 = 700 \quad x_1 = 250$

Sample 2: $n_2 = 800 \quad x_2 = 425$

where x is the number of desired characteristics of interest in the sample.

The ratio of two sample variances $\frac{s_1^2}{s_2^2}$ taken from two samples is termed as F value and follows F distribution.

In F distribution, degrees of freedom are attached to the numerator and denominator, which decide the shape of the F distribution. F distribution is based on the assumption that the populations from which samples are drawn are normally distributed.

The F distribution is neither symmetric nor does it have a zero mean value. So, the simple procedure of obtaining the upper-tail value and merely placing a minus sign besides to the upper-tail value for obtaining the lower tail value is not applicable here.

The F value is always positive because it is a ratio of two variances (two squared quantities). The lower-tail value is obtained by using the reciprocal property of the F distribution.

13.6 HYPOTHESIS TESTING ABOUT TWO POPULATION VARIANCES (F DISTRIBUTION)

A decision maker might want to know the difference in two population variances. For example, a decision maker may want to know the variances in product quality on account of two different production processes or the variances in the product characteristics between products manufactured by two different machines. In the field of finance, variances are used to measure financial risk. The greater the variance in the stock market, the higher the risk. In testing the hypotheses about the difference in two population variances, sample variances are used. The ratio of two sample variances $\frac{s_1^2}{s_2^2}$ taken from two samples is termed as ***F* value** and follows the F distribution. So, F value can be defined as:

***F* test for the difference in two population variances**

$$F = \frac{s_1^2}{s_2^2}$$

with $df = v_1 = n_1 - 1$ (for numerator)

and $df = v_2 = n_2 - 1$ (for denominator)

where n_1 is the size of the sample taken from Population 1, n_2 the size of the sample taken from Population 2, s_1^2 the variance of Sample 1, and s_2^2 the variance of Sample 2.

13.6.1 F Distribution

F distribution is based on the assumption that the populations from which samples are drawn are normally distributed. It is named in honour of the famous statistician R. A. Fisher and is also termed as the "variance–ratio distribution." It is not symmetric. In the F distribution, the degrees of freedoms are attached to the numerator and denominator, which decide the shape of the distribution. A typical F distribution with acceptance and rejection region is shown in Figure 13.1.

From Figure 13.1, it is very clear that the F distribution is neither symmetric nor does it have a zero mean value. So, the simple procedure of obtaining the upper-tail value and merely placing a minus sign besides the upper-tail value for obtaining the lower tail value is

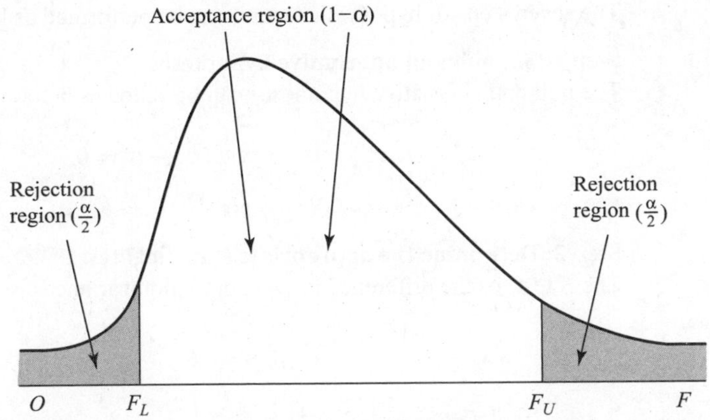

FIGURE 13.1
Acceptance and rejection regions for a two-tailed F test

not applicable here. The F value is always positive because it is a ratio of two variances (two squared quantities). The value of the lower tail is obtained by using the reciprocal property of the F distribution. The reciprocal property can be stated as

$$F_{1-\alpha\,(v_2,\,v_1)} = \frac{1}{F_{\alpha\,(v_1,\,v_2)}}$$

This property helps in determining the lower-tail value of the F distribution. For example, if $\alpha = 0.05$, then for $v_1 = 10$ and $v_2 = 8$ (for a two-tailed test), the upper F value is $F_{0.025(10,\,8)} = 4.30$.

Thus, the F value for the lower tail is $F_{0.975(8,\,10)} = \dfrac{1}{F_{0.025(10,\,8)}} = \dfrac{1}{4.30} = 0.23$.

The total area under the F distribution is equal to unity. The F distribution is positively skewed with a range from 0 to ∞, because sample variances s_1^2 and s_2^2 are the unbiased estimates of population variances and ($s_1 > s_2$). Its degree of skewness decreases with the numerator degree of freedom v_1 and denominator degree of freedom v_2. It is important to note that for $v_2 \geq 30$, the F distribution is approximately normal.

The total area under the F distribution is equal to unity. F distribution is positively skewed with a range from 0 to ∞, because sample variances s_1^2 and s_2^2 are the unbiased estimate of population variances and ($s_1 > s_2$). Its degree of skewness decreases with the numerator degree of freedom v_1 and denominator degree of freedom v_2. It is important to note that for $v_2 \geq 30$, the F distribution is approximately normal.

Example 13.5

A plant has installed two machines producing polythene bags. During the installation, the manufacturer of the machine has stated that the capacity of the machine is to produce 20 bags in a day. Owing to various factors such as different operators working on these machines, raw material, etc. there is a variation in the number of bags produced at the end of the day. The company researcher has taken a random sample of bags produced in 10 days for Machine 1 and 13 days for Machine 2, respectively. The following data gives the number of units of an item produced on a sampled day by the two machines:

Machine 1	18	19	19	18	17	19	18	19	18	19			
Machine 2	16	17	17	17	16	18	16	16	17	17	16	16	17

How can the researcher determine whether the variance is from the same population (population variances are equal) or it comes from different populations (population variances are not equal)? Take $\alpha = 0.05$ as the level of significance.

Solution

The seven steps of hypothesis testing can be performed as below:

Step 1: Set null and alternative hypotheses

The null and alternative hypotheses can be stated as below:

$$H_0: \sigma_1^2 = \sigma_2^2 \qquad H_0: \sigma_1^2 - \sigma_2^2 = 0$$
$$\text{or}$$
$$H_1: \sigma_1^2 \neq \sigma_2^2 \qquad H_1: \sigma_1^2 - \sigma_2^2 \neq 0$$

Step 2: Determine the appropriate statistical test

The F test for the difference in two population variances is

$$F = \frac{s_1^2}{s_2^2}$$

with $df = v_1 = n_1 - 1$ (for numerator)
and $df = v_2 = n_2 - 1$ (for denominator)

Step 3: Set the level of significance

α has been specified as 0.05.

Step 4: Set the decision rule

Value of $\alpha = 0.05$. We are conducting a two-tailed test; hence, $\frac{\alpha}{2} = 0.025$. For $v_1 = 9$ and $v_2 = 12$, upper F value is $F_{0.025(9,\,12)} = 3.44$. Thus, the lower F value is $F_{0.975(12,\,9)} = \frac{1}{F_{.025(9,\,12)}} = \frac{1}{3.44} = 0.29$. The null hypothesis will be accepted if the observed value of F lies in between 0.29 and 3.44, otherwise it will be rejected.

Step 5: Collect the sample data

The sample information is as below:
Variance for the first sample $s_1^2 = 0.4888$
Variance for the second sample $s_2^2 = 0.4230$
n_1 = Size of the sample taken from Population 1 = 10
n_2 = Size of the sample taken from Population 2 = 13

Step 6: Analyse the data

The F test for the difference in two population variances is given as

$$F = \frac{s_1^2}{s_2^2} = \frac{0.4888}{0.4230} = 1.15$$

with $df = v_1 = n_1 - 1 = 10 - 1 = 9$ (for numerator)
and $df = v_2 = n_2 - 1 = 13 - 1 = 12$ (for denominator)

Step 7: Arrive at a statistical conclusion and business implication

The observed F value 1.15 lies in between the lower value $F_L = 0.29$ and upper value $F_U = 3.44$. Hence, the null hypothesis is accepted and the alternative hypothesis is rejected. So, it can be concluded that there is no significant difference between the production capacity of the two machines. The results obtained by the sample may be due to chance.

SELF-PRACTICE PROBLEMS

13E1. Test the hypotheses mentioned below:

$$H_0: \sigma_1^2 = \sigma_2^2$$
$$H_1: \sigma_1^2 \neq \sigma_2^2$$

Use $\alpha = 0.05$ and the following information related to samples:

Sample 1: $n_1 = 10 \quad s_1^2 = 85$

Sample 2: $n_2 = 13 \quad s_2^2 = 165$

Assume that the populations are normally distributed.

13E2. Test the hypotheses mentioned below:

$$H_0: \sigma_1^2 = \sigma_2^2$$
$$H_1: \sigma_1^2 < \sigma_2^2$$

Use $\alpha = 0.10$ and the following information related to samples:

Sample 1: $n_1 = 9 \quad s_1^2 = 70$

Sample 2: $n_2 = 15 \quad s_2^2 = 120$

Assume that the populations are normally distributed.

13E3. Two bottle filling plants are supposed to fill 5 litres of water in each bottle. A researcher has taken a random sample of 10 bottles from Plant 1 and 15 bottles from Plant 2.The data collected are provided in the table below: How can the researcher determine whether the variance is from the same population (population variances are equal) or it comes from different populations (population variances are not equal)? Take $\alpha = 0.05$ as the confidence level.

Plant 1	5.1	5.2	5.2	5.2	5.3	5.4	5.3	4.9	4.8	4.9					
Plant 2	4.9	4.8	4.7	5.1	5.2	5.3	5.4	4.9	4.8	5.1	5.2	4.8	4.9	5.1	5.2

SUMMARY |

This chapter discusses various techniques of analysing data that come from two samples. It also focuses on four techniques of analysing data for two populations. It is important to note that out of the four techniques, three are based on the assumption that the samples are independent and the fourth is based on related samples. These techniques are related to means and proportions. We already know that for a large sample, the *z* statistic is used and for a small sample, the *t* statistic is used. The concept of central limit theorem can also be applied for testing the difference between two population means because the difference in two sample means, $\bar{x}_1$ $\bar{x}_2$ is normally distributed for large samples (both n_1 and $n_2 \geq 30$) irrespective of the shape of the population.

For large samples, *z* statistic is applied when sample size is small (n_1, $n_2 < 30$) and independent (not related) and population standard deviation is unknown; *t* statistic can be used to test the hypotheses for the difference between two population means. This technique is based on the assumption that the characteristic being studied is normally distributed for both the populations.

The *t* test can also be applied for dependent samples or related samples. The procedure of testing hypotheses is also referred to as "matched paired test or *t* test for related samples." In matched paired test or *t* test for related samples, observations in Sample 1 are related to the observations in Sample 2.

Hypothesis testing can also be carried out for sample proportions. On the basis of the difference in sample proportions, a researcher can estimate the difference in population proportions. The statistic used for comparing the difference in sample proportions is $\bar{p}_1 - \bar{p}_2$ where $\bar{p}_1$ and $\bar{p}_2$ are the sample proportions from Sample 1 and Sample 2, respectively. The difference in sample proportions, $\bar{p}_1 - \bar{p}_2$, is based on the assumption that the difference between two population proportions, $p_1 - p_2$, is normally distributed.

For comparing the difference in two population variances, *F* test can be used. The ratio of two sample variances $\frac{s_1^2}{s_2^2}$ taken from two samples is termed as "*F* value" and follows *F* distribution.

KEY TERMS |

F Value, 322

Related populations, 316

NOTES |

1. www.jkpaper.com/index.php?option = com_content&task = view&id = 34&Itemid, accessed August 2008.
2. Prowess (V. 3.1), Centre for Monitoring Indian Economy Pvt. Ltd, Mumbai, August 2008, reproduced with permission.
3. http://economictimes.indiatimes.com/Interview/Harshpat_Singhania_MD_JK_Paper_Ltd/, accessed August 2008.

DISCUSSION QUESTIONS |

1. Discuss the concept of hypothesis testing for two populations?
2. What is the procedure of using z formula for hypothesis testing for two populations?
3. How can we test hypothesis for the difference between two population means using the t statistic?
4. Explain the procedure of testing hypothesis for the difference between the means of two related populations (matched samples).
5. Which populations are called "related populations"?
6. Explain the procedure of testing hypothesis for the difference in two population proportions.
7. Explain the properties and importance of the F distribution.
8. Explain the procedure of testing hypothesis for two population variances.

NUMERICAL PROBLEMS |

1. Suppose the mean of Population 1 is accepted to be the same as that of Population 2. However, it is now believed that Population 2 has a higher mean than Population 1. The randomly selected observations of Population 1 and Population 2 are given below. Assume that both the populations have equal variances and x is normally distributed. Take 95% as the confidence level and test this belief.

Observations from Population 1

51	52	53	52	54
52	53	53	52	51
50	51	52	54	53
53	52	52	52	54
53	57	54	51	51
51	55	52	50	51
54	52	55	53	53

Observations from Population 2

62	63	58	53	65
64	63	63	65	63
61	63	54	55	63
62	55	61	63	62
54	54	64	62	63
63	61	62	63	62
62	62	65	61	67
61	62	58	55	58

2. Bright Career Academy is a reputed educational group in North India. It wants to launch a good public school in a town in Madhya Pradesh. It has the option of launching the school in two cities. The group wants to estimate the expenditure pattern of the families in two cities. Five years ago, another group had launched a school in City 1, based on the information that the average expenditure on school education was higher in City 1 as compared to City 2. Bright Career Academy realizes that these data might have changed in five years. For testing this belief, the company has

appointed a researcher who collected information from a random sample of 40 families from City 1 and 45 families from City 2. Information gathered by the researcher is presented in the following two tables:

Average expenditure of 40 families on education in City 1			
35,000	34,000	39,000	34,500
36,000	33,000	42,000	34,000
35,500	37,500	41,000	36,600
36,000	38,000	36,000	32,500
37,000	32,000	37,500	38,500
35,400	33,500	32,000	40,000
38,000	35,500	31,000	32,500
42,000	34,000	34,000	33,400
36,000	33,000	35,000	40,500
32,000	38,000	36,000	42,000

Average expenditure of 45 families on education in City 2				
30,000	27,000	23,500	24,000	28,000
25,000	24,000	26,000	22,000	24,500
26,500	22,000	25,000	25,400	22,000
26,400	22,500	23,500	27,500	23,500
28,000	24,500	27,500	23,000	24,000
22,500	25,000	23,400	22,000	
25,500	24,400	25,600	24,500	
26,600	25,500	23,400	23,500	
29,000	22,300	25,000	22,500	
27,500	24,500	27,500	26,500	

Assuming that the populations have equal variances and x is normally distributed, test the belief using 90% as the confidence level.

3. Nitrozen is a leading fertilizer company based in Madhya Pradesh and has two plants in Bhopal and Indore. The company produces fertilizers in bags of 100 kg. The company mixes 6 kg phosphate per 100 kg bag by using a newly purchased mixing machine installed in both the plants. A quality control officer of the company has taken a random sample of 10 bags from the Bhopal plant and 12 bags from the Indore plant. The quantity of phosphate in each bag (in kg) is given below:

Bhopal plant:	5.5	5.5	4.5	5.5	5.75
	5.5	5.2	5.3	5.2	5.4
Indore plant:	5.2	4.8	4.9	5.1	4.75
	5.2	4.75	4.2	4.3	4.8
	4.7	4.5			

On the basis of the information given above, can we say that there is a significant difference in the average quantity of phosphate in the bags produced by the two plants? Take 95% as the confidence level.

4. A researcher wants to measure the job satisfaction levels of the employees of two cement manufacturing plants located at Chhattisgarh. The researcher has used a questionnaire consisting of 10 questions related to job satisfaction levels of the employees. The researcher has used a rating scale from 1 to 4, where 1 is the lowest score and 4 is the highest score. So, a maximum score of 40 and a minimum score of 10 can be obtained. The researcher has randomly selected 15 employees from the first plant and 17 employees from the second plant. The scores obtained from these employees are given below:

First plant:	32	29	31	33	32
	31	30	32	33	32
	34	32	33	32	28
Second plant:	25	28	26	27	24
	26	27	22	25	26
	24	22	23	22	28
	27	24			

Taking 95% as the confidence level, examine the significant mean difference in terms of job satisfaction levels between the employees of the two plants.

5. A company is concerned about the decline in its sales revenues. After an analysis, the management concluded that the employee attitudes had become negative due to increased competition and excessive workload. The management organized a 7-day special motivational programme. In order to analyse the effectiveness of the motivational programme, the company researchers have administered a well-designed questionnaire to 12 employees selected randomly.

The scores obtained by the employees are as follows:

Scores before the programme	25	26	25	27	28
	25	29	27	30	28
	29	25			
Scores after the programme	29	30	31	30	31
	32	33	31	32	30
	31	32			

Take 90% as the confidence level and examine whether the motivational programme has changed the attitude of the employees.

6. Mega Furniture Ltd is a leading manufacturer in the furniture industry. It had been using an old advertisement to promote its product. In order to enhance the effectiveness of the advertisement, it makes a few changes to the advertisement. For measuring the effectiveness of the advertisement it has taken a random sample of 8 customers. The scores obtained are as follows:

Scores before the change in advertisement:	27	28	26	25
	32	31	32	27
Scores after the change in advertisement:	26	27	28	30
	31	30	32	29

Using 95% as the confidence level, examine whether the advertisement has become more effective after the changes made to it.

7. Modern Bicycles has conducted a survey among 100 randomly selected men and 120 randomly selected women. As per the findings, 25 men and 35 women say that the size of the wheel is a very important factor in purchasing a bicycle. On the basis of this data, can the company claim that a significantly higher proportion of women when compared to men believe that the size of wheel is a very important factor? Take 95% as the confidence level.

8. Magnus is a leading metal products manufacturer in India. The company has installed two machines at its Nagpur plant and Jalandhar plant. The company wants to test the efficiency of the new machine in terms of thickness of the product manufactured by two machines. It has taken a random sample of 10 products from the Nagpur plant and 13 products from the Jalandhar plant. The thickness of the products in millimeters is noted as follows:

Nagpur plant	15	22	24	23	25	23	25	26	24	27			
Jalandhar plant	18	29	27	28	26	29	28	30	31	25	27	27	27

Can we determine that the variance comes from the same populations (population variances are equal) or it comes from different populations (population variances are not equal)? Take $\alpha = 0.05$.

9. A researcher wants to estimate the difference in sugar prices in two towns of Punjab. The researcher has taken a random sample of 10 shops from City 1 and 11 shops from City 2. Use F test to determine whether there is a significant difference in the variance of the prices. Sugar prices per kilogram in these shops are given below:

City 1	12.5	12.3	12.6	13.0	13.5	12.8	12.7	12.5	13.2	12.3	
City 2	11.5	11.4	12.2	11.8	11.9	11.9	11.9	11.2	12.3	12.0	12.3

Take 95% as the confidence level.

CASE STUDY |

Case 13: *Crompton Greaves Ltd: A Global Enterprise*

Introduction

The history of Crompton Greaves Ltd goes back to the year 1878 when R. E. B. Crompton founded R. E. B. Crompton & Company. The company merged with F.A Parkinson to form Crompton Parkinson Ltd in 1927. In 1937, Crompton Parkinson Ltd, established its wholly-owned Indian subsidiary, namely Crompton Parkinson Works Ltd in Bombay, along with a sales organization, Greaves Cotton & Crompton Parkinson Ltd, in collaboration with GCC. The company was taken over by an eminent Indian industrialist, Lala Karamchand Thapar, in 1947.[1]

The company is organized into three business groups, namely, power systems, industrial systems, and consumer products. It offers a wide range of products such as power and industrial transformers, HT circuit breakers, LT and HT motors, DC motors, traction motors, alternators/generators, railway signaling equipment, lighting products, fans, pumps and public switching, transmission, and access products. It also undertakes turnkey projects from concept to commissioning.[1]

Becoming Global Through Major Acquisitions

Crompton Greaves acquired the Belgium-based Pauwels group, a company internationally known for its transformer manufacturing and service capabilities in 2005. In its continuous quest for expansion, the company also acquired Ganz Transelektro Villamossagi Zrt. and its associate company, Transverticum Kft, in Hungary in 2006–2007 for an enterprise value of approximately Euro 35 million. In May 2007, Crompton Greaves purchased the shares of Microsol Holding Ltd for an enterprise value of Euro 10.5 million. The company has adopted a deliberate "transformational policy" since 2000–2001 in three stages. These were: (1) turning around the company's fortunes through operational excellence, (2) leveraging the gains from operational excellence to generate significantly greater all-around growth in revenues and profits, and (3) building on international acquisitions to achieve global leadership.[2]

The company has clearly laid down its goal: to be a global leader in the power transmission and distribution business; to lead most of Asia-Pacific in motors and drives; and to be the South-Asian leader in consumer electrical products and appliances. The third phase of its transformation story has just begun. In order to judge the company's performance, it would be better to analyse some of its financial parameters such as sales and profit after tax from 1997–2007 (exhibited in Table 13. 01).

The company has recovered from its negative financial performance in 1999–2000 and 2000–2001 when its sales dropped down and profit after tax became negative. It is now in the third stage of reconstruction and making successful international acquisitions in order to achieve its goal of becoming a global leader.

TABLE 13.01
Sales and profit after tax from 1997-2007

Year	*Sales (in million rupees)*	*Profit after tax*
1997	15351.8	307.6
1998	16064.5	215.2
1999	16557.7	231.2
2000	16650.6	–1465.7
2001	14048.8	–731.6
2002	17594.6	41.3
2003	16978.3	281.7
2004	18708.6	708.3
2005	22546.5	1147.9
2006	28021.1	1630.5
2007	37006.7	1923.7

Source: Prowess (V. 3.1), Centre for Monitoring Indian Economy Pvt. Ltd, Mumbai, accessed August 2008, reproduced with permission.

1. The management believes that customer satisfaction is crucial to Crompton's success. Suppose customer satisfaction surveys were undertaken in 2004 and 2006. A random sample of 35 customers was used for the survey in 2004, while a random sample of 40 customers was used in 2006. The same questionnaire consisting of one question on a rating scale of 1 to 5 was used in both the surveys. The following table exhibits the scores obtained by customers in two years, that is, in 2004 and in 2006. Analyse the data relating to the two years and submit a report to the company management on the basis of your findings.

Year 2004				*Year 2006*			
3	2	4	3	4	3	4	4
2	3	3	3	4	3	3	4
4	4	3	3	4	4	3	3
3	4	3	2	4	4	2	3
3	3	2	3	3	3	4	4
4	3	2		3	2	4	4
3	2	3		3	2	3	4
3	2	3		3	4	3	4
4	4	4		2	4	4	3
2	4	4		2	4	4	3

2. Crompton Greaves places great emphasis on employee satisfaction. Suppose the company conducted a survey in 2003 to measure the job satisfaction level of its employees. It used a random sample of 25 employees and administered a questionnaire based on a seven-point rating scale. The average score obtained by the employees was 32.10. Sample standard deviation for the first sample is computed as 3.25. In order to measure the degree of job satisfaction of employees after the company's spate of acquisitions, it conducted another survey in 2006 with the same questionnaire and with a sample size of 28. The average score obtained by the employees was 41.20. Sample standard deviation for the second sample is computed as 2.41. The output generated by Minitab assuming unequal variance is given below. On the basis of this output, how would you interpret the data?
3. Suppose Crompton Greaves uses iron plates produced by a thirdparty vendor to manufacture its water pumps. The vendor makes these plates in two different shifts. The company's quality control department has noticed some variation in the diameter of iron plates. For verifying this, company has taken a random sample of 8 iron plates from the first shift and a random sample of 12 ironplates from the second shift. The diameter of the plates is given in the table below:

Diameter in shift 1 (in cm)	*Diameter in shift 2 (in cm)*
5	5.25
5.1	5.20
5.12	5.21
4.95	5.26
4.97	5.27
4.98	5.26
4.98	5.29
5.02	5.24
	5.22
	5.23
	5.26
	5.27

Conduct an a propriate test to determine the difference in the variance of plates in two populations. On the basis of the test, present a report to the management, stating full interpretation of the software output.

Two-Sample T-Test and CI

```
Sample   N    Mean  StDev  SE Mean
1       25   32.10   3.25     0.65
2       28   41.20   2.41     0.46

Difference = mu (1) - mu (2)
Estimate for difference:   -9.10000
95% CI for difference:   (-10.70061, -7.49939)
T-Test of difference = 0 (vs not =): T-Value = -11.47  P-Value = 0.000  DF = 43
```

NOTES |

1. www.cglonline.com/overview.htm, accessed August 2008.
2. Prowess (V. 3.1), Centre for Monitoring Indian Economy Pvt. Ltd, Mumbai, August 2008, reproduced with permission.

CHAPTER 14

Analysis of Variance and Experimental Designs

LEARNING OBJECTIVES

Upon completion of this chapter, you will be able to:

- Understand the concept of ANOVA and experimental designs
- Compute and interpret the result of completely randomized design (one-way ANOVA)
- Compute and interpret the result of randomized block design
- Compute and interpret the result of factorial design (two-way ANOVA)

STATISTICS IN ACTION: TATA MOTORS LTD

Tata Motors Ltd, widely known as TELCO, established in 1945, is one of India's oldest automobile manufacturing companies. It is the leader in commercial vehicles in each segment, and is one among the top three in the passenger vehicles market with winning products in the compact, midsize car, and utility-vehicles segments. The company is the world's fourth largest truck manufacturer and the world's second largest bus manufacturer.[1]

Tata Motors acquired the Daewoo Commercial Vehicles Company, South Korea's second largest truck maker, in 2004. The next year, it acquired a 21% stake in Hispano Carrocera, a reputed Spanish bus and coach manufacturer, with an option to acquire the remaining stake as well. In 2006, the company entered into a joint venture with the Brazil-based Marcopolo. In the same year it also entered into a joint venture with the Thonburi Automotive Assembly Plant Company of Thailand to manufacture and market the company's pick-up vehicles in Thailand.[1] Table 14.1 shows the profit after tax of the company from 1995 to 2007.

TABLE 14.1
Profit after tax of Tata Motors Ltd from 1995–2007 (in million rupees)

Year	*1995*	*1996*	*1997*	*1998*	*1999*	*2000*	*2001*	*2002*	*2003*	*2004*	*2005*	*2006*	*2007*
Profit after tax (in million rupees)	3189.5	5058.2	7623.6	2946.6	978.5	712.0	–5003.4	–537.3	3001.1	8103.4	12,369.5	15,288.8	19,134.6

Source: Prowess (V. 3.1), Centre for Monitoring Indian Economy Pvt. Ltd, Mumbai accessed August 2008, reproduced with permission.

Tata Motors unveiled "Tata Nano," a Rs one-lakh car (excluding VAT and transportation costs) in January 2008. The Tata Nano is expected to shift thousands of two-wheeler owners into car owners because of its affordable price. The market segmentation of the passenger car segment by region is as shown in Table 14.2.

Suppose Tata Motors wants to ascertain the purchase behaviour of the future consumers of Tata Nano in four segments of the country. The company has used a questionnaire consisting of 10 questions and used a 5-point rating scale with 1 as 'strongly disagree' and 5 as 'strongly agree'. It has taken a random sample of 3000 potential customers from each region with the objective of finding out the difference in the mean scores of each region. In order to find out the significant mean difference of potential consumer purchase behaviour in the four regions taken for the study, the company can analyse the data adopting a statistical technique commonly known as ANOVA. This chapter focuses on the concept of ANOVA and experimental designs; completely randomized design (one-way ANOVA); randomized block design, and factorial design (two-way ANOVA).

TABLE 14.2
Region wise market share of passenger cars

Segment	*Share (%)*
North	43
East	8
West	26
South	23

Source: www.indiastat.com, accessed August 2008, reproduced with permission.

14.1 INTRODUCTION

In the previous chapter, we discussed the various techniques of analysing data from two samples (taken from two populations). These techniques were related to means and proportions. In real life, there may be situations when instead of comparing two sample means, a researcher has to compare three or more than three sample means (specifically, more than two). A researcher may have to test whether the three or more sample means computed from the three populations are equal. In other words, the null hypothesis can be, that three or more population means are equal as against the alternative hypothesis that these population means are not equal. For example, suppose that a researcher wants to measure work attitude of the employees in four organizations. The researcher has prepared a questionnaire consisting of 10 questions for measuring the work attitude of employees. A five-point rating scale is used with 1 being the lowest score and 5 being the highest score. So, an employee can score 10 as the minimum score and 50 as the maximum score. The null hypothesis can be set as all the means are equal (there is no difference in the degree of work attitude of the employees) as against the alternative hypothesis that at least one of the means is different from the others (there is a significant difference in the degree of work attitude of the employees).

14.2 INTRODUCTION TO EXPERIMENTAL DESIGNS

An experimental design is the logical construction of an experiment to test hypothesis in which the researcher either controls or manipulates one or more variables.

An **experimental design** is the logical construction of an experiment to test hypothesis in which the researcher either controls or manipulates one or more variables. Some of the widely used terms while discussing experimental designs are as follows:

Independent variable: In an experimental design, the independent variable may be either a **treatment variable** or a **classification variable**.

Treatment variable: This is a variable which is controlled or modified by the researcher in the experiment. For example, in agriculture, the different fertilizers or the different methods of cultivation are the treatments.

Classification variable: Classification variable can be defined as the characteristics of the experimental subject that are present prior to the experiment and not a result of the researcher's manipulation or control.

Experimental Units: The smallest division of the experimental material to which treatments are applied and observations are made are referred to as experimental units.

Dependent variable: In experimental design, a dependent variable is the response to the different levels of independent variables. This is also called response variable.

Factor: A factor can be referred to as a set of treatments of a single type. In most situations, a researcher may be interested in studying more than one factor. For example, a researcher in the field of advertising may be interested in studying the impact of colour and size of advertisements on consumers. In addition, the researcher may be interested in knowing the difference in average responses to three different colours and four different sizes of the advertisement. This is referred to as two-factor ANOVA.

14.3 ANALYSIS OF VARIANCE

Analysis of variance or ANOVA is a technique of testing hypotheses about the significant difference in several population means. This technique was developed by R. A. Fisher. In this chapter, experimental designs will be analysed by using ANOVA. The main purpose of analysis of variance is to detect the difference among various population means based on the information gathered from the samples (sample means) of the respective populations.

Analysis of variance or ANOVA is a technique of testing hypotheses about the significant difference in several population means.

Analysis of variance is also based on some assumptions. Each population should have a normal distribution with equal variances. For example, if there are n populations, variances of each population, that is, $\sigma_1^2 = \sigma_2^2 = \sigma_3^2 = \cdots = \sigma_n^2$. Each sample taken from the population should be randomly drawn and should be independent of each other.

In analysis of variance, the total variation in the sample data can be on account of two components, namely, **variance between the samples and variance within the samples**. Variance between samples is attributed to the difference among the sample means. This variance is due to some assignable causes. Variance within the samples is the difference due to chance or experimental errors. For the sake of clarity, the techniques of analysis of variance can be broadly classified into one-way classification and two-way classification. In fact, many different types of experimental designs are available to the researchers. This chapter will focus on three specific types of experimental designs, namely, **completely randomized design**, **randomized block design**, and **factorial design**. ANOVA is based on the following assumptions:

In analysis of variance, the total variation in the sample data can be on account of two components, namely, variance between the samples and variance within the samples. Variance between the samples is attributed to the difference among the sample means. This variance is due to some assignable causes. Variance within the samples is the difference due to chance or experimental errors.

- Samples are drawn from normally distributed populations.
- Samples are randomly drawn from populations and are independent of each other.
- Populations from which samples are drawn have equal variances.

14.4 COMPLETELY RANDOMIZED DESIGN (ONE-WAY ANOVA)

Completely randomized design contains only one independent variable, with two or more treatment levels or classifications. In case of only two treatment levels or classifications, the design would be the same as that used for hypothesis testing for two populations

Completely randomized design contains only one independent variable, with two or more treatment levels or classifications.

in Chapter 13. When there is a case of three or more classification levels, analysis of variance is used to analyse the data.

Suppose a researcher wants to test the stress level of employees in three different organizations. For conducting this research, he has prepared a questionnaire with a five-point rating scale with 1 being the minimum score and 5 being the maximum score. The researcher has administered the questionnaire and obtained the mean score for three organizations. The researcher could have used the *z*-test or *t* test for two populations if there had been only two populations. In this case, there are three populations, so there is no scope of using *z*-test or *t* test for testing the hypotheses. In this case, one-way analysis of variance technique can be effectively used to analyse the data. One-way analysis of variance can also be used very effectively in the case of comparison among sample means taken from more than two populations.

In one-way analysis of variance, testing of hypothesis can be carried out by partitioning the total variation of the data in two parts. The first part is the variance between the samples and the second part is the variance within the samples. The variance between the samples can be attributed to treatment effects and variance within the samples can be attributed to experimental errors.

Suppose if *k* samples are being analysed by a researcher, then the null and alternative hypotheses can be set as below:

$$H_0: \mu_1 = \mu_2 = \mu_3 = \cdots = \mu_k$$

The alternative hypothesis can be set as below:

$$H_1: \text{Not all } \mu_j s \text{ are equal } (j = 1, 2, 3, \ldots, k)$$

The null hypothesis indicates that all population means for all levels of treatments are equal. If one population mean is different from another, the null hypothesis is rejected and the alternative hypothesis is accepted.

In one-way analysis of variance, testing of hypothesis is carried out by partitioning the total variation of the data in two parts. **The first part is the variance between the samples and the second part is the variance within the samples**. The variance between the samples can be attributed to treatment effects and variance within the samples can be attributed to experimental errors. As part of this process, the total sum of squares can be divided into two additive and independent parts as shown in Figure 14.1:

SST (total sum of squares) = SSC (sum of squares between columns) + SSE (sum of squares within samples)

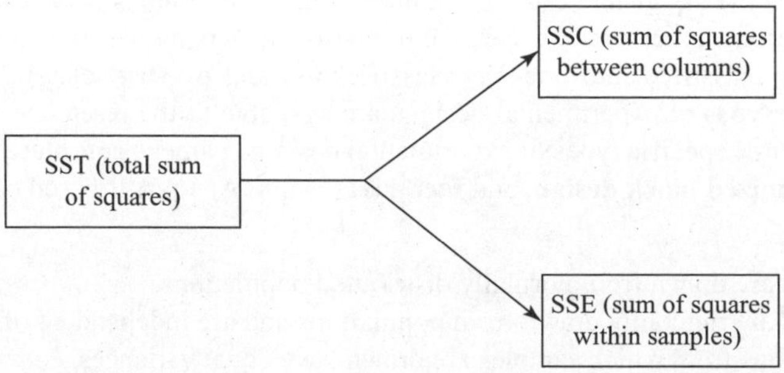

FIGURE 14.1
Partitioning the total sum of squares of the variation for completely randomized design (one-way ANOVA)

14.4.1 Steps in Calculating SST (Total Sum of Squares) and Mean Squares in One-Way Analysis of Variance

As discussed above, the total sum of squares can be partitioned in two parts: sum of squares between columns and sum of squares within samples. So, there are two steps in calculating SST (total sum of squares) in one-way analysis of variance, in terms of calculating sum of

TABLE 14.3
Observations obtained for k independent samples based on one-criterion classification

Observations	*Numbers of samples*					
	1	*2*	*3*	*j*	…	*k*
1	x_{11}	x_{12}	x_{13}	x_{1j}	…	x_{1k}
2	x_{21}	x_{22}	x_{23}	x_{2j}	…	x_{2k}
3	x_{31}	x_{32}	x_{33}	x_{3j}	…	x_{3k}
⋮	⋮	⋮	⋮	⋮	…	
i	x_{i1}	x_{i2}	x_{i3}	x_{ij}	…	x_{ik}
⋮	⋮	⋮	⋮	⋮	…	
n	x_{n1}	x_{n2}	x_{n3}	x_{nj}	…	x_{nk}
Sum	T_1	T_2	T_3	T_j	…	T_k
A.M.	$\overline{x}_1$	$\overline{x}_2$	$\overline{x}_3$	$\overline{x}_i$	…	$\overline{x}_k$

squares between columns and sum of squares within samples. Let us say that the observations obtained for k independent samples is based on one-criterion classification and can be arranged as shown in the Table 14.3 above:

where $$T = \sum_{j=1}^{k} T_j$$

$$\overline{x}_i = \frac{1}{n}\sum_{i=1}^{n} x_{i1} \quad \text{and} \quad \overline{\overline{x}} = \frac{1}{nk}\sum_{j=1}^{k} \overline{x}_j = \frac{1}{n}\sum_{i=1}^{n}\sum_{j=1}^{k} x_{ij}$$

The variance between columns measures the difference between the sample mean of each group and the grand mean. The grand mean is the overall mean and can be obtained by adding all the individual observations of the columns and then dividing this total by the number of total observations.

1. **Calculate variance between columns (samples):** This is usually referred to as **sum of squares between samples** and is usually denoted by *SSC*. The variance between columns measures the difference between the sample mean of each group and the grand mean. **Grand mean** is the **overall mean** and can be obtained by adding all the individual observations of the columns and then dividing this total by the total number of observations. The procedure of calculating the variance between the samples is as below:
   (a) In the first step, we need to calculate the mean of each sample. From Table 14.3, the means are $\overline{x}_1, \overline{x}_2, \ldots, \overline{x}_k$.
   (b) Next, the grand mean is calculated. The grand mean is calculated as
   $$\overline{\overline{x}} = \frac{1}{n}\sum_{i=1}^{n}\sum_{j=1}^{k} x_{ij}$$
   (c) In Step 3, the difference between the mean of each sample and grand mean is calculated, that is, we calculate $\overline{x}_1 - \overline{\overline{x}}, \overline{x}_2 - \overline{\overline{x}}, \ldots, \overline{x}_k - \overline{\overline{x}}$.
   (d) In Step 4, we multiply each of these by the number of observations in the corresponding sample, square each of these deviations and add them. This will give the sum of the squares between samples.
   (e) In the last step, the total obtained in Step 4 is divided by the degrees of freedom. The degrees of freedom is one less than the total number of samples. If there are

k samples, the degrees of freedom will be $v = k - 1$. When the sum of squares obtained in Step 4 is divided by the number of degrees of freedom, the result is called mean square (MSC) and is an alternative term for sample variance.

$$\text{SSC (sum of squares between columns)} = \sum_{j=1}^{k} n_j(\bar{x}_j - \bar{\bar{x}})^2$$

where k is the number of groups being compared, n_j the number of observations in Group j, $\bar{x}_j$ the sample mean of Group j, and $\bar{\bar{x}}$ the grand mean.

and $$\text{MSC (mean square)} = \frac{\text{SSC}}{k-1}$$

where SSC is the sum of squares between columns and $k - 1$ the degrees of freedom (number of samples – 1).

The variance within columns (samples) measures the difference within the samples (intra-sample difference) due to chance. This is usually denoted by SSE.

2. **Calculate variance within columns (samples):** This is usually referred to as the sum of squares within samples. The variance within columns (samples) measures the difference within the samples (intra-sample difference) due to chance. This is usually denoted by SSE. The procedure of calculating the variance within the samples is as below:
   (a) In calculating the variance within samples, the first step is to calculate the mean of each sample. From Table 14.3 this is $\bar{x}_1, \bar{x}_2, ..., \bar{x}_k$
   (b) Second step is to calculate the deviation of each observation in k samples from the mean values of the respective samples.
   (c) As a third step, square all the deviations obtained in Step 2 and calculate the total of all these squared deviations.
   (d) As the last step, divide the total squared deviations obtained in Step 3 by the degrees of freedom and obtain the mean square. The number of degrees of freedom can be calculated as the difference between the total number of observations and the number of samples. If there are n observations and k samples then the degrees of freedom is $v = n - k$

$$\text{SSE (sum of squares within samples)} = \sum_{i=1}^{n}\sum_{j=1}^{k}(x_{ij} - \bar{x}_j)^2$$

where x_{ij} is the ith observation in Group j, $\bar{x}_j$ the sample mean of Group j, k the number of groups being compared, and n the total number of observations in all the groups.

and $$\text{MSE (mean square)} = \frac{\text{SSE}}{n-k}$$

where *SSE* is the sum of squares within columns and $n - k$ the degrees of freedom (total number of observations – number of samples).

The total variation is equal to the sum of the difference between each observation (sample value) and the grand mean $\bar{\bar{x}}$. This is often referred to as SST (total sum of squares).

3. **Calculate total sum of squares:** The total variation is equal to the sum of the squared difference between each observation (sample value) and the grand mean $\bar{\bar{x}}$. This is often referred to as SST (total sum of squares). So, the total sum of squares can be calculated as below:

SST (total sum of squares) = SSC (sum of squares between columns) + SSE (sum of squares within samples)

$$\sum_{i=1}^{n}\sum_{j=1}^{k}(x_{ij}-\bar{\bar{x}})^2=\sum_{j=1}^{k}n_j(\bar{x}_j-\bar{\bar{x}})^2+\sum_{i=1}^{n}\sum_{j=1}^{k}(x_{ij}-\bar{x}_j)^2$$

$$\text{SST (total sum of squares)} = \sum_{i=1}^{n}\sum_{j=1}^{k}(x_{ij}-\bar{\bar{x}})^2$$

where x_{ij} is the *ith* observation in Group *j*, $\bar{\bar{x}}$ the grand mean, *k* the number of groups being compared, and *n* the total number of observations in all the groups

and $$\text{MST (mean square)} = \frac{\text{SST}}{n-1}$$

where SST is the total sum of squares and
$n-1$ the degrees of freedom (number of observations – 1).

14.4.2 Applying the *F*-Test Statistic

As discussed, ANOVA can be computed with three sums of squares: SSC (sum of squares between columns), SSE (sum of squares within samples), and SST (total sum of squares). As discussed in the previous chapter (Chapter 13), *F* is the ratio of two variances. In case of ANOVA, *F* value is obtained by dividing the treatment variance (MSC) by the error variance (MSE). So, in case of ANOVA, *F* value is calculated as below:

In case of ANOVA, *F* value is obtained by dividing the treatment variance (MSC) by the error variance (MSE).

F test statistic in one-way ANOVA

$$F=\frac{\text{MSC}}{\text{MSE}}$$

where MSC is the mean square column and MSE the mean square error.

The *F* test statistic follows *F* distribution with $k-1$ degrees of freedom corresponding to MSC in the numerator and $n-k$ degrees of freedom corresponding to MSE in the denominator. The null hypothesis is rejected if the calculated value of *F* is greater than the upper-tail critical value F_U with $k-1$ degrees of freedom in the numerator and $n-k$ degrees of freedom in the denominator. For a given level of significance α, the rules for acceptance or rejection of the null hypothesis are shown below:

For a given level of significance α, the rules for acceptance or rejection of the null hypothesis

Reject H_0, if calculated $F > F_U$ (Upper tail value of *F*),
otherwise do not reject H_0.

Figure 14.2 exhibits the rejection and non-rejection region (acceptance region) when using ANOVA to test the null hypothesis.

14.4.3 The ANOVA Summary Table

The result of ANOVA is usually presented in an ANOVA table (shown in Table 14.4). The entries in the table consist of SSC (sum of squares between columns), SSE (sum of squares within samples) and SST(total sum of squares); corresponding degrees of freedom $k-1$, $n-k$ and, $n-1$; MSC (mean square column) and MSE (mean square error); and *F* value. When using software programs such as MS Excel, Minitab, and SPSS, the summary table also includes the *p* value. The *p* value allows a researcher to make inferences directly without taking help from the critical values of the *F* distribution.

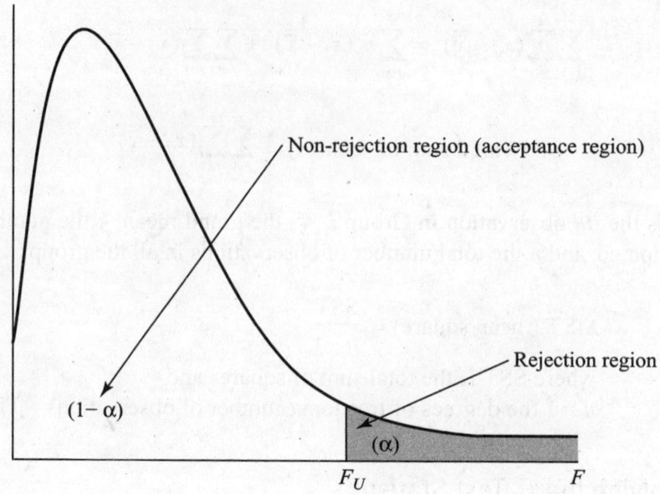

FIGURE 14.2
Rejection and non-rejection region (acceptance region) when using ANOVA to test null hypothesis

TABLE 14.4
ANOVA Summary Table

Source of variation	*Sum of squares*	*Degrees of freedom*	*Mean squares*	*F Value*
Between Columns (Treatment)	SSC	$k-1$	$MSC = \frac{SSC}{k-1}$	$F = \frac{MSC}{MSE}$
Within Columns (Error)	SSE	$n-k$	$MSE = \frac{SSE}{n-k}$	
Total	SST	$n-1$		

Example 14.1

Vishal Foods Ltd is a leading manufacturer of biscuits. The company has launched a new brand in the four metros; Delhi, Mumbai, Kolkata, and Chennai. After one month, the company realizes that there is a difference in the retail price per pack of biscuits across cities. Before the launch, the company had promised its employees and newly-appointed retailers that the biscuits would be sold at a uniform price in the country. The difference in price can tarnish the image of the company. In order to make a quick inference, the company collected data about the price from six randomly selected stores across the four cities. Based on the sample information, the price per pack of the biscuits (in rupees) is given in Table 14.5:

TABLE 14.5
Price per pack of the biscuits (in rupees)

Delhi	*Mumbai*	*Kolkata*	*Chennai*
22	19	18	21
22.5	19.5	17	20
21.5	19	18.5	21.5
22	20	17	20
22.5	19	18.5	21
21.5	21	17	20

Use one-way ANOVA to analyse the significant difference in the prices. Take 95% as the confidence level.

Solution The seven steps of hypothesis testing can be performed as below:

Step 1: Set null and alternative hypotheses
The null and alternative hypothesis can be stated as below:

$$H_0 : \mu_1 = \mu_2 = \mu_3 = \mu_4$$

and H_1: All the means are not equal

Step 2: Determine the appropriate statistical test
The appropriate test statistic is F test statistic in one-way ANOVA given as below

$$F = \frac{\text{MSC}}{\text{MSE}}$$

where MSC = mean square column
MSE = mean square error

Step 3: Set the level of significance
Alpha has been specified as 0.05.

Step 4: Set the decision rule
For a given level of significance 0.05, the rules for acceptance or rejection of null hypothesis are as follows:

Reject H_0 if calculated $F > F_U$ (upper-tail value of F),
otherwise, do not reject H_0.

In this problem, for the numerator and the denominator the degrees of freedom are 3 and 20 respectively. The critical F-value is $F_{0.05, 3, 20} = 3.10$.

Step 5: Collect the sample data
The sample data is as shown in Table 14.6.

Step 6: Analyse the data
From the table

$$T = T_1 + T_2 + T_3 + T_4 = 132 + 117.5 + 106 + 123.5 = 479;$$

$$\bar{\bar{x}} = (\bar{x}_1 + \bar{x}_2 + \bar{x}_3 + \bar{x}_4)/4 = 19.95833$$

TABLE 14.6
Sample data for Example 14.1

Delhi	*Mumbai*	*Kolkata*	*Chennai*
22	19	18	21
22.5	19.5	17	20
21.5	19	18.5	21.5
22	20	17	20
22.5	19	18.5	21
21.5	21	17	20
$T_1 = 132$	$T_2 = 117.5$	$T_3 = 106$	$T_4 = 123.5$
$\bar{x}_1 = 22$	$\bar{x}_2 = 19.5833$	$\bar{x}_3 = 17.6666$	$\bar{x}_4 = 20.5833$

and $n_1 = n_2 = n_3 = n_4 = 6$

$$\text{SSC (sum of squares between columns)} = \sum_{j=1}^{k} n_j(\bar{x}_j - \bar{\bar{x}})^2$$

$$= \begin{bmatrix} 6(22-19.9583)^2 + 6(19.5833-19.9583)^2 + 6(17.6666-19.9583)^2 \\ + 6(20.5833-19.9583)^2 \end{bmatrix}$$

$$= 25.0104 + 0.8437 + 31.5104 + 2.3437 = 59.7083$$

$$\text{SSE (sum of squares within samples)} = \sum_{i=1}^{n}\sum_{j=1}^{k}(x_{ij} - \bar{x}_j)^2$$

$$= \begin{bmatrix} (22-22)^2 + (22.5-22)^2 + (21.5-22)^2 + (22-22)^2 \\ + (22.5-22)^2 + (21.5-22)^2 + \cdots + (21-20.5833)^2 + \\ (20-20.5833)^2 + (21.5-20.5833)^2 + (20-20.5833)^2 \\ + (21-20.5833)^2 + (20-20.5833)^2 \end{bmatrix}$$

$$= 9.25$$

$$\text{SST (total sum of squares)} = \sum_{i=1}^{n}\sum_{j=1}^{k}(x_{ij} - \bar{\bar{x}})^2$$

$$\begin{bmatrix} (22-19.95833)^2 + (22.5-19.95833)^2 + (21.5-19.95833)^2 + \cdots \\ + (20 - 19.95833)^2 + (21-19.95833)^2 + (20-19.95833)^2 \end{bmatrix}$$

$$= 68.9583$$

$$\text{MSC (mean square)} = \frac{\text{SSC}}{k-1} = \frac{59.7083}{3} = 19.9027$$

$$\text{MSE (mean square)} = \frac{\text{SSE}}{n-k} = \frac{9.25}{20} = 0.4625$$

$$F = \frac{\text{MSC}}{\text{MSE}} = \frac{19.9025}{0.4625} = 43.03$$

Table 14.7 exhibits the ANOVA table for Example 14.1

TABLE 14.7
ANOVA table for Example 14.1

Source of variation	*Sum of squares*	*Degrees of freedom*	*Mean squares*	*F Value*
Between columns (treatment)	SSC	$4 - 1 = 3$	$MSC = \frac{59.7083}{3} = 19.9027$	$F = \frac{MSC}{MSE} = 43.03$
Within columns (error)	SSE	$24 - 4 = 20$	$MSE = \frac{9.25}{20} = 0.4625$	
Total	SST	$24 - 1 = 23$		

Step 7: Arrive at a statistical conclusion and business implication
At 95% confidence level, the critical value obtained from the F table is $F_{0.05, 3, 20} = 3.10$. The calculated value of F is 43.03, which is greater than the tabular value (critical value) and falls in the rejection region. Hence, the null hypothesis is rejected and the alternative hypothesis is accepted.

There is enough evidence to believe that there is a significant difference in the prices across four cities. So, the management must initiate corrective steps to ensure that the prices should remain uniform. This must be done urgently to protect the credibility of the firm.

SELF-PRACTICE PROBLEMS

14A1. Use the following data to perform one-way ANOVA

Factor 1	*Factor 2*	*Factor 3*	*Factor 4*
13	17	22	18
12	15	26	17
13	18	27	16
14	16	28	15
15	17	29	16
13	18	30	17

Use $\alpha = 0.05$ to test the hypotheses for the difference in means.

14A2. Use the following data to perform one-way ANOVA

Factor 1	*Factor 2*	*Factor 3*	*Factor 4*	*Factor 5*
115	122	113	110	121
118	120	115	115	117
119	122	110	117	120
112	123	119	118	121
110	125	122	120	122
	123		121	123
			122	

Use $\alpha = 0.01$ to test the hypotheses for the difference in means.

14A3. A company is in the process of launching a new product. Before launching, the company wants to ascertain the status of its product as a second alternative. For doing so, the company prepared a questionnaire consisting of 20 questions on a five-point rating scale with 1 being "strongly disagree" and 5 being "strongly agree." The company administered this questionnaire to 8 randomly selected respondents from five potential sales zones. The scores obtained from the respondents are given in the table. Use one-way ANOVA to analyse the significant difference in the scores. Take 90% as the confidence level.

Sales zone 1	*Sales zone 2*	*Sales zone 3*	*Sales zone 4*	*Sales zone 5*
65	70	63	70	65
67	65	65	60	64
68	68	65	62	67
70	67	67	63	68
66	65	68	65	62
64	68	63	67	65
63	67	62	68	67
60	62	60	62	68

14.5 RANDOMIZED BLOCK DESIGN

We have already discussed that in one-way ANOVA the total variation is divided into two components: variations between the samples or columns, due to treatments and variation within the samples, due to error. There is a possibility that some of the variation, which was attributed to random error may not be due to random error, but may be due to some other measurable factors. If this measurable factor is included in the MSE, it will result in an increase in the MSE. Any increase in the MSE would result in a small F value (MSE being a denominator in the F-value formula), which would ultimately lead to the acceptance of the null hypothesis.

Like the completely randomized design, the randomized block design also focuses on one independent variable of interest (treatment variable). Additionally, in randomized block design, we also include one more variable referred to as "blocking variable." This blocking variable is used to control the confounding variable. Confounding variables though not controlled by the researcher can have an impact on the outcome of the treatment being studied.

Like the completely randomized design, **randomized block design** also focuses on one independent variable of interest (treatment variable). Additionally, in randomized block design, we also include one more variable referred to as "blocking variable." This blocking variable is used to control the confounding variable. Confounding variables, though not controlled by the researcher, can have an impact on the outcome of the treatment being studied. In Example 14.1, the selling price was different in the four metros. In this example, some other variable which is not controlled by the researcher may have an impact on the varying prices. This may be the tax policy of the state, transportation cost, etc. By including these variables in the experimental design, the possibility of controlling these variables can be explored. The blocking variable is a variable which a researcher wants to control but is not a treatment variable of interest. The term blocking has an agriculture origin where "blocking" refers to a block of land. For example, if we apply blocking in Example 14.1, under a given circumstance, each set of the four prices related to four metropolitan cities will constitute a block of sample data. Blocking provides the opportunity for a researcher to compare prices one to one.

Blocking variable is a variable which a researcher wants to control but is not a treatment variable of interest.

In case of a randomized block design, variation within the samples can be partitioned into two parts as shown in Figure 14.3.

So, in randomized block design, the total sum of squares consists of three parts:
SST (total sum of squares) = SSC (sum of squares between columns) + SSR (sum of squares between rows) + SSE (sum of squares of errors)

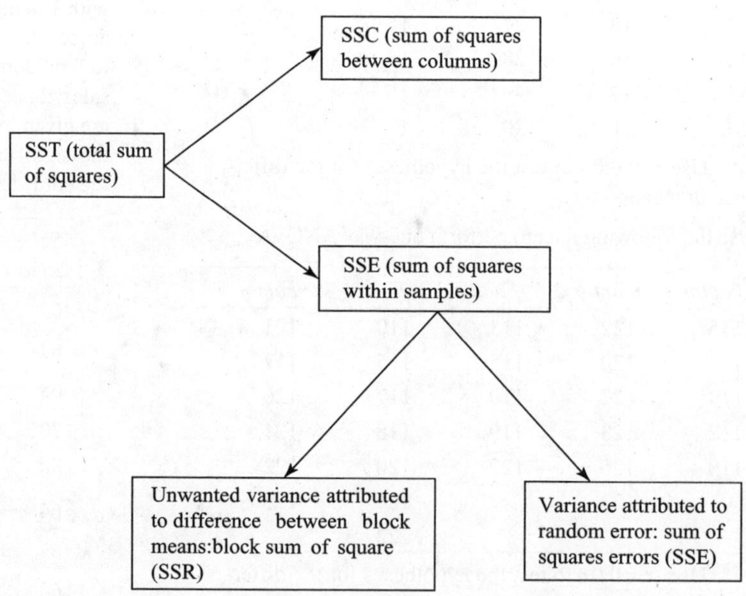

FIGURE 14.3
Partitioning the SSE in randomized block design

14.5.1 Null and Alternative Hypotheses in a Randomized Block Design

It has already been discussed that in a randomized block design the total sum of squares consists of three parts. In light of this, the null and alternative hypotheses for the treatment effect can be stated as below:

Suppose if c samples are being analysed by a researcher then null hypothesis can be stated as:

$$H_0: \mu_1 = \mu_2 = \mu_3 = \cdots = \mu_c$$

The alternative hypothesis can be set as below:

H_1: All treatment means are not equal

For blocking effect, the null and alternative hypotheses can be stated as below (when r rows are being analysed by a researcher):

$$H_0: \mu_1 = \mu_2 = \mu_3 = \cdots = \mu_r$$

The alternative hypothesis can be set as below:

H_1: All blocking means are not equal

Formulas for calculating SST (total sum of squares) and mean squares in a randomized block design

$$\text{SSC (sum of squares between columns)} = r\sum_{j=1}^{c}(\bar{x}_j - \bar{\bar{x}})^2$$

where c is the number of treatment levels (columns), r the number of observations in each treatment level (number of blocks), $\bar{x}_j$ the sample mean of Group j (Column means), and $\bar{\bar{x}}$. the grand mean

and $$\text{MSC(mean square)} = \frac{\text{SSC}}{c-1}$$

where SSC is the sum of squares between columns and $c - 1$ the degrees of freedom (number of columns – 1).

$$\text{SSR (sum of squares between rows)} = c\sum_{i=1}^{r}(\bar{x}_i - \bar{\bar{x}})^2$$

where c is the number of treatment levels (columns), r the number of observations in each treatment level (number of blocks), $\bar{x}_i$ the sample mean of Group i (row means), and $\bar{\bar{x}}$. the grand mean

and $$\text{MSR(mean square)} = \frac{\text{SSR}}{r-1}$$

where SSE is the sum of squares within columns, and $r - 1$ the degrees of freedom (number of rows – 1).

$$\text{SSE (sum of squares of errors)} = \sum_{i=1}^{r}\sum_{j=1}^{c}(x_{ij} - \bar{x}_j - \bar{x}_i + \bar{\bar{x}})^2$$

where c is the number of treatment levels (columns), r the number of observations in each treatment level (number of blocks), $\bar{x}_i$ the sample mean of Group i (row means), x_j the sample mean of Group j (column means), x_{ij} the *ith* observation in Group j, and $\bar{\bar{x}}$. the grand mean

and $$\text{MSE (mean square)} = \frac{\text{SSE}}{n-r-c+1}$$

where SSE is the sum of squares of errors and $n - r - c + 1 = (c - 1)(r - 1)$ = degrees of freedom (number of observations – number of rows – number of columns + 1). Here, $rc = n$ =number of observations.

14.5.2 Applying the *F*-Test Statistic

As discussed, the total sum of squares consists of three parts: SST(total sum of squares) = SSC (sum of squares between columns) + SSR (sum of squares between rows) + SSE (sum of squares of errors)

In case of two-way ANOVA, *F* value can be obtained as below:

F-test statistic in randomized block design

$$F_{treatment(columns)} = \frac{\text{MSC}}{\text{MSE}}$$

where MSC is the mean square column and MSE the mean square error.

with $c - 1$, degrees of freedom for numerator

$n - r - c + 1 = (c - 1)(r - 1)$, degrees of freedom for denominator

and

$$F_{blocks(rows)} = \frac{\text{MSR}}{\text{MSE}}$$

where MSR is the mean square row and MSE the mean square error.

with $r - 1$ = degrees of freedom for numerator and

$n - r - c + 1 = (c - 1)(r - 1)$, degrees of freedom for denominator.

For a given level of significance α, rules for acceptance or rejection of null hypothesis are as below:

For a given level of significance α, rules for acceptance or rejection of null hypothesis

Reject H_0 if , $F_{calculated} > F_{critical}$. Otherwise, do not reject H_0.

14.5.3 ANOVA Summary Table for Two-Way Classification

The results of ANOVA are usually presented in an ANOVA table (shown in Table 14.8). The entries in the table consist of SSC(sum of squares between columns), SSR (sum of squares between rows), SSE (sum of squares of errors), SST (total sum of squares); corresponding degrees of freedom $(c - 1)$; $(r - 1)$; $(c - 1)(r - 1)$, and $(n - 1)$; MSC (mean square column); MSR (mean square row) and MSE (mean square error); *F* values in terms of $F_{treatment}$ and F_{block}. As discussed, in randomized block design when using software programs such as MS Excel, Minitab, and SPSS, summary table also includes *p* value. The *p* value allows a researcher to make inferences directly without taking help from the critical values of the *F* distribution.

TABLE 14.8
ANOVA Summary table for two-way classification

Source of variation	*Sum of squares*	*Degrees of freedom*	*Mean squares*	*F-Value*
Sum of squares between columns	SSC	$c - 1$	$\text{MSC} = \frac{\text{SSC}}{c-1}$	$F_{treatment} = \frac{\text{MSC}}{\text{MSE}}$
Sum of squares between rows	SSR	$r - 1$	$\text{MSR} = \frac{\text{SSR}}{r-1}$	$F_{block} = \frac{\text{MSR}}{\text{MSE}}$
Sum of squares of errors	SSE	$(c - 1)(r - 1)$	$\text{MSE} = \frac{\text{SSE}}{(c-1)(r-1)}$	
Total	SST	$n - 1$		

Example 14.2

A company which produces stationary items wants to diversify into the photocopy paper manufacturing business. The company has decided to first test market the product in three areas termed as the north area, central area, and the south area. The company takes a random sample of five salesmen S1, S2, S3, S4, and S5 for this purpose. The sales volume generated by these five salesmen (in thousand rupees) and total sales in different regions is given in Table 14.9:

TABLE 14.9
Sales volume generated by five salesmen (in thousand rupees) and total sales in different regions (in thousand rupees)

Region	*Salesmen*					
	S1	*S2*	*S3*	*S4*	*S5*	*Region's total*
North	24	30	26	23	32	135
Central	22	32	27	25	31	137
South	23	28	25	22	32	130
Salesmen's Total	69	90	78	70	95	402

Use a randomized block design analysis to examine:

1. Whether the salesmen significantly differ in performance?
2. Whether there is a significant difference in terms of sales capacity between the regions?

Take 95% as confidence level for testing the hypotheses.

Solution

The seven steps of hypothesis testing can be performed as below:

Step 1: Set null and alternative hypotheses

The null and alternative hypotheses can be divided into two parts: For treatments (columns) and for blocks (rows).

For treatments (columns), null and alternative hypotheses can be stated as below:

$$H_0: \mu_1 = \mu_2 = \mu_3 = \mu_4 = \mu_5$$

and H_1: All the treatment means are not equal

For blocks (rows), null and alternative hypotheses can be stated as below:

$$H_0: \mu_1 = \mu_2 = \mu_3$$

and H_1: All the block means are not equal

Step 2: Determine the appropriate statistical test

F-test statistic in randomized block design

$$F_{treatment(columns)} = \frac{\text{MSC}}{\text{MSE}}$$

where MSC is the mean square column and MSE the mean square error.

with $c-1$, degrees of freedom for numerator

$n-r-c+1=(c-1)(r-1)$, degrees of freedom for denominator

and $$F_{blocks(rows)}=\frac{\text{MSR}}{\text{MSE}}$$

where MSR is the mean square row and MSE the mean square error.

with $r-1$, degrees of freedom for numerator

$n-r-c+1=(c-1)(r-1)$, degrees of freedom for denominator.

Step 3: Set the level of significance

Let $\alpha = 0.05$.

Step 4: Set the decision rule

For a given level of significance 0.05, the rules for acceptance or rejection of null hypothesis are as follows

Reject H_0, if $F_{calculated} > F_{critical}$, otherwise do not reject H_0.

For treatments, degrees of freedom = $(c-1)=(5-1)=4$

For blocks, degrees of freedom = $(r-1)=(3-1)=2$

For error, degrees of freedom = $(c-1)(r-1)=4\times 2=8$

Step 5: Collect the sample data

Sample data is given in Example 14.2. The treatment means and block means are shown in Table 14.10 as follows:

TABLE 14.10

Treatment means and block means for sales data

Region	*S1*	*S2*	*S3*	*S4*	*S5*	*Block means*
North	24	30	26	23	32	27
Central	22	32	27	25	31	27.4
South	23	28	25	22	32	26
Treatment means $\bar{x}_j$	23	30	26	23.33	31.66	26.3

Step 6: Analyse the data

SSC (sum of squares between columns) = $r\sum_{j=1}^{c}(\bar{x}_j-\bar{\bar{x}})^2$

$$=3\left[\begin{array}{r}(23-26.8)^2+(30-26.8)^2+(26-26.8)^2+(23.33-26.8)^2\\+(31.66-26.8)^2\end{array}\right]$$

$= 183.066$

SSR (sum of squares between rows) = $c\sum_{i=1}^{r}(\bar{x}_i-\bar{\bar{x}})^2$

$$=5\left[(27-26.8)^2+(27.4-26.8)^2+(26-26.8)^2\right]$$

$= 5.2$

SSE (sum of squares of errors) = $\sum_{i=1}^{r}\sum_{j=1}^{c}(x_{ij}-\bar{x}_j-\bar{x}_i+\bar{\bar{x}})^2$

$$= \begin{bmatrix} (24 - 23 - 27 + 26.8)^2 + (22 - 23 - 27.4 + 26.8)^2 \\ + (23 - 23 - 26 + 26.8)^2 + \cdots + \\ (32 - 31.6666 - 27 + 26.8)^2 + (31 - 31.6666 - 27.4 + 26.8)^2 \\ + (32 - 31.6666 - 26 + 26.8)^2 \end{bmatrix}$$

$= 12.1333$

$$\text{SST (total sum of squares of errors)} = \sum_{i=1}^{r}\sum_{j=1}^{c}(x_{ij} - \bar{\bar{x}})^2$$

$$\begin{bmatrix} (24 - 26.8)^2 + (22 - 26.8)^2 + (23 - 26.8)^2 + \cdots + (32 - 26.8)^2 \\ + (31 - 26.8)^2 + (32 - 26.8)^2 \end{bmatrix}$$

$= 200.40$

$$\text{MSC} = \frac{\text{SSC}}{c-1} = \frac{183.066}{5-1} = 45.766$$

$$\text{MSR} = \frac{\text{SSR}}{r-1} = \frac{5.2}{3-1} = \frac{5.2}{2} = 2.6$$

$$\text{MSE} = \frac{\text{SSE}}{n-r-c+1} = \frac{12.1333}{15-5-3+1} = 1.5166$$

$$F_{treatment(columns)} = \frac{\text{MSC}}{\text{MSE}} = \frac{45.766}{1.5166} = 30.17$$

$$F_{blocks(rows)} = \frac{\text{MSR}}{\text{MSE}} = \frac{2.6}{1.5166} = 1.71$$

The ANOVA summary table for Example 14.2 is shown in Table 14.11.

TABLE 14.11
ANOVA Summary table for Example 14.2

Source of variation	*Sum of squares*	*Degrees of freedom*	*Mean squares*	*F Value*
Sum of squares between columns	SSC	$5 - 1 = 4$	MSC = 45.766	$F_{treatment} = \frac{\text{MSC}}{\text{MSE}} = 30.17$
Sum of squares between rows	SSR	$3 - 1 = 2$	MSR = 2.6	$F_{block} = \frac{\text{MSR}}{\text{MSE}} = 1.71$
Sum of squares of errors	SSE	$(5 - 1)(3 - 1) = 8$	MSE = 1.5166	
Total	SST	$n - 1 = 15 - 1 = 14$		

Step 7: Arrive at a statistical conclusion and business implication
At 95% confidence level, critical value obtained from the F table is $F_{0.05, 4, 8} = 3.84$ and $F_{0.05, 2, 8} = 4.46$.

The calculated value of F for columns is 30.17. This is greater than the tabular value (3.84) and falls in the rejection region. Hence, the null hypothesis is rejected and alternative hypothesis is accepted.

The calculated value of F for rows is 1.71. This is less than the tabular value (4.46) and falls in the acceptance region. Hence, the null hypothesis is accepted and alternative hypothesis is rejected.

There is enough evidence to believe that there is a significant difference in the performance of five salesmen in terms of generation of sales. On the other hand, there is no significant difference in the capacity of generating sales for the three regions. The result that indicates a difference in the sales volume generation capacity of the three regions may be due to chance. Therefore, the management should concentrate on individual salesmen rather than concentrating on regions.

SELF-PRACTICE PROBLEMS

14B1. The table below shows data in the form of a randomized block design.

Block level	*Treatment level* 1	2	3	4	5
1	16	18	19	19	24
2	18	19	22	23	23
3	19	20	23	23	22
4	22	21	21	22	25
5	24	22	24	21	21

Use a randomized block design analysis to examine:

(1) Significant difference in the treatment level.
(2) Significant difference in the block level.

Take 95% as confidence level for testing the hypotheses.

14B2. The table below shows data in form of a randomized block design

Block level	*Treatment level* 1	2	3	4	5
1	30	45	45	63	80
2	32	46	49	65	82
3	33	43	52	68	85
4	31	47	55	70	90

Use a randomized block design analysis to examine:

(1) Significant difference in the treatment level.
(2) Significant difference in the block level.

Take 90% as the confidence level for testing the hypotheses.

14B3. A researcher has obtained randomly selected sales data (in thousand rupees) of four companies: Company 1, Company 2, Company 3, and Company 4. These data are arranged in a randomized block design with respect to company and region. Use a randomized block design analysis to examine:

(1) Significant difference in average sales of four different companies.
(2) Significant difference in average sales of three different regions.

Take $\alpha = 0.05$ for testing the hypotheses.

	Company 1	*Company 2*	*Company 3*	*Company 4*
Region 1	26	32	40	12
Region 2	28	35	45	17
Region 3	30	38	50	21

14.6 FACTORIAL DESIGN (TWO-WAY ANOVA)

In some real-life situations, a researcher has to explore two or more treatments simultaneously. This type of experimental design is referred to as factorial design.

In some real-life situations, a researcher has to explore two or more treatments simultaneously. This type of experimental design is referred to as factorial design. In a factorial design, two or more treatment variables are studied simultaneously. For example, in the previous example, we had discussed the variation in performance of salesmen due to one blocking variable, region. Salesmen performance may also depend upon various other variables such as support provided by the company, attitude of a particular salesman, support from the dealer network, support from the retailer, etc. All these four variables (and many other variables depending upon the situation) can be included in the experimental design and can be studied simultaneously. In this section, we will study the factorial design with two treatment variables.

Factorial design has many advantages over completely randomized design. If we use completely randomized design for measuring the effect of two treatment variables, we will have to apply two complete randomized designs. Factorial design provides a platform to analyse both the treatment variables simultaneously in one experimental design. In a factorial design, a researcher can control the effect of multiple treatment variables. In addition, factorial design provides an opportunity to study the interaction effect of two treatment variables. It is important to understand that the randomized block design concentrates on one treatment (column) and control for a blocking effect (row effect). Randomized block design does not provide the opportunity to study the interaction effect of treatment and block. This facility is available only in factorial design.

Factorial design provides an opportunity to study the interaction effect of two treatment variables.

14.6.1 Null and Alternative Hypotheses in a Factorial Design

A two-way analysis of variance is used to test the hypothesis of a factorial design having two factors. In light of this, the null and alternative hypotheses for the treatment effect can be stated as below:

Row effect: H_0: All the row means are equal.
H_1: All the row means are not equal.

Column effect: H_0: All the column means are equal.
H_1: All the column means are not equal.

Interaction effect: H_0: Interaction effects are zero.
H_1: Interaction effect is not zero (present).

14.6.2 Formulas for Calculating SST (Total Sum of Squares) and Mean Squares in a Factorial Design (Two-Way Analysis of Variance)

$$\text{SSC (sum of squares between columns)} = nr\sum_{j=1}^{c}(\bar{x}_j - \bar{\bar{x}})^2$$

where c is the number of column treatments, r the number of row treatments, n the number of observations in each cell, $\bar{x}_j$ the sample mean of Group j, and $\bar{\bar{x}}$ the grand mean

and $$\text{MSC (mean square)} = \frac{\text{SSC}}{c-1}$$

where SSC is the sum of squares between columns and $c - 1$ the degrees of freedom (number of columns – 1).

$$\text{SSR (sum of squares between rows)} = nc\sum_{i=1}^{r}(\bar{x}_i - \bar{\bar{x}})^2$$

where c is the number of column treatments, r the number of row treatments, n the number of observations in each cell, $\bar{x}_i$ the sample mean of Group i (row means), and $\bar{\bar{x}}$ the grand mean

and $$\text{MSR (mean square)} = \frac{\text{SSR}}{r-1}$$

where SSR is the sum of squares between rows and $r - 1$ the degrees of freedom (number of rows – 1).

$$\text{SSI (sum of squares interaction)} = n\sum_{i=1}^{r}\sum_{j=1}^{c}(\bar{x}_{ij} - \bar{x}_j - \bar{x}_i + \bar{\bar{x}})^2$$

where c is the number of column treatments, r the number of row treatments, n the number of observations in each cell, $\bar{x}_i$ the sample mean of Group i (row means), $\bar{x}_j$ the sample mean of Group j (column means), $\bar{x}_{ij}$ the mean of the cell corresponding to *ith* row and *jth* column (cell mean), and $\bar{\bar{x}}$ the grand mean

and $$\text{MSI (mean square)} = \frac{\text{SSI}}{(r-1)(c-1)}$$

where SSI is the sum of squares interaction and $(r-1)(c-1)$ the degrees of freedom.

$$\text{SSE (sum of squares errors)} = \sum_{i=1}^{r}\sum_{j=1}^{c}\sum_{k=1}^{n}(x_{ijk} - \bar{x}_{ij})^2$$

where c is the number of column treatments, r the number of row treatments, n the number of observations in each cell, x_{ijk} the individual observation, $\bar{x}_{ij}$ the mean of the cell corresponding to *ith* row and *jth* column (cell mean)

and $$\text{MSE (mean square)} = \frac{\text{SSE}}{rc(n-1)}$$

where SSE is the sum of squares of errors and $rc(n-1)$ the degrees of freedom.

$$\text{SST (total sum of squares)} = \sum_{i=1}^{r}\sum_{j=1}^{c}\sum_{k=1}^{n}(x_{ijk} - \bar{\bar{x}})^2$$

where c is the number of column treatments, r the number of row treatments, n the number of observations in each cell, x_{ijk} the individual observation, $\bar{\bar{x}}$. the grand mean.

and $$\text{MST (mean square)} = \frac{\text{SST}}{N-1}$$

where SST is the total sum of squares and $N-1$ the degrees of freedom (total number of observations – 1).

14.6.3 Applying the *F*-Test Statistic

As discussed, the total sum of squares consists of four parts: SST (total sum of squares) = SSC (sum of squares between columns) + SSR (sum of squares between rows) + SSI (sum of squares interaction) + SSE (sum of squares of errors)

In case of two-wayANOVA, the F value can be obtained as below:

F-test statistic in two-way ANOVA

$$F_{treatment\,(columns)} = \frac{\text{MSC}}{\text{MSE}}$$

where MSC is the mean square column and MSE the mean square error
with $c-1$, degrees of freedom for numerator and
$rc(n-1)$ degrees of freedom for denominator.

$$F_{blocks\,(rows)} = \frac{\text{MSR}}{\text{MSE}}$$

where MSR is the mean square row and MSE the mean square error
with $r-1$, degrees of freedom for numerator and
$rc(n-1)$ degrees of freedom for denominator.

$$F_{\text{int}\,eraction\,(column \times row)} = \frac{\text{MSI}}{\text{MSE}}$$

where MSI is the mean square interaction and MSE the mean square error

with $(r-1)(c-1)$, degrees of freedom for numerator and

$rc(n-1)$, degrees of freedom for denominator.

For a given level of significance α, rules for acceptance or rejection of null hypothesis are as below:

For a given level of significance α, rules for acceptance or rejection of null hypothesis

Reject H_0, if $F_{calculated} > F_{critical}$, otherwise, do not reject H_0.

14.6.4 ANOVA Summary Table for Two-Way ANOVA

The result of ANOVA for a factorial design is usually presented in an ANOVA table (shown in Table 14.12). The entries in the table consist of SSC (sum of squares between columns), SSR (sum of squares between rows), SSI (sum of squares interaction), SSE (sum of squares of errors), SST (total sum of squares); corresponding degrees of freedom $(c-1)$; $(r-1)$; $(c-1)(r-1)$; $rc(n-1)$ and $(N-1)$; MSC (mean square column); MSR (mean square row); MSI (mean square interaction) and MSE (mean square error); F values in terms of $F_{treatment}$; F_{block}, and $F_{interaction}$. Software programs such as MS Excel, Minitab, and SPSS, calculate p-value test in the ANOVA table, which allows a researcher to make inferences directly without taking help from the critical values of the F distribution.

TABLE 14.12
ANOVA Summary table for two-way ANOVA

Source of variation	*Sum of squares*	*Degrees of freedom*	*Mean squares*	*F-Value*
Sum of squares between columns	SSC	$c-1$	$\text{MSC} = \dfrac{\text{SSC}}{c-1}$	$F_{treatment} = \dfrac{\text{MSC}}{\text{MSE}}$
Sum of squares between rows	SSR	$r-1$	$\text{MSR} = \dfrac{\text{SSR}}{r-1}$	$F_{block} = \dfrac{\text{MSR}}{\text{MSE}}$
Sum of squares interaction	SSI	$(c-1)(r-1)$	$\text{MSI} = \dfrac{\text{SSI}}{(c-1)(r-1)}$	$F_{interaction} = \dfrac{\text{MSI}}{\text{MSE}}$
Sum of squares of errors	SSE	$rc(n-1)$	$\text{MSE} = \dfrac{\text{SSE}}{rc(n-1)}$	
Total	SST	$N-1$		

Example 14.3

Chhattisgarh Steel and Iron Mills is a leading steel rod manufacturing company of Chhattisgarh. The company produces 8-metre long steel rods, which are used in the construction of buildings. The company has four machines which manufacture steel rods in three shifts. The company's quality control officer wants to test whether there is any difference in the average length of the iron rods by shifts or by machines. Data given in Table 14.13 is organized by machines and shifts obtained through a random sampling process. Employ a two-way analysis of variance and determine whether there are any significant differences in effects. Take $\alpha = 0.05$.

TABLE 14.13
Length of the iron rod in different shifts and produced by different machines

Machines	*Length of the iron rod*		
	Shift 1	*Shift 2*	*Shift 3*
1	8.12	8.11	8.04
	8.01	8.12	8.06
	8.05	8.06	8.11
2	7.98	7.88	7.89
	7.89	7.77	7.96
	7.99	7.95	7.98
3	8.22	8.24	8.17
	8.25	8.20	8.19
	8.26	8.18	8.16
4	7.79	7.88	7.73
	7.75	7.77	7.74
	7.73	7.72	7.71

Solution

The seven steps of hypothesis testing can be performed as below:

Step 1: Set null and alternative hypotheses

The null and alternative hypotheses can be stated as below:

Row effect: H_0: All the row means are equal.
H_1: All the row means are not equal.

Column effect: H_0: All the column means are equal.
H_1: All the column means are not equal.

Interaction effect: H_0: Interaction effects are zero.
H_1: Interaction effect is not zero (present).

Step 2: Determine the appropriate statistical test

F-test statistic in two-way ANOVA

$$F_{treatment(columns)} = \frac{\text{MSC}}{\text{MSE}}$$

where MSC is the mean square column and MSE the mean square error with $c - 1$, degrees of freedom for numerator and $rc(n - 1)$ degrees of freedom for denominator.

$$F_{blocks(rows)} = \frac{\text{MSR}}{\text{MSE}}$$

where MSR is the mean square row and MSE the mean square error with $r - 1$, degrees of freedom for numerator and $rc(n - 1)$ degrees of freedom for denominator.

$$F_{interaction(column \times row)} = \frac{\text{MSI}}{\text{MSE}}$$

where MSI is the mean square interaction and MSE is the mean square error. with $(r-1)(c-1)$, degrees of freedom for numerator and $rc(n-1)$ degrees of freedom for denominator.

Step 3: Set the level of significance

Let $\alpha = 0.05$.

Step 4: Set the decision rule

For a given level of significance α, the rules for acceptance or rejection of the null hypothesis are

Reject H_0 if $F_{calculated} > F_{critical}$, otherwise, do not reject H_0.

For treatments, degrees of freedom $= (c-1) = (3-1) = 2$
For blocks, degrees of freedom $= (r-1) = (4-1) = 3$
For interaction, degrees of freedom $= (c-1)(r-1) = 2 \times 3 = 6$
For error, degrees of freedom $rc(n-1) = 4 \times 3 \times 2 = 24$

Step 5: Collect the sample data

The sample data is given in Table 14.14:

TABLE 14.14
Sample data for Example 14.3 and computation of different means

Machines	*Length of the iron rod*			
	Shift 1	*Shift 2*	*Shift 3*	$\bar{x}_i$
1	8.12	8.11	8.04	
	8.01	8.12	8.06	
	8.05	8.06	8.11	
	$\bar{x}_{11} = 8.06$	$\bar{x}_{12} = 8.0966$	$\bar{x}_{13} = 8.07$	8.0755
2	7.98	7.88	7.89	
	7.89	7.77	7.96	
	7.99	7.95	7.98	
	$\bar{x}_{21} = 7.9533$	$\bar{x}_{22} = 7.8666$	$\bar{x}_{23} = 7.9433$	7.9211
3	8.22	8.24	8.17	
	8.25	8.20	8.19	
	8.26	8.18	8.16	
	$\bar{x}_{31} = 8.2433$	$\bar{x}_{32} = 8.2066$	$\bar{x}_{33} = 8.1733$	8.2077
4	7.79	7.88	7.73	
	7.75	7.77	7.74	
	7.73	7.72	7.71	
	$\bar{x}_{41} = 7.7566$	$\bar{x}_{42} = 7.79$	$\bar{x}_{43} = 7.7266$	7.7577
$\bar{x}_j$	8.0033	7.99	7.9783	

$\bar{\bar{x}}$ = Grand mean = 7.99055

Step 6: Analyse the data

$$\text{SSR (sum of squares between rows)} = nc\sum_{i=1}^{r}(\bar{x}_i - \bar{\bar{x}})^2$$

$$= (3\times 3)\left[\begin{array}{r}(8.0755 - 7.99055)^2 + (7.9211 - 7.99055)^2 + (8.2077 \\ - 7.99055)^2 + (7.7577 - 7.99055)^2\end{array}\right]$$

$$= 1.02077$$

$$\text{SSC (sum of squares between columns)} = nr\sum_{j=1}^{c}(\bar{x}_j - \bar{\bar{x}})^2$$

$$= (3\times 4)\left[\begin{array}{r}(8.003 - 7.99055)^2 + (7.99 - 7.99055)^2 + (7.9783 \\ - 7.99055)^2\end{array}\right]$$

$$= 0.00376$$

$$\text{SSI (sum of squares interaction)} = n\sum_{i=1}^{r}\sum_{j=1}^{c}(\bar{x}_{ij} - \bar{x}_j - \bar{x}_i + \bar{\bar{x}})^2$$

$$= 3\times\left[\begin{array}{l}(8.06 - 8.0755 - 8.003 + 7.99055)^2 + (8.0966 - 8.0755 - 7.99 \\ + 7.99055)^2 + \cdots + (7.7266 - 7.7577 - 7.9783 + 7.99055)^2\end{array}\right]$$

$$= 0.02527$$

$$\text{SSE (sum of squares errors)} = \sum_{i=1}^{r}\sum_{j=1}^{c}\sum_{k=1}^{n}(x_{ijk} - \bar{x}_{ij})^2$$

$$= \left[\begin{array}{r}(8.12 - 8.06)^2 + (8.01 - 8.06)^2 + \cdots + (7.74 - 7.7266)^2 \\ + (7.71 - 7.7266)^2\end{array}\right]$$

$$= 0.0568$$

$$\text{SST (total sum of squares)} = \sum_{i=1}^{r}\sum_{j=1}^{c}\sum_{k=1}^{n}(x_{ijk} - \bar{\bar{x}})^2$$

$$= \left[\begin{array}{r}(8.12 - 7.99055)^2 + (8.01 - 7.99055)^2 + \cdots + (7.74 - 7.99055)^2 \\ + (7.71 - 7.99055)^2\end{array}\right]$$

$$= 1.106589$$

$$\text{MSR (mean square)} = \frac{\text{SSR}}{r-1} = \frac{1.02077}{3} = 0.340256$$

$$\text{MSC (mean square)} = \frac{\text{SSC}}{c-1} = \frac{0.00376}{2} = 0.00188$$

$$\text{MSI (mean square)} = \frac{\text{SSI}}{(r-1)(c-1)} = \frac{0.02527}{6} = 0.00421$$

$$\text{MSE (mean square)} = \frac{\text{SSE}}{rc(n-1)} = \frac{0.05680}{24} = 0.002367$$

$$F_{treatment} = \frac{\text{MSC}}{\text{MSE}} = \frac{0.00188}{0.002367} = 0.79$$

$$F_{block} = \frac{\text{MSR}}{\text{MSE}} = \frac{0.340256}{0.002367} = 143.7$$

$$F_{interaction} = \frac{MSI}{MSE} = \frac{0.004211}{0.002367} = 1.78$$

TABLE 14.15
ANOVA Summary table for Example 14.3

Source of variation	*Sum of squares*	*Degrees of freedom*	*Mean squares*	*F Value*
Sum of squares between columns	SSC	3 – 1 = 2	MSC = 0.00188	$F_{treatment}$ = 0.79
Sum of squares between rows	SSR	4 – 1 = 3	MSR = 0.340256	F_{block} = 143.7
Sum of squares interaction	SSI	(3 – 1)(4 – 1) = 6	MSI = 0.004211	$F_{interaction}$ = 1.78
Sum of squares of errors	SSE	$rc(n-1) = 24$	MSE = 0.002367	
Total	SST	$N - 1 = 35$		

Table 14.15 presents the ANOVA summary table for Example 14.3.

Step 7: Arrive at a statistical conclusion and business implication
At 95% confidence level, the critical value obtained from the table is $F_{0.05,\,2,\,24} = 3.40$, $F_{0.05,\,3,\,24} = 3.01$ and $F_{0.05,\,6,\,24} = 2.51$.

The calculated value of F for columns is 0.79. This is less than the tabular value (3.40) and falls in the acceptance region. Hence, the null hypothesis is accepted and the alternative hypothesis is rejected.

The calculated value of F for rows is 143.77. This is greater than the tabular value (3.01) and falls in the rejection region. Hence, the null hypothesis is rejected and alternative hypothesis is accepted.

The calculated value of F for interaction is 1.78. This is less than the tabular value (2.51) and falls in the acceptance region. Hence, the null hypothesis is accepted and the alternative hypothesis is rejected.

The result indicates that there is a significant difference in the steel rods produced by different machines. The results also indicate that the difference in the length of the steel rods produced in three shifts are not significant and the differences obtained (as exhibited from the sample result) are due to chance. Additionally, interaction between machines and shifts is also not significant and differences (as exhibited from the sample result) are due to chance. Therefore, the management must focus on the machines to ensure that the steel rods produced by all the machines are uniform.

SELF-PRACTICE PROBLEMS

14C1. Perform two-way ANOVA on the data arranged in the form of a two-way factorial design below:

		Treatment 1		
		A	B	C
Treatment 2	D	23	24	25
		25	27	24
		27	29	22
	E	28	25	29
		30	30	32
		31	32	34

14C2. Perform two-way ANOVA analysis on the data arranged in form of a two-way factorial design as below:

		Treatment 1		
		A	B	C
Treatment 2	D	1.3	2.1	3.8
		1.5	2.9	3.9
	E	1.8	3.0	4.3
		1.7	3.2	4.8
	F	1.9	5.1	5.8
		2.1	5.3	5.9

14C3. A company organized a training programme for three categories of officers: sales managers, zonal managers, and regional managers. The company also considered the education level of the employees. Based on their qualifications, officers were also divided into three categories: graduate, post graduates, and doctorates. The company wants to ascertain the effectiveness of the training programme on employees across designation and educational levels. The scores obtained from randomly selected employees across different categories are given below:

	Designation	Sales managers	Zonal managers	Regional managers
Qualification	Graduate	30	34	38
		40	40	39
		42	42	40
		33	45	42
	Post graduates	35	36	40
		39	38	43
		41	42	41
		39	43	32
	Doctorate	34	44	30
		38	45	28
		39	37	32
		35	38	29

Employ a two-way analysis of variance and determine whether there are significant differences in effects. Take $\alpha = 0.05$

SUMMARY |

An experimental design is the logical construction of the experiment to test hypotheses in which researcher either controls or manipulates one or more variables. Analysis of variance or ANOVA is a technique of testing a hypothesis about the significant difference in several population means. In analysis of variance (one-way classification), the total variation in the sample data can be divided into two components, namely variance between the samples and variance within the samples. Variance between the samples is attributed to the difference among the sample means. This variance is due to some assignable causes. One-way ANOVA is used to analyse the data from completely randomized designs.

Like completely randomized design, randomized block design also focuses on one independent variable of interest (treatment variable). Additionally, in randomized block design, we also include one more variable referred to as "blocking variable." This blocking variable is used to control the confounding variable. Confounding variables are not being controlled by the researcher but can have an impact on the outcome of the treatment being studied. In case of a randomized block design, variation within the samples can be partitioned in two parts: unwanted variance attributed to difference between block means (block sum of square) (SSR); variance attributed to random error sum of squares errors) (SSE).

In some real-life situations, a researcher has to explore two or more treatments simultaneously. This type of experimental design is referred to as factorial design. In a factorial design, two or more treatment variables are studied simultaneously. Factorial design provides a platform to analyse both the treatment variables simultaneously at the same time in one experimental design. In a factorial design, a researcher can control the effect of multiple treatment variables. In addition, factorial design provides an opportunity to study the interaction effect of two treatment variables. The total sum of squares consists of four parts: SSC (sum of squares between columns), SSR (sum of squares between rows), SSI (sum of squares interaction), and SSE (sum of squares of errors).

KEY TERMS |

Analysis of variance, 333
Classification variable, 332
Completely randomized design, 333
Dependent variable, 333
Experimental design, 332
Experimental units, 333
Factor, 333
Factorial design, 333
Independent variable, 332
Randomized block design, 333
Treatment variable, 332

NOTE |

1. www.tatamotors.com/our_world/profile.php, accessed August 2008.

DISCUSSION QUESTIONS |

1. Explain the concept of using experimental designs for hypothesis testing.
2. Define the following terms:
   - Independent variable
   - Treatment variable
   - Classification variable
   - Experimental units
   - Dependent variable
3. What do you understand by ANOVA? What are the major assumptions of ANOVA?
4. What is the concept of completely randomized design and under what circumstances can we use completely randomized design for hypothesis testing?
5. Explain the procedure for calculating SSC (sum of squares between columns) and SSE (sum of squares within samples) in a completely randomized design.
6. Discuss the concept of randomized block design? Under what circumstances can we adopt randomized block design? Explain your answer in light of blocking variable and confounding variable.
7. Explain the procedure of calculating SSC (sum of squares between columns), SSR(sum of squares between rows), and SSE (sum of squares of errors) in a randomized block design.
8. Explain the difference between completely randomized design and randomized block design.
9. What do you understand by factorial design? Explain the concept of interaction in a factorial design.
10. Explain the procedure of calculating SSC (sum of squares between columns), SSR (sum of squares between rows), SSI (sum of squares interaction), and SSE (sum of squares of errors).

NUMERICAL PROBLEMS |

1. There are four cement companies A, B, C, and D in Chhattisgarh. Company "A" is facing a problem of high employee turnover. The personnel manager of this company believes that the low job satisfaction levels of employees may be one of the reasons for the high employee turnover. He has decided to compare the job satisfaction levels of the employees of his plant with those of the three other plants. He has used a questionnaire with 10 questions on a Likert rating scale of 1 to 5. The maximum scores that can be obtained is 50 and the minimum score is 10. The personnel manager has taken a random sample of 10 employees from each of the organizations with the help of a professional research organization. The scores obtained by the employees are given in the table below.

Organization A	*Organization B*	*Organization C*	*Organization D*
28	34	38	38
26	35	36	40
27	33	35	39
24	32	38	38
29	34	39	37
28	33	37	41
32	34	36	38
28	32	35	38
29	33	38	39
30	34	39	37

Use one-way ANOVA to analyse the significant difference in the job satisfaction scores. Take 99% as the confidence level.

2. A company has launched a new brand of soap Brand 1 in the market. Three different brands of three different companies already exist in the market. The company wants to know the consumer preference for these four brands. The company has randomly selected 10 consumers of each of the four brands and used a 1 to 4 rating scale, with 1 being the minimum and 4 being the maximum. The scores obtained are tabulated below:

Brand 1	*Brand 2*	*Brand 3*	*Brand 4*
25	24	30	32
26	28	31	33
24	29	30	31
25	23	32	32
26	29	31	33
25	28	29	34
26	24	28	28
25	26	29	30
23	27	30	31
26	24	31	30

Use one-way ANOVA to analyse the significant difference in the consumer preference scores. Take 95% as the confidence level.

3. A consumer durable company located at New Delhi has launched a new advertisement campaign for a product. The company wants to estimate the impact of this campaign on different classes of consumers. For the same purpose, the company has divided consumer groups into three classes based on occupations. These are service class, business class, and consultants. For measuring the impact of the advertisement campaign, the company has used a questionnaire, which consists of 10 questions, on a 1 to 7 rating scale with 1 being minimum and 7 being maximum. The company has randomly selected 8 subjects (respondents) from each of the classes. So, a subject can score a minimum of 10 and maximum of 70. The scores obtained from the three classes of consumers are given below:

Subject	*Service class*	*Business class*	*Consultants*
1	40	42	38
2	42	43	40
3	43	45	43
4	48	45	44
5	45	48	47
6	44	42	48
7	46	46	45
8	42	44	46

Use one-way ANOVA to determine the significant difference in the mean scores obtained by different consumers. Assume $\alpha = 0.05$

4. A company has employed five different machines with five different operators working on it turn-by-turn. The table given below shows the number of units produced on randomly selected days by five machines with the concerned operator working on it:

Machine \ *Operator*	*O1*	*O2*	*O3*	*O4*	*O5*
M1	25	27	26	28	27
M2	27	28	28	27	28
M3	28	29	27	26	27
M4	32	33	32	35	34
M5	33	32	33	33	34

Use a randomized block design analysis to examine:

(1) Whether the operators significantly differ in performance?

(2) Whether there is a significant difference between the machines?

Take 90% as the confidence level.

5. A woolen threads manufacturer recently purchased three new machines. The company wants to measure the performance of these three machines at three different temperatures (in terms of unit production per day). The following table depicts the performance of the three machines at three different temperatures on randomly selected days:

Temperature \ Machines	M1	M2	M3
T1	12	13	12
T2	14	15	15
T3	16	17	18

Use a randomized block design analysis to examine:

(1) Whether the machines are significantly different in terms of performance?
(2) Whether there is a significant difference between the three different temperatures in terms of production?

Take 95% as the confidence level.

6. A company wants to ascertain the month wise productivity of its salesmen. The sales volume generated by five randomly selected salesmen in the first five months is given in the following table:

Month \ Salesmen	S1	S2	S3	S4	S5
Jan	24	27	26	28	29
Feb	25	28	28	32	31
Mar	28	32	30	34	33
Apr	32	34	32	40	42
May	26	35	30	36	35

Use a randomized block design analysis to examine:

(1) Whether the salesmen are significantly different in terms of performance?
(2) Whether there is a significant difference between five months in terms of production?

Take 90% as the confidence level.

7. A company wants to measure the satisfaction level of consumers for a particular product. For this purpose, the company has selected respondents belonging to four age groups and asked a simple question, "Are you satisfied with this product?" Respondents were also classified into four regions. On the basis of four different age groups and regions, 48 customers were randomly selected. The company used a nine-point rating scale. The data given below represents the responses of the consumers:

		Regions			
		North	West	East	South
Age groups	20+	6	8	5	3
		7	7	3	5
		6	8	4	6
	30+	5	8	5	4
		6	7	4	5
		5	6	3	3
	40+	6	6	4	5
		7	8	4	6
		6	6	5	5
	50+	5	8	6	6
		6	7	5	7
		6	8	5	6

Employ two-way ANOVA to determine whether there are any significant differences in effects. Take $\alpha = 0.05$.

9. A water purifier company wants to launch a new model of its popular product. The company has divided its potential customers into three categories, "middle class," "upper-middle class," and "upper class." Potential customers are further divided among three states of India, "Gujarat," "Delhi," and "Punjab." For determining the purchase intention of the potential randomly selected consumers, the company has used a simple question, "Does this new product appeal to you?" The questionnaire is administered to 36 randomly selected customers from different classes and states. The company has used a five-point rating scale. The table given below depicts the responses of these randomly selected potential consumers:

Region		Gujarat	Delhi	Punjab
Customer classes	Upper class	3	4	1
		4	5	2
		4	4	3
		3	5	2
	Upper middle class	3	4	2
		5	5	3
		4	5	3
		3	5	2
	Middle class	4	4	1
		4	3	3
		5	4	2
		3	4	2

Employ a two-way ANOVA and determine whether there are any significant differences in effects. Take $\alpha = 0.01$.

10. Black Pearl is a leading tyre manufacturing company in Pune. In the last 10 years, the company has achieved success in terms of branding, profitability, and market share. As a downside, the management has realized that the highly competitive and stressful environment has reduced its employee morale. For boosting employee morale, the company has opted for three methods: motivational speeches, meditation, and holidays with pay. The company researchers measure the success of the three-point programme after taking random samples from three departments, marketing, finance, and production. The researchers have used a questionnaire (10 questions) on a five-point rating scale. So, the maximum score can be 50 and minimum score can be 10. The scores obtained from 36 randomly selected employees are as shown in the given table:

Methods		Motivational speeches	Meditation	Holidays with pay
		35	38	39
	Marketing	40	34	40
		35	38	39
		35	35	38
		36	40	35
		30	28	29
Departments	Finance	31	29	30
		29	30	28
		32	29	31
		32	33	31
	Production	31	33	32
		33	32	33
		29	29	35

Employ a two-way ANOVA and determine whether there are any significant differences in effects. Take $\alpha = 0.05$.

CASE STUDY |

Case 14: *Tyre Industry in India: A History of Over 75 Years*

Introduction

The Indian government has been placing high emphasis on the building of infrastructure in the country. This has given a tremendous fillip to the development of road infrastructure and transport. After liberalization, there has been a remarkable increase in the numbers of vehicles on Indian roads. As a direct result of this, a heavy demand for tyres has been forecast in the near future. Indian tyre manufacturing companies have started re-engineering their businesses and are looking at strategic tie-ups worldwide to meet this demand.[1] Table 14.01 shows the market segmentation for different categories of tyres.

TABLE 14.01
Market segmentation for different categories of tyres

Segment	*Share by No. (%)*
Commercial vehicles	30
Passenger car	13
Utility vehicles	4
Farm tyres	8
2/3 wheelers	45

Source: www.indiastat.com, accessed August 2008, reproduced with permission.

Major Players in the Market

MRF Ltd, Apollo Tyres Ltd, Ceat Ltd, JK Industries Ltd, GoodYear, Dunlop, etc. are some of the major players in the market. MRF Ltd is the leader in the market. The company is involved in the manufacturing, distribution, and the sales of tyres, tubes, and flaps for various vehicles. CEAT, established in 1958, is a part of the PRG group. CEAT is also a key player in the market and offers a wide range of tyres for almost all segments like heavy-duty trucks and buses, light commercial vehicles, earthmovers, forklifts, tractors, trailers, cars, motorcycles, and scooters, etc.

Apollo Tyres Ltd is also a dominant player in the truck, bus, and light commercial vehicle categories. In January 2008, the company announced an investment of ₹12,000 million to set up a passenger car radial plant in Hungary to cater to the needs of the European and the North American market. It acquired Dunlop Tyre International along with its subsidiaries in Zimbabwe and the UK in April 2006[1]. Apollo Tyres CMD, Mr Onkar Singh Kanwar, optimistically stated, "We believe that alliances offer the power of many companies working together for the benefit of the customer. This ultimately is for the greater good of the market and the individual companies."[2]

JK Industries Ltd is the pioneer in launching radial tyres in India. Radial tyres cost 30% more but are technologically superior to conventional tyres. JK Tyres is the key player in the four-wheeler tyre market. In 1922, Goodyear tyre and rubber company Akron, Ohio, USA, entered the Indian market. Goodyear India has pioneered the introduction of tubeless radial tyres in the passenger car segment. Dunlop India Ltd is also a leading player in the market.

Worry Over Chinese Imports

Between April and December 2006, 550,000 trucks and bus tyres were imported from China when compared to just over 3 lakh units during the financial year 2005–2006. The increase in imports of low-priced tyres from China has become a sore point for Indian tyre manufacturers. Indian manufacturers are relying on the superior quality of Indian tyres to fight this battle. Mr Arun K. Bajoria, President, JK Tyre and Industries Ltd argued, "The quality of an Indian tyre and Chinese tyre cannot be compared. Indian tyres are exported to around 80 countries around the world and we have no complaints from anywhere on the quality."[3]

With world class products under its stable, Indian tyre companies are getting ready to cater to an estimated demand of 22 million units of car and jeep tyres; 57 million units of two-wheelers tyres; 6.5 million units of LCV tyres; 17 million units of HCV tyres by 2014–2015.[4]

Let us assume that a researcher wants to compare the mean net sales of four leading companies Apollo Tyres Ltd, Ceat Ltd, JK Industries Ltd and MRF Ltd. The researcher is unable to access the complete net sales data of these companies and has taken a random sample of net sales for six quarters of the four companies taken for the study. Table 14.02 shows the net sales (in million rupees) of four leading tyre manufacturers in randomly selected quarters. Apply techniques presented in this chapter to find out whether:

1. The companies significantly differ in performance?
2. There is a significant difference between the quarterly sales of these companies?

TABLE 14.02
Net sales of four leading tyre manufacturers for six randomly selected quarters

Net sales (in million rupees)	*Apollo tyres Ltd*	*Ceat Ltd*	*J K Industries Ltd*	*M R F Ltd*
Jun 1998	1689.7	2708.4	3221.3	5578.7
Sep 2000	2983.1	2432.1	2675.4	2854.7
Dec 2002	4041.6	2722.8	3871.4	5189.8
Mar 2004	5147.9	3926.4	4611.5	6208.7
Jun 2005	5680.9	4027.7	5626.7	7951.2
Mar 2006	7458.5	4843.6	6250.4	8796

Source: Prowess (V. 3.1), Centre for Monitoring Indian Economy Pvt. Ltd, Mumbai, accessed August 2008, reproduced with permission.

NOTES |

1. Prowess (V. 3.1), Centre for Monitoring Indian Economy Pvt. Ltd, Mumbai, accessed August 2008, reproduced with permission.
2. www.tribuneindia.com/2003/200330901/biz.htm, accessed August 2008.
3. www.thehindubusinessline.com/2007/07/20/stories/2007072050461400.htm, accessed August 2008.
4. www.indiastat.com, accessed August 2008, reproduced with permission.

CHAPTER 15

Hypothesis Testing for Categorical Data (Chi-Square Test)

LEARNING OBJECTIVES

Upon completion of this chapter, you will be able to:

- Understand the concept of chi-square statistic and chi-square distribution
- Understand the concept of chi-square goodness-of-fit test
- Understand the concept of chi-square test of independence: two-way contingency analysis
- Understand the concept of chi-square test for population variance and chi-square test of homogeneity

STATISTICS IN ACTION: STATE BANK OF INDIA (SBI)

The State Bank of India (SBI) is the country's oldest and leading bank in terms of balance sheet size, number of branches, market capitalization, and profits. This two hundred year-old public sector behemoth is today stirring out of its public sector legacy and moving with an agility to give the private and foreign banks a run for their money. The bank has ventured into many new businesses such as pension funds, mobile banking, point-of-sale merchant acquisition, advisory services, and structured products. All these initiatives have a huge potential for growth.[1]

Suppose SBI wants to find out whether its new services such as mobile banking and internet banking will only be used by its younger customers or by customers across all age groups. Let us assume that the management has a perception that personal banking would be more popular with middle-aged and older customers. Suppose it hires the services of a marketing research firm, which conducts a survey among customers from five different age groups to find out an answer. This marketing research firm has randomly selected 2413 customers across the age groups: 17 to 27, 28 to 35, 36 to 44, 45 to 57, and 58 to 70. The observations made by the marketing research firm about the type of banking opted by different age groups are given in Table 15.1.

TABLE 15.1
Preferences of type of banking across different age groups

Age \ *Product*	*Mobile banking*	*Internet banking*	*Personal banking*	*Row total*
17 to 27	125	175	145	445
28 to 35	155	180	197	532
36 to 44	167	210	150	527
45 to 57	146	156	142	444
58 to 70	133	156	176	465
Column total	726	877	810	2413

The marketing research group wants to determine whether the type of product usage in the population is independent of age group. The bank can resolve this confusion by applying the chi-square test of independence which is discussed in detail in this chapter. Apart from chi-square test of independence, the chapter mainly focuses on the concept of chi-square statistic and chi-square distribution. The chapter also focuses on concepts such as chi-square goodness-of-fit test, chi-square test for population variance, and chi-square test of homogeneity.

15.1 INTRODUCTION

In the previous chapters, we have discussed that under various circumstances z, t, and F tests are used to test the hypothesis about the population parameters. In this chapter, we will discuss some tests related to categorical data. Categorical data is defined as the counting of frequencies from one or more variables. Let us take the example of a special seminar organized by a company for its officers. The company has a total of 40,000 officers and it selected a random sample of 650 officers across four departments to assess the representativeness across departments in the seminar. Out of 650 randomly selected officers, 150 officers are from the production department, 200 officers are from the marketing department, 160 from the finance department, and remaining 140 from the human resources department. A research variable "representatives from the departments" does not require any rating scale to be used. Here, the research question is the frequency count from each department and can be analysed using the chi-square technique.

Some researchers place the chi-square technique in the category of non-parametric tests for testing of the hypothesis.

Some researchers place the chi-square technique in the category of **non-parametric tests** for the testing of hypothesis. The tests described in previous chapters for testing the hypothesis such as z, t, and F tests are based on the assumption that the samples are drawn from a normally distributed population. In some cases, the researcher may not be sure of whether the population distribution is normal. The statistical tests that do not require prior knowledge about the population are termed as non-parametric tests. This chapter will focus on only χ^2 (chi-square) test.

15.2 DEFINING χ^2-TEST STATISTIC

χ^2 distribution is the family of curves with each distribution defined by the degree of freedom associated to it. In fact χ^2 is a continuous probability distribution with range 0 to ∞.

χ^2 test was developed by Karl Pearson in 1900. The symbol χ stands for the Greek letter "chi." We have discussed that t and F distributions are functions of their degree of freedom. Likewise χ^2distribution is also a function of its degree of freedom (Figure 15.1). The distribution is skewed to the right. Being a sum of square quantities, χ^2 distribution can never be a negative value. In other words, **χ^2 distribution** is the family of curves with each distribution defined by the degree of freedom associated with it. In fact, χ^2 is a continuous probability distribution with range 0 to ∞ (Figure 15.1). The probability density function of a χ^2 distribution is given by

$$f(\chi^2) = C(\chi^2)^{\frac{v}{2}-1} e^{-\frac{\chi^2}{2}}$$

where v is the degree of freedom, C is a constant depending upon the degrees of freedom, and $e = 2.71828$.

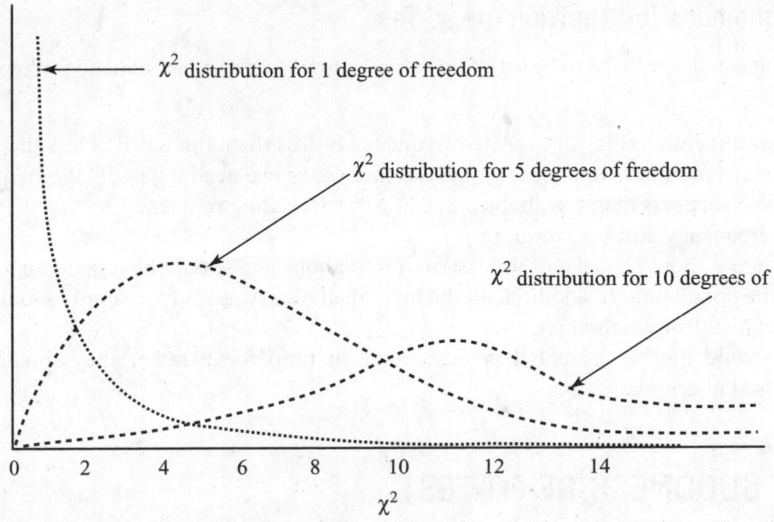

FIGURE 15.1
χ^2 distribution with 1, 5 and 10 degrees of freedom

χ^2-test statistic can be defined as below:

χ^2-test statistic

$$\chi^2 = \sum \frac{(f_o - f_e)^2}{f_e} \quad \text{with } df = k - 1 - c$$

where f_o is the observed frequency, f_e the expected or theoretical frequency, k the number of categories, and c the number of parameters being estimated from the sample data.

At a particular level of significance, the calculated value of χ^2 is compared with the critical value of χ^2. Decision rules are as below:

If $\chi^2_{cal} > \chi^2_{critical}$, reject the null hypothesis, otherwise do not reject the null hypothesis. This is shown in Figure 15.2.

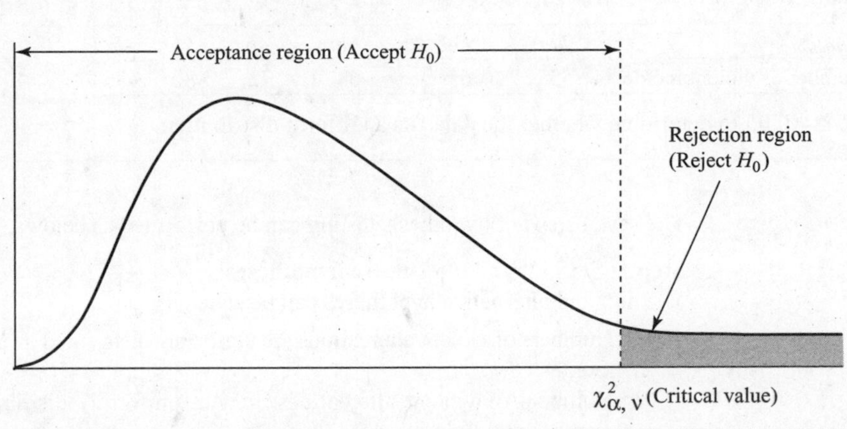

FIGURE 15.2
Acceptance or rejection region in a χ^2 test

15.2.1 Conditions for Applying the χ^2 Test

The following conditions need to be satisfied before applying χ^2 as a test statistic for hypothesis testing:

- In a **contingency table**, an expected frequency of less than 5 in a cell is less than the frequency required to apply the χ^2 test. In such cases, we need to "pool" the frequencies which are less than 5 with the preceding or succeeding frequency, so that the sum of the frequency will be 5 or more.
- The sample should consist of at least 50 observations and should be drawn randomly from the population. In addition, all the individual observations in a sample should be independent from each other.
- Data should not be presented in percentage or ratio form, rather they should be expressed in original units.

15.3 χ^2 GOODNESS-OF-FIT TEST

χ^2 test provides a platform that can be used to ascertain whether theoretical probability distributions coincide with empirical sample distributions.

χ^2 test is very popular as a goodness-of-fit test. χ^2 test enables us to ascertain whether the known probability distributions such as binomial, Poisson, and normal distributions fit or match with an actual sample distribution. In other words, we can say the **χ^2 test** provides a platform that can be used to ascertain whether theoretical probability distributions coincide with empirical sample distributions. χ^2 test compares the theoretical (expected) frequencies with the observed (actual) to determine the difference between theoretical and observed frequencies.

For applying χ^2 test, first a theoretical distribution is hypothesized for a given population. As the next step, the χ^2 test is applied to make sure whether the sample distribution is from the population with the hypothesized theoretical probability distribution. The seven steps for hypothesis testing can also be performed using the **χ^2 goodness-of-fit test**.

Example 15.1

A company is concerned about the increasing violent altercations between its employees. The number of violent incidents recorded by the management during six randomly selected months is given in Table 15.2.

TABLE 15.2
Record of violent incidents in six randomly selected months

Months	*Jan*	*Feb*	*Mar*	*Apr*	*May*	*Jun*
Number of violent incidents	55	65	68	72	80	85

Use $\alpha = 0.05$ to determine whether the data fits a uniform distribution.

Solution The seven steps of hypothesis testing can be performed as below:

Step 1: Set null and alternative hypotheses
The null and alternative hypotheses can be stated as:

H_0: Numbers of violent altercations are uniformly distributed over the months.

H_1: Numbers of violent altercations are not uniformly distributed over the months.

Step 2: Determine the appropriate statistical test
The appropriate test statistic is

$$\chi^2 = \sum \frac{(f_o - f_e)^2}{f_e}$$

with $df = k - 1 - c$

Step 3: Set the level of significance
Alpha has been specified as 0.05.

Step 4: Set the decision rule
For a given level of significance 0.05, rules for acceptance or rejection of null hypothesis are as below:

If $\chi^2_{cal} > \chi^2_{critical}$, reject the null hypothesis, otherwise, do not reject the null hypothesis.

The critical χ^2 value is $\chi^2_{0.05,\,5} = 11.07$ where degrees of freedom $= n - 1 = 6 - 1 = 5$

Step 5: Collect the sample data
The sample data are given in Table 15.2.

Step 6: Analyse the data
Expected frequencies can be computed by dividing total observed frequencies by number of months. In this case, expected frequency = $\frac{\sum f_o}{6} = \frac{420}{6} = 70$

Table 15.3 exhibits expected frequencies and chi-square statistic for the data relating to violent altercations.

TABLE 15.3
Computation of expected frequencies and chi-square statistic for Example 15.1

Months	f_o	f_e	$\frac{(f_o - f_e)^2}{f_e}$
Jan	55	70	3.2142
Feb	65	70	0.3571
Mar	68	70	0.0571
Apr	72	70	0.0571
May	78	70	0.9142
Jun	82	70	2.0571
	$\sum f_o = 420$		$\sum \frac{(f_o - f_e)^2}{f_e} = 6.65$

So, $\chi^2 = \sum \frac{(f_o - f_e)^2}{f_e} = 6.6571$

Step 7: Arrive at a statistical conclusion and business implication
At 95% confidence level, the critical value obtained from the table is $\chi^2_{0.05,\,5} = 11.07$. χ^2 value is calculated as 6.65, which is less than the

tabular value and falls in the acceptance region. Hence, the null hypothesis is accepted and the alternative hypothesis is rejected.

There is enough evidence to indicate that the number of violent altercations is uniformly distributed over the months. Hence, the management must realise that due to some unexplained reasons, incidents of violence are uniformly distributed over the months. So, the reasons must be explored and corrective measures must be initiated as early as possible.

15.3.1 Hypothesis Testing for a Population Proportion Using χ^2 Goodness-of-Fit Test as an Alternative Technique to the z-Test

In Chapter 12, we discussed the z-test for a population proportion for $np \geq 5$ and $nq \geq 5$. This formula can be presented as below:

The z-test for a population proportion for $np \geq 5$ and $nq \geq 5$ is given as

$$z = \frac{\bar{p} - p}{\sqrt{\frac{pq}{n}}}$$

where $\bar{p}$ is the sample proportion, n the sample size, p the population proportion, and $q = 1 - p$.

The χ^2 goodness-of-fit test can be used to test the hypothesis about the population proportion as a special case when the number of classifications are two.

Let us reconsider Example 12.5 discussed in Chapter 12 for understanding the concept. The null and alternative hypotheses were stated as below:

$$H_0: p = 0.10$$
$$H_1: p \neq 0.10$$

In this section, we will reconsider this problem by using the χ^2 goodness-of-fit test to test a hypothesis about population proportion. This problem can be reframed as a two-category expected distribution in which there are 0.10 defective items and 0.90 non-defective items. Samples (in this case frequencies) are 100, so the expected frequencies for defective items are ($0.10 \times 100 = 10$) and expected frequencies for non-defective items are ($0.90 \times 100 = 90$). The observed frequencies for defective and non-defective items are 12 and 88, respectively. On the basis of these observations, a contingency table can be constructed (Table 15.4).

TABLE 15.4
Contingency table of defective and non-defective Items

Category	f_o	f_e
Defective items	12	10
Non-defective items	88	90

The confidence level is 95%, which shows that on both sides of the distribution, the rejection region will be 0.025%, that is, $\chi^2_{0.025,\,1} = 5.0239$. χ^2 statistic can be calculated as below:

$$\chi^2 = \sum \frac{(f_o - f_e)^2}{f_e} = \frac{(12 - 10)^2}{10} + \frac{(88 - 90)^2}{90} = 0.44$$

The calculated value of χ^2 is in the acceptance region ($0.44 < 5.0239$), so the null hypothesis that the population proportion is 0.10 can be accepted. If we examine this result in the light of the result that we have obtained in Example 12.5 (Chapter 12), approximate similarities can be observed. In that example, the calculated value of z is in the acceptance region ($0.67 < 1.96$), so the null hypothesis that the population proportion is 0.10 is accepted.

SELF-PRACTICE PROBLEMS

15A1. Use the data given in the table for determining whether the observed frequencies represent a uniform distribution. Take $\alpha = 0.05$.

Category	f_o
1	19
2	15
3	12
4	17
5	20
6	21
7	22
8	15
9	14
10	13

15A2. Use the data given in the table for determining whether the observed frequencies represent a uniform distribution. Take $\alpha = 0.01$.

Category	f_o
1	50
2	55
3	58
4	52
5	50
6	49
7	47
8	45

15A3. The table below shows the sales of a company (in thousand rupees) for eight years. Use $\alpha = 0.05$ to determine whether the data fit a uniform distribution.

Year	*Sales (in thousand rupees)*
1	75
2	80
3	73
4	70
5	67
6	82
7	81
8	83

15.4 χ^2 TEST OF INDEPENDENCE: TWO-WAY CONTINGENCY ANALYSIS

In many business situations, a market researcher might be interested in understanding the relationship between two variables or to check whether they are independent of each other. For example, an edible oil company may be interested in knowing whether the purchase of oil is independent of the customer's age or whether it is dependent on the customer's age. These are two different situations and the company has to frame a production and selling strategy accordingly. Another example is that of the HRD manager of a company who is interested in ascertaining whether the rate of employee turnover is independent of employee qualification.

When observations are classified on the basis of two variables and arranged in a table, the resulting table is referred to as a contingency table. χ^2 test of independence uses this contingency table for determining independence of two variables; this is why this test is sometimes referred to as contingency analysis.

When observations are classified on the basis of two variables and arranged in a table, the resulting table is referred to as a contingency table (Table 15.5). **χ^2 test of independence** uses this contingency table for determining independence of two variables; this is why this test is sometimes referred to as contingency analysis.

When we add the row or column totals, the grand total (*N*) is obtained. This grand total is the sum of all the frequencies and represents the sample size.

It can be observed that in the contingency table (Table 15.5), Variable *X* and Variable *Y* are classified into mutually exclusive categories. Observations in each cell represent the frequency of observations that are common to the respective row and column. R_j is the row total of the *j*th row and C_k is the total of the *k*th column. When we add row or column totals, the grand total (*N*) is obtained. This grand total is the sum of all the frequencies and

TABLE 15.5
Contingency table

Variable Y	*Variable X*					*Row total*
	X_1	X_2	X_3	...	X_k	
Y_1	O_{11}	O_{21}	O_{31}	...	O_{1k}	R_1
Y_2	O_{21}	O_{22}	O_{32}	...	O_{2k}	R_2
Y_3	O_{31}	O_{32}	O_{33}	...	O_{3k}	R_3
.	.	.	.		.	.
.	.	.	.		.	.
.	.	.	.		.	.
Y_j	O_{j1}	O_{j2}	O_{j3}	...	O_{jk}	R_j
Column total	C_1	C_2	C_3	...	C_k	N

represents the sample size. It is very important to calculate the expected frequencies to apply the χ^2-test.

The calculation of the expected frequency for any cell is based on the concept of multiplicative law of probability. Probability theory suggests that if two events are independent, then the probability of their joint occurrence is equal to the product of their individual probabilities. This concept of probability can be used to calculate the expected frequency in *j*th row and *k*th column. So, the expected frequency of cell *jk* is

$$f_{e(jk)} = \frac{\text{Total of the } j\text{th row}}{\text{Total number of frequencies}} \times \frac{\text{Total of the } k\text{th column}}{\text{Total number of frequencies}} \times \text{Total number of frequencies}$$

We know (from Table 15.5) that R_j is the row total of the *j*th row, C_k is the total of the *k*th column, and the total number of frequencies are N. Placing these values in the equation above, we get

$$f_{e(jk)} = \frac{R_j}{N} \times \frac{C_k}{N} \times N = \frac{R_j \times C_k}{N}$$

The expected frequency for any cell can be obtained by applying the formula discussed as under:

Expected frequency for any cell

$$f_e = \frac{RT \times CT}{N}$$

where RT is the row total, CT the column total, and N the total number of frequencies.

χ^2 test statistic

$$\chi^2 = \sum_{\text{all cells}} \frac{(f_o - f_e)^2}{f_e}$$

where f_o is the observed frequency and f_e the expected or theoretical frequency.

Degrees of freedom in a χ^2 test of independence

Degrees of freedom = (Number of rows – 1) (Number of columns – 1)

Example 15.2

The Vice President (Sales) of a garment company wants to determine whether sales of the company's brand of jeans is independent of age group. He has appointed a marketing researcher for this purpose. This marketing researcher has taken a random sample of 703 consumers who have purchased jeans. The researcher conducted survey for three brands of the jeans, namely Brand 1, Brand 2, and Brand 3. The researcher has also divided the age groups into four categories: 15 to 25, 26 to 35, 36 to 45, and 46 to 55. The observations of the researcher are provided in Table 15.6:

TABLE 15.6
Contingency table for Example 15.2

Age \ *Brand*	*Brand 1*	*Brand 2*	*Brand 3*	*Row total*
15 to 25	65	75	72	212
26 to 35	60	40	64	164
36 to 45	45	52	50	147
46 to 55	55	65	60	180
Column total	225	232	246	703

Determine whether brand preference is independent of age group. Use $\alpha = 0.05$.

Solution The seven steps of hypothesis testing can be performed as below:

Step 1: Set null and alternative hypotheses

The null and alternative hypotheses can be stated as below:

H_0: Brand preference is independent of age group

and H_1: Brand preference is not independent of age group

Step 2: Determine the appropriate statistical test

The appropriate test statistic is

$$\chi^2 = \sum_{\text{all cells}} \frac{(f_o - f_e)^2}{f_e}$$

with degrees of freedom = (number of rows – 1) × (number of columns – 1)

Step 3: Set the level of significance

Alpha has been specified as 0.05.

Step 4: Set the decision rule

For a given level of significance 0.05, the rules for the acceptance or rejection of the null hypothesis are as follows:

If $\chi^2_{cal} > \chi^2_{critical}$, reject the null hypothesis, otherwise, do not reject the null hypothesis.

The critical χ^2 value is $\chi^2_{0.05,\,6} = 12.59$

where degrees of freedom = (number of rows – 1) (number of columns – 1)
= (4 – 1) × (3 – 1) = 6

Step 5: Collect the sample data

The sample data are given in Table 15.6.

Step 6: Analyse the data

The contingency table with the observed and expected frequencies is shown in Table 15.7.

TABLE 15.7
Contingency table of the observed and expected frequencies for Example 15.2

Age \ *Brand*	*Brand 1*	*Brand 2*	*Brand 3*	*Row total*
15 to 25	65 (67.8520)	75 (69.9630)	72 (74.1849)	212
26 to 35	60 (52.4893)	40 (54.1223)	64 (57.3883)	164
36 to 45	45 (47.0483)	52 (48.5120)	50 (51.4395)	147
46 to 55	55 (57.6102)	65 (59.4025)	60 (62.9872)	180
Column total	225	232	246	703

Expected frequency for cell (1, 1) can be calculated as below:

$$f_{e11} = \frac{RT \times CT}{N} = \frac{212 \times 225}{703} = 67.8520$$

Similarly, the expected frequencies for other cells can be calculated. Table 15.8 exhibits the computation of expected frequencies and chi-square statistic for Example 15.2.

TABLE 15.8
Computation of expected frequencies and chi-square statistic for Example 15.2

f_o *(Observed frequency)*	f_e *(Expected frequency)*	$\frac{(f_o - f_e)^2}{f_e}$
65	67.8520	0.1198
60	52.4893	1.0746
45	47.0483	0.0891

55	57.6102	0.1182
75	69.9630	0.3626
40	54.1223	3.6849
52	48.5120	0.2507
65	59.4025	0.5274
72	74.1849	0.0643
64	57.3883	0.7617
50	51.4395	0.0402
60	62.9872	0.1416
		$\sum\frac{(f_o-f_e)^2}{f_e}=7.23$

So, $\chi^2=\sum\frac{(f_o-f_e)^2}{f_e}=7.23$

Step 7: Arrive at a statistical conclusion and business implication

At 95% confidence level, the critical value obtained from the chi-square table is $\chi^2_{0.05,\,6}=12.59$. χ^2 is calculated as 7.23, which is less than the tabular value and falls in the acceptance region. Hence, the null hypothesis is accepted and the alternative hypothesis is rejected.

There is enough evidence to indicate that brand preference is independent of age group. So, the management can go in for a uniform sales and marketing policy.

15.5 χ^2 TEST FOR POPULATION VARIANCE

χ^2 test is based on the assumption that the population from which the samples are drawn is normally distributed. From a normal population, if a sample of size n is drawn, then the variance of sampling distribution of mean $\bar{x}$ is given by $s^2=\sum(x-\bar{x})^2/n-1$. The value of χ^2-test statistic is determined as below:

$$\chi^2=\frac{1}{\sigma^2}\times\sum(x-\bar{x})^2$$

$$\chi^2=\frac{1}{\sigma^2}\times\sum(x-\bar{x})^2=\frac{(n-1)s^2}{\sigma^2}\quad\text{where, } s^2=\left[\sum(x-\bar{x})^2/n-1\right]$$

with degrees of freedom $= n-1$

If $\chi^2_{cal}>\chi^2_{critical}$, reject the null hypothesis, otherwise, do not reject the null hypothesis.

Example 15.3

A researcher draws a random sample of size 51 from the population. The sample standard deviation is calculated as 15. Use $\alpha=0.05$ and test the hypothesis that the population standard deviation is 20.

Solution

The null and alternative hypotheses can be described as below:

H_0: Population standard deviation is 20.

and H_1: Population standard deviation is not 20.

As described above, χ^2-test statistic can be given by the formula below:

$$\chi^2 = \frac{1}{\sigma^2} \times \sum (x - \bar{x})^2 = \frac{(n-1)s^2}{\sigma^2} = \frac{(51-1)\times(15)^2}{(20)^2} = \frac{50 \times 225}{400} = 28.12$$

The critical χ^2 value is $\chi^2_{0.05,\,50} = 67.50$

At 95% confidence level, the critical value obtained from the table is $\chi^2_{0.05,\,50} = 67.50$. Calculated value of χ^2 is 28.12. Decision rules are

If $\chi^2_{cal} > \chi^2_{critical}$, reject the null hypothesis, otherwise, do not reject the null hypothesis.

In this case, $\chi^2_{cal}(= 28.12) < \chi^2_{critical}(= 67.50)$

Hence, the null hypothesis is accepted and the alternative hypothesis is rejected. On this basis, it can be concluded that the population standard deviation is 20.

15.6 χ^2 TEST OF HOMOGENEITY

χ^2 test of homogeneity is used to determine whether two or more independent variables are drawn from the same population or from different populations. In other words, we can say that χ^2 test of homogeneity is used to determine whether two or more populations are homogenous with respect to some characteristic of interest.

χ^2 test of homogeneity is used to determine whether two or more independent variables are drawn from the same population or from different populations. In other words, we can say that χ^2 test of homogeneity is used to determine whether two or more populations are homogenous with respect to some characteristics of interest. For example, a researcher may be interested in knowing whether the employees from three departments, production, finance, and personnel, feel the same about the requirements of the top management in terms of hard work expected from employees. The amount of hard work can also be classified into three groups, namely, very hard, hard, and easy going. In this case, we can set a null hypothesis that the opinion of all the groups is the same about the requirement of hard work. In other words, the null hypothesis states that the three classifications are homogenous in terms of their opinion about the amount of hard work required by the top management.

This test is different from the previously discussed χ^2 test of independence in a few aspects. In χ^2 test of independence, a researcher determines whether two attributes are independent. In χ^2 test of homogeneity, a researcher determines whether two or more populations are homogenous with respect to some characteristic of interest. Additionally, in χ^2 test of homogeneity two or more independent samples are drawn from each population as against the test of independence in which we draw a single sample from a population. There are some similarities also between the two tests. In both the tests, a researcher is concerned with the cross tabulation of the data. The procedure of testing hypotheses is also the same for the two tests.

Example 15.4

A television company has launched a new product with some advanced features. The company wants to know the opinion of consumers about this product with respect to four characteristics: preferred brand with new features, did not prefer brand with new features, preferred only a few new features, and indifferent. The company has divided consumers into three groups—executives/officers; businessmen, and private consultants. It has taken a random sample of size 459 and obtained results are presented in Table 15.9.

TABLE 15.9
Consumer responses for a new product with some advanced features

Opinion \ *Consumers*	*Executives/Officers*	*Businessmen*	*Private consultants*	*Row total*
Preferred brand with new features	35	25	40	100
Did not prefer brand with new features	30	45	34	109
Preferred only a few new features	45	50	25	120
Indifferent	25	55	50	130
Column total	135	175	149	459

Use χ^2 test of homogeneity and draw inference from the data.

Solution The seven steps of hypothesis testing can be performed as below:

Step 1: Set null and alternative hypotheses
The null and alternative hypotheses can be stated as below:

H_0: Opinion of all the groups is the same about the product with new features

and H_1: Opinion of all the groups is not the same about the product with new features

Step 2: Determine the appropriate statistical test
The appropriate test statistic is

$$\chi^2 = \sum_{\text{all cells}} \frac{(f_o - f_e)^2}{f_e}$$

with degrees of freedom = (number of rows – 1) × (number of columns – 1)

Step 3: Set the level of significance
α is taken as 0.05.

Step 4: Set the decision rule
For a given value of $\alpha = 0.05$, rules for acceptance or rejection of null hypothesis are as below:

If $\chi^2_{cal} > \chi^2_{critical}$, reject the null hypothesis, otherwise, do not reject the null hypothesis.

The critical χ^2 value is $\chi^2_{0.05,\,6} = 12.59$

where degrees of freedom = (number of rows – 1) (number of columns – 1)
= (4 – 1) × (3 – 1) = 6

Step 5: Collect the sample data
The sample data are given in Table 15.9.

Step 6: Analyse the data

The contingency table with observed and expected frequencies is shown in Table 15.10.

TABLE 15.10
Computation of expected frequencies for Example 15.4

Opinion \ *Consumers*	*Executives/ Officers*	*Business-men*	*Private consultants*
Preferred brand with new features	35(29.41)	25(38.13)	40(32.46)
Did not prefer brand with new features	30(32.06)	45(41.56)	34(35.38)
Preferred only a few new features	45(35.29)	50(45.75)	25(38.95)
Indifferent	25(38.24)	55(49.56)	50(42.20)

Expected frequency for cell (1, 1) can be calculated as below:

$$f_{e11} = \frac{RT \times CT}{N} = \frac{135 \times 100}{459} = 29.41$$

The procedure of computating chi-square statistic is indicated in Table 15.11

TABLE 15.11
Computation of chi-square statistic for Example 15.4

f_o	f_e	$\frac{(f_o - f_e)^2}{f_e}$
35	29.41	1.0617
30	32.06	0.1322
45	35.29	2.6691
25	38.24	4.5814
25	38.13	4.5192
45	41.56	0.2851
50	45.75	0.3944
55	49.56	0.5961
40	32.46	1.7504
34	35.38	0.0540
25	38.95	4.9987
50	42.20	1.4415
$\sum f_o = 420$		$\sum \frac{(f_o - f_e)^2}{f_e} = 22.48$

So, $\chi^2 = \sum \frac{(f_o - f_e)^2}{f_e} = 22.48$

Step 7: Arrive at a statistical conclusion and business implication

At 95% confidence level, the critical value obtained from the table is $\chi^2_{0.05,\,6} = 12.59$. χ^2 is calculated as 22.48, which is greater than the tabu-

Chi-Square Test: Executives/Officers, Businessmen, Private consultants

```
Expected counts are printed below observed counts
Chi-Square contributions are printed below expected counts

        Executives/                Private
          Officers Businessmen  consultants  Total
   1            35          25           40    100
             29.41       38.13        32.46
             1.062       4.519        1.750

   2            30          45           34    109
             32.06       41.56        35.38
             0.132       0.285        0.054

   3            45          50           25    120
             35.29       45.75        38.95
             2.669       0.394        4.999

   4            25          55           50    130
             38.24       49.56        42.20
             4.581       0.596        1.442

Total          135         175          149    459

Chi-Sq = 22.484, DF = 6, P-Value = 0.001
```

FIGURE 15.3
Minitab output for Example 15.4

lar value and falls in the rejection region. Hence, the null hypothesis is rejected and the alternative hypothesis is accepted.

There is enough evidence to indicate that the opinion of all the groups is not the same about the product with the new features. Hence, the company has to consider different groups and their needs separately. The Minitab output for Example 15.4 is shown in Figure 15.3

SELF-PRACTICE PROBLEMS

15B1. Use the following contingency table to test whether Variable 1 is independent of Variable 2. Take $\alpha = 0.05$

	Variable 1		
Variable 2	20	40	52
	23	43	45
	34	37	38

15B2. Use the following contingency table to test whether Variable 1 is independent of Variable 2. Take $\alpha = 0.01$.

	Variable 1			
	105	110	120	125
	100	95	103	112
Variable 2	110	98	92	105
	95	98	103	107

15B3. A firm is interested in knowing whether preference for its three brands: Brand 1, Brand 2, and Brand 3 is independent of type of occupation: government job, private job, and own business. Data collected from the consumers are given in the following contingency table. Use $\alpha = 0.05$ to test whether brand preference is independent of type of occupation.

Brand / *Type of occupation*	*Brand 1*	*Brand 2*	*Brand 3*
Government job	78	87	90
Private job	110	120	125
Own business	111	123	127

SUMMARY |

Statistical tests that do not require any prior information about the population are termed as non-parametric tests. This chapter focuses on only χ^2 (chi-square) distribution and the related χ^2 test. χ^2 distribution is the family of curves with each distribution being defined by the degree of freedom associated to it.

χ^2 test can be used for a variety of purposes. χ^2 test provides a platform that can be used to ascertain whether the theoretical probability distribution coincides with the empirical sample distribution. This is commonly known as χ^2 goodness-of-fit test. χ^2 test can also be used to test the independence of two variables. χ^2 test of independence uses contingency table for determining the independence of two variables. χ^2 test is also used for estimating the population variance. χ^2 test of homogeneity is used to determine whether two or more populations are homogenous with respect to some characteristics of interest.

KEY TERMS |

χ^2 distribution, 364
χ^2 goodness-of-fit test, 366
χ^2 test, 364
χ^2 test of independence, 369
χ^2 test of homogeneity, 374
Contingency table, 366

NOTE |

1. www.statebankofindia.com/viewsection.jsp?lang=0&id=0,11,670, accessed November 2008.

DISCUSSION QUESTIONS |

1. What is the importance of χ^2 distribution in decision making?
2. Explain the conceptual framework of χ^2 test with respect to expected and observed frequencies.
3. Under what circumstances is the χ^2 test used for decision making?
4. What is the χ^2 goodness-of-fit test and what are its applications in decision making?
5. Discuss the concept of contingency table.
6. Under what circumstances is the χ^2 test of independence used?
7. What is the χ^2 test of homogeneity and when do we use it?
8. Explain the differences and similarities between χ^2 test of independence and χ^2 test of homogeneity.
9. How can we use the χ^2 test for population variance?

NUMERICAL PROBLEMS |

1. Due to certain unknown reasons, employees of a company have started availing sick leave frequently. The management has a record of the number of employees who have availed sick leave in the past 6 months from a randomly selected department. Data are presented in the table below:

Months	Jul	Aug	Sep	Oct	Nov	Dec
Number of sick leaves	75	108	75	85	82	97

Use $\alpha = 0.05$ to determine whether the data fit a uniform distribution.

2. "Milky" is a newly launched mineral water company. The company wants to know whether the sale of mineral water bottles is uniformly distributed during a week. The company wants to know whether the demand for the number of mineral water bottles is the same for each day. The company collected data in terms of the number of bottles sold per day from a randomly selected departmental store. Data are presented in the table below:

Week days	Mon	Tue	Wed	Thu	Fri	Sat	Sun
Numbers of bottles sold	110	108	135	175	182	178	183

Use $\alpha = 0.01$ to determine whether sales are uniformly distributed over the week.

3. National Highway Ltd is a road construction company. The company was involved in the construction of a 230 km road with special features designed to prevent road accidents. The company collected data about the number of road accidents per month from a randomly selected 0.5 km stretch of the road. Data are presented in the table below:

Months	Jan	Feb	Mar	Apr	May	Jun
Numbers of accidents	49	58	63	48	65	59

Use $\alpha = 0.05$ to determine whether the number of accidents are uniformly distributed over the months.

4. The production manager of a printing paper company believes that at least 15% of the products are defective. For testing his belief, he takes a random sample of 100 products and finds that 20 pieces are defective. Taking 95% as the confidence level, use χ^2 goodness-of-fit test to test the hypothesis.

5. "Flat TV" is a company that produces coloured televisions with flat screens. The company wants to launch a new brand with special features, with a complete built-in audio-sound system in the television set. The company wants to estimate the potential market for this. The company has taken a random sample of 495 households who purchased "Flat TV" to ascertain the demand. These households are divided into three groups on the basis of income; middle-income group, upper-middle income group, and upper-income group. Consumer opinion is also divided into three categories: preferred brand with new features, did not prefer brand with new features and indifferent. The observations made by the researcher are given in the following table:

Income group / *Consumer Opinion*	*Middle-income group*	*Upper-middle income group*	*Upper-income group*	*Row total*
Preferred brand with new features	55	65	45	165
Did not prefer brand with new features	65	25	55	145
Indifferent	65	45	75	185
Column total	185	135	175	495

Determine whether consumer opinion is independent of income group. Use $\alpha = 0.05$.

6. A scientific calculator company has developed a new model. The company test marketed it in a particular geographic region. The consumer opinion (obtained through a randomly selected sample of 511 consumers) of different age groups is given in the following table:

Age group / *Consumer opinion*	*Above 15*	*Above 20*	*Above 25*	*Row Total*
Liked new brand	95	85	70	250
Did not like new brand	35	55	72	162
Indifferent	30	34	35	99
Column total	160	174	177	511

Examine whether the consumer opinion for a new brand is independent of age groups. Use $\alpha = 0.10$.

7. "XYZ pharmaceuticals" has launched a new drug to fight seasonal infections that affect people during winter. This drug is given to randomly selected 790 persons from a population of 4990 persons. The number of infections is shown in the table below:

Treatment / *Drug*	*Fever*	*No fever*	*Row total*
Drug given	40	750	790
No drug	300	3900	4200
Column total	340	4650	4990

Discuss the effectiveness of the new drug. Use $\alpha = 0.05$.

8. The personnel manager of an industrial goods company wants to know whether the years of experience is independent of professional positions occupied by various employees. He conducted a survey among 193 randomly selected employees. Data gathered are shown below:

Determine whether years of experience is independent of professional positions occupied by various employees. Use $\alpha = 0.05$.

Professional positions / *Experience*	*Assistant manager*	*Regional manager*	*Vice president*	*Row total*
Up to 7 years	25	15	3	43
Between 8 years and 14 years	20	40	8	68
Above 14 years	15	55	12	82
Column total	60	110	23	193

CASE STUDY

Case 15: *Indian Bicycle Industry: Second Largest in the World*

Introduction

Bicycles are an important mode of transportation in the rural areas of India. The country is the second-largest producer of bicycles in the world. The Indian bicycle market is primarily dominated by branded players. Low income and the large population had been responsible for the steady growth of the industry after independence. With the passage of time, the usage and importance of the bicycle has changed across urban India. By 2014–2015, the demand for bicycles is estimated to reach about 37.1 million units.[1]

Major Players in the Market

Hero Cycles Ltd, Tube Investment of India Ltd, Atlas Cycles Ltd, Avon Cycles, and Hamilton Ltd are the major players in the Indian bicycle industry. Hero Cycles Ltd is the market leader and started operations in Ludhiana (1956) with just 639 bicycles in a year. Hero Cycles now produces over 18,500 cycles per day, which is the highest in the world.[2] Tube Investment of India Ltd is the second largest player in the Indian bicycle market. TI Cycles President G. Hari says, "The company reckons repositioning its cycles on the health platform will be one of the ways to interest a consumer who has more choices and less time than before."[3] Atlas Cycles Ltd, Avon Cycles, and Hamilton Ltd are also key players in the market with 18%, 11% and 2% of the total market share, respectively.[1]

Changing Nature of the Bicycle Market

Indian bicycle brands are divided into two categories: standard and special. "Standard" caters to the needs of the common man while "special" caters to the needs and aspirations of urban and semi-urban kids and youths. The changing life style needs of consumers have lead to the growth of the "special" segment. Indian bicycle manufacturers are specifically targeting the health concerns of consumers in order to cater to the changing needs of consumers.

Sunil Kant Munjal, Managing Director and CEO Hero Cycles said, "There is certainly a change in the demand pattern linked to consumers' changing aspirations and choices. The bicycle industry (like many other industries) has also pooled together its resources to ensure that the benefits of these changes are shared by all concerned; and as a result of this, the marketers have promoted the fitness plank."[3] Indian bicycles manufacturers are hopeful that the fancy segment of bicycleswill grow by 70% by 2010. There is a thin line between standard and special segment in bicycles and standard customers will be asking for special features in his or her bicycle.

Like any other industry, the threat from Chinese manufacturers is a matter of concern for Indian bicycle manufacturers. Sunil Kant Munjal, Managing Director and CEO, Hero Cycles optimistically stresses on quality of Indian bicycles to counter-attack this threat. He says, "with protection being a thing of the past, the onslaught of the Chinese cycle-makers is surely a challenge. However, the Indian bicycle industry due to its inherent strength of quality, customer services, and fast launching of new products is all set to face the Chinese bicycle industry successfully."[3] However, the fact that China and Taiwan are the world leaders in the international bicycle market cannot be ignored. Indian players have to focus on research and design development in order to face the future challenges.

1. Suppose a leading bicycle manufacturer has divided its products into six brands. Price of these brands and unit sold for 2005 and 2006 are shown in Table 15.01. Use the techniques presented in this chapter and examine whether the distribution of unit sales has changed from 2005–2006.

TABLE 15.01
Prices of bicycle brands and units sold by a leading bicycle manufacturer in 2005 and 2006

Brand	*Price category (in rupees)*	*2005 (in thousands)*	*2006 (in thousands)*
1	Less than 1200	110	120
2	1200–1400	95	105
3	1400–1800	105	102
4	1800–2000	102	98
5	2000–2200	90	102
6	2200–2500	80	88

2. Suppose Hero Cycles has launched three brands—Hero Premium, Hero Passion, and Hero Smart. Let us assume the Vice President (Sales) of the Hero Cycles company wants to determine whether the sales of bicycle brands are independent of age group. He has appointed a marketing researcher for this purpose. This researcher has taken a random sample of the consumers who have purchased bicycles in 2005. The market researcher has conducted a survey for analysing the consumer preference for the three brands of bicycles. The researcher has also divided the age groups into four categories; 05 to 07, 07 to 09, 09 to 12, and 12 to 17. The observations made by the researcher are given in Table 15.02:

TABLE 15.02
Consumer preference for three leading bicycle brands

Age group \ Brand	*Hero premium*	*Hero passion*	*Hero smart*	*Row total*
05 to 07	20	25	32	77
07 to 09	10	20	22	52
09 to 12	15	12	10	37
12 to 17	25	22	23	70
Column total	70	79	87	236

Determine whether brand preference is independent of age group. Use $\alpha = 0.05$.

NOTES |

1. www.indiastat.com, accessed September 2008, reproduced with permission.
2. www.herocycles.com/about.php, accessed September 2008.
3. www.hindubusinessline.com/catalyst/2004/05/20/stories/2004052000120100.htm, accessed September 2008.

CHAPTER 16

Correlation and Simple Linear Regression Analysis

LEARNING OBJECTIVES

Upon completion of this chapter, you will be able to:

- Use the simple linear regression equation
- Understand the concept of measures of variation, coefficient of determination, and standard error of the estimate
- Understand and use residual analysis for testing the assumptions of regression
- Measure autocorrelation by using the Durbin-Watson statistic
- Understand statistical inference about slope, correlation coefficient of the regression model, and testing the overall model

STATISTICS IN ACTION: TATA STEEL

Tata Steel, established in 1907, is the world's sixth-largest steel company with an existing annual crude steel capacity of 30 million tonnes. It is Asia's first integrated steel plant and India's largest integrated private-sector steel company with operations in 26 countries and commercial presence in 50 countries.[1]

In line with its vision of becoming a global company with a 50 million tonne steel capacity by 2015, the company has expanded through the acquisition route. Tracing the company's history of inorganic growth in recent years, Tata Steel acquired Natsteel in February 2005 and Millennium Steel Company renaming it as Tata Steel Thailand in April 2006. In April 2007, the company acquired Corus, the second-largest steel producer in Europe and the ninth-largest steel producer in the world for USD 13.7 billion. With the acquisition of Corus, Tata Steel has become the world's sixth-largest steel company.[2] Tata Steel made its maiden entry in the list of Global 500 Companies released by *Fortune* in 2008. Table 16.1 shows the sales volumes and marketing expenses of Tata Steel from 1995 to 2007.

The sales volume of the company has increased over the years. The increase in marketing expenses (includes commissions, rebates, discounts, sales promotional expenses on direct selling agents, and entertainment expenses) could be one of the factors that have contributed to the increasing sales. A researcher may like to analyse the relationship between sales and marketing expenses. If there is a relationship, what is the proportion of change in sales that can be attributed to marketing expenses? How can we develop a model to predict the relationship between sales volume and marketing expenses? This chapter focuses on the answer to all these questions. The chapter focuses on the concept of simple linear regression equation measures of variation, coefficient of determination, standard error of the estimate and the use of residual analysis for testing the assumptions of regression. The chapter also deals with the concept of autocorrelation by using the Durbin-Watson statistic and explains the understanding of statistical inference about slope, correlation coefficient of the regression model, and testing the overall model.

TABLE 16.1
Sales volumes and marketing expenses of Tata Steel from 1995-2007

Year	*Sales (in million rupees)*	*Marketing expenses (in million rupees)*
1995	46,274.1	576.4
1996	58,541.2	571.5
1997	63,485.0	916.8
1998	64,292.7	781.4
1999	55,160.0	747.9
2000	61,562.8	895.6
2001	71,966.3	332.2
2002	75,954.1	709.3
2003	97,884.9	871.9
2004	119,178.8	819
2005	158,676.2	861.8
2006	171,329.4	807.5
2007	197,711.9	647.1

Source: Prowess (V. 3.1), Centre for Monitoring Indian Economy Pvt. Ltd, Mumbai, accessed September 2008, reproduced with permission.

16.1 MEASURES OF ASSOCIATION

Measures of association are statistics for measuring the strength of relationship between two variables.

Measures of association are statistics for measuring the strength of a relationship between two variables. This chapter focuses on only one measure of association, that is, **correlation** for two numerical variables.

16.1.1 Correlation

Correlation measures the degree of association between two variables.

Correlation measures the degree of association between two variables. For example, a marketing manager may be interested in knowing the degree of relationship between two variables: sales and advertisement. In this section, we focus on one method of determining correlation between two variables: Karl Pearson's coefficient of correlation.

16.1.2 Karl Pearson's Coefficient of Correlation

Karl Pearson's coefficient of correlation is a quantitative measure of the degree of relationship between two variables. Coefficient of correlation lies between +1 and -1.

Karl Pearson's coefficient of correlation is a quantitative measure of the degree of relationship between two variables. Suppose these variables are x and y, then Karl Pearson's coefficient of correlation is defined as

$$r = \frac{n\sum xy - \left(\sum x\right)\left(\sum y\right)}{\sqrt{n\left(\sum x^2\right) - \left(\sum x\right)^2}\sqrt{n\left(\sum y^2\right) - \left(\sum y\right)^2}}$$

The coefficient of correlation lies in between +1 and –1. Figure 16.1 explains how coefficient of correlation measures the extent of relationship between two variables. Figure 16.2 exhibits five examples of correlation coefficient.

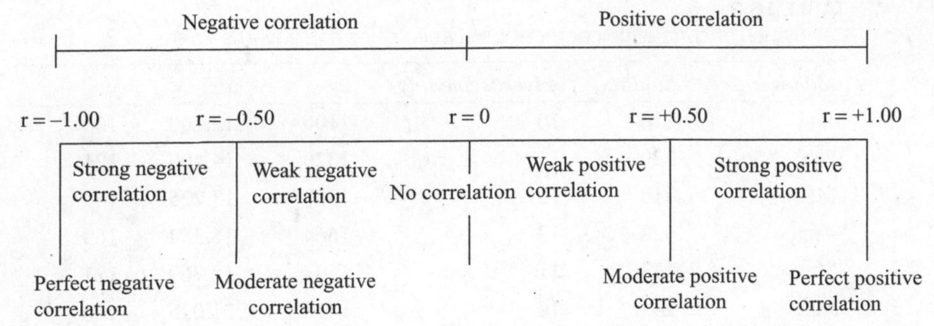

FIGURE 16.1
Interpretation of correlation coefficient

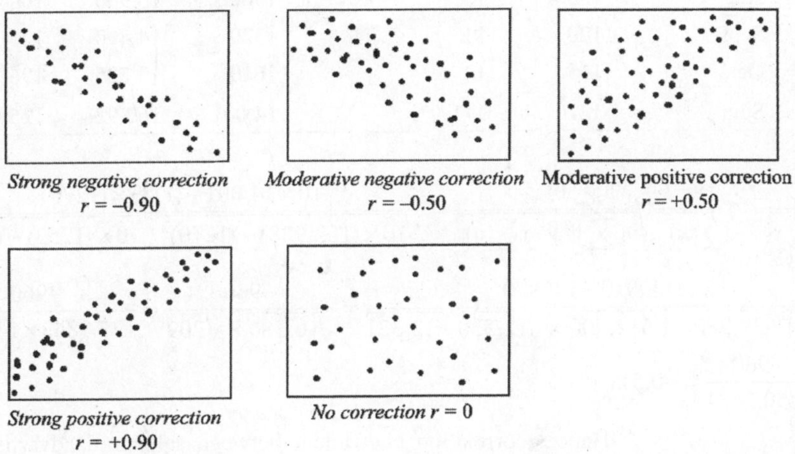

FIGURE 16.2
Five examples of correlation coefficient

Example 16.1

Table 16.2 shows the sales revenue and advertisement expenses of a company for the past 10 months. Find the coefficient of correlation between sales and advertisement.

TABLE 16.2
Sales and advertisement for 10 months

Month	*Jan*	*Feb*	*Mar*	*Apr*	*May*	*Jun*	*Jul*	*Aug*	*Sept*	*Oct*
Advertisement (in thousand rupees)	10	11	12	13	11	10	9	10	11	14
Sales (in thousand rupees)	110	120	115	128	137	145	150	130	120	115

Solution As discussed, the correlation coefficient between sales and advertisement can be obtained by applying Karl Pearson's coefficient of correlation formula as shown in Table 16.3.

$$r = \frac{n\sum xy - \left(\sum x\right)\left(\sum y\right)}{\sqrt{n\left(\sum x^2\right) - \left(\sum x\right)^2}\sqrt{n\left(\sum y^2\right) - \left(\sum y\right)^2}}$$

TABLE 16.3
Calculation of correlation coefficient between sales and advertisement

Month	*Sales (x)*	*Advertisement (y)*	*xy*	x^2	y^2
Jan	110	10	1100	12,100	100
Feb	120	11	1320	14,400	121
Mar	115	12	1380	13,225	144
Apr	128	13	1664	16,384	169
May	137	11	1507	18,769	121
June	145	10	1450	21,025	100
July	150	9	1350	22,500	81
Aug	130	10	1300	16,900	100
Sept	120	11	1320	14,400	121
Oct	115	14	1610	13,225	196
Sum	1270	111	14,001	162,928	1253

$$r = \frac{n\sum xy - (\sum x)(\sum y)}{\sqrt{n(\sum x^2) - (\sum x)^2}\sqrt{n(\sum y^2) - (\sum y)^2}} = \frac{10 \times 14{,}001 - (111) \times (1270)}{\sqrt{10 \times (162{,}928) - (1270)^2}\sqrt{10 \times (1253) - (111)^2}}$$

$$= \frac{140010 - 140970}{\sqrt{1{,}629{,}280 - 1{,}612{,}900} \times \sqrt{12{,}530 - 12{,}321}} = \frac{-960}{\sqrt{16{,}380} \times \sqrt{209}} = \frac{-960}{127.9843 \times 14.4568}$$

$$= \frac{-960}{1850.2434} = -0.51$$

Hence, correlation coefficient between sales and advertisement is –0.51. This indicates that sales and advertisement are negatively correlated to the extent of –0.51. We can conclude that an increase in the expenditure on advertisements will not result in an increase in sales.

Regression analysis is the process of developing a statistical model, which is used to predict the value of a dependent variable by at least one independent variable. In simple linear regression analysis, there are two types of variables. The variable whose value is influenced or to be predicted is called dependent variable and the variable which influences the value or is used for prediction is called independent variable.

In regression analysis, independent variable is also known as regressor or predictor, or explanatory while the dependent variable is also known as regressed or explained variable. In a simple linear regression analysis, only a straight line relationship between two variables is examined.

16.2 INTRODUCTION TO SIMPLE LINEAR REGRESSION

Regression analysis is the process of developing a statistical model, which is used to predict the value of a **dependent variable** by at least one **independent variable**. In simple linear regression analysis, there are two types of variables. The variable whose value is influenced or is to be predicted is called the **dependent variable** and the variable which influences the value or is used for prediction is called the **independent variable**. In regression analysis, the independent variable is also known as regressor or predictor or explanatory while the dependent variable is also known as regressed or explained variable. In a simple linear regression analysis, only a straight line relationship between two variables is examined. In fact, simple linear regression analysis is focused on developing a regression model by which the value of the dependent variable can be predicted with the help of the independent variable, based on the linear relationship between these two. This does not mean that the value of a dependent variable cannot be predicted with the help of a group of independent variables. This concept will be discussed in the next chapter (Chapter 17). In the next chapter, we will focus on non-linear relationship and regression models with more than one independent variable. Determining the impact of advertisement on sales is an example of simple linear regression. Determining the impact of other variables such as personal selling, distribution support and advertisement on sales in an example of multiple regression.

16.3 DETERMINING THE EQUATION OF A REGRESSION LINE

Simple linear regression is based on the slope–intercept equation of a line. This equation is given as

$$y = ax + b$$

where a is the slope of the line and b the y intercept of the line.

The straight line regression model with respect to population parameters β_0 and β_1 can be given as

$$y = \beta_0 + \beta_1 x$$

where β_0 is the population y intercept which represents the average value of the dependent variable when $x = 0$ and β_1 the slope of the regression line which indicates expected change in the value of y for per unit change in the value of x.

In case of specific dependent variable y_i

$$y_i = \beta_0 + \beta_1 x_i + \varepsilon_i$$

where β_0 is the population y intercept, β_1 the slope of the regression line, y_i the value of the dependent variable for ith value, x_i the value of the independent variable for ith value, and ε_i the random error in y for observation i (ε is the Greek letter *epsilon*).

ε is the error of the regression line in fitting the points of the regression equation. If a point is on the regression line, the corresponding value of ε is equal to zero. If the point is not on the regression line, the value of ε measures the error. This concept leads to two models in regression; deterministic model and probabilistic model.

ε is the error of the regression line in fitting the points of the regression equation. If a point is on the regression line, the corresponding value of ε is equal to zero. If the point is not on the regression line, the value of ε measures the error.

A deterministic model is given as

$$y = \beta_0 + \beta_1 x$$

A probabilistic model is given as

$$y = \beta_0 + \beta_1 x + \varepsilon$$

It can be noticed that in the deterministic model, all the points are assumed to be on the regression line and hence, in all the cases random error ε is equal to zero. Probabilistic model includes an error term which allows the value of y to vary for any given value of x. Figure 16.3 presents error in simple regression.

In order to predict the value of y, a researcher has to calculate the value of β_0 and β_1. In this process, difficulty occurs in terms of observing the entire population. This difficulty can be handled by taking a sample data and ultimately developing a sample regression model. This sample regression model can be used to make predictions about population parameters. So, β_0 and β_1 (population parameters) are estimated on the basis of the sample statistics b_0 and b_1. Thus, the simple regression equation (based on samples) is used to estimate the linear regression model.

It can be noticed that in the deterministic model, all the points are assumed to be on the regression line and hence, in all the cases random error ε is equal to zero. Probabilistic model includes an error term which allows the value of y to vary for any given value of x.

The equation of the simple regression line is given as

$$\hat{y} = b_0 + b_1 x$$

where b_0 is the sample y intercept which represent the average value of the dependent variable when $x = 0$ and b_1 the slope of the sample regression line, which indicates expected change in the value of y for per unit change in the value of x.

For determining the equation of the simple regression line, values of b_0 (sample y intercept) and b_1 (slope of the sample regression line) must be determined. Once b_0 and b_1 are determined, a researcher can plot a straight line and the comparison of this straight line with the original data can be performed very easily. The main focus of simple regression analysis is on finding the straight line that fits the data best. In other words, we need to minimize the

The main focus of the simple regression analysis is on finding the straight line that fits the data best. In other words, we need to minimize the difference between the actual values (y_i) and the regressed values ($\hat{y}_i$). This difference between the actual values (y_i) and the regressed values ($\hat{y}_i$) is referred to as residual (ε).

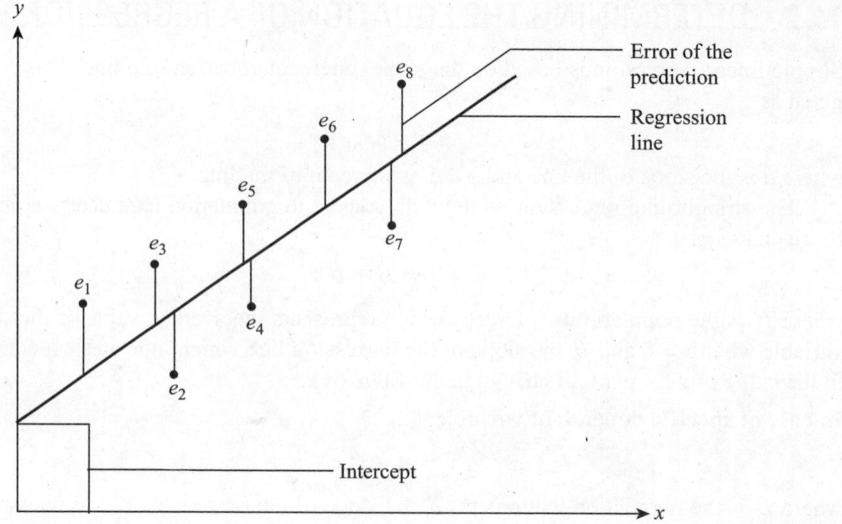

FIGURE 16.3
Error in simple regression

The sample data are used in the least squares method to determine the values of b_0 and b_1 that minimizes the sum of squared differences between the actual values (y_i) and the regressed values ($\hat{y}_i$).

difference between the actual values (y_i) and the regressed values ($\hat{y}_i$). This difference between the actual values (y_i) and the regressed values ($\hat{y}_i$) is referred to as **residual** (ε). In order to minimize this difference, a mathematical technique "**least-squares method**" developed by Carl Friedrich Gauss is applied. The sample data are used in the least squares method to determine the values of b_0 and b_1 that minimizes the sum of squared differences between the actual values (y_i) and the regressed values ($\hat{y}_i$). Least squares criterion is given by

$$\sum (y_i - \hat{y}_i)^2$$

where y_i is the actual value of y for observation i and ($\hat{y}_i$) the regressed (predicted) value of y for observation i.

An equation for computing the slope of a regression line is given below:

Slope of a regression line

$$b_1 = \frac{\sum (x-\bar{x})(y-\bar{y})}{\sum (x-\bar{x})^2} = \frac{\sum xy - n(\bar{x}\times\bar{y})}{\sum x^2 - n\bar{x}^2} = \frac{\sum xy - \frac{\left(\sum x\right)\left(\sum y\right)}{n}}{\sum x^2 - \frac{\left(\sum x\right)^2}{n}}$$

where

$$SS_{xy} = \sum (x-\bar{x})(y-\bar{y}) = \sum xy - \frac{\left(\sum x\right)\left(\sum y\right)}{n}$$

and

$$SS_{xx} = \sum (x-\bar{x})^2 = \sum x^2 - \frac{\left(\sum x\right)^2}{n}$$

$$b_1 = \frac{SS_{xy}}{SS_{xx}}$$

The sample y intercept of the regression line is given as

$$b_0 = \bar{y} - b_1\bar{x} = \frac{\sum y}{n} - b_1\frac{\left(\sum x\right)}{n}$$

It has already been discussed that in the estimation process through a simple linear regression, unknown population parameters, β_0 and β_1, are estimated by sample statistics b_0 and b_1. Figure 16.4 exhibits the summary of the estimation process for simple linear regression.

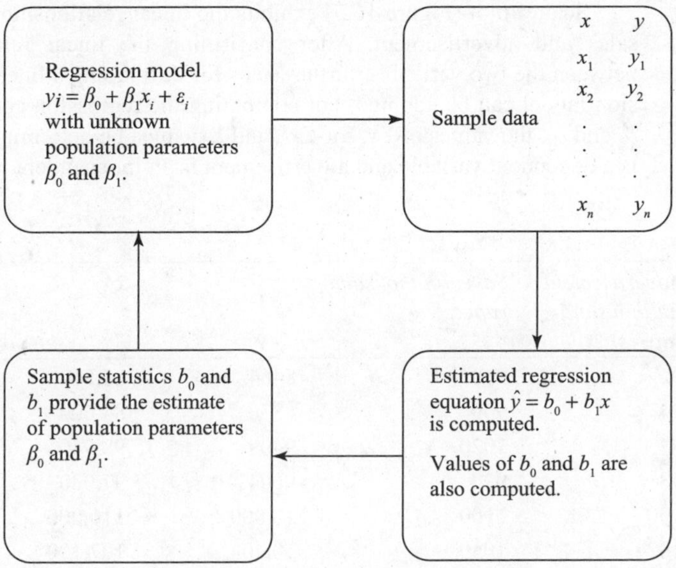

FIGURE 16.4
Summary of the estimation process for simple linear regression.

Example 16.2

A cable wire company has spent heavily on advertisements. The sales and advertisement expenses (in thousand rupees) for the 12 randomly selected months are given in Table 16.4. Develop a regression model to predict the impact of advertisement on sales.

TABLE 16.4
Sales and advertisement expenses (in thousand rupees) of a cable wire company

Months	*Advertisement (in thousand rupees)*	*Sales (in thousand rupees)*
Jan	92	930
Feb	94	900
Mar	97	1020
Apr	98	990
May	100	1100
Jun	102	1050
Jul	104	1150
Aug	105	1120
Sep	105	1130
Oct	107	1200
Nov	107	1250
Dec	110	1220

Solution

The first step is to determine whether the relationship between two variables is linear. For doing this, a scatter plot, drawn by any of the statistical software programs (MS Excel, Minitab, or SPSS) can be used. Figure 16.5 is the scatter plot produced using Minitab.

Scatter plot (Figure 16.5) exhibits the linear relationship between sales and advertisement. After confirming the linear relationship between the two variables, further steps for developing a linear regression model can be adopted. For computing the regression coefficient, b_0 and b_1, the values of Σx, Σy, Σx^2, and Σxy must be determined. Sales is a dependent variable and advertisement is an independent variable.

Computation of Σx, Σy, Σx^2, and Σxy for Example 16.2

Months	*Advertisement (in thousand rupees): x*	*Sales (in thousand rupees): y*	x^2	*xy*
Jan	92	930	8464	85,560
Feb	94	900	8836	84,600
Mar	97	1020	9409	98,940
Apr	98	990	9604	97,020
May	100	1100	10,000	110,000
Jun	102	1050	10,404	107,100
Jul	104	1150	10,816	119,600
Aug	105	1120	11,025	117,600
Sep	105	1130	11,025	118,650
Oct	107	1200	11,449	128,400
Nov	107	1250	11,449	133,750
Dec	110	1220	12,100	134,200
	$\Sigma x = 1221$	$\Sigma y = 13,060$	$\Sigma x^2 = 124,581$	$\Sigma xy = 1,335,420$

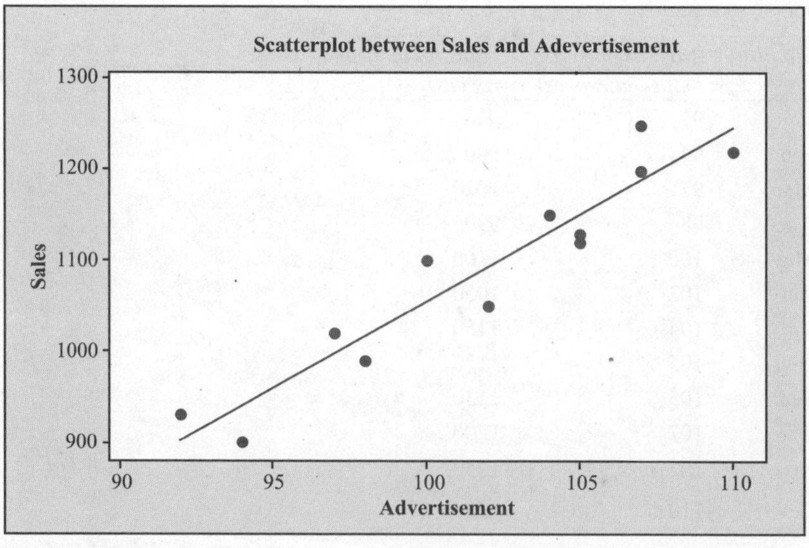

FIGURE 16.5
Scatter plot between sales and advertisement produced using Minitab

$$SS_{xy} = \sum xy - \frac{(\sum x)(\sum y)}{n} = 1{,}335{,}420 - \frac{(1221) \times (13{,}060)}{12} = 6565$$

$$SS_{xx} = \sum x^2 - \frac{(\sum x)^2}{n} = 124{,}581 - \frac{(1221)^2}{12} = 344.25$$

$$b_1 = \frac{SS_{xy}}{SS_{xx}} = \frac{6565}{344.25} = 19.0704$$

$$b_0 = \frac{\sum y}{n} - b_1\frac{(\sum x)}{n} = \frac{13{,}060}{12} - (19.0704) \times \frac{1221}{12} = -852.08$$

Equation of the simple regression line

$$\hat{y} = b_0 + b_1 x = (-852.08) + (19.07)x$$

This result indicates that for each unit increase in x (advertisement), y (sales) is predicted to increase by 19.07 units. b_0 (Sample y intercept) indicates the value of y when $x = 0$. It indicates that when there is no expenditure on advertisement, sales is predicted to decrease by 852.08 thousand rupees.

16.4 USING MS EXCEL FOR SIMPLE LINEAR REGRESSION

The first step is to select **Data** from the menu bar. Then select **Data Analysis** from this menu bar. The **Data Analysis** dialog box will appear on the screen as shown in Figure 16.6. From the **Data Analysis** dialog box, select **Regression** and click **OK** (Figure 16.6). The **Regression** dialog box will appear on the screen (Figure 16.7). Place independent variable in **Input X Range** and place dependent variable in **Input Y range**. Place appropriate confidence level in the **Confidence Level** box. In the **Residuals** box, check **Residuals, Residual Plots, Standardized Residuals**, and **Line Fit Plot**. From **Normal Probability**, select **Normal Probability Plots** and click **OK** (Figure 16.7). The MS Excel output (partial) as shown in (Figure 16.8) will appear on the screen.

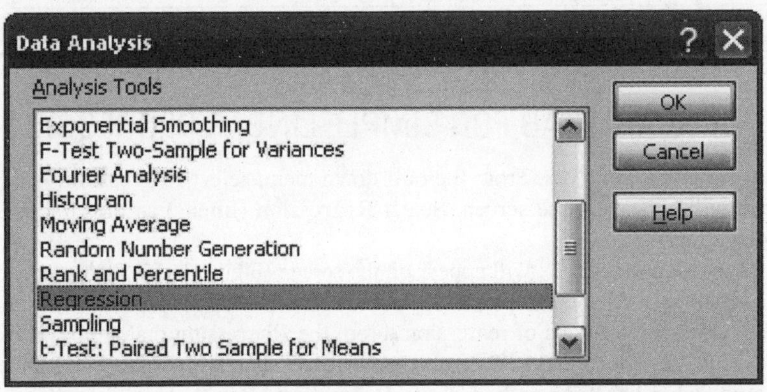

FIGURE 16.6
MS Excel Data Analysis dialog box

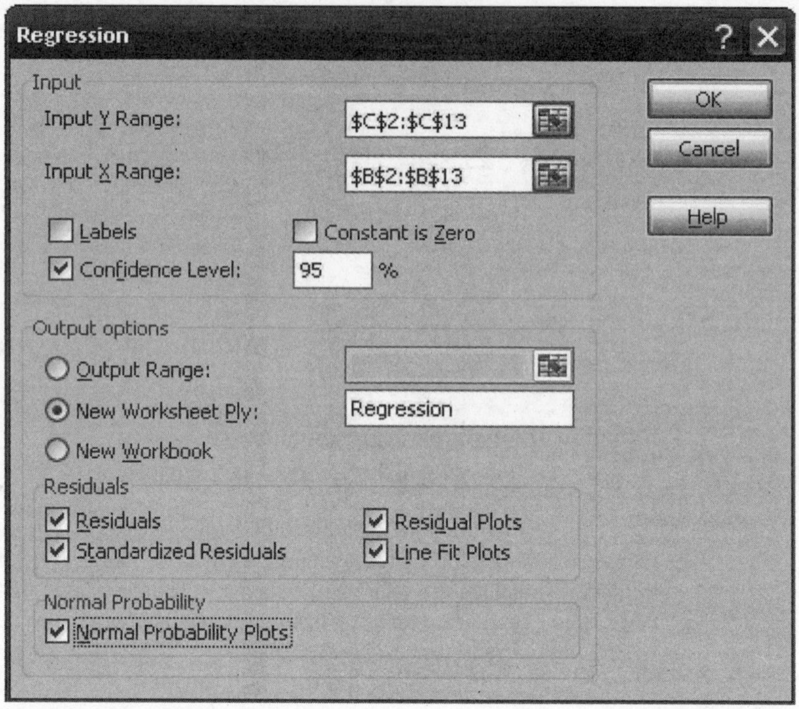

FIGURE 16.7
MS Excel Regression dialog box

	A	B	C	D	E	F	G
1	SUMMARY OUTPUT						
2							
3	*Regression Statistics*						
4	Multiple R	0.94916657					
5	R Square	0.90091719					
6	Adjusted R Square	0.8910089					
7	Standard Error	37.106884					
8	Observations	12					
9							
10	ANOVA						
11		*df*	*SS*	*MS*	*F*	*Significance F*	
12	Regression	1	125197.4582	125197.4582	90.92568	2.45382E-06	
13	Residual	10	13769.20842	1376.920842			
14	Total	11	138966.6667				
15							
16		*Coefficients*	*Standard Error*	*t Stat*	*P-value*	*Lower 95%*	*Upper 95%*
17	Intercept	-852.08424	203.7758887	-4.181477243	0.001883	-1306.125214	-398.0432684
18	X Variable 1	19.070443	1.999942514	9.535495577	2.45E-06	14.61429339	23.52659259

FIGURE 16.8
MS Excel output (partial) for Example 16.2

16.5 USING MINITAB FOR SIMPLE LINEAR REGRESSION

Select **Stat** from the menu bar. From the pull-down menu select **Regression.** Another pull-down menu will appear on the screen. Select **Regression (linear)** as the first option from this pull down menu.

The **Regression** dialog box will appear on the screen (Figure 16.9). Place dependent variable in the **Response** box and independent variable in the **Predictors** box. Minitab has the ability to open various dimensions of regression. From the **Regression** dialog box, click **Graph, Options**, **Result**, and **Storage**. The **Regression-Graphs** dialog box (Figure 16.10), the **Regression-Options** dialog box (Figure 16.11), the **Regression-Results** dialog box (Figure 16.12),

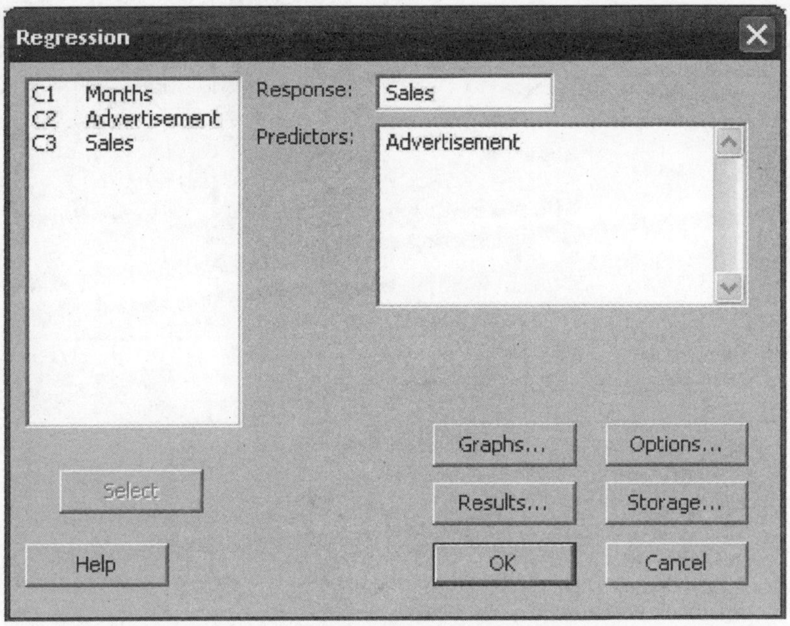

FIGURE 16.9
Minitab Regression dialog box

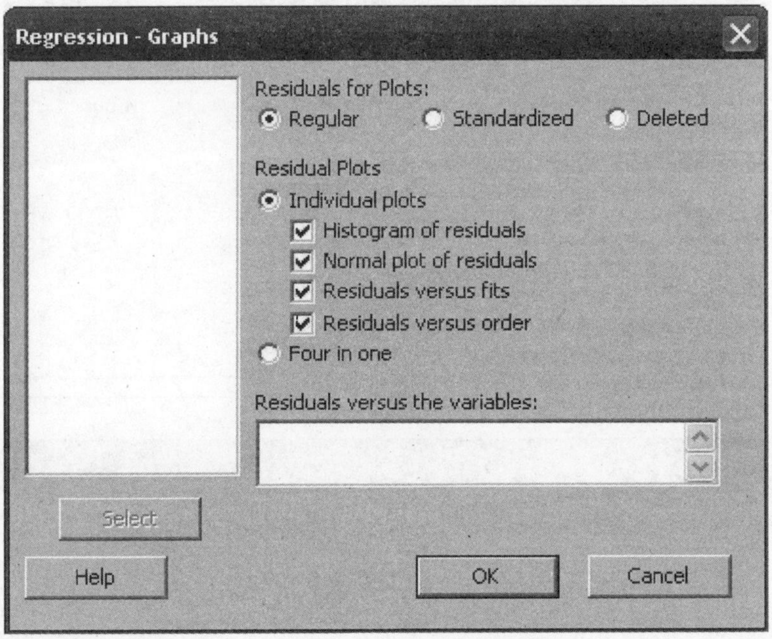

FIGURE 16.10
Minitab Regression-Graphs dialog box

and the **Regression-Storage** dialog box (Figure 16.13) will appear on the screen. The required output range can be selected from these dialog boxes. After selecting required options from each of the four dialog boxes, click **OK**. The **Regression** dialog box will reappear on the screen. Click **OK**. The partial regression output produced using Minitab will appear on the screen as shown in Figure 16.14.

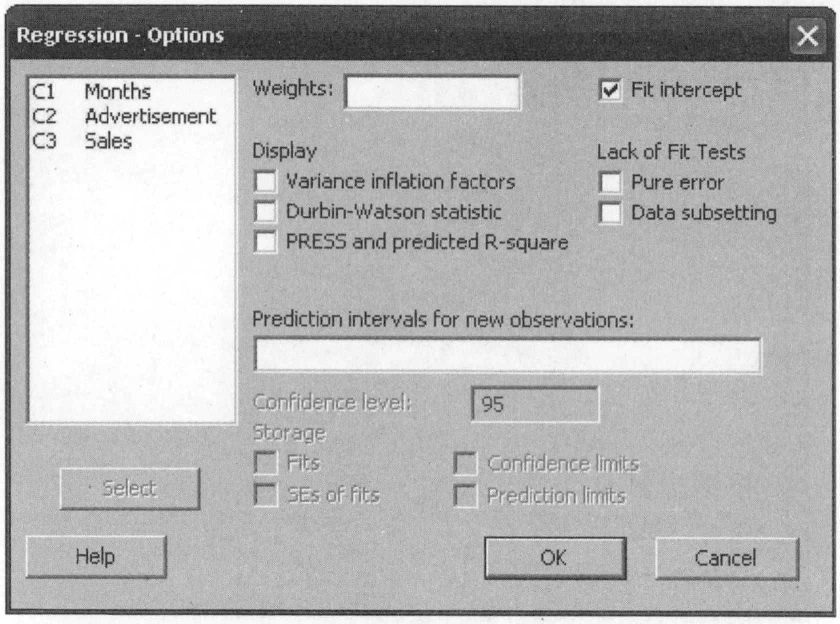

FIGURE 16.11
Minitab Regression-Options dialog box

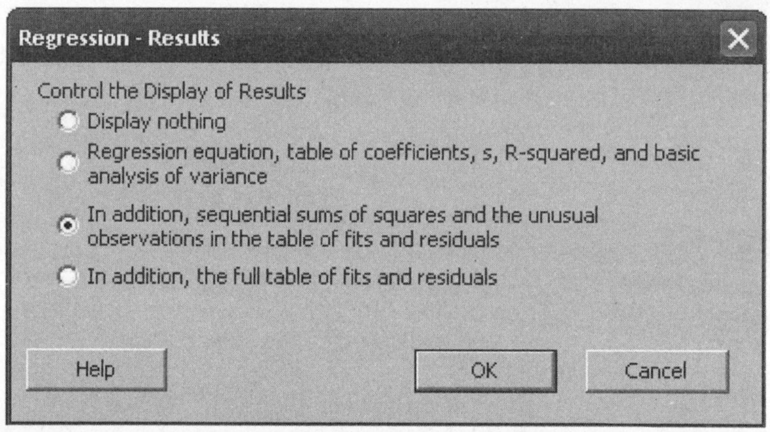

FIGURE 16.12
Minitab Regression-Results dialog box

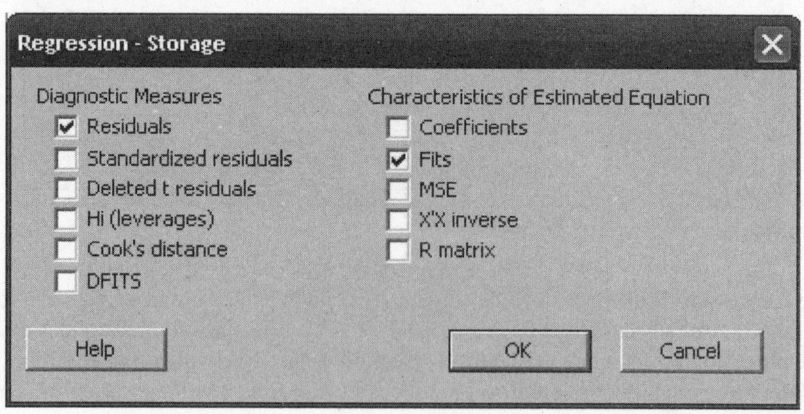

FIGURE 16.13
Minitab Regression-Storage dialog box

```
Regression Analysis: Sales versus Advertisement

The regression equation is
Sales = - 852 + 19.1 Advertisement


Predictor          Coef  SE Coef      T      P
Constant         -852.1    203.8  -4.18  0.002
Advertisement    19.070    2.000   9.54  0.000


S = 37.1069   R-Sq = 90.1%   R-Sq(adj) = 89.1%


Analysis of Variance

Source           DF      SS      MS      F      P
Regression        1  125197  125197  90.93  0.000
Residual Error   10   13769    1377
Total            11  138967
```

FIGURE 16.14 Minitab output (partial) for Example 16.2

16.6 USING SPSS FOR SIMPLE LINEAR REGRESSION

Select **Analyze** from the menu bar. Select **Regression** from the pull-down menu. Another pull-down menu will appear on the screen. Select **Linear** from this menu.

The **Linear Regression** dialog box will appear on the screen (Figure 16.15). Place dependent variable in the **Dependent** box and independent variable in the **Independent(s)** box. Like Minitab, SPSS also has the ability to open various dimensions of regression. From

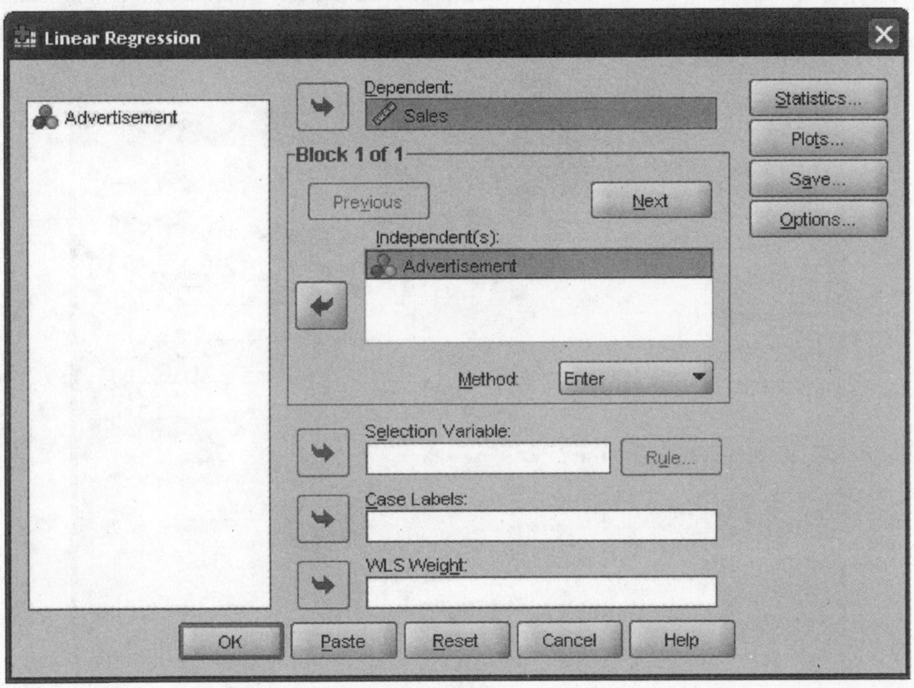

FIGURE 16.15 SPSS Linear Regression dialog box

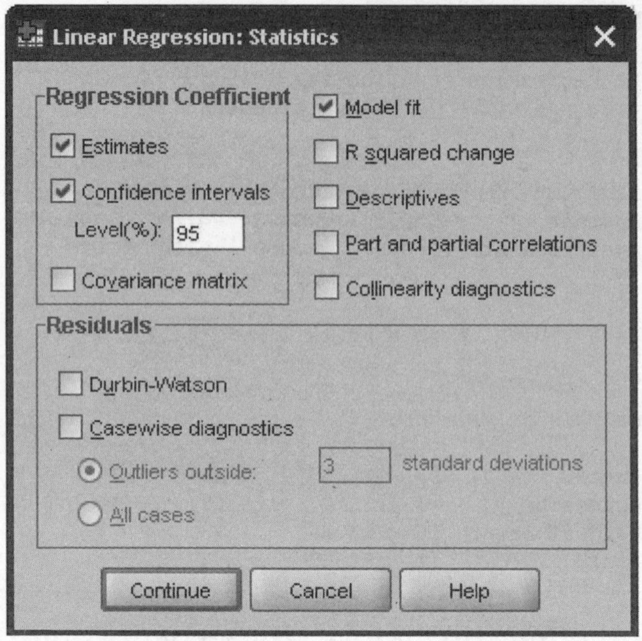

FIGURE 16.16
SPSS Linear Regression: Statistics dialog box

the **Regression** dialog box, click **Statistics**, **Plots**, **Options**, and **Save**. The **Linear Regression**: **Statistics** dialog box (Figure 16.16), the **Linear Regression**: **Plots** dialog box (Figure 16.17), the **Linear Regression**: **Options** dialog box (Figure 16.18), and the **Linear Regression**: **Save** dialog box (Figure 16.19) will appear on the screen. The required output range can be selected from these dialog boxes. After selecting required options from each of the four dialog boxes, click **OK**. The **Linear Regression** dialog box will reappear on the screen. Click **OK**. The regression output (partial) produced using SPSS will appear on the screen as shown in Figure 16.20.

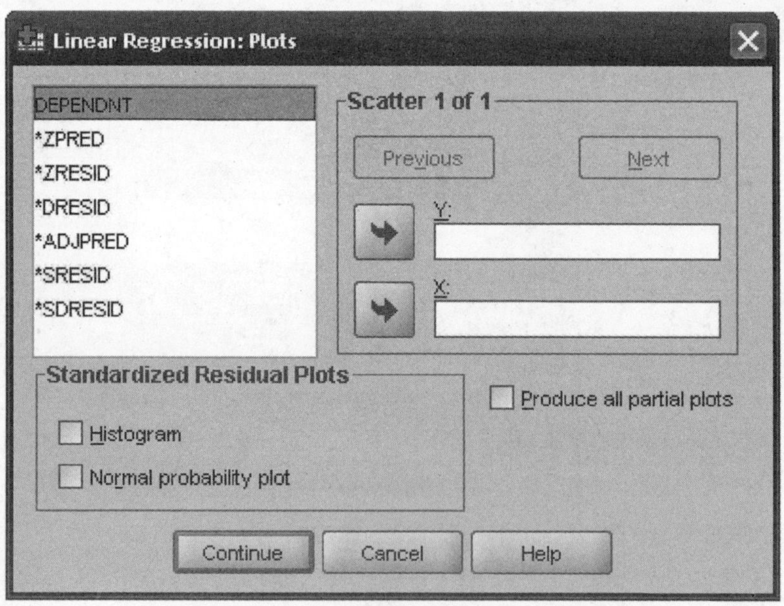

FIGURE 16.17
SPSS Linear Regression: Plots dialog box

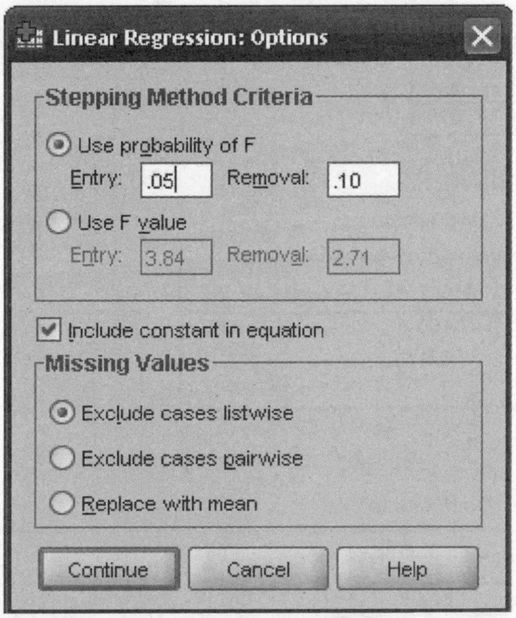

FIGURE 16.18
SPSS Linear Regression; Options dialog box

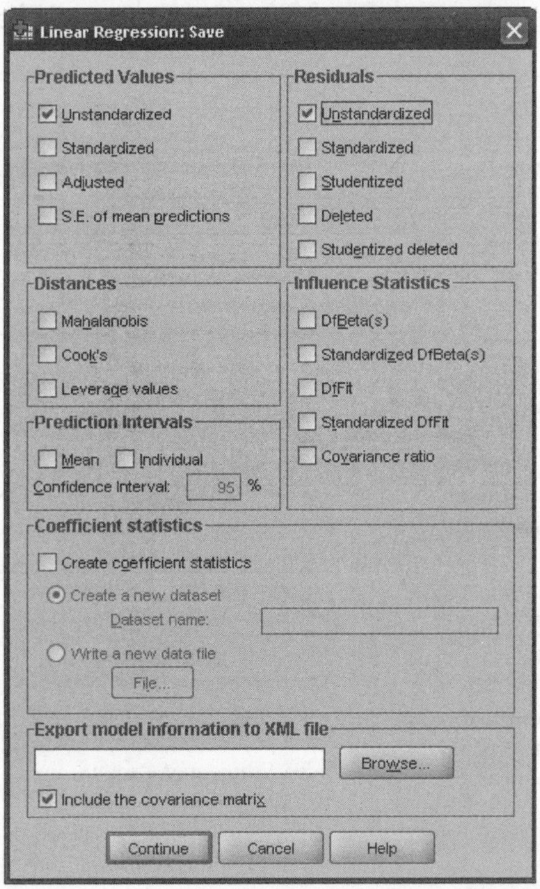

FIGURE 16.19
SPSS Linear Regression: Save dialog box

FIGURE 16.20
SPSS output (partial) for Example 16.2

Model Summary[b]

Model	R	R Square	Adjusted R Square	Std. Error of the Estimate
1	.949[a]	.901	.891	37.10688

a. Predictors: (Constant), Advertisement
b. Dependent Variable: Sales

ANOVA[b]

Model		Sum of Squares	df	Mean Square	F	Sig.
1	Regression	125197.458	1	125197.458	90.926	.000[a]
	Residual	13769.208	10	1376.921		
	Total	138966.667	11			

a. Predictors: (Constant), Advertisement
b. Dependent Variable: Sales

Coefficients[a]

Model		Unstandardized Coefficients		Standardized Coefficients	t	Sig.	95.0% Confidence Interval for B	
		B	Std. Error	Beta			Lower Bound	Upper Bound
1	(Constant)	-852.084	203.776		-4.181	.002	-1306.125	-398.043
	Advertisement	19.070	2.000	.949	9.535	.000	14.614	23.527

a. Dependent Variable: Sales

SELF-PRACTICE PROBLEMS

16A1. Taking x as the independent variable and y as the dependent variable from the following data, determine the line of regression. Let $\alpha = 0.05$.

x	12	21	28	25	32	42	43	39	55
y	14	22	12	28	35	37	32	44	49

16A2. Taking x as the independent variable and y as the dependent variable from the following data, construct a scatter plot and determine the line of regression. Let $\alpha = 0.05$.

x	13	18	25	30	22	24	40
y	14	16	17	18	15	22	38

16A3. A company believes that the number of salespersons employed is a good predictor of sales. The following table exhibits sales (in thousand rupees) and number of salespersons employed for different years.

Sales (in thousand rupees)	120	125	118	115	100	130	140	135	130	123
Number of sales-persons employed	10	15	12	18	20	21	22	20	15	19

Develop a simple regression model to predict sales based on the number of salespersons employed.

16A4. Cadbury India Ltd, incorporated in 1948, is the wholly owned Indian subsidiary of the UK-based Cadbury Schweppes Plc., which is a global confectionary and beverages company. Cadbury India Ltd operates in India in the segments of chocolates, sugar confectionary, and food drinks.[2] The following table provides data relating to the profit after tax and advertisement of Cadbury India Ltd from 1989–1990 to 2006–2007.

Year	Advertisement (in million rupees)	Profit after tax (in million rupees)
Mar 1990	73.4	55.5
Mar 1991	101.8	55.1
Mar 1992	99	37.1
Mar 1993	110.9	13.6
Mar 1994	145.3	86.8
Mar 1995	127.7	95.9
Mar 1996	190.3	200.8
Mar 1997	255.9	196.3
Mar 1998	296.2	185.7
Mar 1999	394.1	262.1
Mar 2000	532.8	367
Mar 2001	577.8	520.2
Mar 2002	731.6	574
Mar 2003	876.7	749.1
Mar 2004	904.4	456.5
Mar 2005	910.2	462.1
Mar 2006	958.2	459.6
Mar 2007	1218.5	688.1

Source: Prowess (V. 3.1), Centre for Monitoring Indian Economy Pvt. Ltd, Mumbai, accessed December 2008, reproduced with permission.

Develop a simple regression line to predict the profit after tax from advertisement.

16.7 MEASURES OF VARIATION

While developing a regression model to predict the dependent variable with the help of the independent variable, we need to focus on a few measures of variations. Total variation (SST) can be partitioned into two parts: variation which can be attributed to the relationship between x and y and unexplained variation. The first part of variation, which can be attributed to the relationship between x and y is referred to as explained variation or **regression sum of squares (SSR)**. The second part of variation, which is unexplained can be attributed to factors other than the relationship between x and y, and is referred to as **error sum of squares (SSE)**. So, in a simple linear regression model, total variation, that is, the total sum of squares is given as:

While developing a regression model to predict the dependent variable with the help of the independent variable, we need to focus on a few measures of variation. Total variation (SST) can be partitioned into two parts: variation which can be attributed to the relationship between x and y and unexplained variation.

Total sum of squares (SST) = Regression sum of squares (SSR) + Error sum of squares (SSE)

Total sum of squares (SST) is the sum of squared differences between each observed value (y_i) and the average value of y.

$$\text{Total sum of squares} = (\text{SST}) = \sum (y_i - \bar{y}_i)^2$$

The first part of variation, which can be attributed to the relationship between x and y, is referred to as explained variation or regression sum of squares (SSR). The second part of the variation, which is unexplained can be attributed to factors other than the relationship between x and y, and is referred to as error sum of squares (SSE).

Regression sum of squares (SSR) is the sum of squared differences between regressed (predicted) values and the average value of y.

$$\text{Regression sum of squares} = (\text{SSR}) = \sum (\hat{y}_i - \bar{y})^2$$

Error sum of squares (SSE) is the sum of squared differences between each observed value (y_i) and regressed (predicted) value of y.

$$\text{Error sum of squares} = (\text{SSE}) = \sum (y_i - \hat{y}_i)^2$$

Figure 16.21 exhibits the measures of variation in simple linear regression. It can be seen easily that Total sum of squares (SST) = regression sum of squares (SSR) + error sum of squares (SSE), that is, 138,966.6667(SST) = 125,197.4582 (SSR) +13,769.20842 (SSE)

Figure 16.22 is the ANOVA table produced using MS Excel exhibiting values of SST, SSR and SSE and other values for Example 16.2. The same ANOVA table as shown in Figure 16.22 can be obtained using Minitab and SPSS. Figures 16.14 and 16.20 exhibit this ANOVA table containing SST, SSR, and SSE values obtained from Minitab and SPSS, respectively.

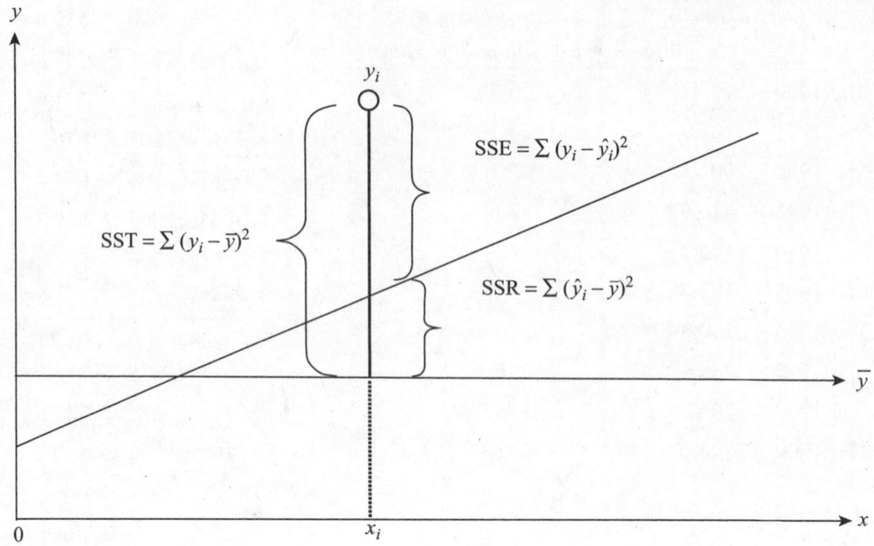

FIGURE 16.21
Measures of variation in simple linear regression

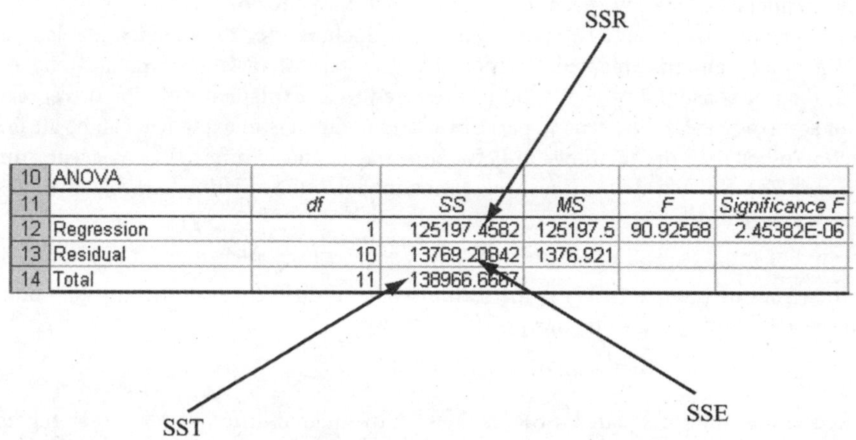

10	ANOVA					
11		*df*	*SS*	*MS*	*F*	*Significance F*
12	Regression	1	125197.4582	125197.5	90.92568	2.45382E-06
13	Residual	10	13769.20842	1376.921		
14	Total	11	138966.6667			

FIGURE 16.22
Values of SST, SSR and SSE for Example 16.2 produced using MS Excel

16.7.1 Coefficient of Determination

The ratio of regression sum of squares (SSR) to total sum of squares (SST) leads to a very important result which is referred to as coefficient of determination. The values of coefficient of determination ranges from 0 to 1.

Coefficient of determination is a very commonly used measure of fit for regression models and is denoted by r^2. The utility of SST, SSR, and SSE is limited in terms of direct interpretation. The ratio of regression sum of squares (SSR) to total sum of squares (SST) leads to a very important result, which is referred to as coefficient of determination. In a regression model, the coefficient of determination measures the proportion of variation in y that can be attributed to the independent variable x. The values of coefficient of determination range from 0 to 1. Coefficient of determination can be defined as

$$r^2 = \frac{\text{Regression sum of squares}}{\text{Total sum of squares}} = \frac{\text{SSR}}{\text{SST}}$$

In Example 16.2, coefficient of determination r^2 can be calculated as

$$r^2 = \frac{\text{Regression sum of squares}}{\text{Total sum of squares}} = \frac{\text{SSR}}{\text{SST}} = \frac{125{,}197.4582}{138{,}966.6667} = 0.9009$$

As discussed, the coefficient of determination leads to an important interpretation of the regression model. In Example 16.2, r^2 is calculated as 0.9009. This indicates that 90.09% of the variation in sales can be explained by the independent variable, that is, advertisement. This result also explains that 9.91% of the variation in sales is explained by factors other than advertisement.

Figures 16.23, 16.24, and 16.25, are the partial regression outputs from MS Excel, Minitab, and SPSS respectively, exhibiting coefficient of determination and other important results.

A residual is the difference between actual values (y_i) and the regressed values $(\hat{y}_i)$, determined by the regression equation for a given value of the independent variable x.

16.7.2 Standard Error of the Estimate

It has already been discussed that sample data are used in the least squares method to determine the values of b_0 and b_1 that minimize the sum of squared differences between the actual values

3	Regression Statistics	
4	Multiple R	0.949166574
5	R Square	0.900917186
6	Adjusted R Square	0.891008904
7	Standard Error	37.10688403
8	Observations	12

r^2(coefficient of determination)

S_{yx}(Standard error)

FIGURE 16.23
Partial regression output from MS Excel showing coefficient of determination and other important results

S_{yx}(Standard error)

```
S = 37.1069   R - Sq = 90.1%   R - Sq(adj) = 89.1%
```

r^2(Coefficient of determination)

FIGURE 16.24
Partial regression output from Minitab showing coefficient of determination and other important results

r^2(Coefficient of determination)

Model Summary[b]

Model	R	R Square	Adjusted R Square	Std. Error of the Estimate
1	.949[a]	.901	.891	37.10688

a. Predictors: (Constant), Advertisement

b. Dependent Variable: Sales

S_{yx} Standard error

FIGURE 16.25
Partial regression output from SPSS showing coefficient of determination and other important results

(y_i) and the regressed values $(\hat{y}_i)$. Variability in actual values (y_i) and the regressed values $(\hat{y}_i)$ is measured in terms of residuals. A residual is the difference between the actual values (y_i) and the regressed values $(\hat{y}_i)$, determined by the regression equation for a given value of the independent variable x. The residual around the regression line is given as

$$\text{Residual } (e_i) = \text{actual values } (y_i) - \text{regressed values } (\hat{y}_i)$$

Standard deviation measures the deviation of data around the arithmetic mean; similarly, standard error can be understood as the standard deviation around the regression line.

Variation of the dots around the regression line represents the degree of relationship between two variables x and y. Though the least squares method results in a regression line that fits the data best, all the observed data points do not fall exactly on the regression line. There is an obvious variation of the observed data points around the regression line. So, there is a need to develop a statistic which can measure the differences between the actual values (y_i) and the regressed values $(\hat{y}_i)$. **Standard error** fulfils this need. Standard error measures the amount by which the regressed values $(\hat{y}_i)$ are away from the actual values (y_i). This is the same as the concept of standard deviation that we developed in Chapter 11. Standard deviation measures the deviation of data around the arithmetic mean; similarly, standard error can be understood as the standard deviation around the regression line. Standard error of the estimate can be defined as

Standard error of the estimate

$$S_{yx} = \sqrt{\frac{SSE}{n-2}} = \sqrt{\frac{\sum (y_i - \hat{y}_i)^2}{n-2}}$$

A large standard error indicates a large amount of variation or scatter around the regression line and a small standard error indicates small amount of variation or scatter around the regression line. A standard error equal to zero indicates that all the observed data points fall exactly on the regression line.

where y_i is the actual value of y, for observation i and $\hat{y}_i$ the regressed (predicted) value of y, for observation i.

In the above formula, the numerator is the error sum of squares and the denominator is degrees of freedom determined by subtracting the number of parameters, β_0 and β_1, that is, 2 from sample size n. Hence, the degrees of freedom is $n - 2$. In Example 16.2, the sample size is 12 and there are two parameters. Therefore, the degrees of freedom can be computed as $12 - 2 = 10$. A large standard error indicates a large amount of variation or scatter around the regression line and a small standard error indicates small amount of variation or scatter around the regression line. A standard error equal to zero indicates that all the observed data points fall exactly on the regression line.

For Example 16.2, standard error of the estimate can be computed as

$$S_{yx} = \sqrt{\frac{SSE}{n-2}} = \sqrt{\frac{13769.20842}{12-2}} = 37.1068$$

Figures 16.23, 16.24, and 16.25 exhibit the computation of standard error from MS Excel, Minitab, and SPSS, respectively. Figure 16.26 is the scatter plot exhibiting actual values and the regression line for Example 16.2.

Table 16.5 indicates the predicted (regressed) values and residuals for Example 16.2.

Figures 16.27, 16.28, and 16.29 exhibit the computation of predicted values (fits) and residuals, and are the part of the regression outputs obtained from MS Excel, Minitab, and SPSS, respectively.

It is important to note that the sum of residuals is approximately zero. Ignoring some rounding off errors, the sum of residuals is always equal to zero. The logic behind this is very simple. Residuals are geometrically the vertical distance from the regression line to the data point. The regression equation used to solve for the intercept and slope place the line of

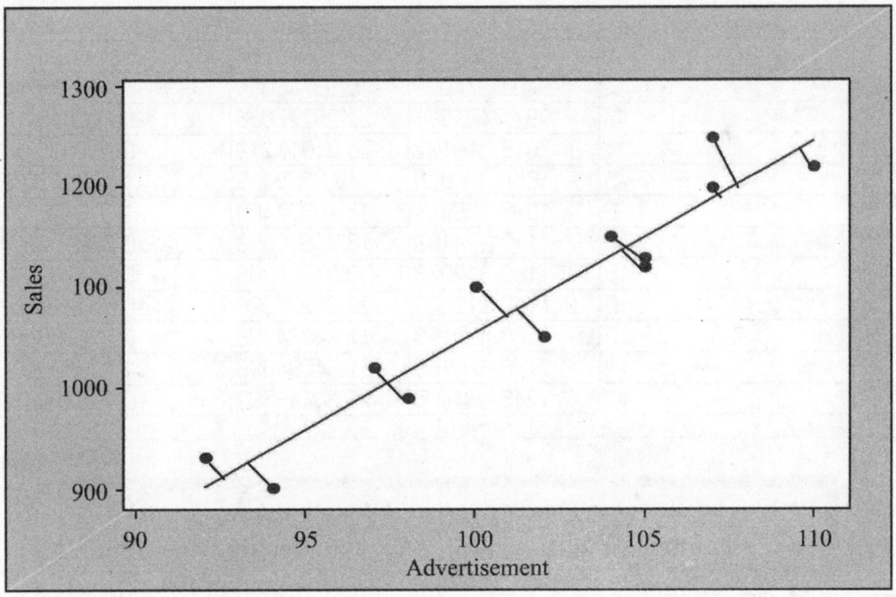

FIGURE 16.26
Scatter plot exhibiting actual values and the regression line for Example 16.2

TABLE 16.5
Predicted (regressed) values and residuals for Example 16.2

Months	*Advertisement (in thousand rupees): x*	*Sales (in thousand rupees): y*	*Predicted values:* $\hat{y}$	*Residuals* $(y_i - \hat{y}_i)$
Jan	92	930	902.39651	27.60349
Feb	94	900	940.53740	–40.53740
Mar	97	1020	997.74873	22.25127
Apr	98	990	1016.81917	–26.81917
May	100	1100	1054.96006	45.03994
Jun	102	1050	1093.10094	–43.10094
Jul	104	1150	1131.24183	18.75817
Aug	105	1120	1150.31227	–30.31227
Sep	105	1130	1150.31227	–20.31227
Oct	107	1200	1188.45316	11.54684
Nov	107	1250	1188.45316	61.54684
Dec	110	1220	1245.66449	–25.66449
				$\Sigma(y_i - \hat{y}_i) = 0.000$

24	Observation	Predicted Y	Residuals	Standard Residuals
25	1	902.3965142	27.60348584	0.780199711
26	2	940.5374001	-40.53740015	-1.145770793
27	3	997.7487291	22.25127088	0.62892184
28	4	1016.819172	-26.81917211	-0.758031447
29	5	1054.960058	45.0399419	1.273033046
30	6	1093.100944	-43.10094408	-1.218228172
31	7	1131.24183	18.75816993	0.530190964
32	8	1150.312273	-30.31227306	-0.856762324
33	9	1150.312273	-20.31227306	-0.574116967
34	10	1188.453159	11.54684096	0.326366098
35	11	1188.453159	61.54684096	1.739592883
36	12	1245.664488	-25.66448802	-0.725394838

FIGURE 16.27
MS Excel output (partial) exhibiting the computation of predicted values, residuals, and standardized residuals for Example 16.2

↓	C1-D	C2	C3	C4	C5
	Months	Advertisement	Sales	Residuals	Fits
1	Jan	92	930	27.6035	902.40
2	Feb	94	900	-40.5374	940.54
3	Mar	97	1020	22.2513	997.75
4	Apr	98	990	-26.8192	1016.82
5	May	100	1100	45.0399	1054.96
6	Jun	102	1050	-43.1009	1093.10
7	Jul	104	1150	18.7582	1131.24
8	Aug	105	1120	-30.3123	1150.31
9	Sep	105	1130	-20.3123	1150.31
10	Oct	107	1200	11.5468	1188.45
11	Nov	107	1250	61.5468	1188.45
12	Dec	110	1220	-25.6645	1245.66

FIGURE 16.28
Minitab output (partial) exhibiting the computation of residuals and predicted values (fits) for Example 16.2

It is important to note that the sum of residuals is approximately zero. The logic behind this is very simple. In fact, residuals are geometrically the vertical distance from the regression line to data point. The regression equation which we solve for intercept and slope, place the line of regression in the middle of all the data points. So, the vertical distance from the line to data points cancel each other and lead to a sum that is approximately equal to zero.

regression in the middle of all the data points. So, the vertical distance from the line to data points cancel each other and lead to a sum that is approximately equal to zero. Figure 16.26 is the scatter plot with residuals (distance between actual values and predicted values) for Example 16.2. This figure clearly exhibits that that the line of regression is geometrically in the middle of all the data points. This also exhibits that the residuals with (+) sign fall above the regression line and residuals with (–) sign fall below the regression line. Table 16.5 clearly exhibits that the sum of residuals is approximately equal to zero. Residuals are also used to find out outliers in the data set. This can be done by examining the scatter plot. Outliers can produce residuals with large magnitudes. These outliers may be due to misreported or miscoded data. These outliers sometimes pull the regression line towards them and hence put undue influence on the regression line. A researcher after identifying the origin of the outlier can decide whether the outlier should be retained in the regression equation or regression line should be computed without it.

	Advertisement	Sales	PRE_1	RES_1
1	92.00	930.00	902.39651	27.60349
2	94.00	900.00	940.53740	-40.53740
3	97.00	1020.00	997.74873	22.25127
4	98.00	990.00	1016.81917	-26.81917
5	100.00	1100.00	1054.96006	45.03994
6	102.00	1050.00	1093.10094	-43.10094
7	104.00	1150.00	1131.24183	18.75817
8	105.00	1120.00	1150.31227	-30.31227
9	105.00	1130.00	1150.31227	-20.31227
10	107.00	1200.00	1188.45316	11.54684
11	107.00	1250.00	1188.45316	61.54684
12	110.00	1220.00	1245.66449	-25.66449

FIGURE 16.29 SPSS output (partial) exhibiting the computation of predicted values (fits) and residuals for Example 16.2

SELF-PRACTICE PROBLEMS

16B1. Compute the value of r^2 and standard error for Problem 15A1. Discuss the meaning of the value of r^2 and standard error in developing a regression model.

16B2. Compute the value of r^2 and standard error for Problem 15A2. Discuss the meaning of the value of r^2 and standard error in developing a regression model.

16B3. Nestle India Ltd, incorporated in 1959, is one of the largest dairy product companies in India. The company has a broad product portfolio comprising of milk products, beverages, prepared dishes, cooking aids, chocolate, and confectionary. The following table shows the net sales (in million rupees) and salaries and wages (in million rupees) of the company for different quarters.

Develop a simple regression line to predict net sales from salaries and wages. Discuss the meaning of the value of r^2 and standard error in developing a regression model.

Quarters	*Net sales (in million rupees)*	*Salaries and wages (in million rupees)*
Jun 1999	3639	220
Sep 1999	4169	211
Dec 1999	4230	277
Mar 2000	3478	243
Jun 2000	4198	259
Sep 2000	4694	264
Dec 2000	4403	284
Mar 2001	4516	308
Jun 2001	4683	314
Sep 2001	5329.6	329.7
Dec 2001	4681	369
Mar 2002	5300.1	321.9
Jun 2002	5114.8	336.9
Sep 2002	5235	500.3
Dec 2002	4827.1	303
Mar 2003	5981	388.3

Quarters	*Net sales (in million rupees)*	*Salaries and wages (in million rupees)*
Jun 2003	5460.7	380.7
Sep 2003	5326.1	390.7
Dec 2003	5305	424.4
Mar 2004	6200.7	413.1
Jun 2004	5143.9	412
Sep 2004	5600.2	390.3
Dec 2004	5719.8	427.1
Mar 2005	6135.3	443.9
Jun 2005	6157.7	475
Sep 2005	6248.1	473.3
Dec 2005	6227.9	440.7
Mar 2006	6759.2	542.8
Jun 2006	6811.8	565.1
Sep 2006	7226.6	566.1
Dec 2006	7362.9	569.4
Mar 2007	8630.8	1399.8

Source: Prowess (V. 3.1), Centre for Monitoring Indian Economy Pvt. Ltd, Mumbai, accessed September 2008, reproduced with permission.

16.8 STATISTICAL INFERENCE ABOUT SLOPE, CORRELATION COEFFICIENT OF THE REGRESSION MODEL, AND TESTING THE OVERALL MODEL

If there is no serious violation of the assumption of linear regression and residual analysis has confirmed that the straight line regression model is appropriate, an inference about the linear relationship between variables can be obtained on the basis of sample results.

16.8.1 *t* Test for the Slope of the Regression Line

After verifying the assumptions of linear regression, a researcher has to determine whether a significant linear relationship exists between the independent variable x and the dependent variable y. This is determined by performing a hypothesis test to check whether the population slope (β_1) is zero. The hypotheses for the test can be stated as below:

$$H_0: \beta_1 = 0 \text{ (There is no linear relationship)}$$
$$H_1: \beta_1 \neq 0 \text{ (There is a linear relationship)}$$

Any negative or positive value of the slope will lead to the rejection of the null hypothesis and acceptance of the alternative hypothesis (as the above hypothesis test is two-tailed). A negative value of the slope indicates the inverse relationship between the independent variable x and the dependent variable y. This means that larger values of the independent variable x are related to smaller values of the dependent variable y and vice versa. In order to test the significant positive relationship between the two variables, the null and alternative hypotheses can be stated as below:

$$H_0: \beta_1 = 0 \text{ (There is no linear relationship)}$$
$$H_1: \beta_1 > 0 \text{ (There is a positive relationship)}$$

To test the significant negative relationship between the two variables, the null and alternative hypotheses can be stated as below:

$$H_0: \beta_1 = 0 \text{ (There is no linear relationship)}$$
$$H_1: \beta_1 > 0 \text{ (There is a negative relationship)}$$

The test statistic *t* can be defined as below:

$$t = \frac{b_1 - \beta_1}{S_b}$$

where

$$S_b = \frac{S_{yx}}{\sqrt{SS_{xx}}}$$

$$S_{yx} = \sqrt{\frac{\text{SSE}}{n-2}}$$

$$SS_{xx} = \sum x^2 - \frac{\left(\sum x\right)^2}{n}$$

The test statistic t follows a t distribution with $n - 2$ degrees of freedom and β_1 as the hypothesized population slope.

On the basis of above formula, the t statistic for Example 16.2 can be computed as

$$t = \frac{b_1 - \beta_1}{S_b} = \frac{19.07 - 0}{\dfrac{37.1068}{\sqrt{344.25}}} = 9.53$$

where $$SS_{xx} = \sum x^2 - \frac{\left(\sum x\right)^2}{n} = 124{,}581 - \frac{(1221)^2}{12} = 344.25$$

$$S_{yx} = \sqrt{\frac{\text{SSE}}{n-2}} = \sqrt{\frac{13{,}769.20842}{12-2}} = 37.1068$$

Figures 16.30(A), 16.30(B), and 16.30(C) show the computation of the t statistic using MS Excel, Minitab, and SPSS, respectively.

Using the p value from the above outputs, the null hypothesis is rejected and the alternative hypothesis is accepted at 5% level of significance. In light of the positive value of b_1 and p value = 0.000, it can be concluded that a significant positive linear relationship exists between the independent variable x and the dependent variable y.

16.8.2 Testing the Overall Model

The F test is used to determine the significance of overall regression model in regression analysis. More specifically, in case of a multiple regression model, the F test determines that at least one of the regression coefficients is different from zero. In case of simple

16		Coefficients	Standard Error	t Stat	P-value	Lower 95%	Upper 95%
17	Intercept	−852.0842411	203.7758887	−4.18148	0.001883	−1306.125214	−398.043
18	X Variable 1	19.07044299	1.999942514	9.535496	2.45E–06	14.61429339	23.52659

← t statistic

FIGURE 16.30(A)
Computation of the t statistic for Example 16.2 using MS Excel

Predictor	Coef	SE Coef	T	P
Constant	-852.1	203.8	-4.18	0.002
Advertisement	19.070	2.000	9.54	0.000

← t statistic

FIGURE 16.30(B)
Computation of t statistic for Example 16.2 using Minitab

Model		Unstandardized Coefficeints		Standardized Coefficeints			95% Confidence Interval for B	
		B	Std. error	Beta	t	Sig.	Lower Bound	Upper Bound
1	(Constant)	−852.084	203.776		−4.181	.002	−1306.125	−398.043
	advertisement	19.070	2.000	.949	9.535	.000	14.614	23.527

← t statistic

FIGURE 16.30(C)
Computation of the t statistic for Example 16.2 using SPSS

regression, where there is only one predictor the F test for overall significance tests the same phenomenon as the t-statistic test in simple regression. The F statistic can be defined as the ratio of regression mean square (MSR) and error mean square (MSE).

***F* statistic for testing the slope**

$$F = \frac{MSR}{MSE}$$

where $MSR = \frac{SSR}{k}$, $MSE = \frac{SSE}{n-k-1}$, and k is the number of independent (explanatory) variables in regression model (In case of simple regression $k = 1$).
The F statistic follows the F distribution with degrees of freedom k and $n - k - 1$.

Figures 16.31(A), 16.31(B), and 16.31(C) illustrate the computation of F statistic using MS Excel, Minitab, and SPSS, respectively. On the basis of the p value obtained from the outputs, it can be concluded that expenses on advertisement is significantly (at 5% level of significance) related to sales. If we compare the p value obtained from Figures 16.30 and 16.31, we find that the p values are the same in both the cases.

16.8.3 Estimate of Confidence Interval for the Population Slope (β_1)

Estimate of confidence interval for the population slope (β_1) provides an alternative approach to test the linear relationship between the independent variable x and the dependent variable y. This can be done by determining whether the hypothesized value of β_1 ($\beta_1 = 0$) is within the interval or outside the interval. For understanding the concept, we will take Example 16.2 again. Confidence interval for the population slope (β_1) is defined as

10	ANOVA					
11		*df*	*SS*	*MS*	*F*	*Significance F*
12	Regression	1	125197.4582	125197.5	90.92568	2.45382E-06
13	Residual	10	13769.20842	1376.921		
14	Total	11	138966.6667			

F statistic

FIGURE 16.31(A)
Computation of the *F* statistic from MS Excel for Example 16.2

```
Analysis of Variance

Source           DF      SS      MS      F      P
Regression        1  125197  125197  90.93  0.000
Residual Error   10   13769    1377
Total            11  138967
```

F statistic

FIGURE 16.31(B)
Computation of *F* statistic for Example 16.2 using Minitab

ANOVA[b]

Model		Sum of Squares	df	Mean Square	F	Sig.
1	Regression	125197.5	1	125197.458	90.926	.000[a]
	Residual	13769.208	10	1376.921		
	Total	138966.7	11			

a. Predictors: (Constant), advertisement

b. Dependent Variable: sales

F statistic

FIGURE 16.31(C) Computation of *F* statistic for Example 16.2 using SPSS

Estimate of confidence interval for the population slope (β_1)

$$b_1 \pm t_{n-2} S_b$$

From the outputs given in Figures 16.8, 16.14, and 16.20, the following values can be obtained

$$b_1 = 19.0704 \quad n = 12, \quad \text{and} \quad S_b = 1.9999$$

From the table, for $\alpha = 0.05 \left(\frac{\alpha}{2} = 0.025\right)$ and degrees of freedom $= n - 2 = 10$, the value of t is 2.2281. By substituting all these values in the formula of confidence interval estimate for the population slope, we get

$$b_1 \pm t_{n-2} S_b = 19.0704 \pm 2.2281\ (1.9999) = 19.0704 \pm (4.4559)$$

So, the upper limit is 23.5263 (19.0704 + 4.4559) and the lower limit is 14.6145 (19.0704 − 4.4559).

So, population slope β_1 is estimated with 95% confidence to be in the interval of 14.6145 and 23.5263. Hence,

$$14.6145 \le \beta_1 \le 23.5263$$

The upper limit as well as the lower limit is greater than 0 and population slope lies in between these two limits. So, it can be concluded with 95% confidence that there exists a significant linear relationship between advertisement and sales. If the interval would have included 0, the inference would have been different. In this situation, the existence of a significant linear relationship between the two variables could not have been concluded. This confidence interval also indicates that for each thousand rupee increase in the advertisement expenditure, sales will increase by at least ₹14,614.50 but less than ₹23,526.30 (with 95% confidence).

16.8.4 Statistical Inference about Correlation Coefficient of the Regression Model

From Figures 16.8, 16.14, and 16.20, it can be seen that the value of correlation coefficient is a part of the output. **Correlation coefficient (*r*)** measures the strength of the relationship between two variables. Correlation coefficient (*r*) specifies whether there is a statistically significant relationship between two variables. The *t* test can be applied to check this. The population correlation coefficient (ρ) can be hypothesized as equal to zero. In this case, the null and the alternative hypotheses can be stated as follows:

Correlation coefficient (*r*) measures the strength of the relationship between two variables.

$$H_0: \rho = 0$$
$$H_1: \rho \ne 0$$

In order to test the significant relationship between two numerical variables statistically, the t statistic can be defined as

The t statistic for testing the statistical significant correlation coefficient

$$t = \frac{r - \rho}{\sqrt{\frac{1 - r^2}{n - 2}}}$$

where

$$r = +\sqrt{r^2}, \quad \text{if } b_1 \geq 0$$

$$r = -\sqrt{r^2}, \quad \text{if } b_1 < 0$$

The t statistic follows the t distribution with $n - 2$ degrees of freedom. From Figures 16.8, 16.14, and 16.20, the following values can be obtained:

$$r = 0.9491 \quad \text{and} \quad b_1 = 19.0704$$

By substituting these values in the above formula, we get

$$t = \frac{0.9491 - 0}{\sqrt{\frac{1 - 0.9009}{10}}} = 9.53$$

From the table, for $a = 0.05 \left(\frac{a}{2} = 0.025\right)$ and degrees of freedom $= n - 2 = 10$, the value of t is 2.2281. The calculated value of t is 9.53. The calculated value of t (= 9.53) > tabular value of t (= 2.2281). Hence, the null hypothesis is rejected and the alternative hypothesis is accepted. So, it can be concluded there is a significant relationship between two variables. It is important to note that the value of t is the same as calculated in Figures 16.8, 16.14, and 16.20.

The statistical significance of correlation coefficient can be directly inferred using Minitab and SPSS.

SUMMARY |

Regression analysis is the process of developing a statistical model which is used to predict the value of a dependent variable by at least one independent variable. In simple linear regression analysis, there are two types of variables. The variable whose value is influenced or is to be predicted is called dependent variable and the variable which influences the value or is used for prediction is called independent variable. Simple linear regression is based on the slope–intercept equation of a line. In regression analysis, sample regression model can be used to make predictions about population parameters. So, β_0 and β_1 (population parameters) are estimated on the basis of sample statistics b_0 and b_1. For this purpose, least squares method is used. Least-squares method use the sample data to determine the values of b_0 and b_1 that minimizes the sum of squared differences between actual values (y_i) and the regressed values ($\hat{y}_i$). Once line of regression is developed, by substituting the required variable values and values of regression coefficient, regressed values, or predicted values can be obtained.

While developing a regression model to predict the dependent variable with the help of independent variable, we need to focus on a few measures of variations. Total variation (SST) can be partitioned in two parts: variation which can be attributed to the relationship between x and y and unexplained variation. First part of variation which can be attributed to the relationship between x and y is referred to as explained variation or regression sum of squares (SSR). The second part of the variation, which is unexplained can be attributed to factors other than the relationship between x and y is referred to as error sum of squares (SSE). Coefficient of determination is also a very important phenomenon in regression analysis. Coefficient of determination measures the proportion of variation in y that can be attributed to independent variable x. A residual is the difference between actual values (y_i) and the regressed values ($\hat{y}_i$) and is used to examine the magnitude of the errors produced by the regression model. In addition, residual analysis can be used to verify the assumptions of regression analysis. These assumptions are (1) linearity of the regression model (2) constant error variance (homoscedasticity) (3) independence of error (4) normality of error.

After verifying the assumptions of linear regression, a researcher determines whether a significant linear relationship between independent variable x and dependent variable y exists. This can be done by performing a hypothesis test to check whether the population slope (β_1) is zero or not. The t test is applied for this purpose. A significant p value for the t statistic establishes the linear relationship between the independent variable x and the dependent variable y. In regression analysis, the F test is used to determine the significance of the overall regression model. More specifically, in case of a multiple regression model, the F test determines that at least one of the regression coefficients is different from zero. In case of simple regression, where predictor is only one, the F test for overall significance tests the same phenomenon as the t-statistic test in simple regression. Apart from coefficient of determination (r^2), regression analysis also provides the correlation coefficient (r), which measures the strength of the relationship between two variables. Correlation coefficient (r) specifies whether there is a significant relationship between two variables. Again t statistic is used to determine the significant relationship between two variables.

KEY TERMS |

NOTES |

1. www.tatasteel.com/Company/profile.asp,accessed September 2008.
2. Prowess (V. 3.1), Centre for Monitoring Indian Economy Pvt. Ltd, Mumbai, accessed September 2008, reproduced with permission.

DISCUSSION QUESTIONS |

1. What is the conceptual framework of simple linear regression and how can we use it for marketing decision making?
2. Regression analysis is an important tool for forecasting. Explain this statement.
3. Explain the concept of regression sum of squares (SSR) and error sum of squares (SSE) in a regression model.
4. Explain the concept of coefficient of determination and standard error of the estimate in a regression model.
5. How can we use the t test for determining the statistical significance of the slope of the regression line?
6. How can we test the significance of the overall regression model?
7. How can we use correlation coefficient (r) for determining the statistical significance of the relationship between two variables in a regression model?

NUMERICAL PROBLEMS |

1. A large supermarket has adopted a new strategy to increase its sales. It has adopted a few consumer friendly policies and is using video clips of 15 minutes to propagate the new policies. The following table provides data about the number of video clips shown in a randomly selected day and the sales turnover of the supermarket in the corresponding day.

Days	*No. of video clips shown*	*Sales (in thousand rupees)*
1	25	150
2	25	210
3	25	140
4	35	180
5	35	230
6	35	270
7	40	310
8	40	330
9	40	300
10	50	270
11	50	310
12	50	340

(1) Develop a regression model to predict sales from the number of video clips shown.
(2) Calculate the coefficient of determination and interpret it.
(3) Calculate the standard error of the estimate.

2. The HR manager of a multinational company wants to determine the relationship between experience and income of employees. The following data are collected from 14 randomly selected employees.

Employees	*Experience (in years)*	*Income (in thousand rupees)*
1	2	30
2	4	40
3	5	45
4	6	35
5	7	50
6	8	60
7	9	70
8	10	65
9	12	60
10	13	55
11	14	75
12	15	80
13	16	85
14	18	75

(1) Develop a regression model to predict income based on the years of experience.
(2) Calculate the coefficient of determination and interpret it.
(3) Calculate the standard error of the estimate.
(4) Predict the income of an employee who has 22 years of experience.

3. A dealer of a motorcycle company believes that there is a positive relationship between the number of salespeople employed and the increase in the sales of bikes. Data for 14 randomly selected weeks are given in the following table.

Weeks	*No. of salespeople employed*	*Sales (in units)*
1	17	34
2	14	39
3	25	60
4	40	80
5	15	38
6	18	50
7	13	35
8	11	25
9	27	51
10	12	29
11	38	89
12	36	85
13	41	90
14	28	63

(1) Develop a regression model to predict sales from the number of salespeople employed.
(2) Calculate the coefficient of determination and interpret it.
(3) Calculate the standard error of the estimate.
(4) Predict sales when number of salespeople employed are 100.

4. For Problem 3, estimate the following:
(1) *t* Test for the slope of the regression line
(2) Testing the overall model
(3) Statistical inference about the correlation coefficient of the regression model

5. For Problem 2, estimate the following:
(1) *t* Test for the slope of the regression line

(2) Testing the overall model
(3) Statistical inference about the correlation coefficient of the regression model

6. The municipal corporation of a newly formed capital city is planning to launch a new water supply scheme for the city. For this, the Municipal Corporation has considered past data on water consumption in 16 randomly selected weeks of the previous summer and the average temperature in the corresponding week. On the basis of the data, the corporation wants to estimate the water requirement for the current year. Data are given as below:

Weeks	*Temperature (in °F)*	*Water consumption (in million gallons)*
1	37	150
2	38	160
3	39	168
4	35	145
5	34	140
6	33	142
7	37	155
8	40	165
9	41	167
10	42	175
11	44	185
12	42	180
13	40	170
14	38	165
15	42	170
16	44	173

(1) Develop a regression model to predict water consumption from the temperature of the corresponding week.
(2) Calculate the coefficient of determination and interpret it.
(3) Calculate the standard error of the estimate.
(4) Predict the water consumption when temperature is 47 °F.
(5) *t* Test for the slope of the regression line
(6) Test the overall model
(7) Statistical inference about correlation coefficient of the regression model

7. A company is concerned about the high rates of absenteeism among its employees. It organized a training programme to boost the morale of its employees. The following table gives the number of days that sixteen randomly selected employees have received training, and the number of days they have availed leave.

Employee	*Training days*	*Leave*
1	12	20
2	14	18
3	16	16
4	13	22
5	11	18
6	10	19
7	15	14
8	17	12
9	18	10
10	19	9
11	17	11
12	15	16
13	13	19
14	15	17
15	17	15
16	12	21

(1) Develop a regression model to predict leaves based on training days.
(2) Calculate the coefficient of determination and state its interpretation.
(3) Calculate the standard error of the estimate.
(4) Predict the leaves when training days are 25.
(5) *t* Test for the slope of the regression line
(6) Test the overall model
(7) Statistical inference about the correlation coefficient of the regression model
(8) Calculate Durbin–Watson statistic and interpret it.

CASE STUDY |

Case 16: *Boom in the Indian Cement Industry: ACC's Role*

Introduction

The Indian cement industry was delicensed in 1991. After China, India is the second largest producer of cement. The estimated demand for cement is 265 million metric tonnes by 2114–2115.[1] The Indian cement industry saw a growth of 11.6% in 2006. The financial year 2007 also witnessed a muted growth of 7.1%. In order to meet the increasing demand, several manufacturers have embarked on significant capacity expansion plans.[2]

ACC—A Pioneer in the Indian Cement Industry

Associated Cement Companies Ltd (ACC) came into existence in 1936, after the merger of 10 companies belonging to four important business groups: Tatas, Khataus, Killick Nixon, and F E Dinshaw. The Tata group was associated with ACC since its inception. It sold

14.45% of its share to Gujarat Ambuja Cements Ltd between 1999 and 2000. After this strategic alliance, Gujarat Ambuja Cements Ltd became the largest single stakeholder in ACC. In 2005, ACC entered into a strategic relationship with the Holcim group of Switzerland, a world leader in cement as well as a large supplier of concrete, aggregates, and certain construction related services. These global strategic alliances have strengthened the company.[3]

ACC is India's foremost manufacturer of cement and concrete. The company has a wide range of operations with 14 modern cement factories, more than 30 ready mix concrete plants, 20 sales offices, and several zonal offices. ACC's research and development facility has a unique track record of innovative research, product development, and specialized consultancy services. ACC's brand name is synonymous with cement and it enjoys a high level of equity in the Indian market.[4]

The Impact of Cartelization

Cartelization is one of the major problems in the cement industry. Cartelization takes place when dominant players of the industry join together to control prices and limit competition. In the Indian market, manufacturers have been known to enter into agreements to artificially limit the supply of cement so that the price remains high. When markets are not sufficiently regulated, large companies may be tempted to collude instead of competing with each other. For example, in May 2006, the Competition Council of Romania imposed a combined fine of 27 million euros on France's Lafarge, Switzerland's Holcim, and Germany's Carpatcement for being involved in the cement cartel in the Romanian market. These three companies share 98% of Romanian cement capacity.[4] The government should take appropriate action to check acts of cartelization.

Escalating input and fuel costs have forced manufacturers to tap new sources of supply and increase the quest for alternative fuels and raw materials. The cement industry is faced with the challenge of optimizing the utilization of scare basic raw materials and fossil fuels while simultaneously protecting the environment and maintaining emission levels within acceptable limits. It is vital for the cement industry to achieve high levels of energy utilization efficiencies and to sustain them continuously.[2] Table 16.01 exhibits sales turnover and advertisement expenses of ACC from 1995 to 2007.

TABLE 16.01
Sales turnover and advertisement expenditure of ACC from 1995–2007

Year	*Sales (in million rupees)*	*Advertisement (in million rupees)*
1995	20,427.0	58.6
1996	23,294.6	72.6
1997	24,510.5	122.3
1998	23,731.1	61.9
1999	25,858.3	144.7
2000	26,792.2	132.2
2001	29,361.2	172.6
2002	32,260.0	184.3
2003	33,718.8	259.8
2004	39,003.7	334.8
2005	45,498.0	321.9
2006	37,235.1	336.0
2007	64,680.6	442.3

1. Develop an appropriate regression model to predict sales from advertisement.
2. Calculate the coefficient of determination and state its interpretation.
3. Calculate the standard error of the estimate.
4. Predict the sales when advertisement is ₹ 500 million.
5. Test the significance of the overall model.

NOTES

1. www.indiastat.com, accessed September 2008, reproduced with permission.
2. Prowess (V. 3.1), Centre for Monitoring Indian Economy Pvt. Ltd, accessed September 2008, reproduced with permission.
3. www.acclimited.com/newsite/heritage.asp, accessed September 2008.
4. www.acclimited.com/newsite/corprofile.asp, accessed September 2008.
5. ww.businesstoday.org/index.php?option=com_content&task=viewed&id=370&Itemi, accessed September 2008.

CHAPTER 17

Multivariate Analysis I: Multiple Regression Analysis

LEARNING OBJECTIVES

Upon completion of this chapter, you will be able to:

- Understand the applications of the multiple regression model
- Understand the concept of coefficient of multiple determination, adjusted coefficient of multiple determination, and standard error of the estimate
- Understand and use residual analysis for testing the assumptions of multiple regression
- Use statistical significance tests for the regression model and coefficients of regression
- Test portions of the multiple regression model
- Understand non-linear regression model and the quadratic regression model, and test the statistical significance of the overall quadratic regression model
- Understand the concept of model transformation in regression models
- Understand the concept of collinearity and the use of variance inflationary factors in multiple regression
- Understand the conceptual framework of model building in multiple regression

STATISTICS IN ACTION: HINDUSTAN PETROLEUM CORPORATION LTD (HPCL)

Indian oil major Hindustan Petroleum Corporation Ltd (HPCL) secured the 336th rank in the *Fortune* 500 list of 2007. It operates two major refineries producing a wide variety of petroleum fuels and specialities, one in Mumbai and the other in Vishakapatṇam. HPCL also owns and operates the largest lube refinery in the country producing lube-based oils of international standard. This refinery accounts for over 40% of India's *total lube*-based oil production.[1]

HPCL has a number of retail outlets launched on the platform of "outstanding customer and vehicle care" and are branded as "Club HP" outlets. In order to cater to the rural market, HPCL operates through *"Hamara Pump"* which not only sells fuel but also sells seeds, pesticides, and fertilizers to farmers through *"Kisan Vikas Kendras"* set up at selected *"Hamara Pump"* outlets. The company remains firmly committed to meeting fuel requirements without compromising on quality and quantity, extending the refining capacity through brown field and green field additions, maintaining, and improving its market share across segments and its growth in the organic and inorganic growth areas of the value chain. With the growth in the Indian economy and rising income levels, the demand for petroleum products is expected to increase presenting opportunities to companies in the petroleum and refining segment.[2]

>>>

Table 17.1 presents compensation paid to employees, marketing expenses, travel expenses, and the profit after tax for HPCL from 2000 to 2007. Suppose that a researcher wants to develop a model to find the impact of marketing expenses, travel expenses, and profit after tax on compensation paid to employees. How can this be done? This chapter provides the answer to this question. Additionally, residual analysis, statistical significance test for regression model and coefficients of regression, non-linear regression model, model transformation, collinearity, variance inflationary factors, and model building in multiple regression are also discussed in this chapter.

TABLE 17.1
Compensation to employees, marketing expenses, travel expenses, and profit after tax (in million rupees) from 2000–2007 for HPCL

Year	*Compensation to employees (in million rupees)*	*Marketing expenses (in million rupees)*	*Travel expenses (in million rupees)*	*Profit after tax (in million rupees)*
2000	4023.6	152.9	301.7	10,574.1
2001	5323.7	1129.7	291.5	10,880.1
2002	5603.0	1437.2	335.6	7876.8
2003	5528.9	2148.0	377.4	15,373.6
2004	5753.2	3159.4	559.7	19,039.4
2005	7179.5	4626.0	593.9	12,773.3
2006	6956.2	5646.7	680.9	4055.5
2007	7312.3	7289.8	742.5	15,709.8

Source: Prowess (V. 3.1), Centre for Monitoring Indian Economy Pvt. Ltd, Mumbai, accessed September 2008, reproduced with permission.

17.1 INTRODUCTION

Regression analysis with two or more independent variables or at least one non-linear predictor is referred to as multiple regression analysis

In Chapter 16, we discussed simple regression analysis in which one independent variable, x, was used to predict the dependent variable, y. Even in case of more than one independent variable, a best-fit model can be developed using regression analysis. So, **regression analysis** with two or more independent variables or at least one non-linear predictor is referred to as multiple regression analysis. In this chapter, we will discuss cases of multiple regression analysis where several independent or explanatory variables can be used to predict one dependent variable.

17.2 THE MULTIPLE REGRESSION MODEL

In Chapter 16, we discussed that a probabilistic regression model for any specific dependent variable y_i can be given as

$$y_i = \beta_0 + \beta_1 x_i + \varepsilon_i$$

where β_0 is the population y intercept, β_1 the slope of the regression line, y_i the value of the dependent variable for ith value, x_i the value of the independent variable for ith value, and ε_i the random error in y for observation i (ε is the Greek letter epsilon).

In case of multiple regression analysis where more than one explanatory variable is used, the above probabilistic model can be extended to more than one independent variable and the probabilistic model can be presented as multiple probabilistic regression model as:

Multiple regression model with *k* independent variables

$$y_i = \beta_0 + \beta_1 x_1 + \beta_2 x_2 + \beta_3 x_3 + \cdots + \beta_k x_k + \varepsilon_i$$

where y_i is the value of the dependent variable for *i*th value, β_0 the *y* intercept, β_1 the slope of *y* with independent variable x_1 holding variables $x_2, x_3, \ldots, x_k$ constant, β_2 the slope of *y* with independent variable x_2 holding variables $x_1, x_3, \ldots, x_k$ constant, β_3 the slope of *y* with independent variable x_3 holding variables $x_1, x_2, x_4, \ldots, x_k$ constant, β_k the slope of *y* with independent variable x_k holding variables $x_1, x_2, x_3, \ldots, x_{k-1}$ constant, and ε the random error in *y* for observation *i* (ε is the Greek letter epsilon).

In a multiple regression analysis, β_i is the slope of *y* with independent variable x_i holding all other independent variables constant. This is also referred to as a **partial regression coefficient for the independent variable x_i**. β_i indicates increase in dependent variable *y*, for unit increase in independent variable x_i holding all other independent variables constant.

In a multiple regression analysis, β_i is slope of *y* with independent variable x_i holding all other independent variables constant. This is also referred to as partial regression coefficient for independent variable x_i.

In order to predict the value of *y*, a researcher has to calculate the values of $\beta_0, \beta_1, \beta_2, \beta_3, \ldots, \beta_k$. Like simple regression analysis, challenges lie in observing the entire population. So, sample data is used to develop a sample regression model. This sample regression model can be used to make predictions about population parameters. So, an equation for estimating *y* with the sample information is given as

Multiple regression equation

$$\hat{y} = b_0 + b_1 x_1 + b_2 x_2 + b_3 x_3 + \cdots + b_k x_k$$

where $\hat{y}$ is the predicted value of dependent variable *y*, b_0 the estimate of regression constant, b_1 the estimate of regression coefficient β_1, b_2 the estimate of regression coefficient β_2, b_3 the estimate of regression coefficient β_3, b_k the estimate of regression coefficient β_k, and *k* the number of independent variables. Figure 17.1 shows the summary of the estimation process for multiple regression.

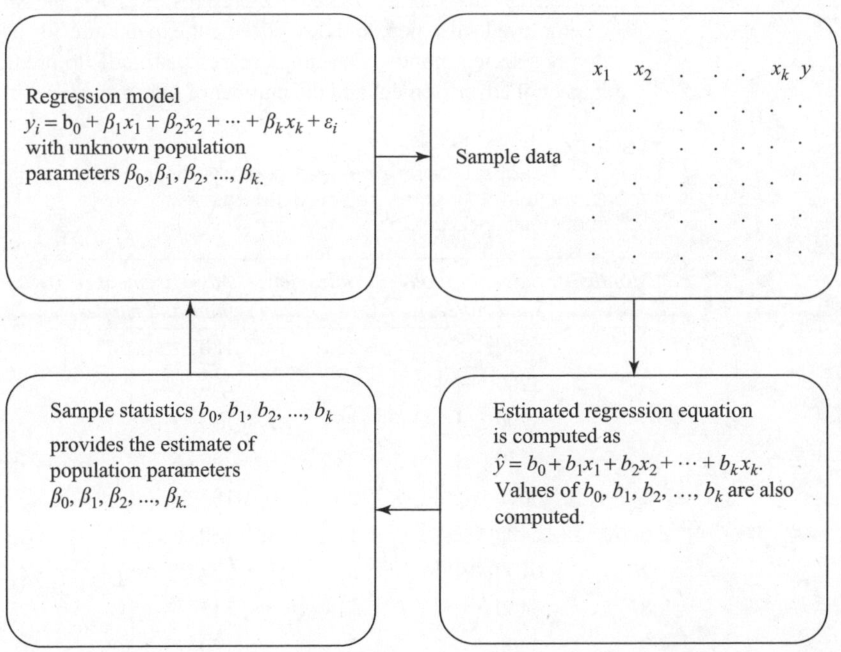

FIGURE 17.1
Summary of the estimation process for multiple regression

17.3 MULTIPLE REGRESSION MODEL WITH TWO INDEPENDENT VARIABLES

Multiple regression model with two independent variables is the simplest multiple regression model where highest power of any of the variables is equal to one.

Multiple regression model with two independent variables is the simplest multiple regression model where the highest power of any of the variables is equal to one. Multiple regression model with two independent variables is given as

Multiple regression model with two independent variables:

$$y_i = \beta_0 + \beta_1 x_1 + \beta_2 x_2 + \varepsilon_i$$

where y_i is the value of the dependent variable for ith value, β_0 the y intercept, β_1 the slope of y, with independent variable x_1 holding variable x_2 constant, β_2 the slope of y with independent variable x_2 holding variable x_1 constant, and ε_i the random error in y, for observation i.

Like simple regression analysis in a multiple regression analysis, sample regression coefficients (b_0, b_1, and b_2) are used to estimate population parameters (β_0, β_1, and β_2).

In a multiple regression analysis, sample regression coefficients (b_0, b_1, and b_2) are used to estimate population parameters (β_0, β_1, and β_2). Multiple regression equation with two independent variables is given as

Multiple regression equation with two independent variables:

$$\hat{y} = b_0 + b_1 x_1 + b_2 x_2$$

where $\hat{y}$ is the predicted value of dependent variable y, b_0 the estimate of regression constant, b_1 the estimate of regression coefficient β_1, and b_2 the estimate of regression coefficient β_2.

Example 17.1

A consumer electronics company has adopted an aggressive policy to increase sales of a newly launched product. The company has invested in advertisements as well as employed salesmen for increasing sales rapidly. Table 17.2 presents the sales, the number of employed salesmen, and advertisement expenditure for 24 randomly selected months. Develop a regression model to predict the impact of advertisement and the number of salesmen on sales.

TABLE 17.2
Sales, number of salesmen employed, and advertisement expenditure for 24 randomly selected months of a consumer electronics company

Months	*Sales (in thousand rupees)*	*Salesmen*	*Advertisement (in thousand rupees)*
1	5000	25	180
2	5200	35	250
3	5700	15	150
4	6300	27	240
5	6000	20	185
6	6400	11	160
7	6100	8	177
8	6400	11	315
9	6900	29	170

Months	*Sales (in thousand rupees)*	*Salesmen*	*Advertisement (in thousand rupees)*
10	7300	31	240
11	6950	6	184
12	7350	10	218
13	6920	14	216
14	8450	8	246
15	9600	18	229
16	10,900	7	269
17	10,200	9	244
18	12,200	10	305
19	10,500	6	303
20	12,800	8	320
21	12,600	12	322
22	11,500	14	460
23	13,800	11	430
24	14,000	9	422

On the basis of the multiple regression model, predict the sales of a given month when the number of salesmen employed are 35 and advertisement expenditure is 500 thousand rupees.

Solution

Figures 17.2 and 17.3 depict the three-dimensional graphs between sales, salesmen, and advertisement produced using Minitab. Recall that in a simple regression analysis, we obtained a regression line that was the best-fit line through data points in the xy plane. In case of multiple regression analysis, the resulting model produces a response surface. In multiple regression analysis, the regression surface is a response plane (shown in Figures 17.2 and 17.3).

In case of multiple regression analysis, the resulting model produces a response surface and very specifically, in a multiple regression analysis the regression surface is a response plane.

The process of using MS Excel for multiple regression is almost the same as that for simple regression analysis. In case of using MS Excel for multiple regression, instead of

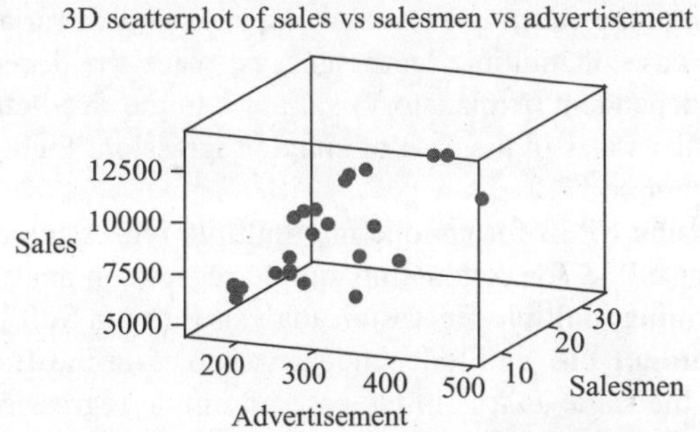

FIGURE 17.2
Three-dimensional graph connecting sales, salesmen, and advertisement (scatter plot) produced using Minitab

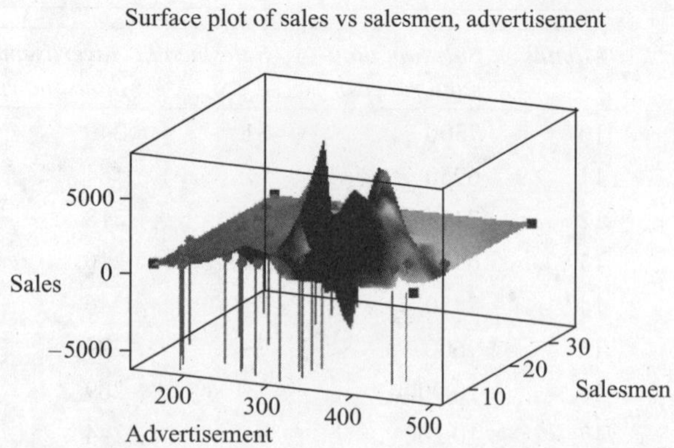

FIGURE 17.3
Three-dimensional graph between sales, salesmen, and advertisement (surface plot) produced using Minitab.

	A	B	C	D	E	F	G
1	SUMMARY OUTPUT						
2							
3	*Regression Statistics*						
4	Multiple R	0.8596888					
5	R Square	0.7390649					
6	Adjusted R Square	0.714214					
7	Standard Error	1560.5465					
8	Observations	24					
9							
10	ANOVA						
11		*df*	*SS*	*MS*	*F*	*Significance F*	
12	Regression	2	144851448.6	72425724	29.73989	7.47465E-07	
13	Residual	21	51141413.94	2435305			
14	Total	23	195992862.5				
15							
16		*Coefficients*	*Standard Error*	*t Stat*	*P-value*	*Lower 95%*	*Upper 95%*
17	Intercept	3856.6927	1340.772104	2.876471	0.009033	1068.404453	6644.98089
18	X Variable 1	-104.32061	39.48937978	-2.64174	0.015252	-186.443271	-22.19795
19	X Variable 2	24.609282	3.923141041	6.272852	3.2E-06	16.45066339	32.7679002

FIGURE 17.4
MS Excel output (partial) for Example 17.1

placing one independent variable in Input X Range, place independent variables in Input X Range. The remaining process is the same as in the case of simple regression. Figure 17.4 is the MS Excel output (partial) for Example 17.1.

The process of using Minitab for multiple regression is also almost the same as for simple regression analysis. In case of using Minitab for simple regression analysis, we place the dependent variable in the **Response** box and one independent variable in the **Predictors** box. Whereas, in the case of multiple regression, we place the dependent variable in the **Response** box and independent (explanatory) variables in the **Predictors** box. The remaining process is the same as it is in the case of simple regression. Figure 17.5 is the Minitab output (partial) for Example 17.1.

The method of using SPSS for conducting multiple regression analysis is analogous to the method of using SPSS for conducting simple regression analysis with a slight difference. While performing multiple regression analysis through SPSS, we place dependent variable in the **Dependent box** and independent variables in the **Independent box**. The remaining process is the same as it is in the case of simple regression. Figure 17.6 is the SPSS output (partial) for Example 17.1.

Regression Analysis: Sales versus Salesmen, Advertisement

```
The regression equation is
Sales = 3857 - 104 Salesmen + 24.6 Advertisement

Predictor         Coef  SE Coef      T      P  VIF
Constant          3857     1341   2.88  0.009
Salesmen       -104.32    39.49  -2.64  0.015  1.1
Advertisement   24.609    3.923   6.27  0.000  1.1

S = 1560.55   R-Sq = 73.9%   R-Sq(adj) = 71.4%

Analysis of Variance

Source          DF         SS        MS      F      P
Regression       2  144851449  72425724  29.74  0.000
Residual Error  21   51141414   2435305
Total           23  195992862
```

FIGURE 17.5
Minitab output (partial) for Example 17.1

Model Summary[b]

Model	R	R Square	Adjusted R Square	Std. Error of the Estimate	Durbin-Watson
1	.860[a]	.739	.714	1560.54652	1.791

a. Predictors: (Constant), Advertisement, Salesmen

b. Dependent Variable: Sales

ANOVA[b]

Model		Sum of Squares	df	Mean Square	F	Sig.
1	Regression	1.449E8	2	7.243E7	29.740	.000[a]
	Residual	5.114E7	21	2435305.426		
	Total	1.960E8	23			

a. Predictors: (Constant), Advertisement, Salesmen

b. Dependent Variable: Sales

Coefficients[a]

Model		Unstandardized Coefficients		Standardized Coefficients	t	Sig.	95.0% Confidence Interval for B		Collinearity Statistics	
		B	Std. Error	Beta			Lower Bound	Upper Bound	Tolerance	VIF
1	(Constant)	3856.693	1340.772		2.876	.009	1068.404	6644.981		
	Salesmen	-104.321	39.489	-.306	-2.642	.015	-186.443	-22.198	.928	1.077
	Advertisement	24.609	3.923	.726	6.273	.000	16.451	32.768	.928	1.077

a. Dependent Variable: Sales

FIGURE 17.6
SPSS output (partial) for Example 17.1

From Figures 17.4, 17.5, and 17.6, the regression coefficients are

$$b_0 = 3856.69, \quad b_1 = -104.32, \quad b_2 = 24.60$$

So, multiple regression equation can be expressed as

$$\hat{y} = b_0 + b_1 x_1 + b_2 x_2$$

or

$$\hat{y} = 3856.69 - 104.32x_1 + 24.60x_2$$

or

Sales = 3856.69 – (104.32) Salesmen + (24.6) Advertisement.

Interpretation: The sample y intercept b_0 is computed as 3856.69. This indicates expected sales when zero salesmen are employed and expenditure in advertisement is also zero. In other words, this is the sales when x_1(number of salesmen employed) and x_2 (advertisement expenditure) is equal to zero. In general, the practical interpretation of b_0 is limited.

b_1 is the slope of y with independent variable x_1 holding variable x_2 constant. That is, b_1 is the slope of sales (y) with independent variable salesmen (x_1) holding advertisement expenditure (x_2) constant. b_1 is computed as –104.32. The negative sign of the coefficient b_1 indicates an inverse relationship between the dependent variable, sales (y) and the independent variable salesmen (x_1). This means that holding advertisement expenditure (x_2) constant, unit increase in the number of salesmen employed (x_1) will result in –104.32(1000) = –10,432 thousand rupees predicted decline in sales.

b_2 is the slope of y with independent variable x_2 holding the variable x_1 constant. In other words, b_2 is the slope of sales (y) with independent variable advertisement (x_2) holding the number of salesmen employed (x_1) constant. In Example 17.1, the computed value of b_2 is 24.6. This indicates that holding salesmen employed (x_1) constant, the unit increase in advertisement expenditure (thousand rupees) will result in a 24.6(1000), that is, ₹24,600 predicted increase in sales.

On the basis of the regression model developed above, the predicted sales of a given month when number of salesmen employed are 35 and advertisement expenditure is ₹500,000 can be calculated very easily. As explained earlier, regression equation is developed as

$$\hat{y} = 3856.69 - 104.32x_1 + 24.60x_2$$

or

Sales = 3856.69 – (104.32) Salesmen + (24.6) Advertisement. When $x_1 = 35$ and $x_2 = 500$, by placing the values in the equation, the predicted sales of a given month can be obtained as below:

$$\hat{y} = 3856.69 - 104.32 \times (35) + 24.60 \times (500)$$
$$= 12{,}505.49$$

Therefore, when the number of salesmen employed is 35 and advertisement expenditure is ₹500,000, the sales of the consumer electronics company is predicted to be ₹12,505.49 thousand.

17.4 DETERMINATION OF COEFFICIENT OF MULTIPLE DETERMINATION (R^2), ADJUSTED R^2, AND STANDARD ERROR OF THE ESTIMATE

This section will focus on the concept of **coefficient of multiple determination** (R^2), **adjusted** R^2, and standard error of the estimate.

17.4.1 Determination of Coefficient of Multiple Determination (R^2)

In Chapter 16, we discussed the coefficient of determination (r^2). The coefficient of determination (r^2) measures the proportion of variation in dependent variable y that can be attributed to the independent variable x. This is valid for one independent and one dependent variable in case of a simple linear regression. In multiple regression, there are at least two independent variables and one dependent variable. Therefore, in case of multiple regression, the coefficient of multiple determination (R^2) is the proportion of variation in the dependent variable y that is explained by the combination of independent (explanatory) variables. The coefficient of multiple determination is denoted by $r^2_{y.12}$ (for two explanatory variables). Therefore, coefficient of multiple determination can be computed as

$$r^2_{y.12} = \frac{\text{Regression sum of squares}}{\text{Total sum of squares}} = \frac{\text{SSR}}{\text{SST}}$$

From Figures 17.4, 17.5 and 17.6

$$r^2_{y.12} = \frac{\text{Regression sum of squares}}{\text{Total sum of squares}} = \frac{\text{SSR}}{\text{SST}} = \frac{144{,}851{,}448.6}{195{,}992{,}862.5} = 0.7390$$

The coefficient of multiple determination $r^2_{y.12}$ is computed as 0.7390. This implies that 73.90% of the variation in sales is explained by the variation in the number of salesmen employed and the variation in the advertisement expenditure.

In case of multiple regression, the coefficient of multiple determination (R^2) is the proportion of variation in the dependent variable y that is explained by the combination of independent (explanatory) variables.

17.4.2 Adjusted R^2

While computing the coefficient of multiple determination R^2, we use the formula

$$R^2 = \frac{\text{SSR}}{\text{SST}} = 1 - \frac{\text{SSE}}{\text{SST}}$$

If we add independent variables in the regression analysis, the total sum of squares will not change. Inclusion of independent variables is likely to increase SSR by an amount, which may result in an increase in the value of R^2. In some cases, additional independent variables do not add any new information to the regression model though it increases the value of R^2. In this manner, sometimes, we may obtain an inflated value of R^2. This difficulty can be solved by taking adjusted R^2 into account which considers both the factors, that is, the additional information that an additional independent variable brings to the regression model and the changed degrees of freedom. The adjusted R^2 formula can be given as adjusted coefficient of multiple determination (adjusted R^2).

$$\text{Adjusted } R^2 = 1 - \frac{\text{SSE}/n-k-1}{\text{SST}/n-1}$$

For Example 17.1, the value of adjusted R^2 can be computed as

$$\text{Adjusted } R^2 = 1 - \frac{\text{SSE}/n-k-1}{\text{SST}/n-1} = 1 - \frac{51{,}141{,}413.94/21}{195{,}992{,}862.5/23} = 1 - 0.285786 = 0.714214$$

Adjusted R^2 is commonly used when a researcher wants to compare two or more regression models having the same dependent variable but different number of independent variables. If we compare the values of R^2 and adjusted R^2, we find that the value of R^2 is 0.024 or 2.4% more than the value of adjusted R^2. This indicates that adjusted R^2 has reduced the overall proportion of the explained variation of the dependent variable attributed to independent

Adjusted R^2 is commonly used when a researcher wants to compare two or more regression models having the same dependent variable but different number of independent variables.

variables by 2.4%. If more insignificant variables are added in the regression model, the gap between R^2 and adjusted R^2 tends to widen.

If we analyse the formula of computing the adjusted R^2, we find that it reflects both the number of independent variables and the sample size. For Example 17.1, the value of adjusted R^2 is computed as 0.714214. This indicates that 71.42% of the total variation in sales can be explained by the multiple regression model adjusted for the number of independent variables and sample size.

17.4.3 Standard Error of the Estimate

In Chapter 16, it has been discussed that in a regression model the residual is the difference between actual values (y_i) and the regressed values ($\hat{y}_i$). Using statistical software programs such as MS Excel, Minitab, and SPSS, the regressed (predicted) values can be obtained very easily. Figure 17.7 is the MS Excel output showing y, predicted y, and residuals. Figure 17.8 is the partial regression output from MS Excel showing the co-efficient of multiple determination, adjusted R^2, and standard error. Figures 17.9 and 17.10 are partial regression outputs produced

y	*Predicted Y*	*Residuals*
5000	5678.348135	-678.3481348
5200	6357.791756	-1157.791756
5700	5983.275785	-283.2757851
6300	6946.263821	-646.263821
6000	6322.997596	-322.9975956
6400	6646.651044	-246.6510444
6100	7377.970666	-1277.970666
6400	10461.08972	-4061.089721
6900	5014.972876	1885.027124
7300	6528.981379	771.0186205
6950	7758.876859	-808.876859
7350	8178.309998	-828.3099981
6920	7711.808993	-791.8089931
8450	9076.011109	-626.0111088
9600	7614.447215	1985.552785
10900	9746.3452	1153.6548
10200	8922.471935	1277.528065
12200	10319.31751	1880.682487
10500	10687.38139	-187.3813911
12800	10897.09796	1902.902039
12600	10529.03408	2070.965917
11500	13716.47375	-2216.473748
13800	13291.15713	508.8428745
14000	13302.92409	697.075908

FIGURE 17.7
MS Excel output showing y, predicted y, and residuals

3	*Regression statistics*		
4	Multiple R	0.859688849	
5	R Square	0.739064916	← Coefficienct of multiple determination (R^2)
6	Adjusted R Square	0.714213956	← Adjusted R^2
7	Standard Error	1560.546515	← Standard error
8	Observations	24	

FIGURE 17.8
Partial regression output from MS Excel showing coefficient of multiple determination, adjusted R^2, and standard error

Standard error — Coefficient of multiple determination (R^2) — Adjusted R^2

```
S = 1560.55     R-Sq = 73.9%     R-Sq(adj) = 71.4%
```

FIGURE 17.9 Partial regression output from Minitab showing coefficient of multiple determination, adjusted R^2, and standard error

Coefficient of multiple determination (R^2) — Adjusted R^2 — Standard error

Model summary[b]

Model	R	R Square	Adjusted R Square	Std. Error of the Estimate
1	.860[a]	.739	.714	1560.54652

a. Predictors: (Constant), Advertisement, Salesmen

b. Dependent Variable: Sales

FIGURE 17.10 Partial regression output from SPSS showing coefficient of multiple determination, adjusted R^2, and standard error

using Minitab and SPSS, respectively. Similarly, in Minitab and SPSS, using the storage dialog box (discussed in detail in the Chapter 16), predicted y and residuals can be obtained easily.

As discussed in Chapter 16, standard error can be understood as the standard deviation of errors (residuals) around the regression line. In a multiple regression model, the standard error of the estimate can be computed as

$$\text{Standard error} = \sqrt{\frac{\text{SSE}}{n-k-1}}$$

where n is the number of observations and k the number of independent (explanatory) variables.

For Example 17.1, standard error can be computed as

$$\text{Standard error} = \sqrt{\frac{\text{SSE}}{n-k-1}} = \sqrt{\frac{51{,}141{,}413.94}{24-2-1}} = 1560.5465$$

SELF-PRACTICE PROBLEMS

17A1. Assume that x_1 and x_2 are the independent variables and y the dependent variable in the data provided in the table below. Determine the line of regression. Comment on the coefficient of multiple determination (R^2) and the standard error of the model. Let $\alpha = 0.05$.

x_1	14	16	17	19	15	13	21	20	19
x_2	16	17	20	22	18	20	23	22	19
y	15	17	16	14	18	20	22	25	23

17A2. Assume that x_1 and x_2 are the independent variables and y the dependent variable in the data provided in the table below. Determine the line of regression. Comment on the coefficient of multiple determination (R^2) and the standard error of the model. Let $\alpha = 0.10$.

x_1	15	25	30	35	38	35	50	55	48	70	72
x_2	10	13	17	21	28	22	37	40	43	50	52
y	200	210	220	230	240	235	250	260	255	270	290

17A3. Mahindra & Mahindra, the flagship company of the Mahindra group manufactures utility vehicles and tractors. Data relating to sales, compensation to employees and advertisement expenses of Mahindra & Mahindra from March 1990 to March 2007 are given in the following table. Taking sales as the dependent variable and compensation to employees and advertisement expenses as independent variables, determine the line of regression. Comment on the coefficient of multiple determination (R^2) and the standard error of the model. Let $\alpha = 0.05$.

Year	*Sales (in million rupees)*	*Compensation to employees (in million rupees)*	*Advertisement expenses (in million rupees)*
Mar 1990	9028.1	1105.5	22
Mar 1991	9983	1283.9	18.5
Mar 1992	11,967.3	1481.4	24
Mar 1993	14,584.5	1813.4	52.3
Mar 1994	16,741.8	2077.9	32.5
Mar 1995	20,391.4	2335.4	54.3
Mar 1996	27,831.4	2950.5	91.2
Mar 1997	35,214.4	3416.7	124.1
Mar 1998	39,976.3	3874.8	158.6
Mar 1999	41,020.3	3853.4	158.3
Mar 2000	43,207.9	3975.7	349.2
Mar 2001	42,778.7	4250.3	402.3
Mar 2002	39,360.5	3907.6	307.9
Mar 2003	44,997.1	3851.9	289.6
Mar 2004	58,888.4	4278.4	523.8
Mar 2005	76,547.7	4695.1	576.1
Mar 2006	92,764.9	5587.6	548.7
Mar 2007	112,384.9	7024.1	822.7

Source: Prowess (V. 3.1), Centre for Monitoring Indian Economy Pvt. Ltd, Mumbai, accessed September 2008, reproduced with permission.

17.5 STATISTICAL SIGNIFICANCE TEST FOR THE REGRESSION MODEL AND THE COEFFICIENT OF REGRESSION

After developing a regression model with a set of appropriate data, checking the adequacy of the regression model is of paramount importance. The adequacy of the regression model can be verified by testing the significance of the overall regression model and coefficients of regression; residual analysis for verifying the assumptions of regression; standard error of the estimate; examining the coefficients of determination and variance inflationary factor (VIF) (will be discussed later in this chapter). In the previous sections, we have discussed residual analysis for verifying the assumptions of regression; standard error of the estimate, and coefficient of multiple determination. This section will focus on the statistical significance test for regression model and the coefficients of regression.

17.5.1 Testing the Statistical Significance of the Overall Regression Model

Testing the statistical significance of the overall regression model can be performed by setting the following hypotheses:

$$H_0 : \beta_1 = \beta_2 = \beta_3 = \cdots = \beta_k = 0$$

H_1 : At least one regression coefficient is $\neq 0$

or

H_0 : A linear relationship does not exist between the dependent and independent variables.

H_1 : A linear relationship exists between dependent variable and at least one of the independent variables.

In the previous chapter (Chapter 16), we have discussed that in regression analysis the F test is used to determine the significance of the overall regression model. More specifically, in case of a multiple regression model, the F test determines that at least one of the regression coefficients is different from zero. Most statistical software programs such as MS Excel, Minitab, and SPSS provide F test as a part of the regression output in terms of the ANOVA table. For multiple regression analysis, F statistic can be defined as

***F* statistic for testing the statistical significance of the overall regression model**

$$F = \frac{\text{MSR}}{\text{MSE}}$$

where,

$$\text{MSR} = \frac{\text{SSR}}{k}$$

$$\text{MSE} = \frac{\text{SSE}}{n-k-1}$$

where k is the number of independent (explanatory) variables in the regression model F statistic follows the F distribution with degrees of freedom k and $n-k-1$. Figures 17.11(a), 17.11(b), and 17.11(c) indicate the computation of the F statistic from MS Excel, Minitab, and SPSS, respectively. On the basis of the p value obtained from the outputs, it can be concluded that at least one of the independent variables (salesmen and/or advertisement) is significantly (at 5% level of significance) related to sales.

10	ANOVA					
11		*df*	*SS*	*MS*	*F*	*Significance F*
12	Regression	2	144851448.6	72425724.28	29.7398936	7.47465E-07
13	Residual	21	51141413.94	2435305.426		
14	Total	23	195992862.5			

FIGURE 17.11(a) Computation of the F statistic using MS Excel (partial output for Example 17.1)

Analysis of Variance

Source	DF	SS	MS	F	P
Regression	2	144851449	72425724	29.74	0.000
Residual Error	21	51141414	2435305		
Total	23	195992862			

FIGURE 17.11(b) Computation of the F statistic using Minitab (partial output for Example 17.1)

ANOVA[b]

Model		Sum of Squares	df	Mean Square	F	Sig.
1	Regression	1.45E+08	2	72425724.28	29.740	.000[a]
	Residual	51141414	21	2435305.426		
	Total	1.96E+08	23			

a. Predictors: (Constant), Advertisement, Salesmen

b. Dependent Variable: Sales

FIGURE 17.11(c) Computation of the F statistic using SPSS (partial output for Example 17.1)

17.5.2 *t* Test for Testing the Statistical Significance of Regression Coefficients

In the previous chapter, we examined the significant linear relationship between the independent variable *x* and the dependent variable *y* by applying the *t* test. The same concept can be applied in an extended form, for testing the statistical significance of regression coefficients for multiple regression. In a simple regression model, the *t* statistic is defined as

$$t = \frac{b_1 - \beta_1}{S_b}$$

In case of multiple regression, this concept can be generalized and the *t* statistic can be defined as

The test statistic *t* for multiple regression

$$t = \frac{b_j - \beta_j}{S_{b_j}}$$

where b_j is the slope of the variable j with dependent variable y holding all other independent variables constant, S_{b_j} the standard error of the regression coefficient b_j, and β_j the hypothesized population slope for variable j holding all other independent variables constant.

The test statistic *t* follows a *t* distribution with $n - k - 1$ degrees of freedom, where *k* is the number of independent variables.

The hypotheses for testing the regression coefficient of each independent variable can be set as

$$H_0: \beta_1 = 0$$
$$H_1: \beta_1 \neq 0$$
$$H_0: \beta_2 = 0$$
$$H_1: \beta_2 \neq 0$$

.

.

.

$$H_0: \beta_k = 0$$
$$H_1: \beta_k \neq 0$$

Most statistical software programs such as MS Excel, Minitab, and SPSS provide the *t* test as a part of the regression output.

Figures 17.12(a), 17.12(b), and 17.12(c) illustrate the computation of the *t* statistic using MS Excel, Minitab, and SPSS, respectively. The *p* value indicates the rejection of the null hypothesis and the acceptance of the alternative hypothesis. On the basis of the *p* value obtained from the outputs, it can be concluded that at 95% confidence level, a significant linear relationship exists between salesmen and sales. Similarly, at 95% confidence level, a significant linear relationship exists between advertisement and sales.

FIGURE 17.12(a) Computation of the *t* statistic using MS Excel (partial output for Example 17.1)

16		Coefficients	Standard Error	t Stat	P-value	Lower 95%	Upper 95%
17	Intercept	3856.692673	1340.772104	2.876471446	0.00903293	1068.404453	6644.981
18	X Variable 1	-104.3206104	39.48937978	-2.641738385	0.01525211	-186.443271	-22.1979
19	X Variable 2	24.60928178	3.923141041	6.272851658	3.2006E-06	16.45066339	32.7679

```
Predictor          Coef   SE Coef      T      P
Constant           3857      1341   2.88  0.009
Salesmen        -104.32     39.49  -2.64  0.015
Advertisement    24.609     3.923   6.27  0.000
```

FIGURE 17.12(b) Computation of the *t* statistic using Minitab (partial output for Example 17.1)

Coefficients[a]

Model		Unstandardized Coefficients B	Unstandardized Coefficients Std. Error	Standardized Coefficients Beta	t	Sig.
1	(Constant)	3856.693	1340.772		2.876	.009
	Salesmen	-104.321	39.489	-.306	-2.642	.015
	Advertisement	24.609	3.923	.726	6.273	.000

a. Dependent Variable: Sales

FIGURE 17.12(c) Computation of the *t* statistic using SPSS (partial output for Example 17.1)

SELF-PRACTICE PROBLEMS

17B1. Test the significance of the overall regression model and the statistical significance of regression coefficients for Problem 17A1.

17B2. Test the significance of the overall regression model and the statistical significance of regression coefficients for Problem 17A2.

17B3. Test the significance of the overall regression model and the statistical significance of regression coefficients for Problem 17A3.

17.6 INDICATOR (DUMMY VARIABLE MODEL)

Regression models are based on the assumption that all independent variables (explanatory) are numerical in nature. There may be cases when some of the variables are qualitative in nature. These variables generate nominal or ordinal information and are used in multiple regression. These variables are referred to as indicator or **dummy variables**. For example, we have taken advertisement as the explanatory variable to predict sales in previous sections. A researcher may want to include one more variable "display arrangement of products" in retail stores as another variable to predict sales. In most cases, researchers collect demographic information such as gender, educational background, marital status, religion, etc. In order to include these in the multiple regression model, a researcher has to use indicator or dummy variable techniques. In other words, the use of the dummy variable gives a firm grounding to researchers for including categorical variables in the multiple regression model.

Regression models are based on the assumption that all the independent variables (explanatory) are numerical in nature. There may be cases when some of the variables are qualitative in nature. These variables generate nominal or ordinal information and are used in multiple regression. These variables are referred to as indicator or dummy variables.

Researchers usually assign 0 or 1 to code dummy variables in their study. Here, it is important to note that the assignment of the codes 0 or 1 are arbitrary and the numbers merely represent a place for the category. In many situations, indicator or dummy variables are dichotomous (dummy variables have two categories such as male/female; graduate/non-graduate; married/unmarried, etc). A particular dummy variable x_d is defined as

$x_d = 0$, if the observation belongs to category 1

$x_d = 1$, if the observation belongs to category 2

Example 17.2 clarifies the use of dummy variables in regression analysis.

Researchers usually assign 0 or 1 to code dummy variables in their study. Here, it is important to note that the assignment of code 0 or 1 is arbitrary and the numbers merely represent a place for the category.

Example 17.2

A company wants to test the effect of age and gender on the productivity (in terms of units produced by the employees per month) of its employees. The HR manager has taken a random sample of 15 employees and collected information about their age and gender. Table 17.3 provides data about the productivity, age, and gender of 15 randomly selected employees. Fit a regression model considering productivity as the dependent variable and age and gender as the explanatory variables.

TABLE 17.3
Data about productivity, age, and gender of 15 randomly selected employees.

Employees	*Productivity (in units)*	*Age*	*Gender*
1	850	40	male
2	760	34	female
3	750	28	female
4	860	34	male
5	800	38	female
6	710	26	male
7	760	31	male
8	860	38	male
9	770	31	male
10	800	30	male
11	870	38	male
12	800	28	male
13	750	31	female
14	840	37	male
15	760	31	female

Predict the productivity of male and female employees at 45 years of age.

Solution

We need to define a dummy variable for gender for Example 17.2. A dummy variable for gender can be defined as

$$x_2 = 0 \text{ (For female)}$$

$$x_2 = 1 \text{ (For male)}$$

After assigning code numbers 0 to females and 1 to males, the data obtained from 15 employees is rearranged, as shown in Table 17.4.

The multiple regression model is based on the assumption that the slope of productivity with age is the same for gender, that is, for both males and females. Based on this assumption multiple regression model can be defined as

Multiple regression model with two independent variables

$$y_i = \beta_0 + \beta_1 x_1 + \beta_2 x_2 + \varepsilon_i$$

where y_i is the value of the dependent variable for the *i*th value, β_0 the y intercept, β_1 the slope of productivity with independent variable age holding the variable gender constant, β_2 the slope of productivity with independent variable gender holding the variable age constant, and ε_i the random error in y, for employee *i*.

TABLE 17.4
Data about productivity, age, and gender of 15 randomly selected employees (after coding)

Employees	*Productivity*	*Age*	*Gender*
1	850	40	1
2	760	34	0
3	750	28	0
4	860	34	1
5	800	38	0
6	710	26	1
7	760	31	1
8	860	38	1
9	770	31	1
10	800	30	1
11	870	38	1
12	800	28	1
13	750	31	0
14	840	37	1
15	760	31	0

After coding of the second explanatory variable, gender, the model takes the form of multiple regression with two explanatory variables—age and gender. The solution can be presented in the form of regression output using any of the software applications.

Note Figures 17.13, 17.14, and 17.15 are the MS Excel, Minitab, and SPSS outputs, respectively for Example 17.2. The procedure of using MS Excel, Minitab, and SPSS is exactly the same as used for performing multiple regression analysis for two explanatory variables.

	A	B	C	D	E	F	G
1	SUMMARY OUTPUT						
2							
3	*Regression Statistics*						
4	Multiple R	0.875911345					
5	R Square	0.767220684					
6	Adjusted R Square	0.728424131					
7	Standard Error	25.9669807					
8	Observations	15					
9							
10	ANOVA						
11		*df*	*SS*	*MS*	*F*	*Significance F*	
12	Regression	2	26668.59096	13334.3	19.77549	0.000159099	
13	Residual	12	8091.409039	674.2841			
14	Total	14	34760				
15							
16		*Coefficients*	*Standard Error*	*t Stat*	*P-value*	*Lower 95%*	*Upper 95%*
17	Intercept	488.8522598	53.13363981	9.200429	8.74E-07	373.0840038	604.620516
18	X Variable 1	8.492214204	1.600280177	5.306705	0.000186	5.005503228	11.9789252
19	X Variable 2	40.35700722	14.29543816	2.823069	0.015372	9.209923178	71.5040913

FIGURE 17.13
MS Excel output for Example 17.2

Regression Analysis: Productivity versus Age, Gender

```
The regression equation is
Productivity = 489 + 8.49 Age + 40.4 Gender

Predictor     Coef  SE Coef     T      P
Constant    488.85    53.13  9.20  0.000
Age          8.492    1.600  5.31  0.000
Gender       40.36    14.30  2.82  0.015


S = 25.9670    R-Sq = 76.7%    R-Sq(adj) = 72.8%


Analysis of Variance

Source          DF     SS     MS      F      P
Regression       2  26669  13334  19.78  0.000
Residual Error  12   8091    674
Total           14  34760
```

FIGURE17.14
Minitab output for Example 17.2

Model Summary

Model	R	R Square	Adjusted R Square	Std. Error of the Estimate
1	.876[a]	.767	.728	25.96698

a. Predictors: (Constant), Gender, Age

ANOVA[b]

Model		Sum of Squares	df	Mean Square	F	Sig.
1	Regression	26668.591	2	13334.295	19.775	.000[a]
	Residual	8091.409	12	674.284		
	Total	34760.000	14			

a. Predictors: (Constant), Gender, Age
b. Dependent Variable: Productivity

Coefficients[a]

Model		Unstandardized Coefficients		Standardized Coefficients	t	Sig.
		B	Std. Error	Beta		
1	(Constant)	488.852	53.134		9.200	.000
	Age	8.492	1.600	.743	5.307	.000
	Gender	40.357	14.295	.395	2.823	.015

a. Dependent Variable: Productivity

FIGURE 17.15
SPSS output for Example 17.2

In multiple regression, for dummy variables, we take the second column (column with 0 and 1 assignment) as the second explanatory variable. The remaining procedure is exactly the same as for multiple regression with two explanatory variables. The following procedure can be used to create a dummy variable column in MS Excel.

17.7 COLLINEARITY

A researcher may face problems because of the collinearity of independent (explanatory) variables while performing multiple regression. This situation occurs when two or more independent variables are highly correlated with each other. In a multiple regression analysis, when two independent variables are correlated, it is referred to as collinearity and when three or more variables are correlated, it is referred to as multicollinearity.

In multiple regression analysis, when two independent variables are correlated, it is referred to as collinearity and when three or more variables are correlated, it is referred to as multicollinearity.

In situations when two independent variables are correlated, obtaining new information and the measurement of separate effects of these on the dependent variable will be very difficult. Additionally, it can generate an opposite algebraic sign of the regression coefficient that will be expected for a particular explanatory variable. For identifying the correlated variables, a correlation matrix with the help of statistical software programs can be constructed. This correlation matrix identifies the pair of variables which are highly correlated. In case of extreme collinearity between two explanatory variables, software programs such as Minitab automatically drop the collinear variable. For example, consider Table 17.5 with sales (in thousand rupees) as the dependent variable and advertisement (in thousand rupees), and number of showrooms as the independent variables. Figure 17.16 is the regression output produced using Minitab for the data given in Table 17.5. From the output (Figure 17.16), it can be seen that number of showrooms which is a collinear variable is identified and is automatically dropped from the model. The final output contains only one independent variable that is advertisement.

TABLE 17.5
Sales as the dependent variable and advertisement and number of showrooms as the independent variables

Sales (in thousand rupees)	*Advertisement (in thousand rupees)*	*Number of showrooms*
10	5	3
13	3	1
15	4	2
16	7	5
17	9	7
18	6	4
20	8	6
22	10	8
26	12	10
29	11	9
30	10	8
35	9	7

Collinearity is measured by the **variance inflationary factor (VIF)** for each explanatory variable. Variance inflationary factor (VIF) for an explanatory variable i can be defined as

Collinearity is measured by variance inflationary factor (VIF) for each explanatory variable.

Variance inflationary factor (VIF) is given as

$$VIF_i = \frac{1}{1-R_i^2}$$

where R_i^2 is the coefficient of multiple determination of explanatory variable x_i with all other x variables.

Regression Analysis: Sales versus Advertisement, Number of showrooms

```
* Number of showrooms is highly correlated with other X variables
* Number of showrooms has been removed from the equation.

The regression equation is
Sales = 5.03 + 2.03 Advertisement

Predictor        Coef  SE Coef     T      P  VIF
Constant        5.032    4.554  1.10  0.295
Advertisement  2.0279   0.5489  3.69  0.004  1.0

S = 5.19789   R-Sq = 57.7%   R-Sq(adj) = 53.5%

Analysis of Variance

Source          DF      SS      MS      F      P
Regression       1  368.74  368.74  13.65  0.004
Residual Error  10  270.18   27.02
```

FIGURE 17.16
Minitab output (partial) for sales versus advertisement, number of showrooms

In a multiple regression analysis, if there are only two explanatory variables, R_1^2 is the coefficient of multiple determination of explanatory variables x_1 and x_2. Similarly, R_2^2 is the coefficient of multiple determination of explanatory variables x_2 and x_1 (same as R_1^2). In case of a multiple regression analysis when there are three explanatory variables, R_1^2 is the coefficient of multiple determination of explanatory variable x_1 with x_2 and x_3. R_2^2 is the coefficient of multiple determination of explanatory variables x_2 with x_1 and x_3. R_3^2 is the coefficient of multiple determination of explanatory variable x_3 with x_2 and x_1. Figure 17.17 and 17.18 are Minitab and SPSS output (partial) respectively, indicating VIF for Example 17.1.

If explanatory variables are uncorrelated, then variance inflationary factor (VIF) will be equal to 1. Variance inflationary factor (VIF) being greater than 10 is an indication of serious multicollinearity problems.

If explanatory variables are uncorrelated, then variance inflationary factor (VIF) is equal to 1. Variance inflationary factor (VIF) being greater than 10 is an indication of serious multicollinearity problems. For example, if the correlation coefficient between two explanatory variables is –0.2679. Hence, the variance inflationary factor (VIF) can be computed as

$$VIF_1 = VIF_2 = \frac{1}{1-(-0.2679)^2} = 1.077$$

This value of the variance inflationary factor (VIF) indicates that collinearity does not exist between the explanatory variables.

Collinearity is not very simple to handle in multiple regression. One of the best solutions to overcome the problem of collinearity is to drop collinear variables from the regression equation.

In multiple regression, collinearity is not very simple to handle. A solution to overcome the problem of collinearity is to drop the collinear variable from the regression equation. For example, let as assume that we are measuring the impact of three independent variables x_1, x_2, and x_3 on a dependent variable y. During the analysis, we find that the explanatory variable x_1 is highly correlated with the explanatory variable x_2. By dropping one of these variables from the multiple regression analysis, we will be able to solve the problem of collinearity. How to determine which variable should be dropped from the multiple regression analysis? This can be achieved comparing R^2 and adjusted R^2 with and without one of these variables. For example, suppose with all the

```
Predictor         Coef  SE Coef      T      P    VIF
Constant          3857     1341   2.88  0.009
Salesmen       -104.32    39.49  -2.64  0.015  1.077
Advertisement   24.609    3.923   6.27  0.000  1.077
```

FIGURE 17.17
Minitab output (partial) indicating VIF for Example 17.1

Coefficients[a]

Model		Unstandardized Coefficients		Standardized Coefficients	t	Sig.	Collinearity Statistics	
		B	Std. Error	Beta			Tolerance	VIF
1	(Constant)	3856.693	1340.772		2.876	.009		
	Salesmen	-104.321	39.489	-.306	-2.642	.015	.928	1.077
	Advertisement	24.609	3.923	.726	6.273	.000	.928	1.077

a. Dependent Variable: Sales

FIGURE 17.18 SPSS output (partial) indicating VIF for Example 17.1

three explanatory variables included in the analysis, R^2 is computed as 0.95. When x_1 is removed from the model, R^2 is computed as 0.89, and when x_2 is removed from the model, R^2 is computed as 0.93. In this situation, we can drop the variable x_2 from the regression model and variable x_1 should remain in the model. If adjusted R^2 increases after dropping the independent variable, we can certainly drop the variable from the regression model.

In some cases, due to the importance of the concerned explanatory variable in the study, a researcher is not able to drop the variable from the study. In this situation, some other methods are suggested to overcome the problem of collinearity. One way is to form a new combination of explanatory variables, which are uncorrelated with one another and then run the regression on the new uncorrelated combination of explanatory variables instead of running the regression on original variables. In this manner, the information content of the original variables is maintained; however, the collinearity is removed. Another method is to centre the data. This can be done by subtracting the means from the variables and then running the regression on newly obtained variables.

SUMMARY

Multiple regression analysis is a statistical tool where several independent or explanatory variables can be used to predict one dependent variable. In multiple regression, sample statistics b_0, $b_1, b_2, \ldots, b_k$ provide the estimate of population parameters β_0, $\beta_1, \beta_2, \ldots, \beta_k$. In multiple regression, the coefficient of multiple determination (R^2) is the proportion of variation in the dependent variable y that is explained by the combination of independent (explanatory) variables. In multiple regression, adjusted R^2 is used when a researcher wants to compare two or more regression models with the same dependent variable but having different independent variables. Standard error is the standard deviation of errors (residuals) around the regression line.

For residual analysis, in a multiple regression model, we test the linearity of the regression model, constant error variance (homoscedasticity), independence of error, and normality of error. The adequacy of the regression model can be verified by testing the significance of the overall regression model and coefficients of regression. The contribution of an independent variable can be determined by applying partial F criterion. This provides a platform to estimate the contribution of each explanatory (independent) variable in the multiple regression model. The coefficient of partial determination measures the proportion of variation in the dependent variable that is explained by each independent variable holding all other independent (explanatory) variables constant.

In case of the existence of a non-linear relationship between two explanatory variables, we have to consider the next option in terms of quadratic relationship (most common non-linear relationship) between two variables. There are cases when some of the variables are qualitative in nature. These variables generate nominal or ordinal information and are used in multiple regressions. These variables are referred to as indicator or dummy variables. A technique referred to as the dummy variable technique is adopted for using these variables in the multiple regression model.

In many situations, in regression analysis, the assumptions of regression are violated or researchers find that the model is not linear. In both the cases, either the dependent variable y, or the independent variable x, or both the variables are transformed to avoid the violation of regression assumptions or to make the regression model linear. There are many transformation techniques available such as the square root transformation and the log transformation techniques.

In multiple regression when two independent variables are correlated, it is referred to as collinearity and when three or more variables are correlated, it is referred to as multicollinearity. Collinearity can be identified either by correlation matrix or by **variance inflationary factors** (VIF).

Search procedure is used for model development in multiple regression. In this procedure, more than one regression model is developed for a given data base. These models are compared on the basis of different criteria depending upon the procedure opted. Various search procedures including all possible regressions, stepwise regression, forward selection, and backward elimination are available in multiple regression.

KEY TERMS |

Adjusted R^2, 422

Coefficient of multiple determination, 422

Dummy variables, 429

Variance inflationary factors, 436

NOTES |

1. www.hindustanpetroleum.com/aboutsus.htm, accessed October 2008.
2. Prowess (V. 3.1), Centre for Monitoring Indian Economy Pvt. Ltd, Mumbai, accessed October 2008, reproduced with permission.

DISCUSSION QUESTIONS |

1. Explain the concept of multiple regression and explain its importance in managerial decision making.
2. Explain the use and importance of coefficient of multiple determination (R^2) in interpreting the output of multiple regression.
3. Discuss the concept of adjusted coefficient of multiple determination (adjusted R^2) and standard error in multiple regression?
4. How can we test the significance of regression coefficients and the overall significance of the regression model?
5. When does a researcher use the dummy variable technique in multiple regression analysis?
6. What is collinearity in multiple regression analysis? Explain variance inflationary factor (VIF) and its use in diagnosing collinearity in multiple regression analysis.

NUMERICAL PROBLEMS |

1. A consultancy wants to examine the relationship between the income of employees and their age and experience. The company takes a random sample of 15 employees and the data collected from these 15 employees are presented in the table below:

Employees	*Income*	*Age*	*Experience*
1	25,000	30	10
2	30,000	30	10
3	38,000	30	10
4	44,000	30	10
5	50,000	30	10
6	58,000	35	15
7	65,000	35	15
8	73,000	35	15
9	87,000	35	15
10	96,000	35	15
11	104,000	40	18
12	110,000	40	18
13	120,000	40	18
14	128,000	40	18
15	136,000	40	18

Taking income as the dependent variable and age and experience as the independent variables, develop a regression model based on the data provided.

2. A cement manufacturing company has discovered that sales turnover of cement is largely dependent on advertisements on hoardings and wall paintings and not on advertisements in the print media. The company has invested heavily on the first two modes of advertisement. The company's research team wants to study the impact of these two modes of advertisement on sales. The research team has collected a random sample of the sales for 22 days (given in the table below). Develop a regression model to predict the impact of the two different modes of advertising: hoardings and wallpaintings on sales.

Days	*Sales (in thousand rupees)*	*Hoardings (in thousand rupees)*	*Wall paintings (in thousand rupees)*
1	1000	10	50
2	1130	10	50
3	920	20	30
4	700	20	30
5	920	30	37
6	990	30	37
7	930	40	40
8	1250	40	40
9	960	50	30
10	1100	50	30
11	1720	60	60
12	1600	60	60
13	1100	70	10
14	1000	70	10
15	1450	80	30
16	1460	80	30
17	1570	90	37
18	1590	90	37
19	1700	100	40
20	1900	100	40
21	2000	110	50
22	1650	110	50

On the basis of the regression model, predict the sales on a given day when advertisement expenditure on hoardings and wall paintings are 130 thousand and 70 thousand rupees, respectively.

3. A company wants to predict the demand for a particular product by using the price of the product, the income of households, and the savings of households as related factors. The company has collected data for 15 randomly selected months (given in the table below). Fit a multiple regression model for the data and interpret the results.

Months	*Demand (in units)*	*Price (in hundred rupees per unit)*	*Income of the household (in hundred rupees)*	*Savings of the household (in hundred rupees)*
1	50	15	100	17
2	55	13	200	25

3	62	15	300	21
4	70	13	400	23
5	77	11	500	19
6	85	9	600	25
7	68	9	700	27
8	68	13	800	29
9	75	7	900	39
10	75	7	1000	33
11	85	7	1100	35
12	100	2	1200	41
13	80	4	1300	31
14	87	2	1400	45
15	82	4	1500	39

4. The sales data of a fast food company for 20 weeks selected randomly are given below. Fit an appropriate regression model taking sales as the dependent variable and sales executives as the independent variable and jutify the model based on these data.

Weeks	*Sales (in thousand rupees)*	*Sales executives*
1	150	6
2	160	6
3	170	6
4	180	6
5	190	6
6	200	6
7	210	6
8	90	14
9	100	14
10	110	14
11	118	14
12	127	14
13	138	14
14	146	14
15	75	23
16	87	23
17	97	23
18	107	23
19	118	23
20	127	23

5. The Vice President (Sales) of a computer software company wants to know the relationship between the generation of sales volumes and the age of employees. He believes that some of the variation in sales may be owing to differences in gender. He has randomly selected 12 employees and collected the following data.

Employees	*Sales (in thousand rupees)*	*Age*	*Gender*
1	250	40	Male
2	240	42	Female
3	260	40	Female
4	270	38	Male
5	290	36	Female
6	210	44	Male
7	196	42	Male
8	240	36	Male
9	265	36	Female
10	225	38	Male
11	255	38	Female
12	200	44	Male

Fit a regression model, considering the generation of sales volume as the dependent variable and the age of employees and gender as the explanatory variables.

6. A consumer electronics company has 150 showrooms across the country. The Vice President (Marketing) wants to predict sales by using four explanatory variables—show room space (in square feet), electronic display boards in showrooms, number of salesmen, and showroom age. He has taken a random sample of 15 showrooms and collected data with respect to the four explanatory variables. Develop an appropriate regression model using the data given below.

Sl. No.	*Sales (in thousand Rupees)*	*Show-room space (in square feet)*	*Electronic display boards in showrooms*	*Number of sales-men*	*Show-room age (in years)*
1	1000	30	18	10	12
2	1300	40	25	12	13
3	1700	20	15	14	14
4	2100	30	24	12	15
5	2500	22	18	10	13
6	2900	11	16	11	10
7	3300	7	17	8	9

8	3900	11	31	10	8
9	4500	31	17	12	6
10	5100	35	24	14	14
11	5600	8	18	11	15
12	6100	13	21	9	16
13	6500	19	21	13	15
14	6900	11	24	14	14
15	7300	21	22	16	16

CASE STUDY |

Case 17: *Maruti Udyog Ltd—The Wheels of India*

Introduction

The passenger car industry in India was characterized by limited production owing to limited demand before the entry of Maruti Udyog Ltd. The real transformation of the industry took place after Maruti Udyog started operations in 1981. After liberalization, global players such as General Motors, Ford, Suzuki, Toyota, Mitsubishi, Honda, Fiat, Hyundai, Mercedes, and Skoda entered the passenger car segment in India. The sales volumes in the passenger car segment is estimated to touch 2,235,000 units by 2014–2015[1].

Many factors have contributed to the increase in demand in the Indian passenger car industry. In India, car penetration is low at 7 cars per 1000 persons as compared to developed countries. This has opened a host of opportunities for car manufacturers. The increasing disposable incomes, possible upgradation from a two wheeler to a four wheeler because of the launch of low priced cars, the aspirations of Indians to have a better lifestyle, etc. are factors that have expanded demand in the passenger car segment. The challenges ahead of the industry are the high fuel prices and interest rates, increasing input costs, and growth in mass transit systems, etc.[2] Apart from these factors, the overall scenario seems to be positive for the Indian passenger car industry.

Maruti Suzuki—A Leader in the Passenger Car Segment

Maruti Suzuki, earlier known as Maruti Udyog, is one of India's leading automobile manufacturers and is the market leader in the passenger car segment. The company was established in February 1981 through an Act of Parliament, as a government company in technological collaboration with Suzuki Motor Corporation of Japan. In its initial years, the government had the major controlling major stake. In the post-liberalization era, the Indian government completely divested its stake in the company and exited it completely in May 2007. Maruti's first product—the Maruti 800 was launched in India in December 1983. After its humble beginning, the company dominated the Indian car market for over two decades and became the first Indian car company to mass produce and sell more than a million cars by 1994. Till March 2007, the company had produced and sold over six million cars.[2]

Unique Maruti Culture

Maruti strongly believes in the strength of its employees and on account of this underlying philosophy has moduled its workforce into teams with common goals and objectives. Maruti's employee-management relationship is characterized by participative management, team work and kaizen, communication and information sharing, and open office culture for easy accessibility. Maruti has also taken steps to implement a flat organizational structure. There are only three levels of responsibilities in the company's structure—board of directors, division heads, and department heads. As a firm believer in this philosophy, Maruti has an open office, common uniform (at all levels), and a common canteen for all.[3]

On the Road to Becoming Global

Maruti Suzuki India is a major contributor to Suzuki's global turnover and profits and has ambitious plans to capture the global automobile market. Maruti Suzuki India, Managing Director and CEO, Mr Shinzo Nakanishi said, "When we exported 53,000 cars in 2007–2008 that was the highest ever in our history. But we now want to take it to 2, 00,000 cars annually by 2010–2011." [4]

Maruti is aware that the passenger car market in India is highly competitive. Changing lifestyles and increasing incomes of Indian customers have attracted world players to the Indian market. These MNCs are widening the product range in order to expand the market. Confident of its strategies Chairman of Maruti Suzuki India R. C. Bhargava said, "The car market is growing increasingly competitive. This is not surprising as global manufacturers are bound to come where they see a growing market. Maruti has a strategy for the future."[5]

Table 17.01 presents the sales turnover, advertising expenses, marketing expenses, and distribution expenses of the company from 1989–2007. Fit a regression model considering sales volume generation as the dependent variable and advertising expenses, marketing expenses and distribution expenses as explanatory variables.

TABLE 17.01
Sales turnover, advertising expenses, marketing expenses, and distribution expenses of Maruti Udyog from 1989-2007

Year	*Sales (in million rupees)*	*Advertising expenses (in million rupees)*	*Marketing expenses (in million rupees)*	*Distribution expenses (in million rupees)*
1989	9324.6	9.0	129.8	139.9
1990	11,870.8	20.2	206.1	124.7
1991	15,118.6	9.8	105.1	169.9
1992	19,406.4	17.2	53.0	483.9
1993	21,715.4	11.5	65.0	495.0
1994	28,270.2	38.9	68.5	618.4
1995	41,960.1	41.9	81.0	850.3
1996	64,647.5	139.9	203.0	1273.2
1997	77,826.3	344.9	439.6	1624.6
1998	83,059.5	451.6	767.7	1538.3
1999	78,855.6	656.3	1680.0	1474.9
2000	94,407.0	882.0	1638.0	1732.0
2001	90,615.0	1051.0	1376.0	1594.0
2002	92,313.0	1170.0	2063.0	1588.0
2003	92,038.0	1676.0	2361.0	2041.0
2004	111,281.0	2518.0	354.0	1188.0
2005	134,859.0	2044.0	195.0	1133.0
2006	151,252.0	2257.0	234.0	1069.0
2007	174,580.0	3389.0	234.0	1376.0

Source: Prowess (V. 3.1), Centre for Monitoring Indian Economy Pvt. Ltd, Mumbai accessed September 2008, reproduced with permission.

NOTES |

1. www.indiastat.com, accessed September 2008, reproduced with permission.
2. Prowess (V. 3.1), Centre for Monitoring Indian Economy Pvt. Ltd, Mumbai, accessed September 2008, reproduced with permission.
3. www.maruti.co.in/ab/careers.asp?ch=1&ct=9&sc=1, accessed September 2008, reproduced with permission.
4. www.hinduonnet.com/businessline/blnus/02201806.htm, accessed September 2008.
5. www.thehindubusinessline.com/2008/08/21/stories/2008082152240200.htm, accessed September 2008.

CHAPTER 18

Multivariate Analysis II: Discriminant Analysis and Conjoint Analysis

LEARNING OBJECTIVES

Upon completion of this chapter, you will be able to:

- Understand the concept and application of discriminant analysis and multiple discriminant analysis
- Interpret the discriminant analysis output obtained from statistical software
- Use Minitab and SPSS to perform discriminant analysis
- Understand the concept and application of conjoint analysis
- Interpret the conjoint analysis output obtained from the statistical software
- Use SPSS to perform conjoint analysis

RESEARCH IN ACTION: CAMLIN LTD

The Indian stationery market can be categorized into school stationery, office stationery, paper products, and computer stationery. Increased spending on the educational sector by the government, improvement in educational standards and introduction of new categories of specialized education, and concentration on overall development of students have led to the speedy growth of the stationery market in India. The office-supplies segment is also growing rapidly. Opening of new commercial offices having multi-locational presence has helped organized players with scalability to serve across locations and offer diverse range of products. These factors have not only contributed to increased demand but also shifted sales from unorganized to organized sector with premium-quality products.[1]

Mr D. P. Dandekar started Camlin in 1931. Camlin has come a long way from a company manufacturing ink powder in 1931 to a company manufacturing more than 2000 products, operating in various diverse fields. With more than 50,000 strong retailer network, prestigious foreign collaborations, large customer base, regular interaction with consumers by the sales force, and participation in international trade fairs, such as Paperworld in Frankfurt, it has now become a trusted household name all over India. It first launched the hobby range of colours in India. It has also introduced colour categories such as fine art colours, hobby colours, and fashion colours in India.[2] Table 18.1 gives the income and profit after tax (in million rupees) of Camlin Ltd from 1994–1995 to 2008–2009.

Camlin, through its wholly owned arm Camlin Alfakids, plans to set up 200 preschools throughout the country within the next 5 years. Mr Nitin Pitale, President-Projects (New Business Development), told *Business Line*, "We have been looking to diversify into a new line of business for some time now. As we have strong brand equity among

>>>

parents and children for our stationery and art products, we decided to get into the business of setting up and managing play schools." The company is in the process of deciding whether these preschools will be company owned or franchised. Each proposed preschool will have an area over 8000 ft^2 with facilities such as gardens, swimming pools, sandpits, and so on.[3]

Suppose Camlin Ltd wants to assess parent's preference for the new playschool compared with two other established playschools and researchers have collected data on a categorical dependent variable (preference for three playschools including Camlin's playschool). The independent variables have also been identified and data are collected on an interval scale. How will the researcher analyse the data? We have already discussed in the previous chapter that for applying multiple regression technique both the dependent and the independent variables should be interval scaled. In this case, the dependent variable is not interval scaled; hence, we are supposed to find another way of analysing the data. Discriminant analysis is a statistical technique to analyse the data when the dependent variable is categorical scaled and the independent variable is interval scaled. This chapter deals with the concept and application of discriminant analysis and also discusses an important and a widely applied multivariate technique—conjoint analysis.

TABLE 18.1
Income and profit after tax (in million rupees) of Camlin Ltd from 1994–1995 to 2008–2009

Year	*Income*	*Profit after tax*
Mar-95	1042.9	16.6
Mar-96	1081.3	–6.7
Mar-97	1166.6	10.5
Mar-98	1367.7	23.5
Mar-99	1466.4	23.3
Mar-00	1616.3	19.7
Mar-01	1601.5	20.7
Mar-02	1879.1	30.8
Mar-03	1895.2	44.4
Mar-04	1945.3	18.9
Mar-05	2065.6	–48.8
Mar-06	2080.8	–15.3
Mar-07	2424.4	360.7
Mar-08	2245	38.3
Mar-09	2924.7	61.1

Source: Prowess (V. 3.1): Centre for Monitoring Indian Economy Pvt. Ltd, Mumbai, accessed September 2009, reprinted with permission.

18.1 DISCRIMINANT ANALYSIS

This chapter focuses on **discriminant analysis** and **conjoint analysis**. Use of these two multivariate techniques in marketing research is increasing day by day. Let us start the discussion by taking discriminant analysis first.

18.1.1 Introduction

Discriminant analysis is a technique of analysing data when the dependent variable is categorical and the independent variables are interval in nature.

We have already discussed that multiple regression analysis is used when both the dependent and independent variables are **interval scaled**. In real-life situations, there may be cases where the independent variables are interval scaled but the dependent variable is **categorical scaled**. **Discriminant analysis** is a technique of analysing data of this nature. For example, the dependent variable may be choice of a brand of refrigerator (Brand 1, Brand 2, and Brand 3) and the independent variables are ratings of attributes of the refrigerator on a 5-point Likert rating scale. As another example, a marketing research analyst may be interested in classifying a group of consumers into '**satisfied with the product**' or '**not satisfied with the product**' on the basis of few characteristics such as age, income, education, or any other characteristics that can be measured on a rating scale. Apart from the multiple regression technique, another technique that is becoming familiar and useful, especially in marketing applications, is the use of discriminant analysis in which an attempt is made to separate the observations into groups or clusters that have discriminating characteristics (Hallaq 1975).

18.1.2 Objectives of Discriminant Analysis

The following are the major objectives of discriminant analysis:

- Developing a **discriminant function** or determining a linear combination of independent variables to separate groups (of dependent variable) by maximizing between-group variance relative to within-group variance.
- Examining significant difference among the groups in light of the independent variables.
- Developing procedures for assigning new entrants whose characteristics are known but group identity is not known to one of the groups.
- Determining independent variables that contribute to most of the difference among the groups (of dependent variable).

Similar to multiple regression analysis, discriminant analysis also explores the relationship between the independent and the dependent variables. The difference between multiple regression and discriminant analyses can be examined in the light of the **nature of the dependent variable** that is categorical, when compared with metric, as in the case of multiple regression analysis. The independent variables are metric in both the cases of multiple regression and discriminant analyses. Thus, the dependent variable in discriminant analysis is categorical, and there are as many prescribed subgroups as there are categories (Parasuraman et al. 2004).

The difference between multiple regression and discriminant analyses can be examined in the light of the nature of the dependent variable that is categorical, when compared with metric, as in the case of multiple regression analysis. The independent variables are metric in both the cases of multiple regression and discriminant analyses.

18.1.3 Discriminant Analysis Model

Discriminant analysis model derives a linear combination of independent variables that discriminates best between groups on the value of a discriminant function. Discriminant analysis model can be presented in the following form:

Discriminant analysis model derives a linear combination of independent variables that discriminates best between groups on the value of a discriminant function.

$$D = b_0 + b_1x_1 + b_2x_2 + b_3x_3 + \cdots b_nx_n,$$

where D is the discriminant score; $b_0, b_1, b_2,\ldots b_n$ are the discriminant coefficients; and $x_1, x_2, x_3,\ldots x_n$ are independent variables. The discriminant coefficients $b_0, b_1, b_2,\ldots b_n$ are estimated in such a way that the difference among the groups (of dependent variable) will be as high as possible by maximizing the between-group variance relative to the within-group variance.

18.1.4 Some Statistics Associated with Discriminant Analysis

Several statistical terms associated with discriminant analysis are described as follows:

Canonical correlation: It measures the degree of association between the **discriminant scores** and the groups (levels of dependent variable).

Centroids: The average (mean) value of the discriminant Score D for a particular category or group is referred as **centroids**. There will be one centroid for each group. For a two-group discriminant analysis, there will be two centroids, and for a three-group discriminant analysis, there will be three centroids. The averages for a group of all the functions are the **group centroids**.

Classification matrix: It gives a list of correctly classified and misclassified cases. The diagonal of the matrix exhibits correctly classified cases.

Unstandardized discriminant coefficients: These are multipliers of the independent variables in the discriminant function.

Discriminant function: Discriminant analysis generated linear combination of independent variables that best discriminate between the categories of dependent variable.

Discriminant scores: These can be computed by multiplying unstandardized discriminant coefficients by values of the independent variables and a constant term of the discriminant function is added to their sum.

Eigenvalue: For each discriminant function, **Eigenvalues** are computed by dividing between-group sum of squares by within-group sum of squares. A large eigenvalue implies a strong function.

***F* values and its significance:** *F* values are same as it is computed in one-way analysis of variance (ANOVA). Its significance is tested by corresponding *p* values, which is the likelihood that the observed *F* value could occur by chance.

Pooled within-group correlation matrix: This is constructed by averaging the correlation matrices for all the groups.

Structure correlation: It is also known as **discriminant loading** and is the correlation between the independent variables and the discriminant function.

Wilks' lambda (λ): For each predictor variable, the ratio of within-group to total-group sum of squares is called **Wilks' lambda**. This is the proportion of total variance in the discriminant scores not explained by differences among groups. The value of Wilks' lambda varies between 0 and 1. The value of lambda equal to 1 indicates that the group means are equal. This means that all the variance is explained by the factors other than the difference between these means. A small value of lambda indicates that the group means are apparently different.

Chi-square (χ^2): It measures whether the two levels of the function significantly differ from each other based on the discriminant function. A high value of χ^2 indicates that the functions significantly differ from each other.

18.1.5 Steps in Conducting Discriminant Analysis

Two-group discriminant analysis is conducted through a five-step procedure as follows: formulating problem, computing discriminant function coefficients, testing the statistical significance of the discriminant function, interpreting results generally obtained through statistical software, and concluding comments by performing classification and validating discriminant analysis. Figure 18.1 shows the five-step procedure of conducting discriminant analysis.

18.1.5.1 Formulating a Problem

Discriminant analysis starts with problem formulation by identifying the objective, the dependent variable, and the independent variables. The main feature of discriminant analysis is that the dependent variable must consist of two or more mutually exclusive and collectively exhaustive groups (categories). If the dependent variable is an interval or a ratio, it must first

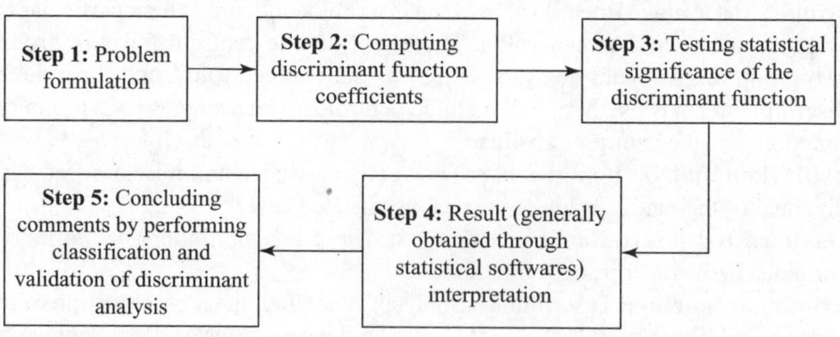

FIGURE 18.1
Five steps in conducting discriminant analysis

be categorised. For example, the dependent variable may be consumer satisfaction and is measured on a 5-point rating scale (strongly disagree to strongly agree with either agree or disagree in the middle). This can be further divided into three categories: dissatisfied (1, 2); neutral (3); and satisfied (4, 5).

As a next step, the sample is divided into two parts. First part of the sample is referred as **estimation or analysis sample** and is used for the estimation of the discriminant function. Second part of the sample is referred as **hold-out or validation sample** and is used for validating the discriminant function. To avoid data specific conclusions, validation of the discriminant function is important. The number of subjects (cases) in analysis and hold-out samples should be in proportion with the total sample. For example, if in the total sample 50% of the consumers are in the "satisfied" category and 50% of the consumers are in the "dissatisfied" category then the analysis and hold-out samples should also contain 50% consumers in the satisfied category and 50% in the dissatisfied category.

First part of the sample is referred as estimation or analysis sample and is used for the estimation of the discriminant function. Second part of the sample is referred as hold-out or validation sample and is used for the validation of the discriminant function.

The procedure of conducting discriminant analysis can be better explained by Example 18.1. In this example, four independent variables, such as age of the consumers, income of the consumers, attitude of the consumers towards shopping (measured on a 7-point rating scale), and occupation have been identified. The dependent variable is categorical and has two categories (groups): "satisfied" and "not satisfied." Hence, this is a case of two-group discriminant analysis.

Example 18.1

A garment company has launched a new brand of shirt. The company wants to categorize consumers into two groups—satisfied and not satisfied—related to some characteristics of the consumers during the last 2 years. The company conducted a survey and data were obtained from 36 consumers on the age of the consumers, income of the consumers, attitude of the consumers towards shopping (measured on a 7-point rating scale), and occupation. The data are given in Tables 18.2 (analysis sample) and 18.3 (hold-out sample).

TABLE 18.2
Data obtained for the garment company (analysis sample)

Subject no.	*Groups*	*Age*	*Income (in thousand rupees)*	*Attitude*	*Occupation*
1	1	53	164	4.00	4
2	1	61	152	4.00	3
3	1	51	135	5.00	5
4	1	35	108	5.00	4
5	1	56	118	4.00	3
6	1	70	160	6.00	4
7	1	64	105	5.00	2
8	1	52	130	6.00	5
9	1	58	145	6.00	3
10	1	46	154	6.00	4
11	1	43	164	5.00	4

(Continued)

TABLE 18.2 *(Continued)*

Subject no.	*Groups*	*Age*	*Income (in thousand rupees)*	*Attitude*	*Occupation*
12	1	63	160	4.00	3
13	1	52	128	1.00	5
14	2	54	78	5.00	2
15	2	50	86	4.00	1
16	2	53	99	1.00	1
17	2	52	95	1.00	2
18	2	43	98	6.00	2
19	2	45	86	6.00	1
20	2	56	120	2.00	1
21	2	50	100	4.00	3
22	2	65	80	6.00	4
23	2	52	84	3.00	3
24	2	55	92	5.00	2
25	2	33	124	6.00	1
26	2	50	73	5.00	1

TABLE 18.3
Data obtained for the garment company (hold-out sample)

Subject no.	*Groups*	*Age*	*Income (in thousand rupees)*	*Attitude*	*Occupation*
1	1	48	149	4	5
2	1	57	131	6	3
3	1	59	115	5	5
4	1	61	161	4	3
5	1	46	148	5	5
6	2	55	114	3	2
7	2	38	143	4	2
8	2	45	125	5	4
9	2	52	120	2	5
10	2	36	165	2	3

Perform a discriminant analysis to identify the variables that are relatively better in discriminating between the satisfied and the not satisfied consumers.

Solution SPSS generated output for Example 18.1 is shown in Figure 18.2.

Analysis case processing summary

Unweighted Cases		N	Percent
Valid		26	100.0
Excluded	Missing or out-of-range group codes	0	0.0
	At least one missing discriminating variable	0	0.0
	Both missing or our-of-range group codes and at least one missing discriminating variable	0	0.0
	Total	0	0.0
Total		26	100.0

(a)

Group Statistics

Group		Mean	Std. Deviation	Valid N (listwise)	
				Unweighted	Weighted
1.00	Age	54.1538	9.44145	13	13.000
	Income	140.2308	21.05213	13	13.000
	Attitude	4.6923	1.37747	13	13.000
	Occupation	3.7692	0.92681	13	13.000
2.00	Age	50.6154	7.51153	13	13.000
	Income	93.4615	15.20754	13	13.000
	Attitude	4.1538	1.86396	13	13.000
	Occupation	1.8462	0.98710	13	13.000
Total	Age	52.3846	8.55138	26	26.000
	Income	116.8462	29.87399	26	26.000
	Attitude	4.4231	1.62906	26	26.000
	Occupation	2.8077	1.35703	26	26.000

(b)

Tests of Equity of Group Means

	Wilks' Lambda	F	df1	df2	Sig.
Age	0.955	1.118	1	24	0.301
Income	0.363	42.161	1	24	0.000
Attitude	0.972	0.702	1	24	0.410
Occupation	0.478	26.224	1	24	0.000

(c)

FIGURE 18.2
(a) Analysis case processing summary table, (b) Group statistics table, (c) Test of equity of group means table

Pooled Within-Groups Matrices

		Age	Income	Attitude	Occupation
Correlation	Age	1.000	-0.039	-0.142	-0.012
	Income	-0.039	1.000	-0.042	-0.067
	Attitude	-0.142	-0.042	1.000	0.037
	Occupation	-0.012	-0.067	0.037	1.000

(d)

Eigenvalues

Function	Eigenvalue	% of Variance	Cumulative %	Canonical Correlation
1	3.184[a]	100.0	100.0	0.872

a. First 1 canonical discriminant functions were used in the analysis.

(e)

Wilk's Lambda

Test of Function(s)	Wilks' Lambda	Chi-square	df	Sig.
1	0.239	31.487	4	0.000

(f)

Standardized Canonical Discriminant Function Coefficients

	Function
	1
Age	0.178
Income	0.798
Attitude	0.131
Occupation	0.637

(g)

Structure Matrix

	Function
	1
Income	0.743
Occupation	0.586
Age	0.121
Attitude	0.096

Pooled within-groups correlations between discriminating variables and standardized canonical discriminant functions
Variables ordered by absolute size of correlation within function.

(h)

Canonical Discriminant Function Coefficients

	Function
	1
Age	0.021
Income	0.043
Attitude	0.080
Occupation	0.665
(Constant)	-8.395

Unstandardized coefficients

(i)

Functions at Group Centroids

Group	Function 1
1.00	1.714
2.00	-1.714

Unstandardized canonical discriminant functions evaluated at group means

(j)

FIGURE 18.2
(d) Pooled within-group matrices table, (e) Eigenvalues table, (f) Wilks' lambda table, (g) Standardized canonical discriminant function coefficients, (h) Structure matrix table, (i) Canonical discriminant function coefficients table, (j) Function at group centroids table

Classification Processing Summary

Processed		26
Excluded	Missing or out-of-range group codes	0
	At least one missing discriminating variable	0
Used in Output		26

(k)

Prior Probabilities for Groups

		Cases Used in Analysis	
Group	Prior	Unweighted	Weighted
1.00	0.500	13	13.000
2.00	0.500	13	13.000
Total	1.000	26	26.000

(l)

Classification Results[b,c]

			Predicted Group Membership		
		Group	1.00	2.00	Total
Original	Count	1.00	12	1	13
		2.00	0	13	13
	%	1.00	92.3	7.7	100.0
		2.00	0.0	100.0	100.0
Cross-validated[a]	Count	1.00	11	2	13
		2.00	1	12	13
	%	1.00	84.6	15.4	100.0
		2.00	7.7	92.3	100.0

a. Cross-validation is done only for those cases in the analysis. In cross-validation, each case is classified by the functions derived from all cases other than that case.

b. 96.2% of original grouped cases correctly classified.

c. 88.5% of cross-validated grouped cases correctly classified.

(m)

FIGURE 18.2
(k) Classification processing summary table, (l) Prior probabilities for groups table, (m) Classification results table

18.1.5.2 Computing Discriminant Function Coefficient

After identifying the analysis sample, discriminant function coefficients are estimated. There are two methods to determine the discriminant function coefficients: **direct method and stepwise method**. This process is similar to the process of least square adopted for multiple regression. In the direct method, all the independent variables are included simultaneously, regardless of their discriminant power to estimate the discriminant function. In the stepwise method, the independent variables are entered sequentially based on their capacity to discriminate among groups.

There are two methods to determine the discriminant function coefficients: direct method and stepwise method.

As discussed earlier, there are four independent variables in Example 18.1, and each respondent's individual discriminant score can be obtained by substituting his or her values for each of the four variables in the discriminant equation as below.

$$D = -8.395 + 0.021(\text{age}) + 0.043(\text{income}) + 0.080(\text{attitude}) + 0.665(\text{occupation}).$$

18.1.5.3 Testing Statistical Significance of the Discriminant Function

It is important to verify the significant level of the discriminant function. Null hypothesis can be statistically tested. Here, null hypothesis is framed as in the population; means of all discriminant functions in all the groups are equal. As discussed earlier, Wilks' lambda (λ) is used for this purpose, which is the ratio of within-group sum of squares to the total group sum of squares. The Wilks' lambda is a statistic that assesses whether the discriminant analysis is statistically significant (Hair et al. 2002). To test the significance of each independent variable, the corresponding F value is used. To test the significance of the **discriminant function**, chi-square transformation of Wilks' λ is used. A high value of χ^2 indicates that the functions significantly differ from each other. In Example 18.1, χ^2 value is found to be 31.487 with the corresponding p value as 0. This value is significant at 99% confidence level. Hence, it can be concluded that the population means of all the discriminant functions in all the groups are not equal (acceptance of alternative hypothesis). It indicates that the discriminant function is statistically significant and further interpretation of the function can be proceeded.

To test the significance of each independent variable, the corresponding F value is used. To test the significance of the discriminant function, chi-square transformation of Wilks' λ is used. A high value of χ^2 indicates that the functions significantly differ from each other.

18.1.5.4 Result (Generally Obtained through Statistical Software) Interpretation

Figure 18.2(a) shows **analysis case processing summary table**. This is the first part of the discriminant analysis output. This gives a summary of the number of cases (weighted and unweighted) for each level (category) of the dependent variable and the values for each level.

Figure 18.2(b) shows **group statistics**, which gives the means and standard deviations for both the groups. From this figure, few preliminary observations about the groups can be made, and it clearly shows that the two groups are widely separated with respect to two variables: **income and occupation**. With respect to age, the difference between the two groups is minimal. A visible difference can also be observed in terms of the standard deviation of the two groups.

Figure 18.2(c) shows **test of equity of group means**. F statistic determines the variable that should be included in the model (Riveiro-Valino et al. 2009) and describes that when predictors (independent variables) are considered individually, **only income and occupation significantly differ** between the two groups. The last column of Table 18.2(c) is the p value corresponding to the F value and confirms that only income and occupation differ significantly between the two groups.

Figure 18.2(d) shows **pooled within-group matrices** and indicates the degree of correlation between the predictors. From the figure, it can be observed clearly that there exist weak correlations (0 is no correlation) between the predictors. Thus, multi-collinearity will not be a problem.

Figure 18.2(e) shows **Eigenvalues table**, a large eigenvalue is an indication of a strong function. In Example 18.1, only one function is created with two levels of dependent variables. If there are three levels of dependent variables (a case of multiple discriminant analysis), $3 - 1 = 2$ functions will be created. A maximum of $n - 1$ discriminant functions are mathematically possible when there are n groups (Raghunathan and Raghunathan 1999). The function always accounts for 100% of the variance. As discussed earlier, canonical correlation measures the degree of association between the discriminant scores and the groups (levels of dependent variable). A high value of the canonical correlation indicates that a function discriminates well between the groups. Canonical correlation associated with the function is 0.872. Square of this value is given as $(0.872)^2 = 0.7603$. This indicates that 76.03% of variance in the dependent variable can be attributed to this model.

Figure 18.2(f) shows **Wilks' lambda table**. This is already described in the significance of the discriminant function determination (Section 18.1.5.3).

Figure 18.2(g) shows **standardized canonical discriminant function coefficients**. From the figure, it can be noted that **income** is the most important predictor in discriminating between the groups followed by **occupation, age, and attitude towards shopping**, and note that *F* values associated with **income and occupation** are significant (see Figure 18.2(c)).

Figure 18.2(h) shows **structure matrix table**. The following line appears in the output of SPSS, "Pooled within-group correlations between discriminating variables and standardized canonical discriminant function variable ordered by absolute size of correlation within function." Pooled values are the average of the group correlations. These structured correlations are referred as **canonical loadings or discriminant loadings**. The importance of a predictor variable can be judged by the magnitude of correlations. Higher the value of correlations, higher is the importance of the corresponding predictor.

Pooled values are the average of the group correlations. These structured correlations are referred as canonical loadings or discriminant loadings.

Figure 18.2(i) shows **canonical discriminant function coefficients table**, which gives an **unstandardized coefficient** and a **constant value** for the discriminant equation. As discussed earlier, after substituting the unstandardized coefficient values with the corresponding predictor and constant values, the discriminant equation can be written as

$$D = -8.395 + 0.021(\text{age}) + 0.043(\text{income}) + 0.080(\text{attitude}) + 0.665(\text{occupation}).$$

Figure 18.2(j) shows **function at group centroids table**. These are unstandardized canonical discriminant functions evaluated at group means and are obtained by placing the variable means for each group in the discriminant equation rather than placing the individual variable values. For the first group—satisfied—the group centroid is a positive value (1.714), and for the second group, it is an equal negative value (−1.714). The two scores are equal in absolute value but have opposite signs. From the discriminant equation, it can be noted that all the coefficients associated with the predictors have a positive sign. These results show that higher age, higher income, higher attitude towards shopping, and higher level of occupation are likely to result in satisfied consumers. Of the four predictors, only two have got a significant *p* value. Hence, it will be useful to develop a profile with these two statistically significant predictors.

Figure 18.2(k) shows **classification processing summary table.**

Figure 18.2(l) shows **prior probability for groups table**. In the second column, the value 0.5 indicates that the groups are weighted equally.

18.1.5.5 Concluding Comments by Performing Classification and Validation of Discriminant Analysis

Classification results table is a simple table of the number and percentage of subjects classified correctly and incorrectly.

Figure 18.2(m) shows **classification results table**, which is a simple table of the number and percentage of subjects classified correctly and incorrectly. Both SPSS and Minitab offer cross-validation option. In leave-one-out-classification, the discriminant model is re-estimated as many times as the number of subjects in the sample. Each model leaves one subject and is used to predict that respondent. In other words, each subject in the analysis is classified from the function derived from all cases except itself. This is referred as *U* method.

In the **classification matrix**, the diagonal elements of the matrix represent correct classification. The **hit ratio**, which is the percentage of cases correctly classified, can be obtained by summing the diagonal elements and dividing it by the total number of subjects. From Figure 18.2(m), it can be noted that the sum of the diagonal elements is 25 (i.e., 12 + 13 = 25), hence the hit ratio can be computed as 25/26 = 0.9615, and a line can be seen as a part of the SPSS output that "96.2% of the original grouped cases correctly classified." This 96.2% is the hit ratio. One has to determine a **good hit ratio**. When the groups are

In the classification matrix, the diagonal elements of the matrix represent correct classification. The hit ratio, which is the percentage of cases correctly classified, can be obtained by summing the diagonal elements and dividing it by the total number of subjects.

Classification Results[b,c]

		Group	Predicted Group Membership 1.00	2.00	Total
Original	Count	1.00	5	0	5
		2.00	0	5	5
	%	1.00	100.0	0.0	100.0
		2.00	0.0	100.0	100.0
Cross-validated[a]	Count	1.00	4	1	5
		2.00	1	4	5
	%	1.00	80.0	20.0	100.0
		2.00	20.0	80.0	100.0

a. Cross-validation is done only for those cases in the analysis. In cross validation, each case is classified by the functions derived from all cases other than that case.

b. 100.0% of original grouped cases correctly classified.

c. 80.0% of cross-validated grouped cases correctly classified.

FIGURE 18.3
SPSS classification results table for hold-out sample

equal in size (as in our case), the percentage of chance classification is one divided by the number of groups. Thus, in Example 18.1, the percentage of chance classification is 0.5 (i.e., 1/2 = 0.5). As a thumb rule, if the classification accuracy obtained from the discriminant analysis is 25% greater than that obtained from chance then the validity of the discriminant analysis is judged as satisfactory.

As discussed, in the classification matrix, the numbers of cases correctly classified are 96.2%. One can argue that this figure is inflated, as the data for estimation are also used for validation. Leave-one-out-classification (cross-validation) correctly classifies 88.5% of the cases. The classification matrix of the hold-out sample (Figure 18.3) indicates that 100% of the cases are correctly classified and cross-validation indicates that 80% of the cases are correctly classified. Improvement over chance is more than 25%; hence, validity of the discriminant analysis is judged as satisfactory (no clear guideline is available for this, but few authors have suggested that the classification accuracy obtained from the discriminant analysis should be 25% more than the classification accuracy obtained by chance).

In the maximum chance criterion, a randomly selected subject should be assigned to a larger group to maximize the proportion of cases correctly classified. The proportional chance criterion allows the assignment of randomly selected subjects to a group on the basis of the original proportion in the sample.

When the two groups considered in the discriminant analysis are of **unequal size**, then two criteria—the **maximum chance criterion** and the **proportional chance criterion**—can be used to judge the validity of the discriminant analysis. In the **maximum chance criterion**, a randomly selected subject should be assigned to a larger group to maximize the proportion of cases correctly classified. The **proportional chance criterion** allows the assignment of randomly selected subjects to a group on the basis of the original proportion in the sample. The formula used for this purpose is as follows: (proportion of individuals in Group 1)^2 + (1 − proportion of individuals in Group 2)^2.

For example, a sample of size 100 is divided into two groups with 70 and 30 subjects in Groups 1 and 2, respectively. In this case, the proportional chance criterion will be equal to $(0.70)^2 + (0.30)^2 = 0.58$. Thus, a classification accuracy of 80% seems to have a good improvement over chance.

18.2 CONJOINT ANALYSIS

In the field of management, **conjoint analysis** has got wide applications in marketing research and product development. A marketing manager faces a common problem—how do customers evaluate various tangible or intangible attributes offered by a particular product? For example, a customer may wish to purchase a colour television. Now, he or she will have to make a judgement about his preference for various attribute combinations such as brand image, flat screen, screen size, sound quality, picture quality, price of different models, and so on. Conjoint analysis provides an answer to this question. The main objective of **conjoint analysis** is to find out the attributes of the product that a respondent prefers most.

The main objective of conjoint analysis is to find out the attributes of the product that a respondent prefers most.

18.2.1 Introduction

The word '**conjoint**' refers to the notion that relative value of any phenomenon (product in most of the cases) can be measured jointly, which may not be measured when taken individually. People tend to be better at giving well-ordered preferences when evaluating options together (conjointly) rather than in isolation; this method relieves a respondent from the difficult task of accurately introspecting the relative importance of individual attributes for a particular decision (Green and Rao 1971). Conjoint analysis determines the relative importance of various product attributes (attached by the consumers to different product attributes) and values (utilities) attached to different levels of these attributes. It is an attempt to measure the value of each attribute on the basis of the responses provided by the customers in a systematic way. It uses the customer's responses to infer their value system about the attributes of a product instead of using self-evaluation of the consumer's preference of different product attributes. In fact, conjoint analysis asks the participants to give an overall evaluation of the product that vary systematically on a number of attributes (Caruso et al. 2009).

The word conjoint refers to the notion that relative value of any phenomenon (product in most of the cases) can be measured jointly, which may not be measured when taken individually.

18.2.2 Concept of Performing Conjoint Analysis

To understand the concept of conjoint analysis, let us consider the colour television example once again. Suppose the consumer has got two choices in terms of two different brands: "Brand A" and "Brand B." The consumer is willing to consider three attributes—brand image, sound quality, and picture quality. The consumer is supposed to provide his preference for these three attributes on a 5-point rating scale (where 5 indicates very high degree of preference and 1 indicates very low degree of preference). The consumer's preference is given in Table 18.4.

The general tendency of the respondents is to indicate that all the attributes are important. In conjoint analysis, the respondent is supposed to make trade-off judgements. In Table 18.4, he or she is willing to trade-off the superiority of Brand B on brand image and sound quality over the superiority of Brand A on picture quality because utility may be attached to "picture quality." The conjoint analysis is based on the assumption that subjects evaluate the value or utility of a product or service or idea (real or hypothetical) by combining the separate amount of utility provided by each attribute (Schaupp and Belanger 2005). It works on the simple principle of developing a **part-worth or utility function** stating the utility consumers attach to the levels of each attribute.

Conjoint analysis works on the simple principal of developing a part-worth or utility function stating the utility consumers attach to the levels of each attribute.

TABLE 18.4
Consumer's preference for the attributes of two brands of television

Attributes	*Brand A*	*Brand B*
Brand image	3	4
Sound quality	3	5
Picture quality	5	2

As discussed, the conjoint analysis has a wide range of application in the field of marketing. It can be effectively used in situations when alternative products or services have a large number of attributes with each having two or more levels. The example of the consumer's preference for the attributes of two brands of television is the simplest one in terms of comparison of the attributes of the product. In real-life situations, the attributes offered to consumers to indicate their preference may be conflicting in nature. For example, a consumer has to select between mileage and pick-up capacity of a motorbike. The main issue of focus in conjoint analysis is to find out compromise set of attribute levels. The procedure of using conjoint analysis can be better explained by the steps in conducting the conjoint analysis, which are discussed in the next section.

18.2.3 Steps in Conducting Conjoint Analysis

The conjoint analysis is performed using the following five steps: problem formulation, trade-off data collection, metric versus non-metric input data, result analysis and interpretation, and reliability and validity check. These steps are explained in Figure 18.4.

18.2.3.1 Problem Formulation

To formulate a problem, as a first step, a researcher must identify the various attributes and attribute levels.

To formulate a problem, as a first step, a researcher must identify the various attributes and attribute levels. These attributes can be identified from discussion with the management or industry expert, secondary data, pilot survey, and so on. While selecting an attribute, the researcher should keep in mind that the selected attribute should be actionable. An actionable attribute means that the company or management can do something about the attribute based on the result of conjoint analysis.

As a thumb rule, the number of attributes used in a typical conjoint analysis study averages six or seven.

The number of attributes used in the conjoint analysis should be selected with care. As a thumb rule, the number of attributes used in a typical conjoint analysis study averages six or seven. After identification of the salient attributes to be used, appropriate (actual) levels of each attributes should be specified. The number of attribute levels determines the number of parameters that will be estimated, and consequently, it affects the consumer's preference of an attribute and level. To minimize the consumer's evaluation task and to estimate the parameter with reasonable degree of accuracy, it is desirable to have a check on the number of attribute levels. It is important to understand that the model is linear depending on the number of the most desired attributes. In other cases, the model may be non-linear or there may not be any systematic relationship between the consumer's preference and the attribute level. For example, while purchasing an air conditioner, most of the consumers would like to prefer a low price or less electricity bill indicating a linear relationship between the utilities and the attribute level. In the same situation, many consumers may prefer a medium price range rather than high or low, indicating a non-linear relationship.

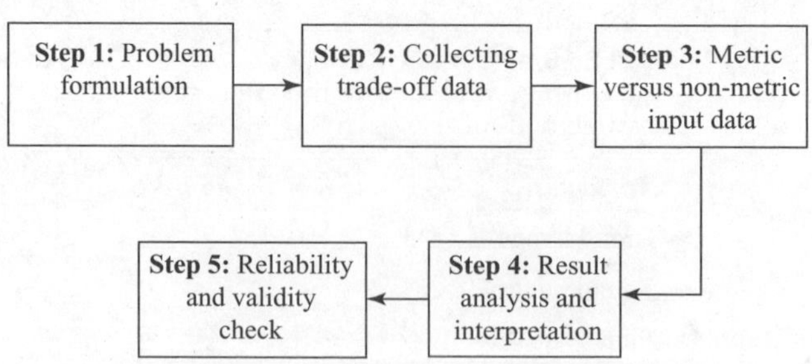

FIGURE 18.4
Five steps of conducting conjoint analysis

TABLE 18.5
Attributes and levels of colour television

Attribute	*Level no.*	*Details*
Screen	3	Flat
	2	Semi-flat
	1	No flat
Sound quality	3	Superior quality
	2	High quality
	1	Average quality
Price	3	10,000
	2	15,000
	1	20,000

It is obvious that the attribute level selected will affect the consumer's process of evaluation. For example, if the price of the colour television varies at ₹500, ₹700, and ₹900, the price will be relatively unimportant as compared with the situation when the price varies at ₹1000, ₹2500, and ₹4000. A researcher should consider the attribute levels that exist in the market to enhance the consumer's believability of the evaluation task. Using attribute levels that are not prevalent in the market will decrease the believability of the consumers but can increase the accuracy with which the parameters are statistically estimated. In this regard, the general recommendation is to select the attribute levels that are larger than the attribute levels prevailing in the market but not as large as it can make the options unbelievable.

To understand the concept of conjoint analysis, let us continue with the colour television example. Suppose the company has conducted a qualitative research and three attributes, such as screen, sound quality, and price, have been identified as salient attributes. Each attribute is defined in terms of three levels that are given in Table 18.5.

18.2.3.2 Trade-off Data Collection

To construct conjoint analysis stimuli, two broad approaches are available: the pair-wise (two-factor) approach and full-profile approach. The respondents can reveal their trade-off judgements by either considering two attributes at a time or making an overall judgement of a full profile of the attributes (Aaker et al. 2000). In the pair-wise approach, the respondents are required to evaluate two attributes at a time until all the possible pairs of attributes have been exhausted. These attributes can be identified through discussion with the management and industry experts, analysis of secondary data, qualitative research, and pilot survey (Malhotra 2004). In the case of the colour television, this approach is illustrated in Tables 18.6, 18.7, and 18.8.

To construct conjoint analysis stimuli, two broad approaches are available: the pair-wise (two-factor) approach and full-profile approach.

TABLE 18.6
Pair-wise (two-factor) approach for comparison between screen and sound quality

Sound quality	*Screen*		
	Flat	*Semi-flat*	*No flat*
Superior quality			
High quality			
Average quality			

TABLE 18.7
Pair-wise (two-factor) approach for comparison between screen and price

Price	*Screen*		
	Flat	*Semi-flat*	*No flat*
10,000			
15,000			
20,000			

TABLE 18.8
Pair-wise (two-factor) approach for comparison between sound quality and price

Price	*Sound quality*		
	Superior quality	*High quality*	*Average quality*
10,000			
15,000			
20,000			

Attribute	Details of level
Screen	Flat
Sound quality	High quality
Price	15000

FIGURE 18.5
Full-profile approach for collecting conjoint data

In full-profile approach, a full profile of the brands is constructed with all the attributes. An index card is used to describe each profile. Figure 18.5 is an example of the full-profile approach.

Both the methods, that is, pair-wise (two-factor) approach and full-profile approach, have their own utility, but full-profile approach is the most widely used method.

It is easy for the respondents to supply information through pair-wise judgement as compared with the judgement based on the full-profile approach. There are some advantages and disadvantages of pair-wise judgement. In the disadvantage side, when the number of attributes and levels are high, the respondent may supply mechanical information (supplying information for the sake of supplying information). In other cases, the task of evaluation may become unrealistic because only two attributes are being compared simultaneously. Apart from these disadvantages, this approach has got few advantages in terms of checking the consistency of the respondents in answering. The respondents who show great deal of inconsistency in answering can be removed from the analysis. Both the methods, that is, pair-wise (two factor) approach and full-profile approach, have their own utility, but full-profile approach is the most widely used method. It gives a more realistic description of stimuli by defining the levels of the factors and possibly taking into account the potential environmental correlation between the factors in real stimuli (Green and Srinivasan 1978).

In the colour television example, three attributes and three levels of each attribute are given. Hence, following full-profile approach, a total of $3 \times 3 \times 3 = 27$ profiles can be constructed.

In the colour television example, three attributes and three levels of each attribute are given. Hence, following full-profile approach, a total of $3 \times 3 \times 3 = 27$ profiles can be constructed. To minimize the evaluation risk of the respondents, fractional factorial design will be used and nine set of responses will be kept in estimation stimuli set and nine set of responses will be kept in the category of validation stimuli. The next step focuses on making decisions about the form of input data.

18.2.3.3 Metric Versus Non-Metric Input Data

Conjoint analysis data can be of both the forms: metric data and non-metric data. For non-metric data, the respondents indicate ranking, and for metric data, the respondents indicate rating. Rating approach has got popularity in recent days. As obvious, in conjoint analysis, the dependent variable is consumer preference or intention to buy a product (rating or ranking provided by the customers for buying a product). In the colour television example, ratings are obtained in a 7-point Likert scale with 1 as not preferred and 7 as highly preferred. These ratings are given in Table 18.9.

18.2.3.4 Result Analysis and Interpretation

In this step, a proper technique is selected to analyse the input data obtained in the previous step and then interpretation is made. The conjoint analysis model can be represented by the following formula:

$$U(x) = \sum_{i=1}^{m} \sum_{j=1}^{k_i} u_{ij} x_{ij},$$

where $U(x)$ is the utility of an alternative, u_{ij} the part-worth contribution (utility of jth level of ith attribute), k_i the number of levels for attribute i, and m the number of attributes. $x_{ij} = 1$ if the jth level of the ith attribute is present and $x_{ij} = 0$ otherwise.

Importance of an attribute R_i can be defined as the range of part-worth contribution, across the levels of attributes.

Importance of an attribute $(R_i) = [\text{maximum}(u_{ij}) - \text{minimum}(u_{ij})]$

The relative importance of the attribute can be computed by dividing the importance of an attribute by the total importance of all the attributes. Symbolically,

$$\text{Relative importance of an attribute} = \frac{R_i}{\sum_{i=1}^{m} R_i},$$

where

$$\sum_{i=1}^{m} R_i = 1.$$

To estimate the model, a variety of techniques are available. The most popular and widely applied technique is dummy variable regression technique. In most of the researches, the researchers **assign 0 or 1 to code** dummy variables. It is important to note that the assignment

To estimate the model, a variety of techniques are available. The most popular and widely applied technique is dummy variable regression technique.

TABLE 18.9
Selected profiles of colour television example

Profile no.	*Screen*	*Sound quality*	*Price*	*Preference rating*
1	1	1	1	5
2	1	2	2	7
3	1	3	3	6
4	2	1	1	4
5	2	2	2	6
6	2	3	3	5
7	3	1	1	3
8	3	2	2	2
9	3	3	3	1

of code 0 or 1 is **arbitrary** and numbers merely represent a **place for the category**. In many situations, indicator or dummy variables are **dichotomous** (dummy variables have two categories such as male or female, graduate or non-graduate, married or unmarried, etc.). A particular dummy variable x_d is defined as

$$x_d = 0, \text{ if the observation belongs to Category 1}$$

and

$$x_d = 1, \text{ if the observation belongs to Category 2.}$$

Another important point in analysing the data is to decide whether the data will be analysed on individual basis or aggregate basis. In terms of individual-level analysis, each respondent (data obtained from the respondent) is analysed separately. To apply aggregate-level analysis on the basis of similarity in part-worth, the respondents can be grouped and then an aggregate-level analysis can be performed for each cluster.

To analyse the conjoint analysis data, dummy variables are treated as independent or explanatory variables and preference rating obtained from the respondent is treated as dependent variable. If the *i*th attribute has k_i levels then it is coded in $k_i - 1$ dummy variables. To analyse the data obtained from the respondent (given in Table 18.4), ordinary least square regression analysis is applied on dummy variables. In the regression model, there will be six dummy variables, two for each attribute. The data converted into dummy variables are listed in Table 18.10.

To estimate utility, regression model can be formed as

$$U = b_0 + b_1x_1 + b_2x_2 + b_3x_3 + b_4x_4 + b_5x_5 + b_6x_6$$

Using any statistical software, regression equation can be obtained as

$$U = 2.42 + 4.16x_1 + 3.53x_2 + 0.842x_3 + 0.632x_4 - 4.74x_5 - 2.26x_6$$

Figure 18.6 exhibits SPSS output (multiple regression) for the conjoint problem.

In this model, x_1 and x_2 are dummy variables representing the attribute "screen," x_3 and x_4 are dummy variables representing the attribute "sound quality," and x_5 and x_6 are dummy variables representing "price." For screen, attribute levels are coded as below:

TABLE 18.10
The colour television data converted into dummy variables on applying regression technique

Preference rating (dependent variable)	*Screen*		*Sound quality*		*Price*	
	x_1	x_2	x_3	x_4	x_5	x_6
5	1	0	0	1	0	1
7	1	0	1	0	1	0
6	1	0	0	0	1	0
4	0	1	1	0	0	1
6	0	1	0	0	0	0
5	0	1	1	0	0	1
3	0	0	0	1	0	0
2	0	0	0	0	1	0
1	0	0	1	0	0	1

Model Summary

Model	R	R Square	Adjusted R Square	Std. Error of the Estimate
1	0.992[a]	0.984	0.934	0.51299

a. Predictors: (Constant), x6, x4, x1, x2, x3, x5

ANOVA[b]

Model		Sum of Squares	df	Mean Square	F	Sig.
1	Regression	31.474	6	5.246	19.933	0.049[a]
	Residual	0.526	2	0.263		
	Total	32.000	8			

a. Predictors: (Constant), x6, x4, x1, x2, x3, x5

b. Dependent Variable: Rating

Coefficients[a]

Model		Unstandardized Coefficients		Standardized Coefficients		
		B	Std. Error	Beta	t	Sig.
1	(Constant)	2.421	0.772		3.137	0.088
	x1	4.158	0.526	1.039	7.900	0.016
	x2	3.526	0.623	0.882	5.663	0.030
	x3	0.842	0.526	0.222	1.600	0.251
	x4	0.632	0.865	0.139	0.730	0.541
	x5	-0.474	0.956	-0.118	-0.495	0.669
	x6	-2.263	0.600	-0.596	-3.771	0.064

a. Dependent Variable: Rating

FIGURE 18.6 SPSS output (multiple regression) for conjoint problem

	x_1	x_2
If screen is flat (Level 1)	1	0
If screen is semi-flat (Level 2)	0	1
If screen is no flat (Level 3)	0	0

Similarly, other attribute levels can also be coded. From the regression equation, we can obtain the regression coefficients, such as $b_0 = 2.42$, $b_1 = 4.16$, $b_2 = 3.53$, $b_3 = 0.842$, $b_4 = 0.632$, $b_5 = -0.474$, and $b_6 = -2.26$.

From the coding pattern of the dummy variables (exhibited from coding of screen), it can be noted that Level 3 is the base level. Each dummy variable coefficient can be represented as the difference between part-worth for the concerned level and the base level. For example, for the **first attribute**, screen

$$b_1 = u_{11} - u_{13}$$

and

$$b_2 = u_{12} - u_{13}.$$

In estimating the part-worth, on an interval scale, the origin is arbitrary. Hence, among the three utilities, the following equation exists.

$$u_{11} + u_{12} + u_{13} = 0.$$

After substituting the values of b_1 and b_2, for screen, the following three equations are obtained.

$$u_{11} - u_{13} = 4.16,$$

$$u_{12} - u_{13} = 3.53,$$

and

$$u_{11} + u_{12} + u_{13} = 0.$$

Solving these equations, we get

$$u_{11} = 1.586667,$$

$$u_{12} = 0.996667,$$

and

$$_{13} = -2.56333.$$

Similarly, for the **second attribute**, sound quality, below equations can be obtained:

$$u_{21} - u_{23} = 0.842,$$

$$u_{22} - u_{23} = 0.632,$$

and

$$u_{21} + u_{22} + u_{23} = 0.$$

Solving these equations, we get

$$u_{21} = -0.350667$$

$$u_{21} = 0.140667,$$

and

$$u_{23} = -0.491333.$$

For the **third attribute,** price, below equations can be obtained:

$$u_{31} - u_{33} = -4.74,$$

$$u_{32} - u_{33} = -2.26,$$

and

$$u_{31} + u_{32} + u_{33} = 0.$$

Solving these equations, we will get

$$u_{31} = 2.33333,$$

$$u_{32} = -2.406667,$$

and

$$u_{33} = 0.07333.$$

As discussed, the importance of an attribute is given as

$$R_i = \left[\text{maximum}\left(u_{ij}\right) - \text{minimum}\left(u_{ij}\right)\right].$$

Thus, importance of the first, second, and third attributes can be computed as

$$R_1 = \left[\text{maximum}\left(u_{ij}\right) - \text{minimum}\left(u_{ij}\right)\right] = [1.586667 - (-2.56333)] = 4.149997,$$

$$R_2 = \left[\text{maximum}\left(u_{ij}\right) - \text{minimum}\left(u_{ij}\right)\right] = [0.350667 - (-0.491333)] = 0.842,$$

and

$$R_3 = \left[\text{maximum}\left(u_{ij}\right) - \text{minimum}\left(u_{ij}\right)\right] = [2.33333 - (-2.406667)] = 4.739967.$$

$$\sum_{i=1}^{3}\left(R_1 + R_2 + R_3\right) = 4.149997 + 0.842 + 4.739967 = 9.731964.$$

The relative importance of the attribute can be computed by dividing the importance of an attribute by the total importance of all the attributes. Symbolically,

$$\text{Relative importance of an attribute} = \frac{R_i}{\sum_{i=1}^{m} R_i},$$

where

$$\sum_{i=1}^{m} R_i = 1.$$

Therefore,

$$\text{Relative importance of screen} = \frac{R_i}{\sum_{i=1}^{3} R_i} = \frac{4.149997}{9.731964} = 0.4264,$$

$$\text{Relative importance of sound quality} = \frac{R_i}{\sum_{i=1}^{3} R_i} = \frac{0.842}{9.731964} = 0.0865,$$

and

$$\text{Relative importance of price} = \frac{R_i}{\sum_{i=1}^{3} R_i} = \frac{4.739967}{9.731964} = 0.4870.$$

TABLE 18.11
Result of the conjoint analysis

Attribute	*Level no.*	*Details*	*Utility*	*Importance*
Screen	3	Flat	1.586667	0.4264
	2	Semi-Flat	0.996667	
	1	No flat	–2.56333	
Sound quality	3	Superior quality	0.350667	0.0865
	2	High quality	0.140667	
	1	Average quality	–0.491333	
Price	3	10,000	2.33333	0.4870
	2	15,000	–2.406667	
	1	20,000	0.07333	

The result of the conjoint analysis is presented in Table 18.11. It can be noted that utilities are given in Column 4 and relative importance of various attributes are given in Column 5.

For easy interpretation of the result obtained from conjoint analysis, it is important to plot a graph of utility functions.

For easy interpretation of the result obtained from conjoint analysis, it is important to plot a graph of utility functions. From Table 18.11, it can be seen that flat screen is mostly preferred by the customer, followed by semi-flat and no-flat screen; in terms of sound quality, superior-quality sound is mostly preferred, followed by high quality and average quality; and in terms of price, low-level price, that is ₹10,000, is mostly preferred by the customer, followed by the price of ₹20,000 and ₹15,000. In terms of relative importance of the attribute, it can be seen that the price is most important for the customers, followed by screen and sound quality.

18.2.3.5 Reliability and Validity Check

The following are some of the points that a researcher should strictly adhere to assess the reliability and validity of conjoint analysis:

- As discussed in regression, to estimate the best-fit model, the value of R^2 is an indicator. In our model, value of R^2 is obtained as 98.4%, which indicates a good-fit model.
- Earlier discussed test–retest method of reliability assessment can be applied.
- In an aggregate level analysis, the total sample can be divided into various sub-samples, and conjoint analysis can be performed on all the sub-samples. Then across-samples results are compared to assess the stability of conjoint analysis.

18.2.4 Assumptions and Limitations of Conjoint Analysis

Conjoint analysis is based on the assumption that all the attributes that contribute to the utility of the product can be identified and are independent. Conjoint analysis also assumes that the consumers evaluate the alternatives and make trade-offs. One limitation of the conjoint analysis is that there may be few situations where brand name is an important factor and then the consumer may not evaluate the brands or alternatives in terms of attribute. For a large number of attributes, collection of data may be difficult.

REFERENCES

Aaker, D. A., V. Kumar and G. S. Day (2000). *Marketing Research*, 7th ed., p. 597. Wiley, Asia.

Caruso, E. M., D. A. Rahnev and M. R. Banaji (2009). "Using Conjoint Analysis to Detect Discrimination: Revealing Covert Preferences from Overt Choices", *Social Cognition*, 27(1): 128–37.

Green, P. E. and V. R. Rao (1971). "Conjoint Measurement for Quantifying Judgmental Data", *Journal of Marketing Research*, 8: 355–63 .

Green, P. E. and V. Srinivasan (1978). "Conjoint Analysis in Consumer Research: Issues and Outlook", *The Journal of Consumer Research*, 5(2): 103–23.

Hair, J. F., R. P. Bush and D. J. Ortinau (2002). *Marketing Research: Within a Changing Information Environment*, p. 615. Tata McGraw-Hill.

Hallaq, J. H. (1975). "Adjustment for Bias in Discriminant Analysis", *Journal of the Academy of Marketing Science*, 3(2): 172–81.

Malhotra, N. K. (2004). *Marketing Research: An Applied Orientation*, 4th ed., p. 623. Pearson Education.

Parasuraman, A., D. Grewal and R. Krishnan (2004). *Marketing Research*, pp. 514–515. Boston, MA: Houghton Mifflin Company.

Raghunathan, B. and T. S. Raghunathan (1999). "A Discriminant Analysis of Organizational Antecedents of is Performance", *Journal of Information Technology Management*, 10(1–2): 1–15.

Riveiro-Valino, J. A., C. J. Alvarez-Lopez and M. F. Marey-Perez (2009). "The Use of Discriminant Analysis to Validate a Methodology for Classifying Farms Based on a Combinatorial Algorithm", *Computer and Electronics in Agriculture*, 66: 113–20.

Sanchez, P. M. (1974). "The Unequal Group Size Problem in Discriminant Analysis", *Journal of Academy of Marketing Science*, 2(4): 629–33.

Schaupp, L. C. and F. Belanger (2005). "A Conjoint Analysis of Online Consumer Satisfaction", *Journal of Electronic Commerce Research*, 6(2): 95–111.

SUMMARY

Discriminant analysis is a technique of analysing data when the dependent variable is categorical and the independent variables are interval in nature. The difference between multiple regression and discriminant analysis can be examined in the light of nature of the dependent variable, which happens to be categorical, as compared with metric, as in the case of multiple regression analysis. Two-group discriminant analysis is conducted through the following five-step procedure: problem formulation, discriminant function coefficient estimation, significance of the discriminant function determination, result interpretation, and validity of the analysis determination. When categorical dependent variable has more than two categories, multiple discriminant analysis is performed.

The main objective of the conjoint analysis is to find the attributes of the product, which a respondent mostly prefers. The word conjoint refers to the notion that relative value of any phenomenon (product in most of the cases) can be measured jointly, which may not be measured when taken individually. Conjoint analysis determines the relative importance of various product attributes (attached by the consumers to different product attributes) and the values (utility) attached to different levels of these attributes. Conjoint analysis is conducted through the following five-step procedure: problem formulation, trade-off-data collection, metric versus non-metric input data, result analysis and interpretation, and reliability and validity check.

KEY TERMS

Canonical correlation, 443
Centroids, 443
Chi-square, 444
Classification matrix, 443
Classification results table, 451
Conjoint analysis, 442
Direct method and stepwise method, 449
Discriminant analysis model, 443
Discriminant analysis, 442
Discriminant function, 443
Discriminant scores, 443
Eigenvalue, 444
Estimation or analysis sample, 445
F values and its significance, 444
Good hit ratio, 451
Group statistics, 450
Hit ratio, 451
Hold-out or validation sample, 445
Maximum chance criterion, 452
Part-worth or utility functions, 453
Pooled within-group correlation matrix, 444
Proportional chance criterion, 452
Structure correlation, 444
Unstandardized discriminant coefficients, 443
Wilks' lambda, 444

NOTES

1. Prowess (V. 3.1): Centre for Monitoring Indian Economy Pvt. Ltd, Mumbai, accessed September 2009, reprinted with permission.
2. http://www.camlin.com/corporate/camlin_today.asp, accessed September 2009.
3. http://www.thehindubusinessline.com/2009/05/13/stories/2009051351771500.htm, accessed September 2009.

DISCUSSION QUESTIONS

1. Explain the difference between multiple regression and discriminant analysis.
2. What is the conceptual framework of discriminant analysis and under what circumstances can discriminant analysis be used for data analysis?
3. Write the steps in conducting discriminant analysis.
4. Write short notes on the following topics related to discriminant analysis.
   (a) Estimation or analysis sample
   (b) Hold-out or validation sample
   (c) Pooled within-group matrices
   (d) Eigenvalues
   (e) Wilks' lambda table
   (f) Standardized canonical discriminant function coefficients
   (g) Structure matrix table
   (h) Canonical loadings or discriminant loadings
   (i) Canonical discriminant function coefficients table
   (j) Unstandardized coefficient
   (k) Classification processing summary table
   (l) Hit ratio
5. Explain the conceptual framework of conjoint analysis and its application in the field of marketing.
6. What is part-worth or utility function in conjoint analysis?

CASE STUDY

Case 18: *Emami Limited: Emerging as a Well-Diversified Business Group*

Introduction

The inception of Emami Group took place way back in mid-seventies when two childhood friends, Mr R. S. Agarwal and Mr R. C. Goenka, left their high profile jobs with the Birla Group to set up Kemco Chemicals, an ayurvedic medicine and cosmetic manufacturing unit, in Kolkata in 1974. In 1978, this young organization has taken over a 100-year-old company, Himani Ltd (incorporated as a private limited company in 1949), with brand equity in Eastern India. It was a highly risky decision to buy a sick unit (Himani Ltd) and was difficult to turn it into a profitable organization. Ultimately, this risky decision was proven to be a turning point for the organization. In the year 1984, the company launched its first flagship brand "Boroplus antiseptic cream," followed by many successful brands in the following years. In 1995, Kemco Chemicals, the partnership firm was converted into a public limited company under the name and style of Emami Ltd. In 1998, Emami Ltd was merged with Himani Ltd and its name was changed to Emami Ltd as per fresh certificate of incorporation dated September 1998.[1] Table 18.01 lists sales and profit after tax (in million rupees) of Emami Ltd from 1994–1995 to 2007–2008.

Looking for Consolidation of the Business Through Brand Extension, Penetration in New Markets, and Launching Fresh Categories of Products

Emami has also planned to launch a ₹4000 million biofuel project in Ethiopia. In an interview to *The Financial Express*, the directors of Emami Group Mr Aditya V. Agarwal and Mr Manish Goenka discussed about the biofuel and inorganic growth options. They said, "We are always on the lookout of financially viable acquisitions. We may even consider acquiring companies outside India, particularly in underdeveloped and developing countries. Our revenue from international operations is currently around ₹1000 million. We expect this to grow to ₹3000 million in 3 years and about ₹7000 millions in 5 years. We are contemplating some regional brand acquisition. There are some heritage brands in Bengal that offers immense growth potential. After the Zandu acquisition, we together have the portfolio of around 350 brands. A restructuring of the brand portfolio is underway, and we will clearly define the exact role and positioning of each brand. For instance, each brand will be categorized as natural, ayurvedic, or synthetic. We will also launch new products. We also plan to launch a men's range, baby range including soap, talc and oil and further expand our FMCG business via brand extensions, penetration in new markets and fresh categories." The directors are optimistic about the future of biofuel business.[2]

The Emami group has plans to consolidate its fast-moving consumer goods (FMCG) business and realty business. It has taken a decision to bring its FMCG business under the flagship of the group Emami and realty company under the separate company Emami infrastructure. Mr N. H. Bhansali, CFO and President of Emami Ltd, highlighted the company's policy as "consolidation of FMCG business under one company, Emami, will also ensure various operational synergies, improve profitability, and lead to optimum utilization of the existing manufacturing facilities. Sales and distribution channels of two companies will also get integrated."[3]

Emami has unveiled ₹55,000 million investment plan for its flagship Emami and other group companies. This is a move to make the group a ₹60,000 million group over 2 years (The plan was unveiled in 2009). Talking about the plan, Mr R. S. Agarwal, Executive Chairman of the company, said, "Following the merger of Zandu Pharmaceuticals Works with Emami, we intend to re-launch the Zandu products as well as launch new products in the hair and skincare segment to boost earnings. These initiatives along with our attempt to streamline the operation of the two companies post-merger will require a lot of investment."[4]

TABLE 18.01
Sales and profit after tax (in million rupees) of Emami Ltd from 1994-1995 to 2007-2008

Year	*Sales*	*Profit after tax*
Mar-95	363.4	36.4
Mar-96	409.4	34
Mar-97	577.2	69.7
Mar-98	594.4	83.2
Mar-99	1004.6	99.2
Mar-00	1469.6	170.5
Mar-01	2100.9	206.3
Mar-02	1826.2	169.7
Mar-03	1986.5	183.8
Mar-04	2230.9	217.1
Mar-05	2255.6	295
Mar-06	3073.8	493.7
Mar-07	5200.7	659.3
Mar-08	5864.2	927.5

Source: Prowess (V. 3.1): Centre for Monitoring Indian Economy Pvt. Ltd, Mumbai, accessed September 2009, reprinted with permission.

Some Growth Drivers of Indian FMCG Industry

In India, some distinct factors seem to have generated a ray of great hope for the FMCG industry. The number of households using FMCG products is increasing day by day. The income of rural India is on increase because of increased irrigation facilities. Higher income and heavy television advertisements have fostered the use of branded products. Increase in disposable income, high aspirations of individuals, and higher spending on personal hygiene are also increasing. Few demographic factors, such as a large number of decisive youths, are in favour of FMCG companies. The retail sector in India is dominated by more than 12 million small outlets (one of the highest in the world in any single country) providing a large base for FMCG companies. The government's initiatives on infrastructure development in rural areas are supportive in providing untapped market of rural India. The development of new products in providing a large range to consumers will also enhance the market for FMCG.[5] Emami Ltd has already unveiled its plan to provide all these favourable factors and become a more than ₹60,000 million company in a couple of years.

Emami Ltd has plans to launch few men's range products. Assume that the company wants to conduct a research programme to understand the influence of various independent variables on three types of customer groups: urban customers, rural customers, and semi-rural customers, then a researcher collects relevant independent variables from the literature and develop a discriminant model to identify the discriminating power of these independent variables on the three categories of the dependent variable, "type of customers." In addition, he or she has to find some actionable attributes and attribute levels for men's range product, collect data, and perform conjoint analysis technique described in this chapter and discuss the obtained result.

NOTES |

1. http://www.emamiltd.in/about.asp?detail=history
2. http://www.financialexpress.com/printer/news/499390
3. http://economictimes.indiatimes.com/articleshow/4685147.cms?prtpage=1
4. http://economictimes.indiatimes.com/articleshow/4888190.cms?prtpage=1
5. Prowess (V. 3.1): Centre for Monitoring Indian Economy Pvt. Ltd, Mumbai, accessed September 2009, reprinted with permission.

CHAPTER **19**

Multivariate Analysis III: Factor Analysis, Cluster Analysis, Multidimensional Scaling and Correspondence Analysis

LEARNING OBJECTIVES

Upon completion of this chapter, you will be able to:

- Understand the concept and application of factor analysis
- Interpret the factor analysis output obtained from the statistical software
- Use Minitab and SPSS to perform factor analysis
- Understand the concept and application of cluster analysis
- Interpret the cluster analysis output obtained from the statistical software
- Use SPSS to perform cluster analysis
- Understand the concept and application of multidimensional scaling
- Interpret the multidimensional scaling output obtained from the statistical software
- Use SPSS to perform multidimensional scaling
- Have an introductory idea about correspondence analysis

RESEARCH IN ACTION: BATA INDIA LTD

In India, a large population demands a large shoe market, and the demand for footwear is continuously increasing. In the year 2000–2001, the demand for footwear was 900 million pairs, which is estimated to increase to 2290 million pairs by 2014–2015. In the time span of 2009–2010 to 2014–2015, the market is estimated to grow with a market growth rate of 7.5%. Despite this rosy scenario, market is highly segmented in favour of the informal market. Organized market has only 18% market share, whereas 82% of the market share is catered by the unorganized market. The footwear market is also diversified with respect to product variation. In the casuals, sports, formulas, and performance categories, footwear products occupy 53%, 32%, 7%, and 8% of the market share, respectively. Low-priced, medium-priced, and high-priced products occupy 65%, 32%, and 3% of the market share and leather, rubber/PVC, and canvas footwear occupy 10%, 35%, and 55% of the market share, respectively. Bata India, Liberty Shoe, Lakhani India, Nikhil Footwear, Graziella Shoes, Mirza Tanners, Relaxo Footwear, Performance Shoes, and so on are some of the leading players of the market.[1]

Bata India Ltd is the largest retailer and leading manufacturer of the footwear products in India and is a part of the Bata Shoe Organization. It was incorporated in 1931 as Bata Shoe Company Pvt. Ltd. The company initially started its business as a small operation in Konnagar in 1932. In January 1934, the company laid a foundation stone for the first building of Bata's operation—now called the Bata. The company went public in 1973 when it changed its name to Bata

>>>

India Ltd. With a wide retailer network of 1250 stores all over the country, today Bata India has established itself as India's largest footwear retailer.[2] Table 19.1 presents sales and profit after tax (in million rupees) of Bata India Ltd from 1994-1995 to 2008-2009.

Bata India Ltd, the largest shoe company in India, is overhauling its retail strategy to cope with the new dynamics of the marketplace after the centre opened up the segment to foreign single-brand stores. The company has taken a decision to be more visible in shopping malls, open up to franchisee models, and create the shop-in-shop experience in a multi-branded store.[3] The company has specific objectives to open showrooms in malls to cater the requirement of modern India. If a company wants to determine the features of an attractive showroom in the eyes of consumers and has appointed you as a researcher for conducting this research, with the help of literature and secondary data how will you determine the list of variables to be included in the study? If this list consists of some 70 statements generated from the literature, then how will you factorize these statements into a few factors?

In addition, if the company wants to group customers on some common attributes to present the different brands for the respective groups, then as a researcher, with the help of literature and secondary data, list down some of the common attributes on which the consumers can be clustered. Use the techniques of clustering presented in the chapter and cluster the customers on the basis of their preference for an attribute and then discuss how many cluster solutions will be an appropriate solution. The chapter deals with some of the commonly used multivariate techniques in the field of business research.

TABLE 19.1
Sales and profit after tax (in million rupees) of Bata India Ltd from 1994-1995 to 2008-2009

Year	*Sales*	*Profit after tax*
Mar-95	5076.8	9.8
Mar-96	5323.6	–421.6
Mar-97	5904.9	41.5
Mar-98	6702.2	167
Mar-99	7431.7	242.5
Mar-00	7736.4	304.6
Mar-01	7601.6	156
Mar-02	7599.9	39.8
Mar-03	6965.4	–74.1
Mar-04	7135.2	–260.5
Mar-05	7266.8	–627.5
Mar-06	7349.7	124.9
Mar-07	7956.5	401.5
Mar-08	8923.4	474.4
Mar-09	10,129.5	607.4

Source: Prowess (V. 3.1), Centre for Monitoring Indian Economy (CMIE) Pvt. Ltd, Mumbai, accessed September 2009, reprinted with permission.

19.1 FACTOR ANALYSIS

Factor analysis is a widely used multivariate technique in the field of marketing research. It has been observed that many new researchers are using this technique without understanding the prerequisites for using it. The following section focuses on the use and application of factor analysis in the field of marketing research.

19.1.1 Introduction

The techniques described in this chapter, namely, factor analysis, cluster analysis, multidimensional scaling, and correspondence analysis are often referred as "interdependence analysis."

The techniques described in this chapter, namely, factor analysis, **cluster analysis**, **multidimensional scaling**, and **correspondence analysis** are often referred as **'interdependence analysis**.' As different from the regression and discriminant analysis, in the factor analysis, there is no concept of predicting the dependent variables through the independent variables. The factor analysis is most widely applied to multivariate technique of research, especially in the field of social and behavioural sciences. The techniques described in this chapter (factor analysis, cluster analysis, and multidimensional scaling) mainly examine the systematic interdependence among the set of observed variables, and the researcher is mainly focused on determining the base of commonality among these variables.

19.1.2 Basic Concept of Using the Factor Analysis

The factor analysis is a proven analytical technique that has been studied extensively by statisticians, mathematicians, and research methodologists (Raven 1990). It is a very useful technique of data reduction and summarization. The main focus of the factor analysis is to summarize the information contained in a large number of variables into a few small number of **factors**. Generally for conducting any kind of research, a researcher has to collect information for a large number of variables. These variables are generally gathered either from the literature or from the experience of a researcher or an executive provides it. Most of these variables are correlated and can be reduced into fewer factors.

The main focus of the factor analysis is to summarize the information contained in a large number of variables into a few small number of factors. Generally for conducting any kind of research, a researcher has to collect information for a large number of variables.

The factor analysis allows a researcher to group the variables into a number of factors based on the degree of correlation among the variables. For example, if a company wishes to examine the degree of satisfaction the consumers are deriving from a launch of a new product, then it can collect variables from different sources such as literature, experience of the company executives, and so on. In fact, the list of these variables may be sufficiently large because this is the discretion of a researcher to include a large number of variables in the research. These variables may then be factor analysed to identify the underlying construct in the data. The name of the new factor (group of correlated variables) or factors can be subjectively defined by the researcher, which can be used for further multivariate analysis (may be regression or discriminant analysis). Thus, the factor analysis is a statistical technique used to determine the prescribed number of uncorrelated factors, where each factor is obtained from a list of correlated variables. The factor analysis can be utilized to examine the underlying patterns or relationships for a large number of variables and to determine whether the information can be condensed or summarized into a smaller set of factors or components (Hair et al. 2009).

The factor analysis allows a researcher to group the variables into a number of factors based on the degree of correlation among the variables.

19.1.3 Factor Analysis Model

It has already been discussed that factor analysis is a statistical technique used to transform the original correlated variables into a new set of uncorrelated variables. These different groups of uncorrelated variables are referred as **factors**. Each factor is a linear combination of correlated original variables. Mathematically, it can be expressed as

$$F_i = a_{i1}X_1 + a_{i2}X_2 + a_{i3}X_3 \ldots\ldots\ldots\ldots\ldots\ldots\ldots\ldots a_{in}X_n,$$

where F_i is the estimate of the *i*th factor, a_i the weights or **factor score** coefficients, and *n* the number of variables.

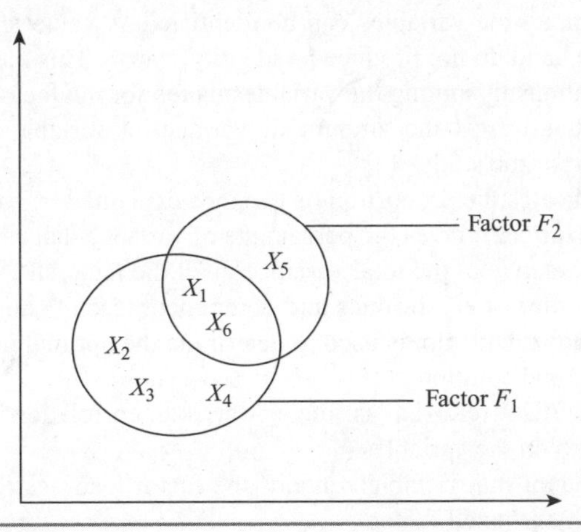

FIGURE 19.1
Joining of various variables to form different factors

It is important to note that for forming a factor F_1, each variable X_i, which is correlated with other variables, shares some variance with these other variables. This is referred as **communality** in the factor analysis.

The variable X_i may then be correlated with another group of variables to form another factor F_2. It may be possible that another group of variables may not be significantly correlated with the variables, which formed Factor F_1. This situation is explained in Figure 19.1. From Figure 19.1, it can be seen that Variable X_1 is highly correlated with Variables X_2, X_3, and X_4 to form Factor F_1. It also clearly shows that Variable X_1 is correlated with Variables X_5 and X_6 to form Factor F_2. However, Variables X_5 and X_6 may not be correlated with Variables X_2, X_3, and X_4. The covariance among the variables can be explained by a small number of common factors and the unique factor for each variable. Such Variable X_i may then be defined as

$$X_i = A_{i1}F_1 + A_{i2}F_2 + A_{i3}F_3 \ldots\ldots\ldots\ldots\ldots A_{im}F_m + V_iU_i,$$

where X_i is the ith standardized variable, A_{ij} the standardized multiple regression coefficient of Variable X_i on common Factor j, F the common factor, V_i the standardized regression coefficient of Variable X_i on U_i, U_i the unique factor in X_i, and m the number of common factors.

19.1.4 Some Basic Terms Used in the Factor Analysis

The following is the list of some basic terms frequently used in the factor analysis:

Correlation matrix: It is a simple correlation matrix of all the pairs of variables included in the factor analysis. It shows a simple correlation (r) between all the possible pairs of variables included in the analysis. In correlation matrix, the diagonal element is always equal to one, which indicates the correlation of any variable with the same variable.

Kaiser-Meyer-Olkin (KMO) measure of sampling adequacy: This statistic shows the proportion of variance, for variables included in the study is the common variance. In other words, this is the common variance, attributed to the underlying factors. A high value of this statistic (from 0.5 to 1) indicates the appropriateness of the factor analysis for the data in hand, whereas a low value of statistic (below 0.5) indicates the inappropriateness of the factor analysis.

Bartlett's test of sphericity: This statistic tests the hypothesis whether the population correlation matrix is an identity matrix. This is important to note that with an identity matrix, the factor analysis is meaningless. Using significance level, the degree of relationship among the variables can be identified. A value less than 0.05 indicates that the data in hand do not produce an identity matrix. This means that there exists a significant relationship among the variables, taken for the factor analysis.

Communality: It indicates the amount of variance a variable shares with all other variables taken for the study.

Eigenvalue: It indicates the proportion of variance explained by each factor.

Percentage of variance: It gives the percentage of variance that can be attributed to each specific factor relative to the total variance in all the factors.

Scree plot: It is a plot of eigenvalues and component (factor) number according to the order of extraction. This plot is used to determine the optimal number of factors to be retained in the final solution.

Factor loadings: Also referred as factor–variable correlation. These are a simple correlation between the variables.

Factor matrix: Factor matrix table contains the factor loadings for each variable taken for the study on unrotated factors.

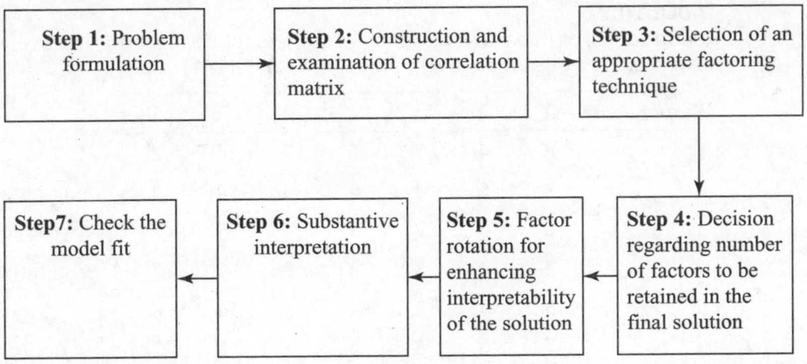

FIGURE 19.2
Seven steps involved in conducting the factor analysis

Factor score: It represents a subject's combined response to various variables representing the factor.

Factor loading plot: It is a plot of original variables, which uses factor loadings as coordinates.

19.1.5 Process of Conducting the Factor Analysis

The factor analysis can be performed using the seven steps as shown in Figure 19.2: problem formulation, construction and examination of correlation matrix, selection of an appropriate factoring technique, a decision regarding the number of factors to be retained in the final solution, factor **rotation** for enhancing the interpretability of the solution, substantive interpretation, and check the model fit.

The following section describes a detailed discussion of these steps with the help of an example that is included in Step 1 as problem formulation.

19.1.5.1 Problem Formulation

The first step in conducting the factor analysis is to formulate the problem of the factor analysis. As discussed earlier, the main focus of the factor analysis is to reduce data. For this purpose, a researcher has to select a list of variables that will be converted into a new set of factors based on the common essence present in each of the variables. For selecting variables, a researcher can take the help of literature, past research, or use the experience of other researchers or executives. It is important to note that the variables should be measurable on an interval scale or a ratio scale. Another important aspect of the factor analysis is to determine the sample size, which will be used for the factor analysis. As a thumb rule, the sample size should be four or five times of the variable included in the factor analysis.

As a thumb rule, the sample size should be four or five times of the variable included in the factor analysis.

For understanding the factor analysis, let us consider an example of a garment company that wishes to assess the changing attitude of its customers towards a well-established product, in light of many competitors presence in the market. The company has taken a list of 25 loyal customers and administered a questionnaire to them. The questionnaire consists of seven statements, which were measured on a 9-point rating scale with 1 as strongly disagree and 9 strongly agree. The description of the seven statements used in the survey is given as follows:

X_1: Price is a very important factor in purchasing.
X_2: For marginal difference in price, quality cannot be compromised.
X_3: Quality is OK, but competitor's price of the same product cannot be ignored.
X_4: Quality products are having a high degree of durability.
X_5: With limited income, one can afford to spend only small portion for cloth purchase.
X_6: In the present world of materialism and commercialization, people are evaluated on the basis of good appearance.
X_7: By paying more if we can get good quality, why not to go for it.

TABLE 19.2
Rating scores obtained by different consumers for the seven statements to determine the changing consumer attitude

Respondents	X_1	X_2	X_3	X_4	X_5	X_6	X_7
1	8	4	7	5	7	4	2
2	3	5	4	4	3	4	7
3	6	6	7	5	7	5	2
4	2	4	3	4	2	5	7
5	3	5	4	4	3	4	8
6	7	6	8	5	7	5	2
7	2	4	2	5	3	4	8
8	8	5	7	6	6	5	2
9	6	5	7	6	5	6	1
10	4	5	5	4	4	5	2
11	8	6	7	5	6	6	2
12	9	5	8	4	9	5	3
13	6	5	6	6	7	6	1
14	6	4	7	3	6	3	2
15	8	5	7	6	7	5	2
16	7	6	6	5	6	5	3
17	3	5	3	6	4	5	8
18	2	4	1	5	3	4	7
19	3	6	5	5	4	5	9
20	9	3	6	4	8	4	2
21	8	2	9	3	7	3	1
22	3	5	2	4	4	4	8
23	6	4	7	5	7	5	2
24	8	4	6	5	7	4	2
25	2	5	3	6	3	5	7

Table 19.2 gives the rating scores obtained by different consumers for the seven statements described earlier.

Figures 19.3(a)–19.3(m) shows the SPSS factor analysis output.

19.1.5.2 Construction and Examination of Correlation Matrix

The following discussion is based on the SPSS output, which is given in the form of Figures 19.3(a)–19.3(m). Figure 19.3(a) is a simple table that shows the descriptive statistics for the variables taken into study. In this figure, the second column shows the mean value for each item for 25 customers, the third column the degree of variability in scores for each item, and the fourth column the number of observations (sample size).

Figure 19.3(b) is the SPSS-produced correlation matrix for the descriptor variables. This is the initial stage of the factor analysis, which gives some initial clues about the patterns of the factor analysis. It is important to note that for the appropriateness of the factor analysis,

FIGURE 19.3 (a) Descriptive statistics, (b) Correlation matrix, (c) KMO and Bartlett's test, (d) Communalities, (e) Total variance explained

Descriptive Statistics

	Mean	Std. Deviation	Analysis N
X1	5.4800	2.50200	25
X2	4.7200	0.97980	25
X3	5.4800	2.16256	25
X4	4.8000	0.91287	25
X5	5.4000	1.93649	25
X6	4.6400	0.81035	25
X7	4.0000	2.87228	25

(a)

Correlation Matrix[a]

		X1	X2	X3	X4	X5	X6	X7
Correlation	X1	1.000	-0.113	0.872	-0.011	0.930	0.068	-0.847
	X2	-0.113	1.000	-0.013	0.447	-0.092	0.655	0.133
	X3	0.872	-0.013	1.000	-0.076	0.838	0.126	-0.845
	X4	-0.011	0.447	-0.076	1.000	0.000	0.687	-0.032
	X5	0.930	-0.092	0.838	0.000	1.000	0.069	-0.802
	X6	0.068	0.655	0.126	0.687	0.069	1.000	-0.179
	X7	-0.847	0.133	-0.845	-0.032	-0.802	-0.179	1.000
Sig. (1-tailed)	X1		0.296	0.000	0.479	0.000	0.373	0.000
	X2	0.296		0.476	0.012	0.331	0.000	0.263
	X3	0.000	0.476		0.359	0.000	0.273	0.000
	X4	0.479	0.012	0.359		0.500	0.000	0.440
	X5	0.000	0.331	0.000	0.500		0.371	0.000
	X6	0.373	0.000	0.273	0.000	0.371		0.196
	X7	0.000	0.263	0.000	0.440	0.000	0.196	

a. Determinant = 0.001

(b)

KMO and Bartlett's Test

Kaiser-Meyer-Olkin Measure of Sampling Adequacy.		0.741
Bartlett's Test of Sphericity	Approx. Chi-Square	135.592
	df	21
	Sig.	0.000

(c)

Communalities

	Initial	Extraction
X1	1.000	0.933
X2	1.000	0.672
X3	1.000	0.882
X4	1.000	0.690
X5	1.000	0.892
X6	1.000	0.863
X7	1.000	0.861

Extraction Method: Principal Component Analysis.

(d)

Total Variance Explained

	Initial Eigenvalues			Extraction Sums of Squared Loadings			Rotation Sums of Squared Loadings		
Component	Total	% of Variance	Cumulative %	Total	% of Variance	Cumulative %	Total	% of Variance	Cumulative %
1	3.592	51.318	51.318	3.592	51.318	51.318	3.592	51.315	51.315
2	2.200	31.433	82.751	2.200	31.433	82.751	2.201	31.436	82.751
3	0.582	8.317	91.069						
4	0.295	4.212	95.281						
5	0.154	2.204	97.485						
6	0.113	1.616	99.100						
7	0.063	0.900	100.000						

Extraction Method: Principal Component Analysis.

(e)

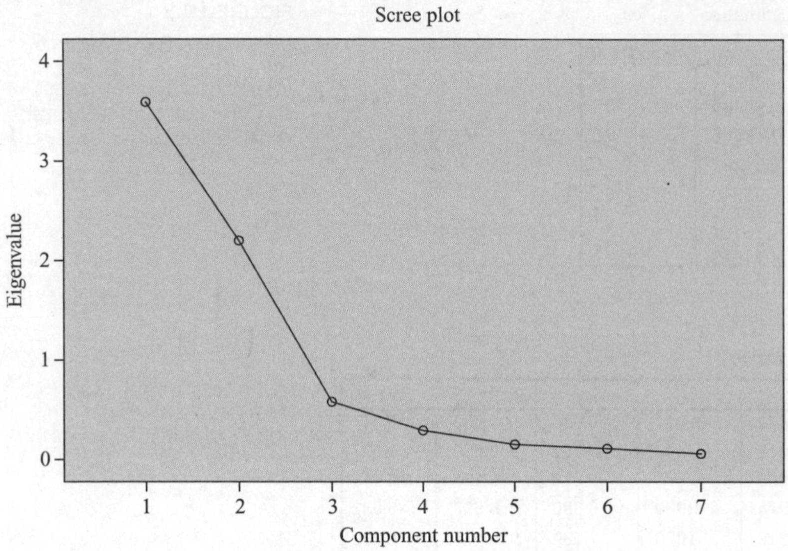

(f)

Component Matrix[a]

	Component	
	1	2
X1	0.965	-0.041
X2	-0.093	0.815
X3	0.939	0.000
X4	-5.190E-5	0.830
X5	0.944	-0.029
X6	0.137	0.919
X7	-0.928	-0.020

Extraction Method: Principal Component Analysis.

a. 2 components extracted.

(g)

Reproduced Correlations

		X1	X2	X3	X4	X5	X6	X7
Reproduced Correlation	X1	0.933[a]	-0.124	0.907	-0.034	0.912	0.094	-0.894
	X2	-0.124	0.672[a]	-0.088	0.677	-0.112	0.736	0.071
	X3	0.907	-0.088	0.882[a]	0.000	0.886	0.128	-0.871
	X4	-0.034	0.677	0.000	0.690[a]	-0.024	0.763	-0.016
	X5	0.912	-0.112	0.886	-0.024	0.892[a]	0.102	-0.875
	X6	0.094	0.736	0.128	0.763	0.102	0.863[a]	-0.145
	X7	-0.894	0.071	-0.871	-0.016	-0.875	-0.145	0.861[a]
Residual[b]	X1		0.011	-0.035	0.023	0.018	-0.026	0.048
	X2	0.011		0.076	-0.229	0.019	-0.081	0.063
	X3	-0.035	0.076		-0.075	-0.049	-0.001	0.026
	X4	0.023	-0.229	-0.075		0.024	-0.076	-0.016
	X5	0.018	0.019	-0.049	0.024		-0.033	0.073
	X6	-0.026	-0.081	-0.001	-0.076	-0.033		-0.034
	X7	0.048	0.063	0.026	-0.016	0.073	-0.034	

Extraction Method: Principal Component Analysis.

a. Reproduced communalities

b. Residuals are computed between observed and reproduced correlations. There are 7 (33.0%) nonredundant residuals with absolute values greater than 0.05.

(h)

FIGURE 19.3
(f) Scree plot,
(g) Component matrix,
(h) Reproduced correlations

Rotated Component Matrix[a]

	Component	
	1	2
X1	0.966	-0.030
X2	-0.103	0.813
X3	0.939	0.011
X4	-0.010	0.830
X5	0.944	-0.018
X6	0.126	0.920
X7	-0.927	-0.031

Extraction Method: Principal Component Analysis.
Rotation Method: Varimax with Kaiser Normalization.

a. Rotation converged in 3 iterations.

(i)

Component Transformation Matrix

Component	1	2
1	1.000	0.012
2	-0.012	1.000

Extraction Method: Principal Component Analysis.
Rotation Method: Varimax with Kaiser Normalization.

(j)

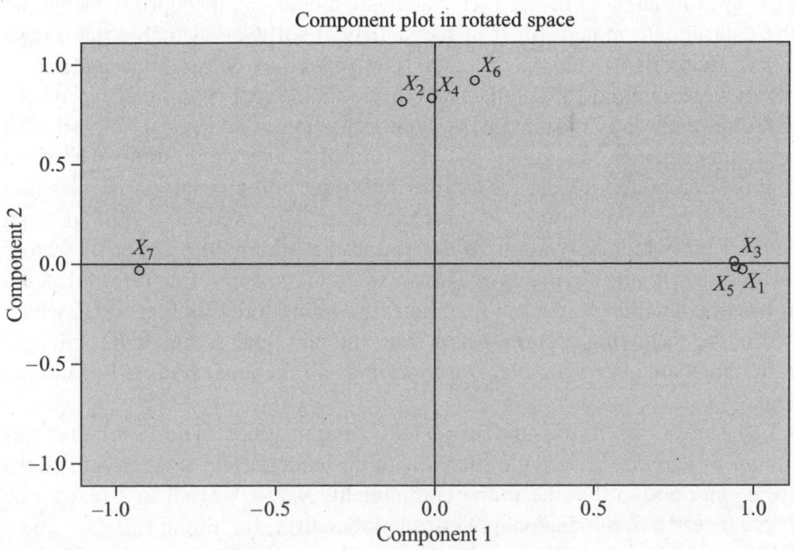

(k)

Component Score Coefficient Matrix

	Component	
	1	2
X1	0.269	-0.015
X2	-0.030	0.370
X3	0.261	0.003
X4	-0.005	0.377
X5	0.263	-0.010
X6	0.033	0.418
X7	-0.258	-0.012

Extraction Method: Principal Component Analysis.
Rotation Method: Varimax with Kaiser Normalization.

(l)

Component Score Covariance Matrix

Component	1	2
1	1.000	0.000
2	0.000	1.000

Extraction Method: Principal Component Analysis.
Rotation Method: Varimax with Kaiser Normalization.

(m)

FIGURE 19.3
(i) Rotated component matrix, (j) Component transformation matrix (k) Component plot in rotated space, (l) Component score coefficient matrix, (m) Component score covariance matrix

If there is no correlation among the variables or if the degree of correlation among the variables is very low, then the appropriateness of the factor analysis will be under serious doubt. In the factor analysis, a researcher expects that some of the variables are highly correlated with each other to form a factor.

Kaiser has presented the range as follows: statistic >0.9 is marvellous, >0.8 meritorious, >0.7 middling, >0.6 mediocre, >0.5 miserable, and <0.5 unacceptable.

Bartlett's test of sphericity tests the hypothesis whether the population correlation matrix is an identity matrix. The existence of the identity matrix puts the correctness of the factor analysis under suspicion.

The main focus of the principal component method is to transform a set of interrelated variables into a set of uncorrelated linear combinations of these variables. This method is applied when the primary focus of the factor analysis is to determine the minimum number of factors that attributes maximum variance in the data.

The communalities describe the amount of variance a variable shares with all other variables taken into study.

% of variance indicates the percentage of variance accounted for by each specific factor or component.

the variables must be correlated. If there is no correlation among the variables or if the degree of correlation among the variables is very low, then the appropriateness of the factor analysis will be under serious doubt. In the factor analysis, a researcher expects that some of the variables are highly correlated with each other to form a factor. Figure 19.3(b) shows that a few variables are relatively highly correlated with each other to form factors.

Figure 19.3(c) shows two important statistics: the **KMO measure of sampling adequacy** and the **Bartlett's test of sphericity** for judging the appropriateness of a factor model. **KMO** statistic compares the magnitude of the observed correlation coefficient with the magnitude of the partial correlation coefficient. As discussed earlier, a high value of this statistic (from 0.5 to 1) indicates the appropriateness of the factor analysis. Kaiser has presented the range as follows: statistic >0.9 is marvellous, >0.8 meritorious, >0.7 middling, >0.6 mediocre, >0.5 miserable, and <0.5 unacceptable. The figure shows that **KMO statistic** is computed as 0.741, which indicates the value in the acceptance region of the factor analysis model.
Bartlett's test of sphericity tests the hypothesis whether the population correlation matrix is an identity matrix. The existence of the identity matrix puts the correctness of the factor analysis under suspicion. Figure 19.3(c) shows that chi square statistic is 135.592 with 21 degrees of freedom. This value is significant at 0.01 level. Both the results, that is, the **KMO statistic** and **Bartlett's test of sphericity,** indicate an appropriate factor analysis model.

19.1.5.3 Selection of an Appropriate Factoring Technique

After deciding the appropriateness of the factor analysis model, an appropriate technique for analysing the data is determined. Most of the statistical software available these days present a variety of methods to analyse the data. **The principal component method** is the most commonly used method of data analysis in the factor analysis model. When the objective of the factor analysis is to summarize the information in a larger set of variables into fewer factors, the principal component analysis is used (Aaker et al. 2000). The main focus of the principal component method is to transform a set of interrelated variables into a set of uncorrelated linear combinations of these variables. This method is applied when the primary focus of the factor analysis is to determine the minimum number of factors that attributes maximum variance in the data. The obtained factors are often referred as the **principal components**. Another important method is the **principal axis factoring**, which will be discussed in the following section. Apart from the principal component method, a variety of other methods are also available. Description of all these methods is beyond the scope of this book.

Figure 19.3(d) shows the initial and extracted communalities. The communalities describe the amount of variance a variable shares with all other variables taken into study. From the figure, it can be seen that the initial communality value is equal to 1 (as can be seen, the unities are inserted in the diagonal of correlation matrix) for all the variables taken into the factor analysis model. The SPSS, by default, assigns a communality value of 1 to all the variables. The extracted communalities as shown in the third column of Figure 19.3(d) is the estimate of variance in each variable, which can be attributed to factors in the factor solution. Relatively small value of the communality suggests that the concerned variable is a misfit for the factor solution and can (should) be dropped out from the factor analysis.

Figure 19.3(e) presents the initial eigenvalues (total, **% of variance**, and cumulative %), extraction sums of squared loadings (total, % of variance, and cumulative %), and the rotation sums of squared loadings (total, % of variance, and cumulative %). In this figure, the "Total" column gives the amount of variance in the variable attributed to the concerned component or factor. The"% of variance" column indicates the percentage of variance accounted for by each specific factor or component. It is important to note that the total variance accounted for by all the seven factors is equal to 7. This is equivalent to the number of variables. The variance attributed to factor 1 is 3.592/7 × 100 = 51.31%. The total variance attributed to factor 2 is 2.200/7 × 100 = 31.43%. Similarly, the total variance attributed to all the factors can be computed. The second part of the figure is the extraction sums of squared loadings that gives information related to the extracted factors or components. If a researcher has adopted the "principal component method" as the method of analysis in a factor model, then the values will remain the same, as shown under the heading "initial eigenvalues." As can be seen from the third part of the figure, rotation sums of squared loadings, the variance accounted for by the rotated factors or components is different from those indicated in the second column of extraction sums of squared loadings. It is important to note that for rotation sums of squared loadings, the cumulative percentage for the set of components (factors) will always remain the same.

19.1.5.4 Decision Regarding the Number of Factors to be Retained in the Final Solution

It is possible to have a number of factors as the number of variables available in the factor analysis. If this is the case, the rationale of applying factor analysis is questionable because the primary objective of the factor analysis is to summarize the information contained in the various variables into a few factors. For this purpose, the basic question in the mind of a researcher while applying factor analysis is that how many factors should be abstracted from the factor analysis. Fabrigar et al. (1999) stated that determining how many factors to include in the model requires the researcher to balance the need for parsimony (i.e., a model with relatively few common factors) against the need for plausibility (i.e., a model with a sufficient number of common factors to adequately account for the correlations among the measured variables). A number of approaches are available to decide the number of factors to be retained in the factor analysis solution. In this section, we will focus on three commonly used criteria for determining the number of factors: eigenvalue criteria, Scree plot criteria, and percentage of variance criteria.

A number of approaches are available to decide the number of factors to be retained in the factor analysis solution.

Eigenvalue Criteria

An eigenvalue is the amount of variance in the variable taken for the study that is associated with a factor. According to the eigenvalue criteria, the factors having more than one eigenvalue are included in the model. A factor that has an eigenvalue of less than 1 is not better than a single variable because due to standardization each variable has a variance of 1.

An eigenvalue is the amount of variance in the variable taken for the study that is associated with a factor. According to eigenvalue criteria, the factors having more than one eigenvalue are included in the model.

Scree Plot Criteria

One of the most popular guides for determining how many factors should be retained in the factor analysis is the Scree test (Cattell 1966). Scree plot is a plot of the eigenvalues and component (factor) number according to the order of extraction [as shown in Figure 19.3(f)]. The shape of the plot is used to determine the optimum number of factors to be retained in the final solution. The objective of the Scree plot is to visually isolate an elbow, which can be defined as the point where the eigenvalues form a liner descending trend (Bentler and Yuan 1998). For an appropriate factor analysis model, this plot looks like an intersection of two lines (Figure 19.4).

Scree plot is a plot of the eigenvalues and component (factor) number according to the order of extraction.

Figure 19.5 clearly shows that the factors on the steep slope should be retained in the model and the factors on the shallow slope can be excluded from the model (as these factors contribute relatively little to the factor model).

Percentage of Variance Criteria

This approach is based on the concept of cumulative percentage of variance. The number of factors should be included in the model for which cumulative percentage of variance reaches

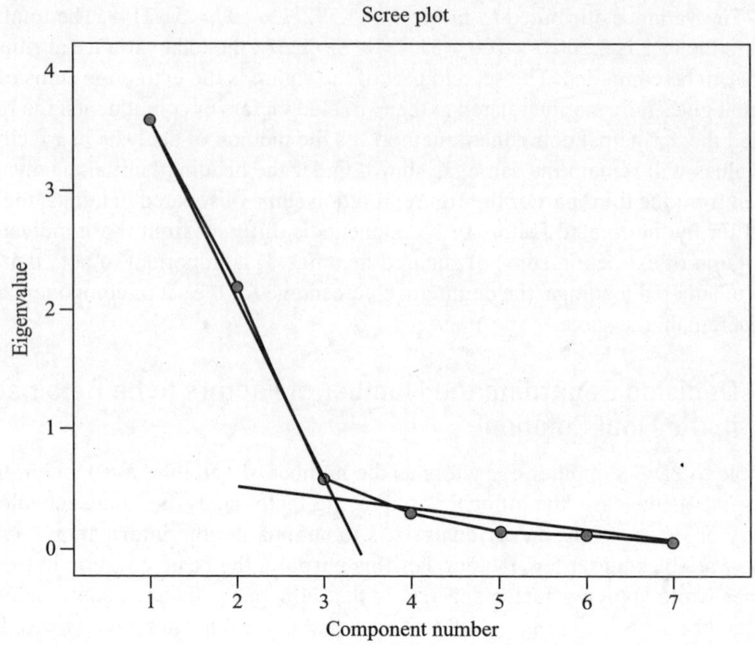

FIGURE 19.4
Scree plot shown as an intersection of two lines

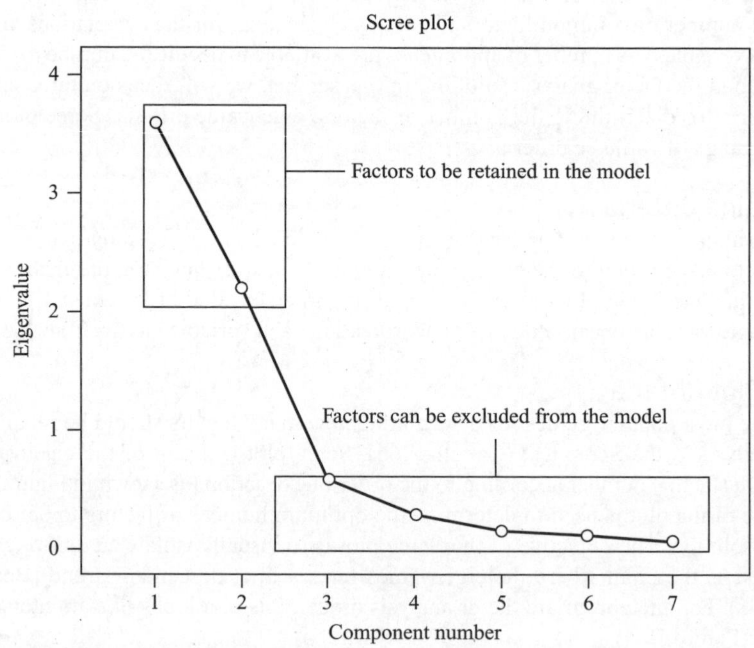

FIGURE 19.5
Scree plot indicating the number of factors to be retained in the model

However, the general recommendation is that the factors explaining 60%–70% of the variance should be retained in the model.

a satisfactory level. Now there is a question that what should be that satisfactory level. However, the general recommendation is that the factors explaining 60%–70% of the variance should be retained in the model.

Considering Figures 19.3(e) and 19.3(f), all the three approaches suggest that the number of factors to be extracted should be only two. According to the eigenvalue approach, only two factors have eigenvalues more than 1. The Scree plot for the problem in hand also shows that only two factors on the steep slope should be retained in the model. The cumulative percentage of variance for the first two factors is 82.751%, which is well within the prescribed limits, which is why only two factors must be retained in the final factor analysis solution. Above are some criteria; however, the number of factors to be retained is a highly subjective matter. The scope of interpretation can be enhanced by rotating the factors and will be described in the following section.

According to the eigenvalue approach, only two factors have eigenvalues more than 1. The Scree plot for the problem in hand also shows that only two factors on the steep slope should be retained in the model. The cumulative percentage of variance for the first two factors is 82.751%, which is well within the prescribed limits, which is why only two factors must be retained in the final factor analysis solution.

Figure 19.3(g) shows the component matrix table that presents the factor loading for each variable on unrotated factors (components). As can be seen from the figure, each value under the heading component (1 or 2) represents the correlation between the concerned variable and the unrotated factors. The values given under **Factor 1** represent the correlation between the concerned variable and Factor 1, and the values given under **Factor 2** represent the correlation between the concerned variable and Factor 2. From this figure, it can be seen that Variables X_1, X_3, X_5, and X_7 are relatively highly correlated (with values 0.965, 0.939, 0.944, and –0.928) with Factor 1, and Variables X_2, X_4, and X_6 are relatively highly correlated with Factor 2 (with values 0.815, 0.830, and 0.919).

Figure 19.3(h) shows the reproduced correlation and residuals for the factor analysis solution. For an assumed appropriate factor analysis solution, the reproduced correlation shows the predicted pattern of relationship. The residuals are the difference between the predicted and observed values. If a factor analysis solution is good enough, then most of the residual values are small.

The residuals are the difference between the predicted and observed values. If a factor analysis solution is good enough, then most of the residual values are small.

19.1.5.5 Factor Rotation for Enhancing the Interpretability of the Solution

After selection of factors, the immediate step is to **rotate** the factors. The rotated simple structure solutions are often easy to interpret, whereas the originally unextracted (unrotated) factors are often difficult to interpret (Reise et al. 2000). A rotation is required because the original factor model may be mathematically correct but may be difficult in terms of interpretation. If various factors have a high loading on the same variable, then interpretation will be extremely difficult. Rotation solves this kind of interpretation difficulty. The main objective of rotation is to produce a relatively simple structure in which there may be a high factor loading on one factor and a low factor loading on all other factors. Similar to correlation, factor loading varies between +1 and –1 and indicates the degree of relationship between a particular factor and the particular variable. It is interesting to note that rotation never affects the communalities and the total variance explained [from Figure 19.3(e), it can be seen that after rotation, the cumulative percentage of variance is not changed (82.751%)].

A rotation is required because the original factor model may be mathematically correct but may be difficult in terms of interpretation.

The main objective of rotation is to produce a relatively simple structure in which there may be a high factor loading on one factor and a low factor loading on all other factors.

Figure 19.6 shows asterisks on the unrotated factor lines, and Figure 19.7 shows asterisks on the rotated factor lines. If we compare both the figures, the rationale of rotation can be easily explained. Rotation enhances the interpretability in terms of association of factor loadings with the concerned factor. When compared with Figure 19.6, Figure 19.7 clearly explains the high factor loading on one factor and the low factor loading on all other factors.

Rotation enhances the interpretability in terms of association of factor loadings with the concerned factor.

Figure 19.3(i) represents the **rotated component matrix** that is often referred as the '**pattern matrix for oblique rotation**.' The columns in this figure represent the factor loading for each variable, for the concerned factor, **after rotation**. The figure clearly shows the interpretability importance of the rotation.

Earlier, the rotation was done manually by the researchers, whereas nowadays, a variety of statistical softwares present a variety of methods of rotation such as **Varimax procedure**, Quartimax procedure, Equamax procedure, Promax procedure, and so on. However, the different rotation procedures more or less reflect the same result about the data; by performing different procedures and later comparing the results of the different schemes, obtaining

Nowadays, a variety of statistical software present a variety of methods of rotation such as Varimax procedure, Quartimax procedure, Equamax procedure, Promax procedure, and so on.

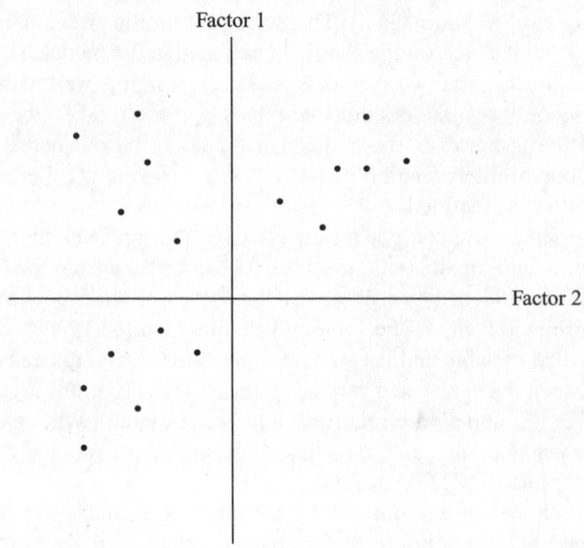

FIGURE 19.6
Asterisks on the unrotated factor lines

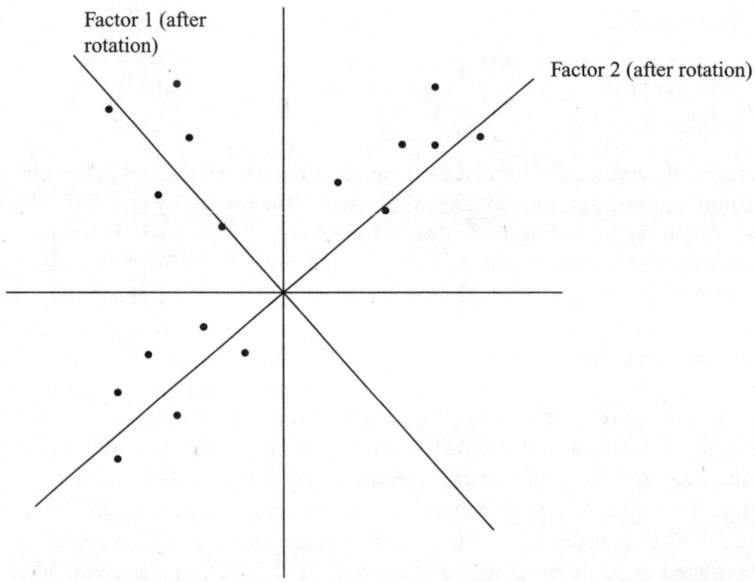

FIGURE 19.7
Asterisks on the rotated factor lines

The widely applied method of rotation is the 'Varimax procedure.'

The rotation is often referred as 'orthogonal rotation' if the axes are maintained at right angles. Varimax procedure is an orthogonal rotation procedure.

the '**most interpretable**' solution will always be beneficial for researchers. The widely applied method of rotation is the '**Varimax procedure**.' Although a number of rotation methods have been developed, varimax has been generally regarded as the best orthogonal rotation and is overwhelmingly the most widely used orthogonal rotation in psychological research (Fabriger et al. 1999). This section focuses on varimax procedure of rotation.

The rotation is often referred as '**orthogonal rotation**' if the axes are maintained at right angles. Varimax procedure is an orthogonal rotation procedure. Orthogonal rotation generates the factors that are uncorrelated. On the other hand, in **oblique rotation,** axes are not rotated at right angle and the factors are correlated. If the factors are truly uncorrelated, orthogonal and oblique rotation produce nearly identical results (Costello and Osborne 2005).

The rotated factor matrix as shown in Figure 19.3(i) shows that the Variables X_1, X_3, X_5, and X_7 are having high loadings on Factor 1 and the Variables X_2, X_4, and X_6 are having high loadings on Factor 2.

19.1.5.6 Substantive Interpretation

At this stage, there is a point to identify the factors with concerned variables as the constituents of the factor. Figure 19.3(k), as the component plot in rotated space, provides this opportunity. Before that, it is important to interpret Figure 19.3(j). Figure 19.3(j) shows the component transformation matrix. The component transformation matrix is used to construct the rotated factor matrix from the unrotated factor matrix by using a simple formula (unrotated factor loading × factor transformation matrix = rotated factor loadings). In the case in which off-diagonal elements are close to zero indicates a relatively smaller rotation and off-diagonal elements are large (greater than ±5) indicates a relatively larger rotation.

As described in the previous paragraph, Figure 19.3(k) is the component plot in rotated space. This plot is a pictorial representation of the factor loadings of the variables taken in the study on the first few factors. The variables near or on the axis show a high factor loading on the concerned factor. Figure 19.3(k) shows that the Variables X_1, X_3, X_5, and X_7 are highly loaded on Factor 1. It is interesting to see here that the Variable X_7 has got the high negative value, and hence, it is in the opposite direction of the three Variables X_1, X_3, and X_5. If a variable is not a part of any factor (neither close to horizontal axis nor close to vertical axis), then it should be treated as an undefined or a general factor. Similarly, the Variables X_2, X_4, and X_6 have high factor loadings on Factor 2.

Factor 1 consists of Variables X_1 (price is important), X_3 (competitor's price cannot be ignored), X_5 (limited affordability), and X_7 (get good quality by paying more). Negative factor loading value of Variable X_7 on Factor 1 indicates that this segment of customers is more concerned about the price even at the cost for compromising quality. Hence, Factor 1 can be named as '**Economy Seekers**.' Similarly, Factor 2 consists of Variables X_2 (quality cannot be compromised), X_4 (quality products are having a high degree of durability), and X_6 (societal evaluation of an individual is based on quality products). Thus, Factor 2 can be named as '**Quality seekers**.' After applying the factor analysis, the original seven variables are categorized into two factors economy seekers and quality seekers.

Figure 19.3(l) shows the **component score coefficient matrix**. For each subject, the factor score is calculated by multiplying the values of variable (can be obtained from Table 19.2) by factor score coefficients. For example, for Subject 1, factor score can be computed as follows:

For Factor 1:

$$(0.269) \times (8) + (-0.030) \times (4) + (0.261) \times (7) + (-0.005) \times (5) + (0.263) \times (7) + (0.033) \times (4) + (-0.258) \times (2) = 4.211.$$

For Factor 2:

$$(-0.015) \times (8) + (0.370) \times (4) + (0.003) \times (7) + (0.377) \times (5) + (-0.010) \times (7) \times (0.418) \times (4) + (-0.012) \times (2) = 4.844.$$

Similarly, using the factor score coefficient, factor scores for other subjects can also be computed. Instead of all the original variables, the factor scores can be used in the

Sometimes instead of computing a factor score, researchers select the substitute variable commonly known as surrogate variable by selecting some of the original variables for further multivariate analysis.

subsequent multivariate analysis. Sometimes instead of computing a factor score, researchers select the substitute variable commonly known as surrogate variable by selecting some of the original variables for further multivariate analysis. It is important to note that a researcher can also select the variables on a discretionary basis. This means that on the basis of experience or literature or any other logical basis, if a researcher believes that the variable with a high factor loading is less important than the variable with a low factor loading, then he or she can select the relatively important variable with a low factor loading as the surrogate variable.

19.1.5.7 Check the Model Fit

For an appropriate factor analysis solution, the difference between the reproduced and observed correlation should be small (less than 0.05).

The last step in the factor analysis is to determine the fitness of the factor analysis model. In factor analysis, the factors are generated on the basis of observed correlation between the variables. The degree of correlation between the variables can be reproduced as shown in Figure 19.3(h). For an appropriate factor analysis solution, the difference between the reproduced and observed correlation should be small (less than 0.05). As can also be seen from Figure 19.3(h), only seven residuals are greater than 0.05, which indicates an appropriate factor analysis model.

19.2 CLUSTER ANALYSIS

This section focuses on a popular multivariate technique known as cluster analysis. It deals with all important dimensions related to the application of cluster analysis. Use of SPSS output for explaining the concept will make its use very convenient for a researcher.

Specifically, in the field of marketing, mangers try to identify a similar group of customers, so that marketing strategies can be chalked out for the concerned similar group of customers. These customers can be grouped or clustered on the basis of a variety of common features such as the benefits the consumers seek from the product, lifestyle of the consumers with special reference to its impact on their purchase behaviour, and so on.

19.2.1 Introduction

In every field of the study, researchers or scientists or marketing executives will like to group the objects on the basis of some similarity. Specifically, in the field of marketing, mangers try to identify a similar group of customers, so that marketing strategies can be chalked out for the concerned similar group of customers. These customers can be grouped or clustered on the basis of a variety of common features such as the benefits the consumers seek from the product, lifestyle of the consumers with special reference to its impact on their purchase behaviour, and so on. The main objective of the marketing executives is to find out a similar group of customers to develop products or services according to their specific need. Thus, the researchers or executives face a common problem in terms of availability of some scientific technique to group the objects on the basis of some similarity. Cluster analysis provides a solution to this kind of problem. It has become a common tool for the marketing researcher (Punj and Stewart 1983). In some aspects, the factor analysis and cluster analysis are similar. In both, a researcher tries to reduce a larger number of variables (in factor analysis) or cases (in cluster analysis) into a smaller number of factors (in factor analysis) or clusters (in cluster analysis) on the basis of some commonality that within-group members share with each other. However, the statistical procedure to do this and the interpretations are different in these two methods.

Cluster analysis is a technique of grouping individuals or objects or cases into relatively homogeneous (similar) groups that are often referred as clusters. The subjects grouped within the cluster are similar to each other, and there is a dissimilarity between the clusters.

19.2.2 Basic Concept of Using the Cluster Analysis

Cluster analysis is a technique of grouping individuals or objects or cases into relatively homogeneous (similar) groups that are often referred as clusters. The subjects grouped

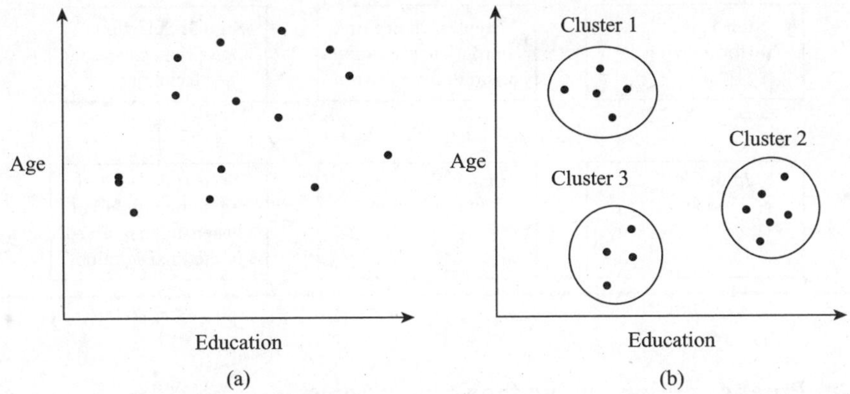

FIGURE 19.8
(a) Before clustering situation, (b) After clustering situation

within the cluster are similar to each other, and there is a dissimilarity between the clusters. In other words, we can say that the individuals or objects or cases when correlated with each other form a cluster. The main focus of the cluster analysis is to determine the number of mutually exclusive and collectively exhaustive clusters in the population, on the basis of similarity of profiles among the subjects. In the field of marketing, cluster analysis is mainly used in **market segmentation, understanding purchase behaviour of the consumers, test marketing**, and so on. A typical use of cluster analysis is to provide market segmentation by identifying subjects or individuals who have similar needs, lifestyles, or responses to marketing strategies (Zikmund 2007). For example, in the process of launching a new product, the CEO of a company wants to group cities of the country on the basis of age group and education of the consumers. If a company has collected data from 15 customers of various cities, then a simple way to group the subjects is to plot the result on two variables, that is, age and education of the consumers. Figures 19.8(a) and 19.8(b) present two different situations: before clustering and after clustering. In most of the cases, the researchers or marketing executives find situations as explained in Figure 19.8(a). This is a situation when there is no clustering and the subjects are scattered with respect to the two variables: age and education. Figure 19.8(b) shows after clustering situation in which subjects join to form different clusters based on some similarity.

The main focus of the cluster analysis is to determine the number of mutually exclusive and collectively exhaustive clusters in the population, on the basis of similarity of profiles among the subjects.

19.2.3 Some Basic Terms Used in the Cluster Analysis

The following list presents some basic terms that are commonly used in the cluster analysis:

Agglomeration Schedule: It presents the information on how the subjects are clustered at each stage of the hierarchical cluster analysis.

Cluster Membership: It indicates the cluster to which each subject belongs according to the number of cluster requested by a researcher.

Icicle plot: It provides a graphical representation on how the subjects are joined at each step of the cluster analysis. This plot is interpreted from bottom to top.

Dendrogram: Also referred as **tree diagram**. It is a graphical representation of relative similarities between the subjects. It is interpreted from left to right in which the cluster distances are rescaled, so that the plot shows the range from 0 to 25.

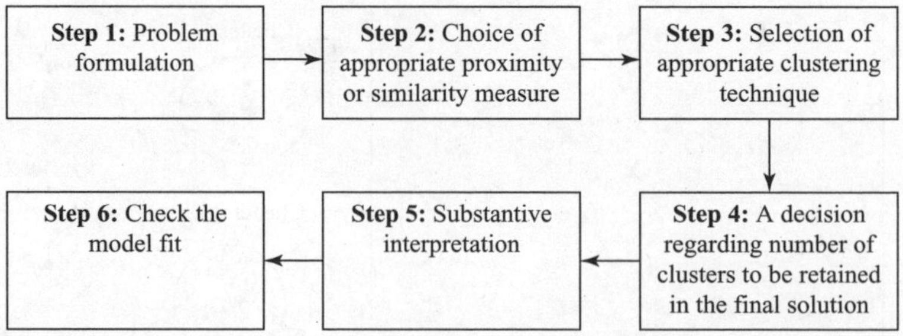

FIGURE 19.9
Six steps involved in conducting the cluster analysis

19.2.4 Process of Conducting the Cluster Analysis

The process of conducting the cluster analysis involves six steps as shown in Figure 19.9: problem formulation, choice of an appropriate proximity or similarity measure, selection of an appropriate clustering technique, a decision regarding the number of clusters to be retained in the final solution, substantive interpretation, and check the model fit.

The following section describes a detailed discussion of these steps with the help of an example that is included in Step 1 as problem formulation.

19.2.4.1 Problem Formulation

The first and most important step in the cluster analysis is to formulate the problem properly in terms of properly defining the variables on which the clustering procedure is to be performed. For understanding the procedure of conducting the cluster analysis, let us formulate a problem. A famous motorbike company wants to launch a new model of motorbike with some additional features. Before launching the product to an entire country, the company has to test market it in select cities. The company is well aware that the majority of the target consumer group consists of urban youth (aged below 45). For understanding the future purchase behaviour of the consumers, the company administered a questionnaire to the potential future customers. The questionnaire consists of seven statements that were measured on a 9-point rating scale with 1 as strongly disagree and 9 as strongly agree. The description of the seven statements used in the survey is given as follows:

X_1: I am trying very hard to understand the loan schemes offered by different banks to purchase the product when it will be coming in the market.

X_2: I am still in confusion whether to sell my old bike or not.

X_3: My old bike is old fashioned; I want to get rid of it.

X_4: My company has promised that it will be releasing a much awaited new incentive scheme; purchase of a new model is based on this factor.

X_5: I will not wait for the product's performance in the market, I know the company is reputed and will certainly launch a quality product.

X_6: Companies always claim high about its product, let the product come in the market only then I will be taking any decision about the purchase.

X_7: I want to purchase a new bike but my kids are growing up and are demanding to purchase a car instead of a bike, which I already have.

Table 19.3 gives the rating scores obtained by different potential consumers for the seven statements, as described earlier, to determine the future purchase behaviour.

For explaining the procedure of conducting cluster analysis, only 25 subjects are selected, but in practice, the cluster analysis is performed on more than or equal to 100 subjects.

TABLE 19.3
Rating scores obtained by different consumers for the seven statements to determine the future purchase behaviour

Subjects	X_1	X_2	X_3	X_4	X_5	X_6	X_7
1	8	5	7	4	8	3	4
2	3	5	2	4	4	8	5
3	5	7	5	8	4	4	7
4	2	4	3	3	3	7	5
5	7	5	8	4	7	2	5
6	8	4	7	5	8	3	4
7	4	8	4	8	4	5	7
8	3	5	3	4	2	8	4
9	7	4	8	5	7	3	5
10	4	7	5	7	4	5	8
11	4	8	4	8	4	5	7
12	8	5	7	4	7	2	4
13	5	7	5	7	5	4	8
14	3	4	2	5	3	8	5
15	7	5	7	4	8	2	5
16	3	4	2	5	3	7	4
17	4	8	4	8	4	5	7
18	2	4	2	5	3	8	4
19	7	5	8	5	8	2	4
20	3	4	3	4	2	7	5
21	5	7	5	8	5	4	8
22	8	5	8	5	8	3	4
23	4	8	5	8	5	4	7
24	3	4	2	4	3	8	5
25	7	5	8	4	7	3	5

19.2.4.2 Choice of an Appropriate Proximity or Similarity Measure

It has already been discussed in the beginning of the chapter that in the cluster analysis, the subjects are grouped on the basis of similarity or commonality. Thus, there is a need to have a measurement of similarity method by which similarity between the subjects can be identified, to group similar subjects in a cluster.

In the cluster analysis, the subjects are grouped on the basis of similarity or commonality. Thus, there is a need to have a measurement of similarity method by which similarity between the subjects can be identified, to group similar subjects in a cluster.

The method that is widely used for measuring the similarity is the **Euclidean distance or its square. The Euclidean distance** is the square root of the sum of squared differences between the values for each variable. The squared Euclidean distance is the sum of squared differences between the values for each variable. This distance measure is used for the interval data. Varieties of other measures are also available, but this section will mainly focus on the squared Euclidean distance method. The Euclidean distance measure also has one disadvantage in terms of varying result with varying units. This disadvantage can be overcome by expressing all the variables in a **standardized form** with a mean value of zero and standard deviation one.

The method that is widely used for measuring the similarity is the Euclidean distance or its square. The Euclidean distance is the square root of the sum of squared differences between the values for each variable. The squared Euclidean distance is the sum of squared differences between the values for each variable.

There are two approaches of clustering: hierarchical clustering approach and non-hierarchical clustering approach. Hierarchical clustering starts with all the subjects in one cluster and then dividing and subdividing them till all the subjects occupy their own single subject cluster. As different from hierarchical clustering, non-hierarchical clustering allows subjects to leave one cluster and join another in the cluster forming process if by doing so the overall clustering criterion will be improved.

19.2.4.3 Selection of an Appropriate Clustering Technique

There are two approaches of clustering: **hierarchical clustering approach and non-hierarchical clustering approach**. Hierarchical clustering starts with all the subjects in one cluster and then dividing and subdividing them till all the subjects occupy their own single-subject cluster. As different from hierarchical clustering, non-hierarchical clustering allows subjects to leave one cluster and join another in the cluster forming process if by doing so the overall clustering criterion will be improved. The various clustering procedures are shown in Figure 19.10.

In the hierarchical clustering method, various approaches are available to cluster the subjects in different clusters. It can mainly be divided into two categories: **agglomerative and divisive**. In agglomerative clustering, initially each subject occupies a separate cluster. In this process of clustering, clusters are created by grouping the subjects into bigger and bigger clusters until all the subjects join a single cluster. In divisive clustering, as clear from

FIGURE 19.10
Different methods of clustering

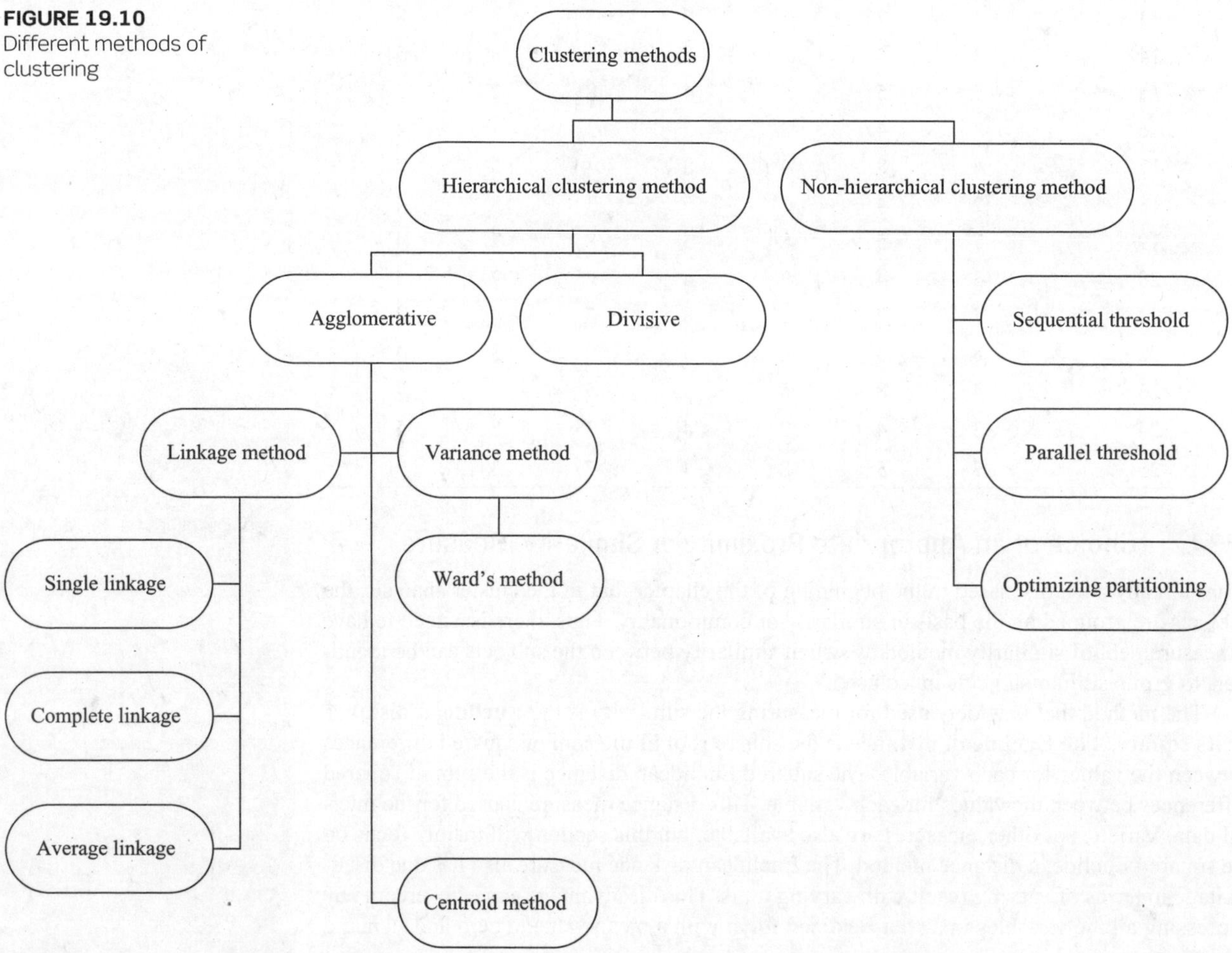

the name itself, initially all the subjects or members are grouped into a single cluster and then the clusters are divided until each subject occupies a single cluster.

The hierarchical clustering method can mainly be divided into two categories: agglomerative and divisive.

As discussed, varieties of clustering methods are available, but in the field of marketing, the agglomerative methods are widely used. From Figure 19.10, we can see that agglomerative methods are categorized into **linkage method, variance method, and centroid method**. Linkage method is based on how the distance between the two clusters is defined. On the basis of the procedure of measuring the distance, it can be categorized into three categories: **single linkage method, complete linkage method, and average linkage method**.

Agglomerative methods are categorized into linkage method, variance method, and centroid method. Linkage method is based on how the distance between the two clusters is defined. On the basis of the procedure of measuring the distance, it can be categorized into three categories: single linkage method, complete linkage method, and average linkage method.

The **single linkage method** also referred as the nearest neighbour approach is based on the principle of the shortest distance. This method measures the shortest distance between the two individual subjects and places them into the first cluster. Then on the basis of the next shortest distance, either the third subject joins the first two or a new subject cluster is constituted [Figure 19.11(a)]. This process continues until all the subjects become a member of one cluster. The **complete linkage method** also referred as the farthest neighbour approach is based on the principle of the longest distance. This method is similar to the single linkage method except the measurement pattern in which the distance between the two clusters is measured as the distance between their two furthest points [Figure 19.11(b)]. As the name indicates, in the **average linkage method**, the distance between the two clusters is defined

The single linkage method also referred as the nearest neighbour approach is based on the principle of the shortest distance. The complete linkage method also referred as the farthest neighbour approach is based on the principle of the longest distance. In average linkage method, the distance between two clusters is defined in terms of the average of the distance between all the pairs of the subjects, in which one subject of the pair is from each of the clusters.

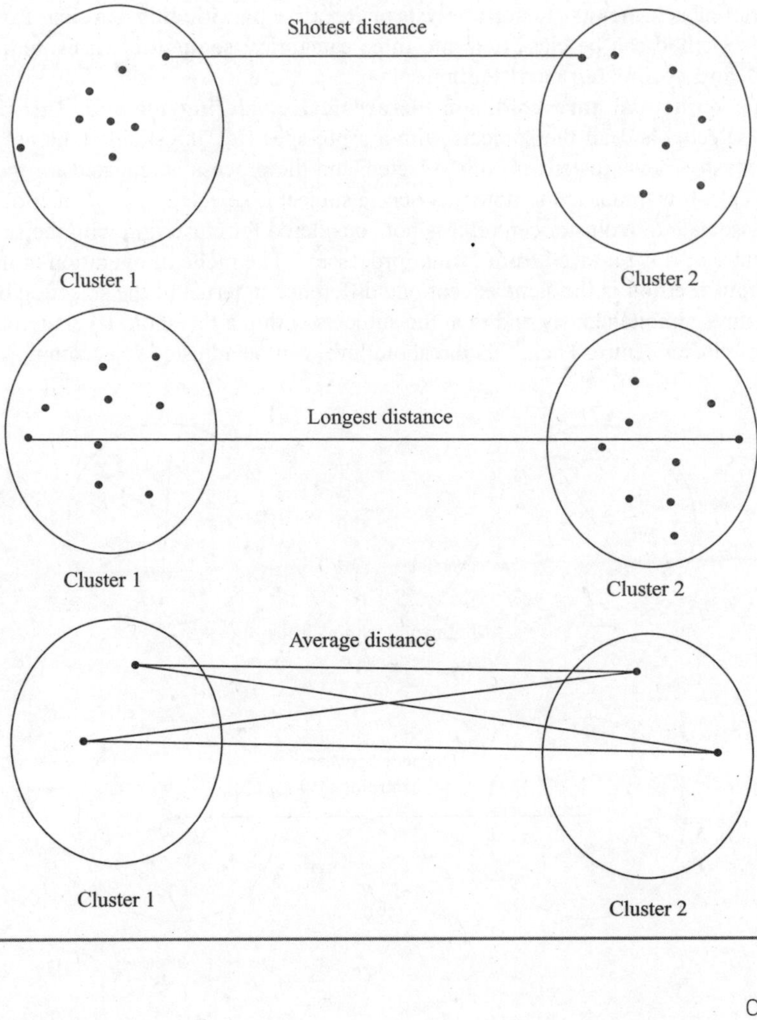

FIGURE 19.11
(a) Single linkage method,
(b) Complete linkage method,
(c) Average linkage method

in terms of the average of the distance between all pairs of the subjects, in which one subject of the pair is from each of the clusters [Figure 19.11(c)]. This method is preferred over the single linkage and complete linkage methods because it avoids taking two extreme members while taking the distance between the two clusters. In fact, this method considers all the members of the cluster rather than the two extreme members of the clusters.

The second type of agglomerative method is the variance method. This method is mainly based on the concept of minimizing within the cluster variance. The most common and widely applied variance method is the Ward's method.

The second type of agglomerative method is the **variance method**. This method is mainly based on the concept of **minimizing within the cluster variance**. The most common and widely applied variance method is the **Ward's method**. In Ward's method, the distance is measured as the total sum of squared deviation from the mean of the concerned cluster to which the subject is allocated. In other words, for each subject, the squared Euclidean distance to cluster means is computed and then these computed distances are summed up for all the subjects. The formation of new clusters tends to increase the total sum of the squared deviations (error sum of squares). At each stage, two clusters are joined to produce the smallest increase in the overall sum of the squared within the cluster distances [Figure 19.12(a)].

The third type of agglomerative method is the centroid method. A cluster centroid is a vector containing one number for each variable, where each number is the mean of the variable for the observations in that cluster.

The third type of agglomerative method is the **centroid method**. A cluster centroid is a vector containing one number for each variable, in which each number is the mean of the variable for the observations in that cluster. In this method, the distance between the two clusters is measured as the distance between their centroid. The two clusters are combined on the basis of the shortest distance between their centroids [Figure 19.12(b)].

The second type of clustering method is the non-hierarchical clustering method that is also referred as k-means cluster analysis or iterative partitioning.

The second type of clustering method is the **non-hierarchical clustering method** that is also referred as **k-means cluster analysis or iterative partitioning**. As clear from Figure 19.10, this method can be classified into three categories: **sequential threshold, parallel threshold, and optimizing partitioning**.

In the sequential threshold non-hierarchical clustering method, first a cluster centre is selected and all the subjects within a pre-specified threshold value are grouped together.

In the **sequential threshold non-hierarchical clustering method**, first a **cluster centre** is selected and all the subjects within a pre-specified threshold value are grouped together. Next, a new cluster centre is selected, and the process is repeated for the unclustered subjects. It is important to note that once a subject is selected as a member of a cluster or as an associate of a cluster centre, it is not considered for clustering with the subsequent cluster centre or it is removed from further processing. The mode of operation in the **parallel threshold method** is the same except one difference in terms of the selection of several cluster centres simultaneously and then the subjects within a threshold level are clubbed to the nearest cluster centre. Then, this threshold level can be adjusted to accommodate some

The mode of operation in the parallel threshold method is the same except one difference in terms of the selection of several cluster centres simultaneously and then the subjects within a threshold level are clubbed to the nearest cluster centre. Then, this threshold level can be adjusted to accommodate some more subject to the concerned cluster. In the optimizing threshold method, the subjects once assigned to a cluster can later be reassigned to another cluster to optimize an overall criterion measure such as the average within the cluster distance.

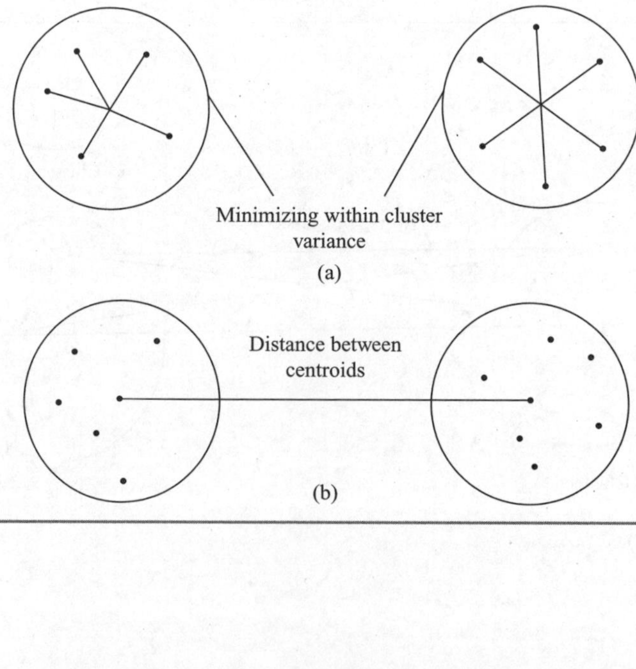

FIGURE 19.12
(a) Ward's method,
(b) Centroid method

more subjects to the concerned cluster. In the **optimizing threshold method**, the subjects once assigned to a cluster can later be reassigned to another cluster to optimize an overall criterion measure such as the average within the cluster distance.

The non-hierarchical clustering method suffers from two major drawbacks. First, one has to pre-specify the number of clusters, and second, the cluster centre selection is arbitrary. This method is recommended when the number of observations is large. It has been recommended to first obtain the initial clustering solution by applying the hierarchical methods (may be Ward's). Next, the number of clusters or cluster centroids can be used as an input material to the optimizing partitioning method. Figures 19.13(a)–19.13(f) present the SPSS output for the problem already defined in the problem formulation stage. To understand the concept of the cluster analysis completely, it is important to understand the interpretation of Figures 19.13(a)–19.13(f).

The non-hierarchical clustering method suffers from two major drawbacks. First, one has to pre-specify the number of clusters, and second, the cluster centre selection is arbitrary.

FIGURE 19.13
(a) Case processing summary,
(b) Proximity matrix

Case Processing Summary[a,b]

Cases					
Valid		Missing		Total	
N	Percent	N	Percent	N	Percent
25	100.0	0	0.0	25	100.0

a. Squared Euclidean Distance used

b. Ward Linkage

(a)

Proximity matrix

	Squared euclidean distance																								
Case	1	2	3	4	5	6	7	8	9	10	11	12	13	14	15	16	17	18	19	20	21	22	23	24	25
1	0.000	92.000	59.000	96.000	5.000	2.000	79.000	102.000	6.000	69.000	79.000	2.000	52.000	103.000	3.000	93.000	79.000	113.000	4.000	95.000	59.000	2.000	64.000	102.000	4.000
2	92.000	0.000	53.000	6.000	97.000	94.000	43.000	6.000	88.000	41.000	43.000	96.000	52.000	3.000	93.000	5.000	43.000	5.000	106.000	7.000	59.000	104.000	56.000	2.000	86.000
3	59.000	53.000	0.000	61.000	50.000	57.000	4.000	57.000	45.000	4.000	4.000	55.000	3.000	52.000	52.000	50.000	4.000	62.000	55.000	50.000	2.000	57.000	3.000	59.000	47.000
4	96.000	6.000	61.000	0.000	93.000	98.000	55.000	6.000	86.000	47.000	55.000	96.000	60.000	7.000	93.000	7.000	55.000	7.000	106.000	3.000	69.000	108.000	66.000	4.000	84.000
5	5.000	97.000	50.000	93.000	0.000	7.000	72.000	103.000	3.000	58.000	72.000	3.000	43.000	106.000	2.000	96.000	72.000	116.000	3.000	92.000	50.000	5.000	55.000	105.000	1.000
6	2.000	94.000	57.000	98.000	7.000	0.000	79.000	104.000	4.000	69.000	79.000	4.000	52.000	101.000	5.000	91.000	79.000	111.000	4.000	95.000	57.000	2.000	64.000	102.000	6.000
7	79.000	43.000	4.000	55.000	72.000	79.000	0.000	49.000	67.000	4.000	0.000	77.000	7.000	44.000	72.000	44.000	0.000	52.000	77.000	46.000	6.000	79.000	3.000	51.000	67.000
8	102.000	6.000	57.000	6.000	103.000	104.000	49.000	0.000	94.000	47.000	49.000	102.000	62.000	5.000	105.000	5.000	49.000	5.000	114.000	3.000	69.000	112.000	64.000	4.000	92.000
9	6.000	88.000	45.000	86.000	3.000	4.000	67.000	94.000	0.000	53.000	67.000	6.000	40.000	93.000	5.000	85.000	67.000	103.000	4.000	83.000	45.000	4.000	52.000	94.000	2.000
10	69.000	41.000	4.000	47.000	58.000	69.000	4.000	47.000	53.000	0.000	4.000	67.000	3.000	42.000	60.000	44.000	4.000	52.000	67.000	40.000	4.000	69.000	5.000	47.000	53.000
11	79.000	43.000	4.000	55.000	72.000	79.000	0.000	49.000	67.000	4.000	0.000	77.000	7.000	44.000	72.000	44.000	0.000	52.000	77.000	46.000	6.000	79.000	3.000	51.000	67.000
12	2.000	96.000	55.000	96.000	3.000	4.000	77.000	102.000	6.000	67.000	77.000	0.000	50.000	105.000	3.000	93.000	77.000	115.000	4.000	93.000	57.000	4.000	62.000	104.000	4.000
13	52.000	52.000	3.000	60.000	43.000	52.000	7.000	62.000	40.000	3.000	7.000	50.000	0.000	55.000	43.000	55.000	7.000	67.000	50.000	53.000	1.000	52.000	4.000	60.000	40.000
14	103.000	3.000	52.000	7.000	106.000	101.000	44.000	5.000	93.000	42.000	44.000	105.000	55.000	0.000	104.000	2.000	44.000	2.000	115.000	4.000	60.000	113.000	59.000	1.000	95.000
15	3.000	93.000	52.000	93.000	2.000	5.000	72.000	105.000	5.000	60.000	72.000	3.000	43.000	104.000	0.000	94.000	72.000	114.000	3.000	94.000	50.000	5.000	55.000	103.000	3.000
16	93.000	5.000	50.000	7.000	96.000	91.000	44.000	5.000	85.000	44.000	44.000	93.000	55.000	2.000	94.000	0.000	44.000	2.000	103.000	4.000	60.000	103.000	57.000	3.000	87.000
17	79.000	43.000	4.000	55.000	72.000	79.000	0.000	49.000	67.000	4.000	0.000	77.000	7.000	44.000	72.000	44.000	0.000	52.000	77.000	46.000	6.000	79.000	3.000	51.000	67.000
18	113.000	5.000	62.000	7.000	116.000	111.000	52.000	5.000	103.000	52.000	52.000	115.000	67.000	2.000	114.000	2.000	52.000	0.000	123.000	6.000	72.000	123.000	67.000	3.000	105.000
19	4.000	106.000	55.000	106.000	3.000	4.000	77.000	114.000	4.000	67.000	77.000	4.000	50.000	115.000	3.000	103.000	77.000	123.000	0.000	105.000	55.000	2.000	58.000	116.000	4.000
20	95.000	7.000	50.000	3.000	92.000	95.000	46.000	3.000	83.000	40.000	46.000	93.000	53.000	4.000	94.000	4.000	46.000	6.000	105.000	0.000	60.000	105.000	59.000	3.000	83.000
21	59.000	59.000	2.000	69.000	50.000	57.000	6.000	69.000	45.000	4.000	6.000	57.000	1.000	60.000	50.000	60.000	6.000	72.000	55.000	60.000	0.000	57.000	3.000	67.000	47.000
22	2.000	104.000	57.000	108.000	5.000	2.000	79.000	112.000	4.000	69.000	79.000	4.000	52.000	113.000	5.000	103.000	79.000	123.000	2.000	105.000	57.000	0.000	62.000	114.000	4.000
23	64.000	56.000	3.000	66.000	55.000	64.000	3.000	64.000	52.000	5.000	3.000	62.000	4.000	59.000	55.000	57.000	3.000	67.000	58.000	59.000	3.000	62.000	0.000	66.000	52.000
24	102.000	2.000	59.000	4.000	105.000	102.000	51.000	4.000	94.000	47.000	51.000	104.000	60.000	1.000	103.000	3.000	51.000	3.000	116.000	3.000	67.000	114.000	66.000	0.000	94.000
25	4.000	86.000	47.000	84.000	1.000	6.000	67.000	92.000	2.000	53.000	67.000	4.000	40.000	95.000	3.000	87.000	67.000	105.000	4.000	83.000	47.000	4.000	52.000	94.000	0.000

This is a dissimilarity matrix

(b)

Agglomeration Schedule

Stage	Cluster Combined		Coefficients	Stage Cluster First Appears		Next Stage
	Cluster 1	Cluster 2		Cluster 1	Cluster 2	
1	11	17	0.000	0	0	2
2	7	11	0.000	0	1	22
3	5	25	0.500	0	0	11
4	14	24	1.000	0	0	12
5	13	21	1.500	0	0	14
6	19	22	2.500	0	0	13
7	16	18	3.500	0	0	19
8	1	12	4.500	0	0	16
9	3	23	6.000	0	0	14
10	8	20	7.500	0	0	18
11	5	15	9.000	3	0	15
12	2	14	10.500	0	4	19
13	6	19	12.167	0	6	16
14	3	13	14.167	9	5	17
15	5	9	16.167	11	0	20
16	1	6	18.500	8	13	20
17	3	10	20.900	14	0	22
18	4	8	23.400	0	10	21
19	2	16	26.000	12	7	21
20	1	5	30.889	16	15	24
21	2	4	36.289	19	18	23
22	3	7	42.889	17	2	23
23	2	3	243.264	21	22	24
24	1	2	619.440	20	23	0

(c)

FIGURE 19.13
(c) Agglomeration schedule

Figure 19.13(a) is the simple statement of the number of cases, missing cases, and total number of cases. Figure 19.13(b) presents the **Proximity matrix** and is the matrix of proximity between subjects. The values in the table represent dissimilarities between each pair of items. The distance measure used in Figure 19.13(b) is the measure of dissimilarities (squared Euclidean distance). In the case of dissimilarities, the larger values indicate items that are very different. This figure gives some initial clues about clustering of subjects.

Agglomeration schedule table gives the information of how subjects are being clustered at each stage of the cluster analysis.

Figure 19.13(c) presents the **agglomeration schedule.** This figure gives the information of how subjects are being clustered at each stage of the cluster analysis. The cluster analysis starts with 24 clusters at Stage 1, where Case 11 and Case 17 are combined (being minimum squared Euclidean distance). The coefficient column in Figure 19.13(c) indicates the squared Euclidean distance between the two clusters (or subjects) joined at each stage. After "coefficient column" "stage cluster first appears column" is shown. When we started the analysis, single cases existed, so it is indicated by zero at the initial stage. The last column "Next stage" indicates the subsequent stage at which the case combined in this cluster will be combined to another case. In the first row of this Column '**2**' can be seen. Its interpretation can be done in Stage 2, where Case 7 is clustered with Case 11. Remember that Case 11 has

Cluster Membership

Case	5 Clusters	4 Clusters	3 Clusters	2 Clusters
1	1	1	1	1
2	2	2	2	2
3	3	3	3	2
4	4	2	2	2
5	1	1	1	1
6	1	1	1	1
7	5	4	3	2
8	4	2	2	2
9	1	1	1	1
10	3	3	3	2
11	5	4	3	2
12	1	1	1	1
13	3	3	3	2
14	2	2	2	2
15	1	1	1	1
16	2	2	2	2
17	5	4	3	2
18	2	2	2	2
19	1	1	1	1
20	4	2	2	2
21	3	3	3	2
22	1	1	1	1
23	3	3	3	2
24	2	2	2	2
25	1	1	1	1

(d)

FIGURE 19.13
(d) Cluster membership

already been clustered with Case 17 in Stage 1. On the basis of the squared Euclidean distance, this process continues until all the cases are clustered in a single group.

The process described in the earlier paragraph can be well explained with the help of three examples in terms of clustering of Case 11 and Case 17 at Stage 1, Case 5 and Case 15 at Stage 11, and Case 3 and Case 13 at Stage 14, and Case 1 and Case 5 at Stage 20.

Cases 11 and 17 are grouped at Stage 1 with minimum squared Euclidean distance. These cases are not clustered before (see two zeros in "stage cluster first appears" below Clusters 1 and 2). In the "Next stage" column, Stage 2 is mentioned. This shows that Case 11 that was grouped with Case 17 in the first stage is grouped again with Case 7, making it a three-case cluster (Case 11, Case 17, and Case 7). This situation is shown in Figure 19.14.

Cases 5 and 15 are grouped at Stage 11. In the "stage cluster first appears," 3 and 0 are mentioned. It means that before clustering at this stage (Stage 11), cluster or Case 5 is first clubbed with Case 25 at Stage 3. Against Stage 11 in the "Next stage" column, Stage 15 is mentioned. This means at Stage 15, Case 5 will be grouped with Case 9 making it a three-case cluster (Case 5, Case 15, and Case 9). This situation is also shown in Figure 19.14.

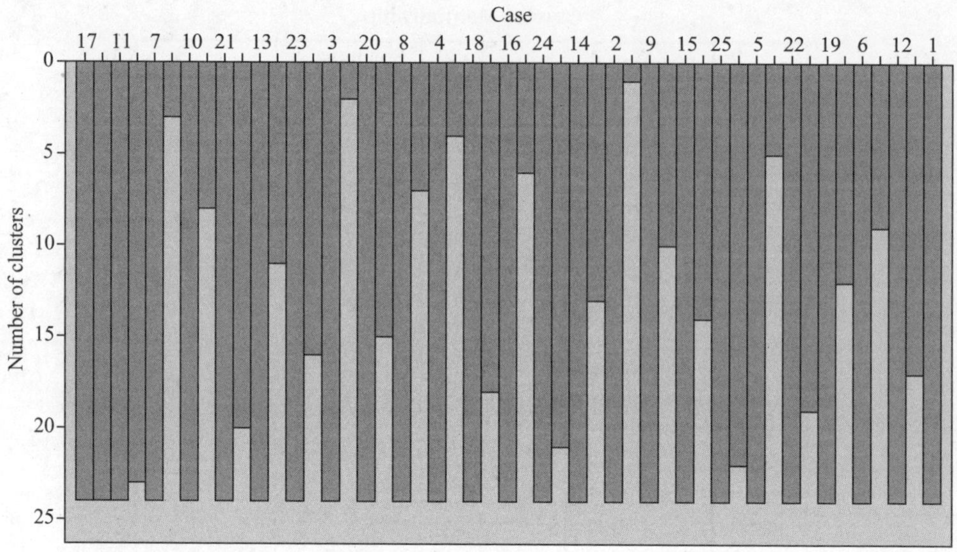

(e)

```
Dendrogram using Ward Method

                       Rescaled Distance Cluster Combine

   C A S E      0         5        10        15        20        25
 Label  Num     +---------+---------+---------+---------+---------+


          11    -+
          17    -+
           7    -+
          13    -+-------------------------+
          21    -+                         |
           3    -+                         |
          23    -+                         +---------------------+
          10    -+                         |                     |
           8    -+                         |                     |
          20    -+                         |                     |
           4    -+-------------------------+                     |
          16    -+                                               |
          18    -+                                               |
          14    -+                                               |
          24    -+                                               |
           2    -+                                               |
           5    -+                                               |
          25    -+                                               |
          15    -+                                               |
           9    -+-----------------------------------------------+
           1    -+
          12    -+
          19    -+
          22    -+
           6    -+
```

(f)

FIGURE 19.13
(e) Vertical icicle plot,
(f) Dendrogram

Agglomeration Schedule

Stage	Cluster Combined		Coefficients	Stage Cluster First Appears		Next Stage
	Cluster 1	Cluster 2		Cluster 1	Cluster 2	
1	11	17	0.000	0	0	2
2	7	11	0.000	0	1	22
3	5	25	0.500	0	0	11
4	14	24	1.000	0	0	12
5	13	21	1.500	0	0	14
6	19	22	2.500	0	0	13
7	16	18	3.500	0	0	19
8	1	12	4.500	0	0	16
9	3	23	6.000	0	0	14
10	8	20	7.500	0	0	18
11	5	15	9.000	3	0	15
12	2	14	10.500	0	4	19
13	6	19	12.167	0	6	16
14	3	13	14.167	9	5	17
15	5	9	16.167	11	0	20
16	1	6	18.500	8	13	20
17	3	10	20.900	14	0	22
18	4	8	23.400	0	10	21
19	2	16	26.000	12	7	21
20	1	5	30.889	16	15	24
21	2	4	36.289	19	18	23
22	3	7	42.889	17	2	23
23	2	3	243.264	21	22	24
24	1	2	619.440	20	23	0

FIGURE 19.14
Joining of the cases or clusters at different stages

At Stage 14, in the case of grouping of Case 3 and Case 13, it can be seen from Figure 19.14 that in the column "stages cluster first appears," 9 and 5 are mentioned. It means that before clustering at this stage (Stage 14), cluster or Case 3 is first clubbed with Case 23 at Stage 9. Similarly, before clustering at this stage (Stage 14), cluster or Case 13 is first grouped with Case 21 at Stage 5. Thus, at Stage 14 there is a four-case cluster (Case 3, Case 13, Case 21, and Case 23). Against Stage 14 in the "Next stage" column Stage 17 is mentioned. This means at Stage 17, Case 3 will be grouped with Case 10 making it a five-case cluster. Interpretation of the other parts of the agglomeration schedule can be done on the same lines.

Figure 19.13(d) indicates '**Cluster membership**' for each case. The SPSS has presented "two- to five-cluster" solutions as requested (is described in using the SPSS for Cluster analysis section). For example, if we take a three-cluster solution, Cases 1, 5, 6, 9, 12, 15, 19, 22, and 25 are the members of '**Cluster 1**.' Cases 2, 4, 8, 14, 16, 18, 20, and 24 are the members of '**Cluster 2**.' Cases 3, 7, 10, 11, 13, 17, 21, and 23 are the members of '**Cluster 3**.' Similar interpretation can be done for other cluster solutions as well.

Figure 19.13(e) exhibits '**Vertical icicle plot**' that displays some important information graphically. In fact, this plot generates the same information as generated by agglomeration schedule except that the values of distant measures are not shown in this plot. As can be seen from the first column of Figure 19.13(e), rows indicates "number of clusters." Most importantly, this plot is interpreted from '**bottom to top**.' In this problem, there are 25 subjects, and in the beginning, each subject is considered as individual cluster, so there are

Vertical icicle plot that displays some important information graphically.

25 initial clusters. At the first stage, two nearest subjects are combined (here these objects are Case 11 and Case 17) that results in 24 clusters. The bottom line of Figure 19.13(e) indicates that 24 clusters (as the plot is interpreted from "bottom to top"). As can also be seen from the agglomeration schedule, in the second stage two subjects Cases 7 and 11 are combined. Figure 19.13(e) shows that the column between 7 and 11 is of maximum length after the column between 11 and 17. In the next stage, Cases 5 and 25 are combined. See Figure 19.13(e), column between 5 and 25 is the third in length (from bottom to top) after "7 and 11" and "11 and 17". In a similar manner, interpretation of other stages can be obtained.

The "dendrogram" exhibits a relative similarity between subjects considered for cluster analysis.

Figure 19.13(f) is another graphical display as an output part of cluster analysis from the SPSS. This graphical plot is referred to as "dendrogram." This tree diagram is a critical component of hierarchical clustering output (Lehmann, Gupta, and Steckel 1998).The dendrogram exhibits a relative similarity between subjects considered for cluster analysis. Dendrogram is interpreted from "left to right" in the form of "branches" that merge together as can be seen from Figure 19.13(f). On the upper part of the plot, one can see "Rescaled Distance Cluster Combine." This indicates that cluster distances are rescaled to get the range of the output from "0 to 25" with 0 representing no distance and 25 representing the highest distance. Cases or clusters that are joined by nearest vertical line (from the left) are very similar, and cases or clusters that are joined by relative distant vertical line (from the left) are very dissimilar (Figure 19.15).

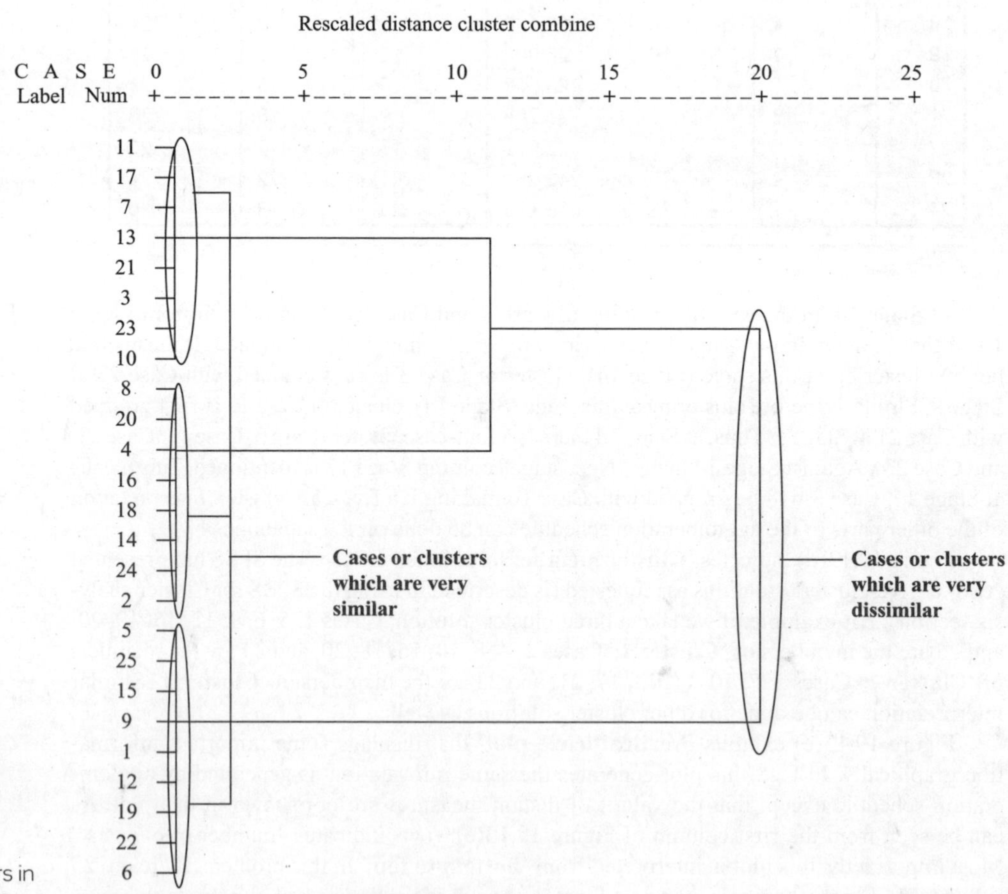

FIGURE 19.15
Joining of cases or clusters in a rescaled cluster distance

19.2.4.4 A Decision Regarding Number of Clusters to be Retained in the Final Solution

A very important question in the cluster analysis is to determine the number of clusters. Virtually all clustering procedures provide little if any information as to the number of clusters present in the data (Milligan and Cooper 1985). In fact, there is no strict rule to adhere to determine the number of clusters in cluster analysis. There are few guidelines that can be followed when determining the number of clusters. A brief discussion of these guidelines is given below:

> In fact, there is no strict rule to adhere, to determine the number of clusters in cluster analysis.

- On the basis of theoretical considerations or experience of an executive, number of clusters can be prespecified.
- Agglomeration schedule and dendrogram can also be used to determine the required number of clusters in cluster analysis in terms of the distance measurement at which the clusters are combined. While reading agglomeration schedule, in a good cluster solution, a **sudden jump** appears. The stage just before the sudden jump point indicates the stopping point for merging of clusters. In the example taken for this chapter, at Stage 22 a sudden jump can be seen. So, this is a stopping point, and **three-cluster solution** will be a good solution in our case (Figure 19.16).

Dendrogram can also be used to determine the number of clusters in cluster analysis. Drawing an imaginary vertical line through dendrogram will present different cluster solutions. The first line in Figure 19.17 presents a three-cluster solution, one for each cut point where the branch of the dendrogram intersects the imaginary drawn vertical line. By considering different cut points, different number of cluster solutions can be obtained (as can be seen that second vertical line presents a two-cluster solution). A good cluster solution can be obtained

> Dendrogram can also be used to determine number of clusters in cluster analysis. Drawing an imaginary vertical line through the dendrogram will present different cluster solutions.

Agglomeration Schedule

Stage	Cluster Combined		Coefficients	Stage Cluster First Appears		Next Stage
	Cluster 1	Cluster 2		Cluster 1	Cluster 2	
1	11	17	0.000	0	0	2
2	7	11	0.000	0	1	22
3	5	25	0.500	0	0	11
4	14	24	1.000	0	0	12
5	13	21	1.500	0	0	14
6	19	22	2.500	0	0	13
7	16	18	3.500	0	0	19
8	1	12	4.500	0	0	16
9	3	23	6.000	0	0	14
10	8	20	7.500	0	0	18
11	5	15	9.000	3	0	15
12	2	14	10.500	0	4	19
13	6	19	12.167	0	6	16
14	3	13	14.167	9	5	17
15	5	9	16.167	11	0	20
16	1	6	18.500	8	13	20
17	3	10	20.900	14	0	22
18	4	8	23.400	0	10	21
19	2	16	26.000	12	7	21
20	1	5	30.889	16	15	24
21	2	4	36.289	19	18	23
22	3	7	42.889	17	2	23
23	2	3	243.264	21	22	24
24	1	2	619.440	20	23	0

Sudden jump in distance from stage 22 to 23

3 clusters after stage 21

FIGURE 19.16 Determining number of clusters through agglomeration schedule

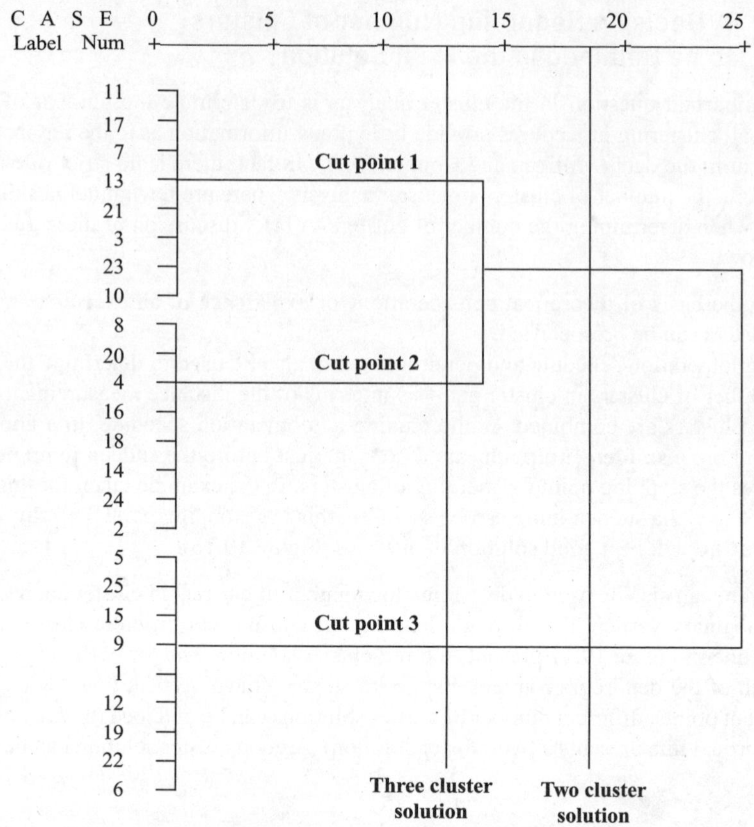

FIGURE 19.17
Determining number of clusters through dendrogram

TABLE 19.4
Different number of cluster solutions with number of subjects in the concerned cluster

Cluster membership	*Five-cluster solution*	*Four-cluster solution*	*Three-cluster solution*	*Two-cluster solution*
Cluster 1	9	9	9	9
Cluster 2	5	8	8	16
Cluster 3	5	5	8	—
Cluster 4	3	3	—	—
Cluster 5	3	—	—	—

by considering small within-cluster distances and large between-cluster distances. By tracing backward down the branches, cluster membership can be obtained.

Number of clusters can also be determined by simply considering relative cluster size.

Number of clusters can also be determined by simply considering **relative cluster size.** From Figure 19.13(d) if we take simple frequency count of the cluster membership, then the number of clusters can be determined. Table 19.4 presents different number of cluster solutions with the number of subjects in the concerned cluster.

So, it can be seen from the table that a three-cluster solution presents a **meaningful cluster solution** with relative equal distribution of the subjects in concerned clusters.

19.2.4.5 Substantive Interpretation

After clustering, it is important to find the meaning of the concerned clusters in terms of finding some natural or compelling structure in the data. For this purpose, cluster centroid can be a useful tool. Remember that cluster centroid can be obtained through discriminant analysis. Figure 19.18 exhibits these cluster centroids. From the figure, it can be seen that Cluster 1 is associated with high values on Variables X_1 (I am trying very hard to understand the loan schemes offered by different banks to purchase the product when it will be coming in the market), X_3 (my old bike is old fashioned; I want to get rid of it), and X_5 (I will not wait for product's performance in the market, I know company is reputed and will certainly launch quality product). This cluster (Cluster 1) can be named as '**desperate consumers.**' Cases 1, 5, 6, 9, 12, 15, 19, 22, and 25 are the members of '**Cluster 1**' [see Figure 19.13(d)]. Cluster 2 has relatively low values on Variables X_1, X_3, and X_5 and relative high value on Variable X_6. Variable X_6 is "companies always claim high about its product, let the product come in the market then only

Group Statistics

ClusterNo		Mean	Std. Deviation	Valid N (listwise) Unweighted	Weighted
1.00	X1	7.4444	0.52705	9	9.000
	X2	4.7778	0.44096	9	9.000
	X3	7.5556	0.52705	9	9.000
	X4	4.4444	0.52705	9	9.000
	X5	7.5556	0.52705	9	9.000
	X6	2.5556	0.52705	9	9.000
	X7	4.4444	0.52705	9	9.000
2.00	X1	2.7500	0.46291	8	8.000
	X2	4.2500	0.46291	8	8.000
	X3	2.3750	0.51755	8	8.000
	X4	4.2500	0.70711	8	8.000
	X5	2.8750	0.64087	8	8.000
	X6	7.6250	0.51755	8	8.000
	X7	4.6250	0.51755	8	8.000
3.00	X1	4.3750	0.51755	8	8.000
	X2	7.5000	0.53452	8	8.000
	X3	4.6250	0.51755	8	8.000
	X4	7.7500	0.46291	8	8.000
	X5	4.3750	0.51755	8	8.000
	X6	4.5000	0.53452	8	8.000
	X7	7.3750	0.51755	8	8.000
Total	X1	4.9600	2.07123	25	25.000
	X2	5.4800	1.50333	25	25.000
	X3	4.9600	2.24499	25	25.000
	X4	5.4400	1.70978	25	25.000
	X5	5.0400	2.09125	25	25.000
	X6	4.8000	2.19848	25	25.000
	X7	5.4400	1.44568	25	25.000

FIGURE 19.18
Cluster centroids obtained through discriminant analysis

I will be taking any decision about the purchase." This cluster (Cluster 2) can be named as **'patient consumers.'** Cases 2, 4, 8, 14, 16, 18, 20, and 24 are the members of **'Cluster 2'**. Cluster 3 has relative high values on Variables X_2 (I am still in confusion whether to sell my old bike), X_4 (my company has promised that it will be releasing a much awaited new incentive scheme; purchase of new model is based on this factor), and X_7 (I want to purchase a new bike but my kids are growing up and are demanding to purchase a car instead of bike, which I already have). This cluster (Cluster 3) can be named **'perplexed consumers.'** Cases 3, 7, 10, 11, 13, 17, 21, and 23 are the members of **'Cluster 3'** [see Figure 19.13(d)].

19.2.4.6 Check the Model Fit

Formal procedures for testing statistical reliability of clusters are not fully defensible. Following are some ad hoc procedures to put a rough check on the quality of cluster analysis.

- Perform the cluster analysis on same data using different distance measures and compare the results across distance measures. In addition, different methods of clustering for the same data can be used and the result can be compared.
- Split the data into halves and perform the cluster analysis on the halves. Obtained cluster centroid can be compared across subsamples.
- Delete various variables from the original sets of variables and perform the cluster analysis on remaining set of variables. Obtained result should be compared with the result obtained from the original set of variables.

19.2.5 Non-Hierarchical Clustering

First, the hierarchical clustering procedure must be used to obtain the number of clusters and then these numbers of clusters can be used as the basis of initial information to perform the k-means cluster analysis (non-hierarchical clustering procedure).

As discussed earlier, to get the optimum cluster solution, hierarchical clustering procedure must be used first to obtain the number of clusters and then these number of clusters can be used as the basis of initial information to perform k-means cluster analysis (non-hierarchical clustering procedure). The k-means cluster analysis typically involves minimizing the within-cluster variation or, equivalently, maximizing the between-cluster variation (Magidson and Vermunt 2002). In the hierarchical clustering method, a three-cluster solution is obtained for the motorbike company example discussed in the beginning of this section. Using this information, the SPPS output for the problem at the beginning of this section through k-means cluster analysis (non-hierarchical clustering procedure) is presented in the form of Figure 19.19(a) to 19.19(g).

Figure 19.19(a) exhibits **Initial cluster centers**. These initial cluster centers are the values of three randomly selected cases. The SPSS by default selects the cases that are dissimilar and then cases join these initial values (based on similarity) to make distinct clusters. Each subject joins nearest classification cluster center and the process continues until the stopping criteria is reached.

Initial Cluster Centers

	Cluster		
	1	2	3
X1	8.00	2.00	4.00
X2	5.00	4.00	8.00
X3	7.00	2.00	5.00
X4	4.00	5.00	8.00
X5	8.00	3.00	5.00
X6	3.00	8.00	4.00
X7	4.00	4.00	7.00

(a)

Iteration History[a]

	Change in Cluster Centers		
Iteration	1	2	3
1	1.207	1.369	1.173
2	0.000	0.000	0.000

a. Convergence achieved due to no or small change in cluster centers. The maximum absolute coordinate change for any center is 0.000. The current iteration is 2. The minimum distance between initial centers is 8.000.

(b)

FIGURE 19.19
(a) Initial cluster centers,
(b) Iteration history

Cluster Membership

Case Number	Cluster	Distance
1	1	1.207
2	2	1.541
3	3	1.173
4	2	1.768
5	1	1.252
6	1	1.457
7	3	1.173
8	2	1.541
9	1	1.457
10	3	1.369
11	3	1.173
12	1	1.296
13	3	1.541
14	2	1.061
15	1	1.252
16	2	1.275
17	3	1.173
18	2	1.369
19	1	1.207
20	2	1.369
21	3	1.369
22	1	1.207
23	3	1.173
24	2	0.791
25	1	1.207

(c)

Final Cluster Centers

	Cluster		
	1	2	3
X1	7.44	2.75	4.38
X2	4.78	4.25	7.50
X3	7.56	2.38	4.63
X4	4.44	4.25	7.75
X5	7.56	2.88	4.38
X6	2.56	7.63	4.50
X7	4.44	4.63	7.38

(d)

Distances between Final Cluster Centers

Cluster	1	2	3
1		9.840	7.670
2	9.840		7.078
3	7.670	7.078	

(e)

ANOVA

	Cluster		Error			
	Mean Square	df	Mean Square	df	F	Sig.
X1	48.681	2	0.254	22	191.343	0.000
X2	24.592	2	0.230	22	107.017	0.000
X3	57.494	2	0.271	22	211.791	0.000
X4	31.469	2	0.328	22	95.859	0.000
X5	48.994	2	0.317	22	154.594	0.000
X6	54.951	2	0.277	22	198.276	0.000
X7	22.094	2	0.271	22	81.388	0.000

The F tests should be used only for descriptive purposes because the clusters have been chosen to maximize the differences among cases in different clusters. The observed significance levels are not corrected for this and thus cannot be interpreted as tests of the hypothesis that the cluster means are equal.

(f)

Number of Cases in each Cluster

Cluster	1	9.000
	2	8.000
	3	8.000
Valid		25.000
Missing		0.000

(g)

FIGURE 19.19
(c) Cluster membership, (d) Final cluster centers, (e) Distance between final cluster centers, (f) ANOVA table, (g) Number of cases in each cluster

Figure 19.19(b) presents **Iteration history** and is the progress of estimation process for each iteration. In each iteration, cases join different clusters, as a result cluster center changes. Any number in the second row of Figure 19.19(b) against "iteration 2" indicates the distance of new cluster center (after joining of cases) from the previous cluster center. When a zero appears in the rows against iteration, change in distance is very small, and stopping criteria is achieved to obtain final solution.

Figure 19.19(c) presents **Cluster membership**. As the name indicates, this figure shows the cluster membership information for each case. In the "Distance" column, distance between the subject and cluster center is given. This distance can be used to obtain some knowledge about the "representativeness" of the case for the concerned cluster. A small distance indicates that the cases are good representative of the cluster and a large distance indicates the cases are not good representative of the cluster.

Figure 19.19(d) shows '**Final cluster centers**'. Values in the figure indicate means for each variable within each final cluster. It can be seen that first cluster has high cluster-center values on Variables X_1, X_3, and X_5. This cluster has also a relatively low value for Variable X_6. Second cluster has relatively high cluster-center value for Variable X_6. Third cluster has relatively high cluster-center value on Variables X_2, X_4, and X_7.

Figure 19.19(e) shows **Distance between final cluster centers** and the "Euclidean Distances" between the final cluster centers. Relatively large values indicate that clusters are different from each other. However, relatively small values indicate that clusters are not so different from each other.

Figure 19.19(f) exhibits **ANOVA table.** This figure indicates the variables that are most important in cluster solution and cluster analysis. Mean square in the Cluster column indicates the variance in the variable that can be attributed to clusters. Mean square in the Error column indicates the variance in the variable that cannot be attributed to clusters. *F* ratio indicates the ratio of cluster variance to error variance. Large *F* value indicates variables that are important for segregating the clusters. Small *F* value (close to 1) indicates variables that are not very useful in identifying the membership of the clusters. *F* statistic should not be interpreted in the traditional way and hence the significance value associated with *F* value cannot be interpreted in the traditional manner, in terms of acceptance or rejection of null hypothesis.

Large *F* value indicates variables that are important for segregating the clusters. Small *F* value (close to 1) indicates variables that are not very useful in identifying the membership of cluster.

Figure 19.19(g) presents **Number of cases in each cluster**. This figure shows number of cases assigned to each cluster. A big mismatch in the proportional size of the cluster is an indication of some problem in the cluster solution. For example, if Cluster 1 has got 18 members and Clusters 2 and 3 have only 3 and 4 members, respectively, then there is some problem with the cluster solution. In this kind of situation, the number of clusters requested should be rechecked, and included list of variables in the cluster analysis must be re-examined in light of its importance in the cluster analysis.

F statistic should not be interpreted in the traditional way and hence the significance value associated with *F* value cannot be interpreted in the traditional manner, in terms of acceptance or rejection of null hypothesis.

19.3 MULTIDIMENSIONAL SCALING

This section deals with a famous multivariate technique known as multidimensional scaling. It presents some basic understanding about the multidimensional scaling procedure and deals with the use of SPSS for performing multidimensional scaling.

19.3.1 Introduction

In the field of marketing, companies are generally concerned with the issue of positioning a product. Management of a company is always interested in knowing the position of its products as compared with the position of competitor's product in the market.

Multidimensional scaling commonly known as MDS is a technique to measure and represent perception and preferences of respondents in a perceptual space as a visual display.

Multidimensional scaling is an attempt to answer such questions. **Multidimensional scaling** commonly known as **MDS** is a technique to measure and represent the perception and preferences of respondents in a perceptual space as a visual display. The goal of multidimensional scaling is to represent the relationships among objects by constructing a configuration of *n* points in low dimension from pair-wise comparison of similarities/dissimilarities among a set of *n* object (Huang et al. 2006). Multidimensional scaling handles two marketing decision parameters. As a first case, the dimension on which respondents evaluate objects must be determined. As a convenient option, only two dimensions are worked out as the evaluation objects are graphically portrayed. As a second case, objects are to be positioned on these dimensions. The output of multidimensional scaling happens to be in the form of location of objects on the dimensions and is termed as **spatial map** or **perceptual map**.

The output of multidimensional scaling happens to be in the form of location of objects on the dimensions and is termed as spatial map or perceptual map.

As discussed, cluster analysis groups individuals or objects or cases into relatively homogeneous (similar) groups on the basis of similarity. Subjects grouped within the cluster are similar to each other and there is dissimilarity between the clusters. Multidimensional scaling attempts to infer the underlying dimensions from the preference judgment provided by the customers. This is done by assigning responses of the respondents to a specific location in a perceptual space in a manner that the distances in the space match the given dissimilarity as closely as possible. In fact, cluster analysis ends with grouping subjects into clusters, whereas multidimensional scaling ends with the construction of a graph in which the distance between objects can visually and quantitatively be examined. Data obtained from the respondents can be metric or non-metric. As a case of metric data, rating of respondent's preference can be obtained and as a non-metric data, ranking of the respondent's relative preference can also be obtained. Multidimensional approaches are available for analyzing metric as well as non-metric data.

Multidimensional scaling attempts to infer the underlying dimensions from the preference judgment provided by the customers.

19.3.2 Some Basic Terms Used in Multidimensional Scaling

Following list presents some basic terms quite commonly used in multidimensional scaling:

Stress: Stress measures lack of fit in multidimensional scaling. A higher value for stress is an indication of poorer fit.

***R*-square (squared correlation):** R^2 value indicates how much of the variance in the original **dissimilarity matrix** can be attributed to multidimensional scaling model. Higher value for R^2 is desirable in multidimensional scaling model. In fact, R^2 is a goodness-of-fit measure in multidimensional scaling model.

Perceptual map: Perceptual map is a tool to visually display perceived relationship among various stimuli or objects in a multidimensional attribute space.

19.3.3 The Process of Conducting Multidimensional Scaling

For conducting multidimensional scaling, a researcher usually follows six steps as exhibited in Figure 19.20. These six steps are as follows: problem formulation, input data collection, selection of multidimensional scaling procedure, determining number of dimensions for perceptual map, substantive interpretation, and check the model fit. A step-by-step description of performing multidimensional scaling is presented in the following section.

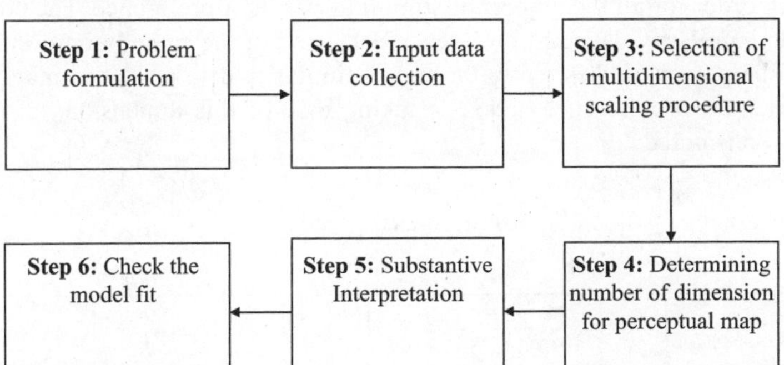

FIGURE 19.20
Steps involved in conducting multidimensional scaling

19.3.3.1 Problem Formulation

As a first step of conducting multidimensional scaling, brand or stimuli that are to be compared are selected. The number of brands that are to be selected is a matter of researcher's discretion, but as a matter of understanding, too few brands like three of four will not be able to produce the desired perceptual map and using too many brands will be difficult to interpret through perceptual map. So there exists a question as to how many brands should be included in multidimensional scaling procedure. A minimum of 8 to 10 brands can be included to construct a well-defined perceptual map, and a maximum of 25 to 30 brands can be included in multidimensional scaling model. In fact, the number of brands or stimuli to be included is based on some factors such as research objective, past researches, decision of researchers, or requirement of management.

A minimum of 8 to 10 brands can be included to construct a well-defined perceptual map, and a maximum of 25 to 30 brands can be included in multidimensional scaling model. In fact, the number of brands or stimuli to be included is based on some factors such as research objective, past researches, decision of researchers, or requirement of management.

We will take a hypothetical example of 10 edible oil brands for better understanding the concept of multidimensional scaling with special reference to obtaining a perceptual map. These 10 edible oil brands are Fortune, Sundrop, Saffola, Gemini, Nutrela, Dhara, Ginni, Maharaja, Vital, and Nature Fresh. Step 2 of performing multidimensional scaling provides discussions on how we can collect data for theses 10 brands of edible oil.

19.3.3.2 Input Data Collection

The input data used for multidimensional scaling may be connected with the **similarity data** or the **preference data**. As a first case, similarity data are described as follows:

Similarity Data: Similarity data are collected through the respondents by just noting the perceived similarity between the two brands or objects. While collecting similarity data, the respondents are not provided with a set of attribute list to judge the similarity or dissimilarity, rather they make their own assessment about similarity or dissimilarity between two objects. These data are often referred to as **similarity judgment**. Figure 19.21 provides respondent's similarity judgment between two pairs (Fortune–Saffola) of edible oil brands.

Number of pairs required to be judged based on similarity judgment are $n(n \quad 1)/2$. Hence, in the edible oil example, number of pairs to be judged are $10(10-1)/2 = 45$. This approach of data collection is referred to as the direct approach.

Number of pairs required to be judged based on similarity judgment are $n(n-1)/2$.

As a second way, derived approach for data collection in terms of conducting multidimensional scaling can also be used. Using this approach, the respondents are supposed to rate the brands for identified attributes on a rating scale. Responses obtained from a single respondent are summarized in Table 19.5 above.

Preference Data: In some cases, a researcher may be interested in knowing the respondent's preference for a stimuli or object. In such situations, the respondent is asked to provide rank order for all the objects or stimuli as per their preference. The configuration derived from similarity data and preference data are not the same but are different. Two objects can be perceived differently through a similarity data produced map but may be close together for a preference data. For taking care of this dimension, an ideal object approach is considered.

The configuration derived from similarity data and preference data are not the same but are different.

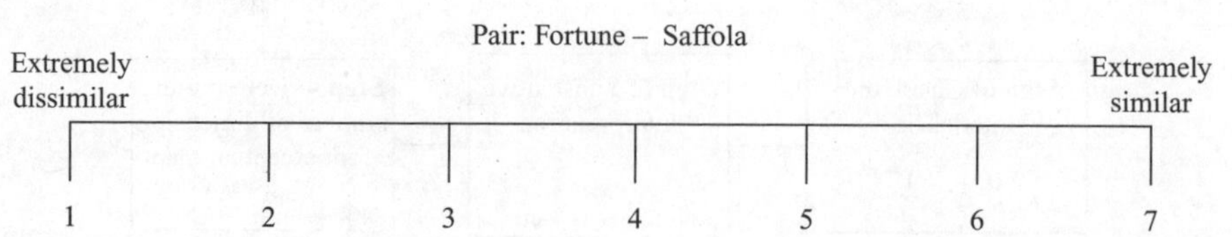

FIGURE 19.21
Respondent's similarity judgment between two pairs of edible oil brands

TABLE 19.5
Similarity score data for different brands of edible oil (data that will be used for multidimensional scaling)

Brands	*Fortune*	*Sundrop*	*Saffola*	*Gemini*	*Nutrela*	*Dhara*	*Ginni*	*Maharaja*	*Vital*	*Nature Fresh*
Fortune										
Sundrop	4.00									
Saffola	1.00	4.00								
Gemini	3.00	3.00	2.00							
Nutrela	5.00	1.00	4.00	2.00						
Dhara	5.00	1.00	5.00	4.00	1.00					
Ginni	4.00	5.00	3.00	1.00	5.00	6.00				
Maharaja	4.00	6.00	3.00	2.00	6.00	6.00	1.00			
Vital	2.00	6.00	3.00	2.00	6.00	7.00	2.00	1.00		
Nature Fresh	1.00	4.00	1.00	2.00	5.00	5.00	3.00	2.00	2.00	

An ideal object is the object that a respondent will like to prefer over all other objects included in the study. It is very interesting to note that this ideal object is actually a hypothetical object. This object can be conceptualized in the map but does not really exist. Respondents may be having similar perception about objects but their preference may vary considerably. Ideal objects are of two types. These two ideal objects can be explained with the help of two examples. As a first example, the respondent is required to rate his preference on an attribute scale related to the "smell of the edible oil when boiling." As his response, suppose the respondent has not selected extreme points but selected some middle point in the scale. The scale is given below:

Good smelled — — — — — — — — Bad odoured

As a second example, a respondent is required to rate his preference for edible oil on a scale (for three attributes) given below:

Very good packaging — — — — — — — — Not at all good packaging
Health friendly — — — — — — — — Not health friendly
Fat free — — — — — — — — Containing fat

In the second case, suppose the respondent has preferred an extreme point of the scale as very good packaging. This case is different from the first case. In the first case, when the respondent has selected some middle point, the ideal object lies within the perceptual map. In the second case, when the respondent has selected an extreme point as his point of preference, the ideal point is reflected by a direction or vector in the perceptual map.

19.3.3.3 Selection of Multidimensional Scaling Procedure

While selecting multidimensional scaling procedure, a researcher should focus on two important issues. The first issue is related to the nature of the data and the second point is related to using multidimensional scaling procedure for average similarity ratings. The input data play a key role in determining multidimensional scaling procedure. Non-metric multidimensional scaling procedure is based on the ordinal nature of input data, whereas metric multidimensional scaling procedure is based on the assumption that the input data are interval scaled. In multidimensional scaling procedure, ordinal or non-metric information is preferred. It is important to learn that non-metric multidimensional scaling procedure results in a metric output. Obviously, metric multidimensional scaling procedure produces a metric output. Here, it is important to note that metric and non-metric multidimensional scaling procedure both produce similar type of results.

Non-metric multidimensional scaling procedure is based on the ordinal nature of the input data, whereas metric multidimensional scaling procedure is based on the assumption that the input data are interval scaled.

Individual-level multidimensional scaling procedure results in a perceptual map for each respondent. While performing multidimensional scaling procedure on aggregate data, a perceptual map on the basis of average similarity rating can be obtained very easily.

As a second issue, a researcher has to determine whether multidimensional scaling procedure should be performed on an individual or an aggregate data is required. Individual-level multidimensional scaling procedure results in a perceptual map for each respondent. While performing multidimensional scaling procedure on aggregate data, a perceptual map on the basis of average similarity rating can be obtained very easily. When using multidimensional scaling procedure for aggregate data instead of an individual's ranking, an aggregate ranking for various individuals is obtained. Aggregating of multidimensional scaling input data is based on the assumption that all the respondents included in the study use the same dimension to evaluate the objects, but these common dimensions are weighted differently by different respondents. Our discussion of multidimensional scaling is based on the edible oil brands example for which data are rank ordered (ordinal) and the adopted procedure is non-metric.

19.3.3.4 Determining Number of Dimensions for Perceptual Map

In the light of the visual interpretation objective of multidimensional scaling procedure, a two-dimensional or at most a three-dimensional perceptual map is desirable.

The focus of multidimensional scaling is to develop a perceptual map with smallest number of dimensions for which there is a "best-fit" between the similarity ranking as input data and resulting perceptual map. In the light of the visual interpretation objective of multidimensional scaling procedure, a two-dimensional or at most a three-dimensional perceptual map is desirable. As discussed in the beginning of the discussion of multidimensional scaling, a statistic "stress" is used. Stress measures lack of fit in multidimensional scaling as the higher value for stress is an indication of poorer fit. Stress measure indicates the proportion of the variance of the disparities (differences in distances between objects on the perceptual map and the similarity judgment of the respondents) not accounted for by multidimensional scaling model (Hair et al. 2009). A widely used criteria to determine the number of dimensions in multidimensional scaling is to construct a plot between stress values (obtained as the SPSS output) and dimensionality. An elbow in the plot indicates number of dimensions to be included in the study to construct a perceptual map.

19.3.3.5 Substantive Interpretation

For generating a perceptual map, we will use the SPSS. The SPSS output for edible oil data is presented from Figures 19.22(a) to 19.22(d). Figure 19.22(a) is the SPSS output exhibiting iteration for stress-value improvement, stress value, and R^2 value. Figure 19.22(b) is the SPSS output exhibiting stimulus coordinates. Figure 19.22(c) is a SPSS-produced two-dimensional perceptual map. Figure 19.22(d) is a SPSS-produced three-dimensional perceptual map.

In fact, stress value is based on the type of multidimensional scaling procedure adopted and the data on which multidimensional scaling is performed.

As discussed, Figure 19.22(a) is the SPSS output exhibiting iteration for stress-value improvement, stress value, and R^2 value. As discussed, this stress index indicates lack of fit in multidimensional scaling. This stress value is commonly known as S-stress or Kruskal's stress. This value ranges from the worst fit (stress value as 1) to best fit (stress value as 0). In fact, stress value is based on the type of multidimensional scaling procedure adopted and the data on which multidimensional scaling is performed. Now, we will analyse the acceptable stress value in multidimensional scaling. The acceptable stress value is suggested by Kruskal (1964) as given below:

Stress (%)	*Goodness of fit*
20.0	Poor
10.0	Fair
5.0	Good
2.5	Excellent
0.0	Perfect

```
Iteration history for the 2 dimensional solution (in squared distances)

          Young's S-stress formula 1 is used.

         Iteration      S-stress       Improvement

             1           0.10166
             2           0.09229          0.00937
             3           0.09174          0.00054

                    Iterations stopped because
          S-stress improvement is less than   0.001000

                    Stress and squared correlation (RSQ) in distances

          RSQ values are the proportion of variance of the scaled data (disparities)
                  in the partition (row, matrix, or entire data) which
                   is accounted for by their corresponding distances.
                    Stress values are Kruskal's stress formula 1.

         For  matrix
Stress  =   0.07469         RSQ = 0.97074
```

(a)

Stimulus Coordinates

Stimulus Number	Stimulus Name	Dimension 1	Dimension 2
1	Fortune	0.4236	1.210
2	Sundrop	-1.6314	0.1112
3	Saffola	0.4314	0.8298
4	Gemini	0.0569	-0.5867
5	Nutrela	-1.6949	-0.3801
6	Dhara	-1.9859	-0.0726
7	Ginni	0.9091	-1.0189
8	Maharaja	1.3333	-0.7384
9	Vital	1.5287	-0.1047
10	NatureFr	0.6292	0.7504

(b)

FIGURE 19.22
(a) SPSS output exhibiting iteration for stress value improvement, stress value, and R^2 value, (b) SPSS output exhibiting stimulus coordinates

As a second step, we are required to examine the value of R^2. As discussed, R^2 value indicates how much of the variance in the original dissimilarity matrix can be attributed to multidimensional scaling model. Higher value for R^2 (close to 1) is desirable in multidimensional scaling. An R^2 value greater than or equal to 60% is considered acceptable.

As a second step, we are required to examine the value of R^2. As discussed R^2 value indicates how much of the variance in the original dissimilarity matrix can be attributed to multidimensional scaling model. Higher value for R^2 (close to 1) is desirable in multidimensional scaling. An R^2 value greater than or equal to 60% is considered acceptable.

Figure 19.22(b) exhibits the stimulus number (brands) and their scores on different dimensions. Figure 19.22(c) is the desired SPSS-produced perceptual map (two dimensional). Spatial map may be interpreted by examining the coordinates of the map and relative position of the brands with respect to these coordinates. The labelling of horizontal axis (*X*-axis) and vertical axis (*Y*-axis) is a matter of researcher's judgment and depends on factors such as researcher's insight, obtained information parameters, and so on. In some cases, the

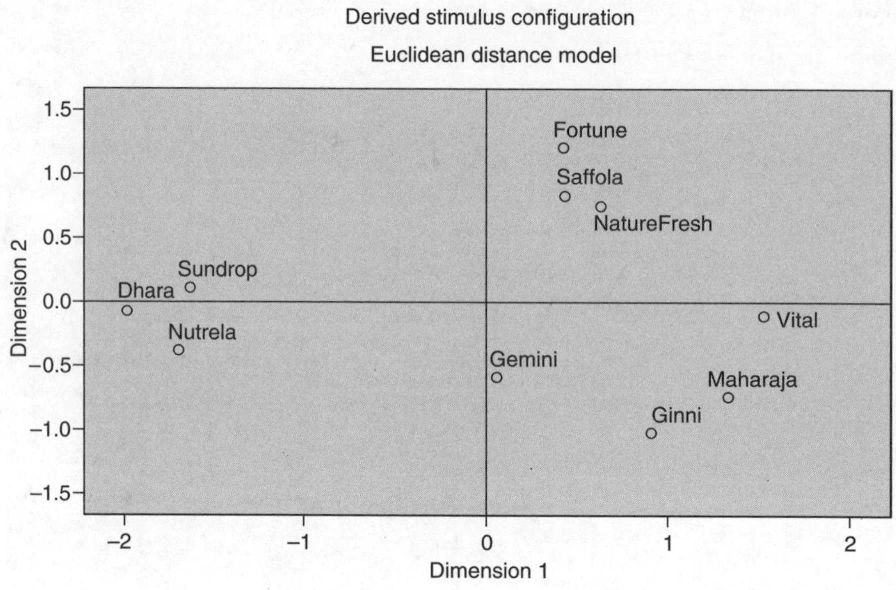

(c)

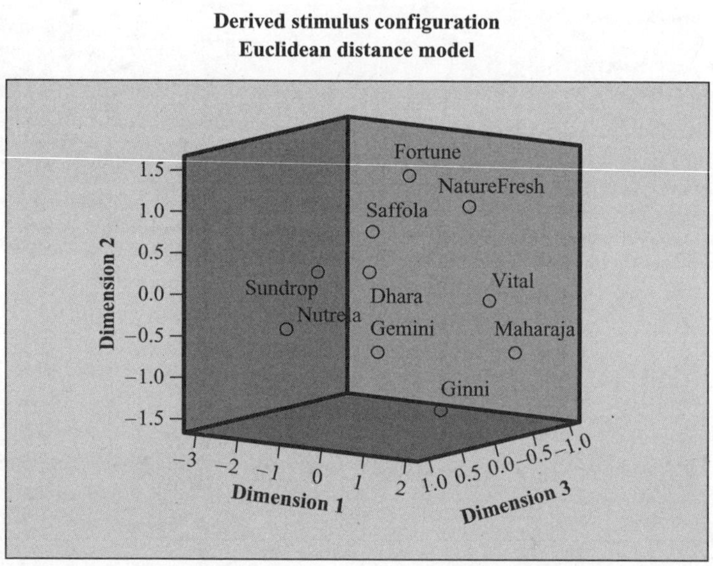

(d)

FIGURE 19.22
(c) SPSS-produced perceptual map (two dimensional),
(d) SPSS-produced perceptual map (three dimensional)

Spatial map may be interpreted by examining the coordinates of the map and relative position of the brands with respect to these coordinates.

respondents are often asked to provide the base of similarity they have used for judging the different brands or objects.

Figure 19.23 exhibits perceptual map (two dimensional) with labelling of dimensions. Brands located close to each other may have competitive nature on related dimension. A brand located in isolation may have unique image. This perceptual map is based on the similarity judgment of a single respondent. If we take an aggregate score of the responses, a perceptual map based on multiple responses (when taken as aggregate) can also be constructed

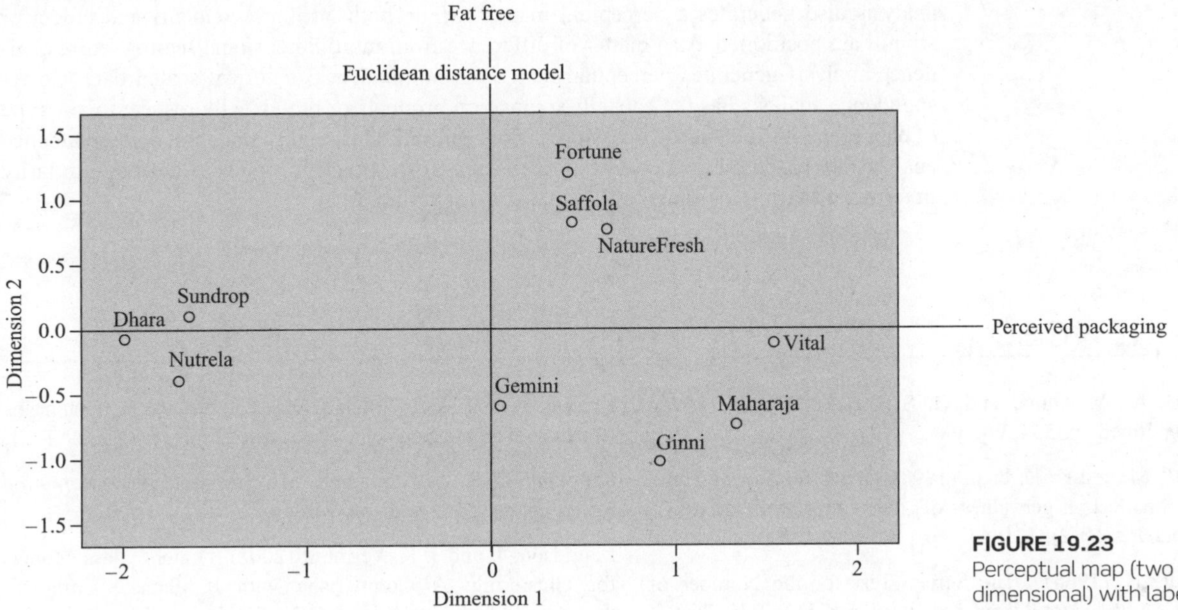

FIGURE 19.23 Perceptual map (two dimensional) with labelling of dimensions

and is very helpful for marketing managers to assess the positioning of their own brand as compared with different brands on some defined attributes.

> Brands located close to each other may have competitive nature on related dimension. A brand located in isolation may have unique image.

19.3.3.6 Check the Model Fit

After performing multidimensional scaling, it is very important for a researcher to assess the reliability and validity of multidimensional scaling model. As a first step of checking reliability and validity of the model, the value of R^2 must be examined. As discussed, an R^2 value greater than or equal to 60% is considered acceptable. In edible oil multidimensional scaling model, R^2 value comes to 0.9707 (97.07%), which is very close to 1 and hence the model is very well acceptable. As a second step, stress value must be examined. In the previous section, the interpretation of an S-stress or Kruskal's stress is already presented. In edible oil multidimensional scaling model, stress value comes to 0.0746 (close to 5%). This is an indication of a good-fit multidimensional scaling model. As a usual approach for performing multidimensional scaling, the original data should be divided in two or parts and obtained results must be compared. As another measure, input data must be gathered at two different points of time and test–retest reliability must be computed.

> As usual approach for performing multidimensional scaling, the original data should be divided in two or parts and obtained results must be compared. As another measure, input data must be gathered at two different points of time and test-retest reliability must be computed.

19.4 CORRESPONDENCE ANALYSIS

> Correspondence analysis has the capacity to position products or brands with respect to any type of data (e.g., attitude, usage occasions). Both multidimensional scaling and correspondence analysis both are based on the concept of similarity. Correspondence analysis defines similarity in terms of sharing the same level of categorical variables.

Discriminant analysis and factor analysis both are based on the assumption of interval-scaled data, which generally is rated on a 1- to 7-point rating scale. However, there are situations when the input data are only binary or categorical when the respondents are simply asked to state which attribute apply to a list of several brands. In this case, respondents are supposed to present their answer in "Yes" and "No" only. "Yes" indicates that the attribute is applicable to the concerned brand and "No" indicates that the attribute is not applicable to the concerned brand. Correspondence analysis is a technique that looks like multidimensional scaling and is used to scale qualitative data in the field of marketing research. Correspondence analysis also generates a perceptual map in which both attribute elements and object or stimuli are positioned. As a matter of difference from multidimensional scaling, correspondence analysis generates perceptual map from nominal or categorical scaled data. Correspondence analysis has the capacity to position products or brands with respect to any type of data (e.g., attitude, usage occasions). Both multidimensional scaling and correspondence analysis are based on the concept of similarity. Correspondence analysis defines similarity in terms of sharing the same level of categorical variables.

REFERENCES

Aaker, D. A., V. Kumar and G. S. Day (2000). *Marketing Research*, 7th ed., p. 554. Wiley.

Bentler, P. M. and K. H. Yuan (1998). "Tests for Linear Trend in the Smallest Eigenvalues of the Correlation Matrix", *Psychometrica*, 63(2): 131–44.

Cattell, R. B. (1966). "The Screen Test for the Number of Factors", *Multivariate Behavioural Research*, 1(2): 245–76.

Costello, A. B. and J. W. Osborne (2005). "Best Practices in Exploratory Factor Analysis: Four Recommendations for Getting the Most from Your Analysis", *Practical Assessment, Research & Evaluation*, 10(7): 1–9.

Fabrigar, L. R., D. T. Wegener, R. C. MacCallum and E. J. Strahan (1999). "Evaluating the Use of Exploratory Factor Analysis in Psychological Research", *Psychological Methods*, 4(3): 272–99.

Hair, J. F., W. C. Black, B. J. Babin, R. E. Anderson and R. L. Tatham (2009). *Multivariate Data Analysis*, 6th ed., p. 125. Pearson Education.

Huang, J., C. Ong and G. Tzeng (2006). "Interval Multi-Dimensional Scaling for Group Decision Using Rough Set Concept", *Expert System with Applications*, 31(3): 525–30.

Kruskal J. B. (1964). "Multidimensional Scaling by Optimizing Goodness of Fit to a Nonmetric Hypothesis", *Psychometrica*, 29: 1–27.

Lehmann, D. R., S. Gupta and J. H. Steckel (1998). *Marketing Research,* pp. 575. Addison-Wesley.

Magidson, J. and J. K. Vermunt (2002). "Latent Class Models for Clustering: A Comparison with K-Means", *Canadian Journal of Marketing Research*, 20: 37–44.

Milligan, G. W. and M. C. Cooper (1985). "An Examination of Procedures for Determining the Number of Clusters in a Data Set", *Psychometrica*, 50(2): 159–79.

Punj, G. and D. W. Stewart (1983). "Cluster Analysis in Marketing Research: Review and Suggestions for Applications", *Journal of Marketing Research*, 20: 134–48.

Raven, M. R. (1990). "The Application of Exploratory Factor Analysis in Agriculture Education Research", *Journal of Agriculture Education,* 35(4): 9–14.

Reise, S. P., N. G. Waller and A. L. Comrey (2000). "Factor Analysis and Scale Revision", *Psychological Assesment*, 12(3): 287–97.

Zikmund, W. G. (2007). *Business Research Methods*, 7th ed., p. 589. South-Western Thomson Learning.

SUMMARY

The techniques described in this chapter, namely, factor analysis, cluster analysis, multidimensional scaling, and correspondence analysis are often referred to as "interdependence analysis." Factor analysis is a very useful technique of data reduction and summarization. The main focus of factor analysis is to summarize the information contained in a large number of variables into few small numbers of factors. Factor analysis is performed using the following steps: problem formulation, construction and examination of correlation matrix, selection of an appropriate factoring technique, a decision regarding the number of factors to be retained in the final solution, factor rotation for enhancing the interpretability of the solution, substantive interpretation, and check the model fit.

Cluster analysis is a technique of grouping individuals or objects or cases into relatively homogeneous (similar) groups. These homogeneous groups are often referred to as clusters. The subjects grouped within the cluster are similar to each other, and there is dissimilarity between the clusters. Cluster analysis is performed using six steps. These six steps are as follows: problem formulation, choice of an appropriate proximity or similarity measure, selection of an appropriate clustering technique, a decision regarding the number of clusters to be retained in the final solution, substantive interpretation, and check the model fit. To get the optimum cluster solution, first hierarchical clustering procedure must be used to obtain the number of clusters and then this number of clusters can be used as the basis of initial information to perform k-means cluster analysis (non-hierarchical clustering procedure).

Multidimensional scaling commonly known as MDS is a technique to measure and represent perception and preferences of respondents in a perceptual space as a visual display. Multidimensional scaling handles two marketing decision parameters. As a first case, the dimension on which the respondents evaluate objects must be determined. As a convenient option, only two dimensions are worked out as the evaluation objects are graphically portrayed. As a second case, the objects are to be positioned on these dimensions. The output of multidimensional scaling happens to be in the form of location of the objects on the dimensions and is termed as spatial map or perceptual map. Multidimensional scaling is performed using six steps. These six steps are as follows: problem formulation, input data collection, selection of multidimensional scaling procedure, determining number of dimensions for perceptual map, substantive interpretation, and check the model fit.

Correspondence analysis is a technique that looks like multidimensional scaling and is used to scale qualitative data in the field of marketing research. Correspondence analysis also generates a perceptual map in which both attribute elements and object or stimuli are positioned. As a matter of difference from multidimensional scaling, correspondence analysis generates perceptual map from nominal or categorical scaled data. Correspondence analysis has the capacity to position products or brand with respect to any type of data (e.g., attitude, usage occasions). Both multidimensional scaling and correspondence analysis are based on the concept of similarity. Correspondence analysis defines similarity in terms of sharing the same level of categorical variables.

KEY TERMS

% of variance, 476
Agglomeration schedule, 483
ANOVA table, 500
Average linkage method, 487
Bartlett's test of sphericity, 470
Centroid method, 487
Cluster analysis, 468
Cluster membership, 483
Communality, 470
Complete linkage method, 487
Correlation matrix, 470
Correspondence analysis, 468
Dendrogram, 483
Dissimilarity matrix, 501
Distance between final cluster centers, 500
Euclidean distance, 485
Eigenvalue, 470
Factor loading plot, 471
Factor loadings, 470
Factor matrix, 470
Factor score, 469
Factors, 469
Final cluster center, 500
Hierarchical clustering approach, 486
Icicle plot, 483
Initial cluster centres, 498
Interdependence analysis, 468
Iteration history, 499
Kaiser-Mayer-Olkin measure of sampling adequacy, 470
Linkage method, 487
Multidimensional scaling, 468
Non-hierarchical clustering approach, 486
Number of cases in each cluster, 500
Oblique rotation, 480
Orthogonal rotation, 480
Parallel threshold optimizing partitioning, 488
Preference data, 502
Principal axis factoring, 476
Rotation, 471
R-square (squared correlation), 501
Scree plot, 470
Sequential threshold, 488
Similarity data, 502
Single linkage method, 487
Spatial map or perceptual map, 501
Stress, 501
Sudden jump, 495
The principal component method, 476
Variance method, 487
Variance methods and centroid method, 487
Varimax procedure, 479
Ward's method, 488

NOTES

1. www.indiastat.com, accessed September 2009, reprinted with permission.
2. http://www.bata.in/page.php?kon=5_2_1, accessed October 2009.
3. http://www.telegraphindia.com/1060331/asp/others/print.html.

DISCUSSION QUESTIONS

1. What is the conceptual framework of factor analysis? Under what circumstances a researcher should apply factor analysis.
2. What are the steps used in performing factor analysis?
3. Write short note on following topics related to factor analysis:
   (a) Estimation or analysis sample
   (b) Communality
   (c) Correlation matrix
   (d) Kaiser-Mayer-Olkin measure of sampling adequacy
   (e) Bartlett's test of sphericity
   (f) Eigenvalue, % of variance
   (g) Scree plot, factor loadings
   (h) Factor matrix and factor score
   (i) Factor loading plot
   (j) The principal component method
   (k) Principal axis factoring
   (l) Varimax procedure
   (m) Orthogonal rotation
   (n) Oblique rotation
4. What is the conceptual framework of cluster analysis? Under what circumstances a researcher should apply cluster analysis.
5. What are the steps used in performing cluster analysis?
6. Explain the difference between hierarchical clustering technique and non-hierarchical clustering technique. What is the use and application of clustering technique in making managerial decisions.
7. Write short note on following topics related to cluster analysis:
   (a) Agglomeration schedule
   (b) Cluster membership
   (c) Icicle plot
   (d) Dendrogram
   (e) Euclidean distance
   (f) Linkage method
   (g) Variance methods and centroid method
   (h) Single linkage method
   (i) Complete linkage method
   (j) Average linkage method
   (k) Variance method
   (l) Ward's method
   (m) Centroid method
   (n) Dissimilarity matrix
   (o) Cluster membership
   (p) Final cluster centre
   (q) Distance between final cluster centres
   (r) ANOVA table in clustering
8. What is the conceptual framework of multidimensional scaling? Under what circumstances a researcher should apply multidimensional scaling.
9. What are the steps used in performing multidimensional scaling?
10. Write short note on following topics related to multidimensional scaling:
    (a) Spatial map or perceptual map
    (b) Stress, R^2 (squared correlation)
    (c) Similarity data
    (d) Preference data
11. What do you understand by correspondence analysis? Under what conditions a researcher should be applying correspondence analysis.

CASE STUDY

Case 19: *Britannia Industries Ltd: A leading player in Indian Bakery Industry*

Introduction: An Overview of Indian Bakery Industry

Indian bakery industry is mainly dominated by small-scale sector. In India, bakery products primarily include biscuits and bread. The two major bakery products in India are biscuits and bread that accounts for 82% of all bakery production. For all the leading companies producing bakery products, biscuits have got the lion's share in total sales. In the year 2001–2002, demand for biscuits was 1188 thousand metric tonnes, which is estimated to increase to 2758 thousand metric tonnes in the year 2014–2015. Market segmentation wise organized and unorganized market secure 50% of the total market size. In the time span of 2009–2010 to 2014–2015, the market is estimated to grow at a rate of 6.2%. Biscuit market is also segmented with respect to product line. Glucose, Milk, Marie, Cream, Crackers, and others occupy 60%, 10%, 10%, 5%, 7%, and 8% of the total market, respectively. Britannia and Parle are two major players in the biscuit market. In the year 2001–2002, demand for bread was 12.85 billion rupees, which is estimated to increase to 26.90 billion rupees in the year 2014–2015. For bread, only 15% market is occupied by the organized players and 85% market is captured by unorganized players. In the time span of 2009–2010 to 2014–2015, bread market is estimated to grow at a rate of 5.0%. Milk bread has got the lion's share with 85% of share of the total market. Modern food and Britannia are two major producers of bread.[1]

Britannia Industries Limited: A Leading Player in Indian Bakery Industry

Britannia Industries Ltd is a leading bakery products company in India with a predominant focus on the sale of branded biscuits. The company's history goes back to 1892, when it was incorporated in Kolkata under the name of Britannia Biscuit Company. BIL got its current name in 1979. In 1993, the Nusli Wadia group acquired a stake in BIL's parent company, Associated Biscuits International Ltd, UK and became an equal partner in BIL with the French Major Groupe Danone. The company is engaged in the business of biscuits, bread, cakes, and rusks. It caters to diverse needs and tastes of the Indian consumer across age groups through its optimum range of biscuit brands. Some of its popular brands are Tiger, Good Day, Marigold, Milk Bikis, Treat, 50:50, Little Heart, Bourbon, Pure Magic, Snax, Premium Bake, and Nutrichoice. The company's strategy of consistently renovating its existing brands and launching new ones has helped it to garner larger share of the Indian biscuits market every year. In the year 2005–2006, the company's market share stood at 37.2%. Britannia is the pioneer in the sliced bread business in India. Today, it caters to almost half the branded bread market in India. Its cake and rusk business, albeit small, has been growing at a healthy pace. However, the bread, cakes, and rusk business together accounts for only 8.9% of the company's total turnover. It is essentially a biscuit company with 90.2% revenue coming from the sale of biscuits.[2]

The company has also been following the inorganic route of expansion quite actively in the recent past. It made its first international acquisition in March 2007 by buying 70% stake in Strategic Food International Co LLC, Dubai, a leading company in the biscuits and cookies segment in the GCC (Gulf Cooperation Council) markets. In July 2005, it acquired 50% stake in Bangalore-based Daily Bread. The company believes that this acquisition will help increase its presence in select markets with a range of gourmet sold under the brand names Daily Bread and Deluca. In addition to the bakery business, Britannia runs its dairy operations through its joint venture Britannia New Zealand Foods Pvt. Ltd. This joint venture with Fonterra of New Zealand was formed in 2002 by demerging the dairy products business from the Britannia Industries Limited.[2] TABLE 19.01 below exhibits sales and profit after tax (in million rupees) of the Britannia Industries Limited from 1994–1995 to 2007–2008. The company has registered encouraging profit after tax figure in the financial year 2007–2008.

TABLE 19.01
Sales and profit after tax (in million rupees) of Britannia Industries Limited from 1994-1995 to 2007-2008

Year	*Sales*	*Profit after tax*
Mar-95	5655.8	183.9
Mar-96	6591.6	160.1
Mar-97	8203.6	178.8
Mar-98	8478.4	289.2
Mar-99	10,301.4	395.6
Mar-00	11,698.4	510.2
Mar-01	13,325.2	705.4
Mar-02	14,509.8	2031.7
Mar-03	13,490.5	991.6
Mar-04	14,705.3	1188
Mar-05	16,154.5	1498.6
Mar-06	18,179.2	1464.3
Mar-07	23,830.7	1076.5
Mar-08	26,786.4	1910

Source: Prowess (V. 3.1): Centre for Monitoring Indian Economy Pvt. Ltd, Mumbai, accessed September 2009, reprinted with permission.

Britannia Plans to Consolidate Factories, Realign Operations

Britannia's non-biscuit business like breads, rusks, cakes, and dairy business is gaining in size. In the light of this development, biscuit giant Britannia is working on operational realignment aimed at streamlining the number of manufacturing locations as well as reworking its distribution strategy. Company's Managing Director Ms Vinita Bali told *The Economic Times*, "Britannia's bread, cake and rusk portfolio has quadrupled in the past four years with a run rate of about Rs 4000 million right now. We will consolidate factories across our bakery products and realign operations wherever it makes sense." Ms Bali added about the realignment strategy of the Britannia Industries, "The realignment is being done to increase cost effectiveness, reduce complexity and to adopt a synergistic go-to-market strategy." Britannia has also strategies to streamline its marketing play into four key paths, namely, modern trade, general trade, rural markets, and transit routes. In the line of this segment, Britannia has introduced smaller SKUs at more buoyant price points over the past 2–3 months. Company has plans to sale through confectionary selling points by offering small packets of biscuits. This is a strategy to shift from grocery segment to confectionary segment. Vice President and COO of Britannia Industries Mr Neeraj Chandra said, "By positioning it as a single serve offering, we have made the range more accessible. It will bring a larger section of the customer base into our ambit."[3]

Suppose the Britannia Industries wants to introduce a very small packet of a famous brand of biscuits to stick to its policy of catering market through grocery stores. For this purpose, suppose the company wants to ascertain consumer perception about the policy of launching very small packets of biscuits. Take the help of literature to list down the statements that can be used to ascertain consumer perception. Use the techniques presented in the chapter to factorize (group) these statements into some variables. Use any software output to determine the required factors and discuss the result in the light of launching a research plan indicating required multivariate analysis to treat the independent variables and dependent variable (consumer perception).

Suppose the company wants to place few products as per the preference or taste of the consumers. Use literature to list down some attributes (statements) related to the taste of the customers for biscuits. These statements can be collected on some taste attributes like salty, light salty, spicy, sweet, light sweet, mix of sweet and salt, and so on. Collect data on these statements on a 7-point rating scale from randomly selected consumers. Apply the clustering techniques (using any statistical software) presented in this chapter to group individuals on common clustering attributes. Discuss the result to present a suitable strategy to the company on the basis of clustering of the consumers.

Collect similarity data with respect to nine brands available in the market, select an appropriate multidimensional scaling procedure, construct a two-dimensional perceptual map, check the model fit, and discuss the result.

NOTES

1. www.indiastat.com, accessed September 2009, reprinted with permission.
2. Prowess (V. 3.1): Centre for Monitoring Indian Economy Pvt. Ltd, Mumbai, accessed September 2009, reprinted with permission.
3. http://economictimes.indiatimes.com/articleshow/4553714.cms?prtpage=1, accessed September 2009, reprinted with permission.

CHAPTER **20**

Sales Forecasting

Look to the future, because that is where you'll spend the rest of your life.

– GEORGE BURNS

LEARNING OBJECTIVES

Upon completion of this chapter, you will be able to:

- Understand the types of forecasting methods (qualitative and quantitative)
- Understand the concept, importance, and components of time series
- Understand the concept of measurement of errors in forecasting
- Understand how to use regression model for trend analysis
- Understand the concept of autocorrelation and autoregression and the use of autoregression in forecasting
- Understand the concept and importance of index numbers

STATISTICS IN ACTION: HINDUSTAN SANITARYWARE & INDUSTRIES LTD

The real estate sector in India has grown at an average rate of 30% over the last few years. The increase in disposable incomes, decline in interest rates, easy and flexible financing, superior real estate options, and relocation of foreign direct investment in construction and real estate are some of the factors responsible for the speedy growth. Apart from sustained economic growth, urbanization, high aspiration levels, and the increase in the number of nuclear families have also been responsible for the surge in housing demand. This trend is likely to sustain. The sanitaryware industry in India has witnessed accelerated growth rates as a result of the boom in the real estate sector.[1]

Hindustan Sanitaryware & Industries Ltd is the flagship company of the Somany group and was established in 1962 as a joint venture with Twyfords of the UK. In India, it soon pioneered vitreous china sanitaryware and gave the concept of sanitaryware a new meaning. The company's brand, "Hindware" commands more than one-third share of the Indian sanitaryware market and is a leader in several categories. It is recognized among the top 300 companies in the country and is also rated among the 100 best small- and medium-sized companies in the world by *Forbes* Magazine.[2] Table 20.1 provides the net income of the company from 1995-2007.

It is possible to forecast the sales of the company in the forthcoming years using statistical forecasting techniques. This chapter mainly focuses on the different types of forecasting methods; concept of time series and measurement of error in forecasting; use of regression models for trend analysis; concept of autocorrelation and autoregression, and the use of autoregression in forecasting. The concept and importance of index numbers is also discussed in detail.

TABLE 20.1
Net income of Hindustan Sanitaryware & Industries Ltd from 1995-2007

Year	*Net income (in million rupees)*
1995	789.6
1996	967.5
1997	1021.3
1998	1161.8
1999	1446.2
2000	1556.9
2001	1698.3
2002	1862.8
2003	2244.0
2004	2744.9
2005	2972.0
2006	3939.1
2007	4797.7

Source: Prowess (V. 3.1), Centre for Monitoring Indian Economy Pvt. Ltd, Mumbai, accessed September 2008, reproduced with permission.

20.1 INTRODUCTION

In today's highly dynamic business environment, managers have to forecast the future and design strategies accordingly. Managers use forecasting (the art or science of predicting the future) techniques to make strategic decisions about selling, buying, hiring, etc every day. The past data are used by managers to make predictions about the future. For example, let us assume that a company wants to order raw material in advance for its production processes in the current year. The demand for the finished product is uncertain in the current year. In this situation, the company can take the help of forecasting techniques (with the help of past data) to order inventory for the current year. These techniques are discussed in detail in this chapter.

In modern organizations, managers believe in being proactive. This proactive approach is based on future planning. **Forecasting** is a technique which can aid in future planning. **Time series** is an important tool that can be used to predict the future. The future is always uncertain, but with the help of past data, an assessment of the future can be made. That is precisely why time series analysis is very important in the fields of economics, sales, and production. Time series analysis is also helpful in making predictions about population, national income, capital formation, etc. The main objective in analysing time series is to understand, interpret, and evaluate changes in economic phenomena in the hope of anticipating the course of future events correctly.

20.2 TYPES OF FORECASTING METHODS

In general, there are two common ways of forecasting. These are—**qualitative forecasting and quantitative forecasting methods**. Figure 20.1 exhibits these methods of forecasting.

20.3 QUALITATIVE METHODS OF FORECASTING

Companies have to rely on **qualitative methods of forecasting** when historical data are not available. These methods are subjective and judgemental in nature. As described in Figure 20.1, executive opinion, panel judgement, **delphi method**, marketing research, and **past analogy** methods can be included in this category.

In the **executive opinion method**, the experience of executives is used to predict the future. For example, if past data are unavailable, the experience of sales executives in the market can be used to forecast sales in the future. Executive opinion method may suffer from errors due to individual bias. The **panel judgement method** is used to tackle problems that result on account of individual bias. In the panel judgement method, a panel of individuals who are

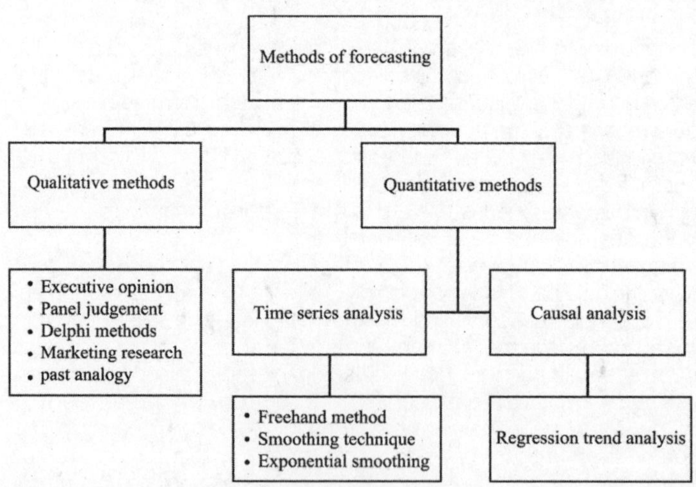

FIGURE 20.1
Methods of forecasting

knowledgeable about the subject is constituted. This panel of individuals share information and opinions about the matter under study and arrive at a conclusion. In the Delphi method, a group of experts who may be stationed at different locations and who do not interact with each other is constituted. After this, a questionnaire is sent to each expert to seek his opinion about the matter under investigation. A summary is prepared on the basis of the returned questionnaire. On the basis of this summary, a few more questions are included in the questionnaire and this modified questionnaire is again sent back to each expert. This process is repeated until a desired consensus is arrived. In the **marketing research method**, a well-designed questionnaire is prepared and distributed among respondents. On the basis of response obtained, a summary is prepared and the survey result is developed. In the past analogy method, the past sales trends of other products are used to forecast sales. These other products may be substitute products, complementary products, or products belonging to consumers in the same income group.

Quantitative methods of forecasting can be broadly divided into two categories: Time series analysis and Causal analysis. Time series analysis involves the projection of the future on the basis of the information available currently. Causal analysis is based on the cause and effect relationship between the two or more variables under study.

Quantitative methods of forecasting can be broadly divided into two categories: Time series analysis and Causal analysis. Time series analysis involves the projection of the future on the basis of the information available currently. Causal analysis is based on the cause and effect relationship between two or more variables under study.

20.4 TIME SERIES ANALYSIS

There are various methods of arranging statistical data. Data can be arranged according to size, geographic area, time of occurrence, etc. The arrangement of statistical data in accordance with the time of occurrence or the arrangement of data in chronological order is known as a time series. This time span may be an hour, a week, a month, a year or several years, depending upon the type of event to which the data refers. In other words, a time series may be defined as a collection of numerical values of variables obtained over regular periods of time.

Mathematically, a time series can be defined by the functional relationship

$$y_t = f(t)$$

where y_t is the value of a variable (or phenomenon) over time period t. For example, (i) sales (y_t) of a consumer durables company in different months (t) of the year (ii) the temperature of a place (y_t) on different days (t) of the week. Thus, if the values of a variable at time period $t_1, t_2, t_3, \ldots, t_n$ are $y_1, y_2, y_3, \ldots, y_n$, then the series

$$t = t_1, t_2, t_3, \ldots, t_n$$

$$y_t = y_1, y_2, y_3, \ldots, y_n$$

constitute a time series. For example, sales (y_t) of a consumer durables company in different years (t) constitute a time series. Table 20.2 gives the sales of a consumer durable company from 1995–2004.

TABLE 20.2
Sales (y_t) of a consumer durables company in different years (t)

Years (t)	*Sales (y_t) (in million rupees)*
1995	50
1996	55
1997	72
1998	66
1999	60
2000	85
2001	90
2002	95
2003	90
2004	100

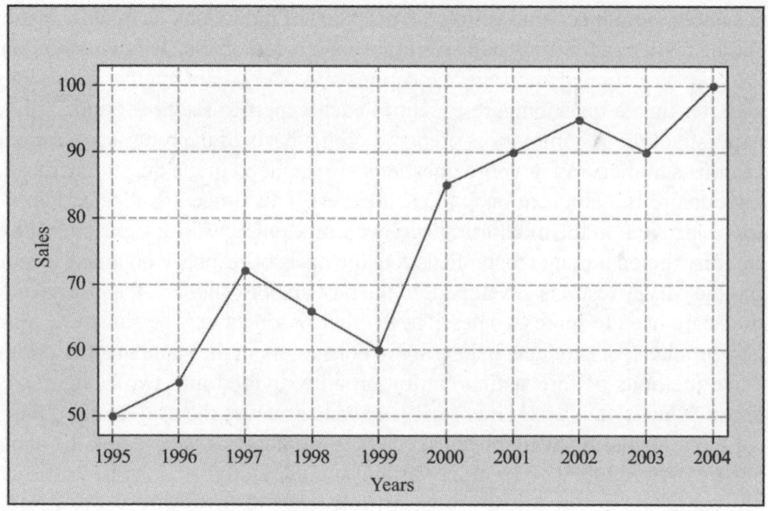

FIGURE 20.2
Time series plot of sales for a consumer durables company produced using Minitab

A time series may be defined as a collection of numerical values of some variable obtained over regular periods of time.

Thus, a time series is a bivariate distribution, in which one variable is time and the other variable is the value of a variable (or phenomenon) for different time periods. Figure 20.2 exhibits the time series plot of sales for a consumer durables company produced using Minitab.

20.5 COMPONENTS OF TIME SERIES

In a time series, data are based on time. Therefore, it is natural that the variable under consideration will change from time to time. A single force cannot be held responsible for fluctuations in data. On the other hand, the net effect of multiplicity of forces seem to be responsible for fluctuations in data. If these forces remain in equilibrium, the resulting time series will remain constant. For example, the sales of a consumer electronics company is influenced by a number of forces rather than a single force. These forces may be a change in the purchasing power of an individual, supply of the finished product by the company, advertising campaigns at a particular time, effort of the sales force, price and quantity discounts offered by the company, etc. The factors that cause fluctuations may be classified into four different categories called the components of time series. Generally in a long time series, the following four components are found to be present.

1. Secular trend or long term movements
2. **Seasonal variations**
3. **Cyclic variations**
4. Random or irregular movements

20.5.1 Secular Trend

Secular trend or simple trend indicates the general tendency of the data to increase or decrease over a long period of time. For example, an upward tendency is usually observed in the data pertaining to population, production, sales, price or income. On the other hand, a downward tendency can be observed in the data pertaining to the rate of infant mortality, the decrease in deaths due to epidemics owing to advancements in medical facilities, etc.

It is not necessary that the increase or decrease be in the same direction throughout the given time period. Different tendencies of increase or decrease or stability can be observed over different periods of time; however, the overall tendency may be upward downward or stable.

This does not mean that all the series must show upward or downward trend. In some cases, values may fluctuate around a constant reading, which does not change with time. For example, the temperature of a particular place does not vary too much with time, instead it remains constant (fluctuates mildly) with time (when the temperature for the different days of a week are considered).

The term "long period of time" is a relative term and cannot be defined exactly. In some cases, 2 weeks may be a long period of time. On the other hand, in some case 2 weeks may not be considered a long period. For example, in order to control an epidemic, 1 week is considered a fairly "long period of time," however, for a census, 1 week cannot be considered a "long period of time."

If the values of a time series are plotted on a graph and these values cluster more or less around a straight line, then the trend shown by the straight line is termed as linear, otherwise the trend is termed as a non-linear trend.

Secular trend or simply trend indicates the general tendency of the data to increase or decrease over a long period of time.

20.5.2 Seasonal Variations

There are variations in a time series due to rhythmic forces which operate in a repetitive, predictable, and periodic manner in a time span of one year or less. Thus, seasonal fluctuations can be measured only if the data are recorded hourly, daily, weekly, monthly, quarterly (every three months). In seasonal variations, the time period should not exceed one year. Most economic series are influenced by seasonal variations. For example, sales of umbrellas and rain coats pick up in the rainy season, sales of ice-cream pick up in the summer, the sales of gold ornaments zoom up during the wedding season, etc.

The study of seasonal variations are important for three reasons. First, we can establish the pattern of past changes. Second, the projection of past patterns into the future is a useful technique of prediction. Third, the effects of seasonal variations can be eliminated from the time series after their presence is established.

Seasonal variations can be of two types:

(i) Seasonal variations due to natural forces: There are **seasonal variations** in the time series due to weather conditions and climatic changes. For example, sales of umbrellas and rain coats zoom up during the rainy reason, sale of ice-creams zoom up in summer, sales of woollen clothes pick up during the winter, the demand for electric fans and air-conditioners goes up during summer, etc. All these variations are due to seasons and can be predicted up to an extent.

Seasonal variations are the variations in time series due to rhythmic forces which operate in a repetitive, predictable, and periodic manner in a time span of one year or less.

(ii) Seasonal variations due to customs: There are seasonal variations due to customs, habits, lifestyle, and conventions of the people in a society. For example, sales of paints and distempers pick up just before Diwali, sales of jewellery and ornaments go up around the marriage season, sales of sweets go up during festivals such as Diwali, Dushera, Holi, Rakshabandhan, etc.

The study of seasonal variations is of paramount importance for businessmen and sales managers. For example, the sales manager of a fast moving consumer goods company has to make policies for purchase, production, inventory control, personnel requirement, advertising, and sales promotion techniques. In order to formulate policies, the knowledge of seasonal variations is very important. Without the knowledge of these seasonal fluctuations, the sales manager may commit mistakes in judging seasonal upswings and seasonal slumps that may affect demand. Therefore, for understanding the behaviour of the phenomenon in a time series, the data must be adjusted for seasonal variations. This technique is called depersonalization and will be discussed later in this chapter.

20.5.3 Cyclical Variations

Cyclical variations refer to oscillatory movements in a time series with a period of oscillation of more than a year. Cyclical variations are the components of a time series that tend to oscillate

Cyclical variations refer to oscillatory movements of time series with a period of oscillation of more than a year.

above and below the secular trend line for periods longer than 1 year or 12 months. Cyclical variations are not as regular as seasonal variations. Instead they exhibit semi-regular periodicity. Most business and economic series represent intervals of prosperity, recession, depression, and recovery, which may also be referred as the "four phase cycle." Each phase changes gradually into the phase that follows it in the given order. In a business activity, these phases follow one another with steady regularity. The period from the peak of one boom to the peak of the next boom is called a complete cycle. Most economic and commercial series relating to prices, production, income, etc. show this tendency. Cyclical variations are not periodic but more or less regular in nature.

20.5.4 Random or Erratic or Irregular Variations

Random or irregular variations are factors in a time series that do not repeat in a definite pattern and are random, unforeseen, unstoppable, and unpredictable.

Apart from the three types of variations discussed above, a time series contains another factor which does not repeat in a definite pattern. These are called random or erratic or **irregular variations**. These variations are purely random, unforeseen, unstoppable, and unpredictable. Variations on account of calamities such as earthquakes, floods, famines, epidemics, etc. are beyond human control. Variations that arise in a time series due to specific events or episodes are called episodic variations. For example, natural calamities, fire, flood, etc. can be placed in the category of episodic variations. Figure 20.3 exhibits all the four components of a time series.

20.6 TIME SERIES DECOMPOSITION MODELS

The analysis of time series includes the decomposition of the time series into trend (*T*), seasonal variations (*S*), cyclical variations, (*C*) and irregular or random variation (*R*). The main objective of time series decomposition is to isolate, study, analyse, and measure the components of time series independently and to determine the relative impact of each on the overall behaviour of the time series.

The analysis of time series includes the **decomposition** of the time series into trend (*T*), seasonal variations (*S*), cyclical variations (*C*), and irregular or random variation (*R*). The main objective of time series decomposition is to isolate, study, analyse, and measure the components of time series independently and to determine the relative impact of each on the overall behaviour of the time series. Many models are available by which a time series can be analysed. Two models, commonly used for decomposing the time series into its components are the **additive model** and the **multiplicative model**.

20.6.1 The Additive Model

The additive model is used when it is assumed that the four components of a time series are independent of one another. This assumption may not hold true in a real-life time series. These components are considered independent of one another when the occurrence and the magnitude of movements in a particular component do not affect the other components. According to the additive model, a time series can be expressed as

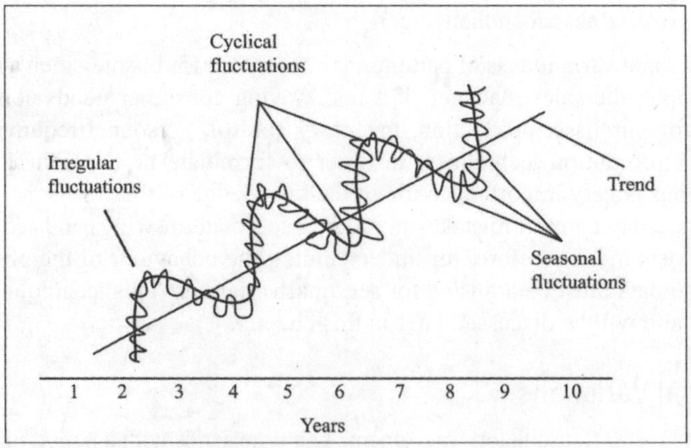

FIGURE 20.3
Components of a time series

$$Y_i = T_i + S_i + C_i + R_i$$

where Y_i is the time series value at time i and T_i, S_i, C_i, and R_i represent the values of trend, seasonal, cyclic, and random components of the time series at time i. This model also assumes that the different components are absolute quantities expressed in original units and can take positive and negative values. The cyclical variations will take positive or negative signs subject to their positions in terms of above or below the corresponding trend values. Positive values of cyclical variations during the upswing will wipe out the negative values, so that the net result over a period of the cycle is zero. Likewise, the net result of a seasonal variation in a year would also be zero.

The additive model is used when it is assumed that the four components of a time series are independent of one another. These components are termed independent of one another when the occurrence and the magnitude of movements in any particular component do not affect the other components.

20.6.2 The Multiplicative Model

In a multiplicative model, it is assumed that all the four components of time series are not independent and the overall variation in the time series is the combined result of the interaction of all the forces operating on the time series. According to the multiplicative model:

$$Y_i = T_i \times S_i \times C_i \times R_i$$

where Y_i is the time series value at time i and T_i, S_i, C_i, and R_i represent the values of trend, seasonal, cyclic, and random components at time i.
By taking logarithms on both the sides of the above equation, we get

$$\text{Log } Y_i = \text{Log } T_i + \text{Log } S_i + \text{Log } C_i + \text{Log } R_i$$

In a multiplicative model, it is assumed that all the four components of a time series are not independent and the overall variation in the time series is the combined result of the interaction of all the forces operating on the time series.

Therefore, it is very clear that the multiplicative decomposition of time series is the same as the additive decomposition of time series with logarithmic values. In the multiplicative model, the geometric means of S_i in a year, C_i in a cycle, and R_i in a long period of time are unity. S_i, C_i, and R_i are index values fluctuating above or below unity. It is not necessary that all the four components be present in a time series. For example, in case of annual data, seasonal component is not present; likewise cyclical component is not present for relatively short period data. In the first case, the multiplicative model is $Y_i = T_i \times C_i \times R_i$ and in the second case, the multiplicative model is $Y_i = T_i \times S_i \times R_i$.

20.7 THE MEASUREMENT OF ERRORS IN FORECASTING

This chapter focuses on several forecasting techniques. In real life, a decision maker encounters the problem of selecting the best technique out of several available techniques. A decision maker has to select a technique that predicts the future well. One method of selecting a best technique is to compare the actual values with the forecasted values and compute the error in estimation. The techniques used to measure errors in forecasting are: mean absolute deviation (MAD), mean absolute percentage error (MAPE), and mean squared deviation (MSD).

The error of a forecast is the difference between the actual value and the forecasted value. Mathematically, an error in forecasting can be explained by

$$e_i = y_i - \hat{y}_i$$

where e_i is the error of the forecast, y_i the actual value, and $\hat{y}_i$ the forecasted value.

The three measures of accuracy—mean absolute deviation (MAD), mean absolute percentage error (MAPE), and mean squared deviation (MSD) can be computed as below:

$$\text{Mean absolute deviation (MAD)} = \frac{\sum_{i=1}^{n} |e_i|}{\text{Number of forecasts (n)}}$$

In real life, a decision maker encounters the problem of selecting the best technique out of several available techniques. A decision maker has to select a technique that predicts the future well. One method of selecting a best technique is to compare the actual values with the forecasted values and compute the error in estimation. The techniques used to measure errors in forecasting are: mean absolute deviation (MAD), mean absolute percentage error (MAPE), and mean squared deviation (MSD).

$$\text{Mean absolute percentage error (MAPE)} = \frac{\sum_{i=1}^{n}\left|\frac{e_i}{y_i}\right|}{\text{Number of forecasts (n)}} \times 100$$

$$\text{Mean squared deviation (MSD)} = \frac{\sum_{i=1}^{n}(e_i)^2}{\text{Number of forecasts (n)}}$$

Let us take the example of the consumer durables company again for understanding the concept of errors in forecasting. Table 20.3 exhibits the computation of the mean absolute deviation (MAD), the mean absolute percentage error (MAPE), and the mean squared deviation (MSD) for the consumer durables company.

TABLE 20.3
Computation of the mean absolute deviation (MAD), the mean absolute percentage error (MAPE), and the mean squared deviation (MSD) for the example relating to the consumer durables company

Years (i)	*Actual sales (y_i) (in million rupees)*	*Forecasted value ($\hat{y}_i$)*	*Error ($e_i = y_i - \hat{y}_i$)*	$\lvert e_i \rvert$	$\left\lvert \frac{e_i}{y_i} \right\rvert$	$(e_i)^2$
1995	50	51.5636	–1.5636	1.5636	0.0312	2.4448
1996	55	57.0606	–2.0606	2.0606	0.0374	4.2460
1997	72	62.5576	9.4424	9.4424	0.1311	89.1589
1998	66	68.0545	–2.0545	2.0545	0.0311	4.2209
1999	60	73.5515	–13.5515	13.5515	0.2258	183.6431
2000	85	79.0485	5.9515	5.9515	0.0700	35.4203
2001	90	84.5455	5.4545	5.4545	0.0606	29.7515
2002	95	90.0424	4.9576	4.9576	0.0521	24.5777
2003	90	95.5394	–5.5394	5.5394	0.0615	30.6849
2004	100	101.0364	–1.0364	1.0364	0.0103	1.0741
Sum				51.612	0.71159	405.22

$$\sum|e_i| = 51.612 \qquad \sum\left|\frac{e_i}{y_i}\right| = 0.71159 \qquad \sum(e_i)^2 = 405.22$$

$$\text{Mean absolute deviation (MAD)} = \frac{51.612}{10} = 5.1612$$

$$\text{Mean absolute percentage error (MAPE)} = \frac{0.71159}{10} \times 100 = 7.1159$$

$$\text{Mean squared deviation (MSD)} = \frac{405.22}{10} = 40.522$$

Note: In Table 20.3, the third column indicates the forecasted value ($\hat{y}_i$). The procedure of computing forecasted value ($\hat{y}_i$) is discussed later in this chapter. Mean absolute percentage error measures accuracy in terms of percentage values.

20.8 QUANTITATIVE METHODS OF FORECASTING

Quantitative methods of forecasting are based on projecting past patterns of data to obtain a future forecast using some mathematical formulae. This method fails to describe the cause–effect relationship between variables. This drawback can be overcome by using causal analysis, which is based on the cause and effect relationship between two or more variables under study. Quantitative methods of time series forecasting can be broadly classified into three categories: free hand methods, smoothing methods, and exponential smoothing methods.

Quantitative methods of time series forecasting can be broadly classified into three categories: free hand methods, smoothing methods, and exponential smoothing methods.

20.9 FREEHAND METHOD

The **freehand method** is the simplest method of determining trend. A freehand smooth curve is obtained by plotting the values y_i against time i as shown in Figure 20.4. Smoothing of the time series with the freehand curve eliminates the seasonal and irregular components. This method is free from mathematical complexities and saves time. Therefore, results can be obtained very quickly. Though this method is very simple, it is not free from demerits. This method is too subjective. If same data is provided to two different persons, two different trend lines may be obtained. For drawing a best-fit trend line, experienced and skilled people are required. Since the trend line depends on human hands, human bias in drawing a trend line cannot be eliminated. In addition, this method does not measure trend mathematically.

While drawing a trend line by the freehand method, one should keep the following points in mind. First, the sum of vertical deviation of the observations above the trend line should be equal to the sum of the vertical deviation of the observations below the trend line. Second, the sum of squares of the vertical deviations of the observations from the trend line should be as less as possible. Third, the trend line should be drawn in such a way so that the trend line bisects the same area above and below a cycle.

The freehand method is the simplest method of determining trend. A freehand smooth curve is obtained by plotting the values y_i against time i.

20.10 SMOOTHING TECHNIQUES

The main objective of the smoothing technique is to "smooth out" the random variations due to the irregular fluctuation in the time-series data. Various methods are available to smooth out the random variations due to irregular fluctuations, so that the resulting series may have a better overall impression of the pattern of movement in the data over a specified period. In this section, we will focus on three methods of smoothing: moving averages method, weighted moving averages method, and semi- averages method.

The main objective of the smoothing technique is to smooth out the random variations due to the irregular fluctuations in the time-series data.

20.10.1 Moving Averages Method

The method of averages is used in the moving average technique to smooth out the irregularities in a time-series data. This method is highly subjective and depends upon the length of the period (L) selected for constructing the averages. For example, if we want to compute a

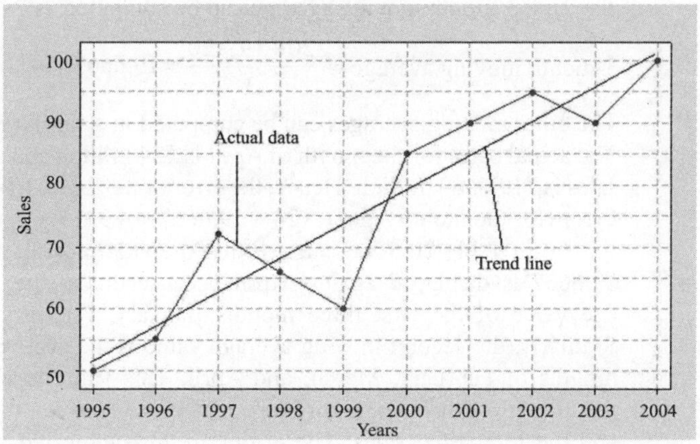

FIGURE 20.4
Freehand graph of sales with trend line for the example on the consumer durables company

3-year moving average from a time series which contains 9 years, that is, $n = 9$, we have to add the first three values pertaining to the first three years as shown below:

$$MA(3) = \frac{y_1 + y_2 + y_3}{3}$$

Similarly, the second-moving average can be computed by taking the average pertaining to the next three values leaving the first one, that is,

$$MA(3) = \frac{y_2 + y_3 + y_4}{3}$$

This process continues until the computation of the last moving average as

$$MA(3) = \frac{y_7 + y_8 + y_9}{3}$$

Example 20.1 explains this process clearly.

Example 20.1

Table 20.4 provides the sales of a manufacturing company in all the 12 months of 2006. Compute a three-month moving average for this time series.

TABLE 20.4
Sales turnover of a manufacturing company for 12 months in 2006

Months	*Sales (in million rupees)*
Jan	20
Feb	19
Mar	20
Apr	24
May	25
Jun	21
Jul	22
Aug	23
Sep	29
Oct	30
Nov	32
Dec	28

Solution

The first 3-month moving average can be computed as

$$\text{3-month moving average} = \frac{20 + 19 + 20}{3} = 19.6667$$

The other moving averages can be computed in a similar manner. The actual sales for the month of April is ₹24 million and the forecasted sales is ₹19.6667 million. Hence, the error of the forecast is computed as Error (for the month April) = 24 – 19.6667 = 4.3333

From Table 20.5 we can see that the first moving average value 19.6667 is displayed against April because this is the moving average value of the first three months: January, February, and March. Similarly, the second moving average value is the average sales in the months of February, March, and April. This value is placed against the month of May. The error is the difference between the actual sales and the forecasted sales. The errors are also indicated in Table 20.5.

The 3-month moving average plot for Example 20.1 produced using Minitab is depicted in Figure 20.5.

TABLE 20.5
Computation of three-month moving average for Example 20.1

Months	*Sales (in million rupees)*	*3-year moving average*	*Fits*	*Error*
Jan	20		-----	-----
Feb	19	19.6667	-----	-----
Mar	20	21.0000	-----	-----
Apr	24	23.0000	19.6667	4.3333
May	25	23.3333	21.0000	4.0000
Jun	21	22.6667	23.0000	–2.0000
Jul	22	22.0000	23.3333	–1.3333
Aug	23	24.6667	22.6667	0.3333
Sep	29	27.3333	22.0000	7.0000
Oct	30	30.3333	24.6667	5.3333
Nov	32	30.0000	27.3333	4.6667
Dec	28		30.3333	–2.33333

20.10.2 Weighted Moving Averages Method

We have already noticed that in the moving averages method, equal weights are assigned to all the time periods. There may be cases when a forecaster may want to attach different weights to different time periods according to their importance. Weighted moving averages method provides a forecaster the opportunity to weigh time periods based on their importance. So, in weighted moving averages method, the weight assignments to different time periods are somewhat arbitrary. In the absence of any specific formula for determining the weights, a general rule is used. As per this rule, the most recent observation of a time series receives more weight and the weights decrease for older values of the data.

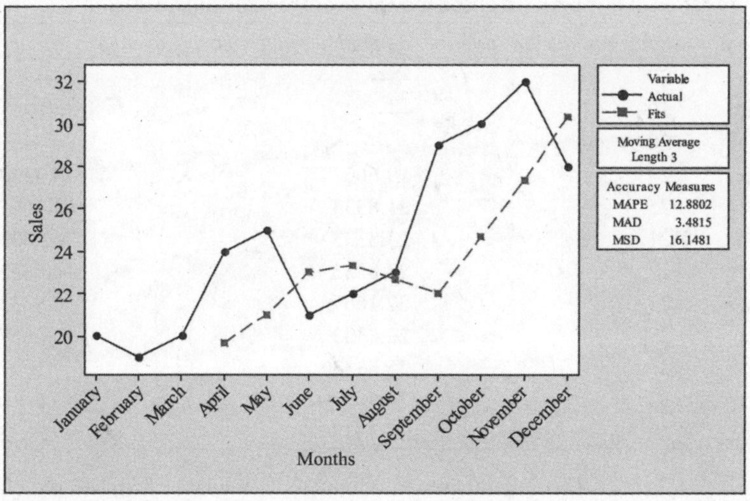

FIGURE 20.5
3-month moving average plot for Example 20.1 produced using Minitab

For example, for computing the 3-month weighted moving average (the value which is placed against April) in Example 20.1, the value corresponding to March is multiplied by 3, the value corresponding to February is multiplied by 2, and the value corresponding to January is multiplied by 1. This weighted moving averages is computed as

$$\bar{x}_{weighted} = \frac{3(M_{t-1}) + 2(M_{t-2}) + 1(M_{t-3})}{6}$$

where M_{t-1} is most recent month's value, M_{t-2} the value for the previous month, M_{t-3} the value for the month before the previous month.

In the above formula, the denominator 6 is the sum of three weights, that is, the denominator is $(3 + 2 + 1 = 6)$.

Example 20.2 Compute the 3-month weighted moving average value for the data given in Example 20.1. Weight the most recent month by 3, the previous month by 2, and the month before the previous month by 1.

Solution The weighted moving average can be computed by using the formula

$$\bar{x}_{weighted} = \frac{3(M_{t-1}) + 2(M_{t-2}) + 1(M_{t-3})}{6}$$

For April, the weighted moving average can be computed as

$$\bar{x}_{weighted} = \frac{3(20) + 2(19) + 1(20)}{6} = 19.6667$$

Similarly, for May, the weighted moving average can be computed as

$$\bar{x}_{weighted} = \frac{3(24) + 2(20) + 1(19)}{6} = 21.8333$$

In a similar manner, the weighted moving average for other months can be computed. These weighted moving averages are shown in Table 20.6.

TABLE 20.6
Computation of 3-month weighted moving average for Example 20.2

Months	*Sales (in million rupees)*	*3-month weighted moving average*	*Error*
Jan	20	-----	-----
Feb	19	-----	-----
Mar	20	-----	-----
Apr	24	19.6667	4.3333
May	25	21.8333	3.1667
Jun	21	23.8333	–2.8333
Jul	22	22.8333	–0.8333
Aug	23	22.1667	0.8333
Sep	29	22.3333	6.6667
Oct	30	25.8333	4.1667
Nov	32	28.5	3.5
Dec	28	30.8333	–2.8333

The general computational tools available with MS Excel, Minitab, and SPSS can be used for calculating weighted moving average.

20.10.2 Semi-Averages Method

In the semi-averages method, data are divided into two equal parts with respect to time. For example, consider a time series *i*, given from 1991–2000, that is, time is given over a period of 10 years. Then, the two equal parts of the data will be the time period from 1991–1995 and the time period from 1996–2000. If the time units in a time series are odd, then two equal parts would be obtained by dropping the value corresponding to the middle year and then dividing the remaining data into two equal parts. For example, for any time series *i*, given from 1991–1999, that is, time is given for a period of 9 years. The two equal parts would be the time period from 1991–1994 and time period from 1996–1999. The value corresponding to the middle year 1995 is dropped. The next step is to calculate the arithmetic mean for each part. Then this mean is plotted against the mid values of the respective time periods for each part. The line which is obtained by joining these two points is known as the trend line and can be extended to estimate future value. For even number of years, that is, for $n = 12$, (say time period from 1991–2002), data can be divided into two equal parts, that is, time slot from 1991–1996 and time slot from 1997–2002. The mean values for 1991–1996 and 1997–2002 are obtained and the first mean value is plotted against middle point of 1991–1996. This middle point will be the middle point of 1993 and 1994, that is, this middle point would be 1st July 1993. The same process should be followed for the second part of the data, that is, for the time span 1997–2002.

The intercept and slope of the trend line can also be obtained using this method. The arithmetic mean of the first part is the intercept value of the trend line. The slope of the trend line can be obtained by taking the ratio of the difference between two arithmetic means computed for two parts and the difference between years (against which arithmetic means are plotted).

In the semi-averages method, data is divided into two equal parts with respect to time.

Example 20.3

Determine straight line trend by semi-averages method for the time-series data related to production of a toy manufacturing company provided in Table 20.7. Also determine the projected production for 2005.

TABLE 20.7
Time-series data related to production of a toy manufacturing company

Year	1991	1992	1993	1994	1995	1996	1997	1998	1999	2000
Production (in 1000 units)	109	119	129	140	153	152	151	163	175	184

Solution

According to the semi-averages method, the times series is divided into two equal parts. Here, the number of years are 10; hence, the first part would be the time slot from 1991–1995 and second part would be the time slot from 1996–2000.

The average of the first five years (from 1991–1995)

$$= \frac{1}{5}(109 + 119 + 129 + 140 + 153)$$

$$= 130$$

The average of the second five years (from 1996–2000)

$$= \frac{1}{5}(152 + 151 + 163 + 175 + 184)$$

$$= 165$$

The first average value is plotted against the middle year between 1991 and 1995, that is, against 1993 and the second average value is

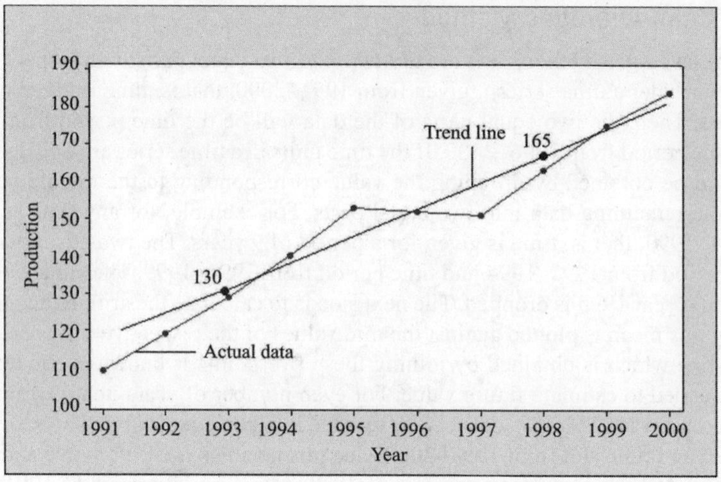

FIGURE 20.6
Time series plot of production (trend line obtained by the method of semi-averages) for Example 20.3

plotted against middle year between 1996–2000, that is, against 1998. For computing the time series $y = a + bx$, we need to compute the values of intercept a and slope b as under:

$$\text{Slope of the trend line } (b) = \frac{\text{Change in production}}{\text{Change in year}} = \frac{165-130}{1998-1993} = \frac{35}{5} = 7$$

As discussed earlier intercept (a) = 130 units (arithmetic mean of the first part)

The resultant trend line can be obtained by substituting the values of a and b in the equation $y = a + bx$. Thus, the required trend line is

$$y = 130 + 7 \times (x)$$

For the year 2005 (which is 12 years away from the origin year 1993) the projected production can be computed as:

$$y = 130 + 7 \times (12) = 214$$

Figure 20.6 exhibits the time series plot of production (trend line obtained by the method of semi-averages).

20.11 EXPONENTIAL SMOOTHING METHOD

Exponential smoothing methods weigh data from the previous time period with expo nentially decreasing importance in the forecast.

Exponential smoothing is another technique used to "smooth" a time series. Exponential smoothing is a type of moving average technique which consists of a series of exponentially weighted moving averages. The **exponential smoothing method** weigh data from the previous time period with exponentially decreasing importance in the forecast. This method has a relative advantage over the methods of moving averages discussed previously. First, this method focuses upon the most recent data (data from the previous time period with exponentially decreasing importance in the forecast). Second, during forecasting, this method takes into account all the observed values because each smoothing value is based upon the values observed previously. In this manner, the values observed most recently receive the highest weight; the previously observed value receives the second highest weight and so on.

In exponential smoothing method, forecasting is carried out by multiplying the actual value for the present time period, X_t, by a value between 0 and 1 (the exponential smoothing constant). This exponential constant is referred to as α (not the same α used in Type I error).

So, the resultant value is $\alpha \cdot X_t$. This value $\alpha \cdot X_t$ is added to the product of the present time period forecast F_t and $(1-\alpha)$. Algebraically, this formula can be stated as below:

$$F_{t+1} = \alpha \cdot X_t + (1-\alpha) \cdot F_t$$

where F_{t+1} is the forecast for the next time period $(t+1)$, F_t the forecast for the present time period (t), α the exponential smoothing constant $(0 \le \alpha \le 1)$, and X_t the actual value for the present time period (t).

The choice of exponential smoothing constant is a very critical step because it directly affects the result. The selection of the exponential smoothing constant is subjective. From the formula given above, we see that the forecast for the next time period is a combination of the actual value for the present time period and the forecast for the present time period. If a forecaster selects α less than 0.5, less weight is placed on the actual value for the present time period and greater weight is placed on the forecast for the present time period. If a forecaster wants to eliminate unwanted cyclical and irregular fluctuations, he or she should select a small value of α (closer to 0). In this case, the overall long term tendencies of the series will be more apparent. If the objective is only forecasting, large value of α (close to 1) should be selected. In this manner, future short-term directions may be more accurately predicted.

In order to understand why this procedure is called exponential smoothing, the formula for forecasting the value of the next time period $(t+1)$ is taken once more as

$$F_{t+1} = \alpha \cdot X_t + (1-\alpha) \cdot F_t$$

If we want to forecast the value of the present time period (t), the forecast F_t is obtained by

$$F_t = \alpha . X_{t-1} + (1-\alpha) \cdot F_{t-1}$$

By substituting the value of F_t in the above equation of forecasting F_{t+1}, we get

$$F_{t+1} = \alpha \cdot X_t + (1-\alpha) \cdot [\alpha . X_{t-1} + (1-\alpha) \cdot F_{t-1}]$$

We know that $F_{t-1} = \alpha \cdot X_{t-2} + (1-\alpha) \cdot F_{t-2}$

Substituting this value of F_{t-1} in the preceding equation for F_{t+1}, we get

$$F_{t+1} = a \cdot X_t + a \cdot (1-a) \cdot X_{t-1} + (1-a)^2 \cdot [a \cdot X_{t-2} + (1-a) \cdot F_{t-2}]$$

$$= a \cdot X_t + a \cdot (1-a) \cdot X_{t-1} + a \cdot (1-a)^2 X_{t-2} + (1-a)^3 F_{t-2}$$

We have discussed that exponential smoothing method weigh data from the previous time period with exponentially decreasing importance in the forecast. This concept is explained by Table 20.8 which contains different values of α and related changes in the values of $a \cdot (1-a)$; $a \cdot (1-a)^2$; $a \cdot (1-a)^3$, and $a \cdot (1-a)^4$.

TABLE 20.8
Different values of α and related changes in the values of $\alpha \cdot (1-\alpha)$; $\alpha \cdot (1-\alpha)^2$; $\alpha \cdot (1-\alpha)^3$, and $\alpha \cdot (1-\alpha)^4$

α	$\alpha \cdot (1-\alpha)$	$\alpha \cdot (1-\alpha)^2$	$\alpha \cdot (1-\alpha)^3$	$\alpha \cdot (1-\alpha)^4$
0.3	0.21	0.147	0.1029	0.0720
0.5	0.25	0.125	0.0625	0.0312
0.7	0.21	0.063	0.0189	0.0056

The exponential formula $F_{t+1} = \alpha \cdot X_t + (1-\alpha) \cdot F_t$ can be rearranged as F_{t+1} $F_{t+1} = F_t + a \cdot (X_t - F_t)$. In this type of arrangement $(X_t - F_t)$, that is, the difference between actual values and forecasted values is referred to as the forecast error. The formula given above clearly shows that the new forecast is equal to the old forecast F_t, plus an adjustment based on α times forecasted error.

Example 20.4

Table 20.9 gives the number of units produced by a watch manufacturing company in different years.

TABLE 20.9
Units produced by a watch manufacturing company in different years

Year	*Production (in thousand units)*
1996	120
1997	112
1998	136
1999	125
2000	155
2001	159
2002	165
2003	150
2004	145
2005	167
2006	170
2007	180

Use exponential smoothing method with $\alpha = 0.3$, $\alpha = 0.5$, and $\alpha = 0.7$ to forecast the production of watches.

Solution

Table 20.10 provides the production forecast for three different values of α. It can be seen from the table that since no forecast is given for the first time period, the forecast based on exponential smoothing method for the second time period cannot be computed. The actual value of the first time period is used to forecast the value of second time period to initiate the procedure. Figure 20.7 shows the Minitab time series plot of production for Example 20.4.

TABLE 20.10
Production forecasts for three different values of α

Year	*Production*	*$\alpha = 0.3$*		*$\alpha = 0.5$*		*$\alpha = 0.7$*	
		Forecast	*Error*	*Forecast*	*Error*	*Forecast*	*Error*
1996	120	-----	-----	-----	-----	----	-----
1997	112	120	–8	120	–8	120	–8
1998	136	117.6	18.4	116	20	114.4	21.6
1999	125	123.12	1.88	126	–1	129.52	–4.52
2000	155	123.68	31.31	125.5	29.5	126.35	28.64
2001	159	133.07	25.92	140.25	18.75	146.40	12.59
2002	165	140.85	24.14	149.62	15.37	155.22	9.77
2003	150	148.09	1.90	157.31	–7.31	162.06	–12.06
2004	145	148.66	–3.66	153.65	–8.65	153.62	–8.61
2005	167	147.56	19.43	149.32	17.67	147.58	19.41
2006	170	153.39	16.60	158.16	11.83	161.17	8.824
2007	180	158.37	21.62	164.08	15.91	167.35	12.64

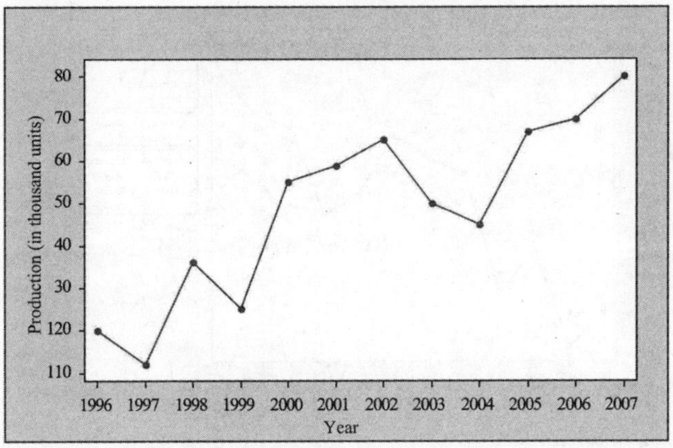

FIGURE 20.7
Time series plot of production (actual values) for Example 20.4 produced using Minitab

Figure 20.8, 20.9 and 20.10 exhibit the Minitab produced exponential smoothing plots for different values of α ($\alpha = 0.3$, $\alpha = 0.5$, and $\alpha = 0.7$). If we compare the three accuracy measures given with the three plots, we find that all the three measures are less for the highest value of α, that is, for 0.7. Figure 20.10 clearly exhibits that the actual values vary considerably with the largest value of α seeming to forecast the best.

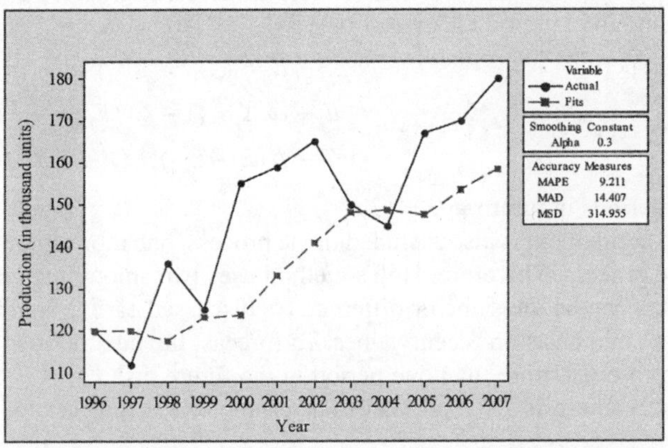

FIGURE 20.8
Exponential smoothing plot for Example 20.4 when $\alpha = 0.3$, produced using Minitab

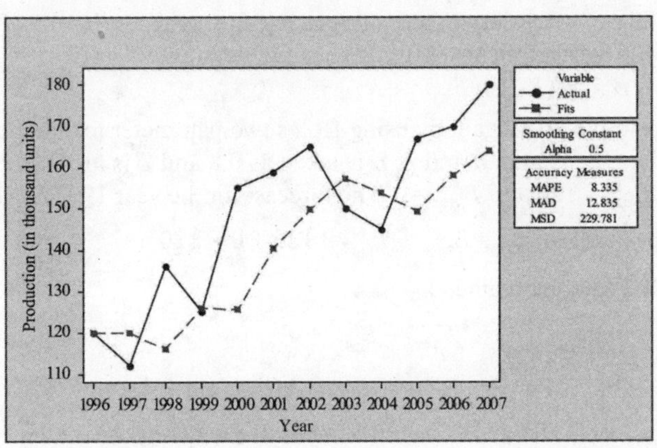

FIGURE 20.9
Exponential smoothing plot for Example 20.4 when $\alpha = 0.5$, produced using Minitab

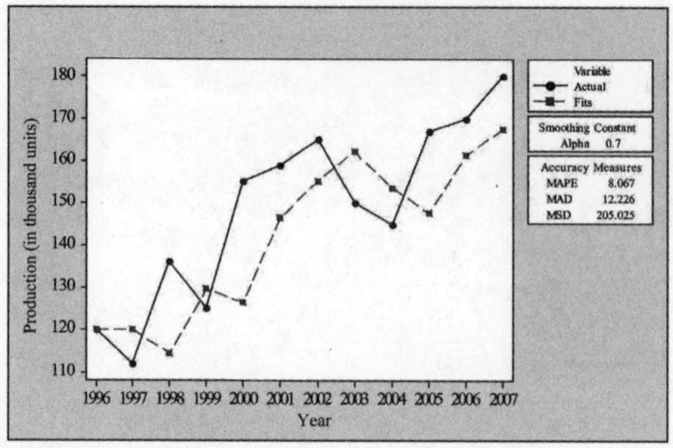

FIGURE 20.10
Exponential smoothing plot for Example 20.4 when $\alpha = 0.7$, produced using Minitab

20.12 DOUBLE EXPONENTIAL SMOOTHING

Single exponential smoothing does not incorporate trend and seasonal components of time series data. There are techniques by which trend and seasonal components can be incorporated in a time series, subject to their existence. In this section, we will focus upon the exponential smoothing method which considers trend effects in forecasting. Holt's two parameter technique is a technique which includes trend effects in forecasting. Holt's double exponential smoothing method for a period *t* is given by

Forecast for the next period $(F_{t+1}) = E_t + T_t$

where, $E_t = \alpha \cdot X_t + (1 - \alpha)(E_{t-1} + T_{t-1})$

and $T_t = \beta(E_t - E_{t-1}) + (1 - \beta) T_{t-1}$

Forecast for *k* periods in future = $E_t + kT_t$

Single exponential smoothing does not incorporate trend and seasonal components of time series data. Holt's two parameter technique is a technique which includes trend effects in forecasting.

Since the trend component is also included in the process, one more smoothing constant β is included in the process. Therefore, Holt's method uses two smoothing constants α and β. These two weights can be the same or different. As discussed earlier, higher values of α and β will give more emphasis on recent values. To forecast the next period $(F_{t+1}) = E_t + T_t$ is used. In order to forecast more than one period in the future, use $E_t + kT_t$, where *k* is the number of periods in future to be forecasted. For example, the forecast for the next four periods is given by

$$F_{t+1} = E_t + 4T_t$$

While calculating the new smoothed value using $E_t = \alpha X_t + (1 - \alpha)(E_{t-1} + T_{t-1})$, the last term is simply a forecast for this period. When we substitute $F_t = E_{t-1} + T_{t-1}$ in the above formula, we get $E_t = \alpha X_t + (1 - \alpha) F_t$.

Let us solve Example 20.4 again by using Holt's two parameter technique. Holt's method uses two smoothing constants α and β, α is taken as 0.8 and β is taken as 0.4. The initial values are taken as $E_{1996} = 120$ and $T_{1996} = 0$. The forecast for the year 1997 can be obtained as

$$F_{1997} = E_{1996} + T_{1996} = 120 + 0 = 120$$

The forecast for 1998 can be obtained as

$$F_{1998} = E_{1997} + T_{1997}$$

where E_{1997} can be computed as

$$E_{1997} = (0.8) \times X_{1997} + (1 - 0.8) \times F_{1997} = (0.8) \times (112) + (0.2) \times 120 = 89.6 + 24 = 113.6$$

T_{1997} can be computed as

$$T_{1997} = (0.4) \times (E_{1997} - E_{1996}) + (1 - 0.4)\, T_{1996} = (0.4) \times (113.6 - 120) + (0.6) \times 0 = -2.56$$

Hence, $$F_{1998} = E_{1997} + T_{1997} = 113.6 - 2.56 = 111.04$$

The forecast for 1999 can be obtained as

$$F_{1999} = E_{1998} + T_{1998}$$

E_{1998} can be computed as

$$E_{1998} = (0.8) \times X_{1998} + (1 - 0.8) \times F_{1998} = (0.8) \times (136) + (0.2) \times (111.04)$$

$$= 108.8 + 22.208 = 131.008$$

T_{1998} can be computed as

$$T_{1998} = (0.4) \times (E_{1998} - E_{1997}) + (1 - 0.4)\, T_{1997} = (0.4) \times (131.008 - 113.6) + (0.6) \times (-2.56) = 5.42$$

Hence, $$F_{1999} = E_{1998} + T_{1998} = 131.008 + 5.42$$

$$= 136.428$$

Other forecasted values can be calculated similarly.

20.11.1 Using SPSS for Holt's Method

Click **Analyze/Time Series/Exponential Smoothing**. The **Exponential Smoothing** dialog box will appear on the screen (Figure 20.13). Place **Production** in the **Variables** box. From **Model**, select **Holt** and click **Parameters**. The **Exponential Smoothing: Parameters** dialog box will appear on the screen (Figure 20.14). From **General (Alpha)** box, select **Value** and place the value of $\alpha = 0.8$ in the box. From **Trend (Gamma) box,** select **Value** and place the value of $\beta = 0.4$ in the box. From the **"Initial Values"** box, click **Custom** and place 120 in the **Starting** box and 0 in the **Trend** box. Click **Continue**, the **Exponential Smoothing** dialog box will reappear on the screen. Click **OK**, SPSS output as shown in Figures 20.11 and 20.12 will appear on the screen. Fits and errors will be attached with the data sheet as shown in Figure 20.11.

	Year	Production	FIT_1	ERR_1
1	1996.00	120.00	120.00000	.00000
2	1997.00	112.00	120.00000	-8.00000
3	1998.00	136.00	111.04000	24.96000
4	1999.00	125.00	136.43520	-11.43520
5	2000.00	155.00	129.05498	25.94502
6	2001.00	159.00	159.88134	-.88134
7	2002.00	165.00	168.96458	-3.96458
8	2003.00	150.00	174.31257	-24.31257
9	2004.00	145.00	155.60214	-10.60214
10	2005.00	167.00	144.46737	22.53263
11	2006.00	170.00	167.05086	2.94914
12	2007.00	180.00	174.91128	5.08872

FIGURE 20.11
SPSS output with data sheet for Example 20.4 (using Holt's method)

```
Results of EXSMOOTH procedure for Variable production
MODEL= HOLT (Linear trend, no seasonality)

 Initial values:        Series              Trend
                     120.00000             .00000

DFE = 10.

The SSE is:     Alpha       Gamma              SSE
             .8000000    .4000000       2753.22244

The following new variables are being created:

  NAME        LABEL

  FIT_1     Fit for production from EXSMOOTH, MOD_2 HO A .80 G .40
  ERR_1     Error for production from EXSMOOTH, MOD_2 HO A .80 G .40
```

FIGURE 20.12
SPSS output for Example 20.4 (using Holt's method)

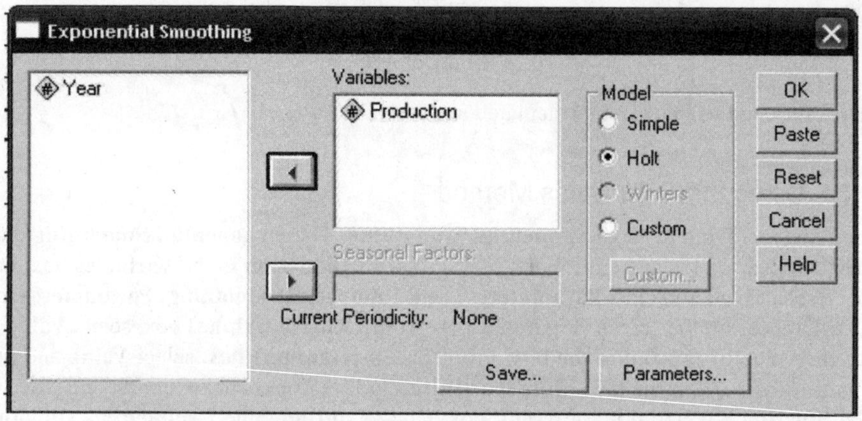

FIGURE 20.13
SPSS Exponential Smoothing dialog box

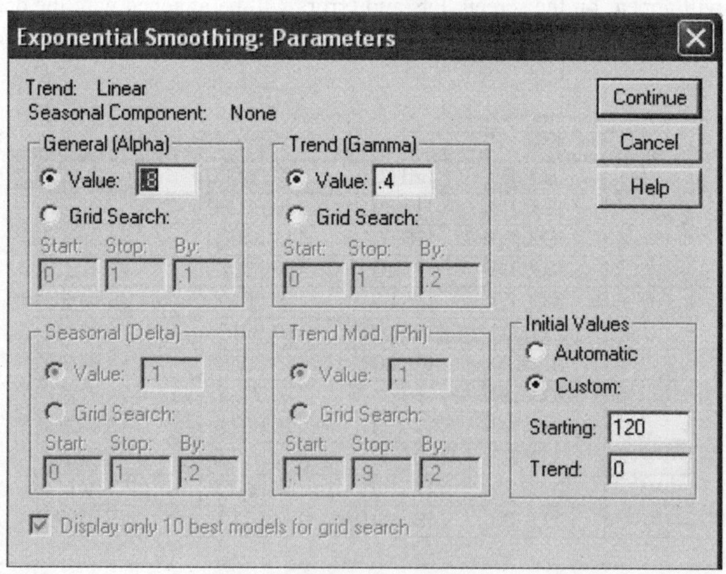

FIGURE 20.14
SPSS Exponential Smoothing: Parameters dialog box

SELF-PRACTICE PROBLEMS

20A1. The following data provides the sales of a consumer durable company from 1992–2003. Compute a 3-year moving average for this time series.

Years	*Sales (in million rupees)*
1992	43
1993	47
1994	51
1995	52
1996	49
1997	62
1998	45
1999	67
2000	78
2001	91
2002	89
2003	95

20A2. Compute 3-year weighted moving average values for Example 20A1. Use weight 3 for last year's value, weight 2 for the previous year's value, and weight 1 for the year before the previous year's value.

20A3. Pfizer Ltd, a US-based company, commenced operations in India in 1950 as private ltd company under the name Dumex Ltd in Mumbai. Pfizer India's business is segregated into three different groups. Pharmaceuticals accounted for the bulk (87%) of the company's revenues in 2007 while its animal health business chipped in 10%. Its service business contributed the remaining 3%.[1] The table below provides the expenses incurred by Pfizer Ltd (India) from 1992–93 to 2006–07. Compute a 3-year moving average for this time series.

Year	*Expenses (in million rupees)*
1992–1993	1727.9
1993–1994	2176
1994–1995	2376
1995–1996	2439.7
1996–1997	2686.1
1997–1998	1570.6
1998–1999	2681.4
1999–2000	3069
2000–2001	3481.8
2001–2002	3829.6
2002–2003	6705.7
2003–2004	5688.3
2004–2005	6366.2
2005–2006	7047.6
2006–2007	7299.3

Source: Prowess (V. 3.1), Centre for Monitoring Indian Economy P. Ltd, Mumbai, accessed December 2008, reproduced with permission.

20A4. Use exponential smoothing method with $\alpha = 0.6$ to forecast expenses for the data given in 20A3.

20A5. Use Holt's two parameter technique with $\alpha = 0.8$ and $\alpha = 0.5$ to forecast expenses for the data given in 20A3.

20.13 REGRESSION TREND ANALYSIS

As discussed earlier, a trend indicates the general tendency of data to increase or decrease over a long period of time. In time series regression trend analysis, the same concept of dependent and independent variables discussed in Chapter 16 is used. In time series regression trend analysis, the dependent variable y is the value being forecasted and x is the independent variable; time.

In time series regression trend analysis, the dependent variable y is the value being forecasted and x is the independent variable, time.

Several methods of trend fit can be explored with time series data. This section will focus on two methods: Linear trend model and quadratic trend model.

20.13.1 Linear Regression Trend Model

Simple linear regression is based on the slope–intercept equation of a line. This equation is given as

$$y = ax + b$$

where a is the slope of the line and b the y intercept of the line.

With respect to population parameters β_0 and β_1, a straight line regression model can be given as

$$y = \beta_0 + \beta_1 x$$

where β_0 is the population y intercept which represents the average value of the dependent variable when $x = 0$, and β_1 the slope of the regression line which indicates expected change in the value of y for per unit change in the value of x.

In case of a specific dependent variable y_i and independent variable x_i, the simple linear regression model is given by

$$y_i = \beta_0 + \beta_1 x_{ti} + \varepsilon_i$$

where β_0 is the population y intercept, β_1 the slope of the regression line, y_i the value of the dependent variable for the ith value, x_{ti} the value of the independent variable (in this case it is time, that is, ith time period) for the ith value, and ε_i the random error in y for observation i (ε is the Greek letter epsilon).

Example 20.5

Table 20.11 lists the sales turnover of a water purifier company for 16 years. Fit a straight line trend by the method of least squares and estimate the sales in 2011.

TABLE 20.11
Sales turnover of a water purifier company for 16 years

Years	*Sales (in million rupees)*
1992	950
1993	920
1994	880
1995	1020
1996	1050
1997	1010
1998	1100
1999	1150
2000	1200
2001	1250
2002	1300
2003	1220
2004	1180
2005	1330
2006	1400
2007	1250

Solution

The time periods are consecutive, so these can be numbered from 1 to 16 and entered along with the time series data (y) in the regression analysis. Table 20.12 indicates the sales turnover of a water purifier company for 16 years with coded time period.

TABLE 20.12
Sales turnover of a water purifier company for 16 years with coded time period

Years	*Time period (coded)*	*Sales (in million rupees)*
1992	1	950
1993	2	920
1994	3	880
1995	4	1020
1996	5	1050
1997	6	1010
1998	7	1100
1999	8	1150
2000	9	1200
2001	10	1250
2002	11	1300
2003	12	1220
2004	13	1180
2005	14	1330
2006	15	1400
2007	16	1250

Figures 20.15, 20.16, and 20.17 are the regression outputs for Example 20.5 using MS Excel, Minitab and SPSS, respectively.

From the Figures 20.15, 20.16, and 20.17, it can be seen that the linear trend forecasting equation can be mentioned as below:

$$\text{Sales} = 884.8 + 29.81(\text{Time period})$$

The estimated sales 2011 can be obtained by substituting $x = 20$, that is, time period = 20 in the above linear trend forecasting equation. So, the estimated sales for 2011 is

$$\text{Sales} = 884.8 + 29.81(20) = ₹1481 \text{ million}$$

The y intercept $b_0 = 884.8$ indicates that in the year prior to the first time period in the data given in Table 20.12, the average sales was ₹884.8 million. The slope $b_1 = 29.81$ indicates that the sales turnover is predicted to increase by ₹29.81 million per year.

	A	B	C	D	E	F	G
1	SUMMARY OUTPUT						
2							
3	*Regression Statistics*						
4	Multiple R	0.918321989					
5	R Square	0.843315275					
6	Adjusted R Square	0.832123509					
7	Standard Error	63.31966718					
8	Observations	16					
9							
10	ANOVA						
11		*df*	*SS*	*MS*	*F*	*Significance F*	
12	Regression	1	302112.4265	302112.4	75.3514	5.22874E-07	
13	Residual	14	56131.32353	4009.38			
14	Total	15	358243.75				
15							
16		*Coefficients*	*Standard Error*	*t Stat*	*P-value*	*Lower 95%*	*Upper 95%*
17	Intercept	884.75	33.2051136	26.64499	2.14E-13	813.5321146	955.9678854
18	X Variable 1	29.80882353	3.433991098	8.680519	5.23E-07	22.44364516	37.1740019

FIGURE 20.15
MS Excel output for Example 20.5

Regression Analysis: Sales versus Time period

```
The regression equation is
Sales = 884.8 + 29.81 Time period

S = 63.3197   R-Sq = 84.3%   R-Sq(adj) = 83.2%

Analysis of Variance

Source      DF      SS      MS      F      P
Regression   1  302112  302112  75.35  0.000
Error       14   56131    4009
Total       15  358244
```

FIGURE 20.16
Minitab output for Example 20.5

Model Summary

Model	R	R Square	Adjusted R Square	Std. Error of the Estimate
1	.918a	.843	.832	63.31967

a. Predictors: (Constant), Timeperiod

ANOVAb

Model		Sum of Squares	df	Mean Square	F	Sig.
1	Regression	302112.4	1	302112.426	75.351	.000a
	Residual	56131.324	14	4009.380		
	Total	358243.8	15			

a. Predictors: (Constant), Timeperiod

b. Dependent Variable: Sales

Coefficientsa

Model		Unstandardized Coefficients		Standardized Coefficients		
		B	Std. Error	Beta	t	Sig.
1	(Constant)	884.750	33.205		26.645	.000
	Timeperiod	29.809	3.434	.918	8.681	.000

a. Dependent Variable: Sales

FIGURE 20.17
SPSS output for Example 20.5

SELF-PRACTICE PROBLEMS

20B1. The following table provides the sales of a departmental store in nine years. Develop a linear and quadratic regression model with the help of the data given in the table and compare the obtained result from both the models.

Year	*Sales (in thousand rupees)*
1998	45
1999	46
2000	48
2001	75
2002	76
2003	76
2004	95
2005	95
2006	96

20B2. Dena Bank was founded on 26th May 1938, under the name Devkaran Nanjee Banking Company Ltd. The bank became a public limited company in 1939 and its name was changed to Dena Bank Ltd. In 1969, Dena Bank Ltd along with 13 other major banks was nationalized.[1] The following table shows the expenses incurred by Dena Bank Ltd from 1994–1995 to 2006–2007. Develop a linear and quadratic regression model with the help of the data given in the table and compare the results obtained from both the models. Predict the expenses that Dena Bank Ltd will incur in 2012–2013 using the appropriate model.

Year	*Expenses (in million rupees)*
1994–1995	7144.6
1995–1996	8819.1
1996–1997	10728.8
1997–1998	13307.2
1998–1999	15797.8
1999–2000	18009.5
2000–2001	21816.9
2001–2002	22200.3
2002–2003	21217
2003–2004	21510.7
2004–2005	20370.3
2005–2006	21832.5
2006–2007	24374.4

Source: Prowess (V. 31), Centre for Monitoring Indian Economy Pvt. Ltd, Mumbai, accessed December 2008, reproduced with permission.

20.14 SEASONAL VARIATION

We discussed in an earlier section in this chapter that time series data consists of four components: secular trend; seasonal variations; cyclic variations, and irregular (random) movements. As discussed, seasonal variations are due to rhythmic forces which operate in a repetitive, predictable, and periodic manner in a time span of one year or less. This section focuses on the techniques that can be used for identifying the seasonal variations. For long run forecasts, trend analysis may be an adequate technique. However, for short run forecasts, awareness about the seasonal effect on the time series data is of paramount importance. Once these seasonal patterns are identified, these can be eliminated from the time series in order to analyse the impact of other components on the time series data. This process of eliminating the seasonal effect from the time series data is referred to as **deseasonalization**. Time series decomposition is a widely used technique to eliminate the effects of seasonality. The decomposition technique is based on the multiplicative model concept of time series.

For long run forecasts, trend analysis may be an adequate technique. However, for short run forecast awareness about the seasonal effect on the time series data is of paramount importance. Once these seasonal patterns are identified, these can be eliminated from the time series data in order to analyse the impact of other components on the time series data. This process of eliminating the seasonal effect from the time series data is referred to as deseasonalization.

According to the multiplicative model

$$Y_i = T_i \times S_i \times C_i \times R_i$$

where Y_i is the time series value at time *i* and T_i, S_i, C_i, and R_i represent the values of trend, seasonal, cyclic, and random components, respectively at time *i*. Data can be deseasonalized by dividing the actual values, which consists of all four components, that is, secular trend; seasonal variations; cyclic variations, and irregular movements by the seasonal variations. In other words, deseasonalized data can be obtained as

$$\text{Deseasonalized data} = \frac{T_i \times S_i \times C_i \times R_i}{S_i} = T_i \times C_i \times R_i$$

In order to eliminate the seasonal variations from the data, we will use the most widely used technique referred to as ratio-to-**moving average method**. Example 20.6 explains this technique clearly.

Example 20.6

The number of units produced by a company for five years for all four quarters of the year is given in Table 20.13. Calculate the seasonal indexes and deseasonalize the data.

TABLE 20.13
Production (in units) of a company for five years (for all four quarters of each year)

Year	*Quarter*	*Production*
2001	1	2022
	2	2100

	3	2150
	4	2120
2002	1	2200
	2	2250
	3	2150
	4	2340
2003	1	2250
	2	2300
	3	2350
	4	2250
2004	1	2400
	2	2450
	3	2300
	4	2270
2005	1	2500
	2	2560
	3	2400
	4	2350

Solution The process of deseasonalizing data starts by computing the 4-quarter moving total for the first year as below:

First moving total = 2022 + 2100 + 2150 + 2120 = 8392

This moving total is the sum of the values of four quarters. Hence, this value is placed as the mid point of theses values, that is, this value is placed in between the second and the third values (Table 20.14). Similarly, the second moving total can be obtained by leaving the first value of 2001 and then adding the remaining values of three quarters of 2001 and the value of the first quarter of 2002 as below:

Second moving total = 2100 + 2150 + 2120 + 2200 = 8570

In this manner, other 4-quarter moving totals can be obtained as indicated in the fourth column of Table 20.14. The fifth column of Table 20.14 is the 4-quarter 2-year moving total and can be obtained by adding two 4-quarter moving totals

4-quarter 2-year moving total = 8392+ 8570 = 16962

Similarly, other 4-quarter 2-year moving totals can be obtained as shown in Table 20.14. From Table 20.14, it can be seen that the value (16,962) is placed besides quarter 3 of 2001 because it is between two adjacent 4-quarter-moving-totals. These values are shown in column 5 of Table 20.14. In column 6, the values of column 5 are divided by 8. This value (2120.25) is the 4-quarter moving average and placed besides quarter 3 of 2001 as shown in Table 20.14. Simlarly, other values of column 6 can be obtained. The values shown in column 6 consist of trend and cyclical components because by adding across the 4-quarter periods of original data, the seasonal effects have been removed. During the same process, irregular effects have also been smoothed. In this manner, column 6 contains only trend and cyclical components ($T_i \times C_i$).

Column 2 consists of the actual values of data which include trend, seasonal, cyclic, and random components ($T_i \times S_i \times C_i \times R_i$). If the values of column 2 consisting of ($T_i \times S_i \times C_i \times R_i$) are divided by values of column 6 consisting of ($T_i \times C_i$), the resulting values consist of seasonal and irregular components and are displayed in column 7 of Table 20.14. These values are multiplied by 100 to index then and are referred to as seasonal *indexes*. These values are shown in Table 20.15.

The next step is to eliminate extreme values from each quarter (these values are in bold in Table 20.15). Then, the remaining two

TABLE 20.14
Calculation of values to moving average for Example 20.6

Col 1	*Col 2*	*Col 3*	*Col 4*	*Col 5*	*Col 6*	*Col 7*
Year	*Quarter*	*Production (Actual values) ($T_i \times S_i \times C_i \times R_i$)*	*4-Quarter moving total*	*4-Quarter 2-year moving total*	*Ratio of actual centered moving average ($T_i \times C_i$)*	*Values to moving average ($S_i \times R_i$) · 100*
2001	1	2022				
	2	2100				
			8392			
	3	2150		16,962	2120.25	101.4031
			8570			
	4	2120		17,290	2161.25	98.0913
			8720			
2002	1	2200		17,440	2180	100.9174
			8720			
	2	2250		17,660	2207.5	101.9252
			8940			
	3	2150		17,930	2241.25	95.9286
			8990			
	4	2340		18,030	2253.75	103.8269
			9040			
2003	1	2250		18,280	2285	98.4682
			9240			
	2	2300		18,390	2298.75	100.0543
			9150			
	3	2350		18,450	2306.25	101.8970
			9300			
	4	2250		18,750	2343.75	96
			9450			
2004	1	2400		18,850	2356.25	101.8567
			9400			
	2	2450		18,820	2352.5	104.1445
			9420			
	3	2300		18,940	2367.5	97.1488
			9520			
	4	2270		19,150	2393.75	94.8302

			9630			
2005	1	2500		19,360	2420	103.3057
			9730			
	2	2560		19,540	2442.5	104.8106
			9810			
	3	2400				
	4	2350				

TABLE 20.15
Seasonal indexes for Example 20.6

Quarter	*Year 1*	*Year 2*	*Year 3*	*Year 4*	*Year 5*
Quarter 1	–	100.9174	**98.4682**	101.8567	**103.3057**
Quarter 2	–	101.9252	**100.0543**	104.1445	**104.8106**
Quarter 3	101.4031	**95.9286**	**101.8970**	97.1488	–
Quarter 4	98.0913	**103.8269**	96	**94.8302**	–

indexes are averaged, as the average index for the respective quarter. Now we take the sum of the indexes obtained for four quarters. It can be seen that this sum is more than 400, that is, 400.7436. The sum of four quarterly indexes should be 400 and their mean should be equal to 100. Here, sum is computed as 400.7436 instead of 400. To correct this error, we multiply each index value by an adjusting constant. This constant can be obtained by dividing 400 by 400.7436. This procedure is shown in Table 20.16.

Seasonal variations are in the form of index numbers, so before deseasonalization these indexes are divided by 100 as shown in column 4 of Table 20.17. For obtaining the deseasonalized values (shown in column 5) of column 3, actual values are divided by the seasonal indexes given in column 4 of Table 20.17. Final deseasonalized values are given in column 5 of Table 20.17. Since the production of units cannot be in decimals as shown in column 5 of Table 20.17 the deseasonalized values are rounded off to the nearest integer values.

After eliminating the extreme values from quarters, the index values are:

$$\text{Quarter 1: } \frac{100.9174 + 101.8567}{2} = 101.3871$$

$$\text{Quarter 2: } \frac{101.9252 + 104.1445}{2} = 103.0349$$

$$\text{Quarter 3: } \frac{101.4031 + 97.1488}{2} = 99.2760$$

$$\text{Quarter 4: } \frac{98.0913 + 96}{2} = 97.0456$$

Sum of indexes = 101.3871 + 103.0349 + 99.2760 + 97.0456 = 400.7436

$$\text{Adjusting constant} = \frac{400}{400.7436} = 0.998144$$

TABLE 20.16
Final seasonal indexes for Example 20.6

Quarter	*Unadjusted indexes (modified mean)*	×	*Adjusting constant*	=	*Seasonal index*
Quarter 1	101.3871	×	0.998144	=	101.19
Quarter 2	103.0349	×	0.998144	=	102.84
Quarter 3	99.2760	×	0.998144	=	99.092
Quarter 4	97.0456	×	0.998144	=	96.866

TABLE 20.17
Deseasonalized data for Example 20.6

Col 1	*Col 2*	*Col 3*	*Col 4*	*Col 5*	*Col 6*
Year	*Quarter*	*Production*	*Seasonal indexes (S)*	*Desonalized data (T . C . R)*	*Desonalized data (rounded) (T . C . R)*
2001	1	2022	1.0119	1998.221168	1998
	2	2100	1.0284	2042.007001	2042
	3	2150	0.9909	2169.744677	2170
	4	2120	0.9686	2188.725996	2189
2002	1	2200	1.0119	2174.127878	2174
	2	2250	1.0284	2187.864644	2188
	3	2150	0.9909	2169.744677	2170
	4	2340	0.9686	2415.857939	2416
2003	1	2250	1.0119	2223.539875	2224
	2	2300	1.0284	2236.483858	2236
	3	2350	0.9909	2371.581391	2372
	4	2250	0.9686	2322.940326	2323
2004	1	2400	1.0119	2371.775867	2372
	2	2450	1.0284	2382.341501	2382
	3	2300	0.9909	2321.122212	2321
	4	2270	0.9686	2343.588685	2344
2005	1	2500	1.0119	2470.599862	2471
	2	2560	1.0284	2489.303773	2489
	3	2400	0.9909	2422.040569	2422
	4	2350	0.9686	2426.182119	2426

20.15 SOLVING PROBLEMS INVOLVING ALL FOUR COMPONENTS OF TIME SERIES

Figure 20.18 exhibits a part of the Minitab output. This output is based on the deseasonalization and detrending of the time series data. In fact, the procedure of describing a time series with all the four components consists of three stages:

- Deseasonalization of time series
- Developing a trend line
- Finding the cyclical variation around the trend line

The process of deseasonalization has been explained earlier. In this section, we will discuss the process of detrending the data. The final predicted values are obtained on the basis of

Time	production	Trend	Seasonal	Detrend	Deseason	Predict	Error
1	2022	2087.61	1.01199	0.96857	1998.04	2112.64	-90.635
2	2100	2108.52	1.02844	0.99596	2041.93	2168.48	-68.478
3	2150	2129.43	0.99092	1.00966	2169.71	2110.09	39.909
4	2120	2150.34	0.96866	0.98589	2188.60	2082.94	37.057
1	2200	2171.26	1.01199	1.01324	2173.94	2197.29	2.712
2	2250	2192.17	1.02844	1.02638	2187.79	2254.51	-4.507
3	2150	2213.08	0.99092	0.97150	2169.71	2192.98	-42.982
4	2340	2233.99	0.96866	1.04745	2415.72	2163.97	176.028
1	2250	2254.91	1.01199	0.99782	2223.34	2281.94	-31.942
2	2300	2275.82	1.02844	1.01063	2236.40	2340.54	-40.536
3	2350	2296.73	0.99092	1.02319	2371.54	2275.87	74.127
4	2250	2317.64	0.96866	0.97081	2322.81	2245.00	5.000
1	2400	2338.56	1.01199	1.02627	2371.57	2366.60	33.405
2	2450	2359.47	1.02844	1.03837	2382.26	2426.57	23.434
3	2300	2380.38	0.99092	0.96623	2321.08	2358.76	-58.763
4	2270	2401.30	0.96866	0.94532	2343.45	2326.03	-56.029
1	2500	2422.21	1.01199	1.03212	2470.38	2451.25	48.751
2	2560	2443.12	1.02844	1.04784	2489.21	2512.59	47.405
3	2400	2464.03	0.99092	0.97401	2422.00	2441.65	-41.654
4	2350	2484.95	0.96866	0.94569	2426.04	2407.06	-57.057

FIGURE 20.18
Minitab output with trend plus seasonal decomposition

deseasonalized and detrended values. Here, it is important to note that final values do not take into account the cyclical and irregular components. Irregular treatments cannot be predicted mathematically and treatment of cyclical variation is descriptive of past behaviour and not predictive of future behaviour.

The process of deseasonalization has been described in the previous section. In this section, we will focus on detrending the data and identifying the cyclical variations around the trend line. We need to identify the trend component first for this. The least squares method, as described in Chapters 16 and 17 is used to identify the trend component. First, we have to code the time variable by assigning a mean 0 to the middle of the data, that is, after 10 quarters (entire time series contains 20 quarters). After this, we measure the translated time, x, by $\frac{1}{2}$ quarters because the number of periods are even. We know that the simple regression trend line equation is $\hat{y} = a + bx$ where a is the y intercept and b is the slope of the regression line. Using computations of Table 20.18, the slope of the regression line can be computed as:

$$b = \frac{\sum xy}{\sum x^2} = \frac{27813.7}{2660} = 10.45628 \text{ and}$$

$$a = \bar{y} = \frac{45725.52}{20} = 2286.276$$

So, the required trend line is $\hat{y} = 2286.276 + 10.45628 \times (x)$. By substituting different values of x, the predicted production based on the trend line can be obtained.

TABLE 20.18
Identifying the trend component

Year	*Quarter*	*Production*	*Deseasonalized production (y)*	*Coding time*	*x = Col 5 × 2*	*xy*	x^2	*Predicted values* ($\hat{y}$)
2001	1	2022	1998.04	–9.5	–19	–37962.8	361	2087.6067
	2	2100	2041.93	–8.5	–17	–34712.8	289	2108.5192
	3	2150	2169.71	–7.5	–15	–32545.7	225	2129.4318
	4	2120	2188.6	–6.5	–13	–28451.8	169	2150.3443
2002	1	2200	2173.94	–5.5	–11	–23913.3	121	2171.2569
	2	2250	2187.79	–4.5	–9	–19690.1	81	2192.1694
	3	2150	2169.71	–3.5	–7	–15188	49	2213.0820
	4	2340	2415.72	–2.5	–5	–12078.6	25	2233.9946
2003	1	2250	2223.34	–1.5	–3	–6670.02	9	2254.9071
	2	2300	2236.4	–0.5	–1	–2236.4	1	2275.8197
				0				

	3	2350	2371.54	0.5	1	2371.54	1	2296.7322
	4	2250	2322.81	1.5	3	6968.43	9	2317.6448
2004	1	2400	2371.57	2.5	5	11857.85	25	2338.5573
	2	2450	2382.26	3.5	7	16675.82	49	2359.4699
	3	2300	2321.08	4.5	9	20889.72	81	2380.3825
	4	2270	2343.45	5.5	11	25777.95	121	2401.2950
2005	1	2500	2470.38	6.5	13	32114.94	169	2422.2076
	2	2560	2489.21	7.5	15	37338.15	225	2443.1201
	3	2400	2422	8.5	17	41174	289	2464.0327
	4	2350	2426.04	9.5	19	46094.76	361	2484.9452
Sum			45725.52			27813.7	2660	

Note that the trend values in the last column of Table 20.18 and the values in column 3 of Figure 20.18 are the same. The detrend values in column 5 of Figure 20.18 can be obtained by dividing the values in column 2 (actual production values) by the values in column 3. From Figure 20.18 first value of column 5 can be obtained as:

$$\text{First value of column 5} = \frac{2022}{2087.61} = 0.96857$$

Similarly, other values in column 5 can be obtained (in Figure 20.18).

When deseasonalized values are divided by the predicted values and the result is multiplied by 100, the trend percent can be obtained. Table 20.19 exhibits the percent of trend computation.

TABLE 20.19
Percent of trend computation

Year	*Quarter*	*Production (A)*	*Deseasonalized production (y)*	*Predicted values* ($\hat{y}$)	*Percent of trend* $\left(\frac{A}{\hat{y}} \times 100\right)$
2001	1	2022	1998.04	2087.61	96.85
	2	2100	2041.93	2108.52	99.59
	3	2150	2169.71	2129.43	100.96
	4	2120	2188.6	2150.34	98.58
2002	1	2200	2173.94	2171.26	101.32
	2	2250	2187.79	2192.17	102.63
	3	2150	2169.71	2213.08	97.14
	4	2340	2415.72	2233.99	104.74
2003	1	2250	2223.34	2254.91	99.78
	2	2300	2236.4	2275.82	101.06
	3	2350	2371.54	2296.73	102.31
	4	2250	2322.81	2317.64	97.08
2004	1	2400	2371.57	2338.56	102.62
	2	2450	2382.26	2359.47	103.83
	3	2300	2321.08	2380.38	96.62
	4	2270	2343.45	2401.30	94.53
2005	1	2500	2470.38	2422.21	103.21
	2	2560	2489.21	2443.12	104.78
	3	2400	2422	2464.03	97.40
	4	2350	2426.04	2484.95	94.56

The seventh column of Figure 20.18 gives the predicted values and can be obtained by multiplying the seasonal index values by the predicted trend values as shown in Table 20.20.

TABLE 20.20
Predicted values after deseasonalization and detrending

Year	*Quarter*	*Production*	*Seasonal indexes*	*Deseasonalized production (y)*	*Predicted trend values* ($\hat{y}$)	*Predicted values after deseasonalization and detrending*
2001	1	2022	1.0119	1998.04	2087.6067	2112.44
	2	2100	1.0284	2041.93	2108.5192	2168.40
	3	2150	0.9909	2169.71	2129.4318	2110.05
	4	2120	0.9686	2188.6	2150.3443	2082.82
2002	1	2200	1.0119	2173.94	2171.2569	2197.09
	2	2250	1.0284	2187.79	2192.1694	2254.42
	3	2150	0.9909	2169.71	2213.0820	2192.94
	4	2340	0.9686	2415.72	2233.9946	2163.84
2003	1	2250	1.0119	2223.34	2254.9071	2281.74
	2	2300	1.0284	2236.4	2275.8197	2340.45
	3	2350	0.9909	2371.54	2296.7322	2275.83
	4	2250	0.9686	2322.81	2317.6448	2244.87
2004	1	2400	1.0119	2371.57	2338.5573	2366.38
	2	2450	1.0284	2382.26	2359.4699	2426.47
	3	2300	0.9909	2321.08	2380.3825	2358.72
	4	2270	0.9686	2343.45	2401.2950	2325.89
2005	1	2500	1.0119	2470.38	2422.2076	2451.03
	2	2560	1.0284	2489.21	2443.1201	2512.50
	3	2400	0.9909	2422	2464.0327	2441.61
	4	2350	0.9686	2426.04	2484.9452	2406.91

For obtaining the exact first value of Column 7 (2112.64) in Figure 20.18, predicted trend value 2087.60671428571... is multiplied by seasonal index 1.01199, which will result in the value 2112.6371. This value is rounded off to 2112.64 and is the first value in column 7 of Figure 20.18. Similarly, other values in column 7 of Figure 20.18 can be obtained.

Figure 20.19 is the time series decomposition plot for production data produced using Minitab. Figure 20.20 exhibits the graph produced using Minitab indicating component analysis for production data.

20.16 AUTOCORRELATION AND AUTOREGRESSION

In some cases, data values are correlated with values from the past time period. During regression analysis these characteristics of data can create some problems. **Autocorrelation** is a problem that occurs when data are regressed.

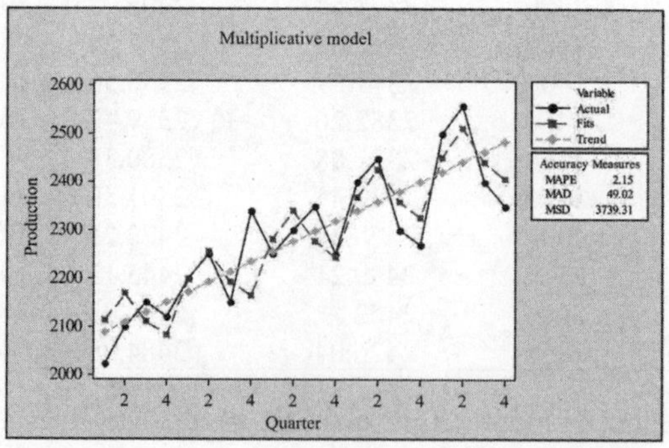

FIGURE 20.19
Minitab produced time series decomposition plot for production data

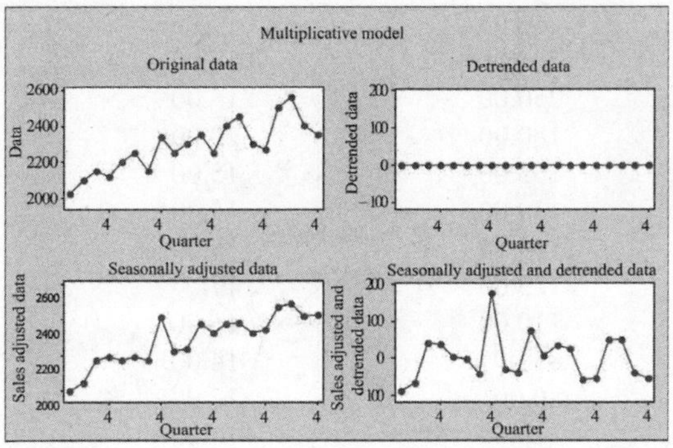

FIGURE 20.20
Minitab produced graph (Component analysis for production data)

20.16.1 Autocorrelation

Autocorrelation occurs when the error terms of a regression model are correlated. We have already discussed the assumptions of regression and we know that independence of error is one of the assumptions of regression. The presence of autocorrelation in a time series data violates this assumption of regression, hence, it affects the authenticity of the regression model. A first order autocorrelation results from the degree of correlation between the error terms of adjacent time periods. Durbin–Watson test is used to identify the presence of autocorrelation in a time series data (discussed in Chapter 14 of *Business Statistics* by Naval Bajpai). The Durbin–Watson formula for testing the autocorrelation in time series can be stated as

Autocorrelation occurs when the error terms of a regression model are correlated.

Durbin–Watson statistic

$$D = \frac{\sum_{i=2}^{n}(e_i - e_{i-1})^2}{\sum_{i=1}^{n} e_i^2}$$

where e_i is the residual for the time period i and e_{i-1} the residual for the time period $i - 1$.

Example 20.7

Table 20.21 provides the sales turnover and the expenditure on sales promotion of a company for different years.

TABLE 20.21
Sales turnover and the expenditure on sales promotion of a company for different years

Years	*Sales (in million rupees)*	*Expenditure on sales promotion (in million rupees)*
1982	140.00	6.00
1983	150.00	7.00
1984	180.00	8.00
1985	210.00	8.00
1986	220.00	9.00
1987	235.00	10.00
1988	240.00	12.00
1989	250.00	14.00
1990	270.00	16.00
1991	300.00	18.00
1992	270.00	21.00

1993	260.00	19.00
1994	285.00	16.00
1995	250.00	15.00
1996	180.00	20.00
1997	165.00	15.00
1998	130.00	15.00
1999	110.00	15.00
2000	125.00	17.00
2001	110.00	15.00
2002	85.00	14.00
2003	80.00	17.00
2004	120.00	16.00
2005	110.00	20.00

Fit a line of regression and also determine whether autocorrelation is present.

Solution In Chapter 14 of *Business Statistics* by Naval Bajpai, we discussed the procedure of using Minitab and SPSS for computing the Durbin–Watson statistic in order to measure autocorrelation. Figures 20.53 and 20.54 are the Minitab and SPSS outputs (partial), respectively for Example 20.7.

From Figures 20.21 and 20.22, it is clear that the Durbin–Watson statistic is calculated as 0.151. From the Durbin–Watson statistic table, for the given level of significance (0.05); sample size (24) and number of indepen-

```
The regression equation is
Sales = 169 + 1.23 Sales Promotion

Durbin-Watson statistic = 0.150972
```

FIGURE 20.21
Minitab output (partial) for Example 20.7

Model Summary[b]

Model	R	R Square	Adjusted R Square	Std. Error of the Estimate	Durbin-Watson
1	.076[a]	.006	-.039	70.99164	.151

a. Predictors: (Constant), salespromotion

b. Dependent Variable: sales

FIGURE 20.22
SPSS output (partial) for Example 20.7

dent variables in the model (1), the lower critical value (d_L) and the upper critical value (d_U) are observed as 1.27 and 1.45 respectively. By substituting the value of lower critical value (d_L) and the upper critical value (d_U) the acceptance and rejection range can be determined easily. The Durbin–Watson statistic for the example is computed as 0.151. This value (0.151) is less than the lower critical value ($d_L = 1.08$). Hence, it can be concluded that there exists a significant positive autocorrelation between the residuals.

20.16.2 Autoregression

Autoregression is a forecasting technique which takes advantage of the relationship of the value (y_i) to the previous values ($y_{i-1}, y_{i-2}, y_{i-3}, \ldots$). The first order autoregression model is similar to simple regression technique and is given by

$$\hat{y}_i = b_0 + b_1 y_{i-1}$$

A second order autoregression model is similar to multiple regression technique and is given by

$$\hat{y}_i = b_0 + b_1 y_{i-1} + b_2 y_{i-2}$$

A *p*th order autoregression model is similar to multiple regression technique and is given by

$$\hat{y}_i = b_0 + b_1 y_{i-1} + b_2 y_{i-2} + \cdots + b_p y_{i-p}$$

Autoregression is a forecasting technique which takes advantage of the relationship of the value (y_i) to the previous values ($y_{i-1}, y_{i-2}, y_{i-3}, \ldots$).

where y_i is the observed value of the time series at time *i*, y_{i-1} the observed value of the time series at time $i-1$, y_{i-2} the observed value of the time series at time $i-2$, y_{i-p} the observed value of the time series at time $i-p$, b_0 the fixed parameter (estimated by least squares method), and $b_1, b_2, \ldots b_p$ the regression parameters (estimated by least squares method).

Autoregression is a multiple regression technique in which the dependent variable is the actual (observed) value of the time series and independent variables are the time-lagged versions of the dependent variable. Independent variables can be lagged into one, two, three, or more time periods.

In short, we can say autoregression is a multiple regression technique in which the dependent variable is the actual (observed) value of the time series and independent variables are time-lagged versions of the dependent variable. Independent variables can be lagged into one, two, three, or more time periods. Let us reconsider Example 20.7 with two time-lagged values to understand the concept of autoregression. Table 20.22 exhibits the actual values with two time-lagged values of Example 20.7.

Figure 20.23 is the Minitab autoregression output (with both the predicters included in the model) and Figure 20.24 is the Minitab autoregression output (with only one predictor included in the model).

TABLE 20.22
Actual values with two time-lagged values for Example 20.7

Years	*Sales (in million rupees)*	*One-period lagged* y_{i-1}	*Two-period lagged* y_{i-2}
1982	140.00	------	-------
1983	150.00	140.00	-------
1984	180.00	150.00	140.00
1985	210.00	180.00	150.00
1986	220.00	210.00	180.00
1987	235.00	220.00	210.00
1988	240.00	235.00	220.00
1989	250.00	240.00	235.00
1990	270.00	250.00	240.00
1991	300.00	270.00	250.00
1992	270.00	300.00	270.00
1993	260.00	270.00	300.00
1994	285.00	260.00	270.00
1995	250.00	285.00	260.00
1996	180.00	250.00	285.00
1997	165.00	180.00	250.00
1998	130.00	165.00	180.00
1999	110.00	130.00	165.00
2000	125.00	110.00	130.00
2001	110.00	125.00	110.00
2002	85.00	110.00	125.00
2003	80.00	85.00	110.00
2004	120.00	80.00	85.00
2005	110.00	120.00	80.00

From Figure 20.23, it is clear that the *p* value related to second predictor is not significant. Hence, we will try an autoregression model with only one-time lagged value, that is, with only one predictor.

From Figure 20.24, it is clear that the *p* value related to the first predictor is significant. The ANOVA table indicates that the overall regression model is also significant. Hence, an autoregression model with only one-time lagged value, that is, with only one predictor seems

Regression Analysis: Sales(in Million versus One period l, Two period l)

```
The regression equation is
Sales(in Million Rupees) = 14.9 + 1.27 One period lagged values
                           - 0.358 Two period lagged values

22 cases used, 2 cases contain missing values

Predictor                    Coef  SE Coef      T      P
Constant                    14.93    17.49   0.85  0.404
One period lagged values   1.2724   0.2154   5.91  0.000
Two period lagged values  -0.3579   0.2181  -1.64  0.117

S = 26.8026   R-Sq = 87.3%   R-Sq(adj) = 86.0%

Analysis of Variance

Source          DF      SS     MS      F      P
Regression       2   94075  47037  65.48  0.000
Residual Error  19   13649    718
Total           21  107724
```

FIGURE 20.23 Minitab autoregression output (with both the predictors included in the model) for Example 20.7

Regression Analysis: Sales(in Million versus One period lagge

```
The regression equation is
Sales(in Million Rupees) = 9.6 + 0.942 One period lagged values

23 cases used, 1 cases contain missing values

Predictor                    Coef  SE Coef      T      P
Constant                     9.64    16.95   0.57  0.575
One period lagged values  0.94231  0.08410  11.20  0.000

S = 27.3078   R-Sq = 85.7%   R-Sq(adj) = 85.0%

Analysis of Variance

Source          DF      SS     MS       F      P
Regression       1   93612  93612  125.53  0.000
Residual Error  21   15660    746
Total           22  109272
```

FIGURE 20.24 Minitab autoregression output (with one predictor included in the model) for Example 20.7

to be a good predictor model. Data are given up to 2005. If we want to forecast sales for 2006, the above regression equation can be used as below:

Sales $(\hat{y}_i) = 9.6 + 0.942\ y_{i-1}$

Projected sales for 2006 $(\hat{y}_{i2006}) = 9.6 + 0.942\ (110)$

$= 113.22$ million rupees

Projected sales for 2007 $(\hat{y}_{i2007}) = 9.6 + 0.942\ (113.22)$

$= 116.25$ million rupees

SELF-PRACTICE PROBLEMS

20C1. Hindustan Copper Ltd was incorporated in 1967 to take over the plants and mines at Rajasthan and Jharkhand from National Development Corporation Limited. Subsequently, it merged with Copper Corporation Limited. The company is engaged in activities ranging from mining, benefication, smelting, refining and production of cathodes, wire bars, and continuous cast rods.[1] The following table provides the income of Hindustan Copper Ltd in different quarters from 2002–2006. Use Minitab to deseasonalize and detrend the data and forecast income of the next 6 quarters.

Year	*Quarter*	*Income (in million rupees)*
2002	Mar 2002	1400.9
	Jun 2002	1274.7
	Sep 2002	1432.2
	Dec 2002	1282
2003	Mar 2003	1145.4
	Jun 2003	1254.2
	Sep 2003	1269.6
	Dec 2003	1361.9

2004	Mar 2004	1588.9
	Jun 2004	1591.5
	Sep 2004	1280.5
	Dec 2004	1303.2
2005	Mar 2005	1299.1
	Jun 2005	1270.2
	Sep 2005	2277.7
	Dec 2005	2641.9
2006	Mar 2006	3389.2
	Jun 2006	3321.4
	Sep 2006	3054.5
	Dec 2006	4831.8

Source: Prowess (V. 3.1), Centre for Monitoring Indian Economy Pvt. Ltd, Mumbai, accessed December 2008, reproduced with permission.

20C2. Reckitt Benckiser (India) Ltd, formerly known as Reckitt and Coleman is a subsidiary of Reckitt Benckiser Plc. The company is engaged in the manufacture and marketing of several consumer products in many segments such household care, toiletories, laundry products, and over-the-counter pharmaceutical products.[1] The table below shows the profit after tax of Reckitt Benckiser (India) Ltd in million rupees. Fit a first order, second order, and third-order autoregressive model. Test the significance of first order, second order, and third-order autoregressive parameters by using $\alpha = 0.05$ Discuss which autoregressive model is appropriate for prediction. With the help of the appropriate autoregressive model, predict the profit after tax of the years 2007–2008, 2008–2009, and 2009–2010.

Year	*Profit after tax (in million rupees)*
1994–1995	177.6
1995–1996	237.3
1996–1997	197.1
1997–1998	300.7
1998–1999	314.7
1999–2000	140.2
2000–2001	212.5
2001–2002	214.4
2002–2003	166.9
2003–2004	589.1
2004–2005	951.9
2005–2006	1025.3
2006–2007	1560.7

Source: Prowess (V. 3.1), Centre for Monitoring Indian Economy Pvt. Ltd, Mumbai, accessed December 2008 reproduced with permission.

SUMMARY |

Forecasting is a technique that can aid in future planning. Time series is an important tool for prediction. In general, there are two common ways of forecasting. These are: qualitative forecasting and quantitative forecasting techniques. Executive opinion, panel judgement, delphi methods, marketing research, and past analogy methods are some of the important methods of qualitative forecasting. Quantitative method of forecasting can be broadly divided into two categories: time series analysis and causal analysis.

The arrangement of statistical data in accordance with the occurrence of time or the arrangement of data in chronological order is known as time series. Generally in a long time series, four components are found to be present: (1) secular trend or long term movements (2) seasonal variations (3) cyclic variations, and (4) random or irregular movements. Time series methods can be broadly classified into three categories: freehand method, average methods, and exponential smoothing methods. In the freehand method, a smooth curve is obtained by plotting the values y_i against time i. There are mainly three methods of smoothing through averages: moving averages method, weighted moving average method, and semi-averages method. In the moving averages method, equal weights are assigned to all the time periods whereas in the weighed moving average method, some time periods are weighed differently as compared to others. In the semi-averages method, data is divided into two equal parts with respect to time.

Exponential smoothing method weigh data from previous time period with exponentially decreasing importance in the forecast. Single exponential smoothing does not incorporate trend and seasonal components of a time series data. Holt's **double smoothing method** is an exponential smoothing method, which considers trend effects in forecasting.

In time series regression trend analysis, dependent variable y is the value being forecasted and x is the independent variable time. Several methods of trend fit can be explored with a time series data. This book focuses on two methods: linear trend model and quadratic trend model. Simple linear regression is based on the slope–intercept equation of a line whereas quadratic relationship between two variables can be analysed by applying quadratic regression model.

For long run forecasts, trend analysis may be an adequate technique. However for short run forecasting, awareness about the seasonal effect on time series data is of paramount importance. Once these seasonal patterns are identified, these can be eliminated from the time series data, in order to analyse the impact of other components on time series data. This process of eliminating the seasonal effect from the time series data is referred to as deseasonalization. One of the widely used techniques to eliminate the effect of seasonality is decomposition. The decomposition technique is based on the multiplicative model concept in time series analysis. In order to eliminate the seasonal variations from the data, this chapter describes a widely used technique referred to as ratio-to- moving average method.

Autocorrelation is a problem that occurs when data is regressed. When error terms of a regression model are correlated, autocorrelation occurs. Autoregression is a forecasting technique, which takes into account the advantage of the relationship of the value (y_i) to the previous values ($y_{i-1}, y_{i-2}, y_{i-3} \ldots$).

KEY TERMS |

Additive model, 518
Autocorrelation, 544
Autoregression, 546
Cyclic variations, 516
Decomposition, 518
Delphi method, 514
Deseasonalization, 537
Double smoothing method, 549
Executive opinion method, 514
Exponential smoothing method, 526
Freehand method, 521
Irregular variations, 518
Marketing research method, 515
Moving average method, 537
Multiplicative model, 518
Panel judgement method, 514
Past analogy, 514
Qualitative methods of forecasting, 514
Seasonal Variations, 516
Secular trend, 516
Single exponential smoothing, 530
Time Series, 514

NOTES |

1. Prowess (V. 3.1), Centre for Monitoring Indian Economy Pvt. Ltd, Mumbai, accessed September 2008, reproduced with permission.
2. http://www.hindwarebathrooms.com, accessed September 2008.

DISCUSSION QUESTIONS |

1. What are the various methods of forecasting?
2. Explain qualitative and quantitative methods of forecasting.
3. What are the various components of a time series?
4. Explain additive and multiplicative models of time series.
5. Describe the methods use to measure errors in forecasting.
6. Explain the concept of freehand method, average method, and exponential smoothing method.
7. Explain the concept and application of the double exponential smoothing method. Also explain the concept of double exponential smoothing using Holt's method.
8. Explain the regression method of forecasting with special reference to two methods: linear trend model and quadratic trend model.
9. What is the process of obtaining deseasonalized data from a time series? Also explain the method of obtaining de-seasonalized and detrended values.
10. Explain the concept of autocorrelation and autoregression. How can the concept of autoregression be used in fore-casting?

NUMERICAL PROBLEMS |

1. The following table provides the travelling expenses incurred by the sales executive of a company from 1993 to 2004. Prepare a time series plot with these figures.

Years	*Travelling expenses (in million rupees)*
1993	10
1994	12
1995	14
1996	13
1997	15
1998	17
1999	16
2000	18
2001	19
2002	17
2003	21
2004	23

2. Compute a 3-yearly moving average for the data given in Problem 1.

3. Compute a four yearly moving average for the data given in Problem 1.

4. Determine the straight line trend by semi-averages method for the following time series data related to the sales of a cement manufacturing company. Also determine the projected sales for 2008.

Year	*Sales (in thousand rupees)*
1998	2000
1999	2100
2000	2150
2001	2300
2002	2200
2003	2400
2004	2500
2005	2400
2006	2700
2007	2670

5. The following table provides the number of units produced by a calculator manufacturer in different years.

Year	*Production (in thousand units)*
1996	200
1997	220

1998	250
1999	210
2000	270
2001	280
2002	290
2003	260
2004	250
2005	295
2006	300
2007	310

Use exponential smoothing method with $\alpha = 0.3$; $\alpha = 0.5$, and $\alpha = 0.7$ to forecast the production of calculators.

6. Use exponential smoothing method with α=0.2; α=0.5, and α= 0.8 to forecast the sales of a company. The sales values for 14 years are given in the table below:

Year	*Sales (in thousand rupees)*
1994	240
1995	250
1996	260
1997	245
1998	240
1999	270
2000	280
2001	265
2002	290
2003	310
2004	320
2005	280
2006	315
2007	325

7. The following table lists the number of units manufactured by a company in 12 years. Fit a straight line trend by the method of least squares and estimate the sales in 2010.

Years	*Production (number of units)*
1996	1050
1997	1010
1998	1100
1999	1150
2000	1200
2001	1250
2002	1300
2003	1220
2004	1180
2005	1330
2006	1400
2007	1250

8. The following table lists the sales values of a company for five years for all the four quarters of the year. Calculate the seasonal indexes. In addition, detrend and deseasonalize the data and obtain the projected values after deseasonalization and detrending.

Year	*Quarter*	*Sales (in thousand rupees)*
2002	1	200
	2	210
	3	215
	4	210
2003	1	225
	2	230
	3	213
	4	238
2004	1	228
	2	232
	3	237
	4	222
2005	1	242
	2	247
	3	229
	4	226
2006	1	255
	2	257
	3	240
	4	235

CASE STUDY |

Case 20: *Nicholas Piramal India Ltd: Success Through Innovation*

Introduction: An Overview of the Domestic Pharmaceutical Market

The domestic pharmaceutical market has witnessed high growth as a result of rising income levels and increasing penetration of modern medicine. As per the ORG-IMS MAT report for March 2008, the growth for the financial year 2007–2008 was 14.8%. Chronic therapies continue to grow faster than acute. The domestic pharmaceutical industry is centered on branded generics and is intensely competitive. The top 10 companies account for only 36% of the market share. Pharmaceutical industry continues to be highly fragmented with has more than 20,000 registered units.[1] The industry expanded drastically in the last two decades. The leading 250 pharmaceutical companies control

70% of the market with the market leader holding nearly 7% of the market share.[2] The demand for drug and pharmaceuticals is estimated to be ₹ 1675 billion by 2014–2015.[3]

Nicholas Piramal India Ltd: India's Second Largest Pharmaceutical Healthcare Company

Nicholas Piramal India Ltd is India's second largest pharmaceutical healthcare company and is a leader in the cardio-vascular segment. The company came into existence after its acquisition of Nicholas Laboratories from Sara Lee in 1988. It has a strong presence in the antibiotics and respiratory segment, pain management, neuro-psychiatry, and anti-diabetis segments. The company has also made forays into biotechnology in key therapeutic areas for which it has formed several global alliances. Nicholas Piramal India Ltd is a part of the USD 500 million Piramal Enterprises (PIL), which is one of India's largest diversified business houses.[4]

Rebranding Exercise at Nicholas Piramal

Nicholas Piramal has worked out a complex internal rebranding exercise for creating a common brand identity across its various divisions such as Wellquest (clinical trials division), Wellspring (pathlabs), and Actics. The company wants to adopt a common name and a new logo that can be easily identified by its clients across businesses. Discussing this exercise, Swati Piramal, Director, Strategic Alliance and Communications, NPIL told *Financial Express* in January 2008, "Yes, we have been discussing a common brand identity, including a change in the company logo. This is an effort to rationalize the various entities and for the ease of the regulatory process.[5]" As a result of this exercise in April 2008, Nicholas Piramal India Ltd Chairman Ajay Piramal announced, "It has been a decade since Nicholas Piramal India Ltd was established. There was no association of Nicholas in Nicholas Piramal India Ltd and moreover it was the name of a multinational. With the emergence of India globally, Nicholas lost its relevance, so we have decided to rechristen the company as Piramal Healthcare Ltd.[6]"

Great People Create Great Organizations

For Piramal Healthcare Ltd, its employees are vital. The belief that "great people create great organizations" has been at the core of the company's approach to its people. It has created a favourable work environment that encourages innovation and meritocracy. It has introduced a Career Opportunity Programme (COP) to promote internal talent. The learning and development cell of the company is dedicated to developing managerial skills and inspiring them to grow as business leaders. The company has also invested in enhancing the size of the sales. As a result, during the financial year 2007–2008, it increased its sales force from 3154 people to 3789 people.[1]

Table 20.01 lists the sales figures of the company from 1990 to 2007:

TABLE 20.01
Sales of Nicholas Piramal India Ltd from 1990–2007

Year	*Sales (in million rupees)*
1990	291.4
1991	587.3
1992	836.2
1993	895.1
1994	1243.5
1995	1558.9
1996	1853.7
1997	5035.8
1998	5346.4
1999	4417.9
2000	4897.1
2001	5746.3
2002	9608.0
2003	11,539.2
2004	14,445.1
2005	13,096.1
2006	15,084.6
2007	17,087.9

Source: Prowess (V. 3.1), Centre for Monitoring Indian Economy Pvt. Ltd, Mumbai, accessed September 2008, reproduced with permission.

1. Prepare a time series plot with the help of the data given in Table 20.01.
2. Compute a 3-year-moving average for this time series.
3. Use exponential smoothing method with $\alpha=0.3$; $\alpha=0.5$ to forecast sales.
4. Use Holt's two parameter ($\alpha=0.3$, $\beta=0.5$) method to forecast sales.

NOTES |

1. Prowess (V. 3.1), Centre for Monitoring Indian Economy Pvt. Ltd. Mumbai, accessed September 2008, reproduced with permission.
2. www.pharmaceutical-drug-manufactures.com/pharmacu-itical-industry/, accessed September 2008.
3. http://wwwindiastat.com, accessed September 2008, reproduced with permission.
4. www.nicholaspiramal.com/media_companyprofile.htm, accessed September 2008.
5. www.financialexpress.com/news/Nicholas-Piramal-joins-rebranding-jitterbug/257357, accessed September 2008.
6. www.expressindia.com/latest-news/nicholas-piramal-rechristened-piramal-healthcare/293233/, accessed September 2008.

PART V
Result Presentation

CHAPTER

21

Presentation of Result: Report Writing

LEARNING OBJECTIVES

Upon completion of this chapter, you will be able to:

- Understand the importance of a written report
- Understand the organization of a written report
- Learn the use of different types of charts and graphs in a research report
- Understand the importance of oral presentation

RESEARCH IN ACTION: BLUE STAR LTD

Mr Mohan T. Advani, an entrepreneur of exemplary vision and drive, founded Blue Star in 1943. In 1949, the proprietorship company set its sight on bigger expansion, took on shareholders, and became Blue Star Engineering Company Private Ltd. Blue Star went public in 1969 to become Blue Star Ltd as it continues to be called today.[1] At present, it is India's largest central air conditioning company with an annual turnover of ₹25,740 million, a network of 29 offices, 5 modern manufacturing facilities, 700 dealers, and around 2600 employees. The company is fulfilling the air conditioning needs of a large number of corporate and commercial customers and has established leadership in the field of commercial refrigeration equipment ranging from water coolers to cold storages. With respect to the nature of products and markets, business drivers, and competitive positioning, the areas of operation of Blue Star can be segmented into three categories: electromechanical projects and packaged air conditioning systems, cooling products, and professional electronics and industrial system. The first category comprises central and packaged air conditioning as well as electrical, plumbing, and firefighting projects. In the second category, it provides a wide range of contemporary window and split air conditioners and a comprehensive range of commercial refrigeration products and services. In the third category, it manufactures analytical instruments, medical electronics, data communication products, material testing, and testing and measuring instruments.[2]

In 2008–2009, the estimated total market size for air conditioning in India was around ₹1,02,500 millions. Of this, the market for central air conditioning, including central plants, packaged/ducted systems, and VRF systems was about ₹57,500 millions, whereas the market for room air conditioners comprised the balance of ₹45,000 millions. The commercial air conditioning segment catering to corporate and commercial customers amounted to around ₹80,000 millions.[3] Blue Star has ambitious plans to cater to this market. Table 21.1 provides a view of the sales and profit after tax (in million Rupees) of Blue Star Ltd from 1994–1995 to 2008–2009. Profit after tax status of the company has crossed ₹1800 million during the financial year 2008–2009, which is almost 2.5 times the profit after tax of the company during

>>>

the financial year 2006-2007. This exhibits the remarkable growth status of Blue Star Ltd in recent years.

The company has made substantial investments in building brand equity over the past few years. During the year 2008-2009, as a measure of economy, there was a moderate reduction in advertising. Within the lower advertising budget, the value proposition of Blue Star as "Experts in cooling," the corporate image-building campaign, the room air conditioners and refrigeration products campaign as well as the packaged air conditioning capabilities campaign continued. Apart from the mass media, the company also made affordable investments in field marketing. This included participation in trade exhibitions; better relationship management with Interior Designers, Architects, and Consultants (IDEAC); participation in customer events; and development of public relation through the press. These field activities are critical and have gone a long way in complementing mass media campaigns and strengthening brand equity.[3]

Suppose that the company wants to ascertain "brand equity" of its products through a well-structured questionnaire and a well-designed research process and a professional research body has conducted this research (taking the help from all the chapters of this book) and is in the process of presenting the findings of the research, then how will the professional research body summarize the result? Is there any scientific way of writing a report on the insights and findings? What should be the ideal research report format? What should be the considerations for presentation of the results and discussion? How can the professional research body use charts and graphs for the presentations? This chapter is an attempt to answer all such questions. It discusses an ideal research report format and focuses on the dimensions of oral presentation.

TABLE 21.1
Sales and profit after tax (in million rupees) of Blue Star Ltd from 1994-1995 to 2008-2009

Year	*Sales*	*Profit after tax*
Mar-95	3062.4	163.8
Mar-96	3863.4	251.8
Mar-97	4317.9	147.7
Mar-98	4449.5	155.1
Mar-99	4717.4	162.7
Mar-00	4749.8	232.4
Mar-01	5039.2	235.4
Mar-02	5010.4	274.5
Mar-03	5818.3	314.1
Mar-04	7015.1	325.5
Mar-05	9225.4	391.6
Mar-06	11,729	489
Mar-07	15,945.8	711.8
Mar-08	22,215.8	1740.9
Mar-09	25,522.9	1802.9

Source: Prowess (V. 3.1): Centre for Monitoring Indian Economy Pvt. Ltd, Mumbai, accessed September 2009, reprinted with permission.

21.1 INTRODUCTION

There exists a difficulty in communicating the researcher's mind to a common person or a person who does not have a solid research background.

It is important for any researcher to present the research material in a systematic and predefined manner. A good research is diluted if it is not presented well by the researcher. A researcher knows what he or she has done and what the ingredients of his or her research work are. There exists a difficulty in communicating the researcher's mind to a common person or a person who does not have a solid research background. It is possible that the company that sponsored the research programme may not be interested in knowing the type of test statistics used to test the hypothesis. The company may only be interested in the research findings that they would apply to either solve the problem in hand or for exploring the opportunity. For a researcher, a test statistics is of paramount importance and he or she would like to discuss it elaborately. Hence, a proper balance between the thinking of the researcher and the requirement of the sponsoring agency is of paramount importance. In a nutshell, the report must contain all the important ingredients of the research in a systematic and predetermined manner. The following section focuses on the organization of the written report.

21.2 ORGANIZATION OF THE WRITTEN REPORT

After conducting any research, the researcher needs to draft the work. Drafting is a scientific procedure and needs a systematic and careful articulation. When the organization for which the researcher is conducting the research has provided guidelines to prepare the research report, one has to follow them. However, if there is no guideline available from the sponsoring organization, then the researcher can follow a reasonable pattern of presenting a written research report. In fact, there is no single universally acceptable guideline available for organization of a written report. In fact, the organization of the written report depends on the type of the target group that it addresses. However, following is the format for a written report organization. Although this format presents a broad guideline for report organization, in real sense, the researcher enjoys flexibility to either include the required items or exclude the items from the list.

In fact, there is no single universally acceptable guideline available for the organization of a written report.

1. Title page
2. Letter of transmittal
3. Letter of authorization
4. **Table of contents (including list of figures and tables)**
5. Executive summary
    - 5.1 Objective
    - 5.2 Concise statement of the methodology
    - 5.3 Results
    - 5.4 Conclusions
    - 5.5 Recommendations
6. Body
    - 6.1 Introduction
    - 6.2 Research objective
    - 6.3 Research methodology (sample, sample size, sample profile, sampling techniques, scaling techniques, questionnaire, test statistic, and fieldwork)
    - 6.4 Results and findings
    - 6.5 Conclusions and recommendations
    - 6.6 Limitations of the research
7. Appendix
    - 7.1 Copies of data collection forms
    - 7.2 Statistical output details
    - 7.3 General tables that are not included in the body
    - 7.4 Bibliography
    - 7.5 Other required support material

21.2.1 Title Page

A **title page** includes the title of the study, the name and affiliation of the researcher, the month and year of the study, and the name of the client for whom the report is being prepared. An attractively laid out title page is important for making a good first impression on the reader (Parasuraman et al. 2004). In general, the title remains in capital letters and is placed at the centre of the title page along with other information, as exhibited in Figure 21.1.

A title page includes the title of the study, the name and affiliation of the researcher, the month and year of the study, and the name of the client for whom the report is being prepared.

21.2.2 Letter of Transmittal

A **letter of transmittal** is an important ingredient of a formal research report. It delivers the report to the client and has a brief description of the report's highlights. It is written

A letter of transmittal is an important ingredient of a formal research report. It delivers the report to the client and has a brief description of the report's highlights.

CHANGE IN CONSUMER ATTITUDE: A COMPARATIVE STUDY IN PRE AND POST LIBERALIZATION PERIOD

Prepared for
Consumer Federation
New Delhi

Prepared by
Research India Ltd
45, Vasant Vihar
New Delhi

July 2010

FIGURE 21.1
Title page

in a personal and slightly informal way. It may include some personal observations by the researcher during the research, which is not generally supported by any data. Figure 21.2 presents an example of a letter of transmittal. It is noticeable that this is not the standard format of a letter of transmittal. The pattern adopted to address the research-sponsoring agency depends purely on the research-conducting agency.

Mr Rajan Pandey   Date: 18-07-2010
President
Consumer Federation
New Delhi

Dear Mr Pandey
With reference to your letter of authorization dated 10-01-2010, I am to inform you that I have completed the job assigned by you. I am also sending you the results contained in a research report entitled, "Change in consumer attitude: A comparative study in pre and post liberalization period."
As already discussed with you, the said report is based on the inputs obtained from 450 subjects taken from three states. Report is arranged in five chapters and explains all the details pertaining to the research conducted by our firm. We have followed the standard pattern of conducting the marketing research. I sincerely hope that the results presented in the report are of great use to you in making some decisions.
Please feel free to call me or e-mail me any time in case of any questions.
Sincerely,

Virendra Kapoor
President
Research India Ltd
45, Vasant Vihar
New Delhi

FIGURE 21.2
Letter of transmittal

21.2.3 Letter of Authorization

A **letter of authorization** is issued by the research-sponsoring agency to the research-conducting agency before the actual start of the research. It is a formal letter that authorizes the research-conducting agency to conduct the research. It generally includes the name and title of the person(s) who authorizes the researcher to conduct the research. It may include a general description of the nature of the research project, the completion date, the terms of payment, and any special condition of the research project requested by the client or research user (Burns and Bush 1999).

> A letter of authorization is issued by the research-sponsoring agency to the research-conducting agency before the actual start of the research. It is a formal letter that authorizes the research-conducting agency to conduct the research.

21.2.4 Table of Contents

The **table of contents** presents the list of topics included in the research report and the corresponding page numbers. It helps the researchers in locating the required information through relevant page numbers. The title page, letter of transmittal, letter of authorization, and table of contents are generally numbered with roman numerals such as i, ii, iii, and so on. Arabic numerals are used from the **executive summary** part of the research report.

> The table of contents presents the list of topics included in the research report and the corresponding page numbers. It helps the researchers in locating the required information through relevant page numbers.

21.2.5 Executive Summary

The executive summary is the most important part of the research report. Very often, executives go through the executive summary only. Thus, it must be capable of providing the information presented in the report in a summarized form. As it is the summarized form of the research report, it must contain the objective, the summarized methodology and findings, the conclusions, and the recommendations in a short form. It should be carefully drafted, so that it conveys the information as briefly as possible.

> The executive summary must be capable of providing the information presented in the report in a summarized form.

As the first part of the executive summary, the objective of the research work must be clearly highlighted. The research objective can also be supplemented with the research questions, question components, and research hypotheses. As the second part, in the category of concise statement of the methodology sampling, the sampling technique, the research design, or any other procedural aspects must be incorporated in one or two paragraphs. As the third part, the results should be incorporated in a brief format. It is really difficult to summarize the results. The researcher must include the results that specifically address the research questions or the hypotheses. In the fourth category, conclusions of the study should be arranged. Conclusions are merely statements of what the research generated and what meaning can be attributed to the findings (Hair et al. 2002). Recommendations are included as the next item in the research report. They are actually suggestions provided to the research-sponsoring firm by the research-conducting agency to address the problem or opportunity in hand, for which the research was launched.

21.2.6 Body

The **body** presents a broad and detailed study of the research. It consists of six sections: background, research objective, research methodology (sample, sample size, sample profile, sampling techniques, scaling techniques, questionnaire, test statistic, and fieldwork), results, conclusions and recommendations, and limitations of the research. If researcher finds that one of the sections is becoming lengthier, he or she can introduce suitable subsections to make the chapters convenient to read.

> The body presents a broad and detailed study of the research.

21.2.6.1 Introduction

This section, also referred to as the background, contains some basic background information that describes the problem, and it focuses mainly on the specific circumstances, in the light of which the researcher has launched the study. It connects the reader with the background circumstances that led to conducting the research. For example, a researcher, comparing the difference in consumer attitude in pre and post liberalization period in India, has to first present the basic information about the consumer attitude in India, impact of liberalization, some visible changes in consumer attitude due to liberalization, and the Indian economy before and after liberalization. There is no rigid guideline available to decide what should be incorporated in the introduction part and this is left to the discretion of individual researchers; what he or she feels is important to be included in this part of the written report.

The introduction section contains some basic background information that describes the problem at hand.

The introduction also contains some similar studies conducted by other researchers on the same topic in different parts of the world. It opens the discussion dimension of the findings of these studies and highlights how the present study may have similar or different dimensions.

21.2.6.2 Research Objective

The research objective may be incorporated in the introduction section or it can be a separate section.

The research objective may be incorporated in the introduction section or it can be a separate section. This section must contain the general problem, which the proposed research is going to address and the specific objectives of the research. It must also contain a brief discussion about the rationale of the specific objectives and their relevance to the problem at hand. Specific hypotheses constructed in relation to the problem must also be included in this section.

21.2.6.3 Research Methodology

The research methodology contains a detailed discussion of the sample, sample size, sample profile, sampling techniques, scaling techniques, questionnaire, test statistics, and the fieldwork.

The research methodology contains a detailed discussion of sample, sample size, sample profile, sampling techniques, scaling techniques, questionnaire, test statistic, and fieldwork. This section focuses on the sample group and how these samples should be selected. Chapter 5 provides the details of sample and sampling techniques, the sample size and its rationale, and the sample size profile. The research methodology section also focuses on scaling techniques, as described in Chapter 3. In this connection, the questionnaire and its format are also discussed. The test statistics, which are used to test the hypotheses, and the rationale of using it to test the hypotheses is dealt with. This section also incorporates some discussion about the fieldwork, that is, the manner in which respondents are contacted and difficulties are overcome to get the questionnaire filled.

The type of research, that is, exploratory, descriptive, or conclusive and the type of data used in the study, that is, whether only primary or secondary data are to be used or a combination of both are to be used are also discussed in this section. Secondary data sources are also mentioned.

21.2.6.4 Results and Findings

The results and findings section mainly discusses the outcome of the statistical analyses performed to test different hypotheses.

The results and findings section mainly discusses the outcome of the statistical analyses performed to test different hypotheses. For example, if a researcher is using the one-way Analysis of Variance (ANOVA) technique to compare various means, ANOVA tables must be incorporated. In addition, the rationale of using this technique must also be discussed. All the tables must be logically arranged to address the research question and hypotheses. Statistical interpretation of the result must also be presented along with the tables. Acceptance or rejection of null or alternative hypothesis with the concerned level of significance must also be mentioned.

21.2.6.5 Conclusions and Recommendations

The conclusion is the meaning derived from the acceptance or rejection of the hypothesis.

The conclusion is derived from the acceptance or rejection of the hypothesis. As discussed in the results and findings section, statistical tests are performed to test the hypothesis. The researcher may either accept the null hypothesis or he or she may reject the null hypothesis and accept the alternative hypothesis. The acceptance or rejection of null hypothesis is very important for results and leads to a non-statistical conclusion in which the researcher or readers of the reports are mainly interested. Thus, the conclusion is the non-statistical explanation of the statistical result. The conclusions are supported by some previous research or existing studies and are made with direct reference to the research objective.

Recommendations are slightly different from that of conclusions. The recommendations are generated from the critical thinking of the researcher. The researcher examines every conclusion and suggests the actual course of action to address the problem or opportunity at hand. The conclusions happen in the form of non-action statements, whereas the recommendations are action statements and guide the research sponsor agency to take action to solve the problem or to take action to explore the untapped opportunity.

The recommendations are generated from the critical thinking of the researcher.

21.2.6.6 Limitations of the Research

Every researcher attempts to conduct a flawless research, free from all limitations. However, this is possible only in theory, real-life circumstances are entirely different and limitations are bound to be observed while conducting any research. Some of the most common limitations of marketing research are sampling bias, sample size, time and cost problems, and measurement error, to name a few. The limitations of the research should not be overemphasized rather the aim should be to aid the decision maker in taking the appropriate action.

The limitations of the research should not be overemphasized rather the aim should be to aid the decision maker in taking the appropriate action.

21.2.7 Appendix

Any information that is of significance to the researcher and reader but cannot be placed in the body part of the research report is placed in the **appendix**. There is no fixed universally accepted rule regarding the information, which should be included in the appendix, rather it is the researcher's discretion, what he or she feels is important to be included in the appendix. In general, the appendix includes copies of data collection forms, statistical output details, general tables which are not included in the body, bibliography, and other required support material.

Any information that is of significance to the researcher and reader but cannot be placed in the body part of the research report is placed in the appendix.

21.3 TABULAR PRESENTATION OF DATA

Tables are very effective tools of presenting data when the aim is to have a quick understanding about the facts and figures, which are arranged in descriptive paragraphs. Usage of tables allows the writer to point out significant features without getting bogged down by details (Zikmund 2007).

It is advisable to use only relevant and important tables in the body of the report. Other important tables must be incorporated in the appendix part of the report. Each table should have a proper table number, so that the reader does not face any difficulty in referring to the table, while going through the text. Every table should have an appropriate title for ready reference. Explanation of the table entries should be properly supported by the footnotes. It is very important to provide the source from where the table is taken. For example, Table 21.2 shows the sales of four leading cement companies: Ambuja, L&T, Madras Cement, and ACC from 1994–1995 to 2006–2007, which is taken from the data source Prowess (V3.1): Centre for Monitoring Indian Economy Pvt. Ltd. Table 21.2 clearly presents the comparative analysis of the sales of the four leading cement companies at a glance, which if arranged in descriptive paragraphs will be very difficult to understand.

Tables are very effective tools of presenting data, when the aim is to have a quick understanding about the facts and figures, which, if arranged in descriptive paragraphs, will be very difficult to understand.

TABLE 21.2
Sales of Ambuja, L&T, Madras cement, and ACC from 1994-1995 to 2006-2007

Year	*Ambuja*	*L&T*	*Madras Cement*	*ACC*
1994–1995	3209.1	32,747.4	2973.2	20,427
1995–1996	4292.3	42,876.2	3901.8	23,294.6
1996–1997	7305.6	53,477.6	4171.4	24,510.5
1997–1998	9303.5	56,914	4886.7	23,731.1
1998–1999	11,457.8	73,030.2	5223.8	25,858.3
1999–2000	12,523.4	74,336.6	5180.9	26,792.2
2000–2001	13,027.8	75,549.9	6192.6	29,361.2
2001–2002	14,473.2	81,199.3	8166.6	32,260
2002–2003	15,826.3	87,762.9	7506.9	33,718.8
2003–2004	20,251	98,945.2	8451.9	39,003.7
2004–2005	23,012.8	133,781	8852.8	45,498
2005–2006	30,258.4	150,290.3	11,909.7	37,235.1
2006–2007	70,167	179,713.1	18,024.8	64,680.6

Source: Prowess (V. 3.1): Centre for Monitoring Indian Economy Pvt. Ltd, Mumbai, accessed November 2008, reprinted with permission.

21.4 GRAPHICAL PRESENTATION OF DATA

While reading magazines and books, we come across charts and graphs. In most presentations, graphs are used as supporting materials for presenting facts and figures. Marketing managers prepare presentations by including a large number of suitable graphs. Graphical presentation of data seems to be more appealing when we simply want to convey the trend of data. It creates an effective visual impact and presents the important features of the data to the viewers. Graphical presentation of statistics helps the researcher understand the shape of the distribution. Software applications, such as MS Excel, Minitab, SPSS, SAS, and so on, have made graphical presentation of data easy. They provide a wide range of options to present data graphically. Some of the basic and most commonly used methods of presenting data in graphs and charts are as follows:

- **Bar chart**
- **Pie chart**
- **Histogram**
- **Frequency polygon**
- **Ogive**
- **Scatter plot**

A bar chart is a graphical device used in depicting data that have been summarized as frequency, relative frequency, or percentage frequency.

21.4.1 Bar Chart

A **bar chart** is a graphical device used in depicting data that have been summarized as frequency, relative frequency, or percentage frequency. The class intervals are specified on the horizontal axis or the *x*-axis of the graph. The frequencies are specified on the vertical axis or the *y*-axis of the graph. Let us take Example 21.1 to understand the procedure of constructing a bar chart.

Example 21.1

Table 21.3 shows the inflow of foreign direct investment (FDI) in the food processing sector in India from 2000–2001 to 2006–2007. With the help of this data, prepare a bar chart.

TABLE 21.3
FDI in the food processing industries sector in India from 2000-2001 to 2006-2007 Year

FDI in the food processing industries sector in India from 2000–2001 to 2006–2007 Year	*FDI in million rupees*
2000–2001	1981.3
2001–2002	10,361.2
2002–2003	1765.3
2003–2004	5108.5
2004–2005	1740.0
2005–2006	1829.4
2006–2007	4410.0

Source: www.indiastat.com, accessed October 2008, reproduced with permission.

Solution Figure 21.3 exhibits the Minitab output (bar chart) for inflow of FDI in the food processing sector in India from 2000–2001 to 2006–2007.

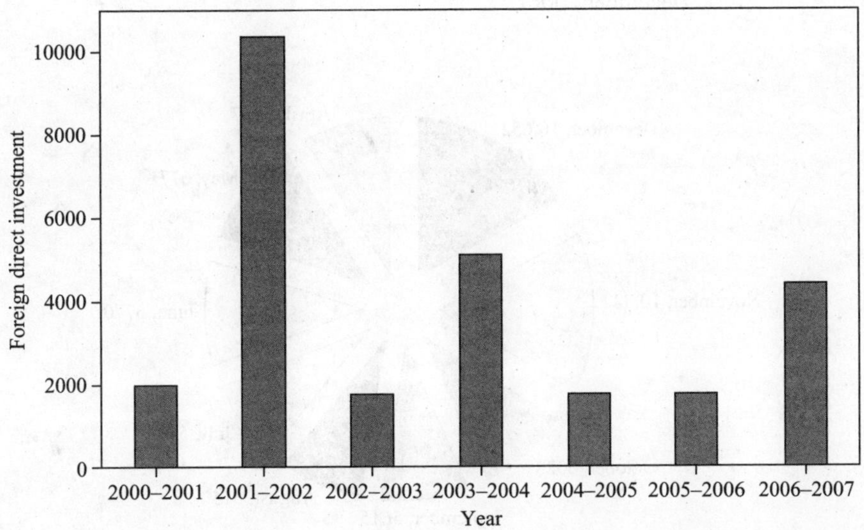

FIGURE 21.3
Minitab output (bar chart) for inflow of FDI in the food processing industries sector in India from 2000-2001 to 2006-2007

A pie chart is a circular representation of data in which a circle is divided into sectors, with areas equal to the corresponding component. These sectors are called slices and represent the percentage breakdown of the corresponding component.

21.4.2 Pie Chart

A **pie chart** is a circular representation of data in which a circle is divided into sectors, with areas equal to the corresponding component. These sectors are called slices and represent the percentage breakdown of the corresponding component. The pie chart is the most common way of data presentation in today's business scenario. They are used for representing market share, budget categories, time and resource allocation, and so on. The construction of the pie chart begins with determining the proportion of the component to the whole. As the pie chart is a circular representation, each component proportion is multiplied by 360 (a circle measures 360° totally), to get the correct number of degrees to represent each component. Let us take Example 21.2 to understand the procedure for constructing a pie chart.

Example 21.2

A travel and tourism company opened a new office in Singapore based on the tourist arrival data from Singapore to India in 2006. Table 21.4 exhibits data related to the number of tourists who arrived from Singapore to India in 2006 (from April 2006 to December 2006). Construct a pie chart for this data.

TABLE 21.4
Number of tourists who arrived from Singapore to India in 2006 (from April 2006 to December 2006)

Month (in 2006)	*Apr*	*May*	*Jun*	*Jul*	*Aug*	*Sep*	*Oct*	*Nov*	*Dec*
Number of tourists who arrived from Singapore	5567	6771	6770	5102	5150	5615	6028	10,322	10,652

Solution

Figure 21.4 exhibits the Excel output (pie chart) for the number of tourists who arrived from Singapore to India in 2006 (from April 2006 to December 2006).

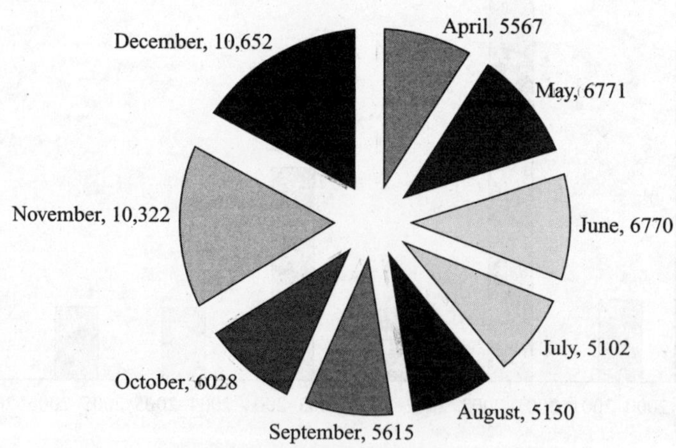

FIGURE 21.4
Excel output (pie chart) for number of tourists who arrived from Singapore to India in 2006 (from April 2006 to December 2006)

21.4.3 Histogram

The histogram is one of the most popular and widely used methods of presenting the frequency distribution graphically. A **histogram** can be defined as a set of rectangles, each proportional in width to the range of the values within a class and proportional in height to the class frequencies of the respective class interval. When plotting a histogram, the variable of interest is displayed on the *x*-axis and the number, proportion, or percentage of observations per class interval is represented on the *y*-axis. Let us take Example 21.3 to understand the procedure for constructing a histogram.

A histogram can be defined as a set of rectangles, each proportional in width to the range of the values within a class and proportional in height to the class frequencies of the respective class interval.

Example 21.3

The demand for tractors in India is zooming up. Many new multinational companies are joining the race. Table 21.5 shows the production of tractors in India from 1998–1999 to 2006–2007. With the help of the data given in the table, prepare a histogram.

TABLE 21.5
Production of tractors in India from 1998–1999 to 2006–2007

Year	*Production (in numbers)*
1998–1999	253,850
1999–2000	266,385
2000–2001	234,575
2001–2002	215,000
2002–2003	162,000
2003–2004	191,633
2004–2005	248,976
2005–2006	292,908
2006–2007	352,827

Solution Figure 21.5 exhibits the MS Excel output (histogram) for production of tractors in India from 1998–1999 to 2006–2007.

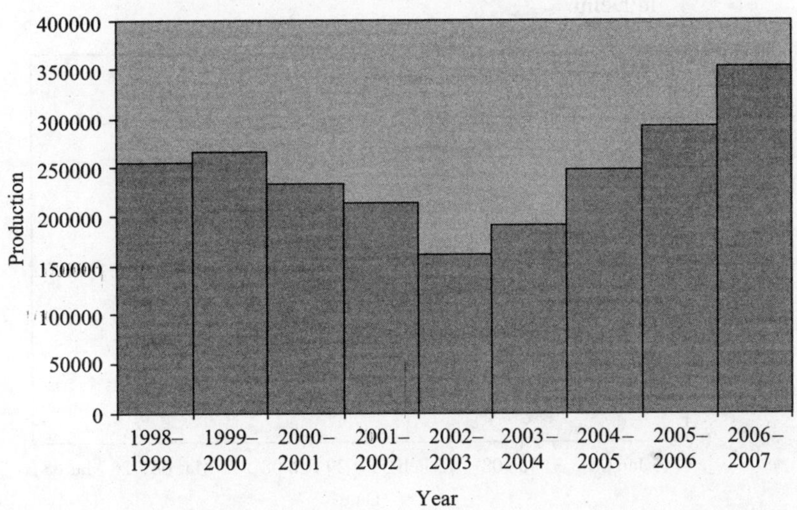

FIGURE 21.5
MS Excel output (Histogram) for production of tractors in India from 1998–1999 to 2006–2007

21.4.4 Frequency Polygon

A frequency polygon is a graphical device for understanding the shape of the distribution.

A **frequency polygon** is a graphical device for understanding the shape of the distribution. To construct a frequency polygon, we take frequencies on the vertical axis, that is, on the *y*- axis and the value of the variable on the horizontal axis or the *x-axis*. A dot is plotted for the frequency value at the midpoint of each class interval. These midpoints are called class midpoints. By connecting these midpoints through a line, the frequency polygon can be constructed easily. The information generated from the histogram and frequency polygon is similar. A frequency polygon can also be constructed by connecting midpoints of individual bars of a histogram. Let us take Example 21.4 to understand the procedure for constructing a frequency polygon.

Example 21.4

In India, vanaspati oil prices have gone up as a result of rising inflation. Table 21.6 gives the price of oil on some specific dates from January 2008 to March 2008 in Delhi. Construct a line graph to observe the trend of oil prices.

TABLE 21.6
Price of vanaspati oil on specific dates between January 2008 and March 2008 in Delhi

Date	*Price unit (Rs 15 kg tin/jar)*
15.01.2008	900
31.01.2008	925
15.02.2008	930
29.02.2008	1000
13.03.2008	1095
28.03.2008	990

Source: www.indiastat.com, accessed October 2008, reproduced with permission.

Solution

Figure 21.6 exhibits the Minitab output (line graph) for the price of vanaspati oil on specific dates between January 2008 and March 2008 in Delhi.

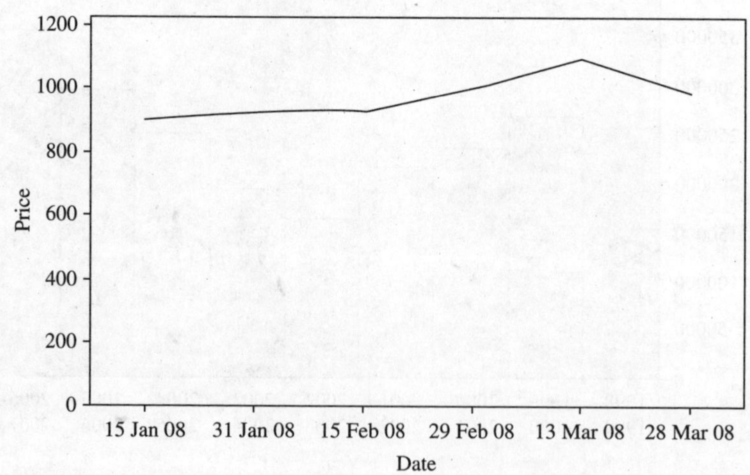

FIGURE 21.6
Minitab output (line graph) for the price of vanaspati oil on specific dates between January 2008 and March 2008 in Delhi

21.4.5 Ogive

An **ogive** (pronounced O-jive) is a cumulative frequency curve. In other words, an ogive is a cumulative frequency polygon. The data values are shown on the horizontal axis and cumulative frequencies are shown on the vertical axis. Once cumulative frequencies are recorded, the remaining procedure for drawing a curve is the same as that followed for other curves. The only difference exists in terms of scaling the y-axis to accommodate the cumulative frequencies. Let us take Example 21.5 to understand the procedure for constructing an ogive.

An Ogive (pronounced O-jive) is a cumulative frequency curve. In other words, an ogive is a cumulative frequency polygon.

Example 21.5

A construction firm has allowed its employees to participate in a private consultancy in order to create an autonomous environment. The firm has decided that the employees will contribute 10% of their income earned from the consultancy to the organization. After 1 year of launching this programme, the data collected by the firm related to the additional income earned by the employees is given in Table 21.7. Construct a frequency polygon and an ogive with the help of this data.

TABLE 21.7
Number of employees under different additional income intervals

Income interval (in thousand rupees)	*Number of employees (frequency)*
10 under 20	25
20 under 30	35
30 under 40	40
40 under 50	47
50 under 60	28
60 under 70	20

Solution

The frequency polygon can be constructed with the help of frequencies given in the Table 21.7. For constructing an ogive, we have to first construct cumulative frequencies as show in Table 21.8. Figure 21.7 is the MS Excel-produced frequency polygon for Example 21.5 and Figure 21.8 is the MS Excel-produced ogive for Example 21.5.

TABLE 21.8
Cumulative frequency distribution

Income interval (in thousand rupees)	*Number of employees (frequency)*	*Cumulative frequency*
10 under 20	25	25
20 under 30	35	60
30 under 40	40	100
40 under 50	47	147
50 under 60	28	175
60 under 70	20	195

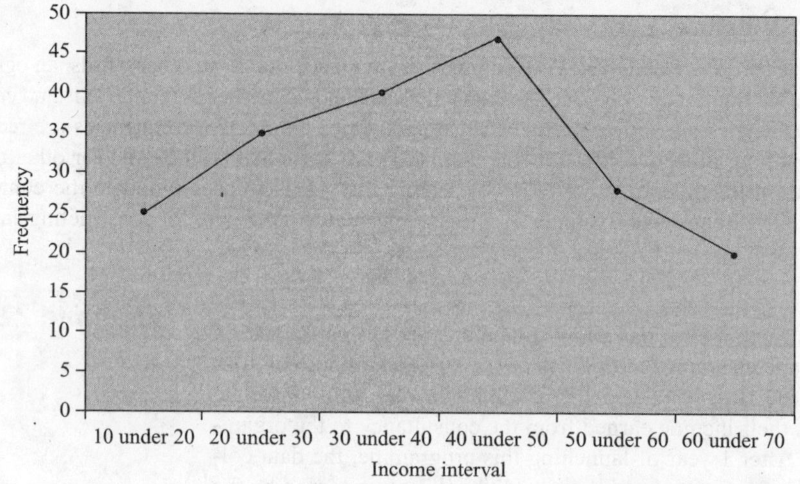

FIGURE 21.7
MS Excel-produced frequency polygon for Example 21.5

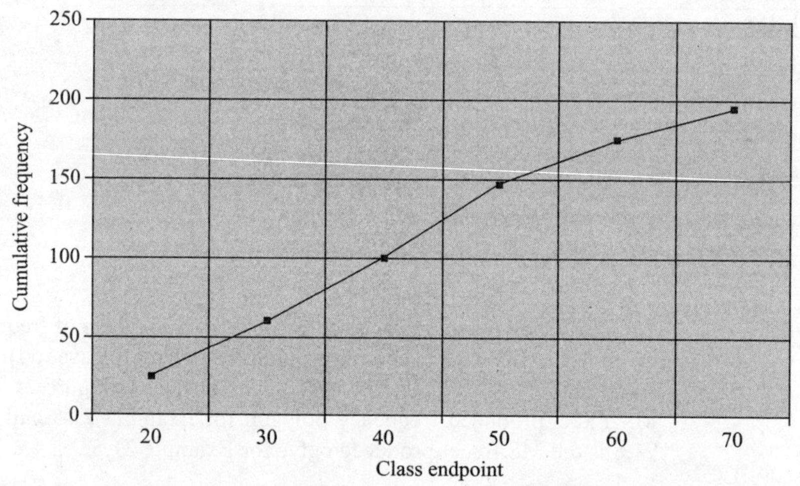

FIGURE 21.8
MS Excel-produced ogive for Example 21.5

A scatter plot is a graphical presentation of the relationship between two numerical variables. It is also widely used in statistical analysis. It generally shows the nature of the relationship between two variables.

21.4.6 Scatter Plot

A **scatter plot** is a graphical presentation of the relationship between two numerical variables. It is also widely used in statistical analysis. It generally shows the nature of the relationship between two variables. The application of a scatter plot is very common in regression, multiple regressions, correlation, and so on. Let us take Example 21.6 to understand the procedure for constructing a scatter plot.

Example 21.6

HDFC Bank was incorporated in 1994 and operates in three core areas: retail banking, wholesale banking, and treasury. By 2007, the bank increased its business in all functional areas especially in the home loans segment. Table 21.9 gives the net income and advertising expenses of the HDFC Bank from 2000 to 2007. Construct a scatter plot with the data given in the table.

TABLE 21.9
Net income and advertising expenses of HDFC Bank from 2000 to 2007

Year	*Net income (in million rupees)*	*Advertising expenses (in million rupees)*
2000	8052.4	113.7
2001	14,449.2	46.3
2002	20,354.1	187.8
2003	24,778.4	175.1
2004	30,359.2	370.6
2005	38,240.1	549.5
2006	56,765.4	808.5
2007	84,676.5	748.8

Source: Prowess (V. 3.1): Centre for Monitoring Indian Economy Pvt. Ltd, Mumbai, accessed November 2008, reprinted with permission.

Solution Figure 21.9 exhibits the Minitab output (scatter plot) for net income and advertising expenses.

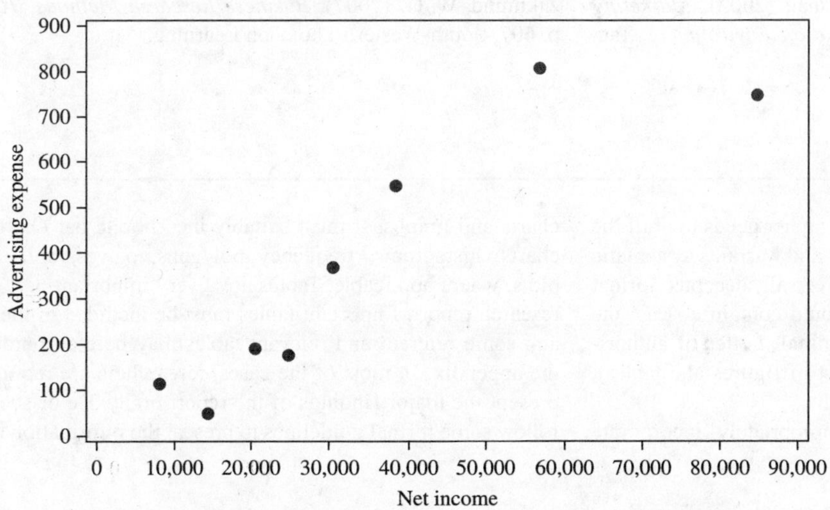

FIGURE 21.9 Minitab output (scatter plot) for net income and advertising expenses

21.5 ORAL PRESENTATION

Along with the written presentation, most research reports are also presented orally. The main purpose of oral presentation is to provide a glimpse of the major findings of the research to the client audience orally, so that any query or ambiguity may be clarified. It can be organized as an exclusive meeting involving the clients and the research sponsors only, or it may be an open presentation, where every person concerned with the research project is invited to attend and ask questions.

Following are some of the guidelines to organize the oral presentation:

- Identify the audience and arrange the presentation in accordance with their understanding capacity.
- Make the presentation in bulleted points and highlight major findings separately.
- A summary of the written report can be distributed to the audience before starting the presentation for their reference.
- Simple charts and graphs can also be used to make the audience comfortable with the data.
- Do not try to read the material rather make an eye contact with the audience and explain the major facts and figures.
- Nowadays many software are available to make the presentation strong and audience friendly. MS Powerpoint is a widely used presentation tool. It provides many attractive presentation features.
- If a researcher is using some software for presentation, important data, figures, and graphs can be exhibited through the hyperlink facility.
- It is important for a person who is involved in the presentation to at least rehearse it three or four times before going for the final presentation.

REFERENCES

Burns, A. C. and R. F. Bush (1999). *Marketing Research*, 3rd ed., p. 651. Upper Saddle River, NJ: Prentice-Hall.

Hair, J. F., R. P. Bush and D. J. Ortinau (2002). *Marketing Research: Within a Changing Information Environment*, Tata McGraw-Hill Publishing.

Parasuraman, A., D. Grewal and R. Krishnan (2004). *Marketing Research*, p. 550. Boston, NY: Houghton Mifflin Company.

Zikmund, W. G. (2007). *Business Research Methods*, 7th ed., p. 607. South-Western Thomson Learning.

SUMMARY

After conducting any research, the researcher needs to draft the work. Drafting is a scientific procedure and warrants systematic and careful articulation. There is no universally accepted format for the written report. However, it should contain at least the following: Title page, Letter of transmittal, Letter of authorization, Table of contents (including list of figures and tables), Executive summary, Body, and Appendix.

The Research report should appropriately incorporate charts and graphs. It must suitably incorporate bar charts, pie charts, histograms, frequency polygons, ogives, and scatter plots, where applicable. Tables are a very important part of the research report. Important tables must be included in the body and some referent and relevant tables may be incorporated in the appendix. In most of the cases, researchers are required to present the major findings of the report orally. He or she must follow some formal guidelines to present the information orally.

KEY TERMS

Appendix, 561
Bar chart, 562
Body, 559
Executive summary, 559
Frequency polygon, 562
Histogram, 562
Letter of authorization, 559
Letter of transmittal, 557
Ogive, 562
Pie chart, 564
Scatter plot, 568
Table of contents (including list of figures and tables), 557
Title page, 557

NOTES |

1. http://www.bluestarindia.com/about/history.asp
2. http://www.bluestarindia.com/about/default.asp
3. Prowess (V3.1), Centre for Monitoring Indian Economy Pvt. Ltd, Mumbai, accessed September 2009, reprinted with permission.

DISCUSSION QUESTIONS |

1. What is the importance of the research report for a researcher?
2. What are the important components of a good research report?
3. Why one should include the letter of transmittal and letter of authorization in the research report?
4. What is the appropriate way of presenting tables and graphs in the research report?
5. Why does a researcher have to incorporate an executive summary in the research report? Is there any significance in omitting the executive summary from the research report?
6. What should be the components of the body part of the research report?
7. How should a researcher incorporate different types of charts and graphs in the research report?
8. What should be the ingredients of the appendix of the research report?

CASE STUDY |

Case 21: *Eicher Motors: A Strategic View to Focus on the Commercial Vehicles Segment*

Introduction: Commercial Vehicles Industry in India

Commercial Vehicles (CV) can be broadly classified into two categories: Medium and heavy commercial vehicles (M & HCVs) and light commercial vehicle (LCVs). Buses and trucks come under the category of M & HCVs and vans, station wagons, and some lightweight vehicles come under the category of LCVs. Road transport, more specifically quality road transport, has gained popularity in the last few decades. The demand for LCVs in the year 2003–2004 was 1,05,000 in numbers which is projected to increase to 1,92,000 by the year 2014–2015. Northern, eastern, western, and southern regions of the country secure 18%, 9%, 33%, and 40% of the total market size, respectively. Telco, Mahindra & Mahindra, Bajaj Tempo, Swaraj Mazda, and Eicher Motors are the major players in the market. With a record growth of 13.8% in the year span 2001–2002 to 2006–2007, the market is estimated to grow at the rate of 6.0% by the year span 2009–2010 to 2014–2015.[1]

Eicher Motors: Aspiring to Excel in Commercial Vehicle Category

Eicher Motors started operations in 1959, with the roll-out of India's first tractor. It is today one of the significant players in the Indian automobile industry. The Eicher group has diversified business interests in the areas of: design and development, manufacturing, and local/international marketing of trucks and buses, motorcycles, automotive gears and components. Activities of the group in business units like Eicher Motors Ltd (Eicher Motors, Royal Enfield, and Eicher Engineering Components), Eicher Engineering Solutions, and Good Earth Publication.[2]

Eicher Motors has taken a strategic decision to take CVs as a major growth driver. The group chairman and CEO Mr S. Sandilya has stated, "The Eicher Group has made significant progress over the last several years in strengthening the financial performance of its various automotive businesses. In order to propel ourselves on to next trajectory of growth, we have reviewed our portfolio with the objective of focusing on selected businesses in which we can achieve strong market positions." He added, "In particular, we believe we have the potential to grow aggressively and reach a leadership position in commercial vehicles."[3] Table 21.01 shows the sales, net income and profit after tax of Eicher Motors Ltd from 1994–1995 to 2008–2009.

Opportunities and Threats for the Company

In the CVs category, the opportunities to be explored are: the development of infrastructure and building of highways, quicker and efficient servicing of demand from the consumers, technical upgradation of the CVs, and increased awareness on overloading of vehicles. The issues of concern in this category are:

TABLE 21.01

Sales, net income and profit after tax (in million rupees) of Eicher Motors Ltd from 1994–1995 to 2008–2009

Year	*Sales*	*Net income*	*Profit after tax*
Mar-95	2085.7	1926	122.4
Mar-96	2604.1	2401.8	123.5
Mar-97	3263.3	2927.4	116.8
Mar-98	2670.3	2385.6	30.2
Mar-99	2699.7	2414.9	78.2
Mar-00	3526.6	3120.5	158.6
Mar-01	4492.7	3965.2	235.3
Mar-02	5318.2	4812.6	178.8
Mar-03	7004.2	6297.1	374.6
Mar-04	15715	13735.1	336.2
Mar-05	22207	19915.5	588.5
Mar-06	18701.2	16605.4	2168.8
Mar-07	22381.9	19816.7	612.6
Mar-08	25331.9	22332.5	630.5
Mar-09	7775.5	7170.8	390

Source: Prowess (V. 3.1): Centre for Monitoring Indian Economy Pvt. Ltd, Mumbai, accessed September 2009, reprinted with permission.

the increasing interest rates, the rising inflation which tends to an increase in prices, continuing rise in crude oil prices, etc. In the two-wheeler category, the customer's preference for "power/style/leisure and cruiser" bikes, increasing the customer base for 350cc bikes, and production of more bikes are some of the opportunities, whereas the small size of the customer base for the Royal Enfield bikes is perceived to be a big threat for the company. The company's growth focus on the CV category will automatically give an impetus to the auto component, including gears, business as this segment is a strategic supplier for the in-house CV business. In addition, the company is also widening its product portfolio to increase the size of orders from export customers. In the view of the company, increasing interest rate is the only threat for the domestic auto-component business, whereas increasing steel prices poses a challenge for its export segment. The Engineering-solutions segment of the company is also grooming very fast. Appreciation of the rupee to US dollars may reduce the profit margin of the company.[4]

Eicher Motors have decided to be focused on growing the LCV category to generate voluminous sales. There is no doubt that the LCV market has been growing rapidly and has many well-established players with a major share of the market. In a multiplayer environment, customers shifting from one brand to another are not very uncommon. All the companies are in the process of coming up with unique offers not only to retain its customers but also to encroach the customer base of other companies. Suppose that Eicher Motors is wishes to examine the "brand shift" from Eicher Motors to other companies and vice versa. What kind of research strategy should it opt for? What should be the steps of this research programme? Make a blue print of this research programme. Supposing that you have completed the research task, how will you present the results in a written-report format? What should be the important components in writing a research report? Suppose the company asks you to present the report orally in front of its executives, what will be your preparation to present the major parts of the results? How will you make your oral presentation effective?

NOTES |

1. www.indiastat.com, accessed September 2009. Reprinted with permission.
2. http://www.eicherworld.com/about.aspx?toplink=About+Us&id=1&mid=1, accessed September 2009.
3. http://timesofindia.indiatimes.com/articleshow/1032894.cms, accessed September 2009.
4. Prowess (V. 3.1): Centre for Monitoring Indian Economy Pvt. Ltd, Mumbai, accessed September 2009, reprinted with permission.

PART VI

Applications of Marketing Research

CHAPTER 22

Marketing Mix Research: Product, Price, Place and Promotion Research

LEARNING OBJECTIVES

Upon completion of this chapter, you will be able to:

- Understand the application aspects of market research.
- Understand the meaning of marketing mix and its connection with marketing research.
- Understand the issues pertaining to new-product development research.
- Understand the role of marketing research with respect to pricing dimensions.
- Understand the marketing research inputs required to take different distribution decisions.
- Understand the use of marketing research in making different promotional decisions.

RESEARCH IN ACTION: MAHINDRA RISE

Established in 1945 as a steel trading company, Mahindra & Mahindra (M&M) entered automotive manufacturing in 1947 to bring the iconic Willys Jeep to Indian roads. Over the years, M&M has diversified into many new businesses in order to meet the needs of its customers. M&M follows a unique business model of creating empowered companies that enjoy the best of entrepreneurial independence and group-wide synergies. This principle has led the company's growth into a USD 16.7 billion multinational group with more than 180,000 employees in over 100 countries across the globe.[1]

The company initiated a social marketing movement termed "Spark the Rise," which Anand Mahindra, the chairman and managing director of M&M, termed as Version 3.0 of corporate brand building. Anand Mahindra described "Spark the Rise" as an endeavour to build a 21st century corporation by energizing people and giving them a core purpose to be part of. The focus of "Spark the Rise" is on co-creating with surrounding communities. Highlighting the importance of this philosophy, Anand Mahindra said, "I will take responsibility of this movement. I remain on it. This is much more important than selling four more Scorpios. There are other people who do that better than me at Mahindra."[2]

Mahindra & Mahindra's success story was narrated by Ratan Tata in an address at the Annual General Meeting of Tata Motors. Tata said that he had great respect for the new initiative and achievements of M&M and exhorted his employees to not let a competitor overtake them but to strive hard to be the first in everything that they do.[3]

Let us assume that Mahindra & Mahindra wants to launch a new four-wheeler to cater to the space available in the market. It needs to first determine the marketing mix for placing the product correctly in the market. What steps will it follow to develop an innovative product in the light of the fact that many companies are doing the same exercise? What is the competitive price that the company can offer? How can it make the best use of its existing channels of distribution? Will the company use only existing members of the distribution channel or will it appoint some new channel members for better penetration in the market? What promotional policy will it adopt to promote these products? How will the company assess the effectiveness of the advertisement campaign and other promotional programmes? This chapter is an attempt to develop a knowledge base that will enable us answer all such questions. It deals with issues pertaining to the marketing mix and focuses on product, price, place and promotion as integral parts of the marketing mix.

22.1 INTRODUCTION

We have discussed the different aspects of making and presenting decisions in marketing in the previous chapters. We have also discussed how marketing research is a sequential and interlinked exercise that is difficult to execute without following a defined sequence. Traditionally, the 4Ps of marketing defined by McCarthy in 1964 include **product**, **price**, **place** and **promotion**. This chapter focuses on the information required by a decision maker to take decisions regarding product, price, place and promotion.

Traditionally, the 4Ps of marketing include product, price, place and promotion.

Companies invest heavily on new product development. Marketing research provides companies with inputs to take objective decisions. The pricing of a product is also an important consideration to place and penetrate a product effectively in the market. Information pertaining to various aspects of pricing can also be generated by engaging in marketing research. The place indicates a distribution channel required to make the product available in the market. Distribution involves determining the number and location of warehouses, retail stores and sales personnel. Promotion caters to decisions pertaining to communication with users or potential users or non-users of the product. These aspects are very important for any marketer to take informed decisions to optimize profit and customer satisfaction.

22.2 MARKETING MIX: MEANING

Product particulars incorporate product variety, quality, design, features, brand name, packaging, sizes, services, warranties and returns. Price includes list price discounts, allowances, payment period and credit terms. Place covers channels, coverage, assortments, locations, inventory and transport. Promotion includes sales promotion, advertising, sales force public relations and direct marketing.

McCarthy (1964) first defined **marketing mix** with the help of a combination of four tools, which he called the four Ps of marketing—product, price, place and promotion. Product variables include product variety, quality, design, features, brand name, packaging, sizes, services, warranties and returns. Price includes list price, discounts, allowances, payment period and credit terms. Place covers channels, coverage, assortments, locations, inventory and transport. Promotion includes **sales promotion**, **advertising**, sales force **public relations** and **direct marketing** (Kotler et al. 2009). A marketer always seeks the latest information related to the tools of marketing discussed above. The marketing environment is highly dynamic and inputs from market research is essential for marketers to understand the changing needs of the market. Marketing research acts as a facilitating tool to make effective decisions.

Though the four Ps present a comprehensive discussion of the various elements of marketing, there has been debate on the extension of the concept to include more Ps. Researchers who can be referred to as "traditionalists" argue that the original four Ps are sufficient for dealing with the various dimensions of marketing activity as the addition or deletion of factors is always possible within each P. Another group of researchers who can be referred to as "modernists" suggest that since these Ps were developed way back in 1964, many aspects of each P has completely changed. Hence, there is an urgent need to enhance the traditional list of four Ps. Researchers and academicians claim that during the evolution of the four Ps, the approach was manufacturing focused and customer focus was minimal. They also argue that after the evolution of the four Ps, every decade has been marked by changes in the marketing arena. For example, the use of the Internet for marketing was unimaginable at the time of the development of the traditional four Ps of marketing. Over a period of time, new concepts such as total quality management, services marketing, customer relationship management and e-marketing have also emerged. The inclusion of all these concepts in the traditional four Ps did not seem appropriate and the need was felt to include a few more Ps to make this discussion complete. There has been a lot of debate and research about the sufficiency of the four Ps as a marketing management tool in its original form. Many researchers have proposed alternative approaches by adding new parameters to the original mix or replacing it with alternative frameworks altogether (Goi 2009).

Researchers who can be referred to as "traditionalists" argue that the original four Ps are sufficient for dealing with the various dimensions of marketing activity as the addition or deletion of factors is always possible within each P. Another group of researchers who can be referred to as "modernists" suggest that since these Ps were developed way back in 1964, many aspects of each P has completely changed.

From a **services marketing** perspective, Booms and Bitner (1981) have added three more Ps—**physical evidence, participants and process**. **Physical evidence** refers to physical surroundings and all tangible issues. **Participants** reflect all **people** including employees, channel members, customers, etc. directly or indirectly involved in the marketing or consumption process. **Process** is also a comprehensive phenomenon that involves all the procedures, mechanisms or flow of activities pertaining to the environment where the service is being delivered. Many researchers and experts claim that a list of the four traditional Ps and three more Ps derived from the services marketing point of view make the study and discussion more exhaustive. They felt that there was no need to add another P to cover the wide scope of marketing activities. Over a period of time, importance was given to the customer relationship aspects in marketing. Scholars of **relationship marketing** felt that the list of seven Ps would become more comprehensive with the addition of a tool to factor in the long-term relationships with customers. In order to make the list complete from the relationship marketing point of view, Goldsmith (1999) added one more P (**Personalization)** to make the list of Ps more complete. Theories of marketing management and strategy need to evolve and change to keep pace with the changes in the marketplace and in marketing practice. As the next century draws closer, it is apparent that some marketing managers are basing their relationships with customers on policies and procedures called either "individualization", "mass-customization", or as we prefer, "personalization". The core of this practice involves tailoring goods and services to the individual needs and wants of specific consumers, just the opposite of one-size-fits-all. Personalization is so important to marketing strategy that it should become one of the featured elements of the marketing mix, alongside product, price, promotion, place, personnel, physical assets, and procedures, to form a new marketing mix, the 8Ps (Goldsmith, 1999).

From a services marketing perspective, Booms and Bitner (1981) have added three more Ps—physical evidence, participants and process.

An argument has also emerged to make the list complete from a relationship marketing point of view and Goldsmith has added one more P—Personalization—to make the list of Ps more complete.

The journey of adding more Ps to cover all the dimensions of marketing does not stop over here. The additional three Ps were based on services marketing. Balmer (1998) proposed a list of 11 Ps in the field of **corporate marketing**. Balmer and Greyser (2005) listed it as **Philosophy and Ethos, Product, Price, Place, Performance, Positioning, Personality, Promotion, People, Perception and Promise.** Their scholarly research paper further explains all these 11 components making 11 Ps in the field of corporate marketing. **Philosophy and Ethos** indicates how the organization is constituted and how it executes its work activities to address different issues. **Product** refers to what the organization is making and doing. **Price** is beautifully explained as the emotional and capital asset of the organization. It also includes a valuation of the organization's brands, share price and staff salaries. **Place** widely covers distribution and organizational relationships in terms of the selling and distribution of product and services. **Performance** not only focuses on the quality of product and services but also covers issues related to governance, ethics and social responsibility. **Positioning** indicates the organization's position relative to its competitors in the market. **Personality** is related to the critical role of personnel for corporate marketing activities. **Promotion** incorporates coordinated corporate communications including corporate advertising, corporate PR, visual identification and the like. **People** defines the organization's internal and external constituencies and communities in addition to customers. **Perception** is the image and reputation of the organization by groups, communities and by

The journey of adding more Ps to cover all the dimensions of marketing does not stop over here. The additional three Ps were based on services marketing. Balmer (1998) proposed a list of 11 Ps in the field of corporate marketing. Balmer and Greyser (2005) listed it as Philosophy and Ethos, Product, Price, Place, Performance, Positioning, Personality, Promotion, People, Perception and Promise.

individuals. **Promise** includes fulfilling stakeholder's expectations as well as satisfying the expectation from the organization's point of view.

Understanding marketing from a discussion of Ps sometimes presents a great simplification but some authors tried to make the concept of marketing mix more elaborative. The marketing mix can be explained as the specific collection of actions and associated instruments employed by an organization to stimulate acceptance of its ideas, products, or services. The basic functions included in the mix are product development and policymaking, pricing, channel selection and control, and marketing communications, personal selling, direct marketing, and advertising (Dalrymple and Parsons 2000). This definition is more elaborate as it addresses different issues in marketing management and focuses not only on products but also ideas and services. This stimulus can include any effort done by the marketer to make a product, an idea or services acceptable to customers. This definition travels from developing a marketing mix to ultimately making it acceptable to all the potential customers.

Over a period of time, the understanding of marketing mix has included one more dimension of framing strategy to cater to the needs and demands of customers. The undue focus on the four Ps or many Ps has diverted the attention of the marketer and the market researcher. In a powerful earlier incarnation lodged firmly in the marketing department, marketing essentially referred to the "marketing mix," the set of implementation programs that the firm would develop to address a particular market or market segment. Later, in the era of "strategic marketing", it became clear that the choice of markets and market segments, and the manner in which the firm would position its offerings in those markets and segments, were logically decisions that had to be made prior to designing the marketing mix (Capon and Hulbert 2001). This definition opens the strategic dimension of understanding the marketing mix. This concept focuses on making logical decisions related to the markets. The market segments comes first and then the marketing mix comes into the picture.

Over a period of time, the understanding of marketing mix has included one more dimension of framing strategy to cater to the needs and demands of customers. The undue focus on the four Ps or many Ps has diverted the attention of a marketer and the market researcher.

The four Ps act as the basis of understanding marketing activity and the various dimensions of marketing. A market researcher has to provide inputs to the marketer or organization pertaining to the various decision dimensions mainly emerging from the four Ps. As discussed, the concept of seven Ps, eight Ps and 11 Ps emerged over the years (Table 22.1). Even after the emergence of many Ps in different streams of marketing, the importance of the four Ps remain intact. The four Ps are still the focal point of discussion in many popular books of marketing. The four Ps concept has also been criticized by many experts. As discussed, there has been debate to make the four Ps more extensive and wide. Some experts suggest that each category must be subdivided into more categories. For example, promotion can be subdivided into sales promotion and advertising. Nevertheless, the four Ps offer a memorable,

Since 1964, many researchers and marketers have talked about expanding the scope of the study beyond the four Ps. However, the importance and application of four Ps for study and discussion is unchanged.

TABLE 22.1
Evolution of different Ps with the evolution of different branches of marketing

Orientation	*Number of Ps*	*Description of Ps*	*Authors*
Basic marketing	Four	Product, price, place and promotion	McCarthy (1964)
Services marketing	Seven	Four Ps and physical evidence, participants and process	Booms and Bitner (1981)
Relationship marketing	Eight	Seven Ps and personalization	Goldsmith (1999)
Corporate marketing	Eleven	Philosophy and ethos, product, price, place, performance, positioning, personality, promotion, people, perception and promise	Balmer (1998)

useful guide to the major categories of marketing activity, as well as a framework within which they can be used (Czinkota and Kotabe 2002). Since 1964, many researchers and marketers have talked about expanding the scope of the study beyond the four Ps. However, the importance and application of four Ps for study and discussion is unchanged. After almost 50 years, it is apparent that despite the controversies between the "conservatives" and "revisionists", the basic construction of the four Ps is still valid and, with some extension and adjustment, is still the core of operative decisions (Dominici 2009). In this chapter, we will focus our discussion on the combination of four Ps product, price, place and promotion proposed by McCarthy (1964). The chapter will focus on **new product research**, **pricing research**, place (distribution) research and **promotion research**.

22.3 NEW PRODUCT RESEARCH

Managers hesitate to define a policy to develop a new product as they feel that it is a creative process that should not be shackled by definition or policy. Their hesitation seems to be genuine as any pre-specified policy may disturb the creative and innovative process of new product development. Though the literature related to new product development presents some formal stages in new product development, a strict policy to adhere to is not readily available in the literature. Within the new product development literature, there are a number of studies that seek to identify the factors that determine the outcome of new product development. Generally, a distinction can be made between "generalist" and "specialist" studies. Generalist studies typically include a broad range of possible determinants of new product success and aim at identifying the most important ones among them within an exploratory research design. On the other hand, specialist studies focus on an in-depth analysis of a limited range of determinants of new product success (Gruner and Homburg 2000). Figure 22.1 presents a roadmap to develop a new product. As shown in Figure 22.1, generally, there are eight steps in the new-product development process. These are: new product **idea generation** (need identification and concept identification); **strategic screening of ideas** (revenue and cost analysis); **concept development and testing**; **product development and marketing strategy**; **product testing**; **test marketing, commercialization and post-launch evaluation** (short term and/or long term). The very first step in new product development process is the generation of ideas with two inherent components: need identification and concept identification. Need identification propels need identification research. Concept identification is an activity that is launched to develop a concept for fulfilling the identified need.

> Generalist studies typically include a broad range of possible determinants of new product success and aim at identifying the most important ones among them within an exploratory research design. On the other hand, specialist studies focus on an in-depth analysis of a limited range of determinants of new product success.

> Generally, there are eight steps in the new product development process.

22.3.1 New Product Idea Generation (Need Identification and Concept Identification)

Need identification requires inputs from marketing research. A systematic market research effort is required to cater to the needs of customers. A technique known as **multidimensional scaling** (discussed in Chapter 19) can be used to identify the needs of customers. As discussed in Chapter 19, multidimensional scaling is the process of positioning products in a spatial map or perceptual map with the defined dimensions. This map can be used to generate gaps, which can be used to fit in a potential new product. Though multidimensional scaling is a widely applied technique of need identification, it also suffers from one major drawback. This method can be used to frame user perceptions and preferences in terms of attributes. However, it does not offer the means of going beyond the experience of the users interviewed. First, for reasons discussed above, user subjects are not well positioned to accurately evaluate novel product attributes or "amounts" of familiar product attributes that lie

> Need identification requires inputs from marketing research. A systematic market research effort is required to cater to the needs of customers. A technique known as multidimensional scaling can be used to identify the needs of customers.

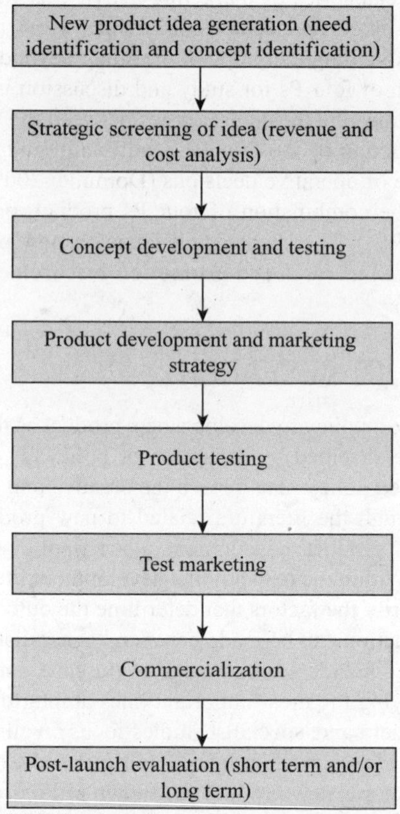

FIGURE 22.1
Stages in new product development research

outside the range of their real-world experience. Second, and more specific to these techniques, there is no mechanism to induce users to identify all product attributes potentially relevant to a product category, especially attributes that are currently not present in any extant category member (Hippel 1986).

In recent years, the **lead user analysis** technique has been adopted to identify customer needs.

In recent years, the **lead user analysis** technique has been adopted to identify customer needs. Hippel (1986) defined "lead users" of a novel or enhanced product, process or service as those who display two characteristics with respect to it:

- Lead users face needs that will be general in a marketplace but face them months or years before the bulk of that marketplace encounters them.
- Lead users are positioned to benefit significantly by obtaining a solution to those needs.

After the identification of lead users, their need data is collected and analysed. The analysed data is then used for addressing the market needs strategically and not directly. This means that the data obtained from the lead users is specified and examined for a special market need and then it is appropriately used for catering to the needs of the customers. Over the past decade, empirical research has shown that, in many fields, users have a great deal more to contribute to the marketing researcher than data regarding their unfilled needs. Often, they can contribute insights regarding solutions responsive to their needs as well. This "solution" data can range from rich insights to working and tested prototypes of the desired novel product, process or service. In some fields, users have been shown to be the actual developers of most of the successful new products eventually commercialized by manufacturers (Urban and Hippel 1988).

The **focus group method** is another technique to identify the needs of customers. In the focus group method, a market researcher calls a group of customers who are familiar with the product and its features for a discussion whose duration is specified in advance. The market researcher acts as a moderator and ensures that the discussion is recorded for later analysis. The issue to be discussed is also specified earlier and it is generally is related to the problems and issues associated with a particular aspect of a product. For example, a market researcher can organize a discussion on some issues related to the launch of a new feature in the product. In this method, sometimes the discussed issues go beyond the issues specified earlier with the deliberate silent approval of the moderator. This kind of discussion provides an opportunity to uncover respondents' feelings not only regarding the existing attributes of the product but also to analyse their opinion about the future requirement of the product or product attributes. Focus group method is largely dependent on the analytical ability of the analyst or researcher, which sometimes makes it very subjective. If issues are perceived correctly by the researcher, the process is effective. Otherwise, the situation becomes very complex for a decision maker.

The **focus group method** is another technique to identify the needs of customers. In the focus group method, a market researcher calls a group of customers who are familiar with the product and its features for a discussion whose duration is specified in advance.

An approach termed as **benefit structure analysis** is also being used to determine the needs of customers in the market, A benefit structure analysis study indicated what types of product characteristics are seen by respondents as being the most closely associated with any single benefit or any group of related benefits. This provides a linkage between benefits and the product characteristics that produce the desired benefits. This provides a "structure" for a particular type of consumer product or service market (Myers 1976). Benefit structure analysis helps in identifying the benefits that a current product is not able to provide. This is very important for a market researcher as it provides a base for the development of a new product.

A benefit structure analysis study shows what types of product characteristics are seen by respondents as being most closely associated with any single benefit or any group of related benefits.

A market researcher has to identify the product needs correctly as heavy investment is incurred by the company on the initial identification. This is a great responsibility and needs to be done at the outset. If the product needs are identified wrongly and the process reaches the commercialization stage, the company will have to bear heavy losses. Figure 22.2 exhibits the cost of failure in new product development research. Marketing researchers face serious difficulties if they attempt to determine new product needs falling outside the real-world experiences of the users they analyse (Hippel 1986).

Marketing researchers face serious difficulties if they attempt to determine new product needs falling outside the real-world experiences of the users they analyse.

Concept identification is also a very important step in new-product development research. A market researcher has to keep a strict surveillance on the changing marketing dimensions and environment to identify the right concept at the right time. For example, the Indian two-wheeler industry is witnessing a shift in terms of consumer preferences for a two-wheeler. The scooter market is shrinking and the motorcycle market is expanding. So, companies are placing more emphasis on the production of motorcycles as compared to scooters and are focusing on features such as the mileage. It is a well-known fact that Indians are very particular about the mileage they receive from their two-wheelers. Hence, most two-wheeler companies are focusing on mileage and their advertisement campaigns also mainly address this issue. So, in this case, the concept identification must not only focus on the production of motorcycles but should also be able to take care of the mileage issue.

Concept identification is also a very important step in new-product development research. A market researcher has to keep a strict surveillance on the changing marketing dimensions and environment to identify the right concept at the right time.

In the concept identification stage, the needs are being identified and a broad concept emerges to cater to the identified needs. An initial idea for new product development is generated. On the basis of the information generated, the researcher can decide whether the concept can be sent for development or whether it must be further refined before it is developed further. In the field of marketing research, conjoint analysis (discussed in Chapter 18) is typically used for concept generation related to the combination of different product attributes. Concept identification generally addresses issues such as the correct identification of the concept; removal of initial flaws and making it appropriate for further processing in terms of the various stages in new product development. A marketing research firm can also

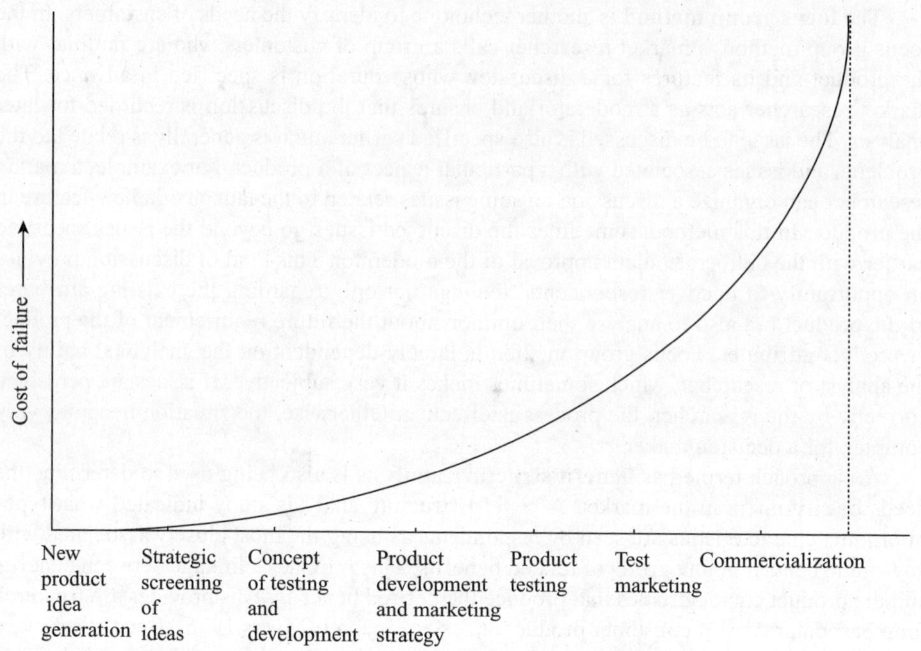

FIGURE 22.2
Cost of failure in new product development

Concept identification generally addresses issues such as the correct identification of the concept; removal of initial flaws and making it appropriate for further processing in terms of the various stages in new product development.

introduce the concept to potential customers to make it more concrete. This will be a type of exploratory research in which a market researcher tries to obtain a potential customer's views and suggestions on the identified concept. The traditional methods of concept identification sometimes make the respondents aware about the concept without considering environment in which the new product will be used. Sometimes, the market researcher finds it difficult to present the complete information. This hinders the process. In some cases, respondents can provide information only after using the product. In such a situation, the presentation of the concept may not generate much information. Nowadays market researchers have also started using modern techniques such as exposing consumers to a virtual buying environment. The new market measurement system combines existing methods with a multi-media virtual buying environment that conditions respondents to future situations, simulates user experiences and encourages consumers to actively search for information on the product (Urban et al. 1996).

The new market measurement system combines existing methods with a multi-media virtual buying environment that conditions respondents to future situations, simulates user experiences and encourages consumers to actively search for information on the product.

22.3.2 Strategic Screening of Ideas (Revenue and Cost Analysis)

Before the concept testing and development stage, the idea generated in stage one has to pass the strategic screening of ideas phase.

Before the concept testing and development stage, the idea generated in stage one has to pass the strategic screening of ideas phase. Among the criteria employed at this point are those related to fit with the business unit's strategy, its core competencies, and the potential of the idea to meet or exceed the unit's growth and profitability objectives (Capon and Hulbert 2001). This stage is termed as the strategic screening of ideas stage as the idea may also be related with the enhanced potential of the company. There is a possibility that a company may be willing to enhance its existing potential with the introduction of the new product in the market. The introduction of a new product may be a part of its development and growth strategy. The ideas generated vary widely in scope and are filtered out to meet the firm's strategy and vision.

The strategic screening of the idea also includes a detailed revenue and cost analysis. This is the stage where the potential of the market must be assessed and a detailed study must be launched to understand the potential profitability of the new product. At this stage, if a market researcher has any doubts about the success of the product, it must be immediately communicated to the firm as the cost incurred up to this stage is not very high and further losses can be prevented. A simple mathematical approach can be adopted to assess market potential. This can be computed using a simple formula

This stage is termed as the strategic screening of ideas stage as the idea may also be related with the enhanced potential of the company.

$$PMP = NPB \times ASP \times ANPB$$

Where

$$PMP = \text{Projected market potential}$$
$$NPB = \text{Number of potential buyers}$$
$$ASP = \text{Average selling price}$$
$$ANPB = \text{Average number purchased by each buyer}$$

For example, a microwave oven company plans to launch a new product in 2015. The company has estimated the number of potential buyers as 50,000; average selling price per unit as ₹7,000 and average number purchased by each buyer as one. For such a situation, the projected market potential can be computed as:

$$PMP = 50{,}000 \times 7{,}000 \times 1 = 35{,}00{,}00{,}000$$

Hence, the project market potential is computed as ₹35 crore. The figure obtained from such a simple method of projection may contain some errors. This figure can be further adjusted by ±10% or ±20% or the adjustment margin decided by the company officials or experts. This stage is extremely important as a wrong estimation will lead to heavy losses for the company. For example, a company realises that the product will not work in the market after investing a huge amount in research and development. This realisation could prove to be very costly for the company because it has already come out with the new product and there is no way to undo the losses that it has started incurring.

The next step is to estimate the cost of new product development. At this stage, where the product has just passed through the initial stage of idea generation, the determination of accurate and actual costs is a difficult exercise. However, it is a very essential part of the product development stage. The cost includes development cost, cost related to new product penetration efforts, cost related to promotional efforts including advertisement and selling expenses, distribution expenses, overheads and many miscellaneous expenses. The right estimation of costs is important at this stage before the company moves to the next stage of concept testing and development. Marketing researchers provide inputs to ensure that the costs estimated are close to the real cost. An analysis of the competitors' costs incurred in developing a similar type of product is also a helpful technique in determining the cost of new product development. Cost estimation is the start of the cost management process and influences the "go," or "no go" decisions concerning new product development (Rush and Roy 2000). The various cost estimation techniques can be broadly divided into qualitative and quantitative techniques. Qualitative techniques are helpful either in furnishing rough cost estimates or serve as a decision-aid tool for designers or estimators especially during the early phases of the design process. However, when the detailed design becomes available, quantitative techniques provide more accurate estimates, which are necessary for factors such as design rationalization, determination of profit margins, etc. (Niazi et al. 2006). Qualitative techniques use past information and are very helpful in generating cost estimates when detailed information about the product is not available. Qualitative techniques can be further divided into intuitive cost estimation techniques and analogical cost

At this stage, where the product has just passed through the initial stage of idea generation, the determination of accurate and actual costs is a difficult exercise. However, it is a very essential part of the product development stage.

The cost includes development cost, cost related to new product penetration efforts, cost related to promotional efforts including advertisement and selling expenses, distribution expenses, overheads and many miscellaneous expenses.

estimation techniques. Intuitive techniques covers case-based methodology and decision-support systems. The case-based methodology uses the design of an old product, which is similar to the new product for estimating the cost of the new product. Decision-support systems are helpful in evaluating design alternatives. The main purpose of these systems is to assist estimators in making better judgments and decisions at different levels of the estimation process by making use of the stored knowledge of experts in the field (Niazi et al. 2006). The analogical cost estimation technique covers a traditional approach known as regression technique. This technique is based on the linear relationship between the cost of a product and some independent variable. This relationship and the information available for the past product is used to forecast the cost of a new product.

22.3.3 Concept Development and Testing

Concept development and testing is different from idea generation. A product idea refers to the possible product that a company can offer to the market. On the other hand, concept development is an extended version of the idea that is presented to a consumer in his or her own way of understanding.

Concept development and testing is different from idea generation. A product idea refers to the possible product that a company can offer to the market. On the other hand, concept development is an extended version of the idea that is presented to a consumer according to his or her understanding. Concept development and testing is also an important stage of the new product development process. The difference between an idea and a concept can be explained with the help of an example. Suppose a four-wheeler manufacturer is looking to launch an SUV at an affordable price for a new segment of customers. This is the idea generated by the company. This product development idea can be categorized in many ways. A market researcher has to address many issues. The first and most important issue is to identify the segment of customers who will buy the product. Second, how will the proposed new product be different from the existing products in the market? Third, why will the potential customer buy this new product when there are already many established products in the market? Fourth, what will be the right time to introduce the product in the market? Hence, a basic idea concerning the introduction of a new product has been categorized in several addressable concepts. The first concept explores the exact customer segment that will be mainly attracted by the new product. A market researcher can provide information on this issue. A systematic market study can reveal that after liberalization and globalization, an affluent middle class has emerged in India, which is looking out to buy an SUV. The second concept may address the issue of discovering the difference that this new product can offer. A market researcher can provide the input that even with fewer features, customers may like to purchase a vehicle that looks like an SUV in a reasonable price range and with enhanced mileage. This leads to the brand positioning concept. A perceptual map can be used to compare the offering of this new brands with other available brands. The third concept forces a market researcher to establish the notable difference between the new proposed product and the existing products in the market. A market researcher may discover that price and mileage may be the two major differentiating features of the new product that can be used to penetrate the market. The market researcher can also provide information regarding the right time to introduce the product in the market. A systematic study should be undertaken for discovering the right time for product introduction. A market researcher can reveal that Indians have the tendency to purchase products during the festive season especially during Diwali. There are regional differences even in the festive season across the country. A market researcher can advice the company about these regional differences.

Concept testing is the presentation of the product concept symbolically or physically to potential consumers to obtain their feedback on the different characteristics of the product.

Concept testing is the presentation of the product concept symbolically or physically to potential consumers to obtain their feedback on the different characteristics of the product. Concept testing must relate to the proposed new product so that it is an effective exercise. This is the stage when many cost considerations come into the picture. Allocating resources at this early stage poses quite a challenge considering the inherent uncertainty. In particular, uncertainty arises from imperfect information about customers and markets, undiscovered or untested product designs and technologies, and the challenges of perfectly executing and delivering even an ideal design. Concept tests help resolve this uncertainty and encompass most methods used to measure the performance of new products and processes along with the dimensions affecting profitability (Dahan and Mendelson 2001).

As discussed, concept testing is an exercise in which a market researcher presents an elaborate version of an idea that has already been generated in stage one. For example, a market researcher can select a group of potential purchasers and interact with them in a virtual environment for discussing the special features offered by the company. For an easy to manufacture and bulk retail selling capacity product, a physical experience can also be provided. Market researchers collect information on different dimensions of the product and use it for testing the viability of the product. Market researchers collect information to analyse the acceptability of the product, the need for the product and purchase intentions for the product. Market researchers also undertake a gap analysis to fill the gap between consumer's expectations and the new product.

Market researchers collect information to analyse the acceptability of the product, the need for the product and purchase intentions for the product. Market researchers also undertake a gap analysis to fill the gap between consumer's expectations and the new product.

22.3.4 Product Development and Marketing Strategy

After passing through the first three stages of product development, a company reaches a very important stage of development. Even in the 1990s, scholars clearly identified the importance of bringing products early in the market. In today's highly competitive environment, those who are slow in bringing new products to market often lose out to those with a more agile development process (Smith 1990). This is a crucial stage where a firm has to make heavy investments. In the hurry to release products as early as possible in the market, the probability of committing mistakes (in terms of producing lower quality products) also become very high. The speedy development of products can also lead to more expenses in research and development leading to high costs of development. Hence, a careful approach needs to be adopted.

In today's highly competitive environment, those who are slow in bringing new products to market often lose out to those with a more agile development process.

A defined gap exists between idea generation and the final development of the product. This gap may consist of many years and millions of rupees in research expenses. It is very important for a market researcher to provide authentic and accurate information in the initial stages as the product is developed on the basis of these inputs only. Any misappropriation in providing quality information can lead to a disaster for the firm developing a new product. If a company's problems earlier were due to little new product development activity, problems now arise due to too much or rather too much unstructured and uncontrolled new product development activity (Bessant and Francis 1997). Every industry nowadays has become technological driven and technology is changing very fast. The firm launching a new product must learn to cope up with the changing technology. The unpredictability of customer requirements and competitor strategies in high-tech industries would require: (1) use of step-wise new-product development processes, (2) establishment of a stable though not exhaustive business case, (3) full integration of customers, and (4) higher specialization as opposed to cross-functional collaboration (Harmancioglu et al. 2007).

Any misappropriation in providing quality information can lead to a disaster for the firm developing a new product.

It is important to understand that in a rush to launch a new product as early as possible companies should not discard the organized and systematic way of introducing a product to the market. It is also true that products now have a shorter life cycle as compared to some 20–30 years ago. India, especially after liberalization, has witnessed a tremendous change in the buying and consumption pattern. The demand of people has also been changing rapidly. For example, in the early and late nineties, there were only a few players in the consumer electronics segment. Liberalization, globalization and privatization has opened up opportunities in the market and the market scenario has completely changed. This has posed new challenges and opportunities for indigenous firms. So, the environment itself is fostering the speedy development of new products. Takeuchi and Nonaka (1986), in their article published in the *Harvard Business Review* clearly stated that speed and flexibility are essential in today's fast-paced, fiercely competitive world of commercial new product development. Companies are increasingly realising that the old, sequential approach to developing new products simply won't get the job done. Instead, companies in Japan and the United States are using a holistic method—as in rugby, the ball gets passed within the team as it moves as a unit up the field. This holistic approach has six characteristics: built-in instability, self-organizing project teams, overlapping development phases, multilearning, subtle control and organizational transfer of learning.

In the market strategy stage, the idea has completed its transformation into a physical product. Technical and design problems are resolved and consumer reaction is gauged in order to develop entry strategies.

In the **market strategy stage**, the idea has completed its transformation into a physical product. Technical and design problems are resolved and consumer reaction is gauged in order to develop entry strategies. During this stage, the emphasis shifts from technical to market concerns as the product approaches commercialization (Yelkur and Herbig 1996). After passing through the product development stage, a firm has to make a sound marketing strategy to gain a competitive advantage in the market. Marketing strategy is not only focused on the internal environment that is controllable up to one extent. Rather, a sound marketing strategy has to deal with many uncontrollable external marketing variables. Innovation in marketing strategies is the key to gain success in the marketplace. However, this is also not a guarantee for success in the market. New ventures must develop innovative strategies but the possession of an innovative strategy does not assure commercial success of a product. Rather, consistent with the contingent resource-based view of the firm, the productive capacity of marketing strategy innovativeness (MSI) is determined by its congruency with other organizational capabilities and the environmental conditions (Atuahene-Gima et al. 2006). Hence, the marketing strategy actually relates to how a firm appropriately positions its product in the market in the light of many intervening and impacting internal and external constraints. A market researcher can provide information for making a sound marketing strategy and ultimately implementing it. Marketing strategy for a new product can broadly be divided into three parts (Kotler et al. 2009). A broad marketing strategy covers target market, size of the target market, positioning of the product, its sales plans, market share, penetration strategy, and profit generation for the initial few years as the first part. The second part covers planned price, distribution strategy and marketing budget. The third part includes long-run sales, profit goals and marketing mix strategies. The level of relative efficiency of the firm's marketing strategy influences the new product's performance level not only directly but also by interacting with market condition variables, such as the degree of competitiveness of the market, stage of the product life cycle, and market growth rate (Yoon and Lilien 1985).

22.3.5 Product Testing

After a successful journey passing through the first four stages, the product is launched in the market in the product testing stage. Market researchers investigate the feedback of the customers regarding the new product. Customer acceptance is the key and this must be assessed thoroughly. It is critical at this stage to measure whether the product is acceptable to the customer, to measure the customer's level of interest, liking, preferences, and intent to purchase, and to determine those benefits, attributes, and features of the product to which the customer responds (Bhuiyan 2011). Even though a lot of expenditure has been incurred by the firm at this stage, customer approval is vital. This is vital as non-approval will give a signal to a firm to either modify or completely stop the production process. It has been observed that many products fail at this stage due to non-approval or low approval by the customers.

It is also important that there should not be any hurry to make any new product a success. A market researcher has to spend a considerable amount of time to determine customer approval as sometimes an initial non-response gets converted into a huge response after some time. A market researcher may face several problems at this stage. There is the possibility of respondents providing misleading opinions about the product due to their lack of awareness about the product. Sometimes a free sample provided by the firm during the introduction stage may have distorted customer opinion. There is also the possibility of customers providing an inflated opinion about the purchase. Customers can provide random answers about their purchase intention and in the end they may not even purchase the product. Marketing strategy is not only focused on the internal environment, which is controllable only up to some extent. Rather, a sound marketing strategy has to deal with many uncontrollable external marketing variables. Innovation in marketing strategies is the key to gain success in the marketplace. A rational customer opinion about purchase intention is also very important as any wrong estimate about future purchase intention may lead to a misleading projection of future purchase.

Marketing strategy is not only focused on the internal environment that is controllable up to one extent. Rather, a sound marketing strategy has to deal with many uncontrollable external marketing variables. Innovation in marketing strategies is the key to gain success in the marketplace.

In order to determine consistency in purchase intention, a market researcher has to take a consistent approach after analysing trial purchase, repeat purchase, final adoption and frequency purchase. This is important to avoid speedy conclusions about the purchase of the new product and making blunders on the basis of conclusions drawn from premature marketing research. Some techniques like sales-wave research and simulated store techniques are often used to determine repeat purchase pattern of the customers. In the sales-wave technique, the firm offering the new product offer some incentives (may be some discount in price) as compared to the competitor's product and observes repeat purchase behaviour by the customers. In a simulated store technique, purchasers are allowed to purchase and are asked about their intention to repeat the purchase. These purchasers can also be interviewed to judge their future purchase or repeat purchase.

In order to determine consistency in purchase intention, a market researcher has to take a consistent approach after analysing trial purchase, repeat purchase, final adoption and frequency purchase. This is important to avoid speedy conclusions about the purchase of the new product and making blunders on the basis of conclusions drawn from premature marketing research.

22.3.6 Test Marketing

Test marketing is the process of conducting an experiment in a field setting. Companies generally launch test market strategy in selected parts of the market referred to as the test markets. Test marketing is discussed in detail in Section 8.11 of Chapter 8.

22.3.7 Commercialization

Figure 22.2 clearly indicates that this stage involves the highest risk among the product development stages. The commercialization stage consists of a list of all the activities that need to be undertaken for moving a product to market after it successfully passes through the first six stages of product development. Time is a major consideration when a new product needs to be introduced in the market. For example, the introduction of a new statistical software program in the market may be a really difficult exercise for the producer. Like any other product, this product has to pass through several phases of development. Obviously, it will take a long time to make a novel product that is acceptable in the market. In such a case, there is a severe threat of the product becoming obsolete in the market as it has to go through different stages of development that could involve several months or years. Such problems are very common in the fashion industry, software and hardware industry and many such industries. It has to be noted that the problem of obsolescence can prove to be very challenging for more stable industries such as the consumer electronics industry and the automobile industry. For example, almost two decades ago, the Indian automobile industry was dominated by a few major Indian players like Maruti, Tata and Mahindra. This situation changed completely when the Indian markets were liberalized. The market was thrown open to all the leading automobile companies of the world. Global auto giants were keen to cater to the large and ever expanding customer base of the country. Though this was an opportunity for Indian players, it also posed a threat with respect to the new product development time

The commercialization stage consists of a list of all the activities that need to be undertaken for moving a product to market after it successfully passes through the first six stages of product development.

available with the Indian players. The leading global players were ready to capture the market with their established research and development departments. So, the timing of placement of the product in the market is also an extremely important factor. Most of the commercialization failures occurred because the idea or its timing was wrong (Griffin 1997).

A firm has two popular options when it plans to enter a market. It can either act as an initiator or as a follower. An initiator has to spend a lot of energy and resources to enter the market. There is also a considerable amount of risk associated with failure in the market. This also gives the firm an opportunity to become the market leader and generate great profits over a long period. The firm also gets to keep the technical know-how and obtain the copyright or patent for it. The follower approach presents the reverse opportunity. The initiator firm has already explored the market and the viability of the product has already been established in the market. Hence, the risk is now minimized and the follower firm can enter the market in relative comfort.

Another consideration related to product commercialization is the market to be targeted. The firm has to decide whether it would like to launch the new product for a small market, a regional market or the national market. This depends upon the size and the capacity of the firm launching the new product. A small firm may launch the product in a few selected markets whereas a large firm may to cater to the national market. For example, Maruti has a strong dealer network in all parts of India. So, launching a product nationally is a routine exercise for the company as it has the strength to do so. The firm also has to decide to whom the product should be targeted. Some companies fix a specific target group for facilitating early penetration in the market. This helps them in attracting early adopters who can actually become opinion leaders for the relatively late adopters. Last, the firm developing the new product has to chalk out an effective marketing strategy to make the product acceptable and adoptable in the market.

Though commercialization is an important stage in the established process of new product development, the stage cannot be independently assessed or evaluated without considering the previously interlinked stages. By understanding the contribution of each potential driver in the product development decision process, an organization can assess the strengths and weaknesses of the organization, the new product development technology itself, and the environmental surrounding the technology to drive effective new product development. The iterative assessment of each of these factors on a continual basis is necessary throughout the product development process to ensure that logical, effective and efficient decisions are made (Baltz et al. 2012). The market researcher here can provide valuable information for making an optimum decision.

22.3.8 Post-Launch Evaluation (Short Term and/or Long Term)

After the launch, the evaluation of the launch is also a critical step in the new-product development process. This is treated differently by different authors. Some authors treat it as an interlinked stage while some others do not consider it as an interlinked stage in new product development and tend to treat it separately. Evaluation can be short term as well as long term. A short-term evaluation is important to find out easily identifiable shortcomings of the product, which can be corrected easily. A long-term evaluation is important to identify the gaps in customers' needs, wants and product offerings. This may be an important factor for launching a new product again or extending an existing product line.

> Evaluation can be short term as well as long term. A short-term evaluation is important to find out easily identifiable shortcomings of the product, which can be corrected easily. A long-term evaluation is important to identify the gaps in customers' needs, wants and product offerings.

A review of the recent business and other publications suggests that companies are also using the following new-product evaluation methods: (1) brand-equity analysis, (2) need/usage context analysis, (3) environmental scanning, (4) portfolio approach, (5) pattern recognition, (6) the Internet, (7) alliances, (8) value-chain approach, and (9) straight judgment/vicarious input (Ozer 1999). In brand-equity analysis, the firm focuses on assessing the brand equity of the new product. New products are developed taking into account the needs of customers and tend to satisfy these needs. Need/usage context analysis is done to assess whether the new product is able to satisfy the needs of customers or not. Environment scanning can also provide valuable inputs for the evaluation of the new product. This can identify gaps that can be used to further refine the new product. Companies generally generate a product line with the use of the same technology. It is important for the firm to evaluate new products on a different product line portfolio. This approach can also provide information about the need for a better product line, which can be developed using the same technology. The access to information through various sources of information is not as difficult as it was may be some 30 years ago. This pool of information can be used to forecast emerging patterns in the market. For example, Indian companies have realised that scooters are becoming obsolete in the two-wheeler market. As a result, the scooter manufacturers in India are now focusing on the motor-cycle market. Similarly, the SUVs have become popular in the Indian four-wheeler market. As a result, Mahindra has come out with many affordable mini SUVs such as the different variants of "Quanto" to create a new market segment. The Internet has also become an important tool for new product evaluation. For example, many software companies use the Internet to test their new software prototypes. Market alliances help a firm to operate successfully in the uncertain new product launch environment. Alliances also allow a firm to minimize the risk of launching a product by sharing the risk of launching a product. As part of the value chain, the opinions of wholesale **distributors**, distributors, dealers and **retailers** must be sought to evaluate a new product in the market. The discussion presents the market researcher with an opportunity to provide relevant, authentic and accurate information at all the stages.

22.4 PRICING RESEARCH

Pricing is a very important topic in the current tough economic environment. It is a vital part of framing a market strategy. As discussed earlier, price is one of the four elements of the traditional marketing mix. Price is not only an important element of marketing mix, it is also different from the other three elements of the marketing mix. Product, place and promotion are the activities mainly linked with providing value to a customer. Value can be defined broadly as the benefits or satisfaction that a customer derives from the product. So, these three elements of the marketing mix actively create value for the product or services. In fact, price harvests the value created by the other three elements of the marketing mix. Therefore, price is an important parameter that the firm should deal with effectively. Among the four elements of the marketing mix, product, place, promotion and price, only price creates income while the other three elements generate costs. Price, besides creating income, plays a major role as a strategic factor in developing competitive advantage in the market. The income of a company and its position in the mind of customers are related to suitable pricing strategies (Zaribaf 2008).

> Price is not only an important element of marketing mix, it is also different from the other three elements of the marketing mix.

There are many factors affecting the pricing policies of firms. These factors are different from new-product pricing strategies. Broadly, the factors influencing the pricing strategy of a firm can be categorized into **organizational factors**, **customer factors** and **market factors**. The organizational factors can further be grouped into product life cycle pricing, **product portfolio pricing**, **product line pricing** and **pricing for market segmentation**. Customer factors can be grouped into **demand pricing**, **benefit pricing**, **value pricing** and **place pricing**. The factors related to the market can also be grouped into **competitive pricing**, **pricing in economic and regulatory environment**, **exchange rate pricing** and **geographical pricing** (Czinkota and Kotabe 2002). Most firms adopt a different approach to price their new products. The popular pricing techniques for a new product are: **skimming pricing**, **penetration pricing** and **value-in-use pricing**.

> Broadly, the factors influencing the pricing strategy of a firm can be categorized into organizational factors, customer factors and market factors.

22.4.1 Organizational Factors

Organizational factors are related to the life cycle of a product, product portfolio, product line, and segmentation and positioning.

While taking a decision on pricing a product, many factors remain beyond the control of a firm. However, some factors are related to organizations and can be controlled by the firm relatively. These factors are related to the life cycle of a product, product portfolio, product line, and segmentation and positioning. This section focuses on these four controllable organizational factors related to pricing.

22.4.1.1 Product Life Cycle Pricing

Every product passes through different stages in the product life cycle as exhibited in Figure 22.3. Traditionally, these stages include introduction, growth, maturity and decline. A firm has to take these stages into consideration when fixing a price. At the introduction stage, a firm can fix a high price and obtain the initial market share. At the growth and maturity stage, the price can be relatively lower than the introduction period. At the stage of decline, the firm can either a fix higher price to milk the product revenue or it can fix a low price to ensure maximum purchase of the product. At the stage of decline, the firm can also offer a discount to cater to the closing stages of the product life cycle. The pricing strategy adopted by a firm is usually situation specific. It has to change its strategy according to the different stages in the product life cycle. The main application suggested for the product life cycle is to plan changes in marketing strategy as the product moves from one stage to another. It follows that the product life cycle would be more useful in strategy planning if one could more accurately forecast the time when a product moves across the different phases of the product life cycle (Rink and Swan 1979).

Product life-cycle management enables companies to leverage their investments in product-related intellectual and physical assets and are the vehicles to reduce cost, provide solid return on investment and enable product and process innovation.

It is obvious that a firm has to chalk down a specific pricing strategy to cater to the market according to the different stages of the product life cycle. Some authors have questioned the stages in the product life cycle described above and have proposed the new stages: Innovation, Imitation, Repetition and Substitution. This approach defines the new **product life-cycle** phases based on some key consumer trends during product market evolution, resulting in a four-phased product life cycle model: Innovation → Imitation → Repetition → Substitution. New marketing strategy implications emerge for each phase due to this additional focus on consumers (Steffens 2002). The market researcher can provide valuable information that

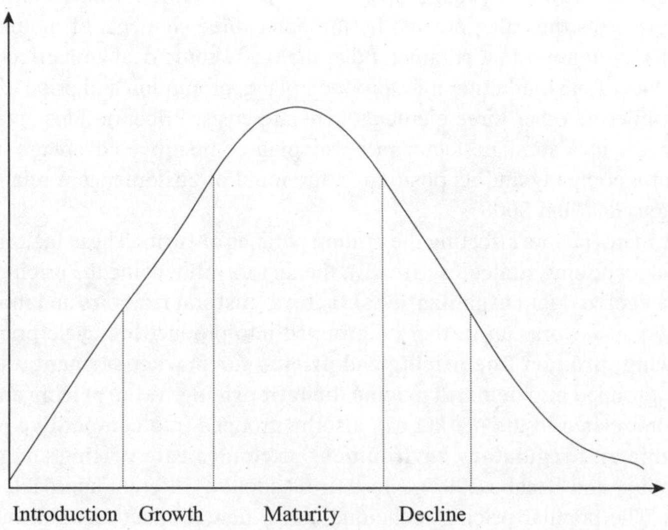

FIGURE 22.3
Stages in the product life cycle

will help the firm tackle the market during the different stages of the product life cycle. Pricing is the key to manage the product life cycle. Today, product life-cycle management is widely recognized as a business necessity. Product life-cycle management enables companies to leverage their investments in product-related intellectual and physical assets and are the vehicles to reduce cost, provide solid return on investment and enable product and process innovation (Liu and Maletz 2009).

22.4.1.2 Product Portfolio Pricing

Product portfolio pricing enables a firm to practice a balanced pricing strategy by fixing different prices for the different products available in its portfolio so that the overall combined impact is optimal. A firm can adopt the approach of fixing a relatively higher price for a product that is popular and a relatively lower price for a product that is not so popular. For example, companies that manufacture air conditioners come out with a variety of models with slight differences in features in the summer. Pricing is also a factor when a varied option is given to consumers. All leading companies showcase their different models with prices on their Web sites.

22.4.1.3 Product Line Pricing

It is widely believed that product variety increases a firm's market power, which further increases a firm's profit margin and market share (Hopp and Xu 2005). While deciding the pricing of different product lines, a firm has to be careful about demand switch in the same product line. For example, consumer electronics companies these days come out with a number of variants of the same product. If there is a big difference in the price, then there is the possibility of a customer picking the product with the lower price or the higher price perceiving a better quality at the higher price. This impacts the demand or acceptance of the other products in the product line. There is a common feeling that the profit margins are higher if a firm is able to offer a variety of products in the market. However, a few scholars have termed product proliferation as double-edged sword. A firm with a long product line may be able to obtain a high market share, but it can also end up with higher prices (due to the higher costs of the broad product line). These higher prices, in turn, put downward pressure on the firm's market share (Bayus and Putsis 1999). Market research can provide information about customer perceptions and behaviour for the different price ranges fixed for the different products of a product line.

Market research can provide information about customer perceptions and behaviour for the different price ranges fixed for the different products of a product line.

22.4.1.4 Pricing for Market Segmentation and Brand Positioning

Market segmentation is a crucial marketing strategy. It enables the marketing manager to divide total demand into relatively homogeneous segments identified by geographic, demographic, psychological or behavioural variables. These characteristics are relevant in explaining and in predicting the response of consumers, in a given segment, to marketing stimuli (Tynan and Drayton 1987). A firm should not segment a market just for the sake of convenience. The rational of segmentation must first be analysed and only then must it be taken as a strategic alternative. All market segmentation strategies are based on three basic assumptions(Hunt and Arnett 2004):

Market segmentation is a crucial marketing strategy. It enables the marketing manager to divide total demand into relatively homogeneous segments identified by geographic, demographic, psychological or behavioural variables.

- Many markets are significantly, but not completely, heterogeneous regarding consumers' needs, wants, use requirements, tastes, and preferences, and, therefore, can be divided into smaller, meaningful, relatively homogeneous segments of consumers.
- A firm's market offerings (here, including price, promotion, and channels) can often be designed to meet the needs, wants, tastes, and preferences of such segments.

- For many firms, a strategy of targeting specific segments can lead to competitive advantages in the marketplace and, in turn, superior financial performance.

Market segmentation can be based on different parameters. Segmentation can be carried out on the basis of a specific category of buyers and prices can be fixed by keeping the needs and demands of this category of customers in mind.

Market segmentation can be based on different parameters. Segmentation can be carried out on the basis of a specific category of buyers and prices can be fixed by keeping the needs and demands of this category of customers in mind. The location can also be used to segment markets and different pricing strategies can be framed for different locations. For example, a cement manufacturing company can fix a lower price for a city that is close to its plant as the freight charges will be lower. Obviously, freight is the main determinant of price in cement marketing. The timing of purchase can also acts as the basis for segmentation. In India, all leading companies come out with lucrative price discount offers during the festive season. The quantity of purchase also offers another method of segmentation and pricing. Many Indian national banks offer different interest rates according to the amount invested. Many industrial product manufacturers often offer a discount price for bulk purchases. Product design is also an important basis of segmentation. For example, water purifier companies fix different prices for home users and industrial users. For all segmentation strategies, market researchers can provide important information to decide the pricing strategy that can effectively cater to the market.

Positioning is a subjective activity that is based on the perception of consumers and not the reality that the consumer encounters.

Brand positioning relates to creating a perception about the brand in the customer's mind, which differentiates it from the offerings of the competitors and also meets the consumer's needs/expectations. A brand marketer's main objective should be to create the desired perception in the target consumer's mind (Ghodeswar 2008). Clearly, positioning is a subjective activity that is based on the perception of consumers and not the reality that the consumer encounters. An important aspect of a brand's positioning in a product category is how similar or different the brand is perceived to be in comparison with other brands in a product category (Sujan and Bettman 1989). A company can adopt different measures to position its brand in the minds of consumers. It has to ensure that its customers are positively influenced by its brand. This should be done in a systematic manner. Thought it is difficult to make a positive perception about a product, it is difficult for a competitor to break it once it is made. Positioning is the way company wants customers to perceive, think and feel about its brand versus competitive entries. According to such a perspective, brand positioning is highly subjective since it refers to the customer's individual perceptions (Janiszewska and Insch 2012).

A brand is a distinguishing name and/or symbol (such as logo, trademark, or package design) intended to identify the goods or services of either one seller or a group of sellers, and to differentiate those goods or services from those of competitors.

A brand is a distinguishing name and/or symbol (such as logo, trademark, or package design) intended to identify the goods or services of either one seller or a group of sellers, and to differentiate those goods or services from those of competitors (Ghodeswar 2008). As discussed earlier, brand positioning is an individual's perception about the brand and is not linked with the features or importance of product or services offerings. It is not an activity based on developing better products, rather it is a managerial activity to position a product properly in the mind of a customer. So, positioning is a managerial activity shaping the perceived value of a product prevalent in society. For example, companies are adopting an environment friendly approach to position a brand. This is referred to as green branding A green brand identity is defined by a specific set of brand attributes and benefits related to the reduced environmental impact of the brand and its perception as being environmentally sound. A well-implemented green branding identity should provide benefits to environmentally conscious consumers (Hartmann et al. 2005). Green branding offers a differentiation to customers and highlights the special positioning effort of the brand as more environment friendly. Green branding is a systematic effort to position a product differently by highlighting its environment friendly attributes.

For sound positioning, the evaluation of the positioning efforts is an important factor that cannot be ignored. Managers will have to develop some tools to measure the effectiveness of positioning. Positioning effectiveness can be defined as the extent to which consumers perceive a brand to occupy a favorable, differentiated and credible position in the minds of consumers (Fuchs and Dianantopoulos 2010). For measuring the effectiveness of positioning, the behavior pattern of consumers can be constantly observed. A consumer influenced by the positioning effort of a company will be less likely to shift to a competitor's product irrespective of the efforts undertaken by the competitor which produces a similar type of product. The mindset of brand users may be another way of assessing the effectiveness of the positioning effort. A customer's mindset refers to his or her's assessment about the features and quality of the product and services as compared to the offerings provided by competitors. A positive mindset indicates good positioning for the brand in the minds of customers. A customer's dependency on the brand is also an indicator for measuring brand effectiveness. When a brand provides high value, it occupies a place in the customer's life and the customer develops an emotional bonding with the brand. Brand equity can also be a very good measure of positioning effectiveness.

For sound positioning, the evaluation of the positioning efforts is an important factor that cannot be ignored. Managers will have to develop some tools to measure the effectiveness of positioning.

22.4.2 Customer Factors

One of the main considerations for price determination is to know how much a customer is willing to pay for a particular product. For example, many studies in India are suggesting that the disposable income levels have increased. This presents an opportunity to a manufacturer for offering different products to effectively explore different levels of disposable income customers available in the market. This section will focus discussion on demand pricing, benefit pricing, value pricing and place pricing.

One of the main considerations for price determination is to know how much a customer is willing to pay for a particular product.

22.4.2.1 Demand Pricing

Price fixing on the basis of customer demand is a very simple and widely applied phenomenon. When demand is high, a high price can be fixed and a low demand will force a firm to fix a low price. For example, many companies launch mega housing projects in India and abroad. It is obvious that the demand is high for housing projects in the premium locations of any city. This opportunity is used by the service provider to fix a higher price. Such a high price cannot be fixed for a non-premium location even with the same construction cost. Hence, a high demand gives a firm the freedom to leverage profit. A careful approach must be adopted as an extremely high price will put off customers and they will start looking for alternative options.

Price fixing on the basis of customer demand is a very simple and widely applied phenomenon.

22.4.2.2 Benefit Pricing

Benefit pricing is based on the assumption that the customer will be ready to pay an additional price for additional product features that he sees or perceives are not available in the other products. Here, it is important to understand that sometimes the benefit is actually a perception of the customer and he is ready to pay extra for the perceived benefit. A firm has to discover what a consumer perceives as an extra benefit. Sometimes, customers believe that a particular brand provides extra benefits such as quality and they readily pay more for this extra benefit.

Benefit pricing is based on the assumption that the customer will be ready to pay an additional price for additional product features that he sees or perceives are not available in the other products.

22.4.2.3 Value Pricing

A benefit is the value that a customer seeks from a product and is ready to pay for. Customer value-based pricing approaches use the value a product or service delivers to a predefined segment of customers as the main factor for setting prices. The key to sustained profitability

Customer value-based pricing approaches use the value a product or service delivers to a predefined segment of customers as the main factor for setting prices.

lies in the essential features of customer value-based pricing, including understanding the sources of value for customers; designing products, services, and solutions that meet customers' needs; setting prices as a function of value; and implementing consistent pricing policies (Hinterhuber 2008).

Value pricing is also based on the theory of "perceived value" that a product derives in the eyes of potential customers.

Value pricing is also based on the theory of "perceived value" that a product derives in the eyes of potential customers. For generating differential value-based pricing, it is very important that a firm creates a specific, differential value for the product. A firm has to generate capacity to obtain the advantage of value-based pricing. The implementation of value-based pricing is contingent on five distinct types of capabilities working together to understand and communicate value: capabilities in value assessment, capabilities in value communication, capabilities in market segmentation, capabilities in sales force management, and, finally, capabilities in leadership (Hinterhuber and Bertini 2011).

22.4.2.4 Place Pricing

The place or in other words the distribution channel plays a key role in determining the final price that is offered to a customer.

In some cases, a manufacturing firm alone cannot decide on the pricing of a product. The place, or in other words, the distribution channel plays a key role in determining the final price offered to a customer. For example, we see that in many purchase transactions, the distributer or even the retailer sells the product at a price that is different from the displayed MRP (maximum retail price). Though the product displays the MRP, the minimum price of selling is not indicated. This price is a localized type of price and varies from one shop to another. Some companies offer special incentive plans for distributors for bulk sales. In order to avail this benefit, distributors pass some discount to retailers and retailers also pass some price discount to the end users. Therefore, there is a possibility that different end users are being offered different prices.

22.4.3 Market Factors

Market factors can broadly be categorized as competitive pricing; pricing in economic and regulatory environment; exchange rate pricing and geographical pricing.

As discussed, pricing cannot be determined in isolation and many factors play a decisive role in determining the price of a product in the market. The first two sections focused on organizational factors and customer factors as the determinants of a firm's pricing policy. This section will focus on the market itself as a key determinant of pricing strategies. Market factors can broadly be categorized as competitive pricing; pricing in economic and regulatory environment; exchange rate pricing and geographical pricing.

22.4.3.1 Competitive Pricing

The competitor's price for a product is a compelling factor that needs to be taken into consideration for fixing the final price.

The competitor's price for a product is a compelling factor that needs to be taken into consideration for fixing the final price. In a competitive marketplace, the effectiveness of any element of the marketing mix is determined not only by its absolute value, but also by its relative value with respect to the competition. For example, the effectiveness of a price cut in increasing demand is critically related to competitors' reaction to the price change (Sudhir 2001).

A firm has to devise a strategy related to pricing after taking the competitors' strategy into consideration. No firm can operate in isolation by ignoring the price strategy of a rival firm. A competitive strategy requires a firm to be positioned in the marketplace in such a way that the value of its most outstanding capabilities is maximized (Natter and Hruschka 1998). The rivalry in the market creates the need for competitive strategies including pricing strategies that can be used to defend a firm's position in the industry (Fratto et al. 2006).

22.4.3.2 Pricing in Economic and Regulatory Environment

The prevailing economic environment of the country is a determining factor in deciding the price of a product. Liberalization, privatization and globalization in India have opened the markets for firms from across the globe. This has really benefitted the Indian consumer as many options from across the globe are available to them. Such an environment has also impacted the price regime of many firms as the high competition in the market has forced these firms to fix prizes considering the pricing strategies adopted by competing firms. In addition, the flow of easily available products in the market has also fostered a free purchase and sell environment that was not available in the market earlier. For example, many four-wheeler and two-wheeler companies are offering replacement schemes for old vehicles and adjusting the price of the new vehicle accordingly.

Prevailing economic environment of the country also is determining factor in deciding price of a product.

The regulatory economic environment in the country also prevents firms from freely fixing prices. Government regulation in India can broadly be grouped into two categories: economic regulation and regulation in the public interest. Economic regulation is broadly applied by the Government to check market failure. For example, firms providing electricity in many states cannot fix tariffs independently. They will have to fix tariffs in compulsory consultation with some consulting bodies formed by the Government. Public interest regulation covers the actions taken by the Government to protect the interests of the common people. For example, the Indian government provides subsidies for diesel and gas cylinder purchase. Petroleum companies cannot can fix prices ignoring the guidelines provided by the government irrespective of the losses that they may incur. In order to safeguard the interests of poor people, the Indian government sells essential grains at heavily subsidized prices through the public distribution system. The paying capacity of ordinary citizens are taken into account when the Indian Railways fixes train fares. In India, even after liberalization many Government regulators are working to safeguard the interests of the public.

The prevailing economic environment of the country is a determining factor in deciding the price of a product.

22.4.3.3 Exchange Rate Pricing

Exchange rates fluctuate on a regular basis and have a decisive impact on products qualified for import and export. Exchange rate pricing is beyond the control of a firm and they will have to adopt compulsory price changes in the light of global changes in the exchange rates.

22.4.3.4 Geographical Pricing

The transport cost is also an important element in deciding the price of a product. Obviously, a place that is remotely located will have to bear a high price as compared to a place that is close to the manufacturing plant. State imposed taxes also play a key role in making prices slightly different in different states. For example, a four-wheeler company markets the same product in different parts of the country with a slight varying price considering factors such as the distance and the state tax policy. Similarly, petrol and diesel prices differ from town to town though there is a national policy available to fix the price uniformly for the entire country. Hence, many or almost all the products have price variations according to the geographical location.

Many or almost all products have price variations according to the geographical location.

22.4.4 New Product Pricing

Companies have to adopt a careful strategy to determine the pricing strategy for a new product. The price decided for a new product will definitely act as a direct comparison referral when the company changes the price in later stages. So, the initial price set by the company itself will become a point of consideration. The price movement from low to high or high to low will be scrutinized by the customer and the price will be assessed by the customer based on his perception. The three accepted pricing techniques for a new product: skimming pricing, penetration pricing and value-in-use pricing are discussed in the following section.

22.4.4.1 Skimming Pricing

This skimming price strategy is used when a new and innovative product is launched in the market. Firms try to set a higher price for the new product in order to generate high initial revenues. This strategy is used to "skim" early users of the product.

A common pricing strategy employed by managers in new and growing markets is price skimming–setting high prices during introduction and dropping them over time. As product life cycles become shorter and the number of new products and services increase every year, managerial use of price skimming appears to be increasing (Gebhardt 2006). This strategy is used when a new and innovative product is launched in the market. Firms try to set a higher price for this new product in order to generate a high initial revenue. This strategy is used to "skim" of early users of the product. The price goes down when the demand from these early users start declining. The price also starts to decline when competitors start entering the market with similar products. This approach obviously generates high revenue for a firm but is not free from some inherent drawbacks. High prices attract competitors and they also try to enter the market as soon as possible. There is a possibility that by the time the innovative firm decides to reduce the prices; competitors will enter the market and sometimes destroy the innovative firm's dream to exploit early market share. Hence, timing is a crucial factor in the skimming price strategy. A market research firm can conduct a small-scale survey to provide information about the trends in the market status. This information may be extremely useful for a firm which plans to use a skimming price strategy.

22.4.4.2 Penetration Pricing

Penetration pricing is the strategy of offering a lower price (even below cost) while entering the market with the expectation that a mass market will open quickly.

Penetration pricing is the strategy of offering a lower price (even below cost) while entering the market with the expectation that a mass market will open quickly. The users of this strategy sacrifice potential profits in the early stages of the product life cycle with the expectation to sell higher volumes in the later stages. The strategy is based on some assumptions. First, firms believe that the chances of product modifications are low. Second, the initial low price and high cost technical knowhow will keep potential competitors away from the market. Demand is highly elastic and the initial low price will help in expanding the market base. The penetration pricing strategy requires accurate information about the market as in the later stages companies will have to cope up with the low price set initially. Market researchers may be able to provide useful information to firms using this pricing strategy.

22.4.4.3 Value-in-Use Pricing

The theory believes in offering complete value pricing to its potential customers in the long run. Value-in-use pricing firms provide a complete value package including warranty, post-purchase service, delivery on time, service and maintenance on time, etc.

This theory of pricing does not follow an initial low or high pricing strategy. The theory believes in offering complete value pricing to its potential customers in the long run. Value-in-use pricing firms provide a complete value package including warranty, post-purchase service, delivery on time, service and maintenance on time, etc. Using such a strategy, firms try to understand the value that a customer expects from the product. After understanding customer needs completely and modifying the product accordingly, the firm is in a position to fix the price. A market researcher can provide the necessary information by conducting an organized survey. It is not an easy job to decide the value package for a potential customer and a systematic study is required to decide on the value proposition that will work for both customers and the company.

22.5 DISTRIBUTION (PLACE) RESEARCH

Distribution research is a vast topic and researchers are continuously working on it. Distribution channel decisions involve well-specified procedures to reach the end consumers in the light of the marketing strategy. A firm has to first decide whether it will approach the end consumer directly or indirectly. The direct approach is widely used nowadays to reach the end consumer. Direct approach can be grouped into **direct selling**, direct marketing, **company owned or sponsored special retail outlets** and **Internet marketing**. Firms can also reach customers indirectly through some intermediaries. In the indirect approach, the common distribution channel members are distributors, **wholesalers** and retailers. Some distributors appoint wholesalers and help wholesalers in appointing retailers. Wholesalers appoint retailers who directly reach the end consumers. Figure 22.4 presents this common distribution network. Market research is necessary to make effective decisions about channel members as unethical practices by the last member in channel, i.e. by a retailer is capable of tarnishing the image of the company. These channel members act as a link between the firm and the consumer and their behaviour has a direct impact on the firm's image and sales.

Direct approach can be grouped in direct selling, direct marketing, company owned or sponsored special retail outlets and internet marketing.

In an indirect approach, common distribution channel members are distributors, wholesalers and retailers.

22.5.1 Direct Approach

Direct approach is based on the concept of contacting the potential buyer directly. As exhibited in Figure 22.4, the direct approach of contacting customers can be generally grouped

FIGURE 22.4
A common distribution network

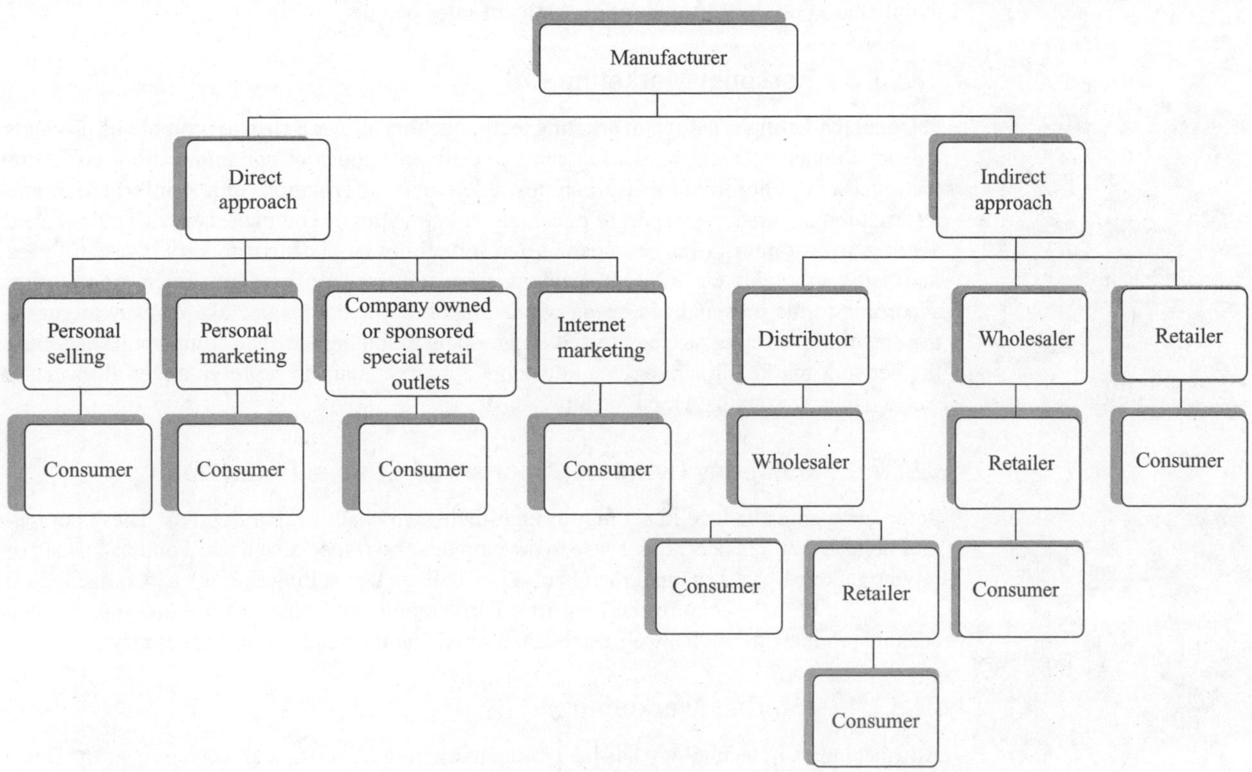

into personal selling, personal (direct) marketing, company owned or sponsored special retail outlets and Internet marketing.

22.5.1.1 Personal Selling

Personal selling is also an important method of reaching customers directly. It allows face-to-face communication for both buyers and sellers.

Personal selling is also an important method of reaching customers directly. It allows face-to- face communication for both buyers and sellers. The strength of personal selling lies in the fact that it allows communication interchange, a process more subtle but, at the same time, more hazardous than classical methods such as advertising that rely on one-way communication. In terms of efficiency, communication interchange results in the reduction of reach losses. It is of primary importance in the marketing of commodities that have to be explained or demonstrated to the buyer and particularly, therefore, in industrial marketing and the marketing of services (Hammann 1979). Personal selling allows a seller to form an individualized personal relationship with the buyer in the process of selling, which otherwise seems to be an expensive activity.

Marketing research acts as the facilitator for certain specific forms of personal selling. In recent times, the scope of personal selling has expanded and many new dimensions of contacting a customer directly have emerged. A recent research study emphasizes the role of personal selling as a partnering activity in the selling process. This partnering role provides the opportunity for a firm to resolve the inherent conflicts between the buyer and seller. For salespeople in the partnering role, personal selling shifts the focus from influencing buyer behaviour to managing the conflict inherent in buyer-seller relationships. The emphasis on building relationships rather than making short-term sales and the use of sales teams dictate changes in the way firms select, train, evaluate, and compensate salespeople and members of sales teams (Weitz and Bradford 1999). Many companies like Eureka Forbes in India are mainly based on the personal selling skills of sales people.

22.5.1.2 Personal Marketing

Personal marketing is a direct marketing technique that allows a firm to promote its products by direct contact. Direct marketing can use different modes of communication like informational letters, informational brochures, telephonic information, online information and information in person.

Personal marketing is a direct marketing technique that allows a firm to promote its products by direct contact. Direct marketing can use different modes of communication like informational letters, informational brochures, telephonic information, online information and information in person. As a part of personal marketing, many companies provide customized services to customers. Many companies and sometimes large distributors try to use different marketing strategies for different segments of customers by offering different programmes according to the personalized needs of customers. Some companies like Amway are using the network marketing strategy to sell its products in the market. The company has adopted the network marketing strategy and developed a large chain of representatives all over the world using personalized relationships.

22.5.1.3 Company Owned or Sponsored Special Retail Outlets

Some companies believe in selling through their own chain of retail outlets. These companies believe that it makes more sense to develop their own specialized retail outlets instead of relying on third-party channel members.

Some companies believe in selling through their own chain of retail outlets. These companies believe that it makes more sense to develop their own specialized retail outlets instead of relying on third-party channel members. They believe that selling through specialized retail outlets will be beneficial in the long run. For example, the major footwear company Bata sells its products through a well-established retail chain spread across the country.

22.5.1.4 Internet Marketing

Advancements in technology has lead to the marketing of goods and services over the Internet (Corley et al. 2013). Internet marketing is able to overcome some of the drawbacks of traditional marketing activities. Internet marketing is able to provide 24 hours access to customers; is capable of eliminating geographical boundaries and allows immediate communication with customers. Firms have to be very careful about the web experience a potential customer gets from its web site. Web site nowadays is the first forum of interaction between a firm and the customer. The Web experience as a major parameter of customer influence is crucial for dot.com-type firms but also for multi-channel vendors (Constantinides 2004). Internet marketing presents an opportunity to use diverse channel of communication. Internet marketing presents an opportunity to have communication one to one or many to many, synchronous or asynchronous and local or global. With exiting opportunities for creativity and innovation, variable costs tend to zero (Lawton and Gregor 2003).

Internet marketing is able to overcome some shackles of traditional marketing activities. Internet marketing is able to provide 24 hours access to all the customers; is capable to eliminate geographical boundaries and is able to facilitate immediate communication to customers.

22.5.2 Indirect Approach

Designing a marketing channel can be a complex task because it involves dealing with a large number of issues such as analysing the markets to be served, specifying the distribution function that needs to be performed, deciding on the number of levels in the channel, the intensity of the distribution, the type of middlemen to be used, as well as in determining the availability of middlemen and examining financial considerations (Rosenbloom and Anderson 1985). Some producers use a direct channel of reaching customers whereas many manufacturers adopt an indirect way of reaching customers through some intermediaries. The most common and simple method used by firms is the appointment of distributors, wholesalers and retailers. Some products cannot capture the market without the presence of distributors, wholesalers and retailers. Let us take the example of cement marketing. The direct methods discussed previously can facilitate the firm's desired communication but cannot provide the product to the end user. For making the product available in all urban and rural areas, a firm has to create a strong channel network. In contemporary marketing, firms will also have to cater to global requirements. This is a compelling factor for the firms to develop a solid channel network. Visualizing, tracking, and managing supply chains become more complicated as firms pursue outsourcing strategies and as the supply and delivery systems used by firms become increasingly global (Gardner and Cooper 2003). The following sections focus on three common indirect parties used to reach customers: distributors, wholesalers and retailers.

Some producers use a direct channel of reaching customers whereas many manufacturers adopt an indirect way of reaching customers through some intermediaries. The most common and simple method used by firms is the appointment of distributors, wholesalers and retailers.

22.5.2.1 Distributors

A distributor serves the multiple roles of being an independent representative of a manufacturer and a collector of orders from retailers for the manufacturer's products (Lau 2012). Distributors stock goods and pass it to intermediaries like wholesalers and retailers. Some distributors are large in size and take care of the firm's overseas distribution. Traditionally, distributors were confined to their defined geographical territory but in contemporary marketing practice their traditional role has enlarged. In a conventional setting, one party controls the functioning of the channel by controlling the activities of another party through the use of power (Weitz and Jap 1995). Distributors generally due to their large size compared to other channel members acquire the highest controlling power. In a traditional set up, over a period of time, distributors acquire a sound reputation, goodwill and prestige in a particular territory as an associate of any company. This provides benefits to both the distributor as well as the producer. Marketing research can help a firm maintain a healthy channel relationship between channel members.

Distributors stock goods and pass it to intermediaries like wholesalers and retailers. Some distributors are large in size and take care of the firm's overseas distribution.

22.5.2.2 Wholesalers

A wholesaler typically buys goods from different manufacturers, stocks them in warehouses, and resells them to retailers as one combined order under one invoice (Lau 2012).

Generally, the term distributor and wholesaler refers to the same entity and the names are used interchangeably.

Generally, the term distributor and wholesaler refers to the same entity and the names are used interchangeably. In operating terms, distributors are generally one more intermediary link between the manufacturer and wholesalers. As discussed, distributors are experienced and important players in marketing and selling and soon acquire a superior position in the channel relationship. Firms generally complain that the channel partner wholesaler is not providing the required support and wholesalers complain that the firm is ignorant about the margins of the wholesaler. Conflicts are bound to arise in their relationship. Market research can also act as a conflict resolution agent in the channel network as conflict is an inherent part of channel functioning. Marketing research can act as a facilitator in understanding the channel relationship and its use for maximizing the firm's profit.

22.5.2.3 Retailers

Retailing involves all the activities in selling goods and services to the end consumer.

Research, specifically, marketing research can act as an enabler in discovering new dimensions in the manufacturer → distributor → wholesaler → retailer → consumer relationship.

Retailing involves all the activities in selling goods and services to the end consumer. Companies make products for national or international markets and retailers act as the last member of a specific distribution channel. Large companies go in for advertising the product across the country. However, even a small retailer helps a company generate strong goodwill for its brands. Retailers are the first point of contact for a firm and act as not only a sales facilitator but also as an image creator for the company. The manufacturer acts as a channel leader mainly responsible for making the strategy and the retailer acts as a follower responsible for implementing the strategy effectively (Jorgensen et al. 2006). So, a retailer acts as a follower and helps the manufacturer to implement its ambitious sales plan. It is the responsibility of a firm as a leader to provide the correct direction and roadmap to a retailer to keep the retailer on the correct sales track. Retailers can adopt a short-term profit generation tactic but firms will have to keep a vigilant eye to ensure that the retailer understands the importance of a long-term vision and strategy. In fact, the manufacturer has to the check myopic vision of a retailer. Myopia refers to the lack of recognition of the impact of today's decisions on tomorrow's performance. A myopic retailer hurts the manufacturer's performance. (Taboubi and Zaccour 2002). In the light of the focus on customers, the traditional approach of maintaining a good relationship between a producer and the last member of the channel, the retailer, is getting momentum. Research, specifically, marketing research can act as an enabler in discovering new dimensions in the manufacturer → distributor → wholesaler→ retailer → consumer relationship.

22.6 PROMOTIONAL RESEARCH

After a new product is developed and even for the old products, companies will have to adopt some consumer awareness programmes commonly known as promotional activities.

After a new product is developed and even for the old products, companies will have to adopt some consumer awareness programmes commonly known as promotional activities. Firms can adopt any strategy for making consumers aware about its products or services. Some of the commonly used and established strategies are advertising, sales promotion and public relations. Figure 22.5 shows these commonly applied promotional tools in the field of marketing. This section will focus on the three important elements of promotion: advertising, sales promotion and public relations. Marketing research can help a firm use these tools effectively and appropriately.

22.6.1 Advertising Research

Advertising has been called the "the cave art" of contemporary society that makes consumption a top of mind behaviour (McMullan and Miller 2009). Advertising is a widely applied promotional tool used by many companies. It is often rated as the most powerful and

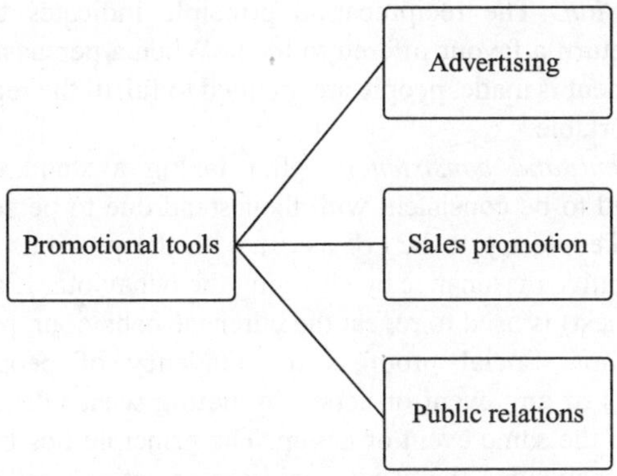

FIGURE 22.5
Commonly used promotional tools

reachable tool of promotion. In a free market economy characterized by a variety of similar products, the role of advertising consists of influencing consumers by creating a preference for one product in comparison with another of the same kind. In the present system of standardized production, an improvement in advertising technique and effort is often easier and more profitable for the entrepreneur than a price or quality variation (Ghidini 1978). It is undoubtedly a powerful tool of communication but is risky and costly in practice. Advertising is a creative exercise where most of decisions pertain to advertising copy. Advertising agencies have expertise in the technical aspects of advertising. An effective advertising message:

In a free market economy characterized by a variety of similar products, the role of advertising consists of influencing consumers by creating a preference for one product in comparison with another of the same kind.

(a) Creates awareness among the unaware
(b) Creates preferences among the undecided
(c) Provides reinforcement among those positively predisposed, and
(d) Provides conversion among those negatively predisposed (Holmes and Crocker 1987)

Marketing research is mainly used for measuring the effectiveness of advertising. Recall and recognition are two memory-based advertising effectiveness techniques, which evaluate the ability of an advertisement to attract the attention of the individual and make him/her aware of the existence of the brand being advertised and the benefits that it provides (Palacio and Santana 1998). Recall is based on the understanding that the more an advertisement is recalled the better it is. This theory believes that since an advertisement is better in recall, it is able to influence the target. As a result, it is more likely to change the attitude and to achieve the desired purchase behavior. After an exposure to the advertisement, recall techniques can be used to systematically investigate interest, clarity of message delivered, understanding of the message and attitude (positive, negative or neutral) toward the concept of the message. Recall is widely used by market researchers as can be used for direct measurement after respondents are exposed to an advertisement. In addition, recall technique provides an objective measurement technique other than a subjective technique. A direct comparison with similar advertisements provides the market researcher with an opportunity to objectively judge which advertisement is more effective. On the other hand, **recognition** is a test to determine whether respondents can recognize an advertisement that they have seen before.

Recall is based on the understanding that the more an advertisement is recalled the better it is.

Recognition is a test to determine whether respondents can recognize an advertisement that they have seen before.

Other than recall and recognition, **persuasive messages** are also a tool for measuring advertising effectiveness. Persuasive advertisement are based on some basic principles of human behaviour. There are seven persuasion principles: namely; reciprocation; commitment and consistency; social proof; liking; authority; scarcity and instant influence (Cialdini 2001). A brief discussion about these principles and its relation with persuasive advertisements is given below:

(i) *Reciprocation:* The reciprocation principle indicates that people feel obligated to return a favour offered to them. When a persuasive request through an advertisement is made, people are inclined to fulfill the request as and when they feel comfortable.

(ii) *Commitment and consistency*: After taking a stand on a particular issue people tend to be consistent with their stand due to personal and interpersonal pressure. People try to be consistent with the previous behaviour in order to avoid cognitive dissonance by changing the behaviour. If a persuasive advertisement (request) is used to repeat the purchase behaviour, people tend to do it.

(iii) *Social proof:* Social proof is the tendency of people to determine the correctness of any event or action by noting what others think about the correctness of the same event or action. The principle lies in the fact when lots of people acknowledge the event, incidents or actions get social approval if it is acknowledged by a majority. Persuasive advertisements sometimes use a number of people who have already used the product in order to influence a person (or a potential buyer) by the sheer number of the approvers.

(iv) *Liking*: Liking is based on the concept that we tend to say "yes" to the people whom we like. When we like someone, we are inclined to say yes to their request.

(v) *Authority*: The authority principle is based on the fact that when a message or a request is being delivered by an authority (may be social, business, sports or films), people tend to follow that. It is not very rare to see why companies are ready to pay a large amount to celebrities from different fields.

(vi) *Scarcity*: People tend to value things that are scare in the environment. Advertising can also use such a phenomenon for promotion by informing buyers about the limited number of products available.

(vii) *Instant influence*: While making a decision, people tend to avoid analysing all the alternatives and are inclined towards taking a quick, instant decision on the basis of some initial and necessary information.

Other than recall and recognition, **persuasive messages** are also a tool for measuring advertising effectiveness.

A market researcher can obtain relevant information on the parameters discussed above as the primary task of an advertisement campaign is to mobilize potential customers for purchase by influencing them.

22.6.2 Sales Promotion

Sales promotion consists of temporary incentives offered to customers for promoting sales. Sales promotion activities are generally classified as consumer promotion, retailer promotion and trade promotion.

Sales promotion consists of temporary incentives offered to customers for promoting sales. Sales promotion activities are generally classified as consumer promotion, retailer promotion and trade promotion. Sales promotion aimed at consumers include coupons, rebates, in-store temporary price cuts, feature advertising, and in-store displays. The impact of these promotions can be categorized as immediate sales promotion bump and effect beyond the immediate bump (Heerde and Neslin 2008). In the consumer promotion model, a manufacturer offers promotional schemes directly to consumers and in retail promotion, customers are offered a lower price through a retail store with advertising support for a definite time period (Martin and Lowe 1986). Trade promotion is an activity where a manufacturer offers different schemes to members of the distribution channel in order to boost sales for a definite time period. For example, sometimes manufacturers offer discount schemes to big distributors on bulk sales. The distributors then pass on discounts to wholesalers and retailers to sell in pre-specified quantities for availing the quantity discount. Pre-specified quantity is a selling quantity decided by the seller in mutual agreement with the producer to avail some discount on bulk selling.

Sales promotions provide an increased sale during the time of promotion; referred to as promotional bump. Its impact on sales can be seen even after the promotions in terms of some brand shift activity, which was actually being initiated during the sales promotion tenure. In some cases, various manufacturers or distributors or retailers join hands for promotion referred to as promotion partnership. We have seen that for promotion many small products are bundled free for the purchase of a relative big product. Whether it is consumer promotion or retailer promotion or trade promotion; the manufacturer has to use some incentive or benefit providing scheme to give a push to sales. Marketing research can have a pivotal role in determining the means of promotion. Researchers have focused on some limited and widely applied tools of promotion like price cut, displays, free sample distribution and the like whereas a lot is required to be explored as any list of promotional activities cannot be completely exhaustive and no doubt it is also not mutually exclusive.

Sales promotion provides an increased sale during the time of promotion; referred to as promotional bump. Its impact on sales can be seen even after the promotions in terms of some brand shift activity, which was actually being initiated during the sales promotion tenure.

22.6.3 Public Relations

Public relations, a common term used in marketing, consists of a list of programmes for promoting a company's image in order to achieve its long-term objectives. Public relations consists of a set of activities designed to influence people in a polite and persuasive manner as one cannot use coercive power for influencing potential customers. It is sometimes defined as soft power that operates through influence and attraction (Vercic 2008). Most organizations have a public relations department commonly known as the PR department, which is mainly responsible for maintaining and developing a sound relationship with the public. The term public includes members of the organization as well as the general public. The main role of the public relations department is to protect the company's image.

Public relations, a common term used in marketing, consists of a list of programmes for promoting a company's image in order to achieve its long-term objectives.

Companies show their concern for non-profit objectives as part of their public relations activities. Exhibiting concern for the welfare of the society helps a company create a responsible image in the long run. Public relation activities cover the aspects mentioned above by promoting the non-profit activities of a company. It is not rare to see many companies participating in local welfare programmes and indirectly showing their concern for the welfare of the society. The journey that starts with social welfare activities ends in creating a sound public image for the company. This ultimately results in profit generation for the company. Through public relations, companies can demonstrate altruistic and non-profit-oriented objectives, indicate a sincere concern for consumer benefits, and establish consumer trust in order to enhance customer loyalty (Hsieh and Li 2007).

Public relations activities involve many activities for promoting products or services or the image of a company in a positive manner. The public relations department of a firm uses the press for generating information about product and services. The media is used not only for providing information; it is also used for disseminating information about the firm's welfare activities. Public relation also deals with maintaining good relations with the government and other agencies with which the company may have to interact in a routine manner. During good times, the public relations department of a firm promotes the image of a company and in bad times, the public relations department of a firm protects the image of a company. Marketing research has an integral role in such activities. Marketing research can be used to generate the required information for product or image promotion.

REFERENCES

Atuahene-Gima, K., H. Li and L. M. De Luca (2006). "The Contingent Value of Marketing Strategy Innovativeness for Product Development Performance in Chinese New Technology Ventures", *Industrial Marketing Management,* 35: 359–72.

Balmer, J. M. T. (1998). "Corporate Identity and the Advent of Corporate Marketing", *Journal of Marketing Management,* 14(8): 963–96.

Balmer, J. M. T. and S. A. Greyser (2005). "Integrating Corporate Identity, Corporate Branding, Corporate Communications, Corporate Image and Corporate Reputation", *European Journal of Marketing*, 40(7/8): 730–41.

Baltz, A., A. Bobek, T. Combs, C. Imondi and M. Trippel (2012). "A Comprehensive Strategic Model for the Commercialization of New Product Development Technologies", *Proceedings of PICMET'12: Technology Management for Emerging Technologies,* 770–84.

Bayus, B. L. and W. P. Putsis Jr. (1999). "Product Proliferation: An Empirical Analysis of Product Line Determinants and Market Outcomes", *Marketing Science*, 18(2): 137–53.

Bessant, J. and D. Francis (1997). "Implementing the New Product Development Process", *Technovation,* 17(4): 189–97.

Bhuiyan, N. (2011). "A Framework for Successful New Product Development", *Journal of Industrial Engineering and Management,* 4(4): 746–70.

Booms, B. H. and B. J. Bitner (1981). "Marketing Strategies and Organization Structures for Service Firms", in Donnelly, J. and W. R. George (eds.), *Marketing of Services*, pp. 47–51. American Marketing Association.

Capon, N. and J. M. Hulbert (2001). *Marketing Management in the 21st Century*, pp. 6, 345. Upper Saddle River, NJ: Prentice-Hall.

Cialdini, R. B. (2001). *Influence, Science and Practice*, pp. 1–257. Boston, MA: Allyn & Bacon .

Constantinides, E. (2004). Influencing the Online Consumer's Behavior: The Web Experience, *Internet Research,* 14(2): 111–26.

Corley II, J. K., Z. Jourdan and W. R. Ingram (2013). "Internet Marketing: A Content Analysis of the Research", *Electron Markets,* 23: 177–204.

Czinkota, M. R. and M. Kotabe (2002). *Marketing Management*, 2nd ed., pp. 14–15. Singapore: Thomson Asia Pte. Ltd.

Dahan, E. and H. Mendelson (2001). "An Extreme-Value Model of Concept Testing", *Management Science*, 47(1): 102–16.

Dalrymple, D. J. and L. J. Parsons (2000). *Marketing Management: Text and Cases,* 7th ed., pp. 13–14. Wiley.

Dominici, G. (2009). "From Marketing Mix to E-Marketing Mix: A Literature Overview and Classification", *International Journal of Business and Management,* 4(9): 17–24.

Fratto, G. M., M. R. Jones and N. L. Cassill (2006). "An Investigation of Competitive Pricing Among Apparel Retailers and Brands", *Journal of Fashion Marketing and Management*, 10(4): 387–404.

Fuchs, C. and A. Dianantopoulos (2010). "Evaluating the Effectiveness of Brand-Positioning Strategies from A Consumer Perspective", *European Journal of Marketing,* 44(11/12): 1763–86.

Gardner, J. T. and M. C. Cooper (2003). "Strategic Supply Chain Mapping Approaches", *Journal of Business Logistics,* 24(2): 37–64.

Gebhardt, G. F. (2006). "Price Skimming Paradoxes", *Advances in Consumer Research*, 33: 242–43.

Ghidini, G. (1978). "Problems of Consumer Protection Against Unfair Advertising Under Italian Law", *Journal of Consumer Policy*, 2(4): 316–25.

Ghodeswar, B. M. (2008). "Building Brand Identity in Competitive Markets: A Conceptual Model", *Journal of Product & Brand Management,* 17(1): 4–12.

Goi, C. L. (2009). "A Review of Marketing Mix: 4Ps or More", *International Journal of Marketing Studies,* 1(1): 1–15.

Goldsmith, R. E. (1999). "The Personalized Marketplace: Beyond the 4Ps", *Marketing Intelligence & Planning,* 17(4): 178–185.

Griffin, A. (1997). "PDMA Research on New Product Development Practices: Updating Trends and Benchmarking Best Practices", *Journal of Product Innovation Management*, 14: 429–58.

Gruner, K. J. and C. Homburg (2000). "Does Customer Interaction Enhance New Product Success?", *Journal of Business Research*, 49: 1–14.

Hammann, P. (1979). "Personal Selling", *European Journal of Marketing*, 13(6): 141–76.

Harmancioglu, N., R. C. McNally, R. J. Calantone and S. S. Durmusoglu (2007). "Your NPD is Only as Good as Your Process", *R&D Management,* 37(5): 400–24.

Hartmann, P., V. A. Ibanez and F. J. F. Sainz (2005). "Green Branding Effectiveness on Attitude: Functions versus Emotional

Positioning Strategies", *Marketing Intelligence & Planning,* 23(1): 9–29.

Heerde, H. J. V. and S. A. Neslin (2008). "Sales Promotion Models", *International Series in Operations Research and Management Science,* 121: 107–62.

Hinterhuber, A. (2008). "Customer Value-Based Pricing Strategies: Why Companies Resist", *Journal of Business Strategy,* 29(4): 41–50.

Hinterhuber, A. and M. Bertini (2011). "Profiting When Customers Choose Value Over Price", *Business Strategy Review*, 1: 46–9.

Hippel, E. (1986). "Lead Users: A Source of Novel Product Concepts", *Management Science,* 32(7): 791–805.

Holmes, J. H. and K. E. Crocker (1987). "Predispositions and the Comparative Effectiveness of Rational, Emotional and Discrepant Appeals for Both High Involvement and Low Involvement Products", *Academy of Marketing Science*, 15(1): 27–35.

Hopp, W. J. and X. Xu (2005). "Product Line Selection and Pricing with Modularity in Design", *Manufacturing & Service Operations Management,* 7(3): 172–87.

Hsieh, A. and C. Li (2007). "The moderating effect of brand image on public relations perception and customer loyalty", *Marketing Intelligence & Planning*, 26(1): 26–42.

Hunt, S. D. and D. B. Arnett (2004). "Market Segmentation Strategy, Competitive Advantage, and Public Policy: Grounding Segmentation Strategy in Resource-Advantage Theory", *Australasian Marketing Journal*, 12(1): 7–25.

Janiszewska, K. and A. Insch (2012). "The Strategic Importance of Brand Positioning in the Place Brand Concept: Elements, Structure and Application Capabilities", *Journal of International Studies*, 5(1): 9–19.

Jorgensen, S., S. Taboubi and G. Zaccour (2006). "Incentives for Retailer Promotion in a Marketing Channel", *Advances in Dynamic Games*, 8: 365–78.

Kotler, P., K. L. Keller, A. Koshey and M. Jha (2009). *Marketing Management: A South Asian Perspective*, 13th ed., pp. 24–25. India: Dorling Kindersley Pvt. Ltd.

Lau, K. H. (2012). "Demand Management In Downstream Wholesale and Retail Distribution: A Case Study", *Supply Chain Management: An International Journal,* 17(6): 638–54.

Lawton, B. and S. Gregor (2003). "Internet Marketing Communications: Interactivity and Integration", *The International Federation for Information Processing*, 23: 239–57.

Liu, W. and M. Maletz (2009). "Product Lifecycle Management: A Review", *International Design Engineering Technical Conferences & Computers and Information in Engineering Conference IDETC/CIE*, pp. 1–13. Proceedings of the ASME, San Diego, USA.

Martin, R. P. and P. H. Lowe (1986). "Production and Inventory Control: Effect of Sales Promotion", *Advances in Manufacturing Technology,* 33–7.

McCharty, E. J. (1964). *Basic Marketing: A Managerial Approach,* 2nd ed. IL: Richard D. Irwin.

McMullan, J. L. and D. Miller (2009). "Wins, Winning and Winners: The Commercial Advertising of Lottery Gambling", *Journal of Gambling Studies,* 25: 273–95.

Myers, J. H. (1976). "Benefit Structure Analysis: A New Tool for Product Planning", *Journal of Marketing,* 40: 23–32.

Natter, M. and H. Hruschka (1998). "Evaluation of Aggressive Competitive Pricing Strategies", *Marketing Letters,* 9(4): 337–47.

Niazi, A., J. S. Dai, S. Balabani and S. Seneviratne (2006). "Product Cost Estimation: Technique Classification and Methodology Review", *Journal of Manufacturing Science and Engineering*, 128: 563–75.

Ozer, M. (1999). "A Survey of New Product Evaluation Models", *Journal of Product Innovation Management*, 16: 77–94.

Palacio, A. B. and J. D. M. Santana (1998). "Memory-Based Advertisement Effectiveness Techniques: Recall versus Recognition", *Managing in Uncertainty: Theory and Practice,* 19: 183–201.

Rink, D. R. and J. E. Swan (1979). "Product Life Cycle Research: A Literature Review", *Journal of Business Research,* 9: 219–42.

Rosenbloom, B. and R. Anderson (1985). "Channel Management and Sales Management: Some Key Interfaces", *Journal of the Academy of Marketing Science,* 13(3): 97–106.

Rush, C. and R. Roy (2000). "Analysis of Cost Estimating Processes Used within A Concurrent Engineering Environment Throughout A Product Life Cycle*", 7th ISPE International Conference on Concurrent Engineering: Research and Applications*, Lyon, France, 17th–20th July, pp. 58–67. Pennsylvania, USA: *Technomic Inc.*

Smith, P. G. (1990). "Fast-Cycle Product Development", *Engineering Management Journal*, 2(2): 11–6.

Steffens, P. R. (2002). "The Product Life Cycle Concept: Buried or Resurrected by the Diffusion Literature?", *Academy of Management Conference*, Technology and Innovation Management Division, pp. 1–29.

Sudhir, K. (2001). "Competitive Pricing Behavior in the Auto Market: A Structural Analysis", *Marketing Science*, 20(1): 42–60.

Sujan, M. and J. R. Bettman (1989). "The Effect of Brand Positioning Strategies on Consumer's Brand and Category Perceptions: Some Insights from Schema Research", *Journal of Marketing Research,* 26: 554–67 .

Taboubi, S. and G. Zaccour (2002). "Impact of Retailer's Myopia on Channel's Strategies, Optimal Control and Differential Games", *Advances in Computation Management Science,* 5: 179–92.

Takeuchi, H. and I. Nonaka (1986). "The New Product Development Game", *Harvard Business Review,* (January–February): 137–46.

Tynan, A. C. and J. Drayton (1987). "Market Segmentation", *Journal of Marketing Management*, 2(3): 301–35.

Urban, E. L., B. D. Weinberg and J. R. Hauser (1996). "Premarket Forecasting of Really New Products", *Journal of Marketing,* 60: 47–60.

Urban, G. L. and E. Hippel (1988). "Lead User Analyses for the Development of New Industrial Products", *Management Science,* 34(5): 569–82.

Vercic, D. (2008). "Public Relations and Power: How Hard is Soft Power?", *Public Relation Research,* 3: 271–9 .

Weitz, B. A. and S. D. Jap (1995). "Relationship Marketing and Distribution Channel", *Journal of the Academy of Marketing Science*, 23(4): 305–20.

Weitz, B. A. and K. D. Bradford (1999). "Personal Selling and Sales Management: A Relationship Marketing Perspective", *Journal of the Academy of Marketing Sciences*, 27(2): 241–54.

Yelkur, R. and P. Herbig (1996). "Global Markets and The New Product Development Process", *Journal of Product and Brand Management*, 5(6): 38–47.

Yoon, E. and G. L. Lilien (1985). "New Industrial Product Performance: The Effects of Market Characteristics and Strategy", *Journal of Product Innovation Management*, 3: 134–44.

Zaribaf, M. (2008). "Pricing Challenges in Global Marketing: A Model for Export Pricing", *International Business and Tourism Society,* 2 (1): 18–31.

SUMMARY

This chapter focuses on the information required by a decision maker to take decisions regarding product, price, place and promotion. McCarthy first defined marketing mix with the help of a combination of 4 Ps—product, price, place and promotion to satisfy market needs. Booms and Bitner added three more Ps—physical evidence, participants and process. Goldsmith added one more P—Personalization—to make the list of Ps more complete. Balmer came out with a list of 11 Ps in the field of corporate marketing in 1998.

Generally, there are eight steps in the new product development process. These are: new product idea generation (need identification and concept identification); strategic screening of ideas (revenue and cost analysis); concept development and testing; product development and marketing strategy; product testing; test marketing, commercialization and post-launch evaluation (short term and/or long term).

Pricing is a very important concept in the current tough marketing environment and is a vital part of framing a marketing strategy. Price in not only an important element of the marketing mix, it is also different from the other three elements of the marketing mix. Product, place and promotion are the activities mainly linked with providing value to a customer. There are many factors affecting the pricing policies of firms. These factors are different from new product pricing strategies. Broadly, factors influencing the pricing strategy of a firm can be categorized as organizational factors, customer factors and market factors. Organizational factors can further be grouped into product life cycle pricing, product portfolio pricing, product line pricing and pricing for market segmentation. Customer factors can be grouped into demand pricing, benefit pricing, value pricing and place pricing. Factors related to market can also be grouped into competitive pricing, pricing in economic and regulatory environment, exchange rate pricing and geographical pricing. Firms adopt different approaches for pricing new products. The popular pricing techniques for a new product are skimming pricing, penetration pricing and value-in-use pricing.

Distribution channel decisions involve a well-specified procedure to reach the end consumers. A firm has to first decide whether it will approach the end consumer directly or indirectly. Nowadays, the direct approach technique is widely used to reach the end consumer. Direct approach techniques can be classified as direct selling, direct marketing, company owned or sponsored special retail outlets and Internet marketing. Other than reaching consumers directly, firms can also reach them indirectly through some intermediaries. In the indirect approach, the common distribution channel members are distributors, wholesalers and retailers.

Firms can adopt many strategies for making consumers aware about its products or services but strategies such as advertising, sales promotion and public relations are commonly used and established strategies.

KEY TERMS |

Advertising, 576
Benefit pricing, 589
Benefit structure analysis, 581
Commercialization and post-launch evaluation, 579
Company owned or sponsored special retail outlets, 597
Competitive pricing, 589
Concept development and testing, 579
Corporate marketing, 577
Customer factors, 589
Demand pricing, 589
Direct marketing, 576
Direct selling, 597
Distribution research, 597
Distributors, 589
Exchange rate pricing, 589
Focus group, 581
Geographical pricing, 589
Idea generation, 579
Internet marketing, 597
Market factors, 589
Marketing mix, 576
New product research, 579
Organizational factors, 589
Participants and process, 577
Penetration pricing, 589
People, 577
Perception, 577
Performance, 577
Personality, 577
Personalization, 577
Philosophy and ethos, 577
Physical evidence, 577
Place, 576
Place pricing, 589
Positioning, 577
Price, 576
Pricing for market segmentation, 589
Pricing in economic and regulatory environment, 589
Pricing research, 579
Product, 576
Product development and marketing strategy, 579
Product life-cycle pricing, 590
Product line pricing, 589
Product portfolio pricing, 589
Product testing, 579
Promise, 577
Promotion, 576
Promotion research, 579
Public relations, 576
Relationship marketing, 577
Retailers, 589
Sales promotion, 576
Service marketing, 577
Skimming pricing, 589
Strategic screening of ideas, 579
Test marketing, 579
Value pricing, 589
Value-in-use pricing, 589
Wholesalers, 597

NOTES |

1. www.mahindra.com, accessed March 2014.
2. http://www.thehindubusinessline.com/feature/brand-line/mahindra/, accessed March 2014.
3. http://blogs.hindustantimes.com/car-nama/2012/10/05/tata-mahindras-sibling-rivalry-set-to-turn-ugly/, accessed March 2014.

DISCUSSION QUESTIONS |

1. What do you understand by marketing mix?
2. How many Ps does the traditional marketing mix consist of ?
3. Write a short note on the evolution of various Ps in marketing.
4. What is new product development research?
5. What are the stages involved in new product development?
6. What is lead-user analysis and benefit-structure analysis?
7. Write a short note on revenue and cost analysis of new-product development.
8. Explain the role of concept development and concept testing in new-product development.
9. Write a short note on commercialization and post-launch status of new-product development.
10. What are organizational factors, customer factors and market factors in making sound pricing strategies?
11. Write a note on the life cycle of a product, product portfolio, product line and segmentation and positioning with reference to pricing.
12. What are demand pricing, benefit pricing, value pricing and place pricing?
13. What is competitive pricing, pricing in economic and regulatory environment, exchange rate pricing and geographical pricing?
14. What is skimming pricing, penetration pricing and value-in-use pricing? How is it used in decisions regarding new product pricing?
15. Write short notes on:
    - Direct selling
    - Direct marketing
    - Company owned or sponsored special retail outlets
    - Internet marketing
16. Explain the role of distributors, wholesalers and retailers as an integral part of the distribution channel.
17. Explain the role of advertising, sales promotion and public relations in promotional research.

CASE STUDY |

Case 22: *Ford EcoSport: A Game Changer for Ford India*

Introduction

The history of the passenger car industry in India can be divided into five phases. The regulated and restrained market in the country up to 1984 can be considered phase one. Phase two consists of the period between 1985 and 1992 when the country witnessed the exploration of new technology. Phase three arrived from 1995–2000 when there was a hurried entry of many world players in India. Phase four was the time duration from 2001 to 2004 when market has started maturing with intense competition. The period from 2005 and after when the market become completely global can be considered phase five.[1] Ford India (started in 1995) entered the market soon after the Indian economy started seeing the impact of globalization, liberalization and privatization specifically after 1995–96. Previously, the industry was completely dominated by Maruti Udyog Limited. The competition for the Indian four-wheeler segment leader Maruti Udyog was very limited and fragmented. Multinational players started entering the market after the announcement of the new industrial policy in 1991. There was an influx of global brands in almost all industries such as automobiles, consumer electronics, consumer durables, etc. There was intense competition between the players and the enhanced purchasing power of the Indian population resulted in the creation of a new, informed and powerful consumer base.

Ford India was established in 1995 as a wholly-owned subsidiary of the Ford Motor Company, a global automotive industrial leader. Ford has invested more than USD 2 Billion in India to meet the requirements of the country's rapidly growing automotive market. The investment has gone into expanding the company's manufacturing facilities and dealership network in the country. Ford India currently operates a modern, integrated manufacturing facility at Maraimalai Nagar, near Chennai, which produces its award-winning range of products including the Ford Figo, Ford Fiesta, Ford Classic, Ford Endeavour and Ford EcoSport.[2] The launch of its game changer brand, the Ford EcoSport, has given fresh impetus to Ford's efforts to become a market leader in the Indian auto segment.

During the time that the EcoSport was launched, market studies clearly indicated that Indian consumers were inclined towards sports utility vehicles (SUVs). Therefore, many auto companies launched SUVs in the Indian market to cash in on consumer sentiments. Compact SUVs were also launched to create a new consumer segment. Indian auto companies came out with similar products, but the response that the EcoSport received was unmatched and the brand was able to set a new example in the Indian automobile segment.

Game Changer Impact of the EcoSport

Since it entered India in 1996, Ford has struggled to get a grip on Indian roads. Despite the occasional and fleeting successes like the Ford Ikon and the Ford Figo, Ford's India journey has remained lacklustre. The launch of the EcoSport has created a buzz around the brand and resulted in a reversal in fortunes of sorts. The compact SUV now contributes over 55% of Ford's total sales in India.[3] EcoSport is trying to create a new customer segment using low price in the industry as the weapon in the sub-four metre vehicle category.

According to the company's marketing director Vinay Piparsania, prices were decided by keeping the target customers in mind. The target customer for the EcoSport is someone who is in his early 30s, urban dweller, brand conscious, adventure-lover, and is practical with a sense of contemporariness about him.[4]

No Impact of Recall

Ford recalled 972 units of the EcoSport within two weeks of its launch because of a fault in the glow plug module of its diesel version. Joginder Singh, President and Managing Director of Ford India, in an interview with the *Business Standard* reiterated Ford's focus on quality and said that the company was working on a skill development programme and strengthening its research and development team to avoid such issues in the future.[5] The recall just after the launch was very unusual for an Indian automobile manufacturer and opened up many discussions regarding its negative impact on consumer sentiments. Many critics felt that this move may invite brand shift as many similar brands are available in the market. However, the recall of the vehicles had no impact on the demand for the EcoSport. Rather, the company had to stop taking bookings to clear the backlog of already booked vehicles.

Existing Product Portfolio

Ford India is also working closely with its suppliers to increase the output of the EcoSport to meet the high demand. Its manufacturing facililty at Chennai is working overtime to meet the high demand for the model. The company is also encouraging customers to choose a product from its existing portfolio so that they can avoid the inconvenience of the long waiting period.[5]

This smart strategy followed by Ford will definitely help it to position other brands using the "unprecedented demand" for the EcoSport as an instrument. Considering the "long queue," Ford is now encouraging its EcoSport customers to go for models such as Figo, Ford Classic, Endeavour or Fiesta with an additional discount.[6]

Let us assume that Ford India has appointed you as a business analyst and consultant and asked you to prepare a report on the marketing mix of its products. The launch of the EcoSport, a game changer for Ford India, has witnessed an unprecedented response from the market. As an analyst, what will you do to prepare a report on the marketing mix for different products of the company? What improvements will you suggest for this new product? What will be your suggestions for promoting Ford's product portfolio? It is also expected that the competitors will launch similar products after seeing the huge demand for the EcoSport. What pricing strategy will you suggest to the company to address this issue. Will you suggest a skimming or a penetration pricing strategy? Ford India is also looking for new partners as channel members to capitalize on this demand. What suggestions will you make to enhance the dealer network in different cities of the country? The company will also be looking for promotional strategies to promote its products. What promotional strategies will you suggest to the company for promoting its different models?

Based on the facts discussed in the case, prepare a detailed report on the marketing mix for the company. Use secondary data and exploratory research for substantiating your findings. Develop a detailed proposal for the company to enhance its market share in the Indian market.

NOTES |

1. www.indiastat.com, accessed March 2014.
2. www.india.ford.com/about, accessed March 2014.
3. http//www.articles.economictimes.indiatimes.com/2013-12-01/news/445... accessed March 2014.
4. http//www.telegraphindia.com/1130627/jsp/business/story_170532..., accessed March 2014.
5. http//www.business-standard.com/article/companies/we-have-stop..., accessed March 2014.
6. http//www.thehindubusinessline.com/companies/its-a-long-wait-for..., accessed March 2014.

Appendix

TABLE A.1
Random numbers

12651	61646	11769	75109	86996	97669	25757	32535	07122	76763
81769	74436	02630	72310	45049	18029	07469	42341	98173	79260
36737	98863	77240	76251	00654	64688	09343	70278	67331	98729
82861	54371	76610	94934	72748	44124	05610	53750	95938	01485
21325	15732	24127	37431	09723	63529	73977	95218	96074	42138
74146	47887	62463	23045	41490	07954	22597	60012	98866	90959
90759	64410	54179	66075	61051	75385	51378	08360	95946	95547
55683	98078	02238	91540	21219	17720	87817	41705	95785	12563
79686	17969	76061	83748	55920	83612	41540	86492	06447	60568
70333	00201	86201	69716	78185	62154	77930	67663	29529	75116
14042	53536	07779	04157	41172	36473	42123	43929	50533	33437
59911	08256	06596	48416	69770	68797	56080	14223	59199	30162
62368	62623	62742	14891	39247	52242	98832	69533	91174	57979
57529	97751	54976	48957	74599	08759	78494	52785	68526	64618
15469	90574	78033	66885	13936	42117	71831	22961	94225	31816
18625	23674	53850	32827	81647	80820	00420	63555	74489	80141
74626	68394	88562	70745	23701	45630	65891	58220	35442	60414
11119	16519	27384	90199	79210	76965	99546	30323	31664	22845
41101	17336	48951	53674	17880	45260	08575	49321	36191	17095
32123	91576	84221	78902	82010	30847	62329	63898	23268	74283
26091	68409	69704	82267	14751	13151	93115	01437	56945	89661
67680	79790	48462	59278	44185	29616	76531	19589	83139	28454
15184	19260	14073	07026	25264	08388	27182	22557	61501	67481
58010	45039	57181	10238	36874	28546	37444	80824	63981	39942
56425	53996	86245	32623	78858	08143	60377	42925	42815	11159
82630	84066	13592	60642	17904	99718	63432	88642	37858	25431
14927	40909	23900	48761	44860	92467	31742	87142	03607	32059
23740	22505	07489	85986	74420	21744	97711	36648	35620	97949
32990	97446	03711	63824	07953	85965	87089	11687	92414	67257
05310	24058	91946	78437	34365	82469	12430	84754	19354	72745
21839	39937	27534	88913	49055	19218	47712	67677	51889	70926
08833	42549	93981	94051	28382	83725	72643	64233	97252	17133
58336	11139	47479	00931	91560	95372	97642	33856	54825	55680
62032	91144	75478	47431	52726	30289	42411	91886	51818	78292
45171	30557	53116	04118	58301	24375	65609	85810	18620	49198
91611	62656	60128	35609	63698	78356	50682	22505	01692	36291
55472	63819	86314	49174	93582	73604	78614	78849	23096	72825
18573	09729	74091	53994	10970	86557	65661	41854	26037	53296
60866	02955	90288	82136	83644	94455	06560	78029	98768	71296

45043	55608	82767	60890	74646	79485	13619	98868	40857	19415
17831	09737	79473	75945	28394	79334	70577	38048	03607	06932
40137	03981	07585	18128	11178	32601	27994	05641	22600	86064
77776	31343	14576	97706	16039	47517	43300	59080	80392	63189
69605	44104	40103	95635	05635	81673	68657	09559	23510	95875
19916	52934	26499	09821	97331	80993	61299	36979	73599	35055
02606	58552	07678	56619	65325	30705	99582	53390	46357	13244
65183	73160	87131	35530	47946	09854	18080	02321	05809	04893
10740	98914	44916	11322	89717	88189	30143	52687	19420	60061
98642	89822	71691	51573	83666	61642	46683	33761	47542	23551
60139	25601	93663	25547	02654	94829	48672	28736	84994	13071

Source: Partially extracted from The RAND Corporation, *A Million Random Digits with 100,000 Normal Deviates* (Glencoe, IL, The Free Press, 1955).

TABLE A.2

Areas of the standard normal distribution

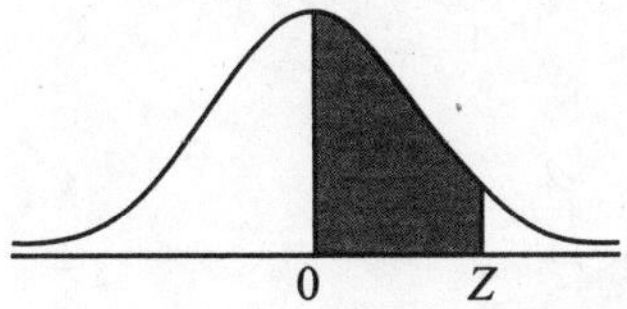

The entries in this table are the probabilities that a standard normal random variable is between 0 and Z (the shaded area).

Z	0.00	0.01	0.02	0.03	0.04	0.05	0.06	0.07	0.08	0.09
0.0	0.0000	0.0040	0.0080	0.0120	0.0160	0.0199	0.0239	0.0279	0.0319	0.0359
0.1	0.0398	0.0438	0.0478	0.0517	0.0557	0.0596	0.0636	0.0675	0.0714	0.0753
0.2	0.0793	0.0832	0.0871	0.0910	0.0948	0.0987	0.1026	0.1064	0.1103	0.1141
0.3	0.1179	0.1217	0.1255	0.1293	0.1331	0.1368	0.1406	0.1443	0.1480	0.1517
0.4	0.1554	0.1591	0.1628	0.1664	0.1700	0.1736	0.1772	0.1808	0.1844	0.1879
0.5	0.1915	0.1950	0.1985	0.2019	0.2054	0.2088	0.2123	0.2157	0.2190	0.2224
0.6	0.2257	0.2291	0.2324	0.2357	0.2389	0.2422	0.2454	0.2486	0.2517	0.2549
0.7	0.2580	0.2611	0.2642	0.2673	0.2704	0.2734	0.2764	0.2794	0.2823	0.2852
0.8	0.2881	0.2910	0.2939	0.2967	0.2995	0.3023	0.3051	0.3078	0.3106	0.3133
0.9	0.3159	0.3186	0.3212	0.3238	0.3264	0.3289	0.3315	0.3340	0.3365	0.3389
1.0	0.3413	0.3438	0.3461	0.3485	0.3508	0.3531	0.3554	0.3577	0.3599	0.3621
1.1	0.3643	0.3665	0.3686	0.3708	0.3729	0.3749	0.3770	0.3790	0.3810	0.3830
1.2	0.3849	0.3869	0.3888	0.3907	0.3925	0.3944	0.3962	0.3980	0.3997	0.4015
1.3	0.4032	0.4049	0.4066	0.4082	0.4099	0.4115	0.4131	0.4147	0.4162	0.4177
1.4	0.4192	0.4207	0.4222	0.4236	0.4251	0.4265	0.4279	0.4292	0.4306	0.4319
1.5	0.4332	0.4345	0.4357	0.4370	0.4382	0.4394	0.4406	0.4418	0.4429	0.4441
1.6	0.4452	0.4463	0.4474	0.4484	0.4495	0.4505	0.4515	0.4525	0.4535	0.4545
1.7	0.4554	0.4564	0.4573	0.4582	0.4591	0.4599	0.4608	0.4616	0.4625	0.4633
1.8	0.4641	0.4649	0.4656	0.4664	0.4671	0.4678	0.4686	0.4693	0.4699	0.4706
1.9	0.4713	0.4719	0.4726	0.4732	0.4738	0.4744	0.4750	0.4756	0.4761	0.4767
2.0	0.4772	0.4778	0.4783	0.4788	0.4793	0.4798	0.4803	0.4808	0.4812	0.4817
2.1	0.4821	0.4826	0.4830	0.4834	0.4838	0.4842	0.4846	0.4850	0.4854	0.4857
2.2	0.4861	0.4864	0.4868	0.4871	0.4875	0.4878	0.4881	0.4884	0.4887	0.4890
2.3	0.4893	0.4896	0.4898	0.4901	0.4904	0.4906	0.4909	0.4911	0.4913	0.4916
2.4	0.4918	0.4920	0.4922	0.4925	0.4927	0.4929	0.4931	0.4932	0.4934	0.4936
2.5	0.4938	0.4940	0.4941	0.4943	0.4945	0.4946	0.4948	0.4949	0.4951	0.4952
2.6	0.4953	0.4955	0.4956	0.4957	0.4959	0.4960	0.4961	0.4962	0.4963	0.4964
2.7	0.4965	0.4966	0.4967	0.4968	0.4969	0.4970	0.4971	0.4972	0.4973	0.4974
2.8	0.4974	0.4975	0.4976	0.4977	0.4977	0.4978	0.4979	0.4979	0.4980	0.4981
2.9	0.4981	0.4982	0.4982	0.4983	0.4984	0.4984	0.4985	0.4985	0.4986	0.4986
3.0	0.4987	0.4987	0.4987	0.4988	0.4988	0.4989	0.4989	0.4989	0.4990	0.4990
3.1	0.4990	0.4991	0.4991	0.4991	0.4992	0.4992	0.4992	0.4992	0.4993	0.4993
3.2	0.4993	0.4993	0.4994	0.4994	0.4994	0.4994	0.4994	0.4995	0.4995	0.4995
3.3	0.4995	0.4995	0.4995	0.4996	0.4996	0.4996	0.4996	0.4996	0.4996	0.4997
3.4	0.4997	0.4997	0.4997	0.4997	0.4997	0.4997	0.4997	0.4997	0.4997	0.4998
3.5	0.4998									
4.0	0.49997									
4.5	0.499997									
5.0	0.4999997									
6.0	0.499999999									

TABLE A.3

Critical values from the t distribution

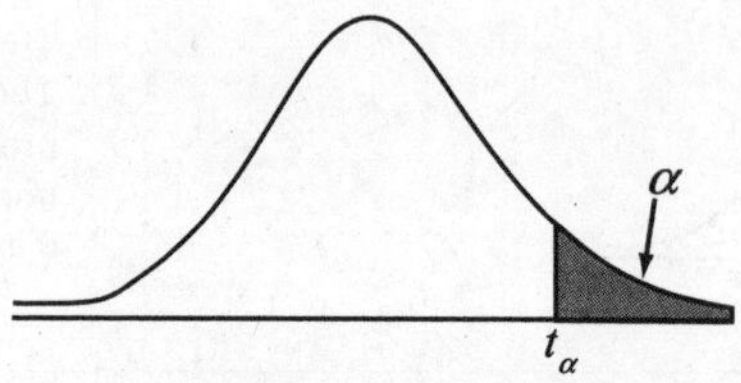

	Values of α for one-tailed test and $\alpha/2$ for two-tailed test					
df	$t_{0.100}$	$t_{0.050}$	$t_{0.025}$	$t_{0.010}$	$t_{0.005}$	$t_{0.001}$
1	3.078	6.314	12.706	31.821	63.656	318.289
2	1.886	2.920	4.303	6.965	9.925	22.328
3	1.638	2 353	3.182	4.541	5.841	10.214
4	1.533	2.132	2.776	3.747	4.604	7.173
5	1.476	2.015	2.571	3.365	4.032	5.894
6	1.440	1.943	2.447	3.143	3.707	5.208
7	1.415	1.895	2.365	2.998	3.499	4.785
8	1.397	1.860	2.306	2.896	3.355	4.501
9	1.383	1.833	2.262	2.821	3.250	4.297
10	1.372	1.812	2.228	2.764	3.169	4.144
11	1.363	1.796	2.201	2.718	3.106	4.025
12	1.356	1.782	2.179	2.681	3.055	3.930
13	1.350	1.771	2.160	2.650	3.012	3.852
14	1.345	1.761	2.145	2.624	2.977	3.787
15	1.341	1.753	2.131	2.602	2.947	3.733
16	1.337	1.746	2.120	2.583	2.921	3.686
17	1.333	1.740	2.110	2.567	2.898	3.646
18	1.330	1.734	2.101	2.552	2.878	3.610
19	1.328	1.729	2.093	2.539	2.861	3.579
20	1.325	1.725	2.086	2.528	2.845	3.552
21	1.323	1.721	2.080	2.518	2.831	3.527
22	1.321	1.717	2.074	2.508	2.819	3.505
23	1.319	1.714	2.069	2.500	2.807	3.485
24	1.318	1.711	2.064	2.492	2.797	3.467
25	1.316	1.708	2.060	2.485	2.787	3.450
26	1.315	1.706	2.056	2.479	2.779	3.435
27	1.314	1.703	2.052	2.473	2.771	3.421
28	1.313	1.701	2.048	2.467	2.763	3.408
29	1.311	1.699	2.045	2.462	2.756	3.396
30	1.310	1.697	2.042	2.457	2.750	3.385
40	1.303	1.684	2.021	2.423	2.704	3.307
50	1.299	1.676	2.009	2.403	2.678	3.261
60	1.296	1.671	2.000	2.390	2.660	3.232
70	1.294	1.667	1.994	2.381	2.648	3.211
80	1.292	1.664	1.990	2.374	2.639	3.195
90	1.291	1.662	1.987	2.368	2.632	3.183
100	1.290	1.660	1.984	2.364	2.626	3.174
150	1.287	1.655	1.976	2.351	2.609	3.145
200	1.286	1.653	1.972	2.345	2.601	3.131
∞	1.282	1.645	1.960	2.326	2.576	3.090

TABLE A.4

Percentage points of the F distribution

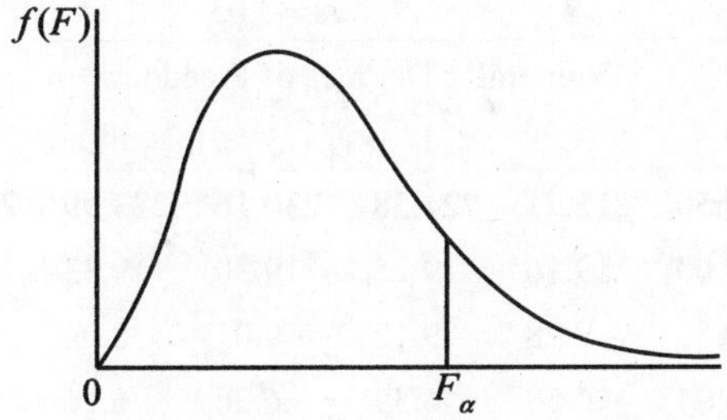

ν_2 \ ν_1	$\alpha = 0.10$ Numerator Degrees of Freedom																		
	1	2	3	4	5	6	7	8	9	10	12	15	20	24	30	40	60	120	∞
1	39.86	49.50	53.59	55.83	57.24	58.20	58.91	59.44	59.86	60.19	60.71	61.22	61.74	62.00	62.26	62.53	62.79	63.06	63.33
2	8.53	9.00	9.16	9.24	9.29	9.33	9.35	9.37	9.38	9.39	9.41	9.42	9.44	9.45	9.46	9.47	9.47	9.48	9.49
3	5.54	5.46	5.39	5.34	5.31	5.28	5.27	5.25	5.24	5.23	5.22	5.20	5.18	5.18	5.17	5.16	5.15	5.14	5.13
4	4.54	4.32	4.19	4.11	4.05	4.01	3.98	3.95	3.94	3.92	3.90	3.87	3.84	3.83	3.82	3.80	3.79	3.78	3.76
5	4.06	3.78	3.62	3.52	3.45	3.40	3.37	3.34	3.32	3.30	3.27	3.24	3.21	3.19	3.17	3.16	3.14	3.12	3.10
6	3.78	3.46	3.29	3.18	3.11	3.05	3.01	2.98	2.96	2.94	2.90	2.87	2.84	2.82	2.80	2.78	2.76	2.74	2.72
7	3.59	3.26	3.07	2.96	2.88	2.83	2.78	2.75	2.72	2.70	2.67	2.63	2.59	2.58	2.56	2.54	2.51	2.49	2.47
8	3.46	3.11	2.92	2.81	2.73	2.67	2.62	2.59	2.56	2.54	2.50	2.46	2.42	2.40	2.38	2.36	2.34	2.32	2.29
9	3.36	3.01	2.81	2.69	2.61	2.55	2.51	2.47	2.44	2.42	2.38	2.34	2.30	2.28	2.25	2.23	2.21	2.18	2.16
10	3.29	2.92	2.73	2.61	2.52	2.46	2.41	2.38	2.35	2.32	2.28	2.24	2.20	2.18	2.16	2.13	2.11	2.08	2.06
11	3.23	2.86	2.66	2.54	2.45	2.39	2.34	2.30	2.27	2.25	2.21	2.17	2.12	2.10	2.08	2.05	2.03	2.00	1.97
12	3.18	2.81	2.61	2.48	2.39	2.33	2.28	2.24	2.21	2.19	2.15	2.10	2.06	2.04	2.01	1.99	1.96	1.93	1.90
13	3.14	2.76	2.56	2.43	2.35	2.28	2.23	2.20	2.16	2.14	2.10	2.05	2.01	1.98	1.96	1.93	1.90	1.88	1.85
14	3.10	2.73	2.52	2.39	2.31	2.24	2.19	2.15	2.12	2.10	2.05	2.01	1.96	1.94	1.91	1.89	1.86	1.83	1.80
15	3.07	2.70	2.49	2.36	2.27	2.21	2.16	2.12	2.09	2.06	2.02	1.97	1.92	1.90	1.87	1.85	1.82	1.79	1.76
16	3.05	2.67	2.46	2.33	2.24	2.18	2.13	2.09	2.06	2.03	1.99	1.94	1.89	1.87	1.84	1.81	1.78	1.75	1.72
17	3.03	2.64	2.44	2.31	2.22	2.15	2.10	2.06	2.03	2.00	1.96	1.91	1.86	1.84	1.81	1.78	1.75	1.72	1.69
18	3.01	2.62	2.42	2.29	2.20	2.13	2.08	2.04	2.00	1.98	1.93	1.89	1.84	1.81	1.78	1.75	1.72	1.69	1.66
19	2.99	2.61	2.40	2.27	2.18	2.11	2.06	2.02	1.98	1.96	1.91	1.86	1.81	1.79	1.76	1.73	1.70	1.67	1.63
20	2.97	2.59	2.38	2.25	2.16	2.09	2.04	2.00	1.96	1.94	1.89	1.84	1.79	1.77	1.74	1.71	1.68	1.64	1.61
21	2.96	2.57	2.36	2.23	2.14	2.08	2.02	1.98	1.95	1.92	1.87	1.83	1.78	1.75	1.72	1.69	1.66	1.62	1.59
22	2.95	2.56	2.35	2.22	2.13	2.06	2.01	1.97	1.93	1.90	1.86	1.81	1.76	1.73	1.70	1.67	1.64	1.60	1.57
23	2.94	2.55	2.34	2.21	2.11	2.05	1.99	1.95	1.92	1.89	1.84	1.80	1.74	1.72	1.69	1.66	1.62	1.59	1.55
24	2.93	2.54	2.33	2.19	2.10	2.04	1.98	1.94	1.91	1.88	1.83	1.78	1.73	1.70	1.67	1.64	1.61	1.57	1.53
25	2.92	2.53	2.32	2.18	2.09	2.02	1.97	1.93	1.89	1.87	1.82	1.77	1.72	1.69	1.66	1.63	1.59	1.56	1.52
26	2.91	2.52	2.31	2.17	2.08	2.01	1.96	1.92	1.88	1.86	1.81	1.76	1.71	1.68	1.65	1.61	1.58	1.54	1.50
27	2.90	2.51	2.30	2.17	2.07	2.00	1.95	1.91	1.87	1.85	1.80	1.75	1.70	1.67	1.64	1.60	1.57	1.53	1.49
28	2.89	2.50	2.29	2.16	2.06	2.00	1.94	1.90	1.87	1.84	1.79	1.74	1.69	1.66	1.63	1.59	1.56	1.52	1.48
29	2.89	2.50	2.28	2.15	2.06	1.99	1.93	1.89	1.86	1.83	1.78	1.73	1.68	1.65	1.62	1.58	1.55	1.51	1.47
30	2.88	2.49	2.28	2.14	2.05	1.98	1.93	1.88	1.85	1.82	1.77	1.72	1.67	1.64	1.61	1.57	1.54	1.50	1.46
40	2.84	2.44	2.23	2.09	2.00	1.93	1.87	1.83	1.79	1.76	1.71	1.66	1.61	1.57	1.54	1.51	1.47	1.42	1.38
60	2.79	2.39	2.18	2.04	1.95	1.87	1.82	1.77	1.74	1.71	1.66	1.60	1.54	1.51	1.48	1.44	1.40	1.35	1.29
120	2.75	2.35	2.13	1.99	1.90	1.82	1.77	1.72	1.68	1.65	1.60	1.55	1.48	1.45	1.41	1.37	1.32	1.26	1.19
∞	2.71	2.30	2.08	1.94	1.85	1.77	1.72	1.67	1.63	1.60	1.55	1.49	1.42	1.38	1.34	1.30	1.24	1.17	1.00

TABLE A.4 *(Continued)*
Percentage points of the *F* distribution

v_2 \ v_1	$\alpha = 0.05$								
	Numerator Degrees of Freedom								
Denominator Degrees of Freedom	1	2	3	4	5	6	7	8	9
1	161.45	199.50	215.71	224.58	230.16	233.99	236.77	238.88	240.54
2	18.51	19.00	19.16	19.25	19.30	19.33	19.35	19.37	19.38
3	10.13	9.55	9.28	9.12	9.01	8.94	8.89	8.85	8.81
4	7.71	6.94	6.59	6.39	6.26	6.16	6.09	6.04	6.00
5	6.61	5.79	5.41	5.19	5.05	4.95	4.88	4.82	4.77
6	5.99	5.14	4.76	4.53	4.39	4.28	4.21	4.15	4.10
7	5.59	4.74	4.35	4.12	3.97	3.87	3.79	3.73	3.68
8	5.32	4.46	4.07	3.84	3.69	3.58	3.50	3.44	3.39
9	5.12	4.26	3.86	3.63	3.48	3.37	3.29	3.23	3.18
10	4.96	4.10	3.71	3.48	3.33	3.22	3.14	3.07	3.02
11	4.84	3.98	3.59	3.36	3.20	3.09	3.01	2.95	2.90
12	4.75	3.89	3.49	3.26	3.11	3.00	2.91	2.85	2.80
13	4.67	3.81	3.41	3.18	3.03	2.92	2.83	2.77	2.71
14	4.60	3.74	3.34	3.11	2.96	2.85	2.76	2.70	2.65
15	4.54	3.68	3.29	3.06	2.90	2.79	2.71	2.64	2.59
16	4.49	3.63	3.24	3.01	2.85	2.74	2.66	2.59	2.54
17	4.45	3.59	3.20	2.96	2.81	2.70	2.61	2.55	2.49
18	4.41	3.55	3.16	2.93	2.77	2.66	2.58	2.51	2.46
19	4.38	3.52	3.13	2.90	2.74	2.63	2.54	2.48	2.42
20	4.35	3.49	3.10	2.87	2.71	2.60	2.51	2.45	2.39
21	4.32	3.47	3.07	2.84	2.68	2.57	2.49	2.42	2.37
22	4.30	3.44	3.05	2.82	2.66	2.55	2.46	2.40	2.34
23	4.28	3.42	3.03	2.80	2.64	2.53	2.44	2.37	2.32
24	4.26	3.40	3.01	2.78	2.62	2.51	2.42	2.36	2.30
25	4.24	3.39	2.99	2.76	2.60	2.49	2.40	2.34	2.28
26	4.23	3.37	2.98	2.74	2.59	2.47	2.39	2.32	2.27
27	4.21	3.35	2.96	2.73	2.57	2.46	2.37	2.31	2.25
28	4.20	3.34	2.95	2.71	2.56	2.45	2.36	2.29	2.24
29	4.18	3.33	2.93	2.70	2.55	2.43	2.35	2.28	2.22
30	4.17	3.32	2.92	2.69	2.53	2.42	2.33	2.27	2.21
40	4.08	3.23	2.84	2.61	2.45	2.34	2.25	2.18	2.12
60	4.00	3.15	2.76	2.53	2.37	2.25	2.17	2.10	2.04
120	3.92	3.07	2.68	2.45	2.29	2.18	2.09	2.02	1.96
∞	3.84	3.00	2.60	2.37	2.21	2.10	2.01	1.94	1.88

$\alpha = 0.05$

Numerator Degrees of Freedom										v_1 / v_2
10	12	15	20	24	30	40	60	120	∞	
241.88	243.90	245.90	248.00	249.10	250.10	251.10	252.20	253.30	254.30	1
19.40	19.41	19.43	19.45	19.45	19.46	19.47	19.48	19.49	19.50	2
8.79	8.74	8.70	8.66	8.64	8.62	8.59	8.57	8.55	8.53	3
5.96	5.91	5.86	5.80	5.77	5.75	5.72	5.69	5.66	5.63	4
4.74	4.68	4.62	4.56	4.53	4.50	4.46	4.43	4.40	4.36	5
4.06	4.00	3.94	3.87	3.84	3.81	3.77	3.74	3.70	3.67	6
3.64	3.57	3.51	3.44	3.41	3.38	3.34	3.30	3.27	3.23	7
3.35	3.28	3.22	3.15	3.12	3.08	3.04	3.01	2.97	2.93	8
3.14	3.07	3.01	2.94	2.90	2.86	2.83	2.79	2.75	2.71	9
2.98	2.91	2.85	2.77	2.74	2.70	2.66	2.62	2.58	2.54	10
2.85	2.79	2.72	2.65	2.61	2.57	2.53	2.49	2.45	2.40	11
2.75	2.69	2.62	2.54	2.51	2.47	2.43	2.38	2.34	2.30	12
2.67	2.60	2.53	2.46	2.42	2.38	2.34	2.30	2.25	2.21	13
2.60	2.53	2.46	2.39	2.35	2.31	2.27	2.22	2.18	2.13	14
2.54	2.48	2.40	2.33	2.29	2.25	2.20	2.16	2.11	2.07	15
2.49	2.42	2.35	2.28	2.24	2.19	2.15	2.11	2.06	2.01	16
2.45	2.38	2.31	2.23	2.19	2.15	2.10	2.06	2.01	1.96	17
2.41	2.34	2.27	2.19	2.15	2.11	2.06	2.02	1.97	1.92	18
2.38	2.31	2.23	2.16	2.11	2.07	2.03	1.98	1.93	1.88	19
2.35	2.28	2.20	2.12	2.08	2.04	1.99	1.95	1.90	1.84	20
2.32	2.25	2.18	2.10	2.05	2.01	1.96	1.92	1.87	1.81	21
2.30	2.23	2.15	2.07	2.03	1.98	1.94	1.89	1.84	1.78	22
2.27	2.20	2.13	2.05	2.01	1.96	1.91	1.86	1.81	1.76	23
2.25	2.18	2.11	2.03	1.98	1.94	1.89	1.84	1.79	1.73	24
2.24	2.16	2.09	2.01	1.96	1.92	1.87	1.82	1.77	1.71	25
2.22	2.15	2.07	1.99	1.95	1.90	1.85	1.80	1.75	1.69	26
2.20	2.13	2.06	1.97	1.93	1.88	1.84	1.79	1.73	1.67	27
2.19	2.12	2.04	1.96	1.91	1.87	1.82	1.77	1.71	1.65	28
2.18	2.10	2.03	1.94	1.90	1.85	1.81	1.75	1.70	1.64	29
2.16	2.09	2.01	1.93	1.89	1.84	1.79	1.74	1.68	1.62	30
2.08	2.00	1.92	1.84	1.79	1.74	1.69	1.64	1.58	1.51	40
1.99	1.92	1.84	1.75	1.70	1.65	1.59	1.53	1.47	1.39	60
1.91	1.83	1.75	1.66	1.61	1.55	1.50	1.43	1.35	1.25	120
1.83	1.75	1.67	1.57	1.52	1.46	1.39	1.32	1.22	1.00	∞

Denominator Degrees of Freedom

(Continued)

TABLE A.4 *(Continued)*
Percentage points of the *F* distribution

v_2 \ v_1	$\alpha = 0.025$								
	Numerator Degrees of Freedom								
Denominator Degrees of Freedom	1	2	3	4	5	6	7	8	9
1	647.79	799.48	864.15	899.60	921.83	937.11	948.20	956.64	963.28
2	38.51	39.00	39.17	39.25	39.30	39.33	39.36	39.37	39.39
3	17.44	16.04	15.44	15.10	14.88	14.73	14.62	14.54	14.47
4	12.22	10.65	9.98	9.60	9.36	9.20	9.07	8.98	8.90
5	10.01	8.43	7.76	7.39	7.15	6.98	6.85	6.76	6.68
6	8.81	7.26	6.60	6.23	5.99	5.82	5.70	5.60	5.52
7	8.07	6.54	5.89	5.52	5.29	5.12	4.99	4.90	4.82
8	7.57	6.06	5.42	5.05	4.82	4.65	4.53	4.43	4.36
9	7.21	5.71	5.08	4.72	4.48	4.32	4.20	4.10	4.03
10	6.94	5.46	4.83	4.47	4.24	4.07	3.95	3.85	3.78
11	6.72	5.26	4.63	4.28	4.04	3.88	3.76	3.66	3.59
12	6.55	5.10	4.47	4.12	3.89	3.73	3.61	3.51	3.44
13	6.41	4.97	4.35	4.00	3.77	3.60	3.48	3.39	3.31
14	6.30	4.86	4.24	3.89	3.66	3.50	3.38	3.29	3.21
15	6.20	4.77	4.15	3.80	3.58	3.41	3.29	3.20	3.12
16	6.12	4.69	4.08	3.73	3.50	3.34	3.22	3.12	3.05
17	6.04	4.62	4.01	3.66	3.44	3.28	3.16	3.06	2.98
18	5.98	4.56	3.95	3.61	3.38	3.22	3.10	3.01	2.93
19	5.92	4.51	3.90	3.56	3.33	3.17	3.05	2.96	2.88
20	5.87	4.46	3.86	3.51	3.29	3.13	3.01	2.91	2.84
21	5.83	4.42	3.82	3.48	3.25	3.09	2.97	2.87	2.80
22	5.79	4.38	3.78	3.44	3.22	3.05	2.93	2.84	2.76
23	5.75	4.35	3.75	3.41	3.18	3.02	2.90	2.81	2.73
24	5.72	4.32	3.72	3.38	3.15	2.99	2.87	2.78	2.70
25	5.69	4.29	3.69	3.35	3.13	2.97	2.85	2.75	2.68
26	5.66	4.27	3.67	3.33	3.10	2.94	2.82	2.73	2.65
27	5.63	4.24	3.65	3.31	3.08	2.92	2.80	2.71	2.63
28	5.61	4.22	3.63	3.29	3.06	2.90	2.78	2.69	2.61
29	5.59	4.20	3.61	3.27	3.04	2.88	2.76	2.67	2.59
30	5.57	4.18	3.59	3.25	3.03	2.87	2.75	2.65	2.57
40	5.42	4.05	3.46	3.13	2.90	2.74	2.62	2.53	2.45
60	5.29	3.93	3.34	3.01	2.79	2.63	2.51	2.41	2.33
120	5.15	3.80	3.23	2.89	2.67	2.52	2.39	2.30	2.22
∞	5.02	3.69	3.12	2.79	2.57	2.41	2.29	2.19	2.11

$\alpha = 0.025$										
Numerator Degrees of Freedom										v_1 / v_2
10	12	15	20	24	30	40	60	120	∞	Denominator Degrees of Freedom
968.63	976.72	984.87	993.08	997.27	1001.40	1005.60	1009.79	1014.04	1018.00	1
9.40	39.41	39.43	39.45	39.46	39.46	39.47	39.48	39.49	39.50	2
14.42	14.34	14.25	14.17	14.12	14.08	14.04	13.99	13.95	13.90	3
8.84	8.75	8.66	8.56	8.51	8.46	8.41	8.36	8.31	8.26	4
6.62	6.52	6.43	6.33	6.28	6.23	6.18	6.12	6.07	6.02	5
5.46	5.37	5.27	5.17	5.12	5.07	5.01	4.96	4.90	4.85	6
4.76	4.67	4.57	4.47	4.41	4.36	4.31	4.25	4.20	4.14	7
4.30	4.20	4.10	4.00	3.95	3.89	3.84	3.78	3.73	3.67	8
3.96	3.87	3.77	3.67	3.61	3.56	3.51	3.45	3.39	3.33	9
3.72	3.62	3.52	3.42	3.37	3.31	3.26	3.20	3.14	3.08	10
3.53	3.43	3.33	3.23	3.17	3.12	3.06	3.00	2.94	2.88	11
3.37	3.28	3.18	3.07	3.02	2.96	2.91	2.85	2.79	2.72	12
3.25	3.15	3.05	2.95	2.89	2.84	2.78	2.72	2.66	2.60	13
3.15	3.05	2.95	2.84	2.79	2.73	2.67	2.61	2.55	2.49	14
3.06	2.96	2.86	2.76	2.70	2.64	2.59	2.52	2.46	2.40	15
2.99	2.89	2.79	2.68	2.63	2.57	2.51	2.45	2.38	2.32	16
2.92	2.82	2.72	2.62	2.56	2.50	2.44	2.38	2.32	2.25	17
2.87	2.77	2.67	2.56	2.50	2.44	2.38	2.32	2.26	2.19	18
2.82	2.72	2.62	2.51	2.45	2.39	2.33	2.27	2.20	2.13	19
2.77	2.68	2.57	2.46	2.41	2.35	2.29	2.22	2.16	2.09	20
2.73	2.64	2.53	2.42	2.37	2.31	2.25	2.18	2.11	2.04	21
2.70	2.60	2.50	2.39	2.33	2.27	2.21	2.14	2.08	2.00	22
2.67	2.57	2.47	2.36	2.30	2.24	2.18	2.11	2.04	1.97	23
2.64	2.54	2.44	2.33	2.27	2.21	2.15	2.08	2.01	1.94	24
2.61	2.51	2.41	2.30	2.24	2.18	2.12	2.05	1.98	1.91	25
2.59	2.49	2.39	2.28	2.22	2.16	2.09	2.03	1.95	1.88	26
2.57	2.47	2.36	2.25	2.19	2.13	2.07	2.00	1.93	1.85	27
2.55	2.45	2.34	2.23	2.17	2.11	2.05	1.98	1.91	1.83	28
2.53	2.43	2.32	2.21	2.15	2.09	2.03	1.96	1.89	1.81	29
2.51	2.41	2.31	2.20	2.14	2.07	2.01	1.94	1.87	1.79	30
2.39	2.29	2.18	2.07	2.01	1.94	1.88	1.80	1.72	1.64	40
2.27	2.17	2.06	1.94	1.88	1.82	1.74	1.67	1.58	1.48	60
2.16	2.05	1.94	1.82	1.76	1.69	1.61	1.53	1.43	1.31	120
2.05	1.94	1.83	1.71	1.64	1.57	1.48	1.39	1.27	1.00	∞

(Continued)

TABLE A.4 *(Continued)*
Percentage points of the *F* distribution

$\alpha = 0.01$

Numerator Degrees of Freedom (v_1); Denominator Degrees of Freedom (v_2)

v_2 \ v_1	1	2	3	4	5	6	7	8	9
1	4052.18	4999.34	5403.53	5624.26	5763.96	5858.95	5928.33	5980.95	6022.40
2	98.50	99.00	99.16	99.25	99.30	99.33	99.36	99.38	99.39
3	34.12	30.82	29.46	28.71	28.24	27.91	27.67	27.49	27.34
4	21.20	18.00	16.69	15.98	15.52	15.21	14.98	14.80	14.66
5	16.26	13.27	12.06	11.39	10.97	10.67	10.46	10.29	10.16
6	13.75	10.92	9.78	9.15	8.75	8.47	8.26	8.10	7.98
7	12.25	9.55	8.45	7.85	7.46	7.19	6.99	6.84	6.72
8	11.26	8.65	7.59	7.01	6.63	6.37	6.18	6.03	5.91
9	10.56	8.02	6.99	6.42	6.06	5.80	5.61	5.47	5.35
10	10.04	7.56	6.55	5.99	5.64	5.39	5.20	5.06	4.94
11	9.65	7.21	6.22	5.67	5.32	5.07	4.89	4.74	4.63
12	9.33	6.93	5.95	5.41	5.06	4.82	4.64	4.50	4.39
13	9.07	6.70	5.74	5.21	4.86	4.62	4.44	4.30	4.19
14	8.86	6.51	5.56	5.04	4.69	4.46	4.28	4.14	4.03
15	8.68	6.36	5.42	4.89	4.56	4.32	4.14	4.00	3.89
16	8.53	6.23	5.29	4.77	4.44	4.20	4.03	3.89	3.78
17	8.40	6.11	5.19	4.67	4.34	4.10	3.93	3.79	3.68
18	8.29	6.01	5.09	4.58	4.25	4.01	3.84	3.71	3.60
19	8.18	5.93	5.01	4.50	4.17	3.94	3.77	3.63	3.52
20	8.10	5.85	4.94	4.43	4.10	3.87	3.70	3.56	3.46
21	8.02	5.78	4.87	4.37	4.04	3.81	3.64	3.51	3.40
22	7.95	5.72	4.82	4.31	3.99	3.76	3.59	3.45	3.35
23	7.88	5.66	4.76	4.26	3.94	3.71	3.54	3.41	3.30
24	7.82	5.61	4.72	4.22	3.90	3.67	3.50	3.36	3.26
25	7.77	5.57	4.68	4.18	3.85	3.63	3.46	3.32	3.22
26	7.72	5.53	4.64	4.14	3.82	3.59	3.42	3.29	3.18
27	7.68	5.49	4.60	4.11	3.78	3.56	3.39	3.26	3.15
28	7.64	5.45	4.57	4.07	3.75	3.53	3.36	3.23	3.12
29	7.60	5.42	4.54	4.04	3.73	3.50	3.33	3.20	3.09
30	7.56	5.39	4.51	4.02	3.70	3.47	3.30	3.17	3.07
40	7.31	5.18	4.31	3.83	3.51	3.29	3.12	2.99	2.89
60	7.08	4.98	4.13	3.65	3.34	3.12	2.95	2.82	2.72
120	6.85	4.79	3.95	3.48	3.17	2.96	2.79	2.66	2.56
∞	6.63	4.61	3.78	3.32	3.02	2.80	2.64	2.51	2.41

$\alpha = 0.01$										
Numerator Degrees of Freedom										v_1 / v_2
10	12	15	20	24	30	40	60	120	∞	Denominator Degrees of Freedom
6055.93	6106.68	6156.97	6208.66	6234.27	6260.35	6286.43	6312.97	6339.51	6366.00	1
99.40	99.42	99.43	99.45	99.46	99.47	99.48	99.48	99.49	99.50	2
27.23	27.05	26.87	26.69	26.60	26.50	26.41	26.32	26.22	26.13	3
14.55	14.37	14.20	14.02	13.93	13.84	13.75	13.65	13.56	13.46	4
10.05	9.89	9.72	9.55	9.47	9.38	9.29	9.20	9.11	9.02	5
7.87	7.72	7.56	7.40	7.31	7.23	7.14	7.06	6.97	6.88	6
6.62	6.47	6.31	6.16	6.07	5.99	5.91	5.82	5.74	5.65	7
5.81	5.67	5.52	5.36	5.28	5.20	5.12	5.03	4.95	4.86	8
5.26	5.11	4.96	4.81	4.73	4.65	4.57	4.48	4.40	4.31	9
4.85	4.71	4.56	4.41	4.33	4.25	4.17	4.08	4.00	3.91	10
4.54	4.40	4.25	4.10	4.02	3.94	3.86	3.78	3.69	3.60	11
4.30	4.16	4.01	3.86	3.78	3.70	3.62	3.54	3.45	3.36	12
4.10	3.96	3.82	3.66	3.59	331	3.43	3.34	3.25	3.17	13
3.94	3.80	3.66	3.51	3.43	3.35	3.27	3.18	3.09	3.00	14
3.80	3.67	3.52	3.37	3.29	3.21	3.13	3.05	2.96	2.87	15
3.69	3.55	3.41	3.26	3.18	3.10	3.02	2.93	2.84	2.75	16
3.59	3.46	3.31	3.16	3.08	3.00	2.92	2.83	2.75	2.65	17
3.51	3.37	3.23	3.08	3.00	2.92	2.84	2.75	2.66	2.57	18
3.43	3.30	3.15	3.00	2.92	2.84	2.76	2.67	2.58	2.49	19
3.37	3.23	3.09	2.94	2.86	2.78	2.69	2.61	2.S2	2.42	20
3.31	3.17	3.03	2.88	2.80	2.72	2.64	2.55	2.46	2J6	21
3.26	3.12	2.98	2.83	2.75	2.67	2.58	2.50	2.40	2.31	22
3.21	3.07	2.93	2.78	2.70	2.62	2.54	2.45	2.35	2.26	23
3.17	3.03	2.89	2.74	2.66	2.58	2.49	2.40	2.31	2.21	24
3.13	2.99	2.85	2.70	2.62	2.54	2.45	2.36	2.27	2.17	25
3.09	2.96	2.81	2.66	2.58	2.50	2.42	2.33	2.23	2.13	26
3.06	2.93	2.78	2.63	2.55	2.47	2.38	2.29	2.20	2.10	27
3.03	2.90	2.75	2.60	2.52	2.44	2.35	2.26	2.17	2.06	28
3.00	2.87	2.73	2.57	2.49	2.41	2.33	2.23	2.14	2.03	29
2.98	2.84	2.70	2.55	2.47	2.39	2.30	2.21	2.11	2.01	30
2.80	2.66	2.52	2.37	2.29	2.20	2.11	2.02	1.92	1.80	40
2.63	2.50	2.35	2.20	2.12	2.03	1.94	1.84	1.73	1.60	60
2.47	2.34	2.19	2.03	1.95	1.86	1.76	1.66	1.53	1.38	120
2.32	2.18	2.04	1.88	1.79	1.70	1.59	1.47	1.32	1.00	∞

(Continued)

TABLE A.4 *(Continued)*
Percentage points of the *F* distribution

v_2 \ v_1	1	2	3	4	5	6	7	8	9
	$\alpha = 0.005$								
	Numerator Degrees of Freedom								
Denominator Degrees of Freedom									
1	16212.46	19997.36	21614.13	22500.75	23055.82	23439.53	23715.20	23923.81	24091.45
2	198.50	199.01	199.16	199.24	199.30	199.33	199.36	199.38	199.39
3	55.55	49.80	47.47	46.20	45.39	44.84	44.43	44.13	43.88
4	31.33	26.28	24.26	23.15	22.46	21.98	21.62	21.35	21.14
5	22.78	18.31	16.53	15.56	14.94	14.51	14.20	13.96	13.77
6	18.63	14.54	12.92	12.03	11.46	11.07	10.79	10.57	10.39
7	16.24	12.40	10.88	10.05	9.52	9.16	8.89	8.68	8.51
8	14.69	11.04	9.60	8.81	8.30	7.95	7.69	7.50	7.34
9	13.61	10.11	8.72	7.96	7.47	7.13	6.88	6.69	6.54
10	12.83	9.43	8.08	7.34	6.87	6.54	6.30	6.12	5.97
11	12.23	8.91	7.60	6.88	6.42	6.10	5.86	5.68	5.54
12	11.75	8.51	7.23	6.52	6.07	5.76	5.52	5.35	5.20
13	11.37	8.19	6.93	6.23	5.79	5.48	5.25	5.08	4.94
14	11.06	7.92	6.68	6.00	5.56	5.26	5.03	4.86	4.72
15	10.80	7:70	6.48	5.80	5.37	5.07	4.85	4.67	4.54
16	10.58	7.51	6.30	5.64	5.21	4.91	4.69	4.52	4.38
17	10.38	7.35	6.16	5.50	5.07	4.78	4.56	4.39	4.25
18	10.22	7.21	6.03	5.37	4.96	4.66	4.44	4.28	4.14
19	10.07	7.09	5.92	5.27	4.85	4.56	4.34	4.18	4.04
20	9.94	6.99	5.82	5.17	4.76	4.47	4.26	4.09	3.96
21	9.83	6.89	5.73	5.09	4.68	4.39	4.18	4.01	3.88
22	9.73	6.81	5.65	5.02	4.61	4.32	4.11	3.94	3.81
23	9.63	6.73	5.58	4.95	4.54	4.26	4.05	3.88	3.75
24	9.55	6.66	5.52	4.89	4.49	4.20	3.99	3.83	3.69
25	9.48	6.60	5.46	4.84	4.43	4.15	3.94	3.78	3.64
26	9.41	6.54	5.41	4.79	4.38	4.10	3.89	3.73	3.60
27	9.34	6.49	5.36	4.74	4.34	4.06	3.85	3.69	3.56
28	9.28	6.44	5.32	4.70	4.30	4.02	3.81	3.65	3.52
29	9.23	6.40	5.28	4.66	4.26	3.98	3.77	3.61	3.48
30	9.18	6.35	5.24	4.62	4.23	3.95	3.74	3.58	3.45
40	8.83	6.07	4.98	4.37	3.99	3.71	3.51	3.35	3.22
60	8.49	5.79	4.73	4.14	3.76	3.49	3.29	3.13	3.01
120	8.18	5.54	4.50	3.92	3.55	3.28	3.09	2.93	2.81
∞	7.88	5.30	4.28	3.72	3.35	3.09	2.90	2.74	2.62

$\alpha = 0.005$										ν_1 / ν_2
Numerator Degrees of Freedom										
10	12	15	20	24	30	40	60	120	∞	ν_2
24221.84	24426.73	24631.62	24836.51	24937.09	25041.40	25145.71	25253.74	25358.05	25465.00	1
199.39	199.42	199.43	199.45	199.45	199.48	199.48	199.48	199.49	199.50	2
43.68	43.39	43.08	42.78	42.62	42.47	42.31	42.15	41.99	41.83	3
20.97	20.70	20.44	20.17	20.03	19.89	19.75	19.61	19.47	19.32	4
13.62	13.38	13.15	12.90	12.78	12.66	12.53	12.40	12.27	12.14	5
10.25	10.03	9.81	9.59	9.47	9.36	9.24	9.12	9.00	8.88	6
8.38	8.18	7.97	7.75	7.64	7.53	7.42	7.31	7.19	7.08	7
7.21	7.01	6.81	6.61	6.50	6.40	6.29	6.18	6.06	5.95	8
6.42	6.23	6.03	5.83	5.73	5.62	5.52	5.41	5.30	5.19	9
5.85	5.66	5.47	5.27	5.17	5.07	4.97	4.86	4.75	4.64	10
5.42	5.24	5.05	4.86	4.76	4.65	4.55	4.45	4.34	4.23	11
5.09	4.91	4.72	4.53	4.43	4.33	4.23	4.12	4.01	3.90	12
4.82	4.64	4.46	4.27	4.17	4.07	3.97	3.87	3.76	3.65	13
4.60	4.43	4.25	4.06	3.96	3.86	3.76	3.66	3.55	3.44	14
4.42	4.25	4.07	3.88	3.79	3.69	3.59	3.48	3.37	3.26	15
4.27	4.10	3.92	3.73	3.64	3.54	3.44	3.33	3.22	3.11	16
4.14	3.97	3.79	3.61	3.51	3.41	3.31	3.21	3.10	2.98	17
4.03	3.86	3.68	3.50	3.40	3.30	3.20	3.10	2.99	2.87	18
3.93	3.76	3.59	3.40	3.31	3.21	3.11	3.00	2.89	2.78	19
3.85	3.68	3.50	3.32	3.22	3.12	3.02	2.92	2.81	2.69	20
3.77	3.60	3.43	3.24	3.15	3.05	2.95	2.84	2.73	2.61	21
3.70	3.54	3.36	3.18	3.08	2.98	2.88	2.77	2.66	2.55	22
3.64	3.47	3.30	3.12	3.02	2.92	2.82	2.71	2.60	2.48	23
3.59	3.42	3.25	3.06	2.97	2.87	2.77	2.66	2.55	2.43	24
3.54	3.37	3.20	3.01	2.92	2.82	2.72	2.61	2.50	2.38	25
3.49	3.33	3.15	2.97	2.87	2.77	2.67	2.56	2.45	2.33	26
3.45	3.28	3.11	2.93	2.83	2.73	2.63	2.52	2.41	2.29	27
3.41	3.25	3.07	2.89	2.79	2.69	2.59	2.48	2.37	2.25	28
3.38	3.21	3.04	2.86	2.76	2.66	2.56	2.45	2.33	2.21	29
3.34	3.18	3.01	2.82	2.73	2.63	2.52	2.42	2.30	2.18	30
3.12	2.95	2.78	2.60	2.50	2.40	2.30	2.18	2.06	1.93	40
2.90	2.74	2.57	2.39	2.29	2.19	2.08	1.96	1.83	1.69	60
2.71	2.54	2.37	2.19	2.09	1.98	1.87	1.75	1.61	1.43	120
2.52	2.36	2.19	2.00	1.90	1.79	1.67	1.53	1.36	1.00	∞

Denominator Degrees of Freedom

TABLE A.5
The Chi-Square table

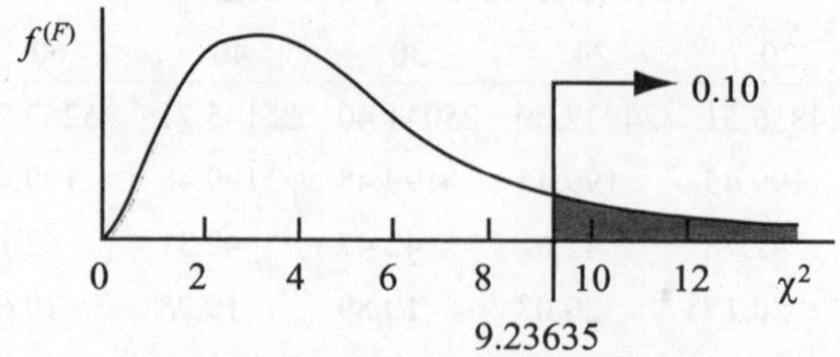

Example df (number of degrees of freedom) = 5, the tail above $\chi^2 = 9.23635$ represents 0.10 or 10% of the area under the curve

Degrees of Freedom	Area in Upper Tail									
	0.995	0.99	0.975	0.95	0.9	0.1	0.05	0.025	0.01	0.005
1	0.0000393	0.0001571	0.0009821	0.0039322	0.0157907	2.7055	3.8415	5.0239	6.6349	7.8794
2	0.010025	0.020100	0.050636	0.102586	0.210721	4.6052	5.9915	7.3778	9.2104	10.5965
3	0.07172	0.11483	0.21579	0.35185	0.58438	6.2514	7.8147	9.3484	11.3449	12.8381
4	0.20698	0.29711	0.48442	0.71072	1.06362	7.7794	9.4877	11.1433	13.2767	14.8602
5	0.41175	0.55430	0.83121	1.14548	1.61031	9.2363	11.0705	12.8325	15.0863	16.7496
6	0.67573	0.87208	1.23734	1.63538	2.20413	10.6446	12.5916	14.4494	16.8119	18.5475
7	0.98925	1.23903	1.68986	2.16735	2.83311	12.0170	14.0671	16.0128	18.4753	20.2777
8	1.34440	1.64651	2.17972	2.73263	3.48954	13.3616	15.5073	17.5345	20.0902	21.9549
9	1.73491	2.08789	2.70039	3.32512	4.16816	14.6837	16.9190	19.0228	21.6660	23.5893
10	2.15585	2.55820	3.24696	3.94030	4.86518	15.9872	18.3070	20.4832	23.2093	25.1881
11	2.60320	3.05350	3.81574	4.57481	5.57779	17.2750	19.6752	21.9200	24.7250	26.7569
12	3.07379	3.57055	4.40378	5.22603	6.30380	18.5493	21.0261	23.3367	26.2170	28.2997
13	3.56504	4.10690	5.00874	5.8') 186	7.04150	19.8119	22.3620	24.7356	27.6882	29.8193
14	4.07466	4.66042	5.62872	6.57063	7.78954	21.0641	23.6848	26.1189	29.1412	31.3194
15	4.60087	5.22936	6.26212	7..26093	8.54675	22.3071	24.9958	27.4884	30.5780	32.8015
16	5.14216	5.81220	6.90766	7.96164	9.31224	23.5418	26.2962	28.8453	31.9999	34.2671
17	5.69727	6.40774	7.56418	8.67175	10.08518	24.7690	27.5871	30.1910	33.4087	35.7184
18	6.26477	7.01490	8.23074	9.39045	10.86494	25.9894	28.8693	31.5264	34.8052	37.1564
19	6.84392	7.63270	8.90651	10.11701	11.65091	27.2036	30.1435	32.8523	36.1908	38.5821
20	7.43381	8.26037	9.59077	10.85080	12.44260	28.4120	31.4104	34.1696	37.5663	39.9969
21	8.03360	8.89717	10.28291	11.59132	13.23960	29.6151	32.6706	35.4789	38.9322	41.4009
22	8.64268	9.54249	10.98233	12.33801	14.04149	30.8133	33.9245	36.7807	40.2894	42.7957
23	9.26038	10.19569	11.68853	13.09051	14.84795	32.0069	35.1725	38.0756	41.6383	44.1814
24	9.88620	10.85635	12.40115	13.84842	15.65868	33.1962	36.4150	39.3641	42.9798	45.5584
25	10.51965	11.52395	13.11971	14.61140	16.47341	34.3816	37.6525	40.6465	44.3140	46.9280
26	11.16022	12.19818	13.84388	15.37916	17.29188	35.5632	38.8851	41.9231	45.6416	48.2898
27	11.80765	12.87847	14.57337	16.15139	18.11389	36.7412	40.1133	43.1945	46.9628	49.6450
28	12.46128	13.56467	15.30785	16.92788	18.93924	37.9159	41.3372	44.4608	48.2782	50.9936
29	13.12107	14.25641	16.04705	17.70838	19.76774	39.0875	42.5569	45.7223	49.5878	52.3355
30	13.78668	14.95346	16.79076	18.49267	20.59924	40.2560	43.7730	46.9792	50.8922	53.6719
40	20.70658	22.16420	24.43306	26.50930	29.05052	51.8050	55.7585	59.3417	63.6908	66.7660
50	27.99082	29.70673	32.35738	34.76424	37.68864	63.1671	67.5048	71.4202	76.1538	79.4898
60	35.53440	37.48480	40.48171	43.18797	46.45888	74.3970	79.0820	83.2977	88.3794	91.9518
70	43.27531	45.44170	48.75754	51.73926	55.32894	85.5270	90.5313	95.0231	100.4251	104.2148
80	51.17193	53.53998	57.15315	60.39146	64.27784	96.5782	101.8795	106.6285	112.3288	116.3209
90	59.19633	61.75402	65.64659	69.12602	73.29108	107.5650	113.1452	118.1359	124.1162	128.2987
100	67.32753	70.06500	74.22188	77.92944	82.35813	118.4980	124.3421	129.5613	135.8069	140.1697

TABLE A.6

Critical values for the Durbin-Watson test

	$\alpha = 0.05$										$\alpha = 0.01$									
	$k=1$		$k=2$		$k=3$		$k=4$		$k=5$		$k=1$		$k=2$		$k=3$		$k=4$		$k=5$	
n	d_L	d_u	d_L	d_u	d_L	d_u	d_L	d_u	d_L	d_U	d_L	d_U	d_L	d_U	d_L	d_U	d_L	d_U	d_L	d_U
15	1.08	1.36	0.95	1.54	0.82	1.75	0.69	1.97	0.56	2.21	0.81	1.07	0.70	1.25	0.59	1.46	0.49	1.70	0.39	1.96
16	1.10	1.37	0.98	1.54	0.86	1.73	0.74	1.93	0.62	2.15	0.84	1.09	0.74	1.25	0.63	1.44	0.53	1.66	0.44	1.90
17	1.13	1.38	1.02	1.54	0.90	1.71	0.78	1.90	0.67	2.10	0.87	1.10	0.77	1.25	0.67	1.43	0.57	1.63	0.48	1.85
18	1.16	1.39	1.05	1.53	0.93	1.69	0.82	1.87	0.71	2.06	0.90	1.12	0.80	1.26	0.71	1.42	0.61	1.60	0.52	1.80
19	1.18	1.40	1.08	1.53	0.97	1.68	0.86	1.85	0.75	2.02	0.93	1.13	0.83	1.26	0.74	1.41	0.65	1.58	0.56	1.77
20	1.20	1.41	1.10	1.54	1.00	1.68	0.90	1.83	0.79	1.99	0.95	1.15	0.86	1.27	0.77	1.41	0.68	1.57	0.60	1.74
21	1.22	1.42	1.13	1.54	1.03	1.67	0.93	1.81	0.83	1.96	0.97	1.16	0.89	1.27	0.80	1.41	0.72	1.55	0.63	1.71
22	1.24	1.43	1.15	1.54	1.05	1.66	0.96	1.80	0.86	1.94	1.00	1.17	0.91	1.28	0.83	1.40	0.75	1.54	0.66	1.69
23	1.26	1.44	1.17	1.54	1.08	1.66	0.99	1.79	0.90	1.92	1.02	1.19	0.94	1.29	0.86	1.40	0.77	1.53	0.70	1.67
24	1.27	1.45	1.19	1.55	1.10	1.66	1.01	1.78	0.93	1.90	1.04	1.20	0.96	1.30	0.88	1.41	0.80	1.53	0.72	1.66
25	1.29	1.45	1.21	1.55	1.12	1.66	1.04	1.77	0.95	1.89	1.05	1.21	0.98	1.30	0.90	1.41	0.83	1.52	0.75	1.65
26	1.30	1.46	1.22	1.55	1.14	1.65	1.06	1.76	0.98	1.88	1.07	1.22	1.00	1.31	0.93	1.41	0.85	1.52	0.78	1.64
27	1.32	1.47	1.24	1.56	1.16	1.65	1.08	1.76	1.01	1.86	1.09	1.23	1.02	1.32	0.95	1.41	0.88	1.51	0.81	1.63
28	1.33	1.48	1.26	1.56	1.18	1.65	1.10	1.75	1.03	1.85	1.10	1.24	1.04	1.32	0.97	1.41	0.90	1.51	0.83	1.62
29	1.34	1.48	1.27	1.56	1.20	1.65	1.12	1.74	1.05	1.84	1.12	1.25	1.05	1.33	0.99	1.42	0.92	1.51	0.85	1.61
30	1.35	1.49	1.28	1.57	1.21	1.65	1.14	1.74	1.07	1.83	1.13	1.26	1.07	1.34	1.01	1.42	0.94	1.51	0.88	1.61
31	1.36	1.50	1.30	1.57	1.23	1.65	1.16	1.74	1.09	1.82	1.15	1.27	1.08	1.34	1.02	1.42	0.96	1.51	0.90	1.60
32	1.37	1.50	1.31	1.57	1.24	1.65	1.18	1.73	1.11	1.81	1.16	1.28	1.10	1.35	1.04	1.43	0.98	1.51	0.92	1.60
33	1.38	1.51	1.32	1.58	1.26	1.65	1.19	1.73	1.13	1.81	1.17	1.29	1.11	1.36	1.05	1.43	1.00	1.51	0.94	1.59
34	1.39	1.51	1.33	1.58	1.27	1.65	1.21	1.73	1.15	1.80	1.18	1.30	1.13	1.36	1.07	1.43	1.01	1.51	0.95	1.59
35	1.40	1.52	1.34	1.58	1.28	1.65	1.22	1.73	1.16	1.80	1.19	1.31	1.14	1.37	1.08	1.43	1.03	1.51	0.97	1.59
36	1.41	1.52	1.35	1.59	1.29	1.65	1.24	1.73	1.18	1.80	1.21	1.32	1.15	1.38	1.10	1.43	1.04	1.51	0.99	1.59
37	1.42	1.53	1.36	1.59	1.31	1.66	1.25	1.72	1.19	1.79	1.22	1.33	1.16	1.38	1.11	1.44	1.06	1.51	1.00	1.59
38	1.43	1.54	1.37	1.59	1.32	1.66	1.26	1.72	1.21	1.79	1.23	1.34	1.18	1.39	1.12	1.44	1.07	1.52	1.02	1.58
39	1.43	1.54	1.38	1.60	1.33	1.66	1.27	1.72	1.22	1.79	1.24	1.34	1.19	1.39	1.14	1.45	1.09	1.52	1.03	1.58
40	1.44	1.54	1.39	1.60	1.34	1.66	1.29	1.72	1.23	1.78	1.25	1.38	1.20	1.40	1.15	1.46	1.10	1.52	1.05	1.58
45	1.48	1.57	1.43	1.62	1.38	1.67	1.34	1.72	1.29	1.77	1.29	1.40	1.24	1.42	1.20	1.48	1.16	1.53	1.11	1.58
50	1.50	1.59	1.46	1.63	1.42	1.67	1.38	1.72	1.34	1.77	1.32	1.43	1.28	1.45	1.24	1.49	1.20	1.54	1.16	1.59
55	1.53	1.60	1.49	1.64	1.45	1.68	1.41	1.72	1.38	1.77	1.36	1.45	1.32	1.47	1.28	1.51	1.25	1.55	1.21	1.59
60	1.55	1.62	1.51	1.65	1.48	1.69	1.44	1.73	1.41	1.77	1.38	1.47	1.35	1.48	1.32	1.52	1.28	1.56	1.25	1.60
65	1.57	1.63	1.54	1.66	1.50	1.70	1.47	1.73	1.44	1.77	1.41	1.49	1.38	1.50	1.35	1.53	1.31	1.57	1.28	1.61
70	1.58	1.64	1.55	1.67	1.52	1.70	1.49	1.74	1.46	1.77	1.43	1.50	1.40	1.52	1.37	1.55	1.34	1.58	1.31	1.61
75	1.60	1.65	1.57	1.68	1.54	1.71	1.51	1.74	1.49	1.77	1.45	1.51	1.42	1.23	1.39	1.56	1.37	1.59	1.34	1.62
80	1.61	1.66	1.59	1.69	1.56	1.72	1.53	1.74	1.51	1.77	1.47	1.52	1.44	1.54	1.42	1.57	1.39	1.60	1.36	1.62
85	1.62	1.67	1.60	1.70	1.57	1.72	1.55	1.75	1.52	1.77	1.48	1.53	1.46	1.55	1.43	1.58	1.41	1.60	1.39	1.63
90	1.63	1.68	1.61	1.70	1.59	1.73	1.57	1.75	1.54	1.78	1.50	1.54	1.47	1.56	1.45	1.59	1.43	1.61	1.41	1.64
95	1.64	1.69	1.62	1.71	1.60	1.73	1.58	1.75	1.56	1.78	1.51	1.55	1.49	1.57	1.47	1.60	1.45	1.62	1.42	1.64
100	1.65	1.69	1.63	1.72	1.61	1.74	1.59	1.76	1.57	1.78	1.52	1.56	1.50	1.58	1.48	1.60	1.46	1.63	1.44	1.65

a_n = *number of observations*; k = *number of independent variables.*

Index

T

U

V